ANDERSON'S
Law School Publications

ADMINISTRATIVE LAW: CASES AND MATERIALS
by Daniel J. Gifford

APPELLATE ADVOCACY: PRINCIPLES AND PRACTICE
Cases and Materials
by Ursula Bentele and Eve Cary

A CAPITAL PUNISHMENT ANTHOLOGY
by Victor L. Streib

CASES AND PROBLEMS IN CRIMINAL LAW
by Myron Moskovitz

THE CITATION WORKBOOK
by Maria L. Ciampi, Rivka Widerman and Vicki Lutz

COMMERCIAL TRANSACTIONS: PROBLEMS AND MATERIALS
Vol. 1: Secured Transactions Under the Uniform Commercial Code
Vol. 2: Sales Under the Uniform Commercial Code and the Convention on International Sale of Goods
Vol. 3: Negotiable Instruments Under the Uniform Commercial Code and the United Nations Convention on International Bills of Exchange and International Promissory Notes
by Louis F. Del Duca, Egon Guttman and Alphonse M. Squillante

A CONSTITUTIONAL LAW ANTHOLOGY
by Michael J. Glennon

CONTRACTS
Contemporary Cases, Comments, and Problems
by Michael L. Closen, Richard M. Perlmutter and Jeffrey D. Wittenberg

A CONTRACTS ANTHOLOGY
by Peter Linzer

A CRIMINAL LAW ANTHOLOGY
by Arnold H. Loewy

CRIMINAL LAW: CASES AND MATERIALS
by Arnold H. Loewy

EFFECTIVE INTERVIEWING
by Fred E. Jandt

ECONOMIC REGULATION
Cases and Materials
by Richard J. Pierce, Jr.

ENDING IT: DISPUTE RESOLUTION IN AMERICA
Descriptions, Examples, Cases and Questions
by Susan M. Leeson and Bryan M. Johnston

ENVIRONMENTAL LAW
Vol. 1: Environmental Decisionmaking and NEPA
Vol. 2: Water Pollution
Vol. 3: Air Pollution
Vol. 4: Hazardous Wastes
by Jackson B. Battle, Mark Squillace and Maxine Lipeles

FEDERAL INCOME TAXATION OF PARTNERSHIPS AND OTHER PASS-THRU ENTITIES
by Howard E. Abrams

FEDERAL RULES OF EVIDENCE
Rules, Legislative History, Commentary and Authority
by Glen Weissenberger

Continued

INTERNATIONAL HUMAN RIGHTS: LAW, POLICY AND PROCESS
Problems and Materials
by Frank Newman and David Weissbrodt

INTERNATIONAL LAW ANTHOLOGY
by Anthony D'Amato

INTRODUCTION TO THE STUDY OF LAW: CASES AND MATERIALS
by John Makdisi

JUSTICE AND THE LEGAL SYSTEM
A Coursebook
by Anthony D'Amato and Arthur J. Jacobson

THE LAW OF MODERN PAYMENT SYSTEMS AND NOTES
by Fred H. Miller and Alvin C. Harrell

PATIENTS, PSYCHIATRISTS AND LAWYERS
Law and the Mental Health System
by Raymond L. Spring, Roy B. Lacoursiere, M.D., and Glen Weissenberger

PROBLEMS AND SIMULATIONS IN EVIDENCE
by Thomas F. Guernsey

A PROPERTY ANTHOLOGY
by Richard H. Chused

THE REGULATION OF BANKING
Cases and Materials on Depository Institutions and Their Regulators
by Michael P. Malloy

A SECTION 1983 CIVIL RIGHTS ANTHOLOGY
by Sheldon H. Nahmod

SPORTS LAW: CASES AND MATERIALS
by Raymond L. Yasser, James R. McCurdy and C. Peter Goplerud

A TORTS ANTHOLOGY
by Lawrence C. Levine, Julie A. Davies and Ted Kionka

TRIAL PRACTICE
Text by Lawrence A. Dubin and Thomas F. Guernsey
Problems and Case Files with *Video* Presentation
by Edward R. Stein and Lawrence A. Dubin

International Law Anthology

International Law Anthology

Edited by
Anthony D'Amato

Leighton Professor of Law

Northwestern University

Anderson Publishing Company

INTERNATIONAL LAW ANTHOLOGY

Contents

PART II
PROFESSIONAL TOOLS

Contributing Authors

Kenneth W. Abbott
Michael Akehurst
Philip Allott
Jill R. Applebaum

Elizabeth Bartholet
M. Cherif Bassiouni
Michael J. Bazyler
David J. Bederman
Richard B. Bilder
Guyora Binder
Virginia Black
Christopher L. Blakesley
Edwin M. Borchard
Henry J. Bourguignon
D.W. Bowett
Francis Anthony Boyle
James D. Boyle
Herbert W. Briggs
Lea Brilmayer
Thomas Buergenthal

Michael Cardozo
David D. Caron
Hilary Charlesworth
Jonathan I. Charney
Abram Chayes
Antonia Handler Chayes
Lung-Chu Chen
Christine Chinkin
Hungdah Chiu
Sudhir K. Chopra
Gordon A. Christenson
Cynthia Price Cohen
Susan Connor
Maurice Copithorne
Christine Alice Corcos
James Crawford

Kenneth Dam
Anthony D'Amato
Lori Fisler Damrosch
Ingrid Detter De Lupis
Tracy Dobson
Karl Doehring
Isaak Dore

Richard W. Edwards, Jr.
Kirsten Engel

Richard Falk
Tom J. Farer
Roger Fisher
Joan Fitzpatrick

Gregory Fox
Thomas M. Franck

John King Gamble, Jr.
David J. Gerber
Michael J. Glennon
W. Paul Gormley
Gidon Gottlieb

Malvina Halberstam
Gunther Handl
Hurst Hannum
John Lawrence Hargrove
Louis Henkin
John T. Holmes

Catherine J. Iorns

John H. Jackson
Mark W. Janis
Anna Jenefsky
Ian Johnstone
Christopher C. Joyner
Friedrich K. Juenger

Hans Kelsen
David Kennedy
Ingrid Kircher
Frederic L. Kirgis, Jr.
Alexandre Charles Kiss

Hersch Lauterpacht
Virginia A. Leary
Richard B. Lillich
Charles Lipson
Andreas F. Lowenfeld
Steven Lubet
Ellen Lutz

Jacques MacChesney
Harold G. Maier
H.W. Malkin
Charles Marvin
Steven C. McCaffrey
Myres McDougal
Theodor Meron
William B.T. Mock, Jr.
John Norton Moore
Fred L. Morrison
Rein Mullerson
John F. Murphy

James A.R. Nafziger
Ved P. Nanda
Terry Nardin

Babacar Ndiaye
Arthur Nussbaum

Nicholas Onuf
Lassa Oppenheim
Bernard H. Oxman

Jordan J. Paust
Catherine Logan Piper
Istvan Pogany
Michla Pomerance
Daniel M. Price

W. Michael Reisman
Alfred P. Rubin
Sarah A. Rumage

Claudia Saladin
Philippe Sands
Oscar Schachter
Norbert A. Schlei
Hans Schultz
Stephen M. Schwebel
Georg Schwarzenberger
Dinah Shelton
Bruno Simma
Anne-Marie Slaughter Burley
Louis Sohn
Barbara Stark
Ted L. Stein
Julius Stone
E.C. Stowell

Fernando R. Teson
Phillip R. Trimble
Grigori Tunkin
Jonathan Turley
Mary Ellen Turpel

Detlev F. Vagts
Christine VanDer Wijngaert
Jon Van Dyke

Prosper Weil
Paul Weis
Edith Brown Weiss
Peter Weiss
Burns H. Weston
Quincy Wright
Shelley Wright

Christopher Yuen

Elisabeth Zoller

Preface

As I was busy nailing together the various planks of this International Law Anthology, I stopped for a moment and thought to myself: Hey, this is really terrific! I'm getting to choose the most intellectually provocative writings from the vast realm of international law. No book will ever be more exciting – to students, to teachers, to readers in general. It's going to rocket to the top of the New York Times' Non-Fiction Best Seller List, get optioned for a major motion picture, set off a hot bidding war for a prime-time TV miniseries . . . .

O.K., you're working hard, you're alone, you obviously need to pump yourself up. Relax. Take a tranquility break. How did you get into this thing in the first place?

The fact is the project never occurred to me. The Anderson Publishing Company called up out of the blue and offered me the job of editing a volume in their extraordinarily successful Anthology series. I spent the greater part of three seconds agonizing over whether I should accept.

And so I plunged into writings that grapple with the deep issues and fascinating underpinnings of international law, writings that test the foundations of the discipline in light of today's and tomorrow's problems and issues. I avoided works that focused on particular rules of law relating to particular disputes, or works that summarized and explained important treaties. The controversies of international law come at you like a mud slide, shifting constantly. To be sure, focusing on a particular dispute can sometimes be quite suitable for a case study or debate – we'll have a few of those – so long as the issues raised are of general and enduring interest. You'll also find a few essays that are published here for the first time; these are "gap-filling" pieces that help round out the presentation of various issues. Over-all, in the tradition of other anthologies in the Anderson Anthology series, I've taken a "highlights" approach to the subject-matter rather than a "comprehensive" approach. This has forced me to make some hard choices. I take complete personal responsibility, and apologize, for negligent omissions as well as errors of judgment.

The bottom line is that what you're holding in your hands is an Anthology dedicated to the groundwork, the structural foundations of international law. Despite its paper cover, it's designed to last for years and years. You'll want to carry it with you and refer to it wherever you go, especially on airplanes.

No book can take the place of classroom learning. This Anthology is at best a supplement to, and not a substitute for, the dialogue between student and professor that characterizes the best way to learn anything. Socrates, the master teacher, cautioned against books in his Phaedrus dialogue:

> Written words seem to talk to you as if they were intelligent, but if you ask them anything about what they say, from a desire to be instructed, they go on telling you just the same thing forever.

The best thing a textbook can do is to provide appropriate material for dialogic dissection by teacher and student.

I should add a brief word about my user-friendly approach to editing. I've simply cut out all digressions and unnecessary footnotes, and have not even indicated omissions by elision marks (. . . .) or brackets [sick] or asterisks (* * * *) because I didn't want to clutter up our little vessel with nail-heads and sawdust. I have done my utmost to be meticulously faithful to the authors' intent. In all cases the original publication source of each excerpt is duly noted, and I urge you to look up the full articles and books whenever you want the bigger picture or just to check up on what I left out.

My international law students at Northwestern are the greatest people in the world, and I would like to thank two of them for the wonderful help they gave me in this editing project: Jacques MacChesney and Patience Marime. With students like them going into the field, I know that international law has a future. I'd also like to thank my former secretary Jim DeLorenzo. I want to thank my colleagues around the country who responded to my appeal for suggestions regarding topics and sources for inclusion in this Anthology: Kenneth Abbott, Richard Bilder, Virginia Black, Christopher Blakesley, Francis Boyle, Lea Brilmayer, Isaak Dore, Richard Falk, Joan Fitzpatrick, David Gerber, David Kennedy, Malvina Halberstam, Harold Maier, Stephen McCaffrey, James Nafziger, Daniel Partan, Jordan Paust, John M. Rogers, Alfred Rubin, Barbara Stark, Henry Steiner, and Burns Weston. In addition, thanks to all who have sent me reprints of their articles over the years; although I have not always been able to acknowledge receipt, I turned to those reprints first in my quest for suitable materials for this Anthology. Finally, my enduring thanks to the great scholars who taught me international law when I was a student at Cornell, Harvard, and Columbia: the late Richard Baxter, the late Herbert Briggs, Roger Fisher, Louis Henkin, Milton Katz, Oliver Lissitzyn, and Louis Sohn – and to my wife the famous mystery novelist Barbara D'Amato who thinks international law is in its infancy.

Acknowledgments

We would like to thank all the authors and publishers who have kindly given their permission to us to reprint excerpts from their published works. Permissions are acknowledged in the first footnote to each article.

In the case of each excerpt from the *American Journal of International Law* and *The Proceedings of the American Society of International Law*, the copyright © is held by the American Society of International Law and is used here by permission.

In the case of each excerpt from the *North Carolina Journal of International Law & Commercial Regulation*, the copyright © is held by the North Carolina Journal of International Law & Commercial Regulation and is used here by permission.

In the case of each excerpt from the *Vanderbilt Journal of Transnational Law*, the copyright © is held by the Vanderbilt Journal of Transnational Law and is used here by permission.

The excerpt from *Criminal Justice Ethics* is reprinted by permission of The Institute for Criminal Justice Ethics.

In the case of each excerpt from the *Harvard International Law Journal*, the copyright © is held by the President and Fellows of Harvard College and is used here by permission.

Part I
Introduction to International Law

1

The Domain of International Law[1]

"What does international law cover?" a student might ask on the first day of the course in International Law. I usually suppress a facetious answer: "Oh, let's see, the world?" Instead, I hear myself saying something like, "Sit back and let me bore you with my patented five-cent lecture." If I go on to tell it right, the impression should soon be conveyed that international law impacts, directly or indirectly, every human activity and endeavor. When I conclude, someone usually asks why such a vast topic is tucked away in the elective part of the curriculum. I don't know, I reply, but that question is related to one that bothers me even more: why, in a shrinking and interdependent world, is there no international law question on the United States multistate bar examination?

So here's the lecture – my aerial view of the domain of international law. If nothing else, it should demolish the skeptic's question "Does international law exist?" It may also serve as a partial corrective to a related skeptical view – rather rife these days in American law schools, I'm afraid – that international law exists only to the extent that it is recognized as a rule of decision by American courts.[2]

As we cruise over the topography of our subject, we might easily miss the enormous depth below the surface. It is only a slight exaggeration to say that, for nearly every topic, sub-topic, or sub-sub-topic I shall mention, there exists a book or a doctoral dissertation somewhere in the world devoted entirely to it. Indeed, every word and every concept in the following survey has a rich and fascinating supporting literature. And the foreign office of each country in the world contains thousands of documents – state letters, diplomatic correspondence, cables, position papers – referring to most of the topics in this brief survey, and to many more that could be mentioned.

A last preliminary word: the survey that follows can only be a present-day snapshot of international law. Our subject undergoes constant revision in content and in scope. A hundred years ago, the topics of belligerency, neutrality, and state acquisition of territory loomed much larger than they do today. On the other hand, a hundred years ago you could find very little in the international law literature on human rights and practically nothing on the global environment. What will international law look like a hundred years from now (if the human race hasn't blown itself up by then)? The one thing I'm sure of is that someone will write an overview of international law, compare it to today's, and conclude that things seemed rather stuffy and medieval back at the close of the twentieth century.

1. STATES. Since states are both subjects and objects of international law, we need criteria to identify the more than 190 of them that today lay claim to the land mass of the earth. International law looks to a government's effective control over a defined territory with a permanent population, its capacity to conduct international relations, and its independence from other countries. States, and governments, are "recognized" by other governments and by international organizations. Recognition is de facto, de jure, or both; in some cases it is retroactive, or conditional, or implied. Sometimes a government in exile is recognized, even though it lacks effective control.

International law regards states as juridically equal. It allocates to them jurisdiction over their internal affairs, but the developing law of international human rights constitutes an exception to a state's domestic jurisdiction. A new trend in the law regarding cultural patrimony may give a state some continuing rights of protection over works of art and cultural artifacts that originated in that state but are now located in another state, even if they were sold or looted from their state of origin in the distant past.

International law regulates the question of state continuity, dealing with problems arising from territorial changes (unification or partition), changes in population, changes in government (constitutional or revolutionary), and belligerent occupation by another state. Consider the fact that Yugoslavia has split up into a number a new states: Croatia, Slovenia, Bosnia, Serbia, Montenegro, Macedonia. May two of these states (Serbia and Montenegro) lay full claim to the benefits of the treaties of the Federal Republic of Yugoslavia by virtue of the fact that they retain its capital city, Belgrade? If an old state ends and a new one takes its place, the new state will likely succeed to the obligations of the former state – its contracts, treaties, debts, as well as its intangible assets in foreign banks. Is there a different rule for "territorial treaties"? Hong Kong today presents most of these problems. While it was a colony of Great

---

[1] By ANTHONY D'AMATO, written for this Anthology.

[2] For a debate on this subject, see The *"Domestication" of International Law,* Chapter 16 in this Anthology.

Britain, Hong Kong had entered into numerous treaties. Now that the period of colonization is coming to an end, will Hong Kong be able to retain its treaties or will international law regard its treaties as absorbed by mainland China? This high-stakes question will occupy many international lawyers in the next few years.

Despite the general rules that apply to most states, some kinds of states present exceptional problems that international law has dealt with through the ages: divided states, "micro-states," dependent states (protectorates, satellites, capitulatory regimes, colonies, spheres of influence), and composite states (unions, federations, confederations). And then there are territorial entities other than states: insurgents, territories under military occupation, non-self-governing territories, aboriginal peoples in places such as the Polar regions, "associated states" that are hard to define (such as Puerto Rico, Cook Islands, Western Samoa, the Isle of Man, the Channel Islands), condominia (Andorra), and special regimes (such as the Holy See, Vatican City, Gibralter, and the Aaland Islands).

2. TERRITORY. How do states legally acquire territories, including the initial territory upon which the state was founded? This question was more important in the age of discovery and exploration, but still arises in current (though not usually large-scale) international disputes. Modes of acquisition include discovery, contiguity, occupation, prescription, long and peaceful possession, purchase, accretion, consolidation, cession, and dispositions by multilateral treaty or by international organizations. If there is passage of considerable time, territorial expansion via conquest and annexation may acquire legitimacy. "Territory" of course may also include airspace, subsoil rights, and rights to the continental shelf and deep seabed. In addition to outright dominion over territory, international law is familiar with servitudes, free cities, demilitarized zones, customs-free zones, leases, transit corridors, and various forms of concessions such as territorial privileges and commercial concession agreements.

3. STATE JURISDICTION. Through its judicial and legislative branches, a state may come into conflict with other states in one of two ways. Its courts might assert jurisdiction over the person or property of a national of a foreign state. And its legislation might regulate the activities abroad of its own persons or corporations. The problem of conflict is especially acute when a state's own citizens or corporations have control, through ownership of stock, of foreign subsidiary corporations which nevertheless are incorporated in foreign states. When the parent state tries to regulate the activities of these foreign subsidiaries, the subsidiary state may complain about legislative overreach. Customary international law regulates the "reach" of a state's courts and legislature as well as the interstate conflicts resulting from alleged overreach.

4. STATE RESPONSIBILITY. Under international law, a state can be held responsible (and may have to pay damages) for its torts, whether deliberate or negligent, its contracts, its indebtedness, and generally its "acts." International law regulates whether tort liability can be imputed to a state (and to what degree) for acts or omissions of its executives, legislators, judges, military personnel, insurgents and revolutionaries, and its citizens. Among the types of activities for which a state can be held responsible include failure to prevent harms to aliens (such as foreign tourists or persons temporarily resident in the state), failure to prosecute persons who wrongfully injure aliens, judicial denial of justice to aliens (a venerable concept dating back to Vattel), nationalization, expropriation or confiscation of foreign property, ultrahazardous activities including weapons testing, and military as well as noncombat activities of its armed forces. A state may plead in justification of its acts the consent of another state or its citizens, force majeure, distress, necessity, self-defense, and various kinds of waivers that have been worked out through the centuries including the famous Calvo Doctrine.

5. STATE IMMUNITIES. The doctrine of "sovereign immunity" is a defense that states typically raise against all foreign claims. A threshold question is the extent of the claimed immunity: does it apply to the state itself, to heads of state, to diplomatic and consular personnel, to consular missions, to state organs, subdivisions, and instrumentalities? Is a state's property covered by sovereign immunity, including its property abroad when the property is government-owned? In the category of property abroad, immunity is more likely to be attached to embassies (their offices, archives, documents, and communications), consular offices, special missions, public vessels, and military bases. But these immunities are receding: embassies sometimes have to pay forms of local taxes, and military bases are regulated by "status of forces agreements" that define their particular immunities. Sovereign immunity, of course, can be waived, whether explicitly or implicitly. In general, when a state engages in profit-making (commercial) activities abroad, the immunity it used to enjoy a hundred years ago has all but vanished. Yet in any case or situation involving the attribution of responsibility to a state for its activities, international lawyers must sooner or later contend with rules relating to the scope of sovereign immunity.

6. THE SEA. Seventy-one per cent of our planet's surface is covered by water. International law has become quite detailed in its regulation of this common heritage. It regulates the breadth of the territorial sea, how it is measured from the baseline including delimitations between opposite and adjacent states and questions relating to offshore islands and reefs, and specifies rights of other states in the territorial sea including the right of innocent passage

and problems of distress. Transit through international straits is also a subject of the law of the sea, as is the delimitation of the contiguous zone and the newly defined exclusive economic zone (EEZ). Complications arise from artificial islands and installations, such as oil rigs. Can a state harness the tidal energy, the wave energy, and extract heat, from the oceans? Can it use the oceans as a dump for garbage and chemical and nuclear wastes? The continental shelf (an appendage of most but not all coastal states) is a rich resource for oil and sedentary fisheries. How is the shelf delimited? How extensive are the coastal state's rights to mineral extraction and fishing? What are the coastal state's responsibilities of management and conservation of living resources in the EEZ and on and above the continental shelf? Who has the right to engage in marine scientific research (a seemingly innocuous question which has spawned enormous controversy in recent years)? What may prove even more controversial in years to come is the concept of "common heritage of mankind"—the claim that any state extracting minerals from the ocean floor must pay a portion of the profits to other states.

Few principles of international law are as entrenched as the principle of freedom of the seas. The high seas are free and open to commercial navigation, but any vessel on the high seas that does not display a flag may be detained and searched by any governmental vessel. There must be a "genuine link" between the vessel and its state of origin. Vessels may not engage in slave transport, and rules are increasingly restrictive regarding the transportation of indentured workers (there is indeterminacy regarding the meaning of "indentured"). Piracy, of course, is a violation of international law, and any governmental vessel may capture a pirate vessel. Vessels carrying goods prohibited in certain countries (such as certain drugs) have freedom of navigation on the high seas, but once they enter into a territorial sea they are subject to apprehension by the coastal state—and if they try to escape, the coastal state vessel has a right of "hot pursuit." States generally may engage in conventional weapons testing and "war games" on the high seas, but for a limited time and place only, and with accompanying obligations to warn other vessels and to pay compensation for damages caused by negligence. And of course there are detailed rules of admiralty and conflicts-of-admiralty laws, regulating subjects such as salvage, collisions, labor conditions, and prize captures.

Internal and partially internal waterways are affected by international rules: transboundary rivers, rivers that constitute the boundaries between states, canals, straits, lakes, bays, and ports of all kinds.

7. POLAR REGIONS. Antarctica is a continent, unlike the water mass of the Arctic Circle. International regulation of overflights applies to both arctic regions. But Antarctica presents special problems, and various nations have laid claims to sectors of that continent. The Antarctica regimes are objective as well as treaty-based, involve claims of exclusivities and commons, and implicate environmental management concerns as well as potential mining activities.

8. AIRSPACE. Air travel by balloon in the nineteenth century and by airplane from 1903 to 1914 raised expectations that the global airspace, like the high seas, was free and open. But with the advent of the First World War and the specter of military planes dropping bombs, a rapid international consensus was reached of "national airspace"—each nation has sovereignty of the airspace over its land territory and territorial seas. Only airspace over the oceans and over arctic regions remained open to all states. Soon "special zones" were invented—limited control by the territorial sovereign of airspace over the high seas contiguous to the territory, for distant early warning purposes. These aerial defense zones extend as much as 600 miles out to sea. The international law of unauthorized aerial intrusion in peace and in war has become dense with regulations, both customary and treaty-based. Regulations analogous to vessels have arisen regarding aircraft, airports, and air traffic control. Acts on board aircraft flying over the high seas or over foreign countries can give rise to international conflicts-of-laws issues: births, marriages, deaths, and entering into contracts. State responsibility and damage liability limits extend to passengers, cargo, airmail, transport of dangerous materials or prohibited substances, and damage to third parties resulting from overflight, sonic boom, environmental damage, emergency landings, accidents, crashes, collisions, towing, and salvage.

9. OUTER SPACE. The American flag was placed on the moon on the first manned expedition. Should this be analogized to the "discovery" of the "new world" by explorers in the sixteenth century, who proclaimed ownership of the territories in which they planted their national flag? Or should it be analogized to the high seas—the common heritage of all nations? International law has quickly resolved this question in favor of the latter alternative. There can be exploration, and limited exploitation, but not appropriation, of planets, satellites, and stars. An artificial satellite, however, is owned by the nation that launched it, subject to tort liabilities for injuries resulting either from its placement or if it crashes upon return to earth. There are lively disputes over technological uses of satellites—for broadcast transmission and reception, broadcast blocking and interception, "spy" surveillance, or weapons launching (conventional or nuclear). All the participants in these disputes refer to the rapidly emerging norms of customary international law.

10. THE GLOBAL ENVIRONMENT. States have belatedly come to realize that they share a common, precarious, life-sustaining global ecological system. International

norms increasingly impact upon conservation–of resources, of the ecosystem, and of knowledge. Resources include rain forests, water quality, the atmosphere and ozone layer, soil management, nonrenewable energy sources, and biological and genetic resources. There is an emerging duty to conserve ecosystem diversity and to prevent specific harm to endangered and protected species. At the cutting edge are claims on behalf of sentient animals that they should have minimal rights such as a right not to be needlessly killed or, if killing is a necessity, to be killed without unnecessary suffering. Another duty of ecosystem conservation is the preservation of knowledge, a resource that includes the traditional knowledge of natural systems, traditional cultures, access to scientific information and experimentation, the gathering and maintenance of data in computers and storage disks, and special duties regarding the creation or introduction of alien or new species or new genetic material. Weather modification and climate change is global in scope and impact; international customary law is growing in this vital area. International law also regulates the export of hazardous materials and technology. Air and marine pollution are also globally interconnected. Marine pollution includes topics such as vessel-source pollution, waste disposal and dumping, land-based pollution, pollution from sea-bed mining, salinization, and the by-products of extracting heat and kinetic energy from the oceans.

11. NATIONALITY. International law addresses itself in the outset to nations, just as corporate law addresses itself at the outset to corporations. But nations and corporations are abstractions; it is people and other living things that really count. Thus international law quickly gets down to the level of human beings.

The traditional link–and still the most important connection–between the state and the person is "nationality." International law requires a "genuine link" between a national and her state. Some people have dual nationality; others can be stateless. A person is not the only proper subject of nationality; other possibilities include ships and planes, corporations, groups and associations. Many issues of taxation turn on the question of nationality: for example, a state may tax income earned abroad by its citizens or by the foreign subsidiaries of its corporations. The Calvo Doctrine was an attempt on the part of some countries to force foreign corporations to waive or renounce their nationality protection in order to engage in local business.

12. INTERNATIONAL MOVEMENT OF PERSONS. Persons are generally free to travel within the confines of their own country (a sad exception these days is the denial of freedom of movement to women in some Islamic countries). But as soon as a national of one country wants to travel to or through another country, they are met with a host of international regulations. States use passports and visas as a means of travel control (in the nineteenth century a passport was used only for identification). States sometimes forbid their own citizens to travel to certain other countries ("area restrictions"). States are free to repatriate undesirable aliens, but also to grant territorial asylum to aliens who are fleeing from political persecution. Economic refugees are given far less consideration than political refugees, but sometimes "boat people," displaced persons, and unwanted or abandoned children get special exemptions. In general, states claim an absolute right under present international law to regulate their own immigration and emigration. But inroads are being made on this claim by the burgeoning law of international human rights.

13. HUMAN RIGHTS. The human rights revolution has added a wholly new dimension to the classic view of international law. The way a government treats its own nationals within its own borders is no longer within that government's exclusive "domestic jurisdiction." Certain basic and minimal rights cannot be arbitrarily invaded by governments, including life, liberty, security, nondiscrimination, and equal protection of the law. Certain fundamental human rights are defined by their status as subjects of criminal prohibitions (see the next section). In addition, various multilateral conventions, broadly ratified (though not ratified by all countries), provide additional rights such as the rights to minimal sustenance, freedom of opinion, freedom of peaceful assembly, habeas corpus, public trial if accused of a crime, the right to marry and found a family, the right to education, the right to work, to own property, and to obtain patent and copyright protection. Human rights law is developing most aggressively in the areas of equal rights for women and the rights of children.

14. GROUP RIGHTS. Among "group rights" claims are the right to self-determination, autonomy, secession, the rights of native communities, the right to use the native language, and freedom of religious exercise. Are these "human rights" or could they be in conflict with human rights? If a group asserts the right of freedom for the group, is there an implicit denial of the freedom of its members to opt out from the group in whole or in part? This area of international law is currently in great ferment.

15. INTERNATIONAL CRIMES. Certain human rights are so fundamental as to constitute international crimes, even if the violators are government officials. These include genocide, torture, enslavement, rape, hijacking, terrorism, racial discrimination such as apartheid, unlawful human experimentation, theft of nuclear materials, and crimes against the cultural patrimony. Piracy, which by definition cannot be committed by government officials, has also long been recognized as an international crime–as has counterfeiting (which might conceivably be committed by government officials). The list of interna-

tional crimes is expanding. Certain offenses against the environment are possible candidates (consider: willful destruction of the ozone layer, willful termination of an endangered species). The United States and some other countries want certain drug offenses added to the list of international crimes.

The procedural aspects of international criminal law center largely upon questions of extradition and asylum, and involve concepts such as non-refoulment, the political offense exception, and the doctrine of specialty. Various "due process" rights of persons accused under the laws of their own state may come within the rubric of "general principles" of international law.

16. THE WORLD MARKET. The commercial movement of goods and services across boundaries – the "world market," if you will – is such a huge area of international law that it is normally called "private international law." Yet the line between "public" and "private" international law is amorphous (for example, on which side of the line do you include sovereign immunity or concession agreements?) Moreover, drawing a line often results in a lawyer's failing to see, for instance, that a question of public law may lurk behind any given question of private law (such as a question of public international law as a default rule on choice-of-law).

The international law of trade is largely treaty-based, but the interpretation of the treaties is based on customary law. Import control is largely a question of tariffs, quantitative restrictions, outright barriers of certain goods, medical controls, subsidies, countervailing duties, dumping, customs unions, free trade areas, commodity agreements, and the huge area of discriminatory internal taxation (amounting to an indirect tariff). Export control focuses on weapons, nuclear technology, other dangerous products, hazardous activites, and involves licensing and inspection.

International financing is a huge sub-topic, including the international monetary fund and the World Bank, but also currency exchanges, currency exchange controls and regulation, stock exchanges, international investment funds, international banking, investment guarantees, debt rescheduling, and multilateral investment insurance. Agencies involved in these activities are also enlisted from time to time in assisting in humanitarian and disaster relief.

World tax policy, conflicts among national tax laws and double taxation, and the breadth of national jurisdiction to tax activities, products, and services, are other vast areas of international commerce regulated by treaties and customary law. Similarly, there are conflicting national antitrust policies impacting upon multilateral enterprises.

The list goes on, but worthy of special mention is the growing field of intellectual property: the unification of trademark, patent, and copyright legislation and the international conflicts arising from disparate national standards.

17. GLOBAL COMMUNICATIONS. The earliest topics in this burgeoning field were international postal services and the laying of submarine cables. The invention of radio, television, and facsimile and modem communications technology, have led to explosive growth in this area of international regulation. Jamming and counter-jamming of another nation's radio wave frequencies, channel regulation, remote sensing, and stationary satellite transmission are matters of intense interest. There is a move toward international broadcast standards and transmission quality. But there are also countervailing pressures against freedom of information, with some nations (and religious groups) desiring the suppression of international telecommunications relating to the advocacy of war or revolution, criticism of governmental officials or policies, regulation of commercial messages, and materials depicting real or fictional violence or pornography.

18. NUCLEAR ENERGY AND ARMS CONTROL. There are enough nuclear bombs still stockpiled to terminate all life on this planet. Although, now that the Cold War has ended, the probability of thermonuclear annihilation seems vanishingly small, if we multiply the probability of its occurrence by the gravity of the potential harm, we come out with a huge number – one that warrants exceptional, unremitting precaution.

Obtaining electricity from nuclear power technology is an ultrahazardous activity. There is international regulation of peaceful uses of nuclear energy, and nations arguably are constrained by international quality and liability standards regarding exports of nuclear power plant equipment and technology.

Inspection and verification of peaceful uses of nuclear power is also designed to monitor the international norm against further nuclear weapons proliferation. Other arms control measures include targeting restrictions, nuclear-free zones, the "star wars" controversy, and declarations of no-first-use.

19. REMEDIES FOR VIOLATIONS OF INTERNATIONAL LAW. The first thing, of course, is dispute prevention, and the second is dispute settlement. Vast procedural institutions of international law are devoted to facilitating negotiation, mediation, conciliation, arbitration, and judicial settlement. Even beyond settlement are procedures for reparations, such as international insurance funds and international funds for reparations. But if these don't work out, and an injured state resorts to self-help, international customary law regulates the degree and kind of countermeasure. The kinds of peacetime countermeasures include retorsion, reprisal, reciprocal entitlement deprivations, economic boycotts and trade sanctions. Closer to wartime countermeasures are arms embargoes, blockades, and quarantines. The degree of permissible countermeasures are

regulated by customary rules of necessity and proportionality.

20. USE AND REGULATION OF FORCE. International law regulates the transboundary use of force that exceeds the permissible bounds of remedial countermeasures. Unilateral transboundary intervention by military force depends for its legality upon the kind and purpose of the intervention: to support self-determination uprisings, to suppress crimes against humanity, to support civil war, to protect one's nationals in the target country, or for limited purposes of humanitarian intervention.

Resort to war is now, of course, prohibited. Self-defense is an excuse depending upon customary rules of international law relating to a showing of instant danger, absence of lawful means of protection, necessity, proportionality, reasonableness, and more controversially "anticipatory" self-defense. If war is illegally initiated, international law nevertheless continues to function. The conduct of the war is regulated by a vastly detailed set of prescriptions relating to regular and irregular forces, reprisals, the taking of hostages, and war crimes. The latter concerns bombardment, guerrilla warfare, prohibited weaponry (including chemical and biological weapons), the treatment of prisoners and wounded persons, the use of captured persons for labor, the doctrine of military necessity, and the treatment of property during wartime including cultural treasures. The scope of the war may depend upon whether third states are drawn into the conflict by violating the international law of neutrality. Detailed rules of neutrality regulate the permissibility of furnishing troops or materiel to belligerents, nationals "volunteering" to fight for belligerent forces, the passage of troops and materiel through neutral territory, the use of neutral territory as a base for military operations, granting asylum to fugitive soldiers or deserters or noncombatant members of belligerent forces or shipwrecked personnel. Neutrality law also specifies "war zones," "neutralized zones", blockades, contraband, hostilities by or against neutrals, and rules relating to neutral vessels (visit and search, impressment, angary, navicerts, capture, and prize law). The conclusion of the war is a matter of intense legal concern not just for the framing of a treaty of peace and its legal consequences, but also for topics such as flags of truce, armistice, amnesty, unconditional surrender, capitulations, and post-war compensation.

21. INTERGOVERNMENTAL ORGANIZATIONS. With the end of the Cold War, the United Nations is assuming an ever-larger role in the development of international law on subjects beginning with peacekeeping and peacemaking, and reaching to nearly all the substantive topics of the preceding survey. Also a host of regional intergovernmental organizations, and numerous specialized international organizations (such as the Red Cross, the International Labor Organization, and the Universal Postal Union), are becoming more important. Since all of these organizations are creations of international law, international law regulates their competences (via treaties and the customary law of treaty-interpretation), their functions, and their "legal personalities." The latter includes the capacity of the intergovernmental organization to bring claims against states, to be responsible themselves for violations of international law, to make treaties, and to appear before international tribunals. The extent of their power over non-members is regulated by international law. In addition there is the entire panoply of immunities: immunities for governmental representatives attending meetings of international organizations, agents, invitees, offices and leased premises, and real estate and other property owned by those organizations. An important impact upon international law comes from non-governmental organizations (NGO'S) which are increasingly claiming a participatory voice at international law summit meetings such as Earth Conferences and Human Rights Conferences. Although in one respect the NGO's are lobbyists for their special interests, in another critical respect they are by-passing the state and interfacing the people of the world directly with international law.

22. SOURCES OF INTERNATIONAL LAW. The international legal system has no central legislature and no comprehensive judicial system with compulsory jurisdiction. Therefore the content of customary international law is much harder to determine than the content of domestic law. Yet I for one regard it as more intellectually appealing because the "answers" are not a simple matter of looking something up in statutes and compilations of court decisions, but rather are dependent upon cogent argumentation, creative research into state practice, and persuasiveness of presentation. The "sources" of generally applicable international law include the practice of states (called "custom"), general principles of law, the writings of publicists, decisions of national courts as well as international courts, equity, and the consensus of states. Sources of particular international law – affecting specific states – include treaties, informal understandings (included under the notion of "soft law"), and special customary law. When the meaning of a treaty provision is at issue, international law provides the background of a venerable customary law of treaty interpretation. Especially challenging is the growing customary law of the effect of state reservations to multilateral treaties. A thorough study of the literature devoted to the "sources" of international law is a prerequisite for any serious international lawyer or student of that subject.

23. INTERNATIONAL LAW IN DOMESTIC COURTS. International norms can operate as a limitation

on domestic law. For example, in a given country, capital punishment for minors may be allowable under its Constitution, but not under international human rights law. Whether or not domestic courts will apply the international norm varies from time to time and from country to country. Domestic law also may provide remedies for violations of international law, as well as contribute to the definition of international crimes. Whether treaty provisions are ''self-executing'' is normally a matter of domestic law (against the background of the customary international law of treaty interpretation). International norms are unavoidable in cases of conflict of law between the forum state and the transaction state, and in cases of regulating the foreign conduct of a state's nationals or corporations. The recognition of foreign court judgments in the courts of the forum state is typically covered by broad treaty provisions which have to be interpreted against a customary law background. In fact, all of public international law, in one way or another, can play a part in cases arising under domestic law, and some professors of international law choose to teach international law through the intermediary of domestic judicial decisions.

2

History of the Law of Nations

A. Political and Economic History

1. From Antiquity to the Middle Ages[1]

There is scope for international law whenever two conditions are fulfilled. First, the entities concerned must be prepared to grant each other at least equality of status if not substantially reciprocal treatment. Secondly, there must be sufficient contact between them to make legal regulation of some of their relations desirable.

Thus, in the fourteenth century B.C., Pharaoh Rameses II of Egypt concluded a Treaty of Peace, Alliance and Extradition with the King of Cheta, and Suppiluliuma, King of the Hittites, entered into an alliance with Nigmad, King of Egarit. The second of these treaties contains a passage which, by more than a millennium, anticipates the teachings of Kautilya (Arthasastra, c. 300 B.C.), and by nearly 3,000 years those of Machiavelli (The Prince, 1532): "Just as formerly thy ancestors were friends and not enemies of the Hittite country, now thou, Nigmad, shouldst be the enemy of my enemy and the friend of my friend." Many other treaties were concluded between States in ancient times, whereby, on a footing of at least formal equality, they settled temporarily political and economic issues between each other.

More frequently matters were settled by the sword. Policies of force were encouraged by the disinclination of States in antiquity to consider any community other than those closely related to themselves as civilized and, therefore, worthy of being treated on a footing of equality. The Hebrews waged many of their wars as wars of extermination. The Greek city States were willing to establish close relations only among themselves and, whenever there was a choice, the Romans treated none but their Latin cousins as equals. The rest of the world were barbarians to whom the Roman Empire brought arma et leges. They were merely fit to become incorporated into the Roman world empire or to be objects of policing operations on its fringes.

Although several systems of international law, in various stages of arrested development, existed in antiquity and, simultaneously or subsequently, in other parts of the world, present-day international law has its roots in medieval Europe. It might be thought that the hierarchical order of the Middle Ages was incompatible with the existence of international law, which requires the co-existence of equal and independent communities. Actually, the pyramidal structure of feudalism, culminating in Pope and emperor as spiritual and temporal heads of Western Christendom, was hardly ever fully realized. It left ample scope for relations on a footing of equality between what were often in fact independent States. This applied especially to kingdoms like England and Scotland which existed on the fringe of the Holy Roman Empire. Even within the Empire, relations between the more powerful feudal princes, independent knights and free cities were regulated by rules which in all but form were indistinguishable from those of international law and formed a system of quasi-international law.

In the absence of specific rules, Roman law and canon law, in the guise of natural law, were adapted to the relations between such entities. In a number of treaties, principles and standards were developed which, at a later stage, were taken for granted and gradually grew into rules of international customary law. When the Holy Roman Empire began to crumble and an increasing number of States became independent of the Emperor in law as well as in fact, chancelleries had at their disposal a reasonable number of standard forms of treaties and even fragmentary rules of international customary law which had long been in use, even though they were not yet necessarily considered as a branch of law separate from municipal law. This continuity, as well as the gradual character of the transition from the medieval order to the modern State, deserves being emphasized, as these significant aspects of the evolution of present-day international law have been unduly neglected.

[1] By GEORG SCHWARZENBERGER, excerpted from: 1 A MANUAL OF INTERNATIONAL LAW 3–7 (4th ed. 1960). Reprinted by permission.

2. Medieval Customary Law[2]

At variance with the modern type of commercial treaties, medieval arrangements were little or not at all concerned with tariff problems. The duties and fees charged to foreign merchants were varied and, for the most part, were determined by custom. One-sided and arbitrary increases were a matter of small concern, because protectionist and other mercantilist policies were on the whole foreign to the period; loss of profit to the local ruler through reduction or discontinuance of foreign trade apparently was a sufficient deterrent to such increases. Still, in the practice of Italian city-states duties were sometimes fixed or reduced by way of agreement – an anticipation of modern tariff arrangements.

In addition to commercial conventions in the Middle Ages there were monetary treaties between neighboring princes or municipalities aimed at creating common standards of coinage, or at least rendering the currency of one country legal tender within the other. A multipartite standardizing agreement of this type, the Rappenmunzbund concluded between rulers of the Upper Rhine area, persisted through almost two centuries, a rare phenomenon for the Middle Ages. In the international area monetary understandings between England and Burgundy (for the Netherlands) made their appearance toward the end of the Middle Ages.

The most-favored-nation clause, which grants to a nation rights conceded, or to be conceded in the future, to other nations, is also found in the Middle Ages, though by no means so often as in modern times. It occurred more frequently in unilateral franchises than in treaties, and it differed from the modern type also in that it was little concerned with customs duties; its subject matter was rather the personal rights of the merchants. Moreover, the medieval clauses dealt, on the whole, only with the extending of favors to specific commercial rivals of the grantee, whereas the modern clause encompasses favors granted to any nation whatsoever.

The "national-treatment" clause so common in modern commercial treaties, which confers, in specified matters, upon foreigners the rights enjoyed by nationals, is found here and there in franchises granted by medieval rulers; in a few instances the clause was embodied in treaties.

Across the shipping lanes of the Mediterranean there unfolded a flourishing commerce with the Arabic countries. On the Christian side Pisa, Genoa, Venice, and Aragon were in the fore; among the Moslem countries, Egypt, Syria, Tunis, and Morocco. The ecclesiastical anti-Saracen legislation failed to stop this traffic. As far as Egypt, center of Moslem fighting power, was concerned, the treaties fell little short of betrayal to the cause of Christianity. It was with Egypt that the first important agreement was concluded by Pisa, in 1154; and in 1208 Venice obtained from Egypt special trade facilities in return for her alleged good services in restraining the crusaders from an attack upon Egypt.

The Moslem rulers were perfectly willing to make large concessions. Of course they were greatly interested in the importation of arms and lumber, but they also found victuals, textiles, jewels, and other Western products most valuable, apart from manifold financial profits. Islamic doctrine was no impediment to a grand-scale admission of Christians. In the dawn of antiquity Amasis of Egypt granted autonomous settlement to the Greeks; now, the Italians were in a situation similar to that of the Greeks. These autonomous settlements are ordinarily called "capitulations" – a misleading term explained by the fact that they were divided into numbered *capitula* (brief chapters). In most cases they took the form of a unilateral grant or franchise, which apparently appealed to the Moslem ruler's feeling of grandeur and generosity. Unilateral franchises were revocable – a point which, in later centuries, Western diplomats and jurists contested: it was a good thing to enjoy the advantages of unilaterality but not so good to be bothered with its reverse side. The question, however, was purely academic as the Moslem rulers were by that time too weak to experiment in revocation. In the eighteenth and nineteenth centuries the capitulations were gradually transformed into commercial treaties, but without entirely expunging the lack of reciprocity. That inequality was removed only in the twentieth century.

The capitulations bore witness to the skill of Western draftsmen. They tended to become more and more elaborate in the course of the centuries. Their core was – in this respect the lack of reciprocity is particularly striking – the permission for citizens of the co-contracting country to establish and maintain, under their own law and administration, a settlement in the territory of the Moslem ruler. (The Italian term *fondaco* may refer to the whole settlement, or to an isolated part of it, or to its main building.) The head of the settlement was called "consul." Usually he was appointed by the home government; a consul electus, chosen by the settlers – a rare case – had more limited authority. Generally, the consular powers, which could be delegated, were judicial as well as administrative. Consular jurisdiction encompassed litigation between citizens of the home country; sometimes it extended to litigation between Christians generally, and even to claims raised by a Moslem against a national of the consul. Claims against Moslems had invariably to be submitted to the local cadi. With certain exceptions, criminal proceedings against the co-

---

[2] By ARTHUR NUSSBAUM, excerpted from: A CONCISE HISTORY OF THE LAW OF NATIONS 32–33, 55–58 (rev. ed. 1954). Reprinted by permission.

nationals of the consul were included in his jurisdiction. In addition, he had diplomatic functions inasmuch as he enjoyed the right to appear from time to time before the Moslem ruler. On the other hand, he was long considered—at least by the Egyptian sultans—as a hostage for the good behavior of his countrymen.

Public worship of Christian faith was invariably granted to members of the settlements, and they were permitted to have their own graveyards. If a Christian died, the succession to his property would take place under his home law without any droit d'aubaine on the part of the Moslem ruler. The privileged status of foreigners extended into other fiscal fields. Numerous exceptions in their favor were provided with regard to the customary import taxes (10 percent), export taxes (5 percent), and sundry imports. But there as much uncertainty on this score, for the remarkable reason that the legalitv of customs duties which are not mentioned in the Koran was subject to doubt.

Other typical features of the capitulations were the prohibition of reprisals, especially in the case of a foreigner's insolvency; the abolition of the law of shipwreck; and reciprocal promises of severe measures against pirates—who, nevertheless, remained the curse of Mediterranean commerce far beyond the Middle Ages. Custom was generally called upon to implement the rights and duties established under the capitulation. This created for the Europeans another opportunity to expand their position by representing as "custom" what could not be proved from the texts. Of course no similar rights were accorded to the Moslem party in the European area. That lack of reciprocity, already referred to, is characteristic of the capitulations.

Agreements in many respects similar were concluded by the Italian city-states with the Christian states of the East—the Byzantine Empire, Lesser Armenia and the short-lived crusader states such as the Latin kingdom of Jerusalem. These agreements differed in character from the "capitulations," according to the political factors involved, and were more varied. Privileges in the crusader territory were granted mainly as a reward for naval or other military aid in war, or as a means of obtaining such aid. The Venetians, with their tremendous naval might, sometimes nearly emasculated the local sovereignty by such agreements. In Constantinople and elsewhere they appointed "bailiffs"—political agents with an almost princely status and with functions far exceeding the consular ones; some resembled modern consuls general in being superior to the ordinary Venetian consuls. The Christian rulers in the East generally granted autonomy to the subjects. An interesting detail is presented by a privilege granted to Pisa in 1165 by Amaury (Almarich), Latin King of Jerusalem. Amaury decreed that an area between the port and the city of Tyrus should be held open for all men of the world regardless of language or nationality. This sounds like an early profession of the "open door" principle. The motives behind the decree are not clear. In any event it remained isolated, and nothing is known regarding the effects of his apparent generosity.

While the "capitulations" and their all-Christian counterparts are matters of the past, their sequels still affect the international law of our day. The capitulations are the origin of the consular institution. In medieval Italy the highest officials of cities or guilds, who had both judicial and non-judicial functions, used the title "consul," so august in antiquity. About the middle of the twelfth century, as the tasks of the city governments grew, consuls of a special type appeared—the mercantile consuls, heads of merchant guilds—first in Italian municipalities including Milan and Pisa and later in other Mediterranean trade centers, such as Narbonne and Barcelona. They exercised judicial jurisdiction over the members of their guilds and, on the basis of actual or presumed submission, over foreigners, particularly in maritime cases. The mercantile consuls, then, were originally domestic officials; and it is to them that the name Consolato del Mare refers. When autonomous Italian settlements were founded in Oriental countries, it was only natural to extend the title to the heads of these settlements. Officials of the new "overseas" type soon came to be employed also between Western countries. As early as the thirteenth century consuls were sent, for instance, by Genoa to Spanish Seville, and by Marseilles to Genoa. This suggests the emergence of a new Western type of consul with a narrower range of functions.

3. The New State System[3]

The disintegration of the Christian Commonwealth of Europe greatly stimulated the growth of international law and its development both as a separate branch of law and as an alternative to international anarchy. Two other major trends also contributed to the shaping of international law. Under the impact of political, spiritual, economic and technical revolutions, by which the medieval community was transformed into the capitalist world, strong incentives were created towards greater expansion and centralization of the then existing European inter-State system. Compared with the Europe of the sixteenth century, only a relatively small number of independent States have survived. But, as European States spread their nets all over the globe, other States formed themselves on their pattern in other continents.

In the course of the expansion of international law from

---

[3] by GEORG SCHWARZENBERGER, excerpted from: 1 A MANUAL OF INTERNATIONAL LAW 3–7 (4th ed. 1960). Reprinted by permission.

the "public law of Europe," as it was often called in State papers of the eighteenth and early nineteenth centuries, intermediate stages were frequently preferred to either outright subjection and incorporation of the territories of outsiders or their acceptance as full subjects of international law.

In some cases it was impossible or inopportune to conquer such countries. Nevertheless, it appeared desirable to settle in a binding form questions of interest to European States as, for instance, in their relations with the Barbary States. It was then assumed that such States could be parties to treaties, but that they were not bound by the more intimate rules of international customary law as applied between European powers.

In other cases, European States considered it desirable to establish trade relations or to give protection to what were called appropriately enough merchant adventurers or to missionaries who were sent out to countries with different civilizations in the Near, Middle and Far East. Capitulation treaties provided means of harmonizing discrepancies in standards of conduct, especially in the administration of civil and criminal law. In this way, foreigners resident in Asian and African countries were exempted from local territorial jurisdiction and made amenable to that of their home States, which exercised jurisdiction on the spot through their consular courts or in their own colonial possessions nearby.

Finally, matters might be left in the hands of colonial companies such as the Dutch and English East India Companies. They were not considered as themselves endowed with international personality, but were regarded as organs of the States which had granted them their charters. They had, however, wide discretionary powers and used them in concluding treaties with, or making war on, local rulers. Some of these treaties acknowledged the sovereignty and international personality of the local princes. Others are more akin to public contracts under the municipal law of the colonial power concerned. Today, these aspects of international law are primarily of historical significance. They are by-products of the transition of the European State system from periods of early colonialism and imperialism to the era of slowly maturing world society.

4. Expansion to the Far East[4]

Up through the nineteenth century, the policy of the great Asiatic nations had been based on a strong determination to maintain the integrity of their indigenous culture and religion by rigid preclusion of European and Christian influences. Chinese seclusion was first encroached upon by the Sino-English Treaty of Nanking (1842), which opened five Chinese ports to foreign trade and established a status of equality between Chinese and British officials of the same rank. Similar treaties with other powers followed, gradually augmenting the number of "treaty ports." The system of Sino-European treaties, as it developed during the century, was characterized by marked inequality to the detriment of China, after the model of the Near East "capitulations." The treaties, more or less forcibly imposed upon China, had as their objective the attainment of privileges for foreigners on Chinese territory, without reciprocal concessions to the Chinese. As a result, Chinese independence was heavily impaired. The nationals of the treaty powers in China were placed under the consular jurisdiction of their countries; they obtained self-government in certain Chinese settlements; China had to grant to the foreign powers most-favored-nation treatment without reciprocity; her tariff autonomy was destroyed; Chinese converts to Christianity were placed under treaty protection, etc. As a semblance of reciprocal concession one may list a provision of the Treaty of Nanking which made the consuls responsible to China for the good behavior of their nationals – a feature reminiscent of medieval conditions in the near East. The whole device worked under great strain and under innumerable frictions which, owing to China's weakness, led more and more to virtual seizures of Chinese territory by foreign powers. In this situation, the United States, through Secretary of State Hay, intervened in 1899 by proclaiming the principle of the "Open Door," that is, of equal opportunity for all nations in Chinese trade. The program, involving maintenance of Chinese territorial integrity, was unopposed by the other powers, diplomatically at least, though Russia's answer was ambiguous. Like the Monroe Doctrine, the Open Door principle constituted a settled standard of policy rather than a rule of law.

Japanese seclusion was first shaken in 1853 and 1854 by the famous expedition of the American, Commodore Perry; by heavy pressure, he obtained a restricted treaty of peace and amity from the Shogun, then Japan's actual ruler. As in the Chinese situation, further agreements with other powers followed – all in the Chinese pattern one-sidedly favoring the foreign power. However, the Emperor (Mikado), who still held some authority, showed himself hostile to the treaties, and, in accord with the general mood of the Japanese people, embarked upon the expulsion of the foreigners. Only in 1865, after military and naval measures taken by the powers, did he assent to the treaties. Following the accession to the throne of Emperor Meiji and the breakdown of the shogunate in 1867, Japan resolutely accepted

---

[4] By ARTHUR NUSSBAUM, from: A CONCISE HISTORY OF THE LAW OF NATIONS 194–96 (rev. ed. 1954). Reprinted by permission.

the new situation in order to turn it to the country's advantage. As a result of her general policy of modernization, Japan soon won equal footing with the treaty powers through the abrogation of foreign consular jurisdiction and of other discriminatory features of the treaties. After the victorious peace of Shimonoseki with China in 1895, she rose to the rank of a Great Power, alone among the non-Christian countries.

The unlocking of Siam to Western trade and influence started in 1825 by a narrowly limited treaty with England, which was replaced by one giving England broader powers, along the lines of the Chinese model. The dramatic incidents which marked Chinese and Japanese relations with the Western countries were absent from the Siamese scene.

The expansion of the Western law of nations to the Far East did not involve a fusion of European and Asiatic ideas. The European conception prevailed as to substance and form. The Oriental nations had small success instilling their cherished notions regarding ranks and ceremonials into the new agreements. Nevertheless, the process of expansion in itself divested the law of nations more and more of its "European" character.

5. The United States Looks Outward[5]

The exhilarating feeling of sudden and decisive victory in the Spanish-American War of 1898 stimulated within all sectors of the United States an increased awareness of international affairs. Of course, prior to that brief War, the United States had not been totally dormant within the cocoon of isolationism spun by Washington's Farewell Address and the Monroe Doctrine. The country had engaged in at least two formal international wars with significant hemispheric consequences: the War of 1812 and the Mexican-American War of 1846. The former can be broadly interpreted as an attempt by the new government to consolidate its recently won independence from Great Britain. The latter was an imperialist enterprise designed to seize most of what is today the southwestern section of the United States in an effort to fulfill the country's so-called "manifest destiny" of complete continental expansion. The numerous expeditions against American Indians could also fit neatly within the category of continual imperialist expansion. Yet, the net effect of these disputes was relatively insignificant when compared to the astounding ramifications for the United States and the world at large ensuing from the Spanish-American War of 1898.

The decrepit Spanish Empire was almost instantaneously dissolved, and the United States assumed its imperial mantle in Cuba, Puerto Rico, Guam, and the Philippines. Acquisition of the former two colonial territories situated the United States in the heart of the Caribbean where it could control the gateway to the isthmus of Central America. From there it was an almost inevitable imperial step to American intervention into Colombia in order to instigate and secure the independence of Panama for the purpose of facilitating construction of a canal; to promulgation of the Roosevelt Corollary to the Monroe Doctrine in order to justify U.S. economic receivership for the Dominican Republic, Honduras, Nicaragua, and Haiti; and to repeated military intervention into and occupation of Cuba pursuant to the Platt Amendment. These developments paved the way for the subsequent history of persistent imperialist interventions by the United States into the affairs of Central American and Caribbean countries that has chronically plagued U.S. foreign policy toward the region adjoining the Panama Canal for the past three-quarters of a century.

On the other side of the world, the decision to take over the Philippines propelled the United States directly into the affairs of the Orient and therefore indirectly into the European balance of power system, since the major powers of Europe had already staked out their respective colonial claims in the Far East. American efforts to preserve and extend its geopolitical and economic position in that region of the world, especially the maintenance of its so-called Open Door policy in regard to China, ultimately set the stage for serious and prolonged friction with Japan that culminated forty years later with the latter's sneak attack on Pearl Harbor and thus America's entry into World War II.

6. First Steps Toward Institutional Dispute Resolution[6]

Secretary of State John Hay instructed the American delegation to the First Hague Peace Conference of 1899 to propose a plan for the foundation of a permanent international tribunal organized along the lines of the United States Supreme Court, which would be endowed with the competence to decide all questions of disagreement between states, except those related to political independence or territorial integrity. But there proved to be little support among the conference participants for the conclusion of a

[5] By FRANCIS ANTHONY BOYLE, excepted from: WORLD POLITICS AND INTERNATIONAL LAW 23–24 (Durham: Duke University Press, 1985). Reprinted by permission.

[6] By FRANCIS ANTHONY BOYLE, excepted from: WORLD POLITICS AND INTERNATIONAL LAW 30–32 (Durham: Duke University Press, 1985). Reprinted by permission.

general multilateral pact calling for the obligatory arbitration of all disputes, let alone politically significant disputes, between states. Germany adamantly opposed the conclusion of a general multilateral pact calling for the obligatory arbitration of even a limited number of certain categories of disputes possessed of relatively inconsequential political significance. Consequently, the First Hague Peace Conference had to content itself with the establishment of the purely voluntary system of arbitration known as the Permanent Court of Arbitration. The Permanent Court was (and still is) not a real "court" of arbitration, but only a list of distinguished jurists appointed by the contracting powers to the convention from which parties to a dispute that cannot be settled by means of diplomacy could, if they so desire, choose an arbitrator or panel of arbitrators to settle the dispute in accordance with a fixed set of procedural rules.

Between 1899 and 1908 some seventy-seven arbitration treaties were concluded by the various countries of the world, and all but twelve provided for some sort of reference to the Permanent Court of Arbitration. Such references were generally subject to reservations concerning certain categories of disputes, typically excluding from arbitration matters involving a state's independence, vital interests, honor, sovereignty, or the rights of non-contracting parties.

By the time of the Second Hague Peace Conference in 1907, Germany had dropped its objection to the principle of obligatory arbitration, but then insisted that the proper approach should be the negotiation of a series of bilateral arbitration treaties between interested states instead of the conclusion of a general multilateral pact. Following the Conference, U.S. Secretary of State Elihu Root promptly negotiated a series of twenty-five general arbitration treaties on behalf of the United States, all of which were ratified by the Senate.

Prior to the outbreak of the First World War, several major international disputes were submitted to the Permanent Court of Arbitration at The Hague, and the U.S. government played the lead role of midwife in bringing this institution to life. From the perspective of maintaining international peace and security, the most significant of the Hague Court's arbitrations proved to be the Venezuela Preferential Case pitting Germany, Great Britain and Italy against Venezuela, and the Casablanca Case (France v. Germany). Pressure by President Roosevelt to refer part of the former controversy surrounding Venezuela's default on its public debts to arbitration before the Permanent Court and the rest of the dispute to mixed commissions contributed to the successful termination of on-going military hostilities conducted by Germany, Italy, and Great Britain in an effort to forcefully collect on their respective nationals' monetary claims against the Venezuelan government. Their action threatened to draw the United States directly into the conflict in order to protect Venezuela from this anticipatory breach of the Monroe Doctrine.

Likewise, the Casablanca incident of 1908 was universally considered to have concerned the honor of France and Germany, and given the militaristic tenor of the times could have rapidly escalated into a general war in Europe because of their respective memberships in competing alliance systems. Thus, the resolution of both disputes by the Permanent Court contributed to the termination of one concerted military operation and to the prevention of one war. History must judge it to have been a phenomenal success and recognize the positive role played by international law and organizations in the amelioration of the generally violent conditions of world politics prior to World War I.

B. Illustrative Historical Topics

1. State Jurisdiction[7]

Traditional international law principles relating to jurisdiction became well-established by the eighteenth century. The governing principle was that of territoriality. Based on a conceptual framework developed largely by the Dutch scholar Ulrich Huber in the sixteenth century and embedded in the U.S. legal system by Joseph Story, the scheme was simple enough. The world was carved up into jurisdictional spheres corresponding to the territories of states. A state was entitled to exercise prescriptive jurisdiction regarding any conduct within its territory; conversely, a state could not exercise jurisdiction over conduct occurring outside of its boundaries, except with regard to its own nationals.

Jurisdictional conflicts generally were avoided under this territorial system so long as (1) situations in which conduct in one state would have had significant consequences in other states were comparatively rare, and (2) legal systems generally attached legal consequences to conduct only when the effects that were constituent elements of the offense were closely related both temporally and spatially to the conduct causing them. As long as states generally were content to regulate the conduct of individuals in their direct relations with other individuals, there was little disintegrative pressure on the territorial scheme.

During the late nineteenth century, new factors began to threaten this neat system. Developments in transportation and communications made it possible for persons acting in one state quickly and effectively to cause effects in other states. Moreover, the growing concentration of business and the internationalization of the world economy meant that actions taken in one state could have multiple

---

[7] By DAVID J. GERBER, excerpted from: *Beyond Balancing: International Law Restraints on the Reach of National Law,* 10 YALE JOURNAL OF INTERNATIONAL LAW 185, 194–95 (1985). Reprinted by permission.

effects far beyond that state's borders. A cartel arrangement in one state, for example, could significantly affect prices and even national welfare in distant states.

The factors led to an expansion of the territorial principle to include the so-called "objective" territorial principle. This notion allows states to prosecute and punish for crimes commenced outside its borders but consummated within them. By means of this principle a state in which a criminal act was completed would not be deprived of jurisdiction to prosecute the crime. The objective territorial principle, however, has been the source of extraordinary difficulties. As originally conceived, its application was limited to situations in which some element of a crime actually occurred in the regulating state. But problems were created by the lack of clear conceptual limits to the objective territoriality principle.

Nevertheless, at least as originally conceived, the objective territorial principle was consistent with territoriality, for it was applied only when the consequences of conduct could be "localized." So long as an offense could only be "consummated" in one place, the functional effectiveness of the territorial paradigm was unimpaired. Jurisdiction was generally conferred on only two states – the state in which the conduct occurred and the state in which the consequences were localized. As the consequences of traditional criminal acts by individuals are generally localizable in this respect, use of the objective territoriality principle in relation to such violations created little risk of jurisdictional conflicts and left the territorial framework intact.

The territorial system was undermined only when states began to define crimes in terms of effects which could easily be achieved across significant distances and in many different places at the same time. Such effects were not "localizable" to any particular place because the conduct causing them started a series of consequences that could lead in many directions. For example, cartel arrangements in one country could create distant and multiple effects. Thus, when cartel behavior was proscribed, the territoriality principle could not accommodate the situation, for these effects were not localizable. As a result, it was primarily the advent of economic regulation – specifically, antitrust regulation – which undermined the territorial system.

2. War[8]

In the fourth century B.C., a Chinese writer, Sun Tzu, in a book entitled The Art of War, described the prevailing customs of sparing the wounded, the elderly, and those *hors de combat.* He developed a strikingly comprehensive theory, bordering on what we would now term absolute liability, of command responsibility for breaches. About the same period in the Hindu civilization, a body of rules regulating war on land was embodied in the Book of Manu. In the second millennium B.C., the Egyptians had treaties with certain other peoples such as the Summerians regulating war and the manner in which it was to be initiated. The ancient Greeks and the Romans had rules on sanctuary, the treatment of wounded and that of prisoners. The Muslim practice of war (since 623) is carefully regulated in terms of its conduct, as per the Koran, and has been recorded in Shaybani's teachings in the eighth century. In the Middle Ages the Catholic Church in several landmark councils set forth proscriptions regulating the conduct of war, among which are: the First Lateran Council of 1122, the Second Council of 1139 (which particularly forbade the use of crossbow), the Third Council of 1215, the First Council of Lyon of 1245 and the Second council of Lyon of 1274. These Councils were essentially concerned with the crusades but also regulated the conduct of war.

The ancient Greeks developed an elaborate code based on "universal law" designed to contain the suffering and destruction of warfare. Ironically it was the "barbarian" King Xerxes who, upon learning that the Greeks had murdered some of his envoys, refused a suggestion of retaliation on the ground that the Greeks had violated the law of all mankind, and that he would not do the very thing of which he accused them.

Other diverse and ancient societies have also sought to regulate the use of force in armed conflict. Research has shown strict limitations on the use of force by codes among the Mayas until approximately the sixth century A.D., in tenth century Japan, and among the fifteenth and sixteenth century Incas. In medieval Europe the codes of chivalry and the law of arms restricted violence to the class of knights, as well as prohibiting absolutely such weapons as the crossbow, the arballst, the harquebus, and poison gas.

Even the practice of private reprisal was historically confined. The purpose of reprisal is to make the enemy desist from continuing illegal practices of warfare, by demonstrating a willingness and ability to use such a method in return. Such a practice was not lightly resorted to, however, and the thirteenth-century English practice included ten conditions precedent, one of which was a demand for satisfaction made and refused. Only after the ten conditions were satisfied would the Crown grant letters of reprisal, and even then the authorization was limited and defined.

In 1621, Gustavus Adolphus of Sweden promulgated his "Articles of Military Lawwes to be Observed in the Warres," providing in the general article for example, that, "no Colonel or Captaine shall command his soldiers to do any unlawful thing; which who so does, shall be punished according to the discretion of the Judge."

In the United States, the first Articles of War were

---

[8] By M. CHERIF BASSIOUNI, from: INTERNATIONAL CRIMINAL LAW: A DRAFT INTERNATIONAL CRIMINAL CODE 5–11 (1980). Reprinted by permission.

promulgated in 1775 and contained explicit provision for the punishment of officers who failed to keep "good order" among the troops. This provision was retained and strengthened in the Articles of War of 1806 and served as the basis for prosecutions for conduct against the law of nations. The most noteworthy regulation is the United States Lieber Code of 1863. Since then, all countries with army regulations have promulgated similar regulations particularly after the Geneva conventions of 12 August, 1949, which must be disseminated to military personnel as well as to the general public.

The international criminalization of violations of the laws, rules and regulations of war evolved gradually, and so did the international prosecution of initiators of unjust or aggressive wars and violators of the regulations on the conduct of war.

The first prosecution for initiating an unjust war is reported to have been in Naples in 1268 when Conradin Von Hohenstafen was put to death for that reason, while the first reported international prosecution for war crimes was of one Peter Von Hagenbach in Breisach, Germany, in 1474. Von Hagenbach was tried before a tribunal of twenty-eight judges from the allied states of the Holy Roman Empire. While he was not tried for crimes committed during wars, this trial is significant in that Von Hagenbach was stripped of his knighthood by an international tribunal, which found him guilty of murder, rape, perjury and other crimes "against the law of God and man" in the execution of a military occupation.

In 1689, James II of England, though then in exile, relieved one Count Rosen of all further military duties, not for the failure of his mission, but because his siege of Londonderry was outrageous, and included the murder of innocent civilians.

Among the landmark cases in history are those which occurred during the American Revolution, including the trial of Captain Nathan Hale, by a British military court, and Major John Andre by a board of officers appointed by George Washington. Following the American Civil War, Confederate Major Henry Wirz was tried for his role in the death of several thousand Union prisoners in the Andersonville prison. The United States also convened war crimes tribunals after the Spanish-American War and the occupation of the Philippines.

After World War I, the Treaty of Versailles in 1919 established the punishability of war criminals; ordered Germany to hand over to the Allies all Germans accused of war crimes to be tried by military tribunals; and allowed the Allies to establish national war crimes tribunals. It also ordered the prosecution of Kaiser Wilhelm II by an international tribunal. A special body was created to report on the persons to be prosecuted and the "Commission on the Responsibility of the Authors of the War and on enforcement of Penalties" issued its report on 3 February 1920. In it, 896 names were submitted by the Allies to Germany of alleged war criminals, but for political reasons that list shrank to 45 and, of these, Germany tried only 12 before the Supreme Court of the Reich sitting in Leipzig, six of whom were acquitted. Article 228 was not applied because Germany refused to extradite its nationals.

The period between World War I and World War II witnessed a lull in the efforts to regulate this type of conduct. During World War II it became apparent, particularly after the tide of the war came to favor the Allies, that prosecution of those who initiated the aggressive war, carried it out and committed war crimes (and other atrocities which were later labeled "crimes against humanity") would be prosecuted. The first such indication came in the Allies' Moscow Declaration of 30 October 1943, followed by Agreement for the Prosecution and Punishment of the Major War Criminals of the European Axis (the London Charter of 8 August 1945), which established the first of history's two international military tribunals at Nuremberg; the second at Tokyo was based on a 1946 statute. In addition to these two internationally constituted military tribunals, the Allies established military tribunals in their respective zones of occupation. This was decreed under Control Council Ordinance No. 10 of 20 December 1945, which provided that each occupying power could try lower-level German officials. The Nuremberg War Crimes Trials prosecuted 19 major war criminals. Prior, during and after the Nuremberg Trials the United States convicted 1,814 (450 executed) in its occupying zone; Great Britain 1,085 (240 executed), France 2,107 (109 executed), and the USSR an estimated 10,000 (number of persons executed unavailable). The total numbers of additional prosecutions per allied power as reported by the United Nations War Crimes Commission were: United States, 809; Britain, 524; Australia, 256; France, 254; The Netherlands, 30; Poland, 24; Norway, 9; Canada, 4; China, 1.

In addition, several Allied nationals were prosecuted for collaboration with the enemy and for commission of war crimes and crimes against humanity. Germany has taken on the task of prosecuting war criminals since the end of the Nuremberg trials and continues to handle such cases through its municipal courts. The only landmark case prosecuted outside Germany of a major war criminal since 1946 was the Eichmann case. That prosecution was conducted by the State of Israel on the basis of the theory of universality of jurisdiction in international crimes which were essentially those of the Nuremberg Trials in respect to "crimes against humanity."

The International Military Tribunal for the Far East started its proceedings in 1946, and 28 persons were tried before it, of whom seven were sentenced to death. Some of these decisions were appealed to the United States Supreme

Court, but the appeals failed. In addition to the Tokyo war crimes trials, the United States set up special military commissions in the Philippines to try Japanese officers for war crimes and the United States Supreme Court affirmed the decisions of those commissions. It is noteworthy that the only case brought against one of the World War II Allies for war crimes was brought by Japanese citizens for the use by the USA of atomic weapons but the case was rejected by the Supreme court of Japan on jurisdictional grounds.[9]

In these internationally constituted tribunals as well as in related nationally constituted war crimes prosecutions, the basic principle of accountability was that of individual responsibility stemming from international legal obligations without the benefit of an absolute defense of "obedience to superior orders." The prosecutions occurring after World War I were for (1) violations of laws and customs of war as established in customary international law and compiled in the Hague Conventions, and (2) initiation and waging of aggressive war in violation of international law. The prosecutions occurring after World War II were in the nature of personal and vicarious responsibility for (1) initiating and waging of aggressive war in violation of customary and conventional international law; (2) violation of laws and customs of war; (3) crimes against humanity (which were not specifically proscribed by international law).

In World War I prosecutions, the principal argument against the aggression charge was its lack of enforceability as an international obligation upon Germany. It was argued that these international proscriptions did not constitute normative proscriptions of a criminal nature and that indeed no penalties were ever promulgated.

To circumvent some of the arguments, the 1945 Statute of the International Military Tribunal established in Articles VII and VIII that heads of state would not benefit from the Act of State Doctrine and that it would be no defense to any person to have acted under "superior orders". This did not, however, eliminate the fact that prior to the enactment of the Charter such rules did not exist other than by extrapolation from limited historical practice which did not evidence an international customary practice. Furthermore, there were never any penalties fixed for the proscribed violations. To that extent the penalties imposed violated the principle of nulla poena sine lege. In addition, the prosecution for "crimes against humanity" was a novelty in international criminal law and constituted, therefore, an ex post facto provision. Thus, the main arguments presented for exoneration were that (1) the creation of the tribunal and its composition by Allied decree, since it was not in accordance with pre-existing international law, was invalid, (2) the crimes charged violated the principles of legality of criminal law in that they were ex post facto, and (3) the penalties imposed violated the principles of legality nulla poena sine lege.

Thus, during the prosecutions stemming from World War II, the arguments of ex post facto and nulla poena sine lege were consistently raised and were valid from a criminal law point of view.

To avoid such difficulties there was an effort after World War II to codify some of the principles and norms which had been challenged so as to avoid the recurrence of these arguments if subsequent prosecution were to take place. In 1947, the General Assembly of the United Nations adopted the International Law Commission's draft of a "Formulation of the Nuremberg Principles"; in 1948, the Genocide Convention was drafted; in 1949, the International Committee of the Red Cross opened for signature four Geneva Conventions; in 1953, the United Nations Committee on the Creation of an International Criminal Jurisdiction reported out a "Draft Statute for an International Criminal Court" (tabled); in 1954, the General Assembly was presented with the "Draft Code of Offenses against the Peace and Security of Mankind" (tabled); and in 1968, the General Assembly passed a resolution entitled "Convention on the Non-applicability of Statutes of Limitations to War Crimes and Crimes against Humanity". Events subsequent to these codifications did not, however, result in further prosecutions under the provisions of these rules or on the basis of the Nuremberg and Tokyo precedents. Only the United States prosecuted three officers for violations of United States military law in connection with the My Lai massacre in Vietnam.[10]

3. Humanitarian Intervention[11]

In the thirteenth century, St. Thomas Aquinas referred to the proposition that one sovereign has the right to intervene in the internal affairs of another "when the latter greatly mistreats its subjects."[12] Grotius recognized the doctrine in the seventeenth century:

---

9 Shimoda v. The State, 355 Hanrel Jiho (Supreme Court of Japan 7 December 1963).

10 The three officers were Col. Henderson (acquitted), Capt. Medina (acquitted), Lt. Calley (guilty, but conviction reversed). See TELFORD TAYLOR, NUREMBERG AND VIETNAM: AN AMERICAN TRAGEDY (1970).

11 By MICHAEL J. BAZYLER, excerpted from: *Reexamining the Doctrine of Humanitarian Intervention in Light of the Atrocities in Kampuchea and Ethiopia,* 23 STANFORD JOURNAL OF INTERNATIONAL LAW 547, 570–74 (1987). Reprinted by permission.

12 Fonteyne, *The Customary International Law Doctrine of Humanitarian Intervention: Its Current Validity Under the U.N. Charter,* 4 CAL. W. INT'L L.J. 203, 214 (1974).

> There is also another question, whether a war for the subjects of another be just, for the purpose of defending them from injuries by their ruler. Certainly it is undoubted that ever since civil societies were formed, the ruler of each claimed some especial right over his own subjects. [But if] a tyrant practices atrocities towards his subjects, which no just man can approve, the right of human social connection is not cut off in such case.[13]

Vattel also accepted the doctrine:

> If the prince, attacking the fundamental laws, gives his people a legitimate reason to resist him, if tyranny becomes so unbearable as to cause the Nation to rise, any foreign power is entitled to help an oppressed people that has requested its assistance.[14]

These scholars' pronouncements were based upon recognition of natural rights, which was then the basis of international law. In the nineteenth century, legal positivism replaced natural law as the foundation of international law; however, scholars still recognized the doctrine. Bernard, a British legal scholar, wrote that positive law "prohibits intervention. [However,] there may even be cases in which it becomes a positive duty to transgress positive law."[15] His contemporary, Harcourt, added: "Intervention is a question rather of policy than of [positive] law, and when wisely and equitably handled may be the higher policy of justice and humanity."[16]

In the first part of the twentieth century, a majority of writers continued to recognize the doctrine of humanitarian intervention. In 1904, Edwin Borchard, in an oft-quoted passage dealing with the related topic of the diplomatic protection of citizens abroad, stated: "Where a state under exceptional circumstances disregards certain rights of its own citizens, over whom presumably it has absolute sovereignty, the other states of the family of nations are authorized by international law to intervene on grounds of humanity."[17] And a year later, Oppenheim, whose work became one of the most authoritative and frequently cited treaties on international law, stated:

> Should a State venture to treat its own subjects or a part thereof with such cruelty as would stagger humanity, public opinion of the rest of the world would call upon the Powers to exercise intervention for the purpose of compelling such a State to establish a legal order of things within its boundaries sufficient to guarantee to its citizens an existence more adequate to the ideas of modern civilization.[18]

4. The Seabed[19]

The history of the ocean floor in international law is a very recent history. In the past, nations were not particularly concerned about the seabed. Cables had been laid across the deep seabed since the mid-nineteenth century, but except in coastal areas where they might foul fishing gear, they had spawned no conflicts requiring legal resolution. Some oceanographic research of the deep seabed had occurred; but like cable-laying, these caused no controversies. As a result, writers on international law paid little attention to the deep seabed.

Early writers on the seabed generally did not distinguish between the continental shelf and the deep seabed, although they were usually more concerned with the practical issues that might be posed by the use of the continental shelf. These early writers treated the seabed (including the continental shelf) either as a res nullius or as a res communis. This disagreement resulted from two conflicting analogies for the seabed. If the seabed is like unclaimed land, it is a res nullius; if it is like the high seas, it is a res communis. In practical terms, no nation can claim exclusive rights or sovereignty over a res communis or over the high seas, but a nation can acquire exclusive rights to a res nullius through occupation.

The res nullius theory enjoyed a surge of popularity in the late 1940's and early 1950's, when it was invoked to provide a legal justification for the then-novel national claims to the exclusive right to exploit natural resources, chiefly petroleum, on adjacent continental shelves. These res nullius advocates used as their primary example the longstanding recognition that certain nations had the exclusive right to exploit sedentary fisheries on the seabed contiguous to their territory but outside their territorial limits. These claims included the regulation of pearl fisheries by Ceylon, Australia, Mexico, and Colombia, and the Italian

---

[13] HUGO GROTIUS, DE JURE BELLI ESTI PACIS 438 (Whewell trans. 1853).

[14] 2 E. DE VATTEL, LE DROIT DES GENS, ch IV, para. 55 (Pradier-Fodere ed. 1863). Fonteyne points out that Vattel, in the immediately preceding paragraph, appears to state a contrary view. Fonteyne, supra n.12, at 215.

[15] M. BERNARD, ON THE PRINCIPLE OF NON-INTERVENTION 33–34 (1860).

[16] V. HARCOURT (HISTORICUS), LETTERS ON SOME QUESTIONS OF INTERNATIONAL LAW 14 (1863).

[17] EDWIN BORCHARD, THE DIPLOMATIC PROTECTION OF CITIZENS ABROAD 14 (1916).

[18] LASSA OPPENHEIM, INTERNATIONAL LAW 347 (1st ed. 1905).

[19] By JON VAN DYKE and CHRISTOPHER YUEN, excerpted from: *"Common Heritage" v. "Freedom of the High Seas": Which Governs the Seabed?* 19 SAN DIEGO LAW REVIEW 493, 514–18, 521–24, 529–30 (1982). Reprinted by permission.

and French regulation of coral in the Mediterranean. All of the sedentary fisheries were located in areas that are now juridically considered continental shelves.

The evolution of the "continental shelf doctrine" makes res nullius obsolete as an explanation for the regulation of sedentary species. In fact, occupation of a res nullius was thoroughly considered and emphatically rejected by the 1958 Convention on the Continental Shelf as the basis for national jurisdiction over the continental shelf. The coastal State has jurisdiction over the continental shelf because it is the "natural prolongation of its land territory."[20] The coastal State need make no occupation in order to obtain jurisdiction over the continental shelf; such jurisdiction exists "ipso facto and ab initio."[21] A prior act of occupation by another State cannot defeat the coastal State's jurisdiction.

Res nullius was politically unacceptable to the drafters of the Convention on the Continental Shelf because it would have permitted the first "occupant" to claim a continental shelf—even if the occupying nation was not adjacent to the shelf. For example, had the United States been the first to drill for oil in the North Sea, under a res nullius theory the United States would arguably have been able to claim exclusive rights to the North Sea oil fields. The rejection of res nullius for the continental shelf is now firmly established in international law.

Ambassador Arvid Pardo's famous address to the United Nations General assembly in 1967[22] triggered international concern over the legal status of the deep seabed. Pardo's speech and the publication of "The Mineral Resources of the Sea"[23] by John Mero, describing vast seabed resources as perhaps easily exploited, made the deep seabed an important issue in international law. While the issue of the deep seabed could be ignored in 1958, by the late 1960's it had to be directly confronted.

Within three years of Pardo's initiative, the international community had reached broad agreement, at least on a policy level, on several important principles concerning the seabed. The agreements were symbolized by the "common heritage of mankind" language that came to be employed whenever the seabed was discussed. Considerable disagreement still exists over both the exact meaning of these principles concerning the seabed and the legal authority of the documents in which these principles are expressed. Nevertheless, the international community had achieved an area of shared policy objectives regarding the deep seabed by the early 1970's.

In 1969, the United Nations General Assembly passed the Moratorium Resolution, by a vote of 62 to 28, with 28 abstentions, declaring that States and corporations are "bound to refrain" from seabed mining until an international regime can be established to govern this activity. The following year, the members of the General Assembly worked hard to hammer out a document that could achieve a broader consensus. The result was an ambiguous document, a negotiated compromise carefully worded to achieve the broadest possible consensus, called the "Declaration of Principles Governing the Seabed and the Ocean Floor, and the Subsoil Thereof, Beyond the Limits of National Jurisdiction" (Declaration of Principles). It was passed unanimously, by a vote of 108-0, with only 14 nations from Eastern Europe including the Soviet Union abstaining. Since the mid-1970's, the Soviet Union and the other Eastern European nationals have come to endorse the developing nations' interpretation of the Declaration of Principles.

Although the United States and other nations universally have endorsed the principle that the deep seabed beyond national jurisdiction is "the common heritage of mankind," it is often argued that the "common heritage" principle lacks enough specificity to import legal obligations. It is true that the words "common heritage" and their accompanying concept are not sufficiently detailed to create a seabed regime. The regime must be more fully defined by the current negotiations. But the principle of the "common heritage" does limit the kinds of actions that are currently permissible in the deep seabed.

Nations have agreed in the Declaration of Principles that the deep seabed is presently the common heritage of humankind. Nations have some freedom to negotiate what the common heritage means and its legal significance, but they cannot deny that the seabed is the common heritage of humankind. Minimally, the content of the "common heritage" concept requires that developing nations share genuine benefits from seabed exploitation even if they do not engage in the undersea mining activities themselves.

5. Human Rights

a. Origin and Development[24]

Most students of human rights trace the historical origins of the concept back to ancient Greece and Rome, where it was closely tied to the premodern natural law

---

[20] North Sea Continental Shelf Cases, [1969] I.C.J. 3, 19.

[21] *Id.*

[22] U.N. Doc. A/6695 (1967).

[23] J. MERO, THE MINERAL RESOURCE OF THE SEA (1965).

[24] By BURNS H. WESTON, excerpted from: *Human Rights*, ENCYCLOPEDIA BRITTANICA. Reprinted by permission.

doctrines of Greek Stoicism (the school of philosophy founded by Zeno of Citium, which held that a universal working force pervades all creation and that human conduct therefore should be judged according to, and brought into harmony with, the law of nature). The classic example drawn from the Greek literature, is that of Antigone, who, upon being reproached by Creon for defying his command not to bury her slain brother, asserted that she acted in accordance with the immutable laws of the gods.

In part because Hellenistic Stoicism played a key role in its formation and spread, Roman law may similarly be seen to have allowed for the existence of natural law and, with it, pursuant to the jus gentium ("law of nations"), certain universal rights that extended beyond the rights of citizenship. According to the Roman jurist Ulpian, for example, natural law was that which nature – not the state – assures to all human beings, Roman citizen or not.

It was not until after the Middle Ages, however, that natural law doctrines became closely associated with liberal political theories about natural rights. In Greco-Roman and medieval times, natural law doctrines taught mainly the duties, as distinguished from the rights, of "Man." Moreover, as evident in the writings of Aristotle and St. Thomas Aquinas, these doctrines recognized the legitimacy of slavery and serfdom and, in so doing, excluded perhaps the central most ideas of human rights as they are understood today – the ideas of freedom (or liberty) and equality.

For the idea of human (i.e., natural) rights to take hold as a general social need and reality, it was necessary that basic changes in the beliefs and practices of society take place, changes of the sort that evolved from about the 13th century to the Peace of Westphalia (1648), during the Renaissance and the decline of feudalism. When resistance to religious intolerance and political-economic bondage began the long transition to liberal notions of freedom and equality, particularly in relation to the use and ownership of property, then were the foundations of what today are called human rights truly laid. During this period, reflecting the failure of rulers to meet their natural law obligations as well as the unprecedented commitment to individual expression and worldly experience that was characteristic of the Renaissance, the shift from natural law as duties to natural law as rights was made. The teachings of Aquinas (1224/25-1274) and Hugo Grotius (1583-1645) on the European continent, and the Magna Carta (1215), the Petition of Right of 1628, and the English Bill of Rights (1689) in England, were proof of this change. All testified to the increasingly popular view that human beings are endowed with eternal and inalienable rights, never renounced when humankind "contracted" to enter the social from the primitive state and never diminished by the claim of "the divine right of kings."

It was primarily for the 17th and 18th centuries, however, to elaborate upon this modernist conception of natural law as meaning or implying natural rights. The scientific and intellectual achievements of the 17th century – the discoveries of Galileo and Sir Isaac Newton, the materialism of Thomas Hobbes, the rationalism of Rene Descartes and Gottfried Wilhelm Leibniz, the pantheism of Benedict de Spinoza, the empiricism of Francis Bacon and John Locke – encouraged a belief in natural law and universal order; and during the 18th century, the so-called Age of Enlightenment, a growing confidence in human reason and in the perfectibility of human affairs led to its more comprehensive expression. Particularly to be noted are the writings of the 17th-century English philosopher John Locke – arguably the most important natural law theorist of modern times – and the works of the 18th century Philosophes centered mainly in Paris, including Montesquieu, Voltaire, and Jean-Jacques Rousseau. Locke argued in detail, mainly in writings associated with the Revolution of 1688 (the Glorious Revolution), that certain rights self-evidently pertain to individuals as human beings (because they existed in "the state of nature" before humankind entered civil society); that chief among them are the rights to life, liberty (freedom from arbitrary rule), and property; that, upon entering civil society (pursuant to a "social contract"), humankind surrendered to the state only the right to enforce these natural rights, not the rights themselves; and that the state's failure to secure these reserved natural rights (the state itself being under contract to safeguard the interests of its members) gives rise to a right to responsible, popular revolution. The Philosophes, building on Locke and others and embracing many and varied currents of thought with a common supreme faith in reason, vigorously attacked religious and scientific dogmatism, intolerance, censorship, and social-economic restraints. They sought to discover and act upon universally valid principles harmoniously governing nature, humanity, and society, including the theory of the inalienable "rights of Man" that became their fundamental ethical and social gospel.

All this liberal intellectual ferment had, not surprisingly, great influence on the Western world of the late 18th and early 19th centuries. Together with the practical example of England's Revolution of 1688 and the resulting Bill of Rights, it provided the rationale for the wave of revolutionary agitation that then swept the West, most notably in North America and France. Thomas Jefferson, who had studied Locke and Montesquieu and who asserted that his countrymen were a "free people claiming their rights as derived from the laws of nature and not as the gift of their Chief Magistrate," gave poetic eloquence to the plain prose of the 17th century in the Declaration of Independence proclaimed by the 13 American Colonies on July 4, 1776: "We hold these truths to he self-evident, that all men are created equal, that they are endowed by their

Creator with certain unalienable Rights, that among these are Life, Liberty and the Pursuit of Happiness." Similarly, the Marquis de Lafayette, who won the close friendship of George Washington and who shared the hardships of the American War of Independence, imitated the pronouncements of the English and American revolutions in the Declaration of the Rights of Man and of the Citizen of August 16, 1789. Insisting that "men are born and remain free and equal in rights," the declaration proclaims that "the aim of every political association is the preservation of the natural and imprescriptible rights of man," identifies these rights as "Liberty, Property, Safety and Resistance to oppression," and defines "liberty" so as to include the right to free speech, freedom of association, religious freedom, and freedom from arbitrary arrest and confinement (as if anticipating the Bill of Rights added in 1791 to the Constitution of the United States of 1787).

In sum, the idea of human rights, called by another name, played a key role in the late 18th- and early 19th-century struggles against political absolutism. It was, indeed, the failure of rulers to respect the principles of freedom and equality, which had been central to natural law philosophy almost from the beginning, that was responsible for this development. In the words of Maurice Cranston, a leading student of human rights, "absolutism prompted man to claim rights precisely because it denied them."

The idea of human rights as natural rights was not without its detractors, however, even at this otherwise receptive time. In the first place, being frequently associated with religious orthodoxy, the doctrine of natural rights became less and less acceptable to philosophical and political liberals. Additionally, because they were conceived in essentially absolutist "inalienable," "unalterable," "eternal" terms, natural rights were found increasingly to come into conflict with one another. Most importantly, the doctrine of natural rights came under powerful philosophical and political attack from both the right and the left.

In England, for example, conservatives Edmund Burke and David Hume united with liberal Jeremy Bentham in condemning natural-rights doctrine, the former out of fear that public affirmation of natural rights would lead to social upheaval, the latter out of concern lest declarations and proclamations of natural rights substitute for effective legislation. In his *Reflections on the Revolution in France* (1790), Burke, a believer in natural law who nonetheless denied that the "rights of Man" could be derived from it, criticized the drafters of the Declaration of the Rights of Man and of the Citizen for proclaiming the "monstrous fiction" of human equality, which, he argued, serves but to inspire "false ideas and vain expectations in men destined to travel in the obscure walk of laborious life." Bentham, one of the founders of Utilitarianism and a nonbeliever, was no less scornful. "Rights," he wrote, "is the child of law; from real law come real rights; but from imaginary laws, from 'law of nature,' come imaginary rights. Natural rights is simple nonsense; natural and imprescriptible rights (an American phrase), rhetorical nonsense, nonsense upon stilts." Hume agreed with Bentham; natural law and natural rights. he insisted, are unreal metaphysical phenomena.

This assault upon natural law and natural rights, thus begun during the late 18th century, both intensified and broadened during the 19th and early 20th centuries. John Stuart Mill, despite his vigorous defense of liberty, proclaimed that rights ultimately are founded on utility. The German jurist Friedrich Karl von Savigny, England's Sir Henry Maine, and other historicalists emphasized that rights are a function of cultural and environmental variables unique to particular communities. And the jurist John Austin and the philosopher Ludwig Wittgenstein insisted, respectively, that the only law is "the command of the sovereign" (a phrase of Thomas Hobbes) and that the only truth is that which can be established by verifiable experience. By World War 1, there were scarcely any theorists who would or could defend the "rights of Man" along the lines of natural law. Indeed, under the influence of 19th-century German Idealism and parallel expressions of rising European nationalism, there were some – the Marxists, for example – who, although not rejecting individual rights altogether, maintained that rights, from whatever source derived, belong to communities or whole societies and nations preeminently. Thus did F.H. Bradley, the British Idealist, write in 1894: "The rights of the individual are today not worth serious consideration. The welfare of the community is the end and is the ultimate standard."

Yet, though the heyday of natural rights proved short, the idea of human rights nonetheless endured in one form or another. The abolition of slavery, factory legislation, popular education, trade unionism, the universal suffrage movement – these and other examples of 19th-century reformist impulse – afford ample evidence that the idea was not to be extinguished even if its transempirical derivation had become a matter of general skepticism. But it was not until the rise and fall of Nazi Germany that the idea of rights – human rights – came truly into its own. The laws authorizing the dispossession and extermination of Jews and other minorities, the laws permitting arbitrary police search and seizure, the laws condoning imprisonment, torture, and execution without public trial – these and similar obscenities brought home the realization that law and morality, if they are to be deserving of the name, cannot be grounded in any purely Utilitarian, Idealist, or other consequentialist doctrine. Certain actions are wrong, no matter what: human beings are entitled to simple respect at least.

Today, the vast majority of legal scholars, philosophers,

and moralists agree, irrespective of culture or civilization, that every human being is entitled, at least in theory, to some basic rights. Heir to the Protestant Reformation and to the English, American, French, Mexican, Russian, and Chinese revolutions, the last half of the 20th century has seen, in the words of human rights scholar Louis Henkin, "essentially universal acceptance of human rights in principle" such that "no government dares to dissent from the ideology of human rights today." Indeed, the last half of the 20th century may fairly be said to mark the birth of the international as well as the universal recognition of human rights. In the treaty establishing the United Nations, all members pledged themselves to take joint and separate action for the achievement of "universal respect for, and observance of: human rights and fundamental freedoms for all without distinction as to race, sex, language, or religion." In the Universal Declaration of Human Rights (1948), representatives from many diverse cultures endorsed the rights therein set forth "as a common standard of achievement for all peoples and all nations."

The catalog of rights set out in the Universal Declaration of Human Rights is scarcely less than the sum of all the important traditional political and civil rights of national constitutions and legal systems, including equality before the law; protection against arbitrary arrest; the right to a fair trial; freedom from ex post facto criminal laws; the right to own property; freedom of thought, conscience, and religion; freedom of opinion and expression; and freedom of peaceful assembly and association. Also enumerated are such economic, social, and cultural rights as the right to work and to choose one's work freely, the right to equal pay for equal work, the right to form and join trade unions, the right to rest and leisure, the right to an adequate standard of living, and the right to education.

The Universal Declaration, it must be noted, is not a treaty. It was meant to proclaim "a common standard of achievement for all peoples and all nations" rather than enforceable legal obligations. Nevertheless, it has acquired a status juridically more important than originally intended. It has been widely used, even by national courts, as a means of judging compliance with human rights obligations under the UN Charter.

b. Human Rights and Natural Law[25]

Although the classic international law scholars did not discuss "human rights" as such, the natural law viewpoint adopted by many of them was fertile soil for the modern seeds of human rights theory. Natural law stems from the teleological, nonexistential world-view of Aristotle, which was transmuted into Western moral thought by St. Thomas Aquinas, and taken up in international law by Suarez and Pufendorf, and to a lesser extent by Grotius and Vattel. The nonexistential view of law is simply that law must make sense as applied to human behavior. The notion of teleology in natural law is more than an empty formality to the effect that the mind's imaging of future events can impact upon present behavioral choices. Rather, it views a rule of law as something enacted by humans in order to fulfill certain human purposes.

The opposite view is positivism, which regards laws as equivalent to a program installed on a computer: the computer literally follows the commands, whether or not they make sense.[26] A naturalist does not equate laws with computer programs; he does not strive to obey the words of the law no matter what. A naturalist judge is a peculiarly human interpreter of law; he assumes that the law does not exist for itself but rather is a means toward the attainment of human ends.

No writer of international law has ever claimed that international law applies only to certain countries at certain times. Rather, the very universality of international law coheres with the universality of natural law. Natural law is neither time-specific or place-specific. Similarly, the very notion of "human rights" suggests that it does not vary with historical time or physical location. Anyone's list of basic human rights is invariably universal in its claim. Equality under the law or freedom of speech or equal rights for women, for example, are not claimed for a particular region or a collection of states in a certain economic classification; rather, these and other human rights are asserted to apply to all people whenever situated. The push toward universality in such claims is a natural concomitant of the naturalist perspective as it is of the notion of a general international law.

Were it not for the essential sameness of human nature, so insisted upon by St. Thomas and assumed today in the writings of Myres McDougal, W. Michael Reisman, and Lung-Chu Chen, natural law would be deflated into existentialism, with a person becoming a purposeless being in a world that, as far as anyone knows or cares, could be absurd. To the contrary, natural law is a non-arbitrary set of human standards that retains its meaning for all people at all times in all places. Its claim is, for this reason, arrogant; but any lesser claim sells humanity short.

---

[25] By ANTHONY D'AMATO, excerpted from: *What "Counts" as Law?* in Nicholas G. Onuf (ed.), LAW-MAKING IN THE GLOBAL COMMUNITY 83 (Durham: Carolina Academic Press, 1982). Reprinted by permission.

[26] For a general exposition of this point, see Anthony D'Amato, *On the Connection Between Law and Justice*, 26 U.C. DAVIS L.R. 527 (1993).

C. Intellectual History of the Law of Nations

1. The Classical Period[27]

Probably the most conspicuous evidence of the historic affiliation of Roman and international law is the familiar name "law of nations" (droit des gens, Volkerrecht), which is a literal translation of the Roman jus gentium. This relation requires a somewhat closer inquiry.

The ancestral Roman law, exclusively applicable to Roman citizens, was an extremely rigid, harsh, and narrow law sprung from the needs of a primitive rural community. It was characterized by the requirement of utterly cumbersome formalities for the few typical transactions which it recognized. Non-Romans remained theoretically outside the boundary of the law. This crude and archaic system, the jus civile, could not persist once Rome began to grow into a large emporium and to attract numerous foreigners. Their status was officially recognized in 242 B.C. when a special magistrate (praetor peregrinus) was instituted to take care, by appointed judges, of litigation between foreigners or between a foreigner and a citizen. Through this procedure, new and liberal rules evolved, amalgamating valuable elements of Roman as well as foreign law, and imbued with the principles of fairness and equity. The archaic formalities of the jus civile were to a great extent discarded; for instance, sales and contracts for sale were recognized if made orally, whereas the jus civile required for analogous transactions the presence of five witnesses and the observance of elaborate formalities. Gradually the new liberal body of rules was extended to litigation between Roman citizens and became, as the jus gentium – in contradistinction to the jus civile of old – the core of what we consider today as the classical Roman law.

The evolution of the jus gentium symbolizes Roman liberalism toward foreign culture; but this jus gentium had nothing to do with the modern law of nations, which, we know, means the law governing relations among independent states as such. The jus gentium is a national Roman law – though sometimes borrowed from foreign sources – and it is virtually "private law," that is, it is concerned with relationships among individuals.

At times, however, the Roman sources employ the juxtaposition of jus civile-jus gentium in a somewhat different sense. Particularly the Institutes, the first part of the Corpus Juris, start with an observation of the famous jurist Gaius (second century of the Christian Era), who contrasts the jus civile as a law established by each people (populus) for itself, with the jus gentium which is the law established among all men (homines) by natural reason and observed as it were by all nations (gentes). This amounts to a philosophical generalization of Roman conditions. While the historical jus gentium of the Romans only here and there utilizes foreign experience, the philosophical jus gentium as defined by Gaius is a comprehensive concept which includes rules and legal institutions (allegedly) found everywhere, such as matrimony, protection of property, or the wrongdoer's obligation for damages; it is a universal law. Among its subjects, matters of international character, like the inviolability of envoys or the law on spoils in war, are mentioned in the sources; but this, of course, is not tantamount to equating jus gentium and international law.

The distinction between jus civile and jus gentium was adopted and elaborated by medieval and post-medieval writers with the result that the ambiguity of the concept of jus gentium began to assume the significance of a technical term for the law among independent states. Unfortunately, the translation of this into "law of nations," or even into "international law" has been applied frequently to earlier references to jus gentium, though the former translation is misleading and the latter definitely inaccurate.

The problems of terminology and meaning were aggravated by another conception appearing in the Roman sources; viz., the one of natural law or law of nature (jus naturale). Here Greek tradition enters. The idea of natural law, that is, of universally applicable rules derived from right reason, is owed to Greek, and particularly to Stoic, philosophy of the third century B.C. Stoic philosophy found numerous followers in Rome, among them the jurist Cicero who did much to popularize Greek philosophy in his country. Thus natural law became familiar in Roman jurisprudence. The Corpus Juris itself contains a number of references to natural law and to natural reason as a source of law, though they hardly amount to more than rationalizing and perhaps here and there to amending the inherited law in terms of natural justice. Being unenforceable in itself, natural law was considered by the Romans to be inferior to the law proper. The vagueness of the conception is brought home by the fact that in some utterances, incorporated in the Corpus Juris, of the great Roman jurist Ulpian (d. A.D. 228), natural law is depicted as extending to animals inasmuch as they have in common with man the habits of mating and of breeding and of educating progeny. This tenet, inspired by mystical conceptions of Pythagorean philosophy, was not generally recognized by the Roman jurists. With Ulpian himself it was of no legal consequence and perhaps no more than an ostentation of philosophical profundity, not uncommon with legal writers; still it offered to the scholastics of later times an occasion for learned disquisitions and refutations.

---

[27] By ARTHUR NUSSBAUM, excerpted from: A CONCISE HISTORY OF THE LAW OF NATIONS 13–16 (rev. ed. 1954). Reprinted by permission.

The bearing of the natural-law doctrine upon the history of international law is twofold. For one thing, in Roman sources natural law is frequently identified with the philosophical jus gentium – the universality of a given rule was quite understandably taken as an indication of its naturalness, that is, of its origin from right reason. For instance, inviolability of envoys derived by the sources from jus gentium may just as well serve as an example of natural law. Gaius' definition of jus gentium, with its reference to "natural reason," clearly points to the law of nature. On the other hand, the Roman sources at times contrast jus gentium and jus naturale; slavery, because found everywhere, is declared to be an institution of the jus gentium, but is held not to belong to the jus naturale, since by nature all men are free. Thus the doctrine of natural law has evoked a bewildering controversy about the character of the jus gentium.

2. The Medieval Period[28]

The beginnings of European international relations can be traced back to the microscopic inter-State system of the Italian city States. It is not, therefore, surprising to find here also the first signs of a doctrine of international law.

The Italian post-glossators, especially Bartolus (1314–1357) and Baldus (1327–1400), may claim to be among the first expositors of international law even though their treatment of the subject was fragmentary. They conceived the law of nations as a universal and natural law applicable between independent princes and free commonwealths.

When, in the late fifteenth and early sixteenth centuries, Spain became the leading power in the Western State system, the center of learning in international law shifted to that country. Vitoria (about 1480–1546) became the founder of the Spanish school of international law. In his Relectiones de Indis Noviter Inventis (1532) he maintained the tradition of the post-glossators in insisting on the universal validity of international law. In the face of royal disapprobation, he held that international law applied no less between Spain and the Indian principalities in America than between Christian States.

Elizabethan England adopted Gentili (1552–1608), a Protestant international lawyer of Italian origin. His works, De Legationibus (1588), Commentationes de Jure belli (1589) and De Jure Belli Libri Tres (1598), show the shift in emphasis which is likely to occur when a jurist is not only an academic lawyer, but also is versed in the art of arguing cases in court, and especially in courts relying on precedents. Gentili acted as counsel in several major cases, and his work greatly benefited from this practical experience. Like other naturalists, he relied as authorities on classical writers, the Bible and the church fathers. In addition, he fortified himself by frequent references to Justinian's Institutes and Digest and to State practice. For him international law was not merely a moral standard to which the behavior of States ought to conform, but a living body of law that was actually applied between States.

3. Gentili's Law of War[29]

Gentili's Law of War centers in the traditional manner on the issue of just war. It is divided into three books. The first is concerned with the causes of war, the second with warfare, and the third – a novelty – with peace treaties. He considers as a war only a contest between public armed forces, thus discarding the "private" wars of old. His treatment is far more comprehensive than that of the scholastics, including Suarez, who came after him; and his discussion of the law of treaties, an extremely important matter, which was greatly neglected by his predecessors, is one of the most valuable parts of his work. Gentili does not yet possess a general theory of treaties. He deals separately with peace treaties, alliances, and a few other international agreements, but his analysis allows some general conclusions. For instance, in the Middle Ages treaties were largely considered binding only during the life of the signatory potentates; Gentili, though he admits exceptions, is guided by the notion that treaties are binding upon the successors as well as the peoples of the covenanting rulers. He furthermore shows that a defeated prince cannot annul a peace treaty on the ground that he was induced to agree by fear or duress. This view, which necessarily holds good for treaties of any kind and has been generally accepted in this sense by writers on international law, bespeaks a basic insight of Gentili's; namely, that the law of private contracts which does permit invalidation on the ground of fear or duress cannot simply be carried over to the law of treaties.

Gentili's most important contribution to the latter law consists in his tenet that one has to read into a (peace) treaty always a tacit condition to the effect that the treaty is binding only as long as conditions remain unchanged. The far-reaching consequences of this so-called clausula rebus sic stantibus are evident. Ancient Roman law had

[28] By GEORG SCHWARZENBERGER, excerpted from: 1 A MANUAL OF INTERNATIONAL LAW 14–18 (4th ed. 1960). Reprinted by permission.

[29] By ARTHUR NUSSBAUM, from: A CONCISE HISTORY OF THE LAW OF NATIONS 95–96 (rev. ed. 1954). Reprinted by permission.

not known that clausula. Gentili relies on the authority of Alciatus (1492-1550), an outstanding Italian writer on civil law, but the clausula rebus sic stantibus doctrine was several centuries older. It originated in canon law, which tended to temper with considerations of equity the rigor of the Roman private law. The new tenet was adopted by the "civilians," and Gentili introduced it into international law. There it has stood its ground down to the present, whereas it has generally disappeared in its original province, private law.

4. The Precursors of Grotius[30]

Francisco de Vitoria treated the problems of international law, along with other legal problems, within the ambit of his lectures on theology. With a Thomist background of argument and method, he nevertheless confronted with startling modernity and courage the burning problems of his own age, in particular those arising from the discoveries and conquest of the New World. In an age when national States were still only in course of severing their bonds with the Universal Empire and the Catholic Church, the interrelations of a whole and changing world of independent States, Christian as well as non-Christian, loomed into Vitoria's range of vision. He was led in this context to differentiate international law somewhat from both natural law and municipal law, the international community from Christendom and the limits of theological doctrine. His law of nations was "what natural reason has established among all nations," among which he included even American barbarian principalities. This law of reason (unlike the theological natural law) was, in his view, of immediate human not divine promulgation; and its validity was correspondingly relative, not absolute; supporting natural law but neither a necessary deduction from it, nor necessary to it. Vitoria thus leaned to a view of international law as positive rather than "natural" in the older sense, as consensus of all men. But by the same token, though international law was human and therefore not absolute, that consensus was so difficult to recapture that its abrogation was virtually impossible.

Francisco Suarez (1548-1617), a Spanish Jesuit jurist-theologian, who taught at several Spanish Universities, and finally at the Portuguese University of Coimbra, was in a sense the last Schoolman. He clearly distinguished the jus gentium of the Roman jurists, as a body of common legal principles applied by individual States within their own borders, from the jus gentium as international law. In fixing the latter as a human law, based on usage and acceptance of mankind as a whole, theoretically relative and changeable but in practice scarcely so, intermediate between natural and human law, lacking natural law's intrinsic necessity, though operating in its support—in all this his doctrines come close to those of Vitoria. For him, too, international law presupposed a community of all mankind, united by the natural precepts of mutual love and mercy. Perfect, sovereign and independent as each State community might be, they all had need of mutual assistance, association and intercourse, and of a system of law to order their relations.

Even so brief a summation shows that both Vitoria and Suarez reached a clear notion of a world-wide community ordered by human law long before Grotius. Both had set off international law as against natural law and municipal law. On the other hand, (1) they both rather assumed that international law must be contrived with the few principles for which a universal consensus of mankind could be shown; (2) they both lacked the more fruitful notion of a consensus of States through State practice; (3) despite their sharp logical equipment of scholastic philosophy, neither of them envisaged (much less elaborated) the wide-ranging and complex mass of modern principles which certainly cannot be derived from any consensus of mankind; and (4) both of them still insisted on the intimate connection of international law with natural law, that international law was auxiliary to natural law, and in the final resort, subordinate thereto, the positivist discard of both natural law and theology being still alien to them. On all these points, Vitoria and Suarez were still of the medieval rather than the modern world.

It is because he took his predecessors' work over the watershed to this positivist landscape that Grotius attached to himself the title of "father of international law." He respectfully set theology apart by his position that the law of nature would obtain even if there were no God, or if human affairs did not concern God, insisting, despite much polite and even propagandist reference to older ideas, on the sufficiency of the psychological drive of sociability (appetitus societatis) as foundation for natural law. His use of the practice and other evidence of consensus of States, as distinct from the vague consensus of mankind, belongs to modern positivism. His De Jure Belli ac Pacis (1625) was in both design and performance a more detailed systematic exposition of inter-State relations than any preceding work. Yet Grotius himself still relied too much on the natural law, and was still too vague in his use of State practice, to be a true modern.

The much praised Grotian tolerance is, as a part of his teachings, no greater than that of Vitoria. But the Grotian tolerance went to the tactics, as well as the content of his teaching; and it goes far to explain why, in historical fact (as distinct from intellectual deserts), his work remained

---

[30] By JULIUS STONE, excerpted from: LEGAL CONTROLS OF INTERNATIONAL CONFLICT 9–11 (1954). Reprinted by permission.

noticed when that of Vitoria was not. It enabled him as pious Protestant, writing amid bitter religious controversy and savage religious wars, to refrain from hurt to Catholic feelings, and to eschew discriminations even against Saracens and other infidels, to support his teachings with Greek philosophy and myth, Roman law and history, Old and New Testaments and the writings of the Church Fathers.

Neither Vitoria, nor Suarez, nor Grotius fathered a full-fledged modern system of international law. If we chose to impute paternity to the one who first determined its general boundaries, it is Vitoria not Grotius who is the father. If we reserve it for the thinker who not only had a clear picture of these boundaries, but secured their general recognition, fenced them sturdily around, prescribed and demonstrated the methods of cultivation, and raised a first harvest of detailed precepts, Grotius may remain where earlier generations of publicists have placed him.

5. Vitoria on the Spanish Conquests[31]

The Spanish Dominican Francisco Vitoria did not publish anything. Among posthumous publications of his works, some lectures are outstanding. They are preserved in elaborate notes of his disciples, partly dictated by Vitoria. From the viewpoint of the law of nations, the interrelated lectures on "The Indians Recently Discovered" and "The Law of War Made by the Spaniards on the Barbarians," given in 1532, are paramount. As the titles indicate, the lectures dealt with the Spanish conquest of America. The Dominicans were particularly interested in this matter since immediately after Columbus' discovery their Order, following its old missionary tradition, had embarked upon the evangelization of the American Indians. Bartholomew de las Casas (1474-1566), the "Father of the Indians," is prominent among the Dominicans who sailed to America. It is recorded in the annals of history how this great and noble man, inspired by the highest principles of Christianity, devoted himself to the defense of the Indians against the ruthless exploitation and ferocious cruelty which they had to suffer from the Spanish conquerors. Whether there were any personal relations between Las Casas and Vitoria we do not know, except that in a politico-theological controversy between Las Casas and his Spanish adversaries, Vitoria, on the request of Charles V, rendered an opinion that was favorable to Las Casas. In any case there was a clear kinship of spirit between these two Dominicans. Yet their approach to the American Indian problem was different. Though an eminent scholar, Las Casas was a missionary, the pastor of his flock. Vitoria was a professor; he attacked the problem from a theoretical viewpoint. Inspired by the teaching of Thomas Aquinas, who had also been a Dominican, he undertook a systematic inquiry into whether the war of the Spaniards against the Indiana aborigines was or was not "just." Examining one after another of the various reasons advanced by ecclesiastical or secular authorities and by writers, Vitoria rejected many but finally approved some of them. In their discussion he nearly always followed the line of enlightened humaneness. He also exhibited political courage. Although Emperor Charles V was then his sovereign, Vitoria dauntlessly dismissed imperial claims to world supremacy. This was in line with inveterate Spanish tradition; but opposition to imperial supremacy required resolve when the Emperor was identical with the King of Spain; and criticizing the methods of Spanish conquest was an even greater proof of moral strength. Vitoria took a vigorous stand against the misdeeds of the conquistadors and showed humaneness and intelligent understanding toward the Indians, in respect to whom he felt keenly the missionary obligations of his order. He warned the Spaniards against self-complacency by reminding them that among their peasants many were "not much better than brute beasts." Even where the Indians tried to expel the Spaniards or slay them, Vitoria insisted the Spaniards should confine themselves to self-defense rather than resort to aggressive warfare. In this connection he pointed out that the natives were frightened in their very timidity and dullness by the sight of strange men with powerful weapons, even though the Spaniards might attempt to allay their fears and assure them of their peaceful intentions.

6. Vitoria on "Just Wars"[32]

Vitoria's discussion of just war begins with the assumption that no war may be just on both sides.

> This is too well known to need proof, for otherwise each of the two belligerents might have an equally just cause and so both would be innocent. This in its turn would involve the consequence that it would not be lawful to kill them, and so imply a contradiction, because it would be a just war.[33]

The justness of war can only be determined by a system

[31] By ARTHUR NUSSBAUM, excerpted from: A CONCISE HISTORY OF THE LAW OF NATIONS 79–80 (rev. ed. 1954). Reprinted by permission.

[32] By DAVID KENNEDY, excerpted from: Primitive Legal Scholarship, 27 HARVARD INTERNATIONAL LAW JOURNAL 1, 32–39 (1986). Reprinted by permission.

[33] F. Vitoria, *De Jure Belli Hispanorum in Barbaros,* reprinted in CLASSICS OF INTERNATIONAL LAW 170 (J.B. Scott ed. 1917).

of natural law rights and wrongs. Only a war which rights a "wrong received" is just. A "wrong" is what happens when one sovereign state violates a natural-law-based norm guaranteeing something to another state. Vitoria imagines all sovereigns to be bound by a single set of natural law norms.

In three ways, Vitoria treats just war to extinguish sovereign authority when it does not conform with these moral/legal norms. First, Vitoria equates the sovereign's public authority with justness. The sovereign's private desires for empire or religious conquest are not just causes. Nor does the violation of a private right legitimate war. Thus a sovereign's authority to wage war is coterminous with the justness of his objectives. Vitoria therefore sharply distinguishes the public and private capacities of the sovereign. In his public role he is the instrument of a universal law enforced by the "agreement of the whole world." In his private role he has desires which are not just causes of war.

Second, the special capacity of sovereigns in matters of war is evident in their special responsibility to ensure the justness of their public acts. The sovereign must be sure of the justness of his cause before making war. The sovereign must consult advisers before making war to ensure that the prince's public authority is actually an exercise in justice. In case of doubt about the justness of the cause, the prince must refrain from war, for were he to go forward, a war might be fought which was not just, or both sides might imagine justice to be on their side.

Third, sovereigns have the capacity to exercise extraordinary powers when their cause is just. Once a war is undertaken, the just prince must judge his enemies and the justice of the war itself. This definition of the sovereign's capacity avoids any collision of separate sovereign views about justice: only the views of the just prince are legitimate. After the war, the victor is the judge of his adversary, for the public authority of the vanquished has been fully extinguished. When the sovereign authority of the vanquished has been snuffed out, the victor is responsible as sovereign to the defeated citizenry:

> When victory has been won and the war is over, the victory should be utilized with moderation and Christian humility, and the victor ought to deem that he is sitting as judge between two States, the one which has been wronged and the one which has done the wrong, so that it will be as judge and not as accuser that he will deliver the judgment whereby the injured state can obtain satisfaction, and this, so far as possible should involve the offending state in the least degree of calamity and misfortune, the offending individuals being chastised within lawful limits; and an especial reason for this is that in general among Christians all the fault is to be laid at the door of their princes, for subjects when fighting for their princes act in good faith.[34]

Yet there is an on-off quality in Vitoria's system of rights and wrongs:

> There is no inconsistency, indeed, in holding the war to be a just war on both sides, seeing that on one side there is right and on the other side there is invincible ignorance. For instance, just as the French hold the province of Burgundy with demonstrable ignorance, in the belief that it belongs to them, while our Emperor's right to it is certain, and he may make war to regain it, just as the French may defend it, so it may also befall in the case of the [South American] Indians – a point deserving careful attention. For the rights of war which may be invoked against men who are really guilty and lawless differ from those which may be invoked against the innocent and ignorant.[35]

In a sense, Vitoria's system of sovereign capacity is derived from his holistic notion of absolute standards of justice. Without a clear belief that natural law could elaborate a system of rights and wrongs which could ensure that only one side of any conflict was just, the sharp boundary between sovereign authorities would collapse.

Vitoria has often been misunderstood, particularly by modern historians who seek to discover the source of international law's legitimate binding force. These scholars begin with a doctrinal assumption of sovereign autonomy, and then cannot imagine how autonomy is preserved by the requirement of consent or how community order is preserved by an external normative scheme. The first proposition seems to lead to radical skepticism, the second to idealism. Nor can they imagine that a worldwide law might order and preserve autonomy or that sovereign consensus can support such a community order. The first assumption is associated with oppressive imperium and the latter with destabilizing relativism.

The open spaces in Vitoria's thought that demand analysis and explanation are quite different. His project aims at elaborating a doctrinal structure of power relations consistent with his faith. What needs explaining, in his view, are the detailed entailments of scripture and right reason for princely activity. Although his scheme of just and unjust wars presents the modern historian with a clash of community order and sovereign autonomy, Vitoria does not think of it this way.

Vitoria's scholarship is significant in that it does not

---

[34] F. Vitoria, *De Indis Noviter Inventis*, in CLASSICS IN INTERNATIONAL LAW 187 (J.B. Scott ed. 1917).

[35] *Id.* at 155.

so much resolve as avoid the problem of order among independent sovereigns. The advantage of distance permits us to recognize his text as a technique for avoiding conceptual conflicts. The interesting thing about Vitoria is not the particular mediation mechanism with which he turns our attention from a conflict between sovereign authorities. It is that this conflict structures his entire discussion.

7. Grotius[36]

Grotius (1583–1645) can at least claim to be the expounder of international law on a scale that was not previously reached. In the service of the United Provinces and as Swedish Ambassador in Paris, Grotius had acquired an intimate insight into the diplomatic affairs of his time. Nevertheless, or perhaps for this very reason, Grotius did not pay as much attention to State practice as Gentili had done.

In Mare Liberum (1609), a chapter from the long unpublished major work De Jure Praedae (1605), Grotius advocated the principle of the freedom of the seas. This should be compared with Selden's (1584–1654) Mare Clausum (1618–first printed in 1635), in which the claim of Charles I to sovereignty over the seas adjacent to the British Isles was ably advanced, even though this proposition involved a striking departure from the policy of Elizabethan England in favor of the freedom of the seas. A comparison of Mare Clausum with Mare Liberum shows how closely they reflect the political and economic interests of their respective patrons and how easy it is, in particular with the assistance of enjoyably elastic notions of natural law, to arrive at predestined conclusions.

8. The Grotius-Selden Debate[37]

The classic debate took place in the early part of the seventeenth century. The Netherlands was at that time the dominant maritime country, and its leading international lawyer Hugo Grotius spelled out the arguments in favor of free navigation on all the oceans. John Selden for England countered in favor of a closed sea. (Later, when England became the dominant naval power, England espoused freedom of the seas.) Historically it was of course the Grotian position that prevailed, and today it is even hard to find a copy of Selden's Mare Clausum in a law library. Curiously enough, however, Selden's position at the time had logic on its side. For Grotius' primary argument in favor of open seas was that the seas could not be contained by any nation, that the oceans could not be dominated or set out in metes and bounds as land. This physical impossibility, Grotius argued, led to a legal conclusion that the oceans perforce had to be free for navigation by all powers.

In reply, Selden noted that Grotius made an exception for bays, inlets, and coastal waters, for these were in Grotius' eyes traditionally part of the mainland. But surely, Selden argued, these were open waters just like the high seas, and if they were subject to national domination then too the high seas could be so subject. Moreover, Selden argued that any exercise of sovereignty was relative to the subject matter. Ownership of portions of the high seas would not entail the same characteristics as ownership of land. Instead of milestones and other markers as on land, ownership of the high seas might consist merely of publication of a map indicating enclosures by latitude and longitude.

What was really at issue in this debate was the paying of tariffs to a nation for navigational use of the high seas. Grotius, representing an aspiring naval power, did not want Dutch ships to have to pay for a license to navigate and trade with a distant power; he feared the proliferation of fees from all countries along the route. Selden, on the other hand, felt that England stood to gain more than she would lose by the imposition of such navigational license fees in the waters around England, affecting not only trade with England but also trade through the Straits of Gibraltar.

It is interesting to speculate on what might have been the result had Selden's position prevailed in international law. It is quite possible that trade on the part of the Netherlands and other maritime powers would have continued unabated, with tariffs being paid for the use of the oceans around a number of countries. This would have required, of course, that tariffs never be so high as to block trade entirely. On this assumption the result would have been the continued existence of trade, but with the profits being shared with tariff-charging countries to the extent of their tariffs.

Moreover, we may speculate that the payment of tariffs and license fees for the use of portions of the ocean would necessarily generate expectations on the part of the shippers that the collecting country would perform certain services. When one pays a fee, one generally comes to expect certain reciprocal benefits. Thus it is conceivable that the countries exercising domination over portions of the high seas would sooner or later have found themselves in the position of

---

[36] By GEORG SCHWARZENBERGER, excerpted from: 1 A MANUAL OF INTERNATIONAL LAW 14–18 (4th ed. 1960). Reprinted by permission.

[37] By ANTHONY D'AMATO and JOHN LAWRENCE HARGROVE, excerpted from: *An Overview of the Problem*, in John Lawrence Hargrove (ed.), WHO PROTECTS THE OCEAN? 1 (1975). Reprinted by permission.

custodians, responsible for the upkeep and maintenance of their portions of the high seas. This responsibility might early have manifested itself in the promulgation of fishing conservation decrees; licenses to fish in those portions of the high seas would be restricted as to certain times of year, certain types of boats, certain methods of fishing, and so forth. And, if we still had such national sovereignty in the twentieth century, we might expect the proprietor nations to exercise other forms of responsibility over mineral exploitation, dumping and other forms of pollution.

9. Assessment of Grotius[38]

The two foundations on which Grotius built were neither of them of his devising. He based the law of nations, first, on natural law as a universal order binding all men as individuals and as communities. For men are reasonable beings, partaking in the universal reason; and they are also, as observation shows, social beings as well. By the application of reason to their common life together, men can thus deduce the principles of natural law which bind them by their own inner nature. This line of Grotian thought has already become central in the works of his Catholic predecessors, notably Vitoria and Suarez. With creative ambiguity, however, Grotius also simultaneously based the law of nations on a second foundation, namely the practice of States as evidence of natural law. We must assume, he argued, that States, consisting as they do of rational men, must have manifested the rules of reason in their past practice. This practice was therefore evidence of what their reason then prescribed, and thus of natural law itself. In the stress on practice Grotius also had predecessors, notably Gentili.

The Grotian contributions lay in the closeness of his linking of State practice and natural law, in the systematic elaboration of consequential rules, and in the tactics of persuasion. Paradoxically enough, the logical cogency of his argument for bolstering natural law with the practice of States was small. For if such practice is consistent with natural law, reference to it seems of little import, for reason itself would have yielded the principle without resort to practice; if inconsistent, the practice would but violate natural law, and could not assist in discovering it. The persuasiveness of the Grotian position, however, transcended merely logical cogency. He marshalled as evidence of practice materials drawn from Catholics and Protestants, and from Old and New Testaments, from the ancient and modern worlds, from paganism as well as Christendom, thus joining to the general appeal of natural law the multiple appeals of sectarian pride and loyalties. Though a man of deep conviction, and not all things to all men, Grotius thus conceded enough to all men to win a hearing far wider than that attained by any of his predecessors.

[38] By JULIUS STONE, excerpted from: LEGAL CONTROLS OF INTERNATIONAL CONFLICT 12–13 (1954). Reprinted by permission.

10. The Grotian Tradition[39]

While Grotius lived through a time in which a *jus gentium intra se* of papal and imperial hegemony was giving way to a *jus gentium inter se* of the nation-state system, today's shift away from overweening state sovereignty endows Grotius's times with a special significance. Grotius's chief contribution to our understanding of international order came with his idea that there was an alternative to nations living either in a state of nature or under imperial hegemony. That alternative was to form an international community.

Hersch Lauterpacht's[40] listing of features of the Grotian tradition includes:[41] (1) the central place of natural law, (2) the universality of international society, (3) the role of the individual in a nation-state system, (4) solidarity in the enforcement of international rules of behavior, and (5) the absence of international institutions. Grotius's suppositions for the most part remain valid today.

11. Bynkershoek, Pufendorf, and Vattel[42]

The course taken by international law after Grotius can be viewed as a process of differentiation of the natural law and practice of States strains in his position. Each of these strains, after Grotius, took its own course; the natural law or "naturalist" strain was led by Samuel Pufendorf, and the practice of States strain came to maturity later under Bynkershoek. An interesting twist of the natural law theory by Vattel bridged the two strains, even though he is often thought of as belonging to the "naturalists."

[39] By DAVID J. BEDERMAN, excerpted from: Book Review, 86 AMERICAN JOURNAL OF INTERNATIONAL LAW 411 (1992). Reprinted by permission.

[40] Hersch Lauterpacht, *The Grotian Tradition in International Law*, 23 BYIL 1, 19–51 (1946).

[41] As restated by Hedley Bull, in: HEDLEY BULL, Benedict Kingsbury & Adam Roberts (eds.), HUGO GROTIUS AND INTERNATIONAL RELATIONS 78–91 (1990).

[42] By JULIUS STONE, excerpted from: LEGAL CONTROLS OF INTERNATIONAL CONFLICT 14–18 (1954). Reprinted by permission.

The Grotian concept of natural law was first stripped, by Samuel Pufendorf (1632-1694) and a long line of followers, of the "impure" support of State practice. The "naturalist" tradition of international law is par excellence this Pufendorfian rejection of the decisiveness of practice of States to an international law founded on natural law.

But within this main "naturalist" strain there appeared, with Emmerich de Vattel in the mid-eighteenth century, a concealed schism of momentous consequences for the whole natural law position. In profession Vattel was a natural lawyer; but his interpretation of natural law so far departed from that of his predecessors as to constitute a distinct position; and one which in the final resort surrendered altogether the natural law basis of international law, leaving the field to the positivist strain, and the modern consent theories. While Pufendorf extruded reference to practice from the confused Grotian theory, Vattel's theory had in the long run quite the opposite effect, of extruding from it all decisive reference to natural law, leaving international law resting on consent of States evidenced by treaty and practice. If this were so, it would explain why, though a "naturalist," Vattel nevertheless laid so heavy a stress on State practice, and why his work has stood so high, for this very reason, with the modern Chancelleries.

The starting-point of this remarkable Vattelian detournement lies in Vattel's transformation of the meaning of the term "nature." For Grotius or Pufendorf, or for that matter, for the Greeks or Romans, the dominant conception of the "nature" of a thing was its ideal nature, what a creature is in its fullest development, yielding in the case of mankind the central notion of rational and social beings mutually dependent for survival. For Vattel, however, "nature" rather meant what it meant to Hobbes—the "actual" rather than the "ideal" nature of the creature. For him, as for Hobbes, what is primary is not the restraint of "natural law," but the license of "the state of nature"—of men in their presocial isolation, each self-dependent for survival.

It is, indeed, precisely because "natural law" consists of the principles applicable to men in their presocial isolation that is (on this view) apt for governing the relations of independent States. The condition of such States, recognizing no binding human law over them and no human superior, is precisely that of isolated men before civil society and its law arise. Only this kind of "natural" law can claim to control such civil anarchy. The precepts of the Vattelian natural law, therefore, on which his international law is based, must be derived from contemplation of such independent beings, from their "naturally" sanctioned claims, from the "rights" inherent in independence. The precepts must assure those rights of all States in a manner which allows them to coexist. Vattel's whole system is (on its theoretical side) an analysis of the precepts which (he thought) followed from these "fundamental rights" of States, illustrated by State practice.

The deeper implications of this position, which in the present view bridges the naturalist and positivist strains, may be most clearly seen in connection with the fundamental right of self-preservation. Not only does each State, according to Vattel, have such a right, in pursuance of which any other rules of international law could if necessary be overridden; each State is also its own final judge whether a situation for the exercise of this right had arisen, and what action was necessary to implement it. On such a basis, the binding force of all rules became subject in the final resort to each State's discretion. The manner in which this detournement of natural law pointed towards the "conventional" or "consent" or "positivist" theories of international law, which became dominant in the nineteenth century, is clear in the present perspective.

One sign of this, indeed, was immediately apparent in the destruction of the Grotian theory of "the just war." In war situations, each belligerent's self-preservation is usually invoked: insofar as each is the final judge of what its self-preservation requires, each can in the external world (however it be in foro conscientiae) maintain its cause as just, without possibility of legal challenge. To that extent, the "just"-"unjust" distinction as applied to the causes of war became vacuous; and with it any basis on which third States might discriminate between the belligerents. Vattel's unchallenged position as founder of the modern law of neutrality is thus also seen to be organically related to his version of natural law, and to his mediating role between natural law and positivism.

12. Vattel's Influence[43]

Emmerich de Vattel (1714-1767) was the son of a Protestant minister in the Swiss principality of Neuchatel, which was connected by personal union with the Kingdom of Prussia. Having studied humanities and philosophy at the University of Basle, he found employment in 1746 in the diplomatic service of the Elector of Saxony, who then wore the crown of King of Poland. In 1749 Vattel was sent to Berne as Minister Plenipotentiary for Switzerland, but in 1758 he was recalled to Dresden as a privy councilor in charge of foreign affairs. Owing to illness he returned in 1766 to Neuchatel, where he died the following year. In 1758 his main work appeared: Le Droit des gens; ou, Principes de la loi naturelle appliques a la conduite et aux

---

[43] By ARTHUR NUSSBAUM, excerpted from: A CONCISE HISTORY OF THE LAW OF NATIONS 156–58, 162 (rev. ed. 1954). Reprinted by permission.

affaires des nations et des souverains. As the title indicates, this is a system of international law based on the principles of the law of nature and written with a view to practical application.

Vattel proposes to present the ideas of Christian Wolff (1676-1756) on the law of nations to a public of "sovereigns and their ministers" in an easily understandable fashion. In reality the book is far more than a paraphrase of Wolff's multi-volumed treatise. It is the work of a modern-minded diplomat who, while leaning on Wolff, systematically sets forth his own opinions on the most diverse topics of international and constitutional law. Frequently he develops Wolff's broad propositions into specific issues of actual international interest, viewed with the eyes of a practitioner of statecraft. For instance, where Wolff in general terms recognizes acquisition, by way of occupation, of dominion over a territory, Vattel makes it clear that actual possession is a prerequisite of legally effective occupation. He concludes that papal allotments of newly discovered territories to various rulers lack legal force; he examines the question whether the presence of wandering native tribes is a bar to occupation, and other matters not investigated by Wolff. In the analysis of treaties, a topic dealt with by Wolff in an abstract manner without real knowledge of the subject, he stresses the problems of interpretation, for example, those arising from the language of very old treaties, or from the use of technical terms; and he brings into relief the interpretative significance of the purpose as well as of the interdependence, of treaty provisions. He admits the clausula rebus sic stantibus where conditions have vitally changed.

In respect to neutrality, Vattel, as a Swiss, had the advantage of a keen awareness of the problems involved. He justly takes neutrality as the ipso facto effect of a war in respect to the nonparticipants in the war, whereas Wolff's treatment centers on the then more or less obsolete treaties of neutrality. Among the numerous special problems of neutrality expounded by Vattel but not considered by Wolff are: loans by a neutral to a belligerent; prize law; the right of visit and search; naval attacks within neutral waters; levying of troops and sale of booty in neutral territory. A matter of such importance as arbitration is barely mentioned by Wolff; Vattel, referring to Swiss practice, discusses it at some length, warning against it where "essential rights" of sovereigns are in dispute; but he recommends arbitration where "less important rights" are involved. This opinion suggests the distinction which became signal in the twentieth century between "justiciable" and "nonjusticiable" controversies. Throughout, topics as well as solutions show that Vattel had ideas of his own.

In spirit, too, Vattel's work differs from Wolff's. Vattel's attitude is more humanitarian, more cosmopolitan, and, in a measure, even democratic. Though he makes considerable concessions to absolute monarchy, with which he was linked by birth and employment, he reacts first of all as a citizen of Switzerland, of the "country of which liberty is the soul, the treasure, and the fundamental law; and by my birth I am the friend of all nations." Emphatically he rejects the idea of "patrimonial" kingdoms, that is, of kingdoms based on the idea of monarchical ownership. He even advances views colored by the notion of popular sovereignty, and in some respects treads the same path as his great fellow countryman, Jean-Jacques Rousseau, who published his epochal works after the appearance of Vattel's book. He may well be counted among the writers who contributed to the formation of the ideas of the French Revolution; in fact, Abbe Gregoire's theses were almost entirely drawn from Vattel's treatise. There is also in his language a tinge of excitement and flourish which foreshadows later revolutionary phraseology.

Moreover, the spirit of Vattel's work was well in accord with the principles of the Declaration of Independence. It soon became a textbook in American colleges and, after the establishment of the Republic, the favorite authority in American theory of international law. The following statistics, prepared by Professor Edwin D. Dickinson on the basis of American cases decided from 1789 to 1820, speak for themselves:

	Citations in Pleadings	Court Citations	Court Quotations
Grotius	16	11	2
Pufendorf	9	4	8
Bynkershoek	25	16	2
Vattel	92	38	22

13. The Path to Positivism[44]

In a crude form, the theories of international law now grouped as "positivist", "conventional" or "consent" theories go back well before Grotius. Their maturity is usually attributed to later writers, and notably to Richard Zouche (1590–1660) and his continental successor Cornelius Bynkershoek (1673–1743). With Bynkershoek, central in whose work was a basic collection of State treaties since the twelfth century, the positivist strain is clearly differentiated. Within the next century, natural law (except of the ambivalent Vattelian brand) was to fade from the literature of international law, as well as from practice. The positivist preoccupation with treaties and other evidence of State practice, and the Vattelian preoccupation with each State's

[44] By JULIUS STONE, excerpted from: LEGAL CONTROLS OF INTERNATIONAL CONFLICT 12–13 (1954). Reprinted by permission.

fundamental rights, both pointed to the consent of States as the source of international legal obligations.

Still a third body of thought pressed in the same direction, namely, the growth in Anglo-Saxon countries of the imperative theory of law, associated with the names of Jeremy Bentham and John Austin. Natural law had played a vital role in municipal systems of law as well as in international law. The work of Austin and Bentham, as the nineteenth century opened, marked a sharp reaction against this municipal role of natural law, which they condemned as an irrational and fictitious basis of law and law-making. With the model of conscious creative legislation of the nineteenth century before them, "natural law" was exorcised in favor of "positive law strictly so-called." To merit the name and attention of lawyers, "law" must have been promulgated by a Sovereign (that is, a determinate person or persons habitually obeyed by the bulk of a territorial community, and not themselves obedient to any other authority). It must further be a rule for the general conduct of the subjects; and supported by a threat of evil (a sanction) emanating from the Sovereign in case of disobedience.

Since international law obviously lacked at least two of these requisites, the imperative theory's attack on natural law also became an attack on international law, Austin admitting it at most to the rank of "positive international morality." In thus attacking natural law as a basis of international law, Austinianism merely confirmed the then contemporary trends among publicists. But the great expansion of international treaty-making in the nineteenth century prevented acceptance of his further step in denying that international law was law at all. It seemed absurd for international law to give up its "legal" ghost in the very age when, for the first time, it seemed to be acquiring some of the richness of principle and the constancy of practice which mark a going legal order. The theory of law-creation by agreement of Sovereigns provided a variant of the imperative theory, which converged with the other supports for the modern consent theories of international law.

14. Invention of the Term "International Law"[45]

The year of the French Revolution, 1789, was also the year when the term "international law" was invented. It appeared in the preface to Jeremy Bentham's Introduction to the Principles of Morals and Legislation.[46] Bentham elaborated upon the term in the final chapter of his book where he was interested, inter alia, in defining the science of jurisprudence. He distinguished books on jurisprudence that "ascertain what the law is" (what he called "expository jurisprudence") from those that "ascertain what it ought to be" ("censorial jurisprudence"). He differentiated works on expository jurisprudence between those composed by the legislator himself (thus "authoritative") and those by "any other person at large" ("unauthoritative"). Laws, themselves, he grouped into five "assemblages" based, respectively, on extent, political quality, time, expression and punishment, these five being the "circumstances that have given rise to the principal branches of jurisprudence."[47] It is in this flurry of categorization that Bentham's "international law" emerged. The new term was formed in the part on the "political quality" of laws and was set in counterpoise to "internal" law:

> In the second place, with regard to the political quality of the persons whose conduct is the object of the law. These may, on any given occasion, be considered either as members of the same state, or as members of different states: in the first case, the law may be referred to the head of internal, in the second case, to that of international jurisprudence.[48]

Bentham footnoted "international" as follows:

> The word international, it must be acknowledged, is a new one; though, it is hoped, sufficiently analogous and intelligible. It is calculated to express, in a more significant way, the branch of the law which goes commonly under the name of the law of nations: an appellation so uncharacteristic that, were it not for the force of custom, it would seem rather to refer to internal jurisprudence.

It seems that, in creating the term "international law," Bentham simply meant to replace one term, the "law of nations," with another term, "international law," that he thought better characterized the relevant branch of the law. One might differ here with H. L. A. Hart, who wrote in the Concept of Law: "Bentham, the inventor of the expression 'international law,' defended it simply by saying that it was 'sufficiently analogous' to municipal law."[49] My difference with Hart is twofold. First, there does not seem to be anything defensive in Bentham's invention or use of the term. Second, it is doubtful that Bentham meant the analogy to be to municipal law. Rather, it is clearer to understand him to say that international law is analogous to the law of nations. This is really the substance of Bentham's explanatory footnote.

---

[45] By MARK W. JANIS, excerpted from: *Jeremy Bentham and the Fashioning of "International Law,"* 78 AMERICAN JOURNAL OF INTERNATIONAL LAW 405 (1984). Reprinted by permission.

[46] (1789) (Burns & Hart eds. 1970).

[47] *Id.* at 294.

[48] *Id.* at 296.

[49] H.L.A. HART, THE CONCEPT OF LAW 231 (1961).

Though Bentham asserted that he was just renaming the law of nations, he really went much further. Look at the next paragraph of Bentham's text:

> Now as to any transactions which may take place between individuals who are subjects of different states, these are regulated by the internal laws, and decided upon by the internal tribunals, of the one or the other of these states: the case is the same where the sovereign of the one has any immediate transactions with a private member of the other: the sovereign reducing himself, pro re nata, to the condition of a private person, as often as he submits his cause to either tribunal; whether by claiming a benefit, or defending himself against a burthen. There remain then the mutual transactions between sovereigns as such, for the subject of that branch of jurisprudence which may be properly and exclusively termed international.

Note that Bentham made two important assumptions about international law. First, he assumed that international law was exclusively about the rights and obligations of states inter se and not about rights and obligations of individuals. Second, he assumed that foreign transactions before municipal courts were always decided by internal, not international, rules. Both of these assumptions about international law flew in the face of Bentham's assertion that he was merely substituting the term "international law" for what had previously gone under the description of the "law of nations." More or less inadvertently, he changed the boundaries of the field he sought to define.

Bentham was plainly optimistic that better international laws and lawyering could reduce the chances of war. Perhaps his most idealistic hope was that nations would sacrifice national self-interest in order to establish world peace. This theme was more fully developed in his A Plan for an Universal and Perpetual Peace, where he addressed proposals to all nations and especially to England and France.[50] Concretely, what Bentham suggested was the giving up of all colonies, the breaking off of all alliances, the establishment of free trade, the reduction of navies to what was necessary to protect against pirates, and the mutual reduction of the size of armies.

Bentham recognized that even if his reforms were adopted, there would still be disputes between nations concerning their rights at international law. His solution was the establishment of "a common court of judicature" that could settle such differences of opinion.[51] He visualized this tribunal as a "Congress or Diet" composed of representatives from each country. To enforce its holdings, Bentham saw a system of graduated responses: first, mere reporting of its opinion; second, circulating the opinion "in the dominions of each state" so as to excite public opinion; third, "putting the refractory state under the ban of Europe"; and fourth, "as a last resource," sending armed contingents furnished by the participating states "for enforcing the decrees of the court."

These were grand plans for world peace: renouncing colonies, reducing navies and armies, settling international disputes in an international court. Bentham recognized that it would take a significant change of heart for countries to do all this, but to the English he pleaded: "Oh my countrymen! purge your eyes from the film of prejudice—extirpate from your hearts the black specks of excessive jealousy, false ambition, selfishness, and insolence. The operations may be painful; but the rewards are glorious indeed! As the main difficulty, so will the main honour be with you."[52]

Thus, Bentham the international law visionary! And how different from the 19th-century positivists like John Austin who followed in his wake. Of course, there was a good measure of idealism in much of Bentham's writing. His mission was first and foremost not legal philosophy but law reform. It should be no surprise that Bentham brought his reformatory zeal, albeit briefly, to international, as well as to municipal, law. Realist and idealist—Bentham displayed both the skepticism and the romanticism that still invests the discipline he named.

15. Positivism at the Turn of the Century[53]

At the outset of the twentieth century the classic paradigm for international legal positivism, which still dominates the profession after seventy-five years, was expounded in the second volume of the American Journal of International Law by the renowned Lassa Oppenheim, Whewell Professor of International Law at Cambridge University.[54] According to Oppenheim, a "positive" method required that its foundation be built upon the extant and recognized rules of international law as set forth in the customary practice of states and in the formal conventions concluded between them, instead of upon philosophical speculations about some nonexistent law of nature.

The positivist method did not preach that international

---

[50] J. Bentham, The Works of Jeremy Bentham 535 (Bowring ed. 1843).

[51] *Id.* at 552.

[52] *Id.* at 553.

[53] By FRANCIS ANTHONY BOYLE, excerpted from: World Politics and International Law 18-19 (Durham: Duke University Press 1985). Reprinted by permission.

[54] Lassa Oppenheim, *The Science of International Law: Its Task and Method,* 2 AJIL 313 (1908).

law should never concern itself with the promotion of moral values. Rather, it was premised upon the forthrightly admitted assumption that international legal positivism, as opposed to the Grotian natural law tradition, constituted the superior means to progress toward the Aristotelian "final cause" of international legal studies – preservation of peace among nations to the greatest degree possible under the given historical circumstances. Positivist international legal analysis was more likely to facilitate successful interstate agreement upon current and proposed rules of international behavior than was interminable disputation over the dogma of Grotian natural law morality, whose reputed tenets invariably masked national interests and national prejudices. International legal positivism could, therefore, better serve to diminish the inevitable friction and ameliorate the unavoidable conflict between states in their conduct of international relations.

At this time in world history, imperial conquest, and the threat and use of force were accepted facts[55] of international life to which the rules of public international law were quite readily accommodated. The purpose of international law was not as yet perceived to be the outlawry of these manifestations of interstate violence, but more simply to reduce their incidence, mitigate their fury, and limit their scope so as to protect neutrals and prevent the development of a worldwide conflagration. International law was never viewed as a transcendent end unto itself but only as a means to achieve the ultimate goal of peace in the human condition. The institution of a more just arrangement in the relationships among states would further the maintenance of world peace and thus contribute to the promotion of all human values.

---

[55] [Editor's Note: For a discussion of the "war as fact" concept, see the section entitled *Terrorism and the Laws of War* in Chapter 8 in this Anthology.]

3

Is International Law "Law"?[1]

Many serious students of the law react with a sort of indulgence when they encounter the term "international law," as if to say, "well, we know it isn't really law, but we know that international lawyers and scholars have a vested professional interest in calling it 'law.'" Or they may agree to talk about international law as a sort of quasi-law or near-law. But it cannot be true law, they maintain, because it cannot be enforced: how do you enforce a rule of law against an entire nation?

A. The "Enforcement" Argument

One intriguing answer to these serious students of the law is to attempt to persuade them that enforcement is not, after all, the hallmark of what is meant, or what should be meant, by the term "law." As Roger Fisher observed, much of what we call law in the domestic context is unenforceable.[2] For example, where the defendant is the United States, such as often occurs in cases involving constitutional law or in ordinary situations involving suits for income tax refunds or social security payments, how would the winning private party enforce his or her judgment against the United States? Upon reflection, we see that the United States only complies with the court's judgment because it wants to. The winning private party cannot hold a gun to the head of the United States to enforce compliance. We can go even further than Professor Fisher did and look at criminal cases where the United States, or one of the states in the federal system (in these cases often called the "people"), is plaintiff. If the jury acquits the defendant, what is to stop the governmental plaintiff from saying, "that was a travesty of justice, so we're going to imprison you anyway"? How could a defendant, in handcuffs, stop the state from throwing him in prison? In some countries, at some times, we have heard of dictators or military regimes proceeding with the imprisonment and execution of defendants after they were acquitted in court. The fact is, if we think of "enforcement" in terms of power, there is nothing to stop any country from disregarding adverse judgments of its own courts. Roger Fisher has shown, therefore, that a great deal of what we normally call "law" in the United States is unenforceable by private parties when the state is party to their private litigation. Therefore, as far as "enforcement" is concerned, an international law dispute where a state is the losing party is no more nor less "enforceable" than a private law dispute where the state is the losing party.

It is no objection to this line of reasoning, by the way, to dismiss it as far-fetched. If one objects that the United States, in any event, routinely complies with adverse judgments of its own courts, then the international lawyer can answer that the same is true of rules of international law. As Louis Henkin put it, "almost all nations observe almost all principles of international law and almost all of their obligations almost all of the time."[3]

But a more substantial critique of Professor Fisher's analogy between cases involving the government as a party and international-law cases is that most domestic litigation, after all, does not involve the government as a party. Most cases involve one citizen against another ("citizen" including artificial persons such as corporations), and in those cases the law is enforced by the full sovereign powers of the state against the losing litigant. This majority of cases, then, suggests the paradigm of "law." Therefore, the argument goes, the minority of cases that do involve the state or the United States as a party are, in a sense, parasitic upon the paradigmatic instance. We tend to regard this latter minority of cases as "law" only because they share certain attributes with the majority of private cases. This minority of cases – where the government itself is a party – only appear to involve "law." Thus, conceding Professor Fisher's major premiss – that international-law cases are similar to domestic cases where the government is a party – we can nevertheless deny his minor premiss, that such cases are true instances of "law." Hence, international law is no more "law" than is constitutional law or tax-refund law or even criminal law. As John Austin stated,

---

[1] By ANTHONY D'AMATO, excerpted from: *Is International Law Really "Law"?* 79 NORTHWESTERN UNIVERSITY LAW REVIEW 1293 (1984). Reprinted by permission.

[2] Roger Fisher, *Bringing Law to Bear on Governments*, 74 HARV. L. REV. 1130 (1961).

[3] LOUIS HENKIN, HOW NATIONS BEHAVE 47 (2d ed. 1979). Professor Henkin's assertion follows tautologically from the fact that there is an international system of legal rules. Clearly, the rules that have evolved over time are the ones that nations have found to be in their collective self-interest; this is simply the Darwinian process of survival-of-the-fittest applied to rules of customary international law. If a particular set of rules evolved, then they evolved because almost all nations in fact obeyed those particular rules over a period of time. Therefore, international law consists of those particular rules that nations have obeyed. Although Professor Henkin's statement is tautological, it is not vacuous; after all, the international system might instead have evolved into total anarchy (if that is imaginable).

both constitutional and international law are merely instances of "positive morality."[4]

You could object that it is frivolous to exclude the vast body of constitutional law and criminal law cases from what we mean by "law." If you say that, then you see the force of Professor Fisher's argument, and you are well on your way to accepting the "reality" of international law. Yet we must concede that Professor Fisher's argument rests entirely upon an analogy between international and domestic litigation, and skeptics might simply not concede the force of the analogy. So, to convince them, we may have to try something different.

Let us then consider a second line of reasoning against the proposition that enforcement is the hallmark of law. This argument is not associated with any particular writer, because it relies on early conceptions of law and also on the philosophy of law itself. If we consider what law is *not,* we soon realize that it is not a rationale for the application of force. It is not a system of "might makes right" in the sense that the state constantly has to compel people, at gunpoint, to behave in a certain way. If you look through a volume of cases, or even a volume of statutes or annotations, you will find that most of the matters therein concern the working-out of private arrangements in a complex society. Most of "law" concerns itself with the interpretation and enforcement of private contracts, the redress of intentional and negligent harms, rules regarding sales of goods and sales of securities, rules relating to the family and the rights of members thereof, and other such rules, norms, and cases. The rules are obeyed not out of fear of the state's power, but because the rules by and large are perceived to be right, just, or appropriate – or simply that they exist in the background of private arrangements as "default rules" that are accepted by the parties whenever there is a gap in the parties' own legal arrangements between themselves. No state could possibly compel people to obey all these rules at gunpoint; there would not be enough soldiers and policemen to hold the guns, and they would have to sleep sooner or later. And even if the state could somehow find enough soldiers and policemen and they stayed awake all the time, who would regulate *them?* What happens if conflicts break out among the officials?

Even more fatal to this Orwellian view of extreme enforcement is that the state would need many rules to channel the decision-making of the enforcers themselves. For instance, how would all these police officials and soldiers know what rules they must enforce, and who would make sure that they enforced the rules as written? We would need another phalanx of soldiers to review the enforcers. The whole process would break down of its own weight. Indeed, Orwell in his novel, *1984*, avoided the question of how to coordinate and control the activities of the officials of the state he described. He simply referred to the state in the abstract as exercising monolithic power over the citizenry, finessing the real problem of how to organize such a state so as to control the controllers.

Thus if law is *not* a body of rules that are enforced at gunpoint, what is an individual rule of law? Is it, as the nineteenth century positivists maintained, a command of the state that is backed by the state's enforcement power? To be sure, some individual "laws" might be just that: a dictator issues a command for his personal indulgence or whim, and if he has sufficiently satisfied his close advisers and the military in other areas, they will probably enforce his command. But most laws will not have this characteristic. Indeed, looking at the matter more microscopically, what is it that forces a *judge* to decide the case before her on the basis of precedent and statutes? Is another judge holding a gun to her head? Does she examine whether the law will be enforced to see whether it is law? How does she know, in advance of her own decision, what will be enforced? Logically, enforcement puts the cart before the horse.

These issues came up in the famous case of Marbury v. Madison,[5] familiar to generations of American law students but often misinterpreted. In that case, Chief Justice Marshall's "bottom line" was that the Supreme Court had no original jurisdiction to issue writs of mandamus. In brief, there was no power to enforce the writ of mandamus demanded by the private plaintiff against an official (Madison) of the United States. If "law" were coincident with enforceability, then, since under Marshall's reasoning there was no power of enforcement in the Supreme Court because it lacked jurisdiction, nothing Marshall said in his opinion would have had any legal significance. To put it another way, lacking a "remedy," the plaintiff would have no "right," not even a right to get a decision from the Court on the question of "right"!

But Marshall took an entirely different tack. He did not deal with enforceability first; he dealt with it last. He began with the question: does the plaintiff have a right? He then asked a second question: if the plaintiff has a right, does he have a remedy? Finally, his third question was: if the plaintiff has a remedy, does this Court have the power to give it to him? By putting the questions in this order, Marshall did the opposite of what the positivists would require. Dealing first with the question of "right," Marshall was able to address that question wholly apart from whether there was a remedy or whether the remedy was available from the Supreme Court. As all law students know, Marshall found that there was indeed a right, and secondly, there being a right meant that the plaintiff had a remedy. By going through this reasoning, Marshall was able to establish the groundwork for his path-breaking assertion of judicial review of questions of constitutionality. He held that, *because there were* a right and a remedy, then the question was squarely presented whether the congressional statute purporting to grant that remedy to the Supreme Court as a matter of original jurisdiction violated the Con-

---

[4] John Austin, The Province of Jurisprudence Determined 127 (Hart ed. 1954).

[5] 5 U.S. (1 Cranch) 137 (1803).

stitution. Marshall would not have been able to make his entire assertion of judicial review if he had begun and ended his opinion with the simple sentence, "we have no jurisdiction; case dismissed." Hence, we see that in a case where by the Court's own admission it lacked jurisdiction and the power of enforcement, nevertheless the Court was able to establish a point of fundamental substantive significance. The (legal) horse was put before the (enforcement) cart.

Marshall's persuasiveness was a function of the consensus in the legal community of his era that there could be such a thing as a "right" without a remedy. This was part of a larger conviction in those days that the "law" itself had overtones of "natural law"–it was not something that only works when a policeman is standing by to enforce it.[6] And even today, in the post-positivist era of jurisprudence, it is generally agreed that law is not dependent on force so much as it is opposed to force; right is not the same thing as might. In Continental countries, the word for "law" is, as translated, the word "right." As Abraham Lincoln so well put it, law is the faith that right makes might.

Another way to put this view is to say that the relation of law to enforcement is a contingent and not a necessary relation. We can imagine a society under law where there is no force. People obey the laws, and no one disobeys. There is no need, in this idyllic utopia, for enforcement, because there is universal willing compliance. Surely we cannot claim that such a society does not have "law." Certainly no one would argue that if any given law is so successful that it never needs enforcement, it is not a law. Similarly, if all the laws of a system are successful without the need for enforcement–or at least, as successful as we may reasonably expect[7]–we cannot say that lack of evidence of enforcement strips all those rules and norms of the title "law."

But you might object that enforcement must at least potentially be present, even if it is never, or not often, invoked. It is this potential for enforcement, after all, that the positivists insist upon when they draw our attention to what they regard as the necessary connection between a rule of law and its enforcement.

To take care of the positivist objection, we may simply modify our previous hypothetical of the idyllic utopia. Assume not only that they have never had a need to enforce their laws, but also that they have no enforcement machinery–no police, no jails, no sheriffs, no marshals. They can still have a system of laws, as complex as you please, even without any potential for enforcement.

Yet you might now object that we cannot prove something about the nature of law, an all-too-human institution, by postulating the existence of a utopia where the inhabitants never break the law. Can we modify our utopia to make it seem more realistic? Suppose occasionally someone breaks the law, but is ostracized from society. Suppose one who breaches a contract is considered a moral renegade who should not be entrusted with any further business dealings.[8] These expressions of sharp social disapproval, and occasionally of ostracism, may work to discourage the few people who would disobey the law. They may not always work, but they may be potent enough to deter most of the people (a minority to begin with) who might consider breaking the law. Thus, our not-perfect utopia now consists of a regime where almost all of the laws are obeyed almost all of the time, where occasional disobedience is met with sharp social disapproval, and where occasionally, despite the "mechanism" of social disapproval, occasional violations of the law occur.[9] Is this not, nevertheless, a legal system?

A positivist might happen to object to this concept as follows: the idea of social disapproval, and sometimes social ostracism, is the same thing as a sanction. It constitutes a way of enforcing the law. Hence, by introducing this social-disapproval factor into the utopia, we have simply underscored the original point–that law (except in idyllic utopias which do not exist) depends upon potential enforcement.

But if that is the positivist's position, then the international lawyer should gladly concede the point. For international law recognizes that the social-disapproval factor operates as a sanction. A nation among the community of nations which violates the law, for example, by disregarding a treaty obligation, would certainly be subject to social disapproval by the other nations.[10] In this sense, international law is really "law."

Now it is perhaps the positivist's turn to beat a hasty retreat. The positivist may now want to retract the equation of social disapproval with "sanction." The positivist may retreat to the original position that physical or even violent enforcement is necessary to make law "law," and hence international law is not "law." We may, however, suspect that the positivist is reshaping definitions in order to exclude the international-law case, rather than to arrive at a general definition of law.[11] Consistent with this position,

[6] For a more extended discussion, see Anthony D'Amato, *Lon Fuller and Substantive Natural Law*, 26 AM. J. JURIS. 202 (1981).

[7] No law is perfectly successful: the law against murder is violated every day, but it is still a law.

[8] The late Arthur Leff, in a series of important writings on the law of contract, shows that in the American corporate community, companies who break contracts are typically not sued–they are shunned.

[9] *Compare* M. BARKUN, LAW WITHOUT SANCTION (1968); W. MICHAEL REISMAN, SANCTIONS AND ENFORCEMENT, IN INTERNATIONAL LAW ESSAYS 381, 383–89 (1981).

[10] [Editor's Note: See the discussion on the Alvarez Extradition Case in this Anthology, Chapters 8 and 16.]

[11] This is analogous to H.L.A. Hart's exclusion of international law from "mature" legal systems, because it lacks a "rule of recognition" (Hart's equivalent of the positivist's command-backed-by-sanction). *See* H.L.A. HART, THE CONCEPT OF LAW 208–31 (1961). For a critique along these lines, see Anthony D'Amato, *The Neo-Positivist Concept of International Law*, 59 A.J.I.L. 321 (1965).

the positivist will have to argue that any legal system in which social disapproval functions as the sole sanction (for example, in a peaceful tribal society) does not in fact have "law." "Law" is present only when, in addition to social disapproval, there is physical coercion stemming from the sovereign power of the state. But what if there is no need for this physical coercion? The positivist must then conclude that there is no law.

Such a position would be difficult to defend, for if there is a society where people are so law-abiding that they need nothing more than a social-disapproval sanction, that society manifests a rather good case of "law." It is strange to insist that, for there to be law, physical coercion must also be used even if there is no need for it.

Yet the serious student of law may not be satisfied with the preceding argument in its entirety, because of the problem of what happens if the need for physical coercion should arise. In the international system, at least, we have states which occasionally break the rules of international law and which seem not to be deterred by expressions of social disapproval from the other states.[12] This is a reality of international life. Therefore, unlike the tribal society where social disapproval may constitute an effective sanction, international society needs a physical sanction to underscore its legal rules. Otherwise, the rules will occasionally be flouted. Perhaps they will be ignored most often when the "chips are down," which is exactly when they most need to be enforced. How can we call such a system, dependent for its support on so feeble a mechanism as social approval, a "legal" system?

It is hard to discern the logic behind the preceding objection, even while it is easy to understand it. We all recognize, and regret, that rules of international law are flouted on occasion, and we are all too aware of the fact that an outraged world public opinion simply is incapable of discouraging the violation. But should we jump to the conclusion that the rules of international law are not "law" as we know the term, because "law" involves the concept of physical enforcement? Yet, even in asking this, we acknowledge that physical enforcement is not a necessary characteristic of law (our "utopian" examples). And we also acknowledge that, even in domestic cases, where the state is one of the parties, we cannot meaningfully speak of physical enforcement (Professor Fisher's argument). These two arguments destroy most of the logical force of the contention that international law is not really law, and yet positivists may want to cling to that position.

Some early writers on the law of nations attempted to meet the enforcement objection head-on, by asserting that rules of international law are enforced by the mechanism of war. A nation that violates the rules will be the object of a "just war" initiated precisely to punish the transgressing nation and to enforce the validity of the rules. This neat logical argument sounds hopelessly out of touch with reality, for we know enough about wars to have learned that bad guys can win if they are strong enough. Physical might bears no necessary connection to international right.

Yet there is something about the notion of a "just war" that may point the way toward a compelling case for the proposition that international law is really "law." I will try to show in Section C that "reciprocal-entitlement violation" is a mechanism somewhat reminiscent of the old "just war" notion that may provide a realistic enforcement mechanism for international law.

At present, we may conclude tentatively as follows:

(1) The fact that some states sometimes disobey some rules of international law does not itself mean that those rules are not rules of "law," because even in domestic society some people (e.g., criminals) break the law from time to time.

(2) On the other hand, the fact that most states obey most rules of international law most of the time is not enough to call those rules "legal" because we are especially concerned with "important" cases where states may get away with violating rules of international law. If states can violate rules with impunity when it is in their national interest to do so, how can we call those rules "law"?

(3) We recognize, even though it makes us somewhat uncomfortable, that international law is more properly analogized to domestic cases where the state is a party than to domestic cases where one citizen sues another. Under this conception, we concede that our usual notions of "enforcement" are not appropriately applied to the state. Yet we may not feel that this argument is a clincher.

(4) We further concede that physical coercion is not a necessary component of "law." However, we are reluctant to conclude that it is totally unnecessary, because we have seen too many cases where a nation violates international law and gets away with it because of the lack of an effective enforcement mechanism.

(5) Hence, we are somewhat, though not totally, persuaded that international law can properly be labelled "law" for most purposes. But we may remain unconvinced, at this point, that it is really "law."

B. The "Verbal" Argument

So let's take a different tack. Suppose we were to read all the communications that governments officially make to one another: letters, speeches, proclamations, treaties, agreements, diplomatic initiatives, and so on. Suppose we read these with an eye toward whether the language contained in these communications refers to "law" and is "legal" language. In brief, we would be engaging in a "content analysis" of these communications to see whether what is being asserted and claimed therein can properly be

---

[12] [Editor's Note: The United States' abduction of a Mexican citizen may be an instance of a violation of international law by a superpower that is not deterred by international law. For a discussion, see the debate on "domestication" in Chapter 16 of this Anthology.]

called "legal."[13] We will find that, indeed, much of the content of intergovernmental communications is self-consciously grounded in legal terminology. We should not be surprised, considering the fact that lawyers typically help draft these documents and speeches. We will find, indeed, that the more important the communication, the more likely it is cast in legal terms, and the more likely it is that lawyers have played a role in drafting it.

We might then want to argue that, given the reality of this legal language, it would be rather absurd to maintain that "law" is not involved in these intergovernmental communications. If the relevant actors call it "law," who are we to say that their terminology is incorrect? Rather, is it not our job, as observers or scholars, to employ the terms the way the relevant actors intend those terms to be employed? In this fashion, the very utilization of legal language in intergovernmental communications is an argument for the proposition at least that governments resort to "law" (or what they call "law") in their attempts to influence each other.

We might want to add to this argument the position taken by the "policy-oriented jurisprudence" of Myers McDougal and his colleagues Harold Lasswell, Michael Reisman, Lung-chu Chen, and others. We might collect on a library shelf their voluminous works and ask, "what have they written about?" Surely, we assume, they must be writing about "law"—the word appears in the titles of their books, and their books are catalogued in the "law" section of the library. If we go and take their books down from the shelf and actually read them, we begin to find an extraordinarily broad definition of "law." The concept is so broad, indeed, that we wonder if there is anything which those writers could properly call "non-law." They cite works from the social sciences, from the humanities, as well as works on international law and international politics. Their idea of international law is that it is a process of authoritative decision-making, but then they seem to view the notion of "authoritative" in such broad terms as to encompass just about any decision made by any international decisionmaker for any reason. Finally, they deliberately disassociate law from enforcement. Legal rules, according to Professor McDougal, "exhaust their effective power when they guide a decision-maker to relevant factors and indicate presumptive weightings."[14]

According to the policy-oriented jurisprudence school, therefore, international law is nothing other than international communication. Under the first argument I made in this Section, the prevalence of legal language in international communication indicates that nations are talking about, and believe they are talking about, "law" in the positions they take vis-a-vis each other. Under the second McDougal-type argument, international communication itself is "law" even when it is not couched in legal terms. Taken together, both of these positions may convince the reader that "international law" is really "law."

In the past, I was intrigued by the law-as-communication approach.[15] Recently, I have become uneasy with it, in the first place because it proves too much. Any international contention couched in legal language (or even, following McDougal, *not* couched in legal language) can become "law." Yet surely "law" is not everything.[16] Or if it is, the term "law" has become totally useless.

The second misgiving I have about the verbal argument is that scholars are, after all, not precluded from criticizing the propriety of the use of language by other persons. Even though international communications are typically couched in legal terms, an observer does not have to conclude that the use of the term "law" in those communications is proper usage. For instance, in the insurance business, contracts between insurance companies are called "treaties." An international lawyer surely is not precluded from criticizing this use of the word "treaties" if that criticism might throw some light on what insurance companies are really doing in the contracts they make with each other.[17] Similarly, we might properly criticize the resort to legal terminology in international communications if we can show that it is not properly "law" that is being invoked.

We may therefore conclude this Section by saying, simply, that the prevalence of legal language in international communications may add to our previous conclusions that international law can properly be called "law" for most purposes and in most contexts. Nevertheless, we reserve final judgment on the question whether it is really "law."

C. The "Reciprocal Entitlements Violation" Argument

I believe that a conclusive argument can be fashioned that international law is really law, by showing that international law is enforceable in the same way that domestic

[13] For a demonstration of the technique of content analysis, *see* P. STONE, D. DUNPHY, M. SMITH & D. OGILVIE, THE GENERAL INQUIRER (1966). For an example of content analysis applied to the writings of foreign policy actors in order to derive predictive "general constructs" of their behavior, *see* Anthony D'Amato, *Psychological Constructs in Foreign Policy Prediction,* 11 J. CONFLICT RES. 294 (1967).

[14] MYERS MCDOUGAL & ASSOCIATES, STUDIES IN WORLD PUBLIC ORDER 887 n.109 (1960).

[15] *See, e.g.,* Anthony D'Amato, *The Relation of Theories of Jurisprudence to International Politics and Law,* 27 WASH. & LEE L. REV. 257 (1970); *cf.* Anthony D'Amato, *What "Counts" as Law?,* in Nicholas Onuf (ed.), LAW-MAKING IN THE GLOBAL COMMUNITY 83 (1982) (attempts to put the verbal approach in perspective).

[16] Even life, according to a quip by the playwright Neil Simon, "isn't *everything.*"

[17] For example, does the use of the term "treaty" imply that rules of international law relating to treaty interpretation should be followed in disputes among insurance companies, instead of domestic contract rules? Since the answer in this case is clearly "no," the use of the term "treaty" can be criticized as misleading. (Psychologically, the use of the term "treaties" may make insurance company executives feel important.)

law is enforceable. That kind of showing should be convincing to the most hardened skeptic of international law.

Of course, I won't make the claim that international law is always, invariably enforced. Rather, I'll suggest that we take a closer look at what we mean by enforcement, and then show that our meaning of the term is applicable equally to the domestic and to the international legal systems.

When we examine the concept of enforcement of law, the first thing we notice is that law can be enforced in many ways. For example, a parent might frown upon a child who does not brush his teeth, or might express stern disapproval. This could tend to "enforce" the law, although as we saw in Section A, social disapproval is not quite a satisfactory concept when we think of enforcement. It's not satisfactory because it's too easy for the child (or a nation) to decide to violate the law and pay the mild price of incurring social displeasure.

Thus, we want to narrow the concept of enforcement. Perhaps a good way to begin to narrow it is to exclude all modes of "enforcement" that are extrinsic to the legal system itself. Social disapproval, in this conception, is extrinsic to the legal system. Social disapproval is an external mechanism for enforcing (or more accurately, reinforcing) the law, but we know intuitively that it is not provided by or required by the law itself.[18]

When we look at the internal workings of a legal system, we find provisions for deprivations and disabilities. When a person disobeys the law, the law itself provides for his "punishment." This possibility of punishment, in turn, is supposed to deter a rational person from violating the law in the first place.

Enforcement thus consists of some form of *legally* imposed sanction. Sanctions don't have to be physical: a monetary fine is an example of a punishment that is purely financial. Physical punishments include being deprived of your freedom (for example by being incarcerated or being forced to perform some kind of community service) or physical harm (the old methods of beatings or public whippings). In the extreme, the law may impose capital punishment.

In this spectrum of legally imposed sanctions for violation of the law, we find that what the law has in fact done is to remove one or more of your entitlements. I could use the word "rights" here instead of "entitlements"—for example, your rights to life, to liberty, and to property. But the word "entitlements" is more precise, because it denotes legally recognized rights. If you claim a right that the law does not recognize (for example, a woman's claim to the right to vote before the Constitutional amendment of 1920 providing for universal suffrage), you may have a claim of right but you do not have a claim of entitlement. Since we are talking about enforcement mechanisms intrinsic to the legal system, it is more precise to speak of entitlements than to speak of rights.

In all cases of law violation, the law responds by depriving you of one or more of your entitlements. You have a legal entitlement to liberty; you lose it if you commit a crime punishable by incarceration. You have a legal entitlement to your bank account; you lose it if you have failed to pay your taxes or if someone obtains a judgment against you and attaches it. You have an entitlement to performance under a private contract that you make with someone else; if you fail to perform your part of the bargain, a court may decide that you have forfeited your entitlement under the contract. Some of these entitlement deprivations that you suffer because you have violated the law can be effectuated against you without any need for physical enforcement. Your bank account can be taken away from you by a bookkeeping entry made in the bank pursuant to a court order. Your marriage can be legally dissolved by a court decree without your willing compliance or participation. Thus, when we think of legal enforcement, we need not imagine the use of physical force against the person of the law-violator, although, of course, in some cases physical force is used. The deprivation of your entitlement to life, liberty, or property may be imposed by court order as a result from your conviction of a crime.

In order to deter or punish people by the threat of removal of their entitlements, people have to start out by having entitlements. Accordingly, all legal systems without exception assign certain entitlements to the people—usually but not always life, liberty, and property. With those entitlements, each person becomes vulnerable to their deprivation by law. Thus it comes about that legal systems typically enforce their rules by removing one or more entitlements of rule-violators.

How does the international legal system work in this regard? Let us begin by imagining a simple international situation. Two nations are at war with each other, but are weary of it and are interested in the possibility of peace. The problem now is how to send a peace ambassador from one nation to the other. The war between them is so total and brutal that no one "volunteers" to be an emissary, because of reasonable fear of being killed by the other side. Since we have not assumed any prior history between the two warring nations, we cannot invoke prior prescribed methods of getting the two sides to talk about peace.

Perhaps nation A might find a particularly brave person who would carry a letter saying, "don't kill the bearer of this letter, as we are attempting to set up communications with you, and we promise to give safe conduct to any person you choose to send to us who has a similar letter signed by you. Moreover, as evidence of our good faith, you can hold the bearer of this letter hostage while your emissary is en route to us, and release him upon the safe return of your own emissary." Such a letter, of course, would not guarantee that its bearer would be safe. All we

[18] If the law required social disapproval to be inflicted upon any law-violator, then you would have the problem of how to force people to socially disapprove of a miscreant's behavior. This would entail an infinite regress, because we'd need other people to socially disapprove of those persons who fail to disapprove of the miscreant's behavior.

know is that, in some instances, letters such as this one must have worked. Of course, we don't know much about instances where the letter didn't work, because its bearer was killed and presumably no written record of the event has survived. But in those cases where the letter did work, a primitive entitlement became established between the two nations. We could call that entitlement "limited ambassadorial immunity" or refer to the document as "a letter of safe conduct."

But one entitlement apiece will not suffice. Suppose nation A is furious with the peace terms brought by nation B's emissary, and responds by killing the emissary. A has, of course, violated the "safe conduct" agreement. What can B do? B can, of course, kill A's emissary (the one B held as a guarantee of the safe return of its own emissary). But that act simply plunges A and B back into total war. And the next time around, a new entitlement might have a harder time getting started, because A and B will remember what happened when the first entitlement got started and then was promptly violated.

Peace would have had a better chance of getting started between A and B if there had been a second, different entitlement in the picture. Suppose, in addition to the emissaries, each nation was holding hostage a national of the other nation. Then the newly emerging entitlement of diplomatic immunity might have had a better chance to survive because of the possibility of retaliation not against the other emissary but against the hostage. Increasing the importance of the hostage would serve the cause of peace even better. That is probably why, in early wars, the king of each side would often volunteered personally to go over to the other side and be held hostage. The kings thus served as personal guarantors for the safety of the peace negotiators.

We can see that the more entitlements on the list, the better the chance that peace has to get started. The fact is that international law provides states with a long list of entitlements. Even a newly born state (such as a nation that has just received its independence from a colonial power) immediately gets a gift of these entitlements.

Our new nation receives at its birth a host of entitlements. It has not chosen any of these entitlements; it has not selected any; it has not even consented to receive any.[19] Instead the entitlements are simply thrust upon the new nation. The first entitlement is of fundamental importance: the entitlement of statehood, which means, in the international system, that our new nation is a geographic entity entitled to exert its own legal jurisdiction in the area within its boundaries and to claim the inviolability of those boundaries against all other states. The legal sanctity of its borders signifies that our new state is a state in a community of states, and not merely a gang of thieves subject to the untrammelled degradations of other neighboring gangs. Indeed, the new nation's receipt of the entitlement of statehood is almost a tautology: by becoming a new state, the new state can enjoy the international-law definition of what a state is. A new state would hardly be a "state" without enjoying the sanctity of its borders. But the entitlement of statehood is not wholly tautological. For international law could have evolved in a manner such that a new state (like a human infant) at first does not possess the full entitlement of statehood (like a child not possessing all the rights of an adult). For example, in its early years, a state might be subject to interventions at will from neighboring states. However, that sort of system never evolved. For good or ill, the international system in fact has evolved so as to give a new nation a full, mature set of the very same entitlements that all other states have.

In sum, still considering this first entitlement, our new nation depends for its very identity upon the recognition of other similar states in the community of states. I am not talking about de jure recognition; rather, all that is necessary is a sense in the international community that the new state is enclosed by international boundaries, and those boundaries, like all boundaries, are lines that differentiate the internal affairs of the state from the external affairs and cannot be crossed at will by military forces in either direction. This notion of a boundary is so fundamental that the Vienna Convention on the Law of Treaties specifically excepts boundary-establishing treaties from the normal rules of rebus sic stantibus (article 62), and the World Court in its leading decision in the Continental Shelf Cases

---

[19] Some writers have suggested that the entitlements are based on the "consent" of the new nation. *See, e.g.*, GRIGORI TUNKIN, THEORY OF INTERNATIONAL LAW 123–33 (1974); G. VAN HOOF, RETHINKING THE SOURCES OF INTERNATIONAL LAW 76–82 (1983). For a critique of 'consent' theories, *see* ANTHONY D'AMATO, THE CONCEPT OF CUSTOM IN INTERNATIONAL LAW 187–99 (1971). Even the writers who insist upon consent will accept tacit consent; yet it is a short move from tacit consent to inferred consent, i.e., that given all the other elements that constitute a norm of international law, consent ultimately is inferred even if there is no evidence of it. Even so, the logic of their position compels them to acknowledge that a new nation is not bound by any particular rule of international law until it has consented to that rule. The new nation is then in a preferred position; it can pick and choose among the rules those that it likes. This pick-and-choose position is clearly wrong as a matter of logic as well as history. Logically, if a new nation tried to assert such a position, the reaction of the other nations might well be that the new nation's rights as well as its duties have thus been put up for grabs, placing the new nation in a perilous position vis-a-vis its boundaries and other basic legal entitlements. Perhaps some such calculus has operated to dissuade any new nation from making the claim that these writers assert. Indeed, history bears out this position. No new nation, to my knowledge, has ever asserted that it has the right to pick and choose among existing international entitlements. As summarized by Sir Humphrey Waldock: "No State has ever argued before the World Court that it was exempt from a general customary rule simply because it was a new State that objected to the rule. In the Right of Passage case, for example, it never occurred to India to meet Portugal's contention as to a general customary right of passage to enclaves by saying that she was a new state; nor did Poland, new-born after the First World War, ever make such a claim in any of her many cases before the Permanent Court." Sir Humphrey Waldock, *General Course on Public International Law*, 106 RECUEIL DES COURS 1, 52 (1962).

made it clear that the normal generation of customary international law cannot affect ownership of territory (in those cases, the submerged land areas) absent a showing of consent from the owner.[20]

Our new state might, therefore, look upon the international law of the sanctity of its boundaries as a gift of a valuable entitlement. But the entitlement carries with it reciprocal duties, so that it is not necessarily a gift. Reciprocity entails that our new nation must respect the borders of all the other states. Indeed, reciprocity is inherent in the concept of defining states as separate entities. Viewed from "within" (or "subjectively"), a state may regard itself as entitled to any values or goods it wishes, even if those values and goods are located outside its borders. But a state may also view itself from "without" (or "objectively")– recognizing itself to be one state among many, deserving no more consideration than any other state. Any subjective desire is matched up against recognition of the objective desires of all states including oneself. The result of the subjective-objective dualism is an expectation of reciprocity.

From just a subjective point of view, the entitlement of sanctity of boundaries may seem more a curse than a blessing. If our new state is militarily powerful and expansionist minded, it might want to extend its boundaries at the expense of its neighbor–in other words, it might want to annex its neighbor.[21] Even so, the very contemplation of annexation includes a desire, once annexation is completed,[22] to have all other nations respect the newly enlarged state. Obviously the desire to annex and the desire to have other nations respect the annexation are mutually incompatible when assessed "objectively"–our new state clearly would not want to be annexed by other states. Hence, the reciprocity inherent in the notion of independent states operates not so much as a limitation upon the freedom of action of our new state (even though it may seem that way from the "subjective" point of view), but rather simply as a rule of the game.[23]

The rule of sanctity of boundaries, therefore, is simply imposed upon the new state at birth. The new state has become a player in the game of international relations, and the rules–which were there before the player joined the game–go with the territory. The new state may dislike particular rules, but I suspect that the new state, whatever it may say, welcomes the entirety of the rules. For if it is pressed to make a judgment whether to accept or reject the list of entitlements as a whole, the new nation would most likely accept the list. It is hard to imagine how the new nation could reject the list, because that would entail giving up its standing as a new nation. Moreover, the list of entitlements is not in its entirety onerous; after all, the list was not handed down from a handful of feuding gods on Mount Olympus, but rather evolved slowly over time to serve the collective self-interest of all the states in the international system.

So far I have mentioned only one entitlement–the basic entitlement to sanctity of boundaries. But there are more; in fact, the list is very long indeed. For the list includes every rule of customary international law. Every single norm in the international system is an entitlement, a "rule of the game," which serves to give our new nation a right against all the other states and at the same time to oblige our new state to respect that same right when it is asserted by any other state. Thus, immediately following the initial entitlement of sanctity of boundaries, would be the entitlement of diplomatic immunity (to facilitate negotiations with other states), the entitlement to enter into binding treaties with other nations, to have those treaties construed and applied according to the generally accepted rules of customary international law pertaining to the interpretation of treaties, to enjoy free use of the high seas, to claim rights over the superjacent airspace, to have jurisdiction over its continental shelf (if the new nation happens to have a continental shelf),[24] to have its citizens enjoy the protections of human-rights law when they travel to other countries, to regulate its commercial trade with other states, to enjoy the protections of the laws of war and rules regulating the conduct of hostilities, to exert extraterritorial jurisdiction within the international rules regulating that subject, and so on through the entire list of international norms. Each specific norm works in two ways: to benefit our new nation to the extent that it has any interest in claiming any specific entitlement, and to impose upon our new nation the duty to respect the same entitlement when it is asserted against itself by other nations.

---

[20] North Sea Continental Shelf (W. Ger. v. Den., W. Ger. v. Neth.), 1969 ICJ Rep. 3. This case has been widely misinterpreted; for a full account of the interpretation given in the text, see Anthony D'Amato, *The Concept of Human Rights in International Law,* 82 COLUM. L. REV. 1110, 1142–44 (1982).

[21] A recent example was Iraq's attempted annexation of Kuwait.

[22] If Iraq expected this after it annexed Kuwait, its expectation was rudely disappointed by the international community, which intervened forcibly in the situation, beat the Iraqi armies back, liberated Kuwait, and required Iraq to pay the entire costs of the intervention out of Iraq's future oil revenues.

[23] Nearly all rules of nearly all games are reciprocal; though a rule may temporarily constrain one player, that player knows that the same rule can and will operate to constrain the opposing player. It would be rather absurd for a player in a game to demand to be entitled to violate one of the rules while insisting that the rule be respected by the other side.

[24] Obviously our new nation will be physically endowed in a unique way. Nations are quite different from each other in terms of whether they border on the oceans, whether they have mineral wealth beneath their soil, and so forth. There is no "reciprocity" regarding these physical attributes in the international system any more than there is reciprocity among persons who are born with different physical attributes and talents. The "law" as it has evolved both internationally and domestically may give each unit (a state, a person) "equal protection of the law," but, so far at least (except for the communist experiment in sharing property) does not attempt to redistribute physical assets or personal property.

Taken as a whole, these entitlements define what it is to be a "nation" (or "state") in the modern world. Interestingly, a state is more "vulnerable" to entitlement-deprivation than a person. A person is not *defined* by her legal entitlements; rather, a person can acquire entitlements when she becomes subject to a particular legal system. But states are different. A state is nothing but a bundle of entitlements. If you take away all the state's entitlements, nothing is left,[25] whereas if you take away a person's entitlements, the person remains in a "state of nature." To be sure, if you take away a person's entitlement to life, then nothing is left. But the crucial point is that people were not born into this world with an "entitlement" to life in the legal sense; they were simply born into the world, and entitlements came later. In contrast, in the modern era at least (we don't have to go back now to primitive states in antiquity), a state is only "born" when the international community recognizes it as a state. And that recognition by the international community is simply a shorthand description of the international community's bestowing upon the new state the long list of entitlements that we call customary law.

This conclusion in turn illustrates why, as a matter of its very identity, a state should act in such a manner as to preserve its entitlements. Yet, its identity as a state, its bundle of entitlements, is dependent upon the acquiescence of all the other states in the system. Since every state has the same bundle of entitlements, the other states in the system have an obvious interest in acquiescing in the entitlements of any given state. In this manner, a new state starts out, as we have seen, with its full complement of entitlements.

But just as all the states in the international legal system have a collective interest in acquiescing to all the entitlements for any given state in the system, they also have an interest in preserving the entitlements as they have been defined in the course of the development of international customary law. For ease of illustration, let us consider the previously mentioned entitlement of diplomatic immunity. All the states in the system have an interest in the preservation of this particular entitlement. The existence of this entitlement, like other entitlements, helps define what a state is and what the international legal system is. The system would be something different, perhaps diminished, if the entitlement of diplomatic immunity were undermined.

Prior to 1979, it would have been difficult to come up with a single example of a state which directly violated the entitlement of diplomatic immunity. In nearly every case from the dawn of history down to 1979, whenever a diplomat's life or liberty was threatened, the host state immediately took action against those persons who threatened the diplomat. Safety of the other side's diplomatic representatives was something that was inviolate, even in the darkest days of the two world wars. But then in 1979, the unprecedented happened. After some radical students occupied the American Embassy in Teheran, the government of Iran took the unheard of step of ratifying the action and holding the American diplomatic personnel hostage. This was a case of a blatant violation of a hallowed international entitlement. To allow it to go unremedied would constitute a threat to the existence of the entitlement of diplomatic immunity within the international legal system.

Let us consider the strategies open to the international community to reverse Iran's action. We dismiss at the outset the absurd idea of dropping a nuclear bomb on Iran (even though some outraged Americans suggested doing so), because that would, among other horrible things, kill every diplomatic person who was being held hostage. Moreover, the retaliation would be clearly disproportionate to Iran's initial act.[26] A second strategy would be to allow the United States to violate Iran's diplomatic entitlement by arresting and detaining diplomatic and consular officials of Iran who were physically present in the United States at the time of the takeover of the American embassy in Iran. This tit-for-tat strategy deserves a closer look. In the first place, it is not always effective.[27] As we saw pre-

[25] Like the wonderful cinematic moment in the 1933 film, *The Invisible Man*, when Claude Rains removes the long bandage from around his head and there is no head underneath.

[26] International law has not evolved a specific measure of proportionality, but it is at least clear that the countermeasure cannot be wholly disproportionate to the initial delict. The Air Service Case, quoted in ELISABETH ZOLLER, PEACETIME UNILATERAL REMEDIES: AN ANALYSIS OF COUNTERMEASURES 167 (1984), calls attention to the possibility of a wholly different countermeasure, and states that it should be measured in terms of quality as well as quantity in order to judge proportionality. Interestingly, the social science literature bears out the effectiveness of quantitatively non-measurable responses so long as there is an ordinal ordering of preferences. As ROBERT AXELROD, THE EVOLUTION OF COOPERATION 17–18 (1984) demonstrates, the payoffs of the two players need not be comparable, nor symmetric, nor measurable on an absolute scale, and there is no need to assume rationality on the part of the players. The only ordering of preferences is that a nation prefers there to be no rule violation, and prefers taking a countermeasure in the event of a rule violation rather than letting the violator get away with a rule violation. In turn, taking countermeasures, in an iterated series (which for international purposes can extend over the centuries) is a stable and robust strategy for deterring the initial delict. Nations in their interactions seem to have evolved a tit-for-tat or a tit-for-a-different-tat strategy in their numerous interactions over the centuries, and this probably accounts for the stability of international legal rules. The tit-for-a-different-tat strategy is actually codified in the Vienna Convention on the Law of Treaties, art. 60, allowing a party to suspend any treaty obligation or obligations if the other party commits a material breach of any of its obligations.

[27] For a recent, provocative explication of the tit-for-tat strategy, see AXLEROD, *supra* n.26. See also ANATOL RAPOPORT, STRATEGY AND CONSCIENCE 48–57 (1964); ANATOL RAPOPORT, FIGHTS, GAMES AND DEBATES 166–79 (1960). The most complete analysis of the legality of countermeasures under international law is found in Zoller, op. cit. *supra* n.26. However, Professor Zoller appears to confine her conclusions to countermeasures which do not violate an independent norm of international law (i.e., those which may simply violate a state's treaty commitments or other such obliga-

viously in the idealized example of two states at total war, the tit-for-tat strategy would simply eliminate the incipient ambassadorial-immunity entitlement and plunge the states back into the chaos of total war. Today, under a more developed international legal system, the tit-for-tat strategy might not have as negative an outcome, but it nevertheless could operate to erode rather than to preserve the entitlement in question. For instance, if the United States had jailed all Iranian diplomatic and consular officials, such an action at least in theory could be interpreted not as an attempt to punish Iran for its initial act but rather as a recognition that Iran's act was correct and that in fact diplomats are not entitled to immunity. I say "in theory" because this particular example has too strong a history of diplomatic immunity behind it to be eroded so quickly by the two counterexamples we posit as coming from Iran and the United States. But generally, since the content of international law depends upon the recognition by all the states in the system of what the entitlements are, the action I have just hypothesized by the United States and Iran might well be interpreted as a new understanding of the entitlement of diplomatic immunity, i.e., that such immunity exists no longer. At least it will be an important step along the customary-law route that could lead to the destruction of this particular entitlement. Consider the following more realistic example of the same theoretical process: nation A announces a territorial sea of 300 miles from its coastline; nation B argues that A has illegally infringed upon the high seas by attempting to expropriate part of it, and in a spirit of sheer retaliation, nation B proclaims its *own* 300-mile territorial sea. Despite nation B's claim (that it was issuing its proclamation in retaliation for A's), the action it took tends to *reinforce* A's claim. Thus, rather than challenging A's claim to a 300-mile territorial sea, B has perhaps inadvertently reinforced it. A new rule for territorial seas, giving coastal states a much larger area of jurisdiction over the high seas, may well have been started by A's and B's similar proclamations. Thus, the tit-for-tat strategy, played against the background of customary international law, could not only fail to deter the original entitlement violation but in fact serve to reinforce it and make a new rule of law out of it.

As things turned out, perhaps for the reason I've just suggested as well as other reasons, the United States did not choose to retaliate by jailing Iranian consular and diplomatic officials. That very strategy was considered by the U.S. government and duly reported in the media.[28] Instead, the United States tried a third strategic approach.

The United States "froze"' approximately thirteen billion dollars of Iranian deposits in American banks and in various European banks where the United States, through American corporations, had the power to act.[29] If it were not for the initial Iranian act of holding the American diplomats hostage, the United States would have violated the Iranian entitlement to the use of its own bank deposits abroad. Yet customary international law regarded the U.S. "freeze" as intended to preserve the diplomatic-immunity entitlement that Iran had violated. More was involved than just a temporary freeze; as I review the figures, the United States actually was involved in a taking of Iranian assets. The United States effectively confiscated much of the interest the Iranian bank assets would have earned. I've not seen any real public discussion of this aspect of the matter, but by my own reckoning, at the time the $13 billion of Iranian money was blocked, world interest rates were at approximately 15%. The Iranian assets remained blocked for slightly over one year. At compound interest, this works out to interest earned – and unpaid – of over two billion dollars. Later, when the hostages were returned to the United States, the United States agreed to pay, in partial settlement, interest of $800 million to Iran.[30] Clearly, there is no entitlement under customary international law to confiscate the interest on another nation's bank accounts. Yet, again, there was no condemnation of the American action by the international community, not even from nations that regard the inviolability of their own bank accounts abroad as something more important than life itself. There is only one explanation: the international community did not regard the American action as endangering the status of governmental bank accounts in foreign banks, but rather as *preserving* the entire system of entitlements. The American action was in retaliation for a blatant, historically unprecedented entitlement-violation by Iran. The United States acted to restore that entitlement (diplomatic immunity) by temporarily violating a different entitlement (Iran's property rights in its bank accounts). Significantly, the United States made no claim whatsoever to a general right to invade other nations' bank accounts. Instead, the United States described its invasion of Iran's bank accounts as a "freeze" – the word suggests that the freeze will be lifted as soon as the American diplomats are returned safely to the United States. More than that, the confiscation of some $1.2 billion in interest was generally perceived as a reasonable retaliation, if not punishment, for Iran's violation of the diplomatic-immunity entitlement.

tions owing to a particular state). In the Case Concerning the Air Service Agreement (*U.S. v. France*), appended to Professor Zoller's book, the Arbitral tribunal concludes: "Under the rules of present-day international law, and unless the contrary results from special obligations arising under particular treaties, notably from mechanisms created within the framework of international organisations, each State establishes for itself its legal situation vis-a-vis other States. If a situation arises which, in one State's view, results in the violation of an international obligation by another State, the first State is entitled, within the limits set by the general rules of international law pertaining to the use of armed force, to affirm its rights through counter-measures."

[28] See N.Y. TIMES, Dec. 13, 1979, at Al, col. 5. To some extent, the U.S. government may have believed that Iran would not care very much about the fate of its overseas ambassadors who might have been the subjects of U.S. retaliation.

[29] See Nickel, *Battling for Iran's Frozen Billions,* FORTUNE, Dec. 15, 1980, at 117.

[30] See N.Y. TIMES, Jan. 21, 1981, at s A9, col. 1.

The workings of international law are rarely as explicit as scholars might like them to be, but I believe we are entitled to infer from the reaction of the community of nations that they did not perceive a threat to the shared entitlement of preserving property rights in state-owned deposits in foreign banks as a result of the American action, but rather regarded the U.S. action as a temporary infringement of an Iranian entitlement for the limited purpose of enforcing the original entitlement of diplomatic immunity. I am not just speculating about the reaction of the international community. We have proof of the international reaction in the unanimous decision of the World Court that Iran had violated the diplomatic-immunity entitlement. The panel of judges represented states from all over the world, but not a single judge regarded Iran's action as legitimate.[31] We can safely conclude that the international community accepted the legality of a strategy that violates an offending nation's entitlements in order to repudiate that nation's initial offense. In the Iran-United States case, the strategy worked well, for the American diplomatic personnel were all safely returned to the United States, and the United States lifted the freeze on Iranian assets. There was never any doubt that the U.S. froze the assets solely as an enforcement measure – to protect the international system of entitlements – and not as an act of aggression against Iran. Nor was there ever any doubt that Iran violated a basic entitlement when it held the American diplomats hostage. And when the whole incident was over, Iran did not make any claim that holding diplomats hostage was justified under international law. In short, the entire incident vindicated the notion of the enforcement mechanism that has evolved in international law.

If we need a label for this mechanism, we could call it "tit-for-a-different-tat." While the U.S.-Iranian example is dramatic, the strategy is employed on numerous occasions in the course of the complex interactions among states.[32] The tit-for-a-different-tat strategy makes sense in a legal system that has neither a central court of compulsory jurisdiction, nor a world legislature, nor a world police force. It depends most crucially on international recognition and acceptance of the basic distinction between initial action and enforcement action. If a nation initially violates another nation's entitlement, it has committed a wrongful act (what Kelsen calls a "delict").[33] But if the other nation retaliates by violating one of the violator's entitlements, then no wrongful act is committed. Rather, the retaliation itself is regarded as an enforcement action. It is not only perfectly legal under international law; without it, we might not have international law.

Some people might object that the notion of unilateral enforcement of international law, using a tit-for-a-different-tat strategy, indicates that international law is still a primitive or crude system of law. These people would seem to prefer a world government that enforced international law through a world executive, a world legislature, and a world court system. For my money, it's a cure far worse than the disease. A world government, at this stage in human history, could be stifling. There would be no shortage of bureaucrats at the United Nations willing and anxious to govern the world, but why should we turn over our rights and liberties to them?

I think the international enforcement system works tolerably well as it stands. The strategy of tit-for-a-different-tat seems to provide in most cases the right amount of enforcement. My fear about the strategy is not that it is ineffective, but rather that it could lead to an escalation of retaliation. Nation A commits a delict; nation B retaliates by depriving nation A of one of its entitlements; nation A counter-retaliates by depriving nation B of another of its entitlements; and so on, leading to general war. I have been unable to think of any logical reason why such runaway retaliation might not someday occur. Therefore, I think we have to stay on our guard. Clearly, multilateral enforcement of entitlement violations (through the Security Council enforcement system of the United Nations) is preferable to unilateral enforcement. We are seeing in recent years a far more activist Security Council. I would be satisfied so long as the United Nations confines itself to enforcement of existing international norms without trying to invent too many new norms itself (by becoming a super-legislature).

But the fact that runaway tit-for-a-different-tat entitlement-violation could occur in the future does not disable us from describing the reality of present international law. At the present time, I claim that customary international law is enforced primarily through the tit-for-a-different-tat strategy of entitlement violation. True, the international system could destroy itself through a runaway series of violations of entitlements. But unless and until that happens, the system continues to police itself by allowing unilateral enforcement of entitlements through the tit-for-tat, or more typically, tit-for-a-different-tat system.

On the whole it is an effective system – as effective for international law as is the enforcement of most laws in domestic systems via the state-sanctioned deprivation of one or more entitlements held by individual citizens or corporations. It would be impossible to understand why nations do or refrain from doing the things they do without understanding what entitlements are included in the bundle and how nations act to preserve their full complement of existing entitlements. In this sense, international law is a very realistic component of the picture that political scientists try to draw of how nations behave. The "serious students of law" who claim that international law isn't really

---

[31] United States Diplomatic and Consular Staff in Tehran (U.S. v. Iran), 1980 I.C.J. 3. As for the U.S. retaliatory action in "freezing" Iranian assets, only two judges out of fifteen felt that the blocking of Iranian assets should be set off against any reparations owing to the United States. *See id.* at 51 (Morozov, J., dissenting); *id.* at 58 (Tarazi, J., dissenting). The other thirteen judges apparently felt that even a set-off should be disallowed, so blatant was Iran's violation of a fundamental entitlement.

[32] For examples of numerous "countermeasures," *see* ZOLLER, op. cit. *supra* n.26.

[33] *See* HANS KELSEN, PRINCIPLES OF INTERNATIONAL LAW (1952).

''law'' make the same mistake that some political scientists have made in the past in ignoring norms just to prove that they are being ''scientific'' in their ''descriptions.''[34] A state cannot be described without reference to its entitlements, nor can its actions be fully understood without reference to the steps it takes to preserve those entitlements. In sum, this retaliatory entitlement-deprivation system constitutes the ''physical sanction'' that positivists require for a system of norms to be called a ''legal'' system.

[34] *See The Political Science Critique* in Chapter 16, this Anthology.

Part II
Professional Tools

4

Sources of General International Law

A. Custom

1. Why Do We Need Customary Law?[1]

Many people feel a need to take the uncertainty out of international law. Let us for a moment suppose that, for every international dispute, there were a treaty provision exactly on point. Could we then say that all of international law has at last been written down, in a form that is ascertainable, retrievable, and definitive?

The answer–assuming the question makes sense–is a grudging "maybe." The written words that are presumably on point would still be subject to interpretation. That interpretation would take place against a context of underlying law. That underlying law would either be textual (i.e., other treaty provisions) or customary (unwritten law) or both–and part of the dispute would be, what law should be referred to in order to settle disputes over interpretation? But even if the treaty provision seems transparently clear, the disputing parties would still have to resort to an underlying customary law regarding the bindingness of the treaties, since treaties cannot provide for their own bindingness–it takes something outside the treaty to say that the treaty itself is binding. And along with the question of bindingness is the question whether events subsequent to the entering into force of the treaty somehow change or modify the treaty provisions. Or to put this point more dramatically, a minute after a treaty is signed, its provisions may seem to be clear; but fifty years after it is signed, things in the real world will have changed enough so that doubt is cast upon the continuing application of the old words of the treaty or whether those words should be reinterpreted in light of history. Moreover, subsequent events could even change the treaty provisions under what in international law is known as clausula rebus sic stantibus–the customary law of changed conditions.

The foregoing considerations are all on the assumption that the question makes sense. But does it really make sense to think that treaties can be so fine-meshed that they take into account all future disputes and provide for the unambiguous resolution of all of those future disputes? Consider the best statutory schemes in the most legally advanced countries: no matter what the statute says, the legislature meets more or less continuously and revises the statutes that seem to get out of touch with events. Moreover, a judicial system provides a continuous interpretation of the statutes, providing a gloss of the meaning of the fine-meshed statutory provisions. Is it not folly to expect that, in the international system, a set of treaties can provide for the resolution of all future disputes in the absence of legislatures and courts?

Well, why not have a Treaty Revision Commission in constant session, so as to keep updating the provisions in treaties? Alas, the Treaty Revision Commission usually will not know that it has a problem with a particular treaty until a dispute arises. But as soon as a dispute arises, then the parties will want to have their dispute settled on the basis of the existing treaty language, and not on the basis of new language proposed by the Commission.

But the most important objection to the idea of the assumption that we can have a fine-meshed system of international treaties capable of resolving every dispute is precisely that nearly all disputes that could be settled by resort to a clear treaty provision simply do not become disputes at all! Disputes tend to arise when a treaty provision does *not* cover the dispute, or when its coverage is ambiguous or otherwise contestable. But you might object, taking a cue from Jeremy Bentham's (never-realized) wish, that the more fine-meshed the treaty system, the fewer disputes–or at least, the fewer important disputes–will tend to arise. Alas, this wish is not realizable, at least if a long demonstration I made in 1983 of the concept is sound (and so far, no one has contested it).[2] I believe I was successful in showing that real-world variety outpaces any conceivable attempt by legislators to subsume it under fine-meshed legislation. That real-world variety results in a race between events and statutes, each trying to catch up with the other, a process that if left to itself results in grotesque statutory schemes such as the present Internal Revenue Code and its accompanying Regulations. The most that a detailed statute can do is substitute statutory language for what otherwise would be resort to the underlying common law–in effect, making a change in the material the judge must read (code provisions instead of judicial decisions), but without materially affecting one's ability to order one's affairs or predict the outcome of future disputes. Indeed, the civil law tradition of Continental European countries is a large exemplary demonstration of this thesis. European law is no more predictable or certain than the law in common-law

---

[1] By ANTHONY D'AMATO, written for this Anthology.

[2] *See* Anthony D'Amato, *Legal Uncertainty*, 71 CALIF. L. REV. 1, 4–8 (1983).

countries, despite the presence in the European systems of what appear to be detailed, fine-meshed codes.

Thus, there is no getting away from customary international law even as treaties become more refined and comprehensive. For the ultimate power of customary international law is that it binds all states irrespective of their consent to specific rules. Thus it constitutes a default law—a law that applies to every dispute whenever a more specific treaty provision does not (for whatever reason of interpretation or clausula rebus sic stantibus) provide a sufficiently clear text to settle the dispute. There is no source of international law other than customary law that provides this kind of comprehensive default rule.

In the next section, W. Michael Reisman focuses on "incidents" as providing the basic precedents that incorporate and develop international customary norms. I wholly endorse Professor Reisman's arguments insofar as they apply to what has traditionally been called the "practice" component of international customary law. As I have advised law-review editors on many occasions, the "case note" in international law should really be the "incident note." For what forms the real basis for general international law applicable to all states—that is, for customary international law—is not the occasional judicial decision but rather the typical "incident" that embodies the states' own *resolution of international claim-conflicts.* The real-world "incident" is the full equivalent of a binding judicial decision in domestic law; it embodies the pragmatic resolution of a conflict in the international system by the state actors who are most concerned with the particular incident in question, and hence it has precedential value in customary law.[3] Its value is especially pragmatic, for as Professor Reisman argues, the kinds of results states have previously achieved in resolving their conflicts of claims have profound instructional value for resolving the situation at hand. "Law" in this instructional sense is an application of the trite saying, "there's no use re-inventing the wheel." But it is even more than that. Once the wheel is invented, new technology takes the invention of the wheel into account, so that, in another common saying, "there's no going back." Similarly, in international law, when the ribbons are tied on one "incident," future incidents will never be quite the same. Future incidents will be played out in light of the former incident. Thus there are two reasons for counting "incidents" as formative of customary international law: that they point the way to a resolution that has already "worked" in the past, and that their very position in the history of the development of international customary law has restructured all future reasonable expectations in light of the way they were in fact resolved.

The argument I made previously, that customary international law applies to states irrespective of their consent, follows from treating international "incidents" the same way domestic law treats precedents. If you have a domestic-law case, the court will cite prior cases *in which you played absolutely no part.* This prior law was created without your consent, and now it is binding upon you. What has happened is that you have not consented to the rules of law as they were developed in prior cases; instead you have consented to the *process* of common-law development of legal rules. Similarly, states do not consent to the specific rules of customary law, but only to the "metarule" of customary law formation. There are many proofs of this proposition. For example, customary rules immediately bind new states who come into existence in the international system, yet no state coming into existence has ever, in the history of international law, announced its non-consent to some of the norms of international law. No new state has ever felt entitled to "pick and choose" among the existing norms of custom. Indeed, new states find it to their immense advantage to accept all the rules of the system, because among those rules are basic rules that guarantee to the new state the things it wants most of all—secure borders and acceptance as an equal into the international community. To attempt to pick and choose from among the existing norms of international law would be to risk being declared a non-state or an outlaw state, and no new state has ever wished to be placed in such a position.

The present Chapter is devoted to the metarules of general law-formation. To the extent that any argument in this Chapter is persuasive, its persuasiveness rests on its accurate depiction of the way that states, over time, have in fact accepted the metarule of law formation at issue. It follows, incidentally, that there is nothing to stop states from changing the metarules of customary law formation that are described here; if they do so, then a new description will be needed. Nothing is written in granite.[4] But the metarule of customary formation changes only at a glacier-like pace, and it is therefore unlikely that there will be any substantial changes in the metarule itself in the foreseeable future.

So, what then is custom? I believe that there is a determinate answer to this question, but it is not one that is reducible to a sentence or a sound byte. Rather, the ascertainment of a customary rule of international law requires a certain amount of professional training. The bad news is that there are no short cuts, but that's also the good news. You have to develop an expertise, but once you develop it, you will have it and you can put it to professional use. It will give you an advantage, but it's the right kind of advantage—one that's attained not by money or social class or privilege but by personal effort.

The training I'm talking about would consist of three

---

[3] I also add, on these occasions, that researching an international incident is a lot more fun, and a lot more creative, than the rather sterile job of parsing a given judicial decision. The result is that an analysis of an international law "incident" will have a lasting value for practitioners and scholars; in contrast, the typical student "note" on a case is hardly ever read.

[4] And if I were saying this in the classroom, I would find it impossible to resist adding one of my terrible puns—"Nor should anything be taken for granite."

tasks. First, one should undertake an unhurried perusal of the nature of customary law as it has developed down to the present day, determining for oneself the context in which questions of custom arise and the questions arising from that context that we should ask of any coherent theory of custom. Second, one should engage in some practice, which can take the form of a research paper or a brief that argues for or against an alleged rule of custom – one that involves doing the library work and the thinking that is needed to prove one's case. Third, one should think through the connections between the first and second tasks, calibrating the conclusions in the first task against the conclusions reached in the second task. We should engage in what the philosopher Nelson Goodman called the "delicate process [of] making mutual adjustments between rules and accepted inferences."[5]

The second task – engaging in some form of practice – should be supervised by an experienced professor or practitioner of international law; it cannot be accomplished by just reading a book. But the first task is a scholarly one. I tried my hand at it in a book-length treatment of the subject published in 1971 (it actually took me – I'm ashamed to admit – twelve long years of work.) Some portions of the book are excerpted here, following Professor Reisman's significant discussion of incidents. After that are some critical views and some alternative formulations of customary law. All of these are relevant for testing the view of custom that you will be developing for yourself as you accept, reject, or modify – and above all, make your own – the material that follows.

2. Incidents[6]

The normative expectations that political analysts infer from events are the substance of much of contemporary international law. The fact that the people who are inferring norms from incidents do not refer to the product of their inquiry as "international law" in no way affects the validity of their enterprise, any more than Moliere's M. Jourdain's obliviousness to the fact that he was speaking prose meant that he was not.

Whatever it is called, law it is. Yet, at least on first consideration, it is startlingly inconsistent with our accepted notions of law to suggest that one ought to orient oneself in the international legal system by reference to these incidents rather than primarily by reference to statutes, treaties, venerable custom and judicial and arbitral opinions. Indeed, as we shall see, the jurisprudential implications of this reorganization of focus are profound, in ways going beyond even Jellinek's disquieting observation about the "normative force of the factual."[7]

International lawyers frequently lament the fact that they are rarely consulted by foreign policy decisionmakers. This cannot be attributed to a general, visceral dislike of lawyers, for government officials, when operating in a domestic setting, frequently consult their lawyers. They correctly assume that lawyers are reliable specialists in understanding the expectations of those who are politically and legally effective. Why is it that the same decisionmakers do not resort to their international lawyers with comparable frequency?

There are numerous reasons why international lawyers are increasingly irrelevant in many areas of international politics, not all of them attributable to the lawyers themselves. We cannot ignore the advanced decay of the formal legal system that was painstakingly reconstructed after World War II. One is as unlikely to seek and pay for the advice of the votaries of a demonstrably ineffective legal system as one is to seek and pay for the blessings of the high priests of a sect manifestly out of favor with the pertinent divinity. But the problems we call "legal" continue to present themselves for resolution, whatever the state of the system; someone must perform legal functions even in a decaying system.

The reasons for the diminished relevance of international lawyers are attributable less to the system than to the international lawyers themselves and the jurisprudential framework within which they operate. For key areas of public international law, international lawyers make themselves irrelevant by failing to identify what international law in this context is and by failing to report it to those to whom they are responsible. International lawyers pay relatively little attention to the incidents from which political advisers infer their normative universe. Rather, they persist in constructing their normative universe from texts. They thus confine their attention to sources of international law that were either merely ceremonial at their inception, or that, although animated by more normative intentions when they were created, have ceased to be congruent with expectations of authority and control held by effective elites.

To be sure, some international lawyers try to examine practice but, as we will see, that exercise is quite a different enterprise from the intuitive legal research of the political adviser. Rather than seeing incidents as norm-indicators or norm-generators, as does the political adviser, the international lawyer generally reacts to them in judgmental fashion, assuming that the norm in question is a priori and enduring, and examining the incidents in terms of whether they indicate that a particular norm has been violated.

The question the political analyst will ask, in contrast, is not simply whether the acts at issue have violated some preexisting norm but rather, whether expectations enter-

---

[5] NELSON GOODMAN, FACT, FICTION, AND FORECAST 64 (4th ed. 1983).

[6] By W. MICHAEL REISMAN, excerpted from: *Interrlational Incidents: Introduction to a New Genre in the Study of International Law,* 10 YALE JOURNAL OF INTERNATIONAL LAW [page 1] (1984). Reprinted by permission.

[7] G. JELLINEK, ALLGEMEINE STAATSLEHRE 308 (1900).

tained by effective elites about what is permissible may be inferred from their behavior. The question is eminently practical, for even those who do not regularly use the word "law" in their discourse, and even those who snicker when others use it, must make estimates about the subjectivities of allies and adversaries alike. These subjectivities necessarily include what those actors think is right. In a world in which allies and adversaries do not submit to intensive interviews and rarely volunteer or are permitted to tell the whole truth (if any part of it), deeds–actions and reactions–become one of the few available windows to what others are thinking, either consciously or unconsciously.

All lawyers, whether domestic or international, face the same core problem in seeking to ascertain the law: to identify the operational norms used by those who are politically and legally relevant in projected situations, so that accurate predictions of how they are likely to characterize and react to different behavioral options can be made, and the most promising plans of action can be fashioned and recommended to the client.

In the United States, identifying the law is simple and relatively routinized. For one thing, the lawyer knows who the decisionmakers are. Statutes are reliable guides to legal expectations, but it is court decisions that present the real test: experience has taught American lawyers that for almost all of their purposes, lawmaking is what the courts in fact do. That insight has allowed American legal science to adopt, as its basic unit of knowledge, what we might call its "epistemic" unit, the appellate decision. A tremendous and technologically impressive industry has developed to report, catalogue, and analyze these epistemic units, all of which are made available to practitioners and scholars in retrieval systems of increasing speed and sophistication. The systems of inference called "legal reasoning" or "legal logic" are applied to these epistemic units and become an important part of the repertory of the lawyer in predicting future decisions by courts and in trying to influence them.

Why have judicial decisions in the United States been a fairly accurate indicator of the operational norms entertained by politically relevant strata? Some American lawyers, without comparative or historical perspective, have assumed that the answer to that question can be found in the inherent character of courts. This is a misleading oversimplification, for it looks at a result without reference to the causal factors that produced it. In particular, it evades the important prior question of why courts are effective in this environment. Not surprisingly, those who accept this apparent insight and have sought to apply it in the international sphere have concluded that the unruliness and violence of international politics is attributable to the absence of courts. For instance, the Peace Movement in the United States of the late 19th century was, in large part, a movement to establish an international judicial system. Indeed, it was a major factor in the creation of the international courts of the 20th century. The locus classicus of this view was Andrew Carnegie's bequest establishing the Peace Palace in the Hague as a home for the Permanent Court of Arbitration. So confident was Carnegie that the Court would succeed that he instructed the trustees to use the remainder of the money in ways they thought most likely to serve the interests of mankind.

Since 1899, international courts in one form or another have existed, but the unruliness and violence of the arena have persisted. Plainly, it is not the presence or absence of courts that determines whether minimum order will obtain. Other factors are critical.

Courts have been significant political institutions in the United States not because of something inherent in courts or in the law they process but because of the continuing congruence in U.S. politics of expectations of authority and expectations of control. Expectations of authority are subjective images of how power ought to be exercised; expectations of control are subjective images of how power will in fact be exercised. The more congruent those two sets of expectations, the more effective the legal system in question. This is not the only possible constellation of power and authority. In Venezuela, during the 19th century, to cite only one contrasting example, a type of caudillo system obtained: all of the formal institutions of power–legislature, court, and sometimes even the executive branch–were essentially powerless, and were largely ignored by those holding effective power.[8]

In the United States, the relatively stable political system and the pre-eminent role assigned to courts within it had a striking effect on the sociology of legal knowledge. Coordinately, it was an important factor in stimulating the creation and then in shaping the unique direction of American law schools and the specialized methods developed there for teaching the "science of law." Oliver Wendell Holmes captured the basic spirit of this new legal science when he stated that law was nothing more than the prediction of what courts will do: "The prophecies of what the courts will do in fact, and nothing more pretentious, are what I mean by the law."[9] Obviously, American lawyers were doing and continue to do much more than merely predict what courts will do. But the power of Holmes' insight derived from the regularly validated fact that what courts in the United States were saying was a remarkably reliable indicator of the probable future actions and reactions of effective elites. Given this degree of predictive power, it is hardly surprising that lawyers should have begun to study appellate decisions.

It has been said that a key part of the American genius is the capacity to mass produce and distribute a good idea. Consistent with Holmes's apothegm, Christopher Columbus Langdell established, at the Harvard Law School, a teaching method which assumed that the fundamental epistemic unit of legal science was the appellate opinion. "It seemed to me," Langdell wrote in the introduction to his

---

[8] *See, e.g.*, R. Perez Perdomo, El Formalismo Juridoco y Sus Funciones Sociales en el Siglo XIX Venezolano (1978).

[9] Oliver Wendell Holmes, *The Path of the Law*, in Collected Legal Papers 167, 173 (1921).

casebook on contracts, "to be possible to take such a branch of the law as Contracts, for example, and, without exceeding comparatively moderate limits, to select, classify, and arrange all the cases which had contributed in any important degree to the growth, development, or establishment of any of its essential doctrines."[10] Thus, one could organize these opinions into a coherent body of law, treating each as a self-contained and self-explanatory unit, consistent in its properties with others. The examination of these epistemic units could provide the basis for a thorough and systematic legal education.

Law schools stimulated the development of a new genre of legal literature, the "casebook," to be used in the institutions of legal education. The preoccupation with cases engendered increasingly sophisticated procedures for gathering, processing, analyzing and retrieving appellate opinions on a national scale. All of these developments combined to enculturate, even more intensely, those trained in American law, to think in terms of cases, with all that that implied.

Since the end of the 19th century, great efforts have been mounted to create in the international arena a set of institutions comparable to those to be found in Western Europe and North America. Since 1945, the result of this handiwork has been a complex superstructure and administrative apparatus which bears striking resemblance, at least superficially, to national governments in Western Europe and North America. In the General Assembly of the United Nations, some purport to find something comparable to a legislature. The Secretariat of the United Nations is compared to a domestic Executive Branch, and the specialized agencies of the United Nations are likened to the regulatory agencies of modern industrial government. Most reassuring, the International Court sits in splendor in the Hague, as the "principal judicial organ" of the United Nations, as specified in to Article 92 of the U.N. Charter.

Plainly, it is absurd to assume that the mere existence of this network of international institutions means that it is as effective as a domestic government and that its edicts may be relied upon; Holmes could plausibly direct his readers to do no more than study the behavior of courts so as to predict the development of law because the context within which his courts operated gave them effective power to prescribe legal rules. Professors who gave the same instructions to their students of international law would be leading their charges into a fantasy world. The sad fact is that the apparent governmental network that has been established internationally has little power. What power it has in particular cases is assigned to it by effective elites who have sometimes found it useful to use the United Nations or a related agency in a particular instance.

Students of international law, like their domestic counterparts, frequently tend to define decisions in terms of the institutions rendering them. In the domestic law systems of Western Europe and North America, courts, for historical reasons, have been deemed to be the authoritative appliers of the law. Hence legal decisions are defined essentially as the handicraft of those courts. Insofar as there is a congruence between actual political power in the community and the authority of courts, that focus can provide a cogent indicator of decisions. In fact, such a congruence is rarely perfect, and the identification of judgments as decisions in a larger sense frequently leads to the distortions characteristic of much academic law.[11]

Indeed, even in effectively organized legal systems, which are characterized by a general convergence of authority and control, key parts of "book law" may fail to approximate the actual normative expectations of elites. This may occur for two major reasons, inherent in the very character of law: discrepancies between myth system and operational code and the differential rates of decay of text and context. People who seek legal advice plainly require it with regard to both the myth system and the operational code: myth system because it is applied in part by some control institutions, operational code because it is applied by others. Myth system is readily retrievable through conventional research in the formal repositories of law. Operational code, in contrast, must be sought in elite behavior.

Even if there is little divergence between myth system and operational code, the differing rate of decay of text and context may limit the usefulness of formal sources of law. The proverbial decrees of the Medes and the Persians still exist; the context in which they were created and in which they had legal relevance is gone. Whether a particular exercise of lawmaking seeks to stabilize or change a situation, if it is concerned not with ornamenting myth but with doing what it says it is doing, there must be a minimum congruence between the socio-political context prevailing at the time and the socio-political presumptions of the legislation. Once legislation is expressed in relatively enduring textual form, however, its rate of decay is minimal,[12] while the rate of decay of the environing socio-political situation will always be greater and may, indeed, be extremely rapid.

Where fidelity to text acquires in itself a symbolic politi-

---

[10] Christopher C. Langdell, A Selection of Cases on the Law of Contracts vii (1871).

[11] Constitutional law in American law schools is identified as the work of the Supreme Court in supervising the discharge of "constitutional functions" performed by all other authorized agencies in the national community. But the Constitution is not a document, it is an institution, as Karl Llewellyn put it. As such, it involves a process in which many other formal and informal, authoritative and functional actors participate. These, alas, are never studied under the rubric of constitutional law. In this respect, there is no comprehensive course on constitutional law in any meaningful sense in American law schools.

[12] [Editor's Note: Perhaps Professor Reisman does not intend to suggest that the meaning of the legislation has a minimal rate of decay, but only that the words in which the meaning is initially expressed have a minimal rate of decay. In any event, the discussion raises the question of interpretation of texts; see the section on "Interpretation" in Chapter 5, this Anthology.]

cal value, texts whose literal congruence with the socio-political situation is less than when they were created may misguide those who would rely on them. At the very least, those who would rely on them may need a validation technique for determining their degree of accuracy. Courts may serve this purpose, but if they themselves and the ambit of their jurisdiction are creatures of legislation, a functional and non-institutional test is required.

In the international arena, the law is applied, for the most part, through a variety of informal channels, and rarely benefits from formal appraisal by a court or tribunal. The International Court, with its usual load of two or three cases per year, and public international arbitral tribunals, with scarcely more than that, can hardly be deemed to represent international decision.

Despite the relative inactivity of these institutions, many international scholars continue to view them as the virtual apotheosis and most authoritative expression of international law. The deference given ad hoc arbitral tribunals is symptomatic of this general problem and sometimes takes the most extraordinary form. A tribunal established by one party, in the absence of the other, and composed of a single person, let us say a professor of international law, is treated by other scholars as an authoritative oracle of international law. At the same time, commentators who defer to such an award will insist that a contrary General Assembly vote, supported by virtually every member state, is not indicative of international law but is only a ''recommendation.''

There are, to be sure, certain methodological advantages in using the international case as an epistemic unit. Part of the attraction lies in its relative simplicity, economy, and availability. Once there is fundamental agreement among scholars that the case is an epistemic unit, there need be no detailed investigation of factual material outside of the case, for the case carries its own authoritative factual statement. Alternative methods of research could require extensive field work or culling through thousands of pages of documents of uneven probative value, in order to determine what the decision actually was. A case presents that decision in a neat ''bite-sized'' and easily digestible package, creating in the process an illusion of consensus about the underlying events that probably does not exist.

''Stipulating'' the facts permits students of this epistemic unit to get on with discussions of the law, freed from complicating political issues. For those who confuse clerical tidiness with scientific method, there is the ecstasy of imagining that the case method is ''scientific,'' an enthusiasm apparently animating many of the consumers of Langdell's work. And of course, there is the latent drive among all who have been given professional legal training to view things in terms of courts. Outside of the United States, admiration for the stability and achievements of the American political-legal system leads many scholars to seek to adopt the American legal style, as if the method of observation can bring about qualitative changes in the things observed.

Yielding to these attractions, contemporary international legal science has adopted a decisional unit that is convenient for scholars but ill-tooled for the subject matter. It is reminiscent of the familiar story of a man, out walking one night on a street in Vienna, who happens on another well-dressed and plainly sober citizen who is crawling about on all fours in the light cast by a street lamp. Naturally, the first fellow stops to find out if there is something wrong. When the man on the ground explains that he has lost his watch, the passerby offers to help him find it and asks exactly where it fell. ''Back there,'' the man on the ground motions, pointing into the darkness on the other side of the street. ''Then why aren't you looking there?'' the first fellow asks in exasperation. ''Because,'' the man on the ground explains as if it were perfectly obvious, ''it's dark over there and I can't see. But here it's light.''

The transposition of the case unit to the international arena has permitted international lawyers to dwell in a comforting pool of light. Yet much of the resulting international legal description is patently out of step with elite expectations. The discrepancy is so painfully obvious that, outside the small circle of international lawyers, it brings discredit upon the very notion of international law. An alternative that would take account of the limited cogency in the international arena of the case as an epistemic unit would develop an additional unit which might be referred to generically as the ''incident.'' I define an ''incident'' as an overt conflict between two or more actors in the international system. It must be perceived as such by other key actors and resolved in some nonjudicial fashion.[13] Finally, and of critical importance, its resolution must provide some indications of what elites in a variety of effective processes consider to be acceptable behavior. Though the incident is ''resolved'' in a factual if not authoritative sense, without the judicial imprimatur which routinely indicates law in domestic settings, the incident may often be a more reliable indicator of international law than are codes or case law.[14]

Among the formidable challenges posed by this proposal is the development of criteria by which incidents are to be selected. Napoleon's remark that history is a collec-

---

[13] [Editor's Note: What if a decision of a domestic court is a factor in resolving an international incident? See the section on ''Municipal Decisions'' later in this Chapter.]

[14] Note that the inquiry being proposed here is quite different from the routine examination of ''practice'' in international law. That inquiry seeks to establish the existence of a bilateral or general norm or custom, by examining, ostensibly, a broad pattern of practice of states. There are many intellectual difficulties with the inquiry into practice. Neither the volume nor the degree of uniformity of practice required has ever been stated with precision. Moreover, examinations of practice do not control for the variable of power. They do not seek to identify who, among a large cast of characters, is effective. The incident, in contrast, is not based on a large volume or flow of supposedly ''uniform'' events, but instead takes a single critical event as a prism through which the reactions of elites to particular behavior may be examined and assessed as an indication of their views of law.

tion of lies we all agree upon has an especially wicked relevance when we consider as a source of history the recital of the facts contained in judicial opinions. The statement of "relevant" facts determined by a court would rarely satisfy a historian; indeed, what the court leaves out is often of most interest to the student of politics and history. Consider a few examples.

The Schooner Exchange[15] judgment of Chief Justice Marshall is usually cited as the cornerstone for the doctrine that the public acts of foreign governments will not be reviewed by the courts of another state even if the effects of the act are felt in that other state. Somehow the judgment never states the extraordinary fact that the case was being decided against the background of the War of 1812, in which the British had set fire to Washington. France, the real defendant, was the only ally of the United States. It seems most unlikely under these circumstances that any United States court would have risked imperiling that relationship.

In the Corfu Channel Case (United Kingdom v. Albania),[16] the International Court somehow never mentions the fact that the Greek Civil War was under way, that the United Kingdom was a major supporter of the Royalist cause, and that Albania, as a proxy for another superpower, was supporting the Communist insurgency. The presence of the British ships in the Straits of Corfu unquestionably constituted a manifest military communication to the Albanians and others about the limits of British tolerance, the susceptibility of Albania to coastal attacks, and the capacity of the British fleet to project its force into that arena.

The point need not be belabored. What these cases demonstrate is that there is no authoritative institution to decree or stipulate that the facts which have been assembled in judgments meet the standards of historical accuracy.

Indeed, legal science is often impatient to finish with "the facts" and to get on with "the law." First instance factual determinations are only rarely reviewed. Subsequent instances simplify the facts even further. In American legal education, the tendency of first-year students to seek to learn more about the facts of the case is often characterized as a frivolous interest; students are urged to get on with the legal analysis.

There are some cogent reasons for this cultivated astigmatism. Every science develops its own specialized lens in order to focus more sharply and intensively on that aspect of life of interest to it. The particular focus of legal science distinguishes it from history and sociology and does, indeed, permit it to concentrate more effectively on the normative or policy dimensions of problems. But sometimes, sticky political problems or issues can be concealed under a bare factual statement and the infinitely obscurantist potentialities of legal language. These selective abbreviations, whatever their intra-disciplinary justification, inevitably produce a legal version of the facts which historians and political advisers often see as, at best, thin and brittle, and, at worst, caricatures of what actually transpired. Since a fuller and more accurate understanding of the facts is indispensable to ascertaining what was actually decided, the versions of the facts often presented by judges may undermine the effectiveness of the predictive function of case law.

The sporadic fashion in which the facts become available in incidents presents a special problem. Many facts are concealed for years or even generations. The attack on Pearl Harbor, for example, could not be described with any accuracy until the archives in all the relevant capitals were at last made accessible to historians. It took a generation for scholars to provide a comprehensive picture that could demonstrate the incorrectness of many of their initial conclusions about the incident.[17] Similarly, the extent of U.S. involvement in the overthrow of the Mossadegh government in Iran and the reinstallation of the Pahlavi dynasty in 1953 was not established until years later.[18]

This is not a problem unique to incidents. In some cases, national courts refuse to exercise jurisdiction because information indispensable to judgment cannot be secured. In international law, judgments of the ICJ may be reopened and revised on the basis of new facts or new information (Article 61 of the Court's Statute). If anything, the problem is considerably less severe in the study of incidents. The student of incidents, it will be recalled, is not involved in judging the lawfulness of the behavior of actors in the incident concerned, but rather evaluates the reactions of other relevant actors and, through those reactions, the subjective conceptions of right and/or tolerable behavior entertained by those other actors. Hence what is important in this exercise is not so much what happened as what effective elites think happened and how they react.

A related practical difficulty in constructing the genre of incidents is the question of boundaries: where does a particular incident begin and where does it end? A case presupposes a consensus that critical events begin and end at some point. An incident is not bounded with such precision. Because of this, there is some question as to when it ends, if at all. Territorial losses, for example, may be viewed by the party securing acquisition as completed incidents, with title consolidated by adverse possession. But the losing party may continue to view the lost territories as its own and dream and plan for their repatriation. Hence the two parties to an incident may have diametrically opposite conceptions of when the incident ended. It is the observer of the incident who must, in effect, establish boundaries in time. Those boundaries are determined primarily by the norms the observer chooses to examine.

---

15 11 U.S. (7 Cranch) 116 (1812).

16 1949 I.C.J. 4.

17 *See, e.g,* G. Prange, At Dawn We Slept: The Untold Story of Pearl Harbor (1981).

18 *See* 1 Senate Select Committee to Study Governmental Operations with Respect to Intelligence Activities, Final Report on Foreign and Military Intelligence, S. Rep. No. 755, 94th Cong., 2d Sess. 111 (1976).

In conclusion, an incident genre whose practitioners continue to update and correct the expression of the code of international law is required. If it is established and adopted (and adapted) by a number of other scholars, it can ultimately yield an abundant literature of international appraisal, richer than the limited number of cases decided by courts, more representative of actual decision trends, more indicative of the political context in which decisions are taken and implemented and, most importantly, more accurate in expressing international normative expectations.

3. Finding Custom in An Incident[19]

Between 1935 and 1950, off the coast of Norway, there was a series of encounters between the Norwegian navy and numerous British fishing vessels. The detailed history of these encounters has been meticulously preserved in the documents filed by Norway and Great Britain in the International Court of Justice.[20] This is one ''incident,'' in Professor Michael Reisman's terminology, that we know a great deal about. I refer to it here as an example of how customary international law unfolds in the real-world interactions of states. The customary law of the Anglo-Norwegian fishing encounters was not ''created'' by the resolution of the conflicting claims of the two parties, but rather existed somehow in the nature of their interactions, and manifested itself as the parties groped toward a real-world solution. I want to argue that, in a profoundly important sense, the ''case'' between Norway and Great Britain was over before the judges left the courtroom to deliberate their decision. The World Court's ultimate decision, in my view, simply ratified the result that was already dictated by the workings of customary international law.

Norway's consistent position throughout the years 1935 through 1950 was that its internal (territorial) waters had in many places off its jagged coastline a breadth exceeding three miles. This is, of course, a legal claim: that Norway remains entitled to exclusive jurisdiction in its territorial waters in certain places where the breadth of the territorial sea exceeds the internationally accepted maximum of three miles. Or, in other words, if a fishing vessel of British origin is found fishing four miles off the Norwegian coast in waters regarded by Norway as coming within Norway's territorial sea,[21] then the vessel is engaging in an illegal activity and may be seized or otherwise dealt with by the Norwegian navy.

Norway backed up its position through those years by seizing and turning back numerous British fishing vessels, and in some cases confiscating the catch. The British government lodged several diplomatic protests, asserting that in no instance may a territorial sea extend outwards more than three miles from the low-water baseline mark of any coast. In short, Great Britain's position was that its vessels were fishing in the high seas, and that Norway had no right to encroach upon the high seas beyond the three-mile territorial limit that at the time was accorded generally to all coastal states.

Now suppose a scholar in 1950 examined the customary international law regarding the delimitation of territorial seas. We assume that the scholar has no personal interest in the matter, has no ''burden of proof'' to discharge in any court, etc. Which position would customary law appear to support—Norway's or Great Britain's? My guess is that the legal situation would be pretty even. On the British side is the general rule limiting territorial seas to a breadth of three miles. But on Norway's side is the idea of historic prescription, an idea that can trump a general rule. If Norway over the years asserted title to certain waters adjacent to its coastline, then that title would not lightly be taken away by a general rule of customary law. Rather, the general three-mile rule of the customary law of the territorial sea might itself accommodate, in specific instances, a wider territorial sea that had been established through the time-honored international law processes of claim, prescription and forcible defense of title.[22]

I want to make it clear that I am not taking the position that international customary law is ''fuzzy'' on the question of delimitation of the territorial sea. The three-mile limit as of 1950 was a clear rule of customary law. If nation A had tried to stop a fishing vessel from nation B a tenth of a mile beyond A's three-mile limit, nation B (and other nations as well) could have regarded A's action as an act of war. Recall how in the 1920s various ''rum-runners'' off the American coastline ''hovered'' just outside the delimited area that the United States established for protecting Prohibition. These rum-runners typically waited for the U.S. Coast Guard to depart, and then they might try to make a run for it to the coast, to discharge their cargo of whiskey and rum. So long as they remained outside the

---

19 By ANTHONY D'AMATO, written for this Anthology.

20 Anglo-Norwegian Fisheries Case, 1951 ICJ Rep. 116.

21 Norway did not claim a fixed territorial sea, but rather claimed that its breadth varied depending on the particular place along the Norwegian coastline where it could be measured.

22 Norway *argued* its prescriptive claims by making a number of related assertions: that the jagged nature of the Norwegian coastline, the unique rock formations and small offshore islands, the ''historic'' claims of Norwegian fishermen to exclusivity with respect to certain inland waters and their economic dependence upon such exclusivity, all amounted to a prescriptive title to specific waters.

delimited area, the Coast Guard did not interfere with them – despite high motivation to do so. But the Norwegian situation is quite different. Norway was not claiming any jurisdiction over a portion of the high seas. Norway did not interfere with a British fishing vessel that was, say, eight miles off the Norwegian coast. Instead, Norway's legal position was that it had historic title to certain territorial waters that in certain specific places had a breadth that exceeded three miles. Only in those specific places did the Norwegian navy enforce Norway's claimed jurisdiction over British fishing vessels.

My best guess, as I've said, is that neither Norway nor Great Britain was advantaged by prior customary law. And so, a great deal would turn on the question of which state, in court, would have the burden of proof. If Norway had the burden of proof, it would be quite difficult for Norway to establish, by a preponderance of argument, that it was entitled to its territorial sea claims. By the same token, if Great Britain had the burden of proof, it would be quite difficult for it to establish by a preponderance of argument that the generally accepted three-mile rule trumped Norway's historic claims.

As things turned out in the World Court, Great Britain was in fact the complaining state on the fisheries issue. It was Great Britain that was complaining about Norway's actions in seizing and turning back British fishing vessels. Although this point seems simple and clear, it is nevertheless of great significance. One might say, logically, that Norway should be complaining that British fishing vessels were failing to respect Norway's jurisdiction over its territorial sea. But this is a logical, and not a real-world, complaint. The fact was that Norway simply utilized its navy to turn back all fishing vessels that were found within Norway's territorial sea as delimited by Norway. Norway wasn't making any international law claim; it was simply acting on the real-world stage. It was only Great Britain that made an international law claim. Great Britain claimed that Norway's acts in forcibly turning back the fishing vessels violated international law.

That Great Britain had the burden of persuasion on the fisheries issue is a consequence of the way the incident played itself out on the real-world stage, and not a consequence of the way the parties appeared before the World Court. Domestic lawyers are used to the assignment of the burden of persuasion to the *plaintiff* in a legal controversy. But international law does not typically regard either of two disputing states as the "plaintiff." Instead, the World Court treats states equally and does not disfavor a state that initiates a lawsuit by charging it with the burden of persuasion. Indeed, the World Court welcomes the initiation of lawsuits as a peaceful means for resolving disputes; hence it does not want to assign an a priori burden on the initiator.

The way the incident arose on the real-world stage is that the Norwegian navy turned back British fishing vessels, and Great Britain protested. Norway did not accede to the British protests. Eventually, the case wound up in the World Court. Again, in that Court, it was Great Britain that was protesting Norway's acts. In short, Great Britain wanted to enlist international law – and the power of the World Court – to reverse the real-world activity of the Norwegian navy.

Accordingly, Great Britain had the burden of persuading the Court that the Norwegian navy violated international customary law. The critical point, worth reiterating, is that the way the facts arose, this burden of persuasion would have to be assigned to Great Britain. Norway was not complaining as to this issue; Norway, in effect, was engaged in self-help on the real-world stage. It was Great Britain who was resorting to international law in its conflict with Norway, and hence it was Great Britain that naturally had the burden of persuading the Court that it was legally right and Norway was legally wrong.

But as the lawyers for Great Britain as well as Norway realized, the party with the burden of persuasion in Court is very likely the party that will lose the litigation – for the reasons I mentioned earlier.

As I read through the fascinating documents, briefs, and oral arguments in the case, one particular sentence came shining through. It was a statement made during the course of oral argument by Sir Humphrey Waldock, arguing on behalf of Great Britain. It exemplified the careful preparation, and quiet beauty, of a master lawyer at work. Sir Humphrey said:

> The United Kingdom, exercising a restraint which I hope will be considered commendable, did not send fishery protection vessels to protect our trawlers from interference in areas which the United Kingdom believes to be high seas.[23]

We should carefully note all the things that are "going on" in this sentence:

1. The Norwegian actions are characterized as "interference."
2. The British response is characterized in terms of responsible action: protecting its own trawlers.
3. Attention is called to the commendable "restraint" exercised by Great Britain.
4. By implication, Norway is accused of failing to exercise restraint.
5. Attention is called to the superior naval power of Great Britain, which easily could have sent fishery

---

[23] I.C.J., Pleadings, Oral Arguments, Documents: Fisheries Case, v. 4, at 395 (1951).

protection vessels to the Norwegian coast that would have been militarily effective.

6. By implication, the Court is urged not to issue a ruling that punishes Great Britain for failing to exercise force, for that would encourage other states to resort to force instead of solving their international disputes peacefully and through legal processes.

7. The Court is put on notice that the "facts" of the case could easily have been different: i.e., if Great Britain had sent in its trawlers, then the burden of persuasion would be upon Norway as the party complaining about the British use of force.

8. By implication, assigning the burden of persuasion to Great Britain is unfair because it was Great Britain, and not Norway, that showed restraint.

Sir Humphrey's argument is indeed impressive as a matter of logic, but it fails the test of practical economics. Suppose in the years 1935–1950 Great Britain *had* sent its fishery protection vessels to protect its trawlers. Sir Humphrey would have the Court believe that Norway would have been forced to complain to the Court, and in so doing put itself in the position of having to discharge the burden of persuasion. Would Norway have done that? My guess is that Norway would have done no such thing. Rather, the Norwegian government would have instructed its navy to back off, not to get into any confrontations with the British navy, but just to adopt a wait-and-see attitude. If in any specific case the British navy failed to protect a fishing vessel, then and only then should the Norwegian navy move in and either seize the vessel or forcibly escort it back to the high seas. The international-law message conveyed by such a Norwegian strategy would be: only British fishing trawlers in sight of British naval enforcement vessels are allowed to fish in the disputed waters, and then only so long as the British navy remains in the immediate vicinity.

The economics of such a policy would be to raise the cost of British fishing in the disputed Norwegian waters to intolerably high levels. Fishing is a marginal business at best; add the high cost of constant protection by armed military vessels and the cost would far exceed any revenues derived from the fishing. Over time—and we're talking about a decade and a half of elapsed time between 1935 and 1950—the British navy would have to give up and go home. The British government would have to instruct British fishermen that if they decide to fish in the disputed waters off the Norwegian coast, they would have to run the risk of being seized by the Norwegians and perhaps having their catch confiscated.

Therefore, it was not "commendable restraint" that kept the British navy away from the Norwegian waters, as Sir Humphrey would have it. Rather, it was the fact that the costs of constant protection were far too high for what was at stake. Hence, contrary to the pure logic of Sir Humphrey's argument, I would have to conclude that his notion of changing the facts is not as easy on the high seas as it is on paper. You might say that the real world presented the facts to the court in the most economic fashion. Norway, being a lot closer to the disputed waters (indeed, the disputed waters were roughly within four miles of the Norwegian coastline), could patrol those waters almost routinely and without the expenditure of a lot of money. Great Britain, on the other hand, would have to expend a great deal of money if it put its navy in the business of protecting its fishing vessels.[24] International custom, therefore, developed in the most economical fashion; that is, it developed in the facts of the case as they really happened and not in the scenario imagined by Sir Humphrey Waldock.

I cannot, of course, know the reasoning processes of the judges on the World Court, but I suspect that when they retired to their chamber to deliberate about the case, they rejected Sir Humphrey's scenario. For there was no compelling reason for the judges to adopt a scenario about how the facts *might* have arisen instead of adopting the real facts as they *did* arise. Under the facts as they really happened, the burden of persuasion fell upon Great Britain.

---

24 I hope that readers will not take my remarks out of context. I am definitely not saying that whenever it's cheaper for one nation to use force than it is for another nation, the first nation can get away with departing from the rules of international law. In the present essay, I hope to have shown that Norway did not depart from any rules; rather, its position was that its prescriptive rights were not trumped by the general three-mile rule.

Suppose instead that Norway had claimed a ten-mile territorial sea. One might argue that, even then, it would be cheaper for Norway to enforce its claim than it would for Great Britain to protect its fishing vessels in the disputed waters. But that argument would be faulty. Great Britain might have a huge stake in keeping territorial seas around the world as narrow as possible. The Norwegian claim might thus be perceived as the opening wedge in the creation of a new customary rule of a ten-mile territorial sea. And *that* would impose intolerably high costs upon the British fisheries industry and many of its other mercantile industries that rely on free passage through the high seas. Given *those* costs, Great Britain would opt to protect the three-mile rule itself by providing fishery protection vessels in the disputed waters off the Norwegian coast. The cost of naval protection would be less than the cost of Norway's adopting a ten-mile limit to be followed by similar claims to ten-mile limits around the world. Accordingly, my "economic" argument in the text of this essay should be read as applying only to cases roughly similar to the Anglo-Norwegian fisheries incident where the international law rules at the outset do not favor one side or the other.

Indeed, in the actual "incident," neither the British nor the Norwegians perceived that the Norwegian claims were readily generalizable to other nations' coasts. In fact, the careful manner in which Norway delimited its territorial-sea claims in the first place reflected this lack of easy generalization, along with (perhaps) a realistic assessment that Norway would eventually "get away with it" vis-a-vis Great Britain so long as Norway did not overreach.

Since Great Britain failed to discharge the burden of persuasion, the decision must be awarded to Norway. And, indeed, the World Court ruled in favor of Norway in the case.

Unpacking this particular "incident" shows not only that international customary law *reflects* deep patterns of the logic of interstate accommodations that were present in the international system all along (whether as a matter of economics, national security, sociology, or any other overriding relevant factor), but that the incident itself *contributes* to the development of custom! How can an incident on the international stage both reflect customary law and contribute to its development? The same way a "case" in common law both reflects prior law and contributes to its development. What we have in both custom and common law is that rather mystical blend of ontology and teleology, what Aristotle regarded as the "actualization" of the empirical world. Whatever our differences may be on other aspects of international law, I believe that Professor Reisman and I are in accord in viewing incidents and cases in this Aristotelian fashion.

4. Customary Law Doctrine[25]

a. The Shortcomings of Mainstream Theory

The standard literature of customary law is replete with disagreements and divergencies. We can get an idea of the confusion and illogic by examining the most generally accepted formula for the derivation of a customary rule of law. The author, Judge Manley O. Hudson, one of the most widely respected authorities of his time, announced his prescription after studying the writings of hundreds of legal scholars at the request of the International Law Commission. His formula consists of five "elements" required for the "emergence of a principle or rule of customary international law": "[1] concordant practice by a number of States with reference to a type of situation falling within the domain of international relations; [2] continuation or repetition of the practice over a considerable period of time; [3] conception that the practice is required by, or consistent with, prevailing international law; [4] general acquiescence in the practice by other States"; [5] the establishment of "the presence of each of these elements by a competent international authority."[26] Let us look critically at each of these elements.

[1] To begin with, who is to determine whether a situation falls within the domain of international relations? Many big-power unilateral interventions in the affairs of neighboring countries have been claimed to be "purely internal" affairs; who is to say otherwise? Or, consider a state's treatment of its own nationals. If the treatment amounts to genocide or apartheid, can other states condemn it as a breach of international law? In other words, are a government's acts toward its own citizens capable of "falling within the domain of international relations"? Judge Hudson's formula offers no criteria for such a determination. Additionally, what is meant in the formula by "concordant" practice? Is this a subjective element – that states must be aware that their practice is concordant? If so, how is it proved? Similarly, must they be aware that their practice is "with reference to" the type of domain-of-international-relations situation of Judge Hudson? And how many constitute a "number of States"? Are two states sufficient, or must we have one hundred?

[2] As for "continuation or repetition of the practice over a considerable period of time," the term "considerable period" is unspecified; it could range from a century to a month. And what is "practice"? Must it constitute overt acts? Would it include expressions of view, such as resolutions in the General Assembly? When a state refrains from acting, would such abstinence amount to a "practice"? If a non-act is the equivalent of an act, how can there be repetitions of nonacts?

[3] The third element demands a "conception that the practice is required by, or consistent with, prevailing international law." How can such an element help to explain "the emergence of a principle or rule of customary international law" as Judge Hudson claims it does? Any *new* rule of customary law would be based on practice that by definition could not be "required by" or "consistent with" prior law! More importantly, Judge Hudson's formula can not explain how existing laws could *change*; for a change in the law would again by definition be based on practice that was not "consistent with" prevailing law.

[4] The fourth element, which requires "general acquiescence in the practice by other States," raises further problems. Not only do we have unspecified terms such as "general" and "other States," but the linchpin concept of acquiescence is left undefined. What does it mean for a state to acquiesce in the "practice" of other states? If Chile and Australia are engaging in a certain practice that affects only themselves, has the United States acquiesced in this practice? How could it *not* acquiesce? A note of protest would not only be ineffective, but would be undiplomatic if the situation does not specifically affect the United States. Or, if we changed the situation so that the Chilean-Australian practice *did* affect the interests of the United States, what would be the significance of a note of protest

---

[25] By ANTHONY D'AMATO, excerpted from THE CONCEPT OF CUSTOM IN INTERNATIONAL LAW (Cornell Univ. Press, 1971). Reprinted by permission.

[26] 2 INT'L LAW COMM'N, YEARBOOK 26 (1950).

that did not result in a withdrawal of the practice by Chile and Australia? Would we say that, although it wrote a note of protest, the United States in fact acquiesced in the practice because it did not take effective steps, as a superpower, to compel a termination of the practice?

[5] Judge Hudson concludes, "Of course the presence of each of these elements is to be established as a fact by a competent international authority." This final element does not fulfill its apparent purpose of assuaging those who had doubts about the preceding four. It states that international custom does not exist until a "competent international authority" pronounces it to exist. But such an authority could never make an initial determination of custom without contravening this requirement that a prior determination must have been made by itself or a similar international authority. Certainly international customary law existed well in advance of the Permanent Court of International Justice, and long before states began to have recourse to bilateral arbitral tribunals. Even apart from these considerations, "competent international authorities," in the sense of authoritative decision-makers, are given occasion to pronounce upon only a small fraction of the international norms invoked by states in their international relations.

In sum, the late Judge Hudson's criteria appear to raise more questions than they solve. Let's examine how and why international scholarship arrived at this impasse.

b. Historical Development

Prior to the nineteenth century, no writer had examined in any detail the process of custom formation. But then, in that century, Puchta[27] and Savigny[28] took the first step, aided by earlier works of Hugo[29] and Moser.[30] These writers were concerned with the ultimate foundation of positive law. Puchta and Savigny held that this foundation resided in the spirit of the people; in their view, custom was merely the immediate and spontaneous revelation of the common popular sentiment.[31] The importance of their work to international law lay not in their conclusion but in their emphasis on the cognitive or psychological aspect of custom. Before their time, this aspect had been almost entirely ignored. Yet, typically, the corrective was carried too far. For in the theories of Puchta and Savigny, if "law" is the expression of popular consciousness or will, then the overt or tangible aspect of custom dwindles in relevance and importance. So long as we can discover the popular sentiment, what need is there for an overt act or "precedent"? Indeed, the overt act may be of minimal use as only one kind of evidence of the underlying popular will. And what if there were conflicting overt acts? Which of them would be the true evidence of the *Volksgeist*?

A major step was taken by Francois Geny in his *Methode d'interpretation et sources en droit prive positif*, published in 1899. Although Geny was not writing about international law, his thoughts on custom in French law immediately influenced the great international scholars of his day. He argued that the important question was not whether overt acts ("usage") reflected the psychological element of will or command, but rather *which* overt acts out of many overt acts constitute custom. Many acts "remain outside the positive legal order," such as "the habits of daily life, what we call the mores of the people or of certain social classes, the commercial and other economic usages, the rules of civil behavior, the social conventions, or even moral or religious practices."[32] All of these, in Geny's words, would "claim in vain the character of a source of positive private law." Something clearly was needed to distinguish legal custom from other usages, and this Geny called the "opinio necessitatis," a psychological component which was "truly specific of customary law."[33]

Summing up, Geny offered two elements of custom: usage (repeated practices) and opinio juris seu necessitatis, the latter meaning that the usage must amount to the "exercise of a (subjective) right of those who practice it." Usage is the "material and detectable element" in custom, and opinio juris the "immaterial and psychological element."[34]

Geny's identification of the two elements of custom passed uncritically into international legal thinking. Most writers forgot or overlooked Geny's motivating reason for his theory of opinio juris—that it was necessary for distinguishing legal usage (custom) from social usage. Instead, writers began to debate whether the psychological element of custom (opinio juris) was or was not more important than the material element (usage, or the practice of states).

The leading positivist theorist Hans Kelsen came close to rejecting the psychological component of custom by saying, in an article published in 1939, that its determination

---

[27] *See* 1 PUCHTA, DAS GEWOHNHEITSRECHT 133–43, 148–55 (1828).

[28] *See* SAVIGNY, VOM BERUF UNSERER ZEIT FÜR GESETZGEBUNG UND RECHTSWISSERNSCHAFT 8–11, 13–14 (3d ed. 1840).

[29] *See* 4 HUGO, CIVILISTISCHES MAGAZIN 4 (1813).

[30] *See* MOSER, PATRIOTISCHE PHANTASIEN (1774).

[31] *See also* SAVIGNY, SYSTEM DES HEUTIGEN ROMISCHEN RECHTS (1840–49).

[32] Geny, at § 110. An intellectual historian of international law could find an antecedent of Geny's view in the writings of Suarez in 1612; *see* SUAREZ, A TREATISE ON LAWS AND GOD THE LAWGIVER 446 (Carnegie Series, 1944). Five years prior to Geny, Pillet had remarked upon the linkage between custom and courtesy. Pillet, *Le droit international public: ses elements constitutifs, son domaine, son object,* 1 REVUE GENERALE DE DROIT INTERNATIONAL PUBLIC 12 (1894).

[33] *Ibid.*

[34] *Id.* at § 118.

is a matter for the absolute and arbitrary discretion of an international tribunal.[35] Paul Guggenheim in a leading text in 1953 adopted Kelsen's view, stating that in reality there is only one constitutive element in custom, that of usage. In his view, a court has unfettered discretion to decide whether a prolonged and constant repetition of positive or negative acts amounts to a legally binding custom or merely to a usage having no legal effect.[36]

A more basic objection is that the phrase "opinio juris sive neccessitatis" suggests usage that has taken place, in Oppenheim's phrase, "under the aegis of the conviction" that the usage is, "according to International Law, obligatory or right."[37] But if custom creates law, how can a component of custom require that the creative acts be in accordance with some *prior* right or obligation in international law? If the prior law exists, would not custom therefore be, in Eric Suy's term, "superfluous" as a creative element?[38] This objection was cogently presented in the discussions of the International Law Commission in 1950 over Judge Hudson's draft formulation of customary law.[39] Recall that Judge Hudson had argued that a component of custom is the "conception that the practice is required by, or consistent with, prevailing international law." J M. Yepes objected that the word "required" could not stand, and that if custom must be *consistent* with international law it "ceases to be a source for that law." Georges Scelle agreed that there was a contradiction in arguing that custom on the one hand is the basis of law and on the other that it must be consistent with prior law. Moreover, Yepes observed that, unless custom could depart from prevailing international law, it had no raison d'etre. Against these views Judge Hudson was willing to modify his formulation to read "not inconsistent with prevailing international law" instead of "consistent with," and later offered "practice not forbidden by prevailing international law." But these modifications did not satisfy the logical objections, and the Commission voted 7 to 3 to reject Judge Hudson's formulation of the elements of custom.

c. The Quantitative Element (Usage)

The quantitative element of custom can be broken down into at least three components: (1) duration, (2) density, and (3) continuity.

(1) *Duration.* The temporal element of usage covers the broadest possible range in traditional writings, from the "immemorial custom" of the classicists to "single act" theories. Custom was never really "immemorial"; that was lawyers' talk for purposes of pleading cases. According to Mateesco, France traditionally required custom to be of forty years' duration, whereas in Germany only thirty years was necessary.[40] But then, after the theories of Puchta and Savigny took hold, writers such as Lambert began to argue that if usage reflected the will of the people or the transcendent law, a single act would reveal this law unambiguously; any further acts would be redundant.[41] Under this view, custom need have *no* duration; one act once is enough.

If "immemorial custom" seems too long to establish custom, and a "single act" seems too short, one can expect writers to fudge the issue. Sir Humphrey Waldock's view is that the time needed to form a custom varies "according to the nature of the case."[42] Depending on the case, even "a single precedent could be sufficient to create international custom," according to Gilberto Amado.[43] James L. Brierly argued in the International Law Commission that the principle of national sovereignty over airspace arose "at the moment the 1914 war broke out."[44] Yet no writer has succeeded in specifying which types or areas of law are susceptible of rapid as contrasted to slow development.

Even so, the time factor cannot be ignored. Karol Wolfke has suggested a relevant covariance: the establishment of custom required a long time in the past when international life was slower and communication primitive, but today custom may be formed rapidly since "every event of international importance is universally and immediately known."[45] This argument suggests a communications fac-

---

35 KELSEN, THEORIE DU DROIT INTERNATIONAL COUTUMIER, 1 REVUE INTERNATIONAL DE LA THEORIE DU DROIT (NEW SERIES) 253, 264–66 (1939).

36 1 GUGGENHEIM, TRAITE DE DROIT INTERNATIONAL PUBLIC 46–48 (1953); see Guggenheim, *Les deux elements de la coutume en droit international,* 1 LA TECHNIQUE ET LES PRINCIPES DU DROIT PUBLIC: ETUDES EN L'HONNEUR DE GEORGES SCELLE 275 (1950). But later Guggenheim appears to have modified his views. See Guggenheim, *Lokales Gewohnheitsrecht,* 11 OSTERREICHISCHE ZEITSCHRIFT FUR OFFENTLICHES RECHT 327 (1961).

37 1 OPPENHEIM, INTERNATIONAL LAW 26 (Lauterpacht ed. 1955).

38 SUY, LES ACTES JURIDIQUES UNILATERAUX EN DROIT INTERNATIONAL PUBLIC 266 (1962).

39 See 1 INT'L LAW COMM'N, YEARBOOK 6, 175–76 (1950).

40 MATEESCO, LA COUTUME DANS LES CYCLES JURIDIQUES INTERNATIONAUX 212 (1947).

41 LAMBERT, ETUDES DE DROIT COMMUN LEGISLATIF OU DE DROIT CIVIL COMPARE 140–42 (1903).

42 Waldock, *General Course on Public International Law,* 106 RECUEIL DES COURS 1, 44 (1962); see also Fitzmaurice, *The Law and Procedure of the International Court of Justice, 1951–54: General Principles and Sources of Law,* 30 B.Y.I.L. 1, 31 (1953).

43 1 INT'L LAW COMM'N, YEARBOOK 5 (1950). Karol Wolfke finds the following writers in agreement as to the sufficiency of a single precedent: Cyprian, Sawicki, Rousseau, Tunkin, and Lukin. WOLFKE, CUSTOM IN PRESENT INTERNATIONAL LAW 68 (1964).

44 1 INT'L LAW COMM'N, YEARBOOK 5 (1950). Not all writers agree that a wartime precedent automatically becomes a precedent in time of peace.

45 WOLFKE at 67–68.

tor in custom, reminiscent of Mateesco's observation that in France a custom had to be "notorious" in order to be valid.[46] The idea of communication or notice indeed may be more basic to custom than the mere fact of duration, a point to which I shall return below when I attempt a reformulation of the theory of custom.

(2) *Density.* Some writers have contended that the "density" of usage, in Waldock's term, is more significant than the temporal factor.[47] As Zdenek Slouka put it, what transpires within a certain time is more important than the mere lapse of time.[48] Yet if communication or notice is a basic factor in custom, clearly duration cannot be separated entirely from density, since both serve to call attention to the overt acts making up the usage. Tunkin's observation that "juridically the element of time cannot in itself have a decisive significance" would appear to apply equally well to the element of density.[49]

(3) *Continuity.* Another element suggested by many writers is that of "continuous" usage. Sorensen has argued that the requirement of continuity precludes the single-act theory of custom.[50] Yet many writers have agreed with Basdevant that few if any rules of international law have been created by a practice in which continuity was never interrupted.[51] On the other hand, discontinuity, according to Tunkin, cannot be decisive in destroying a rule of law.[52] And Wolfke even suggests that discontinuity may help establish a rule when the international community observes that the practice is resumed following interruption.[53]

But present discontinuity would appear to be quite different from discontinuity in the past, for one could not know whether a resumption of the former line of conduct would ever take place. Yet, could an argument be made that a single contrary act suffices to overturn a former line of conduct? Or is not the contrary act by definition illegal since it violates the prior custom? If illegal, might it still contain the "seeds" of a new customary rule to the opposite effect? These questions remain largely unexplored in the literature, and I shall address them below in my attempt to reformulate the theory of custom.

Focusing on "continuity" raises the related question: how valid is it at all to speak of "acts" of states? There are to be sure numerous manifestations of discrete state behavior that we may call "acts," such as seizing a pirate ship, declaring war, arresting a diplomat, or expropriating a foreign company. But even more numerous occasions of continuing behavior that we do not normally call "acts" can be identified, such as providing tourists with police protection, maintaining warning signals on offshore drilling rigs, processing millions of pieces of foreign mail through reciprocal postal arrangements, or maintaining a procedure in place for the extradition of criminals. And perhaps the largest class of manifestations of state behavior involves not acts but restraints on action. Louis Henkin observed that the United States' "failure to commit aggression against Canada 'takes place' every day of the year."[54] Surely restraints are no less valid than acts as evidence of state practice. Yet if they are equally valid, then the somewhat arbitrarily rigid prescriptions of many writers with respect to duration, density, and continuity must be revised. What is the meaning of duration and density in the context of non-acts? Jan de Louter in 1920 suggested that the concept of negative practice proves that continuity, and not repetition, is the basic characteristic of custom.[55] Yet we can reply that anything that has never been done has *continuously* never been done, and that therefore continuity can not be a distinguishing characteristic of custom. Indeed, emphasizing continuity or repetition in the context of negative practice would make it difficult to explain how new laws can readily arise in new legal arenas (such as outer space or human rights) if the continuity and repetition notions lead one to the conclusion that centuries of non-acts must have created strong prohibitory rules in these arenas.

The question becomes more complex when we consider that there are two quite different types of reasons a state does not act: (a) discretion or (b) legal obligation. (a) If a state does not send a rocket to the moon, and its reason is either its choice not to do so or its technological incapacity, then its "failure to act" is purely discretionary and can not be evidence of some kind of prohibitive rule of customary law. (b) Quite different is the case when a state has a duty not to act. This case arises frequently; indeed a duty to refrain from acting is the correlative of every rule of international law that lays down a right. For example, the right of freedom of the high seas obliges all states not to act in such a manner as to interfere unreasonably with states that are exercising that freedom in navigation, fishing, or in some other permitted activity.[56] Yet if we are trying to

---

46 Mateesco at 212.

47 Waldock at 44.

48 Z. Slouka, International Custom and the Continental Shelf 13 (1968).

49 G. Tunkin, *Remarks on the Juridical Nature of Customary Norms of International Law,* 49 Cal. L. Rev. 419, 420 (1961).

50 Sorensen, *Principes de droit international public,* 101 Recueil des Cours 1, 39 (1960).

51 Basdevant, *Regles generales du droit de la paix,* 58 Recueil des Cours 471, 518 (1936).

52 Tunkin, *Co-existence and International Law,* 95 Recueil des Cours 1, 10 (1958).

53 Wolfke at 69.

54 L. Henkin, How Nations Behave 43 (1968).

55 Louter, Le droit international public positif 49 (1920).

56 For example, *The Geneva Convention on the High Seas of 1958,* 52 A.J.I.L. 842, 843 (1958), calls upon the parties not to interfere unreasonably with "the interests of other states in their exercise of the freedom of the high seas."

find out whether there is already a duty in place so that a state has a duty to refrain, then we are back in a circularity. For our task is to find evidence of custom; we cannot find evidence if we must presuppose that a customary obligation exists. Thus we have another element that must be revised in a new formulation of customary theory.

d. The Qualitative Element (Opinio Juris)

The fatal defect of the classical view of the psychological component of custom is its circularity: How can custom create law if its psychological component requires action in conscious accordance with preexisting law? One suggested way around this dilemma has been re-introduced by Bin Cheng. During the period of formation of the custom the participants acted in error; they thought that they were acting under a legal obligation which in fact was nonexistent.[57] This attempt to finesse the circularity problem was first suggested by Hans Kelsen in an article published in 1939, but he himself rejected the idea on the basis that a mistake of this nature cannot turn nonexistent law into positive law; there simply *was* no prior positive law.[58] A more obvious reason for rejecting this approach is the difficulty of imagining that all states participating in custom-formation were erroneously advised by their legal counsel as to the requirements of prior international law. Indeed, it may be self-contradictory to imagine this, since states themselves ultimately decide the content of international law. Finally, it would be just as hard to find evidence of "error" as it would be to find opinio juris itself, and thus the "error hypothesis" does not get us farther along.

Kelsen actually adopted a variation of the "error" hypothesis – a theory that the states originally participating in the custom felt that they were acting under the compulsion of some norm which however was not a legal norm. In 1939 Kelsen proposed that the norm could be a sentiment of morality, equity, or justice.[59] In 1945 he added that "it is sufficient that the acting individuals consider themselves bound by any norm whatever."[60] And in 1952 he broadened the idea by requiring individuals "to regard their conduct as obligatory or right," but added that they "need not believe that it is a legal norm which they apply."[61] A fundamental problem with Kelsen's hypothesis is that everyone who acts, whether a private individual or a national decision-maker, tends to rationalize his own behavior by thinking that it is "right" and required even when it contradicts established legal obligations known to him. Thus Kelsen's broad theory would not enable us to distinguish certain kinds of behavior from others, and accordingly amounts to an unnecessary legal fiction. Moreover, Kelsen's suggestions confuse rather than build upon Geny's functional view of opinio juris. Geny, it will be recalled, used that concept only to separate legal from social usage, realizing that usage that constitutes social courtesy or comity may very well be supported by feelings of morality, equity, or justice, or any normative notion. Kelsen's view misunderstands the motivating reason for Geny's invocation of opinio juris, and the confusion persists today among many writers who focus on the "requirements" of opinio juris in the abstract and who try to solve the circularity problem by inventing various norms other than the only relevant norm (international law itself).[62] My reformulation of the theory of custom (below) attempts to deal with the circularity problem without bypassing the relevant international law norm.

5. A Reformulation of Customary Law[63]

As we have seen, the traditional theory of opinio juris specifies the need for a conviction on the part of states that their acts are required by, or consistent with, existing international law. But such a theory cannot explain the formation of new customary law, nor can it explain changes in existing customary law.

Nevertheless, we need not abandon the traditional view of opinio juris in so far as the identification of existing customary law is concerned. Here opinio juris is at least a harmless tautology. For if we can say in any given situation that a state is acting in accordance with its conviction that its behavior is in conformity with prevailing international law, then we must already know what that international law is in order to say what we've just said. And, if we know what the law is, then there is no further need to cite the "evidence" of the state's belief that it is behaving

[57] Bin Cheng, *United Nations Resolutions on Outer Space: "Instant" Customary Law?* 5 INDIAN J. INT'L L. 23, 45 n.107 (1965).

[58] Kelsen, *Theorie du droit international coutumier,* 1 REVUE INTERNATIONAL DE LA THEORIE DU DROIT (NEW SERIES) 263 (1939). Cheng appears to be unaware of this early statement of Kelsen's.

[59] *Ibid.*

[60] KELSEN, GENERAL THEORY OF LAW AND STATE 114 (1945).

[61] KELSEN, PRINCIPLES OF INTERNATIONAL LAW 307 (1952).

[62] Thus, Myres McDougal says: "The subjectivities of oughtness required to attend such uniformities of behavior [custom], which subjectivities may on occasion be proved by mere reference to the uniformities in behavior, may relate to many different systems of norms, such as prior authority, morality, natural law, reason, or religion." McDOUGAL, LASSWELL, & VLASIC, LAW AND PUBLIC ORDER IN SPACE 117 (1963).

[63] By ANTHONY D'AMATO, excerpted from: THE CONCEPT OF CUSTOM IN INTERNATIONAL LAW (Cornell Univ. Press, 1971). Reprinted by permission.

in conformity with that law. We've found opinio juris, all right, but not as a test of whether a rule is a rule of customary law; rather, it emerges as a harmless by-product of the fact that the rule in question is a rule of customary law.

Yet the concept of opinio juris could not have endured simply because it provides us with tautological reassurance. Rather, the concept points to a necessary psychological element in custom creation. As we have seen, its importance arises when states dispute the content of customary law. Well-established rules of custom, almost by definition, are not the subject of dispute. Rather, states tend to dispute the content of customary law when one side or the other argues either that a new custom has replaced the old (i.e., a change in the law) or that a new custom has arisen in a previously unregulated situation (i.e., a new rule). These problems get us directly into the matter of custom-formation, an area which the traditional theory of opinio juris cannot explain.

a. The Qualitative Element (Articulation)

The simplest objective view of opinio juris is a requirement that an objective claim of international legality be articulated in advance of, or concurrently with, the act which will constitute the quantitative element of custom. The idea of articulation has been well stated by Roger Fisher in a different context:

> If the United States were to test a missile by firing it directly toward the Soviet Union but so arrange the missile that it would alter course and drop into the sea thirteen miles off the Soviet coast, would this violate any existing rule? So far as I know, neither country tests its missiles by firing them toward the other, but no rule against it has been mentioned. When the first person, looking at the specific facts on missile testing, articulates the concept of not shooting missiles toward the other country, the rule begins to take life. A significant fact about a rule is the frequency and extent to which the underlying concept is articulated, repeated, and accepted as a valid concept, whether or not it is accepted as a rule to be followed.[64]

Of course, Professor Fisher is talking about a political rule – one that might serve some propagandistic policy or strategy – and not necessarily a rule of international law. In the context of international law, Myres McDougal has laid similar stress on the verbal formulation of "world constitutive prescription" and the "promulgative communication of the prescriptive content to the target audience."[65] Promulgative articulation, according to Lon Fuller, is one of the most basic "inherent" requirements of any system of law-making.[66] It is reflected in Article 38 of the Statute of the World Court defining custom as evidence of a general practice "accepted" as law. The articulation of a rule of international law in advance of or concurrently with a positive act (or omission) of a state gives a state notice that its action or decision will have legal implications. In other words, given such notice, statesmen will be able freely to decide whether or not to pursue various policies, knowing that their acts may create or modify international law. This voluntaristic aspect of international law is precisely what makes it acceptable to nation-state decision-makers. As we shall see with respect to the Lotus Case, the absence of prior notification that acts or abstentions have legal consequences is an effective barrier to the extrapolation of legal norms from patterns of conduct that are noticed ex post facto – that is, after the conduct but prior to the articulation. The correct order to form customary law, therefore, is: articulation followed by action. The reverse – action followed by articulation – would rob articulation of its opinio juris content, for if opinio juris means anything, it means placing a state on notice that its actions have law-creating consequences. Opinio juris cannot mean investing prior actions with law-creating consequences just by virtue of the fact that someone notices those actions and makes up a rule that characterizes them.

Thus, reduced to its simplest form, the qualitative element of custom is the articulation of a rule of international law. Several components of this formula may be usefully examined with reference to concrete illustrations:

(1) There must be a characterization of "legality." An explicit characterization enables states to distinguish legal actions from social habit, courtesy, comity, moral requirements, political expediency, plain "usage," or any other norm. (Recall, this was Geny's classic reason for the requirement of opinio juris.)

Example: Most states do not levy customs duties on articles purchased for the personal use of a diplomatic agent. But this exemption from customs duties is generally regarded as based on comity, not law. A state would thus be legally free to remove this exemption. Nevertheless, a legal rule could be articulated to the effect that, under international customary law, a state is prohibited from levying duties on personal diplomatic purchases. The verbalization might occur in a resolution of the General Assembly or in a convention proposed by the International Law commission and subsequently ratified. In its draft articles on diplomatic intercourse and immunities, the International Law Commission in fact included such a rule.[67] However, in its accompanying commentary, the Commission undercut any "articulation" of the rule (in the sense I have been proposing) by adding that "it should be accepted as a rule

[64] Fisher, *Constructing Rules that Affect Governments*, PREVENTING WORLD WAR III: SOME PROPOSALS 342, 348 (Wright, Evan, & Deutsch eds. 1962).

[65] McDougal, Lasswell, & Reisman, *The World Constitutive Process of Authoritative Decision*, 19 J. LEGAL EDUC. 403, 424 (1967).

[66] FULLER, THE MORALITY OF LAW 49–51 (1964).

[67] *Int'l L. Comm'n, Draft Articles*, 53 A.J.I.L. 179, 196 (1958) (art. 27); adopted Vienna Conv., 55 id. 1064.

of international law.''[68] When any writer says that a rule ''should become'' a rule of international law, the clear implication is that the alleged rule is not at the present time a rule of international law. Hence, the result is a lack of articulation in the sense here discussed–that a given rule is in fact a rule of customary international law.

Inasmuch as personal diplomatic articles are exempt from customs duties by virtue of comity alone–that is, the consensus of states perceives the issue to be one of comity–it would take a significant change in the consensus to change the rule to an issue of law. The ''rule''–if we can call it a rule–is a rule of comity, of courtesy, and not of law. Moving it from comity to law would require a revamping of the perceived articulation. The situation is different if a wholly new rule is involved–one that was not already a rule of comity, but rather a rule on a new subject that had previously not been articulated at all:

Negative Example: Apartheid is generally conceded to be repugnant to the moral law, the natural law, or the Divine law. But that concession does not make apartheid a violation of international law. As the World Court stated in the South West Africa Case: ''Throughout this case it has been suggested, directly or indirectly, that humanitarian considerations are sufficient in themselves to generate legal rights and obligations, and that the Court can and should proceed accordingly. The Court does not think so. It is a court of law, and can take account of moral principles only in so far as these are given a sufficient expression in legal form.''[69]

Negative Example: Many countries give military aid and economic assistance to other countries. Yet no responsible writer or government official has ever claimed that international law requires the giving of economic aid. Rather, foreign aid is generally conceded to be a matter of political expediency.

Negative Example: Tourists travel nearly everywhere, and nearly all states permit tourism. But we cannot derive from this constant and fairly uniform practice any legal requirement that a country may not in its discretion forbid foreign visitors to enter its borders. Tourism has not been articulated to be a matter of international law. It is simply a long-standing practice, perhaps one of comity, courtesy, political expediency, or simply habit.

Of course a practice based on comity or expediency might become a rule of customary law; this is what allegedly occurred in the case of the Paquete Habana.[70] But a necessary ingredient of change is the articulation of the practice as an issue of international law. Simple repetition is insufficient; all matters of comity do not eventually ''harden'' into customary law. Repetition, no matter how frequent, cannot transform tourism or the use of French as a primary language in diplomacy into legally binding obligations.

Example: Although manned exploration of other planets has not yet taken place, we know in advance of ''usage'' or ''practice'' that exploration, exploitation, and ownership of extra-terrestrial bodies are questions of international law and not exclusively of expediency, morality, or comity. For articulation in advance of usage has taken place in a resolution of the General Assembly of December 13, 1963.[71] Though the resolution in terms is future-oriented, it nevertheless makes clear that exploration and use of outer space are matters of international law. The resolution alone does not generate customary international law, but it does provide the element of articulation. If states later behave in a manner consistent with the resolution when exploration and use of outer space become technologically feasible, we may then say that customary law has been established. Right now, we have a reasonable expectation that a rule of custom will arise.

Note that the ''legality'' must be of international, not domestic, law. As Karl Strupp has suggested with respect to the legal consequences of municipal judicial decisions, the decisions must not reflect merely an opinio juris in the framework of internal law, but rather an opinio juris gentium.[72] For without this objective element of internationality, one could not tell whether the rule articulated would pertain to states in their international relations. Judge Nyholm's dissenting opinion in the Lotus Case reflects this concern, in his reference to acts ''accomplished in the domain of international relations.''[73] One of Judge Hudson's elements of custom, cited above, requires the practice to be ''with reference to a type of situation falling within the domain of international relations.'' Since it is by no means self-evident, as the following examples will show, whether a situation falls within the international or the domestic domain, the rule must be articulated to be one of international law.

Example: A classic international rule says that what a state does to its own nationals within its own territorial boundaries is a matter solely of domestic jurisdiction. Yet some inroads have been made by the Nuremberg decisions and the Genocide Convention, which have articulated the general norm (now starting to have an impact in the human-rights area) that a state must treat even its own nationals in a manner that respects their basic human rights. As the World Court held in 1923, ''the question whether a certain matter is or is not solely within the jurisdiction of a State

---

[68] 53 A.J.I.L. 197 (1958).

[69] 1966 I.C.J. REP. 6, 34.

[70] 175 U.S. 677, 694 (1900). Justice Gray's opinion in this famous case contains ample evidence of a well-settled rule of customary law; the idea of ''comity'' growing in the period of 100 years into a rule of custom was introduced solely to help further distinguish dicta in an old British case.

[71] G.A. Res. 1962 (XVIII). A quite different impact on customary law may now obtain with respect to the multilateral convention on outer space, signed at Washington, London, and Moscow on January 27, 1967.

[72] Strupp, *Les regles generales du droit de la paix*, 47 RECUEIL DES COURS 263, 307 (1934).

[73] P.C.I.J. Ser. A, No. 10, at 4, 59 (1927).

is an essentially relative question; it depends upon the development of international relations.''[74]

(2) In the case of abstentions, the articulation must characterize the abstention as legally required. At every moment of time, any state is not acting with respect to innumerable situations. The United States fails to commit aggression against Canada each day of the year.[75] Switzerland refrains from claiming sovereignty over the Atlantic Ocean every minute of every day. Tanzania continually fails to send a manned spaceship to the moon to assert Tanzanian sovereignty there. Belgium does not order its police to arrest all foreign tourists. In the nineteenth century, no state claimed the right to exclusive use of the resources of the continental shelf. Clearly two categories of non-acts are implicit in these examples: acts a state could do but chooses not to do, and acts which a state could not do given the current level of its technology or its geographical position. Only the failure to commit possible acts can have any legal consequence; surely one cannot draw any conclusion from the fact that a state did not do what it was not capable of doing. But even in the class of possible acts, there is still an indefinitely large number that are not committed. Within this class, a state's failure to act when it has been given notice, by virtue of a prior or concurrent articulation of a legal rule to the effect that states have a duty to refrain from acting in such circumstances, is the only kind of non-act that can contribute to the formation of customary international law.

Example: In 1927, could a rule of international law barring criminal jurisdiction over foreign seamen involved in a collision with a flag ship on the high seas have been deduced from the few previous criminal prosecutions in such circumstances? The Permanent Court of International Justice in the Lotus Case accepted the relevance of the contention of the French agent that ''questions of jurisdiction in collision cases, which frequently arise before civil courts, are but rarely encountered in the practice of criminal courts.'' But, accepting the quantitative allegation of abstention, the Court went on to hold that the qualitative element was absent. It stated that the rarity of cases merely showed that states ''had often, in practice, abstained from instituting criminal proceedings, and not that they recognized themselves as being obliged to do so; for only if such abstention were based on their being conscious of having a duty to abstain would it be possible to speak of an international custom.''[76] At first glance, this significant passage seems metaphoric; a state is an artificial entity not capable of being ''conscious'' or ''unconscious.'' Even if we were to substitute for the term ''states'' the ''national decision-makers within those states,'' the task of proving consciousness of a duty would be impossible. First of all, we would have to know which policy-makers decided not to institute criminal proceedings in collision cases. Since the proceedings never took place, how could one track down the various prosecutors and government officials in all the states in the world who in the course of their terms of office had the chance to, but did not, institute criminal prosecutions of foreign seamen? Many of these officials would not be alive; many who were alive might be unreliable witnesses as to their former mental attitudes concerning such cases – if they remembered them at all. But even here, we could not rest with the collection of evidence of mental attitudes of officials directly involved, for any state has a policy-making apparatus which approves or disapproves of policy stances made at lower levels. We cannot discover whether a given official would have advocated criminal prosecutions of foreign seamen but for the fact that he felt that his superior would disapprove. And, if the superior official never had the opportunity to disapprove, we could not tell what his reasons for disapproving would have been had he been given the chance. Moreover, in most states policy is made by committee and not by individuals. If a committee decides in the first, second, or eighth instance to advocate or to disavow a policy of instituting criminal proceedings over a foreign seaman involved in a collision with a flag ship, perhaps some members of the committee may have felt that the policy was required under international law and that other members made their decisions on entirely different grounds. We could not determine whether a majority in any of these various policy-making committees felt conscious of any international obligation. In addition, if the international law point was raised at all in the committee deliberations, some members may have changed their minds in the course of argument, some might have misconstrued the arguments and decided in error that the policy was or was not required by international law, and some might have hidden their reasons if asked by an outsider after the committee meeting why they had voted in favor of the policy or against it. Even diaries and memoirs are notoriously inaccurate as to previous mental attitudes.

However, the passage in the Lotus Case is susceptible of a more objective interpretation. The Court laid stress on whether the states ''recognized'' themselves as being obliged to abstain under international law. From an objective point of view, we can hardly infer recognition if no one had ever previously claimed that states were under an obligation to abstain in these cases. In other words, if no statesman or responsible jurist had ever articulated a legal rule to the effect that states could not exercise criminal jurisdiction in cases involving collision on the high seas between flag ships of different states over seamen of the foreign vessel, then it would be unpersuasive to argue as a matter of international law that states (that is, their decision-makers) could have recognized themselves as being under an obligation to abstain. The fact of their abstention would thus have no legal consequences; they may have abstained for reasons of comity, courtesy, policy, disinterest, or sheer inertia. In the Lotus Case, the French agent could cite no articulation of a legal rule on the point that was promulgated prior to the actual collision between the

---

[74] *Nationality Decrees Issued in Tunis and Morocco*, P.C.I.J. Ser. B, No 4, at 24 (1923).

[75] *See* HENKIN, HOW NATIONS BEHAVE 43 (1968).

[76] P.C.I.J. Ser. A, No. 10, at 4, 28 (1927).

French and Turkish vessels. In this objective sense, the Court was of course correct in holding that there was no proof that the states recognized themselves under an obligation to abstain.

That the Court itself was not thinking in terms of subjective evidence of the qualitative element is demonstrated on the very next page of the opinion with respect to the matter of protests. The fact that no evidence was adduced that France and Germany had protested in two previous instances of criminal prosecutions against their nationals showed, in the Court's judgment, that they had not tacitly consented to a rule of exclusive jurisdiction of the flag state as contended by the French agent. Here the Court was using the objective evidence – the lack of formal diplomatic protests – to infer a subjective attitude on the part of the states concerned. Although this particular inference is substantively questionable,[77] it nevertheless indicates a technique of proof of custom that is significant.[78] For, despite the occasional language that seems to call for subjective evaluation of states' attitudes, the kinds of proof required by the Court were purely objective: in this instance, notes of protest; in the previous instance, by inference, a prior articulation of a legal rule.

(3) The acting or abstaining state must have reason to know of the articulation of the legal rule. There is no need for the acting state itself, through its officials, to have articulated the legal rule. States often do not give official explanations of their conduct, nor should we expect them to do so.[79] A writer on international law, a court, or an international organization may very well provide the qualitative component of custom. But it must be promulgated in a place which nation-state officials or their counsel would have reason to consult. The leading journals in international law, the leading textbooks, reports of legal decisions affecting international law, resolutions of international organizations – all these are likely sources for the articulation of rules. Diplomatic correspondence is similarly a good source; if one state protests the actions of another, the acting state is clearly apprised of the fact that its actions may have legal consequences. At the present stage of the development of international law, the greatest number of articulated rules may be found in treaties, draft conventions of the International Law Commission, and resolutions of the General Assembly of the United Nations. These sources serve to call to the immediate attention of states the rules that are in the process of change, of "progressive development," or in the process of creation (for example, rules relating to outer space).

The standard of "reason to know," often used in domestic law when matters of notice are at issue, is an objective standard. For it depends not on the actual mental state of the person receiving the notice, but on our inference that a reasonable man so situated would have been informed. When applied to states, the "reason to know" standard clearly cannot be given exact content, but must depend on how persuasively one can contend that a state should have been aware that its actions were constitutive of custom. If the applicable rule has been articulated by the General Assembly in one of its resolutions, one can hardly imagine how a state could plead ignorance of its content. On the other hand, if the applicable rule was published in an obscure law journal devoted to domestic law, a state should not be charged with notice of the rule. International law, to reiterate, is a matter of relative persuasion. Customary law is no different; the side that can produce the better arguments for the existence or nonexistence of a rule of custom will prevail in the legal arena. With respect to the qualitative element of custom, a well-articulated rule

---

77 [Editor's Note: See the section on "Protest," *infra*, this Chapter.]

78 The inference seems to be in error; one might equally well infer that states usually refrained because of the effectiveness of threats of protests (delivered orally). In the two cases where jurisdiction was asserted, actual notes protesting the jurisdiction might have been deemed futile as occurring after the event.

As Judge Altamira pointedly said in his dissenting opinion, governments resort to protests in such cases "only when things have developed into a public scandal." Otherwise, either "indolence" or "anxiety to avoid diplomatic complications" keep them from protesting. *Id.* at 98. One should not readily conclude from failure to protest that a state necessarily feels that what the acting state is doing is legal under international law.

79 [Editor's Note: This argument was subsequently criticized as follows: "The difficulty in D'Amato's identification of opinio juris with articulation is that, as he himself writes, 'States often do not give official explanations of their conduct, nor should we expect them to do so' and this means that, if his theory were correct, we should often have to deny the existence of opinio juris in cases where we would not otherwise be inclined to do so. It should also be borne in mind that States, like private individuals, are likely to guard themselves against formal admissions of obligation to carry out the acts which they do in fact perform." Raphael M. Walden, *Customary International Law: A Jurisprudential Analysis*, 13 ISRAEL LAW REVIEW 86, 99 (1978). I agree with Mr. Walden's last sentence; it is a point well worth making. But I frankly do not understand his first sentence. Surely there is no reason that we would "deny the existence of opinio juris" in cases where officials give no explanation of their conduct, because that would lead to the denial of opinio juris in nearly all of the formative cases of custom in the history of international law. It appears to me, from Mr. Walden's essay as a whole and another one that he published a year earlier, that he retains the fixed classical view of opinio juris as something states feel as a subjective obligation. *See, e.g.*, Raphael M. Walden, *The Subjective Element in the Formation of Customary International Law*, 12 ISRAEL LAW REVIEW 344 (1977). In this respect he joins many international law scholars who have the unshakeable belief that they can somehow ascertain when a state feels an obligation to do something or other. My view is that they are employing a magical theory of jurisprudence; they somehow feel they can attribute a human emotion to an abstract entity, and an extraordinarily sophisticated human emotion at that – the emotion of a subjective sense of obligation to obey a rule of law. I don't just think they are wrong; I think their views are dangerously retrogressive, because they give the central problem of international law – the ascertainment of its customary rules – more than a hint of alchemy amd mysticism. For my part, international law needs all the objectivity it can get.]

is certainly preferable to a poorly articulated one, but no hard-and-fast line can be drawn in advance as to what types of articulation meet the test and what types fail. In the future, hopefully the International Law Commission, acting under its general mandate to make the sources of international law more available to states, or some other international organization under U.N. auspices, will install at the United Nations a data bank which can serve as the definitive repository of all articulations of rules of international law (as well as evidence of state actions and abstentions). Meanwhile, the process of determining when a rule has been "articulated" in the sense used in this chapter will be, like any other element of international law, a matter of reasonable persuasion.

b. The Quantitative Element (Act, Abstention or Commitment)

A rule of law is immaterial, psychological; it is a directive addressed to the mind of man, not something tangible. In domestic legal systems, these intangible rules flow from legislatures and courts. In the international legal system, lacking a central legislature and where the few tribunals that exist deal with very few cases out of all the claim-conflict situations that arise among nations, there is no authoritative voice to ascertain which of all the articulated norms are in fact rules of international law. Rather, the states themselves take on the function of creating international law. But states rarely agree unanimously as to the rules of international law; consensus generally occurs with respect to rules that were already well-established. However, there is a consensus, reflected in state practice, as to rules about rules – here, rules about how customary rules are formed. When a rule is alleged to be a rule of "custom," the person asserting the rule must adduce both a qualitative articulation of the rule and a quantitative element. Without the latter, states could not tell which of the numerous and often conflicting articulated norms were actually embodied in customary law.

The necessity for a quantitative element also assures states that the creation of rules of law is in their exclusive province. Many conflicting rules may be articulated, but a state can only act in one way at one time. The act is concrete and usually unambiguous. Once the act takes place, the previously articulated rule that is consistent with the act takes on life as a rule of customary law, while the previously articulated rules contrary to it remain in the realm of speculation. The state's act is visible, real, and significant; it crystallizes policy and demonstrates which of the many possible rules of law the acting state has decided to manifest. Moreover, a state is willing to be responsible for its actions; no state is willing to be responsible for what it says. The acts of a state can cause harm, and a state may be held responsible under international law for redressing the harm. But the words of a state cannot in themselves cause harm.[80] In short, as the old saying has it, "actions speak louder than words." Or as U.S. Attorney General Mitchell said in cautioning the public about the Nixon administration's policies, "Watch what we do, not what we say."

The conjunction of rule and action becomes a powerful precedent for future similar situations; the next state to come along can repeat the act with a certain amount of assurance that it is not violating international law by doing so, and this sense of assurance increases as more states follow the practice. Other states find it increasingly difficult to challenge the practice. In short, the line of practice becomes customary international law.

What is an "act" of a state? In most cases, a state's action is easily recognized. A state sends up an artificial satellite, tests nuclear weapons, receives ambassadors, levies customs duties, expels an alien, captures a pirate vessel, sets up a drilling rig in the continental shelf, visits and searches a neutral ship, and similarly engages in thousands of acts through its citizens and agents. On the other hand, a claim is not an act. As a matter of daily practice, international law is largely concerned with conflicting international claims. But the claims themselves, although they may articulate a legal norm, cannot constitute the material component of custom. For a state has not done anything when it makes a claim; until it takes enforcement action, the claim has little value as a prediction of what the state will actually do.

Harder to recognize as an "act" is a state's decision to refrain from acting in a situation where it could have acted. If states refrain from exercising civil or criminal jurisdiction over foreign diplomats and their families, it is clear that they could have exercised such jurisdiction. The question then is whether the restraint constitutes the material component of customary law. We have seen from the previous section that if a prior rule calling for such restraint has been articulated in the absence of a consensus that the practice is simply one of comity or courtesy, then customary law will have been generated. Another kind of restraint from action often accompanies the positive action of a foreign state. For example, if a state has a right under international law to send up an artificial satellite, other states will have a correlative duty not to shoot it down. If a state sets up a drilling rig in the continental shelf, other states cannot legally destroy the rig or confiscate the oil. But when the first artificial satellite (Sputnik) circled the globe, no one

[80] To be sure, someone might rely to his or her detriment upon what a state says. Thus a state's policies may be misleading to a person who is unsophisticated about international law. Two decades after the above text was published, Saddam Hussein returned from a meeting with the American ambassador to Iraq with the conviction that she had promised that the United States would look the other way if Iraq attacked Kuwait. A subsequently published transcript of the ambassador's conversation provided reasonable support for the impression Saddam had of the conversation. But then, when Saddam decided to follow through and commit aggression against Kuwait, the United States condemned the act and eventually defeated Iraq in the Persian Gulf War. Was Saddam Hussein misled? Perhaps. Should he have been? Not if his advisers knew anything about international law.

knew whether the Soviet Union had a right to send it up. Thus, the reactions of the other states were of critical importance in establishing custom. The fact that the other states chose not to act – chose not to interfere with Sputnik when it passed over their territory – crystallized the quantitative component of custom.[81] When state A does something that affects state B, and state B allows A to do it, then B's noninterference is just as significant for the formation of custom as A's act. For if B had successfully interfered, A may have been unable to complete the act, and thus the quantitative element would not have been perfected.[82]

In addition to ordinary acts and abstentions, a commitment to act should be included in our list of examples of the quantitative element. If a state has made a collateral engagement to act, its promise – whether subsequently kept or broken – can be argued to be the decisive operative element. In domestic law, a person entering into a contract for sale of a house has at that moment committed herself legally to sell the house. If she thereafter refuses to hand over the deed, the law will "order" her to perform either by injunction or by issuing a new valid deed to the purchaser and causing it to be registered. The mere fact that the seller refuses to comply with the transfer of the deed is legally irrelevant. In international law, states have made extensive use of the treaty to lay down requirements for their future actions and restraints. When a state makes a commitment to act under a treaty, the commitment, rather than the subsequent act, is significant in terms of customary law. Of course, repeated violations of a treaty may constitute a treaty abrogation, but short of that it is the "act" of commitment to a treaty, and not the envisioned performance, that is legally decisive. Similarly, if states have agreed to the jurisdiction of the World Court in a particular case, the court's eventual decision is more significant than the compliance or noncompliance of the losing party. All or nearly all states recognize the Corfu Channel Case[83] as expressing valid rules of international law despite the fact that Albania never complied with the judgment.

Just as an act should be distinguished from a claim, so too a treaty must be distinguished from a unilateral declaration. If a state proclaims an intent to act, and even if it passes implementing internal legislation, it has made no international commitment to follow through on its statement of intent. Although several South American states have unilaterally declared their exclusive sovereignty over a territorial sea of 200 miles, other states have disregarded these claims. Some writers have given considerable attention to the theory that unilateral declarations can constitute customary law,[84] but they have failed to adduce instances to support their theory. Some purported instances of unilateral declarations prove, upon inspection, to be international agreements that were simply not put in writing in treaty form.

A more difficult question, insisted upon by many writers, relates to the number of acts (or restraints) necessary to satisfy the material element of custom formation. However, such an inquiry is misleading. There is no metaphysically precise (such as "seventeen repetitions") or vague (such as "in the Court's discretion") answer possible. States simply do not organize their behavior along absolute lines. There is no international "constitution" specifying when acts become law. Rather, states resort to international law in claim-conflict situations. In such instances, counsel for either side will attempt to cite as many acts as possible. Thus we may say that persuasiveness in part depends upon the number of precedents. At the very least, the party asserting the existence of a custom must cite one instance of an act or restraint that followed the articulation of a rule.

If one act, or failure to act, is cited in support of a customary rule of international law, the citation will carry with it some persuasive power. Even so, there may be a significant difference in the threshold of persuasiveness if two (or more) acts can be cited instead of one. Two may be significantly more persuasive than one, whereas three (or four or five) may only be marginally more persuasive than two. In the ordinary leaning of the word, "custom" is something that has repeated itself. Plucknett cites a thirteenth-century source to the effect that "twice makes a custom."[85] Let us examine how this ordinary-language

---

[81] We assume that the states had the technological capacity, then or later, to interfere with the satellite's flight. They might also have threatened to retaliate in some other way against the Soviet Union unless she ceased to launch Sputniks. Simple protest, standing alone, would have simply reinforced the articulation of the act. What actually happened was that states did not attempt to interfere with Sputnik, nor did they take any other measures against the Soviet Union for launching the satellite. At the same time, the Soviet Union made no extravagent claims: *e.g.*, it did not claim ownership of the stratosphere. All it claimed was that it had the right to send up artificial satellites. By implication from the international principle of equality of states, other states immediately acquired the same right as the Soviet Union. Hence, a new rule of customary law was born, one that allows the launching of artificial satellites above the airspace of the earth. For the purposes of international law, therefore, a line exists between airspace (which is "owned" by the territorial state below) and outer space (which is open to all, like the high seas).

[82] Similarly, where B exacts a penalty from A – *e.g.*, freezing the financial assets of A in B's banks – that imposes a higher cost to A than its act is worth, A may also withdraw the act (or decide not to complete it). This, as well, is a way to prevent a permissive customary rule from forming. (It may, on the other hand, be quantitative evidence of a rule of custom prescribing the exact opposite: *i.e.*, a rule saying that a state in A's position may not legally act as A attempted to act.)

[83] 1949 I.C.J. Rep. 4.

[84] *E.g.*, SUY, LES ACTES JURIDIQUES UNILATERAUX EN DROIT INTERNATIONAL PUBLIC (1962), and citations therein.

[85] PLUCKNETT, A CONCISE HISTORY OF THE COMMON LAW 308 n.1 (5th ed. 1956), citing P. DE FONTAINES, CONSEL A UN AMI 492 (c. 1259).

conclusion would apply in some hypothetical conflict-of-custom situations.

Imagine a case of first impression in which none of the states involved has signed any treaty bearing on the subject matter. State A launches an artificial satellite that, after orbiting the earth several times, re-enters the atmosphere, is not consumed by atmospheric friction in its entirety, but instead falls within state B, striking and killing a citizen of B. State B makes a diplomatic request of state A to pay damages to the heirs of the decedent, arguing that international law requires absolute liability in this admittedly accidental situation. State A thereupon pays to B the damages requested, but reserves its position on the question whether it was under an obligation to pay. Now assume that after some time a second case of falling satellite occurs, the satellite having been launched by state C and causing damage in state D. D represents diplomatically to C that C is liable under international law. When C refuses to pay, D argues as follows: (1) A legal rule was articulated by B in its diplomatic request to A. This articulation occurred prior to A's "act," which in this case was A's decision to pay. There was no need for the articulation to occur prior to the accident, since the accident admittedly was out of the control of A. (2) A's decision to pay constituted the material element of the custom. (3) Although there is only a single instance of this custom, one is better than none at all. The A-B act at least stands for the rule contended for by D, whereas C can cite nothing in its favor.

These arguments would appear to be more persuasive than any that C could make. And yet, C might reason as follows: if C refuses to pay and concedes no liability, then a new precedent, the C-D case, would go into history alongside the A-B case. C's refusal to pay is just as much an "act" as A's prior willingness to pay. Therefore, if a future case arises between E and F, F, the plaintiff, will cite the A-B case while E, the defendant in the diplomatic exchange, will cite the C-D case. Since the two cases cited will be opposed to each other, the rule at that point will be indeterminate. From the point of view of E and F, the E-F case will be the same as a case of first impression.

Thus, C's refusal to pay would operate to defeat the A-B custom. Since C knows this, C may refuse to pay on the basis that its very refusal will cancel the previous rule and thus remove, in effect, whatever legal pressure D was able to muster on the basis of the A-B situation.

D might reply that C's refusal to pay was illegal, and thus C's action could not affect the underlying customary rule established by the A-B case. This position, however, fails to look at the facts from the E-F perspective, which sees C's refusal as equally valid as A's decision to pay. Indeed, the fact that C's refusal to pay came later in time might even make it a more persuasive precedent, from E's point of view, than the A-B case.

But might it not be possible to lay down a rule that the first case or first few similar cases generates a customary rule, and that later cases would simply be violations of the customary rule and should be given no legal effect? Although this position does follow from many of the traditional concepts of opinio juris discussed in the preceding section, it ignores the possibility and actuality of change in customary law. The only way customary international law can change—and it certainly has changed significantly in the practice of states over the centuries—is by giving legal effect to departures from preceding customary norms. The contrary course would be logically absurd. It would mean, for instance, that once the A-B case was on the books, then even though the next five hundred similar cases each resulted in a refusal to pay damages, the A-B case would be good law and the five hundred subsequent states refusing to pay would all be acting illegally. No one has ever claimed this; all writers would admit that the similar actions of five hundred states would overwhelm the first, now seemingly quaint, case that reached the opposite result. But if five hundred cases can overturn one, so can a single contrary case cancel a previous one.

C would not have been in this position had there been two prior instances of the A-B variety. If A had previously paid damages to B, and M had paid damages to N, then in the third case of C vs. D, any refusal by C to pay D, would not effectively overweigh the two prior precedents. C's refusal would not become its own justification, and D would clearly have the more persuasive case. In other words, the repetition of an act constituting the quantitative element of custom serves to enhance the rule significantly. Two acts are significantly more persuasive than one, since in the third situation there would be no effective way of canceling the rule by acting differently.

It is important to note that resort to the World Court or to any other international tribunal is, in present international relations, a highly atypical event. States normally make many claims based on their view of international law; other states will evaluate those claims and either comply with them in whole or in part, or ignore them. Let us nevertheless assume that an international tribunal had jurisdiction over the previous hypothetical cases. In the C-D case when the A-B precedent was the only prior instance, if D brought an action against C in an international court, D would probably prevail on the basis of the arguments suggested for D previously. C could not persuasively argue that its refusal to pay D would constitute a negating precedent for future cases, thus canceling the rule of law, for the court would probably react by ordering C to pay, stating that any refusal by C would be illegal and hence of no effect. Yet the court would be justified in reaching this result because C had previously accepted its jurisdiction, thus agreeing to be bound by its judgments. C's "act" of accepting the jurisdiction of the court, therefore, is what might lead to a different result. Of course, C could argue that its freedom to change the customary rule in the absence of a tribunal should not be compromised by the presence of a tribunal. If the court were to accept this argument, it would make no effective difference whether the C-D case were brought before an international tribunal or were handled in the normal give-and-take of diplomatic bargaining. One can only await with interest such a "case of second impression" in an international tribunal.

Much more assurance can go into a prediction that an international tribunal would decide in favor of D, if there had been two precedents (the A-B and M-N cases) in favor of a rule of absolute liability. Conversely, if an international tribunal had to deal with the initial A-B case, it could not justifiably decide the case on the basis of international customary law, assuming that there was no treaty on the subject. The court might find a consensus of all the nations in the world in favor of the rule of absolute liability or its opposite, particularly if the General Assembly had passed a resolution to that effect. Or the court might resort to analogies, "general principles of law," or some other standard for disposing of the case. But it could not persuasively base its decision on custom, since there was no prior custom.

Finally, the hypothetical cases just analyzed have important implications for the concept of change of customary law. Customary law can be changed or modified by divergent acts subsequent to the initial establishment of the rule. Even a rule of custom based on two or more situations can be changed. For instance, let us imagine again that the A-B and M-N cases resulting in absolute liability have taken place. In the subsequent C-D conflict, even though D now has by far the more persuasive case based on custom, C might nevertheless refuse to pay. Moreover, C might not agree to the jurisdiction of any court to settle the dispute. D might be angry with C's position, but might decide to let the matter drop as being unworthy of risking a serious international incident. If that is the result, then in the next case, E would be in a position to make arguments to F similar to the ones C made to D. E would argue that its own refusal to pay would constitute the second disconfirmatory instance which would then serve to negate the two affirmative precedents.

Customary law clearly has changed over the years, and thus any theory must incorporate the possibility of change into its concept of custom. In particular, an "illegal" act by a state contains the seeds of a new legality. When a state violates an existing rule of customary international law, it undoubtedly is "guilty" of an illegal act, but the illegal act itself becomes a disconfirmatory instance of the underlying rule. The next state will find it somewhat easier to disobey the rule, until eventually a new line of conduct will replace the original rule by a new rule. The number of disconfirmatory acts required to replace the original rule is a function partly of the number of acts that established the original rule in the first place, the remoteness in time of the establishing acts, the legal authoritativeness of the participating states, and other possible factors, including the argumentative skill of the proponent or opponent of a claim of custom. At any rate, the theory that has been suggested here allows for the smooth working of change in customary international law. Each deviation contains the seeds of a new rule. Under the classical theory, change was impossible because each deviation was illegal, and hence there could be no opinio juris (no conviction that the actor was acting in conformity with existing law). The present theory, necessitated by the fact of change, has attempted to show how change is theoretically possible.

Many writers have suggested that in assessing custom the acts of a major power have more "weight" than those of a small country.[86] This observation, which undoubtedly contains some truth, might be refined by saying that what gives a nation its voice in forming custom is not necessarily its military might or the amount of real estate it possesses, but rather its degree of sophistication in international law. Great Britain, for instance, probably speaks with a greater authority in international law than its military position might warrant, because it takes care to publish its diplomatic correspondence, because many British writers publish in the world's leading international legal journals, because it is capable of making sophisticated, and not simplistic, legal arguments in international diplomacy, and so forth.

6. A Seminar on Custom[87]

The seminar was convened on April 22, 1988, at 8:30 a.m. by its Moderator, Anthony D'Amato.

PROFESSOR D'AMATO: My starting point for this discussion is an observation: international law is declining in importance in U.S. law schools. There are many reasons this is happening, but one extremely important reason is that our discipline is not considered sufficiently rigorous. We are seen as loose and muddled in our sources of law. We are seen as finding support for our propositions of international law in literature, polemics, debates – almost anything. Indeed, some international lawyers will cite almost any source to support a claim of law. Critics rightfully see this as nothing more than rhetoric and muddled thinking. Our colleagues in other fields are confined to statutes and cases, and must defend their propositions with precise analytic techniques. When they see that we are not similarly restrained, they lose respect for those of us working in the field of international law.

What can we do about this situation? Today we explore the concept of custom, which is often cited as an example of intellectual nebulousness. Grigori Tunkin, who is here today, pioneered in analyzing custom long before I did my work on the subject. Custom is something that is strange to many of our colleagues. While they can look upon treaties as something vaguely familiar, much of international law is nontreaty. Even the interpretation of treaties is generally nontreaty in origin.

ISAAK DORE: There is an additional factor in the decline

---

[86] DEVISSCHER, THEORY AND REALITY IN PUBLIC INTERNATIONAL LAW 149 (1957); Bishop, *op. cit. supra* n.16, at 227.

[87] By ANTHONY D'AMATO, excerpted from: William B.T. Mock (Reporter), *Seminar on the Theory of Customary International Law*, 82 PROCEEDINGS OF THE AMERICAN SOCIETY OF INTERNATIONAL LAW 242 (1988). Reprinted by permission.

in importance and prestige of international law in American law schools. It seems to me that the psychology of the perception is conditioned by the lack of any central law enforcement mechanism, such as our colleagues normally find in their own disciplines.

PROFESSOR D'AMATO: That's true. In addition, they look to our lack of legislation and our scant case law. All of that is endemic to our situation as international lawyers. My conviction is that our colleagues are the ones who should be on the defensive. Their disciplines are generally very mechanical, almost a kind of ersatz law. We, on the other hand, engage in what I would call pure law–law that grows up out of the interactions of states, who both create and enforce the law over time. It is law within a society, not law imposed by authority. According to Hegel, what we have here is that the creator-subjects of the international legal order are unfolding the law as it is manifested in their interactions with other creator-subjects. In the 11th century, the common law was derived in the self-regulatory Hegelian manner. Parliament then stepped in and took over, imposing commands upon the people. Domestic law lost its common law touch. For a long time now, the only pure common law has been international law.

To approach the subject of custom from the simplest starting point, we look at the international scene. We could have expected to see nothing but chaos and anarchy, everybody fighting with each other all the time and nobody having any idea about what's going on–in other words, Hobbes' state of nature. But instead we see regularity. We see for the most part peace and peaceful accommodations. The basic entitlements of each state under international law are not contested and are virtually incontestable.

Looking at the scene in systemic terms we find that these aggregates of units that we call states–but they are really combinations of people who have certain claims to territories–are getting along with each other in some kind of way. We don't yet know how, because we haven't introduced any notion of law. But somehow they're getting along. They're interacting, and they seem to be behaving in some kind of orderly way. So we say to ourselves: "Aha! Something's going on here that's not explained." There is a systemic process here. These units somehow are interacting in a fashion that cannot be explained by the laws of chance or randomness. We are witnessing ordered behavior.

What accounts for this order? What accounts for this sense that certain things are norms that are adhered to? We don't have to attribute any kind of consciousness to the unit-states. It's just that somehow these units are behaving in a purposeful way. They don't clash with each other at all possible points of interaction, although they may clash on some points. And so we say that there must be some laws in the system. There must be something that accounts for the regularities of this behavior. What are these laws?

Well, that's our customary-law problem: to figure out what laws account for these regularities. And so we start looking at what states do and what they claim. The laws can be anything. We don't dictate what international law is; we look for it and find it out there in the real world. International law is implicit in the interactions of these state units. Somehow they're interacting in ways that tell us that there is regularity there. If we were physicists we would say the same thing. If we saw a bunch of microbes, and they were acting in a certain orderly fashion, we would say that there must be some laws regulating their behavior. If we see the planets going around a certain way, we say, well, there are certain laws of gravity, certain quantum theories, that account for planetary behavior. So today we're looking at states, and we say the same thing–that there are certain laws that seem to account for their regular behavior.

Norms of custom are manifested by the behavior of these unit-states and their interactions with each other. Not only do the norms characterize the interactions of the units, but they tend to define the units. In other words, the evolving customary law that we infer from the system defines what a state is. This is hard to convey to outsiders because people who are unfamiliar with Hegelian logic and dialectic theory tend to think too positivistically–they think that law is something that comes down from above. But if you look at law growing out of the interaction of these units, you will see that the very same law that is in the process of always developing is also in the process of always defining, so that a state is defined as a territory that has a right to certain boundaries, and a right to certain claims over the individuals in it, and certain kinds of competences with respect to other states with other boundaries and certain kinds of competences with respect to other individuals who find themselves in that state. And that notion begins to regularize itself and define what it is that these units are doing.

The norms evolve over time as the units modify their behavior. The 19th-century international-law definition of a state that grew out of the interactions was: "Everything that goes on within our borders is our business and international law only applies to those times when we bump up against other units. We bump up against them on the high seas or when there's a war or at a few other times. But our boundaries carve out a certain territory that's our own and doesn't affect other territories."[88] Yet however obvious that definition may have seemed to theorists like Oppenheim, it has deteriorated in the 20th century. We now have a concept of a state that is defined in terms of the state's interests in its own people and their life concerns.

---

[88] There is an interesting parallel in theoretical physics. In the nineteenth century, physicists thought that it was possible to isolate a particular system and study it. Today, physicists concede the impossibility of isolating anything. The slightest movement of your little finger will have a physical effect on distant galaxies. Similarly, the movement of distant galaxies has an effect on our bodies. Of course, the greater the distance, the more minuscule the effect; nevertheless, the effect is there. The entire universe is a "system"–there is nothing in the universe that is detached from anything else. Everything is connected to everything.

Human rights law has necessitated a new idea of permeability of state boundaries. A new customary law has developed that in certain basic areas puts people ahead of states, and thus makes more complex our notion of what a state is.[89]

PETER WEISS: I have a question about your theory of the self-defining nature of customary international law, based on your analogy with the behavior of atoms and planets. Atoms and planets behave in a certain way because, as most people would say today, that is the way nature behaves, and we have to discover the secrets of nature. Other people would say, it is also because that's the way God willed it, and it's a manifestation of the divine plan.

Now, that corresponds to a certain interpretation of customary international law. You can have purely natural customary international law and say the reason these rules are developing as they are is because they correspond to the nature of society or the nature of human beings, or to a working out of the divine will. But then there is another possible interpretation of why things tend to behave in regular ways. It is totally different from what you can say about microbes or atoms or planets: states tend to behave in a certain way because the powerful states impose their rules on the less powerful. That could be either a North-South relationship or a Capitalist-Socialist one, or whatever. What importance do you attach to the element of the more powerful defining the rules to the less powerful?

PROFESSOR D'AMATO: That's something Charles De-Visscher talked about 30 years ago in his *Theory and Reality in Public International Law*, claiming that it was realistic to acknowledge the legal power of the more powerful states. I don't attach too much importance to that argument. It seems to me that international law is very democratic in a strange sense – the participants in the system at minimum all tend to regard all the international rules as applying equally to all of them. It would be quite hard to contend that certain rules only apply to some. It would be hard to give legal advantages to some states and not to others.

Now, this gets very complicated. The notion of a system is one that certainly can tolerate large units as well as small. We can have the planet Jupiter and the planet Mercury and there's a very big difference in size, but they seem to be following the same laws of gravity. There's no exception for one of them as opposed to the other. When we talk about international rules, we seem to be saying that the same rules, the same entitlements that define one state, define all states.

It's very hard to conceive of a bundle of entitlements as defining some units but not others. Professor Myres McDougal tried to get away with something like this conception. He tried to say that there are certain situations where the rules benefit, say, the United States but don't equally benefit the Soviet Union, because the Soviet Union is an outlaw state.[90] And I think that all of us, except for Professor McDougal, found that to be totally unpersuasive. How do you even make a rational argument when you're saying that the other side of the argument isn't entitled to the same debating time, the same rules of the game, that you're entitled to? It's very hard to make those claims when the Soviet Union is a participant in the debate. That doesn't mean that some states aren't more powerful than others. But it's an incredibly interesting fact that whenever one powerful state tries to impose its rules on anyone else, it finds that those rules get reflected back on it.

A sort of a watershed example of this is what happened in Nuremberg. When the victorious Allies decided to prosecute the leaders of the Third Reich, many thoughtful leaders in the United States and in other countries said: "Wait a minute. If we take this step, aren't we committed to the proposition that in the future we might be the ones who are in the dock? As soon as we prosecute Nazi leaders for leading their countries and doing certain kinds of things, we're committing ourselves irrevocably to the proposition that someday we might find ourselves on the losing side of a war and be up there as criminals." And that underlying acceptance of reciprocity was so strong that a lot of people said we shouldn't proceed with the war crimes trials at Nuremberg proceedings for just that reason. But there were very few people – I don't even know if there were any – who tried to say: "No. This is a one-shot deal. This only applies to the Third Reich, and it cannot apply against us in the future." It is very hard to say that, because there's something about the notion of law that makes that an incredible thing to say. As soon as you talk law, as soon as you talk rules, as soon as you talk regularities, you're already opening yourself up to accepting the fact that it can work against you as well as for you. And that to me is more significant than the differences in power.

CHARLES MARVIN: This all makes me think of Luis Bunuel's film *Viridiana*, with too many peasants flocking around the table. Going back to 11th-century England, at least, you had William the Conqueror and the Domesday Book. You had a register. Yet the states are flocking around the table, lacking etiquette, stealing the silverware. From an etiquette point of view, looking back at your casebook of a few years ago and the Waltz of the Toreadors, how are we to deal with one another in an orderly, civilized fashion? To my mind, with the proliferation of nation-states, all the way down to 5,000-person islands, it does pose a problem of scale as well as of values.

PROFESSOR D'AMATO: Yes, we would all like to clean up the system and make it better. We have to start out at least by asking: "What exactly is going on? What are these rules?" Now, if we find out that we don't like some of these rules, then we resort to all the processes that we have

[89] [Editor's Note: For further discussion of the notion of state personality and its relation to human rights, *see* Chapter 6, below.]

[90] [Editor's Note: Professor McDougal's views are presented below in this Chapter, in the section entitled "Custom as Reasonableness."]

invented over the years for straightening up the rules. In the 11th century, leaving it to the courts did not clean up the process. Parliament had to pass some laws to make the common law system fairer.

But what we are not entitled to do is simply to sit back and say: "Well, we would like these rules to be different, so we can cite 20 resolutions and add a lot of footnotes to make them come out the way we want." That kind of argument is what our colleagues from other disciplines rightfully object to. The first thing we should do is say: "Whether we like the rule or not, this is the rule that has evolved."[91] Then it would be like your colleague saying: "Whether we like the statute or not, this is what the statute says. We may not like the result, but as a lawyer I'm telling you that's what the result is." We may not like all the rules we see out there but if we don't first discern and articulate what those rules are, we're not going to get anywhere. Customary rules exist in the real world, not in the mind of the beholder.

GRIGORI TUNKIN: I was struck by your argument in the American Journal of International Law on whether the President of the United States is bound by the rules of international law. Would you speak to that? I can't understand it.

PROFESSOR D'AMATO: Well, of course, that's part of the problem. Actually, Professor Tunkin's question is the deepest possible question in this area. It's one that I don't have an answer to, although I'm working on it as best I can. The problem is, how can any state say that its own leadership might possibly be in violation of an international rule? Let me see if I can break this problem down into some manageable components.

First of all, let's ask a more primitive question: "Can any state ever violate international law?" Yes, but with a qualification. If you have a system that's not statutory and not precedential, but rather a Hegelian developing system of customary law, then every violation contains the seeds of a new rule. Therefore, the development of these rules must consist always of violations of previous rules or else the rules would have been frozen many centuries ago. So, in one sense a state can violate international law but in another sense it creates new law. Now, how can we reconcile these two possibilities? Well, because of the reactions of other states. You try to do certain things. The United States might take a forceful military position and then maybe back off if it turns out that it doesn't wash with the international community. Or, just to take an example of a couple of days ago, the United States goes in and retaliates against certain Iranian oil rigs and boats as a response to Iran's laying of mines in the Persian Gulf.

PROFESSOR TUNKIN: At a certain moment there is an international law in force. It may be changed later on, but we take it as it is at the moment. The action of the state at this moment may contradict international law. I understand your thinking that in the future these violations may become a rule of international law. It has happened in history. In the future it may be accepted as a rule of international law, but at the moment it is a violation.

PROFESSOR D'AMATO: I don't think so—and we may disagree on this—at the moment it's very hard to tell it's a violation until we see what the reactions are.

PROFESSOR TUNKIN: Well, then you accept McDougal's position that international law is something obscure, changing every day?

PROFESSOR D'AMATO: No. Let me finish the analogy with the U.S. reaction in the Persian Gulf. We bomb a couple of oil rigs and justify that action as a measured response to Iran's violation of international law that consisted of Iran's setting mines in international sea lanes. Elisabeth Zoller, who is here, has written a book about countermeasures,[92] and I think that the notions in her book were played out and were realized by this recent event. The United States says going in: "We're not trying to take over Iran. We're not trying to destroy the country. We're not trying to do anything disproportionate. We're acting within our conception of the rules in this retaliatory countermeasure." It may be, Professor Tunkin, that we went a little too far. Maybe we shouldn't have blown up six oil rigs, we should have blown up only three. That's the problem that we're talking about. It may be that the difference between blowing up three oil rigs and six oil rigs is the difference between complying with the law as it is at the moment and pressing that law to something a little beyond what present international law allows as an enforcement measure.[93] But we don't know until we see the reaction of other states.

Yet there is law going on there. This is not lawless behavior.This is not the United States dropping a nuclear weapon on Iran because we're mad. The only way you can even interpret what the United States did is against the background of customary international law. It would be impossible to interpret the U.S. action if there weren't plenty of rules out there that were shaping and constraining what we were doing. The U.S. action is informed by a very lush and detailed contextual background of legal principles.

INGRID DETTER DE LUPIS: I'm not sure you re talking about legal principles. You have one legal rule that is more or less static in the Persian Gulf situation you're referring to. What you're talking about is whether you can subsume certain facts under that rule.

---

91 To be sure, no rule defines itself or applies itself. Every rule is subject to interpretation. But there is a certain degree of "objectivity" in the notion of an interpretive community. When we say that a rule says this and not that, we are really making a prediction that most other people who look at the rule will say that it says this and not that.

92 [Editor's Note: For a citation to her book, and an excerpt from it, see Chapter 11 in this Anthology.]

93 [Editor's Note: For a discussion of the role of enforcement measures in international law, see Chapter 3 in this Anthology.]

PROFESSOR D'AMATO: I don't regard the rule that way. When you say there's a rule, you're talking as if there's a statute, and we can understand it and interpret it. What I'm talking about is the customary rule that's manifesting itself there.

PROFESSOR DE LUPIS: So you think it's always fluid?

PROFESSOR D'AMATO: Yes. In some respect.

PROFESSOR TUNKIN: Then there is no international law any more.

PROFESSOR D'AMATO: No, I don't think Hegel would have said that.

PROFESSOR DE LUPIS: Well, I don't agree with anything Hegel says.

PROFESSOR D'AMATO: You don't have to agree with anything I say, either. I'm trying to do what I do in my classes, which is to be intentionally provocative, and if I send you out of here very mad, very upset, I will feel that we had a useful seminar.

DANIEL M. PRICE: Does your position include any concept of a breach of international law or a violation of international law? If so, how do you identify the elements of a breach?

PROFESSOR D'AMATO: There is no list of elements in any positivistic sense, but you can say that a particular retaliation went too far. Suppose we dropped a small nuclear weapon on Iran in response to its mining of the shipping lanes. I think that clearly would be a breach. It would be a disproportionate response. Everybody would agree that it would be. And it would be a violation of customary international law.

MR. PRICE: So you can judge at any particular moment in time whether a state's conduct violates international law?

PROFESSOR D'AMATO: That's right. The clearest example in recent years was the Iranian taking of the American hostages. It was so clear that every judge on the International Court of Justice agreed. It was a breach of international law. There was no doubt about it.

The way the world works, we normally don't get an Iranian hostage situation. That's a crazy one. That's so far removed from the way that states interact with each other that everybody immediately knew it was a breach. What we get 99.9 percent of the time are interactions that test the system, that are in the area where there's a certain potential for creativity. It's like the United States with the oil rigs. Perhaps we blew up too many, but we certainly did not drop a nuclear weapon. A nuclear weapon would be as illegal as the Iranian taking of the hostages. Normally, states don't take that kind of action because they're conscious of the system within which they're operating. They're conscious of the rules of the game. That, indeed, is why international law seems to work.

JOAN FITZPATRICK: It's not that there can't be dramatic changes in international law. I think that's a difficult question. You can have an incremental change that doesn't provoke a dramatic response. But you could also have a sudden change in behavior that wouldn't provoke a dramatic response, yet that would change the law suddenly. I'm thinking of the switch from a three-mile territorial sea to a 200-mile exclusive economic zone.

PROFESSOR D'AMATO: But international law doesn't change that dramatically. When a state such as Ecuador makes a claim for a 200-mile zone, does anybody respect that? We have to wait and see. Sometimes they do. Sometimes they flout it. Sometimes they have an understanding with Ecuador—you can seize our ships only for delay, but you have to return them to us. Or sometimes the United States gets into these convoluted things where if your fish is taken by a country like Ecuador then the Congress will reimburse the vessel owners for the confiscated fish. There's so much to figure out. The raw claim is simply an opening sally in a very complex diplomatic move.

PROFESSOR DE LUPIS: You're saying that nothing ever happens quickly like that? What about when Gagarin went into space?

PROFESSOR D'AMATO: It was very interesting when the satellites went up that no nation claimed a breach of international law. When the satellites starting circling, no nation said: "Oh, you can't fly over our airspace!" It's almost as if the system had preaccommodated it. This is almost a mystical process. It's not our thinking that's making it happen, it's the way that states react to these events. They react in ways that are lawful. In other words, they made an immediate decision that the satellites were not going over airspace but they were somehow in outer space. Now, that's not a distinction that we made in our own minds; it's an objective decision that nations somehow reached very quickly.

ELISABETH ZOLLER: I have serious doubts whether customary rules may emerge from a succession of breaches. I'd like very much to be made aware of a customary rule that has emerged from a succession of breaches.

PROFESSOR D'AMATO: Well, you see, you're loading the question, Professor Zoller, because you're saying "breaches." But I don't know that they are breaches.

PROFESSOR ZOLLER: But that's precisely the point. I don't think that a new rule may emerge from a succession of breaches. I think that these claims that may lead to the formation of a new rule take place in areas that are not regulated internationally.

PROFESSOR D'AMATO: I don't think so. Take the three-mile limit. For many years the United States was saying there was only a three-mile limit, and everything else was a breach. A whole succession of breaches was going on, from the point of view of the United States. What was happening was that the law was developing beyond three miles.

PROFESSOR TUNKIN: That's what I said about the U.S. position at the time.

PROFESSOR D'AMATO: You certainly did! And the

United States was taking a very bullheaded position, because it wanted to negotiate something with that three-mile limit. The United States wanted to get something for giving up three miles when the nations of the world had already moved beyond three miles. The reality of the situation was precisely what you described it to be at the time.

PROFESSOR ZOLLER: I don't find support for your position in the example of the 3-mile limit that became a 12-mile limit. That was not a breach because no international rule prohibited a state from extending its jurisdiction to the 12-mile limit. If you take the argument of the Lotus case, it is clear that states may do whatever they want provided they do not run up against a rule of international law. There was no prohibitive rule of international law that precluded coastal states from extending their jurisdictions up to 12-mile limits.

PROFESSOR D'AMATO: Professor Zoller, the prohibitive rule that you're talking about is one whose existence we are trying to determine. We don't know yet whether there is a prohibitive rule.

PROFESSOR ZOLLER: In that particular case, there was not one.

PROFESSOR D'AMATO: The Lotus case said that there was nothing to stop jurisdiction from being asserted by Turkey. There were some cases where there were complaints about these kinds of assertions, and there were other cases that went the other way. And the Court said that the rule hadn't developed yet, not that there was no prohibitive rule. So Turkey was, in a sense, in a position to develop the rule further by its assertion of jurisdiction, the same way that we did with the oil rigs the other day. But to return to the three-mile limit, the United States was at least claiming, back in 1958, that any attempt to go beyond three miles violated international law, not that it was a permissive possibility, but that it was a violation.

PROFESSOR ZOLLER: That was the wrong argument in the light of the Lotus case.

PROFESSOR D'AMATO: I disagree. I think that was a developing argument. It developed from what you call a series of breaches. I simply call them a series of developmental stages.

ISTVAN POGANY: Are you not introducing an unfortunate and possibly dangerous element of indeterminacy? I'm thinking of your comments about the situation in the Gulf and the actions of the U.S. forces. Do you characterize them as a reprisal?

PROFESSOR D'AMATO: An enforcement action.

PROFESSOR POGANY: It seems to me that most of us probably would characterize the action as a forcible reprisal. I'm wondering how much elasticity there really is in international law in this area, given that there appears to have been a near consensus on the part of states in the postwar period concerning the illegality of forcible reprisals. And at a purely policy level, if one is to say that you cannot determine the illegality of a state's forcible actions until you have determined the reaction of other states, are you not, in a sense, loosening the bonds that deter states from resorting to such measures of forcible reprisal?

PROFESSOR D'AMATO: Only if you accept the premise that there was a consensus of states against reprisals. But really I'm trying to proceed from the ground level up, and therefore I say that I don't start by asserting anything about consensus, about rules, about theories. I don't know anything about these alleged rules. All I know is that I'm looking openmindedly to see what the rules are that are in fact at work in the system. And I would say that the rules that have been working in the system turn out to contradict all those notions of consensus that you're talking about. The actual rules that states are using have a lot to do with these enforcement actions. We're seeing many enforcement actions these days. They're measured, but I think Professor Zoller is a lot closer to the truth that these things are happening out there in the real world, whereas it is misleading to take at face value the rhetoric that you get in the United Nations and the friendly declarations among nations that these things aren't happening because they shouldn't be happening. The law that's happening out there, the reality that's happening out there, is that there are proportionate, measured responses. They definitely are forcible responses to specific breaches of international law. And I think we have to see through the clouds of rhetoric in order to get at the reality that force is being used in a measured way to reinforce the underlying customary law.

Now, let me return to Professor Tunkin's question: How can the President of the United States violate international law? How can we ask the question: "Can the President violate international law?" This goes to the problem of the state units that we're talking about. Hegel is not very favored, but I think he was getting at something that was very difficult, and so I tend to resort to some of his thinking. It may be that the United States has developed the kind of consciousness that says that our country, in order to comply with international law, has to do certain things and can't do others. For example, suppose the President of the United States says: "Let's drop a nuclear weapon on Iran and teach those people a lesson they'll never forget. Let's just blow them up. We'll just press a button and boom, goodbye." I think we have developed a consciousness in this country to say that the President cannot do that. That would be illegal. We say that if he did it he could be impeached, he could be put in prison. We reach that conclusion through American constitutional law, which is internal to us. But our Constitution has certain parameters that define what the President can do and can't do, and those parameters include aspects of international law. One of those aspects, indeed, is the Nuremberg result. There are certain kinds of things our leaders might try to do that are prohibited by customary international criminal law. (This is what some American leaders in 1945 were worried about when they felt that the war crimes trials at Nuremberg might someday be reflected back on them.)

I have a case against the Soviet Union called the Wallenberg case. The Soviet Union is the defendant and the Wallenberg family is the plaintiff. How could we be suing a sovereign nation in an American court? Because we're saying, in some sense, that international law is so pervasive that it even comes into our courts and is a factor in their decision-making. The United States can be a defendant here in our own courts when it's violating the norms that are pervasive in the system. Even the President can go too far and violate international law contrary to American law, and his action therefore would be illegal.

The sharp question is: can the President violate international law? The answer is, I don't know, because the sharp question is never asked. These things tend to play out in the real world not in terms of verbal debates but in terms of very subtle accommodations. A state can find that its internal mechanisms create something of a friction on its ability to act on the international scene. Customary rules that evolve out of the interaction of states have a lot to do with what goes on inside the states. Interest groups, regular citizens, government officials, professors of international law, may all have something to say about where the state is going, and that is sometimes a braking mechanism on what states wind up doing. And in that respect, what we're talking about under U.S. constitutional law is only a reflection of these internal processes. If a state is the creator of international law as well as the subject and object of it, the internal decision-making processes in that state will have a lot to do with the way the state really behaves on the international front.

It's such a rich area! We're dealing with things here—just from the topics you've raised this morning—that are so much more complicated and so much more interesting than what goes on in the torts class or contracts class that to think that our profession is looked down upon because we're not dealing with "real law" is astounding. We're dealing with real law that is uncluttered by the simplistic straightening processes of legislatures. We're trying to talk about what really is going on when we peel away the directives of comprehensive codes in domestic legal systems.

HILARY CHARLESWORTH: You've relied upon the reactions of states in defining rules of customary international law. Wouldn't you say in the Nicaragua Case, when faced with constant violations of the U.N. Charter, the World Court found principles of international law by which to judge the case?

PROFESSOR D'AMATO: But the Court stopped considerably short of implementing the Charter. The Court held that American aid to the Contras was not a violation. They held that laying mines was a violation. Most Americans already had concluded that, too. There was very little doubt in this country that laying those mines in the harbor was a violation of international law, and many government officials have concluded it one way or another.

PROFESSOR CHARLESWORTH: But the Court went beyond state practice.

PROFESSOR D'AMATO: I tried to deal with that to some extent in a little piece called "Trashing Customary International Law."[94] The International Court of justice, it seems to me, never really examined state practice at all. One reason was that nobody was arguing for the U.S. position. The United States walked out, and the result was that the Court was swayed by all the rhetoric coming from Nicaragua, and it wrote a very slipshod opinion that tended to justify certain kinds of abstract norms. It then cut back a little bit politically.

PROFESSOR TUNKIN: You don't like abstract norms.

PROFESSOR D'AMATO: That's right. Because they don't solve anything.

PROFESSOR TUNKIN: Every rule of international law is an abstract norm. If you do not recognize abstract norms, then you should not complain if international relations specialists do not recognize international law.

PROFESSOR D'AMATO: Professor Tunkin, if you believe that international law is a collection of abstract rules, then you might say to me that I'm not talking about the same thing you're talking about. But I believe that abstract norms never solve anything.

PROFESSOR TUNKIN: The problems are all settled by people, not by the norms.

PROFESSOR D'AMATO: I agree. Abstract norms invariably can be applied to either side of any case. There's no such thing as applying a norm and getting a result.

PROFESSOR TUNKIN: There is no rule of international law?

PROFESSOR D'AMATO: I'm talking about a kind of international law that is not made up of rhetoric and norms.

PROFESSOR DE LUPIS: Are you sure you're not speaking about words? Earlier, you emphasized the importance of the generality of the law. To some of us generality is precisely the same as the abstract law.

PROFESSOR D'AMATO: I don't mean generality in that sense. What I mean by generality is that when you accept a principle such as the Nuremberg prosecution, you are also accepting that it can be applied to you. I'm talking about reciprocal acceptance of whatever rules apply to all the units in the system. I'm not saying that the rules themselves have to be abstract or concrete.

PROFESSOR DE LUPIS: What's the difference between general and abstract?

MR. WEISS: I think what you're giving us here is an invisible hand theory of international law. Actually, I like your Hegelian approach. I like your deemphasizing the totally abstract nature of the law and relating the life of the law to real life out here, but I am troubled by the way your Hegelian dialectic plays itself out. Your thesis is that there really is a customary international law, and it must

---

[94] [Editor's Note: This essay is excerpted in the next section in the present Chapter.]

be taken seriously. Your antithesis is that it really isn't very important most of the time. Look at the examples you've given us. The Iranian hostage-taking was a clear example of a breach of international law, but that was so crazy that it only happens once in a century. It was a clear case where international law applies. But then you say that most of the other examples – Nicaragua, the three-mile limit – are going to take a long time to sort themselves out. Therefore, it isn't possible to say, unequivocally, that international law has been violated. So on the one hand you're saying international law is there and must be obeyed, and on the other hand you're saying the reason it's real is because everybody can agree on the extreme cases, while as to the others there's room for a lot of debate. Is that your synthesis?

PROFESSOR D'AMATO: No. I don't want to say the latter at all. But that may be what you're hearing. And if that's what you're hearing, it's my fault for not making myself clear.

PROFESSOR TUNKIN: At the beginning, you said that international law is downgraded in the United States. Isn't that the fault of American international lawyers who consider international law something that is vague and changing every minute?

PROFESSOR D'AMATO: Well, I don't think so. I think it's more the fault of the people who try to take abstract rules and say that they count.

PROFESSOR TUNKIN: What do you mean by "abstract"?

PROFESSOR DE LUPIS: By definition any rule is abstract.

PROFESSOR TUNKIN: "Abstract" means capable of universal application.

PROFESSOR D'AMATO: In that sense I have no problem with the word. But let me respond to Peter Weiss' statement that my antithesis is that the real rules of customary international law are too ill-defined to be of much importance. We have a dense system of rules, a dense system of custom. In fact, the more you study it, the more particularity you can get out of it. The actions of states are informed by this very strong context, so that the action we took in the Persian Gulf doesn't seem all that problematic. We took a certain response out of an infinite range of possible responses, most of which would have been clearly violative of international law as anybody would have defined it. But what we actually did was clearly within a range of arguably legal responses.

MR. WEISS: What about Grenada? What about Libya?

PROFESSOR D'AMATO: We went into Grenada differently from the way a country might have done it in the 19th or 18th centuries. Back then, once you were in, you annexed the territory. It became a part of your territory and you moved in your own government. We went in and we came out. Now, isn't that amazing?

MR. WEISS: Did we have a right to go in?

PROFESSOR D'AMATO: Yes. The right to go in came from the human right that the people of Grenada should not have a new government take over power by machine-gunning the previous government.

PROFESSOR TUNKIN: So the United States is the supreme judge?

PROFESSOR D'AMATO: In the absence of a collective enforcement mechanism, there are going to be individual autodeterminations. Each state is going to be a judge. Now, I'm not entirely happy with that system. I would prefer a more community-based approach. But, realistically, what is the United States supposed to do? Should it decide that since it cannot be a judge in this case, it should stay away? That would be just as bad.

PROFESSOR TUNKIN: Article 2(4) prohibits the use of force.

PROFESSOR D'AMATO: No. Only against the territorial integrity or political independence of another state.

PROFESSOR TUNKIN: No. Not only. In any other way incompatible with the purposes of the United Nations.

PROFESSOR D'AMATO: That's right. I'm saying that what the United States did was what the United Nations might have done if its mechanisms were in place to do it. Let me put this in very emotional terms: I know you don't see it this way when you think about Grenada, but at least I'll try to make my case as an advocate. The people of a country are very defenseless. They don't have weapons. The government has more or less a monopoly on the instruments of power and death. Given that incredible disparity in power relationship between the people and the government, we don't want to stand idly by and watch a group of thugs come in and assassinate the previous governors and take over all those instruments of power and then oppress the people. I think we want to have a system of international law that says we care enough about the people of those countries that we are willing to assist them with force when situations like this occur.

PROFESSOR TUNKIN: That was the view in the 19th century, and since that time international law has changed greatly. There is the Charter of the United Nations. There is the United Nations, the Security Council, and so on.

PROFESSOR D'AMATO: But Professor Tunkin, as you well know, as soon as you try to do anything, your country or ours is going to veto it.

PROFESSOR TUNKIN: No. That may happen, but not always. You can't say that there is no international enforcement mechanism now. It exists, but it's weak. We should work on strengthening it.

PROFESSOR D'AMATO: Well, you can take that position, but I think it's more realistic to say the United Nations is pretty much a dead letter as far as these enforcement mechanisms are concerned. I'm a supporter of the United Nations. I think when It can move and when it can work, it's wonderful. But when it doesn't work do we simply sit by and do nothing because the United Nations theoretically could step in? I don't think that you say that, and I don't think we say that.

PROFESSOR DE LUPIS: In my 1988 book, I gave a title to this kind of intervention. Because I'm Swedish, I can criticize both superpowers in this area. Both sides are sometimes guilty of what I call "patronizing intervention": you think you know what's best for that state and will help it because it doesn't know its own best interests.

PROFESSOR D'AMATO: I know. It's very hard. Let me put this in personal terms. Suppose I see a mother hitting her child very severely. You might say I would be a patronizing intervener if I stepped into that situation to protect the child. The moral choice is always a very existential one. You see a child being abused, and do you intervene or do you keep away from other people's business? "She's the parent, she can do it." At some point you intervene. I think at some point we say: "Look. Enough is enough. We're not going to allow this. The kid is defenseless. I don't care that it's the parent. The parent doesn't have the right of life or death over even its own child." And we intervene.

PROFESSOR TUNKIN: That situation is quite different, because you are not dealing with international law.

PROFESSOR D'AMATO: But it is not morally different. Why is it morally different if the Pol Pot regime is out there wiping out carloads of individuals? Are we going to sit back and say that we don't want to intervene?

PROFESSOR TUNKIN: Well, the moral situation may be similar. But do you think that the moral rule should justify the violation of international law?

PROFESSOR D'AMATO: They're not necessarily opposed to each other. When we do intervene in those human rights situations, the only way we can account for it in legal terms is to say that it's a reaction – a very deeply felt reaction – to some set of moral principles that is, in a way, even more important than article 2(4).

PROFESSOR DE LUPIS: Couldn't that very often be a cloak for self-interest?

PROFESSOR D'AMATO: Yes.

PROFESSOR DE LUPIS: Well, then we agree. I agree that there are occasions when you have to stop certain kinds of abuses.

PROFESSOR D'AMATO: That's right. We can argue specific cases, but we're not on the opposite sides of the fence. We're saying there can be a case where intervention would be almost compelled. And there are many cases where intervention would be folly and many cases where intervention would be patronizing or just a cloak for an aggressive move. As a matter of fact, at the moment when the United States invaded Grenada, I could not say whether it was legal. Why? Because the situation hadn't finished yet. If the United States had stayed and annexed Grenada, then going back to the very beginning, I would say the whole thing was illegal and would violate article 2(4).

PROFESSOR TUNKIN: So, is it acceptable if a state enters another state and pushes out its existing government and then leaves?

PROFESSOR D'AMATO: It depends on how the existing government came into power. Yes, I know it's the Monroe Doctrine. It's more than that – it's Woodrow Wilson! I'm not necessarily approving it. I'm just trying to describe the formation of customary law as it actually is happening.

MR. WEISS: Does that mean that now that Soviet troops are pulling out of Afghanistan, the sending of Soviet troops into Afghanistan was O.K.?

PROFESSOR D'AMATO: Well, to some extent they were invited in. I don't know enough about the Afghanistan situation to be able to make a judgment. And I say that because I think it's too easy to sit in your armchair and say that all these things are legal or illegal. That's the problem with our discipline. What is needed is a very careful examination of the situation. I want to know whether the people are better off in Afghanistan after the Soviet intervention or worse off. I don't know.

PROFESSOR DE LUPIS: If you come back to your theory of customary law, how do you ever assess whether this is a violation or not? I still don't understand what you think is the legal rule, or what you think is the law.

PROFESSOR D'AMATO: Assessment is something for courts, and we don't have courts in the international system.

PROFESSOR DE LUPIS: Then no one knows what the law is.

PROFESSOR D'AMATO: No. That's not true, because the law certainly is circumscribing a great deal. The actions states take are in a relatively narrow range of legality whereas many potential actions are not being taken.

PROFESSOR JOAN FITZPATRICK: Your theory seems to be that we need to look at what's happening on the ground, what states are really doing.

PROFESSOR D'AMATO: You're right. This is all about custom.

PROFESSOR FITZPATRICK: If we have to wait to see how states react to a particular action to decide whether or not it was a breach or an incremental change in the rules or something within the rules as they presently exist, there seems to be a problem of state equality. When a major power acts, or a small country acts in a way that infringes upon a perceived right of a major power, then you get a major reaction. When Burkina Faso interacts with another small country, the reaction is invisible.

PROFESSOR D'AMATO: It shouldn't be. We should be just as much aware of that as we are of large state interactions. Let me also say that I don't agree that we only know after the event whether it was legal. We seem to know the legal question before it's going to happen, when we advise governments. International law plays a role in the decisions governments make.

PROFESSOR FITZPATRICK: I think that's right. But how do we know if it's an incremental change in a customary rule or a breach? You seemed to say earlier that the violence of the reaction tells you if it's a breach, or an incremental change in the rule. or a sudden change in the rule that's acquiesced in by everybody. If it depends upon the reaction then what about the small states? If there is no reaction, you still don't know if it's a breach. I agree with the thrust of what I think you're saying, which is that international customary law is what is actually happening. It's not what people cast a vote for in the General Assembly. It's what's happening on the ground but it ought to be what's happening on the ground everywhere.

PROFESSOR D'AMATO: It should be, yes.

PROFESSOR FITZPATRICK: But how do we find it? How do international law scholars find it, if that's what we're supposed to be doing?

PROFESSOR D'AMATO: We have to dig it up. When states like England have a disproportionate effect on international law, it's because their yearbooks tell us what those cases are. They are constantly coming out with articles. They're promoting their view of the cases, so it has an effect. And that's very smart. I said to a Chinese delegation: "If you really want to have more of an effect on international law, start publishing yearbooks and cases and notes. Publish them and send them around the world, so people will have access to these materials, because they're just as important as anybody else's." We're talking about a trivial amount of money from a government's point of view compared to the amount of impact it can have in the world. It's trivial to cut back on international law scholarship or the dissemination of international law materials. Major powers are smart enough to be publishing and disseminating their materials.

GREGORY FOX: You have said that in some circumstances, the customary international legality of an act is a post facto judgment. It seems to me that fundamental to any notion of law, and you described international law as pure law, is a concept of notice: that states or actors should be able to regulate their behavior in accord with what they perceive to be the rules. Yet if the legality of any particular act is determined after the fact then how can that self-regulation occur?

PROFESSOR D'AMATO: Because the perception is one that is made as you go along. As I said earlier, states are both the creators and the subjects of customary law. The advisers to the Israeli Government say: "Look, you can go into the Entebbe airport and rescue those people even though it's a technical violation of the sovereignty of Uganda." And other people say: "I don't know if we can do that. What about article 2(4)?" And yet other people say: "Look, they're our citizens. If we can do it surgically enough, we can do it." All of the things that we are all talking about were being played out in the Israeli decision-making process, as Professor Francis Boyle has demonstrated in his study of the Entebbe raid.

Sometimes finding custom requires looking beyond words. I think that right now a great deal of customary law is being made between the United States and the Soviet Union that is almost unknown, having to do with how far states can go in war-games and military maneuvers. How close can the submarines come to the other nation's shores? How much nuclear weaponry can they carry when they engage in war-games? How much notice must they give to each other about the war-games? This is going on now in a very refined way. Does anybody know about it? Custom is being made out there. Perceptions are being formed about hostile intent between the two superpowers of which the Department of Defense, at least, is very aware. Our department and theirs are very much aware of who is playing what war-game maneuvers and whether these are simply war-games or whether these are preparatory to some kind of huge invasion. And every time that one is played, they chip a little closer at the implied rules and restraints. The submarines come a little closer to the shores. Sometimes they give less notice. It's very interesting. But a stability is being worked out in the oceans right now, hidden from our notice. Customary law is being developed there. No amount of verbal proscription is going to tell us what that law is. It's the way custom is happening that someday, if a tense situation arises, the custom that is being fashioned now in the war games under the seas might serve to provide the rules that could stabilize an otherwise runaway escalation to nuclear war.

PROFESSOR TUNKIN: It is a great mistake for American and British lawyers, that they equate their common law with international customary law. They are different.

PROFESSOR D'AMATO: Sir, if that's the mistake, then you should give me an "F" for my performance today, because I have failed miserably. I am equating the two, and I'm saying that the notion of a developing customary law – for good or ill, for better or worse, but just looking at the reality of what it is – is one where the law is in a constant process of unfolding and development. In other words, we can never know 100 percent in advance what the law is.

PROFESSOR TUNKIN: That's going too far.

PROFESSOR D'AMATO: But there is a more radical position that some critical legal studies adherents are now taking that I subscribe to, and that is that even in a codified system, you are just as uncertain as we are. I know you don't think so, because you're used to the certainty of those words in codes and statutes and regulations. But I would assert that in any individual case you're just as uncertain. That's a concept that takes us beyond the current topic of conversation, however.

MR. WEISS: I'd like to ask Professor Fitzpatrick a question. You said before that you agreed with Professor D'Amato that customary law is what is actually happening, not what gets adopted by the General Assembly. Now there are lots of U.N. resolutions on torture, yet almost every state practices torture. What does that mean for the rule against torture?

PROFESSOR FITZPATRICK: I think that you have to bring in opinio juris. I don't think it can be just practice, per se. I think it has to be what they say they do in that case, rather than what they do.

PROFESSOR D'AMATO: I generally agree, but it's more than just "saying." If you focus just on what governments say, then you do what Dr. Michael Akehurst did—you accept what governments say as the reality. But governments can tell you anything. Governments can dissemble and invent just as much as anybody else. What is interesting about torture is that governments don't even admit the facts. They deny the facts and they say: "If you can prove the facts then we will bring these culprits to justice." The Saudis said that. I have a case against the Saudis where they said: "Look, if you can show that any guard was torturing prisoners, we'll dock that guard three days' pay." That's how serious it is to torture a prisoner in Saudi Arabia! And they add: "But of course, nobody would want to lose three days' pay, so they just don't do this sort of thing."

PROFESSOR FITZPATRICK: I think it has to be what they do with a claim of right attached to it. By and large states don't torture people with a claim of right.

PROFESSOR D'AMATO: I agree. Contrast this with the U.S. intervention in Grenada. We intervened in Grenada with a very strong claim of right. We did it openly. In fact, the only thing I didn't like about it was keeping newspapers and media in the dark. That was stupidity. But it was an open intervention. We went in and we came out.

MR. WEISS: Not all scholars agree that state practice is defined with the qualification that you have a claim of right. Some scholars say that state practice is what states do, period.

PROFESSOR D'AMATO: The reason we cannot focus exclusively on practice is because the idea of a rule is itself a construct that we human beings place on activities. We know that when states act, they're acting purposefully in some sense. It's not like the planets that are just going around. States act with a sense of accommodation to other states and with some notion of reciprocity, of what's going to happen to them in the future. Therefore, they're acting in a purposeful and, I would say, normative fashion. The rules that states display in their interactions with each other are the rules that they want the system to have, by and large. So that even if Professor Tunkin and I both think that states can overdo it and intervene in the affairs of other states too much, the fact that they're doing it under some sort of claim that it's the right thing to do is something that we can't close our eyes to. That's really what's happening in international law. Like it or not, that's the way international law is developing.

PROFESSOR TUNKIN: That doesn't mean that's international law itself.

PROFESSOR D'AMATO: Well, I claim that it is. I say that it's international customary law. It may be that you have another norm like consensus, like U.N. resolutions, whatever it might be that would conflict with custom. But in terms of custom, the customary practice of states is what I'm talking about.

PROFESSOR POGANY: You did say earlier that in assessing the legality of the practice of a state, you cannot rely solely on the practice of the individual state. You must also take into account the reaction of other states.

PROFESSOR D'AMATO: It's an interactive process.

PROFESSOR POGANY: Right. You also said just a minute ago that the United States intervened in Grenada with a strong claim of right. Now, my recollection of the reaction of other states, at least as measured in the context of the deliberations in the Security Council, was that no state joined the United States in opposing the draft resolution, and that even the United Kingdom, which traditionally is aligned closely with the United States, abstained in the actual vote on that resolution. Now, doesn't the reaction of other states in that context tend to reduce the presumed legitimacy of the U.S. intervention?

PROFESSOR D'AMATO: No. I would say that the reaction was a purely verbal one. It's much easier to condemn somebody in the United Nations and then afterwards in cocktail parties say to the ambassador: "You know we have to condemn you in the U.N. for reasons of politics, the Third World, and so forth. I'm sure you don't mind because the Security Council can't do anything about it anyway."

PROFESSOR REIN MULLERSON: What action do you mean would be necessary—military action instead of verbal action?

PROFESSOR D'AMATO: Or economic. There could be boycotts. There are many things that you can do to harass U.S. citizens abroad, I suppose. There are many ways you can hurt the United States. But nobody did that. The only thing any state did was engage in verbal condemnation.

PROFESSOR TUNKIN: It's a political action when a state states its position on something. This is not necessarily by taking economic sanctions or something like that. The statement of the position of the state is also in verbal form.

PROFESSOR POGANY: The U.K. abstention was an application of one of your earlier propositions. I think the United Kingdom was aware that if it actually had approved the U.S. intervention that might in fact have legitimated other interventions. There was a normative element.

PROFESSOR D'AMATO: Sure. I don't take the words as significant, but I take them as indicating where people may be going. These declarations may be starting to prepare us for what states are intending to do. If that's so, and it plays out—if customary practice actually follows what was said in the U.N. resolutions—then we really have something. On the other hand, there's the political game: "Let's just issue this resolution and get it off our backs and take care of it, and then go back to business as usual." There's so much of that kind of game-playing going on that I can't take these words all that seriously.

INGRID KIRCHER: If you say that the Americans were right to be in Grenada, couldn't you then look at Haiti? You actually can say the same thing: that there should have been a perceived moral obligation to intervene to prevent innocent people who, in asserting their right to elect their government, were gunned down, if not directly by the government, with the active support of it.

PROFESSOR D'AMATO: My guess is that if the United States and Soviet Union can get closer together, as Professor Tunkin is advocating that we do in these matters, we may find that in years to come there is going to be a certain concerted interventionist policy. Right now, when the United States goes into Grenada, it looks very bad. We're a big, paternalistic bully. But I claim that somebody had to do the job, and we did it. I would have been happier if the United Nations had done it. I would have been happier if two countries had done it instead of one. I would have been happier if 15 countries had done it instead of 2. My guess is the world is going to be moving in that direction: more sensitivity to human rights, more sensitivity to the rights of the people and against the excesses of some of these dictatorships that carry their power too far.

PROFESSOR ZOLLER: Are you suggesting an end to neutrality?

PROFESSOR D'AMATO: That's right. I think that customary law itself is heading in that direction. You see, neutrality is a concept very much like domestic jurisdiction is a concept. You make a rhetorical claim about neutrality because it helps your interest in certain ways. In fact, you're no more neutral than any other country!

PROFESSOR DE LUPIS: I must emphasize strongly that there are Swedes around and other small countries in Europe that begin with "Sw" that would not accept that neutrality is merely a rhetorical claim.

PROFESSOR D'AMATO: Not only won't you accept that, but you don't have to accept anything I've said. I hope, however, that I've stirred you up a little bit.

7. Criticism of the World Court's View of Custom in the Nicaragua Case[95]

The requirement of Article 38 of the Statute of the International Court of Justice is central to its mission: the determination of international custom "as evidence of a general practice accepted as law." Students of the Court's jurisprudence have long been aware that the Court has done a better job of applying customary law than defining it. Yet until the case of Nicaragua v. United States,[96] little harm was done. For in the sharply contested cases prior to Nicaragua, the Court elicited commonalities in argumentative structure that gravitated its rulings toward the customary norms implicit in state practice. The Court's lack of theoretical explicitness simply meant that a career opportunity arose for some observers like me to attempt to supply the missing theory of custom.

The problem with the Nicaragua case was that it was not forged out of the heat of adversarial confrontation. Instead, it reveals the judges of the World Court deciding the content of customary international law on a tabula rasa, uninformed, uninstructed, and unrestrained by sharp adversary argumentation. Sadly, the Judgment reveals that the judges of the World Court have practically no idea about what custom is when they are left on their own.

What makes international custom authoritative is that it consists of the resultants of divergent state vectors (acts, restraints), thus bringing out what the legal system considers a resolution of the underlying state interests. Although the acts of states on the real-world stage often clash, the resultant accommodations have an enduring and authoritative quality because they manifest the latent stability of the system. The role of opinio juris in this process is simply to identify which acts out of many have legal consequence.

The World Court in the Nicaragua case gets it totally backwards. The Court starts with a disembodied rule—for example, the alleged rule of non-intervention found in various treaties, United Nations resolutions and other diverse sources such as the Helsinki Accords. It then decides that state acceptance of such a rule supplies the opinio juris element. Finally, it looks vaguely at state practice for problematic corroboration. Although the practice of states, the Court then ruefully notes, has not been "in absolutely rigorous conformity with the rule," the Court nevertheless "deems it sufficient" that "instances of State conduct inconsistent with a given rule should generally have been treated as breaches of that rule."[97]

In so ruling, the Court demonstrates its complete misunderstanding of customary law. In the first place, a customary rule clearly arises out of state practice, not in UN resolutions and other majoritarian political documents. Second, opinio juris has nothing to do with a metaphysical (and unverifiable) sort of "acceptance" of rules in such documents. Rather, opinio juris is a psychological element associated with the formation of a customary rule as a

95 By ANTHONY D'AMATO, excerpted from: *Trashing Customary International Law*, 81 AMERICAN JOURNAL OF INTERNATIONAL LAW 101 (1987). Reprinted by permission.

96 *Military and Paramilitary Activities in and against Nicaragua* (Nicar. v. U.S.), *Merits*, 1986 ICJ REP. 14 (Judgment of June 27).

97 1986 ICJ REP. at 98, para. 186.

characterization of state practice. To make matters even worse, the Court gives no independent evidence even of its own theory that states have accepted a given alleged rule in various resolutions and documents, except for the question-begging fact that the states subscribed to those documents and resolutions. If voting for a UN resolution means investing it with opinio juris, then the latter has no independent content; one may simply apply the UN resolution as it is, mislabel it "customary law," and decide that the world community has (remarkably and most revolutionarily) opted for UN legislation to solve the world's problems. A final defect is that instead of beginning with state practice, the Court ends with it. Conveniently, the Court finds that whenever state practice conflicts with an alleged rule of custom, the practice must be an illegal breach of that rule. This procedure robs state practice of independent content and undermines the very notion of custom. All we need, in the Court's simplistic view, is the original alleged rule coupled with a theory that any practice inconsistent with it does not count. The judges of the World Court are doing nothing less than legislating from the bench, when instead they should be doing their homework.

The poverty of the Court's theory is matched by the absence of any supporting research into state practice. The only example of practice given by the Court contradicts its own theory: state intervention for the purpose of "decolonization." Lamely, the Court gets around this unwelcome example of state practice by saying that decolonization "is not in issue in the present case."[98] The Court's embarrassment would probably only be increased had it seen fit to mention some of the other categories of intervention that contradict the nonintervention theory, such as humanitarian intervention, antiterrorist reprisals, individual as well as collective enforcement measures, and new uses of transboundary force such as the Israeli raid on the Iraqi nuclear reactor.

The Court's made-up rule of nonintervention is hard to derive from all these examples of state practice that are inconsistent with such a rule, but in any event the Court did not even try. Rather, it purports to give us a rule of customary international law without even looking at what states do and without giving any independent, ascertainable meaning to the concept of opinio juris.

The Court fares no better when it considers the impact of treaties upon custom. To some extent, the Court was misled in this regard by the United States, which argued in the jurisdictional phase of the Nicaragua case that Article 2(4) of the Charter "is customary and general international law."[99] The United States apparently made this strange concession as an attempt to convince the Court that the UN Charter could not be divorced from the case; on this point, the Court was right that the underlying customary law exists in the absence of the Charter. Nevertheless, the Court took the bait and leaped to the simplistic conclusion that the treaty rule of nonintervention was nearly identical to the customary rule.

That conclusion would not have been easily reached had the Court exhibited any understanding of the process by which treaty rules generate customary law. A treaty is obviously not equivalent to custom or interchangeable with it. A treaty binds only its parties, and binds them only according to the enforcement provisions contained in the treaty itself (against the background of custom). However, rules in treaties reach beyond the parties because a treaty itself constitutes state practice. To illustrate this point, let us consider two hypothetical cases: in (a) a rule arises by the pure process of international custom, and in (b) the same rule arises by virtue of its incorporation into a treaty:

(a) Suppose state A attempts to seize narcotics on board a vessel of state B within X miles of B's coast. State B protests on the ground that state A lacks jurisdiction. If state A nevertheless seizes and confiscates the narcotics, and if B takes no retaliatory or enforcement action against state A, then a customary law precedent will be established for the rule that narcotics seizures are permissible at a distance of X or more miles from the coast of the flag state. This "incident" thus has a precedential effect upon international custom.

(b) Suppose states A and B enter into a treaty allowing the seizure of narcotics at a distance of X or more miles off the coast of the flag state. Such a treaty would be as much a resultant of the A and B "vectors" as was the previously described seizure-plus-no-retaliation incident. Treaties were indeed invented to harmonize competing interests without recourse to threats or forcible measures, and in this fashion are a much more civilized way of creating custom than the normal process described in example (a). For international systemic purposes, the outcome is the same in the (a) and (b) cases; namely, the rule characterizing the resolution of the incident is the resultant of the divergent vectors; it is a "customary" rule of state accommodation.

Customary rules, however, are not static. They change in content depending upon the amplitude of new vectors (state interests). Human rights interests, for example, have worked a revolutionary change upon many of the classic rules of international law as a result of the realization by states in their international practice that they have a deep interest in the way other states treat their own citizens. Thus, reverting to our narcotics example, we can modify the A-B rule by a subsequent C-D incident that adds to the distance X; later, an E-F treaty might subtract from the X

---

[98] *Id.* at 108, para. 206.

[99] 1986 ICJ Rep. at 99, para. 187 (quoted by the Court).

distance; yet later, a G-H incident might reinforce the distance established in the C-D interaction. Over the long run, the distance X will express the resultant of all competing international interests. Another way of phrasing this result is to use Darwinian terms: the customary rules that survive the legal evolutionary process are those that are best adapted to serve the mutual and aggregate self-interest of all states.

The process of change and modification over time introduces a complex element that is missing from the Court's handling of Article 2(4). It is true that when 2(4) was adopted as part of the UN Charter in 1945, it had a major impact (by virtue of the fact that it was a treaty) upon customary law. But Article 2(4) did not "freeze" international law for all time subsequent to 1945 (no more than an equivalent customary-law incident would have done). Rather, the rule of Article 2(4) underwent change and modification almost from the beginning.[100] Subsequent customary practice in all the categories mentioned above (humanitarian intervention, antiterrorist reprisals, etc.) has profoundly altered the meaning and content of the nonintervention principle that was articulated in Article 2(4) in 1945.

To be sure, Article 2(4) itself did not just have a once-only impact in 1945. It has been reiterated each time a new state joined the United Nations, because the Charter rules are extended each time to embrace the new member state. But each reiteration does not necessarily reinforce the 1945 meaning, because each new state that joins the United Nations does so in the light of the practice of the Charter from 1945 to the date of its admission. Under the customary rules of interpretation of international treaties, the subsequent practice of states can modify and change the meaning of the original treaty provisions. Hence, state practice since 1945—whether considered as simply formative of customary international law or as constituting interpretation of the Charter under the subsequent-practice rule—has drastically altered the meaning and content of Article 2(4).

The Court's unidimensional approach to Article 2(4) and to other treaties misses all of these considerations. Its lack of understanding, or conscious avoidance, of the theory of the interaction of custom and treaty undermines the legal authority of its Judgment. As a practical matter, only decisions that command respect by virtue of their inherent soundness and scholarly thoroughness are likely to have a real impact on the future development of international law. The Court is encouraged to render such decisions by its own Statute. Article 53 provides that, when one of the parties fails to defend its own case, the Court must "satisfy itself" that the claim of the party appearing in court is well founded in fact and law. That requirement seems to have been overlooked by the judges who participated in the Nicaragua case.

[100] *See* Thomas Franck, *Who Killed Article 2(4)?*, 64 AJIL 809 (1970).

8. The Central Point of Custom[101]

Dear Mr. Byers:

Thank you very much for your critique of my work on custom. Professor James Crawford kindly sent me a letter saying that it would be coming. I would appreciate your extending to him my warmest personal regards.

I want to say at the outset that I am honored to be the recipient of a critical study, and even more than that, delighted that you are delving into this complex yet fascinating field. We must get the basic rules (or "secondary rules") of international law straight before we can assess the worth of competing claims that fill the pages of the law journals. I believe that you share my commitment to this groundwork, and that is most gratifying.

I believe there is a bedrock view about what custom is, a view that you should consider seriously. That view is very close to, if not identical with, the way Lord Mansfield looked at the customary law of the law merchant. The law merchant was, to Mansfield, the *practices* of the business community, not the unilateral claims of merchants. Suppose the following case: Plaintiff offeree sues defendant offeror on a contract, and the defendant offeror pleads that the offer was not accepted within the time he stipulated in the offer. The case will turn on a question of law: is a contract made when the offeree places his acceptance in the mail, or is the contract made when the offeror actually receives the offeree's acceptance?

Lord Mansfield would not have thought about deciding the case according to what the parties in the case thought the law was, because, obviously, they would be expected to have diametrically opposing conceptions of what the law was. Similarly, in international law, if Peru claims a 500 mile territorial sea, we cannot peruse Peru's statements or claims to discover what customary law has to say about the breadth of the territorial sea.[102]

[101] By ANTHONY D'AMATO, from a letter dated March 16, 1993, to Mr. Michael Byers, Queens College, Cambridge, United Kingdom. Mr. Byers, under the direction of Professor James Crawford, is writing a dissertation on customary international law.

[102] This is a large part of what is wrong with the late Dr. Akehurst's position. To be sure, Akehurst was correct that there is no shortage of judicial dicta recognizing statements of states as constitutive of state practice. Yet, not only is dicta not law, but more significantly, much of this dicta occurs in national courts, which are all too prone to take the statements of their own government as constitutive of international law. All of this stuff, in my view, has to be discarded as self-serving and irrelevant.

Neither would Lord Mansfield have decided the case by sending a questionnaire to all the businesspersons in his area, asking them whether a contract is made when the acceptance is placed in the mail or when the acceptance is received by the offeror. For businesspersons who have not encountered this particular problem, or perhaps not even thought about the question, are wholly unreliable sources for determining what the law is. They are apt to speculate about it, or decide the question according to what they would like the law to be. Similarly, in international law, if a number of states are asked what a particular rule of international law is, they are apt to respond on the basis not of their assessment of the status of the alleged rule under existing international law, but on the basis of what they would like the rule to be. In short, they will respond as legislators rather than as judges.

The only sound alternative open to Lord Mansfield was to look at the actual practices of the business community. If he could find instances where contracts were disputed over the question when the acceptance took place, and find instances where those disputes were resolved, even if many of those resolutions were informal, he would have actual data upon which to build the law merchant. This would be data based upon business practices as opposed to business opinions. This is largely the way international customary law proceeds. There is an actual dispute (a fishing vessel goes within Peru's proclaimed 500 mile territorial sea; Peru takes action or does not take action) and the situation is resolved one way or the other. In this sense, the practices of states are transformed into a law requiring that those practices now be observed as a matter of law. This is the "law merchant" process of Lord Mansfield. He was able to find customary practices and elevate them into binding common law. It was a very "democratic" form of law, because the common law that resulted in Lord Mansfield's court was as close as possible to the unwritten norms that were already in practice in the business community.

I hope you see from all this why I am so determined to keep the notion of customary law rooted in the actual practice of states, and so unwilling to accept unilateral claims – even a host of unilateral claims – as constitutive of "custom." Whether an overwhelming host of parallel unilateral claims constitute "consensus" is an interesting question, but however it is resolved, it cannot constitute an answer to the "customary law" question. No single claim, and no bundle of claims, can ever constitute "custom" in international law any more than they could have constituted the law merchant for Lord Mansfield.

In this connection, I feel it was unjustified for Dr. Akehurst to characterize my position, about a state taking concrete action to prevent the act of another state from constituting custom, as having "disastrous consequences for world public order."[103] You quote with approval his polemical statement. If there were any validity to it, I would have no objection. You will see that there is no validity to it if you think of several different hypothetical examples that could come up. For example, if state A acts in such a way as to be a matter of indifference to state B, certainly B would not take retaliatory action against A to the endangerment of world peace. If Russia sent up Sputnik, and other states felt that no right of theirs was infringed, it would certainly have been disastrous for those nations to take retaliatory action against the Soviet Union. On the other hand, if Sputnik were sent up loaded with nuclear weapons that would eventually fall back to earth and detonate somewhere or other, retaliatory action would have been justified. I've put the point carefully – if nations "feel" that any right of theirs is infringed – because new rights can emerge this way. For instance, if women are raped in Bosnia as a deliberate part of the means of conducting warfare, other countries may feel that their rights have been infringed upon, even though the women who are raped are not their nationals or in any other way connected with them. These other countries may decide to take retaliatory action. On the other hand, when a manned satellite of the United States landed on the moon and the American flag was raised, nations took no action against the United States. The rule that was articulated at the time was *not* that the raising of the American flag meant that the United States now owned the moon in fee simple. At best, the rule was only that the first nation that lands on the moon may put up its flag as a symbolic gesture. Or, the articulated rule could be that any nation that ever lands on the moon can raise its flag as a symbolic gesture. These latter rules were not perceived by other nations to infringe upon their rights – whereas the rule that was not articulated (a claim of ownership) might very well have been perceived to infringe upon the rights of other nations. In short, I am not prescribing that nations go to war to protect their no-

---

[103] Michael Akehurst, *Custom as a Source of International Law*, 47 BYIL 1, 40 (1974–75): "The view that protests form part of the quantitative element of State practice has been challenged by D'Amato. According to him, a protest can articulate a rule of international law, but it cannot be cited as part of the quantitative element of State practice. Consequently protests are not enough to prevent a new rule of customary law arising from other States' physical acts. The precedent-creating effect of such physical acts can only be nullified by contrary physical acts on the part of states which are aggrieved by the physical acts of other States. If D'Amato's view were accepted in practice, there would be disastrous consequences for world public order. A state which wished to prevent the formation of a rule allowing overflight of its territory by artificial satellites could no longer achieve its object by making protests; it would have 'to interfere with the satellite's flight' or 'retaliate in some other way against the Soviet Union unless she ceased to launch sputniks'. Thus a polite difference of opinion would be converted into a major international dispute."

tions of the rules of international law, as Akehurst implies. Why would nations want to do *that*? Rather, I am describing what nations do. If they feel their rights are infringed, they take action against the nation asserting a new rule; otherwise, they do nothing, and the acting nation's assertion becomes a component of custom. Of course, there is an important approach that does not require the taking of action that could lead to a conflict with other nations, an approach that formed an important part of my 1971 book. Suppose nation A feels that an act it wants to do might be interpreted by nation B as an infringement upon B's rights. A may then propose to B a bilateral treaty that makes the proposed action legal for both sides. Thus, there is no need to start a war every time a nation wants to change or expand a rule of customary law; rather, the proper way to do it is to propose a treaty. Sometimes an implicit treaty will do the trick–e.g., the acquiescence of other states that was obtained by the United States prior to President Truman's continental shelf proclamation.

I think your criticism of my position will be strengthened if you look again at some of the extreme characterizations that have been made against my position by my previous critics, and ask yourself whether they are scholarly or polemical. To pass the test of scholarship, they must be based either on the real practice of states or on hypothetical cases that nevertheless are realistically inferable from state practice.

Although you are quite right in saying that I insist on a practice component of custom, I think you are less persuasive in assuming that the denial of my position is tantamount to the assertion of a better position. How is the theory of customary law furthered if custom can be anything that states say it is? You should consider the possibility that such a position will amount to making the concept of custom vacuous. The ICJ adopted this sort of kitchen-sink approach to custom in some aspects of the Nicaragua case; I'm enclosing a reprint of an article in which I take the position that the court in effect trashed custom.[104] Apart from the conclusion I reach in the article, I think the article is so far my best condensed statement of what I think customary law is.

Consider the consequences of the position you take with respect to bilateral treaties involving water rights between upper and lower riparians. In a negotiation between U and L, U insists that the eventual bilateral treaty contain a provision that upper riparians retain sovereignty over the water. L is willing to concede this statement in the treaty to U in return for the water rights that L is insisting upon in this particular case. The result is that both sides are satisfied: U gets its upper-riparian doctrine, and L gets its water. U has won "in principle," and L "in practice." Now, suppose every upper and lower riparian in rivers throughout the world execute similar treaties. Wouldn't it be academic in the extreme to insist upon the articulated treaty rule of upper-riparian sovereignty when in fact there isn't a single instance of it? We have to look at what states commit to, when they sign treaties, in addition to the rules that the treaties articulate. Here, as in custom in general, if the rule conflicts with what the states in fact do, then the rule can't be a rule of custom–indeed, the contrary is the rule of custom. The treaty rule–like the operation of "protest" in the teeth of state action–acts to promote the practice into the realm of something covered by international law, but the particular rule is not the rule of custom that emerges–rather, the rule that emerges is the rule that is consistent with the practice. (Protest is very often used for political window-dressing purposes when the real intent is to approve of the action being protested against; e.g., the feeble "protest" of the UN's condemnatory resolution against Israel following Israel's raid on the Iraqi nuclear reactor, as I cited in my essay on the subject–reprint enclosed.[105])

Another way of putting this point is: the treaty between U and L cannot possibly govern the use the international legal community wishes to make of it. The most the treaty can do is create a specific legal regime for U and L. But the treaty cannot set into motion a rule of custom *other than* the treaty practice adopted by the parties. Perhaps the best way to think of this is to imagine a domestic law case. P sues D. The court reaches a decision. Neither P nor D, nor the two of them together, can decide what precedent value their case will have for future cases. Rather, the result in the P-D case will be decided by future courts either to have, or to lack (for some reason), precedent value. P and D cannot control the legal effect of what they do insofar as the rest of the world is concerned. Similarly, U and L cannot control the legal effect the rest of the world will make of the U-L treaty. I know you take the contrary position in your essay, but I urge you to follow it to its logical conclusion and then assess whether you wish to adhere to it.

There are many ways to improve and refine my theory about treaties as a component of custom. Your critique points to aspects of my treatment that need restatement; perhaps certain aspects need to be discarded. Yet I think one must not lose sight of the fact that back in 1971 when I made this claim about treaties, it was made in the teeth of nearly universal scholarship to the contrary. Indeed, before I found a publisher for my book, I sent the complete

---

[104] [Editor's Note: This article was excerpted in the preceding section in this Chapter.]

[105] [Editor's Note: The reference is to Anthony D'Amato, *Israel's Air Strike Upon the Iraqi Nuclear Reactor,* 77 AJIL 584 (1983).]

argument about treaties to the British Year Book of International Law, which rejected it. The book itself, when it came out, was summarily panned in all the leading journals. It would be a source of some gratification to me if you were to begin your essay not so much by saying, as you so kindly do, that I am the "most prominent and prolific" writer on the subject, but rather that I have introduced certain theories – such as the treaty-into-custom theory, the articulation theory, the relative theory about proof of custom (time and repetitions), and the distinction between general and special custom – that have begun to change the nature of the debate. I remain as critical as you are about these theories, and I would like to improve upon them whenever I can. What I view as my mission in international law is not to become a prominent person in the field, but to help make the subject matter more rigorous and hence worthy of greater respect.

Looking back over what I've said in this letter, I suppose the main point I'd like to convince you about is the need for an action-or-commitment component of custom, that the "practice" that makes up the tangible component of custom cannot be satisfied by words or claims alone. This action-or-commitment component of custom is the central difference between the late Dr. Akehurst and me. If you end up adopting Akehurst's position, your criticism of me will largely parallel Akehurst's. However, the tail should not wag the dog; my advice would be that you should adopt whatever position you choose strictly out of intellectual conviction.

9. Alternate Views of Custom

a. DEBATE: Custom As Reasonableness

(1) Affirmative[106]

The first thermonuclear bomb tests conducted by the United States, in March and April of 1954 in the Pacific Proving Grounds, demonstrated the enormous destructive power of the new weapon, and caused great concern the world over. Through a series of miscalculations, a number of Marshallese, Japanese, and Americans were injured by the test of March 1st, and the test series as a whole in some measure disrupted the activities of a segment of the Japanese fishing industry. As might have been foreseen, the Soviet Union denounced the tests, characteristically couching its invective in the vocabulary of law, and appealing to the abhorrence, shared by all peoples of the world, of the destructive power of the weapon. The United States promptly took all possible measures to repair the damage done, and expressed its extreme regret that the mishaps had occurred. After full compensation had been paid or promised to the victims of the test accidents, and the Trusteeship Council had accepted United States assurances that similar accidents could and would be prevented in the future, the spurious legalisms of the Soviet Union might appropriately have been dismissed with a minimum of consideration. Unfortunately, however, certain neutral statesmen and impartial observers also have questioned the legality of these tests, appealing both to certain customary prescriptions of the international law of the sea and to certain provisions of the United Nations Charter and of the Trusteeship Agreement, under which the United States holds the Pacific Islands.

Throughout the centuries of its development, one may observe the regime of the high seas as not a static body of absolute rules but rather a living, growing, customary law, grounded in the claims, practices, and sanctioning expectations of nation-states, and changing as the demands and expectations of decision-makers are changed by the exigencies of new social and economic interests, by the imperatives of an ever-developing technology and by other continually evolving conditions in the world arena. From the perspective of realistic description, the public order of the high seas is not a mere body of rules, but a whole decision-making process, including both a structure of authorized decision-makers and a body of highly flexible, inherited prescriptions: it is a continuous process of interaction in which the decision-makers of individual nation-states unilaterally put forward claims of the most diverse and conflicting character to the use of the world's seas, and in which other decision-makers, external to the demanding nation-state and including both national and international officials, weigh and appraise these competing claims in terms of the interests of the world community and of the rival claimants, and ultimately accept or reject them.

The competing claims asserted by nation-state decision-makers to the use of the high seas, the events to which the "regime of the high seas" is a response, vary enormously in the comprehensiveness and particularly of the interests sought to be secured, in the location and size of area affected, and in the duration of the claim. They range from the comprehensive and continuous claim to all competence in the "territorial sea," through the continuous but limited claims to navigation, fishing, and cable-laying upon the "high seas," to the relatively temporary and limited claims

---

106 By MYRES S. McDOUGAL & NORBERT A. SCHLEI, excerpted from: *The Hydrogen Bomb Tests in Perspective: Lawful Measures for Security*, in MYRES S. McDOUGAL & ASSOCIATES, STUDIES IN WORLD PUBLIC ORDER 763, 764–65, 773–78, 820–24, 842–43 (New Haven: Yale University Press, 1960). Reprinted by permission.

to exercise authority and control beyond territorial boundaries for a vast array of national purposes: security and self-defense, enforcement of health, neutrality, and customs regulations, conservation or monopolization of fisheries, exploitation of the sedentary fisheries and mineral resources of the seabed and continental shelf, the conducting of naval maneuvers, military exercises, and other peacetime defensive activities, and so on.

It need cause no confusion that the authoritative decision-makers put forward by the public order of the high seas to resolve all these competing claims include, in addition to judges of international courts and other international officials, those same nation-state officials who on other occasions are themselves claimants – that, in other words, the same nation-state officials are alternately, in a process of reciprocal interaction, both claimants and external decision-makers passing upon the claims of others. This duality in function ("dedoublement fonctionnel") merely reflects the present lack of specialization and centralization of policy functions in international law generally. Similarly, it may be observed, without cause for deprecation or shocked averting of the eyes, that these authoritative decision-makers projected by nation-states for creating and applying a common public order, honor each other's unilateral claims to the use of the high seas not merely by explicit agreements but also by mutual tolerances – expressed in countless decisions in foreign offices, national courts, and national legislatures – which create expectations that power will be restrained and exercised in certain uniformities of pattern. This, too, is but the process by which in the present state of world organization most decisions about jurisdiction in public and private international law are, and must be, taken.

The overriding policy which infuses this whole decision-making process – perhaps it requires explicit statement – is not the negation of use but the encouragement of use. The major policy purpose which inspires the regime of the high seas is not merely the negation of restrictions upon navigation and fishing but also the promotion of the most advantageous – that is, the most conserving and fully utilizing – peaceful use and development by all peoples of a great common resource, covering two-thirds of the world's surface, for all contemporary values. The concept of a common and reciprocal interest in fullest utilization underlies the whole flow of decision.

For pursuing this major policy purpose in regulating the maze of conflicting claims which confront them, the authoritative decision-makers of the world community have elaborated that comprehensive body of complementary prescriptions which make up "the regime of the high seas." One set of these prescriptions, that generally referred to under the label of "freedom of the seas," was formulated, and is invoked, to honor unilateral claims to navigation, fishing, cable-laying, and other similar uses. The other set, that which includes the prescriptions summed up in a wide variety of technical terms such as "territorial sea," "contiguous zones," "jurisdiction," "continental shelf," was formulated and is invoked, to honor all the great variety of claims, both comprehensive and particular, which may interfere, in greater or less degree, with navigation and fishing. To the initiated it is not surprising that the technical terms in which both sets of these prescriptions are formulated are at the highest level of abstraction and, hence, ambiguous in highest degree. A decision-maker confronted with the task of deciding upon the lawfulness of a challenged claim to the use of the seas must create meaning for these terms and must turn to other sources for detailed policy guidance. The sources to which such a decision-maker, like the judges of the International Court of Justice, is authorized to turn, and may be required by the necessities of policy clarification to do so, include not only "international conventions, whether general or particular, establishing rules expressly recognized by the contesting states," but also "international custom, as evidence of a general practice accepted by law," "the general principles of law recognized by civilized nations," "judicial decision and the teachings of the most highly qualified publicists of the various nations," and considerations "ex aequo et bono."

The great ambiguity of the constituent technical terms in the principal prescriptions and the wide variety of authoritative policy sources accorded to the authorized decision-makers have given and continue to give to such decision-makers a very large discretion to adjust particular controversies in terms of the multiple variables peculiar to each controversy and thus to promote the overriding policy of full utilization. The degree to which decisions for the last century and a half, because of common interest in the sea as an efficient medium of communication and as an abundant source of food, have given a high priority to claims for freedom of navigation and fishing is sufficiently emphasized in conventional literature. It is equally common knowledge, however, though on occasion reluctantly admitted, that a parallel flow of decisions has protected a great variety of claims to authority and control on the high seas for the protection of security, health, revenue laws, economic welfare, and so on, even against protests that they interfere with navigation and fishing, and a still higher priority is accorded to claims of "sovereign" competence in "territorial seas" despite such interference. It has been recognized in decision, if not in the justifications summarized in the textbooks, that all these claims, those to navigation and fishing and those that may interfere, are of a common character: they are all unilateral assertions by particular claimants to individual use of a great common resource, and all such assertions are affected in equal degree – navigation and fishing no more or no less than the others—with community interest in fullest utilization and conservation, and with national interest, which though possibly varying with geographical propinquity in particular instances, is in the sum of all instances common to all claimants. The technical prescriptions of the "freedom of the seas," on the one hand, and of "territorial sea," "contiguous zone," "jurisdiction," and so on, on the other, are not arbitrary, inelastic dogmas, but rather are highly flexible policy preferences invoked by decision-makers to record or justify whatever compromise or adjustment of competing claims they may reach in any particular controversy. And for all types of controversies the one test that is invariably applied by decision-makers is that simple and ubiquitous, but indispensable, standard of what, considering all relevant policies and all variables in context, is reasonable as between the parties.

In accord with the overwhelming demands of all peoples who value not merely human dignity but even human survival, the United States is continuing to make every practicable effort to achieve world disarmament and to outlaw nuclear weapons. In the contemporary context of failure to achieve effective international control of armaments, the United States considers, however, that it has no alternative but to keep itself armed for self-defense as best it can. Fortunately, almost all proponents of the free world—whatever their idiosyncratic views about either strategy or tactics—still agree in this determination, and recognize that to forego the testing and development of the new weapons would amount only to unilateral disarmament, with attendant invitation to destruction.

The facts available as to the extent to which water and fish were made radioactive by the tests, and in what areas, leave much to be desired. Newspaper reports originating with segments of the Japanese press unfriendly to the United States, for various reasons, exaggerated the effects of the tests with "evident malice," and no complete, authoritative reports are yet available. It is not clear whether fish found to be dangerously radioactive were caught within or without the largest warning zone, established after the effects of the March 1st test became apparent, so that it is not possible to say whether safety measures in addition to the establishment of an adequate warning zone would be necessary if and when future tests are conducted. It seems clear that no injuries whatever resulted from consumption or handling of fish rendered radioactive by the tests, or from radioactive sea water. The safety measures taken by the Japanese Government were understandably drastic, resulting in the condemnation of some 176 tons of fish, but were 100 per cent effective. Domestic tuna prices in Japan plummeted to 50 per cent of normal in April 1954, after sensationalized accounts of the test effects were published, but exports were unaffected. In view of all the facts now known, any serious attempt to balance the stake of the free world in the tests against the damage resulting from pollution—damage which has taken the exclusive form of financial damage for which compensation has been paid—must reach, we submit, the conclusion that the tests are reasonable and hence lawful.

It might of course be concluded, by analogy from municipal law, that although under all criteria of reasonableness a nation-state is entitled to conduct such tests under contemporary conditions, it should still be held responsible in damages for any inevitable injuries to innocent parties. In every mature legal system the balancing process which determines whether liability exists is repeated in answering the entirely separate question whether the liability-creating conduct may be continued. No international tribunal has yet unequivocally faced the issue whether a state may continue to carry on conduct for which it is liable in damages, but sound policy decrees that international law should parallel municipal law in this respect. Although no legal issues were formally resolved between Japan and the United States, the settlement in fact reached a desirable legal result. Japan explicitly refused to demand that the United States discontinue its tests, and the United States paid two million dollars in damages "without reference" to questions of legal liability. Only third parties, unembarrassed by responsibilities for the defense and security of the free world, seem unable to perceive the need for an appropriate discrimination between remedy for damage and mutual tolerance for vital interests.

The prospect of the possible use of the hydrogen bomb against human beings is almost too horrible to contemplate. It appears probable that each half of the world now has the capacity quickly to destroy the other: the common analogy of two death-dealing scorpions enclosed in a small bottle has become all too apt. Under these circumstances the need for the peoples of the world to agree upon and enforce workable plans for disarmament and world public order could not be more urgent. We bow to none in recognition of this need and in demand for rational response. We do not, however, regard it as rational for the free world unilaterally to disarm itself by the unnecessary extrapolation of broad prescriptions from the customary international law of the sea, created for other purposes, or by the narrow and technical interpretation apart from the context of selected phrases from great international charters. Until a reasonably secure would public order can be established, the free half of the world has no alternative but to make certain that it remains a scorpion and does not invite transformation into inanimate radioactive dust. It is only by maintaining their capacity to defend their free institution that proponents of human dignity can hope to achieve by peaceful procedures a world public order which can continue to maintain that defense. Without at least a portion of the world defended in its freedom it would be folly to talk of freedom of the seas and the welfare of dependent peoples, both impossible to isolate from the freedom and welfare of a whole interdependent free world. The only rational policy for proponents of human dignity today is to demand, and to demand from a strength which ensures respect, not merely spurious or naive legalisms and not merely freedom for navigation and fishing and the narrowly conceived and unrealistically isolated welfare of a few scattered peoples, but workable prescriptions and institutions for global disarmament and a world public order which will afford opportunity for the increasing freedom and welfare of all peoples in the full exploitation of all the world's riches.

(2) Negative[107]

Professor Myres McDougal and Mr. Norbert Schlei argue that national decision-makers operating in the international environment must constantly make policy choices between complementary prescriptions, while "for all types of controversies the one test that is invariably applied by decision-makers is that simple and ubiquitous, but indispensable, standard of what, considering all relevant policies and all variables in context, is reasonable as between the parties." One of course should not take this statement too literally. Presumably McDougal would not intend it to apply to fixed treaty obligations that in the short run seem to one party to be unreasonable. Nevertheless, he does apparently equate his conception of reasonableness with the traditional concept of custom in international law. By "international custom" McDougal specifically means "that total flow of explicit communications and acts of collaboration among peoples which create community-wide expectations that certain uniformities in decision will successfully survive challenge." This is an overly broad and inclusive statement, one which might well serve as a tautological definition of "law" as well as custom.

Professor McDougal makes a number of arguments for "reasonableness" as the authoritative guide to the prescriptive requirements of international custom. Some contentions are purely descriptive of international claim-conflicts, such as the concepts of reciprocity, retaliation, and dedoublement fonctionnel. As such, they do not prove McDougal's case for reasonableness. For although competing claims are often settled by "mutual tolerances" based on expectations of reciprocity or fear of retaliation, their resolution does not have to be "reasonable"—a larger power may prevail over a smaller one that cannot communicate as credible a threat of retaliation, reciprocity may be nonexistent (e.g., the United States has a continental shelf but Japan does not), or mutual toleration may place the interests of the immediately affected parties ahead of larger community interests. In addition, the idea of dedoublement fonctionnel—where "the same nation-state officials are alternately, in a process of reciprocal interaction, both claimants and external decision-makers passing upon the claims of others"—does not assure that the officials will gradually become fairer and more reasonable by moderating their own country's claims and meeting external claims halfway. Many officials simply become more hardened in a "my country, right or wrong" attitude.

Professor McDougal contends that rules of custom come often in paired opposites, thus affording wide discretion to the policy maker. Although this idea of the complementarity of customary prescriptions does not necessarily mean that the policies selected will be reasonable, nevertheless it renders the impact of customary prescriptions so feeble that the reader is inclined to grab hold of any straw, such as "reasonableness," that might put some meaningful content into international law. Thus it is important to trace McDougal's contention in some detail.

Professor McDougal describes the regime of the high seas, "a living, growing, customary law," as presenting a "maze of conflicting claims" categorizable under two sets of "complementary prescriptions." The first prescription is that of "freedom of the seas," invoked to honor inclusive claims such as navigation, fishing, and cable-laying. The complementary or opposite set of claims is that of exclusive jurisdiction, comprising "a wide variety of technical terms such as 'territorial sea,' 'contiguous zones,' 'jurisdiction,' 'continental shelf,'" and so forth. Out of the dialectics of these antithetical prescriptions, McDougal offers a synthesis justifying the temporary exclusive use of a portion of the high seas for the American hydrogen bomb tests. The complementarity of the prescriptions, in short, forced American decision-makers to consider "security" goals of the United States and the "free world," leading them to decide to infringe temporarily but reasonably upon the set of interests characterized as "freedom of the seas." The hydrogen bomb tests, McDougal concludes, were "reasonable, and hence lawful."

The apparatus of complementary prescriptions proves too much. If national decision-makers are actually subject to complementary prescriptions, they in fact have unfettered discretion to do whatever they desire. Hopefully they will be "reasonable" and perhaps espouse McDougal's own values, but in fact they may often do what they feel is "reasonable" and what McDougal would describe as irrational. Of course, if by his doctrine of complementary prescriptions McDougal is merely trying to say that there

---

107 By ANTHONY D'AMATO, based upon: THE CONCEPT OF CUSTOM IN INTERNATIONAL LAW (Cornell Univ. Press, 1971). Reprinted by permission.

is no international law at all, then he has picked a rather cumbersome way of doing so.

A second, more basic fault of the doctrine of complementary prescriptions is its focus upon rationalization rather than action. Custom in international law depends upon what states do, and, in terms of their practice, contradictory lines of conduct do not arise nearly as frequently as do contradictory explanations. Whereas a proper quantitative focus upon the acts (or omissions) of states sharpens the characterization of customary legal rules, a shift to a subjective notion of complementarity tends to enable any nation to justify anything. Moreover, McDougal unnecessarily complicates the concept of custom by looking at the rationalizations of decision-makers in terms of their interests rather than at the conduct itself. Once these rationalizations are invoked, it becomes easy to find among them many sets of complementary prescriptions. Lawyers the world over are clever enough to articulate a set of values, rationalizations, and interests (particularly those as simple as the "well-being" of the nation they serve, or values as vague and all-inclusive as "security") to justify anything their client states want to do. Indeed, whenever there is a claim-conflict situation, we should not be surprised to find lawyers on each side invoking a set of prescriptions that taken together are complementary. Clearly we cannot resolve the dispute by simply putting the opposite viewpoints side by side and accepting them both. Complementary prescriptions taken together are a recipe for deadlock, not decision. To be sure, when we are presented with complementary prescriptions by both sides, we might be impelled to accept whichever position is "reasonable." But the fact is that each side will assert that its own view of the matter is the only "reasonable" one. If "reasonableness" emerges as the only standard McDougal offers for resolving disputes under international law, then everything will depend on who is the judge in a given dispute. An American judge might be expected to rule that the hydrogen bomb tests were a "reasonable" use of the high seas; a Soviet judge might be expected to rule that they were not reasonable. Disputes will be resolved, under his scheme, according to the formula: whoever has the power to appoint the judge, wins. Perhaps McDougal's entire jurisprudence boils down to power—power that either excludes law entirely or bends it, if necessary to the breaking point, according to its own lust.

(3) Affirmative Reply[108]

The factitious distinction between law and politics is nowhere more preposterous than in discussions of law-making. The making of law, whether at the international or national level, and whether through explicit deliberation or implicit behavior, is quintessentially a political process. Those who have political power use it to achieve their objectives. Rationally, they enhance their power by a variety of techniques including the establishment of community policy as "law" which they enforce through institutions of the state apparatus. The extent to which particular laws advance the common interest of the community, or discriminate in favor of a particular group, is likely to be a function of the distribution of power in the community. Where power is widely shared, and many actors are able to protect their interests in the arenas of decision, law is more likely to reflect the interests of all who are politically relevant. Where power is narrowly shared, it is no surprise that the content of the law protects the power base and other interests of the oligarchy.

Where there is a congruence between the institutions of formal law-making and those of effective power, we encounter legislation. A formal authority lacking effective power produces "semantic law," a caricature of legislation; socially meaningful law is established extra-legislatively by those with sufficient effective power. The explicitly rational and open deliberative aspects of legislation are then lost and the entire promise of legislation is depreciated. Where the possibilities of reaching agreement have been exhausted, the ultimate outcome will be determined by the exercise of power as a function of its equilibrium. Law is made by "custom," a vague term which tells us little more than that certain laws did not derive from a legislative process. The quality or content of the resulting law is a separate matter. From a disengaged observational standpoint, legal scholars and political philosophers may comment on the relative value, ethical content or degree of means-end utility of particular laws. But, unless they are transempirical natural lawyers who have no grasp of reality, there is no question as to what the law is.

Over the next several decades, new norms will continue to be established and existing norms amended or terminated in complex patterns of interaction. This will be referred to increasingly as customary international law, and sometimes extolled as natural democracy, but one should have no illusions as to what it really means. The critical factor in the establishment of custom is the relative power balances, corrected by the context of the issue, of the parties concerned and the intensity of the interest they have in securing certain outcomes. Even a power process is restrained by concerns of reciprocity and log-rolling, with stronger actors making certain concessions in order to secure a vari-

---

[108] By W. MICHAEL REISMAN, excerpted from: *The Cult of Custom in the Late 20th Century*, 17 CALIFORNIA WESTERN INTERNATIONAL LAW JOURNAL 133, 136, 144-45 (1987). Reprinted by permission.

ety of other concessions from weaker but functionally important actors; however, the power of states which have made unilateral determinations as to what serves their interests will be paramount.

Procedurally, this is a sad state of affairs. It is far from the dazzling dreams of the founders of the United Nations forty years ago and is consistent with the alarming decay in many of the international institutional arrangements laboriously created after World War II. The blame can be apportioned among new states which were exhilarated by the illusion of power and did not temper their aspirations with realism; among the old imperial powers which were intransigent about relinquishing a share in power and among many lawyers in more powerful states who permitted themselves the opiate of theories of voodoo jurisprudence, completely severed from the unyielding reality of power in all politics. Custom will not displace legislation. The world community will legislate for itself in the last decades of the twentieth century, perhaps not badly, but not democratically. However, building or rebuilding an international legislative system which is responsive to the policies of power sharing and responsibility will, I fear, be a long and hard task.

b. Chinese Views of Custom[109]

Almost all major Western treatise writers or casebook editors on international law place custom before treaties as a principal source of international law. Except for Professor Zhou Gengsheng,[110] almost all People's Republic of China writers place custom after treaties in their discussions on principal sources of international law. Despite this difference in arrangement, the standard textbook, edited by Professors Wang and Wei, acknowledges that

> within a specific sense, international custom may be considered as the most important source [of international law] despite the existence of many multilateral treaties. This is because international custom still constitutes the greater part of general international law. In the final analysis, all other sources of international law, including international treaties, generally must go through international custom to be effective.[111]

Professor Zhou Gengsheng defines custom as those general practices of various states which have been accepted as law. Long-term practice of various states and the acceptance of this practice as law are thus two inseparable elements for creating custom. The "practice," according to Zhou, refers to the actions or omissions of various states regarding a particular matter. Usually, so-called state conduct concerns only the conduct of the executive branch of a state. However, if various states enact similar laws on certain matters or the courts of various states render similar judgments on certain cases, these factors also will demonstrate the general practice of various states toward such matters or cases.

Wang and Wei generally agree with Professor Zhou on the creation of custom. But they take into consideration the approach of other Western writers to this question by differentiating between the material and psychological elements for creating custom. The former element refers to the repetition of similar conduct by various states; the latter reflects the acceptance of such similar conduct as legally binding.

Western publicists have recognized the role of local custom in international law since the ICJ's decision in the Rights of Passage Case. However, no Chinese writer has yet recognized local custom. Nor has any discussed the question of regional custom, such as the practice of diplomatic asylum in Latin America.

A closely related matter is the Chinese attitude toward codification of customs. Chinese writers generally support codification of customs in order to make those customs more clear and specific. However, the PRC has hardly been active in this area. Despite the fact that the PRC was admitted to the United Nations in October 1971, it did not nominate a candidate to the United Nations International Law Commission until 1982. The Commission is responsible for codification and development of international law. Similarly, the PRC did not nominate a candidate to the United Nations International Trade Commission until 1982.

B. Treaty-Based Rules of Custom[112]

1. Analytical Background

Some years ago when I read the classic works of the "positivist" writers of international law, such as Bynkershoek, Zouche, Wolff, Moser, and Vattel, I was struck by

---

[109] By HUNGDAH CHIU, excerpted from: *Chinese Views on the Sources of International Law,* 28 HARVARD INTERNATIONAL LAW JOURNAL 289, 295–98 (1987). Reprinted by permission.

[110] 1 ZHOU GENGSHENG, GUOJA FA 10–11 (1981).

[111] WANG TIEYA & WEI MING, GUOJI FA 28–29 (1981).

[112] By ANTHONY D'AMATO, adapted from: *The Concept of Human Rights in International Law,* 82 COLUMBIA LAW REVIEW 1110 (1982); THE CONCEPT OF CUSTOM IN INTERNATIONAL LAW 103–66 (Cornell University Press 1971); *Custom and Treaty: A Response to Professor Weisburd,* 21 VAND. J. TRANSNAT'L L. 459 (1988). Reprinted by permission.

the fact that nearly everything they claimed to be rules of customary international law were provisions of various treaties. But none of these writers restricted the rules they described to the parties to those treaties; indeed, the treaties and the parties thereto were almost always not mentioned. A reader simply had to know that the rules of customary international law that they described in fact had their origin in treaties. And if a reader knew that, the reader would also know that the positivists' books would practically be blank if they omitted the rules found in treaties.

The positivists didn't invent the idea of wholesale borrowing of treaty provisions; far from it. Previous writers had done exactly the same thing. The classicists such as Grotius, Suarez, and Gentili unabashedly included treaty provisions as sources of customary law. But their natural-law approach to international law could easily accommodate treaty provisions. In contrast, the positivists' insistence that rules of international law were only binding upon states by virtue of the states' consent, was not at all accommodating to the notion of treaty provisions as a source of customary law of general applicability. As I read the works of the positivists, I thought how conflicted they must have been to deal with treaties that were so clearly binding on the *parties* by virtue of the parties' consent, and yet use those same treaties as a source of general law applicable to non-parties when the latter, by definition, had not consented.

It almost seemed to me that Wolff, Moser, Vattel and the other positivists were better students of international law than their own theory permitted them to be. Their theory of consent was clearly restrictive; rules of international law would be few and far between if states had to consent to them before they could be bound by them. Yet the positivists could not give up their theory of consent, because they would then have been totally unable to explain why sovereign states could be bound by any external rules. My guess is that they kept their theory of consent because they couldn't imagine any other theory to take its place, but when they turned to the descriptive parts of their books, they tucked their theory of consent safely away and simply wrote in the great international law tradition. They must have understood that international customary law was binding on all states, that its content derived from the practice of states, and a significant portion of state "practice" was the practice of concluding treaties with other states. Hence, treaty provisions were clear, convenient, ascertainable expressions of the accommodations states reached in their dealings with each other. Apart from the troublesome theory of consent, treaties seemed like the best place to look for most of the details of customary law.

It is important to note that, even for the positivists, not all provisions in treaties became part of general customary law. Many treaty provisions are simply not generalizable into norms without destroying their content. For instance, a "most-favored-nation" provision if generalized would mean giving most-favored-nation status to all nations, which of course destroys the intended meaning of the provision. Similarly, if two nations trade territory with each other, or agree upon a mapping of the border they share, those provisions of their treaty are simply not generalizable. Additionally, many treaties contain (usually in their final clauses) various provisions for enforcing the substantive treaty provisions. These enforcement clauses are also of particular relevance to the parties, and cannot be generalized into norms of customary international law.

By the same token, not all rules of customary law had their origin in treaties. For example, the personal safety accorded to diplomatic envoys could only have been purely customary in origin, since the conclusion of a treaty presupposes a safe mission of treaty-negotiation. (Even so, the ambit of "safe-conducts" and later that of diplomatic immunities became the subject of detailed provisions in the early treaties.)

These qualifications aside, the interesting historical question became: what would happen to positivism if it retained its influence on writers of international law? Would the theory be discredited (because of its insistence on consent) or would it become more rigorous?

The main theorists at the turn of the twentieth century turned out to be heavily influenced by positivism. William Hall and especially Lassa Oppenheim concluded that positivism provided no theoretical basis for extending treaty provisions to states that were not parties. Yet they did not "disinherit," so to speak, all the norms of international law cited by their predecessors that had originated in treaties. If you read Oppenheim's hugely influential treatise, *International Law*, you will recognize the carryforward of norms found in Vattel and Moser and Wolff, now said to be part of the generally accepted body of public international law. But as for *new* norms originating in newly ratified treaties, Oppenheim cut the umbilical cord. The argument Oppenheim and Hall made[113] can be summarized as follows:

> 1. A treaty binds only its parties.
>
> 2. The provisions in a treaty can either be declaratory of existing customary law, or can be in derogation of it.
>
> 3. If the treaty provisions are declaratory of international law, no significant consequence can be derived from this fact.
>
> 4. If the treaty provisions are in derogation of existing customary law, it means that the parties

[113] WILLIAM HALL, INTERNATIONAL LAW 7–8 (A.P. Higgins 8th ed. 1924); 1 LASSA OPPENHEIM, INTERNATIONAL LAW 28 (H. Lauterpacht 8th ed. 1955).

have simply opted out of the existing customary law regime as far as their own bilateral relations on a particular subject-matter are concerned, and set up a different set of norms (the treaty norms) to govern their own relations.

5. Treaty provisions that derogate from customary law are perfectly legal (indeed, derogation is the main reason why parties feel the need to conclude a treaty—they simply were not happy with the existing customary norms). But those treaty provisions do not *change* the underlying custom for other states; they simply carve out a special regime for the parties to the treaty.

This argument was also incorporated in the dicta of Lord Alverstone of the much-cited turn-of-the-century case of *West Rand Central Gold Mining Co. v. The King*.[114] Although that case is now generally acknowledged to have been wrongly decided, its "restrictive-contract" view of treaties continues to influence many writers who are convinced by the arguments I have just summarized.[115]

Those arguments boil down to one proposition—that a treaty is just a contract. It is a contract between states, to be sure, but otherwise no different from any ordinary contract between persons or corporations. Since we assume that if two persons enter into a contract, the provisions in that contract only apply to them—and have no effect on the general *law of contracts*—the same must be true of two nations that enter into a treaty.

What's wrong with this argument? Two things. First, a treaty isn't a contract. Second, even if it were, contractual provisions in fact find their way into common law just as treaty provisions find their way into customary law.

A treaty isn't a contract. It resembles a contract in that both are examples of express agreements. But other instruments are examples of express agreements that we don't call contracts—such as constitutions, charters, and even statutes (thought of as agreements among legislators). Contracts are circumscribed by laws and code provisions in domestic legal systems, whereas treaties historically have had no such limitations. Treaties in international law have created their own legal consequences. A treaty can create a sovereign state which in turn becomes capable of entering into treaties. A treaty can create mandates and trust territories, international waterways, and other permanent changes in status.[116] Treaties have set up international organizations such as the United Nations, which in turn has contributed to the shaping of customary law including the law of interpretation of treaties. Treaties have set up international courts. No domestic contract between two corporations, for example, can set up a court that would have ultimate legal power over the parties. But treaties can set up such tribunals and much more. Even if we turn from substance and look just at the way treaties and contracts are interpreted, we find huge differences. For example, the law of duress—which in some circumstances can invalidate a domestic contract—cannot be pleaded in regard to a treaty of peace. Even though the vanquished nation might claim that *war itself* is the most egregious form of duress, the fact is that the very war that forced the vanquished nation to enter into a peace treaty cannot later be used by the vanquished nation as an excuse to get out of the onerous terms of the peace treaty. Another example is the doctrine of rebus sic stantibus: it clearly has a broader effect on the interpretation of treaties over time than any analogous doctrine of impossibility, frustration, or relationalism may have on the interpretation of contracts over time.[117] Nor are analogies to other areas of contract law necessarily helpful in dealing with complex questions that arise in the interpretation of treaties, such as the conflict of law-making treaties,[118] the use made of travaux preparatoires,[119] and whether reservations to multilateral conventions operate to include or exclude the reserving party from the treaty-regime.[120]

But let's suppose, contrary to all of these considerations, one insists on equating treaties with contracts. The second part of that person's argument, then, would be that since contractual clauses have no effect on the law of contracts but rather create law just for the parties, so also the provisions in treaties can have no effect on states other than the parties to the treaties. Such an assertion is simply wrong as a matter of history. In the early days of contracts, many of the common-law rules (we now call them "default rules") of contract interpretation had their origin in private contracts. For example, suppose merchants in a community typically included a clause in their offers that "if you don't deposit your acceptance of this offer in the mails within ten days of the above date, the offer will lapse." Now suppose an offer is made that fails to include this typical

---

[114] 2 King's Bench 391, 398 (1905).

[115] *See, e.g.*, Richard Baxter, *Treaties and Custom*, 1970–71 RECUEIL DES COURS 25; CLIVE PARRY, THE SOURCES AND EVIDENCES OF INTERNATIONAL LAW 29–32 (1965).

[116] *See* Arnold McNair, *The Functions and Differing Legal Character of Treaties*, 11 BYIL 100, 103–04 (1930).

[117] According to Arnold McNair, the doctrine of clausula rebus sic stantibus, if applied to commonlaw contracts, "would have a devastating effect." Arnold McNair, *So-called State Servitudes*, 6 BYIL 111, 122 (1925).

[118] *See* Wilfred Jenks, *The Conflict of Law-Making Treaties*, 30 BYIL 401, 406 (1953).

[119] *See* Hersch Lauterpacht, *Some Observations on Preparatory Work in the Interpretation of Treaties*, 48 HARV. L. REV. 549 (1935).

[120] *See* the section on "Reservations to Multilateral Conventions," Chapter 5, this Anthology.

provision. A court, faced with a situation where the offeree claims that she deposited her acceptance in the mails within ten days, and the offeror says that he did not physically receive the offer within ten days, will likely "read into" the contract the provision that was typically used in other contracts, and hold that the contract was duly accepted upon deposit of the acceptance in the mails within the ten-day period. This is but one example of the numerous ways that business practices reverberate in the common law; it has been given the name "law merchant."[121] We don't think of the law merchant these days because of the enormous codification that the law of contracts has been subjected to. Not only are there Uniform Commercial Codes, but there are also Restatements of contracts and numerous comprehensive codes in various states and jurisdictions. If we remove this abundance of legislation, we can see more clearly how the common law of contract interpretation developed. The customary international law of treaty interpretation has proceeded in an international system that does not have universal legislation or codification. Thus, the earliest treaties, as Georg Schwarzenberger tells us, "contained elaborate provisions regarding duration, interpretation, participation of third parties, relations between treaties, and consequences of breach of treaty by one of the contracting parties."[122] Many of these rules today have been telescoped into short phrases or dispensed with altogether, but evidently they originated in misunderstandings in practice that had to be straightened out by explicit elaboration in the treaty instruments themselves. Over time, these interpretative qualifications became understood as normal "default" rules of international law when they were not explicitly specified in a given treaty. Even the principle pacta sunt servanda initially derived from treaties. Early treaties were elaborately signed and sealed, solemn oaths were added, supernatural sanctions invoked in the preambles, and so forth.[123] Over time these were discarded, as customary rule of pacta sunt servanda rendered them unnecessary.

In brief, the classic writers on international law were right in finding norms of customary international law in the provisions of treaties. For these treaty provisions, though they might apply to the parties by virtue of an exchanged bargain (contract), apply to non-parties through the same mechanism that customary law itself develops in international systems, a mechanism parallel to the way that common law itself develops in domestic systems.

The net effect of Oppenheim's refusal to find that treaties can generate new norms of customary law binding on nonparties is that he simply disabled himself from keeping up-to-date with the progressive development of customary law. One rather stark example among many is his refusal to find that the numerous international treaties outlawing the slave trade generated any international customary prohibition to the same effect. His refusal was perpetuated after his own death by the editor of subsequent editions of the Oppenheim treatise. Thus we find Hersch Lauterpacht, in 1955 as editor of the 8th edition of Oppenheim, saying that he "finds it difficult to say that customary International Law condemns" the traffic in slaves![124] International law, of course, had long since gone in precisely the opposite direction. Not only is traffic in slaves prohibited by customary international law, but in fact, well before 1955, it was one of the clearest prohibitions in all of international law, rising to the level (according to the International Law Commission) of a norm of jus cogens.[125]

Oppenheim (and his subsequent editors) clearly felt the tension between his positivist notion of treaty-as-contract and what he saw was happening in the real world. Treaties were adding new norms of custom, and modifying old ones, all the time. There was certainly a glaring inconsistency between Oppenheim's acceptance of all the previous treaty-generated norms that had been cited by his predecessors (Vattel, Moser, Wolff, etc.), and his rejection of any new treaty-generated norms. His rejection of them was a consequence of his steadfast—one might say dogged—insistence that a treaty was nothing more than a contract.

Many writers at the turn of the twentieth century rejected the positivist approach of Hall and Oppenheim. They openly acknowledged that treaties were "a fountain of law to others than the signatory states."[126] They included writers such as Bluntschli, Despagnet, Calvo, Fiore, Fauchille, Hautfeuille, Pradier-Fodere, Phillimore, Nys, Lawrence, Smith, Westlake, Wheaton, Cavaglieri, and more recently Politis.[127] But many important British and American jurists

---

[121] For a more extended discussion of the "law merchant," *see* Section A8, "The Central Point of Custom," above in this Chapter.

[122] GEORG SCHWARZENBERGER, THE FRONTIERS OF INTERNATIONAL LAW 51 (1962).

[123] *Ibid.*

[124] I OPPENHEIM, INTERNATIONAL LAW 733–34 (8th ed. H. Lauterpacht 1955).

[125] *See International Law Commission, commentary to Article 53 of the Vienna Convention on Treaties*, 63 AJIL 875, 887 (1969). Whatever the legal status of "jus cogens" (see the section on "Jus Cogens" below in this Chapter), it certainly designates a prohibitory norm that is so clear as to be beyond question an obligation of international law.

[126] The quotation is from a disparaging comment by WILLIAM HALL, INTERNATIONAL LAW 7 (8th ed. Higgins 1924).

[127] BLUNTSCHLI, LE DROIT INTERNATIONAL CODIFE 5 (4th ed. 1886); DESPAGNET, DROIT INTERNATIONAL PUBLIC 76–77 (4th ed. 1910); 1 CALVO, LE DROIT INTERNATIONAL THEORIQUE ET PRATIQUE 160 (5th ed. 1896); 1 FIORE, TRATTATO DI DIRITTO INTERNAZIONALE PUBBLICO 147 (4th ed. 1904); 1 FAUCHILLE, TRAITE DE DROIT INTERNATIONAL PUBLIC 53–54 (8th ed. Bonfils 1922); 1 HAUTFEUILLE,

continued to cling to the theory that treaties are just contracts and therefore are either declaratory of customary law or in derogation of it. That theory was almost powerful enough to blind them to the massive evidence around them that customary international law was being shaped, as it had been through the centuries, by provisions in treaties. I say ''almost'' because these post-Oppenheim writers reluctantly began to acknowledge that the generation of custom by treaty could *sometimes* happen.

Richard Baxter, for example, said that provisions in treaties could give rise to custom if the parties to the treaties *intended* the provisions to be declaratory of existing customary law.[128] Professor Baxter opened the door to the idea of treaties generating custom, but only by a hair's breadth: the treaties had to be ''declaratory'' of existing custom. How could anyone tell whether the treaties were declaratory of existing custom? By looking at the evidence of custom *dehors* the treaty, and comparing it with the treaty! It appears that if Professor Baxter opened the door very slightly, he quickly closed it. For if we can know what customary law is apart from the treaty, then why look at the treaty at all? Why would we want to determine whether the treaty is ''declaratory'' of customary law? Under Professor Baxter's approach, *if* the treaty is declaratory of custom, and by hypothesis we already knew what that custom was, then we haven't advanced very far. On the other hand, if the treaty is *not* declaratory of custom – by, for example, departing from existing custom – then it is worthless as far as generating custom is concerned. My guess is that Professor Baxter wanted to show that he was not entirely closed to the idea that treaties could generate custom, but his positivist convictions kept him from going any further than acknowledging that a treaty can be declaratory of existing custom so long as independent evidence demonstrates that it is consistent with existing custom.[129]

Recently, Richard Weisburd has picked up Professor Baxter's notion of ''intent.''[130] While conceding that treaties should count as the practice of states, Professor Weisburd qualifies this by saying that the only treaties that count are those that the parties intend should count. He adds – coming perilously close to Professor Baxter's notion that treaties make law only when they are declaratory of the law that already exists – that when the parties to a treaty do not believe that the background customary law would require them to act in the way that the treaty specifies, then such a treaty can have no impact upon custom.[131]

There is a practical reason and a theoretical reason why the ''intent'' theory cannot work. As a matter of practice, it would fail to account for any change in existing customary law. We know that the content of customary law has changed considerably through the years and through the centuries. Professor Weisburd (and Professor Baxter before him) would deny to treaties that depart from existing customary law the possibility of generating new customary law. Additionally, states usually have two reasons for entering into treaties: to restate in clearer form the customary law that already binds them, and to create new norms that depart from existing customary law. The ''restating'' function would hardly account for all the treaties that have ever been made. Parties often want to depart from the existing norms of custom in their relations with each other. It would be hard to find an example of a treaty that simply restates existing customary law; nations would hardly go to all that trouble just to restate the law. Yet it is only the ''restatement'' treaties that Professors Weisburd and Baxter concede have law-making potential!

The theoretical reason why the ''intent'' qualification cannot work is that the international community owes no obligation to the specific intent of the parties to a treaty. If nations A and B wish to enter into a treaty, they certainly have the right to create new norms that bind themselves in their relations to each other. But what right do they have to dictate general norms to the international community? How could they choose between intending that the provi-

DROITS DES NATIONS NEUTRES xiv–xv (3rd ed. 1868); 1 PRADIER-FODERE, TRAITE DE DROIT INTERNATIONAL PUBLIC 82–86 (1885); 1 PHILLIMORE, COMMENTARIES ON INTERNATIONAL LAW 53 (3rd ed. 1879); 1 NYS, LE DROIT INTERNATIONAL 161-66 (2d ed. 1912); LAWRENCE, THE PRINCIPLES OF INTERNATIONAL LAW 99 (7th ed. 1910); SMITH (EARL OF BIRKENHEAD), INTERNATIONAL LAW 25 (6th ed. 1927); 1 WESTLAKE, INTERNATIONAL 16 (2d ed. 1910); WHEATON, ELEMENTS OF INTERNATIONAL LAW 24 (8th ed. Dana, 1866); CAVAGLIERI, LEZIONIDI DIRITTO INTERNAZIONALE 25–27(1925); POLITIS, THE NEW ASPECTS OF INTERNATIONAL LAW 16 (1928).

128 Richard Baxter, *Multilateral Treaties as Evidence of Customary International Law,* 41 BYIL 275 (1965-66).

129 As the late Professor Baxter's student, I believe that I am not misstating his motivation on this issue. When I took his seminar in international law in 1960, I had just begun my twelve-year-long research into the theory of custom in international law that eventuated in a book published in 1971. The paper I wrote for Professor Baxter's seminar was my first cut at the problem. It was entitled *Treaties as a Source of General Rules of International Law,* later published under that title in 3 HARV. INT'L L.J. 1 (1962). Professor Baxter then wrote two articles on the same subject, the second of which acknowledged my previous work: Richard Baxter, *Multilateral Treaties as Evidence of Customary International Law,* 41 BYIL 275 (1965 66); Richard Baxter, *Treaties and Custom,* 1970-71 RECUEIL DES COURS 25.

130 Richard Weisburd, *Customary International Law: The Problem of Treaties,* 21 VAND. J. TRANSNAT'L L. 1 (1988).

131 He cuts back slightly on this qualification later in his article. Professor Weisburd concedes that a little weight might be given to state denials of the practice of torture if such denials ''are not attributable entirely to political motives.'' Id. at 35. This is a very narrow concession, for how could one possibly go about determining whether the motivations of governmental leaders in foreign countries are or are not *entirely political*?

sions in the A-B treaty should apply to other states or should not apply to other states? If they could make such a choice, then A and B, by virtue of a simple treaty they conclude between themselves, would become legislators for the international community as a whole. The only position that makes any sense – logically and historically – is that the intent of the treaty parties has nothing to do with the impact of their treaty upon general norms of customary international law. A simple analogy should make this point clear. Suppose plaintiff P sues defendant D in a domestic court over a domestic matter. Should P and D be able to decide whether the court's final judgment should count as precedent in future cases? Clearly, P and D have nothing to do with the use that the judicial system makes of the P-D case in the future. The decision to use the P-D case as precedent is one that the judicial system as a whole will make, and not P or D (or even the judge who decides the P-D case). Similarly, A and B may enter into a treaty, but the effect of their treaty on general customary law is a matter not for them to decide. As for the international community, it has already decided what use to make of the A-B treaty. Throughout the history of international law, the content of customary law has been shaped and modified by the provisions in treaties. Unless Professor Weisburd wants to return to the precise content of customary law as followed by the ancient Babylonians in their naval encounters with other city-states, he should rethink his wholesale exclusion of the impact of innovative treaties upon customary law.

Perhaps in acknowledgment of the difficulty of ascertaining the "intent" of states that enter into treaties, Professors Baxter and Weisburd attempt to find objective evidence of intent in the language of the treaty. If the treaty itself declares that it is declaratory of existing law, then Professors Baxter and Weisburd might take the treaty at face value. But surely this puts a premium on dishonesty of treaty draftsmanship. If states A and B know that a particular provision in their bilateral treaty is a departure from existing customary law, all they have to do to make the treaty law-generating under the Baxter-Weisburd rules would be to *say* that the provision is *declaratory* of customary law. I don't know of any example where a treaty did just that, but many treaties at least tell a "white lie" in claiming to be declaratory of existing law. For example, the International Covenant on Economic, Social and Cultural Rights refers to the right to work, the right to form trade unions, the right to social security, the right to an adequate standard of living including adequate food, clothing, and housing, and so forth. If some of these "rights" are a departure from existing norms of international human-rights law, you won't find out about it in the treaty. The treaty proclaims them simply as rights. Indeed, the treaty would lose much of its "bite" if it weakened the statement of each of these human rights by qualifying language to the effect that the rights are not yet fully acknowledged as rights under customary international law. The Economic, Social and Cultural Rights Covenant is just one of numerous examples of treaties being couched in declaratory terms even when the drafters know that some of the provisions reach beyond the existing state of customary international law. The rhetorical power of proclaiming a rule to be part of existing law – and not an outright propensity to prevaricate – suggests that most treaties will be couched in declaratory terms no matter how progressive their provisions. Thus the Baxter-Weisburd qualification has little practical value – unless it's a covert acknowledgement by these writers that *all* treaties generate customary law.

A hesitant step of a different kind was taken by Professor Baxter when he argued that multilateral treaties, but not bilateral treaties, are capable of generating customary norms. Yet as I argued in my book on custom in 1971, if we look at the matter mathematically, a multilateral convention among ten states is the equivalent of forty-five similarly worded bilateral treaties among the same ten states.[132] Surely there can be no legal difference between the exact same treaty language contained in a single instrument signed by ten states, and forty-five bilateral treaties all of which contain the exact same language.[133] To be sure, multilateral treaties are more likely than bilateral treaties to contain generalizable provisions that are capable of being subsumed into customary law (witness the recent proliferation of multilateral human-rights conventions.) But there can be no theoretical difference between a multilateral and a bilateral treaty in terms of their effect upon customary law.

---

132 A real-world example was the series of bilateral treaties, known as the "Bancroft treaties," which contained roughly similar substantive provisions. The World Court, in the Nottebohm Case, cited these treaties as evidence of customary law; indeed, it was the Court's only specific reference to state practice. Nottebohm Case, Second Phase, 1955 ICJ Rep. 4, 21–23. The issue in the case was whether Mr. Nottebohm's Liechtenstein nationality could be invoked against Guatemala, a state of which Mr. Nottebohm was not a national. The "Bancroft treaties" cited by the Court dealt with cases of naturalized citizens returning to the country of their birth. The "Bancroft treaties" were bilateral treaties concluded in 1868 between the United States and Wurtenberg, Bavaria, Baden, Hesse, and the North German Federation, and abrogated on April 6, 1917. A main purpose of the "Bancroft treaties" was to limit the power of protecting naturalized persons who became naturalized to avoid military service but later returned to their countries of origin. Since none of the treaties cited by the Court was shown to be in force between the litigating states, the Court clearly relied upon the treaties as precedential facts for deriving a rule of custom that has become known as the "genuine link" rule in cases of nationality.

133 Professor Baxter never replied to this argument, even though it called into question the basic distinction he drew in his major article on multilateral treaties.

A final attempt to salvage the positivist treaties-as-contracts view with the mounting evidence that treaties generate customary law was to say that treaties don't generate custom immediately but rather that treaties in some sense "ripen into" or "harden into" or eventually "are transmuted into" customary international law.[134] But no writer has ever specified how the moment of time should be determined when a treaty provision suddenly generates a rule of custom, or what the rule of custom is while the treaty provision is "ripening," or what the standards could possibly be for determining when the provision has actually "ripened," or why the "ripening" should occur at all.

At least Oppenheim was consistent: treaties don't generate custom, period. The writers of positivist persuasion after Oppenheim have come up with the sub-theories we have examined – the declaratory, intent, multilateral-treaty, and hardening theories – to salvage positivism in the face of real-world evidence. But that evidence in the end proved too strong. It disabled Oppenheim from identifying clear rules of custom, and it introduced subjectivity and uncertainty in the identification of customary rules by the writers who hedged their positivism with the aforementioned sub-theories.

2. Evidence

The best way to characterize the real-world evidence I have been talking about is to take note of the fact that no writer on international law has ever identified a treaty provision – one that meets the test of generalizability that I mentioned above – that has *not* impacted upon the content of customary law. It is particularly noteworthy that when I introduced, in a 1962 article and a 1971 book, the then-radical theory that treaty provisions immediately generate custom, no writer since then, of all those who have criticized or commented upon my work, has found a single disconfirmatory instance of my theory.

As far as positive proof is concerned, I've mentioned the most impressive evidence at the beginning of this section: the works of all the classical writers, down to the end of the nineteenth century, who unabashedly used treaty provisions as the source of the customary rules that they described in their books. Even at the time that Hall and Oppenheim were writing their treatises, they were in the minority; other writers I've listed above openly accepted the proposition that treaties were a "fountain of law" for nonparties.[135] The development of international customary law in the twentieth century furnishes innumerable specific applications of the theory that treaties generate custom. In my 1971 book I examined areas of state practice, decisions of the World Court, and decisions of municipal courts around the world, all of which supported the theory I was suggesting.[136] Michael Akehurst wrote a long article partly supporting and mostly criticizing my work on custom, taking exception in particular to my interpretation of the Continental Shelf Cases.[137] I wrote an essay in reply to Dr. Akehurst, defending among other things my interpretation of the Continental Shelf Cases.[138] I also engaged in a debate on the treaties-into-custom issue with Arthur M. Weisburd.[139] The examples from state practice and judicial decisions that corroborate the treaty-into-custom theory are so numerous that there is no point in revisiting them here. The interested reader is encouraged to consult the sources mentioned in the footnotes to this section; the sources contain numerous additional references to the relevant literature.

3. Theoretical Support

Although I've argued that the international community can make any use it desires of provisions in treaties (just as the judicial community in a state may make any use it desires of prior case decisions), that doesn't answer the question of exactly *why* a provision in a treaty generates customary law for nonparties. The answer is quite straightforward. As we saw earlier in this Chapter, customary law contains a quantitative and a qualitative element. The quantitative element forces us to look at what states *do*. When they act in the domain of international relations, their acts form the basis of the quantitative element in the development of ordinary customary law. But a treaty is also a special form of action: it is a binding commitment

---

134 *See* MANLEY O. HUDSON, THE PERMAENT COURT OF INTERNATIONAL JUSTICE 609 n.38 (1942) ("forms part of"); Percy Corbett, *The Consent of States and the Sources of the Law of Nations*, 6 BYIL 20, 24 (1925) ("hardening into"); Richard Baxter, *Multilateral Treaties as Evidence of Customary International Law*, 41 BYIL 275 (1965–66) ("transmuted into"); Kopelmanas, *Custom as a Means of the Creation of International Law*, 18 BYIL 127, 136–38 (1937); SORENSEN, LES SOURCES DU DROIT INTERNATIONAL 95–98 (1946); Jenks, *State Succession in Respect of Law-Making Treaties*, 29 BYIL 105, 108 (1952); Georg Schwarzenberger, *The Inductive Approach to International Law*, 60 HARV. L. REV. 539, 563 (1946).

135 *See* notes 126 & 127, *supra*.

136 *See* ANTHONY D'AMATO, THE CONCEPT OF CUSTOM IN INTERNATIONAL LAW 103–66 (1971).

137 Michael Akehurst, *Custom as a Source of International Law*, 47 BYIL 1 (1974–75).

138 Anthony D'Amato, *The Concept of Human Rights in International Law*, 82 COLUM. L. REV. 1110 (1982).

139 *See* Arthur M. Weisburd, *Customary International Law: The Problem of Treaties*, 21 VAND. J. TRANSNAT'L L. 1 (1988); Anthony D'Amato, *Custom and Treaty: A Reply to Professor Weisburd*, 21 VAND. J. TRANSNAT'L L. 459 (1988); Arthur M. Weisburd, *A Reply to Professor D'Amato*, 21 VAND. J. TRANSNAT'L L. 473 (1988); Anthony D'Amato, *A Brief Rejoinder*, 21 VAND. J. TRANSNAT'L L. 489 (1988).

to act. Ratifying a treaty means a state is committed to the acts (and abstentions) specified in the treaty.[140] To be sure, the parties may later decide to violate the treaty, but at least the treaty, at the moment it is ratified, constitutes the binding commitment of the parties. (Subsequent violation of the treaty would begin a new line of customary law, one that is built upon the acts of violation; this is no different from the potential custom-generating power of any act that is inconsistent with existing customary law.) In short, ratifying a treaty constitutes "state practice"—one of the traditional components of custom.

The other component of custom is the qualitative element—the characterization of the act as pertaining to the international legal system. Treaties do this better than any other practice of states. Any generalizable provision in a treaty is a statement of a rule of law. As such it meets all the requirements of articulation specified previously.

It is theoretically possible for the parties to a treaty explicitly to disavow that it is a law-creating instrument. This occurred in the draft version of the United States-Mexico treaty of 1906 regarding the apportionment of transboundary rivers; the treaty contained a phrase that the decision of the United States to enter into the treaty "is prompted only by considerations of international comity."[141] This phrase did not survive in the final version of the treaty.[142] What would have happened if it had been included in the treaty itself? It's a kind of paradox.[143] On the one hand, the intention of the parties should not control the use the international community wishes to make of the treaty, for reasons given above. Moreover, the fact is that the parties entered into a treaty apportioning the boundary waters irrespective of what they said they were doing. On the other hand, it is hard to find in the phrase an "articulation" of international law when the statement itself expressly disavows such an articulation. Since the phrase in question did not survive in the final treaty, we really cannot be sure how the international community would have reacted. My guess is that what parties do is always more important than what they say, and hence the treaty (if it had contained the draft phrase) would, in my view, be regarded as impacting upon customary law.

Finally, we should consider the question why the international community would want to regard provisions in treaties as generating customary law. In my view, when two or more states enter into a treaty, they are resolving a potential dispute. The treaty itself may have grown out of a prior dispute, or it simply might be a farsighted way of averting anticipated disputes. The important thing is that an international accommodation—a dispute settlement—is reached by the ratification of a treaty. A treaty is a peaceful way of settling past or anticipated disputes. Customary practice, in contrast, is a potentially nonpeaceful way to resolve disputes. Recall the illustration of custom getting started by sending emissaries back and forth between warring parties. Or recall the Anglo-Norwegian Fisheries Case, where the Norwegian navy was involved and the British navy at least potentially might have escalated the dispute. The formation of custom in the absence of treaty is not necessarily forceful; for example, if two nations are disputing over two "incidents," they might trade winning one for losing the other (thus helping to establish two lines of custom—one for each incident). But treaty-making is clearly the time-honored way of settling disputes in advance. This is why international law—which doesn't "exist" except for its manifestation in the practice of states—has over the centuries derived its content from the increasing number of treaties that have been concluded among various states, as well as from the articulated practices of states that constitute custom. If treaties are rapidly becoming the preferred means of creating customary law among states—as evidenced by the geometric increase in recent years in the number of bilateral and multilateral treaties deposited with the Secretary-General of the United Nations—then the development of "written" law on the international front is an exact parallel to the increase in statutory law on the domestic front. If statutes are rapidly supplanting domestic common law, treaties are rapidly filling up and detailing international customary law.

C. General Principles of Law[144]

A residuary source of international law is, in the language of Article 38 of the Statute of the International Court of Justice, the body of "general principles of law recognized by civilized nations."

140 Some writers say, rather loosely, that customary law can be evidenced by provisions in unratified treaties. This cannot be true with respect to the quantitative element. A draft treaty is something that the parties may accept or reject. The parties have committed nothing until they ratify the treaty. Hence, the law-generative powers of treaties should be confined to treaties that constitute binding commitments—in other words, ratified treaties.

141 *See* William L. Griffin, *The Use of Waters of International Drainage Basins Under Customary International Law*, 53 AJIL 50, 51–52 (1959).

142 USTS No. 455, 34 Stat. 2953 (1906).

143 The paradox of self-referential statements is the subject of a large literature. Take the sentence "This sentence is false." The sentence is true only if it is false, and false only if it is true. *See* DOUGLAS R. HOFSTADTER, GODEL, EXCHER, BACH: AN ETERNAL GOLDEN BRAID 495–548 (1979); RAYMOND SMULLYAN, FOREVER UNDECIDED (1987).

144 By HERSCH LAUTERPACHT, from: 1 INTERNATIONAL LAW 69–70 (1970). Reprinted by permission.

What is the meaning of that expression? These "general principles" are not, as such, principles of moral justice as distinguished from law; they are not rules of "equity" in the ethical sense; nor are they a speculative law conceived by way of deductive reasoning from legal and moral principles. They are, in the first instance, those principles of law, private and public, which contemplation of the legal experience of civilized nations leads one to regard as obvious maxims of jurisprudence of a general and fundamental character—such as the principle that no one can be judge in his own cause, that a breach of a legal duty entails the obligation of restitution, that a person cannot invoke his own wrong as a reason for release from a legal obligation, that the law will not countenance the abuse of a right, that legal obligations must be fulfilled and rights must be exercised in good faith, and the like.

D. Decisions of National Courts[145]

The decision of a national (or "municipal") court on a question of international law is important not so much for what the court says as for what it does. National courts take part in the formation of state practice, so that their permanent, uniform practice renders good arguments for proving the existence of customary law. In regard to state practice, all official activities of state organs, legislative, executive and judicial, are equally instrumental in the formation of law. Thus a national court decision may be classified as an exercise of state sovereignty in the field of international law. Its effect in international law, that is towards third states, is the same as an act of legislation or administration. All these activities of state organs may equally result in wrongful international acts.

It is a matter for municipal law to find a harmonization, a balance or a compromise, if the actions of the individual state organs result in their decisions contradicting each other. In this regard, national systems differ widely. In some legal systems, the courts are bound by the opinion of the executive authority where international affairs are concerned; in others, the government is precluded from interfering with the decisions of the courts, due to the guaranteed independence of the judiciary. In particular, a constitutional court, where it exists, invariably enjoys the competence to supervise the activities of all other state organs, including instances where international law is involved. International law, on the other hand, imputes all those decisions, regardless of their authors in national law, to the state in its capacity as an undivided subject of international law.

Thus, national adjudication must be seen as an expression of state practice's contribution towards the formation of customary international law. When the International Court of Justice tries to discover the existence of rules of customary law—its primary task in terms of article 38 of the Statute—it must return to the decisions of national courts. Here we face the one situation which justifies the designation of the decisions of national courts as a source of international law in the traditional and classical sense, since these decisions, as a result of state practice, not only offer evidence of existing law but practice—together with others—in the creation of international rules.

E. Equity[146]

Equity was used frequently in international law during the 19th century. Many international arbitrations provided for decision according to international law and equity. Then somehow at the beginning of the 20th century things quieted down and equity was used much less. My assistant a few years ago, Russell Gabriel, did some research for me going through the older decisions of the Permanent Court of International Justice and the International Court of Justice and discovered that in fact equity principles were applied in quite a number of cases, although often without express reference to equity. The Court would state it was well known that a particular principle existed as a general principle of international law accepted by most nations and then would apply it, never mentioning equity.

In the 1960's when the World Court began to consider disputes related to maritime boundaries in the North Sea Continental Shelf Cases, it rediscovered equitable principles. The court relied on the Truman Proclamation that said if the United States had any disputes about the continental shelf, they would be solved by agreement with the other country concerned, in accordance with equitable principles. Because the Proclamation was followed by a number of other states, the Court cited it as the beginning of a trend that established the principle the Court would follow.

Of course, in the North Sea Continental Shelf Cases and a number of following cases, various problems arose about what is equity, what are "equitable principles," and what is an equitable result.

---

[145] By KARL DOEHRING, excerpted from: *The Participation of International and National Courts in the Law-Creating Process*, 17 SOUTH AFRICAN YEARBOOK OF INTERNATIONAL LAW 1 (1991/92). Reprinted by permission.

[146] By LOUIS SOHN, excerpted from: *Equity in International Law*, 82 PROCEEDINGS OF THE AMERICAN SOCIETY OF INTERNATIONAL LAW 277, 277–78, 290–91 (1988). Reprinted by permission.

The first problem we have is the old distinction between equity meaning principles of general international law and equity meaning that the court should decide according to what is just and proper, which some call ex aequo et bono, an old well-known phrase.

The phrase "ex aequo et bono" was used in a large number of treaties, starting with the General Act of Geneva in 1928, and the arbitration treaties that followed it. Those treaties provided that, in principle, cases sent to the International Court of Justice should be decided according to article 38, paragraph 1, of the Statute of the Court, namely the four basic sources of international law. There was also article 38, paragraph 2, however, which allows the Court to decide ex aequo et bono when the parties agree and, of course, some of those treaties amounted to such agreement. The majority of those treaties did not provide, however, for the court to decide ex aequo et bono; they provided instead for an arbitral tribunal to deal ex aequo et bono with disputes that were not legal. There was a second group of treaties, including the European Treaty on Peaceful Settlement in the 1950s, that provided that if a tribunal could not find a rule of international law on the subject, it might deal with the subject ex aequo et bono.

This agrees of course with the statement by Hans Kelsen, who always said that on any subject there was a rule of international law, namely, that you either could do something or you could not do something, and the only question was the burden of proof.

Substantive principles present more of a problem, however. Equity under Anglo-American law means one thing, equity under continental law derived from Roman principles means something different, and equity under Soviet law derived at least partially from Byzantine law will have its own somewhat unique connotation. The same is true for equitable principles under Islamic law, Hindu law, Chinese law, and so on.

Therefore, equity under international law is distinguished from equity under any national law. As the Court has said in several cases, equity under international law is different from equity in the domestic system. The fact that the British Chancellor in the 15th century said something was an equitable principle, or that Islamic law, according to the Koran, considers something as an equitable principle, does not make it an equitable principle at international law. In a way the Eastern European bloc of states contributed to this, because they preferred to have equitable principles of international law rather than equitable principles derived from general principles. Thus the Court applies equitable principles of international law as a whole.

In British law, when the King authorized the Chancellor to apply equitable principles, people thought the sky had fallen. That is, the people trained in strict rules of Roman and ecclesiastical law were dismayed because suddenly the Chancellor simply could disregard those laws. It was revolutionary. It took time to get used to it. Once there were enough equity decisions to form patterns, they started to ossify just as had the earlier laws, to become fixed rules that themselves were inapplicable to changed circumstances. Then you have to find new equitable rules that provide an escape from the old equitable rules, just as the old equitable rules provided some escape from the Roman and canon law.

The Court has gone though this already. In the North Sea Continental Shelf Cases, the Court surprised the legal world by stating very clearly that it was going to apply equitable principles, and the only reason that the Court had to give was that it did not want to apply the equidistance principle there, because it would have been so clearly unjust in that case. The Court, in looking for a solution, did not do what it was supposed to do, namely, to apply the law. You remember the Roman principle that said the law shall be applied even if the world should perish. The Court refused to do that. It preferred to save the world by adjusting the law to the necessity of the day. This is why we are living in such interesting times. We are day by day developing international law. In every decision that comes out of the Court, even one relating to something you might not think is of great importance, there are often some fascinating things hidden. This was true, for instance, in the 1958 Case Concerning the Application of the Convention of 1902 Governing the Guardianship of Infants involving the guardianship of a child who was being taken from one country to another. The Court settled that case on the basis of a treaty, but incidentally it applied some very important equitable principles (without saying they were equitable). That is the way the law is being made.

F. Writings of Publicists[147]

The Statute of the International Court of Justice, repeating an authoritative provision that applied to its predecessor court the Permanent Court of International Justice, lists in Article 38 a subsidiary means for the determination of rules of international law: "the teachings of the most highly qualified publicists of the various nations."

People unfamiliar with international law might look at the quoted language and quickly assume that it denotes nothing more than the way American courts use treatise writers or the various restatements. Many courts will cite as "authority" for their decisions a text-writer such as

---

[147] By ANTHONY D'AMATO, excerpted from: *What Does it Mean to be an Internationalist?* 10 MICHIGAN JOURNAL OF INTERNATIONAL LAW 102 (1989). Reprinted by permission.

Prosser on Torts or Wigmore on Evidence. Even more frequently they will cite the Restatement of Contracts or the Restatement of the Foreign Relations Law of the United States. Are such citations equivalent to the way the International Court of Justice might use the teachings of publicists as a subsidiary means for determining rules of law?

There is an important and subtle difference. Wigmore's text on evidence is only as good as the case authority he uses to back it up. A Restatement of the law is only as good as its accuracy in restating black-letter rules from judicial opinions. These texts can be, and are, impeached in adversary debate by argumentation over their accuracy. In such arguments, the ultimate reference is not to the text itself, but to the cases marshaled in its support. If the text goes one way and the cases the other, the cases win.

The foregoing is a simplification. A separate factor exists that, over time, can validate a text like a Restatement. Consider a section in a Restatement that is an "advance" over present law—such as Section 90 of the First Restatement of Contracts, on "promissory estoppel." If that Section is cited (and not rejected) in judicial opinions, soon it becomes authoritative *because* it was cited in those judicial opinions. The Section then begins to live a life of its own. Indeed, this is true of any successful text. If a paragraph of Wigmore on Evidence is cited by many courts, pretty soon the paragraph itself becomes a statement of the law, and there is no need to look behind it to the original supporting case law.

Certainly an international law text can be used in the same way. One consults the book to find a general statement of an international norm; then repairs to the footnote to see what authority supports the statement. But with this similarity the resemblance to domestic legal texts ends. There is a wholly different and added meaning and use for the "teachings of publicists" in international law that is absent from domestic texts.

The difference is that in a sense an international publicist is a judge. He or she writes a book that is like an extended judicial opinion, mentally "adjudicating" thousands of international incidents and events and coming up with a consistent doctrine to explain them. These thousands of incidents that make up the stuff of customary international law are not themselves immediately available to others: digging them out requires extensive research. The research sometimes takes the publicist into materials that have hardly ever been looked at by anyone else—voluminous correspondence between foreign offices housed in diplomatic archives, old cases in forgotten library collections, newspaper reports on microfilm, and so on. Perhaps if all these materials were indexed and retrievable on computers, the status of the writings of international publicists as a source of law would diminish because there would exist accessible external verification for the claims made in texts.

But even if that material were made generally available, the status of writings of publicists in international law would only diminish to a limited extent. The writings of publicists would still be a subsidiary source of law because of the authoritativeness the publicist enjoys by virtue of having made judgments about all the raw material of international practice. Those judgments themselves are, of course, not externally verifiable. By virtue of the scholarly process of becoming absorbed in the accounts of thousands of hotly-debated incidents, events, and cases, the publicist becomes to some extent disinterested and neutral. The jigsaw puzzle of fitting all these events into coherent rules, principles, and generalizations becomes a sort of training in objectivity. And it is this objectivity that ultimately lends a status of authority to the work of the international publicist such that it can be used as a subsidiary source of international law.

To be sure, some writers never become objective. They see everything through nationalistic eyeglasses. But other scholars recognize this sort of bias, and the non-objective scholar usually does not attain a high status or general acceptance in the world community. The biased person is highly unlikely to be thought of or referred to as among the "most highly qualified publicists," in the language of Article 38.

International law, in this sense, rewards true scholarship. It bestows (wonder of wonders!) upon scholars of international law who seek the truth about their subject matter and report it as objectively as possible, an actual status of being a subsidiary source of law. A "most highly qualified publicist" is thus, in international law, not a mere commentator on the law, but an actual "source" of the law. To be sure, this source occupies the bottom rung of the ladder of sources of international law. Courts resort to it only when (a) the evidence from all the other sources cancels out, or (b) it can bolster the authoritativeness of a decision grounded upon the other sources.

G. Consensus[148]

One alleged validator of international rules is the consensus of states. We have come to know the term "consensus" as denoting that situation where a rule or policy is proposed and no one actively opposes it. Some may abstain from voting or may not be willing to endorse the group decision; so long as there is no active opposition, we can say that a consensus has been reached.

---

[148] By ANTHONY D'AMATO, excerpted from: *What Counts as Law?* in NICHOLAS G. ONUF (ED.), LAWMAKING IN THE GLOBAL COMMUNITY, 83, 99–100 (Durham N.C.: Carolina Academic Press, 1982). Reprinted by permission.

Consensus is not the same thing as a majority vote. There is no international mechanism for creating rules by majority of states through some sort of legislative process. For example, a resolution directed against South Africa in the General Assembly of the United Nations, and actively opposed by South Africa, is not in itself a rule of law by virtue of the consensus of states because of South Africa's opposition to it. Of course, the resolution might reflect already existing law, but then it would be the existing law and not the resolution that counts. As much as nations might want to transform General Assembly resolutions into law, we must acknowledge at this state of world law that one actively opposed dissenter is enough to destroy the consensus.[149]

Nearly all rules of international law at present enjoy the status of law by virtue of the consensus of states over time. We tend to regard the settled rules of international law as those rules that are not actively opposed by a state or group of states. But consensus is not a very useful mechanism for introducing new laws directly into the body of international law, because adversely affected states can express their opposition to such rules, and thereby destroy the consensus. (Opposition to *custom* does not destroy a new rule; I am only here talking about *consensus* as a mechanism.)

Where consensus really works is on the level of rule validation – the meta-level of international law. As Louis Jaffe wrote in 1933, "consent is given to international law as a system rather than to each and every relationship contained in it."[150] Where consensus is really found is in the way that norms become validated.[151] Custom is one of these validators of rules. The process of custom is itself rooted in the consensus of states and is a product of that consensus over time.

H. U.N. Resolutions

1. Legal Effect of U.N. Resolutions[152]

It is trite but no less true that the General Assembly of the United Nations lacks legislative powers. Its resolutions are not, generally speaking, binding on the States Members of the United Nations or binding in international law at large. It could hardly be otherwise. We do not have a world legislature. If we had one, hopefully it would not be composed as is the General Assembly on the basis of the unrepresentative principle of the sovereign equality of states, states which in turn are represented by governments so many of which are themselves not representative of their peoples. As the Secretary of State recently put it:

> In considering the decisionmaking process in the United Nations, it is important to bear in mind that, while the one-state, one-vote procedure for expressing the sense of the General assembly is from many points of view unsatisfactory, the incorporation of this principle in the Charter was balanced by giving the Assembly only recommendatory powers.[153]

Thus, at the San Francisco Conference on International Organization, only one state voted for a proposal that would have permitted the General Assembly to enact rules of international law that would become binding for the members of the Organization once they had been approved by a majority vote in the Security Council. A review of the authority of the General Assembly as set forth in the Charter of the United Nations demonstrates that it has the broadest powers to discuss and to recommend; not a phrase of the Charter suggests that it is empowered to enact or alter international law.

The General Assembly does, of course, have certain internal and financial powers which are binding. But, putting resolutions on such subjects aside, and despite the General Assembly's lack of legislative authority, can other resolutions of the General Assembly have effect in international law; in particular, may other resolutions – some of which are termed "Declarations" – create or change international law?

On this, opinion is sharply divided. At one pole are those who maintain that the distinctions between recommendations and binding decisions are fundamental. The General Assembly has recommendatory powers. Its recommendations may and do embrace aspects of international law, but they remain recommendations, which states are legally free to accept and implement or oppose and disregard. Those who deny that the General Assembly enacts or alters international law point out that, in fact, States Members of the United Nations often vote for much with which they actually disagree. They often go along with a consensus when their reservations are not secondary but primary. They often vote casually: their delegates may be instructed or loosely instructed; they may vote because the members of their group have decided or are disposed so to vote rather than because the immediate interests or considered views of their government so suggest. The mem-

---

149 For a fuller exposition, *see* Anthony D'Amato, *On Consensus*, 8 CANADIAN Y.B. INT'L L. 104 (1970).

150 LOUIS JAFFE, JUDICIAL ASPECTS OF FOREIGN RELATIONS 90 (1933).

151 The validation process is, of course, the subject of the present Chapter. The "rules about rules" considered in this Chapter include the operation of custom, the generation of custom by treaty, decisions of municipal courts, equity, general principles, and so forth.

152 By STEPHEN M. SCHWEBEL, excerpted from: *The Effect of Resolutions of the U.N. General Assembly on Customary International Law*, 1979 PROCEEDINGS OF THE AMERICAN SOCIETY OF INTERNATIONAL LAW 301, 301–03. Reprinted by permission.

153 The Secretary's Report To The President On Reform And Restructuring Of The U.N. System, Dept. St. Publ. 8940 (June, 1978).

bers of the General Assembly typically vote in response to political not legal considerations. They do not conceive of themselves as creating or changing international law. It normally is not their intention to affect international law but to make the point which the resolution makes. The issue often is one of image rather than international law: states will vote a given way repeatedly not because they consider that their reiterated votes are evidence of a practice accepted as law but because it is politically unpopular to vote otherwise. The U.N. General Assembly is a forum in which states can express their views; the expressed views of states undeniably may be elements of that state practice which can give rise to customary international law; but what states do is more important than what they say. It is especially more important than what they may say in General Assembly context. General Assembly resolutions are neither legislative nor sufficient to create custom, not only because the General Assembly is not authorized to legislate but also because its members, as Professor Arangio-Ruiz tellingly sums it up, don't "mean it."[154] That is to say, in fact, states often don't meaningfully support what a resolution says and they almost always do not mean that the resolution is law. This may be as true or truer in the case of unanimously adopted resolutions as in the case of majority-adopted resolutions. It may be truer still of resolutions adopted by "consensus."

I confess to much sympathy for the foregoing line of analysis, for my personal experience so fully bears it out. Perhaps, like Moliere's notable character, the representatives of the United States in the General Assembly do not know that they are speaking prose all the time, do not know that they are enunciating or evidencing practice of international law. But what I can attest is that they certainly don't know it; indeed they—and those in Washington who instruct them—constantly say that the United States can vote for this or join in a consensus for that because, after all, it is only a recommendation.

Yet the other pole of this problem also has much to be said for it. It readily acknowledges that the U.N. Charter gives the General Assembly no legislative powers. But it maintains that, in practice, many of its resolutions have had effects in and on international law; and that this practice, this broad construction of the General Assembly's powers, is now accepted and established.

This school of thought, of which Oliver Lissitzyn is an acute exponent, does not accept the contention that, in the development of customary international law, what states do necessarily is more important than what they say. According to the traditional view, it notes, customary international law is created by uniformities in the actual conduct of states if such conduct is accompanied by the conviction that it is required by international law. But it questions whether the emergence of customary international law is confined to this process of reciprocal claims and mutual tolerances. Uniformity of conduct creates expectations of continuation of the same sort of conduct. States and other international actors develop their policies and plan their actions on the basis of such expectations. There is therefore a common interest in the fulfillment of these expectations and in the stability of conduct, an interest which is translated into the doctrine that "custom" or "general practice" creates legally binding rules. But, Professor Lissitzyn maintains, "expectations may rest not only on actual conduct, but also on other forms of communication, including the verbal." He points out that this is clear in the case of treaties. He concludes that:

> Statements or declarations are not binding as treaties may also give rise to reasonable expectations. If such statements or declarations emanate from a large number of States and purport to deal with a legal matter, they may be regarded in some circumstances as indications of a general consensus amounting to a norm of international law.[155]

And accordingly, he assigns legal value to some verbal expressions of consensus by the General Assembly.

2. Discussion[156]

Mr. SCHWEBEL agreed with Professor McDougal that some General Assembly resolutions created certain expectations, but added that one should realize that these resolutions might also create false expectations as well as reasonably based ones. Hence the United States, in voting on U.N. resolutions, should vote in a manner that would indicate how the U.S. Government actually felt about an issue.

Concerning apartheid, Mr. SCHWEBEL noted that, notwithstanding U.N. resolutions, the illegality of apartheid could be demonstrated in the U.N. Charter itself. Articles 1, 55 and 56 in particular challenge the legality of apartheid, without any need for additional General Assembly resolutions.

The Chairman [ANTHONY D'AMATO] observed that Mr. Schwebel's remarks pointed up an interesting consideration for U.S. foreign policy: While the U.S. Government might find adoption of a U.N. resolution to be politically convenient at one time, what would happen if five

---

[154] Arangio-Ruiz, The Normative Role of the General Assembly of the United Nations and the Declaration of Principles of Friendly Relations, 3 RECUEIL DES COURS 431, 457 (1972).

[155] OLIVER LISSITZYN, INTERNATIONAL LAW TODAY AND TOMORROW 34–36 (1965).

[156] By STEPHEN M. SCHWEBEL and ANTHONY D'AMATO, excerpted from: Anthony D'Amato (Chair), *Contemporary Views on the Sources of International Law: The Effect of U.N. Resolutions on Emerging Legal Norms,* 1979 PROCEEDINGS OF THE AMERICAN SOCIETY OF INTERNATIONAL LAW 300, 330. Reprinted by permission.

years later the government decided that such a resolution should be rejected? How could the U.S. Government argue that it really didn't mean what it said when it cast its vote for the resolution, and therefore, it was rescinding its adherence?

Mr. SCHWEBEL answered that at times the United States tended to join a consensus on a resolution in the U.N. General Assembly without genuinely supporting important elements of legal obligation. The United States was not alone in this behavior; the whole of the West tended to react in this manner on most U.N. resolutions.

3. An Example[157]

Israel launched an air strike upon the Iraqi nuclear reactor near Baghdad on the morning of June 7, 1981. The U.N. Security Council on June 19, 1981 resolved that it "strongly condemns the military attack by Israel in clear violation of the Charter of the United Nations and the norms of international conduct."[158]

In terms of Article 2(4), Israel's attack was not a use of force against Iraq's territorial integrity or political independence. No portion of Iraq's territory was taken away; the territorial integrity of Iraq remained intact. Nor was Iraq's political independence compromised, even though its power might have been. Finally, Israel's act was not "inconsistent with the Purposes of the United Nations," in the words of Article 2(4), because one of the explicit purposes of the United Nations, found in Article 11, is "disarmament and the regulation of armaments." Nuclear proliferation constitutes one of the gravest threats to humanity. Although Israel's unilateral, military, and self-interested aerial attack that destroyed the Iraqi reactor is hardly a peaceful or desirable precedent for the purposes of nonproliferation, it is possible to surmise that the community of nations breathed a little easier after the deed was done. The destructive potential of nuclear weapons is so enormous as to call into question any and all received rules of international law regarding the transboundary use of force. Many of the old rationales for these rules no longer apply. At the same time, the shared values underlying the rules apply more emphatically than ever, for the stake is global survival.

How, then, do we interpret the Security Council's condemnatory resolution? It is often politically expedient for the international community to condemn a forceful initiative in explicit terms, yet to approve of it in fact by stopping short of reprisals against the initiator. The very resolution condemning Israel's aerial strike fell noticeably short of imposing any penalty or sanction against Israel. The lack of imposition of a sanction, penalty, or reprisal of any kind tends to support a claim that the act complained of was in fact legal.

157 By ANTHONY D'AMATO, excerpted and adapted from: *Israel's Air Strike Upon the Iraqi Nuclear Reactor,* 77 AMERICAN JOURNAL OF INTERNATIONAL LAW 584 (1983). Reprinted by permission.

158 UNSC Res. 487, reprinted in 75 AJIL 724 (1981).

I. Protests[159]

Every now and then a writer on customary law will become captivated by the neat assumption that if a state lodges a diplomatic protest against an action taken by another state, the protest operates to vitiate the power of the action to start a new rule of customary law.[160] How easy international law would be if this assumption were true!

What these writers have in mind is the following scenario. State A acts—for example, state A's coast guard turns back a fishing vessel from state B that was fishing 300 miles off A's coast. State A explains that, from now on, its exclusive fishing zone will extend 300 miles out to sea. Immediately, the international community recognizes A's act as clearly illegal under present international law. But the international community also knows that if A "gets away with it," the seeds of a new custom may be planted, a custom that would allow all coastline states to proclaim and enforce an exclusive fisheries zone extending 300 miles into the high seas.[161]

159 By ANTHONY D'AMATO, excerpted and adapted from: THE CONCEPT OF CUSTOM IN INTERNATIONAL LAW 96–102 (Cornell University Press, 1971). Reprinted with permission.

160 *See, e.g.*, Michael Akehurst, *Custom as a Source of International Law,* 47 BYIL 1, 40 (1974 75); I.C. MacGibbon, *Customary International Law and Acquiescence,* 33 BYIL 115, 131 (1957); KAROL WOLFKE, CUSTOM IN PRESENT INTERNATIONAL LAW 157–65 (1964).

161 Another fallacy on the part of some writers should be noted at this point. They assume that, by examining the merits of A's claim, we can come to some sort of determination about whether it is capable of constituting a new custom. Alas, in customary international law, the merits of a controversy—as determined by an outside observer—have nothing to do with the question whether an act is constitutive of custom. A moment's reflection will prove this point. Suppose one argues that A's action is illegal because it infringes on the high seas, which are the common heritage of all nations in the world, and therefore A does not have a meritorious claim. This argument could be stalemated by A in any number of ways. For example, A could argue that its people are on the verge of starvation, and the only way to feed them is to extend A's fisheries outward to a total of 300 miles. Otherwise, A says, highly industrialized nations with highly efficient and mechanized fishing vessels will capture nearly all the fish off A's coastline and sell it for profit to people who have a high standard of living and simply wish to have their appetites satiated by "gourmet" seafood. I believe that these arguments, on both sides, *ought* to be made in the "court of world opinion"—through the media, at

One of the first things that nation B is likely to do is to protest A's action. Nation C may also lodge a protest, because A may repeat its act against C's fishing vessels in the near future. (We could assume other similar protests by other nations) What is the effect of the protests? Let us analyze this question in light of the elements of custom that were presented earlier in this Chapter.

Does the protest by nation B and C qualify for the qualitative element of custom? Yes. The protest *articulates* A's act in the sense of stating both that A's act has legal consequences and that A's act applies to the area of international relations typically covered by international law. So, although the answer is "yes," the articulation actually works in A's favor! It helps underline the fact that A's act impacts upon international law.

Second, does the protest by nation B and C qualify for the quantitative element of custom? No. Nations B and C did not *do* anything; they merely *said* something. Customary law consists of the practice of states. A protest is not an act; it's just an expression of a state's wishes. Wishes don't make customary law, acts do.

We find, perhaps surprisingly, that the protests by B and C not only do fail to block A's act from starting a new customary norm of a 300-mile exclusive fisheries zone, but actually help reinforce A's act by "articulating" it. In this particular case, the "articulation" does not materially add to the impact of A's act upon customary law, because A had already proclaimed that it was turning away B's fishing vessel as a matter of legal entitlement. But in some cases, a protest might indeed supply the missing "articulation" element. For example, suppose A turned back B's vessel, but did not explain what it was doing, or tried to excuse its action as a mistake by its coast guard. (Sometimes, when a nation like A wants to "test the waters" of international law, it may take some initial steps and promptly disavow them – just in order to see what will be the reaction of other states.) If A said it was a mistake, and B lodged a protest, we would then wait anxiously for the next move. Suppose A, in the teeth of B's protest, proceeded to turn back other fishing vessels. In a short amount of time, it would be evident that A was not acting inadvertently, but rather was acting deliberately. In this kind of scenario, the protest by B would indeed serve to "articulate" the act by A.

Why shouldn't B's protest have a legal effect as far as the formation of custom is concerned? Suppose your government is considering the passage of a bill, and you call up your representative and protest that the pending legislation will hurt your small business enterprise. Your phone call may have an effect in dissuading your representative from her stated position in support of the bill. But surely your phone call has nothing to do with the legality of the bill itself. Either the bill passes or it doesn't; all you are doing is voicing your opinion. Similarly, in international relations, either A's act will proceed to carve out a new norm of customary law or it won't; all B and C are doing by lodging diplomatic protests is voicing their opinion in the hope to dissuade A from continuing to turn back their fishing vessels.

Now, of course, if A *is* dissuaded by the strenuous protests lodged by B, C, D, and other nations, and A *ceases* to turn back fishing vessels found within 300 miles of A's coastline, *then* the traditional customary rule that this is an area of the high seas open to all is *reinforced.* In other words, A's initial foray into attempting to create a new rule of custom, coupled with A's desisting under pressure, helps reinforce the background customary rule. A's desisting is, after all, an "act" – it is a conscious decision not to do something that A could have done and indeed did do. That non-action by A, coupled with the "articulation" found in the content of the protests lodged by B and C, is a standard way of proving a rule of customary law.

In short, the protest itself is not an "act" that impacts upon custom; it is only an articulation. But the protest, under the right circumstances, might cause the acting nation to back down. Indeed, that may be exactly what the protesting state hopes will happen.[162] If the acting state backs

the U.N., and so forth. Behind every new initiative in international relations can be found "reasons" that may or may not appeal to other countries and their citizens as justifying the initiative. But that's quite a different thing from saying that a writer on international law can assess the merits of competing claims in situations like this one. Certainly a writer on international law may argue the merits in a scholarly publication, but that argument can have nothing to do with *whether* the action of state A constitutes or does not constitute an element in the formation of a new line of customary law. The writer's argument can only be assessed as a contribution to the formation of world public opinion on the question whether nations *ought* to accept or reject A's initiative.

My point may seem obvious, but it is amazing to me how many articles I read in the journals that boil down to highly rationalized wishful thinking. The authors of these articles usually begin by repeating some random, disjointed platitudes about custom, then go on to address the merits of a particular dispute (conclusively proving that right, reason, and justice are all lodged on one side of the question), then compile some superficial linguistic support for their position from various U.N. resolutions, draft treaties, and writings (all obviously found by a word-search computer retrieval program), and then conclude that *customary international law* favors the position they have been advocating! The idea that wishful thinking and lots of footnotes can give rise to a new rule of international law is one of the notions that lead outsiders to disparage international law. No outside observer can respect a legal discipline where the operative rules arise full-blown out of the rhetoric of article writers. Sadly, the International Court of Justice, in my opinion, was guilty of exactly this kind of wishful thinking in the Nicaragua Case. It decided what norms it wanted to apply to the facts and proclaimed that those norms were norms of customary international law – without giving any supporting evidence in hard state practice to back up this proclamation. A mitigating factor is that the Nicaragua litigation was not contested by the defendant (the United States), and so the judges of the Court did not have the benefit of adversary enlightenment. Nevertheless, the judges ought to have known better. For a more complete statement of this critical view of the Nicaragua Case, *see* Section A, part 7, above in this Chapter.]

162 I say "may" because a state may issue notes of protest to cover up demands that it take forcible action, such as the American protests against British naval infringements of American neutrality between 1915 and 1927 when Germany was demanding that the United States use military force to protect its vessels from British searches and seizures.

down, then the backing-down coupled with the articulation generates custom. Everything (as far as custom-formation is concerned) depends on what A does *after* the protests are lodged.

Diplomatic protest is not the only tool that B and C have for defeating A's incipient attempt to create a new norm of a 300-mile exclusive fisheries zone. It is only the first thing that B and C can do. If it is not effective in this case, B and C can try other initiatives. They might resort to the United Nations or to a regional organization. They might attempt to retaliate against A in other ways, such as freezing A's bank accounts, charging an onerous tariff against A's exports, denying visas to A's nationals, reducing foreign economic or military aid to A or its allies or dependents, supporting a third country's hostility toward A, voting against A in the United Nations, and so forth. The vast variety of "countermeasures" open to B and C may eventually convince A to back down. On the other hand, A may eventually prevail and B and C may decide to abandon the countermeasures and accept A's initiative as forming a new rule of custom. Admittedly, in the hypothetical case I have been talking about, it would be unlikely for B and C to back down, because a 300-mile fisheries zone is such a drastic intrusion upon the regime of the high seas that we might very well expect B and C to escalate their countermeasures until the point that A has no rational choice but to back down. But there is an infinite variety of initiatives that nations may take, many of them only slight and incremental departures from prevailing customary law. The less important the departure from prevailing custom, the less likely that other states will resort to countermeasures. And thus, the inevitable "logic" of customary law proceeds: the content of custom is modified and shaped by thousands of incremental moves by states acting in every issue-area of international law. Large, radical departures from existing norms are unlikely to succeed, whereas small changes grow by accretion. The content of custom typically changes by evolution, not revolution.

With respect to any initiative, we cannot determine in advance whether it will "catch hold" and become part of custom, or be retracted and hence serve only to reinforce the prevailing rule of custom. For example, when Norway extended (only incrementally!) its exclusive coastal fishing zone in 1935, any observer would have had to wait to see whether Norway would back down in the face of repeated British diplomatic protests. But Great Britain did not succeed in getting Norway to back down. This interesting "incident" has been discussed above in this Chapter, in the section entitled "Finding Custom in an Incident." It reveals, among other things, the limited role that protest plays in customary law.

A quite different measure of the limited role that protest plays is to observe the amount of "protest activity" in international relations. If a protest could suffice as a way of blocking the formation of new custom (as the writers I cited in a footnote at the beginning of this Section claim), then we would expect the foreign offices of governments around the world to have huge staffs of people who monitor the acts of all the other governments and fire off diplomatic protests as a matter of daily routine. Instead, in a classic, definitive study of the various functions of one of these foreign offices – the office of the Legal Adviser to the U.S. Department of State – Richard Bilder made only inconsequential mention of the function of issuing diplomatic notes of protest.[163] A state cannot block the formation of custom simply by protesting those acts it disapproves. Customary law-formation doesn't work that way.

Dr. Michael Akehurst wrote a critique of my theory of protests:

> The view that protests form part of the quantitative element of State practice has been challenged by D'Amato. According to him, a protest can articulate a rule of international law, but it cannot be cited as part of the quantitative element of State practice. Consequently protests are not enough to prevent a new rule of customary law arising from other States' physical acts. The precedent-creating effect of such physical acts can only be nullified by contrary physical acts on the part of states which are aggrieved by the physical acts of other States.
>
> If D'Amato's view were accepted in practice, there would be disastrous consequences for world public order. A state which wished to prevent the formation of a rule allowing overflight of its territory by artificial satellites could no longer achieve its object by making protests; it would have "to interfere with the satellite's flight" or "retaliate in some other way against the Soviet Union unless she ceased to launch sputniks." Thus a polite difference of opinion would be converted into a major international dispute.[164]

Of course, nobody likes to convert polite differences of opinion into major international disputes. But notice the implicit assumption in Dr. Akehurst's example. He is assuming that the Soviet sputnik is a peaceful satellite (as indeed, the first Sputnik was). Suppose we change the assumption. Suppose that a nation (the Soviet Union no longer exists as such, so let's make it a generic example) launches a satellite containing hydrogen bomb warheads in sufficient quantity to destroy 90% of the United States. The very launching of such a weapons satellite would be enough to start a "major international dispute" – indeed, even the threat of launching one would start a major international dispute. In this event, a diplomatic protest is almost *too polite* a response! The United States could well be expected to interfere with the satellite's flight, or retaliate in some other significant way against the nation that launched or threatened to launch the satellite.

In short, Dr. Akehurst is mixing minor events with

---

[163] Richard Bilder, *The Office of the Legal Adviser: The State Department Lawyer and Foreign Affairs*, 56 AJIL 633 (1962).

[164] Michael Akehurst, *Custom as a Source of International Law*, 47 BYIL 1, 40 (1974–75).

major ones and jumping to the wrong conclusion in each case. If nation A makes a minor incremental initiative, a proportional reaction by nation B may or may not (as we have seen) cause nation A to back down. B's protest is just the first step to put A on notice that A should cease and desist. Or, to put action-and-reaction in proper perspective, what Dr. Akehurst should have noticed is that if A's action is minor and B's retaliation is minor, there will be no "major international dispute" – irrespective of protest! On the other hand, if A's action is major, then we already have the makings of a major international dispute – again, irrespective of protest!

In short, "protest" is at most an articulation of custom; it is not the equivalent of custom. Customary law does not proceed, and has not proceeded in the past, on the basis of what nations say. The state practice called "custom" is a function of acts (or abstentions) coupled with the articulated claim that the act or abstention is a matter of international legality.

J. The Persistent Objector: DEBATE:

1. The Persistent Objector Cannot Block General Custom[165]

The role of the dissenting State in the development of customary international law is difficult to identify. The positivists clearly held that no rule of international law could be binding on a State without its consent. Most modern theories of international law do not require that express consent be found before a rule of customary international law can be held to be binding on a State. Many authorities argue that a State can be bound by a rule of customary international law even though the State neither expressly nor tacitly consented to the rule. The Socialist States appear to require the presence of consent but permit a finding of consent based on the most indirect evidence. No authority would permit a State unilaterally to opt out of an existing rule of customary international law, and few would permit new States to choose to exempt themselves from such rules.

While the overwhelming majority of international law writers accept the persistent objector rule, support for the rule in State practice and judicial decisions is limited. The writers appear to have no difficulty reconciling their acceptance of the persistent objector rule with their rejection of the requirement that a State must consent to a rule of international law.

Brierly both accepted the persistent objector rule and rejected consent as a necessary element of customary law formation:

> The truth is that states do not regard their international legal relations as resulting from consent, except when the consent is express, and that the theory of implied consent is a fiction invented by the theorist; only certain plausibility is given to a consensual explanation of the nature of their obligations by the fact, important indeed to any consideration of the methods by which the system develops, that, in the absence of any international machinery for legislation by majority vote, a new rule of law cannot be imposed upon states merely by the will of other states.[166]

Brierly proceeded from this passage to criticize further the consensual theory of international law without any explanation of why his arguments mandating a rejection of that theory might not also require rejection of the persistent objector rule. He did not provide any examples of State practice that would support his assertion that new customs cannot be imposed on States "merely by the will of other states."

A more recent writer, Brownlie, sought to identify the basis of the persistent objector rule but did not provide a satisfying explanation:

> *The persistent objector*. The way in which, as a matter of practice, custom resolves itself into a question of special relations is illustrated further by the rule that a state may contract out of a custom in the process of formation. Evidence of objection must be clear and there is probably a presumption of acceptance which is to be rebutted. The toleration of the persistent objector is explained by the fact that ultimately custom depends on the consent of states.[167]

Brownlie justified the rule by reference to a dependence of custom on consent. But he cannot mean that custom depends upon the express consent of State since, at the same time, he declares that both passive and subsequent objectors are bound by customary law. Thus, custom must depend on the implied consent of States, but Brownlie does not disclose to us the rules that determine when consent is to be implied and when it is not. Brownlie is of the view that consent is to be implied in the absence of initial active dissent. Without more, however, the passage quoted above does not explain, but merely restates, the persistent objector rule. Many others report the existence of the persistent

---

[165] By JONATHAN I. CHARNEY, excerpted from: *The Persistent Objector Rule and the Development of Customary International Law,* 56 BRITISH YEAR BOOK OF INTERNATIONAL LAW 1, 1–2, 5–9, 16, 18–24 (1986).

[166] JAMES BRIERLY, THE LAW OF NATIONS 52 (6th ed. 1963).

[167] IAN BROWNLIE, PRINCIPLES OF PUBLIC INTERNATIONAL LAW 10–11 (3d ed. 1979).

objector rule but with little explanation and few supporting authorities.

Only D'Amato appears to reject the rule. His argument has two parts. First, he argues that the persistent objector rule is incompatible with the theory that public international law is not founded upon the specific consent of States to rules of law.[168] Secondly, he argues that the authorities cited in support of the persistent objector rule either do not support the rule in fact or are limited to situations in which a special, rather than general, rule of customary international law is relevant. He maintains that the persistent objector rule is appropriate in the case of a special custom since such a custom represents a derogation from generally applicable legal obligations by a limited group of States. To require consent in that limited circumstance would be compatible with the general jurisprudence of public international law.

D'Amato and Akehurst have engaged in a strenuous debate over whether the case authorities that appear to support the persistent objector rule involve only special customs.[169] They have focused particularly on the passage in the Fisheries case where the Court made an alternative finding that a coastline delimitation rule put forward by the United Kingdom "would appear to be inapplicable against Norway, in as much as she has always opposed any attempt to apply it to the Norwegian coast."[170] D'Amato argues that the Court was referring to a theoretical special custom of Norway and the UK forbidding the use of straight baselines. Akehurst argues that the passage addresses the general proposition that Norway's persistent objection to the 10-mile bay rule had immunized it from the obligations under the rule.

D'Amato's analysis is based on the distinction between general and special customs. The classic example of a special custom is found in the Asylum Case which also serves as an authority for the persistent objector rule.[171] In that case, Colombia alleged that Peru was bound by a Latin-American custom permitting the asylum in question. Colombia had the burden of arguing that the relevant group of States had created a special custom:

> The Party which relies on a custom of this kind must prove that this custom is established in such a manner that it has become binding on the other Party. The Colombian Government must prove that the rule invoked by it is in accordance with a constant and uniform usage practiced by the States in question, and that this usage is the expression of a right appertaining to the State granting asylum and a duty incumbent on the territorial State.

Columbia relied on evidence of practice by Latin-American States and certain international agreements in an attempt to establish this regional custom. Nevertheless, the Court concluded that no uniformity of practice had been shown sufficient to find a custom among Latin-American States and continued:

> The Court cannot therefore find that the Colombian Government has proved the existence of such a [regional or local] custom. But even if it could be supposed that such a custom existed between certain Latin-American States only, it could not be invoked against Peru which, far from having by its attitude adhered to it, has, on contrary, repudiated it.

D'Amato uses this case as the prime example of his position that the persistent objector, although bound by general customary law, is not bound by special, here regional, custom. Unfortunately, his attempt to impose this limitation on the Anglo-Norwegian fisheries case causes him to define the role of a special custom so broadly that the distinction he seeks to draw lacks significance.

In order to make the distinction between special and general custom, D'Amato has had to find the matter under discussion in the Anglo-Norwegian fisheries case to be a special custom. As the reader will recall, Norway argued that it was not bound to use the conservative baseline rules advocated by the UK. It argued that the 10-mile bay closing line rule advocated by the UK did not have the force of law and that it had a right to use its system of straight baselines. The Court held for Norway.

> [The United Kingdom] has not abandoned its contention that the ten-mile rule is to be regarded as a rule of international law. In these circumstances the Court deems it necessary to point out that although the ten-mile rule had been adopted by certain States both in their national law and in their treaties and conventions, and although certain arbitral decisions have applied it as between these States, other States have adopted a different limit. Consequently, the ten-mile rule has not acquired the authority of a general rule of international law.
>
> In any event the ten-mile rule would appear to be inapplicable as against Norway inasmuch as she has always opposed any attempt to apply it to the Norwegian coast.

D'Amato argues thus:

---

[168] ANTHONY D'AMATO, THE CONCEPT OF CUSTOM IN INTERNATIONAL LAW 261, 187095 (1971).

[169] *See* Michael Akehurst, *Custom as a Source of International Law,* 47 BYIL 1 (1974–75); Anthony D'Amato, *The Concept of Human Rights in International Law,* 82 COLUM. L. REV. 1110 (1982).

[170] 1951 ICJ Rep. 116, 131.

[171] 1950 ICJ Rep. 275.

> The Court considered the ten-mile rule both in general and in special custom. It upheld Norway on the general ground because of the division of state practice throughout the world. And it upheld Norway on the special ground because, as between Norway and Great Britain, Norway had not consented to the practice (indeed she had opposed it). Here the Court was in effect saying that Norway's delimitation of bays was not unreasonable in light of general customary practice, and therefore Great Britain could not limit Norway's rights within the ambit of reasonableness unless Norway consented to the establishment of such a special custom.

Thus, according to D'Amato, there were two grounds for the judgment, general and special custom. The first ground states that under general international law Norway was free to draw a system of straight baselines within a range of reasonableness. The second ground is dependent on the first. It provides that initially Norway had the right to draw its straight baselines unless it consented to relinquish that right in a special custom with the UK. But what was this rule that the UK had put forward? It was a general rule of customary international law that limited straight baselines to 10 mile closing lines of bays for all States. The UK did not seek to apply a special custom to Norway but rather a general rule. Thus under D'Amato's analysis any new general rule put forward by a State can be effectively denied applicability to an objecting State without further inquiry. He calls this process the denial of a special custom, but it is hard to distinguish it from the process of developing rules of general customary international law. The result in either event is that a State can resist a new rule by objecting to it at an early date.

Most writers forbear from claiming that consent is the basis for obligation under international law even though they support the persistent objector rule which permits a State to be exempt from a rule of international law by dissenting in a timely manner. It is difficult to see how the acceptance of this rule does not reflect an acceptance of the consent theory of international law. If a mere objection to an evolving rule of law can prevent application of that rule to the State, then each State has the unilateral power to decide whether or not to be bound by the rule.

When the question of consent is directly addressed, most writers argue that States do not have the free will to decide whether or not to be bound by rules of international law. The obligation to conform to rules of international law is not derived from the voluntary decision of a State to accept or reject the binding force of a rule of law. Rather, it is the societal context which motivates States to have an international law and obligates them to conform to its norms.

If it is the societal context that is the source of the obligation to conform to specific rules of international law, then consent, either express or tacit, is irrelevant to the obligation. It may also appear to follow that if the societal context is the source, then an objection at any time, persistent or not, is irrelevant to the binding effect of a rule of law. If this is true, there is no place in international law for the persistent objector rule. A similar conclusion that the rule has no place in international law is reached if one maintains that consent is the basis of obligation. In that case, a particular persistent objector rule is redundant.

Only if one actually believes in the reality of the tacit consent theory of international legal obligation might there be any room for the persistent objector rule. In that case, it is difficult to limit its application only to overt dissent commenced at the formative stages of law development. One also has to refute the powerful arguments of Kelsen and others that tacit consent is a fiction.

Akehurst focuses on this issue in his defense of the persistent objector rule. His argument is based on the premiss that no rule of international law would ever emerge from a system that requires the unanimous consent of all States to a new rule. He argues that a State must either be able to opt out of a new rule of customary international law, or the system must accept some form of majority voting. Akehurst is unable to accept that such a majority voting system exists (or is workable), because it is impossible to agree about the size of the majority necessary or the degree to which different States' votes should be weighted. Therefore, he accepts the only alternative: namely, that a State may contract out of a new rule. Given the possibility of contracting out by the persistent objector rule, no system of majority voting is required to create new norms, because "practice followed even by a small number of States can create new customary rules, provided the practice be consistent."

Akehurst's rejection of a system of majority voting, however, on which depends his conclusion that dissenting States must be allowed to opt out of developing law, does not appear to be well founded. First, despite Akehurst's assertions that "it would be impossible to reach agreement about the size of the majority required," a system of weighted majority decision-making already seems to be the basis upon which customary international law had traditionally developed. In practice, a weighted majority calculation must be undertaken to determine whether an emerging rule of customary law has attained the level of adherence necessary to qualify it as customary international law. In making these calculations the weight accorded to the behavior of particular States varies according to the power of the State and the significance of its interest in the subject-matter of the rule. It is true that one cannot precisely set out the details of how this weighted system operates, but it is not possible to deny that the system exists. Thus, contrary to the position adopted by Akehurst, the fact that States may disagree on the weight to be given particular "votes" or the size of the "majority" required does not make such a system unacceptable. If it were unacceptable, one would have to deny the legitimacy of the modern international legal system.

Secondly, a system of weighted majority decision-making should not be avoided simply because it requires the imposition of the will of the majority on minority States. To hold that States cannot be bound against their will is simply a return to the discarded consensual theory of international law. In fact, States are often bound against their will. Not only are new States, as well as passive and subsequent objectors, bound, but all States are bound by rules of jus cogens whether they presently consent to be so bound or not. If the weight and power of the majority of the international community can impose duties on States against their will in these situations, there is no reason why the persistent objector should be treated any differently.

Akehurst's defense of the persistent objector rule as a necessary safety valve for the States which are unwilling to go along with the majority also raises the question whether international law requires that States be bound by a single uniform rule. International law is clear that a single unvarying rule of behavior is rarely required. Variations are permitted, but those variations are permissible only with the consent or acquiescence of the interested States. Similarly, in the case of prescriptive rights, the State that maintains rights not included within the rule of law may obtain an exemption from the rule by way of prescription, a process which requires the international community to have acquiesced in the right that is claimed. Prior to the vesting of the prescriptive right the deviating State would be a violator of the law.

It is also well accepted that, with the exception of rules that are jus cogens, States may vary rules of international law in their bilateral and multilateral relations inter se by agreement. Even fewer than all the parties to an international agreement may enter into a special agreement under certain conditions establishing rules applicable to their relations inter se that vary the terms of the primary agreement.

All of the rules identified above have a common attribute. The State or States that seek to vary their behavior from a single uniform standard must have the consent or acquiescence of all other States to be affected by the behavior. The persistent objector rule is different. It would permit the dissenting State by unilateral act to exempt itself from a rule of law in its relations with all other States.

At this point it might be wise to conclude that regardless of one's theory of international law, the persistent objector rule has no legitimate basis in the international legal system. Not only is the rule hard to reconcile with the current theories of international law, but the evidence which might be produced to support the rule is weak indeed. This conclusion does not explain why so many reputable international law authorities explicitly report the existence of the rule. Perhaps its raison d'etre can be found in the dynamics of international law development.

While Akehurst's arguments may be wanting, he has focused on the dynamics of law development. Customary international law is not static. It changes as the patterns of State behavior change and opinio juris evolves to reflect current realities of obligation. Extant rules of law are subjected to change. Nations forge new law by breaking existing law, thereby leading the way for other nations to follow. Ultimately, new patterns of behavior and obligation develop.

In the early stages a number of States may object to the new behavior, but over time social pressures and modern realities will cause those reluctant States to conform to the new norm. On the other hand, some will seek to retain the traditional rule. The persistent objector rule becomes directly relevant when those resisting States continue to dissent from the new norm after it has replaced the old norm. At this stage the persistent objector rule promotes disharmony and discord in international relations. The international community will exert pressure to force the objector to conform to the new normative standard. As Akehurst and Fitzmaurice have pointed out, this pressure will be extreme, and few, if any, objectors will persevere to maintain their status long after the new norm becomes settled. In fact, the two International Court of Justice cases which appear to support the persistent objector rule both arise in circumstances in which the new rule itself was in substantial doubt. Thus, it was significantly easier for the objector to maintain its status. No case is cited for a circumstance in which the objector effectively maintained its status after the rule became well accepted in international law. In fact, it is unlikely that such a status could be maintained in light of the realities of the international legal system. This is certainly the plight that befell the US, the UK and Japan in the law of the sea. Their objections to expanded coastal State jurisdiction were ultimately to no avail, and they have been forced to accede to 12-mile territorial seas and 200-mile exclusive economic zones.

It appears, therefore, that the persistent objector rule, if it really exists, focuses more on the process of law development than on the status of a State under stable international law. Its utility, if any, is to provide the State which objects to the evolution of a new rule of law with a tool it may use over the short term in its direct and indirect negotiations with the proponents of a new rule. The objecting State is armed with the theoretical right to opt out of the new rule. The proponents of the new rule are, as a consequence, encouraged to accommodate the objecting State or to utilize greater power to turn the objecting State to their will. At the same time, the persistent objector rule serves to soften the threat that the force of "law" will impose a new and objectionable rule on the State that is content with the status quo. The persistent objector rule permits the objecting State to feel secure that it is not directly threatened, in an overt legal way, by changes in the law which it opposes. The legal system thereby appears to be fair and to permit an accommodation of views in the evolution of rules of law. It will be the political and social realities of the new status quo that will force the objecting State to conform to the new rule of law or the rest of the international community to accept on the basis of prescription the dissenter's unique status. It will not be a formal rule of uniform obligation that will procure conformity.

Viewed in this light, the persistent objector rule may be seen to be closely linked to the doctrine that in order to determine whether a rule of international law exists, one must examine the views and practices of the States whose interests are particularly affected. If the particularly affected States have not behaved in ways that conform to the purported rule of law, the International Court of Justice will be reluctant to hold in favor of that rule.

If any State will be the persistent objector, it will be the particularly affected State. Such a State will have interests directly at stake in the matter that is the subject of the rule of law under study. If it finds that the new rule is contrary to its interests, it will oppose the rule and will work for its rejection. As a particularly affected State, it will have leverage in determining the evolution of the applicable rule of law and will have the theoretical option of invoking the persistent objector rule. Thus both of these rules have one purpose, to force an accommodation of interests in the international community with respect to the evolution of new rules of law.

It is as such a persistent objector and particularly affected States that the US is seeking to pursue its interest in highly migratory species of tuna. While the developing law may be adverse to the US position, it is using its political and economic leverage to forge a more acceptable result. Its legal status may have some marginal value in this effort but, as in the case of the 12-mile territorial sea and the 200-mile exclusive economic zone, the law will settle and the US can be expected to abandon its positions if they do not prevail.

When the rule does settle, there may be a few States that may continue to maintain an objection to a new rule of law. If they are few, they will not be able to block a finding that the new rule represents international law. While in theory or in a court of law they may invoke the persistent objector rule, the realities of the societal pressure will require either that they conform to the new rule or that a new accommodation be reached.

In conclusion, it appears that the persistent objector rule is, at best, only of temporary or strategic value in the evolution of rules of international law. It cannot serve a permanent role, unless, of course, one really does believe that States have the independence freely to grant or withhold their consent to rules of customary international law.

2. The Persistent Objector Should Be Able to Block the Formation of General Custom[172]

I claim that the principle of the persistent objector may exempt a dissenting state from an otherwise generally applicable rule of customary international law. Professor D'Amato views the matter differently. He treats persistent objection as relevant to the constitution or opposability of local custom. D'Amato argues that since general custom does not rest on true consent, objection cannot prevent the application of a general custom to a dissenting state.[173] Local custom does rest on true consent, however, and so objection can prevent the application of a local custom to a dissenting state. Objection can also be the first step in a process by which a local custom is built up, as states in a particular region accept the modification *inter se* of the generally applicable rule.

Professor D'Amato's view does have the virtue of logical consistency. It is true that the conventional theory of customary international law seeks to appropriate the legitimizing power of consent while employing a notion of consent that is largely fictional. Logical consistency, however, may not be the most important value at stake here. According to Professor Weil, the conventional understanding of the principle of the persistent objector provides a desirable balancing element in the theory of custom.[174] It permits a state unilaterally to opt out of a rule that it cannot tolerate, whether on grounds of principle or expediency, without preventing the general application of the rule.[175] And this

---

[172] By TED L. STEIN, excerpted from: *The Approach of the Different Drummer: The Principle of the Persistent Objector in International Law,* 26 HARVARD INTERNATIONAL LAW JOURNAL 457, 476–77 (1985). Reprinted by permission.

[173] *See* ANTHONY D'AMATO, THE CONCEPT OF CUSTOM IN INTERNATIONAL LAW 252–54, 258–62 (1971). [Editor's Note: This reference is excerpted in the section entitled "Special Custom" in Chapter 5 of this Anthology.]

[174] See Prosper Weil, *Towards Relative Normativity in International Law,* 77 AJIL 413 (1983). [Editor's Note: Professor Weil's article is excerpted in the section entitled "Soft Law" in Chapter 5 of this Anthology.]

[175] [Editor's Note: The term "general application" in international law can have either of two meanings: first, it might mean "applicable to all states," and second, it might mean "applicable

unilateralism may very well be the most important virtue of the principle. The tendency to treat multilateral treaties or resolutions as sources of universally binding and generally applicable rules tends to diminish value of obtaining a dissenter's consent to a treaty and, correspondingly, the need to accommodate his interests. It is at least arguable that an order embracing the conventional understanding of the principle of the persistent objector is more likely to promote a universal law that is truly responsive to divergence. Under Professor D'Amato's approach, persistent objection is unavailing precisely where it may be most useful today, in preventing the automatic universality of what is said to be general custom. His approach, it seems to me, reduces the principle to a near cousin of the doctrine of historic rights and thus fails to recognize the unique function that it can play.

K. Jus Cogens

1. Definition.[176]

Rather close to natural law is the notion of *jus cogens*, compelling law. *Jus cogens* is a norm thought to be so fundamental that it invalidates rules consented to by states in treaties or custom. Needless to say, the very possibility of such a fundamental law is hotly controverted by positivists who rely exclusively on state consent for the making of international law. *Jus cogens* postulates an international public order potent enough to invalidate some norms that particular states might otherwise establish for themselves.

The most notable appearance of *jus cogens* is in Article 53 of the Vienna Convention on the Law of Treaties,[177] where the term, is rendered in English as "peremptory norm":

> A treaty is void if; at the time of its conclusion, it conflicts with a peremptory norm of general international law. For the purposes of the present Convention, a peremptory norm of general international law is a norm accepted and recognized by the international community of States as a whole as a norm from which no derogation is permitted and which can be modified only by a subsequent norm of general international law having the same character.

Article 64 of the Convention provides:

> If a new peremptory norm of general international law emerges, any existing treaty which is in conflict with that norm becomes void and terminates.

Although *jus cogens* is sometimes viewed as a form of customary international law, it is really of a different character. *Jus cogens* is capable of invalidating not only conflicting rules drawn from treaties, but also rules that would otherwise be part of customary international law. Thus it is a sort of international law that, once ensconced, cannot be displaced by states either in their treaties or in their practice. *Jus cogens* therefore functions rather like a natural law that is so fundamental that states, at least for the time being, cannot avoid its force.

Partly because of its perceived potency, a peremptory norm is even more difficult to prove and establish than a usually controversial rule of customary international law. In the *North Sea Continental Shelf* cases, the International Court of Justice explicitly put itself on record as not "attempting to enter into, still less pronounce upon any question of *jus cogens*."[178] There seems to be no example in modern international practice of a treaty being voided by a peremptory norm.

Nonetheless, there have been frequent assertions by states and others that certain principles of law are so fundamental as to be considered *jus cogens*. Probably the least controversial claim is that made for the basic principle, *pacta sunt servanda*, that international agreements are binding. Also well agreed upon in theory, if not so definitely in practice, are those principles in Articles 1 and 2 of the Charter of the United Nations, which guarantee the sovereignty of states. Some human rights, too, are claimed to be protected by rules of *jus cogens*.

2. Applications[179]

For good or ill, the concept of *jus cogens* has survived, at least abstractly. Even after the first waves of skepticism, this category of international law has found acceptance as

to most states." The first meaning is the normal one; it is used to distinguish "general rules of international law" (such as the rules of custom) from "particular rules of international law" (such as the rules in treaties that are binding on the parties thereto). In the sentence in the text, Professor Stein can only be interpreted to be using the second of the two meanings (because he allows a state to "opt out" of the general rule). However, two sentences later, he seems to equate "universally binding" with "generally applicable," which is the first (normal) meaning of the term in international law discourse. Two sentences after that, he appears to shift back again. It is thus possible that Professor Stein has switched from one meaning to another and back in the same paragraph without alerting the reader to that fact.]

176 By MARK W. JANIS, excerpted from: AN INTRODUCTION TO INTERNATIONAL LAW 53 (Little, Brown, 1988).

177 U.N. Doc. A/CONF.39/27 (1969),reprinted in 63 AM. J. INT'L L. 875 (1969). (This footnote was number 78 in the original text).

178 1969 I.C.J. Reports 4, 42. (This footnote was number 81 in the original text).

179 By GORDON A. CHRISTENSON, excerpted from: *The World Court and Jus Cogens,* 81 AMERICAN JOURNAL OF INTERNATIONAL LAW 93 (1987). Reprinted by permission.

a general idea. Through its work on treaties, the International Law Commission developed the concept, which most governments accepted. The American Law Institute has approved and expanded it. A peremptory norm is like a public-order imperative in municipal systems. It is used to override other less powerful norms by an external public authority, and it may not be changed except by a norm having the same quality. A *jus cogens* norm must have great staying power. When used in service of world public order, its structure ought to offer stability, at least theoretically. By structuring a justification from the presence of a superior norm to nullify or invalidate ordinary treaty or customary norms in conflict with it, the *jus cogens* category is useful to a public authority in maintaining a stable order. There are some prescriptions of international law, for example, that sovereign states may not change or agree with others to change by *jus dispositivum*: several states ought not to be able to enter a valid agreement among themselves to enslave a minority people, to use force against another state, to liquidate a race thought particularly noxious or to brutalize dissidents contrary to fundamental human rights. Similarly, a single sovereign state ought not to be free in all cases to seek a change in or a new interpretation of existing customary international law by unilateral action arguably in violation of it, even when accepting the legal consequences of a possible delict.

3. The Challenge to Sovereignty[180]

Sovereignty must be re-imagined in international legal theory for peremptory law to be "peremptory" in any sense. The guidance of international legal theory toward *jus cogens* or peremptory law has been part of an ongoing struggle to move beyond unrestricted state sovereignty (that is, to establish an international rule of law). The introduction of *jus cogens* must limit, at least partially, state sovereignty in the sense that the "general will" of the international community of states, and other actors, will take precedence over the individual wills of states to order their relations. Analyzing the sources of *jus cogens* is not a task which can be undertaken without a sustained and whole-hearted challenge to the traditional notion of sovereignty. Some members of the International Law Commission identified this challenge during deliberations on a draft treaty instrument in 1963. Mr. Pal, the Indian representative, indicated that *jus cogens* was part of a move toward the establishment of an international public order in which states could no longer view themselves as unrestricted total sovereigns. He saw an evolution, in this regard, "from an obligation discerned by the community to a more impartial view, from a simple relationship between self and 'another' to a complex relationship between self and 'others.'"[181] The nature of the relationship between "self" and "others," to borrow Mr. Pal's analysis, is the basis of *jus cogens* or universal law.

4. DEBATE

a. It's a Bird, it's a Plane, it's JUS COGENS![182]

If an International Oscar were awarded for the category of Best Norm, the winner by acclamation would surely be *jus cogens*. Who has not succumbed to its rhetorical power? Who can resist the attraction of a supernorm against which all ordinary norms of international law are mere 97-pound weaklings?

To be sure, a critic may object that *jus cogens* has no substantive content; it is merely an insubstantial image of a norm, lacking flesh and blood. Yet lack of content is far from disabling for a protean supernorm. Indeed, the sheer ephemerality of *jus cogens* is an asset, enabling any writer to christen any ordinary norm of his or her choice as a new *jus cogens* norm, thereby in one stroke investing it with magical power. Nor does there appear to be any limit to the number of norms that a writer may promote to the status of supernorm. Consider the gaggle of substantive norms, sharing in common their newly anointed *jus cogens* status, that have been collected by Karen Parker and Lyn Beth Neylon in a recent article.[183] These authors claim that the right to life is a norm of *jus cogens*, as are the prohibitions against torture and apartheid. Indeed, having attained this measure of momentum – faster than a speeding bullet – the authors end by claiming that the entire body of human rights norms are norms of *jus cogens*.

However, Ms. Parker and Ms. Neylon, perhaps in a

---

180 By MARY ELLEN TURPEL & PHILIPPE SANDS, excerpted from: *Peremptory International Law and Sovereignty: Some Questions*. 3 CONNECTICUT JOURNAL OF INTERNATIONAL LAW 364, 365–6 (1988). Reprinted by permission.

181 [1963] 2 Y.B. INT'L L. COMM'N 59, 65, U.N. Doc. A/CN.4/SER.A/1963/Add.1.

182 By ANTHONY D'AMATO, excerpted from: *It's a Bird, It's a Plane, It'sJus Cogens!*, 6 CONNECTICUT JOURNAL OF INTERNATIONAL LAW 1 (1990). Reprinted by permission.

183 Karen Parker & Lyn Beth Neylon, Jus Cogens: *Compelling the Law of Human Rights*, 12 HASTINGS INT'L & COMP. L. REV. 411 (1989).

moment of weakness, admit that "not all commentators agree that the whole of human rights law presently constitutes imperative rules of *jus cogens*."[184] They cite Rosalyn Higgins' observation that while treaties "undoubtedly contain elements" that are peremptory, that fact alone does not lead to the view that all human rights are *jus cogens*.[185] I confess to breathing a sigh of relief when Professor Higgins' down-to-earth comment was mentioned, for I had feared that the next step Ms. Parker and Ms. Neylon might take would be the investiture of every single norm of international law – not just human rights norms – with the heady status of *jus cogens*. If that had happened, we would have wound up with something perilously close to the popular caricature of German Law: "that which is not expressly prohibited is compulsory."

The long bull market in *jus cogens* stock began when Professor Grigory Tunkin proclaimed in 1974 that the Brezhnev doctrine, which he called "proletarian internationalism," is a norm of *jus cogens*.[186] Shares skyrocketed on all international exchanges when the World Court found in the Nicaragua case that the international prohibition on the use of force was "a conspicuous example of a rule of international law having the character of *jus cogens*."[187] This pronouncement should be taken in context – that of a kitchen-sink approach to the sources of international law.[188] In an expansive decision, the World Court found it just as easy to promote an ordinary norm into an imperative norm as to create out of thin air an ordinary norm. The only requirement for either of these transformative processes of legal legerdemain to be effected was the garnering of a majority vote of the judges present at The Hague.

Demonstrating slightly greater restraint than the judges were the rapporteurs of the Third Restatement of the Foreign Relations Law of the United States who conceded that "not all human rights norms are peremptory norms (*jus cogens*), but those in clauses (a) to (f) of this section are, and an international agreement that violates them is void."[189] As usual, neither the rapporteurs of the Restatement nor the judges of the *Nicaragua* case give the reader the slightest clue as to how they came to know that their favorite norms have become *jus cogens* norms.

What exactly is a norm of *jus cogens*? The Vienna Convention on the law of treaties explains, in Article 53, that "a treaty is void if, at the time of its conclusion, it conflicts with a peremptory norm of general international law." I can imagine a candidate case. Suppose a provision of a treaty of Friendship, Commerce, and Navigation permits either party to launch an unannounced preemptive nuclear strike against the other side's civilian population centers. Such a norm – if two nations would have the temerity and absurdity to include it in a treaty – would undoubtedly conflict with some peremptory norm or other, and as a consequence would be regarded as void. I join partisans of *jus cogens* in applauding the wisdom of a preemptive rule to the effect that if two nations seek the freedom to annihilate each other's population centers, they cannot validly establish their right to do so by treaty. Any subsequent attempt to *rely on the treaty* to justify such an act would surely fail to get a majority vote in any neutral court of competent jurisdiction. By extension, of course, I am arguing that when a putative treaty provision becomes so senseless that it is unimaginable that states would actually include it in a treaty (other examples being an agreement to exchange slaves or the right to torture each other's diplomats), then *jus cogens* theory springs into action to make sure that such senselessness, should it occur, would have no legal effect.

Nevertheless, at least one student of international law has expressed his dissatisfaction with confining *jus cogens* to the task of obliterating provisions in treaties. In a recent book designed to introduce students to the subject of international law, Professor Mark Janis confidently asserts that *jus cogens* also can vanquish customary law.[190] His version of the supernorm reminds us of Pac-Man, swallowing up and stamping out any and all norms that stand in its way.

The implications of the claims of Professors Tunkin and Janis are disconcerting. Assume that Professor Tunkin is correct that the Brezhnev Doctrine is a supernorm, and assume that President Gorbachev decided to repeal it. Suppose he wished to announce – as indeed he more or less announced in the wake of Afghanistan – that the Soviet Union will no longer necessarily intervene militarily in every socialist nation that has a democratic-capitalist revo-

---

[184] *Id.* at 422.

[185] *Id.* (citing Higgins, *Derogation Under Human Rights Treaties*, BRIT. Y.B. INT'L L. 282 (1976–77).

[186] G. TUNKIN, THEORY OF INTERNATIONAL LAW 444 (1974).

[187] *Military and Paramilitary Activities in and Against Nicaragua* (Nicaragua v. United States), 1986 I.C.J. 14 (Judgment on Merits of June 27). The Court was encouraged in this view by the statements of both Nicaragua and the United States, and by an earlier view of the International Law Commission. *Id.* at 100–01.

[188] Or so I have claimed in D'Amato, *Trashing Customary International Law*, 81 A.J.I.L. 101 (1987).

[189] 2 RESTATEMENT OF THE LAW (THIRD) OF THE FOREIGN RELATIONS LAW OF THE UNITED STATES 167 § 702 (1987). Clauses (a) to (f) include prohibitions against genocide, slavery, murder, torture, inhuman or degrading punishment, prolonged arbitrary detention, and systematic racial discrimination. The authors do not indicate how an *agreement* can *violate* a peremptory norm. They apparently find that merely concluding a treaty can "violate" a peremptory norm.

[190] See the excerpt from Professor Janis' book, *above* at Section K1.

lution. Would international *jus cogens* scholars object that it was illegal for Gorbachev to retract the Brezhnev Doctrine? He is after all a mere mortal who dares to divest a supernorm of its power. What good is a supernorm if a head of state can retract it at will? Thus, international scholars who champion the cause of *jus cogens* might have to assert that the Soviet Union be *compelled*, as a matter of the Brezhnev Doctrine's peremptory force in international law, to intervene militarily in other states in order to preserve proletarian internationalism. What would Professor Tunkin himself say? Perhaps as the one who bestowed *jus cogens* status on the Brezhnev Doctrine, he is the only one who is entitled to revoke it.

Professor Tunkin may indeed have anticipated the day when he might be called upon to revoke the *jus cogens* status of the Brezhnev Doctrine when he wrote, in an earlier section of his 1974 book, that "imperative principles obviously are not immutable. As all other principles and norms of general international law, they may be modified by the agreement of states, by means of treaty or custom."[191] But he did not explain to us how, if a *jus cogens* norm *invalidates* treaty provisions, a later treaty may *modify* the *jus cogens* norm itself. The whole idea of *jus cogens*, I thought, was to prohibit a later treaty from doing any such thing. Indeed, if a later treaty can simply ignore the force of the *jus cogens* norm in the first treaty, it would be like saying that Superman is stronger than any criminal in Metropolis with the exception of the next criminal who comes along who in fact is a lot stronger than Superman.

In any event, it appears that Professor Janis was not quite so prudent as Professor Tunkin. When Professor Janis converts a norm into a supernorm, even he as its author appears powerless to demote it. For Professor Janis, a norm of *jus cogens* "is a sort of international law that, once ensconced, cannot be displaced by states, either in their treaties or in their practice."[192] This is at least a forthright position. Once you've created a supernorm, monster or not, you've got to live with it. So, if Professor Janis were to include the Brezhnev Doctrine in his list of supernorms (a purely hypothetical case, of course, designed only to test his logic), he would have to disagree with Professor Tunkin and instead insist that the Soviet Union *must* continue to intervene militarily in the affairs of other states. Neither Brezhnev nor his successors could revoke the Brezhnev doctrine, under this kind of reasoning.

What shall we do with the Pandora's Box approach to supernorms taken by Professor Janis? Can't we find a little weakness in it? Isn't there some kryptonite that will sap the powers of these invincible supernorms? The Vienna Convention on the Law of Treaties made an attempt along these lines. It provides that a norm of *jus cogens* "can be modified only by a subsequent norm of general international law having the same character." At least this introduces a second, competing Pac-Man—one supernorm can be swallowed by a subsequent one. But the drafters of the Convention failed to tell us how such a subsequent norm can itself arise. Perhaps that is no serious omission; after all, they did not tell us how the initial peremptory norm arose, so they should not be faulted for failure to reveal the origins of subsequent norms. But conceding that much to the drafters of the Vienna Convention, would it not be the case that as soon as one of their subsequent peremptory norms starts to arise and attempts to "modify" a previous supernorm, the existing supernorm will do a reverse flip and stomp out the oncoming norm? After all, it is only normal to expect that any established supernorm will be on the lookout for incipient competitive supernorms, turn sharply upon them as soon as they get close, and rub them out.

We seem to be left with two polar positions. On one side, represented by Professor Tunkin, is the idea of a norm of *jus cogens* that can be modified by *any* subsequent norm, conventional or customary. One the other extreme, represented by Professor Janis, is the idea of a norm of *jus cogens* that can *not* be modified by any subsequent norm. These polar opposites thus seem to represent Too Cold and Too Hot. Professor Tunkin's view is Too Cold, because it says in effect that a norm of *jus cogens* is exactly like any other norm; it is imperative so long as it remains in place, but loses its imperativeness whenever it is modified or changed by any other subsequent norm. Professor Janis' view is Too Hot, because once the supernorm arises, there is nothing any group of states or group of persons can ever do to replace it or even whittle it down to size. If the wrong one gets invented, watch out! (And since we are talking about *international* law, there will be no safe haven in which to obtain asylum against the supernorm).

What we require, like the third bowl of soup in the story of the three bears, is a theory of *jus cogens* that is Just Right. I do not know if such a theory is possible. I don't even know if one is conceivable. But if someone conceives it, that person deserves the very next International Oscar. To qualify for the award, the theory must answer the following questions:

(1) What is the utility of a norm of *jus cogens* (apart from its rhetorical value as a sort of exclamation point)?

(2) How does a purported norm of *jus cogens* arise?

(3) Once one arises, how can international law change it or get rid of it?

[191] Tunkin, *supra*, n.186 at 159.

[192] Janis, *supra*, n.176 at 54.

With all that has been written about *jus cogens*, these would appear to be rather elementary questions. I await their answers with keen interest, though I have no current plans to rent a formal outfit for the award ceremony.

b. The Reality of Jus Cogens[193]

In a delightful read on *jus cogens*, Professor Tony D'Amato has "thingified" *jus cogens* as the Superman of norms, if only to question the power of such an heroic creation. He applauds "the wisdom of preemptive rule," speculates about certain examples, and provides an I-know-it-when-it's-senseless-or-unimaginable test. It should provide guidance for all who happen to think like those who use the test. Actually, he has made a telling point, however indirectly, and has provided insight into the answer to the second of his three searching questions: "how does a purported norm of *jus cogens* arise?"

The answer to his first question, which concerns the utility of a norm of *jus cogens*, is that such a norm preempts others of a lesser sort, be they treaty or custom based. The answer to his second question (noted above) about the birth of such a norm is implicit in his speculations regarding certain examples. When Professor D'Amato recognizes that some contradictory practices "would undoubtedly conflict," "would be regarded as void," "would surely fail to get a majority vote," would be "senseless" or "unimaginable," he has come close to the touchstone of any norm's validity and to its ultimate source. Indeed, he has also come close to the answer to his third question: once such a norm arises, can it change or even pass away? The patterns which he seeks are evident, not in some superhero or in some fictitious child's soup, but in patterns of expectation generally shared by real (ordinary and extraordinary) human beings in the real world.

Jus cogens is a form of customary international law.[194] It may be reflected also in treaties but, as custom, it is subject to birth, growth, other change, and death, depending upon patterns of expectation and behavior that are recognizably generally conjoined in the ongoing social process. As one form of custom, *jus cogens* norms have, of course, at least the full power and authority of any customary norm, and when identifying or clarifying a norm of *jus cogens* one should consider the degree and intensity of general acceptance or patterns of expectation and how intensely held or demanded a particular norm is within the community. Yet *jus cogens* norms have an extra feature—unlike custom in general, it must be generally expected that such norms *are* peremptory.

Professor D'Amato knows that textwriters and the International Court of Justice among others, expect that certain norms are peremptory. And rather nervously he accepts the preemptive nature of certain norms.[195] He finds "disconcerting," however, the view of Professor Mark Janis "that *jus cogens* also can vanquish customary law" as opposed to treaties. Yet there need be nothing disconcerting about the fact that a peremptory norm, itself a form of custom, can prevail in a clash with a more ordinary norm of customary international law. Again, a feature of *jus cogens* norms is that they are generally expected to be supreme, and that is how they operate if they are effective.

Thus, Tunkin is correct in stating that "imperative principles obviously are not immutable. As all other principles and norms of general international law, they may be modified." Moreover, they can be modified by changing patterns of expectation and behavior, some of which may be reflected in or conditioned through time by treaties. It is not the norm of custom, thingified, or the treaty, thingified, which modifies (at least directly), but rather the patterns of expectation and relevant behavior which underlie and reach previously identifiable peremptory norms. Actually, more directly, it is you and I who modify any form of human law or, if we prefer, assure its unchanged content. *Jus cogens*, literally, is what we make of it.

In this sense, I agree with Professor D'Amato's criticism of the naturalist-orientated view of Professor Janis that *jus cogens* norms are necessarily continuous and are "really of a different character" than custom. No human law is likely to be so eternal or so certain a guarantee to save us from ourselves. Yet knowing this, one can understand the actual strength of customary *jus cogens* and recognize that those who make claims about the inclusion of certain norms into the matrix of peremptory norms are actually participating in an effort to shape attitudes and, perhaps, human behavior.

---

[193] By JORDAN PAUST, excerpted from: *The Reality of Jus Cogens*, 7 *Connecticut Journal of International Law* 81 (1991). Reprinted by permission.

[194] *See, e.g.*, IAN BROWNLIE, PRINCIPLES OF PUBLIC INTERNATIONAL LAW 513 (3d ed. 1979) (referring to jus cogens as "rules of customary law"); ANTHONY D'AMATO, THE CONCEPT OF CUSTOM IN INTERNATIONAL LAW 111, 132 n.73 (1971) (claiming that it "should be possible to argue that a rule of jus cogens simply means a very strong rule of customary international law"). *See also* Ralph G. Steinhardt, *The Role of International Law As a Canon of Domestic Statutory Construction*, 43 VAND. L. REV. 1103, 1180 (1990) (discussing jus cogens as distinguished from nonperemptory, "merely customary" norms).

[195] *See* ANTHONY D'AMATO, INTERNATIONAL LAW: PROCESS AND PROSPECT 128–29 (1987); Jordan J. Paust, *Congress and Genocide: They're Not Going to Get Away With It*, 11 MICH. J. INT'L L. 90, 93 n.3 (1989).

5

Sources of Particular International Law

A. Treaties

1. Treaty Interpretation[1]

The defining issue in both legal and literary interpretation can be characterized as follows: to what extent does the text have a determinate meaning, and to what extent is the reader free to interpret it as he or she chooses? This question is especially relevant to treaty interpretation where, more often than not, the contracting parties themselves have the final say about the meaning of particular provisions of the agreement in question (a phenomenon that can be labelled "auto-interpretation"). Because many international instruments do not provide for the submission of disputes to impartial tribunals, interpretation is a responsibility of domestic officials who are institutionally predisposed to interpretations preferred by their State and government.

Skepticism about the determinacy of meaning combined with the absence of an impartial interpreter can lead to the discomforting conclusion that treaty auto-interpretation is an unconstrained activity determined entirely by short-term national interests and power politics. In this article, I seek to counter that perception by positing the existence of a structure of constraints embedded in the process of treaty interpretation despite the absence of a disinterested interpreter. Interpretive authority, it will be argued, resides in neither the text nor the reader individually, but with the community of professionals engaged in the enterprise of treaty interpretation and implementation. This "interpretive community" is defined and constituted by a set of conventions and institutional practices that structure the interpretive process.

Of primary importance is the notion that treaties, unlike works of literature, embody a commitment to a distinctive process of interpretation. This commitment is rooted in the fact that a treaty is the product of the consensual activity of two or more States, and its terms embody the collective expectations and interests of the parties. Because the parties to the treaty comprise the collective norm-creating body, the competence of authoritative interpretation is vested in the composite organ they form rather than either of them individually. If the treaty does not provide for a dispute resolution procedure, then an authoritative interpretation can only result from a process that embodies this notion of the parties as a composite law-making entity in some other way. In entering into a treaty, a State binds itself not only to the terms of the instrument (however interpreted) but also a process of intersubjective interpretation: the interpretive task is to ascertain what the text means to the parties collectively rather than to each individually. The activities and perspectives of the interpretive communities associated with this enterprise render treaty auto-interpretation something other than the exercise of unilateral political will.

The interpretive process, then, must be understood as part of an ongoing relationship in which the parties generate, elaborate and refine shared understandings and expectations. McDougal, Lasswell and Miller describe the aim of interpretation as follows:

> It is to discover the shared expectations that the parties to the relevant communication succeeded in creating in each other. It would be an act of distortion on behalf of one party against another to ascertain and to give effect to his version of a supposed agreement if investigation shows that the expectations of this party were not matched by the expectations of the other.[2]

The authors were mainly concerned with articulating a theory of interpretation that international tribunals could adopt in interpreting treaties, and it must be refined in the context of auto-interpretation. The argument being presented in this article is that, in entering into a treaty, the parties assent not only to the terms of the agreement but also to a process of interpretation whose goal is an intersubjective understanding of the treaty terms. In Stanley Fish's terminology, the parties create an "interpretive community."[3] The interpretive task is to "uncover together" the

---

[1] By IAN JOHNSTONE, excerpted from: *Treaty Interpretation: The Authority of Interpretive Communities*, 12 MICHIGAN JOURNAL OF INTERNATIONAL LAW 371–72, 380–82, 385–91, 418–19 (1991). Reprinted by permission.

[2] MYRES McDOUGAL, H. LASSWELL, & J. MILLER, THE INTERPRETATION OF AGREEMENTS AND WORLD PUBLIC ORDER: PRINCIPLES OF CONTENT AND PROCEDURE xvi (1967).

[3] STANLEY FISH, IS THERE A TEXT IN THIS CLASS? THE AUTHORITY OF INTERPRETIVE COMMUNITIES (1980).

meaning of the treaty; while auto-interpretation is carried on by individual participants, the process is essentially interactive. Intersubjective interpretation is not simply a matter of finding the points agreement between the parties; it is to engage in a collectively meaningful activity, in an activity collectively understood.

The parties can be viewed as having implicitly agreed to a process of intersubjective interpretation because, while they expect disagreement over the meaning of terms, they do not expect every disagreement to signify a desire on the part of one or the other to revoke the treaty or terminate the relationship embodied in it. States comply with treaties primarily because they have an interest in reciprocal compliance by the other party or parties. Reciprocity is particularly important to security-related agreements because the parties' mutual interest in preserving them extends beyond the perceived advantages of the treaties themselves. Security relations in the nuclear age thrust every nation into a continuing relationship with every other nation, a relationship that outlives particular agreements.[4] Thus, decisionmakers in each State are conscious of the effects of their immediate actions on future relations. Arms control treaties and other security-related arrangements are important events in the overall relationship, but not the complete embodiment of it. It is precisely because they are situated within a broader relationship that such agreements exist and are complied with even in the absence of enforcement mechanisms.

In understanding how treaty auto-interpretation is constrained, two interpretive communities can be identified: the community interpreters directly responsible for the conclusion and implementation of a particular treaty, and a broader, international community consisting of all experts and officials engaged in the various professional activities associated with treaty practice. The conventions and institutional practices of both interpretive communities have constraining effect, although the contribution of the latter is derivative in that its authority can be traced to the implicit agreement between the parties to engage in intersubjective interpretation.

1. *The Narrow Interpretative Community.* The exercise of formulating, negotiating, ratifying, and implementing a treaty generates an interpretive community of individuals within each contracting party who share what Fish calls "assumed distinctions, categories of understanding, and stipulations of relevance and irrelevance."[5] That is, the process of producing and living under a treaty generates a community (not out of whole cloth but out of already existing communities with an elaborate web of relationships to the new community) of people and institutions associated with the treaty. These people are the officials within each State (from the leader down) who have or had responsibility for any of the various steps involved in producing the treaty.

The constraining effect of this narrow interpretive community is felt, in part, though the expectations and beliefs controlled by the agreement. In the period prior to the making of an agreement, some sort of relationship exists (or the agreement would not have been possible) that generates a body of knowledge shared by the parties. Officials within each State learn about the others' interests, values and assumptions, as well as their perspectives on the various components of the relationship. An agreement "crystallizes the learning of a particular period"[6] and the contacts made help spread common understandings about the precise terms of the agreement as well as its significance to the broader relationship. The agreement becomes a focal point around which expectations converge. Furthermore, by communicating and exchanging information the governments come to *know* their partners in the agreement and not merely *know about* them. The participants in the enterprise come to inhabit a common world – a world that does not simply come out of the shared beliefs and attitudes of it inhabitants but in fact generates those beliefs and attitudes through common participation.

Subjective interpretation is constrained, both in terms of interpretations that are actually proffered and those that become authoritative, not by external rules of interpretation but by the existence of a relatively unified interpretive community. When disputes over the meaning of the text do arise, members of the community operate within a common frame of reference as to how the dispute should be resolve. Furthermore, the members share a predisposition toward arriving at a mutually acceptable interpretation. Agreement is far from automotive, because many words (and the rules, principles, purposes and policies they convey) are ambiguous and manipulable, and the interests of the parties will remain, in some respects, divergent. But the criterion of mutual acceptability sets an outer limit on the extent to which they can be manipulated. The limit is not a rule of interpretation but a convention of the enterprise. The parties can argue with one another about the meaning of words, but the mere fact that they argue with one another (and not only within domestic constituencies) reflects their continuing commitment to the relationship. The debate is constrained because governments are impelled to justify their positions on grounds other than national self-interest. Otherwise their arguments would not be persuasive to others nor accepted by members of the relevant interpretive

---

[4] *See* RICHARD BILDER, MANAGING THE RISKS OF INTERNATIONAL AGREEMENT 11 (1981).

[5] STANLEY FISH, DOING WHAT COMES NATURALLY 141 (1989).

[6] Nye, *Nuclear Learning and U.S.-Soviet Security Regimes,* 41 INT'L ORG. 371, 398 (1987).

communities. The outer limit of an acceptable interpretation is not determined according to transcendent standards but according to the shared standards and expectations of the relevant community.

The process differs from negotiation in that the parties operate within an institutional and intellectual framework already in place, a framework they have implicitly agreed to respect. Failure to respect that framework represents something more serious than a decision not to agree on the specific terms of the relationship embodied in the treaty—it represents a breakdown of the relationship. Obviously, the constraint is not absolute, because, as indicated above, sovereign States can withdraw from the relationship if they perceive that it is in their interest to do so. But the constraint on interpretation does exist insofar as certain interpretive activities and positions will be regarded as inconsistent with the enterprise in which the text and interpreter are situated. States may be able to abrogate a treaty but, as long as the relationship embodied in the treaty continues to exist, the constraints of treaty practice (of being in a relationship) limit interpretive discretion.

The conventions of the enterprise operate within the interpretive community not only through expectations and beliefs, but also at the institutional level. For example, in addition to creating international obligations, a treaty acts as an internal directive guiding bureaucratic behavior. Bureaucracies are notoriously status quo oriented; caution rather than creativity and risk-taking characterizes bureaucratic behavior. Violation of an international agreement is not among the options that would typically be suggested by low-level officials when decisions are being made within bureaucracies. Furthermore, a treaty inhibits not only conduct that is clearly prohibited by its terms, but also activities falling within the doubtful zone. Low-level officials do not normally have an incentive to take responsibility for an action that may become the basis for a charge of treaty violation. Of course high-level officials are not inhibited in this way and the top leadership sets goals priorities and policies. However, subordinates influence policy by providing information which effectively defines the situation for superiors. The information provided by these low-level officials is a product of the climate of opinion that arose from process of negotiating and ratifying the treaty. This climate of opinion pervades the environment within which all political and bureaucratic actors must function. It is not easily overridden and thus the actors must, in some measure, either adapt to the climate of opinion or reject it with serious consequences. In this way, the interpretive community that crystallizes around a treaty perpetuates itself. The decision to break a treaty or withdraw from it will occur at the highest levels, but interpretation is shaped by the underlying bureaucratic and organizational structure of less-than-monolithic government.

2. *The Broader Interpretive Community.* Beyond the immediate interpretive community centered around the treaty itself, interpretation is constrained by an amorphous community of all those regarded as possessing the knowledge of an expert or professional in the relevant field. As Oscar Schachter explains, governments cannot escape legal appraisals of their conduct by other governments (expressed either individually or in collective bodies), political parties, international lawyers, non-governmental organizations and other organs of public opinion.[7] In the realm of military security, this community judgment is influenced by the opinions of governmental and non-governmental experts on international law, world politics and strategic affairs. The competency or expertise comes from training and immersion in some feature of the enterprise in which the experts and immersion in some feature of the enterprise in which the experts are engaged. As participants in the field of practice, they have come to understand its purposes and conventions, learned not merely as a set of abstract rules but through the acquisition of know-how, a mastering of the discipline or technique. Having participated in the techniques and discourse of international law, treaty interpretation and/or the subject matter of the treaty, they have become competent in the field.

The outlying interpretive community represents the institutional mechanism closest to an impartial arbiter that the structure of treaty auto-interpretation provides. It constrains interpretation primarily because States have an interest in maintaining a reputation for good faith adherence to treaties. As Henkin states:

> Every nation's foreign policy depends substantially on its "credit"—on maintaining the expectation that it will live up to international mores and obligations. Considerations of "honor," "prestige," "leadership," "influence," "reputation," which figure prominently in governmental decisions, often weigh in favor of observing law. Nations generally desire a reputation for principled behavior, for propriety and respectability.[8]

This interest combined with the implicit agreement between the parties to engage in intersubjective interpretation means the outlying interpretive community effectively checks and structures the interpretive activities of the parties. An interpretation put forward by an official agent does not acquire authoritative status by that fact alone. Rather, it works as a signal within an interpretive system or "mechanism for the endless negotiation of what will be authorized

---

[7] Oscar Schachter, *Self-Defense and the Rule of Law*, 83 A.J.I.L. 259, 264 (1989).

[8] Louis Henkin, How Nations Behave: Law and Foreign Policy 52 (2d ed. 1979).

or nonauthorized.''[9] It is evaluated by the outlying community and judged in terms of its conformity with the conventions and purposes of the enterprise. In this way, the international interpretive community monitors the parties and provides indirect reassurance to each that the other or others will not engage in subjective interpretation. The influence of this community is felt directly in terms of explicit evaluations of the appropriateness of a particular interpretation and indirectly in the way States measure their own interpretations against anticipated judgment of the international community. Because all States have a stake in maintaining a reputation for good faith compliance with treaty commitments, they will hesitate before publicly announcing a construction likely to be branded as improper or far-fetched. Of course, they may elect to do so,[10] but that only signifies that constraint is not absolute: it does not count as an argument against the existence of a constraint.

Now that the Cold War is over and international affairs, in all probability, will no longer be dominated by superpower conflict, a new era of collective security and international law may be upon us. Future disputes, more than in the recent past, will be disputes over the meaning of legal texts and legal norms. There will continue to be much room for argument, but the form the arguments take will be constrained by the distinctive purposes and practices of the legal enterprise. The existence of a legal text or norm is evidence of a commitment to the relationship embodied therein. The relationship represents, on one level, a set of shared understandings about the terms of the relationship. But the generalized character of words and the elusiveness of meaning indicate that the commitment is and must be something more than an agreement to abide by substantive rules of behavior. It is also a commitment to a process of constructing the meaning of the relationship together.

There are, however, limits to the influence of interpretive communities within the existing international legal system. Many if not most international legal disputes (like domestic legal disputes) turn on facts as opposed to law. Yet access to these facts is much more restricted than access to the legal materials. Thus, while members of a community can often be counted on to interpret a legal norm (written or unwritten) in common, such communities rarely exist when it comes to factual assessments. To the extent that the ''facts'' of international life are not self-evident, what actually happened is less important than what relevant legal authorities think (or say) happened. If the relevant authority is the interpretive community, as I have argued, then the facts that count are those upon which there is consensus among members of the community. While interpretive communities perform the task of authoritative interpretation admirably, their capacity to identify and evaluate relevant facts is much more restricted. The facts that surface in international disputes do so through an imperfect process, dominated by the selective revelations of national governments. Thus, perhaps the most important lesson for the international legal system to be learned from this examination of the role of interpretive communities is the need for new institutions and procedures, not for authoritative legal interpretation, but for fact-finding and fact-assessment.

[9] STANLEY FISH, IS THERE A TEXT IN THIS CLASS? THE AUTHORITY OF INTERPRETIVE COMMUNITIES 357 (1980).

[10] [Editor's Note: See the discussion of whether the U.S.-Mexico Extradition Treaty was violated in Chapter 8 (section on ''Abduction'') and Chapter 16 (section on ''Domestication'' of International Law''), in this Anthology.]

2. Rebus Sic Stantibus[11]

According to a widespread opinion, a treaty ceases to be valid as the effect of a vital change of circumstances; or, as this principle is usually formulated, according to the clausula rebus sic stantibus (''Clause concerning vital change of circumstances''). In order to justify the principle that a contracting party to a treaty can withdraw unilaterally from the treaty or, what amounts to the same, declare that it considers itself no longer bound by the treaty if the circumstances under which it has concluded the treaty or adhered to it have essentially changed, some writers maintain that if the change of circumstances is so essential that compliance with the treaty could impair the very existence of the state, the latter cannot be considered as bound by the treaty. Its fundamental right to existence is stronger than its obligation under the rule pacta sunt sevanda. They sometimes refer to the fact that the principle in question is recognized by many national legal orders which permit a person to cancel a contract for the reason that the circumstances under which it has been concluded have essentially changed.

But there exists an important difference between the clausula rebus sic stantibus as part of national law and the same principle as part of international law. Under national law an objective and impartial authority is established to decide the questions as to whether a vital change of circumstances has taken place, whereas under general international law the parties to the treaty are themselves competent to decide this question. The most serious argument against the doctrine that, according to a rule of international law, a treaty loses it validity when the circumstances under which it had been concluded have essentially changed, is

[11] By HANS KELSEN, excerpted from: PRINCIPLES OF INTERNATIONAL LAW 358–60 (1952). Reprinted by permission.

this: that it is the function of the law in general and treaties in particular to stabilize the legal relations between states in the stream of changing circumstances. If circumstances did not change, the binding force conferred upon treaties by the law would be almost superfluous. The clausula rebus sic stantibus is in opposition to one of the most important purposes of the international legal order, its purpose of stabilizing international relations.

As a matter of fact, it is hardly possible to prove that the clausula is part of positive international law. When in 1870 Russia tried to withdraw unilaterally from the Treaty of Paris of 1856, which imposed upon Russia the obligation not to maintain a fleet in the Black Sea, the parties to the Treaty of Paris in a conference held at London in 1871 adopted the following declaration: "It is an essential principle of international law that no power can free itself from obligations imposed upon it by a treaty or modify its terms, except with the consent of the contracting parties by means of an amicable agreement." This is an open rejection of the clausula rebus sic stantibus. The relatively few cases in which states have referred to essential change of circumstances to justify their noncompliance with treaty obligations may be interpreted simply as violations of international law rather than as evidence of the clausula rebus sic stantibus as a rule of positive international law.

3. Reservations

a. Multilateral Conventions

(1) Background[12]

In 1950, when the European Convention on Human Rights was drafted and ratified, European authors generally adopted a contract view of treaties. Any reservation made by a State at the time of its ratification or accession to a multilateral treaty, therefore, amounted to a counter-offer rather than an acceptance. Ratifications with reservations, according to this approach, required the unanimous consent of all the other parties. The counter-offer had to be accepted. That is, all the parties had to assent to the reservation or else the ratification or accession of the reserving State amounted to a nullity. One State party accordingly could object to the reservation and prevent the reserving State from becoming a party to the treaty. This rule of unanimous consent meticulously preserved the integrity of the treaty text, but at the price of discouraging its wider application.

In the next year, 1951, the International Court of Justice held that the unanimous consent rule had not achieved the status of a rule of international law. In response to a request from the United Nations General Assembly, the Court issued an advisory opinion on the law of reservations as it applied to the Convention on the Prevention and Punishment of Genocide.

The Court's majority framed the principal issue as

> whether a contracting State which has made a reservation can, while still maintaining it, be regarded as being a party to the Convention, when there is a divergence of views between the contracting parties concerning this reservation, some accepting the reservation, others refusing to accept it.

The Court acknowledged the general principles that a State cannot be bound by a treaty without its consent, and likewise that no reservation can be effective against it without its agreement. It also recognized the contractual nature of multilateral conventions, which the parties cannot frustrate by unilateral measures. Notwithstanding these general principles, the Court observed that the universal and humanitarian character of the Genocide Convention merited "a more flexible application.

The Court noted that the desire for a wide degree of participation in multilateral conventions had led to a more liberal resort to reservations, even to the point of regarding as parties to conventions States whose reservations had been objected to by other parties. Whether these flexible principles applied to a given convention depended on that convention's purpose and provisions. According to the Court, the Genocide Convention condemned crimes against humanity and embraced principles binding on States even absent any conventional obligations. The Convention also called for universal cooperation in combating genocide. Thus it justified a more flexible approach to reservations to the treaty. Especially in the case of such multilateral humanitarian conventions, the Court wrote, the contracting States have only a single common interest, and "cannot speak of individual advantages or disadvantages to States, or of the maintenance of perfect contractual balance between rights and duties."[13] The exclusion of one or more States from the Convention because of objections to their reservations would restrict the scope of its application and detract from its moral authority.

The Court therefore constructed a new test for determining when a reservation to a humanitarian treaty bars the

---

[12] By HENRY J. BOURGUIGNON, excerpted from: *The Belios Case: New Light on Reservations to Multilateral Treaties*, 29 VIRGINIA JOURNAL OF INTERNATIONAL LAW 347, 350–55 (1989). Reprinted by permission.

[13] *Reservations to the Convention on the Prevention and Punishment of the Crime of Genocide*, 1951 ICJ 15, 23 (Advisory Opinion of May 28, 1951).

reserving State from participation in the treaty:

> It follows that it is the compatibility of a reservation with the object and purpose of the Convention that must furnish the criterion for the attitude of a State in making the reservation on accession as well as for the appraisal by a State in objecting to the reservation.[14]

Thus at least in the case of multilateral humanitarian conventions such as the Genocide Convention (or the European Convention), a reserving party remains a party so long as its reservation, even if objected to by some of the other parties, is compatible with the convention's object and purpose. The appraisal of a reservation and the effect of objections to it, then, would depend not on a general rule but on the circumstances of a particular case. The Court indicated that States should appraise the validity of reservations by the compatibility criterion. If a State did object, it would not be bound by the reservation, but under the flexible principles its objection would affect only the relationship between the reserving and objecting States, and would not exclude the reserving State from the convention. Multilateral treaties therefore took on the appearance of a matrix of slightly varying bilateral treaties.

In the decade and a half following the Genocide Convention case, the International Law Commission struggled with the problem of reservations. Over the course of the debates, the more flexible system of reservations suggested by the Genocide Convention opinion and followed in inter-American practice was eventually accepted by the Commission. Ultimately in 1969 this more flexible system became the core of the clauses on reservations in the Vienna Convention on the Law of Treaties.

The Vienna Convention sets forth as a general rule the right of States to make reservations to treaties, except in three circumstances:

> (a) the reservation is prohibited by the treaty;
>
> (b) the treaty provides that only specified reservations, which do not include the reservation in question, may be made; or
>
> (c) in cases not falling under sub-paragraphs (a) and (b), the reservation is incompatible with the object and purpose of the treaty.[15]

By this last condition the Vienna Convention thus adopted the compatibility test set forth in the Genocide Convention opinion. The International Court in that case had limited the test to multilateral humanitarian conventions, but the Vienna Convention adopted it as the test for treaties in general.

With regard to the acceptance of and objection to reservations, the Convention constructs a more elaborate framework. Generally, acceptance of a reservation by another contracting State constitutes the reserving State as a party to the treaty in relation to that other State; acceptance is considered tacit if no objection is raised within twelve months.[16] The reservation modifies the relevant provisions of the treaty for both the reserving and accepting State with regard to each other; it does not modify the treaty among the other parties.[17]

(2) A Stricter Rule[18]

At first sight it might be thought that, as no state is obliged to sign any convention unless it wishes to do so, any state is entitled to accept as much or as little of a convention as it may think fit, and is therefore in a position to make any reservations which it considers desirable, irrespective of the views of the other contracting parties and without obtaining their consent. But such a view is not, it is suggested, consistent with sound principle. Multilateral conventions are after all only a form of contract in which the consideration for the acceptance of the contract by any one party is its acceptance by the others. In all conventions of this nature there are probably provisions which do not appeal much to certain signatories but which they are prepared to accept as a return for securing the acceptance of other provisions, to which they attach importance, by the other parties to the convention. If, however, any party is entitled, without the consent of the other signatories, to pick out of the convention any provisions to which it objects and exclude them by means of a reservation from the obligations which it accepts, it is obvious, not only that the object of the convention might be largely defeated, but that the consideration indicated above is impaired or even destroyed; the other signatories are not in fact getting what they bargained for. It would seem, therefore, that in principle a party to a convention is only entitled to make such reservations as the other parties are content that it should make, in which case the offer of the party concerned to accept the convention without these provisions is accepted by the other parties as a sufficient consideration for their

---

[14] *Id.* at 24.

[15] *Vienna Convention on the Law of Treaties, May 23, 1969,* 1155 U.N.R.A. 331, reprinted in BURNS H. WESTON, R.A. FALK, & A. D'AMATO, BASIC DOCUMENTS IN INTERNATIONAL LAW AND WORLD ORDER 93 (2d ed. 1990).

[16] *Id.* art. 20(5).

[17] *Id.* art. 21(1), (2).

[18] By H. W. MALKIN, excerpted from: *Reservations to Multilateral Conventions,* 7 BRITISH YEARBOOK OF INTERNATIONAL LAW 141 (1926). Reprinted by permission.

acceptance of the convention as a whole. Or it may well be that most, if not all of the signatories have reservations which they desire to make, in which case the acceptance by each party of the reservations of the others may be regarded as the consideration for their acceptance of its own.

(3) The Tyranny of Labels[19]

The three major classifications of treaty-qualifying unilateral statements are reservations, understandings, and declarations. A reservation is a formal declaration made by a state when it joins a treaty, a declaration that acts to limit or modify the effect of the treaty in application to the reserving state. A reservation is external to the text of the treaty and is an attempt to alter the negotiated package. Because reservations are made outside of the treaty negotiations, their amendment to the multilateral treaty may conflict with the original text of the treaty. The ultimate effect of the reservation will depend on the practice or rule of reservations applied and the existence or nonexistence of special provisions within the treaty governing inclusion and effect of reservations.

The term "understanding" is used to designate a statement not intended to alter or limit the effect of the treaty, but rather to set forth a state's interpretation or explanation of a treaty provision. In practice, understandings are sometimes used to provide a memorandum of the nation's interpretation at the time of signing in case of future judicial or arbitral proceedings.

A declaration is a unilateral statement of policy or opinion that, like an understanding, is not intended to alter or limit any provision of the treaty. It is considered to have the least effect on the original treaty text and is used primarily to articulate a signatory's purpose, position, or expectation, concerning the treaty in question.

The use of the labels "reservation," "understanding," and "declaration" have created much confusion on both the international level and the domestic level. The problem arises because the label attached is not conclusive as to the substantive effect the statement has on the treaty. This is especially evident when dealing with understandings. A state may condition acceptance of a treaty on a specific interpretation, which may later be found contrary to the plain language of the treaty or the intended meaning of other parties. As such, the understanding in effect alters or modifies the original treaty and amounts to a reservation. If a state were allowed to determine conclusively the treatment of a unilateral statement by attaching a label, the statement could alter the multilateral treaty and negate the application of reservation law. It is necessary, therefore, to distinguish qualifying statements by comparing the substance or contents of the statement with the original text of the treaty. If the qualifying statement in application alters the legal effect of the treaty, the statement should be considered a reservation and be governed by the applicable reservation law.

(4) The Vienna Convention's Approach[20]

The term "reservation" is defined in the Vienna Convention on the Law of Treaties for the purposes of that Convention in Article 2(1)(d) as follows:

> "reservation" means a unilateral statement, however phrased or named, made by a State, when signing, ratifying, accepting, approving or acceding to a treaty, whereby it purports to exclude or to modify the legal effect of certain provisions of the treaty in their application to that State.

Two features of the definition in the Vienna Convention on the Law of Treaties deserve special attention. First, what are the consequences of looking to substance rather than the title of the statement to determine whether a particular statement styled, for example, as a "reservation" is or is not in law a reservation and to determine whether a statement styled as an "interpretative declaration" is or is not in law a reservation? Second, what are the consequences of not specifying in the definition that a reservation is a condition upon the expression of consent to be bound?

The phrase in the Vienna Convention definition above, "however phrased or named," was added at the Vienna Conference on the Law of Treaties in 1968. This was the principal substantive change made in the definition proposed by the International Law Commission, and it was not a radical change.[21] The change incorporated into the

[19] By CATHERINE LOGAN PIPER, excerpted from: *Reservations to Multilateral Treaties: The Goal of Universality*, 71 IOWA LAW REVIEW 295, 298 (1985). Reprinted by permission.

[20] By RICHARD W. EDWARDS, JR., excerpted from: *Reservations to Treaties*, 10 MICHIGAN JOURNAL OF INTERNATIONAL LAW 362 (1989). Reprinted by permission.

[21] For the text of the definition of "reservation" proposed by the International Law Commission, see Art. 2(1)(d) of the Draft Articles on the Law of Treaties with commentaries, adopted by the I.L.C. at its 18th Session (1966). Report of the International Law Commission to the General Assembly on the Work of its 18th Session, 21 U.N. GAOR Supp. (No. 9) at 21, U.N. Doc. A/6309/Rev. 1 (1966), reprinted in [1966] 2 Y.B. INT'L L. COMM'N 172, 178, U.N. Doc. A/CN.4/SER.A/1966/Add.1, and in 1968–

text a concept previously accepted within the International Law Commission. The idea that the definition of "reservation" should encompass interpretative statements when they otherwise meet the definition of a reservation was agreed upon within the International Law Commission at least as early as 1962, and was made explicit in the commentary:

> States, when signing, ratifying, acceding to, accepting or approving a treaty, not infrequently make declarations . . . as to their interpretation of a particular provision. Such a declaration may be a mere clarification of the State's position or it may amount to a reservation, according as it does or does not vary or exclude the application of the terms of the treaty as adopted.[22]

A proposal by Hungary that would have treated all statements of interpretation as reservations died in the Drafting Committee at the Vienna Conference.

The implications of using a test that calls for an examination of the substance of a State's statement as compared to its title may not have been fully appreciated. In the relations of men and nations it always seems rational to look at the substance rather than the form in appraising communications. But, a substance test throws a burden on those at the receiving end (or tribunals that may decide disputes) to recognize a statement for what it is rather than for what it is titled. Sometimes a statement in a ratification instrument (or its equivalent) is not titled; had it been, it would, at least, have provided a starting point in deciding whether the statement is or is not a reservation.

(5) A Liberal Rule[23]

Conceptually, the issue of the desirability of reservations is straightforward. Most arguments in favor of the liberal use of reservations have as their cornerstone the belief that the liberal admissibility of reservations will encourage wider acceptance of treaties. H. G. Knight, in discussing the potential use of reservations to the treaty being negotiated by the Third United Nations Conference on the Law of the Sea, stated: "It can be asserted that the permissive use of reservations encourages adherence to multilateral treaties and thus encourages universality, an objective of the current law of the sea negotiations."[24] The International Law Commission, in its deliberations about the law of treaties, put the issue well:

> A power to formulate reservations must in the nature of things tend to make it easier for some States to execute the act necessary to bind themselves finally to participating in the treaty and therefore tend to promote a greater measure of universality in the application of the treaty. Moreover, in the case of general multilateral treaties, it appears that not infrequently a number of States have, to all appearances, only found it possible to participate in the treaty subject to one or more reservations.[25]

The other edge of the sword, as it were, is that reservations necessarily reduce the uniformity and consistency (if not the integrity) of a treaty. Again, the International Law Commission discussed the issue insightfully:

> It is also desirable to maintain uniformity in the obligations of all the parties to a multilateral convention, and it may often be more important to maintain the integrity of a convention than to aim, at any price, at the widest possible acceptance of it. A reserving State proposes, in effect, to insert into a convention a provision which will exempt that State from certain of the consequences which would otherwise devolve upon it from the convention, while leaving the other States which are or may become parties to it fully subject to those consequences in their relations inter se.[26]

The exact nature of the balance between uniformity/

1969 Vienna Conference Documents, *supra* note 9, at 7. Other changes in the definition made at the Vienna Conference on the Law of Treaties did not have significant substantive implications. In a drafting change, the verb "vary," which was used in the I.L.C. draft, was changed to "modify" in the final version of the Vienna Convention. The change harmonized the terminology in the definition with the terminology used in Art. 21, which sets forth the legal effects of reservations. See Ruda, *supra* note 3, at 107.

[22] Commentary to Art. I(1)(f) of Draft Articles on the Law of Treaties, Report of the International Law Commission to the General Assembly Covering the Work of its 14th Session, 17 U.N. GAOR Supp. (No. 9) at 6, U.N. Doc. A/5209 (1962), reprinted in [1962] 2 Y.B. INT'L L. COMM'N 157, 163, U.N. Doc. A/CN.4/SER.A/1962/Add.1.

[23] By JOHN KING GAMBLE, JR., excerpted from: *Reservations to MultilateralTreaties: A Macroscopic View of State Practice,* 74 AMERICAN JOURNAL OF INTERNATIONAL LAW 372 (1980). Reprinted by permission.

[24] H. G. Knight, *The Potential Use of Reservations to international agreements produced by the Third United Nations Conference on the Law of the Sea*, in POLICY ISSUES IN OCEAN LAW 1, 5 (Studies in Transnational Legal Policy No. 8, 1975).

[25] Reports of the International Law Commission on the second part of its 17th session and on its 18th session, [1966] 2 Y.B. INT'L L. COMM'N 169, 205–06, UN Doc. A/6309/Rev.1 (1966).

[26] Report of the International Law Commission covering the work of its 3d session, [1951] 2 Y.B. INT'L L. COMM'N 123, 129, UN Doc. A/1858 (1951).

consistency and universality may be complex. For example, it is possible that a point exists in the liberal use of reservations beyond which participation will be reduced as those states satisfied with a treaty feel its integrity is being stretched to the breaking point by the permissibility of reservations. This problem may be both latent and practical, i.e., perceived because the treaty does not restrict the use of reservations, and an actual reaction to reservations that have been made. The point is that a direct proportionality between the liberal admissibility of reservations and wider acceptance of a treaty cannot be assumed.

(6) The Effect of Formality on Impermissible Reservations[27]

Assuming that the unilateral statement is a true reservation (and not a mere interpretative declaration), and assuming further that the reservation is impermissible, the question then arises of the effect of such a reservation. Is the reservation a nullity, to be set aside, leaving the State's act of ratification or accession as the effective, binding act of the State? Or does the inclusion of the impermissible reservation operate so as to invalidate and nullify the State's act of ratification or accession?

There is a patent contradiction in the expression of will by the State. There is the expression of a will to be bound by the treaty, as evidenced in the act of ratification or accession or even signature (if that is intended to be binding); and then there is the expression of a will to impose a condition, in the form of a reservation, which is in contradiction with the intention to be bound by the treaty precisely because the reservation is not permissible under the treaty. Which expression of will is to prevail?

In principle, the will which ought to prevail is the will to accept the treaty. For that is evidently the overriding intention, the primary intention of the State, and this view is strengthened by the consideration that the State will presumably not have perceived that its reservation is impermissible, whereas its perception of the effect of its act of ratification or accession is clear and unequivocal.

To support this conclusion by direct authority, or even by analogy, is not an easy matter. No direct authority can be found for the proposition that an impermissible reservation is a nullity and severable from the principal act of ratification or accession. The related, but not strictly analogous,[28] problem of reservations to the Optional Clause is as yet unresolved. However, Judge Lauterpacht's view was that:

> If that reservation is an essential condition of the Acceptance in the sense that without it the declaring State would have been wholly unwilling to undertake the principal obligation, then it is not open to the Court to disregard that reservation and at the same time to hold the accepting State bound by the declaration.[29]

It will be recalled that Judge Lauterpacht took this view having carefully examined the practice of the United States, and having come to the conclusion that the insistence on an "automatic" reservations clause was a positive, intentional and consistent part of United States policy. The case we postulate is scarcely of that kind but more a case when it must be assumed that the State failed to perceive that its particular reservation was impermissible. Moreover, Judge Lauterpacht also stated that "there is no element of illegality involved in a declaration of Acceptance which is inconsistent with the Statute of the Court,"[30] whereas we postulate a reservation prohibited by the treaty, or not permissible under the treaty, or contrary to the object and purpose of the treaty, and thus arguably illegal.

In short, it is important to understand that not all impermissible reservations will be fundamentally inconsistent with the object and purpose of the treaty. Thus, it is possible to assimilate fundamentally incompatible reservations with Lauterpacht's category of reservations which nullify the whole acceptance of the principal obligation (be it the Optional Clause or a treaty); and yet keep distinct those reservations which, though they are not permissible, do not raise the issue of fundamental incompatibility and, therefore, may be severed.

Perhaps the safest conclusion, therefore, is that, given the inconsistency of the two expressions of will, it is essentially a question of construction as to what the State really intended. If it can be objectively, and preferably judicially, determined that the State's paramount intention was to ac-

---

[27] By D. W. BOWETT from: *Reservations to Non-Restricted Multilateral Treaties*, 48 British Yearbook of International Law 67 (1978). Reprinted by permission.

[28] The analogy is not strict because the link between States accepting Article 36 (2) of the Statute of the ICJ is not a treaty link. However, the analogy is certainly close and in the *Interhandel* case, Judgement of 21 March 1959, ICJ Reports, 1959, Judge Lauterpacht thought the invalid reservation of the U.S.A. to be both invalid and non-severable, thereby invalidating the entire acceptance of the Optional Clause by the U.S.A. (see pp. 101, 116–119); whereas Judges Klaestad (pp. 76–8) and Armand-Ugon (pp. 93–4) thought the invalid reservation could be severed, leaving the acceptance of the Optional Clause valid and effective.

[29] *Id.* at 117. [Editor's Note: There is further separate discussion of the Optional Clause later in this Chapter.]

[30] *Id.* at 118.

cept the treaty, as evidenced by the ratification or accession, then an impermissible reservation which is not fundamentally opposed to the object and purpose of the treaty can be struck out and disregarded as a nullity. Conversely, if the State's acceptance of the treaty is clearly dependent upon an impermissible condition of which the terms are such that the two are not severable and the reservation is in fundamental contradiction with the object and purpose of the treaty, then the effect of that impermissible and invalid reservation is to invalidate the act of ratification or accession, nullifying the State's participation in the treaty.

(7) The World Court Strikes Down a Reservation[31]

For the first time, an international court has held a reservation to a treaty invalid. The European Court of Human Rights, on April 29, 1988, treated Switzerland's interpretative declaration to the European Convention on Human Rights as a reservation, and held that it did not comply with the reservations clause of that convention.[32]

The European Convention in Article 6 provides for the right of all persons to a fair trial. When Switzerland ratified the European Convention, it said in its interpretative declaration:

> The Swiss Federal Council considers that the guarantee of fair trial in Article 6, paragraph 1 of the Convention, in the determination of civil rights and obligations or any criminal charge against the person in question is intended solely to ensure ultimate control by the judiciary over the acts or decisions of the public authorities relating to such rights or obligations or the determination of such a charge.

The Swiss attorneys arguing before the European Court asserted that "ultimate control by the judiciary" simply meant review of administrative proceedings restricted to questions of law.

The Court, however, found the interpretative declaration too ambiguous to satisfy the requirements of Article 64(1) of the European Convention, which prohibits "reservations of a general character." The Court said it was left guessing "which categories of dispute are included."[33] Nor could the Court decipher from the phrase "ultimate control by the judiciary" whether the *facts* of a case would be heard and determined by a court. This interpretative declaration, therefore, amounted to a reservation of a general character inconsistent with the requirements of Article 64(1).

Did the Court's judgment mean that Switzerland did not become a party to the European Convention on Human Rights because of the incompatibility of its reservation? The Court fumbled the opportunity to explain the consequences of its determination that the Swiss reservation was invalid. This is the first time an international tribunal has held a reservation invalid. Thus the Court was writing on a clean slate. The Court, after declaring the Swiss reservation invalid, stated, "At the same time, it is beyond doubt that Switzerland is, and regards itself as, bound by the Convention irrespective of the validity of the declaration."[34] A mere one sentence statement hardly illuminated this controversial, unexplored area. At the oral hearing in the Belilos Case, the Swiss spokesman speculated aloud, "In the event of the Swiss interpretative declaration being invalid for purely formal reasons, might we not consider insisting on this defect being remedied *a posteriori* and the declaration reworded accordingly?"[35]

(8) Egypt's Reservations to the Convention on the Elimination of Discrimination Against Women[36]

In most countries of the Middle East, relations between the sexes are guided by Islamic laws and traditions. Like any system of jurisprudence, however, Islamic law (Shari'a) is subject to continuous interpretation and reformulation. Egypt provided both the climate and leadership in the early twentieth century that inspired a reassessment of Islamic law and women's rights throughout the Arab world. Consistent with that tradition, Egypt is among the few Arab countries which have ratified the Convention on the Elimination of All Forms of Discrimination Against Women (Women's Convention).[37] However, because of the

[31] By HENRY J. BOURGUIGNON, from: *The Belios Case: New Light on Reservations to Multilateral Conventions,* 29 VIRGINIA JOURNAL OF INTERNATIONAL LAW 347 (1989). Reprinted by permission.

[32] Belios Case, 132 Eur. Ct. H.R. (ser. A)(1988), reprinted in 10 EUR. HUM. RTS. REP. 466 (1988).

[33] *Id.* at 26, reprinted in 10 EUR. HUM. RTS. REP. at 485.

[34] *Id.* at 28, reprinted in 10 EUR. HUM. RTS. REP. at 487.

[35] Council of Europe, Belilos Case: Notes of the Public Hearing (Morning) 47 (Oct. 26, 1987).

[36] By ANNA JENEFSKY, excerpted from: *Permissibility of Egypt's Reservations to the Convention on the Elimination of All Forms of Discrimination Against Women,* 15 MARYLAND JOURNAL OF INTERNATIONAL LAW AND TRADE 199 (1991). Reprinted by permission.

[37] G.A.Res. 34/180 (Dec. 18, 1979), 1249 U.N.T.S. 13 (entered into force Sept. 3, 1981) [hereinafter Women's Convention].

preeminence of Islamic law in the family law of Egypt, Egypt has made reservations to the Women's Convention. This comment analyzes the permissibility of those reservations under international law.

Part I of this comment provides a general background to the Women's Convention and summarizes Egypt's reservations to that agreement. Part II examines general principles of international law governing treaty reservations and the permissibility of reservations to conventions on human rights. The section then applies those principles to Egypt's reservations to Articles 2 and 9 and concludes that the reservations are impermissible. Part III outlines the legal traditions underlying Egypt's reservation to Article 16.

(a) Egypt and the Convention on the Elimination of All Forms of Discrimination Against Women

The Convention on the Elimination of All Forms of Discrimination Against Women is a comprehensive multilateral human rights agreement designed to achieve and enforce equal rights specifically for women. It was unanimously adopted by the United Nations General Assembly on December 18, 1979, and entered into force on September 3, 1981. As of June 1, 1991, 106 states had become parties to the Women's Convention.

Article 1 of the Women's Convention defines discrimination against women as:

> any distinction, exclusion or restriction made on the basis of sex which has the effect or purpose of impairing or nullifying the recognition, enjoyment or exercise by women, irrespective of their marital status, on a basis of equality of men and women, of human rights and fundamental freedoms in the political, economic, social, cultural, civil or any other field.

Articles 2 through 14 address specific areas of discrimination and suggest various types of remedial measures. These remedial measures include the introduction of legislation to end discrimination in the political, social, economic, and cultural spheres. Article 15 further requires parties to grant women equality in all civil legal matters, including administration of property, execution of contracts, and choice of residence. Article 16 provides for the elimination of discrimination against women in all family matters. Specifically, Article 16 addresses a woman's right to choose a spouse, to make decisions regarding her children, and to administer property on an equal basis with her husband.

Egypt signed the Women's Convention in Copenhagen in 1980, during the World Conference of the U.N. Decade for Women, and the Egyptian Parliament ratified the Convention on September 18, 1981. Egypt made reservations to Articles 2, 9, and 16.

Article 2 provides that parties to the Women's Convention shall generally combat discrimination by taking specific legislative action.[38] This provision delineates the means by which parties to the Convention obligate themselves to implement all other enforceable provisions of the Convention. Egypt's reservation to that article states: "The Arab Republic of Egypt is willing to comply with the content of this article, provided that such compliance does not run counter to the Islamic Shari'a."[39] Thus Egypt agrees to adopt such anti-discriminatory legislation only to the extent that it is consistent with Islamic law.

Article 9, paragraph 2 of the Convention provides, in full, that "States Parties shall grant women equal rights with men with respect to the nationality of their children." The stated purpose of Egypt's reservation to that provision is:

> to prevent a child's acquisition of two nationalities where his parents are of different nationalities, since this may be prejudicial to his future. It is clear that

Countries that have ratified or acceded to an international treaty are called "States Parties" to that treaty. Through ratification or accession a country agrees to be legally bound by the treaty's provisions. As of June 1, 1991, the other Arab States that are also parties to the 1979 Convention are Iraq, Tunisia, and the Republic of Yemen.

[38] The full text of Article 2 provides:
States Parties condemn discrimination against women in all its forms, agree to pursue by all appropriate means and without delay a policy of eliminating discrimination against women and, to this end, undertake:
(a) To embody the principle of the equality of men and women in their national constitutions or other appropriate legislation if not yet incorporated therein and to ensure, through law and other appropriate means, the practical realization of this principle;
(b) To adopt appropriate legislative and other measures, including sanctions where appropriate, prohibiting all discrimination against women;
(c) To establish legal protection of the rights of women on an equal basis with men and to ensure through competent national tribunals and other public institutions the effective protection of women against any act of discrimination;
(d) To refrain from engaging in any act or practice of discrimination against women and to ensure that public authorities and institutions shall act in conformity with this obligation;
(e) To take all appropriate measures to eliminate discrimination against women by any person, organization or enterprise;
(f) To take all appropriate measures, including legislation, to modify or abolish existing laws, regulations, customs and practices which constitute discrimination against women;
(g) To repeal all national penal provisions which constitute discrimination against women.

[39] This sentence comprises the full text of Egypt's reservation.

> the child's acquisition of his father's nationality is the procedure most suitable for the child and that this does not infringe upon the principle of equality between men and women, since it is the custom for a woman to agree, on marrying an alien, that her children shall be of the father's nationality.[40]

The reasoning behind this reservation is that Egyptian women voluntarily agree to relinquish the right bestowed upon them by Article 9 of the Women's Convention when they enter into marriage.

Egypt has also made a reservation to Article 16 of the Convention. Article 16 provides that "States Parties shall take all appropriate measures to eliminate discrimination against women in all matters relating to marriage and family relations . . . ."[41] This provision lists each marital and family right separately and requires that parties grant women equality in each individual aspect of marital and family relations, including marriage, divorce, parenting, family planning, adoption, and ownership of property.

Egypt justifies its reservation to Article 16 by invoking "firm religious beliefs which govern marital relations in Egypt" and "ensure complementarity which guarantees true equality between the spouses."[42] Moreover, the reservation explains that because the Islamic dower system of marriage in Egypt favors women over men, the woman's right to divorce is proportionately restricted: Thus, the Shari'a "restricts the wife's rights to divorce by making it contingent on a judge's ruling, whereas no such restriction is laid down in the case of the husband."

Egypt's reservation to Article 16 implicitly rejects the Convention's segmented approach to the domain of marital and family rights in favor of treating those rights as one organic entity in which one type of right may be balanced against another. Moreover, Egypt's approach to Article 16 fails to acknowledge the presence of non-Muslim populations in Egypt, for whom Islamic family law does not apply.[43]

(b) Egypt's Reservations in the Framework of International Law

The permissibility of Egypt's reservations must be determined within the general framework of international law. The following discussion summarizes the general principles of international law that govern the permissibility of reservations to human rights conventions.

The Vienna Convention on the Law of Treaties (Vienna

---

[40] Multilateral Treaties Deposited with the Secretary-General: Status as at 31 December 1990, at 167.

[41] The full text of Article 16 provides:

> 1. States Parties shall take all appropriate measures to eliminate discrimination against women in all matters relating to marriage and family relations and in particular shall ensure, on a basis of equality of men and women:
> (a) The same right to enter into marriage;
> (b) The same right freely to choose a spouse and to enter into marriage only with their free and full consent;
> (c) The same rights and responsibilities during marriage and at its dissolution;
> (d) The same rights and responsibilities as parents, irrespective of their marital status, in matters relating to their children; in all cases the interests of the children shall be paramount;
> (e) The same rights to decide freely and responsibly on the number and spacing of their children and to have access to the information, education and means to enable them to exercise these rights;
> (f) The same rights and responsibilities with regard to guardianship, wardship, trusteeship and adoption of children, or similar institutions where these concepts exist in national legislation; in all cases the interests of the children shall be paramount;
> (g) The same personal rights as husband and wife, including the right to choose a family name, a profession and an occupation;
> (h) The same rights for both spouses in respect of the ownership, acquisition, management, administration, enjoyment and disposition of property, whether free of charge or for a valuable consideration.
> 2. The betrothal and the marriage of a child shall have no legal effect, and all necessary action, including legislation, shall be taken to specify a minimum age for marriage and to make the registration of marriages in an official registry compulsory.

[42] Multilateral Treaties, *supra* note 40, at 167. The full text of the reservation reads:

> Reservation to the text of article 16 concerning the equality of men and women in all matters relating to marriage and family relations during the marriage and upon its dissolution, without prejudice to the Islamic Sharia's provisions whereby women are accorded rights equivalent to those of their spouses so as to ensure a just balance between them. This is out of respect for the sacrosanct nature of the firm religious beliefs which govern marital relations in Egypt and which may not be called in [sic] question and in view of the fact that one of the most important bases of these relations is an equivalency of rights and duties so as to ensure complementarity which guarantees true equality between the spouses. The provisions of the Sharia lay down that the husband shall pay bridal money to the wife and maintain her fully and shall also make a payment to her upon divorce, whereas the wife retains full rights over her property and is not obliged to spend anything on her keep. The Sharia therefore restricts the wife's rights to divorce by making it contingent on a judge's ruling, whereas no such restriction is laid down in the case of the husband.

[43] It is difficult to obtain information on exactly how many non-Muslims live in Egypt. One source states that about 90% of Egypt's population are Muslim, while most of the remaining 10% are Coptic Christian. The Middle East and North Africa 1991, at 406 (Europa Publications Limited, 37th ed., 1990). Another source states that 94% are Muslim, with the remaining 6% being Coptic Christian. THE MIDDLE EAST 140 (Congressional Quarterly, Inc., 7th ed., 1990).

Convention)sets out the general norms that govern treaty interpretation, including the effect of reservations. Article 2 of the Vienna Convention defines a reservation as "a unilateral statement, however phrased or named, made by a State, when signing, ratifying, accepting, approving or acceding to a treaty, whereby it purports to exclude or to modify the legal effect of certain provisions of the treaty in their application to that State." Article 19 generally permits States to make a reservation unless:

a) the reservation is prohibited by the treaty;

b) the treaty provides that only specified reservations, which do not include the reservation in question, may be made; or

c) in cases not falling under sub-paragraphs (a) and (b), the reservation is incompatible with the object and purpose of the treaty.

The Women's Convention specifically permits parties to make reservations to its arbitration provision. This is consistent with Article 19(b) of the Vienna Convention. The Women's Convention also contains an "object and purpose" provision that is similar to Article 19(c) of the Vienna Convention. That provision embodies the "compatibility rule," which was first articulated in 1951 by the International Court of Justice on reservations to the Convention on Genocide. The rule appears to be a reasonable compromise for determining the permissibility of reservations to a convention. However, in the absence of an authoritative mechanism for assessing the compatibility of a specific reservation with the object and purpose of an agreement, the rule provides little guidance. Consequently, the State that enters a reservation is, in effect, the party that decides whether it is compatible with the object and purpose of a convention. Other States may object to the reservation on grounds that it is inconsistent with a convention's object and purpose, but in many multilateral human rights agreements, such objections have little practical consequence.

Like most multilateral agreements, the Women's Convention does not provide a specific definition of its object and purpose in its text. However, it does provide a general definition of its object and purpose in its title. As the title expressly states, the Convention is dedicated to "the elimination of all forms of discrimination against women." Moreover, the Convention's provisions define what constitutes such discrimination and delineate the means that parties must undertake to eliminate such discrimination. Those provisions are discussed at greater length below in the analysis of Egypt's reservations to the Women's Convention.

Egypt's reservations to Articles 2 and 9 of the Women's Convention are inconsistent with basic principles of international law. Both reservations compromise the integrity of the Convention more than they promote its universal adoption and are therefore incompatible with the object and purpose of the Convention.

As noted previously, Article 2 sets out the means by which parties must implement provisions of the Women's Convention into their domestic law. Thus, Article 2 is the central provision giving actual force to the object and purpose of the Convention. As one commentator has noted, a reservation to Article 2 that excludes the establishment of the means to move towards the Convention's ultimate goals "obstructs and compromises compliance with the object and purpose of the Convention."[44]

Egypt's reservation to Article 2 is based on religion. However, Egypt has failed to provide any explanation for this general reservation. Under the compatibility rule, such a broad reservation to the central provision of the Women's Convention appears to frustrate the Convention's primary purpose of eliminating discrimination against women at the domestic level. Therefore, Egypt's reservation to Article 2 is impermissible because it violates the integrity of the Convention more than it advances universal adoption of the Convention. The argument that permitting Egypt to make its reservation to Article 2 may be the only way to elicit Egypt's adoption of the Convention carries little force because Article 2 is the most important provision of the Convention. Egypt's broad reservation to Article 2 is therefore incompatible with the object and purpose of the Women's Convention.

Because Article 2 applies to the means of implementing each provision of the Convention, it is not necessary for a party to make a general reservation to that provision in order to exempt itself from separate provisions in the agreement. It is possible, therefore, for Egypt to withdraw its general reservation to Article 2 and retain its reservations to individual provisions, to the extent that those reservations are separately permissible under international law.

Egypt's reservation to Article 9 of the Women's Convention is also impermissible under international law. While the reservation to Article 9 is more detailed than the reservation to Article 2, the former fails to invoke any distinguishable religious or legal justification. Egypt merely states that "it is clear" that the nationality of the father is more suitable for the child than that of the mother and that "it is custom" for a woman who marries an alien to agree to this. This reservation is based on the proposition that Egyptian women voluntarily abdicate their right of equality with men with respect to the nationality of their children when they enter into marriage.

The reservation is impermissible because it fails to provide any substantive explanation for its purported inability

---

[44] Rebecca J. Cook, *Reservations to the Convention on the Elimination of All Forms of Discrimination Against Women*, 30 VA. J. INT'L L. 643, 689 (1990).

to grant women the fundamental right, provided by the Women's Convention, of equality with respect to the nationality of their children. A reservation which has the effect of denying women such a fundamental right compromises the integrity of the Convention. Neither the wording nor the tone of Egypt's reservation to Article 9 suggest that Egypt would be unable to maintain its adoption of the Convention if it were to withdraw the reservation. To whatever extent the universal application of the Convention is advanced by Egypt's reservation to Article 9, such advancement is outweighed by the violation of the integrity of the Convention the reservation represents.

In contrast with its other reservations, Egypt supports its reservation to Article 16 by outlining the "equivalency" and "complementarity" of rights and duties of husband and wife provided by Shari'a. In making this reservation, Egypt appears to rely on Article 23 of the Convention, which protects domestic legislation of a party that is more conducive to sexual equality than the provisions of the Women's Convention. Whether provisions of Egyptian family law relevant to this reservation are indeed more conducive to sexual equality underlies the analysis in Part V of this comment, which examines the compatibility of Egypt's reservation to Article 16 with the object and purpose of the Women's Convention. First, however, it is necessary to establish the legal and political contexts which gave impetus to this reservation.

(c) Egypt's Reservation to Article 16 in the Context of Islamic and Egyptian Law

Egyptian jurists and scholars played a crucial role in the general development of Islamic jurisprudence and in the interpretation and reformulation of the marital and family rights of Muslim women throughout the Arab world. The discussion that follows briefly reviews the historical role Islam has played in granting women marital and family rights. The discussion outlines the four primary sources of Islamic law as well as the four principal schools of Islamic law. With that background, the section concludes by tracing the development of personal status law in Egypt.

1. *Sources of Islamic Law*. Historically, Islam improved the lives of Arab women by guaranteeing certain rights and privileges not otherwise recognized in the traditional pre-Islamic cultures of the Arab Middle East. In pre-Islamic Arabia, women were "sold" by their families to their husbands, had no say in the initiation or termination of their marriage, and lost all family inheritance rights upon marriage. Moreover, men were entitled to marry as many wives as they chose.

With the introduction of Islam, a husband was required to give money directly to his wife, rather than to her family, in consideration for the marriage.[45] Moreover, women no longer lost their rights to family property upon marriage. Islam also accorded women the right to have a say in determining the contractual provisions of their marriage. In addition, Islam restricted the right of men to initiate and terminate marriage, although it did not entirely negate male dominance in the area of marital relations. Finally, while the introduction of Islam did not eliminate the pre-Islamic practice of polygamy, it imposed significant restrictions on that practice. In Islam, a man is entitled to marry up to four wives. However, that right is limited by the proviso that he treat all his wives equally.[46]

(a) *Qur'an and Sunna: The Divine Revelations*. There are four primary sources of Islamic law: the Qur'an, the Sunna, Qiyas, and Ijma. The first two sources, the Qur'an and the Sunna, are considered to be the divine revelations of God. The Qur'an consists of a compilation of moral prescriptions. The Sunna consists of the deeds and sayings of the Prophet Muhammad, recorded in what are known as the Hadith.

The first 150 years of Islam were characterized by an "almost untrammeled freedom of juristic reasoning" in the solution of problems not specifically addressed by divine revelation.[47] Thus, when new circumstances posed new problems, they were answered on a case by case basis by individual judges and jurists. Gradually, however, a rift developed between those who believed that the Qur'an and the Sunna must be the direct source of every law, and those who believed in the legitimacy and necessity of human reasoning to interpret those sources and formulate laws.

(b) *Qiyas: Reasoning by Analogy*. To resolve this conflict, in the early ninth century, Shafi'i, a jurist now generally regarded as the father of Islamic jurisprudence, developed what came to be accepted as a third source of Islamic law–Qiyas, or reasoning by analogy from the Qur'an and the Sunna. Previously, divine revelation and human reasoning were treated separately by Islamic scholars. Henceforward, divine revelation and human reasoning became intertwined in Islamic jurisprudence, although human reasoning

---

[45] The Qur'an prescribes, "And give unto the women, (whom ye marry) free gift of their marriage portions." THE MEANING OF THE GLORIOUS QURAN IV:4 (Marmaduke Pickthall, trans., 1983 ed.).

[46] This right and qualification are attributed to the following verse of the Qur'an:

> And if ye fear that ye will not deal fairly by the orphans, marry of the women, who seem good to you, two or three or four; and if ye fear that ye cannot do justice (to so many) then one (only) or (the captives) that your right hands possess. Thus it is more likely that ye will not do injustice. QUR'AN IV:3; *see also* QUR'AN IV:129.

[47] NOEL J. COULSON, CONFLICTS AND TENSIONS IN ISLAMIC JURISPRUDENCE 4 (1969).

remained subordinate in authority to the actual sources of divine revelation.

(c) *Ijma: Consensus*. In addition to establishing Qiyas, Shafi'i founded a "school" of Islamic law that bears his name. The other major schools of Islamic law, also named after the jurists who founded them, are the Hanafi, Maliki, and Hanbali schools.[48] Although these four schools ultimately diverged in methods of interpretation and other matters, by the end of the ninth century, they "mutually regarded their several bodies of doctrine as equally legitimate attempts to define Allah's law, equally authoritative versions of the Shari'a."[49] Thus was born the fourth source of Islamic law, Ijma, or consensus. Ijma is the "unanimous agreement of the jurists of a particular age on a specific issue."[50]

(d) *The Closing of the Gate of Ijtihad*. Both Qiyas and Ijma are forms of Ijtihad, or individual reasoning.[51] In the early tenth century, Islamic jurists declared that, where consensus had been reached, the "gate" of Ijtihad was closed. The teachings of the great jurists were deemed complete and further independent interpretation was considered unnecessary. The practice of Taqlid, or adhering superficially to one of the traditional schools of law, took the place of Ijtihad. The gate of Ijtihad remained closed until the early twentieth century.

2. *Personal Status Law in Egypt*. During the mid-nineteenth century, the Arab world found itself increasingly exposed to European culture and influence. Egypt was part of the Ottoman Empire, which promulgated commercial and penal codes modeled on European laws. Although it achieved independence from the Ottomans in 1874, Egypt enacted civil and criminal codes modeled on French law. Throughout these developments, however, the family law of Egypt remained within the exclusive purview of Islamic law.

In 1875, under official sponsorship, an Egyptian jurist named Muhammad Qadri Pasha compiled a family and inheritance legal code based on the Hanafi school of law. Although never officially adopted, that code would greatly influence the administration of Shari'a in Egypt and other parts of the Middle East by the turn of the century. Family law in Egypt did not undergo significant reform until the 1920's. But from that time forward, Egyptian jurisprudence and legislation gave impetus to modernist legislation throughout the Arab world.

The Shari'a had always required that a husband maintain his wife by providing her with food, clothing, and shelter. In return, the wife was obligated to obey her husband and accord him conjugal rights. Under all four Islamic schools of law, the wife had the right to sue for maintenance if her husband refused to provide it. However, under Hanafi law, that right became meaningless, because the wife had no right to recover maintenance that was past due. Moreover, in contrast with Maliki and Shafi'i law, Hanafi law prohibited a woman from divorcing her husband based on his neglect, inability, or refusal to maintain her.

In 1929, Egypt enacted Law No. 25 by royal decree. That law recognized, for the first time, four grounds on which a woman could sue her husband for divorce: (1) failure to provide maintenance, (2) dangerous or contagious disease, (3) desertion, and (4) mistreatment.[52] Law No. 25 rejected the traditional Hanafi limitations on a woman's marital rights by enabling her to recover past maintenance and permitting her to sue for divorce in cases where her husband had failed to provide maintenance.

Law No. 25 introduced further reform by limiting the husband's unilateral right under Hanafi law to divorce his wife at any time and for any reason. Previously, the husband's simple utterance, "I divorce thee," terminated the marriage, regardless of his intention. Consequently, a pronouncement made in jest, drunkenness, or under compulsion was given legal force. The divorce was also treated as valid regardless of whether the wife had been informed or consulted. Under the Hanafi law, if the husband made the pronouncement fewer than three times, the divorce was revocable. However, if he uttered the words three times, the divorce became irrevocable.[53] Law No. 25 signaled a shift away from an emphasis on form in the Hanafi school towards one on intention in the Maliki and Shafi'i schools. For example, under Law No. 25, a husband's pronouncement made in jest, drunkenness, or under compulsion was presumed to lack true intent and was rendered invalid. Moreover, Law No. 25 made any divorce resulting from the husband's pronouncement revocable, regardless of the number of times uttered.

Although Law No. 25 effected many improvements in the legal rights of Egyptian women, it did not address all areas of marriage and divorce law which were considered

---

48 *Id.* at 21. All of these schools are within the Sunni community. The vast majority of Muslims in Egypt are Sunni.

49 *Id.* at 22.

50 John L. Esposito, Women in Muslim Family Law 7 (1982).

51 Joseph Schacht, An Introduction to Islamic Law 37 (1964).

52 Under the Hanafi school, which is the most rigid in the area of family law, a woman could divorce her husband only if the husband was impotent or if the marriage had been fraudulently arranged for the woman when she was a child. She could exercise this option only upon reaching puberty.

53 This latter form of repudiation, when it consists of three pronouncements in a row at the same time, is generally considered to be contrary to the teachings of Muhammad. A permissible form of irrevocable divorce is effected by three pronouncements which are made at different times.

to be in need of reform.[54] During the next few decades, cabinet ministers and specially appointed committees submitted recommendations and drafted legislation for additional reforms, but no further legislation was actually enacted until 1979. In June of that year, to avoid further resistance against family law reform, President Anwar Sadat enacted Law No. 44 by presidential decree. Sadat issued that law while Parliament was in recess, six months before the UN General Assembly adopted the Women's Convention. Popularly known as "Jihan's Law," after Sadat's wife, Law No. 44 required a husband to obtain a notarized certificate of divorce and gave a wife the right to be informed if her husband divorced her or if he planned to marry an additional wife. It also gave a wife the right to divorce her husband if a subsequent marriage harmed her or if he failed to inform her of that marriage. The law invoked Maliki and Hanbali jurisprudence in granting a woman the right to divorce her husband if she disapproved of a subsequent marriage. Although many orthodox Muslim jurists opposed Law No. 44, there were many other religious figures, including several shaikhs from Al-Azhar University, who approved some of its provisions.

In addition to these reforms, Law No. 44 granted a divorced woman with children the right to remain in her marital home until she remarried or lost custody of her children. That right has particular significance in Egypt, where housing is in short supply. The law also expanded a woman's entitlement to maintenance by her ex-husband following divorce, extended the age at which children of divorced parents are automatically returned to their father's custody, and gave a wife who left her husband the right to appeal to the courts against any attempt by her husband to have her forcibly returned. Despite these and other reforms accomplished by Law No. 44, the husband retained the right to practice polygamy and to obtain a divorce without judicial approval.

On May 4, 1985, the Supreme Court of Egypt struck down Law No. 44 as unconstitutional, holding that the enactment of a personal status law did not fall within Sadat's powers to enact presidential decrees, which are limited to "emergency" situations.[55] This repeal caused widespread opposition and inspired organized groups of women to lobby the Egyptian Parliament to reenact the law. Three weeks later, Law No. 100 was passed.

Law No. 100 largely resembles Law No. 44, with some changes. Moving one step backward, the law provides that a judge, rather than the woman herself, decides whether she has been harmed by her husband's second marriage before she may invoke the marriage as grounds for divorce. Moving a step forward, however, unlike Law No. 44, the new law provides penalties to aid in the enforcement of its provisions. Law No. 100 remains effective today as the legislative basis for the marital rights of Egyptian women.

(d) The Compatibility of Egypt's Reservation to Article 16 with the Object and Purpose of the Convention

The object and purpose of the Women's Convention is to eliminate all forms of discrimination against women. The type of action required of a party to facilitate this objective depends on how "discrimination against women" is defined. Article 1 of the Convention provides that discrimination exists when a woman suffers a limitation in her ability to enjoy or exercise either a "human right" or a "fundamental freedom." Egypt's reservation to Article 16 states that a "wife's rights to divorce are contingent on a judge's ruling, whereas no such restriction is laid down in the case of the husband." As previously noted, the compatibility rule for evaluating the permissibility of a reservation is intended to balance the goal of universal participation in a convention against the preservation of its integrity. Permitting Egypt's reservation would promote universality by encouraging Egypt to adopt the Convention. Whether permitting that reservation would compromise the Convention's integrity, however, rests in part upon whether a woman's right to judicial divorce is viewed as either a human right or a fundamental freedom.

Article 16(1)(c) of the Convention addresses the issue of a woman's right to judicial divorce by ensuring women "the same rights and responsibilities during marriage and at its dissolution." This provision suggests that if one spouse must acquire judicial permission to obtain a divorce, then so must the other. Article 16 mandates equal rights in the area of divorce. Therefore, equality in matters relating to divorce may be considered a fundamental right under the Women's Convention.

Egypt's explanation of its reservation to Article 16 states that Egyptian family law accords "equivalency" and "complementarity" of marital rights, including the right to divorce. Egypt's reservation compromises the integrity of the Women's Convention by imposing an asymmetrical procedure for obtaining divorce. That asymmetry violates the fundamental promotion of sameness mandated by the

[54] In 1926, a government appointed committee submitted draft articles to be integrated into Law No. 25 which recommended (1) that a woman be permitted to include certain stipulations in her marriage contract, such as a provision prohibiting her husband from marrying a second wife; (2) that a man be required to obtain permission from a judge to marry more than one wife before the marriage could be registered; and (3) that before granting such permission, a judge be required to investigate the man's ability to treat all or both of his wives equally. Although the Egyptian Cabinet approved these draft articles, they were not incorporated into Law No. 25 due to their controversial nature. *See* ESPOSITO, *supra* n.50, at 59–60.

[55] NADIA HIJAB, WOMANPOWER: THE ARAB DEBATE ON WOMEN AT WORK 31 (1988). Sadat was assassinated in 1981 and was succeeded by Hosni Mubarak.

Convention under the guise of "complementarity," a notion that the Convention simply does not recognize.

Article 23, however, permits States to apply provisions of their own legislation which may be "more conducive to the achievement of equality between men and women." Indirectly, Egypt invokes that provision by asserting that "equivalency" and "complementarity" of rights and duties "guarantees true equality." The reservation reasons that because a husband is required to maintain his wife, he need not obtain a judicial divorce.

This Egyptian "equivalency" approach fails a "true equality" test. It is based on the assumption that it is possible and proper to balance the economic duties of a husband against the legal entitlements of a wife. It fails to recognize, for example, that an independently wealthy or self-supporting woman does not benefit from her husband's obligation of maintenance. Moreover, the majority of Egyptian women match the economic contribution of their husbands by cooking, cleaning, raising the children, and in the case of women in rural areas, tending to agricultural chores as well.[56]

As previously established, the compatibility rule of reservations requires that considerations of integrity be balanced against the objective of promoting universal adoption of a human rights convention. Proponents of the universality approach to reservations stress that the success of a convention depends on its adoption by as many states as possible. Those proponents focus less on the integration of a convention into the domestic law of individual parties. In the case of an instrument such as the Women's Convention, this interest in universal adoption is inherently at odds with the integrity of the agreement. Where a party adopts a convention but fails to enact internal reforms to implement that convention's provisions, the integrity of the convention is compromised.

Egypt would probably not have adopted the Women's Convention if it had been prohibited from entering its reservation to Article 16. Because Islamic law governs all family law in Egypt, it is unreasonable to expect that Egypt would replace Islamic family law with secular law immediately upon adoption of the Women's Convention. In that context, it is necessary to balance Egypt's adoption of the Convention against its ability to sustain and pursue the general objectives promoted by each of the Convention's provisions.

Given the turbulent history of personal status law in Egypt and the diversity of groups attempting to influence its future, including Islamic jurists, women activists, and politicians, Egypt must proceed cautiously in the reform of its family laws. A skeptic may assert that Egypt adopted the Women's Convention without truly intending to undertake reforms consistent with its provisions. However, in light of the ongoing debate in Egypt regarding women's rights, particularly in the family context, it appears that Egypt took a relatively bold step by adopting the Convention at all. Moreover, Egypt explains its reservation to Article 16 in greater detail than the other Islamic states which made reservations to that provision.[57]

Any meaningful reform of personal status law in Egypt must occur within the framework of Islamic jurisprudence. On its face, Egypt's reservation to Article 16 suggests that prevailing marriage laws will remain unchanged "out of respect for the sacrosanct nature of the firm religious beliefs which govern marital relations in Egypt and which may not be called in [sic] question." However, since the turn of the century, such "firm religious beliefs" have repeatedly been called into question in Egypt.

The introduction of Islam into the Middle East improved the status of Arab women. Moreover, reforms in the personal status law of Egypt have generally developed within the purview of Islamic principles. Accordingly, many traditionalists insist that the current state of Islamic law must be preserved. However, others argue, as did Muhammad Abduh, that a rapidly changing society necessitates reexamination and reinterpretation of that tradition of law. These reformists contend that Islam's improvement of women's lives should be treated as an ongoing process, rather than a calcified historical event.[58] However, as the history of

[56] *See, e.g.*, James Toth, *Pride, Purdah, or Paychecks: What Maintains the Gender Division of Labor in Rural Egypt?*, 23 INT'L J. MIDDLE E. STUD. 213, 213–36 (1991).

[57] Below are the full texts of the reservations of other Islamic states to Article 16, contained in Multilateral Treaties, *supra* n. 40, at 166–71:

> Bangladesh: "The Government of the People's Republic of Bangladesh does not consider as binding upon itself the provisions of articles 2, 13(a) and 16.1(c) and (f) as they conflict with Shari'a law based on Holy Quran and Sunna."
>
> Iraq: "The reservation to [Article 16] shall be without prejudice to the provisions of the Islamic Shariah according women rights equivalent to the rights of their spouses so as to ensure a just balance between them."
>
> Jordan: "A reservation to the wording of article 16, paragraph (1)(c), relating to the rights arising upon the dissolution of marriage with regard to maintenance and compensation."
>
> Tunisia: "The Tunisian Government considers itself not bound by article 16, paragraphs (c), (d) and (f) of the Convention and declares that paragraphs (g) and (h) of that article must not conflict with the provisions of the Personal Status Code concerning the granting of family names to children and the acquisition of property through inheritance."

[58] In the Afterword of her widely acclaimed book, *the Egyptian physician and feminist*, Nawal El Saadawi, summarizes a view held by some Arab feminists on the role of Islam in the advancement of women's rights:

> The oppression of women is not essentially due to religious ideologies, or to whether she is born in a Western or Eastern society, but derives its roots from the class and patriarchal system that has ruled over human beings ever since slavery started to hold sway. In the traditions and culture of the Arabs and Islam, there are positive aspects which must be sought for and emphasized. Negative aspects

family law reform in Egypt clearly demonstrates, the process by which such reforms are enacted is just as important to the longevity and force of their acceptance as the fact that they are enacted.

Egypt's experience with Jihan's Law shows that reforms will not endure when a large segment of the population believes that those reforms have been imposed by a mistrusted leader through undemocratic means. The history of Islamic jurisprudence in Egypt, moreover, demonstrates that some Islamic jurists and traditional Egyptians react strongly against reforms, clinging fiercely to Taqlid, particularly if they perceive such reforms to be manifestations of encroaching western domination. The more Egyptians perceive the call for social reform to be a call from within the Arab, Islamic community, the more they are likely to call for an opening of the gate of Ijtihad to accommodate those reforms.

From their experience with Jihan's Law, Egyptian women learned that true reform of personal status law would require support from within their own country's legal tradition. They also learned that women themselves must be actively involved in future family law reform to ensure its lasting effect. The fact that Egyptian women, with the support of Islamic jurists, were responsible for the democratic enactment of Law No. 100 of 1985 suggests that the law will endure, be widely enforced, and provide the springboard for future reforms. Such future reforms may eventually include the abolition of a husband's unilateral right to extra-judicial divorce, which currently prevents Egypt from withdrawing its reservation to Article 16 of the Women's Convention.

(e) Conclusion

In analyzing whether Egypt's reservations to Articles 2, 9, and 16 of the Women's Convention are permissible, this comment has explored the general framework of international law regarding reservations to human rights conventions. The compatibility rule governing the permissibility of reservations to human rights conventions balances the degree to which a reservation violates the integrity of a convention against the extent to which that reservation facilitates universal adoption.

Under the compatibility rule, Egypt's reservation to Article 2 is impermissible because it is a general reservation to the most important provision of the Convention. Accordingly, that reservation so seriously undermines the integrity of the Convention that it renders meaningless any advancement of its universal adoption. Thus, Egypt's reservation to Article 2 is incompatible with the object and purpose of the Women's Convention.

Egypt's reservation to Article 9 is also impermissible because it does not provide an adequate justification for Egypt's inability to grant women the fundamental right of equality with respect to the nationality of their children. A reservation that has the effect of denying women any fundamental right provided by the Women's Convention compromises the integrity of that instrument. Neither the wording nor the tone of Egypt's reservation to Article 9 support the proposition that Egypt would be unable to maintain its adoption of the Convention if it were to withdraw this reservation. In the absence of such support, any advancement of universal adoption of the Convention served by Egypt's reservation to Article 9 is clearly outweighed by that reservation's violation of the integrity of the agreement.

In contrast, the text of Egypt's reservation to Article 16, as well as the turbulent history of personal status law in Egypt, demonstrate that until the government of Egypt enacts reforms consistent with Article 16 that are religiously and politically acceptable to the Egyptian population, Egypt must maintain its reservation to that article in order to remain a party to the Convention. Moreover, unlike the reservation to Article 9, Egypt's reservation to Article 16 provides specific religious justifications which, Egypt maintains, are superior to the underlying secular rationale of Article 16's provisions promoting marital equality. This reservation implicitly invokes Article 23, which provides that the Convention shall not supersede domestic legislation which is "more conducive to the achievement of equality." Thus, the permissibility of this reservation must be considered in the context of the development of Islamic and Egyptian law and of Egypt's social and political history to ascertain whether Egypt's laws on divorce are, in fact, more conducive to the achievement of equality than is Article 16 of the Women's Convention.

Based on consideration of the legal and political context of Egypt's reservation to Article 16, this comment concludes that Egypt's notion of "complementarity" of rights and obligations between spouses violates the integrity of the Women's Convention by denying women the fundamental right to equality with men in all matters relating to marriage and divorce. Egypt's laws on divorce are not more conducive to sexual equality than is Article 16 of the Convention to the extent that they balance a woman's legal rights against her husband's economic obligations for maintenance. However, because Egypt must maintain its reservation to Article 16 to ensure Egypt's continued participation in the Convention, that reservation is not entirely in-

> should be exposed and discarded without hesitation. Women at the time of the Prophet obtained rights of which today they are deprived in most Arab countries.

NAWAL EL SAADAWI, THE HIDDEN FACE OF EVE 211, 212 (1980).

consistent with the object and purpose of the Convention. The narrow substantive breach of integrity posed by Egypt's reservation to Article 16 is outweighed by the broad promotion of universal application of the Women's Convention served by that reservation.

The debate surrounding personal status law in Egypt during the twentieth century indicates a serious commitment among Egyptian women, jurists, and politicians to strengthen the marital rights of women. The legal and political history of family law reform in Egypt shows strong potential for the abolition of extra-judicial divorce by husbands in that country. If that comes to pass, Egypt will be better able to withdraw its reservation to Article 16 of the Women's Convention.

b. World Court Jurisdiction[59]

The Statute of the International Court of Justice is a multilateral treaty of a special kind. It contains in Article 36 a centrally important provision, called the Optional Clause, specifying that the ICJ's compulsory jurisdiction may be accepted, unconditionally or with modifications, by any party.[60] Since every member state of the United Nations is automatically a party to the Statute, every state has the right to accept, accept with modifications, or reject the compulsory jurisdiction of the Court.

When a state makes a reservation to the compulsory jurisdiction provision of the Statute, that reservation has an immediate reciprocal effect: other states may invoke the reserving state's reservation against the reserving state. For example, suppose state A makes a reservation allowing itself to be sued only on matters of Admiralty. Later, state A decides to sue state B, a state that has accepted the compulsory jurisdiction of the Court without any reservation, on a question of Broadcast Blocking. Despite the fact that state B has not made a narrowing reservation, state B may invoke A's own narrowing reservation. State B duly informs the Court that Broadcast Blocking is not a question of Admiralty, with the result that the Court will dismiss A's suit against B as lacking in jurisdiction. The Optional Clause allows a state to affirm or disclaim the operation of reciprocity, but it is generally understood that reciprocity operates even if a state has not affirmed its operation, and so far no state has actually disclaimed the operation of reciprocity.

Compulsory jurisdiction gives a court real general authority. Without it, a court's power is relegated to voluntary acceptance by both sides to a dispute.[61] Thus, it is of critical importance to examine the strategies available to states in accepting or rejecting the Optional Clause. We can begin with a simple overall strategy: every state presumably wishes to maximize its potential for aggressive use of the ICJ and minimize its defensive exposure against the aggressive recourse to the Court by others. In brief, states want to be plaintiffs but not defendants. Yet the condition of reciprocity means that there can be no imbalance between the roles of plaintiff or defendant with respect to acceptance of the court's jurisdiction. This ground rule raises an interesting strategic question: can states nevertheless rig their Optional-Clause declarations to maximize their offensive capability and minimize their defensive exposure? Looking into this strategic question is useful not only for those infrequent occasions when a government is thinking about accepting the Court's compulsory jurisdiction or modifying its present acceptance, but also for throwing light upon the inner workings of the principle of reciprocity as applicable generally to the making of reservations to multilateral conventions.

Following are eleven strategies that can be taken into account when any nation is confronted with accepting the Optional Clause or revising its acceptance of the Clause:

1. *Don't Be a Sitting Duck.* Suppose state A, which has not accepted the World Court's compulsory jurisdiction,

---

[59] By ANTHONY D'AMATO, adapted from: *Modifying U.S. Acceptance of the Compulsory Jurisdiction of the World Court,* 79 AMERICAN JOURNAL OF INTERNATIONAL LAW 385 (1985). Reprinted by permission.

[60] Article 36 of the Court's Statute reads:

(2) The states parties to the present Statute may at any time declare that they recognize as compulsory ipso facto and without special agreement, in relation to any other state accepting the same obligation, the jurisdiction of the Court in all legal disputes concerning:
(a) the interpretation of a treaty;
(b) any question of international law;
(c) the existence of any fact which, if established, would constitute a breach of an international obligation;
(d) the nature or extent of the reparation to be made for the breach of an international obligation.
(3) The declarations referred to above may be made unconditionally or on condition of reciprocity on the part of several or certain states, or for a certain time.

[61] We even *think* of rules of law in a different way depending on whether a court exists that has compulsory jurisdiction over the dispute. If there is ultimately a court either side can resort to, then we tend to think of the "law" of the dispute, at least in part, as a prediction of what the court might decide. Without compulsory jurisdiction, we don't have to think of the applicable law as a prediction of what any particular court might do. True, in international law the parties still must take into account their best prediction as to how other states might react and what the U.N. might do, but they don't have to think of the rules in terms of what the International Court of Justice (including the philosophies of the individual judges of the court) might do about it.

contemplates bringing suit against state B. There is no need for state A to have accepted the optional clause because A can file its declaration under the optional clause a day or two before instituting its suit. Thus, as long as A has not accepted the Court's compulsory jurisdiction, it cannot be sued by B, but if it wants to sue B, it simply files its acceptance just before filing the suit. Consequently, B is a "sitting duck" for the offensive actions of other states but – as to those states that do not have standing acceptances of compulsory jurisdiction – has no offensive capability of its own.

The problem can be remedied by adding a proviso to B's Declaration similar to the British exception, which excludes from jurisdiction those states that have deposited or ratified their acceptance of the Court's compulsory jurisdiction less than 12 months prior to filing their lawsuit. Not only will this protect B, but it will also serve the international interest in gaining general acceptance of the Court's compulsory jurisdiction by encouraging states such as state A to file their declarations well in advance of a given dispute.

2. *Don't Get Hit By a Single Shot*. Suppose state A, anticipating that it may want to sue B with regard to mineral claims in Antarctica, files an acceptance of the Court's compulsory jurisdiction limited to "disputes involving or regarding Antarctica." Twelve months later, state A sues B without ever having exposed itself to general litigation by B or other states. The British Declaration seems to address such a problem by excepting "disputes in respect of which any other Party to the dispute has accepted the compulsory jurisdiction of the International Court of Justice only in relation to or for the purpose of the dispute." But this language, or even appropriately modified language, probably will not suffice to achieve its purpose. For example, would it exclude the Antarctica hypothetical? Twelve months after the fact, the United States might have a hard time proving that state B had accepted jurisdiction for questions relating to Antarctica to enable it to file that particular suit later. If nothing else, Nicaragua v. United States is a warning that vague language in declarations of acceptance of jurisdiction may meet with unsympathetic interpretation by the Court.

Additionally, subject-matter limitations to declarations of acceptance of jurisdiction should be welcomed as at least partial steps along the road to general acceptance. An Antarctica-question limitation, for instance, is not per se objectionable. Thus, it would probably be unwise to attempt to defeat all such subject-matter limitations in advance by such vague formulas as that of the British exception, "in relation to or for the purpose of the dispute."

Instead, the remedy for B in such a case is not an additional exception to its Declaration, but rather an alertness on the part of its government to react within 6 months to limited acceptances of compulsory jurisdiction. Thus, if state A, 12 months before filing suit against B accepts the compulsory jurisdiction of the World Court only for questions regarding Antarctica, B could modify its own Declaration within the next 6 months to take state A's possible tactics into account. For example, B could amend its Declaration to exclude disputes on questions relating to Antarctica if the other party to the dispute has limited its acceptance of jurisdiction to such questions. Perhaps B might decide, in the actual instance, not to do this; perhaps it might conclude that a case limited to Antarctica brought by state A would be welcome as a way to resolve legal questions vis-a-vis state A. Such an option would be retained by the strategy here indicated.

3. *Don't Be the Victim of a Hit and Run*. Suppose A sues B in the World Court, and then a day or two after filing suit, withdraws its acceptance of compulsory jurisdiction. This hit-and-run tactic is objectionable from B's standpoint, although it is perhaps not a serious problem in any event. For one thing, any counterclaim B may want to make against state A arising out of the litigation instituted by A is permissible under the Court's rules even after A has withdrawn its acceptance of jurisdiction. However, A's withdrawal may well serve to insulate it from related claims of other states. For example, when state A sues B, its legal theory in the litigation may suggest a similar claim that could be asserted against A. State A's withdrawal would bar a lawsuit by C, perhaps to the tactical disadvantage of B in its litigation strategy.

A related strategy that, as far as I know has not been tried, is to add a condition subsequent to B's declaration, providing for the defeat of jurisdiction if a plaintiff state (in this example, state A) withdraws or modifies its own declaration within 6 months after filing its suit. However, the Court might refuse to give effect to such a condition subsequent, on the ground that the Court, once seised of a case, cannot have its jurisdiction vitiated by a subsequent event. To avoid that adverse possibility, a state might consider transforming a condition subsequent into a condition precedent. For example, B might condition its acceptance of compulsory jurisdiction on the presence of at least a 6-month notice-of-withdrawal provision in A's declaration! Yet such a condition could turn out to be draconian in its effect. Since at least 11 states currently accept compulsory jurisdiction with no provision as to termination, and at least 25 other states currently accept compulsory jurisdiction with undefined duration but with the right to terminate upon notice, the effect of such a modification would be to remove all of these states from the possibility of being sued by (or suing) whichever state adopts B's strategy. Since states are notoriously slow to modify their World Court declarations, the negative impact of these disabilities upon the Court's jurisdiction might be long-lasting.

4. *Watch Out for Last-Minute Withdrawal.* Nations don't usually sue other nations "out of the blue." Usually there are meetings, negotiations, diplomatic initiatives, telephone calls, and many other procedures to resolve potential disputes. But suppose these don't work, and state A hints that it might seek resolution of the problem in the World Court. State B therefore is put on notice that a lawsuit is imminent.

Suppose that, to head off the lawsuit, state B summarily exercises its right under the Optional Clause to withdraw from the compulsory jurisdiction of the World Court. Will B thus be insulated against suit? The Court will probably step in and declare that last-minute withdrawal is not allowed. In Nicaragua v. United States, the Court held that a 3-day period of withdrawal would not amount to a reasonable time, drawing upon an analogy to the law of treaties, which requires a reasonable time for withdrawal from treaties that contain no provision regarding the duration of their validity.[62]

Nevertheless, state A cannot count on the Court's reading into B's declaration a reasonable withdrawal time. But the problem for A is that, while it may itself specify a "notice of withdrawal" period (say, six months), if B specifies no period or a very brief period (say, a week), under the "reciprocal" interpretation of the Optional Clause the Court will have to take the shorter of these periods of time as operative. In other words, B would get its week, and A would also get a week to withdraw from a lawsuit initiated by B (even though A's own Declaration provides for six months). But this doesn't do A any good if all it wants is to sue B, and is not worried about a suit by B.

The fact is that A doesn't have an assured strategy. Since B didn't have to accept the Court's compulsory jurisdiction in the first place, B certainly has the right to withdraw its acceptance. The most A can hope for is to set up a rule, like the three-day rule in the Nicaragua case, for reasonable notice prior to withdrawal. The best place for A to do this is in its own Declaration. Thus, if A specifies that it reserves the right to withdraw its Declaration upon giving the Court ten days' notice, the Court might view this as minimally reasonable, and apply it to all states (like B) who do not themselves actually specify a shorter withdrawal period than ten days. Thus, if B specifies no withdrawal period at all (many states in fact specify no withdrawal period), the Court might infer a reasonable notice period of ten days. In that event, once A tips its hand that it may be suing B, A has at least ten days to get its case filed in the Court before B's withdrawal can become effective.

5. *Beware of the Connally Trap.* For many years before the United States withdrew from the compulsory jurisdiction of the World Court, its Declaration accepting that jurisdiction had contained the "Connally reservation" named after Senator Connally who insisted on it at the time the United States ratified the Charter of the United Nations. The Connally reservation excepts from that jurisdiction "disputes with regard to matters which are essentially within the domestic jurisdiction of the United States of America as determined by the United States of America." Because the reservation seems to set up the United States as judge and jury in its own cause, it has been the subject of voluminous scholarly commentary, mostly hostile.[63] President Eisenhower urged the repeal of "our present self-judging reservation" in his State of the Union message in 1960.[64] I argue that, for any state, the costs of a "Connally" reservation exceed its benefits, and in any event it is a reservation that is apt to backfire.

Suppose state A has a Connally reservation. The principle of reciprocity assures that if state A sues state B, B may invoke the Connally reservation in its own defense. The interesting point is that B's invocation of A's Connally reservation will most likely be more effective for B offensively than if A, the maker of the reservation, had used it defensively as A had intended it to be used. For when A, the maker of the reservation, is plaintiff and B invokes A's reservation, the validity of the reservation, as the Court held in the Norwegian Loans case,[65] is not in issue. It is not in issue, presumably, because the Court does not want to be in a position to rule that A's reservation is invalid when A is not invoking the reservation! The net result is that B will have a free ride on A's self-judging reservation, as indeed Norway did in the Norwegian Loans case. The

[62] Military and Paramilitary Activities in and against Nicaragua (Nicar. v. U.S.), Jurisdiction and Admissibility, 1984 ICJ Rep. 392 (Judgment of Nov. 26). The Court's interpretation of a 3-day period as not constituting a reasonable period of time was undoubtedly made easier by the fact that the Nicaraguan Declaration says nothing about withdrawal or termination; hence, by "operation of law" it can be said that a reasonable time should be read into it. The situation would be made more difficult for the Court if it had to construe one of the several declarations that provide expressly for withdrawal to take place from the moment of notification. However, having once determined that 3 days is not a reasonable time, the Court may find it possible, when later confronted with a declaration providing for withdrawal from the "moment" of notification, to say that although withdrawal takes effect as of the moment of notification, the notification process itself must consume a reasonable period of time after preliminary notice is given to other states that the notification process has begun.

[63] *See* the references cited in Crawford, *The Legal Effect of Automatic Reservations to the Jurisdiction of the International Court*, 50 BRIT Y.B. INT'L L. 63, 63 n.3 (1979).

[64] 42 Dep't St. Bull. 111, 118 (1960).

[65] Case of Certain Norwegian Loans (Fr. v. Nor.), 1957 ICJ REP. 9, 27 (Judgment of July 6).

situation is quite different if A wants to use its own reservation defensively. Suppose state C sues state A, and A invokes its "Connally" reservation to say that the case involves a matter within the domestic jurisdiction of A as A has determined it is. As plaintiff, C can make argue, first, that because international law in fact does extend to the particular dispute in question, A's invocation of the reservation has not been done in good faith and thus should be rejected by the Court. Second, C may argue that the self-judging reservation is incompatible with Article 36, paragraph 6 of the Statute of the Court, which provides that "in the event of a dispute as to whether the Court has jurisdiction, the matter shall be settled by a decision of the Court." State C will not want to go so far as Judge Lauterpacht, who said that the presence of a "Connally" self-judging reservation vitiates A's entire declaration of acceptance of compulsory jurisdiction,[66] because that would do C no good in the lawsuit it has instituted against A. Rather, C should argue to the Court that only the Connally reservation itself should be deleted from A's acceptance of compulsory jurisdiction – the rest of A's Declaration should be left intact. This argument – assuming that C's case against A is meritorious and clearly outside A's "domestic jurisdiction" – would have a reasonable chance of succeeding. Third, as a back-up argument, C could contend that A's invocation of its Connally reservation should be interpreted according to a standard of reasonableness in order to preserve the Court's ultimate power under Article 36 to adjudicate questions of its own jurisdiction. Under a reasonableness standard, A's attempt to use its Connally reservation to remove a clearly international case from the Court's docket by spuriously determining it to be a case of domestic jurisdiction, should be summarily rejected by the Court. To be sure, a reasonableness standard would apply to both offensive and defensive uses of the Connally reservation. Even so, the ambit of reasonableness is likely to be larger in a defensive use because there it is applied against the party that initiated and formulated the reservation. Thus, whichever of these three arguments or combination of them is used, there is a substantial probability that A will see its Connally reservation blunted or destroyed when used defensively in the way it was meant to be used, and yet be subject to the humiliation of having it invoked successfully against it when it attempts to sue another state.

There is no substantive need for the Connally reservation. Since the World Court can only deal with questions of international law, anything that is a matter of domestic jurisdiction is ipso facto not a matter of international law. At best, the Connally reservation is a tautology; at worst, it can work against the state that adopts it.

6. *Eschew the Vandenberg Complication.* Senator Vandenberg's reservation to the U.S. Declaration of 1946 withholds from the Court's compulsory jurisdiction disputes arising under a multilateral treaty unless "all parties to the treaty affected by the decision are also parties to the case before the Court." The reservation was added partly out of a sense of excess caution by a nation not familiar with the jurisprudence of the World Court (the United States had not joined the predecessor Permanent Court of International Justice), and partly to ensure that the United States not be the only one of several parties to a multilateral dispute bound by a decision of the Court. The wording of the reservation leaves much to be desired; as the Court asked in Nicaragua v. United States, how can the Court determine who is "affected" until the final decision in the case is reached on the merits?[67]

As a practical matter, there are today many broadly based, fundamental multilateral conventions. It is hard to imagine any lawsuit that would bring fifty or a hundred or more states as parties before the Court. Under the Court's own rules regarding intervention and indispensable party practice, it is clear that Senator Vandenberg's concerns are amply met by the Court's procedures. Despite a valiant attempt by the U.S. litigators in the Nicaragua Case to flesh out and insist upon the validity of the Vandenberg reservation, the Court dispatched it rather handily. In the future, that reservation will only serve to slow down and complicate jurisdictional questions, and – like the Connally reservation – it may hurt the adopting state more when invoked by others than when it invokes the reservation defensively.

7. *Avoid the All-or-None Approach.* A nation might condition its acceptance of the Court's compulsory jurisdiction upon the similar acceptance of all other nations. Although such a universalist sentiment is commendable, it is unrealistic. You can't get all the nations of the world to agree on anything. However, if a nation wishes to dissemble, using an all-or-none clause as a fig leaf to cover its total disinterest in compulsory jurisdiction, then as fig leaves go this is probably not much worse than any other. (It does have the drawback of appearing to pander to the lowest

---

[66] Dissenting in the Interhandel Case (Switz. v. U.S.), 1959 ICJ Rep. 6, 95, 101–02 (Judgment of Mar. 21), Judge Lauterpacht said that the Connally reservation, "being an essential part of the U.S. Declaration of Acceptance, cannot be separated from it so as to remove from the Declaration the vitiating element of inconsistency with the World Court's Statute and of the absence of a legal obligation." In other words, a self-serving acceptance is an illusory acceptance, amounting to no acceptance at all.

[67] Nicaragua Case, paras. 72, 75. The Court cogently posited the hypothetical that "if the Court were to decide to reject the Application of Nicaragua on the facts, there would be no third State's claim to be affected." *Id.*, para. 75.

common denominator: state A is saying in effect that A's policy will be governed by state Z, the worst state in the international community.)

But failing to accept the Optional Clause – whether by a dissembling all-or-none statement or by flat-out non-acceptance – is a poor strategy for any nation that has an interest in the furtherance of the rule of law in the world. Joining in the World Court's compulsory jurisdiction is a net asset for such a nation, not a net liability. If state A believes that it itself is law-abiding, it must also believe that it is less likely to be sued by other states for violating international law than it is likely to want to sue other states for their violations of international law. An aggressive use of the World Court to sue other states can well serve the interests of state A, moving the resolution of international conflicts from the battlefield to the courtroom.

8. *Avoid the Swiss Cheese Fallacy*. Some states have specified certain subjects as being outside the ambit of compulsory jurisdiction. By thus creating "holes" in their acceptance of the Court's jurisdiction, they believe they are protected legal incursions into sensitive matters of national security or high national interest. The approach, however appealing it may appear, is fallacious. To illustrate, let us consider two examples.

First, the Canadian Declaration omits from compulsory jurisdiction

> disputes arising out of or concerning jurisdiction or rights claimed or exercised by Canada in respect of the conservation, management or exploitation of the living resources of the sea, or in respect of the prevention or control of pollution or contamination of the marine environment in marine areas adjacent to the coast of Canada.

However, the definition of what constitutes a dispute "arising out of or concerning" the named areas is a matter for the Court and not for Canada to say (for Canada has not utilized a self-serving "Connally" reservation). What, for example, is a marine area "adjacent" to the coast of Canada? Are the Pacific and Atlantic Oceans in their entirety marine areas adjacent to Canada's coast? If not, how far out does "adjacency" extend? Is the "sea" mentioned in the first clause of Canada's reservation the same as the "marine areas" mentioned in the second clause?

It is clear that Canada is especially concerned about the areas and subject-matters mentioned in its reservation. But the higher the degree of concern, the more it would seem in Canada's interest to be able to litigate questions of law involving those areas and subject-matters. Thus, the Court, in a case involving the marine environment of Africa, might define the customary law of the conservation, exploitation or management of living resources of the sea in a way that would have a negative impact upon the interpretation of all of Canada's claims to the same subject-matters. If Canada, with its expert attorneys in international legal advocacy, were to try to intervene as a party in interest in the hypothetical Africa that I have just mentioned, their own reservation would disable them from doing so. Perhaps a recognition of this disablement led Australia in 1975 to withdraw its Declaration of 1954, which had contained a similar exclusion in respect to Australia's continental shelf. Australia instead accepted the Court's compulsory jurisdiction without any subject-matter reservation.

As a second example, let us consider a possible U.S. reservation excluding disputes involving armed hostilities. In Nicaragua v. United States, such a reservation was argued by the United States to be implied as a limitation upon the judicial process. The Court, however, found by a vote of 16 to 0 that the ongoing armed conflict in Nicaragua was no barrier to judicial resolution of the legal aspects of that conflict. Faced with this decisive rejection of its strenuously argued position, the United States might very well have contemplated adding an explicit exclusion for disputes involving armed hostilities to its declaration on compulsory jurisdiction.

Such a reservation, however, would disable the United States from resorting to the Court in many cases that may arise in the future. For example, if American diplomats are taken hostage, as occurred in Teheran in 1979, the involvement of armed hostilities (the Iranian "students" at that time stormed the American Embassy and took prisoners by force of arms) might well exclude such a dispute from the jurisdiction of the Court. (Recall that the Court will treat a nation's own exclusion more generously when invoked reciprocally by the opposing party!) The same exclusion would apply if American citizens were involved in a terrorist attack abroad, especially one with the apparent complicity of the local government. Another significant and unfortunate effect of such a reservation would be to encourage disputes that have begun peacefully to be escalated by the party opposed to the United States just in order to defeat World Court jurisdiction. Thus, a dispute over fishing rights in a self-proclaimed "exclusive economic zone" might encourage a foreign country to send military vessels to the scene, and perhaps to fire warning shots at the American fishing vessel, so as to bring the dispute under the U.S. exclusion for cases involving armed hostilities. Or a military action that has ceased, and thus becomes subject to a lawsuit for damages, might be revived by intermittent military actions. It would be most ironic if a U.S. reservation regarding armed hostilities would itself lead to an escalation of armed hostilities in the world.

Any attempt to cut a "hole" in the jurisdiction of the Court by a subject-matter exclusion may thus give rise to either or both of the negative effects discussed in the two preceding examples. In any event, it would evoke the image of a nation afraid to trust the Court on certain subjects, an image hardly conductive to the goal of encouraging all nations to settle their disputes in court rather than by resorting to military power.

9. *Should you Deal from a Limited Deck?* The opposite of excluding certain subject-matters from the ambit of a general compulsory jurisdiction would be to decline jurisdiction except for certain specified subject-matters. Thus, for instance, a nation that has not accepted compulsory jurisdiction at all might begin by accepting it solely with respect to questions involving outer space and Antarctica. Later, encouraged by the Court's jurisprudence in dealing with these subjects, that nation might add another card or two to the jurisdictional deck – for example, questions involving the law of the sea or the rights and duties of ambassadors. Gradually over time (hopefully not centuries), enough states would add enough subjects to give the Court almost universal jurisdictional competence.

There is little that is strategically unwise about such a procedure, and indeed it may be a feasible way of introducing reluctant states to the idea of having their disputes settled by the Court. The idea itself is time-honored, dating back to proposals for international arbitration at the end of the 19th century. But what would be a step forward for states that have not subscribed to the optional clause would just as clearly be a step backward for states that currently accept compulsory jurisdiction. For states that now accept the general jurisdiction of the Court, the limited-deck procedure would be retrogressive from the standpoint of the general viability of the international legal system. (Recall that the states that now accept the full jurisdiction of the Court would still be able to invoke defensively the limited-deck restrictions of states that might sue them.)

But the difficulty of drawing bounds and limits of specified named subjects, which I discussed in the "Swiss Cheese" section, continues to apply here when the reverse strategy is utilized. For example, suppose that the United States had modified its acceptance of the Court's compulsory jurisdiction so that the only areas included are the law of the sea and human rights. Would such a limited-deck have blocked the United States from the lawsuit by Nicaragua? By slightly changing its allegations, Nicaragua could have brought exactly the same case against the United States. It could have alleged that the U.S. mining of its harbors violated the law of the sea. It could have added that "law of the sea" jurisdiction was also implicated by the U.S. use of the high seas to ship arms to insurgent groups in Nicaragua. And, to bring the case within the "human rights" area, Nicaragua could have alleged that U.S. military and economic support for the insurgents in Nicaragua resulted directly in violations of the human rights of Nicaraguan citizens committed by the insurgents. In short, not only would the limitation to the law of the sea and human rights have failed to block the Nicaraguan lawsuit against the United States, but, to make matters worse, those limitations might at least arguably block a U.S. defense/counterclaim in the very same case that U.S. military and paramilitary activity in the region was designed to contain Nicaraguan aggression against its neighbors. Attorneys for Nicaragua would certainly be expected to argue that external aggression does not come within the U.S. subject-matter limitations of law of the sea and human rights!

10. *Don't Pass the Buck.* A state could accept the compulsory jurisdiction of the Court except for those matters which are under consideration by the political organs of the United Nations. Consider the old Declaration of the United Kingdom and other Commonwealth countries under Article 36, paragraph 2 of the Statute of the Permanent Court of International Justice (predecessor to the ICJ). The reservation allowed the British Government to suspend judicial proceedings in respect of any dispute "which has been submitted to and is under consideration by the Council of the League of Nations." What would a similar reservation entail, substituting "Security Council" for the Council of the League?

In the first place, under the principle of reciprocity, such a reservation would allow either the plaintiff or the defendant state to suspend judicial proceedings. Second, Article 35 of the UN Charter allows any member state to bring a dispute to the attention of the Security Council, the judicial proceedings would be subject to suspension by the action of any other state. With so many current member states in the United Nations, there will surely be one state that will have an interest, even if only a perverse one, in bringing a litigated case before the Security Council so as to suspend the litigation. Third, either party might bring the case to the attention of the Security Council in order to get out of defending the lawsuit; this gets very close to a self-serving reservation that we saw was self-defeating under the discussion of the Connally Trap. To be sure, under the British reservation to the PCIJ, it would not be enough merely to bring the matter to the attention of the Council; the Council must also decide to take the matter under consideration. Yet we must recall that, under the law of the Charter, procedural questions are not subject to veto, but require only an affirmative vote of 9 out of the 15 members of the Security Council. Nine member states might vote to take a matter under consideration just for the political purpose of helping out whichever party seems to have the weaker case before the ICJ. Such possible disruptive effects upon the Court's judicial processes, including random and nonsensical ones, make this passing-the-buck type of reservation undesirable. We know too much now about the political nature of voting in the United Nations to be as complacent about giving those political organs preemptive jurisdictional powers as were the old members of the League of Nations.

Passing the buck may have seemed desirable to the United States in the aftermath of the Nicaragua litigation. In that case, the United States argued that the Nicaraguan claim was inadmissible before the Court because it was a "political question" as evidenced by Nicaragua's simultaneous appeal to the Security Council for a condemnation of U.S. military and paramilitary activities in and against Nicaragua. The Court held against the United States on this point, again by a vote of 16 to 0. It pointed out that although the Security Council is given "primary responsibility for the maintenance of international peace and security" under Article 24 of the UN Charter, "primary" does not mean "exclusive." But, for the reasons given, the strategy of passing the buck can backfire.

11. *Don't Even Pass a Certified Buck.* A variant on the preceding scheme, that might be of interest to the five Permanent Members of the Security Council, would be a declaration dis-seising the Court of litigation only if the Security Council, including the five permanent members, agrees to consider the dispute. Under such a stipulation, any Permanent Member would be in the self-serving position of having a veto over any potential suspension of litigation. However, the ICJ would probably see through such a declaration as a self-serving reservation, and might invalidate it altogether as an attempt to strip the Court of its statutory right to finally determine disputed questions of jurisdiction. What makes the situation even worse than the Connally Amendment is the inherent lack of reciprocity in the arrangement: if the other party to the dispute is not a Permanent Member of the Security Council, it would not have the same power as the first party. This lack of reciprocity would probably loom large in the Court's deliberation whether to rule that passing a certified buck in this case is a sham. A final argument open to the Court would be that, under the principle that voting rules specified in the Charter cannot be modified by specific treaties, the Court's jurisdiction cannot be modified by a procedure that depends on obtaining a particularly specified majority vote in the Security Council.

Finally, any attempt to attach to a passing-the-buck type of reservation the provision that it applies only to disputes that endanger international peace and security will not suffice to cure the problems previously mentioned. The World Court will undoubtedly itself decide whether the dispute is likely to endanger peace and security, under its statutory power to determine questions regarding its own jurisdiction. We should then not be too surprised if the Court held that the dispute cannot endanger peace and security so long as it is subject to the Court's own jurisdiction and resolvable by the application of accepted principles of customary international law. This would have the perverse effect of possibly stripping the Security Council of its inherent powers to determine whether certain disputes are a threat to the peace or a breach of the peace. Hence, despite the fact that the British declaration seemed to work under the old PCIJ, I doubt whether a similar strategy would pass muster with the ICJ today.

4. Compliance[68]

Our concern is with contemporary agreements of relatively high political salience in fields such as security, economics, and environment, where the treaty is a central structural element in a broader international regulatory regime. We believe that when nations enter into an international agreement of this kind, they alter their behavior, their relationships, and their expectations of one another over time in accordance with its terms. That is, they will to some extent comply with the undertakings they have made.

According to Louis Henkin, "almost all nations observe almost all principles of international law and almost all of their obligations almost all of the time."[69] The observation is frequently repeated without anyone, so far as we know, supplying any empirical evidence to support it. A moment's reflection shows that it would not be easy to devise a statistical protocol that would generate such evidence. For example, how would Iraq's unbroken respect for the borders of Turkey, Jordan, and Saudi Arabia count in the reckoning against the invasions of Iran and Kuwait?

Equally, and for much the same reasons, there is no way to validate empirically the position of mainstream realist international relations theory going back to Machiavelli, that "a prudent ruler cannot keep his word, nor should he, where such fidelity would damage him, and when the reasons that made him promise are no longer relevant." Contemporary realists accept that the interest in reciprocal observation of treaty norms by other parties or a more general interest in the state's reputation as a reliable contractual partner should be counted in the trade-off of costs and benefits on which a decision is based (an extension that detracts considerably from the power and elegance of the realist formula). No calculus, however, will supply a rigorous, nontautological answer to the question whether a state observed a particular treaty obligation, much less its treaty obligations generally, only when it was in its interest to

---

[68] By ABRAM CHAYES and ANTONIA HANDLER CHAYES, from: *On Compliance,* 47 INTERNATIONAL ORGANIZATION 175–84, 186–87, 197–98, 201–02, 204–05 (1993). Reprinted by permission.

[69] LOUIS HENKIN, HOW NATIONS BEHAVE 47 (2d ed. 1979).

do so. Anecdotal evidence abounds for both the normative and the realist propositions, but neither of them, in their general form, is subject to statistical or empirical proof. The difference between the two schools is not one of fact but of the background assumption that informs their approach to the subject.

A critical question for any study of compliance, then, is which background assumption to adopt, and that question is to be resolved not on the basis of whether the assumption is "true" or "false" but whether or not it is helpful for the particular inquiry. Thus, for game-theoretic approaches that focus on the abstract structure of the relationship between states, the realist assumption of a unitary rational actor optimizing utilities distributed along smooth preference curves may have value. As Thomas Schelling said at the beginning of his classic work, "The premise of 'rational behavior' is a potent one for the production of theory. Whether the resulting theory provides good or poor insight into actual behavior is a matter for subsequent judgment."[70]

Organization theory would reach the same result but by a different route. In place of the continuously calculating, maximizing rational actor, it substitutes a "satisficing" model of bounded rationality that reacts to problems as they arise and searches for solutions within a familiar and accustomed repertoire. In this analysis, bureaucratic organizations are viewed as functioning according to routines and standard operating procedure, often specified by authoritative rules and regulations. For Max Weber, this was the defining characteristic of bureaucracy.[71] The adoption of a treaty, like the enactment of any other law, establishes an authoritative rule system. Compliance is the normal organizational presumption.

The bureaucracy is not monolithic, of course, and it will likely contain opponents of the treaty regime as well as supporters. When there is an applicable rule in a treaty or otherwise, opposition ordinarily surfaces in the course of rule implementation and takes the form of argument over interpretation of language and definition of the exact content of the obligation. Such controversies are settled in accordance with normal bureaucratic procedures in which, again, the presumption is in favor of "following" the rule. Casuistry is admissible, though sometimes suspect. An advocate of outright violation bears a heavy burden of persuasion.

The assertion that states carry out treaty commitments only when it is in their interest to do so seems to imply that commitments are somehow unrelated to interests. In fact, the opposite is true. The most basic principle of international law is that states cannot be legally bound except with their own consent.[72] So, in the first instance, the state need not enter into a treaty that does not confirm to its interest.[73]

More important, a treaty does not present the state with a simple binary alternative, to sign or not to sign. Treaties, like other legal arrangements, are artifacts of political choice and social existence. The process by which they are formulated and concluded is designed to ensure that the final result will represent, to some degree, an accommodation of the interests of the negotiating states. Of course, if state interests are taken to be fixed and given, the assertion that states do not conclude treaties except as they embody those interests would add little to the realist position. But modern treaty making, like legislation in a democratic polity, can be seen as a creative enterprise through which the parties weigh the benefits and burdens of commitment to explore, redefine, and sometimes discover their interests. It is at its best a learning process in which not only national positions but also conceptions of national interest evolve.

In contrast to day-to-day foreign policy decision making that is oriented toward current political exigencies and imminent deadlines and is focused heavily on short-term costs and benefits, the more deliberate process employed in treaty making may serve to identify and reinforce longer range interests and values. Officials engaged in developing the negotiating position often have an additional reason to take a long-range view, since they may have operational responsibility under any agreement that is reached. What they say and how they conduct themselves at the negotiating table may return to haunt them once the treaty has gone into effect. Moreover, they are likely to attach considerable importance to the development of governing norms that will operate predictably when applied to the behavior of the parties over time. All these convergent elements tend to influence national positions in the direction of broad-based conceptions of the national interest that, if adequately reflected in the treaty, will help to induce compliance.

It is true that a state's incentives at the treaty-negotiating stage may be different from those it faces when the time for compliance rolls around. Parties on the giving end of the compromise, especially, might have reason to seek to escape the obligations they have undertaken. Nevertheless, the very act of making commitments embodied in an international agreement changes the calculus at the compliance

---

70 THOMAS C. SCHELLING, THE STRATEGY OF CONFLICT 4 (1980).

71 M. RHEINSTEIN (ED.), MAX WEBER ON LAW IN ECONOMY AND SOCIETY 350 (1954).

72 [Editor's Note: The authors, presumably, are referring to treaties, and not to international law in general.]

73 Even in the case of peace treaties, the victor seems to attach importance to the signature of the vanquished on the document. After the Persian Gulf War, for example, the UN Security Council insisted that Iraq accept the terms of Resolution 687 establishing a cease-fire.

stage, if only because it generates expectations of compliance in others that must enter into the equation.

Moreover, although states may know they can violate their treaty commitments in a crunch, they do not negotiate agreements with the idea that they can do so in routine situations. Thus, the shape of the substantive bargain will itself be affected by the parties' estimates of the costs and risks of their own compliance and expectations about the compliance of others. Essential parties may be unwilling to accept or impose stringent regulations if the prospects for compliance are doubtful. The negotiation will not necessarily collapse on that account, however. The result may be a looser, more general engagement. Such an outcome is often deprecated as a lowest-common-denominator outcome, with what is really important left on the cutting room floor. But it may be the beginning of increasingly serious and concerted attention to the problem.

The strongest circumstantial evidence for the sense of an obligation to comply with treaties is the care that states take in negotiating and entering into them. It is not conceivable that foreign ministries and government leaders could devote time and energy on the scale they do to preparing, drafting, negotiating, and monitoring treaty obligations unless there is an assumption that entering into a treaty commitment ought to and does constrain the state's own freedom of action and an expectation that the other parties to the agreement will feel similarly constrained. The care devoted to fashioning a treaty provision no doubt reflects the desire to limit the state's own commitment as much as to make evasion by others more difficult. In either case, the enterprise makes sense only on the assumption that, as a general rule, states acknowledge an obligation to comply with agreements they have signed.

These attitudes are not confined to foreign offices. U.S. Department of Defense testimony during the cold war repeatedly sounded the theme that arms control treaties with the Soviet Union were important in providing the stability of expectations and predictability the Pentagon needed for sound strategic planning. In the United States and other Western countries, the principle that the exercise of governmental power in general is subject to law lends additional force to an ethos of national compliance with international undertakings. And, of course, appeals to legal obligations are staple of foreign policy debate and of the continuous critique and defense of foreign policy actions that account for so much of diplomatic interchange and international political commentary.

All this argues that states, like other subjects of legal rules, operate under a sense of obligation to conform their conduct to governing norms. From the perspective of the system as a whole, however, the central issue is different. For simple prohibitory norms like a highway speed limit, it is in principle a simple matter to determine whether any particular driver is in compliance. Yet most communities and law enforcement organizations in the United States seem to be perfectly comfortable with a situation in which the average speed on interstate highways is perhaps ten miles above the limit. Even in individual cases, the enforcing officer is not likely to pursue a driver operating within that zone. The fundamental problem for the system is not how to induce all drivers to obey the speed limit but how to contain deviance within acceptable levels. So, too, it is for international treaty obligations.

"An acceptable level of compliance" is not an invariant standard. The matter is further complicated because many legal norms are not like the speed limit that permits an on-off judgment as to whether an actor is in compliance. As noted above, questions of compliance are often contestable and call for complex, subtle, and frequently subjective evaluation. What is an acceptable level of compliance will shift according to the type of treaty, the context, the exact behavior involved, and over time.

It would seem, for example, that the acceptable level of compliance would vary with the significance and cost of the reliance that parties place on the others' performance.[74] How is what is "acceptable" to be determined in any particular instance? The economists have a straightforward answer: invest additional resources in enforcement (or other measures to induce compliance) up to the point at which the value of the incremental benefit from an additional unit of compliance exactly equals the cost of the last unit of additional enforcement resources. Unfortunately, the usefulness of this approach is limited by the impossibility of quantifying even approximately, let alone monetizing, any of the relevant factors in the equation–and markets are not normally available to help.

In such circumstances, as Charles Lindblom has told us, the process by which preferences are aggregated is necessarily a political one.[75] It follows that the choice whether to intensify (or slacken) the international enforcement effort is necessarily a political decision. It implicates all the same interests pro and con that were involved in the initial formulation of the treaty norm, as modified by intervening changes of circumstances. Although the balance will to some degree reflect the expectations of compliance that the parties entertained at that time, it is by no means rare, in international as in domestic politics, to find that what the lawmaker has given in the form of substantive regulation is taken away in the implementation. What is "acceptable" in terms of compliance will reflect the perspective and interests of participants in the ongoing political

---

[74] *See* Charles Lipson, *Why Are Some International Agreements Informal?* [excerpted below, this Chapter.]

[75] Charles E. Lindbolm, Politics and Markets 254–55 (1977).

process rather than some external scientific or market-validated standard.

The foregoing discussion reflects a view of noncompliance as a deviant rather than an expected behavior, and as endemic rather than deliberate. This in turn leads to de-emphasis of formal enforcement measures and even, to a degree, of coercive informal sanctions, except in egregious cases. It shifts attention to sources of noncompliance that can be managed by routine international political processes. Thus, the improvement of dispute resolution procedures goes to the problem of ambiguity; technical and financial assistance may help cure the capacity deficit; and transparency will make it likelier that, over time, national policy decisions are brought increasingly into line with agreed international standards.

These approaches merge in the process of jawboning–an effort to persuade the miscreant to change its ways–that is the characteristic form of international enforcement activity. This process exploits the practical necessity for the putative offender to give reasons and justifications for suspect conduct. These reasons and justifications are reviewed and critiqued in a variety of venues, public and private, formal and informal. The tendency is to winnow out reasonably justifiable or unintended failures to fulfill commitments–those that comport with a good-faith compliance standard–and to identify and isolate the few cases of egregious and willful violation. By systematically addressing and eliminating all mitigating circumstances that might possibly be advanced, this process can ultimately demonstrate that what may at first have seemed like ambiguous conduct is a black-and-white case of deliberate violation. The offending state is left with a stark choice between conforming to the rule as defined and applied in the particular circumstances or openly flouting its obligation. This turns out to be a very uncomfortable position for even a powerful state.

Enforcement through these interacting measures of assistance and persuasion is less costly and intrusive and is certainly less dramatic than coercive sanctions, the easy and usual policy elixir for noncompliance. It has the further virtue that it is adapted to the needs and capacities of the contemporary international system.

B. Soft Law

1. Relative Normativity[76]

Alongside "hard law," made up of the norms creating precise legal rights and obligations, the normative system of international law comprises more and more norms whose substance is so vague, so uncompelling, that A's obligation and B's right all but elude the mind. One does not have to look far for examples of this "fragile," "weak," or "soft law," as it is dubbed at times: the 1963 Moscow Treaty banning certain nuclear weapon tests, Article IV of which provides, inter alia, that "each Party shall in exercising its national sovereignty have the right to withdraw from the Treaty if it decides that extraordinary events, related to the subject matter of this Treaty, have jeopardized the supreme interests of its country";[77] the numerous treaty provisions whereby the parties undertake merely to consult together, to open negotiations, to settle certain problems by subsequent agreement; and the purely hortatory or exhortatory provisions whereby they undertake to "seek to," "make efforts to," "promote," "avoid," "examine with understanding," "act as swiftly as possible," "take all due steps with a view to," etc. While particularly common in economic matters, these "precarious" norms are similarly encountered in the political field, as witness, apart from the above-quoted Moscow Treaty provision, a recent Advisory Opinion of the International Court of Justice including obligations "to co-operate in good faith" and "to consult together" among the "legal principles and rules" governing the relations between an international organization and a host country.[78] Whether a rule is "hard" or "soft" does not, of course, affect its normative character. A rule of treaty or customary law may be vague, "soft"; but, as the above examples show, it does not thereby cease to be a legal norm. Yet the fact remains that the proliferation of "soft" norms, of what some also call "hortatory" or "programmatory" law, does not help strengthen the international normative system.

The acts accomplished by subjects of international law are so diverse in character that it is no simple matter for a jurist to determine what may be called the normativity threshold: i.e., the line of transition between the nonlegal and the legal, between what does not constitute a norm and what does. At what point does a "nonbinding agreement" turn into an international agreement, a promise into a unilateral act, fact into custom? Of course, this problem of the transition from nonlaw to law occurs in all legal systems, in particular under the guise of the distinction between moral and legal obligation. But the multiplicity of the forms of action secreted by the needs of international intercourse has rendered it more acute in that field than in any other, since in the international order neither prenormative nor normative acts are as clearly differentiated in their effects as in municipal systems. While prenormative acts do not create rights or obligations on which reliance may be placed before an international court of justice or of arbitration, and failure to live up to them does not give

[76] By PROSPER WEIL, excerpted from: *Towards Relative Normativity in International Law*, 77 AMERICAN JOURNAL OF INTERNATIONAL LAW 413 (1983). Reprinted by permission.

[77] 14 UST 1313, TIAS No. 5433, 480 UNTS 43.

[78] Interpretation of the Agreement of 25 March 1951 between the WHO and Egypt, 1980 ICJ Rep. 73, 95 (Advisory Opinion of Dec. 20).

rise to international responsibility, they do create expectations and exert on the conduct of states an influence that in certain cases may be greater than that of rules of treaty or customary law. Conversely, the sanction visited upon the breach of a legal obligation is sometimes less real than that imposed for failure to honor a purely moral or political obligation.

If there is one field pervaded by this problem, it is surely that of the resolutions of international organizations. Today, the distinction between decisions, as creative of legal rights and obligations, and recommendations, as not creative of any "legal obligation to comply with them,"[79] has been rejected by some in favor of a more flexible conception: without crossing the normativity threshold, certain resolutions, it is said, nevertheless possess a "certain legal value" that may vary not only from one resolution to another but, within the same resolution, from clause to clause." Henceforth, "there are no tangible, clear, juridical criteria that demarcate with precision the zones of binding force"; there are only "hazy, intermediate, transitional, embryonic, inchoate situations." Even if resolutions do not attain full normative stature, they nevertheless constitute "embryonic norms" of "nascent legal force," or "quasi-legal rules."[80] In other words, there is no longer any straightforward either/or answer to the problem of the normative force of the acts of international organizations; it is all a matter of degree.

It is beyond question that we are faced here with a pathological phenomenon of international normativity.

This is so in the first place because the concrete content of this partial or attenuated normativity, said to characterize certain acts, is quite beyond the grasp of intellect. Even recourse to the notion of "soft law" – in a different sense, this time – to summon up the picture of a rule not yet hardened into full normativity, leaves it no less elusive. Some writers have sought to narrow the problem by propounding the notion of "permissive" or "abrogatory" force: without creating any obligation, a resolution is supposed at least to have entitling effects, so that any state acting in conformity with it could not thereby be committing an internationally unlawful act. While powerless to create new norms, the resolution would at least have the power to abrogate existing ones, which would leave states free to cease abiding by them. But this is playing with words, for a permissive norm is a norm like any other norm, and only one norm can abrogate another. Thus, to ascribe permissive or abrogatory force to certain resolutions is tantamount to attributing normative force to them, full and undiluted.

Second, we are faced with a pathological phenomenon because the approach in question is based on a misconception. Nobody would deny that certain resolutions serve to prepare, even accelerate, the abrogation of existing norms or the formation of new ones; and it is understandable that states not desiring change in the existing law should oppose the adoption of such resolutions or attach reservations to them, exactly as one might oppose the voting of a resolution or motion by a learned society in the hope of blocking or delaying some development one wished to avert. Resolutions, as the sociological and political expression of trends, intentions, wishes, may well constitute an important stage in the process of elaborating international norms; in themselves, however, they do not constitute the formal source of new norms. That does not mean, of course, that the jurist should ignore them; but between showing due interest in them and integrating them into the normative system under the cover of a sliding scale of normativity, there is a gap that can be bridged only at the cost of denying the specific nature of the legal phenomenon. Unlike national legislatures, international organizations, though capable of defining the "desired law," do not possess what would be the truly legislative power of themselves transforming it into "established law"; thus, normative force cannot be attributed to resolutions without overriding the distinction between lex lata and lex ferenda. It is inadmissible within, say, "development law" or "environmental law," to give equal status to conventional or customary rules, on the one hand, and non-normative resolutions, on the other. Neither is there any warrant for considering that, by dint of repetition, non-normative resolutions can be transmuted into positive law through a sort of incantatory effect: the accumulation of nonlaw or prelaw is no more sufficient to create law than is thrice nothing to make something.

Finally, we are faced with a pathological phenomenon because, however much some writers deny the difference between norms and non-norms, states continue clearly to perceive that difference. Otherwise, what explanation could there be for the way they hammer home the fact that they are not legally bound by this or that resolution, declaration, or final act of a conference? When they subscribe to such instruments (or refrain from opposing them), governments neither intend to commit themselves legally nor feel they are doing so: "they don't mean it."[81]

---

79 Judge Lauterpacht in South West Africa: Voting Procedure, 1955 ICJ Rep. 67, 115 (Advisory Opinion of June 7) (sep. op. Lauterpacht, J.).

80 These expressions (also to be found, with variants, in the writings of several contemporaries) are borrowed from J. Castaneda, Legal Effects of United Nations Resolutions 176 (1969).

81 Arangio-Ruiz, *The Normative Role of the General Assembly of the United Nations and the Declaration of Principles of Friendly Relations,* 137 Recueil des cours 419, 431 (1972 II). *See also* Schwebel, *The Effect of Resolutions of the U.N. General Assembly on Customary International Law,* 73 ASIL Proc. 301, 302 (1979).

True, it is not always easy to draw the frontier between the prelegal and the legal. This is a problem that recurs every time law resorts to the technique of the threshold: between the reasonable and the nonreasonable, the equitable and the nonequitable, the essential and the nonessential, the appurtenant and the nonappurtenant. "I know it when I see it": this celebrated formula of a Justice of the United States Supreme Court aptly illustrates this difficulty. It is nonetheless true that the threshold does exist: on one side of the line, there is born a legal obligation that can be relied on before a court or arbitrator, the flouting of which constitutes an internationally unlawful act giving rise to international responsibility; on the other side, there is nothing of the kind.

While it has always been difficult to locate the threshold beyond which a legal norm existed, at least there used to be no problem once the threshold could be pronounced crossed: the norm created legal rights and obligations; it was binding, its violation sanctioned with international responsibility. There was no distinction on that score to be made between one legal norm and another. But the theory of jus cogens, with its distinction between peremptory and merely binding norms, and the theory of international crimes and delicts, with its distinction between norms creating obligations essential for the preservation of fundamental interests and norms creating obligations of a less essential kind, are both leading to the fission of this unity. Normativity is becoming a question of "more or less": some norms are now held to be of greater specific gravity than others, to be more binding than others. Thus, the scale of normativity is reemerging in a new guise, its gradations no longer plotted merely between norms and non-norms, but also among those norms most undeniably situated on the positive side of the normativity threshold. Having taken its rise in the subnormative domain, the scale of normativity has now been projected and protracted into the normative domain itself, so that, henceforth, there are "norms and norms."[82]

At the same time, normativity is also tending towards dilution. Traditionally, every international norm has had clearly specifiable passive and active subjects: it creates obligations incumbent upon certain subjects of international law, and rights for the benefit of others. The principles governing the relative effect of treaties, the opposability of customary rules, and the capacity to present international claims reflect this individualization of those owing an obligation and those owed a right. But at present both these categories are tending to become indefinite. Where those enjoying rights are concerned, this trend is exemplified by the concept of obligations erga omnes. The same development is less perceptible where those with obligations are concerned; however, the profound transformations that for some time now have been affecting the substance of the sources of law, and more particularly the theory of custom and the interrelation of conventional and customary rules, have been gradually fostering the idea that there are certain obligations that are incumbent on every state without distinction. We are nowadays witnessing the appearance, alongside obligations erga omnes, of what one is tempted to call obligations omnium.

Without question, this development is a factor of progress in many respects. By placing the emphasis on "legal conscience," it helps to ensure the primacy of ethics over the aridity of positive law. Without higher moral "values," international law is but a soulless contrivance: that, more or less, is the essential message of these new theories. By thrusting the concept of "international community" into the foreground, they reflect the awareness of increased solidarity and the aspiration to a greater unity overspanning ideological and economic differences; they also impart the frustration of a Third World that has long felt itself powerless and aspires to place its new majority position within international organizations at the service of what it sees as a fight for justice. In view of the multiplication of states and their increasing diversity, this will to transcend the traditional international society made up of juxtaposed egoisms, and to forge an international community animated by the quest for the "common good" and common "values," is all the more precious. One could even see in it an unexpected return to the historic sources of international law: to "irreducible natural law," no doubt, but also to that fundamental unity of the human race expressed in the 16th century by Vitoria's famous "Totus orbis, qui aliquo modo est una res publica," of which the "international community of States as a whole" is, after all, simply a modernized version.

Accordingly, the potential negative consequences of the relativization of international normativity must at worst be regarded as secondary effects of changes that in themselves are beneficial. Vigilance, however, is imperative, lest too high a price be paid for the progress of international law towards greater moral substance and greater solidarity. At a time when international society needs more than ever a normative order capable of ensuring the peaceful coexistence, and cooperation in diversity, of equal and equally sovereign entities, the waning of voluntarism in favor of the ascendancy of some, neutrality in favor of ideology,

---

82 [Editor's Note: In a portion of his article too long to be excerpted here, Professor Weil cites norms of jus cogens as an example of norms that have a higher status than regular norms. For analysis and debate, see the section on "Jus Cogens" in Chapter 4 in this Anthology.]

positivity in favor of ill-defined values might well destabilize the whole international normative system and turn it into an instrument that can no longer serve its purpose.

Concurrently with the vertical diversification of normativity, a trend towards its lateral dilution has appeared, in that the subjects of rights and obligations have been growing ever more indeterminate. So much so, that it is growing increasingly difficult to determine not only what a norm consists of, but whom it binds, and in favor of whom. It is in this setting that one has to view the famous passage from the 1970 Barcelona Traction Judgment mentioning that certain obligations exist "towards the international community as a whole." "In view of the importance of the rights involved," the Court declared, "all States can be held to have a legal interest in their protection; they are obligations erga omnes."[83] A few years later, in the Nuclear Tests cases, the Court was to analyze certain unilateral statements by French authorities as having been made "erga omnes." Those statements, the Court said, were not "addressed to a particular State" but "to the international community as a whole," and therefore entailed on the part of the French Government an "undertaking to the international community to which [its] words were addressed."[84]

The intention behind the erga omnes theory, as thus conceived, is to sound the death knell of narrow bilateralism and sanctified egoism for the sake of the universal protection of certain fundamental norms relating, in particular, to human rights. Like the jus cogens doctrine, it is inspired by highly respectable ethical considerations. Yet, here too, subjects of doubt and perplexity come crowding in.

This is so, in the first place, because it is no easier, of course, to identify obligations erga omnes than peremptory norms or essential obligations. But the prime source of perplexity lies in the ambiguity surrounding the precise identity of the omnes to whom the obligations are owed. Have the corresponding rights become vested in the "international community as a whole," or in each of its component states ut singuli? The first alternative would imply the possession by the international community of some organic representation capable of taking legal action for the protection of its rights, which is certainly not the case. The second would signify that any state, acting separately and on its own behalf, could claim the fulfillment of an obligation erga omnes and invoke the international responsibility of any other state committing a breach of it. But then more questions arise. Is it contemplated that there should be some reparation of the classic type? If so, it is hard to see what injury would have been sustained by the applicant or what, apart from a declaratory judgment, an individual constituent of the omnes could claim. Is punishment envisaged? In the absence of any judicial channels organized to that end, that would mean that any state, in the name of higher values as determined by itself, could appoint itself the avenger of the international community. Thus, under the banner of law, chaos and violence would come to reign among states, and international law would turn on and rend itself with the loftiest of intentions.

As one might well expect, the conventional norm has put up greater resistance to this process of increasing indeterminacy of the subjects of international obligations: treaty-conclusion procedures comprise too many tangible signs, and the principle of relative effect is too respectably entrenched, for the distinction between parties and third persons to be easily overcome. Hence, the conventional norm has not been frontally assaulted but cunningly outflanked. The principle remains that an international treaty binds only the states that have become parties to it, and cannot create obligations incumbent upon third states. Yet behind the mask of classicism thus retained there has been a change of substance: in reality, the conventional norm itself may now create obligations incumbent upon all states, including those not parties to the convention in question.

What was needed in order to reach this point was, in the first place, to erode the autonomy of the conventional rule vis-a-vis the customary rule. Admittedly, these two categories have never been divided by an insuperable barrier, and it has always been accepted that a treaty could codify or contribute to the formation of a customary norm. But these once exceptional phenomena are now of such frequent occurrence and far-reaching scope as to have become intrinsically altered. Treaty clauses that are declaratory of preexistent customary norms, or crystallize customary norms in process of formation, or attract concordant practice "like iron filings to a magnet":[85] these three variant erasers of the frontier between conventional and customary norms have been too often discussed to require further comment here.

The relationship between the conventional rule and the customary rule goes much farther, however, than the mere "interaction" or "interpenetration" described by writers. The conventional norm—once regarded as the archetypal rule of international law because the purest expression of classic consensualism—is now considered to be a minor variety unable to attain full stature until it has passed into the general corpus of international law. The decision of the court of arbitration on the Delimitation of the Continental Shelf between France and the United Kingdom bears witness to this tendency towards outright identification of

---

83 1970 ICJ Rep. at 32.

84 Nuclear Tests (Austl. v. Fr.), 1974 ICJ Rep. 253, 269–70 (Judgment of Dec. 20).

85 Richard Baxter, *Treaties and Customs*, 129 RECUEIL DES COURS 25, 73 (1970 I).

the conventional norm (in casu, Article 6 of the Geneva Convention on the Continental Shelf) with the general (understood: customary) norm, since the court regards the former as the "particular expression" of the latter.[86] An even more striking illustration of the premium placed on rules of customary law, held to be of superior quality, was given by the International Court of Justice in the Case concerning United States Diplomatic and Consular Staff in Teheran, where it pointed out that the obligations violated by Iran "are not merely contractual obligations established by the Vienna Conventions of 1961 and 1963, but also obligations under general international law."[87] Time was when no call would have been felt to stray outside the terra firma of the conventional norms that bound the parties; here, apparently, the Court did not regard it as sufficient to take that ground but felt it necessary, in order to underscore the normative character of the rules breached by Iran, to point out that those rules had passed into the general corpus of international law—or, in other words, that they were also rules of customary law. And so we find a veritable de-conventionalization of conventional rules taking place on every hand.

Once the conventional norm had been absorbed into the customary norm and deprived of its specificity, all that remained to be done, in the second place, was to submit it to that increasing indeterminacy of the subjects of international obligations which we have seen affecting the customary norm. Thus, through the relay of the customary norm—itself qualified as a general rule or rule of general international law—the conventional norm, too, comes to be imposed on all states, including those who never became parties to the convention in question or never even signed it.

From this turmoil the law of treaties is emerging profoundly altered. Once hallowed by the prestige of consensualism, now fallen victim to the fascination exerted by the general rule, the conventional norm is being not only devalued against the other sources of law but forced to abandon what hitherto have been the characteristic features of its legal regime. While it is true that the Vienna Convention has confirmed both the classic procedures for the conclusion of treaties and the principle of their relative effect, this confirmation is reduced to an empty shell if a formally conventional provision can be analyzed as being substantively customary, and thus be submitted to the vagaries of a customary rule that, in turn, has become a rule of general international law. In such a situation there is virtually no difference any longer between a state that is a party to the Convention and a state that is not: the norm in question will be applicable to both. Neither will there be any difference between a convention that has entered into force and a convention that has not: did not the International Court of Justice and arbitral tribunals apply provisions of the Vienna Convention on the Law of Treaties many a time before it came into force, and do so in regard to states that had not ratified it, or did not intend to ratify it in future?[88] Whether that Convention is in force or not vis-a-vis a given state is after all, it seems, not so important. Not only that: if it is now possible for a customary rule to spring not merely from an actually adopted convention but even from the "general assent" manifested at an international conference, there no longer remains much difference between "near-agreements" and agreements actually achieved. Many other fundamental aspects of the law of treaties are also being eroded: it is surely out of the question to enter reservations to a treaty provision that has been construed to be a rule of general international law, or to denounce a treaty enshrining such provisions. Besides, what useful purpose would such a denunciation serve, considering that the provisions would continue to be binding on the denouncer as general rules of international law?

In sum, the intention manifested by a state in regard to a given convention is henceforth of little account: whether it signs it or not, becomes party to it or not, enters reservations to such and such a clause or not, it will in any case be bound by any provisions of the convention that are recognized to possess the character of rules of customary or general international law.

2. A Brief Response[89]

Prosper Weil's article of ten years ago, excerpted above, created a minor sensation among international lawyers. It was generally considered to be an important contri-

---

[86] Delimitation of the Continental Shelf, para. 70 (France/United Kingdom) (Cmnd. 7438 (1978)).

[87] 1980 ICJ Rep. at 31.

[88] Legal Consequences for States of the Continued Presence of South Africa in Namibia, 1971 ICJ Rep. 16, 47 (Advisory Opinion of June 21); Fisheries Jurisdiction (UK v. Iceland), Jurisdiction of the Court, 1973 ICJ Rep. 3, 14 (Judgment of Feb. 2); Aegean Sea Continental Shelf (Greece v. Turkey), 1978 ICJ Rep. 3, 39 (Judgment of Dec. 19); Interpretation of the Agreement of 25 March 1951 between the WHO and Egypt, 1980 ICJ Rep. at 92, 95. Cf. awards in Beagle Channel, 17 ILM 645 (1978), para. 7, and German External Debts, 19 ILM 1370 (1980), para. 16. [Editor's Note: Under the theory that a treaty supplies the quantitative component of custom by virtue of—and only by virtue of—the fact that the parties have bound themselves to observe the treaty, it would follow that an unratified treaty cannot be a source of customary international law. However, an unratified treaty certainly can articulate a rule, thus supplying the qualitative component of custom. Hence, an unratified treaty has gone half the distance toward customary law.]

[89] By ANTHONY D'AMATO, written for this Anthology.

bution to international scholarship. The passage of time has perhaps moderated the initial reception accorded his article. Professor Weil's colorful and dramatic prose style continues to give pleasure–and food for thought–to all who encounter his article for the first time. But it is also possible that his prose style has also served to obscure whatever message he may have intended to convey.

For my part, I confess that I am just as skeptical today of the merits of Professor Weil's approach as I was in 1983 when I first read his article. He is essentially casting blame on the looseness and softness of many of the terms and concepts used in present-day international legal communication because those terms and concepts do not fit the sharp and rigid categories defined by international law scholars. In my view this is precisely the wrong way to approach the task of international scholarship. We should not blame the real world for failing to fit neatly into categories that we have invented. Our task as scholars should be to discover truths about the real world. If those truths require us to revise, modify, or even discard the categories we have invented, so much the worse for our categories. The "pathology," to use Professor Weil's term, is not in the real world; it is in ourselves to the extent that we want to deny what is happening in the real world and turn the clock back to the days when things seemed more categorizable and manageable. In my view, to the extent that there is a "soft law" phenomenon going on in the real world, it is our job to try to understand why it is happening and what purposes it serves.

3. Informal Practice As Soft Law[90]

As D'Amato has taken pains to show, the relationship between legal custom and treaties is organic. Perhaps the most visible index of a state's practice in the present day is its treaty obligations. Multilateral treaties in particular show a considerable tendency to have significantly prompted the emergence of coextensive customary norms. D'Amato is inclined to see treaties as the principal means by which states articulate their acceptance of the legal consequences of their practice. Since he regards such articulation as a necessary component of a legal custom, the effect is to make custom nearly synonymous with treaties.

In my view, D'Amato does not go far enough. Not only is much of the vast volume of treaty law coextensive with customary law for which treaties, by virtue of their public and formal nature, are decisive practice, but there also exists a great deal of informal and unarticulated practice which is nonetheless treated as if it were law by those who are exposed to it.

[90] By NICHOLAS ONUF, excerpted from: *Global Law-Making and Legal Thought*, in NICHOLAS GREENWOOD ONUF (ED.), LAW-MAKING IN THE GLOBAL COMMUNITY 1, 23–24 (1982). Reprinted by permission.

4. The Importance of Soft Law[91]

Normal normativity is not, as Professor Weil's very important essay contends, something that is monolithic, or unidimensional. Relative normativity is in no sense exceptional. The ego is constantly bombarded by many different communications in the subjunctive mood, and the ego constantly makes assessments of which ones are important, which ones one can run a risk of violating, and so on. We know that in various ways all the norms we are subjected to as individuals, and the norms that we are subjected to as advisers to more composite entities, are soft in various ways, and we make calculations as to which must be complied with and which must not. We have, in other words, a sliding scale of hardness or softness in all norms.

Many so-called soft international norms are actually intentionally and functionally soft. They would be unworkable were they made much harder. Distinctions between degrees of control intention and severity of sanction are extremely important for scholars and practitioners.

International law classically provides us with many examples of soft law. One may be found in the corpus of comity, or comitas gentium norms in the international system whose violation is not delictual, but is nonetheless seen as an unfriendly act. Violations of comity may serve as a way of communicating displeasure, and indicating the unwillingness of one state to accept the actions or demarches of another. All the actions traditionally grouped under retorsion are essentially norms of comity. They are soft, and yet they perform a very important function within the international system.

Sir Joseph Gold said that it is too easy to be condescending toward soft law.[92] Soft law can overcome deadlocks in the relations of states that result from economic or political differences among them, when efforts at firmer solutions have been unavailing. A substantial amount of soft law can be attributed to differences in the economic structures and economic interests of developed, as opposed to developing, countries. Sometimes, Sir Joseph says, soft law may be the only alternative to anarchy. And though I would dis-

[91] By W. MICHAEL REISMAN, excerpted from: *A Hard Look at Soft Law: Remarks*, 82 PROCEEDINGS OF THE AMERICAN SOCIETY OF INTERNATIONAL LAW 371, 374–75 (1988). Reprinted by permission.

[92] 77 AJIL 443 (1983).

agree with him when he says that soft law has the capacity to become hard law, I disagree because it seems to me to be beside the point. Even if soft law does not harden up, soft law performs important functions, and, given the structure of the international system, we could barely operate without it.

5. Human Rights As Soft Law[93]

I would like to say a few words on the transformation of human rights soft law into customary law. This has become a rather popular topic, especially with American colleagues, even though personally I am not convinced that this popularity has helped to overcome wishful thinking in favor of more careful analysis. What we are observing in the international human rights field is certainly not the emergence of a general, extensive, uniform, consistent, settled practice accompanied by the more or less gradual building up of an opinio juris. Rather, we have been witnessing the steady emergence and broadening through decades of international debate, innumerable expressions of international concern and an impressive number of soft law resolutions, declarations, and the like, of a strong international consensus on certain basic human rights obligations and standards.

Corresponding to these international developments, human rights law has flowered quite impressively in many domestic legal orders. But are we to take all this as something going beyond the formation of an opinio juris? Maybe as the only state practice that really counts? Is it in our context irrelevant that the history of international human rights law also has been a history of widespread, persistent violations of these rights, only too often committed by the very states that speak out in their favor? Against this reality, to confirm the existence of universal customary law is an exercise calling for optimistic emphasis on words and much less attention to deeds.

6. The Many Forms of Agreement[94]

The complexity of global bargaining and its diplomatic modes is compounded by the importance of informal instruments of legal interest. Global and regional bargains are struck in instruments of all shapes and forms. The elusive character of many of these instruments reflects the wish of states to structure not only the substance of obligations, but also their weight, legal effect, and domestic processes. States are intent to structure their freedom to retain, modify or terminate agreements. In a regime of global interdependence, some states find it difficult to end and reduce commitments. The demands of mutually deeply impacting and sustained relationships between the powers give rise to inertial forces that stabilize the agreements which consecrate and define these relationships. This inertial force can make it truly difficult to modify or end them. Less formal instruments give states greater leeway. Informal agreements can be terminated or revised or suspended with greater ease—and this can then be done, in the United States at least, without requiring formal Congressional support. [Thus] it is not surprising that the formality or legal character of international agreements and arrangements can itself become the object of negotiations.

The adoption of conference texts or resolution in parliamentary arenas is pregnant with legitimizing powers even when these texts lack binding power. They are invoked in disputes and in situations in which the legitimacy of a policy is in issue. Quite apart from the question of their binding effect, assembly resolutions tend to have a self-enabling, self-licensing, or self-authorizing power for states supporting them. Formal limitations on the competence of representative parliamentary organs are not an effective restraint in the face of a willful majority.

Emphasis on binding texts has been a costly bias of legal investigation. Preoccupation with binding texts, obligatory resolutions, and enforceable decisions, which are at the core of conventional legal inquiry, has led to the neglect of the authorizing, licensing, recognizing and constitutive properties of resolutions that do not aspire to obligatory status. Concern with binding force and enforcement in the decentralized international system is a relic of legal habits developed in the hierarchical milieu of the state system. It is the licensing, authorizing, recognizing, and constitutive powers of the recommendations of the General Assembly of the United Nations which largely account for its political potency.

7. Why Are Some International Agreements Informal?[95]

"Verbal contracts," Samuel Goldwyn once said, "aren't worth the paper they're written on." Yet informal

[93] By BRUNO SIMMA, excerpted from: *A Hard Look at Soft Law: Remarks*, 82 PROCEEDINGS OF THE AMERICAN SOCIETY OF INTERNATIONAL LAW 372, 378 (1988). Reprinted by permission.

[94] By GIDON GOTTLIEB, excerpted from: *Global Bargaining: The Legal and Diplomatic Framework*, in NICHOLAS G. ONUF (ED.), LAW-MAKING IN THE GLOBAL COMMUNITY 109, 120–21, 122–23 (1982). Reprinted by permission.

[95] By CHARLES LIPSON, excerpted from: *Why Are Some International Agreements Informal?* 45 INTERNATIONAL ORGANIZATION 495, 495–96, 498–501, 511–13 (1991). Reprinted by permission.

agreements and oral bargains suffuse international affairs. They are the form that international cooperation takes in a wide range of issues, from exchange rates to nuclear weapons. Take monetary affairs, for instance. Except for the regional European Monetary System, there have been no formal, comprehensive agreements on exchange rates since the downfall of the Bretton Woods system in 1971. A prolonged effort to resurrect the pegged-rate system failed, although new treaties were drawn up and duly signed. Private financial markets simply overwhelmed these official efforts, and central bankers eventually conceded the point. The one comprehensive agreement since then, concluded in 1976 in Jamaica, merely ratified a system of floating rates that had emerged unplanned. For the past fifteen years, monetary arrangements have been a succession of informal agreements of indefinite duration, most recently the Plaza Communique and the Louvre Accord, designed to cope with volatile currency movements. The Bretton Woods system itself depended on such agreements in its declining years. It was held together by the tacit agreement of European central banks not to convert their major dollar holdings into gold. The system fell apart when Germany and France abandoned that commitment. They did so because they believed that the United States had abandoned its own (tacit) commitment to restrain inflation and to avoid large current account deficits. Put another way, the U.S. formal pledge to convert dollars into gold at $35 per ounce – the very heart of the Bretton Woods system – was sustained only by silent agreements that America would not be called upon to do so.

Such informal agreements are vital in security relationships as well. The U.S. decision to pursue containment rather than "rollback," even at the height of Cold War tensions, was a tacit acknowledgement of the Soviet sphere of influence in Eastern Europe. When popular uprisings broke out during the 1950s, the United States did nothing – nothing to aid resistance movements in Germany, Poland, and Hungary and nothing to deter their forcible suppression.

Informal accords among states and transnational actors are not exceptional. The scale and the diversity of such accords indicate that they are an important feature of world politics, not rare and peripheral. The very informality of so many agreements illuminates basic features of international politics. It highlights the continuing search for international cooperation, the profusion of forms it takes, and the serious obstacles to more durable commitments.

All international agreements, whether formal or informal, are promises about future national behavior. To be considered genuine agreements, they must entail some reciprocal promises or actions, implying future commitments.

Nations still can and do break even their most formal and solemn commitments to other states. Indeed, the unscrupulous may use treaty commitments as a way of deceiving unwary partners, deliberately creating false expectations or simply cheating when the opportunity arises. (Informal agreements are less susceptible to these dangers. They raise expectations less than treaties and so are less likely to dupe the naive.) But states pay a serious price for acting in bad faith and, more generally, for renouncing their commitments. This price comes not so much from adverse judicial decisions at The Hague but from the decline in national reputation as a reliable partner, which impedes future agreements. Indeed, opinions of the World Court gain much of their significance by reinforcing these costs to national reputation.

Put simply, treaties are a conventional way of raising the credibility of promises by staking national reputation on adherence. The price of noncompliance takes several forms. First, there is less of reputation as a reliable partner. A reputation for reliability is important in reaching other cooperative agreements where there is some uncertainty about compliance. Second, the violation or perceived violation of a treaty may give rise to specific, costly retaliation, ranging from simple withdrawal of cooperation in one area to broader forms of noncooperation and specific sanctions. Some formal agreements, such as the General Agreement on Tariffs and Trade (GATT), even establish a limited set of permissible responses to violations, although most treaties do not. Finally, treaty violations may recast national reputation in a still broader and more dramatic way, depicting a nation that is not only untrustworthy but is also a deceitful enemy, one that makes promises in order to deceive.

This logic also suggests circumstances in which treaties – and, indeed, all international agreements – ought to be vulnerable. An actor's reputation for reliability has a value over time. The present value of that reputation is the discounted stream of these current and future benefits. When time horizons are long, even distant benefits are considered valuable now. When horizons are short, these future benefits are worth little, while the gains from breaking an agreement are likely to be more immediate and tangible. Thus, under processing circumstances, such as the looming prospect of war or economic crisis, the long-term value of a reputation for reliability will be sharply discounted. As a consequence, adherence to agreements must be considered less profitable and therefore less reliable. This points to a striking paradox of treaties: they are often used to seal partnerships for vital actions, such as war, but they are weakest at precisely that moment because the present looms larger and the future is more heavily discounted.

This weakness is sometimes recognized, though rarely emphasized, in studies of international law. It has no place at all, however, in the law of treaties. All treaties are treated equally, as legally binding commitments, and typically lumped together with a wide range of informal bargains. Treaties that declare alliances, establish neutral territories, or announce broad policy guidelines are not classified separately. Their status is the same as that of any other treaty. Yet it is also understood, by diplomats and jurists alike, that these three types of treaty are especially vulnerable to violation or renunciation. For this reason, Richard Baxter has characterized them as "soft" or "weak" law, noting that "if a State refuses to come to the aid of another under the terms of an alliance, nothing can force it to. It was never expected that the treaty would be "enforced."[96]

Agreements may be considered informal, to a greater or lesser degree, if they lack the state's fullest and most authoritative imprimatur, which is given most clearly in treaty ratification.

The informality of agreements varies by degrees, along two principal dimensions. The first is the government level at which the agreement is made. A commitment made by the head of state (an executive agreement) is the most visible and credible sign of policy intentions short of a ratified treaty. In important matters, commitments by lower-level bureaucracies are less effective in binding national policy. They are simply less constraining on heads of state, senior political leaders, and other branches of government, partly because they lack a visible impact on national reputation. The second dimension is the form, or means, by which an agreement is expressed. It may be outlined in an elaborate written document, or it may involve a less formal exchange of notes, a joint communique, an oral bargain, or even a tacit bargain. Written agreements allow greater attention to detail and more explicit consideration of the contingencies that might arise. They permit the parties to set the boundaries of their promises, to control them more precisely, or to create deliberate ambiguity and omissions on controversial matters. At the other end of the spectrum – most informal of all – are oral and tacit agreements. Their promises are generally more ambiguous and less clearly delimited, and the very authority to make and execute them may be in doubt. If disputes later arise, it is often difficult to specify what was intended ex ante. Indeed, it may be difficult to show that there was an agreement.

Genuine tacit cooperation is based on shared expectations that each party can improve its own outcome if its strategic choices are modified in expectation of reciprocal changes by others. Shared "understandings" can arise in either case. They are not a unique marker of cooperative agreements. What distinguishes cooperation, whether tacit or explicit, are the subtle forms of mutual reliance and the possibilities of betrayal and regret.

The central point here is not taxonomic, presenting definitions of tacit arrangements and other informal bargains simply to classify them. The goal is to understand how different kinds of agreements can be used to order international relationships. The means of international cooperation are frequently informal, and it is important to explore their rationale, uses, and limitations. At the same time, we should not mistake all shared understandings for voluntary, informal bargains.

Informality is best understood as a device of minimizing the impediments to cooperation, at both the domestic and international levels. What are the impediments? And what are the advantages of informal agreements in addressing them? First, informal bargains are more flexible than treaties. They are willows, not oaks. They can be adapted to meet uncertain conditions and unpredictable shocks. "One of the greatest advantages of an informal instrument," according to a legal counselor in Britain's Foreign Office, "is the ease with which it can be amended."[97] Although treaties often contain clauses permitting renegotiation, the process is slow and cumbersome and is nearly always impractical. This point can be put in another, less obvious way: informal agreements make fewer informational demands on the parties. Negotiators need not try to predict all future states and comprehensively contract for them.

Second, because informal arrangements do not require elaborate ratification, they can be concluded and implemented quickly if need be. In complex, rapidly changing environments, speed is a particular advantage.

Finally, informal agreements are generally less public and prominent, even when they are not secret. This lower profile has important consequences for democratic oversight, bureaucratic control, and diplomatic precedent. Informal agreements can escape the public controversies of a ratification debate. They can avoid the disclosures, unilateral "understandings," and amendments that sometimes arise in that open process. Because of their lower profile, they are also more tightly controlled by the government bureaucracies that negotiate and implement the agreements and less exposed to intrusion by other agencies. Agencies dealing with specific international issues, such as environmental pollution or foreign intelligence, can use informal agreements to seal quiet bargains with their foreign counterparts, avoiding close scrutiny and active involvement by other government agencies with different agendas.

The lower profile and the absence of formal national

---

[96] *See* Baxter, *International Law in "Her Infinite Variety,"* 29 INT'L & COMP. L.Q. 550 (1980).

[97] Anthony Aust, *The Theory and Practice of Informal International Instruments*, 35 INTERNATIONAL AND COMPARATIVE LAW QUARTERLY 791 (1986).

commitment also mean that informal agreements are less constraining as diplomatic precedents. They do not stand as visible and general policy commitments, as treaties so often do. In all these ways, the most sensitive and embarrassing implications of an agreement can remain nebulous or unstated for both domestic and international audiences, or even hidden from them.

Yet all of these diplomatic benefits come at a price, and sometimes a very high one. The flexibility of informal agreements also means that they are more easily abandoned. Avoiding public debates conceals the depth of national support for an agreement. Ratification debates can also serve to mobilize and integrate the multiple constituencies interested in an agreement. These policy networks of public officials (executive, legislative, and bureaucratic) and private actors sustain agreements sidestep these basic democratic processes. This evasion typically means that the final agreements are less reliable for all participants.

C. Special Custom[98]

When an international law case happens to come up in their practice, many lawyers who have never studied the subject will look for a "quick and dirty" way to amass whatever knowledge they may need. Their motives are exemplary: they want to minimize the time spent in research in order to save money for the client. So if their case seems to involve a question of "customary international law" (and I can hardly think of an international law case that does not involve custom, even if it is only the customary law of treaty interpretation), the attorneys will look up "custom" in various international law texts and treatises as well as entering the term "custom" on their computer retrieval system. When they do a word-search of that term in the case law of the World Court, one of the items that will pop up is the following paragraph from one of that Court's leading cases (the *Asylum* case):

> The Party which relies on a custom of this kind must prove that this custom is established in such a manner that it has become binding on the other Party. The Colombian Government must prove that the rule invoked by it is in accordance with a constant and uniform usage practiced by the States in question, and that this usage is the expression of a right appertaining to the State granting asylum and a duty incumbent on the territorial State. This follows from Article 38 of the Statute of the Court, which refers to international custom "as evidence of a general practice accepted as law."[99]

And it is right here that the busy practitioner starts to go seriously wrong. The practitioner thinks: "The World Court, in interpreting Article 38 of its Statute, has obviously held that a rule of customary law must be proved by evidence of a constant and uniform usage."

But as we have seen in Chapter 4 of this Anthology, a constant and uniform usage is only a *sufficient*, not a *necessary*, way to prove a rule of custom. If it were necessary, then a new rule of custom could never get started and an old rule of custom could never get changed, because as soon as a state acts in conflict with the prevailing constant and uniform usage, its act would be deemed illegal and in violation of customary law. So, all that could count as custom would be the *old* constant and uniform usage, and we would never be able to change it. The content of international law would today be exactly the same as it was at the time of the ancient Babylonians.

Something is therefore wrong with the notion that a rule of customary law, binding on all states, must be evidenced by a constant and uniform usage before it becomes binding on them. A "constant and uniform usage" is such a *stringent* requirement that it would defeat finding a rule of custom in all except the most obvious cases where the rule of custom is long established. But it is precisely those obvious cases, where the operative rule is long established and uncontested, that do *not* typically arise in practice. The lawyer who looked up "custom" on the computer would not likely have a case where the applicable rule of custom is so entrenched and clear that the client would not have needed a lawyer to find it. Parties do not tend to contest cases, and hire lawyers, where the operative rule is clear. Hence, the *kinds* of evidence of custom that *typically* arise in the real world of conflicting claims and legal disputes are those kinds where there is an absence of a constant and uniform usage.

This is true as well of the *Asylum* case quoted at the beginning of this section. Clearly the rule of asylum relied upon by Colombia was anything but a well-established rule reflecting a constant and uniform usage. So, we have to be detectives and look for interpretive clues in the above-quoted paragraph from the *Asylum* case. The hasty practitioner is not likely to engage in detective work, especially if the above-quoted paragraph was quoted out of context in some book or word-processing system that did not give the full text of the Court's opinion. But the good practitioner must engage in detective work. We get our clue from the opening words that I have quoted: "The Party which relies on a custom of this kind." What kind of custom is "this kind"? Might "this kind" refer to some-

[98] By ANTHONY D'AMATO, written for this Anthology.

[99] Asylum Case, 1950 ICJ Rep. 266, at 276–77.

thing other than a rule of general customary law? We have to look farther back in the Court's opinion to see what "this" refers to. And we find that the Court was actually quite clear; it said that the Colombian government was relying "on an alleged regional or local custom peculiar to Latin-American States."[100]

"Just so!" reasons the good (not the hasty) practitioner. "The Colombian government obviously would not have tried to rely on a local custom peculiar to the Latin-American region if there had been a general rule of customary law that would have been helpful to Colombia's case." Therefore it makes sense for us to deduce that the applicable general rule of customary law was the *opposite* of what Colombia wanted![101] We deduce that Colombia was arguing for a Latin-American *exception* to the general rule of customary law.

So, the good practitioner might draw up a simple table:

1. General customary rule: favors Peru.
2. Special ("local" or "regional") customary rule: favors Colombia.

Which of these two rules would have the higher burden of proof? Clearly the second one. For Peru would be expected to have relied on the general rule of custom; after all, a general rule of custom is the operant rule of international law. For a country to come along and say, "Despite the general rule, there's an exception in my favor," that country would have to satisfy a high burden of proof. Hence, we would *expect* special custom to have a higher burden of proof than general custom. And indeed, as we analyze it this way, the quoted paragraph of the Court's opinion makes sense. A Party which "relies on a custom of this kind" must make a convincing showing that it accords with a constant and uniform usage. Thus, we may make a second deduction: general customary rules need *not* be proven by reference to a constant and uniform usage! General customary rules need not be subjected to the stringent evidentiary proof required of special customary rules. In short, we have arrived at the opposite result from the one reached by the hasty practitioner when reading the Court's opinion. The hasty practitioner assumed that a "constant and uniform usage" must be applicable to general custom. We find, upon analysis, that it is *not* applicable to general custom. Rather, it is applicable only to special custom—an exception to general custom.

What are the evidentiary requirements we need to prove special custom? The World Court has already given us one: "a constant and uniform usage." Are there others? In my research I found that the earliest notion of a special or local custom that was an *exception* to the otherwise generally prevailing law is found in Roman law. Again, a word-search approach to Roman law would be misleading; the term "custom" had many synonyms and usages.[102] But where the general concept of custom was very important was in the Roman ius gentium. The ius gentium characterized the Roman law that applied to foreigners within the Roman Empire (for example, law that applied to lands we now call France and Spain), whereas the ius civile applied roughly to the territory we now call Italy.[103] As the Roman Empire extended its power, it did not override or trample upon many of the local laws of the lands that came within its dominion. Indeed, many historians have commented upon this aspect of the genius of Roman hegemonical expansion—there was no point in overriding local law just for the sake of doing so. A presumption arose in Roman law to the effect that local customary law remained in place unless expressly canceled by a statute enacted in Rome. When a statute specifically was stated to override local customs within the Empire, then of course it preempted the local or special customs—the ius civile was thus stronger than the ius gentium. Yet, remarkably, Roman law also knew of the concept of *desuetudo*. A Roman statute that preempted custom within the ius gentium could nevertheless wear out through lack of application and enforcement over time. Of course, the statute remained on the books, and its cancellation through desuetude only applied to the particular communities where it was not enforced. Interestingly, the term *desuetudo* is the opposite of *consuetudo*, the latter being one of the terms for "custom." Thus *desuetudo* is a form of "negative custom." For example, if a particular community has successfully resisted the application of a Roman statute over a considerable period of time, we might say that the local community has practiced a form of negative custom. Its *desuetudo* actually has the effect of canceling the operation of the Roman statute. And this is indeed what special custom is all about. It is an exception to the general law of the realm.[104]

---

[100] *Id.* at 276.

[101] Of course, it's also logically possible that the general rule of custom was not the precise opposite of the rule Colombia wanted, but rather substantively indeterminate. Yet, if it were indeterminate, then Colombia might have been better off arguing that the Latin American practice was evidence that the general rule was not really indeterminate but rather had a content that was in Colombia's favor. Hence, it is a reasonable deduction (in the absence of further evidence) that the general rule of custom was the opposite of what Colombia wanted it to be.

[102] For example, in discussing "custom," Roman jurists of the classical period used the following terms more or less interchangeably: *mos*, *mores*, *usus*, *consuetudo*, and *ius non scriptum*.

[103] Some writers have confused ius gentium with natural law, a confusion that apparently dates back to Pufendorf.

[104] Of course, if communities pushed the notion of *desuetudo* too far, it would amount to civil disobedience. The Roman emperors would not have tolerated widespread challenges to their rule. The details are of course buried in antiquity, but as a general

In the eighteenth century, Sir William Blackstone wrote the most influential legal treatise of all time, his *Commentaries*. In this work Blackstone draws a distinction between general custom and special custom (he calls the latter "particular customs"). General custom is simply the source of the common law. Judges "find" it by applying their own experience and study and by following precedent. In sharp contrast, special customs require strict construction because they are or can be in derogation of the common law.[105] Blackstone gives a number of criteria that are necessary to prove special custom. A special custom:

1. Must be specially pleaded.
2. Must be proved by a jury and not just by a judge.
3. Must have been in use "so long that the memory of man runneth not to the contrary."
4. Must have been peaceable.
5. Must have been continuous.
6. Must not be unreasonable.
7. Must be certain (determinable).
8. Must be obligatory (not optional).
9. Must be consistent with each other.[106]

In 1902, Salmond added to the list, claiming that the following criteria were implicit in Blackstone's treatment:

10. Must be based on *opinio juris*, that is, it must have been observed as a matter of right.
11. Must not be contrary to an Act of Parliament.[107]

In 1927, Sir Carleton Allen found another qualification implicit in Blackstone's treatment: that special customs can apply only to "a particular *class* of persons or to a particular *place*."[108]

These items, one and all, historically have served to distinguish special custom from general custom. A number of international law publicists have failed to notice the vast distinction between the two types of custom, and some of them appear to be unaware of special custom at all. The unfortunate consequence of this failure has been to attribute some of the requirements of special custom to general custom. In particular, writers have been intrigued with the notion of opinio juris, and have applied it to the proof of general customary law. Of course, for all the reasons suggested in Chapter 4 above, applying opinio juris to general custom would result in the inability of general custom to change its content over time. Opinio juris, in the stringent sense suggested by Blackstone and Salmond, only applies when a state is seeking an exception to general custom.[109]

The "regional" exception to a rule of customary law that came up in the *Asylum* case is a rather rare example of special custom. Much more frequent in international law are the special customs that are one or another form of prescription. If the case at hand involves a claim to full or partial jurisdiction over a specific piece of the planet, then it is very likely that prescription is involved and that special custom is the relevant methodological tool.[110] As Carleton Allen above quoted said, special custom applies to a "particular place." Indeed, the application of special custom to cases of prescription makes a great deal of sense. A nation does not lightly lose or forfeit its territory. If a portion of its jurisdiction over its territory is to be forfeited, the stringent proofs of special custom must be satisfied.

There are many World Court cases where the Court's opinion only makes sense if the concept of special custom is used to interpret what the Court said. (Interpretation is often necessary because the Court has not always been entirely explicit about what it is doing.) Thus, in the *Anglo-Norwegian Fisheries Case*, the Court said in an oft-quoted sentence, "the ten-mile rule would appear to be inapplicable as against Norway inasmuch as she has always opposed any attempt to apply it to the Norwegian coast."[111] This sentence does not and cannot mean that a state can opt out of a general rule of custom simply by opposing it.[112] What it does mean is that the prescriptive claim of the international community to the high seas is opposed here by a counter prescriptive claim by Norway to certain specific areas of the Norwegian coastline. The burden of proof on Norway

proposition, it appears that the concepts of *ius gentium* and *desuetudo* enabled the Roman emperors to expand their Empire in a flexible manner, tolerating certain practices that were inconsistent with their *ius civile* but probably enforcing—and thus negating the operation of desuetude—all the ones they deemed important.

105 Examples of special custom in Blackstone are the law of gavelkind in the borough of Kent (which is contrary to the general rule of primogeniture—in Kent, all sons alike succeed to the father's estate), and the law of borough-English in a few boroughs (a more radical departure from the general rule of primogeniture, where the youngest son inherits the estate).

106 Blackstone, Commentaries *76–78.

107 Salmond, Jurisprudence 262–64 (9th ed. 1937).

108 Carleton Allen, Law in the Making 126–36 (3d ed. 1939).

109 I have argued, in Chapter 4 above, that even general custom cannot dispense with the qualitative (or psychological) component; in that respect, opinio juris stands for a requirement that the act or omission be articulated as having international-law implications.

110 According to Judge Fitzmaurice, "the acquisition of a historic right by prescriptive means is merely a special case of the creation of right by custom or usage." Sir Gerald Fitzmaurice, *The Law and Procedure of the International Court of Justice, 1951–54: General Principles and Sources of Law*, 30 BYIL 1, 39 (1953).

111 1951 ICJ Rep. 116, 131.

112 *See* the section on "The Persistent Objector" in Chapter 4 in this Anthology.

is stringent; Norway must meet all the requirements for special custom discussed above. The rest of the Court's opinion makes it clear that Norway in fact discharged this stringent burden of proof.[113] In another important case involving off-coast claims, the *North Sea Continental Shelf Cases*,[114] commentators such as Dr. Michael Akehurst have misread the Court's opinion because of a failure to distinguish between general and special custom.[115] A leading casebook on International Law goes so far as to *omit* the portion of the Court's opinion that draws the vital distinction, thus misleading students into thinking that the Court is talking about general custom when in fact the Court is talking about special custom.[116] Denmark and the Netherlands had contended that the North Sea continental shelf delimitation line between themselves and the Federal Republic of Germany should be drawn according to the equidistance method as required by of customary international law. The Court, however, held that the newly developed equidistance method (developed in part by its mention in the Geneva Convention on the Continental Shelf) could not operate to take land away from a nation. The continental shelf, as a natural prolongation of Germany's land territory below sea level, simply belonged to Germany as a matter of prescription. Neither equity, fairness, nor equidistance have any relevance to Germany's title to its own continental shelf.[117] The only way to take away a portion of Germany's title would be for Denmark and the Netherlands to show their own right to the disputed area as a function of special custom. But Denmark and the Netherlands could not have begun to satisfy the stringent requirements of special custom as Blackstone, Salmond, and Allen set forth. They tried to get by with general custom (the equidistance rule), but that was unavailing in light of Germany's title to specific territory.

Another leading World Court case on special custom was the *Right of Passage Case*.[118] Again, what was involved was particular prescriptive rights to a particular territory. Portugal claimed that it had a right of passage over Indian territory to reach the Portuguese enclave of Goa. This was a pure case of special custom, as the Court indeed noted:

> It is objected on behalf of India that no local custom could be established between only two States. It is difficult to see why the number of States between which a local custom may be established on the basis of long practice must necessarily be larger than two. The Court sees no reason why long continued practice between two States accepted by them as regulating their relations should not form the basis of mutual rights and obligations between the two States.[119]

Clearly the Court specifies that "local custom" (what I've been calling "special custom") meets the Blackstone-Salmond-Allen requirements: long practice, continuous practice, and opinio juris ("accepted by them as regulating their relations"). In other sections of its opinion, the Court discusses general custom (which has led some readers to misinterpret the entire distinction drawn by the Court between general and special custom.) Dealing with the question of nonmilitary rights of passage, the Court found it superfluous to inquire whether general custom would yield the same result as special custom. As for alleged military rights, the issue was more complex. Portugal failed to advance any convincing argument either in its briefs or in its oral presentation to the effect that a right of military access to enclaves existed as a matter of general customary international law. Inasmuch as the Court was able to find in the special customary practice between India and Portugal a distinction between military and nonmilitary rights, it refused to reach the question of the alleged general custom of military access. In other words, special custom, once proved, trumped dubious rules of general custom. The Court noted that this was "a concrete case having special features," that the practice between the two states was "clearly established," and that therefore "such a particular practice must prevail over any general rules."[120]

Rounding out the most prominent World Court cases dealing with special custom as distinguished from general custom is the *Nationals in Morocco Case*.[121] This was not quite a case of prescription, although the nearest cousin to it. It involved "capitulatory rights," a medieval forerunner

---

[113] *See* the related discussion of the Anglo-Norwegian Fisheries Case in Chapter 4 in this Anthology, in the section entitled "Finding Custom in an Incident."

[114] (W. Ger. v. Den., W. Ger. v. Neth.) 1969 ICJ Rep. 3.

[115] See Michael Akehurst, *Custom as a Source of International Law*, 47 BYIL 1, 49 (1974–75).

[116] Louis Henkin, Richard Pugh, Oscar Schachter & Hans Smit, International Law Cases and Materials 38 (1980).

[117] The Court said: "What confers the ipso jure title which international law attributes to the coastal State in respect of its continental shelf is the fact that the submarine areas concerned may be deemed to be actually part of the territory over which the coastal State already has dominion – in the sense that, although covered with water, they are a prolongation or continuation of that territory, an extension of it under the sea." 1969 ICJ Rep. at 32. For a further analysis of the way the Court dealt with counter-contentions by Denmark and the Netherlands, *see* Anthony D'Amato, International Law – Process and Prospect 135–42 (1987).

[118] 1960 ICJ Rep. 4.

[119] 1960 ICJ Rep. 4, at 39–40.

[120] 1960 ICJ Rep. 4, at 44.

[121] 1952 ICJ Rep. 176.

of colonialism,[122] called an "old and dying institution" by Verzijl in 1966.[123] Capitulatory rights were extraterritorial rights attached to specific territories, and hence the connection with prescriptive rights. The United States had claimed, on behalf of its nationals in Morocco, certain of these capitulatory rights. But the Court did not find any general customary law on capitulatory rights that would support the U.S. claim. The United States was relegated to special custom if it wanted to win the case. The World Court pointedly cited its previous decision in the *Asylum Case*, indicating that the plaintiff state must prove in a very specific way that the defendant state has expressly or impliedly consented to capitulatory rights as a specific "derogation" from its general "territorial sovereignty."[124] This citation shows that the Court regarded capitulatory rights as a subset of prescriptive rights which can only be established by the stringent criteria of special custom.

---

[122] For the origin and historical instances of "capitulatory rights," see the section of Chapter 2 entitled "Medieval Customary Law" in this Anthology.

[123] 2 VERZIJL, THE JURISPRUDENCE OF THE WORLD COURT 135 (1966).

[124] Citing 1950 ICJ Rep. 266, at 274–75.

Part III
Substantive Law and Theory

6
The State

A. Personality

1. The Classical Conception of State Personality[1]

The conception of International Persons is derived from the conception of the Law of Nations. As this law is the body of rules which the civilized States consider legally binding in their intercourse, every State which belongs to the civilized States, and is, therefore, a member of the Family of Nations, is an International Person. Sovereign States exclusively are International Persons—i.e. subjects of International Law.

In contradistinction to Sovereign States which are real, there are also apparent, but not real, International Persons—namely, Confederations of States, insurgents recognized as a belligerent Power in a civil war, and the Holy See. All these are not real subjects of International Law, but in some points are treated as though they were International Persons, without thereby becoming members of the Family of Nations.

It must be specially mentioned that the character of a subject of the Law of Nations and of an International Person can be attributed neither to monarchs, diplomatic envoys, private individuals, or churches, nor to chartered companies, nations, or races after the loss of their State (as, for instance, the Jews or the Poles), and organized wandering tribes.

A State proper—in contradistinction to so-called Colonial States—is in existence when a people is settled in a country under its own Sovereign Government. The conditions which must obtain for the existence of a State are therefore four:

There must, first, be a people. A people is an aggregate of individuals of both sexes who live together as a community in spite of the fact that they may belong to different races or creeds, or be of different color.

There must, secondly, be a country in which the people has settled down. A wandering people, such as the Jews were whilst in the desert for forty years before their conquest of the Holy Land, is not a State. But it matters not whether the country is small or large; it may consist, as with City States, of one town only.

There must, thirdly, be a Government—that is, one or more persons who are the representatives of the people and rule according to the law of the land. An anarchistic community is not a State.

There must, fourthly and lastly, be a Sovereign Government. Sovereignty is supreme authority, an authority which is independent of any other earthly authority. Sovereignty in the strict and narrowest sense of the term includes, therefore, independence all round, within and without the borders of the country.

The term Sovereignty was introduced into political science by Bodin in his celebrated work, "De la republique," which appeared in 1577. Before Bodin, at the end of the Middle Ages, the word sovereign was used in France for an authority, political or other, which had no other authority above itself. Thus the highest courts were called Cours Souverains. Bodin, however, gave quite a new meaning to the old conception. Being under the influence and in favor of the policy of centralization initiated by Louis XI of France (1461-1483), the founder of French absolutism, he defined sovereignty as "the absolute and perpetual power within a State." Such power is the supreme power within a State without any restriction whatever except the Commandments of God and the Law of Nature. No constitution can limit sovereignty, which is an attribute of the king in a monarchy and of the people in a democracy. A Sovereign is above positive law. A contract only is binding upon the Sovereign, because the Law of Nature commands that a contract shall be binding.

The conception of sovereignty thus introduced was at once accepted by writers on politics of the sixteenth century, but the majority of these writers taught that sovereignty could be restricted by a constitution and by positive law. Thus at once a somewhat weaker conception of sovereignty than that of Bodin made its appearance. On the other hand, in the seventeenth century, Hobbes went even beyond Bodin, maintaining that a Sovereign was not bound by anything and had a right over everything, even over religion. Whereas a good many publicists followed Hobbes, others, especially Pufendorf, denied, in contradistinction to Hobbes, that sovereignty includes omnipotence. Ac-

[1] By LASSA OPPENHEIM, excerpted from: 1 INTERNATIONAL LAW: A TREATISE 107–15 (2d ed. 1912). [Editor's Note: Oppenheim's book is generally acknowledged as the most influential treatise on international law in the twentieth century.]

cording to Pufendorf, sovereignty is the supreme power in a State, but not absolute power, and sovereignty may well be Constitutionally restricted. Yet in spite of all the differences in defining sovereignty, all authors of the sixteenth and seventeenth centuries agree that sovereignty is indivisible and contains the centralization of all power in the hands of the Sovereign, whether a monarch or the people itself in a republic.

2. An Updating of the Classical Conception[2]

Internal acceptance of the legitimacy of acts by a few on behalf of the many is a prerequisite for participation in a consensual international legal system. A state's functional capacity to act as a community member is conditioned on the explicit or implicit acceptance by its own population that some central institution may act in a governmental capacity over and on behalf of that population. If a population group does not recognize the legitimacy of some centralized authority to communicate on its behalf, then indicia of consent to be legally bound to other nations by persons purportedly exercising such authority could never create those reliable expectations of generally conforming conduct that are a prerequisite to any system of law, consensual or otherwise. Recognition of a state by other members of the international community is nothing more than the acknowledgement that this centralized conduit for communication exists and that acceptance of obligation through that conduit is an act recognized as legitimate by the population group on behalf of whom the central communicators speak. Thus, recognition of one state by another is both a pragmatic acknowledgement of a set of real world facts and an agreement that the newly recognized entity will be the beneficiary of legal rights in return for being the obligee of legal duties.

The principle of sovereign equality does not suggest that all sovereign states are equal in wealth, power, or size. The sovereign equality principle does teach that once community recognition of sovereignty identifies a population group as having collective legal rights and duties with respect to other such groups, those rights and duties will be viewed as being reciprocal by other community members who granted such recognition. No consensual legal system could exist without such a principle of reciprocity and equality.[3]

The principle of sovereignty is essential to the continued growth and increasing sophistication of an international legal system. Far from being divisive, that principle represents perhaps the best hope for peace and the ultimate effective protection of international human rights. The corollary of sovereign power is sovereign responsibility. The more exclusive the power over nationals and territory, the more responsibility the international community can reasonably require from the governments that exercise that power.[4]

3. A Normative Critique of State Personality[5]

Hugo Grotius held to a doctrine sometimes called "parallelism." Since individual persons can be virtuous and just, reasonable, dutiful and sociable, keep contracts and obey laws, then corporate organizations like the state can also be virtuous, reasonable and just, can be sociable, obey laws, conform to the same duties as individuals, etc. It seems that Grotius thought such analogous predication an exemplary condition for international peace. As civil law regards and regulates the rights and interests of persons, so should international law regard and regulate the rights and interests of nations. This doctrine of transferable virtue, transferring "up" to a complex organ from a less complex organ – from persons' interactions to nations' interactions – may find its philosophic origin in Plato who thought justice in the state was the same as justice in the person, only on a grander scale.

But justice within the state cannot be the same as justice among states. There is a natural law that serious wrong should be redressed. A person goes to court. Where does a nation go when it believes it has suffered serious wrong? Perhaps it wages a just war. Is a just war, by any stretch of imagination, to be compared to a day in court?

I think that the non-transferability of personal action to state action lies in certain assumptions and inferences. Predictions in the premises harbor implicit ideas about the

---

2 By HAROLD G. MAIER, excerpted from: *The Principles of Sovereignty, Sovereign Equality, and National Self-Determination*, in PAUL B. STEPHAN III & BORIS M. KLIMENKO (eds.), INTERNATIONAL LAW AND INTERNATIONAL SECURITY: MILITARY AND POLITICAL DIMENSIONS 241, 243–44 (M.E. Sharpe: 1991). Reprinted by permission.

3 [Editor's Note: One might ask whether the author offers this last proposition as a matter of logic or as an empirical proposition derived from observation of the international community.]

4 [Editor's Note: Compare the radically different views of Professors Philip Allott and Richard Falk in Chapter 17 below, *The Future of International Law*.]

5 By VIRGINIA BLACK, from: *Why Nations Find it Hard to be Good to Each Other*, 4 VERA LEX 7, 7–9 (1983-84). Reprinted by Permission.

state; these ideas are non-referring and imprecise and so they are incorrectly applied. In short, we carry around a false understanding of what nations are, what are their sustaining attributes, and how upon the basis of these attributes nations are necessitated to "act" in the world.

Perhaps out of man's desire for permanence, he grants the state a monopoly of power to maintain and defend itself; as a consequence the state's necessary and sufficient function is to coerce. The state must therefore regard in a lesser light all other impositions except as they sustain or augment this condition of power. The state is like no other conglomerate. Born out of the human passion for unity and the fear of attack, it is sui generis.

Why are personal virtues and the good actions that they entail not readily transferable to "virtuous actions" among states? Why do the principled, prudent or kindly acts of persons not readily find a similar moral intelligence in nations vis-a-vis their interactions? Treaties are broken. Promised assistance is withdrawn. Barriers to trade are erected. The civil law that regulates the peace within brings no peace without, for civil law, by definition, is non-extendible. Jural decisions that resolve domestic conflict fail utterly to resolve international conflict. No court would even try to adjudicate a vital conflict between states of unequal powers with any prospect of enforcement. A summons to "appear in court" is too foolish to think about. What, then, is the difference between person and nations?

(1) Individuals have one mind: they show unity of consciousness, will, purpose. This imparts meaning and stability to their beliefs so that, acting in light of this meaning, they know when their purposes are effected. Since individuals discern and evaluate situations uniquely, they may assess or try to alter results with good success. Hence they can discriminatingly reject or re-adapt means and methods while formulating their own time frames for calling gains or losses or for shifting "costs" from one preference to another.

(2) When singleness of mind stands behind individuals' values and the meanings persons place on things, effective motivation results. This coincidence of thought, value, drive and action, we call personal freedom. Measuring and using their own resources, persons' discrete perceptions, energies, intentions, and memories can move their will consistently toward a desired end. Successful action, in turn, reinforces useful habituation.

(3) Persons enjoy sentience, empathy, appetitus socialis to shape and forward their motivations toward avoiding the injury of others, and toward benefiting them as well. "Here," said David Hume, "is the difference between kingdoms and individuals. Human nature cannot by any means subsist without the association of individuals. But nations can subsist without intercourse." Nations lack these affectional wellsprings of moral action, and so they have little incentive—nor do they need—to be good to each other. In the long and short run, it is often not clear to them what they gain by it. Officials can break promises, lie, or even innocently falsify, because personal accountability and shame do not exists with states. Only moral persons enjoy a conscience.

(4) Importantly, individuals are shaped by social influence. Social norms and moral and religious teachings educate them. Law guides them. Enforcements restrain them. When these influences exert themselves upon persons' unitary mind and feeling, the product can, in rough measure, be known. Because persons, being free, can respond intelligently in light of these influences in a kind of self-creating spiral, they themselves can use, evaluate, modify, or even disregard the effects upon them of social influences. Reciprocal adaptation results between individuals and the social environment. Since regular reciprocal adaptation reinforces customs, regularities, and rules, interpersonal expectations become habituated. This makes for civil order. Under these conditions of internal accord, personal virtue develops and the moral actions of individuals can emerge.

Nations enjoy none of these qualities and relations of social intelligence—neither personal freedom, meaning, nor motivation. Unlike individuals, nations lack a natural unity of mind, feeling, and continuity of will. They suffer no pain. They have no incentive to develop virtue. Education, critical thinking, parental modeling, moral or religious suasion—none of these norm-responding sensors influences the state toward intelligent habits of action. Law does not dependably deter the state. Enforcements by other nations leave the state not constrained but afraid. How, then, can the state "know" when it has acted wisely or well? If except by fictional extension there is no such thing as a "national will," then the moral and motivational similarities presumed to exist between nations and persons when, say, both are thought to be just or to engage in just interactions, are a vague illusion.

How, then, can we expect association between nations to parallel the delicate adjustments which free persons arrange among themselves, or to submit to universal principles of common good that benefit all nations fairly? The disanalogy is outstanding.

Not all "national acts" are, however, inconceivable. Prisoners can be exchanged between nations. Trade boycotts can work and tariffs can be laid down or lifted by negotiation. States can award money remuneration for damage to the property of another. The judgment of a world court may be listened to if facilitating opinions are in place, if no nation's vital interests are wronged, and if participating parties see gain to themselves. Free trade exchanges work wonderfully between nations, but of course these are the actions of persons and their associations left unfettered by the state.

Let us be clear, though, that in repudiating moral parallelism we are not falling into Hobbes' idea of the state as an absolute and aggressive sovereign power. The state must always be under law. In defining persons as fearful, selfish, and aggrandizing, and also conceiving of the state as an artificial person, Hobbes commits the same error of personalization. The difference between Hobbes and Grotius lies in their view of human nature which is then analogized upon how states act, or should act, toward one another.

We can think of a world society, however, if we mean by this that other peoples, no matter from what nation, deserve our aid and friendship, respect and non-violation of their rights and interests. Moral universalism realized by individuals differs in every way from the idea of a world wide legislative sovereign with enforcement powers or from the notion that the parameters of interstate relations are fashioned upon the parameters of the natural moral inclinations or sociability of man.

4. The Relation Between State and Individual[6]

I would like to address the question of the relation of the individual to the state and, in so doing, invoke Hegel, the preeminent philosopher of relationships. Hegel believed that relationships are real and that everything else is a mere consequence of relationships. A few years ago, a legal problem confronted me that highlighted this interrelatedness that Hegel envisioned. I received a call from a former student that her friend, Lois Frolova, needed advice regarding a press conference she wanted to hold. Lois, an American, was going to announce a hunger strike that she was committed to endure to the death, if necessary, unless the Soviet Union allowed her Soviet husband, Andrei Frolova, to emigrate from Moscow and join Lois in Chicago. Three other "divided spouses" had also recently announced their hunger strikes from an apartment in Moscow along with Andrei, and this announcement had been widely reported in the press.

In examining this case, there are several key relationships to keep in mind. First is the basic spousal relationship between Lois and Andrei. Second is Lois's relationship with her country of nationality, the United States. Third is Andrei Frolov's relationship with his country of nationality, the Soviet Union. Fourth, there is the relationship between the two countries. There are other interesting relationships, such as the attorney-client relationship between Lois and myself, but as you will see as we get into this case, the most interesting and complex relationship turns out to be that between Lois and the United States.

The press conference was held the next morning at Northwestern Law School. The reporters were taken by Lois's obvious dedication and sincerity, and a major "divided families" media event was launched.

The next day Lois came to my office, and before we got down to serious business I asked her about yet another relationship – that between Lois and her parents. How did parents react to her hunger strike? Lois said that her father's reaction was that of a philosophical absolutist: "Are you out of your mind? Do you think you can change the policy of the Soviet Union by threatening suicide? Do you think I've spent twenty years raising you so that you could die for some foreigner?" Her mother's reaction, on the other hand, could be characterized as philosophical pragmatism: "If you must go on a hunger strike, then you must go on a hunger strike. Just be sure to get a little something to eat."

Lois asked me for my estimate of her chances for success, and I was pessimistic. While I was concerned for the couple's health, I felt that Lois's actions and the ensuing publicity[7] would ensure Andrei's personal safety; the Soviet Union probably would not arrest or hurt him in full view of the American public. Lois asked if there was anything else she could do, and I said that we could explore the matter further if she wanted me to represent her. We agreed upon an attorney-client relationship,[8] and I said, "You do have legal rights. International law clearly states that any person has the right to leave his country for any reason.[9] And on top of that, there is a growing body of international human rights law regarding family reunification."[10] Lois was a bright graduate student[11] and asked the right question, "But is there any way to back up these rights in a court?"

"Maybe we can sue the Soviet Union directly," I said.

"I didn't know one could sue the Soviet Union in an international court."

---

[6] By ANTHONY D'AMATO, excerpted from: *The Relation of the Individual to the State in the Era of Human Rights*, 24 TEXAS INTERNATIONAL LAW JOURNAL 1 (1989). Reprinted by permission.

[7] The Chicago coverage soon was picked up nationally, and in a few days Lois and I were on ABC's *Nightline* program. *Nightline* (ABC television broadcast, May 17, 1982).

[8] The arrangement was on a pro bono basis, with Lois paying out-of-pocket expenses and court filing fees.

[9] Universal Declaration of Human Rights, an. 13(1), (2), G.A. Res. 217, 3 U.N GAOR at 71, U.N. Doc. A/810 (1948); International Covenant on Civil and Political Rights, art. 12, G.A. Res. 2200, 21 U.N. GAOR Supp. (No. 16) at 52–58, U.N. Doc. A/ 6316 (1966).

[10] Conference on Security and Cooperation in Europe, Final Act, 14 I.L.M. 1293 (1975).

[11] She later received her Ph.D from Stanford; her thesis was on nineteenth century Russian liberalism.

"You're right as far as that's concerned. Not only isn't the Soviet Union a party to the International Court of Justice,[12] but even if it were, only states can be plaintiffs in that court, and not individual persons."[13]

"Then what?"

"A federal court here in Chicago might be a possibility. But the real problem is that we couldn't even get the case started without serving the Soviet Union, and they would have sixty days to answer service of process."[14] Lois confirmed that no one could hold out on a hunger strike that long.

After Lois left my office, I researched the possibility of an injunction and discussed general strategy with my colleague Steven Lubet and a practicing attorney, Luis Kutner. Why not ask the court for an injunction? An action for injunction can be commenced without formal service of process; if time is of the essence, simple notification will suffice.[15] We could limit the injunction to Chicago, asking the court to bar all Soviet sales of gold and purchases of wheat on the Chicago commodities markets until Andrei was given permission to emigrate. Theoretically we did not have to limit it to Chicago, but I felt that it was more realistic to do so; it might scare Soviet exporters.

We marshaled numerous treaties and other international instruments in support of the injunction, including the United Nations Charter, the Universal Declaration of Human Rights, and the Helsinki Accords. I also included provisions of the Soviet Constitution that recognize the central importance of the family.[16] We sent a telegram to the Soviet embassy in Washington, D.C., notifying the Soviet officials that a motion had been filed in federal court for a temporary restraining order prohibiting Soviet sales of gold and purchases of wheat on the Chicago commodities markets. I was unsure, however, whether this would galvanize the embassy into action. The officials might simply ignore the telegram. Or, more likely, the Soviet government would request the United States to intervene and ask the district judge to dismiss the motion. The Department of State and the Department of Justice had been quite active in recent years in intervening on behalf of foreign sovereigns to oppose American plaintiffs bringing human rights actions in United States courts.[17]

Our twin goals of bringing home the importance of the injunction to the Soviet Union and keeping the United States government from intervening on behalf of the Soviet Union might be accomplished if the United States could be joined as a co-plaintiff in the litigation against the Soviet Union. The problem, however, was that the United States government could certainly not be induced to join Lois on her side of the lawsuit. So we resorted to a little-known rule of federal civil procedure[18] to bring the United States in as a necessary co-plaintiff and, accordingly, served the United States with a copy of the complaint listing the United States as co-plaintiff.

But the critical strategies in the case had much more to do with relationships than with marshaling legal authority and procedure. We joined the United States as a party because of the conception of the nationality relationship under classical international law: an individual lacks standing to sue a state under traditional theory and, hence, when an individual has a grievance against a foreign state, only the individual's state of nationality can bring the claim.[19] Under this view, the United States could "espouse" the claim of its national, Lois Frolova, against the Soviet Union. If the United States chose not to espouse Lois's claim, under traditional international law – and perhaps under more modern conceptions as well – there was no international norm that would compel it to do so. Nationality is thus a necessary, but not a sufficient, condition of the "espousal" doctrine. On this point, I turned to United States law. I argued that Lois had a due process right under the United States Constitution to compel the United States to assert and attempt to vindicate her international human right to live with her husband.

This litigation strategy appeared to produce the desired effect. First, we had started a lawsuit between the two superpowers in a Chicago court, and that in itself was sure to bring Lois and Andrei's plight to the attention of the leadership in Moscow. Second, by placing the Soviet Union and the United States on opposite sides of a lawsuit that neither nation wanted, we hoped that a diplomatic conversation would ensue between the two countries in which the United States might hint that the best way out of the mess

---

12 The U.S.S.R. had not consented to compulsory jurisdiction under article 36(2) of the Statute of the International Court of Justice.

13 It would have been superfluous to tell Lois that, in theory, the United States could espouse her claim and bring an action in the International Court of Justice. Not only would it take months to convince the State Department, but there was practically no chance that the State Department could be convinced.

14 28 U.S.C. § 1608(d) (1982).

15 FED. R. CIV. P. 65(a)(1).

16 *See, e.g.*, Konstitutsiya SSSR arts. 35, 53 (USSR), translated in 17 A. BLAUSTEIN & G. FLANZ, CONSTITUTIONS OF THE COUNTRIES OF THE WORLD 26, 29 (1972).

17 *See, e.g.*, Republic of the Philippines v. Marcos, 806 F.2d 344 (2d Cir. 1986), *cert. denied*, 107 S. Ct. 2178 (1987); Siderman v. Republic of Argentina, No. 82-1772, slip op. (C.D. Cal. Sept. 28, 1984). [*See also* the discussion of Saudi Arabia v. Nelson, in the section on "Espousal of Claims" in Chapter 11, this Anthology.]

18 FED. R. CIV. P. 19(a).

19 [Editor's Note: *See* the section on "Espousal of Claims" in Chapter 11, this Anthology.]

would be for the Soviet Union simply to let Andrei emigrate. Third, the United States, suddenly faced with a novel set of questions under the necessary co-plaintiff procedure, was diverted from intervening on behalf of the Soviet Union by being forced to expend its legal energies on resisting our attempt to bring it into the case as a co-plaintiff. The net result was that the United States was not a threat to Lois's case for a few days – and, considering the hunger strike, a few days were all that we had.[20]

Only five days after our telegram was delivered to the Soviet embassy in Washington, the Soviet secret police visited Andrei Frolova in Moscow and told him that he could leave the country.[21] We received corroboration through a reporter for the Chicago Tribune that Andrei would not meet with any bureaucratic obstacles in getting out of the Soviet Union. Thus, in our view, the United States' role as a necessary co-plaintiff was over. Indeed, if Lois later decided to pursue the case against the Soviet Union for monetary damages, having the United States involved in the case on her side might be awkward. Under classical international law theory, any monetary damages would be paid to the nation espousing its national's claim and not to the individual. In such a situation, Lois might be stuck with the additional problem of suing the United States to retrieve any damages paid by the Soviet Union to the United States. So when the attorney for the Department of Justice showed up in court to argue its motion for dismissal as a co-plaintiff, I surprised her by simply informing the court that I consented.[22]

It took Andrei Frolova almost a month to get all of his exit papers in order, but he duly arrived in the United States. His arrival at O'Hare was pictured on the front page of the Chicago Tribune with the headline "From Russia with Love."

I was criticized in some quarters for using manipulative legal tactics against the Soviet Union, both in asking for an injunction and in joining the United States as a necessary co-plaintiff. Some thought it was frivolous[23] to play on the Soviets' lack of knowledge of American courts and their consequent fear that I might possibly get an injunction against their gold sales and wheat purchases. I think that those who say it was a manipulation of the legal system are implicitly adopting the perspective that nations are the entities of primary concern and that law is meant to serve national interests. My own perspective is quite different; I believe that what counts are the rights of human beings and the primacy of the individual human personality. If there were no nations in the world, Lois and Andrei would naturally have the right to live together in the place of their choosing. We may superimpose national borders on the world, but I don't see how that changes their basic right. Nations themselves, although only recently, have conceded that any person has the right to emigrate from his country and that a married couple has the right to live together in any country they choose. I see nothing wrong in deconstructing a legal system to the extent that it places and maintains barriers between a husband and wife who want to live together. On the contrary, I would argue that those who feel that I manipulated the legal system to help Lois and Andrei have themselves been manipulated by the legal superstructure into believing that people are subordinate to abstract entities.

Hegel believed that persons create legal norms as rules for their interactions with other persons. Unlike the legal positivists[24] who see law as emanating from the legislature at the top and commanding individuals at the bottom, Hegel saw law arising from the bottom, out of the everyday interactions of persons. In this way, persons continuously fill and refill the world with the rights they have created.[25] Persons can only be expected to obey a legal norm if they have participated in the process of creating it. This notion may seems strange to lawyers who deal with national legal systems, but it is familiar to international lawyers as a description of the way customary law develops.[26]

What are the roles of legislatures and courts in Hegel's philosophy? To Hegel, legislation is external to the law-making process; it is a kind of intrusion into that process; the legislator is an outsider commanding you to do that

[20] As an aside, the publicity finally penetrated all the way to the dean's office of Northwestern Law School. Dean David Ruder stopped me in the hall and asked, "What's this about a hunger strike that somebody is conducting in your office?" He must have thought that it was a kind of sit-in or other illegal activity. I replied that Lois Frolova, my client, was conducting a hunger strike wherever she went, and that included my office. I said with a smile that the hunger strike had little choice but to follow her around.

[21] He was the only one of the four hunger strikers in the Moscow apartment who was allowed to leave. Two of the others eventually abandoned their strike, and a third was hospitalized.

[22] The eventual lawsuit for damages was dismissed in district court on the act of state doctrine, and the dismissal was affirmed in the court of appeals on entirely different grounds (sovereign immunity). Frolova v. Union of Soviet Socialist Republics, 558 F. Supp. 358 (N.D. Ill. 1983), *aff'd*, 761 F.2d 370 (7th Cir. 1985).

[23] Oliver, Book Review, 81 AJIL 445, 440 (1987); *see also* Letter from Burns H. Weston and Clarification by Covey T. Oliver, reprinted in 81 AJIL 635–37 (1987).

[24] Legal positivism is the belief that the validity of law is not affected by moral or ethical values; morals do not enter into the definition of law. For a discussion of this point, *see* Anthony D'Amato, *The Moral Dilemma of Positivism*, 20 VAL. U.L. REV. 43 (1985).

[25] *See* Arthur Jacobson, *Hegel's Legal Plenum*, 10 CARDOZO L. REV. 877 (1989).

[26] [Editor's Note: *See* the discussions of "Incidents" in Chapter 4, this Anthology.]

which may or may not be in your interest or in the interest of persons with whom you interact. Courts, for Hegel, are subordinate and incidental to human interaction.[27] Courts simply recognize norms that people have created. A judicial precedent is, therefore, not itself a source of law, but rather a way of recognizing the rule-creating and rule-articulating effect of previous personal interactions. Even when a court cites a rule in its opinion, the rule is not law but rather a way of describing the law.

Jeremy Bentham's positivism is the antithesis of Hegel's view.[28] Bentham was an enthusiastic supporter of overactive legislatures, indeed of comprehensive civil codes. He wanted written rules to govern every aspect of your life. As Arthur Jacobson has noted, positivism strives to eliminate personality from the law.[29] Positivism treats us as the objects of legislative commands rather than as the sources of law, and hence dehumanizes us by subjecting us to a sort of dictatorship of external law.[30] And positivism is the reigning notion of law in the world today. It is at the root of the philosophies of those who want to "protect" legal systems against the human rights claims of individuals who challenge the structure of a given system.

A healthy dose of the study of international law is a good antidote to this prevailing positivist vision. International customary law develops from the bottom up. Through their interactions, nations both create and enforce the evolving norms of custom. Yet the analogy between international customary law and Hegel's view of law is too easy; simply substituting "nation" for "person" in Hegel's philosophy leads to the reification of nations. Although Hegel himself was on occasion guilty of such a substitution, and although he has been thought of as the philosopher whose personification of the state was a precursor of Nazism,[31] I want to make the harder argument that the personification of the state is an outgrowth of Bentham's, not of Hegel's, philosophy. It was Jeremy Bentham who in 1789 helped fashion the term "international law" to mean what it does today.[32] It was Bentham who looked upon the state as a legal and juristic institution, and it was his positivist view that assumed international law to be about the rights and duties of states per se, and not about the rights and duties of individuals. Accordingly, I shall argue that, despite those aspects of Hegel's philosophy that have led some interpreters to say he apotheosized the state, a closer look at Hegel's philosophy reveals a more subtle and complex picture.

Let us consider three possible ways of looking at a state (Hegel was fond of trichotomies): transparent, translucent, and opaque. These words are, of course, very ordinary and no special significance should be attached to them.[33] A state is opaque under the view that I have attributed to Jeremy Bentham.[34] In his philosophy, the state has standing in international law and Lois is not recognized at all; we would see only the United States and could not look through it to see Lois. In Lois's case, it would be not her but the United States that was damaged by the Soviet Union's violation of international law in refusing to let Andrei Frolova emigrate. And an international court could conceivably rule that the remedy for the violation was not to allow Andrei to emigrate, but rather to do something symbolically that would satisfy the United States' national honor (such as firing off a 21-gun salute).

Many advocates of international human rights would view the state as utterly transparent, believing that the state is a completely artificial construct; it really does not exist in any meaningful sense.[35] The only thing of significance in the world is people. People have problems. People can be hurt. People have rights. Any claim that states have separate rights puts a mask on the rights of people within those states and is apt to divert our attention from the legitimate rights of persons.

I believe that neither of these polar views is consistent with Hegel's philosophy. While I am not sure that he would have liked the term, I think Hegel's view of the state is that it is in some sense translucent. The people in the state do not constitute and cannot claim the totality of the rights in the state; this is partly because the state also incorporates rights of people who have lived in the past and people who will live in the future, and partly because the mere sum of the individuals in the state does not fully account for the way those people behave. To some extent, people behave as they do because of the state's particular configuration. As Hegel said,

---

27 T. KNOX, HEGEL'S PHILOSOPHY OF RIGHT 141 (1942).

28 One writer summarized Bentham's view as follows: "Rights proceed from laws, and laws from government: men living without government live without rights." E. KAYSER, THE GRAND SOCIAL ENTERPRISE 38 (1932).

29 Arthur Jacobson, *supra* note 25, at 885.

30 *See* J. BENTHAM, AN INTRODUCTION TO THE PRINCIPLES OF MORALS AND LEGISLATION 8–9 (J. Burns & L. Hart eds. 1970).

31 KARL POPPER, THE OPEN SOCIETY AND ITS ENEMIES 226–73 (1950).

32 [Editor's Note: *See* the section on "Invention of the Term 'International Law' " in Chapter 2, this Anthology.]

33 Indeed, I choose them because they do not come to us already weighted with significance. Other writers have used terms such as "transnationalism," "realism," "utopianism," and "Cosmopolitanism," but I think these terms come to us with too much connotative baggage.

34 The Benthamite view was translated most thoroughly into international law by the supremely influential treatise of Lassa Oppenheim. [*See* the discussion by Oppenheim in the section entitled "The Classical Conception of State Personality," above in this Chapter.]

35 *See* Elfstrom, *On Dilemmas Of Intervention*, 93 Ethics 709, 713 (1983).

> The State, its laws, its arrangements, constitute the rights of its members; its natural features, its mountains, air, and waters, are their country, their fatherland, their outward material property; the history of this State, their deeds; what their ancestors have produced, belongs to them and lives in their memory. All is their possession, just as they are possessed by it; for it constitutes their existence, their being.[36]

Or to put it prosaically, the state is more than the sum of its parts. In representing the individuals within it, the state is in a sense effectuating their moral position in the international community. Their moral position, in turn, is not just the sum of the moral positions of the individuals in the state, but rather what those persons, their ancestors, and their future generations ought to desire and have a right to desire. In a sense the state is the physical manifestation of the collective rights of the people who have lived in it, who are living in it, and who will be born within its territory.

There is a danger that this translucent view of the state can lead to nationalism and national chauvinism. Governments and leaders may be quick to suggest that they know better than the people what is in the interest of the state,[37] and they can rally the people behind them by engaging in adventures abroad. But while the Hegelian position can lead to nationalism, it does not necessarily point in that direction. If we consider the Hegelian view in the context of international law, we find that it suggests some interesting and not intuitively obvious legal positions.

Of the many examples I could choose, let me pick three cases of United States military intervention: Vietnam, Grenada, and Nicaragua. The United States went into Vietnam to fill the power gap left after the French withdrew from Indochina following their defeat at Dien Bien Phu in 1954. The United States's avowed purpose was to prevent the spread of communism. The realization of this goal, however, required supporting the corrupt slumlords of Saigon in their fight against the indigenous revolutionary movement of the Viet Cong. The result was the longest war in United States history, and one that we eventually lost. In the aftermath of our withdrawal, the massive genocide in Cambodia took thousands of lives.

Quite different was our intervention in Grenada. A military group had machine-gunned its way into control, killing the leaders of the democratic government. The United States intervened, restored the democratic government, and then withdrew.

The Nicaraguan intervention was similar in some respects to both of these cases and dissimilar in others. At first, the United States applauded the ascension to power of the Sandinista government, but as it showed signs of becoming a leftist political dictatorship (suppressing opposition newspapers and rigging elections, among other things), the United States shifted its support to the Contras. But the Contras did not represent a democratic movement; not only did they lack indigenous support, they also tortured and murdered defenseless Nicaraguan citizens. Support for the Reagan administration's Nicaraguan policy waned when the American public became aware of the brutal human rights violations by the Contras.

In analyzing these three cases, we should begin with the obvious but often unnoticed proposition that in none of the interventions was annexation a goal of the United States.[38] This itself is historically remarkable. Up through the nineteenth century, a vastly superior military power that intervened in a foreign country was almost certain to annex it and transform it either into a colony or a protectorate. To be sure, our foreign policy purpose might have been akin to the nineteenth century notion of "balance of power" politics. Many political and military thinkers have indeed conceived of our foreign policy in these terms.[39] But this can only be rhetoric designed for domestic public relations, for in our overstock-piled nuclear age, when we can destroy any foreign country by pressing buttons, neither the United States nor the Soviet Union has any strategic military need for third-world allies, nor any need to redress insignificant imbalances among other nations.

Ultimately, the United States respected the nationhood of Vietnam, Grenada, and Nicaragua by not trying to impose upon them permanently its political control. But how

---

[36] G.W.F. Hegel, Introduction to the Philosophy of History 406 (Loewenberg ed. 1929).

[37] Rousseau, for example, considered this view carefully. J.-J. Rousseau, The Social Contract 131–34 (M. Cranston trans. 1968). On a superficial reading, Rousseau's "general will" can be that which is asserted by a totalitarian government and ratified by overwhelming plebiscite; we are familiar with the uses to which Hitler and Mussolini put this "general will." On a deeper reading, Rousseau's philosophy has to be considered in light of the great international lawyers, especially Grotius and Pufendorf, whom he had read and to whom he was reacting. Rousseau's "general will" turns out to reflect natural law, which (in his theory) is not easily manipulated by charismatic leaders. What is most obviously missing from Rousseau is the element later supplied by Hegel: the configuration of the state itself as a physical manifestation of the rights (the general will in the natural-law sense) of the people.

[38] By neither annexing nor colonizing the three nations, the United States arguably did not violate article 2(4) of the United Nations Charter, which prohibits the use of force against the territorial integrity or political independence of another country. Of course, other writers have looked at the language of article 2(4) and concluded the opposite. My purpose here, however, is not to engage in traditional legal analysis. [*See* the section on "Humanitarian Intervention," Chapter 7, this Anthology.]

[39] In particular, Henry Kissinger has emphasized the Metternich approach in his many books and papers contemporary with the Vietnam intervention.

should we assess the United States posture toward these countries in terms of opacity, translucency, and transparency? The Vietnam situation was one in which the United States regarded Vietnam as opaque. The United States considered the Saigon military dictatorship to be the sole legal voice of the state and refused to concern itself with the "democratic" aspirations of the people of that unfortunate country. Instead, a position based on the notion of the translucent state would have dictated that, if we had to intervene at all – and whether or not we should have is not a question that I am addressing here – we should have helped the Viet Cong establish a democratic, even if leftist, government to correspond with the wishes of the Vietnamese people.[40]

Grenada was, I believe, a paradigm of the Hegelian translucent position. The United States intervened on behalf of the Grenadians who otherwise would have been at the mercy of the small group of murderers who usurped power. After restoring the democratic structure of the state, United States military forces left.[41] The United States position might be characterized as supporting the nation of Grenada for the people of Grenada to enjoy, and opposing the capture of that nation by a group of thugs who would have established an authoritarian dictatorship against the wishes of the people.

This brings me to the most difficult case – Nicaragua. If the new Sandinista government were going to do the same thing as the thugs who temporarily took over Grenada, then I think the United States would have a prima facie case for intervening on behalf of the people of Nicaragua. Moreover, the time for intervention in such cases must be before the new government has consolidated its power, destroyed opposing political parties, abolished elections, and put opposition newspapers out of business. Intervention on behalf of the people of Nicaragua against the gradual movement toward totalitarianism of the new government was, therefore, a policy that had to be set in motion before all the evidence was in about the intentions of the new government.

But the problem in Nicaragua was that the United States could not find an opposition movement that represented the wishes of the people. The Contras, whom the United States government backed, were led by deposed officers of the previous Somoza dictatorship. Unlike Castro, who in his guerrilla campaign in the hills of Cuba enjoyed the overwhelming support of the villagers, the Contras in Nicaragua have never had such indigenous support and have turned instead to the arbitrary murder and torture of the citizenry in order to "prove" to them that the existing government is powerless to protect its people and that, therefore, they should support the Contras. Few citizens have been won over by these desperate tactics.

The failure to find an indigenous movement antithetical to the Sandinista government should have signaled to the Reagan administration that the Sandinistas indeed had popular support, and that perhaps it was United States support of the Contras rather than widespread domestic resistance to the new government that was pushing the Sandinistas toward suppression of civil liberties.

Some highly traditionalist writers on international law might agree that the United States should not have supported the Contras or mined Nicaragua's harbors, but only for the reason that no transboundary use of military force is acceptable. Their position is echoed by many leaders of third-world nations who proclaim publicly that under no circumstances should the superpowers intervene in the internal affairs of any nation. These officials take an opaque view of nations as entities on the international scene and cite article 2(4) of the U.N. Charter to support their position. But I think we should regard their position as self-serving. Obviously, these third-world leaders want to be secure in their home countries against all external intervention, especially the kind that would establish a democratic government and maybe remove them from office in the process. These leaders do not necessarily represent the legitimate aspirations of their people.[42]

Furthermore, I think we should always be skeptical about any legal argument that categorically prohibits the use of force, because some uses of force are clearly required in order to protect people against brutality and degradation. If you are walking down a street and someone assaults you, you would expect a nearby police officer to intervene on your behalf. You would expect the police officer to use force if necessary. Or consider a case that is more closely analogous to a nation: Suppose you walk by a house and see through the window a man savagely

---

[40] There is no evidence that a leftist popular revolution would necessarily lead to control by an external power such as the Soviet Union. Certainly China – for all its radical communism under Mao – remained steadfastly independent of Moscow. The lesson of China, however, may not have been perceived in the mid-1960s when the United States began escalating its military commitment in Vietnam. But even apart from these considerations, any revolutionary movement in Vietnam that reflected the aspirations of the majority of the people would by definition have to be "leftist," since the Saigon government was an extreme rightist dictatorship. *Cf.* CHRISTOPHER BEAL & ANTHONY D'AMATO (EDS.), THE REALITIES OF VIETNAM (1968).

[41] I said at the time that I thought that, irrespective of our avowed purpose, our real purpose was humanitarian and fully consistent with international law. Anthony D'Amato, *Intervention in Grenada: Right or Wrong?* N.Y. TIMES, Oct. 30, 1983, at E18, col. 3.

[42] [Editor's Note: *Compare* the views of Professors Philip Allott and Richard Falk in Chapter 17 below, "The Future of International Law."]

beating a woman. Even if they are husband and wife, and even if they are in their own house and on private property, you would have a moral obligation to call the police and would expect the police to intervene forcibly. If the police were not available, you would have a moral right to intervene personally. Why should the situation in the house be any different from the situation within a nation? If the government kidnaps or "disappears" citizens, and continues to do so as a policy, why should that government be immune from outside military intervention? Such a government has no moral claim to be left alone to work its arbitrary will upon the people.[43]

Certainly, if there were a multilateral police force operant in the world today, that force—and not any individual nation acting unilaterally—would be the proper agent to engage in these humanitarian interventions. But there is no such force. In its absence, nations do engage from time to time in humanitarian intervention,[44] and I suggest that the intervention is legal under international law if the use of military force itself is not expected to cause greater suffering or loss of life than that caused by those violations of human rights that it is attempting to remedy (and there is no attempt to annex the target state).

In brief, what goes on in another country should no longer be obscured by an opaque view of the state. International morality, in the form of humanitarian intervention, has caught up with international law. Of course, intervention cannot end in annexation or colonization and must be terminated when the evil has been remedied, but the customary practice of states is now telling us that, within these parameters, governments are no longer insulated from the international legal community if they brutalize their own citizenry. In other words, states should be thought of as translucent entities.

Returning to Lois Frolova's case, I would have preferred to see the United States welcome, not fight, the opportunity to join Lois's lawsuit as co-plaintiff. But the United States is still a long way from supporting the private enforcement of international human rights, even in its own courts. Rather, the government prefers to monopolize all foreign affairs matters and settle them, if at all, on a political basis. Unfortunately, the notion of deregulation and smaller government, although embraced domestically, is far from being actualized in the conduct of United States foreign policy.[45]

Looking ahead, I hope that the new and exciting human rights cases that some American lawyers are initiating in United States courts will help educate our own government as to the proper translucency of our own country. Our government should make every effort to assist its citizens in the assertion of their international human rights. These assertions should become part of what this country stands for. Foreign policy should not be decided solely in Washington, D.C., but rather should be an expression of the legitimate aspirations of all the people, certainly to the extent that these aspirations are articulated in our own court system. And we should welcome, not resist, similar human rights cases being filed in the courts of other nations. Courts throughout the world can be a forum in which people can assert the primacy of their human rights in all situations in which states are impeding the realization of those rights. The United States should welcome this trend and not, by adherence to a principle of the opacity of a state, resist it on the grounds of "sovereignty."

If we reject the state as either opaque or transparent, we are rejecting simplistic approaches and embarking instead on a new vision, albeit one of great complexity. The rules of international law will not seem nearly as clear as they were in the past. The intellectual challenge to students who want to begin a career in international law will be much greater than it was to past generations. But as students of international law, we should look forward to achieving the complex synthesis implicit in Hegel's philosophy: to promote the human rights of all persons in the natural context of the unique nation in which they live.

5. The Torturer Speaks[46]

If a torturer were to defend his work, here is what he might say:

The world is at war, though the war is undeclared. Ferocious battles erupt, often unexpectedly, now in one country, now in another, often in several at once. Battles are won; others are lost. The war goes on. There are grounds neither for compromise nor pity. The stakes are too high for pity. Pity makes you weak. And there cannot be compromise because the antagonists hold utterly incompatible views about the ends of life and the organization of society.

We are defending a social order that has evolved over

---

[43] [For a further development of this position, *see* my response to Professors Nanda and Farer regarding Panama, in the section on "Humanitarian intervention," Chapter 7, this Anthology.]

[44] For a collection and excellent discussion of intervention cases, *see* FERNANDO TESON, HUMANITARIAN INTERVENTION: AN INQUIRY INTO LAW AND MORALITY 155–200 (1987).

[45] For more discussion of this point, *see* Anthony D'Amato, *International Human Rights at the Close of the Twentieth Century*, 22 INT'L LAWYER 167 (1988).

[46] By TOM J. FARER, excerpted from: THE GRAND STRATEGY OF THE UNITED STATES IN LATIN AMERICA 98 (New Brunswick: Transaction Books, 1988). Reprinted by permission.

two millennia. We are defending the fundamental institutions of our civilization: the family, religion, private property, and the whole system of ordered liberty which they support and in turn supports them. The enemy, Marxists of one liturgy or another, are bent on destroying those institutions and abolishing liberty.

Because your societies are richer and more developed, because you have filled out all the empty spaces and imbued most citizens with respect for the civil order into which they are born, you can deal with the problem largely as an external threat. You do not need extraordinary measures. We are not so fortunate.

Your bleeding hearts talk as if we've butchered half of our population and the rest are starving to death. Then how, I ask you, is it that our towns and cities are awash with people, young people for whom we have no houses, no schools, and no jobs? Meanwhile the priests and other agitators, Marxists and their fellow-travelers, go around telling everyone he has a right to these things. The best of them are just irresponsible and dangerous fools throwing sparks onto tinder.

To build up the economy we need capital. To get the capital, we need social peace. To get that peace, we need to insulate the masses from the agitators. When the cancer of subversion has already penetrated into the healthy flesh of society, we have to cut out the cancerous tissue, quickly, before metastasis.

In societies like ours, ordinary measures don't work against clandestine groups. Torture does. You talk about us as if we were animals, subhuman, or you say we use these methods because we're not professionals, not well-trained. As if we invented torture. Were the Gestapo badly trained or the S.D. or other German units? Not on your life. But they knew that when you are dealing with organized political movements capable of energizing much larger groups if they go undetected, if you are dealing with such movements rather than isolated criminals, you need shortcuts, and you need to discourage those who have not yet committed themselves to the life of subversion.

You call us thugs and incompetents. Well, there's nothing unprofessional about the French security services; but they failed to root the terrorist cells out of the Casbah during the Algerian war. Then the paratroop units were sent, the elite of the whole French army, as fine a group of professional troops as exists. And they failed too, at first. Then they turned to torture, and when they finished, the Casbah was secure.

You think the situation in El Salvador is precarious now? How do you think it would be if the death squads hadn't been operating in 1980 and 1981? They annihilated the guerrilla networks in San Salvador. They secured the capital. And they scared the hell out of a lot of potential collaborators.

All right, maybe they also drove some people into the subversion. That is a risk. Terror doesn't always work, particularly if it is applied halfheartedly, as the Salvadorans have been forced by pressure from Washington to apply it. The Guatemalans, on the other hand, told you to go to hell. They butchered everyone they thought needed butchering, terrified the Indians, and they've got the problem under control again.

I know I've been talking about killing, not just torture. Of course, in many cases we do both, particularly when the torture confirms what we suspected, namely the guilt of the detainee. If we fill our jails with them, the next thing you know their friends have seized the American ambassador and want to trade him for imprisoned colleagues.

As far as the killing is concerned, I take it your only possible objection is the lack of due process, not the killing itself. After all, these people are rebels, usually with links of one kind or another to foreign governments. Rebellion is treason. Capital punishment is not unusual in the case of treason. (Need I remind you that you executed the Rosenbergs, husband and wife?) So I take it that you think torture is worse than execution, that torture is something special.

I admit that, as a matter of law, you have a point. Article 3 of the Geneva Conventions of 1949 does ban torture, while not preventing a government from executing its opponents during or after a civil war. All right; that's the law; but is this a morally compelling distinction? You could argue, you know, that torture has a far clearer military justification. The only justification for executing rebels at the end of a civil war or spies in time of peace is some very problematic idea about the long-term deterrent effect. But taking up the gun against the state is such a dangerous gamble to begin with. I doubt people do it unless they expect to win. With torture, on the other hand, you are seeking information directly related to reducing your casualties. The connection between this supposedly illegitimate means and the clearly legitimate end is much closer.

Moreover, society does not normally value freedom-from-prolonged-pain more than it values life. In many of your states, capital punishment has been outlawed. But what is life imprisonment in conditions of maximum security other than torture? Even if a person prefers death, you won't let him have it. Just as your courts wouldn't allow a person in a state of acute pain and humiliating dependence to choose death. Indeed, you are prepared to force-feed a person to keep her alive.

Torture, summary execution, all the apparatus of terror is ugly, no doubt. And as a child of the enlightenment, I share with you a presumption against their use. But like all presumptions, it has exceptions. And we are not the only ones who have carved them out. You North Americans have done your part.

I remember a few years ago, on some anniversary of the atomic bombing of Hiroshima and Nagasaki, the survivors among those who had been involved in the decision to drop the bomb were asked whether they had repented. I can't remember one who admitted he had. Moreover, various eminent intellectuals who had not been involved were prepared with the wisdom of hindsight to defend the incineration of those two Japanese cities. Why? Because it saved lives. Classical utilitarianism: Maximize the sum total of happiness and minimize the pain.

The bomb was indiscriminate, a terror weapon, like torture and disappearance and mutilation and the other instruments we have found it useful to employ in times of grave national emergency. And who among you would not do the same in the right circumstances. Suppose you arrested a man a few days before Christmas who told you mockingly that he had planted a bomb in a department store which would go off in three hours. And suppose you were able to confirm that he had set off bombs in the past. So there was every reason to believe his claim. Maybe some among you would not have the stomach to torture the location of the bomb out of him. But how many would not feel the thrilling hope that there was someone willing to take on the job? As I said earlier, in North America and Europe, these extenuating circumstances don't yet arise very often. We are less fortunate in this respect.

We who preserve order in Latin America and our friends and colleagues faced with similar challenges in other parts of the world – in South Africa, South Korea, Zaire, Indonesia – we recognize that either we are being subjected to some kind of double standard or the alleged concern with our means conceals hostility to our ends, above all, the preservation of a stable anticommunist order with potential for economic growth and ultimate legitimization among the great, volatile masses.

First this matter of a double standard. No doubt you think I am going to insult your intelligence by claiming that human rights organizations and the media dramatize problems in countries like my own far more than in Communist countries. I leave that sort of adolescent mendacity to American supporters of our cause. We see that the mere denial of a visa and discharge from government employment of a single Jewish dissident in the Soviet Union is more likely to galvanize American, particularly congressional, opinion than the execution of a thousand peasants in one of the countries for whom I speak.

But when I speak of a double standard, I have a different comparison in mind. Chile, Guatemala, El Salvador, Argentina before Alfonsin: We are not the only allies of your country facing subversion and terrorism and using means we find not only efficient but necessary. I admit now, perhaps implicitly I have done so already, that in a sense these means are somewhat indiscriminate. Sometimes the people we torture know nothing useful and have no direct connection to the guerrillas. But even in those cases can it be said that there is "innocence?" We do not pick up people who are with us, who support us, who sympathize with our efforts. No, my friends, obviously we pick up people who have identified themselves as at least latent enemies of order: People who fertilize the ground for guerrilla recruitment by telling peasants they have all kinds of economic and social rights (by the way, the Reagan Administration has been quick to recognize this problem and has assisted us by rejecting, as dangerous and statist, the notion that there are such things as economic and social rights); people who give ammunition to international campaigns against our countries by accusing us of human rights violations. We pick them up because objectively they are helping the enemy. Or peasants who choose to live in guerrilla-dominated areas where inevitably they provide cover and food and infrastructure for the subversive delinquents.

I appreciate you will not share my point of view about the dimensions of culpability. And, you doubtless think, since our methods foreseeably subject to torture or death people you deem innocent, they should be condemned. Indeed you go further, urging suspension of the aid we need in some cases to survive the assault against our capitalist and Christian civilization. And this, I respectfully suggest to you, is where the double standard appears. For how many of you or your clones in Congress were demanding a punitive suspension of aid to another friend of the United States faced with terrorist assaults on its society when it has found itself driven to measures you label indiscriminate when we employ them?

Obviously I refer to Israel. You understand that I do so not for the purpose of criticizing Israel or urging you to support sanctions against that country. On the contrary, the Israelis are good friends of ours. When I recently visited my fellow officers in Guatemala, I found practically all the elite troops equipped with Israeli Galil assault rifles, excellent weapons by the way. My old comrade-in-arms Anastasio Somoza probably could not have held out as long as he did, after the Carter administration cut off his arms supply, if Israel had not helped fill the gap. Along with the weapons – for which, to be sure, we pay market rates – we get excellent technical advice. We do not criticize our friends. We ask only for equal understanding.

When the Israelis bombed PLO headquarters in Beirut, before the Lebanese invasion, many so-called civilians were killed. That was foreseeable. The Israelis are excellent pilots; but there are limits to the degree of surgical accuracy anyone can achieve. But most or all of those civilians were Palestinians who probably sympathized with the cause of the PLO and no one forced them to live where the PLO operated.

I know there was criticism of the bombing even in the pages of The New Republic. Well, if it makes you feel better, criticize us. But just as Mr. Peretz, who owns that magazine, did not suggest that Israel should be punished with sanctions that could threaten its existence, he should not call for sanctions against us when we do what is necessary. For us, nothing is excused. For Israel, everything. Some people said it was wrong of the PLO to locate its headquarters and its weapons in refugee camps and civilian buildings. Well, by the same process of reasoning, our guerrillas should not seek to swim in the peasant sea. But that's like asking fish to walk.

When the Phalangists slaughtered the Palestinians in their camps and an Israeli tribunal found Sharon and Eytan "indirectly responsible," The New York Times, which never misses an opportunity to calumniate us, which has never expressed a single word of sympathy or understanding for our difficulties, proclaimed this a vindication of the Israeli political system.

Some of my colleagues were a little bitter. "Indirect responsibility," they snapped at me. As if anyone who had spent one week in that part of the world, as a number of them had, did not know what the Phalangists would do once they were allowed into the camps. Sharon was condemned for failing to take into consideration the danger of a massacre, when the truth is that of course he took it into consideration.

And where is Sharon now? In prison, like some of my Argentine colleagues, or is he still a Minister? Nor is it necessary to look outside the core group of capitalist democracies to find an impulse toward extraordinary measures whenever the social order is threatened. Look at your reaction to Pearl Harbor. You rounded up citizens of Japanese ancestry and dumped them in concentration camps.

I appeal to you to be less unfair in the future, to appreciate that in our minds, we are fighting a war for survival—the survival of the military institution, the survival of the capitalist mode of production, the survival of the small-town values of family and church and order and accepted hierarchy that we were born into, that are the warp and the woof of our identity.

Are you hostile to these ends? Is that what makes us different? Is that what justifies your anger?

We do not torture and kill gratuitously. We are not savages. We act out of a sense of extreme necessity. We feel justified. And we will continue, albeit moderating our operations from time to time to coincide with executive branch certification to your Congress that we are making progress in the human rights realm.

Let me assure you that the efficiency of our means—above all, torture, disappearance, the public exposure of mutilated cadavers, in short, terror—cannot be doubted. Terror, you see, is a strategy of disorientation. It is designed to deprive potential subversives of the ability to calculate and foresee the consequences of their actions. Terror disrupts and dissolves the ability of people to act in concert. The occasional error and the variable definition of the enemy is in this respect immensely useful. For it helps to chill even the most latent opposition; it multiplies the force of each individual blow against the subversive enemy.

Not only torture but the signs of it on randomly distributed cadavers that mark the face of a new day heighten the chill which, if it is successful, will spare us still more extreme measures. As one of our enemies, the scholar Juan Corradi, has so aptly put it, they "remind the provisionally living that they too might fall at any moment," that everyone who is not with us is, ineluctably, a hostage. If, despite that, resistance endures, can you imagine how perilous our cause would be if we fought by rules you announce from the sedated comfort of societies where capitalism has achieved ideological hegemony over the entire population?

We who live in the jungle, and we alone, know the paths that lead to safety. Do not presume to instruct us. For if I may paraphrase another enemy of our cause, you are like the professor who knows a country only from the bare figures in his books about the gross national product or the per capita output of wheat, trying to describe that place to a man who has thirsted in its deserts and shivered on its mountains. You cannot reasonably believe that you have a superior grasp of our tactical requirements.

So at bottom, you must feel hostility to our ends. Assuming you are not Marxists, we believe this hostility stems from a misapprehension of our ends. Do you think we want the poor to be hungry and the upper classes to be obscenely rich? Do you think we are opposed to free institutions? Do you think we want the armed forces to occupy the same omnipotent, all-pervasive position in our societies that the Communist Party occupies in Marxist states? If you believe those propositions, you do misapprehend our ends. And that is because you do not understand our problems.

Here again I see a double standard. For your own society, you accept a marginalized sector of the population because you recognize the costs in material and institutional terms of trying to absorb that sector. But for our societies you postulate millenarian goals and treat them as if they were presently realizable, and as if we did not have constraints far greater than those you coexist with comfortably.

Let me put it very simply. Our population is growing quickly. It is urbanizing even more quickly. Its appetite for material goods may grow quickest of all. The fundamental task of any political order is to regulate the demands of the masses so that they are compatible with the capacity of governing elites to respond without violating the society's values and traditions and long-term security. Overload leads to instability and civil war.

Traditional methods of demand control do not work well under current circumstances. Urbanization debases the symbolic currency in patron-client relations which at one time substituted in part for material benefits. Alien ideas—Marxism, Liberation Theology, so-called economic and social rights—aggravate this tendency to demand material rewards for political support.

Nor is it possible in most cases to mobilize the masses around nationalist issues. In the first place, mobilization is a two-edged sword. While for a time it may distract the population from distributional issues, it also may create a heightened sense of competence, may facilitate communication and the discovery of common concerns and, if actual sacrifices are required, may heighten expectations of improved conditions after the national crisis is resolved. In the second place, wars are dangerous to the social order because only we, the armed forces, stand between civilization and chaos followed by Marxism. The military institutions cannot risk defeat. Thirdly, within the Western Hemisphere, the U.S. has imposed a kind of Pax Americana. Our economies are too vulnerable for us to resist serious economic sanctions. Finally, in our epoch, ideological fraternity is more important than common citizenship. Would it not be grotesque for me to feel hostility toward fellow officers in other countries with whom I have shared the firing range at your training camps, with whom I have exchanged intelligence information, who fight the common enemy, merely because they live on the other side of a geographic frontier? It would be unnatural and it would be dysfunctional.

While on the one hand, then, our traditional control mechanisms are weak, on the other, we need control to create the conditions of economic growth, the ultimate key to a stable social order. Today, capital knows no national loyalties. If we do not create an attractive environment in our countries, indigenous capital flows out and foreign capital stays out. This generation must serve as the cannon fodder of the war against underdevelopment.

A final word to you so that you will better understand us and yourselves. You call us savages, thugs, barbarians. But to us you are weak, pathetic, and decadent. You have lost the capacity even to imagine causes for which it is worthy to torture and to kill, even at the risk of one's immortal soul. Perhaps you never had it. Martyrdom is not native to your history, as it is to ours. In this respect, even the subversive delinquents – the anarchists and the Marxists – are more akin to us than are you, the unworthy beneficiaries of our holy struggle.

So, now you know what is the appeal of torture. Whether you will benefit from this knowledge, whether you can benefit from this knowledge, remains to be seen.

6. Torture as *Raison d'Etat*[47]

We normally assume, with some justification, that law enforcement officers are motivated by a desire to serve the public and to vindicate the interests of victims of crime. Of course, psychologists can find other motives for them (desire for advancement, better salary, lust for power, sadism). But in addition to all of these, I want to suggest a somewhat different motivation that is hard to pinpoint or describe: the feeling of a need to vindicate the interests of the state. If there is such a motivation, it may help to throw some light on the legal creature called the "state," to which we blithely entrust the making and the implementation of all the laws that restrict our individual freedoms.

While we can understand a motivation to vindicate the interests of victims, it is harder to understand what it would be like to vindicate the interests of the state. I would be called mentally unstable if I proclaimed I was acting to vindicate the interests of my apartment or my piece of farm land. Our normal notion of the state is that it is an abstraction – the residual totality of things, the entity that represents the public in a legal but not a corporeal sense. How could vindicating the state's interests be any different from vindicating the interests of any other nonliving or abstract thing?

[47] By ANTHONY D'AMATO, excerpted from: *Torture as Raison D'Etat*, 10 CRIMINAL JUSTICE ETHICS 40 (1991). Reprinted by permission.

Consider an observation made by Lawrence Weschler in a recent book about torture in Brazil and Uruguay.[48] In a brief discussion of a Brazilian security agent who was taking sexual advantage of the female relative of a prisoner under torture, Weschler tells us that the agent led her to believe that he would intercede in some fashion on the prisoner's behalf. And *that*, Weschler reports, "horrified" the other torturers:

> It's very strange. Rape as a part of torture was perfectly OK: that was an effective method of investigation, a way of sparking fear which would provoke confession and elicit information – all very professional. But rape for pleasure – the very thought that the torturer could be doing anything for his own pleasure – that really shook them up.[49]

Thus the torturer, in the eyes of his colleagues, cannot give the appearance of acting for his own pleasure. The fact that he was acting for his own pleasure and not, as it were, at the pleasure of the state, "shook up" the other torturers perhaps because for a moment it unmasked certain pleasurable emotions that they dimly recognized in their own psychologies but were actively sublimating.

Let us look more closely at the emotions of these other torturers (we can leave the rapist now – *his* emotions are those of your ordinary generic rapist). The "horrified" Brazilian security agents may possibly be categorized under either an "entailment" thesis or a "deviationist" thesis.

The deviationist thesis would view torture as pathologically pleasurable – an act of sadism on the part of the torturers. Under this view, torture would not be a necessary part of a state's security apparatus but rather a dark corridor within the apparatus of state officialdom that some states use and other states avoid. Perhaps the states that condone torture are impelled by the particular sort of people who are drawn into security work in that state at a given time. Those people might start out as confirmed sadists; once they attain official status, they find victims and invent statist rationalizations to torture them. To be sure, they often elicit useful information (the word security agents love is "intelligence")[50], and they may also play an important role

[48] LAWRENCE WESCHLER, A MIRACLE, A UNIVERSE: SETTLING ACCOUNTS WITH TORTURERS ((New York: Pantheon, 1990).

[49] *Id.* at 67.

[50] Yet one may doubt how useful all the so-called intelligence really is. Stalin in 1940 got superb intelligence from Switzerland that Hitler was going to betray their alliance and attack the Soviet Union. Stalin simply refused to believe the report, and hence was taken by surprise and nearly annihilated. I am convinced that in the week or two before August 2, 1990, the United States government received intelligence that Saddam Hussein was going to attack Kuwait. The problem, again, was that this evidence was disbelieved (or improperly processed, which amounts to the same thing). The Walker spy case in the United States showed that for

for the state in intimidating political opposition movements. But the deviationist thesis, I would argue, finds most of the alleged utility of torturing to be a rationalization. Perhaps the most cynical view of the deviationist thesis is that in any army, police force, guerrilla band, and so on, there are some useful fighters and colleagues who happen to be sadists. Once the organization attains power in the state, the energy of these people has to be siphoned off somehow, so that they don't turn on their colleagues. Channeling their energies becomes transmuted into a practice of torture that is rationalized as necessary to national security.

The entailment thesis, on the contrary, would view torture not as a pleasurable act but as work that is a necessity from the state's point of view. There is no rationalization about it. It is simply dirty work in a dirty world. Under this view, we would expect to find that all states at one time or another order or permit varying degrees of torture, and indeed anecdotal history seems to corroborate this position.

Between the two theories, if we judge from popular motion pictures, the deviationist thesis has more Hollywood value. The sadist is the "bad guy" whom you can comfortably hate during the movie, after which you leave the theatre with a good feeling that torture is a chance event – a contingent occurrence that is containable and not a functional part of your own state's apparatus but rather something that happens only in other countries or in the movies. The torturers are "sick" people. Nietzsche tells us that everyone was once "sick" in this way, and our implicit question should be whether human nature has changed:

> *Cruelty* constituted the great festival pleasure of more primitive men and was indeed an ingredient of almost every one of their pleasures. . . . It is not long since princely weddings and public festivals of the more magnificent kind were unthinkable without executions, torturings, or perhaps an auto-da-fe. . . . To see others suffer does one good, to make others suffer even more: this is a hard saying but an ancient, mighty, human, all-too-human principle to which even the apes might subscribe; for it has been said that in devising bizarre cruelties they anticipate man and are, as it were, his "prelude." Without cruelty there is no festival; thus the longest and most ancient part of human history teaches – and in punishment there is so much that is *festive.*[51]

As far as overt acceptance of torture is concerned, we have indeed come a long way from the "princely weddings and public festivals" thus spake. Torture today is universally condemned as an international crime. But is it only our culture that has changed? Have we merely driven the "festival" underground? Are the "pleasures" now reserved for a select group of torturers operating in the dimly lit basements of government buildings? Thus speaks the deviationist thesis.

In contrast, the entailment thesis holds that the torturer is a mere agent with an unpleasant job. It may be dirty business, but what is important is that it is the state's business. If a particular torturer does not take his job seriously – if he appears to enjoy it – then he is personalizing what should be an abstract act of state. He is implicitly attacking the justificatory foundations of his colleagues. They will regard *him* as a deviationist because it is essential to their own world-view that *they* are professionals.[52]

Even if the torturer secretly enjoys what he is doing, the statist entailment thesis requires that he not appear to be enjoying it. This requirement was recognized explicitly in 1486 by the notorious church-promulgated *Malleus Malificarum*, a manual of *legal* instructions for dealing with witchcraft. Stating that witches should not be condemned unless convicted by their own confessions, the book in chilling terms tells a judge what to do if a woman accused of being a witch refuses to confess:

> Order the officers to bind her with cords, and apply her to some engine of torture; and then let them obey at once but not joyfully, rather appearing to be disturbed by their duty.[53]

The entailment thesis is supported by what is perhaps the most revealing point about torture in Weschler's book: the meticulous *records* kept by the military courts in Brazil. All cases began with a written confession of guilt signed by the defendant. Twenty-five percent of the cases in the files of the Supreme Military Court contained open-court denunciations by the defendant or his attorney of the torture that was used in extracting the defendant's confession. Weschler writes:

> I asked the lawyers I talked to, and other observers, why the judges had allowed the denunciations of torture to be entered in the record and then allowed the records to be preserved. Alfred Stepan suggested that "record keeping like that is part of a long Ibe-

about a decade all U.S. top-secret codes for all our naval maneuvers were leaked by Walker to the Soviet Union. Did it make any discernible difference – to the Soviets or to us?

[51] F. NIETZSCHE, ON THE GENEALOGY OF MORALS 66–67.

[52] Is there a parallel here to our childhood? Recall a serious parent getting ready to punish you and saying, "This is going to hurt me more than it hurts you," and your being frightened and at the same time incredulous. Somehow your inner disbelief about the veracity of your parent's statement *adds* to your sense of dread.

[53] THE MALLEUS MALEFICARUM OF HEINRICH KARAMER AND JAMES SPRENGER 222–23 (Summers tr. 1971).

rian tradition of thoroughly recording acts of state, which, as acts of state, could not by definition be viewed as suspect or illegal

"They never dreamed that any of this would be used against them," Jaime Wright commented. "They never imagined they'd ever lose power."

"The judges no doubt assumed," one of the lawyers told me, "that the same thing would happen this time that happened in 1945 – the records would all be burned, and they themselves, of course, would be immune."[54]

Jaime Wright added:

> It's amazing, when you think about the risks involved – after all, these prisoners could expect to be given back over to their jailers following the trial – that anybody ever chose to make such a denunciation. But, from what we've been able to ascertain, about 25 percent of the prisoners did. Anyway, in such cases the judge would dutifully listen as the defendants described their tortures; the judges would then summarize these accounts and order the court reporters to enter the summaries into the record. Everything was done by the book. And then the tribunals would hand down their decisions. Once in a while – admittedly, very rarely – they'd actually find the defendant innocent. But it didn't really matter, because either way the losing side would appeal the case to the Supreme Military Court in Brasilia, which would almost invariably find the defendant guilty after all."[55]

Remarkably, all the files of these cases were smuggled out of the Supreme Military Court building, photocopied (there were over one million pages), microfilmed, compiled, and released as a book that turned into a best-seller, *Brasil: Nunca Mais* (1985) ("Brazil: Never Again").[56] What did the people of Brazil and Uruguay do after the torture regimes were deposed and exposed? The public in elections and referenda approved wholesale amnesty for the torturers. Many individual cases were not prosecuted or their cases were dismissed. The few individual trials that took place got caught up in endless litigation delays and ultimately led either to acquittals or to executive pardons.

Many South American liberals anguished about the future of their countries in light of the popular willingness to forgive and forget the tortures. Weschler does not hide his personal disappointment:

> One has to return to the scream welling out of the torture chamber. An old man, a teenage boy, a young woman five months pregnant, is screaming in agony. And what is the torturer saying? As Marcelo Vignar has pointed out, he is saying "Go ahead, scream, scream all you like, scream your lungs out – nobody can hear you, nobody would dare to hear you, nobody cares about you, no one will ever know." That is the primordial moment which has desperately to be addressed – and as desperately by the torture society as by the torture victim: Who was there? Who was screaming? Who were those people standing by the screamer's side? Who, even now, will dare to hear? Who will care to know? Who will be held accountable? And who will hold them to account?[57]

Aryeh Neier told author Weschler:

> "The human capacity to look backward is frail enough. The human capacity to look forward is frailer yet. Rather, punishment is the absolute duty of society to honor and redeem the suffering of the individual victim. In a society of law, we say it is not up to the individual victims to exercise vengeance, but rather up to society to demonstrate respect for the victim, for the one who suffered, by rendering the victimizer accountable."[58]

But why, in light of all this, does Weschler conclude as follows?

> When the torturer assures his victim, "No one will ever know," he is at once trying to break the victim's spirit and to bolster his own. He needs to be certain that no one will ever know; otherwise the entire premise of his own participation in the encounter would quickly come into question.[59]

I can understand that Weschler might *want* to reach this facile conclusion – after all, his book is *about* the importance of exposing torturers. But in light of his own evidence, I fear that Weschler is engaged in wishful thinking. To recapitulate the main points:

(1) The judges kept elaborate records of the tortures.

(2) The records were discovered and published.

(3) The torturers were given amnesty by popular vote.

These points suggest that exposing torturers is not so democratically significant after all.

---

54 Weschler, at 47–49.

55 *Id.* at 15–16.

56 (PETROPOLIS: VOZES, 1985), published in the United States as JOAN DASSIN (ED.), TORTURE IN BRAZIL (Jaime Wright, tr., N.Y.: Random House, 1986).

57 Weschler, at 242.

58 *Id.* at 244.

59 *Id.* at 246.

I submit that the entailment thesis goes a lot deeper than liberal observers are willing or able to admit. The people of Brazil and Uruguay may have perceived that the torturers were doing what needed to be done at the time, and that they were acting selflessly and in the interests of the state at least insofar as they sincerely perceived those interests. The torturers were doing the state's business, not their own. Hence they did not deserve to be held personally accountable for their acts.

Even though the "subversives" during the torture regimes later turned out to be the vanguard of the new democratic regimes, the public apparently was ungrateful to them. Perhaps the public felt that there was something "illegal" about what the subversives did *even though* what they did was to fight dictatorship, cruelty, and oppression.

Law is, of course, the formal ideological clothing of the state. Just as "the clothes make the man," the popular attitude toward law is often indistinguishable from the popular attitude toward the state. Although law seems highly specific in its rules, statutes, and precedents, it also seems less tangible than the state. If I cannot quite visualize the state as an actual player, its legal clothing to a large extent gives it form and substance, much like the clothes and facial bandages worn by the Invisible Man in the 1933 film of that name.

A huge mistake that liberals make is to assume that laws are mutable, changeable, the artifacts of a particular legislature trapped by shifting lobbies, the whims of a particular ruling elite. H.L.A. Hart, a leading positivist, was able to justify his rather dictatorial view of law as the command of a sovereign (in his classic book *The Concept of Law* [1961]) by another book he published at roughly the same time where he said that *whenever* a law conflicts with morality, a person should do what is moral and disobey the law.[60] This austerely British view of "law" underdetermines the impact law itself has upon public morality.[61] The South American public may have been genuinely impressed by the notion that what the torturers were doing was legal and therefore right and that their victims's actions must have been contrary to the interests of the state, illegal, and therefore wrong.

How can we unpack the psychological denial, the cognitive dissonance embedded in this popular conviction of the citizens of Brazil and Uruguay? One possibility is that there is a curious mixture in South American jurisprudence of the idea of natural law (stemming from the Church and suggesting the affinity between moral law and positive law) and Kelsenian positivism (the view that *whatever officials do* is what the law is).[62] Under an extension of Kelsen's perspective,[63] as long as the torturers sincerely acted in their role as state officials, then what they did *constituted* the law. At this moment natural law chimes in to say that if what these state officials did was legal, then it was right.

If torture is *not* supposed to be pleasurable, if it is just a difficult job that must be done, then perhaps it is *entailed by statism* rather than a pathological deviation from statism. This to me is the more frightening alternative. If it is correct, we cannot dismiss torture as a deviation that occurs from time to time. Instead, we have to try to understand and analyze it as one of the things that states do because they are states.[64]

B. Nationality[65]

Nationality, in the sense of membership in a State, the "belonging" of an individual to a State, presupposes the co-existence of States. Nationality is, therefore, a concept not only of municipal law but also of international law. As a concept of municipal law it is defined by municipal law; as a concept of international law it is defined by interna-

---

60 H.L.A. HART, LAW, LIBERTY, AND MORALITY (1962).

61 For general discussion of this point, *see* D'Amato, *The Moral Dilemma of Positivism*, 20 VALPARAISO L. REV. 43 (1985).

62 Hans Kelsen, a German legal theorist who came to the United States as a refugee from the Nazis, is perhaps the leading theorist of law in Latin America, judging from the widespread use of his texts in Latin American law schools and the countless references in Latin American legal literature to his authoritative writings. Kelsen's unbridled positivism was early welcomed as a counterfoil to the entrenched natural law views of the legal estabiishment in these countries. Over the years, however, a curious blending of his views and the natural law school seems to have penetrated the Latin American legal psyche.

63 *See* H. KELSEN, THE PURE THEORY OF LAW (Max Knight trans. 1967). Kelsen viewed pure law as the commands issued to officials. This law is discoverable by the public either by getting hold of a copy of those commands or by inferring them from the actions of officials. For example, there is no law against murder in Kelsen's jurisprudence; rather, there is a command to state officials that asserts: "If a citizen unjustifiably kills another person, then you shall arrest the citizen, try him, and if he is found guilty, imprison him." If a Nazi secret law directs the Gestapo to arrest a citizen if the citizen does X, then in Kelsen's jurisprudence that is a valid law—it is simply up to the citizenry, at their peril, to infer what X is. If Kelsen were alive today and we confronted him with the outrageousness of his theory, I imagine he would reply: "But every law is like that. Every law is more or less secret. Do you know what's in the Internal Revenue Code? Even if you manage to look it up and read it, can you possibly understand it?"

64 [Editor's Note: For further dialogue on the nature of the state, *see* Chapter 17, "The Future of International Law," in this Anthology.]

65 By PAUL WEIS, excerpted from: NATIONALITY AND STATELESSNESS IN INTERNATIONAL LAW 239–45 (The Netherlands: Sijthoff & Noordhoff, 2nd rev. ed. 1979). Reprinted by permission.

tional law. From the aspect of municipal law there is, therefore, no one concept of nationality but as many concepts as there are municipal laws; in fact, however, the concepts of nationality under municipal law have a great many common features and they show a large measure of conformity. Whether conceived as a status or as a relationship between State and individual, nationality has specific functions; in municipal law it confers upon the individual specific rights and imposes upon him specific obligations in relation to his State of nationality.

The function of nationality in international law is usually described as that of providing a link between the individual and the benefits of the Law of Nations. However, in international law, as at present constituted, nationality as a concept can only be defined by reference to the rights and duties of States. Nationality, according to international law, is a specific relationship between an individual and a particular State: it entitles that State to grant permanent and unconditional protection to the national and his property. There are exceptions in which diplomatic protection may not be exercised but they confirm the rule. And it imposes, on the other hand, on the State of nationality the duty, in relation to other States, to admit the individual to its territory.

Nationality has, therefore, according to international law, definite functions. Kelsen, who denies the existence of the principle of personal jurisdiction in international law, considers that the need for the notion of nationality in international law is conditional, not absolute. According to Kelsen, a State is not obliged to have nationals, as all persons in its territory are subject to its territorial jurisdiction. He sees, therefore, no difference of principle between the subjection of nationals abroad and that of aliens abroad to the jurisdiction of the State of sojourn. That State does not, he argues, violate international law if it takes enforcement action against an alien in its territory on the ground of an illegal act committed by the alien abroad. Whether against nationals or against aliens, enforcement action on account of acts committed abroad can only be taken if the person concerned is in the territory of the State. This reasoning leads to an essentially negative concept of nationality, i.e., that nationals are those persons in relation to whom the State does not have the obligations which international law imposes on States as regards aliens and the property of aliens in their territory. In the view of the present writer, however, the functions of nationality in international law are positive functions.

Persons in regard to whom a State has the aforementioned rights and obligations in relation to other States are nationals according to international law, whether they are nationals according to municipal law or not. Persons, or classes of persons, on the other hand, in respect of whom a State does not claim, as a matter of law or policy, the right of diplomatic protection, or to whom it denies, as a matter of law or policy, vis-a-vis other States, a duty of admission to its territory, are not nationals, even if they are defined as nationals by its municipal law.

The problem of an international law of nationality must be distinguished from the question of the determination of the nationality status of individuals. Whether a person has or has not the nationality of a particular State is a question to be determined exclusively in accordance with the law of that State. If such law is inconsistent with customary international law or with treaty obligations, it is an infringement of international law. Such a municipal law need not be recognized by other States: it may be denied extraterritorial effect, and it will be disregarded by tribunals applying international law. If, however, the State concerned does not remedy the situation which is inconsistent with international law, an individual will have the nationality which is ascribed to him by the municipal law, inadmissible from the point of view of international law though that law may be. To ascribe to such an individual a nationality other than that which he possesses under municipal law would be to resort to a legal fiction.

International law confers, in general, rights and obligations on States. International law does not, therefore, directly confer nationality on or withdraw it from individuals. It follows, however, from the rights and duties of States that they are bound by international law to behave in a certain manner when regulating questions of nationality. From the general rules of international law governing the relations between States, a few rules can be derived which limit the freedom of States to confer or withdraw their nationality. While questions of nationality are normally determined by municipal law, this legislative competence of States does not amount to omnipotence. The rules of customary international law relating to nationality are mainly indirect rules, derived from the rules governing the relations between States, particularly from those relating to State jurisdiction; one can, therefore, speak only of a so-called international law of nationality. These rules are mainly negative rules, restricting the freedom of States to confer or withdraw nationality.

There are no rules of customary international law which impose a duty on States to confer their nationality on certain individuals at birth. In so far as rules of international law relating to acquisition of nationality exist, they concern acquisition subsequent to birth, that is, by naturalization in the wider sense. There is no rule of international law which restricts the right of States to grant naturalization in the narrower sense, that is, the conferment of nationality by a formal act to persons residing in its territory, on application, or which stipulates a prior period of residence. The naturalization of persons residing abroad requires, however, recognition by the State of residence in order to have legal effect there. The conditions for naturalization are determined by municipal law. International law, while requiring the existence of personal ties, a social fact of attachment, between naturalizing State and the individual, does not lay down any rules defining the nature of these ties; this is a matter for municipal law.

It is, however, an accepted rule of international law that naturalization of foreign nationals must be based on a voluntary act of the individual. Conferment of nationality by operation of law, without any specific voluntary act on the part of the individual, has therefore to be considered only as an offer of naturalization requiring acceptance; such acceptance may be explicit or implicit. Whether any particular act of the individual is considered as tacit acceptance depends on whether it is recognized as such by the practice of States: it depends on the development of international law. The reason for the rule that naturalization may not be conferred on foreigners against the will of the individual is that such naturalization results in an infringement of the right of protection of the previous State of nationality. It follows, therefore, that the compulsory naturalization of stateless persons is not inconsistent with international law.

The right of States to withdraw their nationality from individuals is, on the whole, not limited by international law. Deprivation of nationality, even mass denationalization, is not prohibited by international law, with the possible exception of the prohibition of discriminatory denationalization. There is no rule of international law in its present state of development which requires a state to admit former nationals to its territory, although a State may be bound to admit a denationalized person in those exceptional cases where deprivation of nationality has been resorted to in order to deprive the State of residence of the possibility of expulsion—as it would, in this case, infringe the right to expel aliens inherent in territorial jurisdiction.

Whether acquisition of another nationality by a national entails the loss of his existing nationality depends on the municipal law of the State concerned. Nationality is no longer considered as inalienable. According to the laws of many countries, release from nationality upon acquisition of another nationality requires special authorization (expatriation permits); but it may be concluded from consistent treaty practice and from the administrative practice of most States that such authorization must not be withheld without valid reasons where the acquisition of foreign nationality has taken place voluntarily, in a manner consistent with international law and in good faith. If authorization is refused in violation of this rule, the person concerned retains his nationality according to municipal law but such nationality need not be recognized by other States and will be disregarded by international tribunals: in other words, it will be denied extraterritorial effect.

The relative freedom of States in the field of nationality law leads to what are usually called conflicts of nationality laws: statelessness and plural nationality. Statelessness is not prohibited by international law and its reduction or elimination can, therefore, only be effected by treaty. Similarly, international law cannot prevent plural nationality, but any nationality held by an individual under municipal law which is inconsistent with international law will be disregarded in international law. In this sense one may speak of rules of international law for the solution of conflicts of nationality laws. Thus, for example, the nationality retained by a naturalized person owing to refusal of an expatriation permit without valid reason, or the nationality of the predecessor State retained by an individual who has become a national of the successor State under its law, consistent with international law, in consequence of transfer of territory based on a valid title, are irrelevant in international law; they do not have to be recognized by other States or by international tribunals.

Apart from the few rules of international law for the solution of conflicts of nationality laws, international law contains only rules for the solution of difficulties arising from plural nationality, for example:

(1) Each of the States whose nationality a person possesses may regard him as a national.

(2) The principle of equality, i.e., that protection may not be afforded by the State of nationality against a State whose nationality the person also possesses, has been embodied in the Hague Convention of 1930 and was considered as well established some time ago. It still reflects the normal practice of States but lately international tribunals have applied the principle of effective or active nationality, the so-called "link concept", i.e., they considered the nationality of the State with which the claimant is more closely connected as determining for the admissibility of the claim.

(3) Different tests are applied as to the nationality which is to be ascribed to plural nationals in a third State, or by an international tribunal in cases where the person on whose behalf the claim is made also holds a nationality other than that of the States between which the tribunal is called upon to adjudicate.

Recently, particularly since the decision of the World Court in the Nottebohm Case, the test of effective nationality has gained ground. It plays an important role when the question of nationality is relevant for the purpose of municipal law of a third State or for purposes of international law.

It is difficult to speak of rules of international law as to evidence of nationality because such rules, if any, have been developed by international tribunals acting on the basis of specific arbitral agreements and because before such tribunals the question of nationality is a question of law rather than one of fact. The principle that international tribunals are not bound by municipal rules of evidence seems, however, to be generally accepted.

It follows from the nature of the question of nationality before international tribunals that they may disregard a nationality possessed according to municipal law, even though conclusively proved, if the municipal law is inconsistent with international law or if the nationality has, in the determination of the tribunal, been acquired by fraud, misrepresentation or concealment of material facts.

While nationality is still the primary link between the individual and international law, it is no longer the only link. There is an increasing tendency to provide the rights of individuals – apart from their international protection by the State of nationality and even in relation to the State of nationality – with the safeguards of international law by the conclusion of plurilateral or multilateral treaties for the protection of human rights. There is, moreover, an increasing tendency to regulate, by the conclusion of multilateral agreements relating to the status of refugees and stateless persons, the status of persons devoid of diplomatic protection, in international law. Such tendencies may to a certain extent reduce the importance of nationality in the international sphere; it is none the less an essential legal attribute of human personality.

C. State Jurisdiction

1. Criminal Jurisdiction

a. Principles[66]

1. *Territorial*. One of the main functions of a State is to maintain order within its own territory, so it is not surprising that the territorial principle is the most frequently invoked ground for criminal jurisdiction; even in continental countries, which also rely on the nationality principle to a far greater extent than common law countries, prosecutions based on the territorial principle far outnumber prosecutions based on the nationality principle.

It often happens that a crime is committed partly in one country and partly in another; the example always given in textbooks is firing a gun across a frontier. At the turn of the century some writers argued in favor of conferring jurisdiction on the State where the crime was initiated, others argued in favor of conferring jurisdiction on the State where the crime was completed. But the arguments were so evenly matched that it was eventually realized that there was no logical reason for preferring the claims of one State over the claims of the other; and the only alternative to granting jurisdiction to neither State (which would have led to intolerable results) was to grant jurisdiction to both States. In some cases jurisdiction may be shared by more than two States, e.g., if X writes a fraudulent letter from State A to Y in State B, and Y, relying on the letter, sends money to X in State C.

Logically a State should be able to claim jurisdiction only if the offense has been committed, in part or in whole, in its territory; it must prove that a constituent element of the offense occurred in its territory. Sometimes this rule has been stretched by using the device of the continuing offense. A thief who steals goods in State A and brings them to State B is regarded as having committed theft in B as well as in A, because theft is a continuing offense. Similarly a couple who commit bigamy in A and subsequently cohabit in B can be prosecuted in B as well as in A, because bigamy is deemed to be a continuing offense as long as the parties bigamously cohabit. This is clearly a legal fiction and goes against the logic of the law; but it is relatively harmless.

Some States, however, go considerably further, and claim jurisdiction over offenses committed abroad which merely produce effects on their territory, even though those effects were not a constituent element of the crime. Moreover, a man can be convicted of a crime in the State where the effects of his act are felt, even though his act was not a crime in the State where it occurred.

Once we abandon the 'constituent elements' approach in favor of the 'effects' approach, we embark on a slippery slope which leads away from the territorial principle towards universal jurisdiction. If, for instance, a man commits arson against a factory and the company owning the factory becomes insolvent as a result, the effects may be felt all over the world – losses may be suffered by the company's suppliers, customers and creditors. Clearly the line must be drawn somewhere. But where?

It is submitted that jurisdiction can be claimed only by the State where the primary effect is felt. In order to determine whether the effects are primary or secondary, it is necessary to take two factors into account: (1) Are the effects felt in one State more direct than the effects felt in other States? (2) Are the effects felt in one State more substantial than the effects felt in other States? This test fits the decided cases, in the sense that jurisdiction has been claimed in practice only by States where the primary effects of an act have been felt. This test enables jurisdiction to be exercised by one or two States which have a legitimate interest in exercising jurisdiction, but it prevents the exercise of jurisdiction by States with no legitimate

---

66 By MICHAEL AKEHURST, excerpted from: *Jurisdiction in International Law*, 46 BRITISH YEAR BOOK OF INTERNATIONAL LAW 1, 152–60, 163–66 (1972–73). Reprinted by permission.

interest. The requirement of directness would, for instance, prevent jurisdiction's being based on the economic effects of a crime on the victim's creditors, dependents or employees. The requirement that effects must be substantial would, for instance, prevent jurisdiction's being exercised over a radio station by every State where the broadcast was heard; jurisdiction could be exercised only by the State where the majority of the listeners lived.

In borderline cases it may be relevant to take the accused's intentions and motives into account. Thus, in the case of broadcasting, it would be legitimate to examine whether the broadcast was aimed at the country claiming jurisdiction. Similarly, if a man built a high building near the frontier of one State which interfered with access by aircraft to an airport on the other side of the frontier, it would be reasonable to suggest that the State in which the airport was situated would have jurisdiction only if the builder's motive was to obstruct the aircraft. But, apart from such borderline cases, intentions and motives are irrelevant; many crimes, after all, do not require mens rea. Thus in the Lotus case Turkey was allowed to assume jurisdiction under the objective territorial principle over a crime of inadvertence.

It is submitted that the 'primary effects' approach provides a better means of keeping the jurisdiction of States within reasonable bounds than the 'constituent elements' approach does. Take the example of broadcasting. The constituent elements of broadcasting a defamatory or seditious statement include, in most legal systems, the reception of the statement by a third person. Under the 'constituent elements' approach, jurisdiction could be claimed by any State where the statement was heard, which would produce absurd results. (One could take other examples besides broadcasting, e.g., polluting the atmosphere.) Moreover, if a State wishes to punish someone for causing certain effects, it can evade the restrictions imposed by the 'constituent elements' approach by creating a new offense, the constituent elements of which include the effects in question. Suppose A kills B in State X, leaving B's widow in State Y destitute. Y cannot try A for murder, but it could create a new offense of causing the destitution of widows by killing their husbands, and try A for that. This would be lawful under the 'constituent elements' approach, because one of the constituent elements of the new offense (the destitution of the widow) has occurred in State Y. But it would not be lawful under the 'primary effects' approach, because the destitution of B's widow is only an indirect and relatively non-substantial effect of A's act.

Finally a few words should be said about liability for omissions. If a man undertakes by contract to do something in a particular State, he can be punished for breaking his contract; if he acquires property in a particular State, he can be punished for not paying taxes on it; by marrying a wife he undertakes to support her and can therefore be punished for not supporting her by the State where she resides. But these examples have one thing in common – a voluntary undertaking (making a contract, acquiring property, marry). In the absence of such an undertaking, it is submitted that a positive duty to act can be imposed only by the State where an individual is present or carrying on business at the time when action is called for – otherwise jurisdiction over omissions, far from being based on the territorial principle, would in practice be based on the universality principle, because an omission cannot be localized and occurs everywhere simultaneously.

2. *Nationality*. A State has jurisdiction over crimes committed by its nationals abroad. Some States require proof that the act is also criminal under the lex loci, or restrict jurisdiction to serious crimes or cases where the injured party or his government requests prosecution (e.g., France, Turkey); others do not (e.g., India, South Korea, Austria, Poland, U.S.S.R.). It would seem that such restrictions are not required by international law; a State has an unlimited right to base jurisdiction on the nationality of the accused. It should be noted, however, that the nationality of each accused must be considered separately; jurisdiction over an accused national does not carry with it jurisdiction over his alien accomplices.

Common law countries claim jurisdiction on this ground over a comparatively small number of offenses, but they have not objected to the wider claims made by continental countries; on the contrary, the United States has (by providing evidence, etc.) aided Greece and Italy to prosecute their nationals for crimes committed in the United States.

Sometimes jurisdiction is based on some other personal link between the accused and the State claiming jurisdiction. For instance, Denmark, Iceland, Liberia, Norway, and Sweden claim jurisdiction over crimes committed abroad by their permanent residents. In a few cases the United Kingdom has also based jurisdiction on residence. States often claim extraterritorial jurisdiction over members of their armed forces and (in connection with crimes committed in the course of their duties) over their civilian officials. The United States and the United Kingdom also claim jurisdiction over crimes committed on foreign territory by members of the crews of their merchant vessels.

3. *Protective*. During the nineteenth century continental countries began to claim jurisdiction over acts committed by aliens abroad which threatened the State. The principle is well established, but the range of acts covered by the principle is not free from controversy. The Harvard Research Draft Convention speaks of crimes against the security, territorial integrity or political independence of the State, and the counterfeiting of the seals, currency, instruments of credit, stamps, passports or public documents issued by the State. The exercise of jurisdiction over these

offenses is unobjectionable, but some States make wider claims to jurisdiction. Article 13 of the Ethiopian Penal Law of 1957 speaks, inter alia, of offenses against the servants or essential interests of the State. The Hungarian Penal Code spoke of offenses against "a fundamental interest relating to the democratic, political and economic order of the Hungarian People's Republic." Laws drafted as widely as this are obviously open to abuse.

The decided cases also reveal examples of abuse. A Jewish alien who had sexual intercourse with a German girl in Czechoslovakia was convicted by a German court under the protective principle, because his act threatened the racial purity of the German nation. Now that such racial ideologies are discredited, this case is unlikely to constitute a precedent for the future. But the cold war has produced other abuses of the protective principle; an American was convicted in Czechoslovakia for doing research work for Radio Free Europe in West Germany, and foreign companies which buy United States goods and undertake not to re-export them to Communist countries can be prosecuted in the United States if they break that undertaking. French and Belgian courts convicted aliens who aided Germany abroad during both world wars; such decisions are defensible in cases where the accused persons were nationals of allied powers, but not in cases where nationals of neutral countries were convicted for acts done in their own countries.

In addition, the protective principle needs to be limited in the same way as the 'effects' doctrine – a State can claim jurisdiction only if the primary effect of the accused's action was to threaten that State. If this were not so, a State would be able to punish the editors of all the newspapers in the world for criticizing its government.

4. *Universality*. For centuries there has been universal jurisdiction to try pirates. War crimes are often mentioned as another example of universal jurisdiction, but until recently universal jurisdiction to try war crimes was a matter of controversy. Courts trying war crimes often used to think that war crimes were subject to the same jurisdictional rules as ordinary crimes; even after the Second World War the Netherlands' courts held that international law authorized a State to try war crimes only if they were committed in its territory, against its nationals or against its national interests. However, in other war crimes trials which resulted from the Second World War, the courts of one allied national frequently tried war crimes committed on foreign territory by foreign nationals against the nationals of other allied nations, or even against the nationals of enemy States themselves. Several commentators explained this by saying that States have a universal jurisdiction to try war crimes, and Israeli courts relied heavily on the universality principle in the Eichmann case.

5. *Passive Personality*. A number of States claim jurisdiction over crimes committed by foreigners in foreign countries if the victim of the crime was one of their own nationals. This "passive personality principle" has always been regarded as totally unacceptable in English-speaking countries. Some writers from English-speaking countries erroneously imagine that the criminal law of all countries was originally based on the territorial principle, and that other bases of jurisdiction are recent (and usually questionable) innovations.

The English-speaking countries are not alone in regarding such jurisdiction as contrary to international law. France is of the same opinion, which was shared by individual judges in the Lotus case and by the arbitrator in the Costa Rica Packet case. It is also significant that many countries believe that international law prohibits a State from trying crimes committed by foreigners on foreign ships within its ports, unless the crime disturbs the peace of the port, which suggests a fortiori that a State cannot try crimes committed by foreigners on foreign territory (unless perhaps the effects of the crime are felt in the State claiming jurisdiction).

In a situation like this, where different States have different ideas about the content of the relevant rules of international law, there are two possible solutions. One is to fall back on the Soviet idea of custom as an implied agreement and to say that there are different rules of customary law in force between different groups of States. The other solution is to try to find some common ground between the two groups of States; and this common ground may be easier to find if we examine the reasons why some States oppose the universality and passive personality principles and why others support them.

One suspects that the unstated reason for the attitude adopted by the United States, United Kingdom and French Governments is that they fear that in some other countries courts are biased and punishments inhuman. However, there are others rules of international law which guarantee a minimum international standard for the treatment of aliens, so one cannot invoke the possibility of jurisdiction's being abused as a reason for denying jurisdiction altogether. A stronger argument is contained in Brierly's famous statement: "The suggestion that every individual is or may be subject to the laws of every State at all times and in all places is intolerable." But surely it is intolerable only if the laws vary from place to place; if they are the same in all countries the individuals suffers little hardship.

Supporters of the universality and passive personality principles argue that States should work together for the punishment of crime and that the presence within a State of an unpunished criminal is socially dangerous. But these arguments (particularly the first) presuppose that the act in question is a crime in all countries (or at least in the State where it was committed as well in the State claiming jurisdiction).

One solution would be for the State claiming jurisdiction to try the accused under the law of the State where the crime was committed. No State has applied this solution in modern times, but a number of States, while applying their own law, do require proof that the act in question was a crime under the law of the State where the act was performed. It is necessary to add a number of corollaries, to make sure that the accused is in the same position as he would have been if he had been tried in the State where the crime was committed. Thus periods of limitation laid down by the lex loci should be respected, and the penalty imposed should not be greater than the penalty imposed by the lex loci. The accused should also be able to plead, as a bar to prosecution, the fact that he has already been tried in the State where the crime was committed.

b. Desirable Limits[67]

The following propositions are not eternal verities but rather a kind of checklist against which further assertions by the United States[68] of jurisdiction to prescribe and enforce criminal law should be tested, whether the assertions are made unilaterally or pursuant to treaty:

(1) The basic principle that crime is territorial remains sound. Departures from that principle are not precluded, but should be justified one by one and not built on a series of increasingly questionable precedents.

(2) Jurisdiction based on the nationality of the accused is sound under international law, but is questionable under the Constitution without some additional link to the United States.

(3) Jurisdiction based on the commission of a crime aboard a ship or aircraft registered in the United States is generally acceptable constitutionally, at least as to specific crimes of violence.

(4) Jurisdiction on the basis of the nationality of the victim may be justified constitutionally if it is exercised in implementation of an international convention widely adhered to, but probably not otherwise.

(5) Jurisdiction on the basis of the presence of the accused is justified constitutionally where that presence is directly related to the offense, as in the first landing of an aircraft diverted (or sought to be diverted) in flight. Where the accused's presence is not directly related to the offense charged, or where the presence of the accused is itself questionable,[69] jurisdiction on that basis seems to self-generated to pass constitutional muster, even if it is in accord with an international convention.

The proposition that compliance with international law is a necessary, but not sufficient, condition for the administration of criminal law in a troubled world is not easy to apply. The interrelation among statute, Constitution and treaty is, to put it charitably, confusing. But the ultimate values of limited government transcend any given triumph of law enforcement.

2. Civil Jurisdiction[70]

A State which denies foreigners access to its courts may be guilty of denial of justice. Conversely a State's jurisdiction is limited by rules about sovereign, diplomatic and other immunities. But, apart from that, are there any rules of public international law which limit the jurisdiction of a State's courts in civil trials?

1. *The Defendant is Temporarily Present.* At common law the court of a State acquired jurisdiction in personam if (and only if) a writ was served on the defendant while he was in the State concerned. Although other bases of jurisdiction have been added by statute, this remains the main basis of jurisdiction in common law countries. What is remarkable is that the court's jurisdiction is not affected by the brevity of the defendant's stay in the country concerned; in theory a visit lasting a few seconds would be sufficient. It is true that an English court can halt proceedings when this is necessary to prevent injustice to the defendant; but the fact that a writ has been served on a foreigner temporarily present in England is not necessarily regarded as a source of injustice.

Service on someone who is present for only a few hours has been held to be sufficient to give jurisdiction in the United States, and the courts have made it clear that this

---

67 By ANDREAS F. LOWENFELD, excerpted from: *U.S. Law Enforcement Abroad: The Constitution and International Law*, 83 AMERICAN JOURNAL OF INTERNATIONAL LAW 880, 892–93 (1989). Reprinted by permission.

68 [Editor's Note: Although Professor Lowenfeld is writing specifically about United States law, his propositions suggest limitations that could be accepted by any nation in the interests of a workable international understanding about the limits of national criminal jurisdiction.]

69 [Editor's Note: Compare the U.S. Supreme Court's subsequent decision in the Alvarez Case, and the debate on that case, in the section on "Abduction" in Chapter 8 of this Anthology.]

70 By MICHAEL AKEHURST, excerpted from: *Jurisdiction in International Law*, 46 BRITISH YEAR BOOK OF INTERNATIONAL LAW 1, 170–75 (1972–73). Reprinted by permission.

rule applies when the party is in the State, however transiently. In one case the defendant was served with process on board an aircraft flying over Arkansas, and this was held to give jurisdiction to the District Court in Arkansas. Recently, however, United States courts have often dismissed such cases on the grounds of forum non conveniens.

In continental countries service of process is often required to give the defendant notice of proceedings, but it does not create jurisdiction; jurisdiction must exist already before a writ can be served (the most common basis of jurisdiction being the habitual residence of the defendant). The practice followed by common law countries is virtually unknown in other countries, and a judgment given by a court which based its jurisdiction solely on the temporary presence of the defendant would almost certainly be refused recognition outside the common law world. However, no State appears to have protested that such jurisdiction is contrary to international law, even though it is obvious that the practice followed in common law countries enables a State to exercise jurisdiction over cases and parties having no real connection with that State.

2. *The Defendant has Assets Within the State*. A number of countries claim jurisdiction whenever the defendant has assets within the State concerned. In some States (the Netherlands, South Africa, many states in the United States) jurisdiction is limited to the value of the assets; in other States (Austria, Belgium, Denmark, Germany, Scotland, Sweden, Japan, parts of Switzerland) it is not so limited. As a result, a tourist who left his slippers behind in a hotel bedroom might find the local court claiming jurisdiction over all sorts of unrelated claims against him, running into millions of pounds. It is obvious that this rule enables a State to exercise jurisdiction over cases and parties having no real connection with that State, but no State seems to have protested that such jurisdiction is contrary to international law.

3. *Nationality or residence of the plaintiff*. Article 14 of the French Civil Code gives French courts jurisdiction if the plaintiff has French nationality. A similar rule existed in medieval Belgium, in the Netherlands until 1940 and in Greece until 1946. At the present day such rules exist in Haiti, Luxembourg, Quebec and Roumaina. Courts in Portugal and the Netherlands claim jurisdiction on the grounds of the plaintiff's domicile.

Judgments given on the basis of such provisions are unlikely to be recognized in other countries. In 1883 an Italian court held that Article 14 of the French Civil Code was contrary to the law of nations, but Italian courts usually hold that it is merely contrary to Italian public policy, as a reason for not recognizing such French judgments. There is no record of diplomatic protests concerning such grounds of jurisdiction.

Such jurisdiction may be unusual in proceedings in personam, but in the case of matrimonial proceedings it is normal. The traditional rule, not only in England but also throughout western Europe, was that jurisdiction was vested in the court of the husband's domicile. This meant that, after the husband and wife had separated, the husband might acquire a new domicile in a country where his wife had never set foot and institute proceedings there against his wife. The tendency of modern legislation is to extend this privilege to the wife, instead of insisting that proceedings must be brought in the court of the defendant's domicile. At the present day the plaintiff's domicile or residence is a basis of jurisdiction in the majority of countries. Jurisdiction is claimed on the basis of the plaintiff's nationality in a number of Eastern European countries, including Greece and Yugoslavia; nationality of either spouse is a ground for recognition under English law.

4. *Title to foreign land*. It has sometimes been suggested that it would be contrary to international law for a municipal court to decide title to foreign land. But courts in Austria, Germany and Italy have done precisely this, without provoking diplomatic protests. English courts refrain from exercising such jurisdiction, probably because they realize the futility of giving judgment which cannot be enforced against the wishes of the local State, but they circumvent this rule by means of the equitable jurisdiction in personam. (French courts have also sometimes dealt indirectly with title to foreign land by exercising jurisdiction in personam.)

The idea that international law prohibits a municipal court from deciding title to foreign land probably arises from confusing ownership of land with sovereignty over territory. The fallacy in this reasoning is too obvious to require demonstration.

5. *Jurisdiction based on subject-matter*. One might imagine that it would be perfectly reasonable for a State to exercise jurisdiction over a case if the subject-matter of the case had a close connection with that State; if a State's courts can try crimes committed on the State's territory, why should they not try torts and breaches of contract committed on the State's territory? But Joseph Story argued, early in the nineteenth century, that jurisdiction in personam must be based on the physical presence of the defendant within the State's territory when proceedings are started. A number of English and American judgments have held that the subject-matter of a case was, by itself, insufficient to confer jurisdiction in personam, and in the Daylight case the United States Government argued that public international law prevented Mexico's hearing a case involving an absent United States citizen whose ship had collided with a Mexican Government ship off the coast of Mexico.[71]

---

[71] Foreign Relations of the U.S. (1884), p. 359. The United States was trying to present a claim on the international plane on

Story's attitude clearly does not represent modern international law, because at the present day a very large number of States claim jurisdiction founded on the subject-matter of cases (e.g., torts committed on the territory of the State concerned, contracts governed by its law, etc.). Moreover, there are obvious advantages in attributing jurisdiction to the State where the facts occurred, and whose law has the closest connection with those facts.

3. Conflicts of jurisdiction[72]

Since several States can exercise concurrent jurisdiction in many cases, it can happen that an individual is forbidden by one law to do an act which is permitted or even required by another law. In extreme cases the actual content of the law of one of the States concerned may be contrary to international law, or it may be possible to show that the law in question represents an abuse of legislative power and thus a breach of international law. United States courts have traditionally refrained from ordering defendants to perform acts which would violate foreign law, but there is no evidence that they regard such restraint as being required by international law.

Some writers have suggested that it is contrary to international law to forbid an individual to behave in a way which is required by the law of the place where the act is performed; a few writers extend this principle to acts which are merely permitted by the lex loci. The result of this suggestion is that the territorial principle would always override the nationality principle and other principles of extraterritorial jurisdiction in the event of conflict. Yet one of the reasons why States claim jurisdiction under the protective principle is precisely because acts which threaten a foreign State are often not illegal in the State where they are performed. The United States required United States companies operating in foreign countries to obey United States laws which prohibit certain kinds of trade with communist countries, even when the law of the country in which the company is operating permits such trade.

behalf of the shipowner, and Mexico was arguing that he ought to exhaust local remedies in Mexico first. If the Mexican contention had prevailed, the United States shipowner would have appeared in the Mexican court as plaintiff, and not (as the United States argument appears to suggest) as defendant – which only confirms the total illogicality of the attitude adopted by the United States Government.

In 1853 Attorney-General Cushing advised that Texas committed 'a usurpation of general sovereignty' by trying a case against a United States army officer who was not domiciled in Texas, had never been personally served, had never appeared before the court and had no property in the State (6 Opinions of the Attorneys-General, p. 75). The case concerned a tort which had been committed, at least in part, in Texas.

It was said in the Idler case (U.S. v. Venezuela (1885), Moore, History and Digest of the International Arbitrations, pp. 3491, 3511–12), that a judgment will be void unless the defendant in a action in personam is domiciled or served with process in the State claiming jurisdiction. But the question at issue was whether Idler's dispute with Venezuela (concerning goods shipped by Idler to Venezuela) was res judicata, not whether Venezuela had broken public international law by instituting proceedings against Idler in its own courts.

[72] By MICHAEL AKEHURST, excerpted from: *Jurisdiction in International Law*, 46 BRITISH YEAR BOOK OF INTERNATIONAL LAW 1, 167–69 (1972–73). Reprinted by permission.

D. State Succession

1. Introduction[73]

State "succession" is a somewhat imprecise term that deals with the transmission or extinction of rights and obligations of a state that no longer exists or has lost part of its territory. State succession is one of the oldest subjects of international law. Even Aristotle speculated in his *Politics* on the problem of continuity when "the state is no longer the same." Grotius and the other founding fathers of international law proposed distinctions on grounds of reason and justice. State practice, as usual in international law, was largely determined by perceived political interests influenced in some degree by conceptions, analogies and metaphors derived from juristic commentary. Underlying the legal discourse we can discern the human dramas: the break-up of age-old empires and the emergence of new identities, new voices, new frontiers separating peoples or uniting them, deeply affecting their personal lives. These events are not only the stuff of history; they foreshadow the future. We can be quite sure, as we look around today, that some states will split, others will be absorbed, frontiers will be moved, and new generations will question old alliances and commitments.

The prevailing legal view in the nineteenth and much of the twentieth century accepted two basic principles relating to succession. One was the critical difference between succession of states and changes in government. The principle of succession was relevant only where one state was replaced by another in the responsibility for the international relations of a territory. The legal problem of succession did not arise when governments – that is, internal political regimes – changed, no matter how profound or revolu-

[73] By OSCAR SCHACHTER, excerpted from: *State Succession: The Once and Future Law*, 33 VIRGINIA JOURNAL OF INTERNATIONAL LAW 253, 253–55 (1993). Reprinted by permission.

tionary a change. This principle, traced by scholars to Grotius, has been generally accepted by scholars, courts, and foreign ministries. It was challenged by the Soviet regime in its early effort to repudiate obligations of the Czarist government, an effort that did not succeed in changing doctrine or practice.

In its origin, the international law of succession drew a basic distinction between obligations that were "personal" (as were the sovereigns) and obligations that were "dispositive" because they were linked to the "land" (or "real"). Only the latter survived the extinction of the personality. This personal-dispositive dichotomy seemed to provide a simple solution. Political treaties, treaties of alliances, and at least some debts not linked to territorial benefits (called "odious debts") did not survive. (When the United States took over Cuba in 1898 and when the British annexed South Africa, neither successor paid the debts of the predecessor states.)

2. Basic Concepts[74]

1. *International legal personality.* The term "international legal personality" has been defined as "the capacity to be bearer of rights and duties under international law."[75] The term "capacity" in this context is perhaps unfortunate: any person or aggregate of persons presumably has capacity to be given rights and duties by States. The question is not "capacity" but the extent to which the entity in question actually has such rights and duties. To say that a particular entity is an international legal person is to say only that the entity is in fact accorded particular rights, or subjected to particular duties, under international law.

2. *Sovereignty.* The term "sovereignty"' has a long and troubled history, and a variety of meanings. In its most common modern usage, sovereignty is the term for the totality of international rights and duties recognized by international law as residing in an independent territorial unit – the State. It is not itself a right nor is it a criterion for statehood. It is a somewhat unhelpful, but firmly established, description of statehood; a brief term for the State's attribute of more-or-less plenary competence. No further legal consequences attach to sovereignty than attach to statehood itself.

3. *State and Government.* The distinction between State and Government has received little attention, although it is a problem of considerable intrinsic difficulty. One of the prerequisites for statehood is the existence of an effective government; and the main, indeed, for most purposes the only, organ by which the State acts in international relations is its (central) government. There would thus seem to be a close relation between the two concepts. According to O'Connell: "Until the middle of the nineteenth century, both types of change [change of State and change of government] were assimilated; and the problems they raised were uniformly solved. With the abstraction of the concept of sovereignty, however, a conceptual chasm was opened between change of sovereignty and change of government."[76] This post-Hegelian development O'Connell criticizes as "dogmatic" and "arbitrary."[77] In the context of succession to obligations – that is, in the context of the legal effects of changes in State or government – it is more useful and more cogent in his view to pay regard not to any such distinction but to the real changes or continuities in political, social and administrative structure. He thus advocates, in effect, a return to the eighteenth-century position of practical assimilation of changes of State and government.

It can readily be admitted that some changes of government have greater and more traumatic effects than many changes of State personality. None the less it seems a fair assumption that changes in State personality are more likely to be of greater social and structural importance than changes in government. In any case international law does distinguish between change of State personality and change of government. Thus, prima facie, the State continues to exist, with concomitant rights and obligations, despite revolutionary changes in government, or despite a period in which there is no, or no effective, government. Belligerent occupation, it is established, does not affect the continuity of the State, even where there exists no government claiming to represent the occupied State. The legal position of governments-in-exile is thus dependent on the distinction between government and State. The concept of representation of States in international organizations also depends upon the distinction.

Moreover, in the context of State succession, it is important to note that, in arguing for a closer identification of State and Government, O'Connell is seeking to maximize the extent to which treaty obligations and the like are legally transmitted from one State to its successor. However, the law of State succession has developed otherwise: it is now generally accepted that successor States, in particular newly independent States, have substantial

---

[74] By JAMES CRAWFORD, excerpted from: *The Creation of States in International Law* 25–30, 36–37, 40–44, 47–49, 71–74, 400–402, 404–08, 417–18 (Oxford: Clarendon Press, 1979). Copyright James Crawford 1979. Reprinted by permission.

[75] GEORG SCHWARZENBERGER, A MANUAL OF INTERNATIONAL LAW 53 (6th ed. 1976).

[76] 1 D.P. O'CONNELL, STATE SUCCESSION IN MUNICIPAL LAW AND INTERNATIONAL LAW 5–6 (1967).

[77] *Id.* at 7.

freedom as to the succession of treaty rights and obligations. To obliterate the distinction between "change of State" and "change of government" would now only decrease the stability of legal relations between governments, and would thus have precisely the opposite effect from that for which O'Connell was arguing.

4. *State Personality and State Succession*. There is then a clear distinction in principle between the legal personality of the State, and the government for the time being of the State. This serves to distinguish in turn the field of State personality (which includes the topics of identity and continuity of States) and that of State succession. State succession depends upon the conclusion reached as to State personality. However, in some areas, the principles and policy considerations involved are the same. In particular the problem of State succession in the case of devolving territories (for example, the British Dominions) is in part a matter of succession and in part a matter of personality. None the less the two areas remain formally distinct.

3. Classical Criteria for Statehood[78]

1. *Defined Territory*. It is evident that States are territorial entities. "Territorial sovereignty. . . involves the exclusive right to display the activities of a State."[79] Conversely, the right to be a State is dependent at least in the first instance upon the exercise of full governmental powers with respect to some area of territory. But, although a State must possess some territory, there appears to be no rule prescribing the minimum area of that territory. States may thus occupy an extremely small area, provided they are independent in the sense to be explained. Monaco and Nauru, for example, are respectively only 1.5 and 21 square kilometers in area.

2. *Permanent Population*. If States are territorial entities, they are also aggregates of individuals. A permanent population is thus necessary for statehood, though, as in the case of territory, no minimum limit is apparently prescribed. For example in 1973 the estimated population of Nauru was 6,500; that of San Marino was 20,000. Of putative States with very small populations, only the Vatican City may be challengeable on this ground, and this as much because of the professional and non-permanent nature of its population as its size.

The rule under discussion requires States to have a permanent population: it is not a rule relating to the nationality of that population. It appears that the grant of nationality is a matter which only States by their municipal law (or by way of treaty) can perform. Nationality is thus dependent upon statehood, not the reverse. Whether the creation of a new State on the territory of another results in statelessness of the nationals of the previous State there resident, or an automatic change in nationality, or in retention of the previous nationality until provision is otherwise made by treaty or the law of the new State, is a matter of some doubt. The problem is made more difficult because of the confusion prevalent between "international nationality" (i.e., nationality under the "effective link" doctrine) and municipal nationality. Persons could very well be regarded as nationals of a particular State for international purposes before the State concerned had established rules for granting or determining its (municipal) nationality. On the other hand, apart from treaty a new State is not obliged to extend its nationality to all persons resident on its territory. Perhaps the international customary law on the subject is best formulated as follows: in the absence of provision to the contrary, persons habitually resident in the territory of the new State automatically acquire the nationality of that State, for all international purposes, and lose their former nationality, but this is subject to a right in the new State to delimit more particularly which persons it will regard as its nationals.

3. *Government*. The requirement that a putative State have an effective government might be regarded as central to its claim to statehood. "Government" is obviously related to "independence." It is also related to "territory" inasmuch as international law defines territory not by adopting private law analogies of real property, but by reference to the extent of governmental power exercised, or capable of being exercised, with respect to some area and population. Territorial sovereignty is not ownership of, but governing power with respect to, territory. There is thus a strong case for regarding government as the most important single criterion of statehood, since all the others depend upon it. The difficulty is, however, that the legal criteria for statehood are of necessity nominal and exclusionary: that is to say, their concern is not with the central, clear cases but with the borderline ones. Hence the application of the criterion of government in practice is much less simple than this analysis might suggest.

A striking modern illustration is that of the former Belgian Congo, granted a hurried independence in 1960 as the Republic of the Congo (now Zaire). No effective preparations had been made; the new government was bankrupt, divided, and in practice hardly able to control even the capital. Belgian and other troops intervened, shortly after independence, under claim of humanitarian intervention; and extensive United Nations financial and military assistance became necessary almost immediately. Among the tasks of the United National force was, or came to be, the

[78] By JAMES CRAWFORD, *supra n.* 74.

[79] Island of Palmas Case (1928), I RIAA 829, 839 (Judge Huber).

suppression of secession in Katanaga, the richest Congolese province. Anything less like effective government would be hard to imagine.

Yet despite this there can be little doubt that the Congo was in 1960 a State in the full sense of the term. It was widely recognized. Its application for United Nations membership was approved without dissent. United Nations action subsequent to admission was of course based on the "sovereign rights of the Republic of the Congo." On no other basis could the attempted secession of the Katanga province have been condemned as illegal.

When then is to be made the criterion of "effective government"? Three views can be taken of the Congo situation in that regard. It may be that international recognition of the Congo was simply premature or wrongful, because, not possessing an effective government, the Congo was not a State. It may be that the recognition of the Congo was a case where an entity not properly qualified as a State is treated as such by other States, for whatever reason; that is, a case of constitutive recognition. Alternatively, it may be that the requirement of "government" is less stringent than has been thought, at least in particular contexts. The last view is to be preferred.[80]

4. *Independence*. Independence is the central criterion of statehood. As Judge Huber stated in the Island of Palmas Case:

> Sovereignty in the relations between States signifies independence. Independence in regard to a portion of the globe is the right to exercise therein, to the exclusion of any other State, the functions of a State. The development of the national organization of States during the last few centuries, and, as a corollary, the development of international law, have established this principle of the exclusive competence of the State in regard to its own territory in such a way as to make it the point of departure in settling most questions that concern international relations.[81]

It must first be said that different legal consequences may be attached to lack of independence in specific cases. Lack of independence can be so complete that the entity concerned is not a State but an internationally indistinguishable part of another dominant State. A grant of "independence" may, in certain circumstances, be a legal nullity, or even an act engaging the responsibility of the grantor, as with so-called "puppet States." Or an entity may be independent in some basic sense but act in a specific matter under the control of another State so that the relation becomes one of agency, and the responsibility of the latter State is attracted for illegal acts of the former.

5. *Sovereignty*. The term "sovereignty" is sometimes used in place of "independence" as a basic criterion for statehood. However it has, as has been seen, another more satisfactory meaning as an incident or consequence of statehood, namely, the plenary competence that States prima facie possess. Since the two meanings are distinct, it seems preferable to restrict "independence" to the prerequisite for statehood, and "sovereignty" to the legal incident.

6. *Permanence*. Despite some claims that a temporary or terminable entity is not a state, in fact States may have a very brief existence, provided only that they have an effective independent government with respect to a certain area and population. Thus the Mali Federation lasted only from 20 June to 20 August 1960, when it united with the former Italian Trust Territory of Somaliland to form the Somali Republic.

This is not to say that permanence is not relevant to issues of statehood in some cases. In particular where another State's rights are involved (for example in a secessionary situation), or where certain criteria for statehood are said to be missing, continuance of an entity over a period of time is of considerable evidential value. In the divided State situations, whatever the original legality of the establishment of certain of those regimes, long continuance has forced effective recognition of their position. Permanence is thus not strictly a criterion of statehood in the sense of an indispensable attribute: it is a sometimes important piece of evidence as to the possession of those attributes.

7. *Willingness and Ability to Observe International Law*. It is sometimes said that "willingness to observe international law" is a criterion for statehood.[82] But it is particularly necessary to distinguish recognition from statehood in this context. Unwillingness or refusal to observe international law may well constitute grounds for refusal of recognition, or for such other sanctions as the law allows, just as unwillingness to observe Charter obligations is a ground for non-admission to the United Nations. Both are however distinct from statehood.

A different, though connected, point is whether inability to observe international law may be grounds for refusal to treat the entity concerned as a State. H.A. Smith puts the point thus: "a State which has fallen into anarchy ceases to be a State to which the normal rules of international intercourse can be applied."[83] But again one must distinguish between permitted sanctions for breach of interna-

---

[80] [Editor's Note: Professor Crawford's analysis in 1979 is strikingly confirmed by the current example of Somalia, a state that exists and whose borders are not threatened, but which at the present time (1993) has no government whatsoever.]

[81] 2 RIAA 829, 838 (1928).

[82] 1 J.B. Moore, A Digest of International Law 6 (1906).

[83] 1 H.A. Smith, Great Britain and the Law of Nations 18–19 (1932).

tional obligations (which used to extend to armed reprisals and war), and a lack of responsibility for public order or government such that the territory concerned ceases to be part of the defaulting State or (if the whole State territory is concerned) such that it ceases to be a State. The former circumstance is clearly distinguishable from the latter and much more common. The latter case concerns not ability to obey international law but a failure to maintain any State authority at all. As such it is referable to the criterion of government; reference to international law is unnecessary and confusing.

8. *A certain degree of civilization.* United States practice, in particular, has on occasions supported the view that, to be a "State of International Law the inhabitants of the territory must have attained a degree of civilization such as to enable them to observe with respect to the outside world those principles of law which are deemed to govern the members of the international society in their relations with each other."[84] But once again this requirement is better formulated as one of government: international law presupposes not any common faith or culture, but a certain minimum of order and stability.

9. *Recognition.* Recognition by other states is not strictly a condition for statehood in international law. The denial of recognition to an entity which otherwise qualifies as a State cannot entitle the non-recognizing States to act as if the entity in question was not a State. On the other hand, in some cases at least, States are not prohibited from recognizing or treating as a State an entity which for some reason does not qualify as a State under the general criteria discussed here. Such recognition may well be constitutive of legal obligation for the recognizing or acquiescing State; but it may also tend to consolidate a general legal status at that time precarious or in statu nascendi. Recognition, while in principle declaratory, may thus be of great importance in particular cases. In any event, at least where the recognizing government is addressing itself to legal rather than purely political considerations, it is important evidence of legal status.

4. State Continuity[85]

There is a fundamental distinction between cases where the 'same' State can be said to continue to exist, despite changes of government, territory, or population, and cases where one State can be said to have replaced another with respect to certain territory. The law of State succession depends on this distinction, and it must therefore, presumably, be possible to distinguish cases of continuity from cases of succession. None the less in many situations in practice the distinction is arbitrary, and it may depend in particular cases not on the substance of a particular transaction but on the way in which that transaction was carried out. The notion of "continuity" has thus been criticized as misleading and over-general. Yet in practice, claims to "continuity" are made and recognized.

Certainly, it is one thing to determine that entity A is a State at a particular time, and another to determine that entity A1, at some other time, is the "same" State, for relevant purposes. However, allowing greater latitude to recognition and the views of the actors concerned, one would have thought that reasonable solutions to problems of identity could have been found by reference to the basic criteria of statehood as affecting the entities at the relevant times. A different approach has been adopted in Marek's leading study:[86] there, identity is defined by reference to the legal obligations of the State in question, rather than by application of the criteria for statehood. Thus Marek defines "the identity of a State" as the identity of its international rights and obligations, before and after the event which called that identity in question, and solely on the basis of the customary norm pacta sunt servanda. Where a State is identical in the sense defined, it is by definition continuous as between the two occasions referred to. State continuity is merely "the dynamic predicate of State identity." It is therefore impossible, in Marek's view, that a State should finally disappear, and then reappear as the "same" State: the extinction of a State puts an end to any possible identity of continuity.

To the view that State identity means identity of legal rights and obligations, several objections may be proposed. In the first place, the existence of a State might seem to be separate from the legal relations of that State, and certainly from its conventional legal relations. This is not to say that the State is some meta-legal "thing": qua legal person it is, in a sense, merely the sum of its rights, duties, and notably, powers and immunities. But the assertion that the customary rights, etc. of entity A are the "same" as those of entity A1, two weeks or two years later, may not be self-evident and is certainly not self-explanatory. To say that a particular entity is the "same" in this context (given that other entities may have equal rights) is merely to say that the relevant rights exist with respect to, or are attributed to, the same State—that is, the same, or substantially the same, territorial governmental entity. Particular rights, duties and powers, in terms of the creation of States, are not criteria for, but rather the consequences of statehood.

---

[84] 1 CHARLES CHENEY HYDE, INTERNATIONAL LAW CHIEFLY AS INTERPRETED AND APPLIED BY THE UNITED STATES 23 (2d ed. 1947).

[85] By JAMES CRAWFORD, *supra n.* 74.

[86] K. MAREK, IDENTITY AND CONTINUITY OF STATES IN PUBLIC INTERNATIONAL LAW 68–76 (1954).

It therefore seems sensible to make continuity, identity, and extinction depend on variants of these basic criteria; that is, primarily, territory, population, and independent government, and, as subsidiary criteria (but criteria which may be particularly important in doubtful or marginal cases), permanence and recognition.

Problems do however arise where the constitutive elements of statehood undergo substantial change. The following rules are established under customary international law.

1. *Territorial changes*. It is established that acquisition or loss of territory does not per se affect the continuity of the State. This may be so even where the territory acquired or lost is substantially greater in area than the original or remaining State territory. The presumption of continuity is particularly strong where the constitutional system of the State prior to acquisition or loss continues in force.

The presumption of continuity despite territorial change is somewhat dramatically illustrated by the case of "imperial" States. The United Kingdom remains the same State despite the loss since 1920 of a massive Empire: indeed its continuity has never been questioned. Turkey was also regarded as a continuation of the Ottoman Empire. The cases of Austria and Hungary are more doubtful.[87]

2. *Changes in population*. Changes in population are of course concomitants of territorial changes (in the absence of a transfer of population), and the same considerations apply.

3. *Changes in government*. It has long been established that, in the case of an internal revolution, merely altering the municipal constitution and form of government, the State remains the same; it neither loses any of its rights, nor is discharged from any of its obligations. Despite the question-begging nature of this and other formulations, the rule that revolution prima facie does not affect the continuity of the State in which it occurs has been consistently applied to the innumerable revolutions, coups d'etat and the like in the nineteen and twentieth centuries. After some hesitation, it was for example established that the Soviet Union was a continuation of Imperial Russia. A fortiori, continuity is not affected by alterations in a municipal constitution according to its own amendment provisions; or by a change in the name of the State; or by non-recognition of the revolutionary government of a State. Although it is sometimes argued that "socialist revolutions," which result in a changed class-structure of the State, bring about a fundamental discontinuity in relations, it is not at all clear whether this claim is directed to the notion of legal continuity of the State, or is a claim to a more liberal regime of succession. Neither the Soviet Union or the People's Republic of China have asserted such discontinuity; while problems of succession of governments in the two cases have tended to be worked out on an ad hoc basis.

4. *Changes in international status*. It is established in practice that, for example, international protectorates or protected States continue the legal personality of the pre-protectorate State. Where there are substantial changes in the entity concerned, continuity may depend upon recognition (as in the case of India after 1947). The predominant view was that Austria and Hungary after 1918 continued the legal personality of the two States of the Dual Monarchy. Where the change in status is a result of external imposition (in particular of a puppet entity), continuity is not to be presumed, since, in the absence of general recognition, such an entity lacks any international status other than as agent of the belligerent.

5. *Belligerent occupation*. It is well established that belligerent occupation does not affect the continuity of the State: as a result, governments-in-exile have frequently been recognized as governments of an enemy-occupied State. The continuity of a State under belligerent occupation remains until the peace settlement, or, probably, until the point when all effective organized resistance to the invader has ceased.

6. *Continuity and illegal annexation*. State practice in the period since 1930 has established, not without some uncertainty, the proposition that annexation of the territory of a State as a result of the illegal use of force does not effect the extinction of the State. The various States (Ethiopia, Austria, Czechoslovakia, Poland, and Albania) effectively submerged by external illegal force in the period 1935-40 were reconstituted by the Allies during, or at the termination of, hostilities. The view was on the whole taken that the legal existence of these States was preserved from extinction.

7. *Identity without continuity*. The case of Syria demonstrates the possibility that a State which has for a time been extinguished may be reestablished on the same or substantially the same territory and be regarded as for relevant purposes the same entity as before extinction. Syria's United Nations membership apparently revived upon its secession from the United Arab Republic in 1961, without the need for readmission. The South African Republic also seems to have been regarded as the same State before and after a period of extinction (1877-81). However, where state existence is terminated either by consent of the entities concerned (as with the United Arab Republic) or validly in accordance with international law at the time (as with the South African Republic), any subsequent assertion of "identity" takes on decidedly fictional overtones. This is especially so where (as with Poland from 1795 to 1918)

[87] The Treaties of Saint-Germain and Trianon assumed continuity of Austria and Hungary with the two kingdoms of the Dual Monarchy. Marek, at 199–236, denies that either Austria or Hungary before 1918 possessed separate international status, and thus denies the possibility of continuity.

the period of extinction lasts for more than a few years.

8. *Extinction*. Effective submersion or disappearance of separate State organs in those of another State, over any considerable period of time, will result in the extinction of the State, so long at least as no substantial international illegality is involved. This is particularly so where the previous State organs voluntarily relinquished separate identity; for example in the case of the union of two States. More difficult is the case of annexation of the entire territory of a State by external force – a situation which occurred with some frequency in the period 1935-40. As we have seen (above, section 6), the international community did not regard those annexations as cases of extinction. The difficulty remains: how long could it be said that the legal identity of the State was preserved, despite its lack of effective control, in face of effective but illegal annexation? Post-1945 practice has been of little assistance in determining this issue, since illegal invasion of a State for the purpose of its annexation has not occurred with any frequency.[88] The most significant case, that of the Baltic States, sheds little light on the problem. Marek seems to regard that case as one of extinction: "the final loss of independence, either by way of a legal settlement or by way of a total obliteration of the entire international delimitation of the State."[89] If, on the other hand, it is concluded that continued recognition of Latvia, Lithuania, and Estonia signifies their continued existence as States, then it may be that the rule protecting State personality against illegal annexation has achieved relatively peremptory, permanent force. The absence of more recent and explicit State practice is hardly regrettable; it would seem to preclude any more conclusive assessment of the effect of continued effective but illegal annexation upon statehood.[90]

5. The Moving Boundary Doctrine[91]

In some transactions, portions of a state are divested and attached to another one. The applicable rule in this situation is most often the "moving boundary" doctrine, the notion that the treaty commitments of the state to which the divested region is transferred apply in that region, while the commitments of the state from which it was divested cease to apply in that area. Thus, as Alsace and Lorraine went back and forth between France and Germany, the treaties of extradition, for example, changed. In general, the old treaty obligations apply as before in the territories that are not affected by the transfer, although one can visualize circumstances under which the commitments undertaken by a state would become too onerous to honor if it suffered a serious diminution in size and wealth.

6. Partition[92]

What is now unfolding in Yugoslavia and what seems to have run its course in the former Soviet Union is the case of one or more new states emerging from what was formerly a single entity. Three alternatives face one attempting to draft a set of rules for treaty succession in cases where the number of states increases. One could emphasize the values of reliability and continuity, thus deciding that all new states would be obligated to maintain the treaty commitments of the predecessor state. This option has not in fact attracted any drafter. Another option would be to enact a clean-slate rule that no newly-formed states would be bound by preexisting obligations. Brownlie argues for this rule, finding in the concept of sovereignty a rationale for permitting new states to begin without the burdens of their predecessor's obligations.[93]

The Vienna Convention on Treaty Succession (1978) chose a third option, a split rule favored by the newly-formed majority of developing states that dominated the U.N. General Assembly after 1960. That rule would burden most new states with the predecessor state's agreements, but would take a clean-slate approach to a limited category of "newly-independent" states: those states that had emerged from colonial domination. Such states, the drafters asserted, did not have the opportunity to share in the decision-making that had created the obligations binding the empire. The peoples of India, Burma or Tanzania, for example, had no voice in the creation or negotiation

---

88 [Editor's Note: Indeed, the attempted annexation of Kuwait by Iraq in 1991 seemed amazingly anachronistic to everyone (except Saddam Hussein). Of course, the international community found his attempt intolerable, and multilateral force was used to drive the Iraqi army out of Kuwait and to impose sanctions upon Iraq for its illegal aggression.]

89 MAREK, IDENTITY AND CONTINUITY 589.

90 [Editor's Note: Profesor Crawford's sense of the law back in 1977 has proved exactly right. With the break-up of the Union of Soviet Socialist Republics, there was vigorous assertion of independent nationhood on the part of Estonia, Latvia, and Lithuania and immediate acceptance by the international community of their membership in the family of nations.]

91 By DETLEV F. VAGTS, excerpted from: *State Succession: The Codifier's View*, 33 VIRGINIA JOURNAL OF INTERNATIONAL LAW 275, 286 (1991). Reprinted by permission.

92 By DETLEV F. VAGTS, excerpted from: *State Succession: The Codifier's View*, 33 VIRGINIA JOURNAL OF INTERNATIONAL LAW 275, 286–89 (1991). Reprinted by permission.

93 IAN BROWNLIE, PRINCIPLES OF PUBLIC INTERNATIONAL LAW 668 (4th ed. 1990). He notes that the United States never recognized treaty obligations of Great Britain after 1776.

of the extradition, dual taxation, and other treaties to which they would have fallen heir under the traditional continuity approach to treaties. This selective clean-slate rule, in favor of one class of developing states, likely contributed to the fact that the Vienna Convention on Treaty Succession has never been ratified.

The drafters of the Restatement (Third) of the Foreign Relations Law of the United States declined to follow the Vienna Convention in this regard. They considered the distinction unworkable and unfair. It was noted that the people of Bangladesh had as little influence on the commitments of Pakistan as the people of Tanzania had upon decision-making in London. Yet, under the Vienna Convention, Bangladesh would be subject to Pakistan's antecedent agreements, but Tanzania would be free of all prior agreements. Application of the Vienna Convention's clean-slate rule would also have had curious reverberations in the case of the dissolution of the Soviet Union. One could make the argument, with considerable force, that some of the Soviet republics were in fact colonial states. This argument would apply with particular force to such ''republics'' as Georgia, Armenia, Tazikistan and others which had been conquered by the armies of the Tsars during the nineteenth century, at much the same time as the armies of France and Britain were spreading their colors around the globe. The mere fact that the Tsars' armies could march overland while the other armies had to travel by sea does not seem to be a relevant distinction. Differentiating the case of Belarus from Tazikistan, of course, would pose serious problems of equity. Why should Tazikistan be free of limitations assumed by the U.S.S.R. on its possession of weapons if Belarus is to be bound by them?

The fact is that in the real world, the number of governments that truly represent all of the people under their sovereignty is minimal and that, consequently, the scope of the clean-slate argument is uncomfortably wide.

7. DEBATE: Secessionist Movements and Self-Determination

a. The Primacy of Territoriality[94]

The principle of self-determination of peoples suggests that every ''people'' has a right to its own nation-state. While the positive law status of this norm and its applicability to the secessionist context are debatable, on a rhetorical level few deny the principle's appeal. Unfortunately, it seems directly contrary to another, equally venerable, principle of international law, which upholds the territorial integrity of existing states. In secessionist struggles, it seems, one principle or the other must give way. Where a secessionist movement establishes that its people do not currently possess a nation-state of their own, the first principle would require that the existing territorial boundaries be redrawn, but this redrawing would violate the territorial integrity of the existing state. If, conversely, territorial integrity takes priority, then minority groups within the existing state will be denied their cherished claims to independence. Or at least, so goes the standard account.

I argue here that, contrary to popular assumptions, the difficult normative issues arising out of secessionist claims do not involve an incompatibility of territorial integrity and rights of peoples. Secessionist claims involve, first and foremost, disputed claims to territory. Ethnicity primarily identifies the people making the disputed territorial claim. The two supposedly competing principles of people and territory actually work in tandem.

This reinterpretation of secessionist movements alters the equities somewhat. The plausibility of a separatist claim does not depend primarily on the degree to which the group in question constitutes a distinct people in accordance with relevant international norms. The normative force behind secessionist arguments derives instead from a different source, namely the right to territory that many ethnic groups claim to possess. Secession typically represents a remedy for past injustices. This historical territorial analysis contrasts sharply with the traditional analysis of ethnic differentiation. The currently accepted interpretation of self-determination claims poses the wrong questions in evaluating the merits of particular secessionist claims. It overlooks an important normative ingredient of the arguments that secessionists make, and for this reason understates their claim.

In addition, the current rhetoric about self-determination in one respect treats secessionists' arguments too generously. It suggests that the right to secede flows naturally from principles of self-government such as those embodied in the American Declaration of Independence and the French Declaration of the Rights of Man and of the Citizen. This distinguished lineage affords secessionist claims an undeserved opportunity to stake out the high moral ground. Focusing secessionist disputes instead on disputed claims to territory puts the competing groups on a more even rhetorical par. The mere fact that the secessionist group constitutes a distinct people does not by itself establish a right to secede. To be persuasive a separatist argument must also present a territorial claim.

---

94 By LEA BRILMAYER, excerpted from: *Secession and Self-Determination: A Territorial Interpretation*, 16 YALE JOURNAL OF INTERNATIONAL LAW 177, 177–79, 183–87, 191–93, 197–202 (1991). Reprinted by permission.

Existing norms of international law do not highlight the territorial claim but focus instead on whether the aggrieved group constitutes a distinct people. The phrase self-determination frames the separatist question in a misleading way; it obscures the territorial aspects of the dispute. At issue is not a relationship between peoples and states, but a relationship between people, states, and territory. Separatist arguments make little sense unless interpreted in a territorial light.

While international law does not provide a right of secession, separatists have nonetheless relied on particular provisions of international law in making their secessionist claims. They have focused on the United Nations' clear recognition of self-determination, while disregarding the accompanying caveats that the principle does not supersede a state's territorial integrity. But the self-determination argument potentially supports an unlimited right to withhold individual consent to state authority. Proponents of secession therefore face a very slippery slope in formulating a right to secede that does not open the door to complete anarchy.

The appeal of a secessionist argument lies in the importance of self-determination, the links between principle and the concept of democratic self-government, and the alleged moral superiority of self-determination over the preservation of territorial boundaries. Ethnic distinctiveness plays an important role in these arguments because the secessionist needs to limit the number of groups entitled to claim a right to secede. Whether or not a positive law right to secede can be established, such arguments have undeniable rhetorical force.

Two important problems mark the way in which separatists frame their claims. First, a straightforward appeal to principles of consent and self-government cannot justify secession. Second, the alleged tension between self-determination and territorial integrity rests on a misconception of the principle of self-determination. These arguments overlap because both concern the importance of territory to political governance. I will first criticize the supposed link between secessionist claims and consent theory, for this argument is far less controversial than the latter.

Traditionally, the self-determination norm on which secessionists base their claims is thought to turn on democratic principles of consent and popular sovereignty. According to this argument, self-determination represents a liberal democratic value (with secession as the liberal democratic alternative), while the principle of territorial integrity remains feudal, undemocratic, and oppressive. The idea that government must stem from the consent of the governed seems to allow a disaffected group the right to opt out of an existing state. If consent is the keystone of legitimacy, then a non-consenting individual must be allowed to leave. In this way, principles of democratic government translate into a right of secession. The only countervailing principle, that of the territorial integrity of existing states, suffers from a suspect historical association with monarchy and feudalism. Therefore, so the argument goes, territoriality must give way to liberal democratic principles and the right of self-determination.

The apparent simplicity of this position is misleading in at least one important way; it places too much weight upon consent as the cornerstone of state legitimacy. Despite the rhetoric of liberal democracy, actual consent is not necessary to political legitimacy. Indeed, theorists have never thought that a refusal to consent exempts an individual from state authority. In the domestic context, actual consent rarely exists, and for this reason political philosophers have fallen back on theories of tacit consent, arguments which are fictitious. Tacit consent theories do not crumble in the face of a citizen's loud protest that a government cannot legitimately represent him or her. Consent makes up an important part of democratic rhetoric, but philosophers have managed to justify state power quite nicely without actual consent. Separatists cannot base their arguments upon a right to opt out because no such right exists in democratic theory.

Government by the consent of the governed does not necessarily encompass a right to opt out. It only requires that within the existing political unit a right to participate through electoral processes be available. Moreover, participatory rights do not entail a right to secede. On the contrary, they suggest that the appropriate solution for dissatisfied groups rests in their full inclusion in the polity, with full participation in its decision-making processes.

Two lines of reasoning explain why one might erroneously link theories of democratic participation with a right of secession. First, in some cases in which secession is sought, the members of the separatist group are also denied democratic participation rights. For example, inhabitants of most colonies were denied both independence and electoral influence on the decision-making processes of the colonizing state. This is not always the case. In some contemporary secession movements, the polity accords members of the minority group the same democratic rights as other citizens. Yet separatists typically would not find satisfaction in rights of democratic participation. What makes them separatist is their desire to leave and form a new state. The fact that some states deny certain groups the right to participate does not explain why secession, rather than full participation, is the appropriate remedy.

The second line of reasoning linking consent to secession proposes that denying a right of secession is directly contrary to the wishes of the separatist group, and thus a violation of the principle of popular sovereignty. If one were to consult the secessionists, in many cases one would find a desire to secede. How then can it be consistent with democracy to deny a right to secede? The fallacy of this argument is obvious; it assumes that the relevant individuals to consult are the members of the secessionist group. In consulting the population of the entire state, one might find that a majority overall wished to remain a single country. What has not been explained is why only the separatists need be consulted. However, this cannot be explained in terms of popular sovereignty of consent. As Michla Pomerance author has put it, who is the "self" in self-determination? Is it the minority group, or is it the state as a whole?[95]

The separatist would argue that the relevant wishes are clearly those of the secessionists themselves. Because it is their preferences that matter, they have a right to withhold consent if they choose and, if they do, then they have a right to secede. A separatist would probably concede that individuals in the dominant ethnic group do not have a right to opt out. They cannot escape political obligations by withholding consent from the government, but if some minority ethnic group withholds consent then it cannot be bound. The argument must be, in other words, that tacit consent can be attributed to members of the dominant ethnic group in the state, but not to members of the secessionist group. As to the latter, only actual consent will suffice.

This raises an argument about the proper unit within which democratic government should operate, for the secessionists have assumed that there are properly two governmental units, while opponents of secession assume that there is only one. Both sides agree that a state has substantial power to infer tacit consent from all those within the governmental unit, but has no such power over those outside the unit. They disagree, however, over how that unit should be defined.

The separatist argument seems to propose that the governmental unit ought to be defined in terms of ethnic or national groupings rather than territory. This view defines political boundaries in terms of peoples. This argument does not follow directly from democratic theory, for the secessionist definition of governing units is no more democratic than the territorial view. Neither argument is based on consent. Indeed, as Professor Cobban argues, ethnic groupings are, if anything, less liberal and consensual than territorial.[96] While, for the most part, a person's residence remains subject to choice, her ethnicity is fixed at birth. Under a territorial view, one can, at least theoretically, withdraw consent simply by leaving the territory. One's geographical location is more nearly voluntary than one's ethnic identity. Democratic theory does not therefore compel the secessionist definition.

Are governmental units better defined in terms of peoples, or in terms of territory? This rephrasing of the separatist argument demonstrates the oft-noted tension between people and territory, but the supposed tension is misconceived. Properly understood, the principle of territorial sovereignty accommodates a right of secession perfectly well, and indeed provides a better account of secessionist claims than a self-determination principle defined in terms of the rights of peoples. The reason is that the territorial principle does not necessarily give a state power when its exercise of territorial sovereignty is illegitimate. If secessionists argue that the current exercise of territorial power is illegitimate, and that territorial sovereignty in fact belongs to the minority group rather than to the majority, then the secessionists can base a right to secede upon a territorial claim, rather than on a personalistic one. In other words, tacit consent can be attributed to a state's inhabitants only when the state has legitimate power over its territory.

This interpretation of the typical separatist argument focuses squarely on a feature of the controversy that has no direct bearing on the ethnic, religious, or racial differences between the group that wishes to secede and the majority group that controls the existing state. Does this mean that ethnic claims are irrelevant under a territorial interpretation of secessionist movements? If so, the territorial version of the separatist argument appears inconsistent with current legal statements, which bestow the right of self-determination only on peoples. But ethnic identity is not irrelevant under a territorialist interpretation, for it explains why historical grievances continue to matter. The territorial interpretation recognizes a significant role for claims of ethnic distinctiveness, although not the role suggested by the standard account.

The important function of ethnic identity under the territorial interpretation is to explain how territorial claims survive, and why particular individuals currently feel aggrieved by past events. Unjust historical occurrences do not automatically give rise to contemporary movements to right past wrongs. Individuals are typically motivated to become involved in secessionist movements because they identify in some way with those who were unjustly treated in the past. Without a reason to identify with the earlier possessors of the territory, the separatists would simply remain disengaged observers. While some might perceive that earlier victims of colonial aggression were unfairly treated, no impetus for action would exist unless a current group identified with those losers and considered itself the heir to their territorial claims. If no such group exists, there are few persons motivated to fight and most probably no one to whom the territory can be returned.

Ethnic identification keeps the historical grievance alive

---

[95] [Editor's Note: *See* the section on "Self-Determination" in Chapter 9, "Group Rights," in this Anthology.]

[96] [Editor's Note: For further discussion of these issues, *see* the section on "Self-Determination" in Chapter 9, in this Anthology.]

by passing the loss from one generation to the next. Old wrongs will not be forgotten so long as an existing group continues to experience the historical wrongs as its own, as part of its heritage. The usual modes of transmission of this shared sense of wrong are precisely the ones that typically define ethnic communities. Wrongs are passed down by recitation within the family, through educational and religious institutions, and by way of shared culture, such as stories, myths, nationalistic songs, and the like. If at any point an individual should ask, "Why should I care about the past?" the answer follows that "These are your people who were wronged. You are one of us, and we all share this wrong and ought to struggle to make it right." If one were as likely to identify with the winners as the loser, then there would be little reason to feel resentment or to fight. Ethnicity answers the question, "Why do people still care about something that occurred such a long time ago?" It constitutes the barrier to assimilation and the guarantee that historical grievances will continue to be relevant in the present day. It gives the current claimants their standing to protest, not in a technical, but in an emotional sense.

My thesis is that every separatist movement is built upon a claim to territory, usually based on an historical grievance, and that without a normatively sound claim to territory, self-determination arguments do not form a plausible basis for secession. Self-determination proves a misleading way to characterize the issue because it focuses attention exclusively on people, not on places. That is not to say that territorial claims are necessary for every kind of minority claim. If a minority experiences discrimination or suffers human rights violations, then it certainly has a grievance even though it claims no historical right to a particular piece of territory. I argue, however, that the minority cannot justifiably claim the remedy of secession unless it can convincingly assert a claim to territory. What distinguishes separatist from other minority claims is the fact that the group wishes to establish a new state on a particular piece of land.

Furthermore, whether a territorial claim exists may prove a better indicator of intuitively acceptable secessionist claims than either the ethnic identities or the preferences of the inhabitants. What are characterized as self-determination claims are instead sometimes simple territorial disputes. Claims are at times framed in terms of self-determination where there exists no ethnic group aspiring to secession, and the secessionist claims are sometimes denied even when such an ethnic group exists. From the perspective of the standard account of self-determination, such cases are anomalous. A claim should stand or fall depending on whether an identifiable people is protesting for the right of self-determination. First let us look at the way that a territorial claim, unaccompanied by a claim on behalf of an aggrieved people, sometimes gives rise to a self-determination argument.

Occasionally, states make self-determination claims on behalf of groups of individuals that have not in fact expressed a wish to exercise their supposed right of self-determination. This anomaly suggests that the self-determination of peoples is not the real issue. For example, India cited the norm of self-determination in ousting the Portuguese from Goa, which Portugal had acquired as a colony. This claim was made despite the fact that the people then inhabiting Goa had not been asked whether they wished to repudiate Portuguese rule. India maintained that the preferences of the people of Goa were simply irrelevant. From the perspective of the standard account, the Indian claim seems puzzling. How can India force the people of Goa to exercise their right of self-determination without first consulting the Goans to determine what they themselves might want? From the territorial perspective, the claim becomes considerably more intelligible. The Indian claim was an historical one about rights to territory. From the Indian government's perspective, Portugal had acquired the land improperly and had no legitimate claim to it. India sought to redress what it saw as an historical wrong, although the rhetoric used to explain its anti-colonial stance proved ill-adapted to the task because it focused on the self-determination rights of the inhabitants.[97]

A theory of secession necessarily depends upon a theory of legitimate sovereignty over territory. Separatists are typically motivated by a perceived historical injustice, in which land that was rightfully theirs was taken by another group. The land was seized either by the dominant group in the current state, or by a third group which then conveyed the territory to the currently dominant group. In evaluating the persuasiveness of separatists' arguments, it is necessary to investigate these historical claims. This may be no easy matter, for in many cases the facts will be in dispute. In few cases will the equities point unambiguously in one direction.

Even if an historically sound evaluation is possible, this will not end the inquiry. A key remaining issue is the extent to which the status quo should be altered to rectify past wrongs. This could be called the problem of "adverse possession." Few would say that the status quo deserves no weight at all. Even a separatist is likely to concede (albeit reluctantly) that the status quo is sometimes important. The separatist group may itself have come by the

---

[97] [Editor's Note: South Africa's "homelands" policy could be another example of a self-determination claim made on behalf of Native South Africans by a white South African government. *See, e.g.*, D'Amato, *Territorial Apartheid*, chapter 8 in ANTHONY D'AMATO, INTERNATIONAL LAW: PROCESS AND PROSPECT 165 (1987).]

territory in question through dubious means. By raising its historical claim the group may be relying upon a previous status quo and ignoring still earlier historical wrongs that had been committed. Even where this is not the case because the separatist group is indigenous to the area, it would seem quite impossible to put everything up for grabs. Hardly a territorial boundary anywhere in the world would survive an effort to correct all historical misdeeds. If protecting the status quo must be balanced against rectifying past injustices, then the obvious question is how much weight to assign each concern. Here, I can only suggest a few of the factors that might be taken into account in determining whether the status quo is currently settled enough to give rise to a defense of "adverse possession."

One obvious factor might be the immediacy of the historical grievance. The further in the past the historical wrong occurred, the more likely that it is better now to let things remain as they are. At one extreme, if an illegitimate annexation occurred only a few months earlier, the proper remedy would be to return the territory to its rightful inhabitants. Certainly, the Kuwaitis would suggest as much. Separatists, undoubtedly, are willing to go back a good deal farther in time. The question is, how long an historical reach is warranted?

Another factor might be the extent to which the separatist group has kept the claim alive. Some groups have managed to keep their controversy alive in world public opinion. In such cases, there has been no adverse possession because the minority group has never acquiesced in the loss of its territory. Expectations cannot become settled around new state boundaries when there are constant reminders of the historical illegitimacy of the annexation. The primary problem with including this factor is that it penalizes groups that have been unable to keep their protest alive because of severe repression. Perhaps in such circumstances, where continued struggle is virtually impossible, the lack of public efforts should not be held against the separatist claim. Another problem with relying on this factor is that publicity is often sought through rather dubious methods, such as bombing airplanes; it might be undesirable to reward such activities.

A third factor, also controversial, is the extent to which the territory has now been settled by members of the dominant group. It is a common strategy to attempt to solidify conquest by moving loyal citizens of the victorious state into the new territory. In the Baltic states, for instance, only twenty percent of the residents of Lithuania are non-Lithuanians, but the analogous percentages for Latvia and Estonia are forty-eight and thirty-nine, respectively. From the point of view of separatists, such new settlement ought to have no significance whatsoever. They did not ask for these new inhabitants. Had the secessionists' territory not been improperly annexed, the newcomers could have been excluded entirely. Taking the newcomers' presence into account compounds the original injury. Yet, as a practical matter, the new settlers tend to legitimize the territorial status quo. The reason that members of the separatist group often resist such migration is precisely because they realize that it undercuts their claim in the forum of world opinion.

Finally, the nature of the historical grievance may itself figure in determining whether a right of secession still exists. There are degrees of wrongfulness. The determination is neither black nor white. It is probably no coincidence that the one case on which most people can agree is the decolonization of the empires of the European powers. The European powers' acquisitions lacked even colorable justification. In contrast, some territorial disputes involve uncertain territorial claims in which a genuine dispute exists over the proper ownership of the land. If the "wrong" state wins the contest through use of force, this is an historical grievance. But such victory is qualitatively different than naked conquest, and for this reason might be thought to establish a claim of adverse possession once a period of time goes by. Good faith may also matter. The degree to which the prevailing party has a sincere belief in a right to the territory may perhaps be inferred from its behavior once the territory is annexed. The European powers, of course, treated their colonies as colonies, giving them a distinct political status and treating the inhabitants as subjects rather than as fellow citizens. One would expect that if a victorious state believes it has a pre-existing claim to the territory, then in annexing the territory it will treat the new land in the same way that it treats other parts of its domain.

Clearly, the territorial interpretation of separatist movements does not supply easy answers to the problem of secession. The question of what amounts to a good claim for maintaining the existing status quo seems especially difficult. Adverse possession claims are hard to evaluate. I would submit, however, that under the territorial view we would at least be asking more of the right questions. Separatist movements cannot be understood or evaluated without reference to claims to territory. Groups do not seek to secede merely because they are ethnically distinct, and if they did, they would probably not get much support. It is hard even to understand what a separatist group would demand absent historical claims to territory. When a group seeks to secede, it is claiming a right to a particular piece of land, and one must necessarily inquire into why it is entitled to that particular piece of land, as opposed to some other piece of land—or to no land at all.

The standard account pits the principle of self-determination against the principle of territorial integrity. The first assumes government is defined as a collection of individuals; the latter, as an area of land. Defining government in terms of land better explains what secessionists are trying to accomplish. When individuals seek to secede, they are making a claim to territory. They wish a piece of land for their future, a piece of land on which they will be able to make their own claims of integrity of territorial borders. Their claim is typically centered on a piece of land that they possessed in the past, and upon which they claimed territorial integrity.

Territorial integrity properly understood accommodates the principle of self-determination. Whatever conflict exists is not between principles, but over land.

b. The Primacy of Human Rights[98]

Lea Brilmayer's requirement of a claim to territory does not pose any particular problems for indigenous peoples who may wish to exercise their right to secede, because their historical ties to the land are typically not in question. Where I differ from Brilmayer is in her description that, because we can regard claimants to territory as making competing claims to territorial integrity, we can say that the human rights claims do not really clash with territorial integrity and that, therefore, territorial integrity does not pose a real barrier to the achievement of self-determination. Yet it is the territorial integrity of *present states* that is a fundamental norm of the present world system of states and state sovereignty. The concept of territorial integrity poses a barrier to secession as long as it is conceived of as protecting the present boundaries of states. Brilmayer is quite correct in arguing that this should not be the case, because everyone is really appealing to territorial integrity. However, a simple appeal to the concept of territorial integrity is not the barrier in question; the real barrier is the assumption that protection of the present boundaries of states is so necessary that no derogation will be permitted unless the state concerned agrees to them. With the present rules of state sovereignty, the achievement of respect for human rights via secession does indeed run hard up against the principle of the territorial integrity of present states.

Charles Beitz argues that the existing distribution of territory and resources in the world is completely *morally* arbitrary.[99] It is at least arguable that there are no principled, moral justifications of the international rule of upholding the territorial integrity of *present* states. Many indigenous peoples challenge the legal justification for the rights of present states to the land and resources that they have acquired through the conquest of indigenous peoples. International law has made might right; therefore, the issue that should be addressed is whether this is justified. If it is concluded that it is not, then the appropriate remedy for the injustices done to indigenous peoples must be considered, which must include discussion of such issues as the application of self-determination and whether the territorial integrity of present states should be upheld today. Such discussion will necessarily entail debate on the interests being protected by the principle of territorial integrity and how the various interests involved, including the human rights of indigenous peoples, should be balanced. I suggest that one of the primary factors included in the discussion must be the justification of all territorial entitlements.

We must reinstate the human rights component of self-determination, and reinstate the belief that the state exists for the benefit of people, rather than the reverse. Only through such changes will indigenous peoples achieve control of their destiny, or their self-determination. Any other approach is tantamount to a rejection of a world order based on principle and an embrace of might as right.

8. Autonomy[100]

"Autonomy" is not a term of art or a concept that has a generally accepted definition in international law. In an effort to ascertain just what has been considered over the years to constitute autonomy, the authors undertook a number of case studies of nonsovereign entities and federal states offering a wide range of examples of varying degrees of governmental autonomy and internal self-government. These studies fell, albeit somewhat arbitrarily, into the three major categories of federal states, internationalized territories, and associated states, along with a fourth, miscellaneous grouping. The entities surveyed were chosen because they represented a wide range of autonomy arrangements which, at least to some extent, have been recognized or seriously considered in international law.

The term "autonomy" should be understood to mean general political or governmental autonomy. More restrictive types of autonomy, e.g., cultural or religious autonomy, also have been considered where appropriate, as in the case of the Aland Islands, the Belgian linguistic communities, Eritrea, Greenland, and the millet system under the Ottoman Empire. Autonomy and self-government are de-

[98] By CATHERINE J. IORNS, excerpted from: *Indigenous Peoples and Self-Determination: Challenging State*, 24 CASE WESTERN RESERVE JOURNAL OF INTERNATIONAL LAW 199, 329–30, 332–35, 347–48 (1992). Reprinted by permission.

[99] CHARLES R. BEITZ, POLITICAL THEORY AND INTERNATIONAL RELATIONS 136–43 (1979).

[100] By HURST HANNUM & RICHARD B. LILLICH, excerpted from: *The Concept of Autonomy in International Law*, 74 AMERICAN JOURNAL OF INTERNATIONAL LAW 858 (1980). Reprinted by permission.

termined primarily by the degree of actual as well as formal independence enjoyed by the autonomous entity in its political decisionmaking process. Generally, autonomy is understood to refer to independence of action on the internal or domestic level, as foreign affairs and defense normally are in the hands of the central or national government, but occasionally power to conclude international agreements concerning cultural or economic matters also may reside with the autonomous entity. In brief, our examination of autonomy in theory and practice provided a description and analysis of the degree of independence and control over its own affairs that an autonomous entity generally enjoys, rather than consider the more abstract, if nonetheless interesting, questions of sovereignty or statehood. Thus we excluded the classical categories of protectorate, vassal state, dependent state, colony, and associated state, which are often overlapping and subject to scholarly disagreement as to their application. We regard autonomy as a relative term that describes the extent or degree of independence of a particular entity rather than defining a particular minimum level of independence that can be designated as the status of "autonomy."

Autonomy does not necessarily imply that a territory must be wholly independent and comparable to a sovereign state. Among those kinds of subordination to a higher or principal governmental entity that clearly do not detract even from a territory's statehood, and that therefore cannot be said to be inconsistent with its full autonomy are: common citizenship or nationality; delegation of competence in the area of foreign relations; delegation of competence in the area of defense, including the retention of other states of limited powers of intervention under specific circumstances (e.g., Cyprus); establishment of a common customs union or currency; and subordination to the highest judicial authority of the sovereign or principal state.

Full autonomy and self-government refer essentially to the internal government of a territory; in the majority of cases, the autonomous territories have no international personality and are not treated as "states" for the purposes of international law. It is true, however, that in some recent instances limited authority has been granted to autonomous territories to join international organizations or to enter into international agreements.

Although arriving at a firm definition that is appropriate in all cases is impossible, it is helpful to identify the minimum governmental powers that a territory would need to possess if it were to be considered fully autonomous and self-governing:

(1) There should exist a locally elected body with some independent legislative power, although the extent of the body's competence will be limited by a constituent document. Within the realm of its competence – which should include authority over local matters such as health, education, social services, local taxation, internal trade and commerce, environmental protection, zoning, and local government structure and organization – the local legislative body should be independent, and its decisions should not be subject to veto by the principal/sovereign government unless those decisions exceed its competence or are otherwise inconsistent with basic constitutional precepts.

(2) There should be a locally chosen chief executive, possibly subject to approval or confirmation by the principal government, who has general responsibility for the administration and execution of local laws or decrees. The local executive may be given the authority to implement appropriate national/federal laws and regulations, although this is not a necessary power to attain autonomy.

(3) There should be an independent local judiciary, some members of which may also be subject to approval or confirmation by the central/principal government, with jurisdiction over purely local matters. Questions involving the scope of local power or the relationship between the autonomous and principal governments may be considered by either local or national courts in the first instance and generally may be appealed to a nonlocal court or a joint commission of some kind for final resolution.

(4) The status of autonomy and at least partial self-government is not inconsistent with the denial of any local authority over specific areas of special concern to the principal/sovereign government, as opposed to the reservation by the sovereign of general discretionary powers. Among the cases we surveyed, specific provision has been made for central governmental participation in or control over matters such as foreign relations; national defense; customs; immigration; security of borders and frontiers; airports and ports; interprovincial water and energy resources; general norms of civil, criminal, corporate, and financial behavior, as expressed in national legislation; restrictions on the taxing or debt-issuing authority of the autonomous entity; monetary, banking, and general economic policy; and interprovincial or extraprovincial commerce. In addition, the central government has the power of eminent domain for public works and must approve any proposed amendment to the constitution or other basic constituent documents.

(5) Full autonomy and self-government also are consistent with power-sharing arrangements between the central and autonomous governments in such areas as control over ports and other aspects of transportation, police powers, exploitation of natural re-

sources, and implementation of national/central legislation and regulations.

The granting of only cultural and religious autonomy, even if coupled with certain administrative responsibilities, would not seem to constitute "full" autonomy or self-government. The degree of religious or cultural independence enjoyed by, e.g., the Ottoman millets, or the authority over education granted to the Aland Islands or the linguistic communities in Belgium, simply does not include sufficient political or legal control over internal matters to constitute full autonomy as that term might be applied to, inter alia, Eritrea, the Swiss cantons, or the "internationalized territories" of Danzig, Memel, Trieste, Shanghai, and the Saar.

Nor does the distinction between personal and territorial jurisdiction appear to be crucial in attempting to define full autonomy. However, since many governmental powers are by their nature territorial, e.g., control over internal trade, public works, zoning, and the exercise of general police powers, it is unlikely that a regime with purely personal jurisdiction over its members would be considered fully autonomous.

A summary can do little more than note the extreme diversity of the entities we surveyed and the wide variations exhibited in the degree of autonomy or internal self-government each one enjoys. Certainly the concept of self-government and the right to participate meaningfully in those decisions that directly affect a local community are of growing importance. Also worthy of note, however, is what may be the beginning of a trend away from independence and full statehood as the only answer to the problems perceived either by ethnic communities within existing states or by non-self-governing territories that have yet to emerge fully on the international stage. The proliferation of "mini-" or "micro-states," independent in name only, has been the subject of much critical comment; in many instances a form of associated statehood, for example, might reflect political realities more accurately.

Growing demands for regional self-government, the proliferation of small, newly independent states, and the increasingly complex interdependence of contemporary world politics no longer correspond to the sovereign nation-state simplicity of the nineteenth century. Autonomy remains a useful, if imprecise, concept within which flexible and unique political structures may be developed to respond to that complexity.

7
Human Rights

A. Introduction

1. Reflections on Human Rights[1]

The installation of human rights in the international constitution after 1945 has been paradoxical. The idea of human rights quickly became perverted by the self-misconceiving of international society. Human rights were quickly appropriated by governments, embodied in treaties, made part of the stuff of primitive international relations, swept up into the maw of an international bureaucracy. The reality of the idea of human rights has been degraded. From being a source of ultimate anxiety of usurping holders of public social power, they were turned into bureaucratic small-change. Human rights, a reservoir of unlimited power in all the self-creating society, became a plaything of governments and lawyers. The game of human rights has been played in international statal organizations by diplomats and bureaucrats, and even their appointees, in the setting and the ethos of traditional international relations.

The result has been that the potential energy of the idea has been dissipated. Alienation, corruption, tyranny, and oppression has continued wholesale in many societies all over the world. And in all societies governments have been reassured in their arrogance by the idea that, if they are not proved actually to be violating the substance of particularized human rights, if they can bring their willing and acting within the wording of this or that formula with its lawyerly qualifications and exceptions, then they are doing well enough. The idea of human rights should intimidate governments or it is worth nothing. If the idea of human rights reassures governments it is worse than nothing.

But there is room for optimism on two grounds. (1) The idea of human rights having been thought, it cannot be unthought. It will not be replaced, unless by some idea which contains and surpasses it. (2) There are tenacious individuals and non-statal societies whose activity on behalf of the idea of human rights is not part of international relations but is part of a new process of international reality-forming.

[1] By PHILIP ALLOTT, excerpted from: EUNOMIA: NEW ORDER FOR A NEW WORLD 287–88 (N.Y.: Oxford Univ. Press 1990). Reprinted by permission.

2. The Human Rights Revolution[2]

It will take a long time before the various international human rights systems in existence today will be able to prevent or put an end to all the many human rights violations that still cause so much suffering in the world. Obviously we cannot and should not close our eyes to that suffering. Moreover, it is quite understandable that some of us look at all the international law on human rights that exists on paper and say that it is nothing but window-dressing to cover up the sins of the killers and torturers and rapists who do the bidding of brutal governments. When you feel that way, when you are tempted to despair – and I am not immune to that feeling – try to remember what has been achieved in a few short decades. The international human rights code that came into being over the last forty years has created an international political climate that is daily more sensitive to the illegality of human rights violations, less and less willing to tolerate them, and ever more responsive to public and private pressure to prevent or stop them. Today more and more Western governments condition their foreign aid on the improvement of human rights in the aid-receiving nations. Human rights violations in one country are debated in the national parliaments of other countries; reports of nongovernmental international human rights groups are taken very seriously by an increasing number of governments; and the political and economic health of many a country depends on the perception that people in other countries have about how it treats its nationals. In short, governments find it increasingly more difficult not to take human rights considerations into account when making foreign policy decisions.

The existence of international human rights law has thus had an important socializing impact on the international community. Governments now know that there is a political and economic price to be paid for large-scale violation of human rights. That knowledge affects their conduct; not because they have suddenly become good or altruistic, but because they need foreign investment or trade, economic or military aid, or because their domestic political power

[2] By THOMAS BUERGENTHAL, excerpted from: *The Human Rights Revolution*, 23 ST. MARY'S LAW JOURNAL 3 (1991). Reprinted by permission.

base will be seriously weakened by international condemnation. The international human rights code also legitimates the struggle of the victims of oppression. It gives them faith that the struggle is just, that they have law and the international community on their side and that they are not alone in their struggle. Their struggle thus acquires an ideology that has a normative basis, an ideology that enjoys universal legitimacy. That is why national political ideologies that foster or tolerate oppression cannot in the long run successfully compete against the new ideology.

When law, whether domestic or international, mirrors the aspirations of society and captures its imagination, it acquires a moral and political force whose impact can rarely be predicted. It often far exceeds the wildest expectations or fears of those responsible for its promulgation or of those who oppose it. The lessons history teaches about the power of ideas and the irony of hypocrisy should be studied very carefully by all of us who are interested in a world in which human beings can live in dignity and peace. These lessons are particularly telling when we look at the role the human rights revolution is playing today in many parts of the world. That revolution is proving ever more convincingly that so-called political realism, which discounts all but military and economic power, has no monopoly on political wisdom nor is it all that realistic. We may need bread to live, but we are sustained as human beings by our dreams and our hopes for a better tomorrow: for freedom, for human dignity. That, ultimately, is what the human rights revolution is all about and why it is succeeding.

3. The Hierarchy of Human Rights[3]

A number of approaches to establishing a hierarchy of human rights have been proposed. Perhaps the most common, certainly among the leading U.S. human rights organizations, is to identify non-derogable human rights, that is, those which cannot be suspended under any circumstances: primarily the right to life, physical security, due process, and non-discrimination on the basis of race and other ascriptive categories.

Enthusiasts of this approach have proposed a number of reasons for locating these rights at the peak of the hierarchy. One reason is the shared intuition that they must be of central importance, because we regard violation of them as particularly evil. Another reason stems from the universal recognition which these rights enjoy. In a system where no central institutions of enforcement exist—no courts of general jurisdiction, police forces or armies—we rely on attitudes concerning the legitimacy or illegitimacy of public institutions and of officials, in order to generate the effective enforcement of rights. Since the threat of delegitimation affects the behavior of officials, the defenses of human rights could be undermined if they lost their aura of universalism. To maintain this aura, some argue, the entire community should emphasize the rights most generally accepted as universal. An emphasis on non-derogable rights maintains this consensus. Conversely, a campaign on behalf of contested rights, like those of participation and development or economic and social rights, undermine the consensus. This is the functional justification for treating non-derogable rights as the apex of the human rights hierarchy.

A third argument for treating non-derogable rights as privileged is functional and deductive: they should be seen as primary because all other rights are dependent on them. A political order in which the rights to life, physical security, and due process are frequently violated generates an intense and pervasive fear which annuls the will to exercise other rights. Despite these arguments, some claim that subsistence rights, sometimes described in terms of basic needs, should be seen as the apex rights. The claim usually is expressed in fairly homely terms. For instance, if people are unable to eat or if they die as a consequence of dysentery and other diseases of the poor, then all the other rights are irrelevant.

The next approach to apex rights is that most frequently identified with Henry Shue.[4] He argues that both subsistence and physical security are basic rights, under which he places all the particular liberties upon which security and subsistence depend, including participation. Thus, participation enters the human rights equation.

Shue states that one must speak not only of subsistence but of a sense of security in the enjoyment of subsistence. In order to obtain this security, you need social protection. Social protection implies a variety of other rights, including participation in directing the institutions and policies which vitally affect security of subsistence. He adds that by virtue of being entitled to invoke the right to subsistence, a person is correspondingly entitled to influence the operation of institutions and the implementation of policies relevant to its realization. The influence, he insists, must be genuine. Thus he presents the question of how to measure genuineness of participation.

Still another approach to identifying the apex rights was the one championed by the Reagan Administration, which emphasized fair elections. The Reagan Administration ar-

---

[3] By TOM J. FARER, excerpted from: *The Hierarchy of Human Rights,* 8 AMERICAN UNIVERSITY JOURNAL OF INTERNATIONAL LAW AND POLICY 115, 115–19 (1992). Reprinted by permission.

[4] *See generally,* HENRY SHUE, BASIC RIGHTS (1980).

gued, presumably in good faith, that as long as people participate in fair elections, then all other rights fall into place, albeit not always as quickly as one would like.

In the editorial pages of the Washington Post, Stephen Rosenfeld compared the approaches of Human Rights Watch and Freedom House on the changed environment of human rights[5]. He noted that Freedom House recognized and extolled the transformation in the world, particularly in Eastern Europe where democratic elections have occurred, while Human Rights Watch emphasized human rights violations that continued to occur in countries after they held elections. Rosenfeld mildly disparaged, unfairly I think, what he took to be the latter's continuing sour-notedness about the worldwide condition of the human race.

The Washington Post also published recently a striking column by Richard Cohen on the Algerian democratic elections.[6] He did not deny that the elections were democratic, but he suggested that even people concerned with human rights could recognize occasions where democratic elections produced undesirable results. He suggested that a government dominated by Islamic fundamentalists would adversely affect such minorities as Western-oriented citizens and women, and generally threaten the pluralist values required for democracy to endure. Hence there was a very respectable case for *not* insisting on deference to majority choice.[7]

Most human rights organizations, particularly non-governmental organizations, have steered clear of development issues and touch only peripherally on participation. Amnesty International looks only at torture plus imprisonment for the exercise of rights such as freedom of speech and association. Human Rights Watch concentrates on first generation rights (civil and political rights), and generally refuses to acknowledge second (social and cultural rights), much less third generation rights (e.g., minority rights, the right to development), due to the view that only first generation rights enjoy a broad consensus. The strength of that consensus must be maintained in order to manipulate the capacity for delegitimation through exposure of human rights violations.

At least two other reasons for an exclusive focus on political and civil rights exist. The first reason is the difficulty in monitoring violations of other kinds of rights, such as the right to participate or the right to development. Even if there was consensus, at some very high level of abstraction, that these were indeed rights, in practice the consensus would break down very quickly into debate about progress. This has been a very important aspect of the reluctance to talk about economic rights.

Second, in the area of first generation rights, you have an infinite opportunity to express them. To be sure, if everyone insists on a right to speak on the same street corner at the same time, equal enjoyment would mean no enjoyment. But with a certain amount of management, roughly equal opportunity is available. When, however, it comes to the division of the gross national product, whether it is inter-generationally or within a single generation, only a finite amount of the valued thing is available. No consensus criteria exist for deciding how to make the requisite allocations. Different societies at different times, even different groups within a society, will disagree about the appropriate criteria.

Allow me to conclude by suggesting that we should try to operationalize the right to participate at the macro-level. The ability to participate through the traditional or classical modality of elected representatives is diminished by two phenomena of our time. First, of course, is privatization. As privatization continues, the state has fewer tools and less opportunity to make decisions on matters that vitally affect the quality of life of the electorate.[8] But even if privatization does not occur, as long as the aspiration to increase the gross national product survives, then the consequent participation of the country in the global economy reduces the ability of national policy makers to influence outcomes.

If we focus on participation on the micro or project level, I believe the key issue is the nature of the right to participation. Is it a right to be informed or to have one's views heard? Is it a right to veto projects when the local deprivation is great and the general benefits are uncertain or modest? Is it a right not to suffer a disproportionate burden in contributing to a possibly very great increase in the economic welfare of the society? Or, is it simply a right to compete for the benefits which result from growth? This question brings us back to the macro-level. Here one might look to demands for more education and training, antitrust laws, harsh taxation of inherited wealth, and so on.

I would say finally that perhaps the deepest element of conflict between rights to development and rights to participation, both of which are group rights, and the classic first-generation concerns of human rights groups, relates to the fundamental question of what human rights are

---

[5] Stephen Rosenfeld, *Democracy First, Then Human Rights*, WASH. POST, Jan. 3, 1992, at A23.

[6] Richard Cohen, *Phony Democracies*, WASH. POST, Jan 2, 1991, at A19.

[7] [Editor's Note: Consider in this connection the discussion on Algeria in the chapter on the Democratic Entitlement, Chapter 15 below.]

[8] [Editor's Question: What impact would a finely graduated system of tax penalties for unwanted business activity, coupled with tax incentives for desirable activity, have on the ability of government to shape the quality of life?]

about. Some people think of human rights ultimately as a means to permit individuals to invent and re-invent themselves or to maintain their peculiar personal identity (to be, in G.K. Chesterton's words, "their own petty little selves.") Others think of these rights as a means for groups to prosper and to maintain their identity or to change their identity. Harsh conflicts arise between individual rights and other kinds of rights. In the process of seeking to maintain their identity, groups often must practice or wish to practice forced inclusion and exclusion, and often such group practices are incompatible with the whole notion of human rights as a basis for individual creation and re-creation.

B. Humanitarian Intervention

1. Introduction[9]

Humanitarian intervention may be defined as the justifiable use of force for the purpose of protecting the inhabitants of another state from treatment so arbitrary and persistently abusive as to exceed the limits within which the sovereign is presumed to act with reason and justice. However, the right of the sovereign state to act without interference within its own territory, even though it be no more than a presumption, is of such importance to the well-being of international society, that the states in their wisdom, as evidenced in their practice, have been jealous of lightly admitting the pleas of humanity as a justification for action against a sister state; and we find the intervention on this ground has been rather rigidly limited to specific cases, and conditioned in each of them upon the existence of a certain state of facts. It is true that the appreciation of the facts and the determination as to the existence of the justifying situation still remains to a certain degree a matter entrusted to the conscientious discretion of the intervening state; nevertheless, the general and salutary attitude of suspicion serves as a rough check upon its abuse. The counterpoise which serves as the sanction to prevent aggression and subsequent conquest under the guise of humanitarian intervention is perhaps to be found in the general readiness of states to act in defense of the balance of power and in order to preserve the society of independent states.

2. Third-State Remedies[10]

The traditional view is that remedies under public international law are bilateral and available only to states that have suffered an injury to their legal interests. This view is not necessarily correct. One can go back to Hugo Grotius to find support for the proposition that certain rules of law are or ought to be enforceable by any state, even in the absence of direct injuries. Early in this century Elihu Root argued that states engaging in the illegal use of force or taking other actions which constitute threats to law and order in the international community should be subject to unilateral remedies by third states. Throughout the history of international law, a role for third states in the enforcement of certain rules of international law has been advocated. Prior to World War II, some limited state practice in support of third state rights and duties may also be found. Situations of third state remedies have, however, been the exception to the general behavior of states, which limited the enforcement of international law by traditional means to states whose legal rights had been damaged directly by other states.

3. DEBATE: Resolved that the U.S. Intervention in Panama Violated International Law

a. Affirmative[11]

Only a few hours after ordering the U.S. military forces to Panama on December 20, 1989, President Bush explained that General Manuel Noriega had declared "a state of war with the United States and publicly threatened the lives of Americans in Panama." This, he said, had been followed by the murder of an unarmed American serviceman by Noriega's forces and beatings and harassment of others. He added that, as General Noriega's "reckless threats and attacks upon Americans in Panama" had created an "imminent danger to the 35,000 American citizens in Panama," he as President was obligated "to safeguard the lives of American citizens."

Subsequently, on January 3, 1990, when Noriega had turned himself in to U.S. military authorities in Panama and was en route to Homestead Air Force Base in Florida, President Bush declared that he had accomplished all four objectives for which he had ordered U.S. troops to Panama. These were: "To safeguard the lives of American citizens,

---

[9] By E.C. STOWELL, excerpted from: INTERNATIONAL LAW 349, 352 (1931). [Editor's Note: This classic statement is notable both for its recognition of humanitarian intervention and its obfuscation of any conceivable legal standard.]

[10] By JONATHAN I. CHARNEY, excerpted from: *Third State Remedies in International Law,* 10 MICHIGAN JOURNAL OF INTERNATIONAL LAW 57, 60–63 (1989). Reprinted by permission.

[11] By VED P. NANDA, excerpted from: *The Validity of United States Intervention in Panama Under International Law,* 84 AMERICAN JOURNAL OF INTERNATIONAL LAW 494 (1990). Reprinted by permission.

to help restore democracy, to protect the integrity of the Panama Canal Treaties, and to bring General Manuel Noriega to justice.'' He considered the return of Noriega to mark ''a significant milestone in Operation Just Cause,'' and said that the United States had ''used its resources in a manner consistent with political, diplomatic and moral principles.'' The failure to include ''legal'' among the other principles mentioned by President Bush may have been inadvertent. Earlier, Secretary of State James A. Baker III had justified the U.S. intervention by invoking Article 51 of the United Nations Charter and Article 21 of the Charter of the Organization of American States (OAS), which entitle the United States to act in self-defense.[12]

The inquiry into the validity of U.S. actions under international law must begin by identifying the relevant international law norms. The starting point is Article 2(4) of the UN Charter, which embodies the authoritative community proscription against ''the threat or use of force against the territorial integrity or political independence of any state or in any other manner inconsistent with the Purposes of the United Nations.''

Equally pertinent is Article 18 of the OAS Charter, which prohibits the use of force in language even more categorical than that of the UN Charter. It unequivocally rejects a state's claim of right to use force in another state's territory, or to ''intervene, directly or indirectly, for any reason whatever, in the internal or external affairs of any other State.'' This prohibition covers not only the use of armed force, but also ''any other form of interference or attempted threat against the personality of the State or against its political, economic, and cultural elements.'' It is noteworthy that in 1970 the UN General Assembly recognized the principle of nonintervention in the Declaration on Principles of International Law concerning Friendly Relations among States.

As to the pertinent principles of customary international law on the subject, the International Court of Justice has recognized nonintervention as an operative principle, founded on the respect for sovereignty and political integrity,[13] and has recently reiterated its rejection of intervention on the grounds of law and policy.[14] The following analysis addresses the inquiry: do the stated purposes of the Panama intervention fall within any of the exceptions under Article 51 of the UN Charter, Article 21 of the OAS Charter, or principles of customary international law prescribing the prohibition on the use of force?

1. *Humanitarian Intervention?* The doctrinal debate on the validity of ''humanitarian intervention'' continues.[15] In light of the normative ambiguities inherent in the concept and the very strong differing positions taken by authorities on questions of law and policy, prospects for an early consensus on the definition and scope of the doctrine, or on the applicable criteria to prevent its abuse, are slim. This much is, however, certain: that even those who advocate the validity and viability of this concept can justify only a limited and temporary unilateral intervention, only as a last resort, and only when it meets the twin criteria of necessity and proportionality in the use of force as required under customary international law. Additionally, such unilateral action is ultimately subject to community review. Thus, notwithstanding the lack of agreement on the proper interpretation of Article 51 of the UN Charter, while rescue operations of one's nationals might be considered permissible, the U.S. invasion of Panama does not satisfy the minimum required standards.

Clearly, tensions between Panama and the United States had been steadily rising even prior to Noriega's annulment of the May 1989 elections, and in the week preceding the armed invasion, the escalation of tensions between the two states was especially dramatic. On December 15, the Panamanian legislative body adopted a resolution formally declaring the country to be in a state of war with the United States. Simultaneously, Noriega was named ''Maximum Leader'' and given sweeping new powers. According to the resolution, the move was prompted by U.S. ''aggression'' and the economic sanctions in effect against Panama since 1988. However, the Bush administration did not seem to take these measures seriously, describing the Assembly's action as ''another hollow step in an attempt to force Noriega's rule on the Panamanian people.''[16] Deputy Secretary of State Eagleburger called it ''a charade and nonsense.'' In another public statement, a White House spokesman announced that U.S. troops had not changed their alert status because of the declaration. Yet tension continued to build in the country as confrontations between Panamanians and Americans increased.

Granted, Noriega's ''declaration of war'' against his powerful neighbor to the north was a clear provocation. Secretary Baker's rhetorical statement following the invasion summarizes the administration's public stance on the issue. After citing an unverified ''intelligence report that General Noriega was considering mounting an urban com-

---

[12] Excerpts from *Statement by Baker on U.S. Policy*, N.Y. TIMES, Dec. 21, 1989, at A9, col. 5.

[13] Corfu Channel case (UK v. Alb.), 1949 ICJ Rep. 4, 34 (Judgment of Apr. 9).

[14] Military and Paramilitary Activities in and against Nicaragua (Nicar. v. U.S.), Merits, 1986 ICJ Rep. 14, paras. 205, 258, 263 (Judgment of June 27).

[15] *See, e.g.*, FERNANDO TESON, HUMANITARIAN INTERVENTION (1988); RICHARD LILLICH (ed.), HUMANITARIAN INTERVENTION AND THE UNITED NATIONS (1973).

[16] *See Opposition Leader in Panama Rejects a Peace Offer from Noriega*, N.Y. TIMES, Dec. 17, 1989, at A5, col. 1.

mando attack on American citizens in a residential neighborhood," Secretary Baker stated:

> I cannot prove to you that this report was absolutely reliable, but I do know that if the President had failed to act as he did and Noriega's Dignity Battalions had killed or terrorized a dozen American families in Panama, you would be asking us today why didn't you act to prevent this kind of violence against our citizens?[17]

The tense situation, however, fails to qualify as a legal justification for the invasion under the test of "necessity." Nor can a full-scale invasion be considered a proportional response. The state of tension existing in Panama did not present an imminent danger to U.S. citizens. The most serious and repeatedly cited incident supposedly precipitating the invasion was a single occurrence on December 15 in which one U.S. Marine officer was killed by members of the Panamanian Defense Force, another was wounded, and a third was beaten and his wife threatened at a roadblock. And while there was no assurance that something similar would not happen again, the most serious incident after this one, and before the invasion, occurred when an American officer shot and wounded a Panamanian police officer, who, the American claimed, appeared to be reaching for a gun.

The incidents are serious, but the question is whether they warranted the launching of "Operation Just Cause"—a full-scale invasion, of a size not seen since the Vietnam War, and eventually consisting of 12,000 American invaders (added to the approximately 12,000 U.S. military personnel already stationed in Panama), helicopter gunships, artillery and other heavy firepower. The military attack resulted in the death of 26 Americans and over 700 Panamanians, mostly civilians, in addition to severe and widespread physical devastation, property damage and dislocation.

The conclusion is inescapable that the United States has failed to provide sufficient evidence to prove that the necessity prerequisite was met. But assuming that some level of intervention to protect U.S. nationals was justified, the scale of the operation and the prolonged period of intervention, coupled with the other objectives cited for the invasion, cast serious doubt on its having been a legitimate case of humanitarian intervention.

2. *Restoration of Democracy?* A second ground given for the United States intervention in Panama was the restoration of democracy. This argument is based upon the well-documented fact that General Noriega had climbed to power by the use of strong-arm tactics and remained in power against the clear expression of the will of the Panamanian people. In May 1989, he nullified the election of the U.S.-supported opposition candidate as Panama's next President.

While no one could deny the ongoing excesses under Noriega's autocratic rule, there is no legal basis for replacing that rule with democracy. No international legal instrument permits intervention to maintain or impose a democratic form of government in another state. Nor does state practice support an expansive interpretation of Article 2(4), which was advocated in the UN Security Council by then U.S. Ambassador Jeanne Kirkpatrick, following the U.S. invasion of Grenada in 1983. She argued that the language used in Article 2(4), "or in any other manner inconsistent with the purposes of the United Nations," provides "ample justification" for the use of force "in pursuit of the other values also inscribed in the Charter—freedom, democracy, peace."[18]

Her expansive reading of Article 2(4) should be rejected on the ground that even if the promotion of a democratic form of government were recognized as an overriding value of the international system, military intervention is unlikely to be an effective means of promoting democratic values. Foreign intervention prevents the genuine development of democracy:[19] if democratic forces are well developed in the target state, they will likely prevail without foreign assistance; if they are underdeveloped or nonexistent, a period of foreign-dominated "tutelage" is likely to follow, which is contrary to the concept of self-determination.

Finally, such a construction is not useful in determining legality or illegality at the time of the intervention. It is unclear whether it is the consequences of the intervention that are determinative of legality, or whether the intervener's intention is determinative, or both. In any case, if consequences are to be determinative, they cannot be judged until long after the fact. And whose standards are to be used to make that judgment? If intentions are to be considered, how are they to be discerned? What of the problem of multiple objectives and changing intentions? These problems create the danger of permitting justification of intervention in almost any case.

Appropriately, the justification of invasion for the sake of the institution of democracy has simply never been accepted. The majority of states does not view the right of self-determination to mean that there is a right of democratic representation or that the government must reflect the will of the majority of the people. The United States stands alone in making such a claim, and the community

---

[17] Excerpts from *Statement by Baker on U.S. Policy,* N.Y. TIMES, Dec. 21, 1989, at A9, col. 3.

[18] Dept. State Bull., No. 2081, December 1983, at 74.

[19] *See* Berry, *The Conflict Between United States Intervention and Promoting Democracy in the Third World,* 60 TEMPLE L.Q. 1015 (1987).

response at the United Nations and the OAS has appropriately been to reject the claim.[20]

3. *Apprehending Noriega?* Noriega's indictment by United States grand juries in Miami and Tampa reflects the longstanding U.S. practice of asserting extraterritorial legislative jurisdiction under the "effects" doctrine, or arguably under the "protective" principle. Accordingly, the U.S. courts are likely to exercise personal jurisdiction over Noriega, based upon his presence, notwithstanding criticism of this reach of U.S. legislative and judicial jurisdiction. This, however, does not justify invading Panama to bring Noriega before the courts. For not all means are permitted to accomplish even a lawful goal.

In light of the constraints on unilateral use of force, with only limited, specific exceptions considered permissible, it is unclear which international law principle the United States was invoking in its attempt to justify its action. Perhaps the United States has confused the domestic legality of bringing Noriega before a U.S. court and the international legality of such an act. The fact that Noriega is charged with drugtrafficking, an international crime, does not mitigate the illegality of the invasion. As the Government of Mexico said in response to the U.S. invasion, "the conduct of international crimes cannot be a motive for intervening in a sovereign nation."[21] Since a state has no authority to violate the territorial integrity of another state in order to apprehend an alleged criminal, the U.S. claim cannot be sustained.

4. *Conclusion.* The conclusion is disconcerting to an international lawyer—that the U.S. action was in disregard of the pertinent norms and principles of international law on the use of force. The intervention was evidently dictated by political considerations, in disregard of faithful adherence to the existing norms on the use of force. The international community's condemnation of the invasion at the United Nations and the OAS appropriately reflects this concern. Whatever political objectives President Bush might have achieved by this intervention, he certainly failed to appreciate that compliance with restraints on the use of force serves the long-term interests of the United States, and the world community as well.

[20] On Dec. 29, 1989, the UN General Assembly criticized the U.S. intervention by an overwhelming majority and in strong terms as "a flagrant violation of international law and of the independence, sovereignty and territorial integrity of States." See GA Res. 44/240 (Dec. 29, 1989). See also Doswald-Beck, *The Legal Validity of Military Intervention by Invitation of the Government,* 56 BYIL 189, 207 (1985). As for the OAS, *see, e.g., Criticism of U.S. Action Is Supported in 20-1 Vote,* N.Y. TIMES, Dec. 23, 1989, at A9, col. 5 (reporting vote of the OAS).

[21] N.Y. TIMES, Dec. 21, 1989, at A14, col. 1.

b. Second Affirmative[22]

In the fall of 1867, a powerful British expeditionary force, dispatched from India under the command of Field Marshall Lord Napier and conveyed by over 250 ships, began deploying on the Red Sea coast of Africa. Its mission: rescue two British emissaries and their several assistants who, together with a brace of other Europeans, had been imprisoned by the volatile Ethiopian Emperor Theodore.

After constructing a port, 20 miles of rail lines and a virtual city in the midst of a torrid wasteland, Napier's army, complete with 44 elephants for hauling the heavy guns, found its way through, up and around the daunting gorges of the Ethiopian highlands. Finally reaching the main base of the emperor after extraordinary exertions, it engaged and decimated his forces, destroyed his citadel, auctioned off the contents of his Treasury to generate bonuses for the troops, released the prisoners, marched 400 miles back to the coast pillaging as it went, dismantled the railroad and piers, and returned to India.

Alan Morehead, the Australian writer on whose account I have relied,[23] though opining that the British should have remained long enough to establish order in the empire, offers no final balance of the human and material costs paid by the British and Ethiopian peoples to support this vindication of Britain's honor, its interests and, of course, its rights. By rights I refer to the claims of those who governed the great imperial states of Europe and their North American progeny and to the pronouncements of the international legal scholars who gave a rational order and legitimacy aura to those claims.

When I heard President George Bush's justification for the invasion of Panama, this obscure historical episode burst from the vault of memory. And with it came the thought that Bush had managed at one and the same time to celebrate the end of one era and to illuminate the normative landscape of the next. In the light he has cast, it looks suspiciously like the landscape of the past, specifically of the Victorian imperial past.

But then the second thoughts marched in. The first of them paraded under the interrogative banner: "Can't we squeeze this case into the Charter paradigm?" The President, after all, implicitly invoked it—albeit in lay language—when he inveighed against Panamanian threats to the virtue of American matrons domiciled in Panama. The physical harassment of U.S. nationals had apparently grown in both gravity and frequency during the year pre-

[22] By TOM J. FARER, excerpted from: *Panama: Beyond the Charter Paradigm,* 84 AMERICAN JOURNAL OF INTERNATIONAL LAW 503 (1990). Reprinted by permission.

[23] *Alan Morehead,* THE BLUE NILE 205–74 (1962).

ceding the invasion. Some incidents were attributable to officials. Others had a more uncertain provenance. In neither case did the Noriega Government exhibit concern for the victims or interest in punishing those responsible. On the contrary, it contributed to an environment in which Panamanians could regard attacks on U.S. citizens as a blow for Panamanian dignity welcomed by the Government at its highest levels of responsibility.

Nothing in the United Nations Charter – the seminal textual source of the postwar paradigm of international order – or in any interpretative declaration of the General Assembly, or in any widely ratified international agreement recognizes defense of nationals as a justification for armed intervention. And on at least one occasion an intervention justified in part on this ground was condemned by the great majority of states. But since in the case of the U.S. invasion of Grenada, the factual predicate for the claim was conspicuously thin, the international response cannot fairly be interpreted as an indictment of the exculpatory theory as distinguished from its particular application.

The United States has consistently construed the Charter to allow rescue expeditions. France, Belgium and Israel are among the other countries that have effectively claimed a right to rescue. Within the international community of states, the expectation that governments enjoying the necessary means will continue to assert such a right is, I think, high. On those occasions when the member states of the United Nations have glossed the text of the Charter, as in the Declaration on Friendly Relations and the Definition of Aggression, they have not repudiated the claim. People being a necessary condition for the existence of a state, the protection of nationals can be assimilated without great strain to the right of self-defense explicitly conceded in the text of the Charter.

Taking these several factors into account, rescue missions cannot be persuasively indicted as violations of international law, as long as they comply with the principles of proportionality and necessity and are not tainted by ulterior motives. The normative problem with Bush's Panamanian end game is precisely his difficulty in demonstrating compliance with the limiting conditions for lawful rescue.

The growing insecurity of U.S. nationals stemmed directly from U.S. efforts to effect the removal of Manuel Noriega as commander of Panama's armed forces and de facto head of state. It therefore seems likely that the United States could have ended the campaign of harassment by agreeing to end its campaign against Noriega. That alternative means being available for protecting the security of U.S. nationals, how could the Bush administration plead necessity? Only by demonstrating that the alternative would require the surrender of another legal right the United States was entitled to maintain.

The point becomes clearer by analogy to a hypothetical municipal law case. Imagine a certain tough and affluent gentleman by the name of Crossdouble, habituated to short cuts in all the realms of life, who chooses to reach his office each day by strolling across a business associate's garden and pushing through a topiary hedge. Despite the wear and tear on his topiary, for many years Crossdouble's associate, a Mr. Beagan, tolerates this eccentricity as one of the costs of doing business. But the time comes when, finding that on balance their dealings are no longer profitable, Beagan withdraws from the association. Crossdouble, indifferent to this change in circumstance, continues his diurnal stroll.

Aggrieved by the ragged state of his topiary and no longer inhibited by avarice, Beagan posts "No Trespassing" signs which deter his former associate not in the least. Neither personal appeals nor appeals addressed through mutual acquaintances alter Crossdouble's habit. Finally, convinced that the man is intractable, Beagan files a complaint with the city attorney, who then has Crossdouble arrested and charged with malicious trespass.

After posting bail, the now-enraged stroller, accompanied by two husky employees, proceeds at dusk to his antagonist's home, kicks in the front door, batters the complainant, sexually threatens his wife, warns of more serious measures unless the complaint is withdrawn forthwith, kicks out the back door, strolls across the garden, and pushes his way with more than usual force through the topiary.

Beagan takes two aspirin, ices down his jaw, and then journeys again to the police station. The officer he consults, though sympathetic, advises him to consider dropping the charges. "We can't guard your house night and day. And who knows what this guy might do: kidnap your children; rape your wife; drain your pool. Be practical: either pay him to walk around rather than through your place or simply ignore the creep. After all, aside from a few bruised bushes and the bruises to your ego from having to put up with the guy, he's not really doing much damage."

Unpersuaded, the man goes home, loads the high-caliber weapon he purchased years before to shoot elephant in Africa, and waits patiently until Crossdouble again arrives and kicks the door open. Whereupon the latter is retired by a bullet that passes through him and, regrettably, two neighbors sitting at home across the street watching television.

The White House presumably sees Panama as an a fortiori case because it occurs within a political system lacking police and courts. In their absence, self-help must be deemed a normal means for vindicating rights. To maintain his plea of necessity, then, President Bush must demonstrate that the United States had a right to force Noriega's expulsion from Panama.

Article 18 of the Charter of the Organization of American States (OAS), to which the United States is a party, provides:

> No State . . . has the right to intervene, directly or indirectly, for any reason whatever, in the internal or external affairs of any other State. The foregoing principle prohibits not only armed force but also any other form of interference or attempted threat against the personality of the State or against its political, economic, and cultural elements.

Taken literally, this language would outlaw diplomacy. Beneath the froth of its hyperbole, however, it expresses the central structural principle of the postwar international legal system – equal sovereignty for all nation-states. If sovereignty means anything, it means that one state cannot compromise another state's territorial integrity or dictate the character or the occupants of its governing institutions. If the law allows any exception to this constraint on state behavior, surely it is only where the exception is required to preserve the rule. In other words, consistent with the structural principle, one state may manipulate the politics of another only where the latter's behavior or internal condition leaves the former with no alternative means for defending its own political independence and territorial integrity. Thus, the trail of the claim of necessity for the invasion leads back to a claim of necessity for efforts to dictate who would govern Panama.

The history of the present era begins with the effective assertion of such a claim by the victorious Allies at the close of World War II, who set about transforming the German and Japanese political orders. Since then its occasional, sometimes implicit, assertion has produced a body of precedent providing very doubtful support for the claim other than in its original context: the aftermath of an all-out war of self-defense.

From the outset of the Cold War, the United States acted as if the emergence anywhere in the hemisphere of a government it deemed Marxist so threatened the sovereignty of this nation or its allies as to justify measures to abort or overthrow the offending regime. A 1954 resolution of the OAS Foreign Ministers, adopted at the instance of the United States, declaring in effect that the appearance of a Marxist regime in the Western Hemisphere would constitute a threat to its peace and security, seemed to endorse this view, an impression reinforced by the Organization's supine response to the CIA-orchestrated overthrow of Guatemala's duly elected government later that year. Nevertheless, the clandestine character of the U.S. role evinced skepticism even in Washington about the legal basis for intervention. Washington's skepticism was underlined in 1961 when President John F. Kennedy was unwilling to authorize an open U.S. commitment to the Bay of Pigs assault on Fidel Castro's Government.

The Soviet Union's undisguised enforcement of a comparable national security claim in Eastern Europe – Hungary (1956) and Czechoslovakia (1968) – evoked large hostile majorities in the United Nations. And the more recent invasion of Afghanistan – resting, if anywhere, on this type of claim – elicited almost universal condemnation. Even when linked plausibly to the alleviation of gross violations of human rights – Tanzania and Uganda; India and East Pakistan; Vietnam and Cambodia – the claim has encountered widespread hostility. Vietnam had a particularly strong case: it intervened to replace an unassuageable, ideologically demented government perpetrating a holocaust against the Khmer majority, brutalizing its Vietnamese minority, and periodically violating Vietnam's territorial integrity through violent incursions. And yet Hanoi has confronted unrelenting antagonism from every regional and ideological voting bloc in the United Nations other than the Soviet Union and its closest allies. The failure of Vietnam to win recognition for the political changes it wrought is probably attributable, however, to its refusal to allow an expression of popular will in the wake of its occupation. Had fair elections been held, I suspect that the resulting government would have been seated at the United Nations (as was the Government of Bangladesh following India's intervention).

If these precedents are not an insuperable, they are at least a formidable, barrier to justifying a campaign for Noriega's ouster, a barrier that Bush himself has not really attempted to scale. Were he inclined to make the attempt, he would have to show three things. First, that shipping narcotics across a frontier is as much a violation of territorial integrity as shipping troops and therefore triggers a right of self-defense; second, that Noriega played a significant, continuing role in facilitating violation; and third, that Noriega was unwilling to end collusion in the narcotics trade even when threatened with a campaign for his ouster (the threat being a less serious affront to domestic jurisdiction than the actual ouster).

The third element in the Bush administration's case for a right to force Noriega's expulsion from Panamanian political life, a more-or-less pure question of fact, poses the fewest difficulties for the administration. True, in his negotiations with Washington, Noriega's overriding concern seemed to be safety from prosecution, not continuance of his illegal enterprise. Would Noriega have rejected an offer to overlook past transgressions on condition that he withdraw from the drug trade, an offer backed by the threat of removing or terminating him should he prove intransigent? The administration has not so alleged. But it might reasonably claim that Noriega's malodorous history offered ample grounds for assuming the worthlessness of any pledge he might make.

The first element, a question of international community

policy that has not yet been openly addressed, poses greater difficulties. An affirmative answer will substantially broaden the legitimate occasions for the use of force: Noriega's is neither the first nor likely to be the last government to become involved in the narcotics trade; pollutants including toxic wastes are other deeply injurious substances that can be pushed across frontiers. The precedent is not easily contained.

The second element is partially a question of fact, partially one of assessment. Accepting as true all the allegations made to date about Noriega's role in the drug trade leads one, I fear ineluctably, to the conclusion that the Panamanian was no more than a small cog, a convenience. Even the White House has not claimed that Noriega's capture will conspicuously affect the quantity of narcotics reaching this country. It appears, moreover, that Noriega was not directly involved in either production or delivery: neither he personally nor persons reporting to him actually launched or guided the narcotics on their trajectory into the United States. The less important and the more indirect his role, the weaker the argument for treating his actions as the equivalent of an ongoing armed attack on United States territory.

Thus, as part of the effort to squeeze its Panama expedition into the Charter paradigm of legality, the Bush administration must defend the proposition that under the Charter, one state can compel a change of government in another for reasons other than defense of its own political independence or territorial integrity. The Brezhnev Doctrine's applications and the U.S. invasion first of Grenada and now of Panama have implicitly tested the proposition's acceptability. One could of course try explaining away the international community's adverse response, expressed through a multitude of unilateral declarations and votes in the political organs of the United Nations and the Organization of American States, by emphasizing the special circumstances of each case. But that ploy is not very effective in an instance like this where one faces a heavy presumption of incompatibility between the proposed doctrine and Charter norms. After all, if most states and scholars find any violent after-the-fact punishment of an armed attack (i.e., a reprisal) to be forbidden by the Charter, a fortiori they will find a breach of Charter norms where a regime guilty of some lesser delinquency is punished by death.

To this point, I have proceeded on the basis of four assumptions adopted for purposes of sharpening the focus on certain of the legal issues raised by the invasion. Those assumptions are: first, that Noriega and his associates were, for purposes of international law, the "legitimate" Government of Panama; second, that President Bush could have ended the harassment of U.S. nationals by ending efforts to overthrow Noriega; third, that no means for protecting U.S. nationals in Panama other than the invasion or negotiation of a modus vivendi with Noriega were available; and fourth, that the only relevant norms for measuring the propriety of United States conduct are those that stem from the Charter.

The first assumption is simply the application to the case of Panama of the virtually uniform practice in international relations of treating any group of nationals in effective control of their state as constituting its legitimate government. One occasionally conceded exception to that practice is where local elements, having ridden to power on the back of an invader (Afghanistan, Cambodia), rely for survival on the invader's continuing occupation of their country.

In the case of Panama, the Permanent Council of the OAS initially refused to accept the credentials of the ambassador dispatched by Guillermo Endara to represent Panama. The Noriega regime's ambassador continued to participate and joined in the vote deploring the invasion. Only after the U.S. occupation was secure and Endara had begun to function as head of local administration did the Council relent. What Endara still had not achieved by the end of January 1990, despite the total rout of Noriega and his supporters, was general recognition, by the Latin governments acting individually, as the legitimate head of state.

For tactical or ideological reasons, many governments have refused to tender formal recognition to well-established regimes. The United States waited more than two decades before recognizing the Communist regime in Beijing as the Government of China. But even Washington did not claim during the preceding two decades that it was thereby free under the Charter to assist the Nationalist remnant on Taiwan in reconquering the mainland. It was, in short, universally conceded that by virtue of having won the civil war, the Communist leaders in Beijing formed the Government of China and therefore enjoyed the protection from foreign intervention afforded to all states by the United Nations Charter. If control were not generally regarded as insulating those exercising it from armed intervention, the United States would presumably have withdrawn recognition from the Sandinista regime so as to facilitate aid to the contras.

The continued felt utility of treating effective control as a sufficient condition of de facto legitimacy can sometimes seem repulsive from a moral perspective. But by allowing legitimacy to turn on a single fact that is relatively easy to verify, the practice serves the important policy of inhibiting intervention. Thus, it protects the central Charter value of national autonomy.

The second assumption is a question of fact. Nothing thus far said by the Bush administration or revealed by any other source provides reason to doubt its correspondence to reality.

The third assumption, conversely, is almost certainly

false. An intimidating display—for example, positioning carrier groups off both Panamanian coasts and tripling the assault forces marshaled on our Panamanian bases—coupled with an unambiguous statement of intention to seize Noriega and to dissolve the Panamanian Defense Forces (PDF) if Noriega were not gone by a specified date, would probably have sufficed to induce either Noriega's resignation or his removal by fellow officers. In the unlikely event he had responded by marshaling loyalists and seizing large numbers of American hostages, setting explosive charges around key mechanical components of the canal, and/or preparing to block the canal by sinking ships at key points, U.S. forces could have been withdrawn, the status quo ante restored, and plans then put in place for the surprise attack we subsequently launched. Noriega's voluntary departure, no doubt to a country where he would enjoy immunity from extradition, would have frustrated the aspiration to convict him in an American court. Departure compelled by fellow officers would have left Panama in their parasitic grip.

The dual objectives of removing Noriega and ending harassment of U.S. nationals might also have been achieved if the principal Latin American governments could have been induced to apply more intense political pressure on Noriega and his colleagues. At no time did the Latin heads of state call unequivocally for Noriega's departure. At no time were they prepared to call his continuance in office a threat to the peace and security of the hemisphere.[24] At no time were they willing to declare that, as a consequence of his theft of the last presidential election, sovereignty had passed to the people themselves or to their evident choice in the 1988 presidential election, Guillermo Endara.

Fear of providing a legal justification for U.S. intervention no doubt lay at the heart of their reluctance. Supplementing it was a perception of Washington's implication in the chain of circumstances that had left Panamanians without the capacity to remove the incubus of Noriega and his colleagues. The United States had fostered the expansion and professional training of the PDF. Noriega, if not other officers, had been on Washington's payroll. The United States had winked at previous electoral charades, including the presidential election of 1984.

Another factor behind Latin reluctance to follow the OAS precedent in the Somoza case and declare Noriega's Government illegitimate was the absence of massive violations of the right to life and personal security. Whatever Noriega might have been willing to do had circumstances required it, his actual delinquencies were modest compared, for example, to those of the Salvadoran and Guatemalan armed forces who have enjoyed Washington's patronage.

Nevertheless, if Washington had informed the Latin governments of its determination to act unilaterally as a last resort but declared its preference for a Latin-led process and its willingness to exercise patience if the Latin governments would commit themselves to Noriega's removal by one means or another, they might have overcome their reluctance in order to abort yet another unilateral intervention. Latin America lost an opportunity to initiate an authentically multilateral operation from which the United States could not easily have withdrawn. The United States lost an opportunity to escape from the traditional, sterile confrontation between claims of absolute nonintervention on one side and an imperious unilateralism on the other. The result is a cloudy prospect for closer collaboration in dealing with transnational issues of ever-growing importance both to Latin America and to the United States.

Withdrawal of U.S. nationals from Panama was, of course, another way of protecting them without recourse to measures—invasion and destruction of the de facto Government—peculiarly hard to reconcile with the Charter paradigm. Was the United States entitled to ignore this alternative on the grounds that (1) it amounted to the surrender of legal rights, and (2) their surrender is not required by the principle that means short of force be exhausted before recourse to violence?

Much could be said, for instance, about the issue of proportionality. While the harassment of U.S. nationals was increasing, the few cases of serious injury or death seem to have occurred from inadvertent encounters with low-level operatives. If the available evidence indicated no more than an intention on the part of the Noriega Government to continue harassment at about the same intensity and the least destructive way of preventing continuation was an invasion calculated to cause death or serious injury to several thousand Panamanians and the destruction of the homes and businesses of many thousands more, can the criterion of proportionality be satisfied? Or is proportionality nothing more than a requirement that the damage imposed not be in excess of that required to attain a lawful objective? Does actual or anticipated resistance progressively expand the quantity of force that may be imposed, so that even if the original objective would not justify the infliction of extensive injuries to persons and property, the permissible degree of damage expands with the resistance, each act of resistance constituting an additional violation of the attacking state's rights?

I happily leave these questions to others, in part because, like the issues I have addressed, they belong more to the kinder and gentler world of legal scholarship than to the austere realm of politics. No fair-minded person can examine the words of the President, his colleagues, and the numerous media mavens who have celebrated this splendid little war without concluding that if they rest their case on any normative paradigm, it surely is not one derivable primarily from the Charter. Their views, identical in substance to those propounded with less polish and pretension in one's neighborhood bar, were nicely summarized by that ne plus ultra of conventional thought, the Washington Post columnist David Broder.

---

[24] [Editor's Note: Compare the silence of many Middle Eastern Islamic leaders as to the leadership of Saddam Hussein in Iraq; they were reluctant to condemn him even after he committed blatant aggression against Kuwait!]

The Panama invasion, he has written, satisfied the six criteria for committing American forces laid down by the former Secretary of Defense, Caspar Weinberger, and, Broder insists, subsequently endorsed in their essence by the foreign policy spokesperson for the last Democratic presidential candidate. The engagement must be "vital to our national interest"; we must commit our troops "wholeheartedly and with the clear intention of winning"; we must have "clearly defined political and military objectives" and know "precisely how our forces can accomplish those objectives"; "the objectives and forces must be consonant in style," that is, we must not get "halfway involved"; there must be "reasonable assurance we will have the support of the American people and their elected representatives in Congress"; and "the commitment of U.S. forces to combat should be a last resort." "The Panama invasion," Broder concludes, "met all of those tests."[25]

Broder's piece nicely illustrates the difficulty of getting frail human intellects to apply any test consistently. To declare Noriega's overthrow a vital national interest is to give new and less meaning to the word "vital." Here in action is the Humpty-Dumpty school of linguistic usage. As for force being the last resort, it can always be made that by the sequential failure to exercise other options. But whatever else one may think of the formula or its application to this case, it clearly has nothing to do with conventional legal norms. Nor does it rest on any evident moral ones other than a kind of crude national utilitarianism. Unlike the powerful Aquinian Just War paradigm, it requires no just cause for the use of force.

The apparent absence of an appealing paradigm in the minds of the officials who launched the war and the pundits who leaped to its defense does not preclude the possibility that one might be found elsewhere. Noriega and his colleagues were ugly parasites who had attached themselves firmly to the body of the Panamanian people. Unlike his predecessor, Omar Torrijos, Noriega was not successful in employing populist themes to build a substantial base in the civilian population; the last election revealed a huge hostile majority. In a moral sense, he was not the country's legitimate ruler.

Unlike many other thugs who currently reign over people imprisoned in their own countries, he employed the power of the state to advance a criminal conspiracy to violate the laws of another country. In short, the United States did have a just cause for caging the tyrant; indeed, it had two: he had violated the rights of this country; he had violated the rights of the Panamanian people. And by its earlier actions – strengthening the PDF; ignoring its delinquencies, and corrupting the man who became its commander – the United States was substantially responsible for his grip on Panama.

The United States is now able during this period of political and economic reconstruction in Panama to demonstrate compliance with certain other necessary conditions of a just war. Let us suppose that the President and the Congress extend aid generously, particularly to those civilians directly injured by the invasion. Let us further suppose that the administration resists the temptation to reassemble the PDF with its conventional Latin American officer corps – self-governing and -perpetuating – for service as a U.S. surrogate maintaining order in the country. And finally let us suppose that the United States takes other steps to give Panamanians a fair chance for the first time in their national history to achieve real democracy and autonomy. In that event, those who for understandable reasons have judged us harshly may look back on the invasion and say that although we acted outside the old law and proposed no new one, at least we intended to do good and were not clearly imprudent in calculating that more good than evil would result from our acts.

Whether George Bush ever attempted such a calculation is, as they say, "a nice question." Even those inclined to give Presidents the benefit of the doubt may wonder whether Alan Morehead's final explanation of the British descent on Ethiopia is not, after all, a fit epitaph for Bush in Panama:

> The British sought no gain of any kind, and they had no quarrel with the Ethiopian people. . . . The whole vast expensive operation was nothing more nor less than a matter of racial pride; Theodore had affronted a great power and now he was to be punished."[26]

c. Negative[27]

What Professors Tom Farer and Ved Nanda do not seem to understand is the positive implication for the development of human rights resulting from the United States intervention in Panama. Their views are so conditioned by a statist conception of international law that they seem unable to see through the abstraction that we call the "state" to the reality of human beings struggling to achieve basic freedoms. I am not talking about the human rights of American "matrons domiciled in Panama," as Professor Farer puts it, who were "rescued" in 19th-century expeditionary-force style. Rather, I am talking about the human rights of Panamanian citizens to be free from oppression by a gang of ruling thugs. My focus is on the basic civil liberties and fundamental freedoms of the people of Panama themselves.

Although I am confident that Professors Farer and

---

25 WASH. POST, Jan. 14, 1990, at B7.

26 ALAN MOREHEAD, THE BLUE NILE 258 (1962).

27 By ANTHONY D'AMATO, excerpted from: *The Invasion of Panama Was a Lawful Response to Tyranny,* 84 AMERICAN JOURNAL OF INTERNATIONAL LAW 516 (1990). Reprinted by permission.

Nanda are personally committed to the cause of human rights, it seems that when they put on their formalistic hats and talk about international law, they revert to the Oppenheimian notion that international law is all about states and not at all about people.

For example, Professor Farer says that "if sovereignty means anything, it means that one state cannot compromise another state's territorial integrity or dictate the character or the occupants of its governing institutions." But why should "sovereignty" mean anything? Who assigns it its meaning? Why should its meaning have legal consequences? How is even its Fareian meaning compatible with the enforcement against states of the evolving rules of international law? Professor Farer—according to his own "Humpty-Dumpty school of linguistic usage"—may proclaim that his words mean only what he wants them to mean, but is he entitled to exercise definitional sovereignty over others?

Professor Nanda joins Professor Farer in relying upon Article 18 of the OAS Charter to say that international law denies to any state the right to intervene directly or indirectly in the internal or external affairs of any other state. I do not doubt that the representatives of states at the OAS in 1948 wanted such a principle—they adopted it without much debate. But I will argue that the wishes of those representatives and their academic apologists are far less important to international law than the actual customary-law-generating behavior of states. The U.S. interventions in Panama and, previously, in Grenada are milestones along the path to a new nonstatist conception of international law that changes previous nonintervention formulas such as Article 18.

Like Professor Farer, I want to illustrate my argument by an analogy. In the 19th century, United States courts refused to intervene when wives applied for judicial help against beatings inflicted by their husbands. Some judges repeated the saying, "A man's home is his castle." Most judges observed that the wife has an adequate remedy if her husband hits her—she can sue for a divorce. And nearly all judges opined that intrusion by the "heavy hand of the state" would provide a cure that was worse than the disease. Simple prudence, according to the judges, required a judicial policy of abstention from domestic problems. And what was considered prudent rapidly became transformed into a "neutral principle"—that the law will not intervene in the home on behalf of either spouse.

Courts now recognize that battered wives need and deserve judicial protection. Historians look back at the 19th century and speculate about how much brutality, how much horror, women had to endure at the hands of physically stronger spouses who treated them like chattel. Law students recognize that 19th-century judicial abstention from battery in the home was not the "neutral principle" it was advertised to be; rather, its apparent evenhandedness served to insulate the physically stronger marriage partner against any external compensatory force that could be provided by the police. And legal philosophers now realize that words found so abundantly in the old opinions such as "home" and "domestic" and "marriage" do not stake out lines of jurisdiction but, rather, beg the question of where and for what purposes there ought to be jurisdiction.

The citizens of Panama were as powerless against Noriega and his henchmen as the 19th-century American wives were against physically stronger husbands. In describing Noriega's rule, we should discard loaded words like "government," "legitimate," "authority," "army," "police," and so forth. These words only serve to dull our senses against the reality of power by begging the very question that is the subject of the present debate—whether Panama's borders should be treated as an exclusive reservation of "domestic jurisdiction" to Noriega or whether those borders should be permeable for some purposes.

Noriega ruled Panama because he and his co-thugs controlled the guns, rockets, mortar, truncheons and tear gas. Any citizen who defied Noriega by rational argument risked being answered by bullets. Jails were used to hold political prisoners—citizens who disagreed too loudly with Noriega. Somehow, miraculously, there was an election in May 1989, and Noriega's candidate was defeated. No matter; Noriega had the power. The opposition candidates appealed to reason, to fairness, to the will of the people; Noriega invoked the logic of brute force, of steel, of gunpowder, of the infliction of imprisonment and disappearance. The electoral victors were crushed.

Did Noriega have any "right" to rape Panama for his own ends, to exult in unrestrained power, to ignore or trample on the rights and needs of the people who were his "subjects"? If he had any "right" under Panamanian law, it was because he made that law. (The 19th-century husband also "made the rules" of the household and was himself "above the law"—if his wife did not like it, he could "*make* her like it" by the application of force.) What about a "right" under international law? Professors Farer and Nanda wish to interpret international law in such a way that it hands Noriega such a right on a silver platter.

Professor Farer makes his argument with commendable half-heartedness. He puts quotation marks around the word "legitimate" when he says that "Noriega and his associates were, for purposes of international law, the 'legitimate' Government of Panama." But it is a crabbed 19th-century interpretation of international law that Professor Farer here invokes, and he signals his reluctance to invoke it by the quotation marks. He concedes that his legitimacy argument "can sometimes seem repulsive from a moral perspective." We may well wonder why so sensitive an observer of international relations as Professor Farer feels compelled to brush morality aside. He writes:

> But by allowing legitimacy to turn on a single fact that is relatively easy to verify, the practice serves the important policy of inhibiting intervention. Thus, it protects the central Charter value of national autonomy.

In other words, Professor Farer has been carried away by the rhetoric of statism. He urges us to treat states tenderly even at the morally repulsive cost of refusing to help the citizenry get out from under tyrannical rule. According to Farer, because we can easily tell that Noriega was in charge of Panama (just look at his guns, his brutality, the fact that he ran local television), this easy identification "serves the important policy of inhibiting intervention." But what connection is there between readily identifying the head of state and inhibiting intervention? Would Professor Farer accept intervention in a country where the people govern themselves through town meetings, because in such a country the fact of who's in charge is not easy to verify? Since when, and by whom, was ease of identification elevated to one of the most important values in the international system? And does not his entire argument of ease of identification presuppose the question whether intervention should be inhibited? What about his last sentence—"the central Charter value of national autonomy"? Who proclaimed this to be the central value of the UN Charter? Whatever happened to human rights? A glance at the Preamble to the UN Charter reveals its affirmation of "faith in fundamental human rights," "social progress," and "economic and social advancement of all peoples"; there is no mention of national autonomy.

Professor Nanda refers more directly than does Professor Farer to the problem of Noriega's "autocratic rule," "strong-arm tactics," and nullification of the election of May 1989. Nevertheless, Professor Nanda can find "no legal basis for replacing that rule with democracy." Here, at least, I agree with the rhetoric of Professor Nanda's statement: surely there is no Wilsonian principle of international law that permits intervention to impose a democratic form of government in another state, any more than there is a Brezhnev Doctrine in international law that permits intervention to impose or restore a socialist or Communist form of government. But concepts such as "democracy" and "socialism" are profoundly beside the point. Again, consider the 19th-century battered wife. She was not appealing to the courts to impose a particular form of government in her household; rather, she sought protection from brutality and enslavement. Analogously, at the governmental level, the question we should ask is not what intervention is for but what it is against. I argue that human rights law demands intervention against tyranny. I do not argue that intervention is justified to establish democracy, aristocracy, socialism, communism or any other form of government. But if any of these forms of government become in the Aristotelian sense corrupted,[28] resulting in tyranny against their populations—and I regard "tyranny" as occurring when those who have monopolistic control of the weapons and instruments of suppression in a country turn those weapons and instruments against their own people[29]—I believe that intervention from outside is not only legally justified but morally required.

However, there are several interim questions that can be raised about the argument I have sketched so far. Among the more conspicuous are the following:

1. What country may intervene? My preference would clearly be in favor of multilateral intervention, such as that of France, Great Britain, and Russia in the Greco-Turkish conflict of 1827, one of the earliest cases of humanitarian intervention.[30] Today, the best "intervener" would be the United Nations. Regional arrangements would be preferable to unilateral action. But my bottom line is that any nation with the will and the resources may intervene to protect the population of another nation against the kind of tyranny that was about to gain a foothold in Grenada in 1983 (when a group of thugs machine-gunned their way into power, murdering the existing democratic rulers), and against the kind of tyranny exhibited by Noriega in Panama. Although I would have preferred other Latin American nations to have joined in the intervention in both these cases, since they declined it was left to the United States to safeguard unilaterally the fundamental freedoms of the people of Grenada and of Panama.

2. Did the United States have a right to invade Panama to arrest Noriega because he was under indictment in Florida for dealing in drugs? Professors Farer and Nanda have rehearsed the reasons given by President Bush for the Panamanian action, but they do not necessarily constitute justification under international law. The only reason he gave that even comes close to the justificatory reason I have suggested in this paper is "to help restore democracy." No matter; a state is not required under international law to cite valid international law reasons for its actions.[31] Inter-

---

28 *See* ARISTOTLE, POLITICA, bk. III, chs. 6–13.

29 A good elaboration of this definition is found in JAMES S. FISHKIN, TYRANNY AND LEGITIMACY: A CRITIQUE OF POLITICAL THEORIES 12–25 (1979).

30 The intervention, claimed to be under the auspices of the Treaty of Locarno, was aimed at protecting Christians who were being persecuted by Turkey. See 1 L. OPPENHEIM, INTERNATIONAL LAW 312–13 (H. Lauterpacht 8th ed. 1955).

31 Nor is there any requirement that the intervention be actuated by a legally proper motive. In the case of governments, it is impossible to tell what motivated the action, and if the government explains its motivation, it is still impossible to tell whether the explanation is accurate. I have attempted to spell this out more fully in A. D'AMATO, THE CONCEPT OF CUSTOM IN INTERNATIONAL LAW 34–39 (1971).

national lawyers may appropriately evaluate the actions states undertake on the basis of customary international law irrespective of verbal rationales proffered by the states themselves.[32]

3. Did the United States violate Article 2(4) of the Charter? There is no doubt that under our present understanding of international law the use of military force for the purpose of territorial aggrandizement or colonialism violates customary international law. Nor is there any doubt that such use of force would not count as humanitarian intervention even if appropriately disguised at the time – rather, it would be regarded as pure aggression. I submit that the core intent of Article 2(4) was to secure these understandings.[33] Accordingly, the U.S. forcible intervention in Panama did not violate Article 2(4) because the United States did not act against the "territorial integrity" of Panama: there was never an intent to annex part or all of Panamanian territory, and hence the intervention left the territorial integrity of Panama intact. Nor was the use of force directed against the "political independence" of Panama: the United States did not intend to, and has not, colonialized, annexed or incorporated Panama. Before and after the intervention, Panama was and remains an independent nation.

4. Who determines whether a target nation is under tyrannical rule? This question is a variant on the formalist objection to any transboundary use of force: the asserted relativity of justification. Scholars such as Professor Oscar Schachter prefer "neutral" rules that totally outlaw transboundary force, despairing of the imagined subjectivity that would be involved in any attempt to determine whether a given use of force was justified.[34] Such a position seems good in theory, but inevitably deconstructs itself. For example, Professor Schachter must admit a loophole for the use of force in self-defense,[35] but it is a loophole that grows wider the more one looks at it. Any state can claim that it has acted in self-defense, and in many cases the mere claim will seem credible. If in some cases it appears strained, the aggressor can cover by using the phrase "anticipatory self-defense." The fact is that we cannot delineate "self-defense" in advance to cover future contingencies of often-increasing complexity. Generally speaking, neutral-sounding formulas are not and cannot be self-interpreting; rather, in any case of real-world aggression, there will be disputes as to the meaning and applicability of such formulas. The end result is that all the facts and circumstances surrounding the alleged aggression will have to be taken into account in assessing whether or not it was an illegal aggression. Hence, Professor Schachter's position does not and cannot do the job it sets out to do – to prevent subjective interpretation of rules of law – but, rather, will only serve to divert scholars from the real values at stake and instead lead them into academic, abstract and formalistic linguistic exercises.

Since the job of looking at the facts and circumstances has to be done by the international lawyer anyway, I claim that my position is certainly no more problematic than Professor Schachter's. I assert that we must inquire into the factual situation whether Noriega was a tyrannical ruler. The term "tyrannical" is almost as vague as the term "aggression,"[36] but not quite – though people may differ on the range of behavior that constitutes tyranny, there is probably consensus both outside and inside Panama that Noriega fits the bill. Certainly neither Professor Farer nor Professor Nanda disputes Noriega's entitlement to the status of "tyrant."

Another way of stating my point is that there is no "objective" language in international law. All rules of law must be interpreted; all interpretation varies with context; all interpretation is necessarily subjective. We are better off with rules of international law that at least point us to important factual and contextual considerations than we are with rules that point us only to an endless series of subrules, explanatory rules and learned commentary regarding the interpretation of all of those rules – commentary that then itself must be interpreted. The important factual and contextual considerations in the present case, I submit, are whether the people of Panama were helpless under a tyrannical rule and deserved, in morality and in law, aid from an outside power to remove the unlawful government that was brutalizing them. The factual situation of the people of Panama cannot be determined by consulting textbooks on the legality and exceptions regarding the use of force in international relations.

5. How can the death of over seven hundred innocent

---

32 *Pace* the curious argument of Michael Akehurst that what states say is more important than what they do. Akehurst, *Custom as a Source of International Law*, 47 BYIL 1 (1974-75). He seems to have forgotten that Professor Henry Higgins' observation in *My Fair Lady* was meant to be *ironic*: "The French don't actually care what you do, as long as you *pronounce* it properly!"

33 The proof is not easy, and requires detailed exegesis of historical developmental texts. I have made an attempt along that line in ANTHONY D'AMATO, INTERNATIONAL LAW: PROCESS AND PROSPECT 57-73 (1987).

34 *See* Oscar Schachter, *International Law in Theory and Practice*, 178 RECUEIL DES COURS 13, 58–60 ("The Quest for Objectivity"), 133–87 (use of force and exceptions) (1982 V).

35 *Id.* at 150–66.

36 The term "aggression" is notoriously vague and ambiguous. Consider the dispute as to which side was the aggressor in the recent Iran-Iraq War or in the Vietnam War (North Vietnam or the United States?). Consider also the various types of aggression that have been seriously suggested in the United Nations, such as cultural aggression and economic aggression. If nation A commits cultural aggression against nation B, may B counter militarily against A and call its response "self-defense"?

Panamanian citizens be justified? I believe that the United States used too *few* troops (some 24,000) in the military attack on Panama, with the result that these troops overcompensated for their small numbers by the disproportionate use of force.[37] If at least ten times that number had been deployed, such an overwhelming presence of military forces would have reduced their felt need for firing their weapons. Moreover, in the presence of such superior numbers, Noriega's defenders may have surrendered much sooner. It is extremely ironic that the legal uneasiness felt by the United States in undertaking the Panamanian operation – reflected in the kinds of arguments Professors Farer and Nanda have put forth, arguments that were surely mooted at the time in top decisional circles – probably led to the deployment of as few troops as possible. There was undoubtedly a fear that a massive use of troops would appear somehow to be a greater violation of international law. If, instead, the position that I am urging had been the consensus position among American international lawyers and advisers to President Bush, more troops may well have been deployed with a consequent reduction in civilian casualties. Thus, the very fear that the Panamanian intervention was illegal became, in the event, ironically self-confirmatory with respect to the unfortunately high number of civilian casualties.

No matter how I interpret Article 2(4) of the UN Charter, Professors Nanda and Farer would say that a different provision of a different multilateral treaty – Article 18 of the OAS Charter – shuts the door tightly against any form of transboundary military intervention. I will not undertake a textual analysis of Article 18, replete though it is with vast ambiguities (as Professor Farer concedes). Rather, let us assume that the text could be cited for the proposition that Professors Nanda and Farer want. I could make, although at the present time it might be unpersuasive to make, the following argument:

Article 18 is the self-interested expression of ruling elites of Latin American countries establishing a nonintervention cartel so that they will each have free rein (reign) in their own nations. Whenever diplomats get together and sign a multilateral treaty, the one thing they can all readily agree upon is noninterference in each other's internal affairs. If we want to take human rights seriously, we cannot give much weight to conspiracies among ruling elites that do not represent the views of their populations. If the international law of human rights springs from the people, and not the elites that run governments, then so much the worse for the nonintervention treaties invented by the latter for their own self-interest. Provisions in those treaties do not constitute real rules of international law but, rather, are quasi-rules, invented by ruling elites to insulate their domestic control against external challenge.[38]

The foregoing is, I repeat, an argument that may be unpersuasive now, although someday in the future – if the human rights revolution in international law continues its present course – the same argument may seem intuitively obvious. At the present time, treaties generate rules of customary law, and one of the customary rules of treaty formation continues to be that the credentials of representatives of governments of the signatory states are taken at face value.

But if treaties generate customary rules when they come into force, treaties do not "freeze" such customary rules forever. Rather, new rules of custom may arise out of the practice of states, and these new rules of custom may alter the previous treaty-generated rules. Although this argument is obvious, scholars are often misled by the unvarying text of treaties. The words of Article 18, although the OAS Charter was signed in 1948, still look the same in 1990. Professors Farer and Nanda cite those words as if they were timeless. But, in fact, customary practice since 1948 has superseded whatever legal impact those words had on international law in 1948.

A major customary law development since 1948 was the intervention by the United States in Grenada in 1983, and a second one is the Panamanian intervention of 1989. I argued at the time of the Grenada intervention that it was a lawful and temporary humanitarian intervention to free the people of Grenada from the tyranny of the thugs who had machine-gunned their way into power.[39] Fortunately for my argument, the U.S. military forces pulled out of Grenada soon after their mission was accomplished, and now the episode can safely be cited as an instance of limited humanitarian intervention on behalf of the citizens of Grenada. Assuming that the U.S. forces continue to pull out of Panama (as they are doing at this writing), the Panamanian intervention will be a reaffirming instance of this new customary rule that changes the previous rule flowing out of Article 18.[40]

---

[37] Additionally, as in the case of the military intervention in Grenada, U.S. troops apparently were ill-trained for "surgical" missions where many innocent civilians are present.

[38] For the argument that human rights law trumps even an explicit intergovernmental waiver of liability, see D'Amato & Engel, *State Responsibility for the Exportation of Nuclear Power Technology*, 74 VA. L. REV. 1011 (1988), excerpted in this Anthology, Chapter 14.

[39] Anthony D'Amato, *Intervention in Grenada: Right or Wrong?*, N.Y. TIMES, Oct. 30, 1983, at E18, col. 3.

[40] Assuming that Article 18 of the OAS Charter generated a customary rule of nonintervention when it came into force, and assuming that I have proven that subsequent customary law development has changed the rule into one of intervention to prevent tyranny, what about the *inter se* obligations of the parties to the OAS Charter? Those obligations, I suggest, could remain the same. It is possible to violate a treaty obligation even though the

The real world is changing faster than the paradigms of scholars. The Berlin Wall has crumbled with a suddenness that surprised everyone, but in fact it was merely a visual manifestation of the dynamic logic of popular sovereignty that is sweeping through Eastern Europe. Tyrannical leaders are being replaced in nation after nation by governing bodies that are more responsive to the citizenry.

Contributing to the momentum of popular sovereignty are the Grenada and Panama interventions. Not only did the United States remove tyrannical leaders from those two countries, but more importantly it set an example that has undoubtedly shaken other ruling elites who enjoy tyrannical control in their own countries. For even if some of those entrenched elites regard themselves as secure against popular uprising in their own countries (usually by the application of torture and brutality against political dissidents), they cannot now feel totally insulated against foreign humanitarian intervention. Thus, Grenada and Panama may very well act as catalysts in the current global revolution of popular sovereignty. In this respect, as well as on their own merits, the two interventions underscore the unraveling of statist conceptions of international law. The arguments of Professors Farer and Nanda, struggling to conform to the tautological jargon of statism, already seem anachronistic.

d. Affirmative Response[41]

I am in agreement with Professor D'Amato's position that human rights spring from the people and not from governing elites; human rights cannot be left to the whim of governing elites, including those of the United States. The content of human rights guarantees must be universal, and must not depend upon the views of leaders who decide to project power to enforce their own interpretations of human rights.

I also agree with Professor D'Amato's point that tyrannies are illegitimate, given the modern evolution of human rights law. Where our two views differ is in the consequence of that illegitimacy. Only in the most extreme cases, such as Cambodia and Uganda, can military intervention be justified. Even then, the intervention must be narrowly tailored to be of as short a duration as possible.

Professor D'Amato chides Professor Farer and me for using "loaded words" such as "government" and "legitimate" in analyzing the situation in Panama only a few lines before he refers to Noriega and "his co-thugs." I agree that Noriega's tactics deprived his regime of a certain legitimacy. The issue, however, is not whether Noriega was a tyrant, but whether his actions could have served as a justification for the U.S. military intervention. It is clear that, shorn of loaded rhetoric and viewed in comparative perspective, the Noriega regime was not a significantly worse violator of human rights than many other existing (and some U.S.-supported) regimes. Therefore, justifying the Panama invasion on such a ground seems likely to open the door to U.S. intervention or intervention by another powerful state in many other cases.

Professor D'Amato compares Panama's preinvasion circumstances to a domestic struggle in which the state is called upon to apply the rule of law objectively and prevent further violence. Of course, this analogy misses its intended point entirely. Unlike spouses who, as citizens of a state, receive benefits from, submit to and are expected to abide by universally agreed-to principles of law and morality derived through a democratically elected legislative process and enforced by an objective justice system and police force, nations such as Panama and the United States (and the USSR and Afghanistan) coexist within an international framework in which legal and moral principles are agreed to on the basis of mutual respect. Disagreements are resolved through dialogue, negotiations and the application, across time, of consensual customary norms and principles. In situations where no consensus obtains, these equal participants are under constraints to comply with principles of international law such as nonintervention.

Professor D'Amato's contention that the United States violated neither the territorial integrity nor the political independence of Panama is weak. It turns on the fact that Panama has not been made a de jure colony of the United States. Under such an analysis, the Soviet invasions of Hungary, Czechoslovakia and Afghanistan, or for that matter the Nazi invasions of several European nations, did not take away their political independence or territorial integrity. Such a proposition must be rejected.

Even accepting, arguendo, that colonization of a territory is the only way to destroy territorial integrity, political independence must be a distinct concept or else the phrasing of Article 2(4) is unnecessarily repetitious. Political independence must refer to the freedom of a state to make

same action is now legal under customary law. But we would not say that such action is illegal under "international law"; rather, it is only "illegal," if at all, under the particular treaty regime and only with respect to the particular sanctions, if any, provided by the treaty itself. To be sure, the parties to the treaty may wish to interpret the subsequent customary law development as constituting a "changed circumstance" so that their interpretation of the treaty is not at variance with the newly formed custom. For a discussion of the analogous case of Article 2(4) of the UN Charter, see D'Amato, *Trashing Customary International Law*, 81 A.J.I.L. 101 (1987).

[41] By VED P. NANDA, excerpted from: *The Validity of United States Intervention in Panama Under International Law*, 84 AMERICAN JOURNAL OF INTERNATIONAL LAW 494 (1990). Reprinted by permission.

choices. While the political choices Panamanians could make under Noriega were constrained, they remain so after the invasion owing to Panama's increased dependence on the United States. Professor D'Amato says that "before and after the intervention, Panama was and remains an independent nation." This avoids the issue. We are concerned with the precedent this invasion sets as a violation of both conventional and customary international law.

Professor D'Amato's interpretation of state practice is curious. He contends that state practice after 1968 has changed the meaning of Article 18 of the OAS Charter. The only support he cites is the U.S. intervention in Grenada, which was actually condemned by most of the international community. The logic of D'Amato's argument would allow George Bush in 1992 to contend that burglarizing Democratic National Headquarters has become acceptable practice since Richard Nixon authorized such action in 1972.

In agreement with Professor Reisman, Professor D'Amato argues that "human rights law demands intervention against tyranny" because it is "morally required." Unfortunately, when all the explanations are given, the reader is still without a reasonable (and just) basis for deciding who the interveners should be. By permitting "any nation with the will and the resources," Professor D'Amato reduces international relations to a situation in which the strong dictates to the weak what the standards for intervening will be. Of course, this permits self-designated judges to decide when they will intervene, i.e., when it is most convenient. Thus, Panama is invaded but China is not. The "lesson" that the United States has taught to tyrannical rulers through the example of Panama is not so much about democracy and human rights, as about the importance of currying the favor of the United States. Unfortunately, U.S. practice in the rest of the world indicates that this favor is indeed for sale to tyrants.

Professor D'Amato concedes the desirability of multilateral rather than unilateral intervention, but ignores both its rationale and the actual circumstances surrounding the intervention in Panama. The preference for multilateral intervention stems from several factors. One is that multilateral efforts may provide a check on intervention by a single state to pursue its own ends (political, military, economic, etc.), rather than merely correcting the international outrage that may have justified the intervention. A second rationale is to assure that the incident that justifies the intervention is indeed viewed by the international community as of sufficient magnitude to warrant intervention. The failure of other nations to participate in the intervention, cited by Professor D'Amato, may therefore indicate that the community thought intervention illegitimate. However, factually, I am unaware that the United States offered such an opportunity to the Latin American states.

e. Second Affirmative Response[42]

I frankly cannot tell from Professor D'Amato's feverish comment whether he believes (1) that there is no widely accepted paradigm with respect to the legitimate use of force, or (2) that there is a paradigm but I have misdescribed it, or (3) that there is a paradigm but it is odious and in a sufficiently advanced state of decrepitude that any scholar truly concerned about human beings should feel free to hasten its demise by writing as if it were already embalmed.

There is ambiguity in Professor D'Amato's interpretation of texts in general and the Charter in particular. When discussing Professor Schachter's work, D'Amato dons his deconstructionist's hat and emphasizes the "necessarily subjective" character of interpretation.[43] Having said that, however, Professor D'Amato seems to concede the capacity of texts to produce an intersubjective consensus: "We are better off with rules of international law that at least point us to important factual and contextual considerations." Presumably we are better off only if those "rules" (i.e., those bits of text) can contribute to that degree of coordinated action and response that makes society possible. In short, the content of the text does matter.

More telling evidence of Professor D'Amato's irresolution about the uses and abuses of interpretation is his splenetic response to my, I thought hackneyed, observation that "the central Charter value is national autonomy." "Who proclaimed this to be the central value of the UN Charter?" D'Amato thunders. "Whatever happened to human rights? A glance at the Preamble reveals its affirmation of 'faith in fundamental human rights'; there is no mention of national autonomy."

Particularly for a self-proclaimed contextualist ("all interpretation varies with context," he writes), this is a remarkably literal approach to interpretation. And I fear that, as literal approaches so often do, it leads Professor D'Amato astray. For the most casual study of the preparatory work and of state behavior in the immediate aftermath of the Charter demonstrates as conclusively as anything of this nature can be demonstrated that the defense of human rights was very much a subordinate concern of the initial UN membership. Surely Professor D'Amato is aware, for instance, that the founding members rejected a proposal sponsored by Chile and Panama to include a bill of rights in the Charter, that a majority led by the United Kingdom blocked inclusion of any reference in the Universal Decla-

---

[42] By TOM J. FARER, excerpted from: *Panama: Beyond the Charter Paradigm*, 84 AMERICAN JOURNAL OF INTERNATIONAL LAW 503 (1990). Reprinted by permission.

[43] As a character in David Lodge's novel *Small World* puts it, every decoding is a new encoding.

ration to a right of individual petition, that at its first session the Human Rights Commission decided that it had no authority to take any action with respect to individual petitions, and so on.

A scholar who emphasizes the inconclusiveness of verbal formulas and the corresponding need to understand rules as doing nothing more than pointing us "to important factual and contextual considerations" has a particular obligation to see the larger context of events and to get his/her facts right. Perhaps because he is driven by the sort of unzipped feelings one often encounters in those who view the agonies of the Third World from a book-lined study in the First, Professor D'Amato does not always satisfy this obligation. For instance, in celebrating the invasion of Grenada, he refers to "the kind of tyranny that was about to gain a foothold in 1983 when a group of thugs machine-gunned their way into power, murdering the existing democratic rulers." Professor D'Amato is presumably unaware that the existing ruler, namely Maurice Bishop, had himself seized power through a putsch and that what in fact occurred was a falling-out between two factions of a Marxist-Leninist party.

Professor D'Amato cites only two precedents – Grenada and Panama. And for some reason or other he fails to note that immediately after the Panama invasion, the Permanent Council of the OAS approved a resolution deploring it. My own exchanges with Latin diplomatic personnel at the OAS, particularly the ambassadors from several of the most influential South American democracies, confirmed my sense that the resolution, rather than being perfunctory, expressed in mild form a widespread sense of outrage among democratic elites. Perhaps they are influenced in part by an awareness of historical context to which Professor D'Amato is insensible. I refer to the fact that the number of instances in which the United States has intervened to restore democracy is offset in some not trivial measure by cases where intervention, albeit by more covert means, has functioned to subvert democratically elected governments.

The moral issue is raised by Professor D'Amato's question why sovereignty, assuming it means anything at all, should interfere with efforts to eliminate tyrants? The issue of whether moral values are better served by prohibiting or authorizing intervention on behalf of insurgents battling in the name of democracy to unseat authoritarian regimes has been elegantly joined by Michael Walzer[44] and Stanley Hoffmann.[45] In taking a negative position, Walzer sees a need to demarcate and protect space where a people with a sense of common identity can work out their own destiny. Neither he nor Hoffmann (who arrives finally at a more qualified, nuanced negative that arguably implies a slim affirmative penumbra) would apparently authorize direct intervention, i.e., invasion and occupation, except in cases of massive human rights violations such as those that marked the rule of Idi Amin in Uganda and the Khmer Rouge in Cambodia. Professor D'Amato does not suggest that the Noriega regime had yet reached that level of delinquency.

[44] MICHAEL WALZER, JUST AND UNJUST WARS 87-100 (1977).

[45] STANLEY HOFFMAN, DUTIES BEYOND BORDERS (1981).

f. In Support of the Affirmative[46]

If Professor D'Amato is to be believed, the U.S. invasion of Panama was akin to a crusade of might making right. In substantiating his thesis, however, he greatly overstates his case. Starting out on a defensive note, he denies that the purpose of the invasion was solely to rescue a bunch of blue-haired matrons being held hostage poolside. In fact, D'Amato is not talking about rescue at all. "I am talking," he assures us, "about the human rights of Panamanians to be free from oppression by a gang of ruling thugs."

"Thug" is a favorite word of both D'Amato and President Bush, and their use of it to justify the invasion of Panama is interesting because it intentionally invokes images of domestic criminality, and low-life criminality, at that. The reference, of course, is to Noriega, and he was an easy target even at the height of his power. Noriega is far from a charismatic caudillo leader; he is short, squat, dark-skinned, pock-marked, rheumy-eyed and inarticulate. His limited English sometimes makes him appear obtuse. In brief, Noriega is ugly and coarse, which is what names like "thug" imply.

Where D'Amato and the Bush administration differed somewhat was in their characterization of Noriega's dangerousness. To invade a sovereign state, kill its citizens, many of whom chose to defend Noriega's regime with their very lives, and destroy their property, calls for fighting more than a mere "thug." Such aggression, to possibly be both justified and justifiable, must be inflicted in the cause of vanquishing a great danger or enormous evil. D'Amato understood this requirement; whereas, President Bush did not.

In fulfillment of his agenda, D'Amato rhapsodizes at length about Noriega's alleged iniquities. He characterizes

[46] By SARAH A. RUMAGE, excerpted from: *Panama and the Myth of Humanitarian Intervention in U.S. Foreign Policy: Neither Legal Nor Moral, Neither Just Nor Right*, 10 ARIZONA JOURNAL OF INTERNATIONAL AND COMPARATIVE LAW 1 (1993). Reprinted by permission.

Noriega as the omnipotent warlord. "Noriega rules Panama because he and his co-thugs controlled the guns, rockets, mortar, truncheons and tear gas." D'Amato also points a Dreyfusian finger at Noriega, the megalomaniacal murderer, when he states, "any citizen who defied Noriega by rational argument risked being answered by bullets."[47] "In the 1989 elections," D'Amato says, "Noriega invoked the logic of brute force, of steel, of gunpowder, of the infliction of imprisonment and disappearance. The electoral victors were crushed." There is Noriega, the tyrant and foe of democracy, an evil in the world as common as rain, almost guaranteed to stir American sentiment when all else fails.

The other necessary players in this drama are the allegedly oppressed people. Without them, a despot is little more than an invention of wishful thinking. These are the people to whom our "humanitarian" impulses are ostensibly addressed. In D'Amato's formula, they are supposedly the rest of the state, apart from "Noriega and his henchmen." They are the weakling, lost lambs, helpless to preserve themselves against Noriega's slaughter. In a passage best described as curious, D'Amato compares them to battered women when he claims "the citizens of Panama were as powerless against Noriega and his henchmen as the 19th century American wives were against physically stronger husbands."

Unfortunately, much of this is simply wrong, and what is not obviously wrong is overblown, indulgent exaggeration. While Noriega's "badness" is not in doubt, he was no Hitler. It is true that the "electoral victors" were beaten up when they and their supporters took to the streets to protest the "nullification" of the May, 1989 elections, but that riot was not the Bloody Sunday D'Amato describes. Protesters, for the most part, were not subdued by "guns, rockets [and] mortar," as D'Amato contends, but by tear gas, birdshot, and clubs, riot control hardly being a novelty in Latin America. In fact, after months of all but ignoring protesters, Noriega had directed his commanders to quell the marches and strikes, but warned them repeatedly not to kill anybody. During the riot-torn summer of 1987, Noriega and the Panamanian Defense Forces (PDF) exercised almost exquisite restraint; despite six weeks of demonstrations and clashes, Panama's death toll was a startling zero. Even on July 10, the "Black Friday" of 1987, during one of the largest demonstrations ever in Central American history, the PDF "battered and stunned" a crowd of several hundred thousand protesters, without causing a single fatality. Between June 1987 and April 1988, total protester fatalities numbered four, a rare slip-up by the well-trained police, who were under strict orders to prevent fatalities, and therefore headlines. The unpleasant reality is that Noriega's PDF were in fact trained primarily by U.S. military personnel at the Southern Command to handle just such exigencies, receiving both arms and aid for this purpose.

The "people" of Panama were not relentlessly gunned down in the streets, as D'Amato implies. One wonders, in fact, exactly who D'Amato thinks are the "powerless citizens" of Panama. He is obviously not talking about the dark-skinned, mixed-race people who live in a putrid slum of Terraplin, where Noriega himself was born, literally a stone's throw from the presidential palace and the elite old Union Club, who were Noriega's most fervent supporters. Nor can he be talking about the wretched homeless dwelling in cardboard shacks on the outskirts of Colon, who survive only by rooting through piles of garbage for food. He is also not talking about the landless poor in the interior, who have no access to medical care and decent education for their children, and who worshipped Torrijos and respected Noriega for the attention these men paid to their ceaseless complaints. And when he invokes the image of battered women, D'Amato is not even thinking about the hundreds, if not thousands, of Panamanian women and men and children, pressed into prostitution through unemployment and poverty, who live lives punctuated daily by violence, drunkenness and disease, who sell to any and all buyers the only thing with which they have left to bargain: their physical bodies. These people are the truly powerless of Panama, but they are not the people to whom D'Amato refers. These, in fact, are Noriega's people, the dark-skinned poor of Panama, the angry, the ugly, the alienated and the unemployed, for whom Noriega's wealth and power were symbols of hope, and incentives to struggle against the whiter "rubiblancos" making up the middle and upper-class oligarchy.

These distinctions are not made to prove any social "truths" or disparage D'Amato's ignorance of Panamanian society. However, in considering the issues raised by humanitarian intervention, it is important to keep in mind that Panamanian society is deeply divided, and that there is an economic and social plateau to which the average Panamanian citizen cannot even aspire.

D'Amato's main thesis is "that human rights law demands intervention against tyranny." Does it really? D'Amato does not specify whether he means all tyranny, wherever located, or just the petty tyrannies next door. D'Amato contends:

> I do not argue that intervention is justified to establish democracy, aristocracy, socialism, communism or any other form of government. But if any of these forms of government become in the Aristotelian sense corrupted, resulting in tyranny against their

---

[47] "Dreyfusian finger" actually refers to Major Henry's finger, which he pointed at Captain Dreyfus during his court marital for espionage, shrieking, "And that traitor is sitting there!" DAVID L. LEWIS, PRISONERS OF HONOR: THE DREYFUS AFFAIR 51 (1973).

> populations, I believe that intervention from outside is not only legally justified but morally required.

The realist response to this was best expressed by Irving Babbitt, who wrote in 1924: "Leaders, good or bad, there will always be, and democracy becomes a menace to civilization when it seeks to evade this truth."[48] This pessimistic view of human nature pervades classical realism, incorporating both Niebuhr's religious view of human sinfulness, and Hobbes' more secular view of human beings as power-grubbing and selfish. For realists, the Noriegas of the world are simply social givens. They are evolutionary creatures, integral and inevitable, and a natural part of the political food chain. As Aldous Huxley put it, "So long as men worship the Caesars and Napoleons, Caesars and Napoleons will arise to make them miserable."[49]

Unilateral intervention is neither legal nor moral, neither just nor right. There is nothing humanitarian about invasions at all. Neither human rights advocacy nor theories of state morality can justify it or explain away intervention's pitfalls. In the deeply abstract world of hypotheticals, unilateral intervention is theoretically possible, although invoking it in reality seems to require historical revisionism that borders on the delusional. Still, history itself is marred by the times we wish we or someone had "done something." As Walzer remarks, "When a people are being massacred, we don't require that they pass the test of self-help before coming to their aid. It is their very incapacity that brings us in."[50] This, at least, is the theory. Unfortunately, it is not what usually happens in the real world. Despite the best intentions of scholars like Reisman, D'Amato and Teson, most massacres are unprevented and, when they occur, are largely ignored and remain unavenged. The reasons for this are more complex than simply bowing to the nonintervention norm. Stalin understood the issue well, for the reluctance to answer the roaring cry of the many seems more a part of human psychology than we care to admit: "One death is a tragedy," Stalin supposedly said, "but a thousand deaths is just a statistic."

[48] IRVING BABBITT, DEMOCRACY AND LEADERSHIP (1924), cited in ARTHUR M. SCHLESINGER, THE CYCLES OF AMERICAN HISTORY 417 (1986).

[49] ALDOUS HUXLEY, ENDS AND MEANS (1937). Realists studying Latin America have ascribed this to a legitimacy vacuum in a system where there is only power and the habit of obedience to whoever successfully claims the power of government. D'Amato intentionally sidesteps the issue of legitimacy in Panamanian politics, claiming that words such as "legitimate" and "authority" only serve to dull our senses against the reality of power." This is an evasive and fatuous response, almost alien to D'Amato's previous scholarship.

[50] MICHAEL WALZER, JUST AND UNJUST WARS 106 (1977).

g. In Support of the Negative[51]

I do not deny that sometimes victimized citizens may prefer domestic tyranny to benign outside intervention. In that case, it is correct to say that foreign states should refrain from intervening. A moral requirement for humanitarian intervention is that victimized citizens welcome the intervention. This requirement follows logically from the characterization of humanitarian intervention as an extension of the domestic right to revolution. But in order to reject the moral propriety of humanitarian intervention on those grounds it is necessary to collect the refusals of each oppressed citizen. This is so because it is morally unacceptable to condone human rights violations just because the majority wants it. Therefore, oppressed minorities are entitled to receive outside help, even if a majority of citizens oppose the intervention.

More important, those citizens who support the tyrants in the repression of a segment of the population do not have any moral claim to defend that government in its criminal enterprise. They have a moral duty to support the benign intervention against the tyrants. If they do not do so, they are almost as responsible as their government for the murders, executions, tortures and imprisonments.

Humanitarian intervention must be regarded as an extension of the right to revolution. If it is morally justified violently to resist oppression, then there is at least a prima facie justification for assisting the revolutionaries in their quest for freedom. Noninterventionists are forced to argue that there is some moral quality of the state, or "communal integrity," or necessary legitimacy, that morally precludes foreign intervention even in cases where violent overthrow is perfectly justified on the merits; that is, even in those cases where revolution is morally justified. But this is pure mysticism. A tyrannical government is no more justified vis-a-vis other governments than it is vis-a-vis its own subjects, and once it loses its legitimacy the subjects may request foreign help for the purposes of restoring free institutions.

[51] By FERNANDO R. TESON, excerpted from: HUMANITARIAN INTERVENTION: AN INQUIRY INTO LAW AND MORALITY 85–88 (N.Y.: Transnational Publishers, 1988). Reprinted by permission.

8

International Criminal Law

A. International Criminal Law as Part of Human Rights[1]

The twentieth century has witnessed an unprecedented expansion in the international protection of human rights. This expansion can be attributed to an ever-increasing sharing of fundamental values and expectations among nations. As a result, the world community now acknowledges the need to protect the individual from a variety of human depredations.

Depredations, while sometimes the result of private conduct, are most frequently committed by persons acting in a public or quasi-public capacity. Governmental policies are thus the primary cause of human rights violations today. Fortunately, the claim that sovereignty prevents scrutiny of a state's human rights practices has been at least partially overcome. This development presents the opportunity to adopt modalities of protection that can directly influence a state's human rights practices.

The rationale for international protection of human rights is that certain forms of depredations become matters of international concern when committed under the aegis of state policy because of the presumed international impact of such behavior. Thus, the rationale posits that collective effort is required to protect against policies that may ultimately affect the entire world community.

Concepts upon which a comprehensive framework for development and enforcement of human rights can be based are as yet poorly defined. Indeed, international human rights are themselves inadequately defined and inconsistently enforced. There is no classification of rights according to the values sought to be advanced or effective enforcement modalities. Proceeding from this observation, natural rights thinkers simply might conclude that human rights are divinely endowed. Nevertheless, despite the dearth of scholarly rights analysis, human rights do emerge and develop as part of a coherent process.

The immediate task is to chart and differentiate the stages through which human rights evolve. The degree to which a given right has attained international acceptance can be assessed by considering the following pattern of emergence and development.

Stage 1 – The Enunciative Stage – The emergence and shaping of internationally perceived shared values through intellectual and social processes.
Stage 2 – The Declarative Stage – The declaration of certain identified human interests or rights in an international document or instrument.
State 3 – The Prescriptive Stage – The articulation of these human rights in some prescriptive form in an international instrument (general or specific) generated by an international body; or the elaboration of specific normative prescriptions in binding international conventions.
State 4 – The Enforcement Stage – The search for, or the development of, modalities of enforcement.
State 5 – The Criminalization Stage – The development of international penal proscriptions.

Rights in the declarative stage (Stage 2) frequently are framed in general terms. In the prescriptive stage (Stage 3), rights are more specifically articulated in general international instruments having some legally binding effect. In the final stage, international criminalization, rights are always expressed in specific international conventions which deal exclusively with the rights and proscribe violation of them.

A particular human right may not necessarily evolve through each of these stages in the order listed above. Nevertheless, there is sufficient similarity in the pattern of development of most international human rights to validate the categorization. Perhaps positioning a right at a given stage is a function of the perception of the significance of the interest protected through the articulation of the right and of the appraisal of the degree of protection that the interest requires. Although it is less structured in the international context, the process of evolutionary development can be analogized to the evolution of social values and the development of civil prescription and penal proscriptions in any organized society.

Throughout the evolutionary process, the enactment of international criminal proscriptions invariably has followed an implementation crisis. Nevertheless, the adoption of criminal proscriptions has not derived from an appraisal of the significance of the right sought to be preserved and protected; rather, it has been caused by the inadequacy of modalities of protection in the first four stages. Thus, the inadequacy of these modalities has compelled the transformation of the protected right into a prohibited crime. Therefore, international criminal proscriptions are the ultima ratio modality of enforcing internationally protected human rights.

---

[1] By M. CHERIF BASSIOUNI, excerpted from: *International Criminal Law and Human Rights*, 9 YALE JOURNAL OF WORLD PUBLIC ORDER 193 (1982), *reprinted* in 1 M. CHERIF BASSIOUNI (ED.), INTERNATIONAL CRIMINAL LAW 1 (Transnational Publishers 1986). Reprinted by Permission.

Following is a conceptual categorization of international crimes and an indication of how each of them protects basic human rights:

1. *Crimes Against Peace*. A crime against peace is committed when a state commits an act of aggression, defined as the use of armed force by a state against the sovereignty, territorial integrity, or political independence of another state, or in any other manner inconsistent with the Charter of the United Nations. Such acts of aggression include invasion, attack, military occupation, annexation of territory, blockade of ports or coasts, and allowing a second state to use one's own territory to attack a third state.

The proscription of these acts of aggression protects the rights to life, liberty, and personal security, the right to property, and more indirectly, the right to be free from torture and from cruel, inhuman or degrading treatment or punishment.

2. *War Crimes*. A war crime is the result of the willful undertaking of conduct where such conduct results in the death, great suffering, or serious injury to any protected person, prisoner, or civilian. The term "war crime" is broad and far-reaching, encompassing many specific acts committed during war. Torture, including the administration of unsound medical procedures and mind-altering drugs, physical mutilation, medical experimentation, or inhuman treatment, is the most obvious. Other war crimes are, inter alia, causing a civilian to be taken hostage; rape or murder of civilians or prisoners;[2] appropriating or causing extensive and unjustifiable destruction of property; willfully and unjustifiably delaying the release and repatriation of prisoners of war after the cessation of hostilities; deporting civilians; and discriminating against civilians or prisoners of war on the basis of race, creed, or religion.

These proscriptions protect the following rights: life, liberty, and personal security; freedom from torture and from cruel, inhuman, or degrading treatment or punishment; freedom from slavery and forced labor; freedom from arbitrary arrest or detention; a fair criminal trial; equal treatment; freedom of movement, religion, opinion, expression, and association; the right to a family; and recognition as a person before the law.

3. *Crimes Against Humanity*. Acts constituting crimes against humanity include murder, extermination, enslavement, deportation, and other inhumane acts done against any civilian population, or persecution on political, racial or religious grounds, when such acts are done or such persecutions are carried out in execution of, or in connection with any crime against peace or any war crime.

These penal proscriptions protect the same human rights listed above in connection with war crimes.

4. *Genocide*. The crime of genocide can be committed in peacetime, as well as during war, when members of a national, ethnic, racial, or religious group are killed, seriously injured, or subjected to conditions calculated to partially or completely destroy the group. Additionally, genocide is committed when the group members are prevented from giving birth, or children of the group are forcibly transferred to another group.

Characterizing these acts as crimes attempts to safeguard the same rights as mentioned above, namely, the rights to life, liberty, personal security, freedom from torture or cruel treatment, freedom from slavery, freedom of religion, movement, opinion, association, and the right to a family.

5. *Apartheid*. Apartheid involves acts committed for the purpose of establishing and maintaining systematic domination over a racial group of persons. Physical harm, killing, torture, arbitrary arrest, imprisonment, imposition of severe living conditions, denial of participation in the political, social, economic, and cultural life of the country, and physical and legislative separation of the group from the rest of the society are all acts constituting apartheid.

Criminalizing apartheid protects the variety of human rights listed above.

6. *Slavery and Slave-Related Practices*. Slavery is the status or the condition of a person over whom any of the powers attaching to ownership are exercised. "Slavery-related institutions" include the institutions or practices of debt bondage, serfdom, marital bondage, slave labor, and sexual bondage.

The criminalization of slavery and related institutions has also protected a variety of human rights.

7. *Torture*. The crime of torture is any conduct by which severe physical or mental pain or suffering is inflicted intentionally on a person at the instigation of, or under the responsibility of, a public official to obtain information or a confession, to humiliate or discredit a person, or to inflict illegal, cruel, inhuman, or degrading punishment.

Freedom from torture and cruel or inhuman punishment, rights to life, liberty and personal security, and to a fair criminal trial are the human rights protected by this proscription.

8. *Unlawful Human Experimentation*. The crime of unlawful human experimentation consists of any nonconsensual physical and/or psychological alterations by means of surgical operations or injections, ingestion, or inhalation of substances inflicted by, or at the instigation of, or under the responsibility of a public official. A person is not deemed to have consented to medical experimentation unless he or she has the capacity to consent and does so freely after being fully informed of the nature of the experiment and its possible consequences.

This proscription protects the rights of life, liberty, per-

---

[2] [Editor's Note: Individual rape and murder are only international crimes when committed during war. International human rights law has not progressed to the point where they are international crimes if committed during peacetime. Thus, for example, if an American murders a private person – even another American – abroad, the American has committed no international crime as well as no crime punishable in the United States. The only applicable law is the law of the territory in which the crime is committed. If the murderer is apprehended in the United States, he or she is subject to possible extradition to the country where the crime took place.]

sonal security, freedom from torture and cruel or inhuman punishment, and the right to a family.

9. *Piracy*. The crime of piracy consists of any illegal act of violence, detention, or any other act of deprivation, committed for private ends by the crew or the passengers of a private ship or a private aircraft, and directed: (i) on the high seas, against another ship or aircraft, or against persons or property on board such ship or aircraft; or (ii) against a ship, aircraft, persons, or property in a place outside the jurisdiction of any state.

Life, liberty, and personal security are protected by this proscription.

10. *Hijacking*. It is a crime intentionally to seize an aircraft by force or threat, to destroy it, or to endanger the safety of an aircraft by threatening the safety of any person on board, or damaging or interfering with its operation in flight.

Life, liberty, and personal security are also protected by this proscription.

11. *Kidnapping and Taking of Civilian Hostages*. This crime is committed by behavior which harms or threatens harm against internationally protected persons. Seizing or detaining a person against his will is included. The same human rights are protected by this proscription as are protected by the proscription against hijacking.

12. *Unlawful Use of the Mails*. The use of mails to kill or inflict harm on anyone handling or receiving mailed materials is a crime. Explosives, dangerous substances, or animals are barred from the mails.

The right to life, liberty, and personal security is protected.

B. Rape[3]

It is a pity that calamitous circumstances are needed to shock the public conscience into focusing on important, but neglected, areas of law. The more offensive the occurrence, the greater the pressure for rapid adjustment. Nazi atrocities, for example, led to the establishment of the Nuremberg Tribunal; the evolution of the concepts of crimes against humanity and the crime of genocide; the shaping of the fourth Geneva Convention; and the birth of the human rights movement. The starvation of Somali children prompted the Security Council to apply chapter VII of the UN Charter to an essentially internal situation, bringing about a revolutionary change in our conception of the authority of the United Nations to enforce peace in such situations. There is nothing new in atrocities or starvation. What is new is the role of the media. Instant reporting from the field has resulted in rapid sensitization of public opinion, greatly reducing the time lapse between the perpetration of such tragedies and responses to them.

It took the repeated and massive atrocities in former Yugoslavia, especially in Bosnia-Herzegovina, to persuade the Security Council that the commission of those atrocities constitutes a threat to international peace, and that the creation of an ad hoc international criminal tribunal would contribute to the restoration of peace. The Security Council therefore decided to establish such a tribunal under chapter VII. For the first time since the founding of the United Nations, the Security Council has become, at least for the moment, a major force for ensuring respect for international humanitarian law. Because the international community has failed in the central task of ending the bloodshed and atrocities, the establishment of the tribunal has become the preferred means to promote justice and effectiveness of international law. I consider only one example of the egregious violations of human dignity in former Yugoslavia – rape.

That the practice of rape has been deliberate, massive and egregious, particularly in Bosnia-Herzegovina, is amply demonstrated in reports of the United Nations, the European Community, the Conference on Security and Cooperation in Europe and various nongovernmental organizations. The special rapporteur appointed by the UN Commission on Human Rights, Tadeusz Mazowiecki, highlighted the role of rape both as an attack on the individual victim and as a method of "ethnic cleansing" "intended to humiliate, shame, degrade and terrify the entire ethnic group." Indescribable abuse of thousands of women in the territory of former Yugoslavia was needed to shock the international community into re-thinking the prohibition of rape as a crime under the laws of war. Important as the decision to establish the tribunal is, institutional process must work in tandem with substantive development of international law. What, then, is the current status of rape as a crime under international humanitarian law?

Rape by soldiers has of course been prohibited by the law of war for centuries, and violators have been subjected to capital punishment under national military codes, such as those of Richard II (1385) and Henry V (1419). Of more immediate influence on the modern law of war was the prohibition of rape as a capital crime by the Lieber Instructions (1863). Indeed, rape committed on an individual soldier's initiative has frequently been prosecuted in national courts. In many cases, however, rape has been given license, either as an encouragement for soldiers or as an instrument of policy. Nazi and Japanese practices of forced prostitution and rape on a large scale before and during the Second World War are among the egregious examples of such policies.

Under a broad construction, Article 46 of the Hague

[3] By THEODOR MERON, excerpted from: *Rape as a Crime Under International Humanitarian Law*, 87 AMERICAN JOURNAL OF INTERNATIONAL LAW 424–28 (1993). Reprinted by permission.

Regulations can be considered to cover rape, but in practice it has seldom been so interpreted. Rape was neither mentioned in the Nuremberg Charter nor prosecuted in Nuremberg as a war crime under customary international law. But it was prosecuted in Tokyo as a war crime.

Another seed for future normative development was sown in Control Council Law No. 10, adopted by the four occupying powers in Germany as a charter for war crimes trials by their own courts in Germany. It expanded the list of crimes against humanity found in the Nuremberg Charter to include rape. Nevertheless, although both the fourth Geneva Convention and the Additional Protocols explicitly and categorically prohibit rape, these instruments did not follow the precedent of Control Council Law No. 10 and do not list rape among the grave breaches subject to universal jurisdiction.

It is time for a change. Indeed, under the weight of the events in former Yugoslavia, the hesitation to recognize that rape can be a war crime or a grave breach has already begun to dissipate. The International Committee of the Red Cross (ICRC) and various states aided this development by adopting a broad construction of existing law. The ICRC declared that the grave breach of "willfully causing great suffering or serious injury to body or health" (Article 147 or the fourth Geneva Convention) covers rape. If so, surely rape – in certain circumstances – can also rise to the level of such other grave breaches as torture or inhuman treatment. Moreover, the massive and systematic practice of rape and its use as a "national" instrument of "ethnic cleansing" qualify it to be defined and prosecuted as a crime against humanity.

Several states have submitted positions and draft charters to the UN Secretary-General pursuant to Security Council Resolution 808. France, in defining the crimes within the jurisdiction of the tribunal under its draft charter, lists "outrages upon personal dignity, in particular humiliating and degrading treatment, rape, forced prostitution and indecent assault."[4] This language draws on Articles 75(2)(b) and 76(1) of Additional Protocol I and upgrades its prohibition of rape – which is not specifically mentioned as a grave breach of the Protocol – to a crime punishable by the tribunal, provided, however, that rape (as well as the other crimes mentioned in Article VI(1)(b)) is "mass and systematic." The United States proposal adapts the definition of crimes against humanity in Control Council Law No. 10 to the Yugoslav circumstances, and lists rape among the punishable crimes. Documents submitted by seven states on behalf of the Organization of the Islamic Conference and by Italy also define rape as a crime against humanity. Most important, the statute of the international tribunal proposed by the UN Secretary-General lists rape among crimes against humanity.

The crimes against humanity specified in the London Agreement were only those committed "against any civilian population," not against individual civilians. Nuremberg case law suggest that war crimes committed in a widespread and systematic manner on political, racial or religious grounds may rise to the level of crimes against humanity. Proof of systematic governmental planning has been considered a necessary element of crimes against humanity, in contrast to war crimes. Crimes against humanity are therefore more difficult to establish. The acquisition of facts supporting policy planning, mass character and command responsibility may present evidentiary hurdles to possible prosecutions.

Confirmation of the principle stated in Control Council Law No. 10, that rape can constitute a crime against humanity, is, both morally and legally, of groundbreaking importance. Nevertheless, the possibility of prosecuting the far more frequent cases of rape that are regarded as the "lesser" crimes of war crimes or grave breaches should not be neglected. The references to war crimes and grave breaches in the proposed charters, together with the recognition that rape can be a war crime or a grave breach, provide a basis for such prosecutions.

Although, formally, the law stated by the Security Council under chapter VII is necessarily contextual and applicable only to former Yugoslavia, the tribunal's charter, like that of Nuremberg, is likely quickly to become a fundamental normative instrument of the general law of war. The approval by the Security Council (Res. 827), acting under chapter VII of the UN Charter, of the tribunal's charter recognizing rape as a punishable offense under international humanitarian law validates this important normative development and, it is hoped, may expedite the recognition of rape, in some circumstances, as torture or inhuman treatment in the international law of human rights as well. Meaningful progress in combating rape can only be made by more vigorous enforcement of the law. The recognition of rape as a crime under international law punishable by the future war crimes tribunal for former Yugoslavia is a step in that direction.

C. A Taxonomy of the Laws of War[5]

It seems desirable that governments and jurists make a detailed examination of the rules of war distinguishing the

---

[4] UN Doc. S/25266, Ann. V, Art. VI(1)(b)(iv) (1993).

[5] By QUINCY WRIGHT, excerpted from: *The Outlawry of War and the Law of War*, 47 AMERICAN JOURNAL OF INTERNATIONAL LAW 365, 374–76 (1953). Reprinted by permission.

applicability of the law of war to action by aggressors, by states engaged in individual or collective self-defense, by states engaged in enforcement action under the United Nations, or by states engaged in military action in a foreign country on the basis of agreement with the sovereign of the state:

1. *Rules which confer new powers on belligerents.* This first category includes rules defining the power of belligerents to occupy enemy territory, to destroy his armed forces, to denounce certain treaties, to visit, search, and, in case of probable cause for condemnation, to capture merchant vessels on the high seas, to condemn enemy and, in some cases, neutral property at sea, to requisition, to sequestrate and, in certain circumstances, to confiscate enemy property in occupied territory or in home territory, and to deter espionage and war treason in occupied territory by punishing individuals who engage in such activities. The aggressor enjoys none of these powers, but states engaged in defense or enforcement may exercise all of them insofar as military necessity requires.

2. *Rules which impose liabilities upon belligerents.* Included are rules defining the conditions which make a state responsible under international law and the duty of states to make reparation for injury to other states of individuals for which they are responsible, and, specifically, the duty of belligerents to make reparation to enemy and neutral states for breaches of the law of war by their forces. Under these rules the aggressor should make reparation for all losses of life and property resulting from its military operations, all of which were in violation of its obligations under international law, while states engaged in defense or enforcement action must make reparation only for injuries resulting from breaches of the law of war, including breaches by their armed forces. States engaged in enforcement action may, however, escape liability for certain acts in violation of the normal rules of war and neutrality in case these acts were authorized by the United Nations (see the fifth category below).

3. *Rules which confer individual rights on soldiers and civilians.* This third category includes the rules defining the rights of individuals, such as those dealing with the treatment of prisoners of war; the treatment of the sick and the wounded; the immunities of parlementaires; the procedural rights of persons accused of war crime, espionage, or war treason; the protection of soldiers against methods or weapons causing unnecessary suffering; the exemption of private property from capture, detention or confiscation; and other so-called "humanitarian" rules. All states engaged in hostilities, whether engaged in aggression, defense or enforcement are obliged to observe these rules.

4. *Rules which impose individual liabilities on soldiers and civilians.* This category includes the rules defining war crimes such as maltreatment of prisoners, maltreatment of persons in occupied territory, killing of hostages, acts of perfidy, use of forbidden weapons, etc. Both the aggressor and the defender are entitled to punish persons guilty of such crimes who come into their power, but are obliged to observe the procedural rules required by international law in the conduct of such trials and to permit the usual defenses such as lack of freedom of choice because of the nature of superior orders or other circumstances. Such crimes against international law, as well as the crime of initiating aggressive war, should in principle be tried by an international tribunal. Espionage and war treason conducted for patriotic reasons or under orders of the state in occupied territory are not believed to be war crimes in this sense. The aggressor has no right to punish individuals carrying out such missions, but states engaged in defense or enforcement are permitted to do so (see the first category above).

5. *Rules which define the extent to which the United Nations can authorize action by states which go beyond belligerent rights.* The fifth category includes specific rights conferred upon states engaged in enforcement action by the United Nations. The United Nations doubtless has considerable discretion to permit action beyond normal belligerent rights but this discretion is not unlimited. The United Nations could not, for example, authorize acts which international law regards as war crimes nor could it deprive individuals, even though acting in behalf of an aggressor state, of human rights protected by international law and the law of war. It may, however, authorize measures to assure isolation of the aggressor and to prevent third-state assistance to the aggressor even though those measures go beyond the normal powers of a belligerent to interfere with commerce at sea. It is believed that a state should be entitled to exercise such exceptional rights only on the basis of explicit United Nations authorization. Such exceptional rights should not be enjoyed by states acting in individual or collective self-defense but only by states engaged in United Nations enforcement action.

It has been suggested that a law of war which attempts to differentiate between belligerents is impossible because the observance of any law during war depends upon mutual self-interest contingent upon reciprocity. The aggressor, it is said, cannot be expected to observe rules unless he believes that the defending or policing Powers will observe the same rules. This is true, but the principles stated require reciprocal observance of the humanitarian rules applicable during hostilities. The differences between the legal position of the aggressor and that of the defender may often be made effective only in respect to claims for reparation or liabilities for criminal prosecution after hostilities. The opportunity to make them effective then is, of course, contingent upon defeat of the aggressor, and consequently upon the successful operation of collective security. Even then economic or political considerations may well urge the relaxation of reparation claims or an amnesty or war crimes trials. A clear understanding of the rules, however, may in themselves contribute both to the deterrence of aggression and to its suppression if it occurs. In respect both to the dependence of law enforcement upon success in hostilities and to the frequent political advisability of relaxing such enforcement by amnesty, aggression – outlawed by international law – is analogous to rebellion which is outlawed by the domestic law of a state.

D. Terrorism[6]

"Terrorism" is a term of uncertain legal content. The late Richard Baxter was particularly doubtful of the desirability and necessity of defining the term. In his view, "we have cause to regret that a legal concept of 'terrorism' was ever inflicted upon us. The term is imprecise; it is ambiguous; and above all, it serves no operative legal purpose."[7]

At the international level, there is no universally accepted definition of "terrorism" and hence no international crime of terrorism. Rather, there are treaty provisions aimed at suppressing aircraft hijacking, unlawful acts against the safety of civil aviation, unlawful acts against internationally protected persons including diplomatic agents, the taking of hostages, and the theft of nuclear material. Although these treaty provisions are often loosely described as "antiterrorist," the acts they cover are criminalized regardless of whether, in any particular case, they could be classified as "terrorism." Similarly, under national law, criminal provisions with respect to murder, assault, theft, illegal detention of persons, taking of hostages, arson, and so on, are normally the basis for prosecution of "terrorist" acts, although they rarely mention terrorism and are applicable notwithstanding the absence of traditional elements of the terrorist act. To be sure, some states have adopted antiterrorist statutes, but these are exceptions to the norm.

Besides being imprecise and ambiguous, the term "terrorism" is emotionally charged, as is demonstrated by the cliche, "One man's terrorist is another man's freedom fighter." Some countries believe that the causes of terrorism or the political motivations of individual terrorists are relevant to the problem of definition. For example, some states, including Libya and Syria, take the position that individual acts of violence can be defined as terrorism only if they are employed solely for personal gain or caprice; acts committed in connection with a political cause, especially against colonialism and for national liberation, fall outside the definition and constitute legitimate measures of self-defense. Under this approach, then, sending letter bombs through the mails, hijacking airplanes, kidnappings of or attacks on diplomats and international business persons, and indiscriminate slaughter of civilians by members of revolutionary groups could never constitute "terrorism" if committed on behalf of a just cause. Another approach is to define as "terrorism" only the use of terror by governments – so-called "state terrorism." (Indeed, the word "terror" was first used in connection with the Jacobin "Reign of Terror" during the French Revolution.) As a result of these and other pejorative and ideologically circumscribed uses of the term "terrorism" in international fora, no general definition has been agreed upon.

E. Terrorism and the Laws of War[8]

The humanitarian laws of war are one of the seven basic strands that together make up an overall set of laws to deal with conflict management. These strands are: first, norms concerning the initiation of coercion; second, the laws of war and neutrality; third, norms concerning the obligation to terminate hostilities once they are engaged – a strand that is undeveloped in international law; fourth, institutions for peaceful and third-party dispute resolution; fifth, the law of personal responsibility for violations of major conflict management norms – essentially the "Nuremberg principles"; sixth, institutional mechanisms for conflict management and collective defense; and seventh, arms control.

The law of war is an important part of this interrelated structure. The application of human rights to settings of armed conflict is a wise and fundamentally important part of any overall approach to conflict management. I note that this law of war strand developed, not surprisingly, during the historical period when we treated war "as fact." Under the prevailing myth, war was simply a phenomenon beyond the law, and international law did not comment on whether it was permissible. In the era of the United Nations, which

---

[6] By JOHN F. MURPHY, excerpted from: *The Future of Multilateralism and Efforts to Combat International Terrorism*, 25 COLUMBIA JOURNAL OF TRANSNATIONAL LAW 35, 37–38 (1986). Reprinted by permission.

[7] Richard R. Baxter, *A Skeptical Look at the Concept of Terrorism*, 7 AKRON L. REV. 380 (1974).

[8] By JOHN NORTON MOORE, excerpted from: *A Theoretical Overview of the Laws of War in a Post-Charter World, with Emphasis on the Challenge of Civil Wars, "Wars of National Liberation," Mixed Civil-International Wars, and Terrorism*, 31 AMERICAN UNIVERSITY LAW REVIEW 841 (1982). Reprinted by permission.

moved away from the "just war" and "war as fact" approaches, we happily are now beyond the failure to address norms concerning the recourse to coercion. "Just war" is dead in international law. The United Nations Charter killed it, and rightly so. Under the Charter, the use of force is lawful in defense, but not as affirmative conduct to seek resolution of issues by force, however just the cause is perceived to be.

Terrorism should be considered in the context of conflict management. It is important to dispel several myths about terrorism. First is the insistence on defining terrorism before taking effective action. The effort to do so merely impedes developing an effective response to the functional problems. A second myth is the insistence on first dealing with the causes of terrorism. We do not do that in the laws of war in general; we do not say that we must deal with the causes of war before we can discuss humanitarian rules. To engage in such a discussion is to invite justification for terrorism on the basis of the terrorists' cause. Another myth, the "evenhanded cop-out," is the argument that state terrorism is an implied justification for private terrorism. Although there is no doubt that states can engage in illegal practices, I have never known what state terrorism was, and certainly, whatever it is, it does not justify other forms of terrorism. Finally, there is the method of employing "operational measures" rather than examining normative issues. Thus, when proponents of this method deal with terrorism, they gather statistics, set up offices, discuss jurisdiction and authority to deal with cases, and inquire into obtaining police cooperation. A preferred approach is to focus on establishing widely accepted rules regarding the illegitimacy of certain terrorist tactics and on human rights norms as important elements in the control of terrorism as well as in insisting on improved operational measures for the control of terrorism.

Terrorism is a form of warfare, and therefore it must be subject to the underlying principles of the laws of war.

F. Defenses to War Crimes[9]

In focusing on violations of the laws of war, we should not forget that persons accused of war crimes have human rights too. Unquestioned is the right to a fair and public trial. In addition, international customary law has evolved certain other human rights of defendants that apply when they are prosecuted for war crimes:

1. *Superior Orders.* Under international customary law, a plea that the defendant was merely carrying out the orders of a military superior has rarely if ever been allowed as a defense to the commission of an international crime. At the same time, it has almost always been allowed in mitigation of punishment. The problem for the defense counsel, therefore, is to introduce the fact of superior orders at the trial level so that it might be taken into account in the tribunal's assessment of the guilt of the accused, rather than postponing the question of superior orders to the post-trial assessment of punishment where its effectiveness will be diminished and where it would be routinely allowed anyway.

In the many trials in the Far East following the Second World War, one may read in the transcripts considerable discussion of the defendants' conduct in obeying the principles of the Empire and the Emperor and of loyalty to the generals in the field without often encountering the phrase "superior orders." What in effect happened was that counsel introduced the concept of superior orders without using the vocabulary, undoubtedly because the tribunals might have ruled such arguments out of order if they came labelled as "superior orders" arguments. This tactic clearly is an important one for the defense in any trial where superior orders could be a factor in assessing guilt.

The plea of superior orders would be far more difficult for a person accused of terrorism, due to the lack of a military command structure. A terrorist seems to be a person acting under his own volition, quite unlike a soldier in the field responding to his commander's orders. On the other hand, a terrorist, like a soldier is presumably acting not out of personal motives but for a general cause. The imperatives of that cause, couched in principles that obviously are important for the terrorist, might be assimilated to "superior orders." The problem for defense counsel is certainly more difficult here, because if counsel says that evidence concerning the imperatives of the cause is relevant as functionally analogous to "superior orders," the court may disallow the evidence on the theory that superior orders, even if proven, is not a defense.

Perhaps the most practical use of "superior orders" is at the plea-bargaining stage. It is clear that the Nuremberg and Far Eastern prosecutions did not descend to the level of the common soldier, presumably because the soldier was "only following orders." Prosecutors therefore must have taken superior orders into account in deciding whom to indict. At this level a potential defendant would do well to stress the conflict between obedience to orders and obedience to the general rules prohibiting international crimes, as it is a conflict that prosecutors might understand better than courts.

2. *Lack of Command Responsibility.* Command responsibility is the other side of the coin of superior orders. The

---

[9] By ANTHONY D'AMATO, excerpted from: *National Prosecutions for International Crimes*, in 3 M. CHERIF BASSIOUNI (ED.), INTERNATIONAL CRIMINAL LAW: ENFORCEMENT 169, 172 (N.Y.: Transnational Publishers, 1987). Reprinted by permission.

military commander is held responsible, under international law, for the crimes of his subordinates if (a) he knew or had reason to know of those activities, and (b) he was in a position to prevent or mitigate them.

Thus, if a defendant is charged with commission of an international crime not because of any of his acts, but because of his position as a commander or person in charge, his defenses under international customary law would have to fall under either (a) or (b) or both. Of these, (a) is far more difficult to sustain. A commander, by virtue of his position alone, is generally charged with knowing or having reason to know of the acts of his subordinates, unless those acts are sporadic and isolated. A court will generally not believe that any widespread pattern of war crimes would not be known to the commander; thus the court did not believe General Yamashita who said at his trial in the Philippines that he did not know of the commission of war crimes by his troops.

A defense under (b) has more promise. Here, the mere fact that the defendant was a commander is not enough for culpability. An inference should not be drawn under (b), as it was under (a), that a commander simply by virtue of his office could have prevented or inhibited the commission of war crimes or other international crimes by his subordinates. In the Far Eastern trial of Admiral Toyoda, although the admiral was charged with the command of 20,000 naval troops in Manila that committed atrocities against Filipino civilians, in fact it was shown that the real command lay in General Yamashita and not in Admiral Toyoda. The admiral was acquitted. The commission in Toyoda's case did not need to reach the issue of knowledge because it found a lack of control.

Sometimes a commander can show that he took steps to prevent or inhibit the commission of crimes by his subordinates. However, a mere "paper record" of orders not to commit crimes will not exonerate a commander who in fact tolerated or even approved of those activities. General Yamashita testified at his trial that he removed his Chief of Military Police because there were reports of abuses that reached his ears. On one level, this testimony hurt Yamashita because it constituted evidence that he knew about the abuses. On a second level, however, the testimony would have helped his case had there not been subsequent abuses by the military police, such as mass executions of prisoners, that occurred after the removal of the Chief of Military Police.

If there is evidence that a military commander actually ordered his subordinates to commit war crimes, and the subordinates committed those war crimes, may the commander nevertheless defend himself in court by arguing that his commands constituted unlawful orders of a superior, that his subordinates were under an international legal obligation to disobey those orders, and therefore the fact that he issued those orders cannot be enough to impute to him the (illegal) acts of his subordinates? So far as I know, this paradoxical-sounding defense has never been attempted.[10]

In the case of terrorists who operate in peacetime and whose victims are innocent persons, a plea of lack of command responsibility on the part of a terrorist leader may be effective. The lack of a military organization may excuse a terrorist "commander" from liability on the theory of command responsibility. At the same time, however, such a commander would undoubtedly be prosecuted under a co-conspirator theory, in which case the prosecution would have to prove that the defendant aided and abetted the plan. This is a somewhat stronger test than command responsibility, and if it had been applicable in General Yamashita's case (it wasn't, because he was a military commander, not a peacetime terrorist), on the evidence available against Yamashita his case might have ended in acquittal.

3. *Tu Quoque*. There are occasions where a defendant may argue to the court that nationals of the prosecuting state have engaged in acts similar to those the defendant is charged with, but have not been prosecuted for them. To the extent that this tu quoque plea is saying that others have committed similar crimes, the prosecution can answer simply that such a fact is irrelevant to the present trial. "Prosecutorial discretion" may account for the lack of persecutions in the other cases, but that does not mean that the present indictment should be dismissed.

Yet there is a strong sense of justice in the defense of tu quoque raised by Admiral Karl Donitz at Nuremberg that Admiral Chester Nimitz of the United States had waged unrestricted submarine warfare in the Pacific, refusing to pick up survivors. Since Donitz was charged with allowing shipwrecked survivors to drown, and for failure to carry out rescue missions, he could well question the impartiality of the proceedings against him. Donitz was eventually sentenced to ten years' imprisonment; the avoidance of a death sentence meant perhaps that his arguments carried some psychological weight.

In any event, a more precise version of tu quoque would be not that others have committed similar crimes, but rather the fact that others have committed similar acts without being prosecuted therefor signifies that the customary international law has changed to a point where such acts are no longer in practice regarded as criminal. The evidence of such a change in the customary law is, of course, the fact that others were not prosecuted for those acts but not that they should have been prosecuted! For example, al-

---

[10] For a full discussion and debate, *see* Anthony D'Amato, *Superior Orders vs. Command Responsibility*, 80 AJIL 604 (1986); Howard S. Levie, *Some Comments on Professor D'Amato's "Paradox,"* 80 AJIL 608 (1986).

though rescuing ship-wrecked survivors is itself a laudable goal and one that might very well be considered a duty under customary international law, conditions regarding submarines in the Second World War may have called for a contrary practice. A submarine that spends time rescuing survivors is vulnerable to air attack, for it is likely that the vessel that was hit radioed to the shore its latitude and longitude. (Indeed, revelations about "Enigma" that came out many years after World War II showed that, on many occasions, the Allies knew in advance of U-boat attacks against Allied ships through decoding of German radio communications, but did not strike immediately for fear of tipping off the enemy that their code had been cracked. One possible incident involved Donitz himself. After sinking the British vessel Laconia, he ordered naval commanders to provide aid to the shipwrecked sailors. British Liberator bombers soon showed up, however, and ignoring the victims in the water the bombers began to bomb the U-boats that had gathered to assist in the rescue operation.) Perhaps Admiral Chester Nimitz in the Pacific theater did not rescue survivors because of the danger to his submarines, and hence one might question whether the pre-second world war norm of rescuing survivors remained intact during that war.

4. *Legitimacy of Reprisals*. A "reprisal" is an act that is illegal in itself, but arguably becomes legal because it is taken in retaliation for a prior illegal act by the other side. In recent years there have been many acts of "reprisal" in the Middle East, some limited and some extensive, but all said to be justified because of prior illegalities.

Although a reprisal is backward-looking in that it seeks its justification in a prior illegal act by the other side, its best legal support is mustered if it can be shown to have forward-looking consequences. In other words, a reprisal taken solely for the purpose of revenge is on extremely weak international grounds, whereas a reprisal that can be said to have a deterrent function is on a much more solid legal foundation. A defendant citing a "reprisal" justification for his violation of international criminal law should make sure that the reprisal is characterized, if it can be, in terms of deterrence and not as revenge.

An illustration of this point can be found in the trial of Hans Albin Rautner before a national tribunal of the Netherlands after the Second World War. Occupied Dutch citizens had engaged in acts of violence against German soldiers. German reprisals were then taken against Dutch citizens at random. The tribunal recognized that the occupying power had a right to answer violent resistance by retributive action, but found that Rautner's reprisals were taken for purposes of revenge and not as a deterrent. The conclusion was based on the fact that Rautner made no attempt to arrest the actual perpetrators of the resistance actions but rather killed hostages at random.

In addition, any defense of the legitimacy of reprisals would have to take into account the questions of military necessity and proportionality, which will now be considered.

5. *Military Necessity*. Many formulae have been advanced to describe the plea of military necessity, but it is my judgment that underlying all of them is a notion of cost-effectiveness. For example, assume there is a war where if one belligerent's capital city can be destroyed there will be capitulation. The other side could destroy the capital city immediately, but instead decides first to destroy one or more other major cities. Prolonging the war in this manner, with no justification, and at increased cost to both sides, would clearly violate military necessity.

Often examples of lack of military necessity serve to prove the underlying offense. Adolf Eichmann, in Budapest in 1945, diverted German troops from their task of defending the city against the approaching Russian army so that they might continue to carry out the program of genocide against Hungarian Jews. The murder of civilians was itself clearly a war crime; its criminal nature serves to be underlined by the fact that there was no possible justification of military necessity. A related example occurred during the atrocities committed under General Yamashita in the Philippines: scarce gasoline was used to burn the bodies of civilians. The murder of civilians was itself a war crime; the use of gasoline rations underscored the lack of military necessity.

Military necessity must either be disproved by the prosecution or proved by the defense. It is part of the prosecution's case to disprove when military necessity is named in the war-crime charge itself. Thus, one of the war crimes specified in the "Nuremberg principles" adopted by the United Nations General Assembly in 1950 is "wanton destruction of cities, towns or villages, or devastation not justified by military necessity." However, most of the time the plea of military necessity is raised by way of justification by the defendant.

The defendant need not prove strict cost-effectiveness. Considerable latitude is given to commanders in the field to judge what appeared to them at the time to be reasonable and prudent from a military standpoint. They are not required to abstain from an act because of its brutality or infliction of grave punishment upon the enemy if the act is justifiable from a military perspective and is not per se a war crime. The bombing of munitions factories is justifiable by military necessity even though many workers and their families will inevitably be killed. On the other hand, the concept of military necessity cannot be stretched so far as to include acts of brutality committed solely to terrorize the opponent. The American fire-bombing of Tokyo on March 10, 1945, one of the most congested urban residential districts in the world, and numerous repeated bombings of other populated areas in the ensuing three months, can hardly be justified in terms of military necessity without scuttling all of the laws of war.

It is difficult to assess at this early stage whether an organization dedicated to overthrowing a government and using terrorist means, such as the Irish Republican Army in Northern Ireland, could employ a defense of military necessity in trials of some of its members. The question whether terrorism should come under the laws of war is at present hotly debated. In addition, there is a question whether the situation is one of "war." And apart from the name, is the I.R.A. a military organization? Despite all these theoretical difficulties, one might still draw a line between terrorist acts that might be justified by "military necessity" and those that have no possible claim to such a defense. Acts of sabotage against government military installations, for example, might conceivably fall under the rubric of military necessity, but random terrorist attacks upon civilians for the purpose of intimidating the population and calling attention to the goals of the terrorists are of an entirely different character. Perhaps "military necessity" might be a useful defense if a terrorist organization is directly attacked by a military unit, and fights back in self-defense. Even though the military unit will claim that it is only exercising a police function against common criminals, there is a possibility for an argument here that resistance is not criminal if it would have been justified by military necessity if the terrorist organization were in fact a belligerent.

The attempt to extrapolate from the international criminal law to situations involving terrorists is a difficult one, partially because the very label "terrorist" suggests someone who is not entitled to any defenses and ought to be summarily executed. But the same reaction was vented in the early days of the establishment of war crimes, where it was generally felt that no act could be legally prohibited if directed against the hated enemy. Yet war crimes became established in international law precisely because of a more enlightened realization that without them wars would become more brutal for no good reason and that both sides would be the losers. Similarly, if the admittedly unjustifiable acts of terrorists could be channeled into areas not involving brutality for brutality's sake against innocent civilians, that might be a worthwhile benefit to justify the cost of giving terrorists some incipient rights under the customary laws of war.

6. *Proportionality*. Under the doctrine of proportionality, anticipated military advantage or antecedent provocation are assessed in terms of the costs of collateral civilian deaths and destruction of property. The concept is close to that of military necessity, but there is a difference. An illustration of the difference is the hypothetical case of a densely populated residential area containing in its midst a small legitimate military target such as an armory or a light-vehicle factory. Bombing the area, with great collateral damage to civilians, might be justified under military necessity but might run afoul of the requirement of proportionality. The latter doctrine conceivably could bar bombing of the military target entirely if the bombs used (for example, nuclear weapons) would create too much civilian destruction in proportion to the worth of the military target that is hit. A second example would be the laws governing reprisals, already considered above. There may be no military necessity at all in an act of reprisal, but even if there is not, the reprisal still must pass the proportionality test.

Proving disproportionality is normally part of the persecution's case. However, if a particular court assigns the burden of proof to the defendant, the defendant should stress the costs and benefits as they reasonably appeared at the time of decision. Not only is second-guessing after the fact an unreasonable burden to place upon the defendant—amounting almost to a retroactive application of law—but more importantly, the laws of war are meant to deter unreasonable conduct while still allowing for the necessarily brutal task of subduing an enemy. An imbalance either way in the application of the laws of war can be counterproductive to their humanitarian origin.

7. *Other Defenses*. The defenses that have been covered here are those that may generally be asserted under international law when a person is accused of war crimes in an international or a national court. They stem not from the laws of the forum state, but rather from the same source that the forum state invokes in its indictment—international criminal law.

However, in national courts, many other defenses may exist under the particular laws of the forum state. The above enumeration and discussion of generally available defenses under customary international law should not be construed as pre-empting or replacing or otherwise diverting recourse to those defenses that are available in any criminal action under the laws of the forum state.

G. Environmental Crimes[11]

Anyone who has seen a sign on the back road reading, "No Dumping—Penal Code Sec. XYZ", or words to that effect, can perhaps understand some of the reasons for criminalizing certain kinds of environmentally harmful conduct. First, a prospective "dumper" would probably

---

[11] By STEPHEN C. McCAFFREY, excerpted from: *Crimes Against the Environment*, in 1 M. CHERIF BASSIOUNI (ED.), INTERNATIONAL CRIMINAL LAW: CRIMES 541, 543–45, 549, (N.Y.: Transnational Publishers, 1986). Reprinted by permission.

be less discouraged if the reference to the penal code did not appear on the sign; that reference tells him not only that the relevant community is serious about keeping the area clean, but also that he may be in for a stiff penalty if he gets caught dumping. Second, the area protected by the sign is most likely a "commons" (or the modern equivalent) from would-be dumpers; as a result, the now well-known "tragedy of the commons" would probably ensue: the value of the area to the dumper as a free means of waste disposal would outweigh its value to him as open, or at least unlittered space, and the community's interest in the area's being free of refuse would be too diffuse to discourage him. Since it is a res communis it is unprotected by private vigilance. Criminalization is an attempt to compensate for this by penalizing conduct which offends the public interest. It focuses the otherwise diffuse community interest and enforces it with sanctions. An early example of this use of the criminal law is the common law doctrine of public nuisance. At common law, a public nuisance was always a crime.

There would thus appear to be several categories of reasons for making criminal certain types of conduct that cause harm to the environment. Certainly a principal reason for criminalization in general is to deter conduct which is particularly harmful to society. An effectively enforced criminal statute raises the cost of certain kinds of conduct and thereby encourages compliance with the laws or regulations that would otherwise be largely ignored. The costs that criminalization raise are both monetary and nonmonetary. Monetary costs take the obvious form of imposing or raising a fine for prescribed violations. Perhaps equally important are the nonmonetary costs that flow from criminalization, foremost among which is the element of societal condemnation – a cost that even businesses capable of absorbing a stiff fine may not be willing to bear because of the damage to their reputation that would result. Imprisonment of individual offenders or corporate officials is another price that many potential violators would be unwilling to pay. There is a certain tendency, however, to think of criminalization as a kind of panacea, or "ultimate weapon:" make it a crime and they will stop doing it. Unfortunately, of course, it is not so simple. Penalties may not be sufficiently high to produce the desired deterrent effect, or enforcement may be so uneven, infrequent or difficult that an otherwise sound penal provision becomes a dead letter.

But despite its drawbacks, there are sound reasons for criminalizing environmentally harmful conduct. And it is submitted that these reasons apply with equal vigor to resources that are shared on the domestic and international levels. In fact, the considerations which support and explain criminalization on the domestic level may apply with even greater force to internationally shared resources. It is not necessary here to enter the debate about whether such resources are res nullius or res communis because many of them are, by their very nature, simply not capable of appropriation and reduction to ownership. They may, however, be used in a manner which forecloses certain uses by others or even leads to their complete destruction; air and water may be polluted, species may be extinguished.

Because it is thus likely that internationally shared resources will often be protected even less by private vigilance than their domestic counterparts, the argument for their protection by penal sanctions would seem to be stronger than that applicable on the domestic level. Furthermore, some internationally shared resources – such as certain species of flora and fauna – may be entirely and forever extinguished because of the "commons" effect, which may be more pronounced when the commons in question overlaps jurisdictions or is beyond the limits of national jurisdiction: to the extent that (a) national laws do not reach the conduct in question, and (b) it is not governed by relevant international regime, it will operate free of both private, and any existing public regulatory constraints.

These considerations have led states, both individually and collectively, to attach penal sanctions to certain kinds of conduct and activities that threaten, damage or destroy those natural resources which represent internationally shard values. Some fifteen multilateral conventions relating to the environment require the parties to enact and enforce criminal legislation to protect the subject-matter of those conventions. A number of conventions contain what might be referred to as "policing provisions" which allow the parties to take action on the spot to enforce the rules of the agreement. For example, the 1911 Convention for the Preservation of Fur Seals in the North Pacific[12] provides that persons violating the Convention's prohibition against pelagic sealing "may be seized" by the authorities in the territory in which the violation occurs. It also provides that each Party maintain a guard or patrol in the waters frequented by the Convention-protected seal herd. The Interim Convention on Conservation of North Pacific Fur Seals of 1957 goes further, allowing a duly authorized official of any of the Parties to board and search any vessel subject to the jurisdiction of any of the Parties if there is reasonable cause to believe that the vessel is offending against the prohibition of sealing, and to seize or arrest such vessel or the offending persons on board.[13] Finally, what might be referred to as a "self-policing provision" is found in the Agreement between Canada and the United States on Great Lakes Water Quality of 1978.[14] Annex 4 to that Agreement provides:

---

[12] 37 Stat. 1542, T.S. 564.

[13] 314 U.N.T.S. 105, T.I.A.S. No. 3948.

[14] 30 U.S.T. 1383, T.I.A.S. No. 9257.

> As soon as any person in charge [of a vessel] has knowledge of any discharge of harmful quantities of oil or hazardous polluting substances, immediate notice of such discharge shall be given to the appropriate agency in the jurisdiction where the discharge occurs; failure to give this notice shall be made subject to appropriate penalties.

While the conventional law of the environment is replete with examples of penal provisions, the international community relies for their enforcement upon municipal rather than international institutions. There seems to be general agreement that individuals should be punished under national law for certain conduct harmful to species or the environment. In the author's judgment, however, it cannot yet be said that there is similar agreement regarding the "criminal" responsibility of states. The entire concept of state criminal responsibility is an extremely controversial one, and even if the general concept were accepted, it would apparently apply only to "environmental" offenses that were so cataclysmic that they would be governed, in the first instance at least, by other normative systems.

H. Extradition

1. Overview[15]

The special procedure of delivering a fugitive criminal from one state to another is termed "extradition." Extradition may be requested in order to bring a fugitive criminal before the court to be tried or in order to execute a sentence already pronounced.

Though history records several instances of extradition of fugitive criminals since ancient times, the law of extradition is of much more recent origin, dating from the nineteenth century when international traffic was greatly facilitated by modern techniques of transport. The law of extradition is the result mainly of extradition treaties and is based upon the concept of sovereignty. Extradition has been generally looked upon as a special favor conceded to the prosecuting state, although according to a view dating to Jean Bodin and Hugo Grotius every state is bound under international law either to deliver a fugitive criminal or to try him.

1. *Reciprocity.* The principle of reciprocity as a general condition of any extradition still has a firm hold in most laws on extradition and is referred to in some recent judgments, but it has to be emphasized that it has been contested for a long time. As early as 1880 the Institute for International Law declared in its Resolutions of Oxford: "La condition de reciprocite, en cette matiere, peut etre commandee par la politique: elle n'est pas exigee par la justice." Although it would be desirable that more states practice extradition without demanding reciprocity. But in so far as extradition treaties are concerned, the condition of reciprocity has to be accepted, for it reflects and ensures the equality of states. However, the obligations of the two states that are bound by a treaty of extradition do not have to be identical. Thus reciprocity is satisfied if one state delivers its own nationals while the other state prosecutes its nationals for crimes committed in the first state.

2. *Extraditable Offenses.* It is an undisputed principle of the law of extradition that only a serious offense may be grounds for extradition. The reason for this restriction is purely technical; the procedure of extradition is always lengthy, cumbersome, and costly. The interests of the two states involved and of the fugitive coincide in excluding extradition for petty offenses.

This principle is effectuated by either of the following techniques: (1) extradition treaties might enumerate crimes for which extradition is granted or (2) they place certain minimum limits on punishment to allow extradition. There is a marked trend to prefer the second system of elimination to the older system of enumeration. The usual limit set by modern treaties is a minimum period of one year of deprivation of liberty. However, under "accessory extradition," the requesting state may grant extradition for an offense which does not fulfill the condition with regard to the minimum limit on punishment, provided the fugitive is prosecuted for another offense which fulfills this condition.

3. *Double Criminality.* According to principle, which is almost universally recognized, extradition is to be granted only if the act the fugitive is sought for is an extraditable crime according to the law of the demanding state as well as that of the requested state. Of course the acts of the fugitive must be punishable according to the law of the demanding state, but it might be questioned if the fugitive must be punishable according to the law of the requested state as well. If extradition is primarily looked upon as a means of facilitating criminal proceedings in another state, it might be inferred that it is of no importance to the requested state if its law sanctions punishment of the fugitive criminal. But if the protection of the individual's rights is of paramount importance, the principle of double criminality makes sense. For it would indeed be odd if a person could be arrested and deprived of his liberty, often for a considerable length of time, as a consequence of an act that would never have been prosecuted

---

[15] By HANS SCHULTZ, excerpted from: *The General Framework of Extradition and Asylum, in* 2 M. CHERIF BASSIOUNI & VED P. NANDA (EDS.), A TREATISE ON INTERNATIONAL CRIMINAL LAW 309 (1973). Reprinted by permission.

had it been committed in the requested state.[16] How could one justify the situation wherein the law of the requested state did exempt from punishment a certain behavior but conceded incarceration in order to grant extradition for it? Therefore, an exception is made only when external factors, for instance geographical conditions, cause a certain behavior to be punished in a certain state.

4. *Specialty.* Extradition being originally conceived as a favor granted by one state to another under certain conditions, it follows that extradition is limited to the offense or offenses for which it has been granted. This is the meaning of the universally accepted principle of specialty, according to which the demanding state is allowed to prosecute or to punish the extradited criminal only for the offenses mentioned in the act of extradition and none others; nor is it permissible to surrender him to a third state.

The exception of specialty is no longer applicable once the fugitive has been free for a certain time, generally one month in the demanding state, or if the requested state subsequently consents to his prosecution for another offense.

5. *Nature of the Offense.* Traditionally, extradition is to be granted only if the fugitive is prosecuted for an offense which is not political, military, or fiscal in nature. New developments are likely to occur in this area.

a. *Political Offenses.* Though extradition was exercised in earlier times in order to get hold of the enemies of a state, it is a heritage of liberalism that for quite some time now, extradition is usually refused for political offenses. The main reason for such refusal is that since political offenses are in the nature of attacks against the political order of a state – and it may be debatable if such an order is justified or not – extradition should be granted only if the attacked political order proves to be justified. This condition, however, presupposes that the requested state will examine the legitimacy of the political organizations of the demanding state, but this would not only endanger the friendly relations between both states but would be termed by the demanding state as an undue intervention in its internal affairs.[17] Besides, it may be feared that political offenders will not be treated impartially by the demanding state, and it would be a travesty of justice if the requested state were to grant extradition for a fugitive criminal who did nothing else but try to introduce in the demanding state the political order of the requested state.

The concept of "political crime" is not easy to define. It may assume various forms. For example, "absolute" political offenses consist of direct attacks upon the existence of a state, such as high treason or espionage. A "complex" political offense is the attempt on the life of the chief of state and his family; it is a combination of an absolute political offense with an ordinary offense that is made a special crime by some states. A "connex" political offense is a crime that has been perpetrated in order to prepare or facilitate an "absolute" or "complex" political crime or in order to protect its perpetrators. A "relative" political offense is an ordinary crime committed under such circumstances that its political character is dominant.

The law and the practice of the states may be divided into three groups. The first group recognizes as a political offense only the "absolute," "complex," and "connex" political offenses. A second group adds to these categories the "relative" political offense. A third group examines the motive of the criminal and holds a crime to be a political offense if any political motive is found.

During the early period of modern extradition law, it was customary to refuse extradition for political offenses. As the persons prosecuted for political offenses in the first decades of the nineteenth century were liberals fighting against the antiquated political organizations of their state, the political offender was looked upon as a champion of modern political ideas and generally an uncritical admiration for political offenders was in vogue. The fact that certain political movements and even isolated criminals resorted to terroristic tactics brought about an attitudinal change in judging political offenders. As early as 1856, a Belgian law declared that the attempt on the life of a chief of state and his family was not to be held a political offense. This famous Belgian clause was widely followed, but its critics were right in saying that it was not justified to exclude all such cases from the sphere of political offenses. It was argued that an attempt on the life of any citizen should never constitute a political offense. As an attempt to deter acts of violence, it was also contended that neither acts forbidden by the law of war nor acts of terrorism should ever be political offenses. And last but not least,

---

[16] [Editor's Note: Professor Bassiouini adds another reason for the principle of double criminality: "The law imposing criminal responsibility must not only be formulated as a law but also contain certain elements of notoriety and notice. These may not hold true in the case of a foreigner who has only entered the country shortly and who does not intend to become a domiciliary. However, if the act deemed an offense constitutes also an offense in his country of origin, then he will be on notice of the prohibited conduct. To hold otherwise may jeopardize the foreigner who will furthermore be universally denied a defense of ignorance of the law." M. Cherif Bassiouni, *International Extradition in American Practice and World Public Order*, in 2 M. Cherif Bassiouni & Ved P. Nanda (eds.), A Treatise on International Criminal Law 347, 360 (1973).]

[17] [Editor's Note: This situation may be changing as a result of the "emerging democratic entitlement"; states may assume that democratic states do not later turn undemocratic, and hence the "political offense objection" may atrophy. On the Democratic Entitlement, see Chapter 15 in this Anthology.]

the same was said of the crimes of war and crimes against humanity.

Future developments are likely to move in both directions: (1) Further attempts to prevent and deter acts of violence will be intensified; (2) the protection of the fugitive against political persecution will be sought by improving procedures of extradition.

b. *Military Offenses.* Extradition is usually not granted for "purely military offenses," i.e., violations of military order and discipline which can be committed only by military persons, for "improper military conduct," and for the offenses which are prohibited only by the military penal code. Extradition will be possible if a soldier commits an ordinary crime, even though the offense is also regulated by the military penal code, and the offender is to be tried by a court-martial. It should be noted that the exclusion of military offenses from extradition is not a fixed rule. Exceptions from it are quite common, especially in the case of states which are bound by military alliances.

c. *Fiscal and Economic Offenses.* The policy reasons for excluding fiscal offenses are based on state sovereignty and are similar to those for excluding military offenses. Thus, tax offenses did not give rise to extradition. Later on, the same principle was adopted concerning the violation of laws regulating economic life, as for instance, statutes prohibiting the transfer of money in a foreign country without the permission of the state authorities.

It is obvious that this way of looking at the fiscal offenses does not fit in with our contemporary world of welfare states and economic interdependence. Therefore modern laws of extradition do not exclude or even prohibit extradition for fiscal or economic offenses per se. Special treaties regulate such offenses, and the future developments are likely to follow the treaty route.

d. *Restriction by Place of Commission.* While some states refuse extradition if the offense is committed on the territory of the requested state, others allow it so long as no proceedings have been initiated by the authorities of the requested state. This much, however, is certain, that the requested state does not violate any principle of extradition law if it refuses extradition on the ground that the offense was committed on its territory or that the requested state is, for some other reason, competent to prosecute the fugitive, for instance, because he or the victim is its national, or because the offense was committed on a ship sailing under its flag.

On the other hand, the requested state is free to grant extradition even if its authorities are competent to prosecute the fugitive for the offense he is sought for, and even if the offense was committed in whole or in part in its territory. As a matter of comity, the requested state should renounce proceedings against a requested person who has committed offenses in its state if the bulk of the offenses the requested person is charged with have been committed in the demanding state.[18]

e. *Restriction Based on the Nature of the Requested Person.* It is an old maxim of continental law of extradition that the requested state does not deliver its own nationals. The reason for this rule is the fear that the offender, being a foreigner in the demanding state, might have some difficulties in defending himself in a proper manner and even otherwise he might not get a fair trial. Some states refuse extradition of persons living permanently in their country as well. The privilege in favor of the nationals is extended to the residents in order to permit the place of domicile to try the case and to apply the sanction that seem to be the best to rehabilitate the delinquent.

The common law countries, however, grant extradition of their nationals. The reason being that if the national has committed an offense abroad, it will be left to him to cope with the difficulties of the proceedings in a foreign country. Besides, extradition of nationals seems desirable for the common law countries who do not, as a rule, prosecute for offenses committed abroad.

Perhaps a desirable development would be to allow each state to decide on the issue of a national's extradition but to require the requested state to prosecute the fugitive offender if he is not extradited.

f. *Restriction Based on the Nature of the Penalty.* Some extradition laws and treaties permit the requested state to refuse extradition if the offense for which extradition is asked is punishable by death under the law of the demanding state and if this penalty is not provided for by the law of the requested state or is normally not carried out, unless the demanding state gives sufficient assurance that the death penalty will not be carried out. So long as the death penalty is retained by some states, this principle seems to be both necessary and desirable.

The same is to be said of the rule that extradition may be refused if the requested person will incur corporal punishment. It may be added that the developing law of human rights may make this question moot by forbidding corporal punishment.

2. The Political Offense Exception[19]

Although most states accept the political offense exception to extradition, there are no common standards as to

[18] [Editor's Note: Compare the problem of intercountry abduction, discussed below in this Chapter.]

[19] By CHRISTINE VAN DER WIJNGAERT, excerpted from: THE POLITICAL EXCEPTION TO EXTRADITION: THE DELICATE PROBLEM OF BALANCING THE RIGHTS OF THE INDIVIDUAL AND THE INTERNATIONAL PUBLIC ORDER 1–4 (1980). Reprinted by permission.

the practical application of the rule. This is due to the fact that extradition laws and treaties almost never define the term "political offense" in abstracto, and consequently the interpretation of the term in concreto is left to judicial and administrative authorities who have to decide, in each particular case, whether or not the facts for which extradition is requested constitute political crimes.

While there is no universally recognized definition of the term "political offense," there are, however, a number of "negative definitions," in that it has been provided that certain offenses are not considered as political crimes for the purposes of extradition. Such negative definitions have been formulated, inter alia, for attempts on the lives of heads of state, war crimes, genocide, collaboration with the enemy, acts of terrorism, etc. As such the scope of the political offense exception has been considerably restricted.

Conversely, the scope of the exception has been extended by means of an additional provision prohibiting extradition, not so much on the grounds of the political character of the facts for which extradition is requested, but on the political character of the extradition request. According to this provision, the exception applies if it appears that the extradition request has been made for the purpose of prosecuting the requested person for a political offense, or if the extradition would subject him to prosecution on account of his race, nationality, political opinions or other reasons.

The rationale of the political offense exception is based on the three interests which converge in the rule: those of the requested person, the states concerned (requesting and requested state) and international public order. Under classic extradition theory, this rationale has been explained as follows:

First, with respect to the requested person, the political offense exception has a humanitarian function. It is meant as a protection against an unfair and retaliatory trial in the requesting state which, being the target of the political crime, would function simultaneously as judge and jury.

Second, as regards the states party in interest, the political offense exception is based upon the principle of neutrality. According to classic extradition theory, extradition of political offenders does not further good relations between the states concerned, as the inquiry into the extraditability of a political crime implies a judgment with respect to the political conflict situation in the requesting state. Such a judgment could amount to the taking of a position which, in turn, could be interpreted as a disguised intervention in the internal affairs of the requesting state. Therefore it is better to refuse extradition of political offenders a priori. Motives of self-interest understandably underlie this reasoning: today's political offenders could be tomorrow's political leaders; consequently, the requesting state is best advised to keep itself neutral with respect to political conflicts in the requesting state.

The third part of the rationale underlying the exception is the assumption that political crimes do not violate international public order and therefore states are supposed not to have a mutual interest in the suppression of such crimes. Political offenses have only a local character because they are directed against the domestic public order of the requesting state, and consequently perpetrators of such acts do not constitute a danger for the public order of other states.[20] In addition, international penal cooperation with respect to political offenses is less essential than with respect to common offenses because political crimes have only a relatively anti-social character. As opposed to common offenses, political crimes are not inherently "criminal" because the perpetrator, in theory, does not act from personal motives, but for the benefit of society as a whole. Consequently, his acts are not anti-social but on the contrary altruistic and "hyper-social" because they are committed for the general well-being. This altruism distinguishes the political offender from other offenders and it makes his acts less reprehensible and in some cases very excusable.

Moreover, the possible "criminality" of the state or of the regime against which the act is directed, can, it is true, not eliminate its criminal character, but can possibly shed another light upon it. The nineteenth century idea that rebellion against suppression is legitimate plays an important role in this reasoning.

Finally, the ultimate "criminal" character of political crimes is in the end only dependent upon the outcome of the political struggle. The remark made by Balzac, "Les conspirateurs vaincus sont des brigands, vainqueurs, ils sont des heros" (vanquished conspirators are villains, victorious, they are heroes), still holds true today: many of today's leaders are the "terrorists" of yesterday, whose acts were only justified because they won their political struggle. However, they could as well have ended their lives as criminals, had they been the losers.

The reasons advanced in support of the political offense exception are not as logical as they may seem on the surface. Are political offenders always likely to be subjected to an unfair and partial trial? Is the non-extradition of political offenders always to be considered as an act of neutrality, or on the contrary, is it an effective support to political adversaries of the requested state? And finally, is the relative anti-social character of political crimes to be taken for granted?

---

20 [Editor's Note: Under a combination of the "Democratic Entitlement" and "Perpetual Peace" theories, *infra* Part IV, would it be possible to argue that an anti-democratic movement in a democratic state constitutes a danger to the public order of other states?]

3. Debate: The U.S.-U.K. Supplementary Treaty Is a Retrogressive Step in Extradition Law

a. Affirmative[21]

The Supplementary Extradition Treaty between the United States and the United Kingdom of 1985,[22] amending the 1972 Extradition treaty between the two countries,[23] lists the following crimes for which the political offense exception shall no longer apply: murder, voluntary manslaughter, assault causing grievous bodily harm, kidnapping, abduction, serious unlawful detention including taking a hostage, offenses involving the use of a bomb, grenade, rocket, firearm, letter or parcel bomb, and attempt to commit any of these offenses or participation as an accomplice of a person who commits them. The crucial point is that these are offenses which could be charged by the winning side against its opponents in virtually any civil war or significant insurrection, even if the conduct was engaged against military targets during armed combat. The Supplementary Treaty eviscerates the political offense exception to extradition. It is an inefficient means of fighting terrorism and is inconsistent with legal traditions and social values.

b. A Second Affirmative[24]

Some governments and writers have taken the position that extradition is predominantly a political process between states that involves their foreign relations, and that it is, therefore, in the nature of a ''contract'' or ''compact'' between states. The Supplementary Treaty reflects this orientation. The implication of that conception is that the individual is only an ''object'' and not a ''subject'' of this legal process. Consequently, the individual would have no rights except those that each of the two states chooses to concede. State-granted concessions to individuals will, of course, depend on the degree of political closeness of the respective states, regardless of the rights of the individual under national or international law. Thus, states desiring to strengthen their respective public orders will make extradition easiest between themselves. They will also reduce or eliminate some or all of the substantive and procedural rights of the relator, which they would otherwise uphold with respect to states not enjoying such favored treatment. Individual rights would thus depend upon state interests, irrespective of the other values and policies that might be at stake.

The better view, however, is that individuals are legal subjects entitled to assert rights that inure to their benefit under international law, applicable treaties, and national laws. This view requires that such rights be afforded to individuals uniformly and consistently and that they not be dependent upon the tergiversations of political interests. Such a view derives from the concept of extradition as a tripartite international process involving the requesting state, the requested state and the relator, whose interests must be taken into account.

The purposes and policies of the ''political offense exception'' and the values embodied therein should be first identified before appraising their significance. They include inter alia: (1) political neutrality in foreign internal conflicts; (2) the individual and collective right of resistance, including armed resistance under certain conditions and subject to certain rules; (3) the application of internationally recognized norms of human rights with respect to the rendition of a requested person; and (4) an international duty to cooperate in the prevention and suppression of international criminality as a means of preserving world order.

The crimes enumerated in the Supplementary Treaty are excluded from the ''political offense exception'' irrespective of their nature, intensity, the harm they produce, the motives and goals of the actor, and the circumstances that may have compelled the actor to commit them. The exclusions are contrary to customary international law.

c. Negative[25]

The philosophy of the Supplementary Treaty is to preclude application of the political offense exception where

---

[21] By CHRISTOPHER L. BLAKESLEY, excerpted from: *The Evisceration of the Political Offense Exception to Jurisdiction*, 15 DENVER JOURNAL OF INTERNATIONAL LAW AND POLICY 109, 118, 121 (1986). Reprinted by permission.

[22] Supplementary Extradition Treaty, June 25, 1985, United States-United Kingdom, 24 ILM 1105 (1985).

[23] Extradition Treaty, June 8, 1972, United States-United Kingdom, 28 U.S.T. 227, T.I.A.S. No. 8468.

[24] By M. CHERIF BASSIOUNI, excerpted from: *The ''Political Offense Exception'' Revisited: Extradition Between the U.S. and the U.K.—A Choice Between Friendly Cooperation Among Allies and Sound Law and Policy*, 15 DENVER JOURNAL OF INTERNATIONAL LAW AND POLICY 255, 259–60 (1987). Reprinted by permission.

[25] By STEVEN LUBET, excerpted from: *International Criminal Law and the ''Ice Nine'' Error: A Discourse on the Fallacy of Universal Solutions*, 28 VIRGINIA JOURNAL OF INTERNATIONAL LAW

(1) the crime involved is one of serious violence; (2) the crime involved was committed against the government or people of a stable democracy; and (3) where the institutions of due process are firmly in place. The Supplementary Treaty changes nothing in the political offense exception as it applies to non-violent crimes; these continue to be protected against extradition where they are incident to a political disturbance, or when they have the character of free-speech activity. Even as to violent crimes, neither government suggests that the approach of the Supplementary Treaty be extended beyond the relatively small circle of nations that qualify as stable democracies with fair and independent judicial systems. The point is obvious: between democracies there is little need to shelter insurrectionaries, in part because the United States repudiates the justification for any acts of insurrection. In other words, we are capable of recognizing our international friends and acting in concert to protect them (and us) from even the most politically virtuous terrorists.

M. Cherif Bassiouni does not and cannot make the argument that violence is a human right. Indeed, even political violence may be subject to extradition depending upon the nature of the offense, victims, and other circumstances. He apparently argues, however, that universality of application is an internationally recognized value which, if not binding as a matter of international law, is at least of sufficient importance to defeat the bilateral approach of the Supplementary Treaty.

Professor Bassiouni considers the extradition process as a tripartite process involving the requesting state, the requested state, and the "relator." Another term for "relator," of course, would be "fugitive." While it certainly is self-evident that the community of international fugitives has an interest in uniform and predictable rules of extradition, it is far less obvious that any particular nation or group of nations should indulge that need.

Country-by-country revision of the political-offense exception is appropriate to distinguish between repressive regimes and democracies that function under the rule of law. Cooperation among nations, and particularly among nations of like political and legal systems, can only aid the fight against international terrorism. The Supplementary Treaty between the United States and the United Kingdom sets a standard for the treatment of the political-offense exception to extradition that ought to be widely emulated among the community of democratic nations.

963, 967–68, 971–72 (1988), and *Taking the Terror Out of Political Terrorism: The Supplementary Treaty of Extradition Between the United States and the United Kingdom*, 19 CONNECTICUT LAW REVIEW 863, 882, 893 (1987). Reprinted by permission.

d. Affirmative Reply[26]

According to Steven Lubet, we should have bilateral exclusions of the political offense exception in treaties with our "democratic" friends on a "country-by-country" basis. The obvious flaw in such a scheme, however, is that there is simply no guarantee that yesterday's democracy will remain so, that a new regime will not be repressive, and that local nationals will not need to engage in certain acts of violence to promote authority and self-determination, to effectuate a lawful revolution, or in defense against serious deprivations of fundamental human rights.

Suppose, for instance, that the exclusions in the Supplementary Treaty had been incorporated in an extradition treaty with the German Weimar Republic and that it was still in force in the 1930s. If German nationals of Jewish faith had used firearms to assassinate Hitler, and had fled to the United States, should we have extradited them back to Nazi Germany? Should they have been extradited if they had merely used firearms in order to escape from a concentration camp and had killed German camp guards and soldiers? And if upon escaping they had blown up trains and train tracks in and outside of Germany, in an effort to stall or stop Nazi extermination of fellow nationals, should they have been extradited because they used bombs and firearms?

Impermissible terrorism clearly poses a threat to human dignity. But the "antiterrorist" statisticians fail to count the many more terrorist deaths that occur in the name of the state and that pose at least as great a threat to human rights and democratic values. What we must ever guard against are extralegal or lawless tactics exercised in the name of antiterrorism.

e. Negative Reply[27]

Jordan Paust says that "there is simply no guarantee that yesterday's democracy will remain so." Apparently he concedes that in the case of today's democracy, no one need engage in certain acts of violence to effect political change. This is the very point of the Supplementary Treaty.

Professor Paust's argument, then, rests upon our pow-

---

[26] By JORDAN J. PAUST, excerpted from: *An Introduction to and Commentary on Terrorism and the Law*, 19 CONNECTICUT LAW REVIEW 697, 741–42, 748 (1987). Reprinted by permission.

[27] By STEVEN LUBET, excerpted from: *International Criminal Law and the "Ice Nine" Error: A Discourse on the Fallacy of Universal Solutions*, 28 VIRGINIA JOURNAL OF INTERNATIONAL LAW 963, 977–84 (1988). Reprinted by permission.

ers of prediction. He apparently lacks faith in our government's ability to identify stable democracies. While there may be "no guarantee" that the United Kingdom will continue to function under the rule of law, we do have several centuries of history and direct experience to reflect upon in making the decision. At some point even law professors must allow that the President and Senate are able to make rational judgments. And indeed, far more momentous decisions than extraditability routinely flow from a governmental assessment of an ally's stability. The decisions, for example, to locate military installations in friendly countries, or to station nuclear weapons in other nations, or to share intelligence with allied regimes, all involve a risk significantly greater than the restriction of the political offense exception. Imagine the potential for harm that results from our sharing sensitive security information with a government that, to our surprise, could overnight become one of an entirely different stripe. Yet we routinely entrust such decisions to the military and the State Department, and without the high level of political scrutiny given the ratification of extradition treaties. Must we really fear that the President and two-thirds of the Senate will err in their judgment of which nations may be entrusted to continue to provide fair trials to violent criminals? And if our government is so unreliable, we obviously have far greater insecurities to attend to than the extraditability of a few offenders each year.

But Professor Paust's argument is weaker even than that. Assume that we really are incapable of making intelligent choices among our extradition partners, and that we may enter into a treaty restricting the political offense exception that we will live to regret. Assume that we wake up one morning to discover that a previously stable democracy to which we are obliged, by virtue of such a treaty, to extradite all violent offenders, has overnight become a tyranny that now "needs" to be overthrown. Have we negotiated ourselves into a corner? Are we now compelled to surrender political offenders whom we would far rather protect?

The answer, of course, is no. In even the most extreme circumstances, several avenues of relief allow us to avoid extradition. Treaties, including extradition treaties, may be abrogated or suspended. This is a drastic step, but where a stable democracy transforms itself into a "repressive regime," it is altogether likely that we will be at least standoffish, if not openly hostile, to the new government. Accordingly, the suspension and/or renegotiation of the extradition arrangement is a reasonable supposition.

The approach of the Supplementary Treaty will cause fewer problems than will a continued expansive view of the political offense exception. More importantly, the problems themselves will be of a very different qualitiative nature. If we follow the standard view of the political offense exception, our problem is that we give shelter to terrorists. The guilty go free, our allies are damaged, and we must somehow explain this result to friendly governments. Under the Supplementary Treaty, however, the "problem," if it arises at all, will be our refusal to render a fugitive in accordance with the terms of the treaty. That is, the governmental discomfort will be caused purposefully by our own determination that a particular offender ought not be extradited. We will trade the problem of intergovernmental tension created by our inability to render the guilty for the far less disruptive problem of intergovernmental tension created by our ability to shield the deserving.

Professor Paust's paradigm case of unpredictability is his Weimar Republic example. His exercise in Holocaust comparativism is pointless at best. Is there any basis other than tendentiousness for comparing the United Kingdom to the Weimar Republic? The situation of Germany in the 1930s was sui generis; it hardly stands as a guide for our future conduct regarding the political offense exception. The very obviousness of the answer to Professor Paust's comparison betrays its usefulness. No doctrine of international relations, and especially no doctrine of international law enforcement, can withstand retrospective comparison to Hitler's Germany. Suppose we had a mutual defense treaty with the Weimar Republic; would we then have invaded Poland? Suppose that we had a treaty regarding the reciprocal enforcement of civil judgments; would we have levied on the Jewish community in order to execute the fine imposed following Kristallnacht?[28] The very quickness of our negative replies to these questions demonstrates their irrelevance to complex problems concerning our contemporary treaty relationships.

In any event, the Weimar Republic was not a stable democracy where the institutions of due process were firmly in place. No modern historian nor any contemporary observer has ever credited the Weimar Republic with stability. There is simply no basis on which to suppose that the United States, only a few years after the defeat of the Kaiser, would have taken the extraordinary step of extending "most favored extraditor" treatment to the Weimar Republic. One might just as usefully suppose that our government entered into extradition treaties purely by lot.

---

[28] Kristallnacht, or the night of the broken windows, occurred on November 9, 1938, starting a week of "spontaneous reprisals" against the Jewish community in Germany following the assassination of a German official in Paris. Despite the murder of 36 Jews and 10,000 Jews sent to Buchenwald, from the Nazis' point of view the only problem was that millions of marks worth of plate glass and other property had been destroyed. The Nazi regime imposed a collective fine on the Jewish community in the amount of a billion marks. The fine was enforced by government-ordered confiscations of property.

The second leg of Professor Paust's syllogism is equally flawed. We cannot suppose that even an improvidently negotiated restriction of the political offense exception would have continued into the 1930s following the rise of Hitler. For all of the reasons that we would abrogate or suspend (or ignore) such a treaty now, were the United Kingdom to take a drastic turn away from the rule of law, we obviously would have taken similar steps to discontinue such a treaty with the Nazis.

The Supplementary Treaty is a valuable, near-term step in the contest against international terrorism. It is an application, not a perfect unified theory. It does not address all problems, but it does solve the problems it addresses.

The unwillingness of academic commentators to see the virtue of such a narrow approach stems from either a grandiosity or a shortness of vision. Perhaps they see the problem of terrorism too broadly, or perhaps they are simply unconcerned with specific resolutions. In either case, a more focused view should result in a wider adoption of the law enforcement approach to international terrorism.

f. Affirmative Rejoinder[29]

Steven Lubet says violence is not a human right. But in some contexts there is a lawful right of revolution—recognized for example in the United States Declaration of Independence.

Professor Lubet says that the United Kingdom is a "stable democracy" with "institutions of due process" that are "firmly in place." But even in the United Kingdom one can find draconian laws, detention without trial, the suspension of "due process" in the name of antiterrorism, and other serious deprivations of human right precepts.[30] One cannot concede that merely because there exists a relative democracy "no one need engage in certain acts of violence." Indeed, it is erroneous to assume that relevant legal policies are at stake only in the circumstances of a sudden and jarring change of a closely allied government. The political offense exception addresses problems posed by tyranny in degrees or human rights deprivations in degrees. Just as there may be a continuum of "stability" (with some democracies more stable than others or at certain times), it is more realistic to recognize that there may be a continuum of "due process" and the enjoyment of other fundamental human rights. With respect to deprivations in degrees, the simplistic list-of-exclusions approach is not merely narrowly focused but blind.

When individuals are in need of protection from extradition, Professor Lubet's solution is that the Executive abrogate, suspend, or simply violate the extradition treaty. Why should an entire treaty process be abandoned or seriously jeopardized? Instead, the political offense exception itself allows a built-in flexibility in the treaty relationship. It allows, moreover, an out for the executive who seeks to avoid undue foreign pressure and who seeks a continuous treaty process.

Professor Lubet's suggestion that an executive simply violate the treaty has additional flaws. It is not "less radical" but shockingly inadequate and generally impermissible. It demonstrates, moreover, some of the dangers posed by a narrow, result-oriented approach which ignores other legal policies and interests at stake, other features of context, and probable short and long-term consequences. In sum, the U.S.-U.K. approach should be abandoned.

[29] By JORDAN J. PAUST, excerpted from: *"Such a Narrow Approach" Indeed*, 19 VIRGINIA JOURNAL OF INTERNATIONAL LAW 413 (1989). Reprinted by permission.

[30] *See, e.g.*, INT'L COMM. JURISTS, STATES OF EMERGENCY—THEIR IMPACT ON HUMAN RIGHTS 217–46 (1983); RICHARD LILLICH AND FRANK NEWMAN (EDS.), INTERNATIONAL HUMAN RIGHTS: PROBLEMS OF LAW AND POLICY 563–627 (1979); Francis Boyle, *Human Rights and Political Resolution in Northern Ireland*, 9 YALE J. WORLD PUB. ORD. 156 (1982).

I. Abduction

1. The Threat to World Order[31]

A serious threat to world public order lies in the practice of unlawful seizure of a person in a foreign state and his abduction. The Eichmann and Tschombe cases will remain landmarks of such abusive practice. The abduction or kidnapping is a transgression against the sovereignty of the state wherein the fugitive was taken by agents of another state. It is an affront of the asylum state and a challenge to the lawfulness of orderly world relations—not to mention the individual's human rights. The most serious consequences can result from such practice on the peaceful relations of the respective states and are a threat to world public order. American courts accept jurisdiction over the person of an accused present in court and exercise it no matter how it was secured. The means by which the presence of the accused was obtained has never inhibited the courts. Practically every category of unlawful methods of securing jurisdictional presence has been used so far; and the courts have tacitly accepted for purposes of jurisdiction such practices as disguised extradition, abduction and kid-

[31] By M. CHERIF BASSIOUNI, from: *International Extradition in American Practice and World Public Order*, in 2 M. CHERIF BASSIOUNI & VED P. NANDA (EDS.), A TREATISE ON INTERNATIONAL CRIMINAL LAW 347, 357–58 (1973). Reprinted by permission.

napping, fraud and false pretenses; all have passed the legal test.

The Eichmann and Tschombe cases gave rise to international clamor and demonstrated how potentially harmful the practice is with respect to the maintenance of world peace and public order. But the practice will continue to go unabated so long as the courts will accept in personam jurisdiction irrespective of how the defendant was brought before the court. The gist of the problem is the violation by a state of the orderly process of legality of conduct.

2. Facts of the Alvarez Case[32]

The facts of the Alvarez Abduction case were unusual, to say the least. In 1985, the U.S. Drug Enforcement Agency [DEA], working with Mexican law enforcement officials, conducted a series of highly successful raids on drug producers and traffickers in and around Guadalajara. That city, site of the recent assassination of Cardinal Juan Jesus Posadas Ocampo, has long been viewed as a bastion for Mexican drug traffickers.[33] Partly in response to the success of these raids, local drug lords arranged for the seizure, torture, and killing of DEA special agent Enrique Camarena-Salazar and his Mexican pilot, Alfredo Zavala-Avelar.[34] Their bodies were recovered one month later at the ranch of local drug lord Rafael Caro Quintero, 60 miles outside of Guadalajara.[35]

Mexican authorities proceeded to investigate the crime, but the United States government was disappointed by their slow pace. Five years passed, during which Mexico prosecuted and convicted twelve men in relation to the case; however, the majority of suspects had not yet been prosecuted.[36] On February 1, 1990, the Justice Department announced the indictment in Federal District court of 19 Mexican nationals connected to the case. Only one person named in the indictment was actually in the United States at the time. The indictment included two high ranking Mexican law enforcement officials and Dr. Humberto Alvarez-Machain, a gynecologist with offices in Guadalajara. Dr. Alvarez was accused of injecting agent Camarena-Salazar with stimulants during torture sessions in order to keep him alive for interrogation.

The United States did not make a formal extradition request for Dr. Alvarez under the 1978 U.S.-Mexico Extradition Treaty. Rather, Mexican police officials quietly approached the DEA to negotiate a trade; Dr. Alvarez for a Mexican national at large in the United States.[37] When these negotiations broke down, several Mexicans, representing themselves as Mexican police, offered to turn over Dr. Alvarez to the DEA for a fee. A $50,000 bounty, plus expenses, was authorized by high level DEA officials.

On April 2, 1990, Dr. Alvarez was abducted from his Guadalajara offices, placed on a private plane, flown to El Paso, Texas, and turned over to waiting DEA agents who took him to Los Angeles for arraignment on the Federal charges.

The abduction occasioned public outcry in Mexico and the anger of Mexican President Salinas. The Mexican government declared the abduction to be in violation of the extradition treaty and Mexican sovereignty. On April 18, 1990, Mexico requested an official report on the role of the United States in the abduction, and on May 16, 1990 and July 19, 1990, it sent diplomatic notes of protest from the Embassy of Mexico to the United States Department of State. In the May 16th note, Mexico said that it believed that the abduction was "carried out with the knowledge of persons working for the U.S. government, in violation of the procedure established in the extradition treaty in force between the two countries," and in the July 19th note, it requested the provisional arrest and extradition of the law enforcement agents allegedly involved in the abduction. Unofficially, Mexican authorities threatened to halt DEA activities in Mexico unless Dr. Alvarez was returned.[38] The government of Mexico stated that it would prosecute and punish Dr. Alvarez upon his remission to Mexico. The United States refused Mexico's demand and denied that the DEA was involved in the actual abduction.[39] Mexican prosecutors quickly detained four officials thought to have been involved with the abduction.[40] The magazine *Proceso* revealed the names of 49 people thought to be DEA agents operating in Mexico.[41]

---

32 By JACQUES MacCHESNEY and ANTHONY D'AMATO, written for this Anthology.

33 Washington Post, July 15, 1993, Tod Robberson, pA20.

34 *Murder Case That Has Strained Ties to Mexico Goes to Jury*, N.Y. Times, July 17, 1990, at A19; *Mexican Doctor Goes on Trial in Agent's Slaying*, N.Y. Times, Dec. 3, 1992, at A17.

35 Robert Reinhold, *Judge Tells U.S. to Free Mexican Abducted in Drug Agent's Death*, N.Y. Times, Aug 11, 1990, §1, at 1.

36 Richard L. Berke, *2 Ex-Mexican Aides Charged in Slaying of U.S. Drug Agent*, N.Y. Times, Feb. 1, 1990, at A1. Mexico had prosecuted and convicted 12 men in relation to the case.

37 Robert Reinhold, *Witness Says U.S. Offered Reward to Get a Suspect*, N.Y. Times, May 26, 1990, §1, at 1.

38 Philip Shenon, *Mexico Says Suspect's Seizure Imperils Aid to U.S. on Drugs*, N.Y. Times, April 20, 1990, at A1.

39 Philip Shenon, *U.S. Says It Won't Return Mexican Doctor Linked to Drug Killing*, N.Y. Times, April 21, 1990, sec. 1, at 3.

40 Larry Rohter, *Mexico Detains 4 Officers in Abduction of Doctor Accused in U.S.*, N.Y. Times, April 27, 1990, at A8.

41 Philip Shenon, *U.S. Agents in Mexico, Listed, Are on Alert*, N.Y. Times, April 24, 1990, at A5. Asked about the accuracy of the list, the DEA called it "too close for comfort."

Nevertheless, federal prosecutors moved ahead with the case against Dr. Alvarez. In light of the situation, Federal District Judge Edward Rafeedie ordered the DEA to disclose all events relating to the abduction.[42] The DEA acknowledged its offer of a $50,000 reward, the approval by high ranking DEA officials, and the payment after the abduction of an additional $20,000 for expenses. Mexico in turn demanded the extradition of two men involved in the abduction – a DEA agent and an informer.

On August 11, 1990, Judge Rafeedie ruled that the abduction of Dr. Alvarez violated the U.S.-Mexico extradition treaty.[43] The judge held that, accordingly, the court lacked criminal jurisdiction over Dr. Alvarez. The judge ordered his return to Mexico pending a seven day stay for the Justice Department to appeal. President Salinas of Mexico hailed the ruling as "a victory for justice and legality." Yet two subsequent rulings ensured that the case did not stop there. The Ninth Circuit granted a stay of the release order, and then Judge Rafeedie denied Dr. Alvarez bail, finding him at risk to flee.[44]

After fourteen months of consideration, the Ninth Circuit affirmed.[45] The Supreme Court granted certiorari. The Department of Justice contended that all 103 extradition treaties that the United States had entered into were negotiated in full view of the Ker-Frisbie doctrine – a nineteenth century American judicial view that an abductee lacked standing to claim lack of jurisdiction because of a violation of an extradition treaty.

The Supreme Court reversed the Ninth Circuit and remanded the case for trial proceedings.[46] Justice Rehnquist, for the majority, said this about international law:

> Respondent and his amici may be correct that respondent's abduction was "shocking," and that it may be in violation of general international law principles.

But in examining the U.S.-Mexico Extradition Treaty, Justice Rehnquist said:

> The Treaty says nothing about the obligations of the United States and Mexico to refrain from forcible abductions of people from the territory of the other nation, or the consequences under the Treaty if such an abduction occurs. . . . Abductions outside of the Treaty do not constitute a violation of the Treaty.

Justice STEVENS, joined by Justice BLACKMUN and Justice O'CONNOR dissented:

> [P]rovisions [of the Treaty] requiring "sufficient" evidence to grant extradition (Art. 3), withholding extradition for political or military offenses (Art. 5), withholding extradition when the person sought has already been tried (Art. 6), withholding extradition when the statute of limitations for the crime has lapsed (Art. 7), and granting the requested State discretion to refuse to extradite an individual who would face the death penalty in the requesting country (Art. 8), would serve little purpose if the requesting country could simply kidnap the person. . . . [T]hese provisions "only make sense if they are understood as requiring each treaty signatory to comply with those procedures whenever it wishes to obtain jurisdiction over an individual who is located in another treaty nation."[47] [The majority's view] is a highly improbable interpretation of a consensual agreement, which on its face appears to have been intended to set forth comprehensive and exclusive rules concerning the subject of extradition.

Justice Stevens cites amicus curiae briefs in the case filed by Mexico and Canada:

> Mexico's understanding is that "the extradition treaty governs comprehensively the delivery of all persons for trial in the requesting state 'for an offense committed outside the territory of the requesting Party.' " And Canada, with whom the United States also shares a large border and with whom the United States also has an extradition treaty, understands the treaty to be "the exclusive means for a requesting government to obtain a removal" of a person from its territory, unless a Nation otherwise gives its consent.

When the Supreme Court handed down its decision, the Mexican Secretariat of Foreign Relations issued a communiqué calling the decision "invalid and unacceptable."[48] Latin American leaders examined a proposal to declare U.S. ambassadors persona non grata in response to the ruling.[49] Mexico further demanded a review of the 1978

[42] *Hearing Ordered in Mexico Arrest*, N.Y. TIMES, May 23, 1990, at A24.

[43] 745 F. Supp. 599 (C.D. Cal. 1990). Robert Reinhold, *Judge Tells U.S. to Free Mexican Abducted in Drug Agent's Death*, N.Y. TIMES, Aug. 11, 1990, §1, at 1.

[44] *2 Court Rulings Prevent Release of Mexican Doctor Held by U.S.*, N.Y. TIMES, Aug 25, 1990, §1, at 9.

[45] 946 F.2d 1466 (9th Cir. 1991). *U.S. Court Orders Mexican's Release*, N.Y. TIMES, Oct. 20, 1991, §1, at 1.

[46] 112 S. Ct. 2188, 119 L. Ed. 2d 441 (June 15, 1992).

[47] United States v. Verdugo-Urquidez, 939 F.2d 1341, 1351 (1991).

[48] Tim Golden, *After Court Ruling, Mexico Tells U.S. Drug Agents to Halt Activity*, N.Y. TIMES, June 15, 1992, at A19.

[49] NOTIMEX (Mexican News Service), June 17, 1992.

extradition treaty, with an eye towards addressing the kidnap issue.[50]

Mexican capital markets fell sharply when the Alvarez case seemed to threaten the NAFTA negotiations.[51] President Salinas' decision not to halt DEA activities was assumed to be closely linked to his hopes for the completion of NAFTA. Mexican analysts commented that former President Luis Echeverria "would have probably broken relations. There was probably pressure at the highest level for a deal on free trade. Clearly Mexico decided not to jeopardize other elements of the relationship [between the two nations]."[52] One analyst went so far as to state that "Mexico is hostage to the Free Trade Agreement."[53]

Other nations expressed displeasure with the new American self-defined right to kidnap. Canada stated that any attempt to abduct a person in Canada would be viewed as "a criminal act." Argentina was equally "shocked."[54] Analysts within the United States pointed out that if this right to kidnap actually existed, then the United States would be subject to abductions as well.

In the fall of 1992, Dr. Alvarez finally went to trial before Judge Rafeedie. There was a report that the U.S. government paid $2.7 million dollars to various prosecution witnesses.[55] Judge Rafeedie then threw out the case against Dr. Alvarez Machain for lack of direct evidence.[56] Dr. Alvarez returned to Mexico where he initiated a $20 million lawsuit against various United States officials who were allegedly involved in his abduction.

President Clinton recently pledged not to abduct anyone from Mexico during the negotiation of modifications to the Extradition Treaty.[57] Secretary of State Warren Christopher, announcing that the matter has been referred to a working group under the auspices of the United States-Mexico Binational Commission, stated the key issue is to make extradition easier.

[50] Tim Golden, *After Court Ruling, Mexico Tells U.S. Drug Agents to Halt Activity*, N.Y. TIMES, June 15, 1992, at A19.

[51] Tim Golden, *Mexicans Mollified Over Drug Ruling*, N.Y. TIMES, June 18, 1992, at A3.

[52] Paul Iredale, *Mexican Free Spirit Takes Back Seat in New U.S. Relationship*, REUTERS, June 18, 1992, AM cycle.

[53] Tim Golden, *After Court Ruling, Mexico Tells U.S. Drug Agents to Halt Activity*, N.Y. TIMES, June 15, 1992, at A19.

[54] Neil A. Lewis, *U.S. Tries to Quiet Storm Abroad Over High Court's Right-to-Kidnap Ruling*, N.Y. TIMES, June 17, 1992, at A8.

[55] *Payments are Detailed in Case of Slain Drug Agent*, N.Y. TIMES, Nov. 8, 1992, at A12.

[56] Seth Mydans, *Judge Clears Mexican in Agent's Killing*, N.Y. Times, Dec. 15, 1992, at A20.

[57] Steven A. Holmes, *U.S. Gives Mexico Abduction Pledge*, N.Y. TIMES, June 22, 1993, at A11.

3. DEBATE: Abduction Does Not Violate the U.S.-Mexico Extradition Treaty

a. Affirmative[58]

In United States v. Alvarez-Machain, the Supreme Court sustained the jurisdiction of a U.S. court to try a Mexican national, charged with various counts of conspiracy, kidnaping and the murder of a U.S. drug enforcement agent in Mexico, even though his presence in the United States was the result of abduction rather than extradition pursuant to the Extradition Treaty between the United States and Mexico. The Court did not hold, as widely reported in the media, that the Treaty permits abduction, that abduction is legal, or that the United States had a right to kidnap criminal suspects abroad. On the contrary, the Court acknowledged that the abduction may have been a violation of international law.

The Court reaffirmed the long-established Ker-Frisbie doctrine[59] that "the power of a court to try a person for a crime is not impaired by the fact that he has been brought within the court's jurisdiction by reason of a 'forcible abduction.'" The Court's holding is consistent with existing international law, with its application of the Fourth Amendment to illegal arrests domestically, and with the broad powers and deference that it has historically accorded to the Executive in the conduct of foreign affairs.

Commentators generally agree that the seizure of a person by agents of one state in the territory of another clearly violates international law. They also agree, however, that that does not deprive the court of jurisdiction over the person illegally seized. F.A. Mann asserts, unequivocally, that a "State which authorizes the abduction of a person from the territory of another sovereign State is guilty of a violation of public international law." He then asks, "does the State have criminal jurisdiction in respect of the abducted person?" and answers that "it would be idle to deny that such jurisdiction exists, and it exists however abhorrent the circumstances of the abduction may be."[60]

This rule has been applied by the courts of a number of states, including Canada, France, Germany, England

[58] By MALVINA HALBERSTAM, excerpted from: *In Defense of the Supreme Court Decision in Alvarez-Machain*, 86 AMERICAN JOURNAL OF INTERNATIONAL LAW 736 (1992). Reprinted by permission.

[59] Ker v. Illinois, 119 U.S. 430 (1886); Frisbie v. Collins, 342 U.S. 519, *reh'g denied*, 343 U.S. 937 (1952).

[60] F.A. Mann, *Reflections on the Prosecution of Persons Abducted in Breach of International Law*, in YORAM DINSTEIN (ED.), INTERNATIONAL LAW AT A TIME OF PERPLEXITY 407, 412 (1989).

and Israel.[61] Professor Henkin stated only two years ago:

> To date, however, international law is wedded to the principle male captus bene detentus: a person arrested in violation of international law, for example by kidnapping from the territory of another State without that State's consent, . . . may nonetheless be brought to trial and the arresting State does not thereby commit an additional violation.[62]

Although agreeing with the defendant that his abduction may have been "shocking" and a violation of customary international law, the Court concluded that it did not violate the Extradition Treaty between the United States and Mexico. As the Court noted, "The Treaty says nothing about the obligations of the United States and Mexico to refrain from forcible abductions of people from the territory of the other nation, or the consequences under the Treaty if such an abduction occurs." It may have been unnecessary to include a provision barring abductions by one state in the territory of another, since that was a violation of customary international law. But a provision divesting the court of jurisdiction as a sanction for abduction clearly should have been included, if that is what the parties intended, since the well-established customary international law was, as noted above, to the contrary.

Although the majority and dissenting Justices disagreed on whether the abduction violated the Extradition Treaty, both apparently agreed that if it violated the Treaty, the defendant could not be tried in the United States. Justice Stevens said so explicitly. He stated in his dissent, "It is clear that Mexico's demand must be honored if this official abduction violated the 1978 Extradition Treaty between the United States and Mexico." Justice Rehnquist, writing for the Court, seemed to agree by implication. He stated that "the decision of whether respondent should be returned to Mexico, as a matter outside of the Treaty, is a matter for the Executive Branch." That is somewhat surprising, since under the broad powers of the Executive in the conduct of foreign affairs, the President could order the trial of the defendant in the United States regardless of whether the abduction violated general principles of international law or a treaty provision. A judicial decision barring the trial would be inconsistent with the Court's traditional deference to the Executive in matters involving foreign affairs.

This is not to suggest that the United States should violate international law. Of course, the United States should comply with international law. The United States, like other states, and perhaps even more than other states, has a great interest in and commitment to the rule of law, domestic and international. International law is the means by which relations between states are regulated. From the earliest times, Supreme Court decisions have stressed the importance and application of international law in the United States. In addition, illegal abduction of persons abroad may have many adverse consequences for the United States. However, under the U.S. Constitution, it is for the President and Congress to decide whether to breach U.S. obligations under international law. Unless and until that is changed, it would be inconsistent with the Executive's power in foreign affairs for the Court to prohibit the trial of someone charged with a serious crime over which the United States has jurisdiction, because the seizure of the accused infringed the territorial sovereignty of another state. The point is not that the United States should engage in abductions in violation of international law, but that in this, as in other matters involving the conduct of foreign affairs, the decision has to be made by the executive and legislative branches of the Government, not by the courts.

Clearly, the traditional rule that how a defendant was brought before the court has no bearing on the validity of the trial is inconsistent with modern developments in the international law of human rights. Equally clearly, a rule that would prohibit trial whenever the defendant is illegally seized, unless coupled with a rule requiring states to extradite, would put terrorists, drug dealers and others who have no regard for human life on notice that they can perpetrate the most monstrous crimes without fear of punishment as long as they can find a state that condones their conduct, or that will – for whatever reason – neither prosecute nor extradite.

b. Negative[63]

The diplomatic setbacks suffered by the United States subsequent to the Supreme Court's decision in the Alvarez case, coupled with the fact that the trial court on remand threw out the case, strongly suggest that this is one the Justice Department should have tried hard to lose. By doing the opposite it won a pyrrhic victory. My assessment is that, apart from egotistic drives in recent Justice Department practice to win every case that finds its way into the Supreme Court regardless of the merits or the consequences for national policy, the case probably got lost in a labyrinth of logic. Its complexity, in my view, defeated counsel on both sides of the litigation as well as the Supreme Court itself. It's a bold proposition, and I shall try to defend it.

A starting point is that we should look closely at any

---

61 For discussion and references, *see id.* at 412–14.

62 Louis Henkin, *International Law: Politics, Values and Functions*, 216 Recueil Des Cours 9, 3310 (1989 IV).

63 By ANTHONY D'AMATO, written for this Anthology.

decision that appears to assert that a governmental action may violate international law but there is nothing that the court can do about it. The Supreme Court said "Respondent and his amici may be correct that respondent's abduction . . . may be in violation of general international law principles," and yet proceeded to remand Dr. Alvarez's case for trial. I will attempt to show that the Supreme Court's reasoning was faulty due to a failure to cope with the underlying logic of the issues, and that the Court in fact did not say it was all right to violate international law.[64]

What was the alleged violation of international law and how did the violation relate to Dr. Alvarez's objection to the trial court's jurisdiction over him? If we answer this question with another one, namely, Did the abduction of Dr. Alvarez violate the Extradition Treaty, we will have asked the question posed by the majority as well as the dissenters on the Supreme Court. It is precisely the wrong question. For if we ask *that* question, we should conclude, with the Court's majority, that the answer is no.

Let me show this by comparing the Extradition Treaty in the case to a hypothetical one. Suppose nations A and B sign an extradition treaty which contains a "nationality" clause. This clause provides, in effect, that if an A-national fugitive is found in state B, state B must extradite the A-national back to state A. However, if a B-national fugitive is found in B (a B-national, that is, who violated A's laws), the treaty bars extradition of the B-national to A.[65] Now suppose that a B-national murders an official of A in B. Although A would like to extradite the murderer and proceed with a trial in A, the A-B extradition treaty bars extradition because the murderer is a national of B. It would be frivolous for the government of A to "invoke" the treaty and ask for extradition, because the treaty explicitly excepts the case of a B-national. Suppose A thereupon abducts the murderer. Has A violated the extradition treaty? This is a slight variant of the question the Supreme Court asked. How indeed could A violate a treaty that by its own terms could not even be invoked by A?

The step from my hypothetical case to Dr. Alvarez's case is a short one. The Supreme Court's majority said that since the United States, for whatever reason, did not invoke the Extradition Treaty, then there could be no violation of that treaty. The Treaty did not specify that it had to be invoked in certain cases; rather, the Treaty simply provided a facilitative mechanism for inter-country transfers of fugitive criminals that the United States or Mexico could invoke or not invoke at their discretion. Similarly, although more conclusively, in my hypothetical case it would be pointless to invoke the extradition treaty because by its own terms it does not apply.

To show that the question the Supreme Court asked was the wrong question, let us step back and see how the Court framed the issue in the case. The first sentence of Justice Rehnquist's opinion for the Court states:

> The issue in this case is whether a criminal defendant, abducted to the United States from a nation with which it has an extradition treaty, thereby acquires a defense to the jurisdiction of this country's courts.

That, I submit, is the wrong issue. Take one more step backward and consider how it got framed that way. Certainly the petitioner in the case – the United States government – wanted the issue and the question to be framed that way, because it gave the government a winning advantage in the litigation. But in my experience as a litigator, if the framing of an issue favors one side, the other side should try very hard to get the issue restated. Counsel for Dr. Alvarez needed to get the Supreme Court to frame the issue in an entirely different way in order to win the case. Since Dr. Alvarez's counsel and amici were all superbly qualified attorneys, it is puzzling at first glance why they apparently conceded the way the Justice Department framed the issue.

My analysis of the litigating strategy is that counsel for Dr. Alvarez failed because they never tried in the first place. Their minds were focused on the question of standing when they should have been focusing on something entirely different. What that different something is I shall suggest below. Let me here address the issue of standing, which obviously stood front and center in the thinking of the attorneys for the respondent.

Dr. Alvarez's attorneys clearly felt that the biggest hurdle in the case was getting the Court to accept Dr. Alvarez's standing to invoke the violation of the Extradition Treaty. They were after all facing the well-established Ker-Frisbee doctrine, reflecting a pragmatic attitude of courts to the effect that "we don't care how the defendant got here; he's here now, and the trial can proceed. If he wants to complain about how he got here, he can file a tort action against somebody."[66] Counsel thought they had at least three im-

---

[64] My argument takes an entirely different tack from anything that I have heard or read about the Alvarez case. *See, e.g.*, Malvina Halberstam, *In Defense of the Supreme Court Decision in Alvarez-Machain*, 86 AM. J. INT'L L. 736 (1992); Michael Glennon, *State-Sponsored Abduction: A Comment on United States v. Alvarez-Machain*, 86 AM. J. INT'L L. 746 (1992).

[65] There are, in fact, many bilateral extradition treaties that contain these nationality clauses; they typically go on to provide that if a B-national violates A's laws, B is under a treaty obligation to prosecute that person in B. *See, e.g.*, Hans Schultz, *The General Framework of Extradition and Asylum*, in 2 M. CHERIF BASSIOUNI & VED P. NANDA (EDS.), A TREATISE ON INTERNATIONAL CRIMINAL LAW 309 (1973).

[66] *See* Ker v. Illinois, 119 U.S. 436 (1886); Frisbie v. Collins, 342 U.S. 519, *reh'g denied*, 343 U.S. 937 (1952).

portant strings on Dr. Alvarez's bow. The first was that Mexico had itself protested the violation of the Treaty. The Mexican protest already had impressed the lower federal courts, which ruled in Dr. Alvarez's favor, and it was certainly an item to parade before the Supreme Court. Indeed, the protest appeared to remove from the case the argument the U.S. government might otherwise make, to the effect that a court should not speculate on the basis of an individual's petition whether his home government itself might or might not view the extradition treaty as having been violated. Indeed, as counsel for Dr. Alvarez correctly argued, Mexico might have, after all, *consented* to the abduction, and that consent could have mooted the question whether the treaty was violated.[67] Thus, counsel obviously felt that it had a very strong position on account of Mexico's diplomatic protest. Secondly, counsel argued that the Extradition Treaty was self-executing. The jurisprudence of what constitutes a self-executing treaty has undergone considerable revision from the Ker-Frisbee days,[68] so perhaps the Supreme Court might be sympathetic. Third, counsel obviously hoped that the Court might overrule the Ker-Frisbee doctrine as an outdated and myopic approach to issues of international law.

What all three of these argumentative strategies have in common is their sharp focus on Dr. Alvarez's standing to complain that the Extradition Treaty was violated. Counsel for Dr. Alvarez must have decided, as a matter of strategy, that it would not be too difficult to prove that the treaty was violated; their real problem was bringing that violation home to Dr. Alvarez's case. A violation of the treaty in the abstract would be an intergovernmental matter between the United States and Mexico. Even if the Supreme Court decided to rule on this abstract question, and even if the ruling was that the Extradition Treaty was violated, counsel for Dr. Alvarez might still have feared that the remedy for the violation might be something other than repatriating their client to Mexico.[69] So they focused on the personal connection of Dr. Alvarez to the violation of the treaty, or in other words, Dr. Alvarez's standing to complain.

The three main argumentative strategies of counsel for Dr. Alvarez, therefore, rested like an inverted pyramid on the apex of the proposition that the Extradition Treaty was itself violated. Hence counsel ended up more or less joining with the Justice Department in framing the issue in the case as whether Dr. Alvarez could object to jurisdiction over him by virtue of the violation of the Extradition Treaty. The Supreme Court was thus asked, in effect by both sides, whether Dr. Alvarez could invoke the Treaty on his behalf and show that it was violated. But as I have attempted to show above, this way of framing the issue opened the door for the Supreme Court to say that the treaty was not in fact violated because it wasn't invoked. As the majority of the Court said, Dr. Alvarez's kidnapping occurred "outside" the treaty.

The "standing" issue thus turns out to have considerable bite, but not in the way counsel for Dr. Alvarez assumed. What the Supreme Court is saying is that, for Dr. Alvarez to have standing to invoke the benefits of the Extradition Treaty in his defense to jurisdiction, the treaty has to apply to his case. But the treaty doesn't apply because the United States government never invoked it. So even if we concede that Dr. Alvarez theoretically might have had standing to use the treaty in his defense if the United States had invoked the treaty (thereby overruling Ker-Frisbee), and although if *that* had happened Dr. Alvarez might have been able to make out a case that the treaty was violated (along the lines, for example, stated by the dissenters in the Supreme Court), and if *that* had happened Dr. Alvarez might have been able to convince the Court that the appropriate remedy would be to repatriate him to Mexico, none of these counterfactuals are part of the present litigation. If they were, they would amount to a request for an advisory

---

[67] To similar effect, nations have voluntarily delivered individuals to a requesting country without going through the extradition process, including rendition by deportation, *see, e.g.*, United States v. Valot, 625 F.2d 308, 310 (9th Cir. 1980) and United States v. Cordero, 668 F.2d 32, 37 (1st Cir. 1982), informal rendition, *see, e.g.*, Stevenson v. United States, 381 F.2d 142 (9th Cir. 1967), or rendition by other irregular means, *cf.* Afouneh v. Attorney-General, 4 Ann. Dig. 327 (Palestine S.Ct. 1942). Another way to obtain a wanted individual is to induce that individual to cross the border by means of trickery or fraud. When that occurs, it is generally believed that there has been no violation of an extradition treaty.

[68] *See* Carlos Manuel Vazquez, *Treaty-Based Rights and Remedies of Individuals*, 92 COLUM. L. REV. 1082, 1117–1121 (1992); Anthony D'Amato, *What Does Tel-Oren Tell Lawyers? Judge Bork's Concept of the Law of Nations is Seriously Mistaken*, 79 AJIL 92, 99 (1985).

[69] When Adolf Eichmann was abducted from Argentina by Israeli officials, Argentina lodged a complaint against Israel with the United Nations Security Council. The Council on June 23, 1960, requested the Government of Israel to make appropriate reparation. Quite pointedly, the Council did not say that Eichmann should be remitted to Argentina. On August 3, 1960, the governments of Argentina and Israel issued a joint communique' acknowledging the Security Council resolution and resolving "to regard as closed the incident which arose out of action taken by citizens of Israel, which infringed the fundamental rights of the State of Argentina." Joint communique' of August 3, 1960, Attorney General v. Eichmann, 36 ILR 5, 58–59 (Dist. Jerusalem 1961), *aff'd*, 36 ILR 277, 305 (S.Ct. Israel 1962). The joint communique' thus constituted the appropriate reparation; it was Argentina's rights that were violated, not Eichmann's. Of course, there was no extradition treaty involved in the Eichmann case. But the point is a broad one: that there are many ways of remedying a breach of an extradition treaty other than the one mandated by the Ninth Circuit in the Alvarez case, which was to order the defendants repatriated.

opinion, something the Supreme Court traditionally shuns. In this respect, I read the Supreme Court's sentence, that "Respondent and his amici may be correct that respondent's abduction . . . may be in violation of general international law principles," as a properly cautious statement. The Court is not "hedging" on the question whether the abduction violated international law; rather, the Court is simply saying that the issue of an international law violation is not part of the case or controversy as presented by Dr. Alvarez. Or, to put it more bluntly, Dr. Alvarez cannot plausibly claim that his abduction occurred both "inside" and "outside" the Extradition Treaty. He has no standing to claim that it occurred "inside" the treaty because the treaty itself was not invoked, and he has no standing to claim that it occurred "outside" the treaty because that is a matter of intergovernmental international law about which Dr. Alvarez, under traditional principles,[70] has no standing to invoke.

In thus going through the logic of the case, we find that Dr. Alvarez's litigating strategies led to a logical cul-de-sac. The Supreme Court in effect said to Dr. Alvarez: "on your theory of the case, you lose." Now, in my view, it is generally insufficient for a court to say something like that. A court should decide a case properly, and not merely relegate itself to the role of an umpire ruling on the adequacy of a proffered theory. But this leads to the main inquiry here: is there a better theory of what was really going on in the Alvarez case that the Court should have chosen or invented?

I would like to suggest that we begin to search for such a theory by asking what appears to be an irrelevant and unlitigated question: *if* the abduction of Dr. Alvarez violated the Extradition Treaty, *when* was the treaty violated? To answer this particular question, we should look at the purpose of an extradition treaty. The general purpose is to facilitate the inter-country transfer of fugitive criminals so that they may be brought to trial. We can test this asserted purpose by supposing that a person is kidnapped and taken to another country where he is held for ransom. There is surely no violation of any extradition treaty. Suppose further that the victim is kidnapped by officials of the country to which he is taken. Even then, we can't say that any extradition treaty has been violated, because the kidnapping may have nothing to do with bringing the victim to trial. In general, cross-country abductions are not necessarily related to extradition. If they are officially sponsored abductions, they might even constitute the first signs of a war between the two countries. Yet as the Supreme Court somewhat sarcastically said in the Alvarez case:

> Respondent would have us find that the Treaty acts as a prohibition against a violation of the general principle of international law that one government may not "exercise its police power in the territory of another state." There are many actions which could be taken by a nation that would violate this principle, including waging war, but it cannot seriously be contended an invasion of the United States by Mexico would violate the terms of the extradition treaty between the two nations.

The one point in time that we can be quite certain that an extradition treaty is violated, *if* it is violated, is when an abducted person is put on trial. Then, in retrospect, the reason for his abduction becomes clear: it was to bypass the extradition process. But until the moment when the trial court decides to assert jurisdiction over the abductee, there must be uncertainty whether the abduction had any relation to any existing extradition treaty. Therefore the exercise of trial court jurisdiction acts as a kind of condition subsequent, confirming the violation of the treaty.

If I am right in saying that the first moment we can know whether an extradition treaty is violated, *if* it is violated, is when a trial court asserts jurisdiction over the abductee, then it follows that it is the trial court itself that perfects, as it were, the violation of the extradition treaty. Under this view, it's not a matter of the abductee's standing to complain of a treaty violation; the question of his standing is irrelevant. Rather, it is the court's own action in asserting jurisdiction that perfects the violation of the extradition treaty—if the treaty is violated at all.

This reasoning gets us into a more activist view of what courts do. But there is substantial precedent for such a view. In the leading case of *Shelley v. Kraemer*,[71] the U.S. Supreme Court found that although it was not unconstitutional for private persons to enter into a racially restrictive covenant in a conveyance of land,[72] as soon as a state court enforced that covenant the state itself was acting through the agency of the court in violation of the Fourteenth Amendment. As Chief Justice Vinson put it, the "full coercive power of government" was applied through the vehi-

70 Under at least the British version of classic international law theory that was rife at the turn of the century, an individual has no standing to complain about international law violations; at best, an individual's case may be "espoused" by his or her government, and even if espoused and eventually successful, the government has no international-law duty to turn over to the individual whatever financial compensation it has received in the case. This British view of classic theory, which also made considerable headway in the United States, may have misinterpreted previous international law jurisprudence and may be similarly misguided today. For a more complete account, *see* ANTHONY D'AMATO, INTERNATIONAL LAW: PROCESS AND PROSPECT 193–222 (1987).

71 334 U.S. 1 (1948).

72 The private parties could, for example, adhere to the racially restrictive covenant on a voluntary basis.

cle of a court's judgment. Herbert Wechsler was not troubled by *Shelley's* proposition that action of the state court is action of the state, but by the inference that the state is charged with unconstitutional discrimination "when it does no more than give effect to an agreement that the individual involved is, by hypothesis, entirely free to make."[73] Yet precisely that inference was validated by the result in *Shelley.*[74] By similar reasoning, if the action by United States officials in causing the abduction of Dr. Alvarez was one that they may have been at liberty to make because the Extradition Treaty was not invoked by them and hence not energized when they acted, nevertheless as soon as the trial court asserts jurisdiction over Dr. Alvarez, the court itself has taken governmental action that recharacterizes the entire sequence of events and places all the events inside the Treaty.

In international law circles, there is no need to resort to *Shelley*. The proposition that national courts are engaged in governmental action is ordinary and uncontroversial. From the international point of view, any state government acts through its executive, legislative, or judicial branches; hence, a decision by a court in that state is as much a governmental act as an executive-ordered seizure of a vessel on the high seas:

> The decision of a national court on a question of international law is important not so much for what the court says as for what it does. National courts take part in the formation of state practice, so that their permanent, uniform practice renders good arguments for proving the existence of customary law. In regard to state practice, all official activities of state organs, legislative, executive and judicial, are equally instrumental in the formation of law. Thus a national court decision may be classified as an exercise of state sovereignty in the field of international law.[75]

My theory of the case is now close to being completed. I would not have advised Dr. Alvarez to claim that his personal rights derived from an extradition treaty that was violated when he was abducted. Rather, I would have made a "suggestion" to the trial court that the trial judge, on his own motion, should decline jurisdiction because asserting it could constitute the last necessary element in a United States governmental violation of the Extradition Treaty. Courts typically will decline jurisdiction *sua sponte*, even when the parties do not formally raise the issue as part of their own case, when it appears that the exercise of jurisdiction would be illegal. Certainly, *if* the extradition treaty would be violated by the assertion of jurisdiction, the treaty itself would be legally binding on the trial judge. As the Supreme Court held in the Alvarez case, "The Extradition Treaty has the force of law."

But it may be objected that my theory of the case, like the "standing" approach of Dr. Alvarez's counsel, rests on a showing of a violation of the Extradition Treaty. Since the Supreme Court after all found that the treaty was not violated, why would my theory be an improvement?

In the context of the Alvarez litigation, as I have argued, the question whether the Extradition Treaty was violated was not an integral part of the case or controversy before the Court. Rather, Dr. Alvarez was seeking to invoke the Treaty when a party to the treaty – the United States – had chosen not to invoke it. Thus, the issue of the violation of the treaty was not squarely placed in litigation. It is true that the Supreme Court said that the Treaty was not violated, but a contextual reading of its opinion suggests that the issue of violation could only be squarely presented in a case where the parties are the United States and Mexico, and not in a case where the parties are the United States and Dr. Alvarez.[76] In other words, in saying that the Treaty was not violated, the Supreme Court was only saying that since the Treaty was not invoked by its parties, Dr. Alvarez could not himself invoke it and use it to defeat jurisdiction, and since he could not invoke it, the question of whether it was violated was not squarely presented – even though, in the Court's dictum, the treaty was not in fact violated.[77]

It is a quite different posture, I suggest, when an organ of the United States government – and a court of law, at that – is itself asked to take an action that would violate a treaty. If the trial court had refused to take jurisdiction over Dr. Alvarez on the theory of the case that I have been suggesting – which, given its disposition of the case, we might well expect it would have done – would the Supreme Court nevertheless have reversed and ordered the trial court

73 Herbert Wechsler, *Toward Neutral Principles of Constitutional Law*, 73 HARV. L. REV. 1, 29 (1959).

74 *See* Louis Henkin, Shelley v. Kraemer: *Notes for a Revised Opinion*, 110 U. PA. L. REV. 473 (1962).

75 Karl Doehring, *The Participation of International and National Courts in the Law-Creating Process*, 17 SOUTH AFRICAN YEARBOOK OF INTERNATIONAL LAW 1 (1991/92).

76 Isn't it sufficient that we know what Mexico's position is on the matter? Why does Mexico have to be a party? The Supreme Court is well aware that nonparties make all kinds of statements out of court for all kinds of self-serving reasons. But in the crucible of litigation, positions can differ radically. In short, Mexico might protest the abduction because of media pressure on the Mexican government. Yet in a litigation between the United States and Mexico, the latter might, on the advice of counsel, take the position that the abduction was outside the treaty. I don't suggest that this is likely, only that it is possible.

77 Was this alleged "dictum" necessary to the Court's holding, and hence not "dictum" at all? Not in my view of the case. It was only necessary to answer the question the Court asked, but in my view of the case that question was the wrong question.

to violate the treaty? Clearly the Supreme Court would not have done that. The Supreme Court would instead be in a position of looking for reasons why the treaty was not violated at all. But the question presented – would the action of the trial court itself perfect the violation of the treaty? – would have been a lot harder for the Supreme Court to handle. Such a question would have placed the violation vel non of the treaty squarely in issue. It is thus a far cry from the question whether asserting jurisdiction over an alleged torturer should be defeated when the torturer is trying to invoke a treaty that wasn't invoked. Indeed, under the posture of the Alvarez case as it was actually litigated, some justices might have felt that they should not be in a position of ruling whether the President of the United States violated or did not violate international law in authorizing the abduction of Dr. Alvarez. Some may have even felt that even if the Executive Branch did in fact violate the treaty, the Judicial Branch should refrain from saying anything about it. But under my theory of the case, these justices could feel comfortable in saying that there was no violation of the treaty by the Executive Branch unless and until a trial court asserts jurisdiction over Dr. Alvarez. And that final step can easily be prevented by action of the Supreme Court itself, since the Court clearly has power over inferior federal courts.

Of course, in suggesting this theory of the case, I cannot say that it would have constituted a winning strategy for Dr. Alvarez. Certainly it would have entailed a massive rethinking on the part of counsel, and given the conservatism of lawyers, the chance of their deciding to bypass an expected fight over the "standing" issue probably would have been minimal. But even though counsel for Dr. Alvarez pursued the traditional "standing" strategy (and we shouldn't lose sight of the fact that they were obviously comforted by Mexico's diplomatic protest), the Supreme Court should have seen through the logical thicket and characterized the case not as a "standing" case at all but a case of whether a governmental organ – the trial court – should be implicated in the violation of a treaty. If the Court had thought of the case in such a light, I dare say the result might have been different, and all the subsequent grief the result caused the United States government could have been avoided.

9
Group Rights

A. Minority Rights[1]

Patrick Thornberry has argued that minority rights are really a form of human right because any system of human rights must recognize that people exist not simply as individuals, but within their cultural settings.[2] Both individual rights and rights addressed to protecting minorities are necessary for the perpetuation of minority cultures and the protection of the human rights of the individual members of those cultures. Others have expressed the relationship between individual and group rights as follows: group rights are necessary to ensure the effective implementation of fundamental individual rights, because if minorities are not given rights specifically designed to defend their culture they will be treated unequally and unjustly. Thus, minorities need special rights to defend their cultures in order to give meaning to other fundamental human rights, such as equality. Without these "special rights," members of the minority possess only the right to assimilation into the dominant culture.

Self-determination and minority rights became prominent in international relations in the aftermath of World War I. President Wilson believed that the concepts of self-determination and democracy were intimately related.[3] He considered external freedom from alien sovereignty meaningless without a continuing process of self-government internally.[4] Conversely, if a regime were democratic, then external self-determination became peripheral. To Wilson's mind the minority regime became necessary only in the absence of true self-government. As he conceived it, the principle of self-determination had the protection of minorities as a corollary. He originally proposed that an article on minorities be inserted in the League of Nations Covenant but, instead, minority rights were dealt with in five territorial treaties guaranteed by the League.[5]

The purpose of the minorities rights guarantee in these treaties, explained by the Permanent Court of International Justice in Minority Schools in Albania,[6] was to put nationals belonging to minorities on an equal footing with other nationals and to assure minorities the means to preserve their traditions and national characteristics. The League guarantee had internal and external aspects. Internally the State was required to regard the treaty provisions as fundamental law that invalidated any laws that conflicted with them. Externally the guarantee applied only to the infringement of rights of persons belonging to racial, religious, or linguistic minorities. The League guarantee meant that the Council of the League could take action in the event of an infraction of the treaty obligation. Members of the Council had a duty to call attention to actual or threatened infractions. Minorities themselves were allowed to petition the League, but in practice the right was exercised primarily by strong minorities, such as the Germans, rather than by weaker minorities, such as the Jews. Minorities were strongest if there was a State in which they constituted the majority and which acted to guarantee their rights in a bilateral treaty. Stateless minorities such as Jews and Gypsies were relatively weak because they lacked such a champion.

The League system was a step forward in human rights law because it developed the notion of rights against the State. In the end, however, the system deteriorated because of State objections to the limitation placed on their sovereignty by the minorities treaties and the instability generated by fractious minorities within their territory; minorities themselves wanted liberalization of the petition proce-

---

[1] By CLAUDIA SALADIN, excerpted from: *Self-Determination, Minority Rights, and Constitutional Accommodation: The Example of the Czech and Slovak Federal Republic*, 13 MICHIGAN JOURNAL OF INTERNATIONAL LAW 172 (1991). Reprinted by permission.

[2] Patrick Thornberry, *Is There a Phoenix in the Ashes?—International Law and Minority Rights*, 15 TEX. INT'L L.J. 421, 445–46 (1980).

[3] 54 Cong. Rec. 1742 (Jan. 22, 1917) (Statement of President Wilson before the Senate) ("No peace can last, or ought to last, which does not recognize and accept the principle that governments derive all their just power from the consent of the governed, and that no right anywhere exists to hand peoples about from sovereignty to sovereignty as if they were property."); President Woodrow Wilson, Address before the League to Enforce Peace (May 27, 1916), reprinted in 53 Cong. Rec. 8854 (May 29, 1916) ("We believe these fundamental things: First, that every people has a right to choose the sovereignty under which they shall live.").

[4] *See generally* MICHLA POMERANCE, SELF-DETERMINATION IN LAW AND PRACTICE 3 (1982).

[5] *See* Mary Gardiner Jones, *National Minorities: A Case Study of International Protection*, 14 LAW & CONTEMP. PROBS. 599, 604–05 (1949).

[6] 1935 P.C.I.J. (ser. A/B) No. 64, at 17.

dure and greater autonomy and assurances against assimilation.

After the Second World War there was a general disenchantment with the League minorities program. This was partly due to the perceived double standard in the League system. Only the rights of minorities were raised to the level of internationally guaranteed rights, whereas the rights of nonminorities remained solely within the domestic sphere. Also, critics of the League system perceived minority rights as privileges. But the World Court in the Minority Schools in Albania case addressed this issue by drawing a distinction between equality in law and equality in fact:

> Equality in law precludes discrimination of any kind; whereas equality in fact may involve the necessity of different treatment in order to attain a result which establishes an equilibrium between different situations. It is easy to imagine cases in which equality of treatment of the majority and of the minority, whose situation and requirements are different, would result in inequality in fact. The equality between members of the majority and of the minority must be an effective, genuine equality.[7]

The United Nations replaced the idea of internationalizing the rights of certain minority groups with the concept of universal human rights on a nondiscriminatory basis. The feeling was that if human rights and fundamental freedoms were respected without discrimination, then protection of minority rights would not be a problem. This was in part due to the influence of the United States, which emphasized its "melting pot" tradition, consistent with the dominant philosophy of the time favoring assimilation.[8]

The Covenant on Civil and Political Rights of 1976 is the first international norm dealing specifically with the rights of ethnic, religious, and linguistic groups that is capable of and intended for universal application. Article 27 of the Covenant on Civil and Political Rights spells out the rights of minorities negatively rather than positively:

> In those States in which ethnic, religious or linguistic minorities exist, persons belonging to such minorities shall not be denied the right, in community with the other members of their group, to enjoy their own culture, to profess and practice their own religion, or to use their own language.

Article 27 appears to require only that States tolerate minorities and refrain from interfering with their cultural or religious practices, rather than impose positive duties, although it is arguable that in order to effectively implement article 27, States would have to move from equality in law, or nondiscrimination, to equality in fact.

B. Self-Determination[9]

"Self-determination," the famous catchword of World War I, has become one of the most potent political slogans of our time. In its name battles continue to be waged, and no continent – and scarcely any country – is immune from its grip. The use of force within the most recent period alone in such diverse places as Grenada, Lebanon, the Falkland Islands, Afghanistan, Chad, Angola, Namibia, Punjab, and Kampuchea was related in some way or other to the issue of self-determination. Within the UN, self-determination is viewed by the majority as a kind of "supernorm", a principle which has been lifted from the realm of politics and morality to the very pinnacle of legal rules. According to this perspective, even the linchpin of the UN Charter, the principle prohibiting the threat or use of force in international relations (Art. 2, para. 4), may be overridden in the name of the more sacred "right of self-determination".

It is perhaps not surprising that discussions of self-determination in the media and the UN have been characterized by confusion, misunderstandings and oversimplification. But woolly thinking on the subject is also common in academic circles, where one might expect more rigorous analysis to prevail. At root, the misunderstandings derive from a common basic premise: that to invoke the right of self-determination is to give the solution to a problem. This premise, however, is fallacious. As Arnold Toynbee wrote in 1925, "self-determination is merely the statement of a problem and not the solution of it".[10] The same proposition was spelled out in 1956, by Sir Ivor Jennings, as follows:

> Nearly forty years ago a Professor of Political Science who was also President of the United States, President Wilson, enunciated a doctrine which was ridiculous, but which was widely accepted as a sensible proposition, the doctrine of self-determination. On the surface it seemed reasonable: let the people decide. It was in fact ridiculous because the people

---

[7] Minority Schools in Albania, 1935 P.C.I.J. (ser. A/B) No. 64, at 19.

[8] [Editor's Note: Less recognized by today's writers on the subject was a hidden, but very real, motivation on the part of many conservative U.S. Senators in 1945 (who would be called upon to ratify the U.N. Charter) that any recognition in the Charter of minority rights might tend to ignite a civil rights movement in the United States.]

[9] By MICHLA POMERANCE, excerpted from: *Self-Determination Today: The Metamorphosis of an Ideal,* 19 ISRAEL LAW REVIEW 310, 310–16 (1984). Reprinted by permission.

[10] Arnold J. Toynbee, *"Self-Determination,"* THE QUARTERLY REVIEW, No. 484 (London, 1925) 319.

> cannot decide until somebody decides who are the people.[11]

In recent years, the UN has purported to be the forum which can and should decide this question. It has claimed for itself the power to separate the goats from the sheep, the meritorious "selves" from those who would suppress their "legitimate aspirations." Beyond that, it has sought to attribute far-reaching consequences to its assessments. The powers thus claimed by the UN are, from a legal standpoint, questionable in the extreme, since they are not readily derivable from the UN Charter or customary international law. However, even if this critical issue of the UN's *competence* to determine self-determination claims in a binding manner were to be left aside, further questions would remain. In particular, how does the UN go about deciding the weighty issues involved in self-determination? Does it have objective neutral principles to guide it?

To answer these questions, it is necessary first to specify in which respects self-determination is, indeed, "the statement of a problem." Only then can the UN solutions be properly judged on their merits.

1. *Defining the "Self"*. First and foremost, there is need to define the bearer of the right. Who is the "self" to whom self-determination attaches? Is it Biafra or Nigeria? Northern Ireland, Ireland, or the United Kingdom together with Northern Ireland? The present population of Taiwan (consisting mainly of Nationalist Chinese), the indigenous islanders, or Communist China? Gibraltar or Spain? The Falkland Islands or the Argentine nation which claims the Islands as part of its patrimony? The Kurds, or, respectively, Iraq, Iran, the Soviet Union, and Turkey?

Very early in the history of self-determination, the question of definition worried U.S. Secretary of State Robert Lansing, who accompanied Wilson to Versailles in 1919. He expressed his doubts in his diary in these terms:

> When the President talks of "self-determination" what unit has he in mind? Does he mean a race, a territorial area, or a community? Without a definite unit which is practical, application of this principle is dangerous to peace and stability. . .[12]

In fact, the problem of definition goes beyond the question which troubled Lansing–whether to adopt a territorial or an ethnographic criterion. It is far more complex. Selection of either criterion necessitates further decisions with respect to delimitation, exclusion and inclusion. What are the boundaries of the area? who are its inhabitants? Who are the members of the "race" or the "community"? The territorial and ethnic criteria are not neatly separable; they are rather inextricably interwoven, and are bound up with yet a third factor, the factor of time. It is necessary to determine which population belongs to which area, an exercise which is particularly delicate where significant population movements, of recent or more ancient origin, have occurred. Such movements complicate the ethnographic map and raise thorny questions regarding the identification and rights of "indigenous" and inescapably enters the calculus. The definition of "self" is clearly not only space-bound and group-bound; it is also time-bound. In Lansing's own time, the population in Alsace-Lorraine in 1919, following fifty years of German rule and colonization, was not considered a "self" whose wishes needed to be consulted. The historic rights of an earlier community were preferred over the desires of the existing inhabitants.

The issue of the "critical date" is, of course, very central in the Middle Eastern arena today, and all of the protagonists recognize this fact. Each, quite naturally, has opted for a different "critical date."

2. *A Non-Universalizable Principle*. Self-determination claims generally do not clash with non-self-determination or anti-self-determination claims but with some countervailing self-determination claims. This is probably the most basic dilemma in the matter of self-determination: recognition of the rights of one "self" almost always entails the denial of the rights of a competing "self." The problem may be formulated in three alternative ways:

a) The demand for secession or separate self-determination by one "self" clashes with the claim to territorial integrity or political independence put forward by the unit of which the first "self" is felt to be a part.

b) "Self-determination" by the smaller unit conflicts with the "self-determination" to which the larger unit claims to be entitled.

c) There is an opposition between two claims to territorial integrity–that of the larger as against that of the smaller unit.

There may also be competing claims by different ethnic groups–Arabs and Jews, immigrant Indians and native Fijians, whites and blacks in South Africa–to the same territorial area.

Inherently, self-determination, in the sense of full independence and sovereignty, cannot be given to all peoples, unless the "self" is reduced to the individual "self" of the term's metaphysical origin. For the very act of fulfilling one claimant's right of self-determination will generally constitute the denial of the claim of another contender to the right.

3. *A One-Time Exercise or a Continuing Process?* What happens when new demands for secession arise? Is a limit to be set to the process of self-determination, or should

---

[11] Sir Ivor Jennings, The Approach to Self-Government (1956) 55–56.

[12] Robert Lansing, *"Self-Determination,"* Saturday Evening Post, 9 April 1921, p. 7.

the process be seen as continuing and open-ended? Did the South of the United States have the right to secede from the North, even as the thirteen colonies severed themselves from England? Could Biafra separate itself from Nigeria, Eritrea from Ethiopia? Are minorities within states – for example, Croats and Albanians in Yugoslavia and the diverse ethnic groups in Lebanon – to be granted separate self-determination? Since the right of self-determination, in the form of full independence, cannot, in practice or in theory, be granted to all claimants, may some other solutions – federal scheme, autonomy, minority rights, guarantees of non-discrimination – be viewed as alternative forms of self-determination? Can the right of option be seen as a way of permitting individuals to "vote with their feet," indicating thereby whether they feel a subjective need to align their political with their ethnic allegiance? Could it be said, then, that the only way to grant self-determination as a universal and continuing right to all people, is by recognizing self-determination as a continuum of rights, rather than as a one-time, all-or-nothing, exercise?

4. *"External" Self-Determination, "Internal" Self-Determination and Democracy.* In Wilsonian thought, "self-determination" was clearly a composite concept involving, chiefly, the following three ideas: a) the right of a people to be free from alien rule and to choose the sovereignty under which it will live (an idea often referred to as "external" self-determination); b) the right of a people to select its own form of government ("internal" self-determination); and c) continuous consent of the governed in the form of representative democratic government.

How are these three components of self-determination to be linked? In the Wilsonian view, which remains the Western view today, self-determination is intimately bound with representative government. Unless there is continuous consent of the governed, the rule of prevailing government will always be experienced as "alien." On the other hand, in the presence of true democracy, the question of who possesses sovereignty ("external" self-determination) is not really so important. (The second part of the proposition is, of course, more debatable, since it ignores the problem of permanent minorities, such as the Turks in Cyprus and the Catholics in Northern Ireland. Apart from democratic regimes, special minority arrangements may be warranted.)

C. Humanitarian Intervention and Self-Determination[13]

In an essay published in 1859, John Stuart Mill argued that self-determination, that is, the situation in which, in a given society, the people themselves resolve their political differences and established their institutions without foreign interference, is a necessary, although not a sufficient, condition for the enjoyment of freedom by those people.[14] One reason offered by Mill in support of his thesis is that "the only test possessing any real value, of a people's having become fit for popular institutions, is that they. . .are willing to brave labor and danger for their liberation."[15] In the prose of Walzer, "self-determination is the more inclusive idea, it describes not only a particular institutional arrangement but also the process by which a community arrives at that arrangement – or does not."[16] According to this theory, no external force can ever set men and women free; they have to attend the "school" of the political process. Without it, freedom either cannot be attained or it is not true freedom. Walzer summarized this idea in a subsequent article: "Against foreigners, individuals have a right to a state of their own. Against state officials they have a right to political and civil liberty. Without the first of these rights, the second is meaningless: as individuals need a home so rights require a location."[17] This notion is apparently embodied in the two United Nations International Covenants on human rights, where the right to self-determination (of peoples) precedes the (individual) rights recognized by the two conventions.

Before discussing this claim any further, it is necessary to clarify in what sense the expression "self-determination" is used here. Following standard international law terminology, it is possible to distinguish between external and internal self-determination.[18] External self-determination is the right of peoples to be free from alien rule, the paradigm of which is colonial domination. Determining the content of external self-determination thus is

---

[13] By FERNANDO R. TESON, excerpted from: HUMANITARIAN INTERVENTION: AN INQUIRY INTO LAW AND MORALITY 26–31 (N.Y.: Transnational Publishers, 1988). Reprinted by permission.

[14] J.S. Mill, *A few Words on Non-Intervention,* in 3 DISSERTATIONS AND DISCUSSIONS 153, 171–176 (1867) (hereinafter "Words").

[15] *Id,* at 173. His second reason, which I discuss below, is that "there can seldom be anything approaching to assurance that intervention, even if successful, would be for the good of the people themselves." *Ibid.*

[16] MICHAEL WALZER, JUST AND UNJUST WARS 87 (1977).

[17] Walzer, *The Moral Standing of States,* 9 PHIL & PUBLIC AFF. 209, 228 (1978–79). The same idea is conveyed by Walzer's reminder that we accord respect and yield room to "the political process itself, with all its messiness and uncertainty, its inevitable compromises and its frequent brutality." *Id,* at 229. Frost arrives at a similar conclusion in a different way: Following Hegel, he argues that the very notion of individual rights is meaningless outside a state framework. *See* M. FROST, TOWARD A NORMATIVE THEORY OF INTERNATIONAL RELATIONS, 173–84 (1986).

[18] *See* MICHLA POMERANCE, SELF-DETERMINATION IN LAW AND PRACTICE 130–138 (1982).

the same as determining under what conditions a community has a right to form a separate state, as well as the processes by which the community exercises such right. This in turn raises complex issues about the definition of "people" and the claims to territorial integrity by the parent state in case of secession.

I am not concerned here with external self-determination in this sense. I use instead the expression "self-determination" in the non-technical sense in which Mill uses it; that is, as the right of peoples to establish their own political, economic, and cultural institutions without interference from other states. This concept, sometimes referred to as "internal" self-determination, is the flip side of the non-intervention principle. I am therefore concerned here, not with the issue of whether a group of individuals has a right to create a political association, thus freeing themselves, as a community, from prior alien domination, but with the kind of political association they are morally entitled to create. Self-determination in this Millian sense thus refers to the right of peoples to reach social arrangements through a political process free of foreign interference.

However, Walzer (but not Mill) seems to confuse the two meanings of self-determination. It is one thing to say that citizens have a right "to a state of their own" and a very different thing to claim that foreigners may never intervene when such intervention is aimed, not at denying that right, but rather at reforming unfree institutions. Foreign states may intervene to uphold human rights without denying citizens their right to "a state of their own," that is, their right to external self-determination. In fact, I argue that interventions aimed at depriving citizens of "a state of their own" (wars of conquest or domination) are always unjust wars, and that in no sense may they be called "humanitarian." We may therefore assume that external self-determination is mandated by an appropriate account of international morality. But that assumption is not inconsistent with the claim that internal self-determination need not be accorded similar respect in cases where the result is a tyranny.

Assuming, then, that the principle of internal self-determination or nonintervention is at issue, the Mill-Walzer claim can be understood in two ways: as an empirical assertion or as a normative proposal. As an empirical claim, the argument holds that foreign nonintervention is a necessary condition for the enjoyment of human rights. In this view, there is a causal connection between the absence of foreign intervention and individual liberty. In support of this claim it is argued that since individuals have rights as members of political communities, international law, by protecting states, indirectly protects individual rights.[19] A further consequence is that in fact people who receive outside help to overthrow tyrants can never conquer the freedom they seek. Mill, for example, suggests that after a humanitarian intervention, "it is only a question in how few years or months that people will be enslaved." In a sense, the argument is appealing because it does not give up the idea that human rights can only be established, enforced and observed as the result of a purely domestic political process. Political processes that do not yield free institutions, while regrettable, are preferable to foreign involvement or intervention in that process. The main reason is that in the latter case individuals do not fight for their rights and therefore do not learn the value of freedom. In short, self-determination is causally related to (is a necessary condition of) the enjoyment of individual rights.

Yet as a matter of history this is simply wrong. Many communities have conquered their freedom with outside help – history abounds in examples. Conversely, all too frequently peoples are subjugated and subject to unspeakable suffering as the result of processes of pure self-determination. Take the example of the 1971 takeover in Uganda by Idi Amin. Surely not even Mill or Walzer would say that this was an instance of the Uganda "people" exercising their right to self-determination. The "self" (the Ugandan people) did not "determine" anything. The "self" here is not the real people, but some mystical entity called the "nation" which "determines itself" through the "political process." Suppose the alternatives for a foreign power were then (a) to let the Ugandan "political process" unfold, with the inevitable success of Amin, or (b) to intervene in order to prevent Amin from coming to power and allow free elections in Uganda. Leaving aside for the moment what the correct course of action may be, if Mill and Walzer are claiming that freedom can never result from alternative (b), then this is simply falsified by experience. Many persons enjoy human rights as a result of liberating foreign intervention. Consequently, the assertion that without self-determination (that is, with foreign intervention) the rest of human rights are meaningless is contradicted by the facts. Surely the Begalis liberated by India did not consider the restoration of their human rights as meaningless. Internal self-determination, then, is not a necessary condition for freedom.

The normative aspect of the Mill-Walzer claim is as follows. Even if self-determination is not a necessary condition for freedom, it nevertheless has philosophical priority over individual human rights. To sustain this claim, noninterventionists must show that there is something about self-determination that overrides the imperative of respect for individual rights. They must make some claims about the moral standing of governments, about the rights of states and about their relationship with the rights of citi-

---

19 *See* TERRY NARDIN, LAW, MORALITY, AND THE RELATIONS OF STATES 238 (1983).

zens. Such claims usually focus on the proposition that the essential characteristic of statehood, sovereignty, gives rise to international rights of states which are held over and above the rights of its citizens.

D. DEBATE: Group Freedom

1. The Primacy of Individual Freedom[20]

I am not here concerned with external self-determination. The colonial phase of world history is nearly over. Rule from abroad – the "logic" of capitalism's quest for markets and cheap labor, as Lenin argued – seems to have faded out in recent years just as Lenin has faded out. Rather, I am concerned with claims of "internal" self-determination – "new" claims that are showing up in many countries as ethnic, religious, or cultural groups claim self-determination and autonomy.[21]

For all the reasons expressed above by Professor Pomerance, these "new" claims of self-determination can *not* be solved by an international rule or norm. The international community might proclaim that "self-determination" is a right of peoples everywhere,[22] yet it is impossible to come up with a general-purpose definition of "peoples."[23]

International law (viewed as a set of rules), therefore, "runs out" at this point. The autonomy claims of groups cannot in principle be solved by rules of law. Many such claims are destined to be resolved through bloodshed, destruction, civil war and genocide. But that does not mean that international law is irrelevant to the assessment of autonomy claims. All that is irrelevant is the misguided notion that "law" is a collection of determinative prescriptive rules. A more sophisticated view of law – law as an institutionalized decisional procedure designed to safeguard the conditions of human flourishing – suggests that the relevance of law to the topic of group autonomy claims lies in the underlying values that a legal system promotes.

The relation of law to freedom is not superficially obvious. Jeremy Bentham rightly observed that "Every law is an infraction of liberty." Yet well-chosen laws surely have the power to enhance liberty. The law that requires me to drive my car on the right-hand side of the road (in the United States, not in Great Britain) curtails my liberty of driving on the other side. Yet in the absence of that traffic law, the resulting vehicular confusion and congestion would inhibit my liberty to drive anywhere. The traffic laws are not an infraction of my over-all liberty; when well-designed, they enhance my liberty. To be sure, some laws seem to be out-and-out infractions of liberty. The laws that criminalize certain nonviolent sexual practices between consenting adults do not appear to enhance liberty but simply to restrain it.

When groups seek autonomy and self-determination, they invoke not only rules of law but also the concept of freedom. Thus, individuals seek freedom, and groups seek freedom. There is agreement on goals. The problem is that groups may have a quite different view of human freedom than individuals have.

Thus we should analyze the central concept of human freedom. Much has been written in the abstract about freedom;[24] let me begin with a concrete example from my experience in advising and representing a group of American women who were married or had been married to

---

20 By ANTHONY D'AMATO, written for this Anthology and based on a draft manuscript previously presented to workshops at Northwestern University School of Law and at New York University School of Law.

21 Perhaps these new claims are taking over the central arena *because* old-fashioned international colonialist aggression has receded. A nation can now "afford" to have internal dissension, even civil war, without fearing, as it might have feared a hundred years ago, that a foreign power would move right in and take over. Indeed, one of the most historically remarkable events that never took place – unnoticed because it didn't take place – was the fact that when the Soviet Union dissolved in the last few years, no other country – not even the superpower United States – made any move to "gobble up" any of the new republics. A hundred years ago, the breakup of any nation, let alone empire, would have immediately led to a scramble by other countries to annex the remnants of the nation or empire.

22 As the United Nations General Assembly did in 1960 when it resolved that "All peoples have the right to self-determination; by virtue of that right, they freely determine their political status and freely pursue their economic, social and cultural development." Para. 2, Declaration on the Granting of Independence to Colonial Countries and Peoples of Dec. 14, 1960, 15 UNGAOR, Supp. (No. 16) 66, UN Doc. A/4684 (1969).

23 To be sure, a particular group has no problem in defining the term for itself: "peoples" simply means members of the group. The claim they make is surely an intelligible one: we know, for example, that the Protestants of Northern Ireland are claiming a right of self-determination. But the conflicting claim of the Irish people as a whole is also intelligible: that everyone in Ireland, including the Protestants, are members of the Irish group – a group which, as a whole, is entitled to self-determination. No *definition* or other general norm can solve such a problem. Even if a definition were formulated that was explicitly addressed to the problem in Northern Ireland, it will assuredly fail if it is applied to any other autonomy claim anywhere else in the world.

24 Among the outstanding works are John Stuart Mill's famous essay *On Liberty* (1859) and Isaiah Berlin's book *Four Essays on Liberty* (1969). Psychologists of course have had much to say about freedom in the past hundred years, the spectrum ranging from B.F. Skinner's denial that the term has any content to Eric Fromm's insistence that freedom is the core concept in explaining human behavior.

Arabian husbands. Jenny (not her real name) said that she met Ahmed (not his real name) when they were students at a technical college in Missouri. He treated her as an equal partner in choosing places to go on a date and other aspects of their relationship. They became engaged, and she agreed to convert to the Muslim religion. They were married in the United States and they both graduated. Then, as agreed, they moved to Saudi Arabia (or Iran, Algeria, or Kuwait). She was welcomed warmly by his parents and relatives. But after a few weeks, he began telling her what to do instead of asking her. Soon he issued orders to her, and raised his voice when she protested. Shortly thereafter, he began hitting her when she did not comply with his wishes. The level of violence gradually escalated; he bruised her and battered her, and locked her up in their apartment whose windows he barricaded with tinfoil so that no light from the outside could come in. Jenny tried to run away but was immediately picked up by the police and brought back home, where her husband beat her severely. (In Saudi Arabia, a wife cannot leave the home without her husband's permission; she cannot travel within or outside the country without his permission; and she is totally forbidden to drive a car or ride a bicycle. When she goes out shopping, she must be completely veiled.) Jenny sought the advice of her women friends, including her husband's mother and an American woman who had married an Arab fifteen years previously. Fariva, her mother-in-law, summed up the opinion of all of them when she said: "He's just disciplining you. It's easy to stop him from hitting you. Just obey him and please him."

My other clients told me similar stories. I learned from them, and from my own research, that in Islamic countries a husband may legally divorce his wife simply by saying three times "I divorce thee," but the only way she can divorce him is by petitioning a court. The court, whose judges are exclusively male, in every case count a man's testimony as equivalent to that of two women.[25] If a man divorces his wife, she is not entitled to alimony; indeed, she will be rendered destitute.[26] A man is also entitled to have up to four wives, but a woman may only have one husband.[27]

From Jenny's point of view, her freedom was greatly curtailed when she moved to Saudi Arabia. A good starting position for analyzing freedom is Isaiah Berlin's concepts of negative freedom and positive freedom.[28] "Negative freedom" consists of the uncoerced opportunity for action.[29] Clearly, if Jenny wants to travel away from her home in Saudi Arabia or drive a car or ride a bicycle, or wear the clothes of her choice, she is inviting punishment. "Negative freedom" does not require that Jenny actually drive the car or ride the bicycle, it only states that if she wants to do so she can without fear of coercion or punishment. Thus, objectively speaking, Jenny's situation is one that is lacking in negative freedom. "Positive freedom" consists of the ability to make one's own choices.[30] Jenny lacks positive freedom because most of her life's choices are made by Ahmed. If Ahmed tells Jenny that she must put on a certain kind of nail polish, presumably Jenny retains the freedom to decide the order in which she will apply the nail polish to her fingers and thumb. In this latter respect she is free to make her own choice. But Jenny certainly would not regard this ambit of choice as being significant. For most of the choices of life that matter to her, she is controlled by her husband.[31]

---

25 For a somewhat polemical view, *see* Sandra Mackey, The Saudis: Inside the Desert Kingdom 131–53 (1990).

26 I hasten to note that the blatant inequality of women in Islamic countries is apparently not what Muhammed intended or prescribed in the Koran. Rather, it is the result of interpretations of the Koran through the centuries by conservative Islamic priests. See Ann E. Mayer, Islam and Human Rights 93–128 (1991).

27 One of my clients told me that her eight-year-old daughter was sexually abused in school by older boys. Her husband only hit her when she complained about this to him. Going to the school board was useless. Finally, through great subterfuge and planning, she managed to get her daughter out of school and escape to the American embassy. There she told the diplomatic staff about her beatings (showing them the bruises), and her daughter told them about the repeated sexual abuse. The staff was very sympathetic; they took notes, made phone calls, and kept my client and her child in the embassy for three days. Finally, a jeep drove up. Her face brightened: "We're going to the airport now, aren't we?" The embassy officer replied, "Just go along with them—we've arranged this for you at great trouble and expense. They'll take care of you."

The jeep took my client and her daughter back to their house where the husband was waiting for them. The soldiers had to push the two women out of the jeep. "We're very sorry," they said, "we don't like this job but we can't do anything about it."

28 Isaiah Berlin, Four Essays on Liberty 122–34 (1969).

29 *Id.* at xlii, 122.

30 Positive and negative freedom are not absolutes but are matters of more or less. Moreover, they overlap with one another. Isaiah Berlin does not claim that the two are always and logically separable, but rather, given their development in the history of ideas, keeping the two types in mind aids us in clarifying the concept of freedom. In a reply to his critics, Berlin said: "Let me say once again that 'positive' and 'negative' liberty, in the sense in which I use these terms, start at no great logical distance from each other. The questions 'Who is master?' and 'Over what area am I master?' cannot be kept wholly distinct." Berlin at xliii.

31 Did Jennifer freely relinquish her positive and negative freedoms when she took the marriage vows with Ahmed? The American wives I've represented explain their situation pretty much the same way. They admit that they heard lots of things before they decided to get married about how they would have to give up a great deal of personal freedom if they moved to their husband's homelands. But they add that the situation as it would become was never realistically portrayed to them. They may have been told that it would be a "very big change of lifestyle" without being told the actual details. Moreover, they invariably add that their

Westerners can readily empathize with Jenny. It's harder to see the situation from Fariva's point of view. Yet Fariva's viewpoint is also entitled to fair consideration.

In the first place, with respect to "negative freedom," Fariva would probably say that she has no desire to travel to other cities or countries, or to wear revealing clothes in public, or to have a job and career. She is perfectly content to stay at home and enjoy the home freedoms, including choosing the sequence in which she dresses herself and applies make-up. Instead of resenting the fact that she is cooped up at home, Fariva rises above and becomes unconscious of the impediments to her freedom of movement. It is akin to the claim Epictetus made that he, a slave, is freer than his master. The ancient Stoics accepted their fate in life, "internalized" it, and gloried in it. Moreover, Fariva could give a rational defense of her position. By not caring about going outside the home or getting a job, she attains security and sustenance. American women, in her view, may wish to work in the marketplace, but when they get married their husbands may not have the same degree of commitment that Arab husbands have to support their wives. Moreover, a business career is a risky enterprise and is hard and demanding. To be chained to an office desk is hardly a desirable alternative to staying at home, from Fariva's viewpoint.[32]

Secondly, with respect to "positive freedom," Fariva would probably say that her husband respects her and has her best interests at heart. She willingly leaves the decision-making to him; it relieves her mind and frees her from risk and uncertainty. She would not wish to trade her subservient marital status to the subservient status of a career woman. For a career woman is also subject to the will of her employer, and her employer is much less likely to know what is best for her than her husband. At the outset of their marriage her husband beat and disciplined her; she now says that the discipline made her a better person and a better wife. He has not beaten her in twenty years and she is happy and content with her position in life. Women were not born the equal of men; as a woman, Fariva has done quite well for herself, as well as could be expected.

How can we decide whether Jenny or Fariva is right? The decision is impossible if we make it on the subjective level: Fariva's viewpoint is as logical as Jenny's. In order to proceed, we must reject the viewpoints, feelings, and beliefs of the persons whose freedom we are considering. Epictetus may sincerely believe that he has more freedom than his master; but when we observe his situation, we would be violating semantics and common sense if we agreed with him or concluded that a slave is a free person. Nor must we confuse Fariva's sense of what makes her happy with whether she is a free person. All her wants and desires may be fulfilled by her marital situation, yet the question of freedom is not decided definitively by the degree of her satisfaction. As Isaiah Berlin pointedly argued:

> If degrees of freedom were a function of the satisfaction of desires, I could increase freedom as effectively by eliminating desires as by satisfying them; I could render men (including myself) free by conditioning them into losing the original desires which I have decided not to satisfy.[33]

We must instead adopt an objectivist stance. "Negative freedom" consists in the ability to choose; the degree of freedom consists in the number of choices available. One does not have to travel to attain the freedom of travel. Jenny and Fariva are not free if it is not open to them to travel to other cities or countries. If they are coerced into staying at home, or beaten if they venture away from the home, the result is the same: they have been deprived of an objective measure of freedom. Suppose Jenny is a "homebody" type; living in the United States, she never leaves her small town. Nevertheless, we can say objectively that she is "free" to travel in the United States. Now suppose she is in Riyadh, and also never leaves her immediate home area. The difference is that she has been deprived of the choice to leave, and hence in Riyadh she is not free.

This objective look at freedom results in our drawing the same conclusion for Jenny and Fariva. Both of them are equally unfree in Saudi Arabia. There is of course the subjective difference: Jenny feels constrained but Fariva does not.

The lasting lesson taught by John Stuart Mill is that human freedom is fostered by variety and tolerance.[34] Al-

husbands tricked them. Their husbands assured them that they would be treated as equals even after they moved to the husbands' countries. But when the women arrived there, the husbands "reverted to type" (as some of them put it) or were "influenced by their relatives" to become authoritarian. They say that they had no idea that their husbands, whom they thought they loved and trusted, would do such things.

[32] Charles Manson, the serial killer, is reported to have actually preferred prison to society – which is why he was not deterred by the law. In prison, he said, you get security, food, drink, shelter, and a predictable existence. Outside there is insecurity, worry about where the next meal is coming from, fear of others who may harm you, and so forth.

[33] Berlin at xxxviii. We find in this thought the central concerns of two of the most thought-provoking novels of the twentieth century: Aldous Huxley's *Brave New World* and B.F. Skinner's *Walden Two*.

[34] The most important philosopher of freedom, according to Hilary Putnam, was Immanuel Kant. "Kant makes the remarkable statement," Putnam says, "that it would be a bad thing if the truths of religion could be deduced by reason, because that would produce fanaticism. Note how Kant is using the term 'fanaticism.' He is saying – and with deep philosophical insight – that what

though freedom of speech is the central focus of his essay *On Liberty*, he has a lot to say about human freedom in general. He was an enemy of enforced social conformity—the conformity that stifles our growth as persons because we are cast into a mold ordained by society. The greatest advances in human civilization are achieved by people who are not constrained, who are free to invent and create. Not only must society *tolerate* the differences among people, but society must also be pluralistic—in the sense of increasing the diversity and variety of choices available to everyone.[35] Communication is the most important way that the diversity and variety of free choice can be made known; hence the importance Mill attaches to freedom of speech. Education is also important; a person who is ignorant of various choices is less free than a person who knows about them.

Fariva of course knew about traveling to other cities or countries, or driving a car or riding a bicycle; she simply accepted the fact that women are not allowed to do those things. But suppose she makes the following argument about "positive freedom":

> An insane person who has no control over her body is certainly not "free"; she is slave to her bodily functions and physical needs. Freedom consists in the ability of our minds to control our bodies. Suppose a person decides to become a monk, takes a vow of poverty, and enters a monastery. We say that he has freely made the choice to become a monk, even though he has become in a sense a slave to the dictates of his religion. If God tells his body what to do, he is just as "free" as if his own mind tells his body what to do. In my case, when I got married I gave up the mental decision-making to my husband. Instead of my mind telling me what to do, now it is my husband's mind that tells me what to do. If he wants me to drive a car or travel to another country, then I will do so. You see, I am actually *free* to travel or drive a car or whatever; like anyone else, I follow the commands of the mind. Now that I am married, the mental command comes from my husband's mind and not my own. It's like the monk following the commands of God.

This argument represents the dualist position, the most articulate expression of which was contained in Plato's *Republic*. Plato and the writers who follow him move easily from the Mind controlling the Body, to Reason controlling the Body, to Social Reason controlling the bodies of every member of society. As Isaiah Berlin so well recounts:

> Have not men had the experience of liberating themselves from spiritual slavery, or slavery to nature, and do they not in the course of it become aware, on the one hand, of a self which dominates, and, on the other, of something in them which is brought to heel? This dominant self is then variously identified with reason, with my 'higher nature', with the self which calculates and aims at what will satisfy it in the long run, with my 'real', or 'ideal', or 'autonomous' self, or with my self 'at its best'; which is then contrasted with irrational impulse, uncontrolled desires, my 'lower' nature, the pursuit of immediate pleasures, my 'empirical' or 'heteronomous' self, swept by every gust of desire and passion, needing to be rigidly disciplined if it is ever to rise to the full height of its 'real' nature. Presently the two selves may be represented as divided by an even larger gap: the real self may be conceived as something wider than the individual (as the term is normally understood), as a social 'whole' of which the individual is an element or aspect: a tribe, a race, a church, a state, the great society of the living and the dead and the yet unborn. This entity is then identified as being the 'true' self which, by imposing its collective, or 'organic', single will upon its recalcitrant 'members', achieves its own, and therefore their, 'higher' freedom.[36]

This is the passage that bridges the gap between "group freedom" and "individual freedom" that I discussed earlier. If the collective will of the group becomes the "mind"

makes the fanatic a fanatic isn't that his beliefs are necessarily wrong or his arguments incorrect. It is possible to have true beliefs supported by correct arguments, and still to be what Kant calls a fanatic; it is possible to have the kind of undesirable intolerance, intensity, in short, hostility to others thinking for themselves, that represented 'fanaticism' to the Enlightenment, and still be perfectly logical. In fact the perfectly logical fanatic, Kant is saying, is the most dangerous kind of fanatic. Fanaticism, Kant is saying, is undesirable in itself. That the truths of religion, which for Kant are the most important truths—should be by their very nature *problematic* is a good thing, not a bad one. This is where Kant's break with the medievals is total." HILARY PUTNAM, THE MANY FACES OF REALISM 49–50 (1987).

[35] A client of mine, a man in his early fifties, came to the United States from the Soviet Union when an exit visa was issued to him as a result of a lawsuit I had initiated against his country. (*See* Anthony D'Amato, *The Frolova Case: A Practitioner's View*, 1 N.Y.L. SCH. HUM. RTS. ANN. 33 (1983)). He told me about his first visit to a shoe store. "There's too much freedom in your country," he said. "In the Soviet Union, you go into a shoe store, they measure your foot, and give you a pair of shoes that you buy and take with you." He liked that system; it relieved him of the necessity of choice. He found the American shoe store bewildering in the vast array of shoes that he could buy, and he disliked the experience. I think his observation is extremely accurate: he may have disliked the freedom to choose in the United States, but he still called it "freedom."

[36] Berlin at 132.

that controls the individual actions of the members of the group, then the group's claim to autonomy resonates with at least the conception of "positive freedom" discussed by Plato and his followers. The members of the group are "free" to the extent that they are controlled by the collective mind of the group. This is said to be a higher freedom than any freedom achievable by the individuals themselves. In this sense, Fariva may truly believe that she has achieved a higher freedom by conforming her behavior to her husband's wishes. His mind is the "collective" mind controlling the two of them. Thus her nature, and destiny, as a woman is realized and achieved by doing what is in the collective interest of her husband and herself—as determined by him.

1. *The Problem of Dissenters*. Although Jenny adopted the Muslim faith when she got married, she is obviously a dissenter within the Muslim community. She rejects the community's basic values, especially the value of subordinating women to men. Is Jenny a "member" of the group or a "nonmember"? It's hard to say; the Shari'a courts would treat her as a member, and indeed rejecting the Muslim religion once one has embraced it is a capital crime. But member or nonmember, Jenny dissents from the group's values.

It is often difficult to discover what percentage of a group's membership is comprised of dissidents or potential dissidents. Consider the problem of determining such a statistic even in a case that is fairly open and documented: that of the Arab minority in Israel. The Shari'a courts were given broad authority in matters of personal status and religion over all Muslims in Israel, but the Muslim law allowing men to wed immature girls was specifically prohibited by the Knesset.[37] How can we tell whether a nine or ten-year-old girl is being forced against her will into a marriage arranged by her parents? Some indication of nonvoluntariness might be whether there is a substantial cash payment to the girl's parents. But even then, the child might say that she wishes that her hitherto worthless self be the occasion of a bountiful reward to her mother and father. Yet on the general question I would have no difficulty in agreeing with the Israeli solution. Surely the minority rights of Muslims in Israel deserve to be trumped by the human rights of immature girls whether or not they themselves are actual or potential dissenters from the Islamic group practice in which they were raised.

The position of dissenters within minority groups is part of the larger issue that I am raising in this essay—whether the unseen price we pay for supporting many group claims for autonomy or special international-law protection is a costly erosion of individual human liberties. My position is like saying that when we look at the pyramids of Egypt we should envision not a brilliant achievement of ancient civilization and culture but rather the work product of slaves under whip and lash dragging blocks of stone across hot desert sands.

The characteristics that define a minority group—ethnicity, race, religion, gender, language, culture, or traditions generally—are also the characteristics that need to be reinforced among the membership if the group wishes to preserve its identity. Because the group is politically nondominant, there is a shared concern that its identifying characteristics may be eroded through assimilation of its members into the general society or simply the opting-out of individual members. Within the group, its leadership has a vested interest in preventing the loss of members. Group leaders enjoy personal power solely because there is a group and they are its leaders; if the group erodes, their personal power base will erode as well. Their much-acclaimed "charisma" may merely be a function of the fact that they lead a well-defined group. Such leaders may be expected to promote conformity to group characteristics. Much of their efforts along these lines consist of education and propaganda. Young persons are taught to treasure the particular group characteristics that make them at least "different" from other people and maybe "better." The "difference" is often a suggestion that outsiders "can never know what it is like" to be a group member, or can never experience the "same" feelings or emotions in the same depth. Only the members of the group can be "true believers."

Even if a group does not claim that it is "better" than outsiders, the outsiders will tend to interpret the group's claim as one of superiority. The natural result is a growing resentment between the minority group and the rest of society. The minority group's leaders will of course strive for political dominance within the society, so as to ensure the group's survival, but in most cases the desire for power falls considerably short of securing it. Thus the group leaders will tend to look beyond the state—to the international community—for support and protection.[38] Their claim for international-law assistance is typically couched in terms of the fear of loss, via assimilation of their membership into the majority culture, of their identifying characteristics.

However, the fear of assimilation can arise even if there is no resentment of the minority group by the politically dominant society. Sometimes a government simply must make a policy choice. For example, a government must

[37] Ori Stendel, *The Arabs of Israel: Between Hammer and Anvil*, 20 Israel YB Hum. Rts. 287, 303 (1990) (no minimum age for minors in Islamic law; Ottoman law has a minimum age of nine years; Israel has a minimum age of seventeen.)

[38] "Although the United Nations has not defined the term 'protection of minorities,' it has come to understand this term in the somewhat technical meaning of 'the protection of non-dominant groups which, while wishing in general for equality of treatment with the majority, wish for a measure of differential treatment in order to preserve basic characteristics which they possess and which distinguish them from the majority of the population." ECOSOC Commission on Human Rights, Activities of the United Nations Relating to the Protection of Minorities p. 4, ¶ 5, E/Cn.4/Sub.2/194 (5 Nov. 1958), citing Report of the First Session of the Sub-Commission on the Prevention of Discrimination and Protection of Minorities (E/CN.4/52), § V.

make some choice of the language to be used in elementary school instruction. Most governments, in order to promote national unity, tend to choose a standard national language throughout the school system.[39] Yet some minority groups may feel that their own culture and linguistic heritage could be eroded unless their own minority language is used as the primary language of instruction in the public school system. Belgium in 1968 is an example of a country which had a remarkably tolerant approach to languages in elementary schools: children would be instructed in whatever language was predominant in the locality. However, a group of French-speaking parents situated in a Dutch speaking community petitioned the European Court of Human Rights to require Belgium to provide or approve local French-language schools for their children.[40] The Court denied the petition, holding that states are not obliged under the European Convention for the Protection of Human Rights and Fundamental Freedoms[41] to respect purely linguistic preferences of minorities in the sphere of education.[42]

If we regard the French-speaking parents in the Belgian Linguistic case as a minority group within a minority group, it is clear that they resorted to international law—specifically, to the European Court of Human Rights—because they lacked the political power within the state of Belgium to achieve their objective. The numerous "minorities treaties" following World War I had given more protection to minorities than the European Convention that was cited in the Belgian Linguistic case. For example, in a "minorities" case in 1935, the Permanent Court of International Justice advised that it would be a treaty violation for the Albanian government to abolish *all* private schools in Albania because such abolition would have a disproportionate impact upon a protected minority group in Albania that relied on private schools to preserve and protect the minority group culture.[43]

2. *Accounting for an Increase in Freedom*. I suggest that giving special protection to minority groups may actually decrease the quantum of individual human freedom in the world. This is partly an empirical question. We see that there is considerable human liberty in the world today, and yet we also see the increasing demands of minority groups for autonomy, self-determination, and ultimate political power. Why haven't groups by now reduced human liberty almost to the vanishing point?

The answer may be largely due to the fortuity of history. If we look at a map of the nations of the world today, and superimpose upon it another map that delineates the zones of autonomy claims of minority groups, we will find little congruence of borders between the two maps. Indeed, the boundaries between nations are clearly more determined by natural topological factors than by the beliefs of the inhabitants. In the continent of Africa where topology does not generally determine boundaries, the boundaries were more or less arbitrarily determined by colonization; those boundaries have persisted even as the colonies have become independent. Surely if the beliefs of cultural groups and tribes had been significant in demarcating national boundaries, the end of colonialism in Africa would have been followed by a radical shifting of boundaries so as to maximize the self-determination of existing groups. The opposite happened; the old oppressive colonial boundaries are still there.

Of course, national governments have had a lot to do with the location of boundaries; geographical topology is certainly not a complete explanation. With the rise of the nation-state in the sixteenth century, governments became increasingly suspicious of minority groups within their territory. France's persecution of the Huguenots in the sixteenth and seventeenth centuries was arguably less the product of religious messianism on the part of the Catholic majority than of kingly suspicion that the Huguenots were potentially disloyal to the throne. This pattern of minority-group suppression has repeated itself in state after state ever since that time. Whenever a minority group wishes to assert and preserve its identity, the dominant forces in society increasingly view that group as disloyal and a potential source of sabotage and secession.

In the modern era, governments have resorted to population relocations to dilute the potential disloyalty of minority groups. Some fifty-five million citizens of the U.S.S.R. were shifted and relocated during the Bolshevik era, clearly part of the policy of Stalin and his successors to dilute the dragging effect of the "nationalities" on central state

[39] However, there can be cases where a government does not want national unity. For instance, a government might require a nondominant minority group to use its own language in order to make it harder for spokespersons of that minority group to enter the ranks of government! This was the case in the recent past in South Africa, where the white majority government promoted a policy of elementary-school instruction in the native Bantu languages. Although the government claimed that its policy was intended to safeguard the cultural identity of the Bantu groups, most observers were not fooled by that claim. Instead, it seemed clear that what was at stake was a policy of dividing and conquering the politically powerless Bantu majority. See Anthony D'Amato, International Law: Process and Prospect 176 (1987) (commenting on the policy of "mother-tongue instruction" as a South African governmental policy that seemed egalitarian but in fact was not).

[40] *Belgian Linguistic case (No. 2), European Court of Human Rights,* Series A, No. 6 (1968), 2 EUR. HUM. RTS. REP. 252.

[41] Europ. T.S. No. 5, 213 U.N.T.S. 221 (1950). By implication, the Court's opinion suggests that a more positive minority rights provision like that of the interwar minorities treaties, had it been part of the European Convention for the Protection of Human Rights and Fundamental Freedoms, could have led to a quite different result.

[42] Series A, No. 6, at paras. I.3 and I.6. A broader, but perhaps unjustified, reading of the opinion might give solace to the Dutch community as a minority group being upheld in their use of the Flemish language against the claims of a yet smaller minority group (the French) within the Dutch community. *See, e.g.*, VAN DYKE, HUMAN RIGHTS, ETHNICITY AND DISCRIMINATION 30 (1985).

[43] Minority Schools in Albania, Advisory Opinion of 6 April 1935, PCIJ, Ser. A/B, no. 64.

control. Today in Latvia, for instance, a resurgent "democratic" movement is attempting to expel citizens of other republics who permanently reside on Latvian territory.[44] The nationalistic forces in favor of expulsion seem to exemplify the draconian solution to dissenters within a society–banish them. The end result could be a severe diminution in human freedoms of all the Latvian people. Even more controversial is the Israeli policy of "settlements" in the West Bank. Despite the overwhelming media opposition to these settlements, we might raise the question whether, after all, the net effect of the settlements might be to increase the scope of human liberties by diluting the minority-group monolithism of the Palestinians. Conversely, if the Palestinians achieve autonomy, the question of the individual liberties of the Palestinians could still be the most important remaining issue (although group leaders may suppress dissemination of information about personal lack of freedom). On the Israeli side there is increasing opposition to immigration to Israel by Jews of cultures strange to the Israelis (such as the Ethiopian Jews). Yet these people may help bring pluralism and freedom to the Judaic culture. A different effect is found in the South and South West African cases. Until recently, population relocations–of blacks into designated "homelands"–was viewed by right-wing whites as the best "solution" to the problem of apartheid.[45] It would have isolated the "minority groups" and unified them, thus curtailing the quantum of human liberty. When the attempt failed, the only alternative left was the dismantling of apartheid and the integration of blacks into the voting ranks. The quantum of individual human liberty will clearly be increased by the intermingling of the races if the intermingling can be accomplished peacefully.

3. *Should All Cultures Be Preserved?* Some observers might argue that a lowering of the quantum of human freedom is a price worth paying if all cultures are preserved. The idea is like saying that although slave labor created the Sphinx and the pyramids, at least we now have cultural monuments instead of just more sand. Since in any particular case the trade-off appears at the margins–whether a slight lowering of the quantum of human freedom is worth a raising of a particular stream of culture that contributes to world civilization–reasonable people may differ. I want to challenge at least one large assumption behind the question.

The assumption is that a particular culture always contributes to the advancement of civilization. Last year a student in my International Human Rights seminar contributed a paper on the Yanomami Indians who inhabit the Brazilian rainforest along the Venezuelan frontier.[46] The paper did not address environmental issues. A by-product of Brazilian development policies is the cultural disintegration of Indian tribes such as the Yanomami.[47] The author of the paper and the fourteen other students in the seminar all deplored the apparently inevitable extinction of Yanomami culture. However, the author acknowledged the importance of fierceness and aggression in Yanomami society:

> Men commonly physically abuse their wives, and cases of female infanticide have been reported.[48] In addition, villages periodically raid one another in a cycle of revenge and in order to steal women.[49]

The question "is *this* a culture *worth* preserving?" might be answered quite differently by (a) outside observers such as the participants in our seminar, (b) Yanomami male tribal leaders, and (c) Yanomami women.[50] My students were sufficiently committed to cultural pluralism that they said they would preserve the Yanomami society despite its abuse of Yanomami women.[51] This was not my reaction; is it yours?

But suppose we decide that a given culture does contribute to the advancement of civilization. The question then becomes: whose civilization? As an outsider, I can certainly say that letting different cultures flourish enriches me because it increases world diversity and my own capacity for choice–the essential elements of human freedom. But what about insiders? To them, the group's culture can be stifling. The monolithic culture that they are offering to the world may be denying them the right to make counter-cultural choices. They may suffer the loss of both

---

[44] *See* Viktor Alksnis, Suffering from Self-Determination, 84 FOR. POL. 61, 63 (1991).

[45] For an early account (originally written in 1966) of the inequalities and inequities of such a proposed solution, *see* ANTHONY D'AMATO, INTERNATIONAL LAW–PROCESS AND PROSPECT 165–92 (1987).

[46] Daniel Kanter, *Brazilian Development and the Yanomami's Right to Cultural Identity* (Northwestern Law School, May 12, 1991).

[47] Mr. Kanter did not claim that the Brazilian government was intentionally seeking the destruction of Yanomami culture; there is no justifiable claim of "genocide" (even though decades ago there were clearly acts of genocide against the Indians). The enticements of modern society have led many members of the tribe to abandon their villages.

[48] [Citing] CHAGNON, YANOMAMO, THE FIERCE PEOPLE 81–82 (1968).

[49] [Citing] Kellman, *The Yanomamis: Their Battle for Survival*, 36 J. INT'L AFF. 15, 24 (1984).

[50] There is always, of course, the complication of "false consciousness." Some Yanomami women may sincerely believe that their lot in life is to be physically abused, and that the Yanomami men are entitled to derive pleasure from delivering such abuse. We discussed in the seminar whether "educating" the Yanomami people so as to combat what we regard as their false consciousness might itself tend to destroy their culture. All the students agreed that introducing ideas about human rights into the Yanomami society was morally justified even though it could change their culture.

[51] This was the consensus of the seminar. The majority of the students in the seminar were women. Two students said they believed in total moral relativism: while they would deplore abuses toward women in our own society, they said that we have no business criticizing Yanomami men for abusing Yanomami women.

negative and positive freedom. My guess is that many otherwise liberal minded people tend to ignore the loss of freedom of persons trapped within a culture, and tend too readily to praise that culture as contributing in its own way toward human progress. No liberal-minded person wants to be a snob; no one wants to condemn foreign practices because they are foreign. Airline advertisements are replete with pictures of "quaint" foreign cultures, and people want to travel to these exotic places. Our "tolerance" (shaped and nurtured by the profit motive of travel companies) may lead us to overlook the impact of the foreign culture on freedom of the members of the cultural group. To be sure, in many cases the group members participate because tourism is good business for them. But at least I think we should retain a certain amount of skepticism that a foreign culture (or our own culture, for that matter) may seem interesting to us because of group conformity that is imposed upon the local inhabitants. Conformity can result in colorful costumes, but those costumes can be fetters to the individuals who must wear them.

2. The Primacy of Group Freedom[52]

I will defend the right of groups to some form of autonomy by attacking the reduction of self-determination to the rights of individuals.

The reductive view of self-determination is a form of moral myopia, involving a sociologically naive reduction of morality to justice. Proponents of reduction say that our moral obligations to one another are pretty much exhausted once we get our rights. This leaves us free autonomously to choose and pursue our own ends.

Yet it is a mistake to suppose that people either choose or pursue their vision of the good autonomously. They do not so much choose ends as choose cultural identities through which they can participate in collective decision and action. Thus, they forgo the autonomy celebrated by philosophers in order to gain access to one another's powers and judgment. They do this because the pursuit of genuinely private ends would be emotionally meaningless and politically ineffectual.

Rather than reduce morality to justice, we should view morality as a form of politics in which each person's ability to identify and pursue worthy goals depends on the cooperation of others. From this view it follows that only when we act together can we be the self-determining moral agents philosophers describe.

My argument against reducing group self-determination claims to instruments for the protection of individual autonomy proceeds in three steps.

1. The protection of cultures is a collective good. Indigenous separatists want to shield shared cultures from homogenization, not just to shield individuals against discrimination. We cannot explain such demands for cultural preservation as indirect means to the pursuit of individual ends. Cultures are not reducible to the shared backgrounds or experience of individuals; cultures also commit individuals to shared conceptions of the good. Since we cannot distinguish individual ends from the cultures that constitute them, we cannot explain the value of cultures to their members by describing them as shared resources permitting the pursuit of individual ends. Instead we must admit that in choosing to preserve a culture, we are thereby shaping the identities and the ends of future individuals.

The choices that culture informs are never merely private, because they affect the identity of every participant in the culture. Why do participants in a culture so often contest the meaning of its constitutive traditions instead of politely agreeing to disagree about future goals? The answer lies in the fact that by contesting a common past they are asserting political claims over one another's powers. They refuse to separate their individual ends from their shared history because they refuse to separate from one another—they refuse to treat the collective determination of their selves as a matter of individual choice.

Any argument for group autonomy based on a right of cultural preservation must acknowledge that cultural traditions are not simply inherited by individuals. They are common property that we can make use of only by invoking—or inventing—a common purpose. Cultures cannot be disentailed.

2. Respecting the moral autonomy of individuals entails respecting the autonomy of the group through which they pursue their moral ends. My second point is not that some particularly attractive moral view requires embodiment in a culturally bounded community; my point is that any moral view demands this. We can only effectively advance any conception of the good in a social world by making a *cause* of it—that is, by consulting and cooperating with like-motivated others. Such causes exclude the uncommitted and entail the collective governance of some of the powers of their members. Thus, any seriously entertained moral end is a reason for bounding and empowering a group.

Common sense tells us that identification with others encourages us to act morally. As vain as we are selfish, we are more likely to behave morally if our obligations to others are incorporated into our sense of identity. People are clannish, and moral argument ignores this truth at its peril.

Nor is this clannishness an unfortunate tendency that

[52] By GUYORA BINDER, excerpted from: *The Kaplan Lecture on Human Rights: The Case for Self-Determination,* 29 STANFORD JOURNAL OF INTERNATIONAL LAW 223, 248–50, 255–57, 263, 267–70 (1993). Reprinted by permission.

morality must work its way around. Morality is inherently a collective enterprise, and inherently intolerant.

Why is morality inherently collective? Suppose you think yourself obliged to bring about a certain state of affairs. While you are concerned about the consequences of your actions, those consequences are going to depend on the actions of others. If you can get others to commit to your moral view, and to cooperate with you in planning action, you can plan more effectively because you have more information. You can also act more effectively because more people will be trying to achieve the results you desire. Therefore, no consequentialist moral view can leave you indifferent to the beliefs and actions of others; indeed, any such moral view gives you compelling reasons to cooperate with others committed to the same view.

Why is morality not just inherently collective, but also inherently intolerant? Because the collective pursuit of a moral end is open only to believers. Cooperators in the pursuit of a moral end will have obligations to one another to share information and fulfill expectations, and perhaps to accede to the majority will about how best to pursue the mutually desired consequences. These are obligations that cooperators don't have towards outsiders and that outsiders don't have towards them.

3. Democracy depends upon group autonomy, while the autonomy rights of groups depend upon their democracy. My characterization of moral action as a kind of politics rests on a conception of politics as collective action, coordinated by such communicative practices as deliberation, persuasion, and negotiation. On this view, politics is more than a matter of opinion privately held. A right to participate in politics therefore means more than the right to answer an opinion poll; it entails a right to coordinate action with others. Accordingly, democracy is more than a mere assemblage of individual rights. It requires a society mobilized for political action—organized, that is, into movements.

But what if the individual members of a moral community simply serve as foot-soldiers subject to the command of a charismatic leader? Can we really say that members are committed to a community's moral ends if they do not themselves reflect on the meaning of those ends and evaluate the community's conduct in light of them? Wouldn't we say that these community members were motivated only by loyalty to the leader rather than by their own moral beliefs? If individuals unquestioningly follow orders, don't they act as mere agents rather than as members of the community? We will feel strongly tempted to say that to exercise moral autonomy an individual must participate in the *decisions* as well as the *actions* of her community. Only if a moral community is democratic in this sense, we might conclude, can it claim a right to autonomy.

The modern philosopher may see freedom in each individual's pursuit of her own conception of the good. But for the philosophical tradition from Rousseau to the young Hegelians, *expressing* oneself in this way was nothing more than a surrender to impulse, an index of necessity rather than freedom. True freedom was to be found in the onerous but creative task of *realizing* one's self. Thus her conception of the good was never simply her own—it was always mediated by some community.

If we see our own best selves as contingent on the existence of a certain sort of community, we won't see the right to pursue our chosen ends as an adequate vision of freedom; we won't see merely respecting this right as an adequate standard of morality; and we won't see the right to approve or disapprove our leaders as an adequate conception of self-rule. We will see our own ability to define ourselves, to act on our moral beliefs, and to govern ourselves as requiring the creation and protection of a particular culture.

"Self-determination of peoples" is more than a misleading euphemism for the political and civil rights of individuals. It rightly asserts the connections among solidarity, self-government, and self-realization.

10
The Global Environment

A. DEBATE: Bioethics

1. Our Duty to Future Generations[1]

Since the beginning of life of Earth, each species has in effect been a steward for future generations. The human species, the latest in this great chain, has inhabited the planet for only three million years, a brief interlude in its history. Because we now have the power to alter the planet irreversibly on a global scale, it is essential to enunciate international norms to govern the use of our natural heritage. These norms must be based in universal human values and be accepted by diverse cultures and political systems.

My thesis is that we, the human species, hold the natural heritage of our planet in trust for future generations and that this fiduciary relationship obligates us to conserve the diversity of the natural resource base (conservation of options) and to pass the planet on to future generations in no worse condition than we receive it (conservation of quality).

2. The Duty We Owe to All Existing Forms of Life[2]

There is a common assumption that the present generation owes a duty to generations yet unborn to preserve the diversity and quality of our planet's life-sustaining environmental resources. This duty is sometimes said to be an emerging norm of customary international law,[3] like the more recently treaty-generated custom of the "common heritage of mankind."[4] Professor Edith Brown Weiss says we owe to future generations a global environment in no worse condition than the one we enjoy.[5]

International law scholars appear to have overlooked the startling thesis put forth by Derek Parfit in 1976.[6] I will state his thesis in a somewhat stronger form than he did by subsuming within it chaos theory, as I shall explain.

Let us picture the people who will be living 100 years from now:[7] they will be specific, identifiable persons. We make the claim that we currently owe an environment-preserving obligation to those particular as-yet-unborn persons. Parfit's paradox arises when we seek to discharge that postulated obligation. Suppose that we undertake a specific environmental act of conservation. For example, we help to pass a law requiring catalytic converters on all automobiles in our state. We will thus have succeeded in intervening in the environment–making the environment slightly different from the way it would have been but for our action. Our intervention will reduce the amount of air pollution that otherwise would have taken place, and increase the utilization of energy and resources in the manufacture of catalytic converters.

Yet this slight difference resulting from our intervention in the environment will affect the ecosphere in the years subsequent to our intervention. In particular, it will affect the conditions under which human procreation takes place. The particular sperm and egg cells from which any human being develops is a highly precarious fact; the slightest difference in the conditions of conception will probably result in fertilization of the egg by a different sperm. Hence, when the environment is disrupted even a slight amount, a different future person will probably be con-

---

[1] By EDITH BROWN WEISS, excerpted from: *Conservation and Equity Between* , in THOMAS BUERGENTHAL (ED.), CONTEMPORARY ISSUES IN INTERNATIONAL LAW: ESSAYS IN HONOR OF LOUIS B. SOHN 245, 246 (1984). Reprinted by permission.

[2] By ANTHONY D'AMATO, excerpted from: *Do We Owe a Duty to Future Generations to Preserve the Global Environment*? 84 AMERICAN JOURNAL OF INTERNATIONAL LAW 190 (1990). Reprinted by permission.

[3] Professor Weiss regards it as an obligation erga omnes that has some support in customary international law. *See* Edith Brown Weiss, *The Planetary Trust: Conservation and Intergenerational Equity*, 11 ECOLOGY L.Q. 495, 540-44 (1984).

[4] *See* D'Amato, *An Alternative to the Law of the Sea Convention*, 77 AJIL 281, 282–83 (1983).

[5] EDITH BROWN WEISS, IN FAIRNESS TO FUTURE GENERATIONS: INTERNATIONAL LAW, COMMON PATRIMONY AND INTERGENERATIONAL EQUITY (1989).

[6] Derek Parfit, *On Doing the Best for Our Children*, in ETHICS AND POPULATION 100 (M. Bayles ed. 1976); Parfit, *Overpopulation: Part One* (ms. 1976), referred to in Parfit, *Future Generations, Further Problems*, 11 PHIL & PUB. AFF. 113 (1982).

[7] In saying this, I do not assume that the human race will necessarily survive the next 100 years. Acts of cosmic stupidity are always possible: self-obliteration by nuclear war, depletion of the ozone layer, and so on.

ceived. According to Parfit's thesis, our intervention in the environment will make a sufficient impact to assure that different sperm cells will probably fertilize the egg cells in all procreations that take place subsequent to our environmental intervention. Different people will be born from those who would have been born if we had not intervened in the environment.

To be sure, in the first few years following our environmental intervention, there is very low probability that many subsequent human conceptions will be affected. But as years go by, the effect of our single environmental intervention increases exponentially (according to chaos theory) until it is a virtual certainty that 100 years from now all human conceptions will have been affected a little bit from our single act of environmental intervention, and that this little effect will actually result in fertilization of egg cells by sperm cells different from those that would have fertilized those egg cells in the absence of our act. Parfit's conclusion is that every single person alive 100 years from now will be an entirely different individual from the person he or she would have been had we not intervened in the environment.

This fact creates a paradox in our attempt to discharge our moral obligation to future generations. How can we owe a duty to future persons if the very act of discharging that duty wipes out the very individuals to whom we allegedly owed that duty? Our attempted environmental altruismwill prevent the birth of the precise intended beneficiaries of our altruism.

It is no answer to argue that the entirely new set of individuals who will replace those we wipe out will themselves greatly benefit from our intervention. For although they may be the beneficiaries of our environmental intervention, we could not have owed a duty to them because they were not probable persons at the time we claimed that we had a duty. Any present duty that we have to future generations can only be a duty to particular future persons who are awaiting their turn to be born. If in exercise of such an alleged duty we commit an act of environmental intervention that denies the opportunity to be born to those very individuals, we cannot possibly be making them better off by virtue of our intervention. They would have preferred to be born in a degraded environment than not to be born at all. Thus, we find that any attempted altruism on our part to intervene in the environment to help future persons will make those persons incomparably worse off than if we had not intervened. They would be better off living in a degraded environment 100 years from now—that is, in an environment that did not benefit from our act of environmental improvement—than not living at all.[8]

Parfit's paradox is uncomfortable and counter intuitive. Is it somehow fallacious? If not, is there any way we can accept Parfit's thesis and still make sense of the notion of "obligation to preserve the environment"?

People encountering Parfit's thesis for the first time are properly skeptical that a minor intervention in the environment can actually result in entirely different individuals in 100 years from those who would have existed then had there been no such intervention. But the result is scientifically accurate, proven by the discovery in recent years of chaos theory. In the 1950s, Edward Lorenz, a meteorologist at the Massachusetts Institute of Technology, discovered that a very slight shift in the initial data about weather conditions fed into a computer will result in drastic differences in simulated weather conditions after a number of iterations.[9] The differences, or perturbations, grow exponentially, doubling every 4 days. Lorenz called this the "butterfly effect." For an environmental intervention as slight as a butterfly flapping its wings near a weather station will change long-term weather predictions. Although 2 weeks after the butterfly's capricious flight the effect will hardly be felt outside an area 16 times the path of the butterfly, after 1 or 2 years the butterfly's flight could actually be the cause of a major storm that otherwise would not have taken place.[10] A weekly quadrupling rate means that an initial perturbation will increase by 4 to the 52d power after just 1 year—enough to make itself felt anywhere on the planet. By my own rough calculations, after 3 years the number of perturbations will have increased by more than the total number of atoms in the universe. Thus, applying chaos theory in support of Parfit's thesis makes clear that any action we take will affect the environment in such a way as to change the conditions of all acts of human procreation several decades hence. Even minor acts in the present can substantially affect which particular sperm cells succeed in fertilizing human ova a hundred years from now.

If there is no valid scientific objection to Parfit's thesis, can we argue that it proves too much? Can we argue that any act that we do, not just acts of environmental preservation, will have a similar exponentially increasing future effect? For instance, a jogger will have this effect on the future, just as will the air-polluting automobile that passes her as she jogs. Can we thus contend that since acts of

---

[8] What if the environment is so bad that even the act of living is a curse? Would any person choose not to have lived at all rather than to be born into a miserable and degraded situation? We can perhaps choose for ourselves, but I doubt that we have a moral right to make that choice for others yet unborn.

[9] *See, e.g.*, Ivars Peterson, The Mathematical Tourist 144–49 (1988); J. Glieck, Chaos: The Making of a New Science (1987).

[10] Ivar Ekeland, Mathematics and the Unexpected 66 (1988).

environmental degradation as well as acts of environmental preservation equally change the composition of future populations, Parfit's thesis is vacuous?

No, because Parfit's thesis is aimed at moral considerations. It is premised on the generally accepted moral obligation not to act in any situation where our action would make others worse off.[11] Hence if we engage in an act of environmental preservation for the reason that we feel an obligation to future persons, our very act will make those persons worse off than if we had not acted at all; indeed, our act will make them totally worse off—they will be deprived of their existence. To be sure, the same is true of any environmentally degrading act that we might take—except that no one claims that we owe an obligation to future generations to degrade the environment! Parfit's thesis is thus pinpointed at only one claim of obligation: that if we act to preserve the environment out of a sense of obligation to future persons, that obligation is nonsensical because in so acting we destroy the obligees.

Indeed, this theme could be embellished by pointing out that all environment-preserving actions are supererogatory in contrast to all selfish uses that we might make of the environment. The argument would proceed as follows. Imagine that we could have a conversation with a lawyer who represents the class of actual persons who will be alive 100 years from now. She tells us that she is prepared to accept just our selfishly motivated environmental acts. For as we act to use up environmental resources just to gratify our immediate desires, we are at least motivated by an understandable reason—the reason of self-interest. True, she adds, those acts will operate to change the conditions of future human procreation in such a way that the class of persons she represents will change its members' identities each time we act. But she accepts this result as inevitable; her clients in the future will do precisely the same thing vis-a-vis potential persons in *their* future. On the other hand, she strenuously objects to any of our acts of environmental intervention that are motivated solely by a sense of obligation to her clients. That is not a good reason to act, she argues, because in so acting we will gratuitously destroy her clients. Our attempt to be altruistic to her clients will result in their destruction. "We don't need friends like you," she might conclude. "My clients would rather live in whatever environment is left to them than not be born at all."

[11] With appropriate caveats. For example, if we bar the establishment of a McDonald's hamburger shop directly next to the geyser Old Faithful in Yellowstone National Park, we are making a McDonald's franchisee worse off. As with any moral consideration, we have to balance that against the aesthetic sensibilities of numerous tourists who want to view Old Faithful without updated reminders of how many billions of hamburgers have so far been produced out of how many millions of cows.

Perhaps we can shift the ground of contention to argue against Parfit's thesis on the ground that our obligation to act to preserve the environment stems from a generic notion of "future generations" and not because we have any particular future individuals in mind. In other words, can we say that we do not care which persons inherit the earth so long as whoever inherits it inherits a habitable planet in no worse condition than the one we enjoy? Of course we can say all this, and in a rather rough way we probably think it and act upon it. But the argument, upon analysis, simply glosses over the problem. Future generations are not an abstraction; they consist of individuals. The particularity of the individuals is apparent when we consider how lucky it is for anyone to be born. The odds of your being born instead of one of your many potential siblings are comparable to the odds of winning the Pennsylvania Lottery in the recent drawing when the first prize was over $100 million. The point is that the winner of the lottery would not be equally content to have any other person win the lottery; similarly, you and I would not be content if a different person had been born instead of us. We may have been extraordinarily lucky to have been born at all, but we are not ready to relinquish the outcome of that lucky break simply on the ground that large numbers and vanishingly small probabilities are involved. The fact that somebody will be born does not mean that the person lucky enough to be born is indifferent about who it is.[12] Future generations cannot be indifferent about whether it is they or other persons who will enjoy the fruits of the earth. If we feel we owe an obligation to them, we, too, cannot be indifferent about the question. We cannot discharge our obligation to them if in the process of doing so we deprive them of life.

At first blush, Parfit's thesis appears to set us back. Yet it is not at all retrogressive. Instead, it may help us to clear the ground of unnecessary conceptual confusion and proceed on a firmer footing with regard to environmental obligations.

I suggest that we begin by noticing that the notion of obligation to future generations is typically located within the developing concept of international human rights. The general argument starts with the claim that human rights are more important than any other value in international law, including the rights of states. And it continues by claiming that future generations also have a human right—the right to inherit an environment no worse than the one we enjoy. These are relatively uncontroversial assertions. But if we look closely, we see that the entire concept of "human rights" is species chauvinistic. This form of chauvinism is illustrated by the following quotation from Judge

[12] *See* the analogous philosophical argument by John Leslie, *No Inverse Gambler's Fallacy in Cosmology*, 97 MIND 269 (1988).

Richard Posner: "Animals count, but only insofar as they enhance wealth. The optimal population of sheep is determined not by speculation on their capacity for contentment relative to people, but by the intersection of the marginal product and marginal cost of keeping sheep."[13] Posner purports to derive these conclusions from his principle of wealth maximization, which for him constitutes the bedrock moral justification for all law.[14] He characterizes "wealth" solely in human terms; the sheep's own wealth, of course, is not to be maximized or even taken into account. Since a sheep's own capacity for enjoying life has by definition nothing to do with maximizing human wealth, it becomes for Posner morally and legally irrelevant.

One of the most articulate opponents of "animal rights" is R. G. Frey, whose species chauvinism is explicit when he writes:

> It is the sheer richness of human life, and in what this richness consists, which gives it its superior quality. Some of the things which give life its richness we share with animals; there are other things, however, which can fill our lives but not theirs. For example, falling in love, marrying, and experiencing with someone what life has to offer; having children and watching and helping them to grow up; working and experiencing satisfaction in one's job; listening to music, looking at pictures, reading books . . .. By comparison with animals, our lives are of an incomparably greater texture and richness[15]

Few persons would quarrel with this statement if Professor Frey has in mind comparing humans to the lowest forms of animal life such as insects and mollusks. But what about whales or chimpanzees? Some whales possess a brain six times bigger than the human brain; Dr. John Lilly has claimed that they are more intelligent than any man or woman.[16] According to Dr. Kenneth Norris, whales see and taste through sounds, and possess many other faculties of which we are only vaguely aware.[17] Chimpanzees, monkeys and gorillas take obvious pleasure in raising their young, and exhibit the same gamut of emotions in the process as do humans. They seem to understand human sign language and, indeed, their "language ability" seems to increase the more researchers take pains to teach them our language.[18]

Are we bound by a notion of "human rights" to consider that the only things that are valuable in the world are those that directly benefit ourselves? Consider the following thought experiment. Suppose Robinson is the last person on earth. When he dies, the human species will have come to an end. During his lifetime, would he have a moral right to kill animals for sport, even knowing that some of those he would kill are the last survivors of their own species? Posner's principle of maximizing wealth would still apply in Robinson's case; it is not dependent upon the existence of other humans. Under that principle, Robinson has a moral right to do whatever would contribute to his own wealth, including the hunting and termination of various animal species for no other reason than the "sport" of it. And under Frey's view, Robinson can do anything he pleases because his life is incomparably richer than any lives of the animals or animal species that he destroys.

Does Professor Weiss's notion of obligation to future generations change the result of Posner and Frey? Since there will be no future generations in our hypothetical case, Robinson has no duty. He may, under the duty-to-future-generations hypothesis, proceed to enjoy sport hunting even if in so doing he terminates entire animal species.[19]

If this result is uncomfortable, it points to the shortcomings of the species chauvinism that underlies all three theories: Posner's, Frey's,and Weiss's. All three are impoverished accounts of our actual sense of moral obligation. They share a common ground: a dependency upon the improvement of the *human* condition.

It is important to recall that Parfit's thesis only deconstructs the notion of obligation to future generations, and not environmental obligations generally. If we have a choice between committing a wasteful act (such as killing

---

13 Richard A. Posner, The Economics of Justice 76 (1983).

14 "Wealth maximization provides a foundation not only for a theory of rights and of remedies but for the concept of law itself." *Id.* at 74.

15 R. G. Frey, Rights, Killing and Suffering 109–10 (1983).

16 J. Lilly, Man and Dolphin (1961).

17 Cited in D. Day, The Whale War 154 (1987).

18 *See* D.M. Rumbaugh (ed.), Language Learning by a Chimpanzee: The Lana Project (1977). Skeptics are still heard to claim that chimpanzees cannot use their vocal chords to form words, and therefore they cannot be said to engage in language activity. A hundred years ago skeptics were saying that chimpanzees can never learn sign language and can never understand the meaning of verbal instructions. These claims have been undermined in recent experiments. So the skeptics continue to define "language" more narrowly as more experimental results come in.

19 To be sure, we can argue that an "enlightened" Robinson might calculate that Darwinian evolution might result, 100 million years after his death, in the creation of a new human species. Hence, by not killing off various animal species, an enlightened Robinson might help speed up the evolutionary development of humans from those very animal species. Perhaps in that extremely attenuated sense Robinson could be said to have a kind of obligation to a future to-be-evolved generation of humans. But the hypothesis is problematic for a reason other than its attenuation. For Robinson cannot be certain that refraining from killing *this* or *that* particular animal will help humans re-evolve in the distant future; perhaps killing a particular animal could help ensure the future re-evolution of humans because that particular animal could be a natural predator of the line of animals that would otherwise evolve into humans.

a whale) or committing an environmentally preserving act (such as planting a tree), either act, under Parfit's thesis, will change the identity of future generations. We need a different, larger notion of bioethics to choose between these acts.

Consider Parfit's own thoughts on the subject:

> We need some new principle of beneficence, which is acceptable in all kinds of case. Though we have not yet found this principle, we know that it cannot take a person-affecting form. It will be about human well-being, and the quality of life, but it will not claim that what is morally most important is whether our acts will affect people for good or bad, better or worse.
>
> Non-religious moral philosophy is a very young subject. We should not be surprised that much of it is still puzzling.[20]

I agree with the sentiment of these thoughts but take slight exception to Parfit's search for a moral principle. In fact, I think the search for moral principles and precepts can indirectly support much immoral conduct, because no matter how a principle is stated, it may be interpreted and construed in such a way as apparently to justify immoral behavior.[21] In my view, it is better to begin with our preverbal sense of morality. That sense, I would suggest, tells us that it is somehow wrong to despoil the environment, to act in ways that waste natural resources and wildlife, and to gratify pleasures of the moment at the expense of living creatures who are no threat to us.

What George F. Will said about whales in a sense is true of all acts of environmental preservation: ''The campaign to save whales is a rare and refreshing example of intelligence in the service of something other than self-interest.'' Natural evolution has produced some prey-specific predatory animals that will hunt their prey to extinction, at which point they will become extinct themselves. Presumably if they had developed a greater intelligence, they would exercise restraint. Humans are lucky in that we are blessed with the intelligence to figure out how to survive in an environment where we are not physically the strongest, fastest or best-protected animals. That same intelligence can be stretched to include a world-based empathy for the environment, ''beneficent'' in Parfit's sense.

We should not limit our actions to those we are able to determine now as directly or indirectly benefiting ourselves or our descendants. Rather, we should cultivate our natural sense of obligation not to act wastefully or wantonly even when we cannot calculate how such acts would make any present or future persons worse off. There is good evidence that customary international law—with various fits and starts and setbacks—is moving generally in this direction, perhaps responding to a deep and inarticulate sense that human beings are not in confrontation with, but rather belong to, their natural environment. Calling it ''human rights'' should not constrict our understanding of what it is or where it is going.

3. Reply[22]

Professor D'Amato in his essay takes issue with the notion of rights of future generations to the planet by invoking Derek Parfit's famous paradox and combining it with the new theory of chaos. He argues that future generations cannot have rights because they are composed of individuals who do not exist yet and every intervention we take today to protect the environment affects the composition of these future individuals, robbing some potential members of future generations of their existence.

It is important to parse this analysis into its two component parts: that future generations cannot have rights because the individuals do not exist yet, and that actions to protect the environment for future generations will destroy the rights of some future individuals because different people will be born as a result of the intervention. The first is that future generations cannot have rights, because rights exist only when there are identifiable interests, which can only happen if we can identify the individuals who have interests to protect. Since we cannot know who the individuals in the future will be, it is not possible for future generations to have rights.

This paradox assumes the traditional conceptual framework of rights as rights of identifiable individuals. The planetary, or intergenerational, rights I propose are not rights possessed by individuals. They are, instead, genera-

---

20 Parfit, *Future Generations, Further Problems*, 11 PHIL. & PUB. AFF. 113 171–72 (1982).

21 In brief, any stated moral principle may be deconstructed. Contexts always exist in which a given moral principle, if strictly applied, would lead to an immoral result. *See* JOSEPH FLETCHER, SITUATION ETHICS: THE NEW MORALITY (n.d.); JOSEPH FLETCHER & J.W. MONTGOMERY, SITUATION ETHICS: TRUE OR FALSE (1972). Consider the most morally repugnant behavior of recent times: Hitler's policy of extermination of minority groups. This was ''justified'' at the time in terms of moral utilitarianism—the need to ''purify'' the human race. Yet even entering into the ''debate'' about the immorality of ''Aryan supremacy'' was to compromise one's moral position—for it amounted to giving some degree of intellectual credence to the Nazi position! In other words, it wasn't the principle of utilitarianism that was ''misapplied'' by the Nazis; rather, any attempt to apply a ''principle'' to their acts was itself perverse.

22 By EDITH BROWN WEISS, excerpted from: *Our Rights and Obligations to Future Generations for the Environment*, 84 AMERICAN JOURNAL OF INTERNATIONAL LAW 198 (1990). Reprinted by permission.

tional rights, which must be conceived of in the temporal context of generations. Generations hold these rights as groups in relation to other generations—past, present and future. This is consistent with other approaches to rights, including the Islamic approach, which treats human rights not only as individual rights, but as "rights of the community of believers as a whole."[23] They can be evaluated by objective criteria and indices applied to the planet from one generation to the next. To evaluate whether the interests represented in planetary rights are being adequately protected does not depend upon knowing the number or kinds of individuals that may ultimately exist in any given future generation.

Enforcement of these intergenerational rights is appropriately done by a guardian or representative of future generations as a group, not of future individuals, who are of necessity indeterminate. While the holder of the right may lack the capacity to bring grievances forward and hence depends upon the representative's decision to do so, this inability does not affect the existence of the right or the obligation associated with it.

Now it may be argued that such rights do depend upon knowing at least the number of individuals in the future, because if the earth's population continues to grow rapidly, the amount of diversity and degree of quality that must be passed on will be higher than if the population in the future were at the same level or less than it is today.

But, if anything, the existence of these generational rights to the planet may constrain the population policies of present and future generations. Whether a generation chooses to meet its obligations by curtailing exploitation, consumption and waste or by constraining population growth is a decision it must make. The fact that future generations have a generational right to receive the planet in a certain condition puts constraints on the extent to which a present generation can ignore this choice.

The second part to Professor D'Amato's argument is that if we intervene to conserve the environment to protect future generations, we cannot succeed in protecting them because our intervention will cause a different group of individuals to emerge. But since the rights of future generations exist only as generational rights, it does not matter who the individuals are or how many they may be. Only at the point where the individuals are born and by definition become members of the present generation do the generational rights attach to individuals.

Professor D'Amato's response is that "future generations are not an abstraction; they consist of individuals." But they do not consist of individuals until they are born, and hence it is necessary and appropriate to speak of future generations qua generations as having rights in relation to the planet. Professor D'Amato correctly points out that the composition of future generations cannot be known in advance, in part because it is affected by actions of the present generation. Indeed, he does not make his own case as strongly as he might. For example, we do not need to limit ourselves to ascribing these effects to subtle changes in the biochemistry of conception, as Professor D'Amato does in his amusing excursion into the dynamics of egg and sperm. Virtually every policy decision of government and business affects the composition of future generations, whether or not they are taken to ensure their rights. Decisions regarding war and peace, economic policy, the relative prosperity of different regions and social groups, transportation, health, education—all influence the demographics and the composition of future generations by affecting the lives and fortunes of the present generation: who will succeed and prosper, who will marry whom, who will have children, and even who will emigrate.

I take the view that our planetary obligations to future generations are owed to all the earth's future human inhabitants, whoever they may be. This opens the possibility that these decisions, too, deserve to be scrutinized from the point of view of their impact on future generations. Professor D'Amato's approach reflects an unnecessarily constrained view of human rights law that would shut off a useful and broadly acceptable theoretical underpinning to sustainable resource development. The possibility that intergenerational equity may place limits on our actions is an important new area of human rights research.

Such limitations should be applied very narrowly, lest the rights of future generations develop into an all-purpose club to beat down any and all proposals for change. But surely long-term environmental damage is a good place to begin. Future generations really do have the right to be assured that we will not pollute ground water, load lake bottoms with toxic wastes, extinguish habitats and species or change the world's climate dramatically—all long-term effects that are difficult or impossible to reverse—unless there are extremely compelling reasons to do so, reasons that go beyond mere profitability.

Professor D'Amato invokes chaos theory to justify his contention that any environmental intervention will produce different individuals in the future than would otherwise have been produced. But he overlooks the most important implication of chaos theory for the environment and for future generations: namely, that systems do not proceed on orderly, linear paths of change, but rather that they will abruptly change.[24] This can be demonstrated on a home computer, using a very simple program. Scientists have suggested that there may be key breaking points in our global environmental system, beyond which systems will reorganize and substantially change their properties. If we are concerned about future generations, it is important to try to predict these breaking points. More importantly, the

[23] M. KHADDURI, THE ISLAMIC CONCEPTION OF JUSTICE 233 (1984).

[24] For catastrophe theory, *see* R. THOM, MATHEMATICAL MODELS OF MORPHOGENESIS (1983); for the theory of complex systems, *see* ILYA PRIGOGINE & ISABELLE STENGERS, ORDER OUT OF CHAOS (1984). For a concise review of the influence of chaos theory, *see* *Chaos Theory: How Big an Advance*?, 245 SCIENCE 26 (1989).

best tool that we could give future generations to respond to abrupt changes and reorganizations is a robust planet, which requires conserving a diversity of resources so that future generations have greater flexibility in designing responses.

Professor D'Amato proposes that there is a "preverbal sense of morality" that tells us not to waste resources, degrade the environment or wantonly kill animals. But, if anything, history in the last few centuries suggests that our natural instincts are self-indulgent. We have desecrated environments, wasted resources and slaughtered animals purely for pleasure or for modest personal gain. It may be that the human species carries both a selfish gene and an altruistic one, as the sociobiologists tell us, but it is hardly sufficient to rely on the generous gene to build a theory of morality to overcome the selfish genes, without more.

I have proposed a fundamental norm of equality among generations of the human species in relation to the care and use of the natural system. But my proposal recognizes that we are part of the natural system and that we, as all other generations, must respect this system. We have a right to use and enjoy the system but no right to destroy its robustness and integrity for those who come after us.

Whether we rely on a beneficent "preverbal sense of morality" toward the planet and its resources or on theories rooted in the welfare of the human condition and the ecological system of which people are a part, there is a shared recognition that the present generation has an obligation to care for the planet and to ensure that all peoples can enjoy its services.

4. Rejoinder[25]

Professor Weiss chides me for failing to make the argument that I made. She says that I did not make my own case as strongly as I might, because "virtually every policy decision of government and business affects the composition of future generations." I did in fact argue that although every policy decision of government and business surely affects the composition of future generations, we are nevertheless entitled to examine each and every one of those policy decisions from a moral point of view. If some are immoral, we reject them for that reason alone. If others are asserted to be morally required solely because they will benefit future generations, then it is just those policy decisions that are subject to the Parfit rejoinder: if you undertake a policy decision only to benefit future generations, and that is its *only* "moral" justification, it is not morally justifiable at all because it destroys the very persons you claim to protect.

Professor Weiss says she is talking about group rights, not individual rights, when she talks about future generations, and hence the composition of the group does not matter too much. The reader can decide whether, if every single member of group A is wiped out and replaced by someone else, we are still entitled to call it "group A" and claim that at least the "group" has been preserved.

Professor Weiss criticizes my "preverbal sense of morality." She interprets it as calling for a return to "our natural instincts." But not everything that is preverbal is instinctual. Our sense of similarity (judging what objects are similar to others) is something we develop prior to learning the language—and may indeed be a prerequisite to language learning—without being a matter of instinct.[26] I suspect that much of the grounding of our developed sense of morality comes from thousands of observations of situations that we analyze morally on the grounds of their similarity to other situations. Sometimes we confuse ourselves trying to reduce our sense of morality to verbal formulas. I am arguing that we should be truer to ourselves, to not get misled by the tyrannical hold that words can have on our thinking processes, to look without verbal rationalization into our human condition and to see how connected it is to other people and to animals, plants, and the natural environment. If we can strip away the layers of misleading theories that have justified man's inhumanity to man and man's inhumanity to animals, we may be able to get closer to our root sense of bioethics. If this must be called "our natural instincts," then I'm in favor of it.

5. Intervention[27]

While it should be self-evident that there is a direct functional relationship between protection of the environment and the promotion of human rights, it is much less obvious that environmental protection ought to be conceptualized in terms of a generic human right. Indeed, the

[25] By ANTHONY D'AMATO, excerpted from: *Do We Owe a Duty to Future Generations to Preserve the Global Environment*? 84 AMERICAN JOURNAL OF INTERNATIONAL LAW 190 (1990). Reprinted by permission.

[26] I have made this argument at considerable length in a non-international law context, drawing upon Rudolf Carnap's great book, THE LOGICAL STRUCTURE OF THE WORLD §§ 67–109 (George tr. 1967). *See* Anthony D'Amato: *Counterintuitive Consequences of "Plain Meaning,"* 33 ARIZ. L. REV. 529 (1991), *Pragmatic Indeterminacy*, 85 NW. L. REV. 148 (1990), *On the Connection Between Law and Justice*, 29 U.C. DAVIS LAW REVIEW 527 (1993).

[27] By GUNTHER HANDL, excerpted from: *Human Rights and Protection of the Environment: A Mildly "Revisionist" View*, in A. Cancado Trindade (ed.), HUMAN RIGHTS, SUSTAINABLE DEVELOPMENT AND THE ENVIRONMENT 117 (Instituto Interamericano de Derechos Humanos, San Jose, 1992). Reprinted by permission.

emphasis on such a perspective on the interrelationship of human rights and environmental protection carries significant costs; it reflects a maximalist position that offers little prospect of becoming reality in the near term while its propagation diverts attention and efforts from other more pressing and promising environmental and human rights objectives. In short, a generic international environmental entitlement, both as an already existing and an emerging human rights concept, is a highly questionable proposition.

Narrowly defined environmental objectives may, of course, be vindicated through the assertion of individual human rights as in a situation in which environmental conditions pose a threat to life or health. Likewise, environmental protection objectives may be incidentally vindicated in human rights complaints.

The proposed generic environmental human right, by contrast, would make broad environmental policy decisions, such as standard-setting – the determination of what is a "healthy environment" or what constitutes an "adequate margin safety" etc. – a central concern of an individual right-based process. This offers the prospect of a too narrowly focused, piecemeal approach to setting general environmental policy. Moreover, a generic environmental human rights proposal would presumably imply that alleged violations be dealt with in international human rights fora, few of which might be able to discharge efficiently the task of deciding whether a human right based on the generic entitlement has been violated. This conflicts with the general recognition that in the field of environmental protection, decision-making – except as regards basic policy parameters – is best entrusted to specialized or technical fora: the domestic administrative agencies, and conferences of the parties as repositories of specialized knowledge, in the case of international environmental regimes.

Moreover, the notion of "environmental human rights" fosters an anthropocentric view of the environment which offers no guarantee against global environmental degradation and instability. For a human-rights based approach to the environment – even one that reflects sensitivity to intergenerational concerns – may well be strictly instrumentalist in the sense of subordinating all aspects of nature to the human enterprise. Besides, the very label of "human rights" connotes "species chauvinism,"[28] no matter how enlightened the underlying definition of the "human right." The legitimacy of, indeed the moral obligation to espouse, a more discriminating environmental point-of-view, i.e., one that recognizes the intrinsic merit of protecting nature for nature's sake, has been endorsed in the literature.[29]

Thus, although the proposal for an environmental human right might have a certain attractiveness in that it may (temporarily) give a high profile to environmental issues, in the end, it would amount to little more than legal window dressing. It is unlikely to promote realistic environmental or human rights objectives. Realism calls instead for a more modest, yet focussed campaign which aims at gaining general international recognition of specific or well-defined environmental rights and at strengthening or building upon existing international environmental review procedures.

B. Biodiversity[30]

Biodiversity can be loosely defined as the variety and variability among the multitude of plant and animal species and the ecological complexes in which they occur. Biodiversity is believed to be an essential component of natural systems, but because it is rapidly diminishing, biodiversity has received growing recognition as a significant environmental issue. Evidence of the value of biodiversity and human dependence on its existence is mounting as its current rate of loss escalates. In this context, concern is translating, albeit slowly and haltingly, into protective policies.

Sudden, large-scale extinction has occurred at least eight times on Earth according to scientific record.[31] With greater knowledge about the value and importance of maintaining diverse flora and fauna, increasing attention is being paid to the rapidly accelerating rate of species extinction. Scientists analyzing potential effects of global climate change predict a much higher annual rate of species loss once the full impact of climate change becomes manifest. Current loss rates amount to 150 species per day.[32] This extraordinary rate of loss of biological diversity plays a major role in the mass extinction hypothesis. Mainstream

---

[28] Anthony D'Amato & Sudhir K. Chopra, *Whales: Their Emerging Right to Life*, 85 AJIL 21, 22 (1991); excerpted *infra*, this Chapter.

[29] *See, e.g.*, D'Amato & Chopra, *id.*; CHRISTOPHER STONE, EARTH AND OTHER ETHICS: THE CASE FOR MORAL PLURALISM (1987); Dinah Shelton, *Human Rights, Environmental Rights, and the Right to the Environment*, 28 STANFORD J. INT'L L. 103, 109 (1991).

[30] By TRACY DOBSON, excerpted from: *Loss of Biodiversity: An International Environmental Policy Perspective*, 17 NORTH CAROLINA JOURNAL OF INTERNATIONAL LAW AND COMMERCIAL REGULATION 277 (1992). Reprinted by permission.

[31] David M. Raup & J. John Sepkoski, Jr., *Periodic Extinction of Families and Genera*, 231 SCIENCE 833, 833–36 (1986). For a discussion of the five major mass extinctions of the Pharezoic period, *see* David Jablonski, *Causes and Consequences of Mass Extinctions: A Comparative Approach*, in DAVID K. ELLIOTT (ED.), DYNAMICS OF EXTINCTION (1986).

[32] Edward O. Wilson, *The Current State of Biological Diversity*, in EDWARD O. WILSON (ED.), BIODIVERSITY 13 (1988).

scientific thought explains the functioning of living organisms in terms of food webs or interconnected, interdependent food chains. Ecology, a relatively new area of scientific study, concerns itself with the relationships between organisms and the ways in which these relations create functioning natural systems, or "ecosystems." It is in this vein of scientific investigation that one finds the now widely accepted notion of interdependency of organisms. Simply put, organism interdependency dictates that harm to or loss of one organism will alter an ecosystem, perhaps in dramatic and irreversible ways. Loss of a single species within an ecosystem, then, means alteration of the system's operations. Loss of several organisms from an ecosystem will most likely result in weakening and even, ultimately, destruction of the ecosystem.[33]

The Convention on International Trade in Endangered Species of Wild Fauna and Flora ("CITES")[34] is viewed as a positive step toward preserving biodiversity by restricting trade in endangered species of plants and animals. Because of the huge international trade in wildlife, and the fact that trade increases pressure on endangered species, CITES seeks to regulate it and thereby protect endangered species through its prohibition and permit system. It prohibits, with a few exceptions, international commercial trade in species that are threatened with extinction. Controlled trade, primarily for scientific and educational purposes, may occur under permit limits set by the treaty that will not endanger the traded species.

CITES' ability to function effectively is hampered, however, by its failure to garner the support of some key parties,[35] although it is universally applauded for the unusually high degree of ratification it has achieved.[36] More importantly, it suffers from substantive flaws.[37] First, it focuses on species and ignores habitat destruction. Second, in order to be protected, a species must be traded internationally, thus omitting protection for species that do not cross international borders. Third, illegal trade cannot be addressed by the treaty, and illegal trade in endangered species is believed to be widespread.[38] Furthermore, as with all endangered species policies, such species are by definition on the brink of extinction. They or their habitat may be beyond help at that point. Thus, commentators argue that endangered species policies are triggered too late, bringing restrictions and resources to bear at a time when the risk of species loss is great, and focusing attention on species when loss of habitat is often the driving force behind the threat or endangerment.

Like the clarion call of Rachel Carson's 1962 *Silent Spring* warning of the effects of DDT, the biological diversity crisis needs global attention to awaken educators, school children, university students, the general public, and policy makers at local, national, and international levels to the importance of diversity and what must be done to preserve it. Following the lead of Canada with a statutory requirement for environmental education, and building on the work of the International Joint Commission (U.S.-Canada) as well as numerous nongovernmental organizations, educational materials to launch this program are available for dissemination to teachers, the media, and concerned citizens.[39]

Widespread knowledge of the critical nature of the accelerating loss of biological diversity around the world will result in the development and more rapid acceptance of governmental species protection policies. Private sector decision making, within multinational corporations for example, could also be positively affected by a better understanding of the negative impacts of certain kinds of economic development.

Existing treaties and laws are inadequate, but they are a promising beginning. Such efforts at international policy development indicate a growing recognition of the inherently global nature of major environmental problems such as loss of biological diversity. Global problems require concerted global action; allegiance to nation-states may of necessity diminish if humankind is to survive. Global concerns generating global goals and global action may be needed to bring about real change. National and local law, as well as international agreements, can also mandate the creation of nature reserves within which biodiversity is to be preserved. In Third World countries where financial resources are sorely stretched, debt-for-nature swaps are being employed to fund the creation of reserves.[40]

Alternatively, as argued by Giagnocavo and Goldstein, our survival may depend on our moving towards a deep ecology approach, abandoning what ultimately will prove

---

33 *See* PAUL R. EHRLICH, THE MACHINERY OF NATURE (1985).

34 27 U.S.T. 1087, 993 U.N.T.S. 243 (Mar. 3, 1973).

35 Jeffrey C. Melick, Note, *Regulation of International Trade in Endangered Wildlife*, 1 B.U. INT'L L.J. 249, 262–63 (1982).

36 SIMON LYSTER, INTERNATIONAL WILDLIFE LAW: AN ANALYSIS OF INTERNATIONAL TREATIES CONCERNED WITH THE CONSERVATION OF WILDLIFE 240 (1985).

37 *See* David S. Favre, *Tension Points within the Language of the CITES Treaty*, 5 B.U.INT'L L.J. 247 (1987).

38 *See* MARC REISNER, GAME WARS: THE UNDERCOVER PURSUIT OF WILDLIFE POACHERS (1991).

39 *The Global Classroom*, GREENPEACE MAGAZINE 20 (Mar./Apr. 1990), reports on an international environmental curriculum created by Greenpeace and being tested in the U.S., Europe, and the former Soviet Union.

40 Barbara Bramble, *The Debt Crisis: The Opportunities*, 17 ECOLOGIST 192 (1987); Robert M. Sadler, Comment, *Debt-for-Nature Swaps: Assessing the Future*, 6 J. CONTEMP.HEALTH L. & POLICY 319 (1990).

to be inadequate legal responses to environmental crises.[41] Societal ends themselves, rather than only environmentally insensitive means, must be changed to recognize more clearly the true human role as a small part of nature and stop seeing nature as some kind of "other" to be used and manipulated. [Former] Senator Albert Gore of Tennessee has said:

> It will not be enough to change our laws, policies and programs. The solutions we seek must stem from a new faith in the future, a faith that justifies sacrifices in the present, and from a new courage to choose higher values in the conduct of human affairs. We must also display new reverence for our place in the natural world.[42]

C. Desertification[43]

Desertification, the phenomenon of encroaching desert lands, is hardly a novel occurrence in the history of mankind. To be sure, it has played a salient role in hastening the decline of civilizations since ancient times. For example, both the Sumerian and Babylonian empires suffered telling blows when their agricultural productivity was destroyed, a gradual process principally attributable to improper drainage practices that allowed excessive salt concentrations to pollute their irrigated lands. Archaeologists also have suggested that prolonged desiccation undercut the agricultural basis of the Harappan culture, a people who lived in the third millennium B.C. in what is now Pakistan. Finally, there seems little question that the Mediterranean littoral of Africa was far more fertile and cultivatable in the Carthaginian era (600-200 B.C.) than it is today.

Nonetheless, while man's experience with desertification may not be new, realization of it and its far-reaching ecological impact is. Worldwide recognition of desertification as a transnational environmental problem did not come about until 1968, when a severe drought struck the Sahel, a region in western Africa lying along the southern margin of the Sahara. For six years, the countries of the Sahel – Mauritania, Senegal, Mali, Upper Volta, Niger, and Chad – were devastated by uninterrupted drought and resultant famine. The natural and human consequences were tragically catastrophic: Lake Chad shrunk to only one-third of its normal size; the Niger and Senegal river systems failed to flood, thus leaving barren much of the most productive croplands in the region; shallow wells dried up, seriously restricting the grazing range of pastoralists; vegetation was denuded as starving animals stripped the land; and, splotches of new desert appeared and ultimately linked up with the great desert to the north. Reasonable rainfall did return to the Sahel in 1974, but not before drought, famine, and disease had killed an estimated 250,000 people and millions of domestic animals. As the tragedy and human suffering of people in the Sahel unfolded between 1968-1974, international attention became focused on their plight and the primary reason behind it: the inability of man to cope with spreading deserts in harsh climes.

Admittedly, while there is no reliable way to calculate precisely just how much land has been lost to or severely degraded by man's hand since agriculture began, there is widespread concurrence that the rate of land degradation through desertification has accelerated appreciably during the past five decades. Indeed, some experts have concluded that the rate is now exceeding 50,000 square kilometers (or 31,000 square miles) annually – a startling figure for a world with growing populations that already confront massive food shortages.

Seen from a vantage point in space, the earth appears to be a blue and green spherical oasis suspended in a black void. However, upon closer inspection, large portions of our planet's green area are all too quickly turning brown as desertification continues to deteriorate the composite ecology of land, water, and vegetative natural resources.

Several causal factors have contributed to desertification, including overgrazing, unregulated deforestation, over-cultivation of marginal lands, unwise farming practices, water resource development without adequate land-impact evaluation, and various local land tenure policies. Thus, desertification is an ecological problem, but even more significant, it is a human problem: people cause it, people suffer from its consequences, and only people can retard or reverse it.

Desertification persists as a self-accelerating process, and with its advance, requisite rehabilitation costs rise exponentially. In many cases, technical solutions are now available, but their application remains impeded by social, legal, cultural, and other institutional factors. Yet, in most less developed countries, a dearth of financial resources constitutes the most serious obstacle to more rapid implementation of local anti-desertification policies.

Desertification is manifestly a transnational problem, susceptible to neither easy nor near-term solutions, though the need for land restoration is already urgent and pressing in many arid areas. The 1977 U.N. Conference on Deserti-

[41] Cynthia Giagnocavo & Howard Goldstein, *Law Reform or World Re-form: The Problem of Environmental Rights*, 35 McGill L.J. 345 (1990).

[42] Al Gore, *The Call for SEI*, N.Y. Times, Apr. 3, 1990, at A23 (reprinted from the April 1990 issue of Scientific American).

[43] By CHRISTOPHER C. JOYNER, excerpted from: *Towards Transnational Management of Desertification: The Eco-Politics of Global Concern*, 16 Int'l Lawyer 67, 67–69, 92–93 (1982). Reprinted by permission.

fication furnished a timely forum wherein concerned nations and international organizations specifically addressed the worldwide threat of encroaching deserts. As such, this Conference became a valuable conduit for fostering constructive dialogue between prospective donor developed countries and the most seriously affected less developed countries. Moreover, in the resultant Plan of Action, the UNCOD conferences clearly articulated what general strategy should be pursued by national governments for alleviating the spread of desertlike conditions in their countries: there must be constant governmental monitoring and assessment of the indigenous environment, complemented by prudent land use planning and management, and underpinned by the support of international collaboration and cooperation. Since the Desertification Conference, however, the task of expeditiously implementing this plan on a global scale has proven to be financially formidable and bureaucratically ensnaring.

D. Common Heritage[44]

The Declaration of Principles adopted by the U.N. General Assembly states: "The sea-bed and ocean floor, and the subsoil thereof, beyond the limits of national jurisdiction, as well as the resources of the area, are the common heritage of mankind."[45] Article 136 of the Convention on the Law of the Sea declares, "The Area and its resources are the common heritage of mankind." It is the only such provision in the Convention, and no similar provision appears in the 1958 Convention on the Law of the Sea.

The debate over the deep seabeds is sometimes presented as a conflict between the "high seas" and "common heritage." This is misleading. The common heritage principle, as incorporated into Article 136 of Part XI (on seabed mineral resources) of the Law of the Sea Convention, exists alongside a significant number of other principles elaborated in Part XI that have their origin in high seas law.

It has been argued that the common heritage principle requires more elaborate institutional and substantive restraints on the "universal use" principle than have been customary on the high seas. Be that as it may, the very idea of negotiated restraints on the exercise of high seas freedoms is not alien to high seas law and tradition; quite to the contrary, it is an integral part of the system.[46] One simply cannot imagine multiple and potentially conflicting uses of the high seas without agreement on ground rules. It is difficult to imagine the absence of an organization such as the International Maritime Organization devoted to the continual elaboration and administration of such ground rules with respect to particular uses. Protection of the marine environment in an area open to use by all requires agreement on environmental restraints by all users, and mechanisms for enforcing and updating those restraints.

In truth, there is nothing in the common heritage principle that is inconsistent with high seas law. States may accept any substantive or institutional restraints on their high seas freedoms that they believe suitable. Were Part XI "generally accepted," there would even be some basis in high seas law for arguing that at least some of the relevant regulations must be respected by all. Certainly in spirit, high seas law is far closer to the idea of a common heritage of mankind than to appropriation by coastal or other states.

As of today. the basic structure of the international law applicable to the seabed beyond coastal state jurisdiction is agreed. National claims are prohibited. The area is open to use by all. Any use of the area must be conducted with reasonable regard for other uses of the marine environment, and other uses of the marine environment must be conducted with reasonable regard for any use of the area. All uses of the area must be conducted in accordance with the duty to protect and preserve the marine environment. The significance of this level of agreement, given the alternatives, should not be obscured by debates over whether the agreed principles derive from high seas law as a legal matter, or purely as a historical matter.

E. Common Concern[47]

In the fall of 1988, the Government of Malta proposed a General Assembly declaration proclaiming the global climate as part of the common heritage of mankind. During negotiations on the Malta proposal, "common heritage" became "common concern." Presumably, this change reflected a desire to avoid the politically charged debate over the full implications of "common heritage" engendered by its use in the deep seabed and outer space contexts. In any event, the General Assembly did adopt a resolution on the protection of the global climate containing the "common concern" language.[48]

The resolution may be "soft law," but it is somewhere beyond the starting point on the continuum from nonlaw to true law. It does not purport to prescribe conduct. Instead, it serves a legitimizing function by recognizing cli-

---

[44] By BERNARD H. OXMAN, excerpted from: *The High Seas and the International Seabed Area*, 10 MICHIGAN JOURNAL OF INTERNATIONAL LAW 526, 539–42 (1989). Reprinted by permission.

[45] *Declaration of Principles Governing the Sea-bed and the Ocean Floor, and the Subsoil Thereof, beyond the Limits of National Jurisdiction*, G.A. Res. 1729, 25 UNGAOR Supp. (no. 28), at 24.

[46] [Editor's note: See the section, "Custom as Reasonableness," in Chapter 4 of this Anthology, for a discussion of these restraints.]

[47] By FREDERIC L. KIRGIS, JR., excerpted from: *Standing to Challenge Human Endeavors That Could Change the Climate*, 84 AMERICAN JOURNAL OF INTERNATIONAL LAW 525 (1990). Reprinted by permission.

[48] G.A. Res. 43/53 (Dec. 6, 1988).

mate change to be a common concern of mankind. Its legal significance does not depend on any quasi-legislative power of the General Assembly; rather, it depends on the strength of the shared governmental conviction it enunciates and on the inferences that may properly be drawn from it. Clearly, if climate change is a matter of "common concern," international regulation of it is legitimate. But that still is not saying much. It is not necessary to identify climate change as a "common concern of mankind" so as to legitimize, today, the international regulation of a phenomenon inherently capable of transcending national boundaries. We may then ask if the concept has some additional significance. It would seem that it does. It implies that–whatever states' obligations may be in the area of climate change–they run *erga omnes*. Consequently, any state should have standing to make representations to any other concerning the latter's climate-affecting policies or activities, without having to allege that it is uniquely affected. The law of standing in the context of climate change thus would complement the law of standing as it is increasingly recognized in relation to the marine environment beyond the limits of national jurisdiction. Moreover, in the context of standing, the "common concern" concept is indistinguishable from the "common heritage" concept applicable to the deep seabed where it is usually regarded as conferring standing on all nations.

Giving all nations standing to object to any activity affecting the global climate is efficient, because the cost to broadly inclusive interests will have escalated, perhaps incalculably, by the time any one or a few states could show unique, nonminimal harm to themselves. Standing to complain without a showing of unique harm would enable not only a single government, but also several like-minded governments acting together, to challenge the climate-affecting activity before the consequences get out of hand.

In the long term, the most efficient mechanism will be an international body functioning on premises maximally scientific and minimally political, with its own standing to protect climate stability. Malta's initiative contemplates that eventuality, but it has also given states a potentially useful instrument in the interim.

F. Elephants[49]

1. *The Largest Land Animal.* If, as Lao-tse said, nature is not anthropomorphic, some fellow creatures nonetheless seem to share the better angels of our character; among these animals, none is grander than the African elephant. Elephants live in close-knit "families" of about ten members that seem to do just about everything synchronously–feeding, walking, resting, drinking or mud wallowing.[50] Each unit has a matriarchal structure: it is headed by the oldest female and consists of younger females and their calves, as male calves tend to leave the family and strike out on their own when they reach sexual maturity between the ages of 10 and 15. Fighting is rare.

Elephants are the largest land animals on earth. They grow for their entire life, weighing up to 6 tons and eating up to 300 pounds of food a day, consisting primarily of grasses and bark. Left alone, they can live past 60. They seem able to communicate with low-frequency calls that carry for 6 miles, which may explain the coordinated movement and behavior of separated groups. On the same day that the culling of elephants began in Hwange National Park in Zimbabwe, elephants 90 miles away fled to the opposite corner of the reserve.[51]

Elephants are quite tactile. They often touch each other with their trunks, and tend to stand and even walk bunched together, leaning on or rubbing each other. After being apart for a while, they greet each other by intertwining trunks, clashing tusks and flapping ears, exhibiting great excitement even if the separation has lasted for only a few days. They aid other members of the group that are threatened or disabled.

Elephants have a haunting sense of death. When a member of the family dies, they touch the carcass gently with their trunks and feet, and cover it with loose earth and branches.

Elephants have no natural enemies; threats come entirely from man. Licensed hunting continues to account for several hundred deaths per year. The Governments of South Africa and Zimbabwe conduct culling programs aimed at maintaining their elephant populations at a level the available habitat can support. As with many other species, loss of habitat to human encroachment is a major problem. Elephants and cattle compete for some of the same food, and as Africa has become increasingly agricultural, the natural range of the elephant has diminished. Certain native groups have engaged in random killing of elephants: the Masai, for example, spear elephants as proof of their bravery and even as a form of political protest. As the Masai began to grow crops, their harassment of elephants increased.

By far the greatest threat to the elephant's survival is poaching. The elephant is killed for its ivory tusks, which are carved and used for dice, jewelry, trinkets, ornaments, billiard balls, piano keys and knife handles. A principal use is for hanko, personalized signature seals considered

[49] By MICHAEL J. GLENNON, excerpted from: *Has International Law Failed the Elephant?* 84 AMERICAN JOURNAL OF INTERNATIONAL LAW 1 (1990). Reprinted by permission.

[50] *See generally* C. MOSS, ELEPHANT MEMORIES: THIRTEEN YEARS IN THE LIFE OF AN ELEPHANT FAMILY (1988).

[51] *Id.* at 314, 316. *See also* Payne, *Elephant Talk*, NAT'L GEOGRAPHIC, August 1989, at 264.

status symbols in Japan. International conservation groups estimate that the illegal killing of elephants for their ivory has reduced Africa's elephant population from 1.5 million to fewer than 500,000 in the last decade.[52] By some estimates, the poachers kill two to three hundred a day;[53] at this rate, the African elephant could be extinct by the end of the century.[54] The New York Times compared the elephant population in 1989 for countries where there were more than 50,000 in 1979:[55]

COUNTRY	1979	1989
Central African Republic	63,000	19,000
Kenya	65,000	19,000
Mozambique	54,800	18,600
Sudan	134,000	40,000
Tanzania	316,300	80,000
Zaire	377,700	85,000
Zambia	150,000	41,000

Numbers, however, do not tell the whole story. They do not convey the brutality of the killing, sometimes by paramilitaristic poachers who spray bullets from semiautomatic weapons over entire herds. They do not disclose the horror burned in the memories of survivors that have witnessed the hacking of parents and siblings they have lived with for decades and afterwards wander aimlessly in despair. Numbers—and dispassionate references to "ivory" and "offtake"—do not reveal what really is at issue:

> The word ivory disassociates it in our minds from the idea of an elephant. One tends to lump it with jade, teak, ebony, amber, even gold and silver, but there is a major difference: The other materials did not come from an animal; an ivory tusk is a modified incisor tooth. When one holds a beautiful ivory bracelet or delicate carving in one's hand, it takes a certain leap of understanding to realize that piece of ivory came from an elephant who once walked around using its tusk for feeding, digging, poking, playing and fighting, and furthermore that the elephant had to be dead in order for that piece of ivory to be sitting in one's hand. "Every 10 minutes, another elephant is slain and its tusks wrenched or cut from its face by poachers intent on delivering more ivory to the marketplace."[56]

2. *Customary International Law*. It was not long ago that the international system placed far greater emphasis on national sovereignty over natural resources than on global interdependence. As recently as 1972, states were thought to have absolute control over all natural resources located within their boundaries. Principle 21 of the Stockholm Declaration on the Human Environment provided that "States have, in accordance with the Charter of the United Nations and the principles of international law, the sovereign right to exploit their own resources."[57] Less-developed countries were particularly vigorous in asserting "permanent sovereignty over natural resources" and a correlative right to dispose of resources fully and freely.[58] Even the new Restatement of Foreign Relations Law cautiously limits its discussion of international environmental law to transfrontier pollution.[59]

Since 1972, however, so many states have adopted laws directed at preserving their environment that it probably is no longer correct to think that states have unlimited authority to injure the environment in any manner so long as the injury is restricted to their own territory.[60] States also have bound themselves increasingly by treaty to protect unique international treasures. The UN General Assembly, in the 1982 World Charter for Nature, affirmed general principles of conservation to which "all areas of the earth" are subject. Professor David Caron criticized the narrow approach of the Restatement and summed up emerging thought as follows:

> As humanity believes increasingly that in a theoretical sense the planet belongs to all . . . , the notion of legitimate interests seems to extend far beyond traditional notions of harm. Consequently, there is a perception that all have an interest in preventing the loss of a species, the destruction of cultural heritage, and the waste of natural resources.[61]

International law has been moving steadily to protect wider humanitarian interests and to prevent environmental degradation, even at the cost of eroding state sovereignty.

---

52 N.Y. TIMES, June 11, 1989, s 1, at 6.

53 About 40% of the deaths are caused by killing mothers with calves under 10 years old. *Saving the Elephant: Nature's Great Masterpiece*, ECONOMIST, July 1, 1989, at 15.

54 *Ibid*.

55 N.Y. TIMES, June 2, 1989, at A9.

56 Brennan, *Ivory Wars; Fighting to Save the Elephants*, WASH. POST, Sept. 24, 1989, at Y7.

57 United Nations Conference on the Human Environment, Report at 3, 5, UN Doc. A/CONF.48/14/Rev.1, UN Sales No. E.73.II.A.14 (1973).

58 *See* General Assembly Resolutions: 1803 (XVII) (Dec. 14, 1962), 2692 (XXV) (Dec. 11, 1970), 3016 (XXVII) (Dec. 18, 1972), 3201 (S-VI), para. 4e (May 1, 1974), 3202 (S-VI), sec. 8 (May 1, 1974).

59 RESTATEMENT (THIRD) OF THE FOREIGN RELATIONS LAW OF THE UNITED STATES pt. VI (1987).

60 "General principles common to the major legal systems" constitute a supplementary source of customary international law. *Id.* § 102(4). *See* Statute of the International Court of Justice, 59 Stat. 1055 (1945), TS No. 993, Art. 38(1)(c) (directing the Court to apply "the general principles of law recognized by civilized nations").

61 David Caron, *The Law of the Environment: A Symbolic Step of Modest Value*, 14 YALE J. INT'L L. 528, 529 (1989).

Where once states were seen to have carte blanche to do what they would to persons within their own territory, later they were viewed as owing certain obligations to aliens, and now they are thought to owe such obligations to their own nationals as well. Where once states were free to pollute the "global commons" and the oceans, today they are enjoined against injuring unoccupied islands, ice floes and Antarctica;[62] and they are obliged to prevent injury to the marine environment by pollution and to protect global wetlands.[63] Indeed, as early as 1974, the UNEP Council viewed certain species as constituting "the common heritage of mankind."[64]

It is now possible to conclude that customary international law requires states to take appropriate steps to protect endangered species. Closely related to this process of norm creation by practice is that of norm creation by convention. Several such agreements are directed at wildlife protection, and CITES with 103 states parties is one of them.[65] Moreover, customary norms are created by "the general principles of law recognized by civilized nations."[66] Because CITES requires domestic implementation by parties to it, and because the overall level of compliance seems quite high, the general principles embodied in states' domestic endangered species laws may be relied upon as another source of customary law.[67] Even apart from the CITES requirements, states that lack laws protecting endangered species seem now to be the clear exception rather than the rule.

While the existence of a norm requiring the protection of endangered species thus seems likely, its scope remains uncertain. To the extent that the norm derives from CITES and laws implementing CITES, that scope would be fairly narrow, for the norm would cover only species in international trade, not those taken for domestic consumption or those endangered by threats to their habitat. Even if it could be shown that major legal systems generally comprise endangered species legislation, more work needs to be done to determine exactly what elements those laws have in common. What constitutes an "endangered species," for example, is debatable. Is it one that is endangered in every state, or only in the state making the assessment? And to what lengths must a state go in protecting a species it finds "endangered"? Must it do everything necessary to protect that species, notwithstanding the cost or the ecological significance of the species?

As to the elephant in particular, it is hard to argue under customary international law that states such as South Africa and Zimbabwe are prohibited from selling ivory by a new customary norm, corresponding generally to the CITES restrictions. The southern African elephant "excess" states might be seen as partaking in a regional custom of the sort considered in the Asylum case.[68] Or they might be seen as "persistent objectors" to an emerging norm during the inchoate stages of its development.[69]

It thus appears doubtful that a customary norm concerning the elephant or any other endangered species can yet play any significant role in its protection. But the trend cannot be doubted; and once its contours are more clear, the customary norm requiring states to protect endangered species ought to take on the character of an obligation erga omnes. Ordinarily, claims for the violation of an international obligation may be made only by the state to which the obligation is owed. Obligations erga omnes, however, run to the international community as a whole; thus, their breach is actionable by any state since such matters are "by their very nature the concern of all States. They are obligations erga omnes."[70]

The action erga omnes has its roots in the Roman law right of any citizen to bring an action (actio popularis) to protect the public interest.[71] So, too, does another concept pertinent to states' environmental responsibilities: the public trust doctrine.[72] Roman law recognized "common proper-

[62] *See* Convention on the Regulation of Antarctic Mineral Resource Activities, Art. 4(2), June 2, 1988, reprinted in 27 ILM 868 (1988).

[63] *See* Convention on Wetlands of International Importance, Especially as Waterfowl Habitat, Feb. 2, 1971, reprinted in 11 ILM 963 (1972).

[64] *See* Nanda & Ris, *The Public Trust Doctrine: Viable Approach to International Environmental Protection*, 5 ECOLOGY L.Q. 291, 294 (1976).

[65] Convention on International Trade in Endangered Species of Wild Fauna and Flora, Mar. 6, 1973, 27 UST 1087, TIAS No. 8249, 993 UNTS 243 [CITES].

[66] *See* Statute of the International Court of Justice, 59 Stat. 1055 (1945), TS No. 993, Art. 38(1)(c).

[67] Several major legal systems contain legislation that protects certain species or sets aside protected areas for certain species. See generally C. Du Saussay, Legislation on Wildlife, Hunting and Protected Areas in Some European Countries (UN Food and Agriculture Organization Legis. Study No. 20, 1980).

[68] Asylum (Colom./Peru), 1950 ICJ REP. 266 (Judgment of Nov. 20).

[69] *See* Stein, *The Principle of the Persistent Objector in International Law*, 26 HARV. INT'L L.J. 457 (1985).

[70] *See* Barcelona Traction, Light & Power Co., Ltd. (Belg. v. Spain), Second Phase, 1970 ICJ Rep. 3, 32 (Judgment of Feb. 5).

[71] The International Court of Justice mentioned, but did not accept, this theory in the earlier South West Africa cases. South West Africa (Ethiopia v. S. Afr.; Liberia v. S. Afr.), Second Phase, 1966 ICJ REP. 6, 47 (Judgment of July 18). For a useful discussion of the origins of the doctrine, *see* THEODOR MERON, HUMAN RIGHTS AND HUMANITARIAN NORMS AS CUSTOMARY LAW 188–93 (1989).

[72] *See* Joseph Sax, *The Public Trust Doctrine in Natural Resource Law: Effective Judicial Intervention*, 68 MICH L. REV. 471

ties'' (res communis); the seashores were ''subject to the guardianship of the Roman people.''[73] ''The central idea of the public trust is preventing the destabilizing disappointment of expectations of use of resources held in common but without formal recognition such as title.''[74] Indeed, a powerful case has been made for regarding natural objects themselves as having legal rights.[75] Influenced by Professor Stone's ground-breaking essay,[76] three Supreme Court Justices [dissenting] in *Sierra Club v. Morton* endorsed that approach.[77]

These considerations suggest the outline of a general framework for the protection of endangered species under customary international law. Although such principles may still represent *lex ferenda* with regard to a particular species (or other resource), they appear to constitute emerging *opinio juris* on a broader structure of global environmental resources, rights and obligations that might be summarized as follows.

A global environmental resource is a natural resource located within the territory of one country but broadly enjoyed, and arguably needed, by the world community as a whole. Tropical rain forests, described as the ''lungs of the world'' by Indonesian President Suharto,[78] are a good example. Unique cultural artifacts are another. That these exist within specific states is largely an accident of geography; but for their presence, the life of all would be diminished. For the reasons outlined in this article, and in light of the tremendous worldwide concern generated recently over its possible extinction, the elephant seems properly regarded as a global environmental resource.

A global environmental right arises in connection with a global environmental resource. It refers to the right of all states to expect that the resource will be protected by the state in which it is found. States are trustees, responsible for the preservation of species within their territories. That obligation runs to the international community as a whole: any state should be regarded as suffering legally cognizable injury when that obligation is breached by another state. That states have a global environmental right to expect that the elephant will be protected is confirmed by emerging norms of customary international law pertaining to endangered species, discussed above. ''The protection of the elephant,'' UNEP has said, ''is an obligation of humankind.''[79]

Global environmental obligation refers to the duty of states to share in preserving global environmental resources. There are two tiers of such obligations: custodial obligations, which refer to the preservation duties of states in which the resource is physically located; and support obligations, which refer to the duties of other states to contribute to the conduct of custodial obligations. First World states often complain about the failure of Third World states to meet their custodial obligations (concerning, for example, their elephant populations, rain forests and archaeological treasures), but few of the complainers have met their support obligations. The Economist put it well: ''Logically, if the rest of the world wants the elephant to survive, then it should not only compensate Africa for $60 million of lost exports, but help to foot the bill—of perhaps $80m–$100m—for an effective war on poachers.''[80]

The point bears elaboration. Support obligations are appropriately seen as applying to two sets of costs incurred by ivory-producing states: the opportunity cost of forgoing the sale of ivory from natural elephant deaths and confiscated poached ivory, as well as the cost of running conservation programs.

East African states such as Tanzania and Kenya should not be forced to shoulder the entire burden of running conservation programs themselves. All who benefit from elephant protection should share the cost. As the international system is structured, they do so indirectly, through assistance by their governments. Such assistance ought to be provided through an international authority able to administer and oversee an aid program to African states. UNEP, which is headquartered in Nairobi, seems to be the logical existing vehicle.

Until a multilateral approach can be instituted, unilateral assistance is appropriate, perhaps in the innovative form of ''debt swaps.'' Debt swaps involve monetary concessions by lenders in exchange for enhanced resource management by borrower states that are unable to keep current on debt payments. Much of the attention paid to the idea has derived from concern about the disappearing tropical rain forests. Conservation International, for example, arranged to have Bolivia's external debt reduced by $650,000 in exchange for that country's protection of 3.7 million acres of Amazonian forest.[81] Costa Rica has also received

(1970); Nanda and Ris, *The Public Trust Doctrine: Viable Approach to International Environmental Protection*, 5 ECOLOGY L.Q. 291, 294 (1976).

[73] T. SANDARS, THE INSTITUTES OF JUSTINIAN 159 (1865).

[74] *See* Joseph Sax, *Liberating the Public Trust Doctrine from Its Historical Shackles*, in THE PUBLIC TRUST DOCTRINE IN NATURAL RESOURCES LAW AND MANAGEMENT: CONFERENCE PROCEEDINGS 7 (H. Dunning ed. 1981).

[75] *See* R. NASH, THE RIGHTS OF NATURE (1989).

[76] Christopher Stone, *Should Trees Have Standing?—Toward Legal Rights for Natural Objects*, 45 S. CAL. L. REV. 450 (1972).

[77] 405 U.S. 727, 741–60 (1972) (Douglas, Blackmun and Brennan, JJ., dissenting).

[78] REUTERS (Aug. 16, 1989).

[79] REUTERS (July 3, 1989).

[80] ECONOMIST, July 1, 1989, at 17.

[81] *See* Spitler, *Exchanging Debt for Conservation*, 37 BIOSCIENCE 781 (1987).

debt reduction in return for setting aside certain tracts of land from development.[82]

It is also appropriate for the international community to reimburse "elephant-excess" states such as Botswana and Zimbabwe for the cost of not selling ivory, if they were persuaded to do so. After all, revenues from the export of ivory help pay for conservation programs (as was noted by the CITES Secretariat in opposing the effort[83] to move the elephant to Appendix I.[84])

3. *What Steps Should Be Taken Now?* (1) The ivory trade must be stopped immediately. Halting the ivory trade requires effective steps to dry up both supply and demand and to cut out middlemen. Kenya's President Moi put it well: "To stop the poacher, the trader must also be stopped and to stop the trader, the final buyer must be convinced not to buy ivory."[85] States that do not comply with the international ban must be appropriately pressured into doing so, at least until the elephant is safe and an internationally controlled ivory-marking system is in place.

(2) Antipoaching squads and other enforcement units must be strengthened. We ought not to be deluded into believing that domestic enforcement of the criminal law in producer countries can easily be tightened up. Corruption among law enforcement authorities is not unknown in those countries where the elephant is most threatened. This problem was exemplified by a 1989 incident involving the Indonesian Ambassador to Tanzania. The ambassador, Joesoef Hussein, was caught trying to leave Dar es Salaam with 184 elephant tusks stowed in his luggage. He apparently expected no problem and claimed diplomatic immunity. Rather than asking the Indonesian Government for a waiver so that Tanzania could prosecute, the local government officials reportedly tried to cover up the incident.[86]

Even when there is a will to succeed, it is hard to take seriously a commitment to elephant conservation that sends game wardens armed with pre-World War I carbines against poachers using machine guns.[87] A multilateral entity such as the CITES Secretariat or UNEP should undertake to arrange appropriate assistance. If that means some form of paramilitary or police training—or operational, down-in-the-trenches participation—that agency ought to be empowered to call upon appropriate countries to help, much as the Security Council may call upon members of the United Nations when military units are needed. The objective should be "united international police action to eliminate the illegal ivory trade."[88]

(3) Environmentally sustainable development must be supported as an essential prerequisite to elephant protection. The elephant simply will not be safe as long as unlawful conduct pays so much more than lawful conduct. In the long term, enhanced law enforcement can only be a stopgap measure unless economic incentives to poach are greatly reduced. It is easy for Americans, watching wildlife programs on color television in air-conditioned homes, to support elephant protection; it is not always so easy where the elephants actually live.[89]

(4) An internationally operated ivory-marking system using the latest technology should be instituted. It is now possible not only to identify ivory by species of origin, but also to mark ivory tusks so that parts of lawfully taken tusks are subsequently identifiable—easily and inexpensively. Modern science seems finally to have eliminated the problem most responsible for the elephant's decline: the indistinguishability of lawfully and unlawfully taken ivory. Yet the integrity of a tagging system depends upon that of the officials who operate it; if they are corrupt and accept bribes to mark poached ivory, or if they permit the tagging technology to fall into the hands of poaches, the

---

82 Arias Sanchez, *For the Globe's Sake, Debt Relief*, N.Y. TIMES, July 14, 1989, at A13.

83 In recommending against movement of the elephant to Appendix I, the CITES Secretary-General warned: "Denied the opportunity to sell ivory through natural mortality, control operations and confiscation, producer states would lose significant revenues which could otherwise be used to finance anti-poaching and enforcement operations." Letter from Eugene Lapointe, Secretary-General, CITES, to all CITES Management Authorities (June 8, 1989) (on file with author).

It has been reported that from 1985 to 1989, the CITES Secretariat has received $200,000 from ivory traders, including at least one alleged poacher. Thornton, *The Ivory Trail*, GREENPEACE, September/October 1989, at 8.

84 Appendix I of CITES provides the highest level of protection; it includes "all species threatened with extinction which are or may be affected by trade." Export is allowed solely pursuant to permit, which is only issued, inter alia, when "a Scientific Authority of the State of export has advised that such export will not be detrimental to the survival of that species." The most restrictive provisions, those governing the trade in species listed in Appendix I, thus apply to producer states, middleman states and consumer states. In net effect, these provisions are intended to close down international trade in the species listed in Appendix I.

85 N.Y. TIMES, July 19, 1989, at A4.

86 *His Excellency the Ivory Smuggler*, NEW AFRICAN, April 1989, at 13. In Kenya, the wildlife department fired or transferred 40 of its own officials suspected of participating in poaching. L.A. TIMES, May 8, 1989, at 6.

87 African Elephant Conservation: Hearing Before the Subcomm. on Fisheries and Wildlife Conservation and the Environment of the House Comm. on Merchant Marine and Fisheries, 100th Cong., 2d Sess. 21 (1988) (testimony of William K. Reilly, President, World Wildlife Fund).

88 *Id.* at 145 (testimony of Iain Douglas-Hamilton).

89 Zimbabwe officials called the drive for a ban on ivory trade "cultural imperialism" by outsiders. CHICAGO TRIB., July 9, 1989, at 21. One Zambian wildlife manager, referring to Western conservationists, said: "The dimension they forget is that of people." REUTERS (July 9, 1989).

system loses its reliability. For this reason, international control at this point seems essential.

(5) The broad-based educational campaign already successfully undertaken by nongovernmental organizations must be continued. It is not enough to educate buyers of ivory to the horrors of its origins. Ultimately, protection of the elephant and other endangered species will require a change in mind set by both individuals and governmental institutions that have viewed concern about animals with a certain derision. [Consider] the Governor's complaint to Laurencot in Gary's *The Roots of Heaven*:

> Don't you think that there are in the world, at the present time, causes, liberties, well let's say values, which have a rather better claim than the elephants to [our] devotion? There are still some of us who refuse to despair, to throw up the sponge and go over to the other species for solace. There are men fighting and dying at this very moment, in the streets, on the barricades and in the prisons. One may still be allowed to prefer to take an interest in them.[90]

Laurencot replies: "But the elephants are part of that fight. Men are dying to preserve a certain splendor of life. Call it freedom, or dignity. They are dying to preserve a certain natural splendor."[91] And Morel says: "Today you say that elephants are archaic and cumbersome, that they interfere with roads and telegraph poles, and tomorrow you'll begin to say that human rights too are obsolete and cumbersome, that they interfere with progress."[92]

The struggle to protect beings without reference to any "objective," mathematically quantifiable utility enriches our spirit. Even if this is not a struggle to ensure our own survival, it is a battle to clarify our character, to define what we hold dear, for ourselves and our descendants. It is the character of our species that is at issue. Who can say, on the day the last elephant dies, that the human race will ever again be the same?

G. Whales: Their Emerging Right to Life[93]

Writers of science fiction have often speculated about what it would be like to discover, on a planet in outer space, a much higher form of intelligence. How would we react to those creatures? Would we be so fearful of them that we would try to kill them? Or would we welcome the opportunity to attempt to understand their language and culture? Stranger than fiction is the fact that there already exists a species of animal life on earth that scientists speculate has higher than human intelligence. The whale has a brain that in some instances is six times bigger than the human brain and its neocortex is more convoluted. Discussing the creative processes of whales, Dr. John Lilly says that a researcher "is struck with the fact that one's current basic assumptions and even one's current expectations determine, within certain limits, the results attained with a particular animal at that particular time."[94] Whales speak to other whales in a language that appears to include abstruse mathematical poetry.[95] They have also developed interspecies communication with dolphins.[96] Whales are the most specialized of all mammals.[97] They are sentient, they are intelligent, they have their own community, and they can suffer. Yet because they have no hands to fashion tools or construct weapons for self-defense – because they "do not have the ability to drive harpoons through living flesh"[98] – they are vulnerable to human predation.[99] Many

---

[90] R. GARY, THE ROOTS OF HEAVEN 60 (J. Griffin trans. 1958).

[91] *Ibid.*

[92] *Id.* at 142.

[93] By ANTHONY D'AMATO & SUDHIR K. CHOPRA, excerpted from: *Whales: Their Emerging Right to Life*, 85 AMERICAN JOURNAL OF INTERNATIONAL LAW 21 (1991). Reprinted by permission.

[94] Lilly, *A Feeling of Weirdness* in MIND IN THE WATERS 71 (J. McIntyre ed. 1974). Dr. Lilly's statement is the best description we have seen about what it is like to be possibly dealing with a superior intelligence.

[95] *See generally* J. Lilly, THE MIND OF THE DOLPHIN: A NONHUMAN INTELLIGENCE (1967).

[96] Humans, of course, have been unable to develop interspecies communication, except for the most rudimentary signals. *See generally* J. LILLY, MAN AND DOLPHIN (1961).

[97] Morgane, *The Whale Brain: The Anatomical Basis of Intelligence*, in McIntyre, *supra* note 94, at 84, 91–92. If all brains are "learning machines," as artificial-intelligence researcher Marvin Minsky suggests (M. MINSKY, THE SOCIETY OF MIND 120 (1986)), and these learning machines constitute an efficacious survival mechanism (as the theory of natural selection indicates), the size of whales' brains may indicate a spectacularly efficient survival mechanism. Dr. Lilly speculates: "If a sperm whale, for example, wants to see-hear-feel any past experience, his huge computer [brain] can reprogram it and run it off again. His huge computer gives him a reliving, as if with a three-dimensional sound-color-taste-emotion-re-experiencing motion picture." After thus reviewing the original experience, the whale "can set up the model of the way he would like to run it the next time, reprogram his computer, run it off, and see how well it works." J. Lilly, *supra* note 95, at 63–64.

[98] Morgane, *supra* note 97, at 93 (quoting LOREN EISELEY, THE LONG LONELINESS). Dr. Lilly asks why sperm whales do not attack humans unprovoked? He suggests that they recognize that "we are the most dangerous animal on this planet" and that if attacked unprovoked, "we would . . . wipe them off the face of the earth. I believe they recognize that we now have the means to do this. A large fraction of our atomic and nuclear weapons testing is done over and in the Pacific Ocean close to the ocean routes of the big whales." J. Lilly, *supra* note 95, at 65.

[99] Indeed, human hunting and killing of whales may have occurred largely *because* whales are vulnerable; if whales could have

species of whales have been savagely hunted to near extinction. Even today, despite the international restrictions that have made the outfitting of new whaling vessels unprofitable, whalers already in the business – using their sunk capital investments – continue to search out and destroy these magnificent creatures.[100]

Professor Richard Falk writes that "it is a late hour on the biological clock that controls cetacean destiny, but hopefully not too late."[101] Australia, a nation that in years past had engaged heavily in whaling, declared in 1979 that "the harpooning of these animals is offensive to many people who regard killing these special and intelligent animals as inconsistent with the ideals of mankind, and without any valid economic purpose in mitigation."[102] Yet national policies do not automatically transmute into international legal restrictions. Neither the present opposition to whaling of an overwhelming number of states nor the ethical revulsion of many people throughout the world protects whales from the whale-hunting minority of states or gives them an international legal entitlement to survive. Even if some observers feel that the burgeoning international law of "human rights" should in principle include the preservation of whales, that very label seems inappropriate because it connotes species chauvinism.

This essay examines the history, and argues for the "presentiation,"[103] of a broadening international consciousness about whaling amounting to an *opinio juris* – the psychological component of international customary law. When this component is added to the evolving practices of states toward whaling, the combination of psychological and material elements arguably constitutes binding customary law. The dynamic element of that custom and its underlying philosophy generate, we conclude, an emergent entitlement *of* whales – not just "*on -behalf of*" whales – to a life of their own.[104]

1. The Moral Claim

A weak claim of environmental awareness is that we must concern ourselves with the integrity of the environment because of a duty to future generations. The asserted "duty to future generations" is subject to Parfit's demonstration that it is self-defeating.[105] We may then choose to move to a stronger claim of environmental awareness – that we owe a duty to living creatures in the environment *per se*, without calculating their utility to future generations of human beings. The dawning of such a sense of duty involves a broadening of humanistic consciousness comparable to the Copernican revolution that changed the Ptolemaic earth-centered conception of the universe to the modern realization that ours is but a minor planet revolving around a minor star in only one of billions of galaxies. We may be at the brink of replacing the view that "nature" exists only to serve people, with a larger ecological awareness that people share and ought to share the planet with many other sentient creatures.

This strong environmental claim requires at a minimum that we pause to consider the effect of certain human activities upon other living creatures. Jeremy Bentham, the founder of legal positivism, wrote in 1789 of the moral status of animals: "The question is not, Can they reason? nor Can they *talk*? but, *Can they suffer*?"[106] When whales are harpooned and dying, their characteristic whistles change dramatically to a low monotone. In contrast, in the normal healthy state, their whistles "are beautiful bird-like sounds with trills and arpeggios, glissandos and sitar-like bends in the notes."[107] This change is clearly analogous to the transformation in human expression from talking (or singing) in the normal state to crying when in pain. Additionally, there can be little physiological doubt that whales feel pain; indeed, the real question is whether they perceive acute pain to an even greater degree than humans. This latter possibility is evidenced by the far wider range of skin sensations apparently registered by the complex cerebral cortex of the whale.[108]

---

fought back successfully, humans might have learned to *respect* them and leave them alone. It is one of the darker aspects of *human* psychology that victims can gain respect by resort to violence. *Cf.* W. M. Reisman, The Art of the Possible: Diplomatic Alternatives in the Middle East 44–58 (1970) (discussing Palestinian self-respect resulting from *fedayeen* terrorism).

[100] "Whales are killed for chicken feed, cattle fodder, fertilizer, car wax, shoe polish, lipstick, cosmetics, margarine, cat and dog food, and to raise minks and foxes for fur coats." McIntyre, *Let us Act*, in McIntyre, *supra* note 94, at 224.

[101] Falk, *Introduction: Preserving Whales in a World of Sovereign States*, 17 Den. J. Int'l L. & Pol'y. 249 (1989).

[102] *Quoted* in D. Day, The Whale War 19 (1987). (statement of Prime Minister Fraser).

[103] We use the term "presentiation" as denoting the present instantiation of legitimately realizable expectation. *See* I. Macneil, The New Social Contract 60 (1980) ("presentiation . . . is the bringing of the future into the present").

[104] For reasons we give later in this essay, we are not invoking whales as a surrogate for all animals, or claiming that animal rights are logically implicated by human rights. However, we sometimes refer to "cetacean rights" when we see no reason to exclude dolphins and porpoises from a general point made about whales.

[105] *See* the debate in this Chapter, *supra*.

[106] Jeremy Bentham, The Principles of Morals and Legislation 311n. (1789, reprint 1948). Immanuel Kant accepted the Cartesian position but tried to modify it by moral pragmatism: "Animals are not self-conscious and are there merely as means to an end. That end is man. . . . Our duties to animals are merely indirect duties to mankind . . . [Man] must practice kindness towards animals, for he who is cruel to animals becomes hard also in his dealings with men" Immanuel Kant, Lectures on Ethics 239–40 (L. Infield trans. 1963).

[107] Warshall, *The Ways of Whales*, in McIntyre, *supra* note 94, at 110, 139–40. The author continues: "The whistle provides a great deal of information: the location of the whistler, the identity of friends, the whereabouts of companions, and the desire to hear a response. Choruses of whistles may be a way to confirm and reconfirm the mood, state of being, or purpose of the group." *Id.* at 140.

Anyone who has watched a mammal in intense pain—a dog, a cat, a rabbit, a horse—knows that the animal is suffering and, moreover, that it is aware of its own suffering. When we consider whales, whose intelligence may be superior to our own, it is nearly impossible to avoid concluding that these majestic creatures are capable of a degree of suffering that we may not be able to fathom.

Yet there is a philosophical tradition going back to Descartes that holds that animals other than humans lack the necessary thought processes for awareness of their own suffering and pain. Noam Chomsky quotes a letter from Descartes of 1647 to Henry More:

> But the principal argument, to my mind, which may convince us that the brutes are devoid of reason, is that . . . it has never yet been observed that any animal has arrived at such a degree of perfection as to make use of a true language; that is to say, as to be able to indicate to us by the voice, or by other signs, anything which could be referred to thought alone, rather than to a movement of mere nature; for the word is the sole sign and the only certain mark of the presence of thought hidden and wrapped up in the body; now all men, the most stupid and the most foolish, those even who are deprived of the organs of speech, make use of signs, whereas the brutes never do anything of the kind; which may be taken for the true distinction between man and brute.[109]

Philosophically, the Cartesian thesis is unpersuasive for two complementary reasons. The first is that it is overinclusive. Philosophers such as Wittgenstein have pointed out that the only basis we have for assuming that even another human being can feel pain is the other's distinctive bodily movements, sounds and cries.[110] We have no guarantee that another person feels "pain" the way we do and, moreover, we are not ourselves sure that by labeling an internal condition "painful" we are able to convey what we internally experience to others.[111] Thus, when a Cartesian philosopher argues that we do not know whether a wounded dog or whale feels pain, similar reasons apply to whether a wounded person feels pain. Descartes' skepticism is therefore overinclusive.

Second, the Cartesian thesis is underinclusive. In the letter quoted above, Descartes says that animals lack the ability to "indicate to us" their thoughts. But why should animals have evolved an ability to indicate anything to human beings? Is it not enough that they may be able to communicate adequately with their own species? Whales evolved their large brains 30 million years ago—25 million years before humans appeared on the scene and 29 million years before the present brain size of humans developed.

Why should whales have evolved with a capacity to communicate their ideas to *homo sapiens* when the latter appeared only at the very end of the 30 million years of the whale's history? There is overwhelming evidence that whales communicate effectively with their own species (and, as previously noted, have even developed interspecies communication). The notion that animals do not think because they have not learned to talk with us is arbitrarily underinclusive. Our failure to converse with whales could well be a matter more of our own limitation than of theirs.

Thus, a combination of overinclusiveness and underinclusiveness renders the Cartesian thesis arbitrary and unpersuasive. Throughout history, the denial that other persons—outsiders, minority groups—as well as other animals, have a consciousness equivalent to our own has been the foundational philosophy for genocide and enslavement. This kind of denial of humanity to minority groups is the clearest form of inhumanity. The base evil of genocide, torture, or enslavement of minority or defenseless groups is matched only by the pseudo-rationalization that the victims are less than human. Charles Darwin saw clearly the empathic connection between opposition to slavery and opposition to cruelty to animals. According to his son, "The two subjects which moved my father perhaps more strongly than any others were cruelty to animals and slavery. His detestation of both was intense, and his indignation was overpowering in case of any levity or want of feeling on these matters."[112]

Those who would deny whales the right to live use a similar rationalization. To be sure, whales are not human, but are they "less" than human? The mind set that exults in the killing of whales and the "sports" hunting of endangered wildlife species overlaps with the mind set that accepts genocide of "inferior" human beings. Conversely, the extension of rights to whales resonates deeply with the historical-legal extensions of equal rights to women and to minority groups. We believe that the phrase "human rights" is only superficially species chauvinistic. In a profound sense, whales and some other sentient mammals are entitled to human rights or at least to *humanist rights*—to the most fundamental entitlements that we regard as part

---

[108] Jacobs, *The Whale Brain: Input and Behavior*, in McIntyre, *supra* note 94, at 78, 83.

[109] NOAM CHOMSKY, CARTESIAN LINGUISTICS 6 (1966) (quoting THE PHILOSOPHY OF DESCARTES 284–87 (Torrey, ed. 1892)). The Cartesians who are still among us today deny that chimpanzees use "language" by increasingly restricting their definition of what "language" is. Thus, as chimpanzees are taught to use sign language, and communicate to us their own spontaneous combinations of thoughts, some Cartesian doubters argue that the only language that counts is speech though vocal cords! Others argue that until chimpanzees display a knowledge of grammatical syntax, they are not using language. For a skeptical view, *see* H. TERRACE, NIM: A CHIMPANZEE WHO LEARNED SIGN LANGUAGE (1979).

[110] LUDWIG WITTGENSTEIN, PHILOSOPHICAL INVESTIGATIONS §§ 293–304 (1953).

[111] *See* LUDWIG WITTGENSTEIN, THE BLUE AND BROWN BOOKS 44–54 (1958); 1 LUDWIG WITTGENSTEIN, REMARKS ON THE PHILOSOPHY OF PSYCHOLOGY §§ 137–54 (1980).

[112] Quoted in R.W. CLARK, THE SURVIVAL OF CHARLES DARWIN: A BIOGRAPHY OF A MAN AND AN IDEA 76 (1984).

of the humanitarian tradition. They are entitled to those fundamental rights not because they are "less" than human but because they are "different" from humans in various respects that do not affect or qualify the rights in question. In this article we argue only for extending the single most fundamental of all human rights – the right to life – to whales.[113]

Finally, let us consider a philosophically intermediate position between according rights to whales and abusing them. One might contend that so long as whales are not intentionally maltreated, there is no need to consider them as rights holders. This position is an echo of David Hume's speculation that creatures otherwise like us but lacking the power to harm us can at most hope to be treated mercifully but cannot expect to be treated justly.[114] But, as Allen Buchanan points out, such a position would also deny rights to persons who are unable to contribute to society, such as those who from birth are severely and permanently incapacitated.[115] Our moral obligations to others cannot be grounded on our expectation of future help from them. Even so, we cannot now know what potential future benefit to persons the continued existence of whales might afford. Medical science is replete with examples of cures derived from animals and plants, many of which seemed useless and some of which were at the point of extinction when the therapeutic discovery was made. Yet morality cannot be a matter of self-interested or prudential calculation, but is rather a deontological obligation that we owe to others even at the possibility of a net cost to ourselves.[116] Unless we acknowledge that sentient creatures such as whales are rights holders – even if those rights are limited to a few fundamental ones – we open the door to acknowledging the propriety of a future technological development that would assure the "painless" mass slaughter of whales, arguably without mistreating or abusing them. The philosophically intermediate position, on analysis, is inconsistent with our moral tradition.

2. The International Law Claim

The entitlement of whales to live and be left alone has arguably resulted from the developing practices of various institutions – international, conventional and national – concerned with whaling – practices that may be organized into six historical-analytical stages.

1. *The Free Resource Stage: Up to World War I.* For centuries, whales were considered a free resource, a gift from nature available to anyone who would hunt and kill them. Through the centuries, unregulated whaling caused the depletion of many species. Industrial whale hunting began with the Basques in the Bay of Biscay in the eleventh century and rapidly developed into a commercial industry that provided lamp oil and whalebones in response to the fashion of that time.

By 1578, Basque vessels had extended their activity to Newfoundland in the North Atlantic. The British and Dutch followed soon thereafter and so expanded their activity that Basque whaling nearly ceased by the end of the sixteenth century. Increased whaling activities led to the near extinction of right whales from the North Atlantic a century later. While the Dutch industry then declined, British whalers continued their activity throughout the nineteenth century around Biscay and Greenland. French and German whalers joined the hunt, causing the near extinction of Greenland bowhead whales and Biscayan right whales.

American whalers entered the industry in the eighteenth and nineteenth centuries. On the East coast, whaling took place off Massachusetts, Connecticut, and New York. In the West, gray and right whales were hunted off the California coast. After depleting the stocks in coastal waters, American whalers moved on to South America, Australia, and New Zealand. By the mid-nineteenth century over seven hundred American vessels and seventy thousand people were employed in the industry. American whaling slowed down during the Civil War and after the introduction of petroleum industry, and gradually came to an end at the beginning of the twentieth century.

At the same time that the American industry began to decline, in the middle of the nineteenth century, the biggest of all the Antarctic and Arctic whaling periods was launched. Advances in technology overcame distance as a prohibitive factor in the pursuit of pelagic whaling. Norwegians developed more effective harpoons and equipped their ships with steam engines. To facilitate processing, land stations were established. In 1904 Norway established its first Antarctic whaling station in Georgia.

The Norwegian lead in technology was soon followed by many other nations. In the twentieth century, commercial fleets have hunted the largest whales, in particular the finbacks, humpbacks, bowheads, and sperm, blue, sei, right and gray whales. In 1910 over ten thousand whales were killed. By 1914–15, Norway alone was responsible for killing 14,917 whales just in Antarctic waters. During

[113] What about the right to vote? The right to shelter? The right of other animals? Of plants? People who ask these kinds of questions may not be sincerely interested in the answers we might offer. Our general answer is that a powerful case can be made on behalf of the entitlement of to a right to life. We make no claim that the entitlements asserted in this essay should apply exclusively to whales, or that these are the only entitlements that should apply to whales. We make a minimal case; it is compatible with reasoned argument for extensions in either of these directions. That much said, a general case can be made on behalf of all sentient animals, including whales, for a right not to be inflicted with unnecessary or arbitrary pain.

[114] David Hume, Enquiries Concerning Human Understanding and Concerning the Principles of Morals 190-91 (Selby-Bigge & Nidditch, 3d ed. 1975) (1777).

[115] Buchanan, *Justice as Reciprocity versus Subject-Centered Justice*, 19 Phil. & Pub. Aff. 227, 230 (1990).

[116] Of course, it is impossible ever to know for sure that we will be incurring a net cost. The question is as old as Glaucon's challenge to Socrates in Plato's Republic. For an illuminating discussion, *see* Robert Nozick, Philosophical Explanations 403–570 (1981).

the First World War the total declined to 9,468 by 1918–19. However, after the war it steadily increased from 11,369 whales in 1919–20 to 43,129 in 1931. Finally, whaling nations perceived – entirely in their own self-interest – that some form of regulation was needed.[117]

2. *The Regulation Stage: 1918–1931.* Even before fears arise of the extinction of a species, the hunting and fishing industries realized that their collective profits depend upon the availability of sizable numbers of that species. For example, if there are only a few whales in the Indian Ocean, the time that any whaling vessel has to spend in finding and capturing a whale will be increased perhaps to the point of making the venture unprofitable. Hence, we might expect the whaling industry to agree to setting up a licensing system imposing temporal and spatial restrictions upon its activities. During the period roughly from 1918 through 1931, there was limited international regulation of the whaling industry for these purposes.

The most important effort was made at the meeting of the Whaling Committee of the International Council for the Exploration of the Sea held in 1927. At this meeting the Norwegian delegate proposed that whaling countries prohibit the further expansion of whaling and institute a licensing system. On the recommendation of the Whaling Committee, the International Bureau of Whaling Statistics was established in 1930;, after further negotiations the Convention for Regulation of Whaling was concluded in 1931.[118] Five years later, this Convention came into force under the auspices of the League of Nations.

The 1931 Convention for the first time set forth whaling regulations covering the waters, including territorial waters within national jurisdictions. Contracting parties undertook to take appropriate measures to license their vessels. Salaries of gunners and crew were required to be based on the size and species of the whale and the value and yield of the oil.

3. *The Conservation Stage: 1931–1945.* The 1931 Convention went beyond mere regulation for the purpose of maintaining abundant harvests. Certain measures of actual conservation were introduced. "Conservation" as we use the term implies taking a long-term view of the health of an industry. It looks beyond immediate economic considerations relating to profit and efficiency, and introduces the notion of longevity for the industry. But, like regulation, it is still aimed at the health of the whaling industry and not at the health of whales.

Along these lines, the 1931 Convention prohibited the taking or killing of calves, immature whales and female whales accompanied by calves. More significantly, the taking of right whales and several other species was flatly prohibited. While the latter prohibitions might be construed as an incipient recognition of a duty not to extinguish a species, from the standpoint of the 1930s this interpretation is probably unjustified. Rather, the flat prohibition on the taking of right whales, for example, was more likely a conservation measure that would be removed in a future convention as soon as right whales became more abundant. All told, despite the theoretical advance toward conservation marked by the 1931 Convention, it was largely ineffective in reducing the overexploitation of whales.

A development of a different nature in the early 1930s had a more substantial effect upon the industry. The 1930-31 catch produced a prodigious 3.6 million barrels of whale oil, an oversupply that lead to a precipitous decline in the market. To control the falling prices of whale oil, the private companies negotiated agreements to restrict and reduce their catch. While these measures were purely economic, they proved to be of great help in conserving whale stocks in the 1930s. However, the agreements between 1932 and 1936 were temporary and, in any event, were not acceptable to Japan, Germany and the Soviet Union.

Another conference was held in 1937, leading to the conclusion of the International Agreement for the Regulation of Whaling.[119] This Agreement was a marked improvement over the 1931 Convention. Under the Agreement, the taking of both gray whales and right whales was prohibited. Included were limitations on hunting areas and the length of the whaling season. For each species of whales, a minimum season was established, thus offered at least formal protection for young and immature whales.

In practice, however, whaling continued largely unabated. By now, whaling operations were so "excessive that it was seriously suggested that all regulations be dropped and indiscriminate whaling allowed until stocks were reduced to the level at which whaling ceased to be remunerative."[120] What that suggestion overlooked was the economic fact, so evident today, that even unremunerative whaling will proceed so long as there is sunk capital in whaling vessels. For although it is uneconomic to build new vessels (because of the low expected return), it is also uneconomic not to use existing ones even when the expected return is minimal. As a result, working whalers may be expected to pursue whales to the point of total extinction. Nor would the level of whaling activity necessarily decline even if the number of whaling nations declined to one or two – for example, when Great Britain and the Netherlands opted out of whaling, Japan purchased many of their factory ships and acceded to the British and Dutch international whaling quotas as well.[121] Moreover, the increasing *scarcity* of whales may also drive up prices

---

[117] Conservation is a more acute problem for whales than for fish, owing to the long life cycle. Whales give birth to live calves and suckle their young. Female sperm whales take about 7–13 years to mature, while males take up to 20 years, and breeding often does not begin until the age of 30. Baleen (or toothless) whales are thought to follow the same pattern, but under reduced population conditions are able to reproduce at the age of 5–6 years.

[118] Convention for the Regulation of Whaling, Sept. 24, 1931, 49 Stat. 3079, TS No. 880, 155 LNTS 349.

[119] June 8, 1937, 52 Stat. 1460, TX No. 933, 190 LNTS 79.

[120] D. Johnston, The International Law of Fisheries 400 (1965).

of whale products, perversely *stimulating* those whalers to pursue whales to extinction.

The extermination of the entire whale species surfaced as a major concern by 1938. The 1938 Protocol banned the taking of humpback whales for two years except in the area South of 40 degrees south latitude, where a one-year ban was imposed. A year later, modifications to the Protocol were adopted that provided minor additional protection for the humpback whale. On the whole, however, the agreements of the 1930s failed to achieve their stated objectives. Professor Birnie sums up the reasons for that failure: "inadequacy of the scope of regulations; inadequate scientific data; non-cooperation by some major whaling nations; poor enforcement of agreements and no international supervision or control; and lack of global interest."[122]

3A. *Conservation Becomes Protection: 1945–1977.* The next historical period is characterized by an admixture of conservationist and protectionist sentiments evolving toward the protectionist end of the spectrum. It is difficult to pinpoint when conservation – undertaken for the health of the whaling industry – starts to become transformed into protective measures undertaken for the survival and longevity of whales as a species. The transition is psychological, even though manifested in legal instruments. Consider the parallel case of United States on forests: originally undertaken for purposes of conservation (to preserve the long-term livelihood of the lumber industry), the conservation movement has transformed itself, through groups like the Sierra Club, into advocates of protecting forests as such. The change in attitude occurs a lot sooner in some people (such as Sierra Club members) than in others, which makes it nearly impossible to draw the line between an era of conservation and an era of protectionism.

In 1945 President Truman issued several proclamations that inaugurated a new era of concern for oceanic and suboceanic conservation. The most important of his proclamations, for present purposes, established the right of the United States to create conservation zones for fisheries beyond the territorial seas.[123] This unilateral act, far from being denounced by other states, started a trend among coastal states toward the establishment of large coastal zones to protect marine resources that hitherto had received no protection under international norms establishing freedom of the seas.

Also at the end of the Second World War, most whaling nations recognized the need for a new international convention. The United States called for a conference in late 1946. A new International Convention for the Regulation of Whaling (ICRW), superseding previous agreements, came into effect on November 10, 1948.[124] The ICRW established the International Whaling Commission (IWC), which meets annually to adopt and revise annual quotas, and to identify protected species.

The ability of the IWC to prescribe and regulate quotas gave the ICRW a flexibility and continuity that the previous treaties lacked. Yet the period 1948–1960 was marked by frequent clashes and threats by nations to withdraw from the Commission. Most of these early years were spent arguing over scientific data and quota allocations pertaining to Antarctic whaling. At the seventh meeting, in 1955, Norway proposed that the IWC appoint international observers for all factory ships. This proposal was prompted by the recognition that the Convention was being poorly enforced. At the tenth meeting, held in 1958, the parties for the first time discussed the humaneness of killing of whales.

Ten years after the establishment of the IWC, the 1958 Geneva Convention on Fishing and Conservation of the Living Resources of the High Seas was signed.[125] The 1958 Geneva Conference on the Law of the Sea adopted two resolutions to strengthen the effectiveness of the international conservation organizations and to further support the use of international conservation conventions. Of particular note is the definition of "conservation of the living resources of the high seas" in the Convention itself. Article 2 explains that the "expression 'conservation of the living resources of the high seas' means the aggregate of the measures rendering possible the optimum sustainable yield from those resources." In short, the Convention defines conservation as maximum sustainable yield (MSY). But MSY came under immediate attack by the proponents of eumetric theory, who charged that MSY pays attention only to the physical output of the whaling industry and is therefore underinclusive regarding the goal of conservation. Because MSY does not take into account the costs to fishermen, to society, and to the environment, it results in too high a figure for yield. Eumetric theory would require quotas to be set below the level of MSY. But eumetric theory was still too radical to be generally accepted in the

---

121 *See* Taylor & Ward, *Chickens, Whales, and Lumpy Goods: Alternative Models of Public-Goods Provisions,* 30 Pol. Stud. 350, 359–60 (1982).

122 1 P. Birnie, International Regulation of Whaling 129–30 (1985).

123 Proclamation on the Continental Shelf, 10 Fed. Reg. 12303, 12304 (1945); Watt, *First Steps in the Enclosure of the Oceans: The Origins of Truman's Proclamation on the Resources of the Continental Shelf,* 28 Marine Pol'y 211 (1979); *See also* Jessup, *The Pacific Coast Fisheries*, 33 AJIL 129 (1939); Bishop, *International Law Commission Draft Articles on Fisheries*, 50 AJIL 627 (1956); Bishop, *Exercise of Jurisdiction for Special Purposes in High Seas Areas Beyond Outer Limit of Territorial Waters*, 99 Cong. Rec. 2493 (1953); Myres McDougal & William Burke, The Public Order of the Oceans 630-33 (1962).

124 December 2, 1946, 62 Stat. 1716, TIAS No. 1849, 161 UNTS 72. The Convention was amended in 1956 to incorporate regulations on methods of inspection, and to extend the definition of "whale catchers" to cover aircraft and helicopters. This amendment has since allowed the IWC to revise its schedule annually. Protocol of November 19, 1956, 10 UST 952, TIAS No. 4228, 338 UNTS 336.

125 Apr. 29, 1958, 17 UST 138, TIAS No. 5969, UNTS 285 (entered into force Mar. 20, 1966).

late 1950s, when the prevailing attitude was that oceanic resources were infinite.

Another significant development at the 1958 Geneva Conference was the adoption of a resolution entitled "Humane Killing of Marine Life," which directly deals with whales: "The United National Conference on the Law of the Sea Requests States to prescribe, by all means available to them, those methods for the capture and killing of marine life, especially of whales and seals, which will spare them suffering to the greatest extend possible."[126] This resolution reflects changing perceptions about whales outside the IWC and recognition of the principle of more humane treatment of whales and other marine life.

As the 1960s began, the mood among IWC member states was to safeguard their national economic interests; they tended to ignore the Commission's scientific advice. The only three developments of some significance were the adoption of the International Observer Scheme in 1963, the prohibition the same year on harvesting the humpback whale, and the prohibition in 1964 on catching of the blue whale—both being endangered species. But the IWC failed in the 1960s to meet its principal objective of conserving whale resources at their 1946 stock levels.

The 1970s witnessed rapidly growing international awareness of the need to protect the environment. In 1970 the IWC established the principle of maximum sustainable yield, which required the recovery of stocks to higher levels. Although this principle was still conservationist, it constituted a bridge toward protectionism inasmuch as it specified no time limit on the recovery period for a badly depleted whale species. (A time-limited recovery period would allow whaling to resume even if recovery were incomplete).

The Stockholm Conference on the Human Environment of 1972 was convened by the UN General Assembly primarily to identify problems and coordinate solutions at that time; it was not meant to develop or endorse an action plan. Committee 2 of the conference, which dealt with the "environmental aspects of natural resource management," recommended a ten-year moratorium on commercial whaling to allow time for whale stocks to recover. Japan opposed the recommendation and labeled the resolution that incorporated it as dramatic and emotional. In response, the Netherlands maintained that the recommendation was based on sound scientific advice. The protectionist spirit that pervaded the conference is evidenced by its emphasis on man's "special responsibility to safeguard and wisely manage the heritage of wildlife"[127] In the end, the resolution was approved and the call for a ten-year moratorium on commercial whaling was included in the action plan adopted by the conference. Yet the IWC's Scientific Committee said that "a blanket moratorium cannot be justified scientifically."

By the early 1970s, stocks of Antarctic whales were so badly depleted that, assuming a total and effective ban on whale catching, it would take fifteen years for fin whales to recover to the optimum and fifty years for blue whales.[128] Serious questions were raised about the ability of the IWC to regulate and restrict whaling, and proposals were made calling for the United Nations to assume jurisdiction and control. Although never formally placed before the IWC, these proposals—together with the resolution calling for a ten-year moratorium on commercial whaling—helped increase the pressure on the IWC to change its policies and even consider amending the Convention. In sum, the Stockholm Conference may be seen as marking a pivotal point between conservationism and protectionism, a view reflected in the words of Dr. Robert M. White, who spoke for the United States: "World whale stocks must be regarded as the heritage of all mankind . . ."[129]

The next five years witnessed a serious conflict between nonwhaling and minor whaling states on the one side and major whaling states on the other side, as the former attempted to change the basic policies of the IWC from conservation to protection.

4. *The Protection Stage: 1977-1982.* At some point the attitude we have been associating with "protection" overtakes the psychology of "conservation." Arguably, this important mental shift occurred sometime during the period from 1948 to 1982—perhaps at the time of the Stockholm Conference of 1972. By 1977, the protectionist sentiment appears to have emerged as dominant over that favoring conservation and its precursor, regulation.

Events outside the IWC catalyzed the change in attitude. As important as the Stockholm Conference of 1972 was the finalization of the concept of the 200-mile fisheries zone at the UN Conference on the Law of the Sea in 1977. Although entitling coastal states to such an extensive exclusive zone for fishing might appear to have set back the cause of international controls, it also gave rise to the possibility that the majority of states might ban whaling in their zones. Faced with this dilemma of internationalization versus nationalization, Japan, a pro-whaling state, decided to champion internationalization. At the IWC it argued at the IWC that international management of whale stocks might collapse if states used the 200-mile zones to implement their own ideas about whale management. Australia met this argument with diplomatic finesse at the 1977 meeting

---

126 Res. V, Humane Killing of Marine Life, 2 *United Nations Conference on the Law of the Sea, Official Records* 144, UN Doc. A/CONF.13/38, UN Sales No. 58.V.4, Vol. II (1958) [hereinafter *Official Records*].

127 Stockholm Declaration on the Human Environment, Principle 4, UN Doc. A/CONF.48/14/Rev.1, *reprinted in* 11 ILM 1416 (1972).

128 Gulland, *The Management of Antarctic Whaling Resources*, 31 J. du CONSEIL INT'L POUR L'EXPLOITATION DE LA MER 330 (1968)]; Gulland, *The Management Regime for Living Resources*, in CHRISTOPHER JOYNER & SUDHIR CHOPRA (EDS)., THE ANTARCTIC LEGAL REGIME 222 (1988).

129 U.S. Dep't of State, U. S. Delegation Press Release No. HE/13/72, at 1–2 (June 9, 1972).

of the IWC. It pointed out that Article 54 of the Revised Single Negotiating Text of the Law of the Sea Convention dealt with highly migratory species and marine mammals, giving coastal states the absolute right to prohibit, regulate and limit the exploitation of marine mammals in their respective proposed 200-mile exclusive economic zones. However, the article gave the same right to an "international organization as appropriate." Thus, the article did not negate the legal role of the IWC. In effect, Australia was saying that coastal nations could restrict whaling and the IWC could impose international restrictions as well without conflict. Obviously, this argument could not satisfy Japan's hidden agenda (to combat the growing prohibitory movement), but it helped isolate the minority of pro-whaling states like Japan that were attempting to play off the causes of internationalization and nationalization against each other.

Also in 1977, other outside influences began to make their presence felt by the IWC. The secretariat of the Convention on International Trade in Endangered Species (CITES)[130] transmitted the report of its first meeting, highlighting the characterization of certain whales as endangered species to the IWC. And the negotiation of the Convention for the Conservation of the Antarctic Marine Living Resources, attended by the IWC as an observer, resulted in the establishment of an organization with competing interests and objectives.

An undramatic, but significant event at the IWC's 1977 meeting was the reporting out of the Scientific Committee of an earlier IUCN resolution that suggested replacing the principle of maximum sustainable yield. The resolution provided in part as follows:

> 1. The eco-system should be maintained in such a state that both consumptive and non-consumptive values can be realized on a continuing basis, ensuring present and future options, minimizing the risk of irreversible change and long-term adverse effects;
>
> 2. Management decisions should include a safety factor to allow for limitation of knowledge and imperfections of management[131]

In short, the eumetric criticism of maximum sustainable yield in 1958 had now osmosed into an official resolution. Clearly, MSY does not adequately take into account long-term adverse effects, limitations of knowledge, and imperfections of management. To the extent that the Scientific Committee reflected the philosophy of the IWC, it was beginning to acknowledge the existence of natural fluctuations and ecosystem effects that throw scientific doubt upon the quantitative approach of MSY. Since any "soft" attack upon a quantitative approach suggests the philosophically alternative qualitative approach, this debate about MSY signaled the scientific equivalent of a movement from the traditional notion of conservation to the more radical notion of protection.

In the eumetric spirit, the 1977 meeting instituted an outright ban on aboriginal whaling of the Arctic bowhead whale, which was acknowledged to be the most endangered whale species. However, this ban lasted only until the next meeting of the IWC, when it was lifted at the request of the United States where various indigenous groups had instituted a legal action in the courts alleging denial of their constitutional rights. Since the United States had been the principal proponent of the moratorium, its request for permission to allow aboriginal whaling weakened its general stance.[132] Peru advanced two proposals for a moratorium; however, these were withdrawn when it became obvious that they would be defeated.

At the next meeting in 1979, when the membership of the IWC had expanded to twenty-three, Australia and the United States proposed a worldwide ban on commercial whaling. In a letter to the Commission, the U.S. President urged it to take "effective action to ensure the survival of the great whales." The Australian commissioner announced the intention of the Australian Government to oppose whaling both domestically and internationally, and to prohibit whaling in its proposed 200-mile fishing zone. The new policy, the commissioner said, represents a "change in emphasis from one of the conservative utilization of whale stocks to promoting a policy of banning whaling and protecting whale populations."[133] The commissioner enumerated as reasons for this change the potentially high intelligence of whales, a growing community conviction of the immorality of whaling, the imminent availability of substitutes for whales products, the inhumane way that whales are killed, and the risks to the maintenance—and even survival—of some species.

Similar positions were taken at the meeting by New Zealand, and the Seychelles, but only one outright ban was imposed—on pelagic whaling—and it excepted minke whales and whaling on land stations.

By 1980, *moratorium* was destined to be the IWC's topic of the decade. That year, at the thirty-second meeting, with twenty-four members attending, three different proposals for moratoriums were introduced: a worldwide moratorium; a moratorium on commercial whaling, and a moratorium on sperm whaling. The first had originally been submitted by Australia in 1979. In the meantime Australia

---

[130] Convention on International Trade in Endangered Species of Wild Faunaand Flora, Mar. 6, 1973, 27 UST 1087, TIAS No.8249, 993 UNTS 243.

[131] 1 P. Birnie, *supra* note 122, at 479–80 n.58.

[132] The bowhead whaling exception continues to tarnish the reputation of the United States. In 1980 the United States claimed that the catch limit should be 18 landed or 26 struck, and a majority of the members of the IWC supported this claim. Despite the severely endangered status of the bowhead, by 1987 the United States was requesting an *increase* in the catch limit to 32 struck for that year and 35 struck for 1988; both of these requests were adopted by the IWC. Sumi, *The "Whale War" Between Japan and the United States: Problems and Prospects*, 17 Den. J. Int'l L. & Pol'y 317, 327 (1989).

[133] IWC/31st Mtg./1979/OS (Australia).

had indeed adopted the Whale Protection Act, which prohibits the killing, capturing, or injuring of cetaceans within its 200-mile fishing zone, and a ban on the importation into Australia of all whale products or goods was to be imposed as of January 1981. The Australian proposal was seriously considered and examined by a working group whose report indicated that a worldwide moratorium could result in a direct loss of over 7,000 jobs and an indirect loss of over 35,000 jobs. Although the report was vigorously debated, no action was taken. Both the U.S. proposal for a moratorium on commercial whaling and the proposed moratorium on sperm whaling failed to receive the requisite majority vote.

Membership in the IWC increased by 33 percent by the next year's meeting in 1981. Such new members as Costa Rica and India made strong statements in favor of preserving the whale. Clearly, the increase in membership had brought extra support for conservation policies. The United Kingdom, with the support of the United States, Sweden, France and New Zealand, once again proposed an indefinite global ban on whaling, and once again it failed to receive a majority. Another UK proposal, for an indefinite moratorium in the North Atlantic, also failed, as did a French proposal for an indefinite moratorium on pelagic whaling for minkes after the 1983–84 season, and an Australian proposal for a worldwide phaseout of commercial whaling over a five-year period.

The only proposal to succeed, which it did overwhelmingly, was submitted by the United Kingdom, France, the Netherlands and the Seychelles. It imposed an indefinite moratorium on the taking of sperm whales, whose fisheries by then were virtually denuded.

In December 1982, the long-awaited, comprehensive United Nations Convention on the Law of the Sea was completed at Montego Bay and opened for signature.[134] Although as of this writing in 1990 it has not yet entered into force, its provisions have had a direct impact upon the content of customary international law.[135] Notable for present purposes is Article 65: ''States shall cooperate with a view to the conservation of marine mammals and in the case of cetaceans shall in particular work through the appropriate international organizations for their conservation, management and study.''[136] This provision shows a marked improvement over the Geneva Convention on Fishing and Conservation, which did not specifically address the plight of marine mammals. Another significant improvement is the conspicuous absence of the ''optimum utilization'' requirement, or MSY. Thus, Article 65 tends to infuse ''conservation'' with a meaning other than MSY and closer to the eumetric conception that we have discussed. The singling out of cetaceans not only suggests a heightened sense of international responsibility toward whales, but also may constitute a legal gesture toward giving whales ''standing'' in international law beyond the limits of the IWC. Article 65 may be interpreted as putting whales first and international organizations second; the article makes the IWC legally significant only to the extent that it is an ''appropriate'' organization devoted to the conservation, management and study of whales.

5. *The Preservation Stage: 1982–1990.* We have attempted to show so far that initial regulation of whaling was transformed into conservation (for the health of the whaling industry), which in turn was overtaken by a drive for protection (for the survival of whales themselves). A protectionist attitude and the conservationist attitude have much in common, even though their psychological motivations are different. Together they account for the momentum seen in the activities of the IWC from 1946 through 1982. The protectionist attitude allows for ''reasonable'' exceptions. For instance, the protectionist will try hardest to protect whale species that are endangered, while making trade offs with whalers on stable and growing species. The protectionist might concede that a certain amount of whaling is commercially necessary, so long as the activity is restricted to stable or even growing species. In this respect, protectionists and conservationists find considerable common ground.

We now introduce a form of protectionism that is largely *incompatible* with conservation. For want of a better label, we call it ''preservationism.'' Unlike the protectionist, a preservationist will not admit of exceptions – reasonable or otherwise. The preservationist wants to ban all whaling, irrespective of whether a particular species is stable or endangered, clearly an attitude that is clearly incompatible with the industry of whaling. Whalers and preservationists view each other as mortal enemies – as is dramatically reflected in the ''whale wars'' that began approximately in 1978 and have escalated since then.

Eight new members, all nonwhaling states, joined the IWC by its thirty-fourth meeting in 1982, making the prospects for moratorium brighter than ever before. The Seychelles announced that it was amending its position in the Commission in favor of a phase-out or negotiated cessation of commercial whaling because this course would ''facilitate the adjustment that whaling nations will have to make if the whale is to be saved from extinction, and at the same time [would] safeguard the future work of the Commission as a growing alliance of nations committed to preserving all cetaceans for posterity.'' A diplomatic move, the Seychelles proposal sought zero quotas for all commercial whaling by the 1986 coastal and 1985–1986 pelagic sea-

---

134 *Opened for signature* Dec. 10, 1982, UN Doc. A/CONF.62/122, *reprinted in* UNITED NATIONS, OFFICIAL TEXT OF THE U.N. CONVENTION ON THE LAW OF THE SEA, UN Sales No. E.83.V.5(1983).

135 *See* Anthony D'Amato, *An Alternative to the Law of the Sea Convention*, 77 AJIL 281 (1983). As of 1990, 125 nations have signed the Convention, 23 have ratified without qualifications, and 14 have ratified with qualifications. For a listing of the states, *see* BURNS WESTON, RICHARD FALK & ANTHONY D'AMATO (EDS.), BASIC DOCUMENTS IN INTERNATIONAL LAW AND WORLD ORDER 946–47 (2d ed. 1990).

136 This provision is extended to the high seas by Article 120 which says that ''Article 65 also applies to the conservation and management of marine mammals on the high seas.''

sons, subject to review thereafter. The proposal was approved by a vote of twenty-five in favor, seven against and five abstentions. A three-year period was allowed to give whaling states an opportunity to phase out their commercial activities gradually and to cope with the economic impact of the moratorium, in accordance with the Preamble to the ICRW. The ban on "commercial" whaling was understood to exempt aboriginal subsistence whaling, especially of the endangered bowhead species by the Inuit in arctic Canada, Alaska, Greenland and Siberia.[137]

The next IWC meeting, in 1983, is important for the responses of states that had opposed the 1982 amendment to the schedule. Of the seven that had opposed the moratorium, four filed formal objections (Japan, Norway, Peru and the USSR) while three others, together with one of the absentees (Brazil, Chile, Iceland and the Republic of Korea) decided not to file objections. After Peru decided to withdraw its objection, only Norway, Japan and the USSR were left as formal objectors. The United States at this time notified both Norway and Japan that it was initiating certification under the Pelly Amendment because they were diminishing the effect of a conservation treaty to which the United States was a party. The amendment required that the United States impose an embargo on the certified nations' fishing rights in its 200-mile economic zone and ban the importation of fishing products from those nations. This drastic step was designed to bring both Norway and Japan in line with the conservation measures implemented by the IWC. However, the Soviet Union was immune from this type of pressure because it did not export fisheries products to the United States.

At the IWC's thirty-sixth meeting in 1984, Brazil reversed its stand of 1982 and decided to support the moratorium. Japan, however, adhered to its earlier position and objected on technical and legal grounds to the imposition of the moratorium. Japan also likened Japanese whaling to subsistence whaling elsewhere and insisted that it needed to be perpetuated in the socioeconomic interest of the Japanese coastal community. Of the other states that had opposed the moratorium of 1982, the Republic of Korea reported that despite internal objections and economic problems, it would comply with the measure; the Soviet Union again objected to the moratorium on technical grounds.

Japan shifted its position at the next year's IWC meeting. While maintaining its informal objection on technical grounds, Japan said that "in order to avoid a head-on conflict" with the United States, it would withdraw its formal objection to the moratorium. The Philippines, however, which the previous year had indicated its wish to continue scientific research on whales, now revealed its plans to resume whaling once it was determined that stocks were not endangered. Another important announcement came from the Soviet Union, which stated that it would temporarily stop commercial whaling in the Antarctic, for technical reasons, though it maintained its objection based on the illegality of the moratorium decision.

Meanwhile, sentiment against commercial whaling continued to mount in the IWC. Speaking as a new member, in a letter to the Commission India Prime Minister Rajiv Gandhi pointed out that India had joined as a nonwhaling member only to "join other nations in their endeavor to save this most fascinating and remarkable member of our planet's living fraternity."

At the next meeting, in 1986, Brazil announced its presidential decree of January 1, 1986 enforcing the moratorium and Japan informed the parties that it would cease its commercial activities the next year. Oman was able to proclaim that "whales are safer from human harm now than in any time since the beginning of modern pelagic whaling some sixty years ago."

6. *The Emerging Entitlement Stage*. The five-year moratorium on commercial whaling was revaluated and renewed by the IWC's annual meeting in Noordwijk, which ended on July 6, 1990. Such traditional whaling nations as Japan, Norway and Iceland pressed for the establishment of quotas on certain species that they argued were at harvestable levels. The IWC, however, refused to alter the moratorium in any way. It also denied Japan's request for an allowance for small-type coastal whaling (i.e., whaling by the use of hand implements, as opposed to "pelagic whaling," which uses factory ships). The Commission condemned as unnecessary the killing of whales for research and it asked Norway and Japan to reconsider their policies in this regard. These actions led to threats by Japan and Iceland to pull out.

Virtually all commercial whaling activity had ceased by 1990.[138] The moratorium, however, only applies to great whales (the ten largest species). For the first time, the IWC agreed to study "small cetaceans" including dolphins, porpoises and small whales. In addition, it passed a resolution supporting the UN General Assembly's initiative to phase out large-scale drift-net fishing within two years.

Although a total moratorium would be a triumph for preservationists, the concept of moratorium does not entitle whales to the right to life, because a moratorium implies temporal limitations (even if extendable) upon whaling ac-

[137] *See* Doubleday, *Aboriginal Subsistence Whaling: The Right of Inuit to Hunt Whales and Implications for International Environmental Law*, 17 DENV. J. INT'L L. & POLICY 373 (1989).

[138] However, Japan and Iceland continue to exploit a large loophole in the name of "scientific research." For example, in 1987, Japan submitted a scientific research program to the IWC Scientific Committee stating that approximately 825 minke whales and 50 sperm whales would be lethally taken. IWC/39th Mtg./1987, at 48–53. Iceland's 1987 research program involved the hunting and killing of 80 fin and 20 sei whales. ICW/40th Mtg./1988, Report of the Scientific Committee, para. 4. Inasmuch as even a single whale, by its sheer size, would overwhelm any modern scientific research laboratory, providing enough material to keep a team of scientists busy for months, the label "scientific research" must be critically examined in light of such claims. It is estimated that some 600 great whales will be slaughtered in 1990 under various "scientific research" programs.

tivities. Thus the preservationist movement cannot be the last stage of our story. It is merely the present stage, but it contains the seeds of the final stage, which we have labeled the "entitlement" stage. Preservation is transmuted into entitlement when the moratorium becomes permanent, at which point it is no longer definitionally a "moratorium" but, rather, may be termed an entitlement to life. Yet the new entitlement stage involves an important shift in philosophy. By claiming that whales are "entitled" to life, the entitlement philosophy recognizes this right as belonging to, or even coming from, the whales themselves. In contrast, the preservationist views the permanent moratorium as bestowed by humankind upon whales; the rights come from the people, and the people are exercising their right to preserve whales. Consequently, the entitlement stage may involve the most radical philosophical shift of the progressive stages that we have recounted in this article, even though historically it represents only an incremental advance over preservationism.

The six stages we have recapitulated – free resource, regulation, conservation, protection, preservation, entitlement – may be viewed as a progression from self-interest to altruism[139] or from individualism to communalism,[140] but we suggest that they are better conceptualized as a broadening of international cultural consciousness. The whalers of the early twentieth century were persuaded to accept the second stage – regulation – even though many of them found that it hindered their individual freedom. They accepted it on the rational grounds that they themselves might destroy their livelihood as a whole unless certain common restrictions were placed on the whaling enterprise. This rational conclusion constituted an increase in breadth of consciousness, from "do anything we want" to "don't do some things that might hurt other whalers and eventually ourselves." Similarly, the step from regulation to conservation met resistance; whalers had to be persuaded that long-term conservation would benefit the industry as a whole, which in turn enhanced the economic interests, or at least prospects, of each whaler. Again, consciousness was broadened. And so it continued with each of our six analytic stages. In the fifth and sixth stages, whalers faced the loss of their entire enterprise, yet the increase in consciousness now embraces the environment as a whole, the planet on which we all live. In this respect, whalers should be no different from anyone else; everyone's self-interest is in a stable and viable ecosystem. Hence, it would be a mistake to conclude that the transition from the first stage to the second, or for that matter from any one stage to the next, has been more difficult or historically important than any other.

Although the distance covered between stage one and stage six amounts to a catastrophic change – from uninhibited freedom to prohibition – the change from any one stage to the next was incremental, depicting the same underlying psychological and philosophical process of increasing breadth of consciousness. For this reason, we contend that what we have denominated as the last stage – entitlement – is not qualitatively different from the others. Rather, it is part of a relentless, historically necessary progression. We may or may not be in the final entitlement stage today – different people will think differently – but its seeds were planted in each of the five preceding stages.

We have been sketching, implicitly, a trend in the component of customary international law called opinio juris. The development of international custom is inevitably a dynamic process, and the seeds of a future conflict-resolving synthesis are always present in the clash of thesis and antithesis that constitutes the claim conflicts among states. To anticipate a customary trend is to argue that, in a sense, it already exists. We have seen, in the history we have recounted, the practice of states (reflected through their whaling activities) moving through six stages that are best characterized as increases in international breadth of consciousness. This combination of practice and consciousness formally constitutes the material and psychological elements of general custom. What states *do* becomes what they legally *ought* to do, by virtue of a growing sense that what they do is right, proper, and natural. The dawning sense of duty to the environment – to protect the ability of our small, green planet to sustain life – is evidence of a sense of obligation that constitutes the opinio juris component of binding customary international law.

Hence, if our argument is accepted, we have sketched more than a political-cultural history of a relentless increase in breadth of consciousness about whales. We have suggested an opinio juris – a growing sense of international legal obligation toward whales. In the current stage of that progression, nearly all nations accept the obligation of preservation. And in this consensus of preservation, we suggest that there is the incipient formation of the final, decisive stage – the entitlement of whales to life. Whether that final stage has already arrived cannot be definitively determined. But we argue that in its inevitability it has already been anticipated in the law.

If we are correct, this anticipation of a stage of entitlement for a nonhuman species in international law is a revolutionary development. It takes seriously the fact that human beings are open systems – that our lives are dependent on our environment. The human race will live or die as the ecosystem lives or dies. International law can no longer be viewed as an artifact exclusively concerned with state and human interactions against a mere background called the environment. Rather, other living creatures in the environment are players in a new and expanded international legal arena.

3. Rights and Entitlements

The middle four stages of the legal progression that we traced in Part II – from (2) regulation to (3) conservation,

---

139 *See* Kennedy, *Form and Substance in Private Law Adjudication*, 89 HARV. L. REV. 1685, 1713–22 (1976).

140 *See* Balkin, *The Rhetoric of Responsibility*, 76 VA. L. REV. 197, 206–12 (1990).

to (4) protection, to (5) preservation–might be thought to serve whales well enough for all practical and legal purposes. What need is there to move to the sixth, entitlement, stage? Specifically, what particular value is added by ascribing rights to whales, as distinct from recognizing a duty of nations and individuals toward whales?

We contend, first, that it is intelligible to regard whales as rights holders, and second, that viewing the rights this way makes a difference. On both these points, we employ the pioneering analysis of Christopher Stone.[141]

History has seen a widening of the circle of rights holders. When infanticide was freely practiced, infants had no rights; now of course their right to life is protected in nearly all countries by the law against murder. Convicted felons used to be stripped of all rights; now they have certain basic protections (e.g., equal medical care). The laws of most countries have seen a gradual progression in ascribing rights to aliens, married women, the mentally enfeebled, and racial minorities. Rights have also been extended to inanimate, intangible entities: trusts, corporations, joint ventures, partnerships and municipalities. In recent years corporations have even been prosecuted and convicted of crimes. International law classically regards nation-states as having rights and responsibilities. In this broad context, there is nothing strange about recognizing rights of whales–creatures that are more animate than corporations, more communicative than infants or mentally enfeebled persons, more communal than the society of nations, and perhaps more intelligent than the smartest human beings.

Professor Stone has suggested the important differences that would accrue if we ascribe rights to natural objects in the environment. The first is what we might call the aspect of generality: that having rights is a generalized legal competence, whereas being the beneficiary of the obligations of others breaks down into a series of specialized, specific rules. For example, suppose a person signs a contract with a corporation, then attempts to avoid his obligations under the contract by pointing to the corporation's charter and showing that the terms of the contract were, strictly construed, ultra vires. Under a strict interpretation of the idea of incorporation, the corporation only exists by virtue of the specific competences listed in its corporate charter. But such an approach would hardly ever be adopted by any court.[142] Instead, the corporation is said to have certain generalized "rights" including the right to enter into contracts.

Second, the idea of having "rights" includes a notion of moral rights that can inform existing law or even push it in a certain direction.[143] Take, for example, a battered wife suing her husband in the nineteenth century. Courts routinely dismissed such cases on the ground that they had no jurisdiction over what happened in the home, and in any event a wife had an adequate remedy under the laws of divorce. But at some point, courts changed their approach and began recognizing tort claims by wives against their husbands. Suppose that just prior to the turning point an attorney advised a wife that she had *no* legal right to sue her husband in tort. The advice, though grounded in precedent, would have been misleading, since, by hypothesis, in the very next case the court "found" such a right. What happened is that the court accepted the powerful moral claim of right and recognized it as somehow subsisting in the common law all along, even though legal precedent was to the contrary. We say that the court "articulated" the preexisting right– much as we argued that an international court could articulate an entitlement of whales arising from the customary law practice of their preservation.

Third, the burden of proof in litigation and negotiation can turn on which party is a rights claimant. Courts may be predisposed to give a far more "liberal" construction of applicable rules to a party who claims to be asserting rights than to one that claims to be a third-party beneficiary of asserted rights. Even the rules regarding burden of proof, Professor Stone suspects, would be more liberally interpreted in favor of a rights claimant.

Fourth, the development of a jurisprudence regarding whales is more likely if whales are perceived by courts as rights-holders, just as a jurisprudence of corporate law has developed as the result of viewing corporations as legal entities entitled to sue and be sued and even to be prosecuted for corporate crime.

Finally, standing is facilitated for rights-holders. Standing may be a lesser problem in American law than in the law of many other countries because of the separation-of-powers tradition of contesting many forms of governmental action in the courts. Yet even in U.S. courts when the protection of whales arises, the need to assert harm to one's own interests, as opposed to the interests of whales, may exert a subtle negative influence upon the petitioners. In *Japan Whaling Association v. American Cetacean Society*,[144] although the Supreme Court found (in a footnote) that the American Cetacean Society, Greenpeace, Friends of the Earth, and other environmental organizations had "alleged a sufficient 'injury in fact' in that the whale watching and studying of their members will be adversely affected by continued whale harvesting,"[145] the Court ultimately held against those organizations on the merits. Watching and studying whales seems a slender reed on

[141] CHRISTOPHER STONE, SHOULD TREES HAVE STANDING? TOWARDS LEGAL RIGHTS FOR NATURAL OBJECTS (1974).

[142] One could *imagine* a highly formalistic court taking such an approach, but even then, only if impelled to do so because of some other extrinsic equitable factor such as the unconscionableness of the contract.

[143] Professor Stone does not argue in these natural-law terms. He makes a comparable argument on the basis of the "force" of "ordinary language." *Id.*

[144] 478 U.S. 221 (1986).

[145] *Id.* at 230 n.4.

which to mount a lawsuit to protect whales.[146] The real party in interest is the whale. Perhaps the very tenuousness of the "standing" the Supreme Court allowed the environmental groups contributed to the lack of empathy toward whales in the Court's ultimate decision on the merits.

For these reasons, and similar ones that can be adduced, the extension of legal rights to whales would have significant legal consequence. To move from "preservation" to "entitlement" is not just a way of talking. Rather, it acknowledges the creation of a new subject of international law.

A "right" may be legal or moral or both. The attempt to draw a sharp distinction between legal and moral rights often founders on two grounds.[147] First, as H.L.A. Hart has demonstrated, moral considerations influence the content of law over time.[148] Second, there may be a deeper connection between law and morality than positivists such as Professor Hart are willing to admit. Although this connection may not be a "necessary" one in the substantive sense of Cicero or in the procedural sense of Lon Fuller,[149] it exists in the claim of legitimacy that the law makes – a claim that surpasses that which can be enforced and spills over into the realm of that which is morally persuasive. For these general reasons, we have not attempted in this article to draw lines between the moral and the legal in our discussion of the emerging rights of whales. Although we have indicated when we are primarily talking about moral rights and when we are primarily talking about legal rights, the considerable degree of overlap between the two, we submit, reflects the way a norm develops over time.

Nevertheless, for our discussion of the final stage of the rights of whales, we deliberately chose the term "entitlements" instead of "rights." By entitlements we mean legally enforceable rights. An entitlement may overlap with morality; but if it is not legally enforceable, it is not an entitlement no matter how strong the moral considerations in its favor. We claim that the whale, as a sentient being, is in the process of being assigned an entitlement to life. If we are correct, then in any conflict between whale and whaler, the latter lacks, or soon will lack, any entitlement to hunt and kill the whale.

4. Counterclaims

The acknowledgement that whales have an entitlement to life directly conflicts with at least two types of counterclaims that have been advanced as justifying the hunting and killing of whales. The serious assertion of these claims – of "scientific research" and "aboriginal subsistence whaling" – indicates that even when ecological consciousness can be assumed, investing whales with an entitlement to life is controversial.

1. *"Scientific Research"*. In the 1980s, Japan, Iceland, and the Soviet Union made claims for exceptions to the whaling moratorium on the ground of scientific research. Perhaps the most articulate justification of this position is an article by Kazuo Sumi, professor of international law at Yokohama City University.[150]

Professor Sumi claims that Japan is deviating from the IWC's moratorium on commercial whaling because its purpose is scientific rather than commercial. Although he does not define "scientific research," he indicates at several places in his article what that term comprises. At one place, he says, "Data and information on the resource state of whales are essential for rational management." Later he indicates that the aim of the Japanese research program is: "to obtain estimates of various biological parameters, especially of age-specific natural mortality. Additionally, it [is] also intended to elucidate the role of whales, (namely, the sperm whale and the minke whale) as a key species in the Antarctic marine ecosystem." Asked why most of this research could not be done with photography and non-lethal tests, Sumi invokes the authority of some members of the IWC's Scientific Committee sympathetic to the Japanese position, who asserted that "the analysis of material (particularly ear plugs, ovaries, and stomach contents collected from dead whales) could not be carried out through non-lethal research."

Sumi's claims clearly demonstrate that the purpose of the scientific research program is not to discover new facts about whales but, rather, to prove to the IWC that the particular whales that Japan is hunting are not an endangered species. Sumi in effect concedes this point by stating that "Japan emphasized that the results to be obtained will provide a scientific basis for resolving problems facing the IWC which have generated confrontation among the

146 The immediate effect of Japan Whaling Ass'n v. American Cetacean Soc'ty was to permit Japan to kill 1,200 sperm whales – a species that is "widely believed" to be "under the threat of extinction." Note, Japan Whaling Association v. American Cetacean Society, 6 WISC. INT'L L.J. 129, 150 (1987). While it might be difficult for the American Cetacean Society or Greenpeace to prove that the removal of 1,200 sperm whales from the oceans of the world would actually result in a diminution of their members' ability to watch and study whales – given the difficulty of finding and studying even one whale not in captivity – the contrasting enormity of the loss to the sperm whale species of 1,200 of their number suggests that perhaps the Justices were not sufficiently empathetic to the asserted "injury in fact" of the environmental organizations.

147 *See* D'Amato, *The Moral Dilemma of Positivism*, 20 VAL. U.L. REV. 43 (1985).

148 H.L.A. HART, THE CONCEPT OF LAW 199–200 (1961).

149 For discussion and references, *see* D'Amato, *Lon Fuller and Substantive Natural Law*, 26 AM. J. JURIS. 202 (1981).

150 Sumi, *supra* note 132.

member nations due to the divergent views on the moratorium.'' Under its program, Japan proposed an ''annual sample size'' of 825 minke whales and 50 sperm whales in Antarctic waters; in the two years of ''sampling'' between 1987 to 1991, this would amount to a kill of 1,650 minke whales and 100 sperm whales. But Sumi does not explain what would happen if the very ''sampling'' process he describes destroyed the species. From a logical point of view, if the ''sampling'' is scientifically necessary to determine the facts about whether certain species of whales should be on the IWC's endangered list, Japan must concede that *in advance of* the sampling no one can be sure *whether* the particular species is endangered. Since Japanese whalers are concededly killing all these whales in a state of a priori uncertainty about whether the species is endangered, one result might be that the very process of lethal ''sampling'' itself could reduce a species of whales below the critical level necessary for reproduction. The Japanese scientists would then have to report that as a result of their research efforts on whether sperm whales (for example) could survive extinction, that particular species has become extinct.

Sumi argues that, at least as far as the minke whale is concerned, it appears to inhabit the oceans in large numbers and is far from the point where it should be listed as an endangered species. Yet when he considers the suggestion that Antarctic whales could be scientifically studied by means of photography, he objects that minke whales ''have quick mobile behavior and a large stock size and it is not known whether they have identifiable individual characteristics.'' Noticeably, Sumi does not consider how Japanese whalers—assuming they are hunting only for minke whales—can be sure that the creatures they shoot with exploding harpoons are minke whales. For if these whales cannot be identified by photographs, and if it is unsure that they have identifiable individual characteristics, how can whalers on a boat know that it is the minke whale they are killing and not the similar-shaped and-sized beaked whale, killer whale, or gray whale?

A different sort of justification advanced by Sumi is Japan's domestic law, which in November 1987 dissolved Nippon Kyodou Hogei Co., the last remaining Japanese whaling company, and within thirty days established the Institute of Cetacean Research, a non-profit organization. This change in domestic legislation did not, however, result in changing the claims for exemptions made by Japan before the IWC; the program of ''scientific research'' continued unabated. Sumi concedes that the Institute of Cetacean Research, after hunting and killing the whales, and after the scientists have conducted their research on the carcasses, sells the whale meat and by-products on the Japanese market. But he adds that any profits resulting from these sales ''revert back to the research program.'' Thus, the new Institute of Cetacean Research may pursue the same whaling program as did Nippon Kyodou Hogei Co., so long as profits are poured back into the institute. Sumi does not tell us whether the Nippon Co. also retained its whaling profits (as it might have done instead of distributing them to shareholders in the form of dividends).[151] Nor are we informed whether the Institute for Cetacean Research will build bigger and better whaling vessels, from the profits of its sales of whale meat, in anticipation of the day that the IWC's moratorium is lifted. All we are told is that, by a stroke of domestic legislation, Japan is no longer engaged in ''commercial whaling'' and thus is not subject to the IWC's moratorium on commercial whaling.[152]

Professor Sumi argues further that the United States, which has taken the lead in criticizing Japan's policy, has been gravely inconsistent. By stressing a ban on ''commercial whaling,'' the United States has managed to exempt Alaskan aboriginal subsistence whaling. The United States has tolerated the hunting by the Inuit of the bowhead whale, a truly endangered species while the minke whale hunted by the Japanese is arguably far from being endangered. In the next section we shall criticize the aboriginal exemption. But even if the policy of the United States is wrong, that is no justification for the Japanese policy. And in any event, the U. S. tolerance of the subsistence hunting of bowhead whales by aboriginal Alaskans has no relationship whatsoever to the claim by the Japanese that their whaling policy is dedicated to scientific research.

Professor Sumi claims that a cultural bias is operating unfairly against Japanese whalers. The eating of whale meat in Japan is a function of ''dietary customs, religious beliefs, cultural backgrounds and emotional sensibilities. For the Japanese people, the whale is not only a food source, but also a basis of culture.'' For example, he says that ''baleens of the right whale have been used as an essential part of 'Bunraku,' Japan's traditional puppet theatre.'' The Japanese whaling industry used all parts of the whale in a productive manner, whereas the U. S. whalers in the eighteenth and nineteenth centuries made use only

[151] Nor are we informed, whether any of the executives of the dissolved Nippon Kyodou Hogei Co. found new employment in the Institute of Cetacean Research or, if they did, whether they retained or even increased their former salaries.

[152] To his credit, Professor Sumi quotes Dr. Roger Payne, representative of Antigua and Barbuda in the IWC: ''There is nothing scientific about killing 875 whales and selling the meat. It's just a scam, cloaked, unfortunately, in pseudo-science.'' Sumi, *supra* note 132, at 360 (quoting World Wildlife Fund, Press Release (Sept. 1, 1987)). Professor Sumi immediately follows this quotation with the observation that ''it is truly regrettable that the WWF, with a worldwide reputation, has been influenced by the narrow-minded and prejudiced view of a radical protectionist.'' *Id.*

of whale oil. When it became less expensive to exploit petroleum, the United States could afford to abandon its wasteful whaling ventures and become conservation-minded.

This last argument is a clear example of an antientitlement perspective. Surely from the point of view of the whale, the fact that all of its bodily parts are exploited cannot make a moral difference.[153] Or to state the matter differently, should the fate of a whale turn on whether its whalebone will be simply discarded or effectively utilized for theatrical purposes? One might argue that discarding the whalebone, "wasteful" though it is, may be preferable from an entitlement perspective. For the cultural use of the baleen in folk theatre may well help to perpetuate and solidify a pervasive attitude among the population that the whale is *meant* to be killed for the artistic and gustatory benefit of humans. This attitude itself can thus contribute to the perpetuation of, or increase in, the hunting and killing of whales. But apart from the perspective one adopts with respect to these questions, this final argument, like Sumi's showing of the inconsistency of the United States policy, surely has nothing to do with whether the Japanese whaling policy is justified as a form of scientific research. Despite the many arguments ably advanced by Professor Sumi, it appears that he has not presented a single reasonable contention in favor of fairly labelling the killing of thousands of whales as a scientific research program.

2. *Aboriginal Subsistence Whaling*. If whales have an entitlement to life, what happens if indigenous people assert a competing entitlement to killing them for subsistence? This need has been asserted on behalf of the Inuit—the indigenous peoples of arctic Canada, Alaska, Greenland, and Siberia, also known as Eskimos. The problem is poignant because the whales they hunt are the bowhead, an endangered species.

The case for the Inuit has been effectively presented by Nancy Doubleday.[154] She cites Article 1(2) of the International Covenant on Economic, Social, and Cultural Rights: "In no case may a people be deprived of its own means of subsistence."[155] She attacks the IWC's quotas on aboriginal hunting of endangered species such as gray whales and bowhead whales on the ground that the IWC "does not have express jurisdiction over subsistence whaling." The Inuit hunt "for food in order to survive, not for sport or pleasure." In the Inuit culture, she writes,

> animals and their spirits are respected and shown honor according to tradition, but it is a dialogue, as the animals allow themselves to be taken only by those who respect them. A hunter who abuses or who fails to show respect to the animals he takes will not be successful in the hunt. Failure in the hunt is failure in life.

From earliest times, Ms. Doubleday contends, the Inuit in practice were conservationists; they only hunted and killed whales as they needed them for subsistence. It was the commercial whalers of the nineteenth and twentieth centuries who severely depleted the bowhead species and endangered its survival. Commercial whalers abandoned arctic waters when the remaining bowheads were too few to make the whaling expeditions profitable. Thus have the exploitative commercial whaling practices of the developed nations victimized the Inuit people. Having endangered the species, the commercial nations are attempting through the IWC to curtail the Inuit's historic right to subsistence whaling.

Doubleday does not go so far to argue that the Inuit should be allowed to hunt the bowhead whale into extinction. She concludes by making the modest claim that "indigenous peoples must be a party to any discussions affecting their aboriginal subsistence rights."

The conflict presented by Doubleday between indigenous peoples' subsistence whaling and what we have claimed is the whale's entitlement to life has so far been addressed only in the political arena. The United States, as we have seen, has taken a retrogressive position in favor of the Inuit, presumably on the basis that the Inuit of Alaska can vote whereas whales cannot. Leading environmental organizations such as the Sierra Club and Friends of the Earth have been, if anything, even less forthcoming than U. S. politicians. Although these organizations claim to be champions of the rights of whales, when it comes to the bowhead whale—a truly endangered species—they are uncharacteristically silent. Undoubtedly, the reason is their respect for the "rights" of indigenous people. These "political solutions" are thus not solutions at all; they are simply policies constructed upon expediency.

If we turn from the political sphere to the legal, some of the murkiness clears up. Doubleday's complaint about the jurisdiction of the IWC, like Sumi's, confuses intraorganizational constitutive rights with the lawmaking effect of the organization's activities in the international legal system. Moreover, she is not convincing in her attempt to justify Inuit hunting practices as showing respect and honor to the whales: no one asked the bowhead whales whether the gangs of men clubbing and harpooning them were dem-

---

153 "We rarely stop to consider that the animal that kills with the least reason to do so is the human animal," observed Professor Singer. "We think of lions and wolves as savage because they kill; but they must kill, or starve. Humans kill other animals for sport, to satisfy their curiosity, to beautify their bodies, and to please their palates." PETER SINGER, ANIMAL LIBERATION: A NEW ETHICS FOR OUR TREATMENT OF ANIMALS 235 (1975).

154 Doubleday, *supra* note 137.

155 Dec. 16, 1966, 999 UNTS 171.

onstrating respect. Nor does it follow that because exploitative commercial whaling practices were primarily responsible for endangering the bowhead, the Inuit are therefore free to pursue the species to extinction. Unfortunate though it may be that the commercial whaling placed the Inuit's source of food in danger of extinction, the fact remains that no further killing of bowhead – whether by commercial fishing vessels or by the less technological methods of the indigenous peoples – can be justified. Finally, there is conflation and confusion in Doubleday's repeated linking of the Inuit's "subsistence needs" to the preservation of their "culture" and "way of life." No one claims that the Inuit would starve to death if they were stopped from killing whales. As Professor Stone's analysis reveals, it is not the *lives* of the Inuit that are at stake but, rather, their traditional life style.[156] It appears that Doubleday has failed to make any rational argument for the exempting the Inuit from the norms of international law, even though in closing she makes the emotional argument that the attempt to include whales in the "common heritage of mankind" under international law is "a kind of intellectual imperialism." In fact, all rules of law are a form of intellectual imperialism.

Many international lawyers are taking up the cause of indigenous peoples. As the statist conceptions of international law exemplified by Oppenheim give way to the humanist conceptions of the present day, overlooked voices deserve the greatest consideration. When the rights of indigenous people are suppressed in favor of exploitative commercial interests – as with the Indians of the Brazilian rain forests – the noblest sentiments of international lawyers should be brought to the service of those rights. But Doubleday's easy coupling of the predicament of the Indians of the Brazilian rain forest and the claims of the Inuit to hunt the great whales of the Arctic, is unpersuasive. The Inuit's claims are at the expense of an overlooked voice – the anguished cry – of the sentient inhabitants of the deep. Doubleday would attempt to convince the reader that only one interest is at stake: that of the Inuit and their right to the "resource" of the great whales. But, in fact, there is a second interest: that of the great whales in the survival of their species or – even short of claims of survival – in their right to live. The whales find their own sustenance in the oceans; by what right do the Inuit expropriate the bodies of the whales to serve as their food?[157]

Yet there is a claim that can reasonably and persuasively be made on behalf of the Inuit: that they have been severely disadvantaged by the exploitative commercial whaling practices of the nineteenth and early twentieth centuries, which resulted in endangering the survival of the bowhead species. Absent these practices, the Inuit might at least be able to continue their subsistence whaling without fear of extinguishing the species. To be sure, our "entitlement" argument does not distinguish between endangered and nonendangered species. But as a practical matter, it might be claimed that the Inuit's whaling practices might have been tolerated by the international community for some additional period of time were it not for the invasion of arctic waters by commercial whalers.

Surely, those who profited from the commercial whaling now owe the Inuit a reasonable alternative means of subsistence. A moral obligation has arisen to feed these people if they choose to remain where they are instead of migrating to a place where other food is available or can be grown. We contend that reparations should be made to the Inuit for the decades of commercial whaling that depleted the bowhead species to the point of endangerment. These reparations should ideally be raised by an environmental tax on all nations whose nationals benefited from that commercial whaling.

An environmental tax is appropriate when the social cost or benefit of a project is not internalized by the persons engaging in that practice. What we label a type I instance of a social cost is exemplified by a polluting factory: if the factory emits sulfur oxides into the atmosphere, or dumps its wastes into a river, part of the cost of its operation is passed onto the public as pollution. This "social cost" is not, but should be, internalized by the factory. Thus, society has begun to impose a pollution tax upon such factories, measured by the level of emissions. The factory itself, by installing catalytic converters, may reduce the amount of air pollution it emits and thus reduce the tax. A type II social benefit occurs in the converse situation: the actor internalizes the costs of a social benefit that should be paid for in part by society as a whole. For example, the Brazilian rain forests contribute significantly to replenishing of the world's atmospheric oxygen through photogenesis. Although everyone benefits from the maintenance of the rain forest, this benefit is financed by Brazil's renunciation of more favorable economic opportunities, such as cutting down the forest for lumber. Another type II example is the wild game preserve in Kenya. Everyone benefits from the maintenance of endangered species in the wild, but Kenya internalizes the cost by forgoing economic exploita-

---

[156] CHRISTOPHER STONE, EARTH AND OTHER ETHICS: THE CASE FOR MORAL PLURALISM 220 (1987).

[157] The Inuit have not "farmed" the whales either. As regards a chicken farm, for instance, the argument can be made that, but for the raising and nurturing of the chickens on the farm, they would never have come into existence; therefore, there is perhaps some justification to use them as human food. To be sure, animal rightists would disagree with such a justification; *See, e.g.*, TOM REGAN, THE CASE FOR ANIMAL RIGHTS 347–49 (1983). But in any event, a similar justification would not apply to indigenous people who hunt and kill wild animals such as whales.

tion of the preserves. If the rest of the world objects to a Kenyan proposal to allow hunting for sport, for a high fee, in the preserves, the rest of the world should try to remove the incentive for such licensing by paying Kenya a subsidy instead.[158]

Building on this type II example, we propose that a tax be levied upon those countries whose nationals have benefited directly or indirectly from the unrestrained commercial hunting of bowhead whales, and that the revenues collected be paid to the Inuit as a form of subsidy or reparation for the endangerment of the bowhead species. With these revenues, the Inuit could migrate to places where food is more plentiful, or set up arctic farms, or—at least for a while—simply purchase food supplies. The tax payments could be made over a limited period (for example, twenty years). Reparations in perpetuity would not be fair because, if our presentation of the whales' entitlement to life is persuasive, the Inuit would be legally disabled from hunting whales sooner or later irrespective of the history of exploitative commercial whaling by other nations. Thus, the "social benefit" payments in our type II example should be in reparation for the destruction of the legitimate expectations of the Inuit prior to the whales' final, "entitlement stage."

5. Conclusion

Whales are entitled to consideration as moral entities. Whether we can move from moral desirability to legal actuality is a matter of analyzing the process of international customary law. We have contended in this essay that the opinio juris of nations has encompassed five, and perhaps six, inexorable qualitative stages: free resource, regulation, conservation, protection, preservation, and entitlement. We have argued that assigning whales an entitlement to life is the consequence of an emerging humanist right in international law—an example of the merging of the "is" and the "ought" of the law in the process of legitimization. Law is ever striving to "work itself pure," in Lord Mansfield's felicitous phrase. The law that "ought to be" is implicit in the law that "is," because it invests the "is" with a purposive sense of fulfillment and self-realization.[159] The law that ought to be gives us reason to obey and respect the law that is. Although morality of course shapes the content of law as a matter of historical contingency, the vital consideration is that one cannot fully explain "law" without reference to normative values—what law is striving to achieve. If we merely take a rigid slice-of-time view of international law and argue that, at this very moment, whales either have or lack certain rights, we impose a pseudo-scientific existentiality on international law that does not and cannot capture the richness of what Thomas Franck has called the power of legitimacy of international law.[160]

Thus, while some may question whether we have "reached" the entitlement stage for whales, the very form of question is misleading. For if the final stage of entitlement results from progression through the previous stages, coupled with a sense that further development is inevitable because it is legitimate, an entitlement to life for whales is already implicit, in a fundamental sense, in international law. As the customary law process unfolds, the implicit can be expected to become explicit.

---

[158] Obviously, as stated, this proposal could lead to a form of social blackmail. To implement it fairly, one would have to take into account not the *continued* threat to allow hunters to hunt wild animals, but rather the *discounted* expectation of how long the animals would remain in existence to be hunted *given* their exploitation at the hands of hunters. The latter is a much more manageable price to pay, and is purely compensatory.

[159] *See* LON L. FULLER, THE LAW IN QUEST OF ITSELF (1940).

[160] *See* THOMAS FRANCK, THE POWER OF LEGITIMACY AMONG NATIONS (1990).

11

International Trade and Investment

A. Legislative Reach

1. General Principles[1]

In criminal law, legislative jurisdiction and judicial jurisdiction are one and the same. States do not apply foreign criminal law. But in civil law, legislative jurisdiction and judicial jurisdiction do not necessarily coincide. A court may have jurisdiction and yet apply foreign law; a State may legislate for cases which fall beyond the jurisdiction of its courts. Consequently the absence of limitations imposed by public international law on the judicial jurisdiction of States in civil cases does not necessarily indicate that there is a similar absence of limitations on legislative jurisdiction.

Limitations clearly exist as regards legislation in certain fields of what might loosely be described as public law, such as laws governing the methods of operating of public bodies. Only the State to which the body belongs can legislate for it. We may refuse to enforce a foreign judgment because we disapprove of the procedure followed by the foreign court, but we do not pass laws ordering the foreign court to follow a different procedure—to do so would be an intervention in the foreign State's domestic jurisdiction and a denial of its sovereignty and independence. For the same reasons, a State may not apply its law to the employment relationship between foreign States and their officials.

Limitations also apply to laws conferring sovereign or prerogative rights on the State, i.e. rights which cannot be exercised by private individuals in the State concerned. Tax is a good example; the power to tax can only be exercised by States, not by private individuals. Such laws can be applied against people who have a close connection with the State concerned. What counts as a close connection will vary from context to context; if a foreigner visits a State for a couple of days, the State would be entitled to require him to register with the police, but not entitled to conscript him into the army.

Customary international law permits a State to levy taxes only if there is a genuine connection between the State and the taxpayer (nationality, domicile, long residence, etc.), or between the State and the transaction or property in respect of which the tax is levied. This rule is necessary to protect States against one another; if a man is forced to pay taxes to a State with which he has little connection, he may not have enough money left to pay taxes to a State with which he has a real connection. The rule does not prevent double taxation (that can only be prevented by treaty), but it does restrict the number of States which may lawfully levy taxes.

The law against restrictive business practices (or, to use the convenient American term, antitrust law) is a source of great controversy and many problems concerning jurisdiction in international law. A preliminary problem concerns the classification of antitrust law. It has been suggested in the previous sections of this study[2] that international law imposes limits on the legislative jurisdiction of States as regards criminal law and laws concerned with the functioning of public bodies or with the sovereign rights of States, but not (at least as a general rule) as regards other areas of municipal law. Antitrust law is difficult to fit into this system, because breaches of its rules are usually sanctioned both by criminal proceedings and by civil proceedings. It is submitted, therefore, that the internationally permissible reach of antitrust law varies according to the nature of the proceedings instituted in any given case.

2. Countermeasures

a. An Expansive View[3]

The international arbitral tribunal in the U.S.-France Air Service Agreement dispute stated:

> In the Tribunal's view, it is essential, in a dispute between States, to take into account not only the

---

[1] By MICHAEL AKEHURST, excerpted from: Jurisdiction in International Law, 46 BRITISH YEAR BOOK OF INTERNATIONAL LAW 1, 179-80 (1972-73). Reprinted by permission.

[2] [Editor's Note: *See* "State Jurisdiction" in Chapter 6 of this Anthology.]

[3] By LORI FISLER DAMROSCH, excerpted from: *Retaliation or Arbitration—or Both? The 1978 United States-France Aviation Dispute*, 74 AMERICAN JOURNAL OF INTERNATIONAL LAW 785, 791-92, 807 (1980). Reprinted by permission.

injuries suffered by the companies concerned but also the importance of the questions of principle arising from the alleged breach. The Tribunal thinks that it will not suffice, in the present case, to compare the losses suffered by Pan Am on account of the suspension of the proposed services with the losses which the French companies would have suffered as a result of the countermeasures; it will also be necessary to take into account the importance of the positions of principle which were taken when the French authorities prohibited changes of gauge in third countries. If the importance of the issue is viewed within the framework of the general air transport policy adopted by the United States Government and implemented by the conclusion of a large number of international agreements with countries other than France, the measures taken by the United States do not appear to be clearly disproportionate when compared to those taken by France.[4]

This passage is interesting on several counts. First, it permits states to apply countermeasures that would be disproportionate in an economic sense, in order to enforce a principle. Second, it implies that considerations of principle are all the more weighty when third countries are watching. Figuring third-country reactions into the proportionality formula is novel but sensible, especially in the aviation context. Because of the worldwide network of essentially similar agreements, the way two states interpret and apply their bilateral agreement can have repercussions far beyond the particular case. And apart from questions of aviation practice or policy, a deliberate and effective response to a treaty violation can have, as the tribunal indicated, "an exemplary character directed at other countries": in other words, "the character of a sanction."[5] An overly niggardly approach to proportionality could conceivably detract from the importance of the retaliatory sanction as a deterrent to potential treaty violators. Under this reasoning, the injured party should have an adequate degree of flexibility in assessing the appropriate level of response and should not be subjected to ex post facto censure for having failed to achieve precise equivalence.

Under traditional doctrine, the legality of a retaliatory breach of treaty is judged by whether it is a proportional response to a prior material breach. Commentators have also suggested that states should refrain from implementing countermeasures until a tribunal rules on the existence of a breach, at least when there is a preexisting commitment to third-party dispute settlement.

But the experience of states must prove or disprove the soundness of propositions urged in legal debate. The actions of the United States and France, and the judgment of the tribunal they created,[6] suggest refinement or reexamination of some of the views put forth in legal literature. Proportionality might appropriately be judged on a flexible scale, with considerations of principle and of impact on the thinking of third countries as factors in the equation. Materiality of breach may not be relevant at all. Indeed, under some circumstances a responsive breach might be justified even absent a prior breach, if the responding party believes in good faith that a breach has occurred. Finally, since the interplay and even escalation of responses before a dispute reaches a tribunal can serve important purposes, that dynamic process should not be stifled by a blanket rule of abstention from self-help measures pending arbitration.

b. A Restrictive View[7]

The principle of sovereign equality gives every state the right to have international rules complied with, i.e., to remain in relation with the other states under the equivalent conditions set by international law. Such an analysis takes us back to a very basic legal idea, justice. Justice is primarily equality. Should this equality be distorted by a breach of law, justice calls for its re-establishment. States may have been placed in relation to each other in different situations, but a proportional equality must be maintained. Should this equality be disturbed, it must be redressed. Of course, it is beyond doubt that such a redress is at best guaranteed by the intervention of a third party as the judge. However, should this third party not be available or resort to this third party not be effective, any state is entitled to restore this proportional equality by using unilateral coercive measures, i.e., "countermeasures."

The main purpose of countermeasures is the exercise of pressure on another party to make it again comply with the law. If the measure precludes any possibility of a return to the status quo ante – that is, if its effects are final – then it cannot be regarded as a countermeasure. As long as the measure cannot be reversed, lifted or stopped, it is not a true countermeasure. Its purpose is no longer coercion, but

[4] *Case Concerning the Air Services Agreement of 27 March 1946, Arbitral Award of 9 December 1978,* 54 ILR 304, at para. 83 (1979).

[5] *Id.* at para. 78.

[6] [Editor's Note: The arbitral tribunal was composed of an arbitrator selected by the United States (Thomas Ehrlich), one selected by France (Paul Reuter), and a third arbitrator chosen by agreement of the parties (Willem Riphagen).]

[7] By ELISABETH ZOLLER, excerpted from: PEACETIME UNILATERAL REMEDIES: AN ANALYSIS OF COUNTERMEASURES 72–73, 96–98 (N.Y.: Transnational Publishers, 1984). Reprinted by permission.

the imposition of a harm which will not be taken back, i.e., a punishment.

The United States has employed countermeasures in its protective legislation, such as in the field of antitrust regulation. It has claimed extraterritorial jurisdiction because of detrimental effects on United States interests of an action implemented or merely contemplated abroad. The American claims rest on a very fragile legal ground. For the exercise of coercive power is authorized under international customary law only as a reaction against a wrongful act; international law does not grant states a coercive jurisdiction in itself. It is doubtful whether states on which the United States wishes to impose the extraterritoriality of its antitrust regulations can seriously be regarded as guilty of an internationally wrongful act; they are not under an obligation to protect United States interests. This means that the United States has no legitimate ground for dispensation from the basic territorial principle of jurisdiction.

3. Antitrust[8]

The friction caused by the international enforcement of American antitrust law is symptomatic of the fact that in this field, as elsewhere, the idea of a territorially-based national sovereignty clashes with the realities of international commerce. The crux of the matter is the lack of a law whose scope would be coterminous with the range of international transactions, and the absence of an international antitrust agency with worldwide jurisdiction. Faute de mieux, the territorial organization of this world leaves the regulation of transactions that are international in scope to national agencies, which apply their own law. In this respect, the problem is similar to that presented in conflict of laws cases, another field in which courts apply state law to international transactions. There is, however, a fundamental difference. While domestic courts can and do apply foreign private law, they do not normally enforce any regulatory legislation other than their own.

The Restatement (Third), like its predecessor, takes it for granted that domestic courts lack the power to apply foreign regulatory law. Accordingly, it purports to circumscribe the reach of domestic legislation, rather than to determine which law would most appropriately apply to a given transaction. In conflict of laws terminology, the Restatements' approach is "unilateralist." It is true that the Reinstatement (Third) makes a concession to multilateralism, attempting to resolve conflicts of regulatory laws by deferring to the state with the greatest interest. Yet, unlike truly multilateral rules, this provision does not call for the enforcement of foreign statutes. Rather, the court of the state having the lesser interest is required either to dismiss the case or to refuse to apply the domestic rule that provokes the conflicts with foreign policies or interests.

In the field of private law conflicts, history has shown that the unilateralist approach is unworkable because rules of decision do not reveal their spatial reach. The old attempt to classify laws into two categories – those that are "personal" (and therefore apply to citizens abroad) and those that are "real" (and therefore only apply to domestic events) – broke down. In Beale's words,

> every law has both a territorial and a personal application: and where a conflict arises, it is because one sovereign wishes to apply his own law to a juridical relation arising on his territory, while another wishes to throw around his subject, who is one of the parties to the relation, the protection of his personal law. Which of the two independent sovereigns should yield is a question not susceptible of a solution upon which all parties would agree).[9]

The foreign relations law restatements have attempted to cope with this predicament by hypothesizing that regulatory laws are both personal and territorial. At the same time, they have stretched the notion of territoriality to embrace the effects doctrine. This response, however, merely creates another predicament: any state that has a modicum of contacts with a given international transaction can, prima facie, regulate the transaction. Such a wide scope of prescriptive jurisdiction inevitably raises the specter of overlapping and conflicting regulation, a phenomenon that imposes burdens on international commerce and those who participate in it. As the experience with extraterritorial antitrust enforcement has shown it also causes friction between nations. Thus, instead of resolving problems, the notion of prescriptive jurisdiction provokes them.

There are two ways of dealing with this self-inflicted difficulty. One is to establish narrower, more specific criteria for prescriptive jurisdiction. In spite of various efforts in this direction, however, there is no general consensus on what jurisdictional bases are proper. On the contrary, the famous Lotus Case suggests that international law imposes few constraints on the permissible reach of domestic legislation and that nations may rely on the objective territorial principle. Looking at state practice, it appears that the effects test – although much maligned – has made headway outside the United States. As the Restatement (Third) notes,

---

[8] By FRIEDRICH K. JUENGER, excerpted from: *The "Extraterritorial" Application of American Antitrust Law and the New Foreign Relations Law Restatement*, 7 WIRTSCHAFT UND WETTBEWERB 602 (1990). Reprinted by permission.

[9] 3 J. BEALE, A TREATISE ON THE CONFLICT OF LAWS 1929 (1935).

the West German Act Against Restraints of Competition has cast this test into statutory form and the Court of Justice of the European Communities, after some hesitation, now apparently endorses the objective territorial principle.[10]

Thus, despite the friction it may cause among nations, it appears that neither international law nor international practice disfavor the effects test. The only alternative, then, is to recognize fairly broad jurisdictional bases, but to avoid conflicts by recognizing countervailing considerations that put a damper on the overly enthusiastic employment of those bases. This, of course, is what the Restatement (Third) attempts to do in section 403. But such an approach merely pushes the problem from one level to another. The attempt to specify sufficiently precise limitations poses the same difficulties as formulating narrower jurisdictional bases in the first place. The wording of section 403 ought to make it apparent just how intractable that task is. Unable to define the scope of the limits, the drafters had to entrust the matter to the decisionmaker's discretion. While they did list a hodgepodge of factors to be taken into account in exercising discretion, these factors are too disparate and open-ended to furnish much guidance in practical application. The restaters' valiant efforts reveal, at best, the uncomfortable truth that that branch of law is unrestatable.

4. The Restatement's New "Balancing Test"[11]

The Restatement of Foreign Relations Law (Third) asserts that balancing is a jurisdictional concept required by international law. According to Section 403:

> (1) A state may not exercise jurisdiction to prescribe a law with respect to the conduct, relations, status, or interests of persons or things having connections with another state or states when the exercise of such jurisdiction is unreasonable.
>
> Whether the exercise of jurisdiction is reasonable or unreasonable is judged by evaluating all the relevant factors, including, where appropriate:
>
> (a) the extent to which the activity (i) takes place within the regulating state, or (ii) has substantial, direct, and foreseeable effect upon or in the regulating state;
>
> (b) the links, such as nationality, residence, or economic activity, between the regulating state and the persons principally responsible for the activity to be regulated, or between that state and those whom the law or regulation is designed to protect;
>
> (c) the character of the activity to be regulated, the importance of regulation to the regulating state, the extent to which other states regulate such activities, and the degree to which the desirability of such regulation is generally accepted;
>
> (d) the existence of justified expectations that might be protected or hurt by the regulation in question;
>
> (e) the importance of the regulation in question to the international political, legal or economic system;
>
> (f) the extent to which such regulation is consistent with the traditions of the international system;
>
> (g) the extent to which such regulation is of the kind adopted by other states;
>
> (h) the extent to which another state may have an interest in regulating the activity;
>
> (i) the likelihood of conflict with regulation by other states.

Thus, under the Restatement, a court does not engage in the political function of deciding whether it should exercise a right which it has; it engages in legal function of determining whether it has that right at all. Decisions are no longer isolated exercises of discretion by individual judges, but are guided by previous decisions and are capable of forming precedent to guide future decisions. Through this process a body of experience can develop to provide predictability in the future application of the balancing principle. Moreover, putting the balancing test in a legal context avoids placing domestic judges in the position of foreign policy referees. Thus jurisdictional balancing remedies the set of problems associated with the non-legal nature of comity balancing.

Assigning to balancing a jurisdictional function, however, does not remedy another set of problems. In order to address the extraterritoriality issues effectively, a legal framework must be accepted and applied by other states as part of international law. In the case of balancing, such acceptance appears unlikely.

First, non-common law jurisdictions are generally reluctant to accord judges the wide discretion that is called for by a balancing approach. Civil law systems therefore are unlikely to accept balancing, at least in this unstructured form.

Moreover, despite the Restatement's attempt to ground balancing in the international law concept of reasonableness, balancing is not internationally derived. Rather, it is an approach borrowed from U.S. conflicts of law theory.

---

[10] *See* Ahlstrom Osakevhtio v. Commission of the European Communities, WuW/E, EWG/MUV 829.

[11] By DAVID J. GERBER, excerpted from: *Beyond Balancing: International Law Restraints on the Reach of National Laws*, 10 YALE JOURNAL OF INTERNATIONAL LAW 185, 206–09 (1985). Reprinted by permission.

The most critical problems of balancing, however, is its vagueness. Balancing national interests on the basis of an amorphous standard of reasonableness is unlikely to produce the predictability that is required to minimize jurisdictional conflicts. Any effective jurisdictional scheme must provide reasonable predictability, for uncertainty about what is permitted by international law is a major source of jurisdictional conflicts. No system can provide complete certainty, but to be effective it must provide reasonably clear guidelines. Balancing provides no such guidelines.

Moreover, balancing does not provide a basis for developing concreteness and predictability over time, because it lacks conceptual structure. It provides minimal guidance concerning the kinds of factors to be taken into consideration. Moreover, it says nothing about how these factors are to be evaluated and provides no standards by which these factors may be weighed against each other.

As a decisional model, balancing is not likely to be effective in the international jurisdictional context. Even in the context of domestic conflicts law, courts have acknowledged great difficulty in isolating policy factors in such a way as to allow predictable decision making. This is true even with respect to specific domestic issues such as the interest of a state in providing recovery in actions for wrongful death. In the international jurisdictional context the situations in which interests must be weighed are substantially more complex. The court must somehow balance one state's interest in regulation of foreign conduct against the right of another state to be free from interference.

It is not an effective solution to the problem to list factors that may have some relationship to an issue and to require a court to decide, after examining those facts, when U.S. interests are strong enough to justify the exercise of extraterritorial jurisdiction; it is only through the creation of a legal structure for evaluating such factors that they can be related to each other and to other cases in other situations and thereby become part of a process of law.

5. A Presumption in Favor of Extraterritoriality[12]

Public choice scholarship views "legislative rent-seeking" as conduct aimed at acquiring affirmative gifts through legislation of some good at a rate that a party could not have obtained in the market. Rent-seekers, however, can often achieve their designs through more surreptitious means, such as by securing the omission of critical legislative elements to negate a statutory objective. Such an opportunity arises in extraterritorial cases, in which a multinational interest can acquire a rent simply by forcing ambiguity in an otherwise transnational statute. Courts then become the unwitting instrument of rent-seeking when they exempt the multinational concern from regulation.

For a representative democracy, multinational interests in many ways embody the worst of Madisonian fears. The multinational acts as a special interest group that seeks legislative rents obtainable as easily through legislative inaction as through legislative action. For example, multinationals can avoid having to comply with environmental statutes by encouraging lawmakers to leave extraterritorial application of the acts ambiguous. A court-made presumption against extraterritoriality[13] will suffice to deliver on the hidden legislative deal.

Multinationals comprise a relatively small group of companies with homogeneous, defined, and concentrated interests. Multinational players have a large stake in securing legislative rents through limitations on employment, environmental, and other remedial statutes. They can easily coordinate their lobbying efforts.[14] They also have an advantage over many domestic groups in that United States citizens generally lack even the most fundamental information about transnational regulation. This information deficiency protects hidden deals by special interest groups. The informational and transactional costs are high when transnational interests are involved. Since most transnational regulatory decisions have very diffuse impacts on the population, there is generally no counteractive faction in Congress to oppose such interests beyond the occasional effort by organized labor or environmentalists. More importantly, the failure to regulate transnationally does not offer the same organizational potential for opposing groups as would an overt congressional decision to allow extraterritorial discrimination or pollution. The informational and transactional barriers severely frustrate attempts by citizens to sift through legislation to discover such hidden deals. Because of these costs, it is entirely possible for legislators to enact transnational special interest legislation without incurring any political backlash.

Eliminating the judicially created presumption against extraterritoriality would close this avenue for rent-seeking.

[12] By JONATHAN TURLEY, excerpted from: *Dualistic Values in the Age of International Legisprudence,* 44 HASTINGS LAW JOURNAL 185, 243-45, 259-60, 271 (1993). Reprinted by permission.

[13] *E.g.*, EEOC v. Arabian Am. Oil Co., 111 S.Ct 1227 (1991).

[14] *See* MANCUR OLSON, JR., THE LOGIC OF COLLECTIVE ACTION: PUBLIC GOODS AND THE THEORY OF GROUPS (1965); Jonathan Turley, *Transnational Discrimination and the Economics of Extraterritorial Regulation,* 70 B.U.L. Rev. 339, 355–56 (1990) (discussion of relation of Olson's work to transnational regulation).

Courts would then perform their traditional role in statutory interpretation. It might be argued that eliminating the presumption would simply create an incentive for the affected groups to seek rents in the courts, but it has never been shown that such rent-seeking is likely or even possible on a significant scale. Federal judges do not receive direct compensation from the parties to disputes, and life tenure reduces the value of such indirect benefits as campaign contributions or political action committee support. While multinational interests would clearly spend money to secure a "judicial rent," such activity would meet with counseled opposition. Any legislation presents the opportunity for some party to gain an advantage outside of either the market or a voluntary exchange. Although judicial rent-seeking is clearly more likely to occur today in the "age of regulation" than in years past, the institutional dangers of such activity pale in comparison to those presented by traditional legislative rent-seeking given the character of the adversarial process.

Courts already deal with extraterritoriality in the context of prescriptive jurisdiction or conflicts review in cases with expressly extraterritorial statutes. Courts now accept a legitimate institutional role of interpreting treaties and statutes in light of international conflicts, obligations, and norms. This recent shift in judicial attitudes is apparent in the narrowing of the political question doctrine as a bar to judicial review, the recognition of extraterritorial regulation in areas like antitrust and securities laws, and the preference given international sources under the last-in-time doctrine. Courts treat many of these "international sources" no differently than municipal sources for the purposes of judicial review. Courts have become the best – and perhaps only – institution for reconciling conflicts between municipal and international values. Thus, eliminating the judicially created presumption against extraterritoriality would simply require courts to deal directly with the international dimensions of statutory interpretation.

6. Export Controls[15]

Since the United States began after World War II to systematically restrict exports in peacetime for national security and foreign policy purposes, foreign opposition to the extraterritorial reach of American export controls has been rife. The most important reason why Canada, France, Britain, and other important trading partners have vigorously opposed the U.S. policy is simply the increasing frequency with which the U.S. has come to rely on export controls as instruments of its foreign policy. More specifically, however, extraterritorial regulation has become a recurrent problem because it reflects a fundamental economic phenomenon of the postwar years – the internationalization of major industrial sectors. Many important industries have come to be characterized by a multiplicity of well-established business networks linking firms in different countries. These networks take three principal (though interrelated) forms: international trading networks, technology transfer networks, and investment networks. American export controls have become enmeshed in all three.

1. *International Trading Networks*. Although foreign firms have been developing their technology and manufacturing capabilities quite rapidly, the United States remains the preferred or sole source for sophisticated components and services in a number of important sectors, including the energy industry. U.S.-origin goods thus flow along vast networks of international trade. The United States has correctly perceived that these trading networks can threaten the effectiveness of unilateral export controls. Without widespread international cooperation in a program of economic sanctions, foreign buyers of U.S.-origin goods are in a position to supply those goods to any target of American controls in direct substitution for restricted American exports. To avoid this result, the United States has long asserted the right to regulate not only exports from its territory but also reexports of goods shipped abroad.

2. *Technology Transfer Networks*. Rather than exporting their products, American manufacturers often find it advantageous to engage in foreign-based production. For example, many firms choose to transfer elements of their technology and "know-how" abroad through inter-firm or market transactions, typically licenses of technology. Licensing constitutes a significant proportion of all transactions by American firms relating to foreign production, with the licensees located overwhelmingly in the industrialized nations. Without governmental restrictions, foreign users of U.S.-origin technology can, to the extent permitted by their license agreements, retransfer the technology itself to countries that are targets of U.S. export controls. Foreign licensees can also supply goods produced with the aid of the technology to target countries, thus effectively supplanting U.S.-based exporters constrained by the controls. The U.S. reaction has been to legislate reexport controls that apply to retransfers of technology as well as transshipment of goods. The regulations also extend the concept of reexport to encompass foreign exports of goods that are products of U.S.-origin technology, even where the goods are manufactured abroad using foreign-source materials.

3. *Investment Networks*. The explosive growth of the

---

[15] By KENNETH W. ABBOTT, excerpted from: *Defining the Extraterritorial Reach of American Export Controls: Congress as Catalyst*, 17 CORNELL INTERNATIONAL LAW JOURNAL 79, 81, 90–99 (1984). Reprinted by permission.

multinational enterprise has been a post-World War II American phenomenon. A U.S. multinational enterprise establishes foreign production facilities by transferring its technology, capital, and organizational skill abroad in intrafirm transactions, primarily the establishment or acquisition of foreign subsidiaries. Subsidiaries are for the most part incorporated in the nations where they will conduct most of their operations, but the majority or entirety of their stock is owned by the U.S. parent company. If a subsidiary possesses the necessary capital and technology, it can substitute its production for that of its parent in the United States, thereby reducing the effectiveness of unilateral American export controls in much the same way as an independent foreign firm. To deal with these challenges, the United States has felt it necessary to extend the reach of its regulations to cover transactions by foreign subsidiaries and other affiliates.

Extraterritorial export controls create political and economic costs both for the nation imposing them and for affected third countries, and tend to reduce world economic welfare. These costs will be incurred as long as the United States continues to claim an extensive jurisdictional reach for its trade controls and foreign firms and governments continue to oppose its claims as improper.

7. Intellectual Property

a. Problems[16]

The products and services that should be protected by intellectual property law account for a significant portion of world trade. Inadequate protection today plays a major distorting role in that trade.

Government and industry estimates evaluate yearly losses from counterfeiters at about six to eight billion dollars, or an amount equivalent to five percent of the U.S. merchandise trade deficit of $175 billion. Individual industry estimates include $200 million lost annually by the agricultural chemical industry due to inadequate patent protection, and one billion dollars a year lost in computer software revenues.

A study demonstrated that, already in 1977, those American industries that marketed products dependent just on copyright protection contributed $55 billion, or 2.8 percent to the nation's GNP. It was recently estimated that $1.3 billion, over two percent of that production, is said to have been lost by these so-called "copyright industries" due to inadequate protection in just ten countries.

Nations often exploit their resources in ways that they believe benefit them, without too much attention to external effects. In the intellectual property arena many countries may fail to provide minimum protection or they may restrict rights obtainable under their domestic patent, copyright, and trademark laws to protect their own interests. Argentina does not grant patents for pharmaceutical products because its indigenous industry depends upon copies of foreign drugs. Brazil's patent law fails to protect food, drugs, and metal alloys for the same reason. Brazil also still limits the use of foreign intellectual property rights in industries such as computers in order to protect its own national computer industry.

A number of countries afford substandard or no copyright or trademark protection. Pirates and counterfeiters thereby find a haven to make and distribute worldwide unauthorized copies of legitimate goods. Because international trade involves multilateral relationships, protection of intellectual property must closely follow that network. For example, a U.S. company's market is affected by intellectual property rights in every country upon which it depends for either supplies or sales. So a U.S. recording company depends upon its U.S. copyrights and trademarks both to prevent infringement domestically and to bar entry of infringing imports. Overseas, that same U.S. company must seek protection against infringers who may market in that country and who may also export infringing manufacture from that country.

Just as the problems are complex, the current vehicles for treating them are inadequate. The concept of nondiscriminatory "national treatment," while generally a valuable concept, today may mean no protection at all in a number of countries. For the only "protection" that foreigners may receive in many countries is whatever minimal protection each country provides to its own nationals, and that is sometimes close to no protection at all.

The World Intellectual Property Organization administers major patent and trademarks, as well as copyright treaties. Although all the treaties on all three forms of protection prescribe how rights are obtained, the patent and trademark treaties do not set meaningful minimum standards for defining the acquisition and enforcement of intellectual property rights.

Current levels of protection and enforcement provided in Argentina, Brazil, Korea, Taiwan, Indonesia, and Singapore are not yet up to the standards available elsewhere. Little by little, one can detect a recognition in these countries that their own long-term interests can be served by stronger laws and enforcement. But the seriousness of the trade distortion caused by a combination of market reservation policies and weak protection of foreign copyright has led the United States to initiate trade countermeasures in some cases, notably Brazil and Korea.

---

[16] By KENNETH DAM, excerpted from: *The Growing Importance of International Protection of Intellectual Property*, 21 INTERNATIONAL LAWYER 627, 628–36 (1987). Reprinted by permission.

b. *Droit Moral*[17]

The doctrine of moral rights (*le droit moral*) protects the artist's spirit as embodied in his or her work. It accomplishes this by arming authors with extraordinary rights, most importantly the right to preserve the integrity of his or her work. In France, where the moral rights doctrine has been most highly developed, it is perceived as a natural and personal right rather than a purely legal right. This perception derives from the French belief that artists pour a part of their soul into their work, creating a personal link between themselves and their creations. Certain characteristics stem from the nature of the right. French law provides that moral rights are perpetual, inalienable, and non-seizable. French law thus differentiates art from other forms of property in order to protect intellectual and moral interests. Foreign artists may invoke the right in France, even if their home nations do not have moral rights laws of their own.

Under the law of droit moral as it has developed in France, authors retain all intellectual rights in a work even after they have sold it. The buyer may not transform or alter a work without the author's authorization. For example, a film distributor may not add a musical soundtrack to a silent film without obtaining the permission of the original author of the film or the author's estate. The author's permission is required in order for a television station to interrupt the film with commercials. In a leading case, a French court ruled, on the complaint of the original artist, that an auction house could not separately sell individual panels of an artwork comprised of six panels.[18]

Difficulties arise most often when authors authorize third parties to create adaptations of their work in other mediums (i.e., writers who permit film adaptations of their books) and are then dissatisfied with the results. While French courts have not found a single solution to this growing problem, courts have generally required the adapter to execute contractual obligations in good faith, and to refrain from distorting the original work with the intention of doing harm. These requirements force the trier of fact to judge aesthetics. By characterizing and comparing the artist's creations, the trier of fact must decide whether an adaptation damages the reputation of the author or the integrity of the author's original work.

[Despite the problems associated with *droit moral*, nations may be moving in the direction staked out by France.]

Commentators agree with the theoretical argument that all works of the mind should receive moral rights protection. Moral rights theory is gaining acceptance in the United States. With the enactment of the Visual Artists Rights Act of 1990, the United States has finally adopted a framework for providing moral rights protection to artists.[19] It is limited to visual works of art, excluding literary and musical works. But it also excludes audiovisual and computer works, as well as reproductions and copies of visual art works. The Act has a waiver provision, affording authors the right to renounce their moral rights. When compared to the French *droit moral*, the Visual Artists Rights Act falls short of its potential. But it may be a step towards eventual acceptance of the doctrine of *droit moral.*

B. Trade and the Environment[20]

Proposition 1: Protection of the environment has become exceedingly important, and promises to be more important for the benefit of future generations. Protecting the environment involves rules of international cooperation, sanction, or both, so that some government actions to enhance environmental protection will not be undermined by the actions of other governments. Sometimes such rules involve trade restricting measures.

Proposition 2: Trade liberalization is important for enhancing world economic welfare and for providing a greater opportunity for billions of individuals to lead satisfying lives. Measures that restrict trade often will decrease the achievement of this goal.

These two propositions state the opposing policy objectives that currently pose important and difficult dilemmas for governments. This type of "policy discord" is not unique; there are many similar policy discords, at both the national and the international levels, that governments must confront. Indeed, there is some evidence that environmental policy and trade policy are complementary, at least in the sense that increasing world welfare can lead to citizen demands and governmental actions to improve protection for the environment. The poorest nations in the world cannot afford such protection, but as welfare increases protection becomes more affordable.

An unfortunate development in public and interest group

---

[17] By JILL R. APPLEBAUM, excerpted from: *The Visual Artists Rights Act of 1990: An Analysis Based on the French* Droit Moral, 8 AMERICAN UNIVERSITY JOURNAL OF INTERNATIONAL LAW AND POLICY 183 (1993). Reprinted by permission.

[18] Buffet v. Fersing, Recueil Dalloz (D. Jur.) 570 (Cours d'appel Paris, May 30, 1962).

[19] 17 U.S.C. §§ 101, 106A. *See* Jane C. Ginsburg, *Copyright in the 101st Congress: Commentary on the Visual Artists Right Act and the Architectural Works Copyright Act of 1990,* 14 COLUM.-VLA J.L. & ARTS 477 (1990).

[20] By JOHN H. JACKSON, excerpted from: *World Trade Rules and Environmental Policies: Congruence or Conflict?* 49 WASHINGTON AND LEE LAW REVIEW 1227, 1227–28, 1255–59 (1992). Reprinted by permission.

attention to trade and the environment is the appearance of hostility between proponents of the two different propositions stated above. The hostility is misplaced because both groups will need the assistance and cooperation of the other group in order to accomplish their respective policy objectives. Of course, some of this tension is typical of political systems. Political participants often seek to achieve opposing objectives and goals. Each side may endorse legitimate goals, but when the goals clash, accommodation is necessary.

To some extent, the conflicts between the trade liberalization proponents and the environmental protection proponents derive from a certain "difference in cultures" between the trade policy experts and the environmental policy experts. Oddly enough, even when operating within the framework of the same society, these different "policy cultures" have developed different attitudes and perceptions of the political and policy processes, and these different outlooks create misunderstandings and conflict between the groups.

Is the relation between world trade system policies and environmental policies one of congruence or conflict? The answer obviously is a bit of both.

In the broader long term perspective there would seem to be a great deal of congruence. Some of that congruence derives from the economic and welfare enhancement of trade liberalization policies. Such welfare enhancement can in turn lead to enhancement of environmental policy objectives.

On the other hand, it is clear that the world trade policies and environmental policies do provide a certain amount of conflict. This conflict is not substantially different from a number of other areas where governmental policies have to accommodate conflicting aims and goals of the policy makers and their constituents. Thus, to some degree it is a question of where the line will be drawn, or how the compromises will be made. In that sense, institutions obviously become very important because the decision making process can tilt the decision results. If the world trade rules are pushed to their limit, for example, free trade with no exceptions for problems raised by environmental policies and actions affecting environments, clearly the trade rules will cause damage to environmental objectives. Likewise, if the environmental policies are pushed to their limit at the expense of the trading rules, so that governments will find it convenient and easy to set up a variety of restrictive trade measures, in some cases under the excuse of environmental policies, world trade will suffer.

Furthermore, there is no doubt that the "cultures" of the two policy communities: that of trade, and that of environment, differ in important ways. The trade policy experts have tended, over decades and perhaps centuries, to operate more under the practices of international diplomacy, which often means secrecy, negotiation, compromise, and to some extent behind the scenes catering to a variety of special economic interests. In addition, at the international level, because there is no over-arching "sovereign leader," the processes are slow, faltering, and lend themselves to lowest common denominator results, or to diplomatic negotiations that agree to language without real agreement on substance.

On the other hand, the environmental policy groups, perhaps partly because they primarily operate on the national scene, have become used to using the processes of publicity and lobbying pressure on Congress or Parliaments, to which they have considerable access. There is, thus, a much broader sense of "participation" in the process, which the international processes have not yet accommodated. Furthermore, the environmental policy groups, like many other groups working on the domestic level, have a sense of power achieved through successes in the legislative and public discussion processes. They feel somewhat frustrated with the international processes because those are sufficiently different to pose puzzling obstacles to the achievement of environmental goals.

This difference in culture is not inevitably permanent, and indeed the international processes need to accommodate more transparency and participation. This is true not only of the environmental case, but it is increasingly an important consideration for the broader way that international economic interdependence is managed. As more and more decisions that affect firms, citizens, and other groups, are made at the international level, it will be necessary for the international decision making process to accommodate the goals of transparency, adequate expertise, and participation in the advocacy and rule making procedures.

To some extent, the rhetoric of some environmental policy advocates has been the rhetoric of antagonism to international organizations and procedures altogether. This, I suggest, is not constructive. The notion that the United States, for example, can, or should impose unilaterally its environmental views and standards on other parts of the world, without any constraint from international rules or international dispute settlement procedures, is not likely to be a viable approach in the longer run. This means that in some cases when the United States submits (as it must, partly so as to reciprocally get other countries to submit) to international dispute settlement procedures, it will sometime lose, and find itself obliged to alter its own domestic policy preferences. This has already been the case, and the United States has a mixed record of compliance with GATT rulings, although for a large powerful nation that record is not too bad.

Apart from these longer run and institutional issues, there are matters that can be undertaken jointly by the trade and environmental policy communities, in the context of the GATT/MTO[21] system. It seems feasible for the international trading system to accommodate some of the following actions or goals:

1) Greater transparency both in the rule making and in the dispute settlement procedures of the trading system. This would call for more participation, greater opportunity for policy advocacy inputs, and for more openness in terms of publication of the relevant documents faster and in a way more accessible to interested parties;

2) Greater access to participation in the processes,

3) Some clarification is needed about the degree to which the international process will be allowed to intrude upon the scope of decision making of national and sub-national governments.

In the longer run, there needs to be some clarification about the rules and exceptions to accommodate national governmental unilateral imposition of environmentally justified rules that require or provide incentive for a higher standard of environmental protection than that for which the international community is able to develop a consensus.

It would be tragic if increased antagonism between the two policy groups occurred in such a way that the essential policy goals of both groups would be damaged unnecessarily.

C. Exhaustion of Local Remedies[22]

The principle of international law by virtue of which the alien is deemed to tacitly submit and to be subject to the local law of the state of residence implies as its corollary that the remedies for a violation of his rights must be sought in the local courts. Almost daily the U.S. Department of State has occasion to reiterate the rule that a claimant against a foreign government is not usually regarded as entitled to the diplomatic interposition of his own government until he has exhausted his legal remedies in the appropriate tribunals of the country against which he makes claim. There are several reasons for this limitation upon diplomatic protection: first, the citizen going abroad is presumed to take into account the means furnished by local law for the redress of wrongs; secondly, the right of sovereignty and independence warrants the local state in demanding for its courts freedom from interference, on the assumption that they are capable of doing justice; thirdly, the home government of the complaining citizen must give the offending government an opportunity of doing justice to the injured party in its own regular way, and thus avoid, if possible, all occasion for international discussion; fourthly, if the injury is committed by an individual or a minor official, the exhaustion of local remedies is necessary to make certain that the wrongful act or denial of justice is the deliberate act of the state; and fifthly, if it is a deliberate act of the state, that the state is willing to leave the wrong unrighted. It is a logical principle that where there is a judicial remedy, it must be sought. Only if a judicial remedy sought in vain and a denial of justice established, does diplomatic protection become proper.

D. The Calvo Doctrine[23]

During the later nineteenth and earlier twentieth centuries, disturbed political conditions in the newer States of Latin America gave rise to a steady stream of complaints of injuries to foreigners, and to occasional resort to armed intervention to enforce demands for redress. Lack of confidence in local standards of justice generated a frequently arrogant refusal by foreigners to resort to local remedies, and increased resort to diplomatic protection by foreign States. To the celebrated Argentine jurist Carlos Calvo, the institution of diplomatic protection seemed a weapon of strong, and frequently expansionist, States against the weak. From his writings were developed practices by which Latin American States attempted by treaty, constitutional provision, statute and contracts with aliens to secure observance of the rule of exhaustion of local remedies and to restrain diplomatic interposition.

Treaties by which Latin American States sought to limit their international responsibility for damage to aliens to a restricted form of denial of justice are exemplified by Article 6 of the treaty of July 16, 1897, between Spain and Peru, which provided:

> Spaniards in Peru and Peruvians in Spain shall enjoy the same civil rights as citizens or subjects. Spaniards in Peru or Peruvians in Spain shall not be entitled to diplomatic intervention except in the event of a manifest denial of justice, that is failure or negligence in the administration of it.

---

[21] [Editor's Note: GATT stands for General Agreement on Tariffs and Trade; MTO stands for Multilateral Trade Organization.]

[22] By EDWIN M. BORCHARD, excerpted from: THE DIPLOMATIC PROTECTION OF CITIZENS ABROAD OR THE LAW OF INTERNATIONAL CLAIMS 817–18 (1915).

[23] By HERBERT W. BRIGGS, excerpted from: THE LAW OF NATIONS 637–39 (2d ed. 1952) (N.Y.: Appleton-Century Crofts). Reprinted by permission.

Constitutional and statutory provisions, ostensibly attempting to secure observance of the rule of exhaustion of local remedies, have frequently gone so far as to repudiate responsibility and to deny the right of diplomatic protection. A Salvadorean law of September 29, 1886, provided, in Article 39, that:

> Foreigners may appeal to diplomatic intervention only in the event of a denial or of a willful delay in the administration of justice,

but then added in Article 40:

> By denial of justice is to be understood only the case where the judicial authority refuses to make a formal declaration upon the principal subject or upon any incident of the suit in which he may have cognizance or which is submitted to his cognizance. Consequently, the fact alone that the Judge may have pronounced a decision or sentence, in whatever sense it may be, although it may be said that the decision is iniquitous or given in express violation of law, cannot be alleged as a denial of justice.

This law was protested by the British Government, the United States Government, and the diplomatic corps in Salvador as at variance with the right of diplomatic protection under international law. Similar constitutional or statutory provisions were characterized by Alwyn V. Freeman as "the congenitally defective spawn of an illegitimate attempt to limit all exercise of diplomatic protection to the single hypothesis of a denial of justice."

E. The Calvo Clause[24]

A contract between an alien and a foreign government may contain a stipulation known as a "Calvo Clause," by which the alien promises that he would have resort only to local remedies and local law in disputes arising out of the contract and that he waives his rights as an alien. A typical clause reads:

> The contractor and all persons who, as employees or in any other capacity may be engaged in the execution of the work under this contract, shall be considered as Mexicans in all matters, within the Republic of Mexico, concerning the execution of such work and the fulfillment of this contract. They shall not claim, nor shall they have, with regard to the interests and the business connected with this contract, any other rights or means to enforce the same than those granted by the laws of the Republic to Mexicans, nor shall they enjoy any other rights than those established in favor of Mexicans. They are consequently deprived of any rights as aliens, and under no conditions shall the intervention of foreign diplomatic agents be permitted, in any matter related to this contract.

To the extent that a Calvo Clause requires resort to local remedies, it is merely confirmatory of the rule of international law requiring exhaustion of local remedies. However, to the extent that it pretends to cause a surrender of the rights of the claimant's State under international law or to oust the jurisdiction of an international tribunal, the Calvo Clause is without legal effect. Thus the Clause is either superfluous or irrelevant.

However, instead of uniformly refusing to uphold the validity of the Clause as a bar to an international claim, international tribunals have exhibited considerable confusion, even to the extent of declining, because of a Calvo Clause, jurisdiction conferred upon the tribunal by international agreement to entertain claims allegedly based on municipal law. Imbued with the not unworthy idea that the individual who makes a contract should be held to its terms, international courts have tended to disregard the fact that by means of a Calvo Clause certain States have unworthily sought to deny their responsibility under international law. Some courts have upheld the validity of the Clause by interpreting it narrowly as a mere obligation to submit matters of private law to the local courts. Since the Clause occurs only in contracts, and the mere breach of contract by a government has not generally been regarded as a violation of international law,[25] it has been easy for international courts to assign the Calvo Clause as a local contractual reason for dismissal of the case, avoiding the question of the international rule requiring the exhaustion of local remedies.

F. Espousal of Claims[26]

The topic of "espousal of claims" is directly related to the Calvo Clause and the Calvo Doctrine, discussed above.

Suppose that Ms. Smith, a citizen of Supra, is invited

---

[24] By HERBERT W. BRIGGS, excerpted from: THE LAW OF NATIONS 639, 648–50 (2d ed. 1952) (N.Y.: Appleton-Century Crofts). Reprinted by permission.

[25] [Editor's Note: While this statement is of course generally true, a contract between an alien and a foreign government is better termed a "concession agreement," pointing up the fact that one of the parties is overwhelmingly more powerful than the other and indeed can make (and change) the local law. As a consequence, international customary law has been moving, hesitantly, in the direction of regarding a concession agreement as something more than a private contract, and its breach as having at least some international law implications.]

[26] By ANTHONY D'AMATO, adapted with modifications from: INTERNATIONAL LAW: PROCESS AND PROSPECT 194–99 (N.Y.: Transnational Publishers, 1987). Reprinted by permission.

by the government of Infra to set up a travel agency in Infra that will handle international travel by government employees. Ms. Smith is offered this exclusive five-year contract because of her expertise in the travel business. Assume further that she is told she will not get the contract unless she signs a contract containing a Calvo Clause similar to the one quoted in the previous excerpt by Professor Briggs. Since she wants the business, she signs the contract with the Government of Infra. There is no arbitration clause or any other dispute resolution mechanism specified in the contract. Ms. Smith moves to Infra and sets up her business there.

After a year and a half, one of her employees who has learned the travel business from Ms. Smith decides to leave and set up his own travel agency. He then begins to get travel business from employees of the Infra government, who used to be customers of Ms. Smith. Although the government of Infra made no announcement that its employees should divert their travel business to the newcomer, the government abruptly stops providing the arrival and departure schedules of its government-owned airline to Ms. Smith. Without this essential information, Ms. Smith slowly loses her entire customer base. She sues Infra in an Infran court for the loss of three and a half years of expected profits under her exclusive contract.

The court holds (and its holding is upheld on appeal) that there was no breach of contract, because the State did not direct its employees to go to a different travel agency. In response to Ms. Smith's plea that the intentional deprivation of travel scheduling information ruined her business, the court finds that there was no explicit clause in her contract requiring the government to provide her with scheduling information for its own airline, and that the government was within its power to withhold such information from any particular person for national security reasons.

Ms. Smith has gotten nowhere in the Infran judicial system. But we can ask: is the state of Supra barred, by virtue of the Calvo Clause that Ms. Smith signed, from espousing her claim against Infra?

An immediate problem is the question itself. What do we mean by "espousing her claim"? Many people, sometimes even international lawyers, get confused by assuming that these words mean what they say. What does "espousing" mean? And even if we figure out what it means, what does "her claim" mean? When we unravel these words, we will find that, under classic international law, whatever Supra may be doing, it is *not* espousing Ms. Smith's claim!

Under the strict logic of classical international law, Ms. Smith's claim has absolutely no legal relation to any claim that Supra might lodge against Infra relating to Ms. Smith's situation. Ms. Smith has her own claim (the one she pursued in the Infran courts); Supra has its own claim; the two are not related legally, even though they may be based on the same set of facts. And this logic furnishes us the answer to the previously asked question. The answer is Yes and No. Yes, Supra may bring its own claim against Infra; the fact that Ms. Smith signs a Calvo Clause cannot bar Supra from bringing its own claim. The reasons are simple: it's Supra's own claim, Supra did not sign any Calvo clause, and Ms. Smith is not an official agent of Supra authorized to waive claims on behalf of her state. So, any claim Supra may have cannot be modified or waived by anything Ms. Smith signs. But the answer is also No. Supra is not espousing Ms. Smith's own claim. Why? Consider for a moment what would be entailed by Supra's taking over Ms. Smith's own claim. Such a take-over would amount to an expropriation of Ms. Smith's property – that is, her property interest in her own claim. Then, under its own Constitution, Supra might have to pay Ms. Smith the fair market value of her expropriated claim. States like Supra do not typically do any such thing, but I am spelling it out to clarify the legal picture. Since Supra has not expropriated Ms. Smith's own claim, Ms. Smith's own claim remains unaffected by anything Supra does. That's why it isn't *her* claim that Supra is "espousing."

We can see, therefore, that "espousal" is a misleading word. Supra doesn't "espouse" Ms. Smith's claim, nor does it take her claim over, or do anything else about her claim. If Supra brings a claim against Infra based on the facts of Ms. Smith's situation, it is Supra's own claim that it brings, and not Ms. Smith's claim.

To be sure, there is no serious harm done if we understand the word "espousal" in this limited, technical and qualified manner. Technically, Supra brings its own claim against Infra based on the facts of its national's claim. But isn't it a strange and misleading way of talking to say that Supra is "espousing Ms. Smith's claim"? Her *own* claim, as we have seen, is not involved at all.

Let's to follow the logic of classical international law to its relentless conclusion. If Supra's claim is its own, and not Ms. Smith's, then surely its damages, if any, are its own damages and not Ms. Smith's damages. So, if it ever collects monetary damages against Infra, Supra can put the damages in its national treasury and say something like "thanks Ms. Smith for providing us with a basis for adding to the national wealth."

Suppose Supra lodges a diplomatic protest with Infra over the treatment Ms. Smith received, and suppose further that Infra – because it needs Supra's support in various important matters of foreign policy – says to Supra, "How much money will solve the problem?" Let's say Supra asks for $150,000 in damages. Infra asks, "Why do you want $150,000?" and Supra replies, "Because that's what we figure to be the contract damages suffered by Ms.

Smith – her reasonably projected profit over the remaining life of the contract if Infra hadn't breached." Suppose that Infra writes a check for that amount payable to Supra, and Supra deposits the check in its national treasury.

You're Ms. Smith's attorney and you complain to the government of Supra that the money should be paid over to your client. You point out that, after all, the damages were measured by Ms. Smith's contractual losses. So, it's really *her* money. But, under the classical theory, Supra can reply, "It's true, we used Ms. Smith's contract losses to measure damages, but that was only because it was a convenient measure to use. Instead we could have asked Infra to fire off a twenty-one gun salute to our country. That would have salvaged our national pride, and would have been adequate damages for *our* claim. Don't forget, Infra paid us for *our* claim and not for Ms. Smith's claim!"

However, a persistent attorney should be able to get the money for Ms. Smith. Most countries in Supra's position will pay over the damages to their national who was injured, even though they are not under any legal requirement to do so.

Finally, is there any way that Infra could have avoided the result of having Supra demand damages on behalf of Ms. Smith? We have seen that a "Calvo Clause" doesn't do the job, because Supra is not bound by anything that Ms. Smith signed. But why, exactly, is Supra allowed to protest at all? Supra's protest is allowed because Ms. Smith is a national of Supra. Therefore, if Infra wants to get Supra entirely out of the picture, it has to do something about Ms. Smith's nationality.

Here's what Infra could do. Infra at the outset of its negotiations with Ms. Smith could have said: "If you move to our country and set up a travel agency business, we require that you make a voluntary renunciation of your Supran nationality, and apply immediately to become a national of Infra. We promise you that you will get your Infran citizenship papers in two weeks." There is nothing wrong with Infra making it a condition of Ms. Smith's contract that Ms. Smith renounce her Supran citizenship and become a citizen of Infra; after all, Ms. Smith doesn't have to accept the deal.

Some Latin American countries, toward the end of the nineteenth century, in fact pushed the Calvo Doctrine to this extreme. They required the foreign contractor, whom they lured by offering an exclusive contract with huge profit potential, to renounce his or her former citizenship and become their national. This tactic actually worked. If, for example, Ms. Smith had renounced her Supran nationality, then Supra would have had no basis to complain about Infra's subsequent treatment of Ms. Smith. There would have been no "nationality link" between Ms. Smith and Supra.

But, historically, the tactic worked too well. It discouraged foreign contractors from applying for jobs. Only under extreme circumstances did anyone wish to renounce his or her citizenship in order to move to a foreign country to take up a business deal. And so, gradually, this extreme version of the Calvo Doctrine atrophied.

G. A Letter Requesting Espousal[27]

April 29, 1991

The Honorable Edwin Williamson
Legal Adviser
United States Department of State
2100 K Street, N.W.
Washington, DC 20037-7180

Re: REQUEST FOR ESPOUSAL OF CLAIMS

Dear Mr. Williamson:

I am writing on behalf of my clients Scott and Vivian Nelson to request espousal of their claims by the United States against the Kingdom of Saudi Arabia.

Their claims are summarized by the Court of Appeals for the Eleventh Circuit in *Nelson v. Saudi Arabia,* 923 F.2d 1528 (11th Cir. 1991), and more particularly in their Complaint contained in the Record Excerpts in that case, copies of which are in the possession of the Department of Justice, c/o Stuart M. Gerson, Esq., and, I believe, in the files of Linda Jacobson, Esq., in your office.

I make this formal request with the clear understanding, as you undoubtedly know better than anyone else in the country, that espousal of the Nelsons' claims is legally irrelevant to their private litigation against Saudi Arabia, King Faisal Specialist Hospital, and Royspec. The espousal of claims on the international level is a government-to-government matter, in which individuals are not parties. Any reparations that you may obtain from the Kingdom of Saudi Arabia are not necessarily measurable under international law by the actual damages incurred by Scott and Vivian Nelson; rather, they reflect the degree of injury suffered by the United States, perhaps approximated by the actual injuries suffered by the Nelsons. Any monies that may be paid over to the United States as a result of your successful espousal of the Nelsons' claims are not, as a matter of international law, required to be paid to the Nelsons. Whether such monies are actually paid over to the injured parties in nation-to-nation claim espousals is relegated by international law to domestic legislation and practice.

---

[27] By ANTHONY D'AMATO, from: Respondent's Brief in Opposition for Petition for Writ of Certiorari, Petition for Writ of Certiorari to the United States Court of Appeals For the Eleventh Circuit, Supreme Court of the United States, Oct. term 1991, No. 91-522, Appendix A, at 1a.

The fact that a government-to-government espousal of the claims of private citizens has no legal relevance to private litigation of the type that the Nelsons are currently pursuing, is in the interest of both parties. The Nelsons will not be legally disadvantaged in their private litigation if, despite your best efforts, you are unable to obtain redress on the diplomatic front from the Kingdom of Saudi Arabia. Similarly, if Saudi Arabia responds to your diplomatic efforts by paying damages to the United States, that fact will have no negative legal implication respecting Saudi Arabia's defenses to the Nelsons' claims in the private litigation.

To be sure, if damages are obtained as the result of your successful espousal of the Nelsons' claims, I will stipulate as follows: Any monies recovered by the United States and actually paid over to the Nelsons will be deducted from the amounts, if any, that the Nelsons may obtain against Saudi Arabia, King Faisal Specialist Hospital, and/or Royspec, by virtue either of a settlement entered into between the parties (whether or not facilitated by your good offices) or by virtue of successful prosecution of the Nelsons' claims upon remand to the federal district court.

As far as the Nelsons' continued pursuit of their claims against Saudi Arabia in American courts is concerned, you have already taken the position that American courts are an inappropriate forum. You are urging the Court of Appeals to reverse its decision in the Nelson Case. In light of your clear position on this question, the Department of State surely cannot delay its decision to espouse the Nelsons' claims on the ground that there is pending litigation in a forum which it regards as inappropriate. Moreover, American courts are not "local remedies" under international law with respect to the principle of exhaustion of local remedies, even though under the Foreign Sovereign Immunities Act the Nelsons are clearly entitled to remedies in a private commercial litigation against a non-immune sovereign defendant. Finally, the United States is not party to the case of *Nelson v. Saudi Arabia* in American courts. Indeed, it is my opinion that the Executive Branch of the United States lacks even a colorable "interest" in that litigation.

The Department of State was made aware of the Nelsons' claims in October, 1984. Considering the number of years that have elapsed, the Department of State has had ample time to assess the Nelsons' claims. May I remind you that you mentioned the possibility that the Department of State may espouse the Nelsons' claims, depending on the resolution of the question of exhaustion of local remedies, in your letter of March 25, 1991, to His Excellency Bandar bin Sultan, Ambassador of the Kingdom of Saudi Arabia.

Please permit me to summarize the requests of Mr. and Mrs. Nelson to the espousal of their claims by the United States, and to comment on the question of the exhaustion of local remedies in each instance. I make the following remarks to some extent on the basis of information conveyed to me by Mr. and Mrs. Nelson, but without detailed study of the voluminous records, memos, and tape recordings currently in their possession. If necessary, I will make such a study. I would expect, however, that the general points that I shall make will accord with the information in your own files. In any event, I make the following representations in good faith, subject to corroboration and correction, if necessary, by the documentary evidence.

1. The Claims of Vivian Nelson

Vivian Nelson's claims are summarized by the Eleventh Circuit, 923 F.2d at 1530. Her claims are detailed in the Complaint to which I referred earlier. While separate and distinct from her husband's claims, Mrs. Nelson's claims arise from similar underlying facts and are inextricably intertwined with the claims of her husband.

On the question of Mrs. Nelson's exhaustion of local remedies, I quote from my recently filed motion to exclude your Statement of Interest in *Nelson v. Saudi Arabia:*

> Vivian Nelson is a co-Appellant in the present case. Her claim is inseparable from that of her husband. The Department of State must be charged with awareness that there is no "appropriate forum" in Saudi Arabia for Mrs. Nelson because she would be deprived of elementary due process of law in any Saudi court. A woman's testimony in a Saudi court is valued at only one-half that of a man's testimony. See Department of State, *Country Reports on Human Rights Practices for 1989* at 1557 (legal practices in Saudi courts).

If Mrs. Nelson were to seek private redress in a Saudi court against the man who told her that he would sponsor her husband's release from prison in return for sexual favors, what chance would she have of prevailing in her claim against him when his testimony is accorded, by Saudi law and practice, double the value of her testimony?

As you know, the Department of State and the Department of Justice filed a Statement in opposition to my motion, taking issue with all of the points I raised except the point about Mrs. Nelson. Your brief is conspicuously and glaringly silent about Mrs. Nelson's claim. Its silence leaves an uncomfortable gap in the Court of Appeals' ability to evaluate the statement your Department made that the Department retains the option of espousing the plaintiffs' claims against Saudi Arabia pending the resolution of the question of exhaustion of local remedies. And it leaves co-plaintiff Mrs. Nelson in the dark as well.

I am confident that the Department of State would agree with me that Mrs. Nelson does not deserve to be treated as a non-person. I am sure that the Department of State will appreciate that her claim, recognized by the Eleventh Circuit in its opinion of February 21, 1991, is as worthy of consideration on the diplomatic level by the government of the United States as is her husband's claim.

In short, I believe that Vivian Nelson, a law-abiding citizen of the United States, is entitled to a yes or no answer to the following question: Does the Department of State insist that Vivian Nelson must first exhaust local remedies in a foreign court system that values her testimony at one-half that of a man's testimony before it will undertake to espouse her claim against the Kingdom of Saudi Arabia?

I would appreciate your letting me know your answer so that I can communicate it to Mrs. Nelson.

I would very much hope that your answer to the question will be in the negative, and that you will undertake forthwith to espouse Mrs. Nelson's claims against Saudi Arabia. In light of the six and a half years that have passed, the full and continuing notice that the Department of State has been given about the Nelsons' claims, the exhaustion of the Nelson's family assets, and their plunge into extreme indebtedness to cover Mr. Nelson's hospital bills, any further delay just for the sake of delay would surely be regrettable.

2. The Claims of Scott Nelson

Scott Nelson's claims, like those of his wife, are summarized in the opinion of the Court of Appeals for the Eleventh Circuit and detailed in his Complaint filed with the district court and incorporated in the Record Excerpts filed with the Court of Appeals.

The Department of State has been aware of his claims ever since he was released from a Saudi prison in 1984 through the intervention of Senator Kennedy. Mr. Nelson has consistently and persistently petitioned your Department for its help and assistance in obtaining redress from the Kingdom of Saudi Arabia.

Upon his return to the United States in 1984, Mr. Nelson obtained from the Department of State a list of seventeen Saudi lawyers or law firms who might pursue his claim in Saudi courts. He wrote to each of them. Five responded by telephone, declining his case. Three responded by letter, declining his case. The others did not respond.

Any attempt by Mr. Nelson to pursue his claims in a Saudi court would be heavily dependent upon the existence of substantial documentary evidence. Many original documents, memos, telegrams, official papers, and other evidence were compiled and stored in the United States Embassy in Riyadh, Saudi Arabia. However, in 1987, that Embassy destroyed Mr. Nelson's entire file. In your Department's opposition to my Motion filed with the Eleventh Circuit, you have claimed that the Riyadh documents "were destroyed pursuant to routine embassy security procedures," and added that the State Department "has maintained files on the Nelson matter in its facilities in Washington, D.C." It would appear, however, that if the Department cared about helping Mr. Nelson it would prevented the occurrence of the purported "routine procedures." Moreover, the files that have been "maintained" in Washington D.C. do not contain copies of the original evidence that was destroyed in Riyadh. It is quite evident that Mr. Nelson's ability to pursue local remedies in Saudi courts has been substantially impaired by the deliberate destruction of his files.

Several years later, your Department again urged Mr. Nelson to get a Saudi lawyer to prosecute his claims. The Department presented to Mr. Nelson a list of seventeen attorneys to contact who might help him in Saudi courts. According to Mr. Nelson, the list was identical to the list that had been given to him years earlier. Nevertheless, he wrote again to each of the attorneys on the list. He obtained the same negative results. All that was accomplished was a further deterioration of his financial assets and human spirit. One attorney Mr. Scott contacted, Haig V. Kalbian, wrote directly to Mr. John Knox of the International Claims section of your Department, on April 6, 1989. Mr. Kalbian said, "No Saudi attorney that I am aware of would jeopardize his practice, and some would argue his life to take on such a case."

Quite apart from the question of exhaustion of local remedies is the issue of whether Mr. Nelson in fact was tortured. In your Statement of Interest filed with the Court of Appeals, there is a statement on page 4 that "The record reveals, however, that there is sharp disagreement regarding the facts underlying plaintiffs' claims." Then after referring to the issue of exhausting local remedies, the Statement of Interest goes on to say, "the United States retains the option of espousing plaintiffs' claims against Saudi Arabia—if it finds them to have merit—as an official matter between the two governments" (at p. 5). The juxtaposition of these two sentences gives rise to the clear inference that your Department is skeptical about whether Mr. Nelson was in fact tortured.

I am at a loss to imagine where that skepticism comes from, since Mr. Nelson has consistently provided you with copies of medical records and reports detailing his medical evaluations and treatments. If your Department has failed to read those reports, then it should not have communicated to the Court of Appeals, even by inference, its skepticism about the merits of Mr. Nelson's claims. Such a communication can be highly prejudicial to the rights of one party in an entirely private litigation. The Court of Appeals might naturally assume that your Department, after six and a half years of persistent appeals for help by Mr. Nelson, would only write the two sentences above quoted, with their skeptical implication, if the Department had some evidence in its possession upon which to base its skepticism. On the other hand, if it was not your intention to convey to the Court of Appeals the suggestion that after six and a half years you have reason to be skeptical about the merits of Mr. Nelson's claims, then I respectfully suggest that you might consider removing the prejudicial impact of that implication by a letter addressed to the Court.

There can be no real question that Mr. Nelson was in fact tortured. The proof is incontrovertible. You have most of it in your possession. Please allow me to recapitulate the main points.

Let us first consider whether there is any medical evidence that Mr. Nelson was *not* tortured. I have asked this question of the attorneys for the Kingdom of Saudi Arabia. They have provided me with the sole document upon which they rest their entire case that Mr. Nelson was not tortured. It is a 7-page report by Ledford Gregory, a doctor hired by Hospital Corporation of America in connection with the case of *Nelson v. Hospital Corp. of America*. Dr. Gregory examined Scott Nelson on January 27, 1990. Mr. Nelson says that the examination lasted fifteen minutes. Dr. Gregory reviewed some of Mr. Nelson's medical records, noting that there were many critical records that he had not read. He reported that there had been arthroscopic procedures in the internal knee joints. Dr. Gregory suggested that Mr. Nelson's pain is exaggerated, but he did not conclude that Mr. Nelson had not been tortured.

In contrast, Mr. Nelson has been examined by at least nine doctors, has undergone invasive reconstitutive knee surgery three times, and is presently diagnosed as requiring additional knee surgery. Mr. Nelson has provided you with the depositions of two doctors who have thoroughly examined him over a period of time. Dr. Dan R. Chartier, a psychologist and psychophysiologist in North Carolina and a clinical assistant professor in the School of Medicine at the University of North Carolina in Chapel Hill, in a 112-page deposition, found that Mr. Nelson experienced post-traumatic stress syndrome such as that of some Vietnam war veterans. This was measured by muscular contractions in terms of microvolt readings, and galvanic skin responses measured in micromode conductance. Dr. Alan Spanos, a physician specializing in the management of chronic pain, graduated from Oxford University and has taught and done research at Duke Medical Center. In his 121-page deposition, he testified that Mr. Nelson has a diffuse nerve injury causing his brain to receive messages of intense pain. He stated that his findings were consistent with the process of torture that Mr. Nelson described. Dr. Spanos said that Mr. Nelson's injuries were unlikely to have been caused by a car accident or a sports injury, because those injuries produce localized, and not diffuse, conditions. Mr. Nelson had gross derangements in the knees, according to Dr. Spanos. In sports injuries, there would be signs of the knee being forcefully struck from the side. In Mr. Nelson's case, however, the internal "clockwork" of the knees was deranged without external evidence of trauma. His injuries would be consistent with a pulling injury to the knee which would not do much damage to the outside structures but which could damage the internal structures. Mr. Nelson had a partially torn lateral meniscus, a partially torn anterior cruciate ligament and chronic synovitis (internal inflammation). Dr. Spanos observed that these injuries were partially corrected by invasive reconstitutive surgery.

Most importantly, there are two wholly objective evaluations—one medical, the other legal—that furnish as convincing a proof of Mr. Nelson's torture as could be furnished for anyone's torture. The first is a report, a copy of which Mr. Nelson sent to your Department, of the Center for Victims of Torture, a Minneapolis non-profit corporation. Mr. Nelson was thoroughly evaluated by the Center in April, 1990. I would like to quote for you the summary report of Dr. Barbara Chester:

> Scott Nelson was initially seen at the Center For Victims of Torture on April 9, 1990. In addition to an initial screening and intake interview conducted by the Center's clinical director (Barbara Chester, Ph.D. LCP), Mr. Nelson completed the Center's entire evaluation procedure which consists of a medical assessment (Neal Holtan M.D.), psychiatric assessment (James Jaranson, M.D.), and psychological testing (Rosa Garcia Peltoniemi, Ph.D. LCP). Mr. Nelson was seen at the Center on Monday, April 9th for intake, screening, and psychiatric assessment, Tuesday, April 10th and Thursday April 12th for psychological testing and interpretation, and Friday, April 13th for medical assessment and a final information session.
>
> The Center For Victims of Torture relies upon the definition of torture developed by the World Medical Association as a guideline for eligibility of prospective clients. According to this definition, which involves the deliberate and systematic infliction of physical and/or mental suffering, Mr. Nelson is qualified to receive services at this Center.
>
> Mr. Nelson's evaluation and interview responses are consistent with his reported history of detention and torture in Saudi Arabia in 1984, and quite similar to the responses and reactions reported by other clients. Mr. Nelson was diagnosed as suffering from Post-traumatic Stress Disorder (delayed) (309.89), and Major Depression (296.2), according to the criteria specified in the Diagnostic and Statistical Manual, Third Edition-Revised, of the American Psychiatric Association (DSM-111-R). These symptoms include severely disturbed sleep pattern, nightmares, unwanted and intrusive recollections of his experience, exaggerated startle response, and difficulty concentrating. The client also describes symptoms of anxiety including discrete panic episodes, including rapid heart rate, sweating, and chest heaviness, most frequently occurring after nightmares. The environmental stressors contributing to these disorders were rated as "catastrophic" according to the same DSM-111-R guidelines.
>
> Mr. Nelson appears to be an intelligent, open and direct person. Although he is well oriented to reality, his symptoms are not likely to improve significantly without appropriate intervention.

There is one other report that I want to call to your attention, because it is the only one that Mr. Nelson has not sent in to your Department. It is the decision of Administrative Law Judge David P. Tennant, dated September 14, 1990, of the Office of Hearings and Appeals of the United States Social Security Administration, Department of Health and Human Services. A full copy of Judge Tennant's decision is appended to this letter.

Judge Tennant held that Scott J. Nelson, claimant, met the disability insured status requirements of the Social Security Act beginning on September 27, 1984, the day he claimed he was tortured. Moreover, the severity of his impairments met the requirements of §§ 12.04, 12.06, and

12.07, Appendix I, Subpart P, Regulations No. 4 of the Act, and has precluded Mr. Nelson from working for at least 12 continuous months (20 CFR 404.1525).

As you are aware, Administrative Law judges in the Department of Health and Human Services must pass upon many disability claims, and a number of them are spurious. Those judges are uniquely qualified by virtue of their specialized experience to evaluate the sincerity of disability claimants. I would like to quote some pertinent sections of Judge Tennant's decision:

> The Administrative Law Judge further finds that the claimant has impairments including chronic low back pain with pain in the lower extremities, an affective disorder, and anxiety related disorder, and a somatoform disorder. The claimant's impairments, in combination, are "severe" because they limit the claimant in his ability to sit, stand, walk, lift and carry, maintain the activities of daily living, maintain social functioning, maintain concentration, persistence, and pace, and avoid deterioration or decompensation in work or work-like settings. . . .
>
> The evidence establishes that the claimant was hospitalized initially in November 1984 for treatment of pain in the left knee. At that time, he was diagnosed as having an internal derangement of the left knee with a partially torn lateral meniscus and a partially torn anterior cruciate ligament. During the hospitalization, an arthroscopy with a partial meniscectomy and partial resection of the cruciate ligament with a partial synovectomy was performed to the left knee. The claimant then received emergency treatment in November 1986 for complaints of chest pain, although an electrocardiogram was normal (Exhibits 14 and 15). . . . An arthrogram of the right knee later that month [August 1986] showed a tear of the medial meniscus. An arthroscopy with a partial meniscectomy and a partial synovectomy was performed to the right knee in September 1986. . . .
>
> The evidence shows that since the alleged onset date of disability the claimant has had a disturbance of mood accompanied by anhedonia, appetite disturbance with change in weight, sleep disturbance, psychomotor agitation, decreased energy, feelings of guilt and worthlessness, difficulty concentrating and thinking, and thoughts of suicide as required by section 12.04; anxiety with generalized persistent anxiety accompanied by autonomic hyperactivity and apprehensive expectation, a persistent irrational fear of a specific object, activity, or situation which results in a compelling desire to avoid the dreaded object, activity, or situation, recurrent severe panic attacks manifested by a sudden unpredictable onset of intense apprehension, fear, terror, and sense of impending doom occurring on the average of at least once a week, recurrent obsessions or compulsions which are a source of marked distress, and recurrent and intrusive recollections of a traumatic experience which are a source of marked distress as required by section 12.06; and physical symptoms for which there are no demonstrable organic findings or known physiological mechanisms as evidenced by unrealistic interpretations of physical signs or sensations associated with the preoccupation or belief that the claimant has a serious disease or injury as required by section 12.07. . . . [T]he Administrative Law Judge finds that the claimant's mental impairments, in combination, produce a marked restriction in the activities of daily living, marked difficulties in maintaining social functioning, frequently occurring deficiencies of concentration, persistence, or pace, and repeated episodes of deterioration or decompensation in work or work-like settings. According to the testimony of the claimant's wife and according to his own testimony, his daily activities are extremely limited and she must assist him with dressing and bathing. In addition, although the claimant was quite active socially prior to his arrest and torture, he engages in few social activities at the present and does not even participate in social activities with his wife and son. He has diminished concentration as documented by his treating mental health professionals and he has had repeated episodes of deterioration or decompensation in work or work-like settings. Therefore, the Administrative Law Judge finds that the claimant's impairments are of a severity to meet the requirements of sections 12.04, 12.06, and 12.07. . .

To all this evidence I wish to add an observation of my own. It concerns a piece of evidence that is conspicuous because it is missing—like the famous Sherlock Holmes story about the hound that did not bark in the night.

The Nelsons took up their new home in Riyadh, Saudi Arabia, in 1983 with their infant son Matthew. Like many American families—like my own family, in fact—the Nelsons wanted two children. But a brutal, inhuman torturing of Mr. Nelson intervened. The Nelsons never had a second child. The neurological explanation can be left to the imagination. The fact is that the absence of that second child in the Nelson family speaks louder than all the self-serving allegations in the world challenging his claim of torture.

For the foregoing reasons, I ask the United States to espouse the claims of Scott and Vivian Nelson with the Kingdom of Saudi Arabia. In your diplomatic representations to the Kingdom, you may wish to point out that some members of the Royal Family were among the patients at the King Faisal Specialist Hospital when Mr. Nelson reported the existence of dangerous grease valves in the patients' oxygen supply lines. For his service to them and to all the patients in the hospital, he deserved a medal of commendation. Instead, he was tortured. By universally acknowledged standards of justice and fairness, the Kingdom of Saudi Arabia should generously compensate the United States for the injuries sustained by Mr. and Mrs.

Nelson, and in addition to financial compensation – which cannot hope to make up for deliberate torture – should express its regrets to the United States of America for the behavior of those persons who, acting under color of law in Saudi Arabia, so shockingly violated Scott and Vivian's fundamental human rights.

Sincerely,

Anthony D'Amato

Counsel for Scott and Vivian Nelson[28]

H. Dispute Resolution

1. Negotiation[29]

Any lobbyist knows that his chances of successfully influencing a government are increased if he has a specific proposal in mind. No one would expect success if he approached his own government and asked them to work out some scheme which reflected various principles. Less widely recognized is the extent to which obtaining an effective decision depends on presenting a proposal in the most readily decidable form. We are more likely both to know what we want and to get it if we try to write out the proposed decision with such clarity that it is in a form to which the single word "yes" would be an effective answer.

Putting our objective in the form of a yesable proposition makes us think through our position and the ways in which we will want to go about exerting influence. Too often our demand – the decision we desire – is vague simply because our own thinking is vague. Events have not forced us to be specific, and we have failed to recognize the impact which a specific offer or requested decision might have. We will almost always have a better chance of getting something we want if we know some specific things we would like to have.

There are costs in trying to develop a yesable proposition. Within the bureaucracy there is resistance to being specific. For the individuals concerned it involves work and risks with no compensating advantage. To reconcile the opinions of various officials and departments within our own government will take time and effort. But the more work we do, the easier time our adversaries will have making a decision we want them to make. Trying to write out some sample decisions which we would like Cuba or China or Algeria or East Germany to make in the next six months or next two years is a highly educational exercise. It should make us think about our conduct toward those countries. It tends to make us be realistic, to understand what is in the realm of the possible, and to bring the limitations of their political reality into the calculations of what we would like to have them do. It should help us reconcile what we want with what we can get. And it should make us think about actions we can take which will make it more likely that they will make some of those decisions. Whether or not we intend to communicate the specifics of our demand to our adversary, there is no excuse for not working out in our minds what it is we would like to have them say or do. To develop a firm governmental position might tend to freeze our position and cause us to be unduly rigid, but surely it is a useful exercise for each officer to write out one or two yesable propositions which he thinks are both desirable and within the realm of the possible. Unless we know what it is we are driving at, it will be pure luck if we are able to get it.

Communicating to another government exactly what it is we would like them to decide also involves costs and risks. We may sound as if we were delivering an ultimatum and fail on that account. To submit one yesable proposition may be effectively to forfeit the opportunity to ask for more favorable terms. By being specific we risk including details which, though unimportant to us, make the entire proposition unacceptable to the other government. Coming forward with draft language too soon may upset another government which would like to feel that they had more participation in the formulation of the decision.

Yet there are strong advantages in communicating a simple and decidable question to the government we are trying to influence. Essentially, these advantages flow from the fact that the more work we do the less work there is for them to do, and the more likely they are to do it.

Even in the simple case of selling, where the only question if "How much?" setting a price makes it easier for the buyer. Buying in an oriental bazaar is likely to be a slow process, particularly if each party waits for the other to make the first move. A supermarket simplifies the buyer's job by putting a price tag on every item in the store.

---

[28] As of the date this Brief in Opposition is filed in the Supreme Court, the Department of State has responded only to the effect that it is studying the foregoing Request for Espousal of Claims. [Editor's Note: The foregoing text of this footnote was in the original Brief in Opposition to Certiorari. What happened subsequently to the Nelsons' case? After winning for the Nelsons in the Eleventh Circuit and defeating an attempt by the United States to ask for a rehearing, Anthony D'Amato, the Nelsons' counsel, was replaced by the Nelsons in favor of new counsel in Washington D.C., who proceeded to write the brief and make the oral argument on behalf of Nelsons in the United States Supreme Court. The Court reversed the Eleventh Circuit Court of Appeals, ending the attempt by the Nelsons to vindicate their claims in American courts. Nevertheless, the Request for Espousal letter remains in the Nelson's active file at the Department of State.]

[29] By ROGER FISHER, excerpted from: INTERNATIONAL CONFLICT FOR BEGINNERS 15–26 (New York: Harper, 1969). Reprinted by permission.

This is work and requires a lot of decisions. It also means abandoning the chance to get a higher price even from someone who would be willing to pay more. The advantage lies in giving each buyer a take-it-or-leave-it choice. Even where it is understood that price is subject to negotiation, the person who sets the first price has the harder task. He must think not only about the price he is prepared to accept but also about the problem of adding or subtracting an amount for the purpose of negotiating strategy. He must formulate a price from an almost unlimited number of possibilities, some of which are indistinguishable for all practical purposes. The second person has a far simpler choice.

For more complicated situations the difference between giving somebody a problem and giving them a yes-or-no choice is even greater. Any lobbyist knows that those he is seeking to influence must have a clear idea of what they are being asked to decide. It is not enough to present a government with alternative consequences: "If you do nothing about your population problem, you will be ruined; if you solve it, you can have economic growth and prosperity." The government will clearly prefer the second set of consequences to the first, but no decision will result. There is nothing to which they can say "yes" which will get them there. A memorandum to a government official which makes a particular proposal and ends

Yes __________
No __________

is far more likely to produce a decision than one which points out a problem and suggests that something ought to be done about it.

What is likely in the case of a decision by an individual is even more likely in the case of a decision by a group of individuals such as those who constitute a government. Here the difficulties which each member of the group would face in reaching a decision by himself. Within a bureaucracy, those who have worked out a specific plan and come forward with a yesable proposition are likely to carry the day.

Foreign governments are no different from our own in finding it difficult to digest abstract wisdom or policy guidance. They, too, have a tendency to decide on those courses of action which are the most decidable – the most digestible – in form. And when communicating to a foreign government it is particularly useful that the communications be clear-cut. Much international communication is like smoke signals in a high wind. The more ambiguous the message the greater the chance for distortion and misunderstanding. The more strained the relationship the more likely that an adversary will interpret an ambiguous proposal or demand in the worst possible light. By presenting another government with a specific draft – a yesable proposition – we can cut through some of the suspicion about our intentions and encourage them to evaluate the real costs and benefits of making the decision we want them to make.

For years, the United States sought to influence the Hanoi government and the Vietcong leadership to abandon the war in Vietnam and to shift the conflict from the battlefield to the bargaining table, yet gave them no mechanically easy way to do so. Although we wanted the firing to stop, we presented our adversaries with no yesable proposition which would have resulted in a cease-fire. We left to them the almost unmanageably difficult task of formulating a cease-fire which might have been acceptable to both sides. We made it clear that the cost of continuing to fight the war would be high. We held out some hope that peace might be reasonably attractive to them – we tried to convince them that there were "carrots in the barn." But we provided no door to the barn. We confronted them with no choice where the simple word "yes" would have ended the fighting on a basis which we might have expected them to accept. Had they wanted a cease-fire, there was none they could have accepted. The frequent request of the United States that North Vietnam indicate what it was prepared to do in order to stop the bombing of North Vietnam amounted to a suggestion that it was up to them to give us a yesable proposition.

We often excuse our failure to present a yesable proposition with the thought that if the other side really wanted to do what we want them to do, they could let us know and something could be worked out. But we are not concerned with assessing the relative moral blame between governments; we are not concerned with which government is more at fault. We are concerned with what we can do to maximize the chance of our success. It may be that at any given time North Vietnam was unlikely to make the kind of decision we wanted. However small the chances were, they were further decreased by the way in which the choice was put to them.

Perhaps the clearest statement of the United States position was in the President's speech of September 29, 1967, the so-called San Antonio formula:

> The United States is willing to stop all aerial and naval bombardment of North Vietnam when this will lead promptly to productive discussion. We, of course, assume that while discussions proceed, North Vietnam would not take advantage of the bombing cessation or limitation.

This was not a casually drafted statement. Walt Rostow, Special Assistant to the President, later explained that every word had a purpose and a meaning: discussions must be held "promptly," they must be "productive," and so forth.

The President's statement was, however, a carefully drafted answer to the wrong question. It was an answer to the question, "What should our policy be?" If we really wanted productive discussions to be held promptly, we should have said something which would have made that event more likely. As it was, it was not enough for North Vietnam to say that talks would be held promptly after attacks on North Vietnam stopped. The United States then engaged in extensive "probes" in an effort to determine what North Vietnam "intended" when it agreed that talks would be promptly held. Diplomacy was used not to influence North Vietnam into doing what we wanted but to search for some nonexistent governmental "intentions." United States conduct appeared to be based on the premise that the government of North Vietnam (contrary to all experience with governments) would not be affected by the choices open to it but had some immutable intentions—intentions that were unresponsive, that is, to anything except military measures.

Rather than identify a posture for us to adopt we should have identified the operational decision which we wanted and could expect from North Vietnam and then given them a yesable proposition. Rather than having confronted North Vietnam with a statement of our "policy," we could have made sure that they were confronted with a choice that both was mechanically simple and stood a good chance of being politically acceptable.

An illustration of the kind of yesable proposition which might have shortened the war in Vietnam would have been an invitation from some legitimate source to a specific conference to be held at a given time and place. For example, India, as Chairman of the International Control Commission, might have sent a note along the following lines:

> The following parties are hereby invited to send representatives to attend a meeting of the International Control Commission in New Delhi at the Ministry of External Affairs Building to be held for three weeks beginning at 10 a.m. local time on Monday, the 4th of next month.
>
> The government of the Democratic Republic of Vietnam, Hanoi
>
> The government of the Republic of Vietnam, Saigon
>
> The National Liberation Front of Vietnam
>
> The United States.
>
> The governments of Poland and of Canada, being the other members of the Control Commission, have each already indicated their willingness to have a representative attend the meeting. The purpose of the meeting is to advise the Commission as to measures which might be undertaken (1) to establish and maintain a cease-fire throughout Vietnam, and (2) to implement the Geneva Accords of 1954.
>
> To facilitate the work of the Commission and to improve the prospects for peace in Vietnam, all parties are hereby requested to implement effective at 2:00 a.m. local time on Sunday, the 3rd of next month, a general reduce-fire throughout all Vietnam, such reduce-fire to include a cessation of all major offensive military action, including a cessation of bombing and other armed attacks against North Vietnam, it being understood that no party should take military advantage of the reduced military activities on the part of an adversary.
>
> Any party not wishing to send a formal representative to the meeting may send an unofficial observer or may designate any person, including the representative of some other party, to convey their views officially or unofficially to the Commission, to others attending the meeting, or to both. The meeting will take place as scheduled whether or not all invited parties decide to attend the opening sessions, provided only that the Commission finds that the general reduce-fire is in effect in Vietnam.
>
> A representative of the government of India will chair the meeting. There will be an opportunity for informal discussions as well as for formal statements of position and advice at scheduled sessions. Attendance at the meeting will be without prejudice to the legal or other position of any party. It is requested that no party make any public statement which might prejudge the work of the meeting and that any question be raised with the chairman on the first day of the meeting.

Such an invitation would have asked each of the parties concerned to do two things: implement a general reduce-fire at 2:00 a.m. on the morning of the third and designate a representative to attend the meeting in New Delhi at 10:00 a.m. on the fourth. Each of the decisions would involve some complicating factors, but each is essentially the kind of decision which a government can make on a yes-or-no basis. No doubt a better draft could have been prepared. Some complexity is required in order to make the decision of the invitees easy. This draft was designed to meet the requirement of the United States that a cessation of the bombing of North Vietnam be accompanied by some reciprocal reduction of fighting on the other side, and the requirement of North Vietnam that it not negotiate while the bombing continued. There is little doubt that with some encouragement the government of India would have been willing to issue such an invitation at almost any time in 1967.

The contrast between the President's statement of September 29, 1967, and the suggested note illustrates the difference between focusing our thinking around our decision and focusing it around the decision of those we are trying to influence. The President's statement was concerned with the simplicity of our decision; the draft note is concerned with the simplicity of their decision. The President's statement was designed to articulate a "policy" which would be defended at home and abroad and which could continue in effect for an indefinite period. The draft note was designed to produce an operational decision. The President's statement could be ignored; a note such as the draft could not be. Or North Vietnam could say that they agreed with the President's statement that productive discussions should be held promptly following the cessation of the bombing, and still nothing would happen.

The above example is not intended to prove that North Vietnam would in fact have accepted such an invitation or to prove that discussions if held would have been productive. It is intended to illustrate what is mean by a yesable proposition. It is intended to illustrate what I mean when I say it is their decision we should think about.

2. Arbitration[30]

In 1914 and 1916, Mr. Mavrommatis obtained concessions from the Ottoman Empire to provide certain public services in Jerusalem and Jaffa. After the First World War, the British Government granted duplicate concessions to a different person. Predictably, a dispute ensued. The Government of Greece eventually espoused the claim of Mavrommatis, its national, against the British Government. Ultimately, the claim was addressed on the public international law level by the Permanent Court of International Justice.[31]

The conventional wisdom is that interstate arbitration, like that involving Mavrommatis, has declined in this century. Clive Parry wrote that the "high noon of international arbitration occurred around the year 1900."[32] Yet further consideration of Mavrommatis' situation tells us that the evolution of international arbitration more generally in this century involves a process far more complex than a mere decline in use.

In the early 1920s, Mavrommatis had few, if any, other options for pursuing his claim. Today, in contrast, he would likely include, as a part of his concession, a clause providing for international commercial arbitration in, for example, Geneva under the UNCITRAL Rules of Arbitration or Paris at the International Chamber of Commerce. In contrast to settlement by the Permanent Court of International Justice, this proceeding would not require the cooperation of the other party and could result in an award enforceable and recognizable around much of the world under the New York Convention.

Many arbitrations at the turn of the century, like the Mavrommatis case, involved claims of individuals based on diplomatic protection. That is, many of the disputes were not truly between the two states named as parties. Today, depending upon the circumstances, similar claims likely would be handled through lump sum settlement or international commercial arbitration. Thus, the aggregate effect of the change in options described for Mavrommatis is that there quite plausibly has been a shift in dockets. Although further empirical study is necessary to establish the historical proposition, international commercial arbitration clearly has the capacity to take over the adjudication of many of the essentially private disputes previously addressed by the more politically contentious interstate mechanism of diplomatic protection.

The change is striking. In approximately half a century, an elaborate system for the resolution of international commercial disputes has evolved quietly and efficiently. When viewed against the history of international dispute resolution, this recent evolution is more accurately a revolution. Interstate arrangements, municipal court systems and private contractual dispute settlement systems reflect distinct doctrinal categories. In practice, however, they reflect different options for the resolution of disputes. Different groups can control the shape of each process, and they naturally shape and develop the process they control so that it addresses the needs of the group. The processes, although conceptually distinct, do not operate in isolation. Each evolves in response to the needs of the community controlling it and each of the other mechanisms may be affected by such changes. This is not to say that interstate arbitration, international commercial arbitration and municipal legal orders collectively are developing in accordance with some master plan or that they are not duplicating one another or not competing with one another. It is to say that the community of commercial actors operating internationally demanded a more efficient and enforceable system than traditional interstate arbitration. That it was primarily businessmen and private lawyers who built the international commercial arbitration system from bottom up, rather than states from the top down, makes it no less of a revolution and all the more striking.

The trend away from classic interstate arbitration is desirable politically because it reduces the significance of the state as a world actor in areas where the sensitivities of the state need not be implicated. Moreover, the flexibility of private arrangements is coupled with the assurance

---

[30] By DAVID D. CARON, excerpted from: *The Nature of the Iran-United States Claims Tribunal and the Evolving Structure of International Dispute Resolution*, 84 AMERICAN JOURNAL OF INTERNATIONAL LAW 104, 151–55 (1990). Reprinted by permission.

[31] Mavrommatis Palestine Concessions, 1924 PCIJ (ser. A) No. 2 (Judgment of Aug. 30, 1924).

[32] Clive Parry, *Some Considerations upon the Protection of Individuals in International Law*, 90 RECUEIL DES COURS 653, 660 (1956 II).

of harmonized municipal enforcement standards. The resulting low-level national permeation supports the rule of law by its implicit reliance on the existence of independent national judiciaries.

Yet the transfer of certain disputes to private arbitration does not leave interstate arbitration bereft of content. Rather, it brings more clearly into focus what have always been the central tasks (and the major limitations) of interstate arbitration. Interstate arbitration has worked very well for resolving boundary disputes but not as well for disputes involving central interests of the state, such as the use of force. Although the volume of interstate arbitration may be less than it was at the turn of the century, international resolution of disputes generally is likely at an all-time high. Since these new mechanisms now address disputes that previously were elevated to the level of interstate arbitration by diplomatic protection, it would not be surprising to learn that true interstate arbitration in fact has remained relatively constant. Understanding this evolution helps strip away the false belief that somehow international arbitration accomplished much more in the past.

3. Third Party Assistance[33]

The best way of dealing with international disputes is by negotiations between the parties themselves, and the most important and useful thing third parties usually can do will be to supplement and assist this process. How can third parties help international disputants achieve a settlement? Pruitt and Rubin describe the type of negotiating impasse which may call for third-party assistance:

> Positions tend towards rigidity because the protagonists are reluctant to budge lest any conciliatory gesture be misconstrued as a sign of weakness. Moreover, the parties may lack the imagination, creativity, and/or experience necessary to work their way out of the pit they have jointly engineered – not because they don't want to but because they don't know how. Thus, for a variety of reasons, disputants are sometimes either unable or unwilling to move toward agreement of their own accord. Under the circumstances, third parties often become involved at the behest of one or more of the disputants, or on their own initiative.[34]

They suggest a variety of ways in which a third party can help the parties break out of such an impasse. One way is by modifying the physical and social structure of the dispute. For example, the third party can structure communication between the principals; open and neutralize the site in which the problem-solving takes place, impose time limits, and infuse resources. Another way is by modifying the issue structure. For example, the third party can assist the disputants to identify existing issues and alternatives; help them to package and sequence issues in ways that lead towards agreement; and introduce new issues and alternatives that did not occur to the disputants themselves. Finally, the third party can increase the disputants' motivation to reach agreement. For example, it can facilitate their making concessions without loss of face, engender mutual trust, encourage their venting and coming to grips with irrational feelings, and respect their desire for autonomy.

I have suggested elsewhere[35] that a principal reason why disputing parties may not be able to reach a settlement agreement is what they distrust each other or are otherwise concerned with what they see as very serious risks potentially involved in such an agreement. In this case, third parties can play a crucial role in dispute settlement by helping the parties in a variety of ways to manage these risks – for example, by monitoring or verifying performance, serving as escrow agents, or providing guarantees. Third party risk management devices of this kind may be particularly useful, for example, in facilitating dispute-settlement arrangements in which distrust is a particularly serious obstacle, such as armistice or peace agreements or agreements seeking to resolve complex and emotional racial, ethnic or religious conflicts.

Recent studies suggest that while third party intervention in international conflicts does not always provide a final settlement to a conflict or dispute, it often seems to keep things from getting worse. For example, Bercovitch, analyzing data involving 310 conflicts from 1945-74, found that in 235 of them, or 82% of the total, there was some form of official third-party intervention, primarily by the U.N. and in the form of mediation, and that it was useful in at least abating conflict in a substantial number of these situations.[36]

Finally, we should not forget that international third party dispute settlement has a symbolic significance as well as practical importance. The concept that disputes and conflicts within a group are not simply the business of those directly involved but are of concern of every member is at the root of civilized and ordered society. Consequently,

---

[33] By RICHARD B. BILDER, excerpted from: *International Third Party Dispute Settlement,* 17 DENVER JOURNAL OF INTERNATIONAL LAW 471, 485, 495–96, 503 (1989). Reprinted by permission.

[34] D.G. PRUITT & J.Z. RUBIN, SOCIAL CONFLICT: ESCALATION, STALEMATE AND SETTLEMENT 165 (1986).

[35] RICHARD B. BILDER, MANAGING THE RISKS OF INTERNATIONAL AGREEMENT (1981).

[36] J. BERCOVITCH, SOCIAL CONFLICTS AND THIRD PARTIES: STRATEGIES OF CONFLICT RESOLUTION 92–93, 113–15 (1984).

third party dispute settlement, and institutions such as the International Court of Justice which implement its use, can encourage growing perceptions of international community and play a crucial role in the development of a more peaceful, just and decent world.

4. Adjudication[37]

The relative success of "other" dispute resolution systems presents optimistic possibilities for the future. Most nations are willing to resolve many of their disputes in peaceful ways, frequently including reference to binding third-party dispute settlement. Given the proper context, this approach can be quite successful. This adjudicating mechanism usually involves the application of relatively specific rules and the delimitation of the issues to avoid the questions of the greatest national sensitivity.

We can expect to see the growth of the alternative dispute resolution tribunals over time. The disputes of the future will increasingly be economic in nature. Such disputes will probably fit more readily into a GATT or GATT-type mold than into the International Court's system, especially if the GATT model offers advantages of time, cost, and privacy. In the alternative, we can expect to see international disputes diverted to regional organizations, such as the European Court or the Canada-United States Arbitration Panels. And, if we believe the advocates of alternative dispute resolution, a strict adherence to the formal mechanisms of adjudication is already obsolete.

What about the World Court itself? Are there ways to enhance its jurisdiction and authority? Whenever this question is posed, an inconclusive debate between "messianists" and "chauvinists" normally ensues. This debate pits those who would accept the Court's jurisdiction as an act of faith against those who would reject it as an act of faith. That dispute has remained unresolved for at least seventy years; it is likely to remain unresolved for seventy years more. It is the argument from the opening lines of Charles Dickens' *A Tale of Two Cities* between those who see an "epoch of belief" and those who see an "epoch of incredulity."

I submit that this argument is irrelevant in the modern world. Adhering to the pragmatic school of jurisprudence, I suggest that we have been asking the wrong questions for seventy years. Asking whether we should (or should not) have absolute confidence in a World Court as an abstract proposition is a vain and futile question. Rather, we should ask how we can build confidence in an International Court, and test that confidence with reasonable degrees of risk. If the confidence is then well-founded, the acceptance of jurisdiction and of the Court's work can grow. If not, the risk will be limited by the manner of submission of the dispute to the Court.

The notion of "confidence-building measures" is not new. It was one of the cornerstones of the Helsinki Agreement that was a precursor to the thawing of the Cold War. It involved, not global leaps of faith, but very limited, tentative steps to test the reactions of others. A similar approach might be taken on the question of international jurisdiction.

Confidence is built, not on grand theories, but on actual practice. Perhaps one of the biggest flaws of the old approach was to save only the largest controversies for the World Court, rather than using smaller ones to build confidence in the Court.

For international adjudication, this is neither the best of times nor the worst of times. It is neither a season of Light, nor a season of Darkness, but rather one of Twilight. Gradually building confidence in the institutions of international adjudication, that Twilight can become the Dawn, offering a future in which adjudication will resolve international conflict.

---

[37] By FRED L. MORRISON, excerpted from: *The Future of International Adjudication*, 75 MINNESOTA LAW REVIEW 827, 845–47 (1991). Reprinted by permission.

12
Emerging Issue Areas

A. Rights of the Child

1. Background[1]

Until recently children's rights have not been a perceptible body of law separable from the greater universe of individual human rights. If lawyers and legal scholars recognized them at all, they considered that children's rights derived from the rights of the parents or from individual human rights recognized by international or domestic law. Indeed, for centuries children did not have rights as we normally understand them; they were property to be disposed of at the whim of their (usually male) parents. During the late eighteenth and early nineteenth centuries reformers began to agitate for the protection of children from exploitation through labor laws, compulsory schooling laws, child abuse and neglect laws and other forms of state protection against parental abuse. As the period of childhood lengthened, children escaped the duties that had traditionally constrained them and prevented them from escaping poverty and ignorance. Conversely, they continued to exist without the rights that adults acquired at majority – the right to choose a domicile, the right to marry, the right to engage in a particular profession, the right to practice a particular religion. Children's rights advocates in Europe and the United States began as early as the late 1880s to demand that children be granted at least some of these rights, in both the civil and criminal legal arenas. Thus, children began to exercise certain rights, without the corresponding responsibilities, creating a tension in the laws expanding the child's expectation of liberty and the legal constraints still in operation.

The United Nations Convention on the Rights of the Child is a bold and innovative document, a consensus of international legal and political opinion concerning those rights which children ought to expect their national governments to recognize. This convention's major focus is the "best interests of the child" standard already familiar in U.S., British and other systems of domestic law. The convention repeats rights already stated in the Universal Declaration of Human Rights, the International Covenant on Civil and Political Rights, and the International Covenant on Economic, Social and Cultural Rights. However, the convention applies these rights directly to the situation of the child in international law. Even so, a close examination of the language of the document reveals the tension still inherent in the area of children's rights between the control that parents, and to a lesser extent the State, maintain over children and the autonomy that children can claim through the rights recognized in this international agreement.

Commentators trace the inception of the international children's rights movement to the work of the British-born Eglantyne Jebb, who founded the Save the Children International Union (SCIU) in Geneva in 1920. In 1923, the SCIU promulgated the Declaration of Geneva, which was later adopted by the League of Nations. Among the children's rights recognized in the Declaration were the right to emotional and physical well-being, the right to a family, the right to aid in time of war or national disaster, the right to an education or training, and the right to recognition of their places and responsibilities in the human family. Between 1923 and 1959, various organizations put forward covenants, declarations and conventions which took into account the human rights of children. In 1959, the United Nations adopted the Declaration of the Rights of the Child[2] and in recognition of the twentieth anniversary of that adoption, named 1979 the International Year of the Child.

As part of the celebration of the International Year of the Child, Poland suggested that the United Nations draft a covenant which would put into legal effect the principles pertaining to children set down in the non-binding Universal Declaration of Human Rights. By authority of the General Assembly, the United Nations Human Rights Commission began drafting a Convention on the Rights of the Child. As part of the thirty-year anniversary of the Universal Declaration, various groups began lobbying for a final version of the convention to be voted by 1989. Some nations, however, saw a covenant on children's rights as redundant, or worse, as a ploy by Eastern bloc nations to create rights out of public policy decisions. Within three years, the Commission on Human Rights, a part of the

---

[1] By CHRISTINE ALICE CORCOS, excerpted from: *The Child in International Law: A Pathfinder and Selected Bibliography*, 23 CASE WESTERN RESERVE JOURNAL OF INTERNATIONAL LAW 171 (1991). Reprinted by permission.

[2] 14 U.N. GAOR Supp. (No. 16), U.N. Doc. A/4054 (1959).

Economic and Social Council of the United Nations, launched a working group whose mission was to study the rights of the child in international law. Other U.N. agencies actively studying the rights of the child included the United Nations Children's Fund and the World Health Organization. A steady stream of reports from the Commission on Human Rights Working Group and from the NGO Ad Hoc Group on the Drafting of the Convention on the Rights of the Child led to the presentation of the convention to the General Assembly in 1989. Some of the rights directly attributable to NGO participation in the drafting process are "protection against 'traditional practices' (i.e. female circumcision), and against sexual exploitation, protection of rights of indigenous children, standards for the administration of school discipline and rehabilitation for victims of various types of abuse and exploitation."

While the United Nations Covenant on the Rights of the Child is a tremendous step forward in the direction of recognition of the problems which the particular legal and economic status of the child may cause, it still does not address some of the issues which involve children or some of the situations which continue to put children at risk, namely juvenile justice, including capital punishment, the rights of child non-citizens, the forced relocation of children and right of the child to refuse medical or scientific experimentation. Another novel idea omitted from the covenant as it was accepted is that of an International Ombudsman for children's rights. Areas which continue to be hotly discussed include the rights of the unborn, the rights to freedom of religion and adoption, and the role of children in war. Cynthia Price Cohen points out that the mechanism for implementation of the covenant is slightly different from those used for previous covenants, in that the emphasis is on reinforcement of the activities of complying states rather than on sanctions of non-complying states.[3] She notes as well that individual children have no means through which to lodge complaints with the Human Rights Committee. All of these areas are likely to repay close study and analysis as the Convention is signed and put into effect by the nations of the world.

2. Discussion of Crosscountry Adoption[4]

MAURICE COPITHORNE: The threshold established in article 21(b)[5] seems to be pretty high in the sense that intercountry adoption is only really approved of or deemed acceptable where there is no alternative available in the country from which the child comes. I am concerned that, as it is still in the hands of the government of the country of origin to determine whether adequate arrangements can be made, this may not in fact be in the best interest of the child. Assuming one has the best interests of the child in mind and desires the integration of the child in a suitable family environment, it may be that this interest is quite different from the norms and standards of the country where the child has been living, especially given the countries where many if not most of the children involved in international adoption come from these days.

JOHN T. HOLMES: Well, I can briefly respond to this question and maybe some of the other panelists could also add some comments. During the last stages of the drafting of the Convention, article 21 proved to be a very controversial provision. A number of problems originated from concerns related to child kidnapping. This has increasingly become a major international problem, and many of the concerns stemming from this problem come primarily from Latin American countries. Professor Copithorne has mentioned that article 21 seems to have a very high standard with regard to the question of intercountry adoption. In fact, the view of some, but not all, Latin American delegations was that intercountry adoption should be prohibited completely. The text that eventually emerged in article 21 was therefore a compromise between a position calling for a prohibition on intercountry adoptions and one permitting such adoptions in exceptional circumstances.

To a large extent, the concerns of many countries on this issue related to the difficulty they experienced in trying to regulate intercountry adoptions. Because of the profits that intermediaries could make in such transactions, there were problems of child kidnapping as well as coercion, where large sums of money were offered to the individual mother involved to give up a newborn child. At a particularly vulnerable time, this mother was offered enough money to feed the remainder of her family for a long period of time. There are a number of unscrupulous lawyers and other intermediaries willing to take advantage of these circumstances in order to reap large profits, and it was these types of situations that created concerns on the part of some of the Latin American countries.

This was not an issue where you simply had the devel-

[3] Cohen, *Introductory Note: United Nations: Convention on the Rights of the Child*, 28 I.L.M. 1448, 1452 (1989).

[4] Excerpts from JOAN FITZPATRICK (moderator), Panel Discussion, United Nations Convention on the Rights of the Child, *in* 83 AMERICAN SOCIETY OF INTERNATIONAL LAW PROCEEDINGS 155 (1989). Reprinted by permission.

[5] Article 21(b) of the Convention on the Rights of the Child reads:

> [States Parties shall]
> 21(b) Recognize that inter-country adoption may be considered as an alternative means of child's care, if the child cannot be placed in a foster or an adoptive family or cannot in any equitable manner be cared for in the child's country of origin.

oping world versus the developed. Members of some Canadian indigenous groups were present at the final drafting session and they were very concerned about the provisions on adoption. They had found that in the Canadian context, there had been instances of native children being sent to the United States, for example. The judges and social workers making the decisions in these cases were, in the view of indigenous groups, using the concept of the best interests of the child in a way that focused solely on an economic perspective and overlooked the importance of cultural continuity.

All of the concerns and positions I mentioned came into play during the negotiation of this compromise text. The standard set for intercountry adoption is high; there is no doubt about it. However, I think that in terms of the unfortunate development of child kidnapping and coercion that standard may be a necessary one.

CYNTHIA PRICE COHEN: Article 21 was one of the articles opposed by Islamic delegations because they do not believe in the concept of adoption. Thus, having any article at all in the Convention on this issue proved to be quite an achievement. It was very controversial and difficult, and the final text is the product of extensive and subtle negotiation. To accommodate Islamic interests, article 20(3) was altered to include a reference to the Kafala of Islamic law, which is not technically adoption. As it was explained to me, it is essentially a form of permanent foster care. While a family may be awarded permanent legal responsibility for the child, the child is never given the name of the family with whom he or she lives. Nor is the child given any inheritance rights. Article 21 mentions states that "recognize and/or permit adoption." That "or" is partially the work of the NGO Group. We came up with cases where children were taken from Islamic countries that do not recognize adoption to countries that do, and were then adopted. Therefore, we said that since they do permit this to happen to the child, this called for the "and/or" language. As you can see it was a very hot topic and because of the strong feelings of the Islamic countries against adoption, it was a delicate compromise which was very well worked out by the Egyptian delegate.

3. The Need for Crosscountry Adoption[6]

The Convention on the Rights of the Child of 1989 relegates international adoptions to last resort status, the preferred options being adoption, foster care, or other "suitable" care in the child's country of origin. It does nothing to establish standards and procedures that might facilitate adoption between nations.

The problems that should be seen central to the international adoption debate have to do with the misery and deprivation that characterize the lives of huge numbers of the children in the world. Countless millions of children die of malnutrition and of diseases that should not kill, and millions more live in miserably inadequate institutions or on the streets. Their situations vary: some institutions are worse than others, and some street children maintain a connection with a family, while others are entirely on their own. But there can be no doubt that overwhelming numbers of children in poor countries are living and dying in conditions involving extreme forms of deprivation, neglect, exploitation, and abuse. These are the real problems of the children of the world.

International adoption should be seen as an opportunity to solve some of these problems for some children. It should be structured to maximize this positive potential—to facilitate the placement of children in need of nurturing homes with people in a position to provide those homes. International adoption can of course play only a very limited role. Long-term solutions lie in reallocating social and economic resources, both between countries and within countries, so that children can more generally be cared for by their birth families. But international adoption can play at least some role. Given the fact that cosmic reordering is not on the immediate horizon, such adoption clearly serves the interests of at least those children for whom parents can be found.

Some have suggested that international adoption might conflict with programs designed to improve the lot of the huge numbers of children now in need or with efforts to accomplish the kind of social reordering that might help the children of the future. For example, some argue that instead of promoting and pursuing adoption, governments and individuals in the well-off industrialized countries should devote increased resources to more cost-effective programs designed to promote well-being of children in their native lands—programs that might range from individual fostering arrangements, to sponsoring orphanages abroad, to a wide variety of UNICEF projects. But there is simply no reason to believe that foreign adoption is inconsistent with such efforts. Indeed, quite the reverse: foreign adoption programs are likely to increase awareness in the United States and other receiving countries of the problems of children in the sending countries. These programs give those who adopt reason to identify, through their children, with the situations of those children not lucky enough to have found homes. Foreign adoption can help create a climate that is more sympathetic to wide-ranging forms of

[6] By ELIZABETH BARTHOLET, excerpted from: FAMILY BONDS: ADOPTION AND THE POLITICS OF PARENTING 145–63 (N.Y.: Houghton Mifflin, 1993). Reprinted by permission.

support for children everywhere. Indeed, there is evidence that it has functioned in just this way to date.

Another argument is that international adoption might relieve pressure within some sending countries to deal with social problems that need attention. But this argument too collapses upon analysis. Sending children abroad for adoption tends to highlight rather than hide the fact that there are problems at home. Indeed, opposition to foreign adoption is based in large part on embarrassment within the sending countries over having their domestic problems revealed by this public confession of inability to take care of their own children. Although speculative arguments can always be mounted, it is hard to believe that there is any real risk that providing some of the world's homeless children with adoptive parents would stand in the way of helping other children in this or even in some future world.

The nations of the world are in general agreement that the best interests of the child should be the paramount principle governing the placement of children outside their biologic families. Given the real problems confronting children, it should be clear that this principle requires laws and policies that are designed to facilitate the international placement of children in need of homes.

Obviously the law should guarantee that international adoption does not create new problems. Adoption should not be used to break up viable birth families. Those who want to adopt should not be allowed to use their financial advantage to induce impoverished birth parents to surrender their children. We need laws that prohibit baby-buying, and we need rules that ensure that birth parents have voluntarily surrendered their child for adoption or have had their parental rights terminated for good reason. Adoption should also not be used simply to transfer children from one miserable situation to another. We need rules to ensure that adoptees receive loving, nurturing adoptive homes—rules protecting the adopted against any form of exploitation.

But it makes no sense to focus solely on the problems that might be created by international adoption while ignoring the very real problems of abuse, neglect, and exploitation suffered by homeless children in the absence of such adoption. It is patently absurd to talk as if the real dangers for children were that they might be stolen or bought from their birth parents to be transferred to other adults for purposes of abuse and exploitation.

Nonetheless, public discourse about international adoption focuses overwhelmingly on its alleged risks and dangers. Some of the concerns that have been voiced have no basis whatsoever in fact. One notorious example is the "baby parts" rumor, prevalent in recent years in a number of sending countries, which involves the claim that people from the United States and other receiving countries are adopting foreign children in order to kill them for their organs, which are then used in organ transplants. The claim is entirely unsubstantiated and has been repeatedly debunked, but it has received widespread circulation in the media of some fifty countries, has been taken seriously by a number of international human rights groups, and is apparently widely believed.

Other concerns about international adoption have some basis in reality but are enormously exaggerated. For example, critics both in this country and abroad focus on the danger that children will be kidnapped or bought from their birth parents for sale to rich North Americans who are desperate to parent. The media in this country give headline coverage to any stories of "kidnapping rings" or "baby trafficking." There are indeed some documented instances of kidnappings and of improper payments to birth parents, but there is no evidence that these practices are widespread or that they are significant in the larger picture. Moreover, it is quite unlikely that they are common. Current law makes it extremely risky for would-be adopters and intermediaries to engage in baby-buying or kidnapping. Even if some people might be willing to undertake such activities if this were the only way or the easiest way to accomplish an adoption, the fact is that it is not. International adoption is unduly difficult to accomplish in a lawful manner, and the legal barriers do create pressures to cut corners, but the fact remains that even those who are willing to break the law in certain respects should feel no need to violate the fundamental rules that prohibit using money to induce birth parents to surrender their children or that prohibit kidnapping. Sadly, the world is all too full of birth parents who are desperately eager to find homes for the children they cannot care for and of children who have already been surrendered or abandoned. When you look beneath the surface of most media and other stories of "child trafficking," it becomes clear that the term trafficking is used very loosely. The stories sometimes involve claims that what is characterized as a bribe may have been paid to an official in a country in which small payments to officials are a part of how official business is traditionally done. Often the stories involve nothing more than allegations that the adoptive parents paid high fees to agencies or other intermediaries for services required to accomplish their adoption. This is entirely legitimate, and is made necessary by the complications of the current legal system. Evidence that birth parents have been paid or that children have been taken from birth parents who are capable of and interested in raising them is extremely rare.

My point here is not to justify everything that has been done in the name of international adoption. Children quite obviously should not be stolen, nor should they be bought and sold; birth parents should not be encouraged by the prospect of payment to give up children whom they are interested in and capable of raising. But if we really care about children, we should be prepared to see even these evils in perspective. They are by no means the worst things that are happening to children or their birth parents today, and they occur relatively rarely. They should not divert us from the basic problems that children face, or cause us to ignore their need for the homes that international adoption can and on a regular basis does provide without any improper payments to or pressures on birth parents.

Recent events involving Rumanian adoptions illustrate my point. The foreign adoptions that followed the fall of the communist regime in Rumania in 1989 became the source of the major adoption scandal story of the early 1990s. This story became a focal point for media discussions of international adoption and was used effectively by forces opposed to such adoption. It described would-be adopters from the United States and other countries wandering through Rumanian villages offering money to baffled villagers to induce them to give up their children for adoption. There undoubtedly were more than a few cases involving illicit payments to Rumanian birth parents, but the real story of the children in Rumania, and the role of international adoption in their lives, is quite different from the scandal story, and it is one in which baby-buying deserves a limited amount of space.

The real story has to do with a country in which tens of thousands of children lived in orphanages and state hospitals, where thousands of them acquired AIDS. A recent documentary film, Lost and Found, is a moving testament to some of the horrors. It shows children lying in the cribs where they have been virtually imprisoned all their lives. Some of these children have learned to bang their heads against the crib or rock their bodies back and forth throughout their waking days as a form of comfort in a life that provides none. The film shows children who look like three-year olds but turn out to be ten- and twelve-year-olds who have "failed to thrive"–and failed to grow and learn to talk or walk–because of the absence of care. Seriously ill children lie in their own filth, waiting for death. The real story also has to do with the fact that once news of the situation in Rumania got out, thousands of people who were eager to adopt some of the children they read about and saw on television came forward. Thousands of children were adopted, some from institutions and some directly from birth parents who were unable to care for them.

International adoption was mishandled in Rumania. But the real scandal is not that some abuses occurred; it is that when would-be adopters presented themselves, there was no system in place to handle adoptions in a way that would have eased placement while preventing abuses. And international adoption has not been a tragedy for the children of Rumania or for their birth parents, although it has been described that way. The tragedy lies in the fact that Rumanian women were forced to produce children they could not care for by the Ceausescu regime's policies, which denied them birth control and abortion rights. It lies in the conditions in which Rumanian children were and are living and dying. And it lies in the current move to restrict international adoption in ways that may or may not eliminate abuses but will almost surely prevent huge numbers of Rumanian children from escaping the desperate situations of their lives to live in loving adoptive homes.

Critics of international adoption often voice concern that children will not receive appropriate care in their new families and countries. They argue that it is unfair to separate children from their racial, cultural, and national groups of origin. Loss of the group link and sense of group heritage is said to be a deprivation in itself, and growing up in a foreign land is said to pose risks of discrimination. Those who raise these issues again ignore the reality of children's current situations.

International adoption clearly represents an extraordinarily positive option for the homeless children of the world, compared to all other realistic options. Most of these children will not be adopted otherwise. They will instead live or die in inadequate institutions or on the streets. To the limited degree that foster care is available in these countries, it is likely to be no better than foster care in our country and is often much worse, resulting in little more than indentured servitude. The critics of international adoption engage in a tremendous amount of false romanticization in talking about the dangers of tearing children from their ethnic and cultural roots and their communities. The children we are talking about do not live in richly supportive communities where they have an opportunity to appreciate their ethnic and cultural heritage; they live in states of near-total deprivation. Those who survive to grow up are apt to face virulent forms of racial and ethnic discrimination in their own countries, based on their racial or ethnic status or simply on the fact that they are illegitimate or orphaned. Similarly false romanticization is involved in much of the talk about the problems inherent in losing one's national identity. The fact is that the United States is seen as the land of opportunity for many, many adults in the countries that have large numbers of homeless children. Life is hard for most of those who live in places devastated by poverty, war, or natural disaster. Large numbers would emigrate to the United States if they could.

This is not to deny that international adoptees, many of whom are children of color and others of whom look "foreign," face a complex challenge in resolving issues of individual and group identity. How important will the parents think it is to affirm a connection to the child's various groups of origin? How will they go about the task, if they see it as important, given that they were not themselves born to those groups and may have limited knowledge of and access to the cultures involved? How should biracial, bicultural, binational families think about issues of group identity?

But it is not clear that there is anything intrinsically negative about growing up in a family whose members come from different racial, ethnic, or national groups. It is simply different in some ways that might be extremely positive. At the same time, it is not so very different from the upbringing that many children have. Many children in this country grow up with parents who have crossed various lines of racial, ethnic, and national difference. Throughout their lives, all children in all countries face issues as to which groups they choose to identify with and what importance they choose to place on their group identities.

The evidence provides no support for the critics of international adoption. The research shows that these children and their families function well and compare well on various measures of emotional adjustment with other adoptive families as well as with biologic families. These are rather striking findings, since the vast majority of international adoptees have had problematic preadoptive histories which could be expected to cause difficulties in adjustment. The studies show that adoption has for the most part been extraordinarily successful in enabling even those children who have suffered extremely severe forms of deprivation and abuse in their early lives to recover and flourish. For instance, one major study involved children who had been caught up in the Vietnam War and who arrived in Norway for adoption at ages ranging from two to five. "Many could not walk. They were passive, apathetic, retarded, and malnourished." At ages seventeen to twenty-two, these children were basically well adjusted and strongly attached to their families.[7]

Some of the studies hint at the complex issues involved in being part of a biracial, bicultural, binational family. But there is no evidence that the challenge of establishing a satisfactory ethnic and cultural identity causes any actual harm to the international adoptee. There is simply no basis for assuming that a multicultural identity is problematic from the perspective of the children involved.

In general, the research has not focused on determining what special positive factors might be inherent in international adoption for the children, their adoptive families, or the larger society. But some studies hint at the rich quality of the experience of being part of an international adoptive family and the special perspective its members may develop on issues of community. One nationwide study found that half of the international adoptees involved felt that as a result of their status, "they may be bridge-builders between the nations."[8] Cheri Register's recent study of U.S. families with children adopted from abroad provides a powerful and moving description of the special qualities that parents and children find in living life as part of an international adoptive family. She writes, "We, like these children whom we claim so adamantly as our kids, have deeper roots than we knew, an enlarged sense of family, another place in the heart, and a rich and varied history of facing life issues we would never have encountered without them." Register concludes that a dual heritage can be seen "not as confusing, but as life-enhancing."[9]

In the end, it is clear that the debate over international adoption has little to do with genuine concerns about risks to children. There can be no doubt that children's interests are served by such adoption. If their interests were actually to govern, as they are supposed to govern, we would eliminate current barriers to international adoption so as to expedite placement of as many children in need of adoptive homes as possible.

The debate has instead to do with how national communities perceive their group interests. Children are the innocent victims, symbolic pawns sacrificed to notions of group pride and honor. "It is argued that the practice is a new form of colonialism, with wealthy Westerners robbing poor countries of their children, and thus their resources. National pride is involved. However poor the country, they find the implication that they cannot care for their own children to be undignified and unacceptable."[10] Thus poor countries feel pressure to hold on to what they term "their precious resources." Rich countries feel embarrassed to do anything that might look like colonialist exploitation.

However, there is no genuine clash here between the interest of the sending nations and those of the receiving nations. International adoption serves a symbolic function for those in power. Sending countries can talk of their homeless children as "precious resources," but it is entirely clear that the last thing they need is more children to care for. Clamping down on international adoption does constitute an easy, relatively cost-free way, though, to stand up to the United States and other industrialized nations. At the same time, the well-off countries of the world have no burning need for these children. These countries are not suffering from underpopulation. Their governments might be willing to permit the entry of adoptees from abroad to enable those struggling with infertility to parent, but international adoption is not seen as serving any significant national interest. So the homeless children end up as "resources" that the receiving countries are quite willing

[7] M. Dalen & B. Saetersdal, "Transracial Adoption in Norway," Adoption and Fostering 11 (1987).

[8] M. Rorbech, Mit land er Danmark 20 (1989).

[9] Cheri Register, Are Those Kids Yours? American Families with Children Adopted from Other Countries 205, 207 (1991).

[10] Barbara Tizard, *Intercountry Adoption: A Review of the Evidence*, 32 J. Child Psychology & Psychiatry 743, 746 (1991).

to give up to further the national interest in improved relations abroad.

We should stop thinking of children as "resources"—as belonging in some fundamental way to their racial or ethnic or national communities of origin. We should take seriously the principles enshrined in international human rights documents that recognize children's rights to a loving, nurturing environment and that purport to make children's best interests determinative in matters relating to adoption.

Receiving countries need to take action to build trust. They must recognize that sending countries harbor deep resentment of the historic oppression and exploitation their peoples have been subjected to by imperialist powers, as well as genuine, even if misguided, fear that adoption abroad puts their children at risk of mistreatment. Receiving countries could demonstrate good faith and a genuine concern for children's interests by offering to develop and fund programs to benefit children's welfare within a sending country, in conjunction with any international adoption programs that are instituted. Mechanisms could be developed to provided sending countries with regular feedback on what has happened to the children who are sent abroad for adoption. Regular reports could help assure sending countries that their children are receiving good treatment and are thriving in their new homes.

Sending and receiving countries need to agree on a legal framework for international adoption that would facilitate placement. The model should be one in which each of the key decisions in the adoptive process is made carefully by a responsible agency and then deferred to by all others. All duplicative processes should be eliminated. Several agreements that already exist between particular sending and receiving countries provide examples of how two nations' laws can be coordinated so as to ease the adoption process. Receiving countries should revise their adoption, immigration, and nationalization laws to remove impediments to international adoption, and to ensure fully protected status to all foreign adoptees.

Powerful forces in today's world are aligned against international adoption. The current tendency to glorify group identity and to emphasize the importance of ethnic and cultural roots combines with nationalism to make international adoption newly suspect in this country, as well as in the world at large. But closing down international adoption does not put poor countries in a better economic position or a better power position with respect to foreign governments. It is simply a symbolic gesture "for" the nation and "against" the foreigners. It is a gesture that is easy and cheap to make because the children at issue have no political clout; their voices are not heard.

The nations of the world need to move beyond political hostilities and symbolic acts and focus on the real needs of children. If they did, they would accept international adoption as a good solution for at least some portion of the world's homeless children and could begin to restructure their laws and policies to make it work more effectively. A side benefit would be that many more people who want to parent would be given the opportunity to do so through adoption. These people now feel under significant pressure to pursue parenthood through high-tech infertility treatment techniques or complicated surrogacy arrangements, things that make little sense in a world suffering in myriad ways from overpopulation. Another side benefit would be enrichment of our understanding of the meaning of family and of community.

B. AIDS[11]

What internationally recognized human rights will be affected by AIDS, its prevention and control? Purification of blood, education and supply of items such as condoms and bleach do not raise significant human rights issues, although they may confront cultural and religious norms in certain societies. Of greater potential impact on human rights are measures for screening, isolation and quarantine, criminalization of intentional AIDS transmission, and restrictions upon personal movement.

I reviewed the Universal Declaration of Human Rights, the International Covenant on Civil and Political Rights, as well as the one on economic, social and cultural rights, the European Convention for Protection of Human Rights and Fundamental Freedoms, the American Declaration of Rights and Duties of Man, the American Convention on Human Rights, the African Charter on Human and Peoples' Rights, as well as the European Social Charter. It is clear that there are three sets of human rights contained in all or most of these international instruments that potentially could be affected by measures to control AIDS. The first set is the concepts of life, liberty and security which, of course, are found in all those instruments and have been defined more specifically to include a right to privacy.

The second is mobility rights, which are also included in all those regional and international declarations. The mobility rights generally apply to the right to reside within or leave one's own country. Rarely do they apply to a right to enter another country, although the European Social Charter does give nationals the right to work in the countries of signatories, subject only to economic and social reasons. Obviously, all these rights are not absolute, and they are subject to various limitations, some of which specifically include public health measures. Prohibitions against discrimination are another set of rights. It is worth

---

[11] By SUSAN CONNOR, excerpted from: *Health, Human Rights and International Law*, 82 PROCEEDINGS OF THE AMERICAN SOCIETY OF INTERNATIONAL LAW 128–30 (1988). Reprinted by permission.

noting that other social conditions or status usually are sort of a savings clause.

The third set of human rights is the right to health protection. I have just finished editing a book, a comparative constitutional survey, on the right to health in the Americas, and I am very interested in this. A right to health protection, in addition to the World Health Organization's constitution and the International Covenant on Economic, Social and Cultural Rights, is declared in the American Declaration, the African Charter, and the European Social Charter.

WHO's response to AIDS has taken these human rights into account. WHO has established a global program that has done an exceedingly good job of pulling together all the interested parties involved in the AIDS response. Moreover, governments, as well as research institutions, have been designated as collaborating centers. We have sponsored a number of international conferences that make the front pages of all the papers when they are completed. We have issued a series of technical reports and a number of specific recommendations on special topics. We have established a global strategy for combating AIDS that has been endorsed by the United Nations and followed by the World Bank and throughout the world. It calls for the establishment of national committees on AIDS.

Human rights are among the chief concerns in the London Declaration on AIDS prevention at World Summit of Ministers of Health, which occurred in January of 1988. Paragraph 6 stated: "We emphasize the need in AIDS prevention programs to protect human rights and human dignity. Discrimination against and stigmatization of HIV infected people and people with AIDS in population groups undermine public health and must be avoided." One other quote from the WHO's statement on social aspect disease, prevention and control programs: "AIDS prevention and control strategy can be implemented effectively and efficiently and evaluated in a manner that reflects and protects human rights."

We have the ability under the WHO Constitution to issue regulations and conventions that can be legally binding in form. We generally do not do that. We have issued only the international health regulations in that format, dealing first with the question of the impact of health regulations that restrict personal movement and other aspects of international travel. I would like to read in part from the report of the Consultation on International Travel and HIV Infection, which concluded that "international health regulations in their current form limit the health measures that national authorities may take with respect to international travelers." No measures and no health documents other than those provided for in the regulations may be imposed on arriving travelers.

The Consultation was aware, however, that some national authorities are considering implementing additional measures designed to limit the entry of HIV positive persons. It makes little sense in public terms to undertake screening of international travelers using clinical aspects of AIDS as criteria for exclusion. WHO is strongly opposed to the screening of international travelers and has set forth a series of recommendations. An important concern is that money spent on screening of international travelers, which is not going to prevent the introduction of AIDS or the HIV virus into a country, is going to divert funding from educational and counseling programs that are the most effective means of preventing the spread of the disease. The health legislation unit in WHO publishes international declarations on health legislation and collects health legislation from all of our member countries. As of March 14, 1988, we had unofficial or official notice of 25 countries that had adopted some form of restriction or requirement of an AIDS certificate. Certification that an individual is free of the AIDS virus is directed not toward the casual traveler, but toward someone who is coming to reside within the country for a sustained period of time either as a student or as a worker. The countries that have adopted this approach can be found in virtually every region of the world, in Socialist countries as well as in the United States.

Mandatory screening could be considered a violation of privacy, and particular concerns are raised about potential breaching of confidentiality. We have recommended no mandatory screening, no universal screening except for donors of blood, blood products, cells, tissues and organs. We have stated that because the other modes of transmission are a consequence of private behavior, the effectiveness of additional public health programs will depend largely on voluntary participation. In particular, there are several legal and ethical considerations involved in HIV screening, because the collection of sensitive medical information may infringe human and legal rights. The person's right to privacy can be infringed if information about HIV test results or the fact that testing was sought or required is disclosed without the person's authorization or without a clear public health benefit. Human rights are best respected by using the least restrictive, least intrusive measures available to accomplish specific public health objectives.

C. The Right to Health[12]

Health issues, as is apparent from current questions about AIDS, have many international implications. My focus is on the international legal aspects of the "right to health." What do I mean by international legal aspects? First, international legal instruments, covenants and treaties have recognized that there is a right to health. The most important of these is the International Covenant on Economic, Social and Cultural Rights, which has been ratified or is in the process of being ratified by 91 countries,

---

[12] By VIRGINIA A. LEARY, excerpted from: *Health, Human Rights, and International Law*, 82 PROCEEDING OF THE AMERICAN SOCIETY OF INTERNATIONAL LAW 122–123 (1988). Reprinted by permission.

unfortunately not including the United States. Article 12 of the covenant says that state parties recognize the right of every person to the highest obtainable standard of physical and mental health. Within the last two years, international committees of independent experts have been assembled to examine the implementation of this covenant. The Charter of the World Health Organization (WHO) says that the enjoyment of the highest attainable standard of health is one of the fundamental rights of every human being without distinction as to race, religion, political belief, economic or social condition.

As international lawyers, I believe we are called upon to give normative content to these general statements of the "right to health" by elaboration and by specification. Most of us are more accustomed to the concept of the right to access to health care, rather than the right to health. The latter term has been ridiculed by those assuming that it means that everyone has a right not to be ill or that everyone has an equal right to the most advanced medical care. These two things are patently impossible for any society to provide no matter how rich it is. But the "right to health" is a shorthand expression that can be given reasonable content.

In legal, philosophical and medical circles today the phrase "right to health" is being used increasingly. Health professionals distinguish clearly between health care and health status, an important distinction when talking about the "right to health" internationally. Let me give you an illustration of this distinction.

I just spent 18 months in Canada, analyzing its universal health care system. It is an extraordinary system and one we should study in the United States. Under the Canadian health care system access to health care is excellent. All Canadians have access to a universal health care system, unlike in the United States, where around 37 million Americans do not have medical insurance or health care insurance. Nevertheless, the health status of Canadians, as distinguished from their access to health care, is far from adequate. There are widespread differences in the rates of illness and mortality among different groups in Canada. The urban poor and native Canadian Indians have inferior health status, inequalities that the Minister of Health in Canada has recently adopted a primary health care approach to address.

Why should we have a rights-based approach to health issues? WHO has not emphasized a rights-based approach, despite the fact that its charter and constitution and other instruments refer to a "right to health." Why do human rights groups now emphasize health care or health status as a right? Louis Henkin recently spoke to the Columbia Human Rights Center on health and medical care, and he clarified why it is important to look at health care and access to health from the "rights" point of view. The rights approach, according to Professor Henkin, begins with the individual and focuses on his or her welfare. It sees welfare of the individual as an object of morality and as a purpose of a just society. According to Professor Henkin, adopting a utilitarian approach would provide the greatest good to the greatest number and not concentrate on individuals or on their rights. Another option would be to adopt a paternal or professional perspective, where the individual as a beneficiary is regarded as receiving advice and assistance from professionals in a paternal sense, particularly from medical professionals who would make decisions for the individuals. Or we could have a market perspective where health care is to be sold as are many other goods.

Human rights are justified claims to freedoms, immunities, and benefits that the individual has upon his or her society, and which the society must respect and insure. Legal and philosophical writings contain technical discussions of the concept of rights, but the language of human rights in normal use is not confined to technical definitions. It is used to express the fundamental importance of the particular issue.

Tom Campbell, a Scottish philosopher, has expressed this well. In an introduction to a collection of essays entitled Human Rights from Rhetoric to Reality, he writes that the rhetoric of human rights draws on the moral resources of our belief in the significance of our underlying common humanity. Human rights discourse then serves both as a potent source of radical critiques of actual social arrangements and also as a powerful basis for working out and presenting alternative institutional practices.

It is in this sense that we should discuss the right to health. It is meant to signify that health is an important social value, a social value so fundamental that it should be given particular protection and promotion within the community.

D. Medical Experimentation[13]

Between October 1946 and August 1947 the International Military Tribunal at Nuremberg tried 23 Nazi physicians, medical administrators and anthropologists for war crimes and crimes against humanity. They were charged with four types of acts. First was unnecessary medical experimentation on victims who had absolutely no choice and under conditions that were truly appalling. Second was the taking of living people and killing them for the purpose of putting their skulls and skeletons in an anthropological museum of racial types. Third was the extermination of thousands of tubercular Poles for no reasons at all. Fourth were acts committed pursuant to the Nazi euthanasia pro-

---

[13] By ELLEN LUTZ, excerpted from: *Health, Human Rights, and International Law*, 82 PROCEEDINGS OF THE AMERICAN SOCIETY OF INTERNATIONAL LAW 133–37 (1988). Reprinted by permission.

gram that was initially designed to eliminate "the insane, sick, and aged people" considered by the Nazis to be "useless eaters," but which ultimately provided the excuse for the extermination of European Jewry.

What were the men and women who participated in such horrendous deeds like? Yale psychiatrist Robert Jay Lifton recently completed a study during which he went to Germany and interviewed 29 health professionals who had been active at high levels in Nazi medicine. He describes them as follows: "Neither brilliant nor stupid, neither inherently evil nor particularly ethically sensitive, they were by no means demonic figures–sadistic, fanatic, lusting to kill–[as] people often thought them to be." What was demonic, remarked a survivor, was that they were not demonic.

Indeed, most Nazi doctors were the product of medical training and part of a professional core that had been thoroughly corrupted by Nazi socialism. This process began in medical school. Beginning in 1933, medical schools were reserved for Aryans; non-Aryans were not allowed. Studies were interrupted regularly for military and paramilitary training. Certain faculties were decimated almost totally. For example, in psychiatry, most of the faculty was dismissed, traditional psychotherapy techniques were abandoned, and teaching was limited to the rehashing of Nazi ideology. Thus, the whole educational process at the outset was altered, and admissions into the profession led to continued obligations with professional societies becoming party organs.

The political ideology itself was recast so as to appeal to Aryan physicians. The Nazis thought of the entire Nazi extermination program as a public health problem. Killing became a "therapeutic imperative." One doctor described his involvement as follows: "Of course, I am a doctor, and I want to preserve life. And out of respect for human life, I would remove a gangrenous appendix from a diseased body. The Jew is the gangrenous appendix in the body of mankind." Given this political environment and the degree of institutional penetration it remains appalling, but not surprising, that many physicians yielded their personal values to those of the dominant political and public opinion, instead of adhering to their oaths as physicians.

The sentences handed down by the Nuremberg Military Tribunal were among the harshest penalties ever imposed on health professionals for human rights violations. Of the 16 convicted, 7 were hanged, 5 were sentenced to life imprisonment, and the remainder received lengthy prison terms. But the trial did not mark the end of health professional participation in human rights abuses. Similar, although perhaps lesser but nonetheless grave, abuses have occurred elsewhere around the world.

By the early 1970s human rights organizations such as Amnesty International were concerned about reports of torture in various countries around the world, and in particular by reports of the participation of health professionals in this torture and in other human rights violations. They heard stories that health professionals had (1) performed medical examinations on subjects prior to interrogation and in effect cleared them for torture; (2) attended torture sessions in order to intervene, as in a boxing ring, when the victim's life was endangered; (3) treated physical effects of torture so as to patch up the victim and send him back into the torture chamber; (4) participated directly in torture through the use of psychotropic drugs or other medical techniques; and (5) helped cover up torture by issuing inaccurate medical reports or autopsies.

Amnesty International convened a conference that resulted in, among others, two very important sets of ethical guidelines for health professionals. First, Amnesty reviewed all the old codes of conduct: the Hippocratic Oath, the Prayer of Maimonides, and other codes that have been generated at different times. Looking for evidence of some sort of guidelines for health professionals who were in state service and potentially at risk, it found that the guidelines were inadequate and published its own set.

Two years later the World Medical Association, the premier international nongovernmental body that is affiliated with many national medical associations, adopted a strong set of ethical guidelines, known as the Declaration of Tokyo. The Declaration of Tokyo prohibits health professionals from participating in the practice of torture in "all situations." The U.N. General Assembly promulgated a similar set of guidelines that had been drafted by the World Health Organization. They are also quite strong and forbid health professionals from participating in torture and doing any of the kinds of activities that I described above.

While these codes of professional conduct set very clear guidelines on how health professionals should act, they lacked, with one exception, effective enforcement mechanisms. Only the nursing code of conduct includes a reporting requirement. Thus, national medical associations or governments are left to implement the content, to make sure health professionals do not act in those ways.

In conclusion, let me return to the Nazi experience. Robert Lifton pointedly noted that the world remembered with pride that the Danish resisted Jewish deportation. But very few Jews were deported from Italy or Bulgaria, and this is attributed not to heroic acts of resistance but to a massive but quiet refusal to cooperate by the entire population. In many instances, it caused the deportation system to break down and even created uncertainty in the minds of the Nazi functionaries working there to the point where they became less zealous about the deportation program overall. It is clear that if an entire profession refuses to participate in human rights abuses, the ability of those who seek to perpetrate those abuses becomes weaker. If no doctor would certify that a person is fit for torture, maybe people would not be sent back into torture chambers. If no pathologist would falsify an autopsy report, perhaps there would be fewer violent clandestine summary executions.

I think the legal profession, like the medical profession, needs to take steps to solidify ethical norms and to implement procedures to support those who uphold such norms and censure those who do not. To give an example, there is no lawyer code conduct that includes a provision requiring a prosecutor to refuse to introduce evidence obtained by torture or other illegal means. Defense attorneys should protest due process abuses and refuse to continue when there is no chance that a defendant would get a fair trial. Judges should investigate habeas corpus petitions thoroughly and should refuse to allow sham trials in their courtrooms. As a profession we need to create such guidelines. I hope we can take an even stronger position than the health professionals, although everyone who works in public international law knows the difficulty of this. By trying to create a mechanism to implement these guidelines, perhaps we can reach the supreme goal of eliminating human rights abuses.

Question from the Floor:

MICHAEL CARDOZO: I was interested in the discussion of the Nazi experiments. Occasionally, the Nazi experiments led to discoveries of great importance in the health field. I wonder if scientists now question their right to use these results in modern-day medical care because of human rights abuses. The example that I know something about was in the field of typhus. The Nazis put out a paper announcing the incubation period for typhus between the bite of the louse and the time that the typhus disease developed. The only way they could have discovered this was by having an infected louse bite a human being. I knew some people in the U.S. Typhus Commission who were very excited when the incubation period for typhus was announced. How bad is it to use that kind of information? Is there any comparable situation in the health field where information was obtained in a very evil way, but is very important to us?

ELLEN LUTZ: I'm certainly no expert in this area, although I was quite fascinated about a month ago to hear a program on National Public Radio discussing the ethical use of Nazi experimentation, particularly the freezing experiments. Apparently, it is quite a sensitive debate in the scientific community, the ethics of which have not yet been resolved. My husband is a physician and a specialist in public health, and we argue about this. This is an issue that has provoked some heated debates even within the context of our family about the proper use of these experiments. His position is that there is no other way to get that information because we could never repeat those experiments. Therefore, the research should not be buried. Humanity should have access to it. I am troubled, however, by the thought that we really could learn something from such gross behavior. It is not resolved ethically.

E. Sale of Human Organs[14]

In Brazilian mythology there is a figure called "Papa Figo." "Papa Figo" terrorizes children. He's a bogeyman, the anti-Santa Claus, the anti-Father Christmas. He has a sack of children over his back, and he haunts them at night. In modern-day Brazil, he is the driver of a hired pickup van cruising the streets searching for teen-age children, even younger children, to buy or otherwise obtain from them their kidneys, for there is a very active market in the buying and selling of human organs in Brazil and many other countries today, both developed and undeveloped countries.

I have spoken now on three continents about this particular topic, and it is amazing to see that even the health organizations that comprehend the magnitude of the problem have not yet come to grips with it, despite the fact that it is a major issue world-wide, and certainly a major issue in the United States. True, in the United States, unlike India, one cannot open a copy of a daily paper and see ads for the buying and selling of kidneys. It is also true that, unlike in England, that has no law on the subject, it is rare that in the luggage checking area of a major airport one finds a suitcase that has 11 frozen kidneys in it. But there are problems in the United States with respect to organ transplantation that we have not addressed. For instance, we seem content to deal with offshore organ transplantation as we have with offshore banking and offshore business: minimally or not at all.

With respect to international human rights norms, neither the Universal Declaration of Human Rights nor any other instrument contains provisions that specifically forbid the buying and selling of human organs. In fact, in giving a similar lecture on this subject in Oxford, I was challenged by a professor who contended that my concerns amounted to an interference with a property right in one's body. If one wanted to sell it, one should be allowed to do so, he argued, and any infringement of such a right was arbitrary, and therefore in violation of article 17 of the Universal Declaration.

---

[14] By RICHARD B. LILLICH, excerpted from: *Health, Human Rights and International Law*, 82 PROCEEDINGS OF THE AMERICAN SOCIETY OF INTERNATIONAL LAW PROCEEDINGS 130–33 (1988). Reprinted by permission.

Let me just mention briefly several of the articles in the Universal Declaration from which I derive general guidance. Article 1, of course, says that all human beings are born free and equal in dignity and rights, are endowed with reason and conscience, and should act toward one another in the spirit of brotherhood. Obviously, by selling an organ one violates the body's integrity, even if it is done supposedly on a voluntary basis, and the individual subsequently could be subjected to mortal or other illnesses. This result offends article 1. Similarly, article 3 provides that everyone shall have the right to security of person. Where, as in many countries, women and children are subject to the male in the family, their security of person would be infringed if they were pressured or coerced into selling body parts for the "good of the family." Article 5 deals with degrading treatment. I hardly can think of anything that would be more degrading than putting individuals in the position of having to sell (or for that matter buy) an organ. Article 25(1) might be violated by disregard for the right to a standard of living adequate for the health and well-being of the individual and the family. Most people are born with two kidneys, with one being the backup to the other. What would happen to the individual who sold a kidney, only to have problems with the remaining one later? (Parenthetically, one of the difficulties caused by the harvesting of kidneys from children in Third World countries is deficient medical aftercare which could lead to serious illness or death). Therefore, I maintain that a basic norm emerges from the Universal Declaration and other international human rights instruments that forbids the selling of human organs, and I seek immediate action to prevent such sales.

Questions from the Floor:

W. PAUL GORMLEY: I have a question for Professor Lillich. I am an author on human rights protection and an attorney. You commented that there is a need to restrict the practice of illegal organ transplants. Could you deal with the other side of this problem, namely, is there an individual human right to receive such organ transplants? Would there be a corresponding duty imposed on states to provide, to the degree possible, organ transplants, particularly to those individuals who lack adequate financial resources? Could there be an expansion of human rights guarantees to this area, or am I a bit unrealistic in terms of attainable objectives?

Professor LILLICH: I think you have raised a general question that cuts across the entire field of health care, on whether there's an international right, as well as a domestic right, to health care and health protection. Obviously, on a high level of abstraction, one can say that all individuals should have a right both to ordinary health care and to some of these new, innovative techniques. The tremendous queue for organ transplants would be shortened greatly by an orderly program for the harvesting of human organs and their distribution in a fair and equitable way. Obviously, this step requires an examination of sensitive health care issues, and advocates of it run the risk of being charged with promoting "socialized medicine."

I would say that your specific question phases in very nicely with the general question of the extent to which we should have some kind of orderly provision of health care services, including organ transplants, to the entire body politic. There is no doubt, of course, that you can buy organs in the United States one way or another. You can jump queues. There is also no doubt, too, that I as an academic at Virginia have received better health care than my relative who lives on welfare in the Shenandoah Valley. That is the system, or lack thereof, that we are dealing with, and I would have to say, as a general principle, that it's a system that's got to be remedied. Certainly, I see no difference, however, to return to your specific question, between the furnishing of organs and the furnishing of ordinary health care.

SUSAN CONNOR. May I be permitted a short comment on organ transplants? The World Health Organization has not done much in this area. Coincidentally, we have just collected the legislation from the hemisphere on organ transplants, and quite frankly most of it is good. It follows the recommendations of the U.S. National Commission on Organ Transplants. It prohibits commercialization. It has brain death criteria and establishes a universal donor system. Sometimes there are even national organ centers provided for. One of the problems that we have found, which you are familiar with as international lawyers, particularly those interested in human rights, is that there is a big slip between cup and lip. The enforcement problem is difficult. One of the international problems in the organ transplant area is that hospitals are importing children from Guatemala to remove their kidneys. The Justice Department is investigating this now. Putting on my hat as a representative of the Third World, I would say that the United States needs to clean its own house first and take steps to ensure that this kind of victimization does not occur. All of this deserves further study, and I am delighted that Professor Lillich is working in this area.

F. International Sports Law[15]

Law guides and constrains international sports events. That should not be surprising. If there is law where there

---

[15] By JAMES A.R. NAFZIGER, excerpted from: INTERNATIONAL SPORTS LAW 1–9 (Transnational Publishers 1988), *and In-*

is society, it is likely that the legal process might play a significant role in helping to meet people's expectations about an activity as prominent and universal as athletics.

The term "international sports law" refers to a more or less distinctive body of rules, principles and procedures that govern the political and social consequences of transnational sports activity. As a body of international law, its general sources are the sources of international law: the United Nations Charter; international custom, as evidence of a general practice accepted as law; general principles (including those articulated in the resolutions of international organizations); and, as subsidiary sources, judicial decisions and scholarly writings. The many legal strands include not only hard law, but ad hoc or ambiguous decisions, lofty principles, and incomplete rules. Together they form a framework of distinctive, significant law.

Within this framework, the dominant institution is the Olympic Movement, which is governed primarily by the International Olympic Committee (IOC). Although it is technically a nongovernmental organization limited to a quadrennial agenda of athletic events, it is nevertheless instrumental in shaping a body of rules and principles that extends far beyond the programmatic activity arranged at the IOC's headquarters in Lausanne, Switzerland. The Olympic Movement deliberately plans association and competition among athletes, and effectively serves as a nucleus or catalyst for the development of international sports law. For example, many of the IOC's rules and practices against political exploitation of sports competition have become customary in the global legal system. The charisma and high visibility of the Olympic Games help explain the IOC's unusual influence in the legal process. It is a good example of the role of some nongovernmental organizations in the functional process of international integration and progressive development of international law.

To achieve the objectives of its Charter, the Olympic Movement relies on a continuous program of planning, supervising and regulating sports activity, culminating in the quadrennial competitions. Its structure embraces the IOC, local organizing committees of each Olympiad's host city, international sports federations, national Olympic committees, national associations and clubs, athletes and other participants, and other organizations and institutions recognized by the IOC. Although the nongovernmental Olympic Movement and its constituent bodies cannot alone compel government compliance, their rules, regulations and decisions help determine state practice and best articulate a customary or autonomous sports law. Thus, "the whole Olympic system operates on the fringe of public international law."[16]

Rules of the Olympic Charter govern decisions of sports federations and national committees to which municipal and regional law often defers. For example, "the sui generis law of the Olympic Movement [is] accepted, respected and applied as a State-independent body of legal rules in a growing number of municipal court decisions."[17] In some countries there is a national governing body for each sport; these bodies are endowed with monolithic control within the authoritative structure of the Olympic Movement, including international sports federations and national Olympic committees. Applicable rules and procedures of the Olympic Movement eventually permeate purely domestic competition as well.

The centrality of Olympic aspirations in the commitment and training of athletes at all levels of development is an essential point in understanding the sources and structure of international sports law. In today's high-technology world of sports, improved performance typically requires professional assistance and money. In response, grass-roots management and funding of training and competition are channeled to aspiring athletes through local and national sports associations. These associations operate at the base of a pyramid of authority with the international sports federations and the IOC at the top. This structure for transmitting the authority and legitimacy of the Olympic process influences even schoolyard and sandlot activities whenever participants receive support from sanctioned sports organizations that are ultimately assisted and governed by organizations within the Olympic Movement. Governments, committed to the Olympic Movement or influenced by it, may also assist directly in this transmission of rules and decisions. The agencies of transmission or permeation of Olympic authority and legitimacy vary among states. In some, the process is confined to a strictly nongovernmental hierarchy, from the IOC down through international sports federations and national Olympic committees to national federations and, finally, local associations. In other states, national legislation, pronouncements of sports ministries or national commissions, and judicial decisions may involve governments more directly. Sometimes, as in the Olympic funding of athletes from developing countries, governance is direct. Through these various channels, Olympic rules and decisions normally constitute either an autonomous regime to which governments defer or international custom practiced by them.

ternational Sports Law: A Replay of Characteristics and Trends, 86 AMERICAN JOURNAL OF INTERNATIONAL LAW 489, 491–95, 500–505, 518 (1992). Reprinted by permission.

[16] Johnson, Book Review, 60 B.Y.I.L. 450, 451 (1989).

[17] Bruno Simma, *The Court of Arbitration for Sport*, in VOLKERRECHT/RECHT DER INTERNATIONALES ORGANISATIONEN/WELTWIRTSCHAFTSRECHT: FESTSCHRIFT FUR IGNAZ SEIDL-HOHENVELDERN 573, 580 (1988).

The governing network or structure of international sports law extends beyond the Olympic Movement. Intergovernmental organizations also formulate and enforce international sports law. Such organizations include UNESCO, the Commonwealth Federation, bilateral arrangements, and regional organizations such as the European Communities and the supreme Council for Sports in Africa. Typically, they recognize the authority of the Olympic Movement but expand its rules and develop new institutions.

The complex network of non-governmental organization, government, and inter-governmental organization authority is still rather fragile. Enforcement depends on principles of reciprocity and good faith. Procedures for implementing decisions includes the disqualification of athletes and national teams by the Olympic Movement and such inter-governmental organizations as the Commonwealth Federation, as in its fight against apartheid and other forms of racial discrimination; and the application of international rules and procedures by sports ministries, courts and other domestic authorities. Specific measures under municipal authority include, for example, exceptions to immigration laws and regulations designed to protect athletes' right to compete in conformity with non-governmental or inter-governmental organizational requirements, and the recognition and enforcement of international arbitral awards on such issues as eligibility, the commercialization of sports, and substance abuse.

The overall process of rule making and enforcement might be classified as an "intentional regime," "true international law," "droit des gens," or perhaps simply "transnational law." The label does not seem to be terribly important. What is important in understanding the structure and force of international sports law is to take account of the interdependence of public and private authority and of the emerging role of complex legal processes that blend governmental and nongovernmental authority. This structure clearly reveals the "declining reliability of formal criteria of international law as guideposts to its constitution and the discrepancy between formal status and legal significance."[18] The most challenging and significant questions do not involve labeling, but rather prioritizing, harmonizing and enforcing pertinent rules and procedures on a more effective, pragmatic basis.

The image of lawyers rushing into the international sports arena is as unappealing as watching them chase after ambulances. Nevertheless, because sports events assume heroic proportions in the public limelight, related problems may be big and complex. Resolving such problems requires the skills of lawyers and policy-makers alike.

The problems are big and complex, in part because the public worships athletics. Sports ministries and nongovernmental sports organizations – regardless of their political character – make important political decisions, often ex cathedra. With customary wit, a distinguished jurist, The Lord Wiberforce, referred to the "excommunication" of offending countries by today's "one true world religion," the Olympic Games.[19] At the least, sports competition could be fairly described as a leading folk religion. Sportswriters often use words such as "sacrifice," "faith," "hope," and "glory." There seems to be at work (or play) some kind of human need to mimic the cosmic combat of Good and Evil. Theistic or not, sports relations among nations merit serious attention.

The significance of sports in global affairs is profound. To Juan Antonio Samaranch, President of the IOC, sports activity is "the largest social force of our time."[20] Whatever its sociological magnitude, international competition certainly has significant politico-legal dimensions and consequences. Several examples will illustrate this point. The terrorist kidnapping and murder of athletes at the 1972 Olympic Games led to a Convention for the Prevention and Punishment of Certain Acts of International Terrorism.[21] Boycotts of the 1980 and 1984 Olympic Games involved a flurry of diplomatic activity and a reconsideration of the efficacy of boycotts as an international sanction. Qualifying matches for the World Cup in soccer became a topic at the 1983 Conference of Nonaligned Nations.[22] In 1985 a wave of violence in the sports world led to several measures, including a European-wide treaty on spectator violence[23] that was drafted and entered into force in the record time of less than three months. The issue of whether to exclude South African nationals from international competition has been a focus of diplomatic attention for many years. The reemergence of China as a sports power has substantial implications for it and for the future of international relations and world order. Proposals for North Korea to host part of the 1988 Games presented difficult issues as they were being considered. Issues of commercialization and drug abuse by athletes cry out for resolution.

The sheer scope of the Olympic Games, in particular,

[18] Gunther Handl, Remarks, 82 ASIL PROC. 372 (1988).

[19] The Lord Wiberforce, *The Age of the International Lawyer*, 76 ASIL PROC. 301, 302 (1082).

[20] OLYMPIC REVIEW 156 (Mar. 1984).

[21] John Murphy, THE UNITED NATIONS AND THE CONTROL OF INTERNATIONAL VIOLENCE: A LEGAL AND POLITICAL ANALYSIS 181 (1982).

[22] Shaplen, *A Reporter at Large* (Conference of Nonaligned Nations), 59 NEW YORKER 82, 94 (May 23, 1983).

[23] *European Convention on Spectator Violence and Misbehavior at Sports Events and in Particular at Football Matches*, 24 I.L.M. 1566 (1985).

demonstrates the significance of international sports competition. Nearly 8,000 athletes from 141 countries took part in the 1984 Games in Los Angeles. Revenue from ticket-sales alone was $90 million. The 1984 Games, breaking with tradition, reaped such a huge profit that the United States Olympic Committee (USOC) had to find a way to make use of it.[24] Two years later USOC announced that it would establish a "Friendship Fund" for the distribution of some $1 million to other national committees in proportion to the number of their athletes at the 1984 Games; in addition, the USOC announced that it would disburse an additional $3.2 million for other use within the Olympic Movement. The quadrennial pageant was clearly not a marche au supplice, as some observers had mistakenly predicted.

In no small measure, the Games and other international sports competition take place on this grand scale and issues are routinely resolved because of a relatively stable, though incomplete, legal framework. Rules and principles indisputably shape the organization and administration of global athletics. International sports law, however soft it may be, offers a well articulated, comprehensive means of promoting and protecting the essential values of sports competition. For example, constituent sports organizations, often sanctioned by municipal law, may "never associate themselves with any undertaking which would be in conflict with the principles of the Olympic Movement and with the Rules of the IOC," and "must be autonomous and must resist all pressures of any kind whatsoever, whether of a political, religious or economic nature."[25] Rules such as these in the Olympic Charter define international custom today.

What about political intervention in international sports, such as boycotts of the Olympic Games? Doesn't such intervention belie the reality of legal constraints? Clearly, political intervention is a major threat to the law. Law has its limits. Even so, it is easy to exaggerate the deficiencies in the law and overlook its efficiencies. Too much can be expected of any body of international law, especially when it is young. If we take a good hard look at the actual practice of states, it is apparent that their actions normally accord with the prescribed rules and procedures of international sports law because they are respected as such. East-West boycotts and other spectacular instances of questionable intervention make the front pages of newspapers, but are the exception, not the rule. Rather, it seems likely that international sports law has helped protect competition against a good deal of political intervention and has ensured a measure of universality, solidarity, fairness and goodwill among athletes.

Can international sports law transcend sports to accomplish larger goals of world order? Generally speaking, regulation of international sports competition has been more concerned with the limited tasks of ensuring maximum participation and maintaining minimum order than with larger goals. Despite the high profile of sports in global affairs and the existence of a corresponding legal framework, there is a good deal of confusion and uncertainty about a larger role for sports in world affairs. That is in no small part because reliable information is skimpy. There has been only marginal empirical analysis of the controversial theory that sports competition inherently promotes world order. Our rather hazy understanding of sports sociology and politics thus inhibits our capacity to define the role of law in accomplishing such goals of the Olympic Movement as "to bring together the athletes of the world [and] to spread the Olympic principles throughout the world, thereby creating international goodwill."[26]

So far, the data do not indicate any inherent contribution of sports competition to world order or integration. The contributions of sports activity to world order seem to have been more the unintended consequences of isolated decisions than the results of a deliberate promotion of organizational goals. Nevertheless, as governments and international organizations become more concerned with sports, as sports bodies grow stronger and take on more juridical functions, and as techniques develop to implement values that transcend the sports arena, the organization of international sports is becoming more oriented toward world order. This trend is, of course, consistent with the original aspirations of modern sports organizations.

The institutional structure of sports competition facilitates this trend. Rules and procedures that were intended primarily to govern only the Games has functioned also in pursuit of larger objectives. For example, the IOC's insistence on racial equality in sports has given greater resonance to global campaigns against racial discrimination. Just hosting major competition may encourage a host state to strengthen the human rights of its citizens in order to avoid foreign criticism that might jeopardize scheduled plans. The imminence of the 1964 Games in Tokyo helps explain Japan's improvement of trade-union protection, and concern about the 1988 Games in Seoul encouraged political reform, including the holding of a presidential election in 1987. Bilateral techniques of utilizing sports competi-

---

24 The Los Angeles Olympic Organizing Committee announced initially a profit of "at least $215 million", from which it offered retroactively to pay the expenses of some foreign participants and to make grants for sports programs. CHRISTIAN SCI. MONITOR, Dec. 21, 1984, at 2, col. 4. Final accounting revealed a $225 million profit. L.A. TIMES, Dec. 10, 1985, at 22, col. 1.

25 Olympic Charter, Rule 24(c).

26 Olympic Charter, Rule 1.

tion, such as the ping-pong diplomacy conducted by the United States and China during the early 1970's, have broader implications. In this way, sports events may sometimes be a vital component of world order.

Legal guidance and constraints are not necessarily more important than political, economic, social or cultural ones. In a world of uncertainty it may always be unclear how these constraints relate to each other and which are more important than others in a particular case. What seems clear, however, is the need to bring together the scattered data, norms, rules, principles and procedures of law that do exist; to analyze these; to identify strengths, weaknesses, and gaps in the legal framework; and to offer some guidance to assist in progressively developing the law. The ongoing revision of the Olympic Charter adds to the timeliness of an inquiry into international sports law. An understanding of the present Charter, as applied, will inform revised versions of it and the development of a larger body of international sports law.

The panorama of international sports competition is constantly changing, and change revitalizes. Consider, for example, the following sports: lawn tennis, rackets, roque, lacrosse, tug-of-war, rope climb, Indian club swinging, the 60-meter sprint, five-mile run, 200-meter hurdles, 4000-meter steeplechase, the shot put with both hands, the javelin throw with both hands, obstacle swimming, underwater swimming, plunge for distance (from a dive, to gain the greatest distance straight forward in the water), polo, rugby, and motor boating. All used to be Olympic events, but no longer are. Individuals and nations come and go, too. Traditional distinctions between amateurs and professionals now seem artificial. New problems emerge. In recent years concerns about racism, violence, and the use of drugs have plagued the sports world as never before. What will certainly keep such constantly changing activity and problems within acceptable limits are stable institutions and at least a measure of law, largely of contemporary origin.

UNESCO's Intergovernmental Committee for Physical Education and Sport has warned against three threats to the implementation of the Olympic charter: "inappropriate" commercialization, drugs and violence. These threats, as well as eligibility issues, dominate the attention of international sports lawyers today.

(1) *Eligibility of athletes.* Long-dominant issues of eligibility centered until recently on attempts to define the hallowed, but increasingly archaic, concept of the "amateur" so as to exclude its antithesis, the "professional," from major sanctioned competition. This dichotomy arose in the nineteenth century, on the bases of European elitism and a fairly widespread revulsion to betting, monetary rewards and other commercialization of sports activity. Today, however, the amateur/professional distinction has less significance; open competition has become the norm, and athletes may enter into lucrative commercial identifications in advertising and public relations so long as they comply with regulations established by their international sports federations in conformity with the Olympic Charter. To the extent that the traditional dichotomy remains, "amateurism" is not antithetical to *commercialization* of an athlete's or organization's name, likeness or reputation, but only to *professionalism*, which means that payment is expected for athletic performance, and even that distinction is no longer as important as it once was. To the extent that the distinction remains important, a new rule of athlete eligibility, governed by the international federations of the Olympic Movement, is determinative. The new rule distinguishes between the taboo of direct compensation for performance and the acceptability of status-related income that athletes may receive from advertising or promotional appearances. This concept of eligibility has expanded to govern not just athletes, but coaches, officials, trainers, managers, administrators and all "participants" in sport.

Explanations for this change include a growing recognition of the hypocrisy of "shamateurism" in turning a blind eye to the rampant employment, subsidy and training of athletes by governments and academic institutions. The ideology of amateurism has also suffered from its identification with Victorian-Edwardian elitism; an erosion of the barriers to commercial exploitation of athletes; perceived inequities in denying remuneration to one class of athletes (amateurs) as salaries skyrocketed for others (professionals); and expanded coverage by the media of sports competition, with all of its financial enticements to promoters and athletes. Within the Olympic framework, strict rules of amateurism have given way to flexible rules of eligibility that accept open as well as regulated compensation. For example, Rule 51 of the International Amateur Athletic Federation, which governs track-and-field competition, now provides simply that "an amateur is one who abides by the eligibility rules of the IAAF."

These rules have become institutionalized, essentially as standards for licensing sports participants to engage in regulated activity, and have greatly influenced the management and regulation of domestic competition. Issues of strict "amateurism" having faded, the dominant issues of eligibility now involve compliance by individual athletes with specific rules of international federations and national sports associations, commercialization and doping. As the IOC and international sports federations consolidate immense resources from sponsorships, advertising and broadcasting rights, and as sponsors, advertisers and broadcasters assume greater leverage over athletes, the force of eligibility rules in their lives cannot be exaggerated.

The rules and institutions of international sports law that have governed "amateur" competition are of heightened relevance to "professional" athletes and events as the amateur/professional distinction disappears and as international sports federations take their place as cartels alongside professional sports leagues. Also, the extension of professional sports leagues into international markets has highlighted the need for international agreements and more uniform third-party machinery to resolve issues of player contracting, antitrust implications of mergers and acquisitions, labor rights of athletes and taxation of income. Efforts to extend international sports law to professional activity, however, face formidable hurdles, ranging from divergent antidoping standards and procedures to the very idea of regulating income from individual sports activity. Nevertheless, as open competition, income management and cartelization of "amateur" sports develop, the common ground of all athletic activity becomes apparent.

(2) *Commercialization of sports and athletes.* The IOC has responded to increasing commercialization of the sports arena and its participants by assuming control over the commercial activity rather than fighting it. The resulting bonanza for the Olympic Movement includes the Olympic Programmes, which are gigantic international marketing schemes for recruiting major corporate sponsors by offering them "one-stop shopping." A sponsor thereby becomes the "official sponsor" of competition and the exclusive licensee of intellectual property rights of the IOC and all national Olympic committees. The system is managed exclusively by International Sports and Leisure, a Swiss corporation. Besides this system, the IOC has negotiated lucrative contracts for the exclusive broadcasting of competition and the development of new techniques for broadcasting, including use of private and public networks, Eurosport channels, satellite transmission, and video cassettes. It has also promoted the creation of trust funds under the supervision of international sports federations for the control of income earned by athletes. The Olympic Movement has thus consolidated a vast array of resources under central, nongovernmental administration. In effort, it has developed a sort of international cartel under the authority of the Olympic Charter and the International Olympic Committee. This development exemplifies the transformation of the international sports regime from a decentralized framework relying on unilateral, ad hoc enforcement, into a vast international administrative authority that relies on routine regulation.

(3) *Substance abuse.* The use of performance-enhancing substances and methods by athletes has generated immense controversy. Attention has centered on anabolic steroids, but many other substances and methods are also prohibited. Exposes of government-sponsored steroid usage have alarmed, though perhaps not surprised, the public.

In response, the IOC prohibits competitors from using specific listed substances and procedures. One of its rules, for example, prohibits doping, provides for a medical code, and provides for enforcement through international sports federations. Laboratories accredited by the Committee conduct both routine and unannounced tests. Although municipal law generally defers to the IOC's system, many legal systems have not dealt adequately with such critical questions as the advisability of extending tests from competition to training and ethical-religious objections to mandatory testing. Unfortunately, the various international sports federations have maintained inconsistent standards and procedures of enforcement, and supervision by the IOC has been haphazard, including its failure to test for blood doping at the 1992 winter games in Albertville. These deficiencies have provoked controversy and called into question the effectiveness and integrity of the Olympic Committee's regime of controls.

At the 1988 games in Seoul, the IOC retracted the gold medal won by Canadian Ben Johnson in the 100-meter sprint after tests revealed the presence of an anabolic steroid in his urine. Johnson's stature as an erstwhile world-record holder served to rivet global attention on substance abuse by athletes, and accelerated efforts to establish a uniform, effective antidoping mechanism. The Canadian Government responded to the Johnson incident and the suspension of four Canadian weightlifters for substance abuse by appointing a blue-ribbon commission of inquiry headed by Ontario's Chief Justice, Charles L. Dubin. The Dubin report highlighted the enormity of drug abuse in the international sports arena and the need for improved supervision and enforcement by the IOC and the international sports federations.

The IOC promptly adopted stiff sanctions against drug trafficking and a comprehensive International Olympic Charter against Doping in Sport, and it entered into an agreement with the association of international sports federations to harmonize and mutually enforce rules, procedures and sanctions under the IOC's medical code. The Johnson incident inspired other accords as well. These included a U.S.-Soviet Mutual Doping Control Agreement providing for mutual testing of athletes and other antidoping cooperation; a trilateral agreement between Australia, Canada and the United Kingdom for information sharing and cooperation in drug testing; a multilateral agreement based on the U.S.-Soviet pact, to be supervised by the IOC's Medical Commission; and the Council of Europe's Anti-Doping Convention. These instruments have helped universalize standards and broaden the jurisdiction of testing bodies, though troublesome inconsistencies remain.

(4) *Other issues.* Spectator violence remains a serious problem despite efforts to improve national and international legal controls. Although events have overtaken the observation that the post-Cold War era began "with less violence than we have come to fear from a single soccer

game,"[27] hooliganism in the stadium continues. The European Convention on Spectator Violence provides one model of judicial cooperation and extradition, but it has limitations. It applies only to international competitions, it is regional, and even in its region it has failed to deter bloodshed in the bleachers, mostly instigated by British soccer fans.

Efforts to equalize opportunity have shifted from a longtime focus on apartheid to concentration on more pervasive forms of discrimination prohibited by Rule 3 of the Olympic Charter. Eliminating gender discrimination and facilitating sport for the disabled have headed the agenda. Special programs to train and equip athletes from developing countries and to improve their physical facilities have helped ensure equality of opportunity for them. UNESCO and the IOC, through its program of Olympic Solidarity, have led these efforts, assisted by bilateral programs.

In conclusion, the regime of control over international sports is still incomplete; it is more of a kaleidoscope than a tight system of law. Nevertheless, it is considered to be authoritative and legitimate. A trend toward more systematic and uniform administration, regulation and dispute resolution is apparent. The task for international and comparative lawyers is to refine, prioritize, harmonize and seek better means of enforcing rules and procedures within this dynamic new body of law, and to improve the institutional structure for administering it.

---

[27] Bundy, From Cold War Toward Trusting Peace, Foreign Affairs 197, 198 (No. 1, 1990).

Part IV
The Normative Dimension

13
Peace[1]

Immanuel Kant's originality stems from having been the first to show the strong links between international peace and personal freedom, and between arbitrary government at home and aggressive behavior abroad.

Perpetual Peace was published in 1795 and was one of Kant's last philosophical works.[2] It is a relatively short essay that was meant for popular reading. Kant was not very good at writing for the general public, however, and the essay suffers as a consequence: the arguments are at times too concise and the writing often obscure. Nonetheless, Kant's genius pervades the essay. It had immediate success, and Kant's authority has been invoked frequently by advocates of pacifism and internationalism throughout the nineteenth and twentieth centuries.

Kant describes his task as follows:

> The state of peace among men living in close proximity is not the natural state (status naturalis); instead, the natural state is one of war, which does not just consist in open hostilities, but also in the constant and enduring threat of them. The state of peace must therefore be established, for the suspension of hostilities does not provide the security of peace, and unless this security is pledged by one neighbor to another (which can happen only in a state of lawfulness), the latter, from whom such security has been requested, can treat the former as an enemy.

The first steps that governments must take to end international lawlessness – the preliminary conditions conducive to definitive peace – are that standing armies must disappear; peace treaties should not contain reservations for future wars; states should not intervene in other states' affairs; states should not be acquired by conquest; and abject means of conducting war should be permanently prohibited.

But the most original part of Kant's theory is that international law and domestic justice are fundamentally connected. What is important for international peace is the establishment of republican forms of government in each member state of the international community: "The civil constitution of every nation should be republican." The requirement of a republican form of government must be read in conjunction with Kant's requirement that "The law of nations shall be based on a federation of free states." Together, these propositions stipulate that international law should be based upon a union of republican states. Kant asserts that adherence to these requirements will result in an alliance of free nations that will maintain itself, prevent wars, and steadily expand. Contrary to the predominant belief of his time, and to conventional present legal thinking, international law and the peace it intends to secure can only be based upon a union or an alliance of participant states that protect freedom internally and whose governments are representative. Kant for the first time linked arbitrary government at home with aggressive foreign policies.

By "republican," Kant means what we would call today a liberal democracy, a form of political organization that provides full respect for human rights. This is so notwithstanding Kant's assertion that a pure democracy is a form of despotism. Kant's explanation of a republican constitution strongly suggests the idea of a constitutional democracy, conceived as a participatory political process constrained by respect for rights. Kant correctly points out that a system of pure democracy, if unconstrained by rights, will result in the tyranny of the majority. Kant writes:

> Among the three forms of government, democracy, in the proper sense of the term, is necessarily a despotism, because it sets up an executive power in which all citizens make decisions about and, if need be, against one (who therefore does not agree); consequently, all, who are not quite all, decide, so that the general will contradicts both itself and freedom.

Plainly, Kant wanted to set constraints upon majoritarian decisions. So, only a pure democracy ("in the proper sense of the term") is despotic. In contrast, the republican constitution is a form of political organization that allows people to govern themselves and to legislate by majority vote, provided that the rights of everyone are respected – in

[1] By FERNANDO R. TESON, excerpted from: *The Kantian Theory of International Law*, 92 Columbia Law Review 53 (1992). Reprinted by permission.

[2] Immanuel Kant, *To Perpetual Peace: A Philosophical Sketch* (1795), in Perpetual Peace and Other Essays 107 (Ted Humphrey trans., 1983). Kant elaborates on his international theory elsewhere; *see Idea for a Universal History with a Cosmopolitan Intent* (1784), in Perpetual Peace and Other Essays, at 29.

short, a constitutional democracy. Thus, the Kantian idea of republicanism is best understood as being in opposition to the idea of despotism, whether exercised by a minority (one person or a junta), or by the majority enforcing its decisions in violation of the rights of dissenters. Kant envisions the republican state as one defined by a constitution based upon three principles: freedom, due process, and equality.

One can hardly overemphasize the importance of freedom – respect for individual autonomy under the rule of law – as the first tenet of international ethics. Kant is not committing the fallacy of transposing the notion of individual freedom into the conceptual framework of nationalism: freedom here is not the right to a nation-state, but primarily claims against it, claims against fellow citizens and against the government established by a social contract to implement social cooperation.

But why must states guarantee internal freedom in order to be legitimate members of the international community? One could argue that, provided international peace and stability are secured – the fundamental goal of international law according to Kant – the internal organization of states is irrelevant. Certainly it ought not be the indispensable starting point of a theory of international law. This argument has been repeatedly made; indeed, it is one of the tenets of the statist or realist school of thought.[3]

Kant gives several reasons why peace is likely to be achieved when individual rights and political participation are secured in the internal organization of all states. His first argument is that if people are self-governed, citizens on both sides of any dispute will be very cautious in bringing about a war whose consequences they themselves must bear. Those who will be eventually exposed to the horrors of the conflagration will decide whether or not to go to war.

In contrast, it is relatively easy for a despot to start a war. As Kant points out, the tyrant does not suffer the consequences; his privileges and prerogatives remain intact. Crucially, the despot does not have the benefit of objective advice and debate. He rules by force, which means that within his own entourage he is feared and vulnerable to adulation. Advisers are not likely to tell the tyrant the harsh truths, but rather only what he wants to hear. More generally, because a despotic regime does not tolerate freedom of expression, public opinion has no significant impact on the government's decisions; consequently, there is no opportunity for public debate on the moral and prudential reasons to make war. Psychologically, insulation of tyrannical rulers from criticism and debate fuels in them a sense of megalomania. Tyrants acquire a feeling of invincibility. They become accustomed to getting away with murder (literally) internally and no doubt reach a point of self-delusion where they become convinced that they can get away with external aggression as well.

Another reason Kant believes that there is an increased likelihood of an enduring peace among free republics is that in a liberal democracy citizens will be educated in the principles of right, and therefore war will appear to them as the evil that every rational person knows it is. Finally, liberal democracies foster free trade and a generous system of freedom of international movement that Kant calls the Cosmopolitan Law. Kant remarks that by observing a rule of hospitality for foreigners facilitating commerce with indigenous peoples, "distant parts of the world can establish with one another peaceful relations that will eventually become matters of public law, and the human race can gradually be brought closer and closer to a cosmopolitan constitution." Kant reaffirms this idea by observing that peoples' mutual interests unite them against violence and war, for "the spirit of trade cannot coexist with war."

Kant was cognizant, of course, that "peace to do business" is a nonmoral reason to want peace, but that such pecuniary interests provide an additional argument for requiring a liberalization of trade and freedom of movement. Free trade and freedom of movement are sufficiently linked to the principles of a liberal constitution to make leaders in liberal democracies much more prone to weigh economic costs before initiating a war. There is no question that free trade is a strong, if not dispositive, influence over external behavior. Free trade inclines diplomacy toward peace because international business transactions require stability and predictability to be successful. Kant's views have been confirmed by the success of the European Economic Community and even by the global system of international trade regulated by GATT and similar institutions. It is not by coincidence that the European Economic Community requires democracy as a prerequisite for membership, as does the more recent Mercosur, the Argentine-Brazilian free market agreement.

Recent research by Michael Doyle and R. J. Rummel bolsters Kant's argument for the causal link between domestic freedom and peace.[4] These modern versions of Kant's argument have shown that Kant's prediction of a

---

[3] Statism and realism overlap but are not coextensive. Statism is the view that the basic unit of analysis is the nation-state, not the individual. Realism is the view that nation-states act in the international arena motivated by national interest. Thus, all realists are statists, but not all statists are realists. For example, the "legalists" would argue that international law conceived in a statist way is a major component of foreign policy, thus rejecting the realist emphasis on national interest.

[4] *See* Michael W. Doyle, *Kant, Liberal Legacies, and Foreign Affairs*, 12 PHIL. & PUB. AFF. 205, 213 (1983); *id.* at pt. 2, 12 PHIL. & PUB. AFF. 323 (1983); Michael W. Doyle, *Liberalism and*

gradual expansion of the liberal alliance has been confirmed by events of the last 200 years, and notably the last 45 years. These authors' research has demonstrated that Kant was essentially right.

Liberal states have shown a definite tendency to maintain peace among themselves, while nonliberal states have shown themselves to be generally prone to make war. The historical data since 1795 seems to indicate that even though liberal states have become involved in numerous wars with nonliberal states, liberal states have yet to engage in war with one another.[5] Doyle concedes that liberal states have behaved aggressively toward nonliberal states, but he attributes this fact precisely to the difference in regimes. Conversely, nonliberal states have frequently behaved aggressively among themselves. Therefore, only a community of liberal states has a chance of securing peace, as Kant thought. Should people ever fulfill the hope of creating such a liberal international community, the likelihood of war will be greatly reduced.[6]

The second Kantian argument for including a requirement of respect for human rights as a foundational principle of international law is even more straightforward: Governments should be required by international law to observe human rights because that is the right thing to do. Kant commentators have overlooked the fact that Kant expressly offers this argument along with the empirical one. In Perpetual Peace, Kant defends the universal requirement of human rights and democracy as grounded in "the purity of its origin, a purity whose source is the pure concept of right." The empirical argument is then offered in addition to this normative one. The normative argument is addressed to those who rank justice over peace; the empirical argument, to those who rank peace over justice. Liberal democracies, ranging from laissez-faire states to welfare states, are the only ones that are likely to secure individual freedom, thereby allowing human beings to develop their potential fully. Therefore, the only way in which international law can be made fully compatible with the freedom of individuals to pursue and act upon rational life plans is if it contains a strong obligation for governments to respect human rights. International law must be congruent with individual autonomy – the trait, for Kant, that sets human beings apart from other species.

But how may we reconcile Kant's respect for human rights within a state with his principle of non-intervention? Kant asserts that "no nation shall forcibly interfere with the constitution and government of another." My reading of Kant is that his nonintervention principle is dependent upon compliance with the primary principle of internal legitimacy. The latter is what gives states the shield of sovereignty against foreign intervention. Since morally autonomous citizens hold rights to liberty, the states and governments that democratically represent them have a right to be politically independent and should be shielded by international law from foreign intervention. In other words, if the only just political arrangement is the republican constitution, state sovereignty reacquires its shielding power only in states that have adopted and implemented such a constitution. Sovereignty is to be respected only when it is justly exercised.

Insofar as international law addresses governments, it does so in their capacity as agents of persons, as representatives. This in turn raises the question of representation as an international matter. The agency relationship itself must be subject to international scrutiny. Individuals who claim to represent a nation but in fact have seized power by brute force should not be accepted as members of the community that makes the law. There is every reason to extend these commonsense notions of justice to international relations and include them in a definition of international legitimacy.

The Kantian theory of international law contends that a morally just world order comprises nation-states that are internally just and whose governments therefore represent individuals. The rights and interests of individuals form the ultimate touchstone of the theory.

It follows from my reading of Kant that citizens in a liberal democracy should be free to argue that, in some admittedly rare cases, the only morally acceptable alternative is to intervene to help the victims of serious human rights deprivations in other countries.

Perhaps there is no necessary link between the recent political triumphs of human rights and democracy and the theoretical foundations of international law and politics. Perhaps all we can say is that the wind is blowing now in the direction of individual freedom and that the historical

World Politics, 80 AM. POL. SCI. REV. 1151, 1162 (1986); R. J. Rummel, *Libertarianism and International Violence*, 27 J. CONFLICT RESOL. 27 (1983).

[5] Michael W. Doyle, *Kant, Liberal Legacies, and Foreign Affairs*, 12 PHIL. & PUB. AFF. 205, 209–17 (1983).

[6] I have not seen serious challenge to the evidence provided by Doyle and Rummel. Doyle's assertion that constitutionally secure liberal states have never engaged in war with one another is indeed bold. Writers who take issue with this view contest only the thesis – held by Rummel but not by Doyle – that liberal democracies are generally peace-prone, regardless of the nature of the other regimes. Nevertheless, everyone concurs in the factual assertion that democratic states rarely go to war amongst one another. To be sure, there are some difficult cases. Two hard cases are the 1812 war between England and the United States, and the First World War. As to the first, arguably the United States became a liberal republic only after 1865; as to the second, Doyle's explanation is that Imperial Germany, although largely a liberal republic for domestic issues, did not allow any popular participation in foreign affairs decisions. Yet, even if those cases are treated as genuine instances of war between liberal states, the correlation is still so strong that it begs explanation. The argument is not that war between liberal states is impossible, but that it is highly unlikely.

cycle will before long see nations return to despotism and gross injustice. It is indeed possible that the optimism caused by the triumph of human rights is hasty and that the celebration is therefore premature. Yet, if the tide is going to turn against individual freedom, it will be the product of human design, not of the forces of nature pushing us around. It follows that we have to construct and defend our global institutions if we want them to last.

Kant's accomplishment in the field of international theory and ethics is magnificent. Few other thinkers have successfully combined so many disparate elements of morality, politics, epistemology, and history in a theory of international law. The community of free nations envisioned by Kant will hopefully expand gradually and maintain itself, as it has done for the past two hundred years, and the aim of perpetual peace will be achieved the moment when the liberal alliance comprises every civil society. It is never too late to replace the grim view of a world order in which naked political power is the standard of legitimacy with Kant's inspired cosmopolitan vision of moral progress in which tribute is paid to the definitive traits of humanity—freedom and reason.

14

Justice

A. The View From Political Theory[1]

The debate on the ethical foundations of international law shows the influence of two familiar traditions of international thought. The first, political realism, postulates the inevitable division of mankind into separate states and proposes a strategy for national survival in the international order created by this division. Its principal thesis is that international relations take place in a state of nature. Lacking collective enforcement, international law is little more than a sham. Since no state can be sure that other states will observe the law, each must rely on self-help to protect its interests and security. Foreign policy must be guided by prudence, not morality or law.

The other tradition, which might be called "cosmopolitanism," assumes the existence of a universal community and questions the moral significance of national boundaries. Cosmopolitan moralists claim to have discovered principles of justice, grounded in the nature of rationality itself, for judging entire societies, and on the basis of those principles they seek to specify the conditions international society must meet to qualify as just. International law as an institution is substantially unjust, according to those principles, because it allows governments to abuse human rights and because it tolerates a global distribution of wealth and power that is unacceptably inegalitarian. International law therefore lacks moral authority, and its obligations are without any special force.

In spite of obvious differences, cosmopolitan and realist theories share one striking similarity. Both adopt an essentially economic attitude toward international relations, evaluating policies, rules, and institutions according to their substantive benefits and costs. In each case both the value and the authority of international law are thought to rest on its contribution to producing a state of affairs regarded as good. For the realist the goal is national security within a stable international system, while for the cosmopolitan it is an imagined just world order. Moreover, because the authority of law is grounded in its instrumental utility, international law is regarded as authoritative to the extent that it furthers the desired goal and as lacking authority to the extent that it does not. As a result, neither tradition thinks there is an obligation to obey international law where this obligation interferes with pursuing the goals it regards as most important. But, I will argue, this instrumental understanding of international authority and obligation reveals a profound misunderstanding of the rule of law.

Before defending this conclusion, I'd like to try to articulate an alternative perspective on these matters, one that will be familiar to any international lawyer. It is one that focuses on the internal or formal qualities of action, rather than on external consequences. To evaluate an activity formally is to consider it in relation to standards of justice or propriety that constitute a moral or legal practice—standards that operate as constraints on action in the pursuit of some goal. Whereas instrumental theories such as utilitarianism judge activities by the contribution they make to producing an imagined overarching good end, the formal perspective postulates no such end. On the contrary, it assumes the existence of individuals pursuing a plurality of ends or goods and judges their activities according to considerations of justice or propriety that constitute the normative order within which they are related. To keep things simple, I'll say that to judge formally is to invoke rules, understanding the word "rule" to stand for a variety of rules, principles, practices, and procedures constraining action.

The distinction between the instrumental and the formal can be brought out by considering the attitude toward the authority of rules that is implicit in the two perspectives. In the formal perspective this authority is taken for granted. Formal argument rests on an appeal to rules, and the validity of these rules must be acknowledged before they can be used in making judgments. In the instrumental perspective, however, the authority of rules is not taken for granted, but rests instead on the contribution the rules make to producing a desired result. To think instrumentally about international law, for example, is to focus exclusively on the advantages and disadvantages of its rules for various individual, national, or supranational interests.

Now it is obviously important to pay attention to consequences, but a normative system can have no independent existence if the authority of its rules depends on approval of their consequences. In order for cooperation to take

[1] By TERRY NARDIN, excerpted from: *Realism, Cosmopolitanism, and the Rule of Law*, 81 PROCEEDINGS OF THE AMERICAN SOCIETY OF INTERNATIONAL LAW 415, 416–20, 444 (1987). Reprinted by permission.

place on the basis of common rules, those who wish to cooperate must acknowledge the authority of the rules, and this in turn means that the rules cannot be interpreted unilaterally or altered as economic or prudential considerations dictate. If the authority of a rule depends on its contribution to the realization of a desired outcome, then the rule has no authority apart from its utility as an instrument for producing that outcome, and the distinction between authority and approval disappears. Those who are related on the basis of rules whose authority is conditional in this way are really related on the basis of those conditions, not on the basis of common rules. It is their joint desire for a certain outcome rather than their joint recognition of the authority of certain restraints that binds them together.

The distinction between recognition and approval is implicit in the very concept of a rule and evident in practices of such fundamental importance to cooperation as promising, contracting, and treatymaking. It is certainly essential to the rule of law. Law entails a surrender of private judgment in the interpretation of the common rules governing a community. If it did not, there would not be one law but many. Law is therefore necessarily authoritative, whatever other properties it may possess. If law is a coercive order, it is an authoritative coercive order; if a mechanism for settling disputes, an authoritative mechanism; if an interpretation of justice, an authoritative interpretation.

The benefits of law may explain the origin and persistence of legal systems, but one cannot give an intelligible account of legal authority by appealing to these benefits. Legal rules facilitate cooperation by defining the practices and procedures through which cooperative agreements can be made, interpreted, enforced, and altered, and they may provide other benefits as well. But law can provide these benefits only because its authority, and therefore its very existence, rests on independent grounds. Authority cannot be attributed to law on the basis of what can be enjoyed only through the prior recognition of authority. For to make the benefits of legal order the ground of legal authority would be to regard that authority as an instrument for producing those benefits, and to view legal obligation as conditional on their successful production. A legal order would then be undistinguishable from a voluntary association that might be disbanded at the discretion of its members. Since those members, in effect, would retain the right to judge how well the association served the ends for which it was established, the distinction between a legal order and a state of nature would disappear. The only way to distinguish the authority of law from private opinion is to distinguish the source of that authority from its benefits.

The application of these ideas to international law is straightforward. International law exists to the extent that its authority is acknowledged in the practice of international relations – that is, by those whose conduct falls within its jurisdiction. In matters regulated by international law, statesmen must be guided by the public judgments embodied in law, not their own private judgments of what is desirable or just. If they ignore or violate international law when it appears expedient to do so, or allow foreign policies to be determined by some other, nonlegal, conception of justice, then it is common interests or a shared conception of justice, if these exist, and not law, that is the basis of international order. International law as an independent institution depends on its authority having some other ground than that it is useful as an instrument for promoting a desired international order.

The rule of law comes about in the following way. When people live together within a framework of moral practices, they learn to make judgments based on these practices, and sometimes these practices harden into law. The concept of morality is not exhausted by rules. When you start to think of the moral realm solely in terms of rules, you immediately must postulate some way of resolving disagreements about rules. You discover the need to interpret rules, to decide who has the right to apply them, and so on. I think the rule of law has meaning only when, among people who interact within a framework of rules, those rules are taken seriously and become the basis of their interaction. They are bound together by the law, not by something else such as convergent interests or shared religious belief. The root notion of the rule of law is the notion that it is law that unites a pluralistic society in which people are pursuing a diversity of ends. To the extent that people actually are living within a framework of common rules, those rules are regarded as authoritative. The rules are accepted, not because people think they are morally right or because prudentially they think that they serve shared values, but because they really recognize them as the rules. The rule of law is quite a third thing, distinct from both morality and prudence. There is prudence, there is morality, and then there is recognition and acknowledgement of the fact that there are certain laws governing society.

The rule of law, in international as in other societies, implies a formal relationship among the members of the society – a relationship constituted as well as regulated by authoritative rules. The rule of law may enable the members of international society to enjoy peace, security, and the fruits of cooperative activity, as well as other substantive benefits, but to imagine that international law is authoritative because it produces such benefits is simply to misunderstand the concept of authority.

If one thinks of international society as a cooperative association of states united on the basis of certain shared ends and of international law as an instrument to help states secure those ends, one has accounted for only part of the reality of international relations. Such a society would still be a state of nature, not a moral or legal order—if by that we mean an order founded on the abandonment of unrestricted liberty and the acknowledgement, in its place, of the authority of a body of common rules and, if need be, of a common umpire. What transforms a number of states, contingently related in terms of shared interests or sympathies, into a society proper is not their agreement to participate in a common enterprise for as long as they desire to participate, but their recognition of the authority of common rules, rules they acknowledge to have the status of laws.

International law includes rules that are the outcome of cooperation to further shared goals as well as rules that make such cooperation possible and which exist even where shared goals are lacking. But rules of the latter sort are fundamental. First, the particular arrangements through which states cooperate to promote shared ends themselves presuppose the existence of authoritative procedures for negotiating such arrangements. These procedures, embodied in customary international law, are logically prior to the treaties and international organizations through which states cooperate to achieve shared goals. And, second, it is the rules of customary international law that ultimately delimit the jurisdiction of states, define and forbid aggression and unlawful intervention, and regulate the activities of treatymaking, diplomacy, and war. They govern the relations of enemies as well as of friends, and thus provide a basis for international order even in the absence of shared beliefs, values, or ends. By requiring restraint in the pursuit of national aims and toleration of national diversity, such rules make possible the coexistence of states pursuing different and often incompatible ends. They reflect the inevitably plural character of international society.

Neither the realist nor the cosmopolitan can accept these conclusions. For the cosmopolitan, to assert the fundamental character of legal authority is to make the claims of justice subordinate to those of the law. Because international law reflects and reinforces an unjust global order, insisting on the supremacy of international law appears to lead to unacceptably conservative conclusions. Moreover, from the cosmopolitan perspective none of the arguments I have made supports the conclusion that respect for law should have moral priority over the claims of human rights or economic justice. In order to reach such a conclusion one would have to provide ulterior or external grounds for the authority of international law, that is, a moral justification for international law as an institution. For cosmopolitanism this justification must rest on a conception of justice as the common good of the world community. Realism, in contrast, emphasizes the need to justify international law in terms of its contribution to protecting the interests and security of the state.

Both, however, miss the point. To say that international law exists only insofar as its rules are authoritative is not to assert its moral supremacy. It is to say no more than that if the relations of states are to be based on the rule of law, then the obligations of international law must be respected, even if that should appear to be undesirable from the standpoint of some particular conception of what is advantageous or just. Similarly, to claim that the procedures of customary international law are logically prior to cooperative agreements among states is simply to point to a characteristic feature of any rule-governed order, not to offer a moral justification for those procedures. Whether the rules of international law are consistent with some particular conception of the national interest or the common good is another question. It is not one that needs to be answered in order to understand the character and structure of international law.

To insist that any adequate account of the authority of international law must rest on a moral argument, or that the legal obligations created by international law need not be taken seriously if they have undesirable consequences, is to deny the significance of international law as an independent institution. The view that laws are binding only if they are expedient or just is one that gives no independent weight to the fact that they are laws. Theoretically speaking, it amounts to an assertion that a satisfactory explanation of the authority of international law must rest on considerations of utility or social justice. On such a view, questions about legal authority and obligation cannot be divorced from questions about the benefits of law. But this confuses analysis of the concepts of authority and obligation with the attempt to discover external grounds for legal obedience. And if one argues that legal rules are binding only if the legal system of which they are part is itself a just or advantageous one, as determined by the application of external criteria, then one makes agreement regarding what is desirable or just, not law, the actual basis of association.

Instrumentalist theories such as realism and cosmopolitanism assume that there is a single correct standard, independent of law, according to which the utility or justice of international law itself, as well as of particular acts and policies, can be judged. But if there is such a standard, its identity and principles are not at all evident. There is not less disagreement about what is desirable or just than about other moral and political issues. Sharp differences divide realists from cosmopolitans, and there is disagreement within each of these camps. Realism spans a wide range of positions from moral skepticism to national egoism. The cosmopolitans are also conspicuously unable to agree among themselves. Utilitarian, Marxist, and liberal-contractarian versions of cosmopolitanism offer many different criteria for identifying a just world order. The Rawlsians alone have generated a multiplicity of principles that now rivals the notorious indeterminacy of utilitarianism.

But even if a determinate set of principles of prudence or justice could be proven to be correct, according to some particular conception of rationality, it is unlikely that it would secure general consent, and so there would still be a need for rules governing the relations of those who, irrationally, disagreed with one another. A society–certainly international society–still requires agreed or generally acknowledged principles of conduct, just in case agreement on what is reasonable is lacking. Such principles, of course, may be quite arbitrary from the standpoint of "rationality" as defined by reason of state, utilitarian calculation, or a Rawlsian hypothetical contract. Law can supply this need for agreed principles only if it is authentic or valid law–a body of common rules whose authority can be established independently of its reasonableness, its moral rightness, or the desirability of its consequences. To the extent that they deny this, realism and cosmopolitanism demonstrate either ignorance of or hostility to the rule of law.

B. The View From Moral Philosophy[2]

The most acclaimed work on justice that has appeared this century is clearly *A Theory of Justice* by John Rawls (1971). He chooses to focus upon justice within a society, characterizing a society as involving "many individuals coexisting together at the same time on a definite geographical territory" (p. 126). Since Rawls does not deal directly with international justice–justice across societies–it might be unfair either to extend his theory in that direction or to criticize its shortcomings if it is extended. Yet when we consider the arbitrariness of national borders–after all, what does the location of a nation's borders have to do with justice?–it may not seem quite so unfair to Rawls' theory to examine it in light of its international extendability.

Such an extension is in part justified by the universalistic approach Rawls takes from time to time. At one point he analogizes a nation to a person, and asserts that ethics among persons may be directly extended to the ethical foundations of international law (pp. 377–82). Also, and more indirectly, he conveys the impression that his theories concern mankind in general: he discusses universal traits of persons (moral sentiments), and suggests that ethical theories cannot be particularistic because they must "hold for everyone in virtue of their being moral persons." (pp. 131–32).

Yet is it possible to work out a universal system of justice, based on the nature of persons, without examining issues that transcend particular national boundaries? Consider the basic Rawlsian principle of social justice that he calls the "difference principle"–that social and economic inequalities are permissible if and only if the arrangements generating them work out better for the most disadvantaged person (the "worst-off" person) than would any more equal structure.[3] This principle gives rise to what has become known as a "transfer tax"–a tax on the most advantaged persons to be paid over to the most disadvantaged, with Rawls' caveat that the transfer tax should not be so large as to provide a disincentive for the most advantaged persons to keep producing for the good of all. Thus, should there be enormous taxes upon the incomes of rich persons in industrialized societies so that the money can be paid over to masses that are near starvation in India, China, and other populous and developing nations? Should there be an "excess profits" tax levied upon individuals and corporations for this purpose? To some extent, of course, the "have-not" nations are making this claim today; it takes the form of demands upon limited United Nations resources and capital, explanations for expropriation of foreign-owned industries; justifications for exploiting oceanic resources (primarily fisheries), and so forth. The "relative deprivation" sensed by disadvantaged nations is put forward as a justification for international measures designed to reduce the disparity of wealth between rich and poor nations.

But can the logical leap across such boundaries be justified? There are two important factors, I believe, that argue against it: one on the "supply" and one on the "demand" side of the picture. On the supply side, we have a world that is not infinitely rich in resources. We cannot talk of a "cowboy economy" internationally; rather, basic minerals, food, and resources are limited and the supplies are being used up. In Rawls' hypothetical society, resources are sufficiently abundant to make it possible for the best situated person to argue that further incentives paid to him will result in increased exploitation of natural resources so that the poor will also benefit from them.[4] But if there are

[2] By ANTHONY D'AMATO, excerpted from: *International Law and Rawls' Theory of Justice*, 5 DENVER JOURNAL OF INTERNATIONAL LAW AND POLICY 525 (1975), reprinted in ANTHONY D'AMATO, JURISPRUDENCE: A DESCRIPTIVE AND NORMATIVE ANALYSIS OF LAW 259 (Martinus Nijhoff 1984). Reprinted by permission. Except for stylistic changes, I've left this essay substantively as I wrote it in 1974. At the time the arguments were, I believe, new; certainly no one at the time had discussed the relation of Rawls' theory to international law and politics. Recently there have been similar critiques of Rawls' theory, most of which have not referenced my prior work.

[3] Rawls at 75–83. "The higher expectations of those better situated are just if and only if they work as part of a scheme which improves the expectations of the least advantaged members of society." *Id.* at 75.

[4] Rawls uses the condition of "moderate scarcity," which means that "natural and other resources are not so abundant that schemes of cooperation become superfluous, nor are conditions so harsh that fruitful ventures must inevitably break down." Id. at 127.

only limited resources, then further exploitation by the rich can only be at the expense of the have-nots; the Rawlsian caveat becomes inapplicable. For example, the United States could not, under this formulation, argue that its consumption of thirty percent of the world's energy is needed to raise the standard of living of the masses in India. Thus, Rawls' difference principle would boil down to a straight tax, taking from the rich and giving to the poor, with little room, if any, for the argument that the tax should stop at a point above that of total equality for everyone so that incentives can be maintained. We therefore arrive at the conclusion that either all economic disparities in the world should be eliminated (as an ethical proposition), or that there are counterarguments that Rawls has omitted which change the ethical calculus.

One counter-argument comes from the "demand" side of the picture. Advantaged nations tend to be less populous than disadvantaged nations. For one thing, they tend to hold down the birth rate voluntarily. Secondly, the very fact of a lower population increases per capital wealth and perhaps is implicit in the concept of an advantaged nation. Now, should a populous disadvantaged nation have an ethical claim to the wealth of a less populous advantaged nation? Or might the latter reply that its own population control undertaken to provide a "better life" for all its citizens should not be undercut by claims for a nation that has not similarly restrained itself? Rawls discusses the population problem only briefly, and from the standpoint of classical utilitarianism and not his own theory of justice.[5] But what is at stake for Rawls' own theory is conceptually fundamental. Look at what happens if we redefine "rich." We might say that a developed, advantaged nation is "rich" in economic terms of material wealth, whereas an underdeveloped, disadvantaged nation is "rich" in terms of its large number of people, its large families. We have often heard the remark: "He may be a rich man, but he has no children, and therefore he's really very poor."

Thus my argument – a politically difficult one – is that one type of "rich" nation has no obvious justice claim to the resources of the other type of "rich" nation. If a nation has chosen to become economically rich in part by limiting its population, so that there is more economic wealth per capita, I am unsure that there is a justice claim on the part of a person-rich disadvantaged nation to a significant portion of the wealth of the economically-rich nation. A family in the United States that has two children may be "poorer" in a very real way compared to a family in India that has twelve children. But why should the Indian family have a just claim against the U.S. family for a portion of the latter's material wealth? Or why should the U.S. family have a just claim against the Indian family to take one or more of that family's children?

To be sure, choosing to have a smaller family not only increases per capita wealth, but also frees the time of individuals to innovate and make large capital improvements in society without having to spend all their time in attempting to feed and take care of the family. In this sense, of course, the "rich get richer," if we are talking about economic wealth. Over many generations, an enormous disparity arises between the less densely populated advantaged nation and the more densely populated economically disadvantaged nation. But this increasing disparity of economic wealth over time is a function in part of deliberate individual choices that we made – choices, for example, to limit the size of one's family, to work hard so that one's children and grandchildren will have a good life, to deprive oneself of material advantages in order to bequeath wealth to one's children and grandchildren, and so forth. When we look at the end result and see, for example, the huge disparity in wealth between the average American and the average Indian, we may think that justice requires a Rawlsian transfer payment. But upon further consideration, taking into account how the two countries arrived at their present state, I think we become less sure that a transfer payment is justified.

If Rawls' theory does not provide a justification for transfer payments across national boundaries, how does Rawls justify a transfer payment from individual M to individual N within a given society? Is there something different between international justice and national justice? I don't think so; I think such a distinction is inherently arbitrary. But then, if Rawls has failed to provide a justification for international transfer payments, we may be able to criticize his theory of justice within a society on exactly the same basis. And this, I think, is where Rawls' theory is unconvincing even on its own chosen turf. Rawls seems to take every individual as if he or she had just come on the scene, straight out of the "original position" that Rawls postulates.[6] There is practically no acknowledgement of the fact that a person can work hard and save so as to pass on his or her wealth to children and grandchildren; in short, the generational dimension is lacking. Not only that, but even the annual dimension is lacking for the most part in Rawls' theory. In any given year, to be sure, we can identify the "most advantaged" and the "most disadvantaged" persons. But what should the society do about it? Should it continue, year after year, to tax the advantaged and give to the disadvantaged? Such a scheme could create a huge

---

[5] He states that the classic principle is inferior to that of the average utility principle in that the former, in maximizing satisfactions over the whole of society, can allow for an indefinitely increasing population so that the sum of utilities added by the greater number of persons makes up for the decline in per capita shares of wealth. Rawls at 162–63.

[6] The "original position" is a postulated situation where no one knows his or her own identity, where everyone is risk-averse, and where everyone is treated equally. Many critics have attacked the assumptions of Rawls' "original position." For my part, I think that, instead of its being a postulate from which social-justice consequences are derived, it is rather a consequence itself of Rawls' social-justice theories. In short, I think the entire construct is a vast, self-serving tautology.

"disadvantaged" class of permanent consumers. Suppose, for example, that Jack, an able-bodied young man, is the poorest of the poor–he owns nothing more than the clothes he wears. On January 1st he receives a substantial transfer payment. He has budgeted this money for a year of tourism. He departs for South America, where he will spend one or two months in various countries, stay at inexpensive hotels, go fishing, and end up back in the United States on December 31st. Then the next day he collects the next transfer payment–because, after all, he remains the poorest of the poor, having saved nothing–and embarks once again on a 365 day trip, this time to Europe. Rawls' theory encourages permanent tourists like Jack. But why is it just to tax the wealthy class (many of whom, after all, are still working hard to preserve or increase their wealth) in order to turn the money over to Jack who would rather travel around the world than work? Why is it just to tax workers in order to transfer their vacations to non-workers?

I am not claiming that poor people are all tourists like Jack; quite to the contrary, my concern is to separate genuinely poor, disadvantaged persons from those who could rush in to take advantage of the status of poverty. I claim that the Rawlsian system can create a class of freeloaders who choose not to work for a living and instead collect Rawlsian transfer payments. There is nothing I have found in Rawls' theory to identify the genuinely poor from the fakers: Rawls presents only economic indicia to identify the most disadvantaged persons. Permanent tourists like Jack therefore can thrust themselves into the same category as the genuinely poor person who may be sick or handicapped or otherwise unable to work–both types receive transfer payments. My criticism is that this is a consequence of the way Rawls' theory would inevitably work in practice, and therefore, the theory falls short of a workable theory of "justice."

Because I arrived at my criticism of Rawls by first extending it to international justice, I want to make clear that rejecting Rawls' theory does not mean that we should reject foreign-aid programs. Rather, we should examine more closely what foreign aid is and where it should go. The justness of an underdeveloped nation's claim to foreign aid must be evaluated in far greater detail than Rawls' ethical theory would seem to require. We might well conclude that a certain amount of "excess profits" tax, perhaps under the label of "foreign aid," should be paid to disadvantaged nations; but if this amount falls short of making everyone in the world equally wealthy in an economic sense, the shortfall should not be viewed as an ethical compromise, as Rawls' theory would seem to suggest.

Moreover, I suggest that a non-Rawlsian point of view would argue in favor of placing conditions upon foreign aid. Without conditions, the net result might be similar to the permanent tourist argument I made above. A receiving nation might simply decide to spend the foreign aid money on luxuries (often, in reality, luxuries for government elites who take most or all of the foreign aid money and immediately deposit it in personal Swiss bank accounts). There is something unjust, I feel, in taking money from a wealthy person who has, to some extent, engaged in self-sacrifice to attain the wealth, and giving it to a poor person whose immediate impulse might be to spend and enjoy the money. I view it as unjust because, other things being equal, I believe that if anyone should be allowed to spend money on luxuries it is the person who earned the money and not the person who did not earn it.

The way to prevent foreign-aid recipients from squandering the money is to place conditions upon it. These conditions can require, among other things, that the recipient use the money for capital-formation projects, for road construction, for hospitals, for projects that really benefit the people instead of the elite, etc. True, the recipient countries will probably object that the conditions are wrong, onerous, and paternalistic. (Often these objections come from government elites who were counting on unconditional aid finding its way into their own Swiss bank accounts.) Yet if donor nations do not place conditions on foreign aid, a substantial injustice may be done to the citizens of the donor countries who are taxed to provide the foreign aid that then is used for "permanent tourist" type spending by elite recipients.

Rawls theory would prescribe the giving of foreign aid as part of a nation's obligation to do justice. Hence it could not be made subject to conditions and withheld if the conditions are not met. I think that justice requires a contrary position. While I think that foreign aid is partly a matter of a wealthy nation's obligation to help people in other countries who are less fortunate, I believe that unless appropriate conditions are attached to that aid, the net result can work an injustice upon the citizens of the donor country who are taxed in order to provide the foreign-aid funds. To be sure, the principles of justice that I have just alluded to have not been worked out in a consistent theory, and certainly they are not as simple as Rawls' principles (such as his "difference principle"). This may be a defect, but my present argument is intended to do no more than to suggest that the Rawlsian idea of justice may, if extended internationally, lead us in an unjust direction.

In only one section of his book does Professor Rawls consider extending his argument explicitly to international law. Assuming that nations will have their representatives participating in the original position to arrange moral principles for their nations, Rawls argues that the nations' representatives would choose the principle of equality as the most important ethical basis of international law. This principle, for Rawls, has the following consequences:

> 1. Each nation has the right of self-determination without the intervention of foreign powers;
>
> 2. Each nation has the right of self-defense against attack, including the right to form defensive alliances to protect this right;
>
> 3. The rule is adopted that treaties are to be honored, provided they are consistent with the other principles governing the relations of states;
>
> 4. Principles are adopted regulating the means that a nation may use to wage war.[7]

Yet we may ask whether these principles really derive from justice as Rawls claims. Suppose there is a country that relentlessly oppresses a minority group within its borders. Suppose leaders of the minority group are abducted by the secret police, tortured, and never heard from again. Suppose the group's places of worship are burned down, its language suppressed, its people constitutionally disabled from occupying political office – in short, imagine as *unjust* a situation for this group as you are able. Surely Rawls could not claim that there is justice in the country in question. Now, suppose further that other nations are willing to intercede on behalf of the oppressed group – first by imposing economic sanctions against the country that is harming them, and if that does not work, by military intervention to protect the group's leaders from being arrested and killed. In this hypothetical situation, surely outside intervention is necessary to prevent further injustice and perhaps to restore justice. Yet Rawls' first principle barring outside intervention would preclude external aid to the oppressed minority group. How, then, can Rawls' first principle be derivable from justice?

Obliquely, Rawls seems to have thought of this objection. In addressing the topic of military conscription and conscientious objectors, he writes:

> Conscription is permissible only if it is demanded for the defense of liberty itself, including here not only the liberties of the citizens of the society in question, but also those of persons in other societies as well.[8]

Thus Rawls has recognized that persons may be justly conscripted to fight in a way that is in defense of the liberties of persons in another society.[9] But this is exactly my hypothetical case: a nation is conscripting soldiers to fight for the liberties of others in another society (the minority group I have postulated). It appears that by condoning this sort of conscription, Rawls contradicts his first principle of non-intervention and thus refutes his own claim that his first principle derives from justice.[10]

The preceding argument is a facet of a deeper problem with Rawls' notion of the equality of states. Recall that the equality of states is the first moral principle he derives from states' representatives bargaining in the original position. The important point is that this equality of states is a moral equality. At first blush, there seems to be nothing wrong with postulating the moral equality of states. But I think that such a postulate leads to retrogressive and ultimately justice-denying consequences for international law.

I believe that states are legally (juridically) equal; without that equality, we could hardly have "international law." But the moral equality of states is quite different, and dangerous. A state that persecutes a minority group of its citizens – my previous example – is surely not the moral equal of a state which treats all its citizens with the same care and consideration. In fact, what Rawls has done by his notion of moral equivalence is to embrace the classic picture of international law that excludes from its ambit all matters within the "domestic jurisdiction" of a state. Under the classic view, a state could torture and kill a minority of its own citizens on its own territory without violating any principle of international law. This classic notion is intolerable in light of the vast developments we have seen in human rights – in particular for the present example, the customary international law against genocide. When Rawls treats states as morally equal, his theory becomes a retrogressive bulwark against the development and spread of human rights.

To be sure, this consequence may not have been intended by Rawls. Obviously he did not pay much attention to international justice in his book. Yet the consequence seems to me to be a fair one to draw, given the theory of justice that Rawls has put forth in such detail. But that isn't the main point. What is important for international legal scholarship is that we have to work out a concept of international justice that (a) cannot begin with a postulated "original position," (b) cannot assume the moral equality of states, and (c) cannot assume that states are moral "entities" the same way persons are moral entities. Instead we have to engage in the much harder task of working out principles of international justice that deliver justice to individuals wherever they are located and not to whatever states the individuals are located in. It seems to me that, when a conceptual foundation for human rights is finally worked out, it will start with the cautionary note that although states may be legally equal under international law, they are not necessarily morally equal. Moral equality is not a

[7] Rawls at 378–79. [Editor's Note: Observe the similarity between these Rawlsian principles and the Kantian ones for Perpetual Peace; *see* Chapter 13 in this Anthology.]

[8] Rawls at 380.

[9] In the quoted passage (written, it will be recalled, at the height of the Vietnam War), Rawls seems to be siding with those Americans who resisted the draft. However, his admission that one may be legally and justly drafted to fight to preserve the liberties of persons in another country seems to undercut his own position. Surely the official justification of conscription was that Americans were being drafted to preserve the liberties of certain South Vietnamese citizens who were resisting communism. Whether this official justification was in fact true is not precisely relevant to the logic or illogic of Rawls' position. I believe in fact that it was true of a very few South Vietnamese citizens, but I think the overwhelming number of those citizens viewed us as the oppressors and not the communists. For my own position at the time, see ANTHONY D'AMATO & ROBERT M. O'NEIL, THE JUDICIARY AND VIETNAM (1971).

[10] Could Rawls argue that the country I have hypothesized is one which is clearly unjust, and thus it is not entitled to the equal treatment accorded to other nations? I fail to see how this argument could be made without destroying Rawls' concept of the original position, because in the original position we know nothing about the composition or policies of the countries whose representatives are supposedly demanding the principle of equality.

status that is bestowed upon a state for the purpose of constructing one's theory of justice; rather, a state should have to earn a status of moral equality. It earns this status by the way it treats human beings – its own citizens as well as foreigners.

C. A Skeptical View[11]

Writers such as John Rawls tend to concentrate on distributive justice at the expense of other types of justice (such as commutative justice – the fairness of voluntary exchanges between parties). But policy-makers, pursuing a "just" redistribution policy with a warm glow of self-satisfaction, could be surprised to find their best efforts regarded as cultural imperialism, paternalism, or worse.

My point is that particular actions that impact on other persons must be perceived by those other persons as "just," whether or not those recipients of action accept the entire system. Failure to include the objects of charity or the other party to a bargain in the equation by which the "justice" of the gift or bargain is measured violates principles of commutative justice.

This is more than a merely academic objection. The UN General Assembly Resolution on Permanent Sovereignty over Natural Resources[12] focused primarily on an issue of commutative justice. The impetus for that resolution was the perceived inadequacy of compensation from multinational corporations and their sponsoring governments to less affluent governments for access to their natural resources, and the belief that such access had on occasion been granted improvidently or under "unjust" economic or political pressures. The concern that a transaction regarding natural resources be fairly negotiated and equitable is a commutative concern wholly distinct from the question whether those natural resources were justly distributed in the first instance. Many statesmen brought up in the Anglo-American and European legal traditions, as well as many raised in Islamic, Chinese, and other influential and sophisticated legal and moral traditions, do not regard a lack of distributive justice as the sole complaint against an allegedly unjust international moral order.

D. A Test Case[13]

Does a nation have a duty under international law to do justice to foreigners? This question may open up one of the most controversial areas in human rights law in the foreseeable future.

We begin by noting the clear duty that a nation has to do justice to citizens of another country if they are temporarily present as visitors, tourists or businesspersons within the nation's own territory. This aspect of the international law of state responsibility was developed and refined in the eighteenth and nineteenth centuries. As far as justice is concerned, there are two classic standards benefiting an alien. First is the "international minimum standard" – an alien may not be treated below the international minimum standard, a standard which rises slowly over time.[14] Second

---

[11] By ALFRED P. RUBIN, excerpted from: Beitz, *Political Theory, and International Relations*, 47 UNIVERSITY OF CHICAGO LAW REVIEW 403, 404–06 (1980). Reprinted by permission.

[12] Res. 1803 (XVII), 17 UN GAOR, 1 Annexes 59–60, UN Doc. A/5344 (1962).

[13] By ANTHONY D'AMATO & KIRSTEN ENGEL, excerpted from: *State Responsibility for the Exportation of Nuclear Power Technology*, 74 VIRGINIA LAW REVIEW 1011 (1988). Reprinted by permission.

[14] The principle of the international minimum standard of treatment stands for the proposition that nonnationals are entitled to a certain minimum standard of treatment by the host state. This principle evolved from the norm referred to as 'denial of justice,' applied in egregious cases involving gross denials of justice: denying the accused the right to defend himself, not allowing the accused to call witnesses in his own behalf, double jeopardy, and control of the tribunal by the executive. *See, e.g.*, France (Fabiani) v. Venezuela, 5 MOORE ARB. 4877 (1903) (failure of court to render a decision); Jones, 4 MOORE DIGEST OF INT'L ARB. 3253 (1898) (excessive bail); Coles and Croswell, 78 BRIT. & FOR. STATE PAPERS 1301 (1885) (unfair trial); Idler v. Venezuela, 4 MOORE ARB. 3491 (1885) (tribunal manipulated by the executive in host nation). Later cases transmuted the 'denial of justice' norm into 'ordinary standards of civilization' and extended it beyond the courtroom.

See e.g., Neer Case (U.S. v. Mex.), 4 R. INT'L ARB. AWARDS 60 (1926) (term extended to lack of adequate police protection of aliens). In Roberts Case (U.S. v. Mex.), 4 R. INT'L ARB. AWARDS 77, 80 (1926), after being arrested with a number of others for an assault on a house, Roberts was confined without charge for at least seven months in a 35' x 20' jail cell occupied by 30 to 40 other prisoners. The cell did not have sanitary accommodations, and the prisoners were ill fed and deprived of exercise. The Commissioner found that both Mexico's unreasonably long detention of Roberts prior to trial without charge and its subjection of Roberts to cruel and unusual punishment while in prison fell well below the minimum international standards. The court stated, 'We do not hesitate to say that the treatment of Roberts was such as to warrant an indemnity on the ground of cruel and inhumane imprisonment.' *Id.* at 80.

In the Kennedy Case, Kennedy, a U.S. Citizen and the assistant manager of a mining company located in Mexico, sued the Mexican government for failure to adequately punish a mine employee known to have assaulted Kennedy in a labor confrontation. Kennedy Case (U.S. v. Mex.), 4 R. INT'L ARB. AWARDS 194, 195–96 (1927). The General Claims Commission held that the two month prison sentence imposed upon Kennedy's aggressor was so out of keeping with the seriousness of the crime, which left Kennedy permanently crippled, that it constituted a denial of justice under the minimum international standards of treatment. *Id.* at 196–99. The same determination was made regarding the United States behavior in the De Galvan Case where the U.S. was held liable for the failure of Texan courts to prosecute the murderer of a Mexican subject. The murderer was indicted by a grand jury but not brought to trial for more than six years. De Galvan Case (Mex. v. U.S.), 4 R. INT'L ARB. AWARDS 273 (1927).

The concept of denial of justice was broadened considerably

is the standard of "national" treatment: an alien is entitled to no worse treatment within the nation's justice enforcement system than a citizen.[15] These are important concepts, and the interested reader is referred to the two preceding footnotes for a more detailed account.

by the inclusion of acts by legislative and administrative branches of government. For instance, the British–Mexican Claims Commission stated that responsibility for the denials of justice or the undue delay of justice should not be limited simply to judicial authorities. Interoceanic Ry. of Mexico Case, (Gr. Brit. v. Mex.), 5 R. INT'L. ARB. AWARDS 178, 185 (1931). Rather, while recognizing that such international delinquencies will usually be an act or an omission of a tribunal, the Commission found that often it will be the work of nonjudicial officers responsible for bringing an alien before the court or enforcing a judgment. In the Mallen Case, the U.S. was held liable for injury to a Mexican consul because U.S. failure to execute the penalty imposed upon the American responsible for the injury constituted a denial of justice. Mallen Case (Mex. v. U.S.), 4 R. INT'L ARB. AWARDS 173 (1927).

Other cases establish that a state can incur liability for illegal arrest, failure to account for a suspect under custody, failure of police to control a civilian riot, and arbitrary control of individual property. Colunje Case (Pan. v. U.S.), 6 R. INT'L ARB. AWARDS 342 (1933) (United States liable for detective's illegal arrest of Panamanian citizen); Baldwin and Others Case (U.S. v. Pan.), 6 R. INT'L ARB. AWARDS 328 (1933) (Panama liable for allowing civilians to attack American soldiers); Quintanilla Case (Mex. v. U.S.), 4 R. INT'L ARB. AWARDS 101 (1926) (United States liable for death of Mexican citizen who after escaping from American custody was found dead). In the De Sabla Case (U.S. v. Pan.), 6 R. INT'L ARB. AWARDS 358 (1933), a U.S. citizen successfully brought suit for damages against Panama alleging that that government's land laws so unreasonably burdened private landowners as to fall below international minimum standards. Panamanian officials interpreted domestic laws as requiring them, upon application of a national, to relinquish the title of or the right to cultivate land already occupied by aliens, should the owner not personally protest each application. *Id.* at 360. As a result, the plaintiff, De Sabla, had lost title and cultivation rights to much of her land since she was unable to personally oppose each individual application to acquire or farm her land. *Id.* at 359–60. Owing to the burdensome nature of this practice, which afforded no real protection of aliens' titles, as well as Panama's knowledge of De Sabla's land ownership, the Commission held that Panama's actions regarding De Sabla's property were 'wrongful acts for which the government of Panama is responsible internationally.' *Id.* at 366.

These administrative cases exemplify the proposition that adequate police protection, such that an alien is neither harassed by the authorities nor left to the mercy of unruly mobs, and respect for land ownership, are necessary for compliance with the international minimum standard. The cases suggest a gradual broadening of the principle of the international minimum standard of treatment from its genesis in the earliest egregious examples of denial of justice to the more inclusive doctrine now known as the international minimum standard of treatment of nonnationals. The principle is still limited by a certain notion of nondeprivation of 'justice' to such persons, but the concept of 'justice' itself has been expanded, in accordance with gradually evolving norms of responsibility to others. Its content is no longer confined to the judicial context, but can now embrace legislative and administrative denials of justice. The term 'justice' is gaining content as the international community perceives a greater degree of civilized treatment as part of its standard conception of 'justice.'

[15] This standard was never meant to accord nonnationals the same rights and privileges accorded citizens. For instance, international law does not require a state to permit all aliens to enter its territory or to afford permanent residence to those that it does. Likewise, a state has no obligation to afford aliens the right to vote, hold political office or public employment. Nor does international law require a state to allow aliens to acquire or inherit certain property or allow access to public facilities or resources. Also, aliens may be subject to certain burdens to which nationals are exempt, such as registration or identification procedures. The common denominator of these 'allowed discriminations' seems to be their political nature. An alien is entitled to the protection afforded by the sovereign, but not participation in determining who the sovereign is, whether that sovereign be the people of the nation, in which case aliens may be barred from the country, or their elected leader, in which case aliens may be denied suffrage. Even discrimination under laws and practices governing the acquisition of property may be related to political rights since real property ownership has been historically related to the ability to exercise political rights.

But the "national standard" has had the operative effect of raising the rights of aliens, because if the level of treatment accorded an alien falls significantly below the level of national treatment, the alien can claim a denial of justice. Hence, due to the relationship between the nondiscriminatory standard and the international minimum standard, an alien is entitled to whichever standard is higher. The legal relationship between the minimum standard and the nondiscrimination principle was given expression by the United States Court of Appeals for the Second Circuit in the context of the nationalization of property. In Banco Nacional de Cuba v. Sabbatino (later reversed on other grounds by the Supreme Court), the Second Circuit held that international law required that a state have a 'reasonable basis' for differential treatment of aliens. Banco Nacional de Cuba v. Sabbatino, 307 F.2d 845, 865–66 (2d Cir. 1962), rev'd on other grounds, 376 U.S. 398 (1964). Cuba gave distinctive treatment to non-Cubans when it nationalized an American sugar company ten weeks before it nationalized Cuban companies in order to retaliate against a reduction in American sugar imports from Cuba. *Id.* at 867. The court held that this was not a 'reasonable basis for a distinction in treatment' of non-Cubans and hence was a violation of international law. *Id.* at 866. Thus we might infer from the court's reasoning that the nondiscriminatory treatment standard in the law of state responsibility creates a presumption in favor of according aliens equal treatment with nationals, except when a 'reasonable basis' can be adduced for according aliens a lower level of treatment. In this fashion, the principle of nondiscrimination appears to give a certain progressive element to the principle of the international minimum standard. *See, e.g.*, Smith v. Compania Urbanizadora Del Parque y Playa De Marianao (U.S. v. Cuba), 24 AM. J. INT'L L. 384, 386–387 (1929) (Cuba held liable for damages for failure to accord American citizen the same protection of private property as is given Cuban nationals); Cadenhead Case (Gr. Brit. v. U.S.), 8 AM. J. INT'L L. 663 (1914) (claim for damages for accidental death of British subject by American soldier denied because no showing subject had been discriminated against in treatment under American law).

A nation may accord international minimum treatment to an alien and nevertheless violate the alien's rights if the alien is blatantly discriminated against in comparison to citizens. In this manner the content of the international minimum standard itself might be raised over time, progressively affected in the Sabbatino fashion by the utilization of the nondiscriminatory treatment standard. Indeed, in some countries the nondiscrimination principle will contain higher standards of treatment than the classic minimum international standard; aliens in those countries will then typically invoke the nondiscrimination standard, which may have the effect of ratcheting up the content of the international minimum standard. Cf. Smith v. Compania Urbanizadora del Parque y Playa de Marianao (U.S. v. Cuba), 24 AM. J. INT'L L. 384 (1929) (American citizen sought equal treatment with nationals under Cuba's constitution).

Similarly, a nation may be guilty of falling below the international minimum standard even though it has complied with the nondiscrimination standard. Accordingly, it is not an adequate defense to a charge of failing to meet the international minimum

But does a nation have a duty to do justice to foreigners who are not located within the nation's own borders? Food and relief missions, humanitarian aid missions, and programs for refugee relief are evidences of a strong *charitable* impulse: that we *here* should aid unfortunate people *there.* Yet charity by definition is not compulsory. Does international law recognize any *obligation* to help people in other countries?

The present state of international law probably does not go that far. Yet we think that a case can be made out under international law that there is an obligation *not to harm* people in other countries. To put it more sharply, if engaging in a positive act has the probability of causing unwarranted harm to people of other countries, then such an act is a denial of justice to those people. Within this limited scope, we contend that today's international law would hold a nation responsible in tort damages to the people of the foreign country harmed by an action taken by that nation.

To take a hard case: suppose an industrialized nation E exports an ultrahazardous technology – the plans and equipment to set up a nuclear power plant – to a developing nation R. Suppose further that the government of the receiving nation (R) agrees to take the technology "as is" and signs an agreement with E waiving all legal claims against E that might result from malfunction of the technology. Indeed, we can suppose that E would never have exported the technology to R unless R signed such a blanket waiver. However, we stipulate that, in this hypothetical case, R is a dictatorship.

We shall assume that the nuclear power plant that E exports to R is one that would have failed E's own safety standards – that is, E would not have allowed such a nuclear power plant to be erected on E's territory. In addition, we make the stronger assumption that the governmental officials of E who decide to export the nuclear technology know, or have reason to know, that the particular technology when erected on the territory of R has a small but not insignificant probability of "melting down" within ten years of its construction, causing catastrophic damage to the people of R. But E has a strong profit motive to export the technology, and the government of R (a dictatorship) may not be looking out primarily for the welfare of its people.[16]

If there is a duty on the part of E not to deny justice to the people of R, then – despite the explicit waiver of liability – we argue that if E goes ahead and exports the power plant, and if the power plant melts down, E is liable in damages to the people of R who are killed or seriously injured by the explosion and the radioactive fallout. This is, of course, a highly controversial thesis, and has the potential to impact severely upon exporter nations.[17] If our argument is persuasive, exporter nations would probably not risk exporting substandard hazardous technology regardless of the price that the importing nation is willing to pay, because the potential damages are so high as to be uninsurable.

Is there a "justice connection" between nation E and the people of nation R such that E violates international law if it engages in an act (in this case, exporting the nuclear technology) that could cause enormous harm to the people of R? In brief, is there a positive obligation under international law to do justice to nonnationals residing outside one's own territory such that failing to do so would be a 'denial of justice' to them within the concept of the law of state responsibility?

Our first inquiry should be whether a state generally has any moral obligation to do justice to the nationals of another state. Clearly, justice, as H.L.A. Hart puts it, is a branch of morality.[18] It shares with morality the notion that factors of time and space are irrelevant.[19] In this respect, a national boundary is an artificial, as well as a morally irrelevant, boundary with respect to moral obligations.

We must next inquire whether there are transboundary moral obligations that also constitute legal obligations arising out of customary law. The international law of war contains moral obligations that are also legal obligations to citizens in foreign countries; most of the prohibitions

standard to say that aliens have received the same treatment as that accorded to nationals. In this respect, one is better off, under the classical view of state responsibility, being an alien than being a citizen. The alien is entitled to the international minimum standard of treatment, even though a citizen under exactly the same circumstances is without standing to claim an entitlement to the international minimum standard. The international law of human rights, however, is evolving to close the gap between alien and citizen in this respect. At least as to certain rights – such as habeas corpus and freedom from torture – the difference has narrowed to the point of disappearance.

[16] [Editor's Note: In the case we examine at length in the original article, the United States agreed to export a nuclear power plant to the Philippines during the reign of President Marcos. There were allegations that Marcos received a substantial personal bribe for agreeing to import the plant. The plant was to be constructed near a volcano!]

[17] [Editor's Note: Many of our colleagues have focused on this waiver provision in criticizing the conclusion we have reached. If R signs a waiver, they say, then it is intolerable to then allow R to sue. What our critics miss, in our opinion, are the facts that (a) the people of R have not signed the waiver – only their dictator did – and (b) the notion of international justice that we develop in the article, if it is persuasive at all, requires informed consent on the part of the people who are the potential victims of a breakdown of the nuclear technology.]

[18] H.L.A. Hart, The Concept of Law 153 (1961).

[19] *Cf.* D'Amato, *Lon Fuller and Substantive Natural Law*, 26 Am. J. Juris. 202, 204 (1981) (discussing 'substantive natural law' which holds that there are certain absolutes in law).

against war crimes fall into this category.[20] It follows that in peacetime, a general moral obligation deriving from customary international law is conceptually possible. Specific examples are the fundamental human-rights prohibitions against torture, genocide, and enslavement.[21]

Our question therefore becomes whether the obligation to do justice is encompassed within the general legal obligations under international law owed to nonnationals in foreign countries. We can only conclude provisionally that the obligation to do justice extraterritorially, although part of our general moral obligation as human beings, may or may not be part of customary international law as it has developed up to the present. Yet, the obligation to do justice extraterritorially is clearly not excluded by any customary international law norm. Moreover, it is consistent with the legal obligation to behave morally toward nonnationals in other countries, with respect to particular moral obligations (again, human rights, humanitarian laws of war) that have developed in customary international law.

Accordingly, we proceed to a third and more particularized inquiry: what conditions must exist to give rise to an extraterritorial obligation to do justice? No such conditions can be found in Aristotle's classic analysis of justice in the Nicomachean Ethics.[22] Aristotle's analysis of justice on its own terms would be contradicted by any thesis that justice is not owed by one person to another because that other person is situated in a different polity.

The post-seventeenth century social contract theorists ostensibly stand for a different proposition: that justice is only relevant within a particular society. True, the writings of Bodin, Hobbes, Locke, and Rousseau do not explicitly confine justice to relationships within a given society or legal system, but their emphasis on 'sovereignty' may be a surrogate for such a view.[23] We will examine this question below in the writings of their modern counterpart, John Rawls.

In contrast, the classic international law publicists—Grotius, Pufendorf, Suarez, and Vattel—contemplated the transnationality of justice. Grotius argued that kings "have the right of demanding punishments not only on account of injuries committed against themselves or their subjects, but also on account of injuries which do not directly affect them but excessively violate the law of nature or of nations in regard to any persons whatsoever."[24]

Although Pufendorf was not prepared to go as far as Grotius in advocating military intervention on behalf of nonnationals in egregious cases, he too recognized situations where subjects, persecuted with no semblance of justice by their own ruler, would have a right of forcible resistance.[25] In such cases foreign kings could lawfully come to the military assistance of such persons.[26] And Suarez, perhaps the greatest of the Catholic jurists, said that war might be waged on behalf of aliens abroad on condition that they would independently be "justified" in avenging themselves.[27]

Although Vattel placed much more emphasis on 'sovereignty' than did Grotius,[28] his view of the duty to do justice was similarly universal:

> The universal society of the human race being an institution of nature herself, that is to say, a necessary consequence of the nature of man, all men, in whatever station they are placed, are bound to cultivate it, and to discharge its duties. They cannot liberate themselves from the obligation by any convention or by any private association. When, therefore, they unite in civil society for the purpose of forming a separate state or nation they may indeed enter into particular engagements towards those with whom they associate themselves; but they remain still bound to the performance of their duties towards the rest of mankind; All the difference consists in this,

---

[20] *See, e.g.*, Bassiouni, *Regulation of Armed Conflicts* in 1 INTERNATIONAL CRIMINAL LAW 199 (M.C. Bassiouni ed. 1986) (describing the development of the concept of war crimes in international law).

[21] *See, e.g.*, Anthony D'Amato, INTERNATIONAL LAW: PROCESS AND PROSPECT 123–31 (1987) (discussing human rights norms that are part of customary international law).

[22] *See* W. F. HARDIE, ARISTOTLE'S ETHICAL THEORY (1980).

[23] It is interesting in this regard to note that Rousseau's greatest scholarly antagonist in The Social Contract was Grotius, whom Rousseau must have correctly regarded as being opposed to a social-contractarian notion of the state due to the inhospitability of that notion to universal justice. *See* Friedmann, *Hugo Grotius* in 3 ENCYCLOPEDIA OF PHILOSOPHY 394.

[24] A. H. GROTIUS, DE JURE BELLI AC PACIS LIBRI TRES, ch. XX, sec. xl (F. Kelsey trans. 1925) (1646).

[25] S. PUFENDORF, ELEMENTORUM JURISPRUDENTIAE UNIVERSALIS LIBRI DUO, obs. V, secs. 21–22, 292–93 (Carnegie trans. 1931) (1672).

[26] S. PUFENDORF, DE JURE NATURAE ET GENTIUM LIBRI OCTO, ch. VI, sec. 14, 1307 (Carnegie trans. 1934) (1688).

[27] SUAREZ, DE TRIPLICI VIRTUE THEOLOGICA, FIDE, SPE, ET CHARITATE 'DE CHARITATE, DISPUTATION XIII: De Bello,' in SELECTIONS FROM THREE WORKS, 817 (Carnegie trans. 1944) (1621). Nevertheless, Catholic writers at that time were less likely to agree to military intervention in general, because, as L.C. Green has observed, they were more concerned with the propagation of the faith and tended to look for papal authorization for military intervention abroad. *See* L.C. Green, *Institutional Protection of Human Rights*, 16 ISRAEL Y.B. HUM. RTS. 69, 71 (1986). Despite the unreality of attempting to divorce religious-ideological motivations from moral ones, it is nevertheless possible to theorize that papal authorization, in the eyes of these writers, was a surrogate for an objective determination that the cause of international justice would be served by intervention.

[28] It is Vattel, especially, who can mistakenly be charged with having a theory of sovereignty that appears to be insensitive to transnational justice. *See, e.g.*, Kahn, *From Nuremberg to the Hague: The United States Position in Nicaragua v. United States and the Development of International Law*, 12 YALE J. INT'L L. 1, 35–36 (1987) (assuming that Vattel's vigorous notion of domestic jurisdiction means that he lacks a concept of denial of justice having transnational implications).

> that having agreed to act in common, and having resigned their rights and submitted their will to the body of the society, in everything that concerns their common welfare, it thenceforth belongs to that body, that state, and its rulers, to fulfill the duties of humanity towards strangers, in every thing that no longer depends upon the liberty of individuals, and it is the state more particularly that is to perform these duties towards other states.[29]

Although Vattel erected a strong presumption against external interference in the affairs of government in a state,[30] he wrote that "if the prince, by violating the fundamental laws, gives his subjects a legal right to resist him, if tyranny, by becoming unsupportable obliges the nation to rise in their own defense, every foreign power has a right to succor an oppressed people who implore their assistance."[31]

After Vattel, leading international law publicists from Wolff to Oppenheim increasingly adopted a statist or Hegelian conception of sovereignty that simply failed to address considerations of transboundary justice. The twentieth century has seen the pendulum swing back, fueled by the revolutionary conception of international human rights.[32] At the present time we may say that the classic positions of Grotius, Pufendorf, Suarez, and Vattel enjoy renewed vitality, after the century or so of dormancy under the statist conception.

Nevertheless, social-contract notions continue to cause problems for advocates of transnational justice, if only for the philosophically contingent circumstance that theorists of the social contract have tended to confine their analyses to particular states or societies. The leading modern example is John Rawls, who in his *A Theory of Justice,* written in 1971, invokes social contract ideology to explicate justice obligations among citizens within a single society. To be sure, his conception of the "original position," in which persons argue for their mutual rights and obligations without knowledge of the social position into which they will be born, could be considered to be equally consistent with lack of knowledge of what country into which they will be born. But when Rawls addresses international law, he unaccountably shifts from a discussion of persons to a discussion of representatives of states.[33] Suddenly he seems to be making the error of discussing states as if they were persons.[34] As a result, there is a tension in Rawls's work between the rights of persons in a just society and the rights of states in a just international society, for states' rights are not the same as the rights of individuals within states.

On the other hand, Rawls's moral imperatives call for an expansion of effect that logically could not stop at a nation's edge. This is evidenced by his characterizations of the universal traits of persons (which he calls "moral sentiments") and his axiom of the universality of principles: "Principles are to be universal in application. They must hold for everyone in virtue of their being moral persons."[35]

Given this tension in Rawls's theory, is there any way to interpret it as addressing the question of whether there is an obligation upon persons or states to do justice internationally? Charles Beitz interestingly points out that Rawls regards justice as applying in situations where benefits and burdens are produced by "social cooperation."[36] But because people within society may not always cooperate in social activity, and each person is not necessarily always advantaged by social activity, Beitz reformulates Rawls's baseline contextual requirement as follows: "The requirements of justice apply to institutions and practices (whether or not they are genuinely cooperative) in which social activity produces relative or absolute benefits or burdens that would not exist if the social activity did not take place."[37] Beitz's reformulation persuasively captures the philosophic underpinnings of Rawls's prescriptions. It is a functional, as opposed to a categoric, definition of the social interactions that Rawls posits as the unit for social justice. As such, it clearly encompasses transboundary relations so long as they in fact produce benefits or burdens that would not exist absent the social activity.

Obviously, the degree to which nations interact will then be a critical determinant of the scope of the justice obligation. Nations that share a common boundary, that constantly exchange goods, services, and visitors, and maintain a high degree of mutual investment in each other's industries, will under this analysis have a much higher degree of duty to do justice than nations that are only casual trading partners. This higher degree can indeed approach a duty of distributive justice for which Professor Beitz has argued. Distributive justice is clearly the most demanding of the forms of justice, requiring persons to share their surplus goods (or services) with the less fortunate. Rawls's book primarily addresses distributive justice in its delineation of the 'difference principle': "Social and economic inequalities are to be arranged so that they are to the greatest benefit of the least advantaged."[38]

---

29 E. Vattel, The Law of Nations, or Principles of the Law of Nature, Applied to the Conduct and Affairs of Nations and Sovereigns, Intro., s 11, at lx-lxi (Chitty trans. 1876).

30 *Id.* at Book II, ch. I, ss 1–3, at 133–35.

31 *Id.* at Book II, ch. IV, s 56, at 155.

32 For a detailed account, *see* Anthony D'Amato, International Law: Process and Prospect 215–22 (1987).

33 John Rawls, A Theory of Justice 378 (1971).

34 For an extended discussion and critique of Rawls' concept of justice as it might be applied internationally, *see* Anthony D'Amato, Jurisprudence: A Descriptive and Normative Analysis of Law 267–68 (1984).

35 Rawls, *supra* at 132.

36 Charles Beitz, Political Theory and International Relations 131 (1979). "Like Hume, Rawls regards society as a 'cooperative venture for mutual advantage.'" *Id.* at 130 (noting the comparison with David Hume, A Treatise of Human Nature III, II, ii (1739–40)).

37 *Id.* at 131.

38 Rawls, *supra*, at 302.

But is such a high level of sacrifice, as exemplified by distributive justice, necessary in state relations under Beitz's theories? The answer seems to us to be no. One of the bedrock conceptions of justice, emphasized by Aristotle and institutionalized in all of the world's legal systems, is *compensatory* justice: the requirement that a person who causes injury to another owes that other person financial compensation.[39] In every legal system of which we are aware, this principle of justice forms the basis for private lawsuits.[40] Its pervasiveness and fundamentality are manifest. The important question for present purposes is, when does compensatory justice apply?

Since the notion of compensatory justice is far more elementary than the notion of distributive justice, and since it requires far less by way of individual sacrifice (indeed, one might argue that it involves no sacrifice at all because it is merely compensation for an advantage taken that harmed another), the level of social interaction upon which such a duty of compensatory justice may be based is far lower than that which would give rise to a duty of distributive justice. Indeed, applying Professor Beitz's analysis of the basis of the social-contractarian system, the social activity of the sale of goods (here, the export of nuclear power plant technology) *necessarily* produces relative or absolute benefits or burdens that would not exist if the social activity did not take place. If that social activity is not taken to give rise to the strong obligation of distributive justice advocated by Beitz, at the very least it gives rise to a more minimal but fundamental obligation to render compensatory justice.

Arguably, even a single export of a nuclear power plant from E to R invokes Beitz's relationship theory. Because of the magnitude of potential harm resulting from malfunction of the technology, the people of R are in a particularly dependent relationship with E; their safety and their lives are potentially in E's hands. In this respect, nuclear power plant exports are distinguishable from most other exports. Even a single export of a nuclear power plant carries with it a greater social responsibility than would a stream of exports of household appliances or television sets.

We have thus argued that the very act of import-export creates a relationship between the parties that on a social-contractarian view of justice – and certainly upon an Aristotelian view – gives rise to expectations of, and a duty of, doing justice, at the very least in the minimal form of compensatory justice. The obligation to compensate the purchasing party for damages resulting from the installation and use of a dangerous product (a nuclear power plant) is an obligation within the modern and generally accepted notion of justice. Thus, it would be a *denial of justice* not to furnish compensation to an injured party in appropriate circumstances.

What would be appropriate circumstances is not a matter of legal or moral philosophy, but rather is a matter of the application of the customary international law of state responsibility to the exportation of nuclear power plant technology. We contend that the applicable law, impelled by the justice considerations we have outlined, is the classic principles of minimum international standard and national treatment.[41] If failure to abide by these standards results in the denial of justice to aliens resident within a nation's own borders, surely failure to abide by these standards in the context of the export of hazardous technology is a denial of justice to human beings who are resident in their home country.

E. DEBATE: Resolved That Peace Is More Important Than Justice[42]

The Charter of the United Nations reflected universal agreement that the status quo prevailing at the end of World War II was not to be changed by force. Even justified grievances and a sincere concern for "national security" or other "vital interests" would not warrant any nation's initiating war. Peace was the paramount value. The Charter and the United Nations organization were dedicated to realizing other values as well – self-determination, respect for human rights, economic and social development, justice, and a just international order. But those purposes could not justify the use of force between states to achieve them; they would have to be pursued by other means. Peace was more important than progress and more important than justice. The purposes of the United Nations could not in fact be achieved by war. War inflicted the greatest injustice, the most serious violations of human rights, and the most violence to self-determination and to economic and social development. War was inherently unjust. In the future, the only "just war" would be war against an aggressor – in self-defense by the victim, in collective defense of the victim by others, or by all. Nations would be assured

---

39 For an excellent historical analysis focusing on Aristotle, see Richard Posner, *The Concept of Corrective Justice in Recent Theories of Tort Law*, 10 J. LEG. STUD. 187 (1981).

40 Judge Posner's statement is beautifully concise: "Law is a means of bringing about an efficient (in the sense of wealth-maximizing) allocation of resources by correcting externalities and other distortions in the market's allocation of resources. The idea of rectification in the Aristotelian sense is implicit in this theory. If A fails to take precautions that would cost less than their expected benefits in accident avoidance, thus causing an accident in which B is injured, and nothing is done to rectify this wrong, the concept of justice as efficiency will be violated." *Id.* at 201.

41 The concrete application of these classic standards is detailed in the original article in the Virginia Law Review.

42 By LOUIS HENKIN, excerpted from: *The Use of Force: Law and U.S. Policy*, in COUNCIL ON FOREIGN RELATIONS, RIGHT V. MIGHT: INTERNATIONAL LAW AND THE USE OF FORCE 37, 38–42, 44, 57–62 (Council on Foreign Relations 1989). Reprinted by permission.

independence, the undisturbed enjoyment of autonomy within their territory, and their right to be let alone. Change–other than internal change through internal forces–would have to be achieved peacefully by international agreement. Henceforth there would be order so that international society could concentrate on meeting better the needs of justice and human welfare.

Virtually every putative justification of a use of force has been rejected. Over the years since the Charter's adoption, even states that have perpetrated acts of force, when seeking to justify their acts, have not commonly urged a relaxed interpretation of the prohibition of Article 2(4). Rather, they have asserted facts and circumstances that might have rendered their actions not unlawful. For example, in 1950, North Korea claimed that the South Korean army had initiated hostilities, permitting North Korea to act in self-defense; in Czechoslovakia in 1948 and 1968, and in Hungary in 1956, the USSR claimed that its troops had been invited by the legitimate authorities to help preserve order.

On several occasions states have claimed the right to use force in "humanitarian intervention." The paradigmatic case was the action of Israel in 1976 to extricate hostages held on a hijacked plane at Entebbe (Uganda). The United States claimed its unsuccessful attempt in 1980 to liberate the diplomatic hostages held in Teheran also came within the exception. States have been reluctant to adopt this exception to Article 2(4) formally, but the legal community has widely accepted that the Charter does not prohibit humanitarian intervention by use of force strictly limited to what is necessary to save lives.

The exception, I believe, is not restricted to actions of a state on behalf of its own nationals. But it is a right to liberate hostages if the territorial state cannot or will not do so. It has not been accepted, however, that a state has a right to intervene by force to topple a government or occupy its territory even if that were necessary to terminate atrocities or to liberate detainees. Entebbe was acceptable, but the occupation of Cambodia by Vietnam was not. The U.S. invasion and occupation of Grenada, even if in fact designed to protect the lives of U.S. nationals, also was widely challenged.

At bottom, all suggestions for exceptions to article 2(4) imply that, contrary to the assumptions of the Charter's framers, there are universally recognized values higher than peace and the autonomy of states. In general, the claim of peace and state autonomy have prevailed.

I dismiss extreme hypothetical options for the United States. In theory, the United States could decide that the law of the Charter has been a mistake; that it is not viable; that one cannot subject the decisions of governments on national security and vital interests to restraints by legal norms; that it is undesirable–indeed, dangerous–to pretend that there is law when in fact there is none. Or the United States might decide that if the law on the use of force is not as it wishes it to be, it would prefer no law on the subject. Or it might decide that the USSR has not in fact been restrained by law and that it is therefore not in U.S. interests to be so restrained.

Whatever some hard-nosed editorial writers may say, scuttling the law of the Charter is not a viable policy for any U.S. government. Even if the United States were persuaded that the law is wholly futile and deceptive, it would not be in U.S. interests to scrap it and, with it, the fruits of the Second World War and the hopes, aspirations, and efforts of half a century. Rejecting the Charter in effect would reject Nuremberg, undermine our national justification in history, and reestablish Adolf Hitler as no worse than anyone else. Such a move would be condemned by the whole world. It would serve no good for the United States. The end of the rule of the Charter's law would not encourage cooperation for other law we seek, such as to outlaw and deny haven to terrorists, or to solve international economic ills.

The law of the Charter is here to stay. For the years ahead the interpretation of that law that renders the prohibition on the use of force most stringent is also here to stay.

Perhaps, over time, by actions and assertions, the United States could move and shape law informally to make it more permissive, even if so doing entailed eroding the rule of law and courting disorder and charges of violation along the way. In fact, it is not clear that the United States would wish to see that view of the law prevail generally. U.S. actions and justifications for them are not an indication that the United States would like to have all states legally free to do as it has done. The United States has asserted rights of intervention and counterintervention, but it has challenged the right of others (Libya, South Africa, Cuba, Syria, Iran, Israel) to follow policies that appear comparable under international law. In Grenada and in Nicaragua, the United States apparently has been asserting the right to use force to impose or restore democracy, but presumably it would continue to oppose a rule that would permit other states to use force to impose their version of democracy, or another ideology (socialism).

Like every country, the United States occasionally is disposed to interpret the Charter in accordance with its own interests as it sees them. But an interpretation that does not accord with text, purpose, design, history, and other accepted principles of treaty construction will persuade nobody and will serve no purpose. Moreover, an interpretation that may appeal to a particular constituency in the United States will not necessarily appeal to others. What will appeal at a particular time may not at a different time. What is popular is not necessarily what is in the interest of the United States. A construction of the law that may be in the immediate interest of the United States may not be in its longer, deeper interests.

The United States is free to promote democracy and human rights around the world by example, by friendship, by economic and other assistance, but not by the use of force. Clearly, it was the original intent of the Charter to forbid the use of force even to promote human rights or to install authentic democracy. Nothing has happened to justify deviations from that commitment. Human rights are indeed violated in every country. In some counties violations are egregious. But the use of force remains itself a most serious – the most serious – violation of human rights. It should not be justified by any claim that it is necessary to safeguard other human rights. Surely the law cannot warrant any state's intervening by force against the political independence and territorial integrity of another on the ground that human rights are being violated, as indeed they are everywhere.

The claims that democracy justifies the use of military force by another state are no stronger. All the framers of the Charter purported to believe in democracy. They were hardly agreed as to what it meant, but they were agreed that force was not to be used against another state even to achieve democracy, however defined. Over forty years later states are still not agreed as to what democracy means, but they are still agreed that it is not to be achieved by force. The Charter would be meaningless if it were construed or rewritten to permit any state to use force to impose its own version of democracy. Such a view of the Charter would permit "aggression for democracy" against any on of 100-150 states by any self-styled democratic champion. That is not the law; it could not become the law; it should not be the law.

2. Negative[43]

Professor Louis Henkin says:

> At bottom, all suggestions for exceptions to article 2(4) imply that, contrary to the assumptions of the Charter's framers, there are universally recognized values higher than peace and the autonomy of states.[44]

But he does not identify these "suggestions for exceptions to article 2(4)." Readers will nevertheless recognize the "suggestions" as coming from younger scholars who may not be committed Chartists. Their arguments are known to go something like this: The Charter attempted to create a monopoly of law-enforcement power in the UN Security Council. The monopoly was a two-sided coin. One side was Article 2(4), prohibiting unilateral uses of force. The other side was the international army under the control of the Security Council specified in Chapter VII of the Charter. Thus, whenever a nation violated Charter norms or other important rules of international law, the Security Council could send in its army to enforce the law.

To "apply" Article 2(4) in isolation from Chapter VII would be to ignore the other side of the coin. This is not to say that Article 2(4) would be meaningless in the absence of Security Council enforcement action; rather, it must be carefully interpreted. Careful scrutiny reveals that it does not outlaw all transboundary uses of military force, but only those directed against a nation's territorial integrity or political independence. A "humanitarian intervention" that does not annex any portion of the target state arguably is allowed by Article 2(4) if the Security Council's enforcement capability is stultified by veto. Thus, since 1945 there have been several successful unilateral humanitarian interventions arguably creating new customary law, such as India in Bangladesh (1971), Tanzania in Uganda (1979), France in Central Africa (1979) and the United States in Grenada (1983) and Panama (1989).

Professor Henkin refuses to recognize this custom, because in his view it violates Article 2(4). He sees no reason to recognize forty-four years of practice that in his view is not justified:

> Clearly, it was the original intent of the Charter to forbid the use of force even to promote human rights or to install authentic democracy. Nothing has happened to justify deviations from that commitment. Human rights are indeed violated in every country. In some countries violations are egregious. But the use of force remains itself a most serious – the most serious – violation of human rights.

Pressed to give his own explanation of customary law since 1945, Henkin proclaims in ringing terms:

> Virtually every use of force in the years since the Charter was signed has been clearly condemned by virtually all states. Virtually every putative justification of a use of force has been rejected. Over the years since the Charter's adoption, even states that have perpetrated acts of force, when seeking to justify their acts, have not commonly urged a relaxed interpretation of the prohibition.[45]

But, we may ask, *which* states "clearly condemned" these

---

[43] By ANTHONY D'AMATO, excerpted from: Book Review: *Right v. Might*, 85 AMERICAN JOURNAL OF INTERNATIONAL LAW 201 (1991). Reprinted by permission.

[44] *Supra* n.42 at 44.

[45] *Supra* n.42 At 40.

acts of force? *Who* rejected all these putative justifications? *How* were they "rejected"? The use by Henkin of the passive voice side-stepped the need for citations or examples. And what about all the exceptions that Henkin concedes? He admits that (a) the many instances of "humanitarian intervention" have "brought wide acquiescence," (b) "intervention to support self-determination" has been supported by "many states," and (c) a "permissive interpretation of article 51" that largely erodes article 2(4) has "found favor with some commentators." Does the sum total of these admitted exceptions still support his original use of "virtually," or is Henkin entitled by virtue of his status to depart from the meaning of his own words without announcing that he is doing so?

In sum, the author of *The Rights of Man Today* and many articles on human rights now claims in effect that if another Hitler should repeat the holocaust against the Jews, so long as the genocide is confined to nationals within the neo-Hitler's country, and so long as that country's allies have a veto in the Security Council, any foreign nation's forcible intervention to prevent the genocide would be illegal under international law as ordained by the Charter. Or if a radically repressive white minority regime were to take over in South Africa and begin a policy of extensive disappearances and murders of black leaders and spokespersons – a fear that fortunately appears to be receding – and if the Security Council were paralyzed, Henkin would have to hold this selective racial genocide to be one of those "egregious" violations of human rights that international law regrettably tolerates. For he values the "autonomy of states" above all considerations of morality and justice that affect real people – above every human value of care, compassion and empathy for neighbors suffering governmental oppression. He is more solicitous of the rights of states than those of persons. So long as genocide, slavery or torture is "official" (government sponsored), the Nuremberg precedent is trumped by the Charter. What he offers us is an interpretation of the Charter that negates Nuremberg, the practice of states since 1945 and elementary considerations of transnational justice.

15

Democracy

A. The Emerging Democratic Entitlement[1]

Increasingly, governments recognize that their legitimacy depends on meeting a normative expectation of the community of states. This recognition has led to the emergence of a community expectation: that those who seek the validation of their empowerment may only govern with the consent of the governed. Democracy, thus, is on the way to becoming a global entitlement, one that increasingly will be promoted and protected by collective international processes.

The transformation of the democratic entitlement from moral prescription to international legal obligation has evolved gradually. In the past decade, however, the tendency has accelerated. Most remarkable is the extent to which an international law-based entitlement is now urged by governments themselves. This is a cosmic, but unmysterious, change. For nations surfacing from long, tragic submergence beneath bogus "people's democracy" or outright dictatorship, the legitimation of power is a basic, but elusive, move in the direction of reform. As of late 1991, there are more than 110 governments, almost all represented in the United Nations, that are legally committed to permitting open, multiparty, secret-ballot elections with a universal franchise. Most joined the trend in the past five years.[2] While a few, arguably, are democracies more in form than in substance, most are, or are becoming, genuinely open to meaningful political choice. Many of these new regimes want, indeed need, to be validated by being seen to comply with global standards for free and open elections.

We are witnessing a sea change in international law, as a result of which the legitimacy of each government someday will be measured definitively by international rules and processes. We are not quite there, but we can see the outlines of this new world in which the citizens of each state will look to international law and organization to guarantee their democratic entitlement.

Citizens, however, will not be the only beneficiaries. We have observed that the engine pulling the democratic entitlement is the craving of governments for validation. Without validation, the task of governance becomes fraught with difficulty. Regimes prize validation, then, as evidence of their legitimacy. Legitimacy, in turn, is the quality of a rule, or a system of rules, or a process for making or interpreting rules that pulls both the rule makers and those addressed by the rules toward voluntary compliance.

Western democracies have achieved legitimacy largely by subjecting the political process to rules, often immutably entrenched in an intrepid constitution. These lucky few nations have succeeded in evolving their own legitimate means of validating the process by which the people choose those they entrust with the exercise of power. To achieve such a system of autochthonous validation (and thus to facilitate governing), those who hold or seek political power have made a farsighted bargain comparable to John Locke's social compact: they have surrendered control over the nation's validation process to various others – to national electoral commissions, judges, an inquisitive press and, above all, the citizenry acting at the ballot box. This collectivity decides whether the standards of the democratic

[1] By THOMAS M. FRANCK, excerpted from: *The Emerging Right to Democratic Governance*, 86 AMERICAN JOURNAL OF INTERNATIONAL LAW 46 (1992). Reprinted by permission.

[2] States that currently make legal provision for determining their governments by recourse to multiparty, secret-ballot elections are: Albania, Angola, Antigua and Barbuda, Argentina, Australia, Austria, the Bahamas, Bangladesh, Barbados, Belgium, Belize, Benin, Byelorussia, Bolivia, Botswana, Brazil, Bulgaria, Canada, Cape Verde, Chile, Colombia, the Comoros, Congo, the Cook Islands, Costa Rica, the Cote d'Ivoire, Cyprus, Czechoslovakia, Denmark, Dominica, the Dominican Republic, Ecuador, Egypt, El Salvador, Estonia, Finland, France, Gabon, Gambia, Germany, Greece, Grenada, Guatemala, Guyana, Hungary, Honduras, Iceland, India, Ireland, Israel, Italy, Jamaica, Japan, Kiribati, Korea (Republic of), Latvia, Liberia, Liechtenstein, Lithuania, Luxembourg, Madagascar, Malaysia, Mali, Malta, the Marshall Islands, Mauritius, Mexico, the Micronesian Federation, Mongolia, Morocco, Mozambique, Namibia, Nauru, Nepal, the Netherlands, New Zealand, Nicaragua, Niger, Norway, Pakistan, Panama, Papua New Guinea, Paraguay, Peru, the Philippines, Poland, Portugal, Romania, Sao Tome, Senegal, Singapore, the Solomon Islands, the Soviet Union, Spain, Sri Lanka, St. Kitts, St. Lucia, St. Vincent, Sweden, Switzerland, Tonga, Trinidad, Tunisia, Turkey, the Ukraine, the United Kingdom, Uruguay, Vanuatu, Venezuela, Western Samoa, Zambia and Zimbabwe. Several more states, such as Nigeria and Ethiopia, are committed to free, multiparty elections but have not yet enacted the necessary constitutional or legislative fiat. It must also be conceded that there are borderline cases, such as Morocco (included) and Jordan (not included), in which the elections are not necessarily decisive, depending on various factors, including the disposition of a monarch with substantial residual powers. In the large majority of cases, however, the decision to include or exclude is not seriously in doubt – though it should be recalled that the test for inclusion is whether the legal system establishes free and secret elections. Whether these are conducted fairly is another question.

entitlement have been met by those who claim the right to govern. In return, the legitimacy bestowed by that process gives back far more power to those who govern than they surrendered.

The capacity of the international community to extend legitimacy to national governments, however, depends not only on its capacity to monitor an election or to recognize the credentials of a regime's delegates to the UN General Assembly, but also on the extent to which such international activity has evolved from the ad hoc to the normative: that is, the degree to which the process of legitimation itself has become legitimate.

In any rule system, national or international, legitimacy has its own modalities. It is to the latter that the international lawyer's creative perspective must turn. Do the global requisites for democratic validation of governments now include, or are they evolving into, rules and procedures that are perceived as legitimate by those to whom they are addressed? In the international context, legitimacy is achieved if – or to the extent that – those addressed by a rule, or by a rule-making institution, perceive the rule or institution to have come into being and to be operating in accordance with generally accepted principles of right process.[3]

In seeking to assess whether an international democratic order is emerging, data will be marshaled from three related generations of rule making and implementation. The oldest and most highly developed is that subset of democratic norms which emerged under the heading of "self-determination." The second subset – freedom of expression – developed as part of the exponential growth of human rights since the mid-1950s and focuses on maintaining an open market-place of ideas. The third and newest subset seeks to establish, define and monitor a right to free and open elections.

1. *Self-Determination.* Self-determination is the historic root from which the democratic entitlement grew. Its deep-rootedness continues to confer important elements of legitimacy on self-determination, as well as on the entitlement's two newer branches, freedom of expression and the electoral right.

Self-determination postulates the right of a people organized in an established territory to determine its collective political destiny in a democratic fashion and is therefore at the core of the democratic entitlement. Symbolically, it is signified by a long-evolving tradition of maintaining observers, on behalf of international and regional organizations, at elections in colonies and trust territories. Early observer missions developed operational procedures. They sent reports to their sponsoring international agency or committee, which helped the community's political organs and individual member governments make deductions about the legitimacy of the decolonization process. Gradually, with many variations, the observer missions' methods became the standard operating procedure for validating an exercise of self-determination. The aspiration that underpins the principle of self-determination is of an antiquity traceable, in the West, at least to the Hebrews' exodus from Egypt, estimated to have been approximately in 1000 B.C. Its modern rise to the status of universal entitlement began when the Versailles Peace Conference undid the work of the Congress of Vienna, which had utterly disregarded ethnic sensibilities in redrawing the map of post-Napoleonic Europe. Embarking on another redesign of Europe after the First World War, President Woodrow Wilson made self-determination his lodestar. To this end, he reinforced the U.S. team of negotiators with an unusual contingent of historians, geographers and ethnologists, the more effectively to argue for the norm's supremacy over power politics and strategic or economic considerations. Consequently, the American delegation summoned up extensive data on demographics and evidence of ethnicity in advocating free choice by "peoples."[4]

Thus prodded, the Versailles Peace Conference authorized twenty-six on-site consultations with different European groups seeking self-determination. The Danes of Schleswig, annexed to Prussia in 1864, were able to secure agreement that "the frontier between Germany and Denmark shall be fixed in conformity with the wishes of the population."[5] Wilson also prevailed in the view "that all branches of the Slav race" in what was to become Czechoslovakia "should be completely freed from German and Austrian rule" in full consultation with Slavic representatives.[6] He resisted efforts by France's Premier Clemenceau to establish an independent Rhenish buffer state consisting of unwilling Germans.[7] Although the Versailles settlement also brought self-determination to Poland as well as Fiume, Wilson reluctantly came to concede that sometimes one had to consider "other principles" – strategic, economic and logistic – that could "clash with the requirements of self-determination."[8]

Remarkably, after the Second World War the principle of self-determination became the most dynamic concept in international relations. Former German, Japanese and Italian colonies were placed under the trusteeship of the victors (and, in one case, the vanquished), with the clear obligation under Article 76 of the United Nations Charter "to promote progressive development towards self-government or independence" in accordance with "the freely expressed

---

[3] THOMAS FRANCK, THE POWER OF LEGITIMACY AMONG NATIONS 19 (1990).

[4] *See* 1 S. WAMBAUGH, PLEBISCITES SINCE THE WORLD WAR 13 (1933).

[5] 2 A HISTORY OF THE PEACE CONFERENCE OF PARIS 203 (H.W.V. Temperley ed. 1920).

[6] *Id.* at 261–62.

[7] 4 THE INTIMATE PAPERS OF COLONEL HOUSE 334–35, 345 (C. Seymour ed. 1928).

[8] M. POMERANCE, SELF-DETERMINATION IN LAW AND PRACTICE 4 (1982). For example, Czechoslovakia ended up with defensible boundaries only by denying self-determination to a large Sudeten-German minority.

wishes of the peoples concerned.'' Conceptual evolution, however, did not stop there. Soon not only was self-determination recognized as a writ for obtaining decolonization but, by the terms of the very first article of the UN Charter, it achieved the status of a fundamental right of all ''peoples'' as a necessary prerequisite to the development of ''friendly relations among nations.'' At least potentially, the concept was thus both universalized and internationalized, for it could now be said to portend a duty owed by all governments to their peoples and by each government to all members of the international community.

In the thirty-five years following the surrender of the Axis powers, self-determination transformed the world's political landscape. Today, the process of decolonization is nearly complete. Nevertheless, the principle of self-determination retains vigor, manifestly having contributed to the decision by the leaders of the Soviet Union, beginning in 1989, to withdraw their military forces and political suzerainty from Eastern Europe and, more recently, from the Baltic States. Its pull prompted South Africa's decision to give independence to Namibia and Morocco's volte-face regarding Western Sahara. When another vestige of imperfect decolonization, the Angolan civil war, ended in 1991, it was on the basis of an agreement to hold free, internationally observed elections, which, nunc pro tunc, would give Angola the legitimate regime it had failed to acquire at the chaotic moment of its independence. Another UN-supervised process of popular consultation was created by the Paris agreement ending the civil war in Cambodia. Thus the idea of self-determination has evolved into a more general notion of internationally validated political consultation, one that is beginning to be applied even to independent (postcolonial) states like Nicaragua and Angola, albeit without implying the community's right to validate secessionist movements within sovereign states.

The International Covenant on Civil and Political Rights clearly intends to make the right of self-determination applicable to the citizens of all nations, entitling them to determine their collective political status through democratic means. This treaty, ratified or acceded to by 113 states as of November 1991, but probably binding on other states as customary law, provides in Article 1: ''All peoples have the right of self-determination. By virtue of that right they freely determine their political status and freely pursue their economic, social and cultural development.'' The Covenant also makes an important distinction between that right of each nation's collective polis and the rights of minorities within each state, which the Covenant elucidates in Article 27. Under Article 27, ''ethnic, religious or linguistic minorities . . . shall not be denied the right, in community with the other members of their group, to enjoy their own culture, to profess and practice their own religion, or to use their own language.'' Notably, Article 27 does not mention any right to secede. When the Covenant came into force, the right of self-determination entered its third phase of enunciation: it ceased to be a rule applicable only to specific territories (at first, the defeated European powers; later, the overseas trust territories and colonies) and became a right of everyone. It also, at least for now, stopped being a principle of exclusion (secession) and became one of inclusion: the right to participate. The right now entitles peoples in all states to free, fair and open participation in the democratic process of governance freely chosen by each state.

How is self-determination to be implemented? Gradually, answers to this question have also emerged. During the first forty years of the United Nations, members responsible for trust territories and colonies were charged with making periodic reports on their progress; these reports were subjected to increasing scrutiny by various UN bodies. Since the coming into force of the Covenant, reporting and scrutiny have been formalized, depoliticized to an extent, and welded to the process of case-by-case norm application. This development will help shape the postcolonial concept of self-determination and give it more determinacy. The Covenant thus foresees a continuing, growing body of law made by means of the interpretation and application of its provisions by an expert, independent, quasi-judicial body.

2. *Free Expression.* The second building block in constructing a normative entitlement to democracy is the right of free political expression. This right originated conceptually in the antitotalitarianism born of World War II and was first enunciated normatively in the Universal Declaration of Human Rights, adopted by the General Assembly on December 10, 1948. As a mere resolution, the Universal Declaration does not have the force of a treaty; yet it was passed with such overwhelming support, and such prestige has accrued to it in succeeding years, that it may be said to have become a customary rule of state obligation.[9] More to the point, its text manifests considerable determinacy, specifically recognizing a universal right to freedom of opinion and expression (Article 19), as well as to peaceful assembly and association (Article 20).

These entitlements reappear with even greater specificity in the legally binding Covenant on Civil and Political Rights. Spelled out in that treaty are specific rights to freedom of thought (Article 18) and freedom of association (Article 22). Article 19(2), an especially important component of the democratic entitlement, provides: ''Everyone shall have the right to freedom of expression; this right shall include freedom to seek, receive and impart information and ideas of all kinds, regardless of frontiers, either orally, in writing or in print, in the form of art, or through any other media of his choice.''

Rights to opinion, expression and association contained in Articles 18, 19 and 22 look both backward and forward. They are a refinement of an aspect of the older right of

---

[9] [Editor's Note: Professor Franck may be saying that the practice of states has confirmed the rule of freedom of political expression. Otherwise, it would be hard to see how a General Assembly resolution itself, even if time-honored, can generate customary law. See the section entitled ''U.N. Resolutions'' in Chapter 4 of this Anthology.]

self-determination; they also constitute the essential preconditions for an open electoral process, which is the newest component of the democratic entitlement. First mooted in the Universal Declaration, they became explicit treaty-based entitlements by incorporation into the Covenant and are likely to be made even more explicitly determinate by the review and monitoring of required national reports on compliance and specific petitions by complainants.

3. *Participatory Political Process.* The third and newest building block in constructing the entitlement to democracy is the emerging normative requirement of a participatory electoral process. As early as 1948, the Universal Declaration of Human Rights, in Article 21, enunciated the right of all persons to take part in government, as well as in "periodic and genuine elections which shall be by universal and equal suffrage and shall be held by secret vote or by equivalent free voting procedures." At the time, only UN members outside the socialist, Arab and Latin American blocs took this as a restatement of conditions already prevailing in their polis. With rapid decolonization, the proportion of UN members actually practicing free and open electoral democracy began to shrink further under the aegis of one-party modernizing authoritarianism in Africa and Asia. Nevertheless, even in that relatively hostile atmosphere, few states were willing openly to block the textual evolution of a specific electoral entitlement, however many mental reservations their regimes may have harbored. Thus, two decades later, the Civil and Political Covenant was opened for signature, entering into force in 1976 as a set of legal obligations now binding on more than two-thirds of all states. With the balance now heavily tilting toward the substantial new majority of states actually practicing a reasonably credible version of electoral democracy, the treaty-based legal entitlement also begins to approximate prevailing practice and thus may be said to be stating what is becoming a customary legal norm applicable to all.

Article 25 extends to every citizen the right:

> (a) To take part in the conduct of public affairs, directly or through freely chosen representatives;
>
> (b) To vote and to be elected at genuine periodic elections which shall be by universal and equal suffrage and shall be held by secret ballot, guaranteeing the free expression of the will of the electors.

Admirable as it is, this standard still needs greater specificity. Textual determinacy, once again, is gradually being augmented by process determinacy under the auspices of the Human Rights Committee, which is authorized to monitor compliance. That body has discussed the implications of Article 25 in connection with its review of national reports on implementation and a small number of petitions lodged under the Optional Protocol. In reviewing two citizens' complaints against the military regime of Uruguay, the Committee concluded that the complainants had been arbitrarily deprived of protected rights by decrees banning their political party and by being barred from running for office.[10]

In 1990, the leaders of the thirty-four states of the Conference on Security and Co-operation in Europe met in Paris and unanimously endorsed an extraordinary Charter, which commits them "to build, consolidate and strengthen democracy as the only system of government of our nations."[11] The Charter restates the older entitlement to free expression but adds the right of every individual, without discrimination, "to participate in free and fair elections," backed by the leaders' pledge to "co-operate and support each other with the aim of making democratic gains irreversible." Although the Charter is not a treaty, its language is deliberately norm creating. In particular, the Charter builds on the assumption that electoral democracy is owed not only by each government to its own people, but also by each CSCE state to all the others.

To safeguard the rights concerned, the Paris Charter establishes an institutionalized process for monitoring compliance with the electoral duties of states. It gives the CSCE several organs, including a secretariat at Prague and an Office for Free Elections at Warsaw.

Most recently, in September to October 1991, these nations' representatives unanimously endorsed the Document of the Moscow Meeting of the Conference on the Human Dimension of the CSCE. It reaffirms "that issues relating to human rights, fundamental freedoms, democracy and the rule of law are of international concern, as respect for these rights and freedoms constitutes one of the foundations of the international order."[12] The participating states "categorically and irrevocably declare that the commitments undertaken in the field of the human dimension of the CSCE are matters of direct and legitimate concern to all participating States and do not belong exclusively to the internal affairs of the State concerned." Most important of all is part II of the Moscow Document, in which the members pledge that they

> will support vigorously, in accordance with the Charter of the United Nations, in case of overthrow or attempted overthrow of a legitimately elected government of a participating State by undemocratic means, the legitimate organs of that State upholding human rights, democracy and the rule of law, recognizing their common commitment to countering any attempt to curb these basic values.

As the entitlement becomes an accepted norm, a drawn-out debate in international law will draw to a close. Do

---

[10] Case 34/1979, 1981 Report of the Human Rights committee, 36 UN GAOR Supp. (No. 40) at 130; Case 44/1979, id., Ann. XVI, at 153.

[11] Conference on Security and Co-operation in Europe, Charter of Paris for a New Europe and Supplementary Document to Give Effect to Certain Provisions of the Charter, Nov. 21, 1990, Preamble, reprinted in 30 ILM 190, 193 (1991).

[12] Conference on Security and Co-operation in Europe, Document of the Moscow Meeting of the Conference on the Human Dimension of the CSCE, Oct. 3, 1991, Preamble, at 2 (unofficial text of the U.S. delegation), reprinted in 30 ILM 1670 (1991).

governments validate international law or does international law validate governments? It is becoming apparent that each legitimates the other.

The capacity of the international system to validate governments in this fashion is rapidly being accepted as an appropriate role of the United Nations, the regional systems and, supplementarily, the NGOs. A recent study conducted by the Netherlands Minister of Foreign Affairs gives expression to the new normative expectation. It asked: what can reasonably be expected of a European state seeking to join the European Communities and the Council of Europe? The study finds that applicant states "must be plural democracies; they must regularly hold free elections by secret ballot; they must respect the rule of law; and they must have signed the European Convention on Human Rights and Fundamental Freedoms."[13] Such a test for validation of governance and entry into a society of nations would have been unthinkable even a decade ago; it is considered unexceptionable in the new Europe. Some comparable rule in future should, and undoubtedly will, become the standard for participation in the multinational institutions of the global community.

4. *Human Rights*. Self-determination, freedom of expression and electoral rights, have much in common and evidently aim at achieving a coherent purpose: creating the opportunity for all persons to assume responsibility for shaping the kind of civil society in which they live and work. There is a large normative canon for promoting that objective: the UN Charter, the Universal Declaration of Human Rights, the International Covenant on Civil and Political Rights, the International Convention on the Elimination of All Forms of Racial Discrimination, the International Convention on the Suppression and Punishment of the Crime of Apartheid, the Declaration on the Elimination of All Forms of Intolerance and of Discrimination Based on Religion or Belief, and the Convention on the Elimination of All Forms of Discrimination against Women. These universally based rights are supplemented by regional instruments such as the European Convention for the Protection of Human Rights and Fundamental Freedoms, the American Convention on Human Rights, the African Charter on Human and Peoples' Rights, the Copenhagen Document and the Paris Charter.

Each of these instruments recognizes related specific entitlements as accruing to individual citizens. These constitute internationally mandated restraints on governments. As we have seen, they embody rights of free and equal participation in governance, a cluster within which electoral rights are a consistent and probably necessary segment. The result is a net of participatory entitlements. The various texts speak of similar goals and deploy, for the most part, a similar range of processes for monitoring compliance, several of which have already become common usage in connection with the democratic entitlement. One can convincingly argue that states which deny their citizens the right to free and open elections are violating a rule that is fast becoming an integral part of the elaborately woven human rights fabric. Thus, the democratic entitlement has acquired a degree of legitimacy by its association with a far broader panoply of laws pertaining to the rights of persons vis-a-vis their governments.

Nevertheless, while we may well be moving in this direction, we may not have arrived. When, in November 1989, the UN Secretary-General was asked by the Nicaraguan Sandinista Government to monitor national elections, he felt compelled to link his acceptance not to the human rights framework but to older, perhaps better-established, norms of the international system. Indeed, he went out of his way to reassure the General Assembly that, while the United Nations had frequently supervised elections in the context of decolonization, "it has not been the practice to do so in respect of independent States." He even noted with pride that, "on a number of occasions over the years, we have declined invitations from Member States to that effect." Nevertheless, the Nicaraguan case could be distinguished because the request was not from "a single Member State, but one which has the support of the Presidents of Costa Rica, El Salvador, Guatemala, Honduras and Nicaragua," and thus "clearly belongs in the context of the Central American peace efforts."[14]

So far, the Secretary-General's choice of the peacemaking linkage strategy has avoided a head-on conflict between proponents and opponents of election monitoring as a general normative democratic entitlement. Sooner or later, however, an unresolved conflict of deep-seated principles—the emerging right to free and fair elections and nonintervention in domestic affairs—is likely to generate a clash of political wills in the global and regional communities unless these dissonant principles are reconciled.

The very idea of general international monitoring of elections in sovereign states still arouses the most passionate ire, not only of the increasingly isolated residue of totalitarian regimes, but also of nations with long memories of humiliating interventions by states bent on "civilizing" missions. While they will accept occasional monitoring of elections to end a civil war or regional conflict, they consider it a necessary exception, not a normal manifestation of a universal democratic entitlement.

Some nations are motivated by fear that monitoring will be used to reimpose a form of neocolonialism under the banner of establishing democracy. That fear must be addressed, but it must also be put in perspective. History has warned, repeatedly, that the natural right of all people to liberty and democracy is too precious, and too vulnerable, to be entrusted entirely to those who govern. John Stuart Mill once observed that the moral fiber of a nation is weak-

---

[13] Letter from the Minister for Foreign Affairs (H. van den Broek) to the Advisory Committee on Human Rights and Foreign Policy (June 20, 1990), reprinted in NETHERLANDS ADVISORY COMMITTEE ON HUMAN RIGHTS AND FOREIGN POLICY, DEMOCRACY AND HUMAN RIGHTS IN EASTERN EUROPE 30-31 (1990).

[14] UN Doc. A/44/210, at 2 (1989).

ened if the intervention of outsiders spares its people the trouble of liberating themselves.[15] In view of the technological edge dictators nowadays enjoy over their people, this proposition is no longer wholly defensible. The opposite case was stated by Uganda's President Godfrey L. Binaisa, who, after the overthrow of Idi Amin's bloody junta, went before the General Assembly to chide its delegates for their indifference to his people's plight. "In the light of the clear commitment set out in provisions of the Charter," he said, "our people naturally looked to the United Nations for solidarity and support in their struggle against the Fascist dictatorship. For eight years they cried out in the wilderness for help; unfortunately, their cries seemed to have fallen on deaf ears." Acerbically, Binaisa observed that, "somehow, it is thought to be in bad taste or contrary to diplomatic etiquette to raise matters of violations of human rights by Member States within the forums of the United Nations."[16]

There are no legal impediments to institutionalizing voluntary international election monitoring as one way to give effect to the emerging right of all peoples to free and open electoral democracy, but this is not to say that states as yet have a duty to submit their elections to international validation. Although the CSCE, in Europe, seems poised to pioneer a generalized duty to be monitored, even it has not made the duty mandatory for all. In the international community, while there may be a duty under Article 25 of the Civil and Political Rights Covenant and its regional and customary law analogues to permit free and open elections and review of national compliance by the Human Rights Committee, there is as yet no obligation to permit actual election monitoring by international or regional organizations.

The coherence of the democratic entitlement ultimately will depend on whether most states, most of the time, freely agree to be monitored: whether, in short, the process is perceived as legitimate. To achieve this normative coherence, monitoring will have to be uncoupled, in the clearest fashion, from a long history of unilateral enforcement of a tainted, colonialist "civilizing" mission. If the duty to be monitored is to develop as customary law, it must be reconciled in the minds of governments with their residual sovereignty. This requires that all states unambiguously renounce the use of unilateral, or even regional, military force to compel compliance with the democratic entitlement in the absence of prior Security Council authorization under Chapter VII of the Charter; such authorization, except for regional action under Article 53, would require a finding that the violation had risen to the level of a threat to the peace. Such a pledge would merely reiterate the existing normative structure of the Charter, Articles 2(4), 51 and 53 in particular. Yet this reiteration is necessary, in view of the history of unilateral interventionism which has undermined that self-denying ordinance.[17] Specifically, states must acknowledge that the evolution of a democratic entitlement cannot entitle a state or group of states to enforce the right by military action under the pretext of invoking Articles 51 or 53. Ca va sans dire is no answer to those demanding that assurance in the light of recent Soviet and U.S.-led unilateral or pseudoregional actions alleged to promote "democracy" in neighboring states and justified as "collective self-defense."

A specific renunciation of unilateralism would obviously not obviate every possibility that some negative consequences might ensue for governments unwilling to be monitored or to hold free elections; nor should it. The international community long has asserted, in the case of South Africa, a right of all states to take hortatory, economic and – in extreme cases – even military action to enforce aspects of the democratic entitlement, but only when duly authorized by the United Nations in accordance with its Charter. Article 2(7), in barring UN intervention "in matters which are essentially within the domestic jurisdiction of any state," stipulates that "this principle shall not prejudice the application of enforcement measures under Chapter VII." Rhodesia's Unilateral Declaration of Independence provoked a UN resolution permitting Britain to use military force. It is no longer arguable that the United Nations cannot exert pressure against governments that oppress their own peoples by egregious racism, denials of self-determination and suppression of freedom of expression. That litany is being augmented by new sins: refusals to permit demonstrably free elections or to implement their results. However, if the sin is committed, the international community may only invoke collective enforcement measures such as sanctions, blockade or military intervention in limited circumstances – as when the Security Council finds that a threat or breach of the peace has occurred – or if it collectively determines that it is not engaging in enforcement against a member but is acting at the request of a legitimate government against a usurper. These prerequisite determinations, however, must be made by the appropriate collective machinery of the community and not by individual members.

This procedure is both legally required and politically essential. To obtain the general consent necessary to render the denial of democracy a cognizable violation of an international community standard, it must be understood that whatever countermeasures are taken must first be authorized collectively by the appropriate UN institutions. Collec-

---

[15] 3 J.S. Mill, Dissertations and Discussions: Political, Philosophical and Historical 238–63 (1873).

[16] UN Doc. A/34/PV.14, at 4–6 (1979).

[17] [Editor's Note: Is there a necessary linkage between Security Council authorization and intervention to restore a democratic government? What if sometime in the future the Security Council, for political reasons of its own, refuses to intervene even though the case for intervention is clear? These questions are intended to raise the issue with the reader whether Professor Franck's main argument is a substantive one (an entitlement to a democracy) or a procedural one (whatever the UN does is right). Note carefully the arguments Professor Franck makes in the paragraphs that follow.]

tive action – so the tremulous must understand and the powerful aver – is not a substitute for, but the opposite of, unilateral enforcement. In this respect, as in many others, the principal enemy of the evolution of a new rule is fear of its vigilante enforcement. For that reason, the entitlement to democracy can only be expected to flourish if it is coupled with a reiterated prohibition on such unilateral initiatives. Only then will the rule enjoy the degree of principled coherence necessary to the widespread perception of its legitimacy.

5. *Peace*. The democratic entitlement is more likely to be perceived as a legitimate rule if it can be seen as a necessary part of a normative hierarchy. As it happens, the right to democracy can readily be shown to be an important subsidiary of the community's most important norm: the right to peace.

With the exception of the principle pacta sunt servanda, no principle of international law has been more firmly established – first by the Kellogg-Briand Pact and, particularly since 1945, by the UN Charter – than that states "shall refrain in their international relations from the threat or use of force against the territorial integrity or political independence of any state" (Article 2 (4)). Not only has this peace principle been featured in treaty law, but it has been resoundingly echoed in the jurisprudence of the International Court of Justice and in key UN resolutions.

Most recently, the Security Council, in its resolutions and actions to reverse Iraq's attack on Kuwait, reiterated the primacy of the entitlement to peace and protection against aggression. More than thirty nations joined in liberating Kuwait because, at last, aggression against one has begun to be seen as a contingent violation of the common peace. Stopping aggression and maintaining the peace has become the central concern of a newly cohesive international community.

If that principle indeed stands at the apex of the global normative system, the democratic governance of states must be recognized as a necessary, although certainly not a sufficient, means to that end. Peace is the consequence of many circumstances: economic well-being, security, and the unimpeded movement of persons, ideas and goods. States' nonaggressiveness, however, depends fundamentally on domestic democracy. Although the argument is not entirely conclusive, historians have emphasized that, in the past 150 years, no liberal democracies have ever fought against each other. It has been argued persuasively that "a democratic society operating under a market economy has a strong predisposition towards peace."[18] This stands to reason: a society that makes its decisions democratically and openly will be reluctant to engage its members' lives and treasure in causes espoused by leaders deluded by fantasies of grievance or grandeur.

No one has stated this position more eloquently than the eighteenth-century German philosopher Immanuel Kant. He examined the correlation between democratic governance and nonaggressiveness in his essay *Perpetual Peace*.[19] He argued that democracy, leading to a "pacific union" among liberal states, would counteract the aggressive tendencies of absolutist monarchies by making government accountable to the majority. In contrast, a state of perpetual war would likely prevail between democracies and totalitarian states.[20] Moreover, Kant discerned a three-way linkage among democracy, peace and human rights.

Neither Kant nor his modern interpreters make the argument that democracies will not fight: only that they are not disposed to fight each other. The historical record bears this out.[21] Consequently, one way to promote universal and perpetual nonaggression – probably the best and, perhaps, the only way – is to make democracy an entitlement of all peoples. This conclusion was eloquently and unanimously accepted as axiomatic by the CSCE representatives at their 1990 Copenhagen meeting. Unanimously, they proclaimed "their conviction that . . . pluralistic democracy" is a prerequisite "for progress in setting up the lasting order of peace, security, justice and co-operation that they seek to establish in Europe."[22]

Both textually and in practice, the international system is moving toward a clearly designated democratic entitlement, with national governance validated by international standards and systematic monitoring of compliance. The task is to perfect what has been so wondrously begun.

B. Democratic Governance: An African Perspective[23]

The involvement of the international community in efforts to promote democracy and protect human rights in individual countries presumes the existence of a certain consensus among members of the community on the essential attributes of democracy, and on those rights that are to be considered as basic human rights. A closer examination of the issue would, however, indicate that while there

---

[18] T. Smith, *Democracy Resurgent*, in SEA CHANGES 152, 157 (N. Rizopoulos ed. 1990).

[19] IMMANUEL KANT, PERPETUAL PEACE 107–39 (T. Humphrey rev. ed. 1983) (1795).

[20] [Editor's Note: For a discussion of Kant's "Perpetual Peace," *see* Chapter 13 in this Anthology.]

[21] The point is well developed by Doyle, *An International Liberal Community*, in RETHINKING AMERICA'S SECURITY (G. Allison ed., forthcoming).

[22] Conference on Security and Co-operation in Europe, Document of the Copenhagen Meeting of the Conference on the Human Dimension, June 29, 1990, preamble, reprinted in 29 ILM 1305, 1307 (1990).

[23] By BABACAR NDIAYE, excerpted from: *International Co-operation to Promote Democracy and Human Rights: Principles and Programmes*, 49 INTERNATIONAL COMMISSION OF JURISTS REVIEW 23, 25–29 (1992). Reprinted by permission.

may be agreement on the desirability of democratic systems, considerable differences still exist on the essential properties of democratic systems of governance. There may, moreover, be greater agreement on what constitutes a *non-democratic* system of governance. In other words, members of the international community may find it easier to agree that a particular system of governance is non-democratic (e.g., as is the case of the apartheid system in South Africa), than to agree on the constitutive elements of a democratic society.

In Western liberal thought, democracy is traditionally identified with two essential attributes: popular sovereignty and individual liberty. These imply that legitimate power rests solely with the people, and that the people have the right to choose or dismiss their government. Complementing this fundamental axiom of popular sovereignty is the inalienability of certain human and political rights, such as the right to free speech and political assembly. Contemporary discourse in the Western world on the notion of democracy is marked by debates on whether rights, other than the purely political, should also be included within the notion of democracy. Many would argue, for example, that the right to basic needs, such as a minimum supply of food and acceptable shelter, as well as the right to work, should be included in the notion of democracy. By contrast, many in the developing countries would argue not only for a hierarchy of rights (with basic material rights often being given higher priority), but would also insist on the reconciliation of the "universal" attributes of democracy with the specific value-systems and cultures of a people.

In considering the historical evolution of democracy, it is also important to note how this notion has expanded progressively over the centuries. It is worthwhile to recall, for instance, that when proponents of natural rights argued passionately for the "rights of man" in the eighteenth and nineteenth centuries, they did not include the rights of women, nor did they refer to the rights of people of color. Even in our own century, it is important to recall the total disregard shown by colonial powers for the democratic and human rights of the peoples that they had subjugated. We should note further that it is only in this century that the notion of "economic rights" as an integral component of democratic rights has gained some ground.

International cooperation and involvement should, in the first instance, be guided by the recognition of the legitimacy of different national political, economic, and cultural systems. The international community can not insist that all countries have identical systems of political organizations or systems of governance, even if there would appear at present to be some convergence towards the ideals of democracy and the protection of human rights. In other words, there is a need to recognize the legitimacy of a national political and cultural space in the determination of systems of governance, and in the recognition and respect of fundamental human rights.

It is clear that a notion such as that of a legitimate "national space" can come in conflict with the broader principle of "shared humanity." It could also be argued that the notion of "national space" is not much different from that of "national sovereignty," which the international community has, in some important respects, already begun to abridge. A way of reconciling these seemingly contradictory principles is by recognizing the higher legitimacy of the principle of "shared humanity" only under certain specific conditions. In other words, it is best done by recognizing that the international community does have the right, and the moral duty, to express its profound concern and even take measures when certain clearly defined conditions prevail. A few can be cited: a case of attempted genocide against a people, be they a religious or ethnic minority; and the occurrence of a humanitarian crisis of unacceptable proportions, either due to the breakdown of law and order, or to criminal negligence on the part of a government. In these types of egregious violations of basic human rights, or unacceptable levels of human suffering, the involvement of the international community could be considered legitimate and clearly called for.

A second principle which should govern international involvement in support of democracy and human rights is when a people clearly expresses a desire to exercise its democratic and human rights, but is thwarted by its own repressive government. The rationale for intervention under such conditions is the coincidence of value-systems between internationally accepted democratic and human rights values and the political and cultural values of a people. Involvement in such a case is called for because of the manifest disregard of the clearly enunciated wishes of a people. Under these types of conditions, the appropriate response of the international community would, in general, be punitive measures such as suspension of resource flows, or, in very serious cases, the imposition of economic and trade embargoes.

The international community will, however, need to observe strictly the obverse of the above type of situation. It will need to accept the principle of non-interference if a people, either due to religious or cultural reasons, genuinely supports a particular system of government, even if such a system may seem to contravene generally accepted democratic principles and even if it would appear to fall short in its observance of human rights principles. In the contemporary context this would, for example, mean accepting political systems based on *Sharia* law, if it is proven that the large majority wish to have their political and social relations governed by such a religious system. But the right of the majority to establish such a political system does not, on the other hand, give it also the liberty to impose forcefully its beliefs or will on a minority that may, for religious or other reasons, not support it.[24]

Finally, a third principle that should be applied is the principle of non-selectivity. The international community, if it is to use the principle of "shared humanity" to justify its involvement in the affairs of individual countries, will need to demonstrate its impartiality in the application of this principle. To date, there are clear cases of selectivity, not only in the actions that individual countries take in response to human rights abuses and violations of democratic principles, but even in the implementation of the resolutions of the United Nations. If the principle of shared humanity is indeed to become a universally-accepted principle and used to justify the involvement of the international community in the affairs of nations, it can only become so if it is applied in a non-discriminatory manner.

C. What Kind of Democracy Do We Want to Export?[25]

Professor Thomas Franck's important argument for an emerging democratic entitlement is based on a vision of democracy that I would call process-based. I contrast it with a rights-based democracy (a third kind, a "general-will-based democracy, will be dealt with below). A process-based democracy is perhaps true to the Aristotelian meaning of the term: absolute rule by the people. But Aristotle deplored democracies – an unenlightened sort of government capable of the worst tyranny, the tyranny of the crowd, mob-rule. Aristotle shared with Plato a preference for elite rule – the rule of educated, enlightened persons.

The ancient Greek philosophers had very little knowledge or experience with rights-based government – government according to a constitution that safeguarded basic human rights. The idea of a rights-based constitutional democracy was first mooted in the eighteenth century. Even the American Constitution reflected mostly the process-based theory. To be sure, the idea of separation of powers borrowed from Montesquieu, combined with a federal system where the states retained significant powers, was an engineering improvement over the direct kind of majority rule that Aristotle feared. By an elaborate system of checks and balances, power was diffused in the American polity. Freedom of the press, freedom of speech, and free elections were vital components of the process-based democracy established by the Framers. Fortunately, some of the Framers of the American Constitution also insisted on a Bill of Rights. It was added to the Constitution in the form of the first ten amendments.

Although almost an afterthought, it is this Bill of Rights that makes the American democracy what I call rights-based. As students of American democracy have come to appreciate, the Bill of Rights is a distinctly minoritarian document. A majority of the public does not need a Constitution that contains enumerated rights, because the majority can protect itself against any unwanted legislation through its dominance over the electoral process. But a minority, by definition, may not be able to protect itself against unwanted legislation. Thus the Bill of Rights is a sort of guarantee[26] to minorities that no legislative majority may tamper with their basic human rights – the rights that are enumerated in the Bill of Rights.

Even with all the historical data at hand today, scholars can still debate whether the American constitutional system has succeeded primarily because of its process-based complex of checks and balances and federalism, or because of its rights-based complex of enumerated rights and inferred rights (one might regard the "right of privacy" as a right inferred from other rights in the Bill of Rights). Perhaps the combination and interaction of both types of democracy has made the American system successful. In any event, as far as the United States is concerned, it's clearly an academic debate.

But the choice between process-based and rights-based democracy is not at all academic when we consider countries that are in the early stages of going democratic. In my view, a process-based democracy – no matter how well engineered – can be a disaster if there are no concurrent rights-based democratic safeguards.

I would have needed a hypothetical case to illustrate my point except for the strange fact that the real world has recently provided an illustration exactly on point – Algeria. Back in 1962, after a long revolutionary war against France, Algeria attained independence. The country, then numbering 7 million people, was ruled by the National Liberation Front (which had led the fight for independence). A quarter of a century later, riots and broad-based

---

[24] [Editor's Note: Many systems based on *Sharia* law do not allow women the freedoms of political speech, expression, petition, or assembly. How may the wishes of these women be ascertained and/or given effect?]

[25] By ANTHONY D'AMATO, written for this Anthology and based on work in progress, drafts of which have been read in the past few years at a meeting of the Board of Editors of the American Journal of International Law, the faculty workshop of Northwestern University School of Law, and Professor Lea Brilmayer's seminar in international law at New York University School of Law.

[26] I say "sort of" because there can be no such thing as a sure-fire guarantee. During World War II, the guarantees of the Bill of Rights did not protect American citizens of Japanese ancestry from being rounded up and placed in detention camps. The detention-camp orders at the time had the full support of Congress and the President, reflecting the clear majority support of the American public. Even so, the Supreme Court, as an independent body, should have struck down the military orders as unconstitutional. Some Justices would have done so, but they were in a minority. Thus, one can never be certain that rights enumerated in a Constitution will prevail in the face of an overwhelmingly popular desire to trample on those rights.

demonstrations led to a government decision to proceed to democratization. Numerous political parties were formed, and a two-stage election was set for December 1991 and January 1992.

By the time of the first national election in 1992, the population of Algeria stood at 26 million. The increase—from 7 million in 1962 to 26 million thirty years later—may be one of the most rapid population explosions in history. The result of the first-round election in December 1991 took the leadership of Algeria by surprise: the fundamentalist Islamic Salvation front won 188 of 231 seats. With more than 200 seats still to be decided in the second-round in January, there were immediate calls by the Algerian government to persons who had not voted in the first round to vote in the second round. Yet it soon became clear that, despite the government's best efforts, the Islamic Front would attain a clear majority of the parliament in the January elections. The Islamic Salvation Front based its campaign on its promise to turn Algeria into a Muslim fundamentalist state and to establish Sharia law. The Algerian middle class and Westernized segments of the society have argued that the Islamic Front's goal is to establish an Islamic theocracy and dictatorship.[27]

Abruptly on January 11, 1992, President Chadli Benjedid of Algeria resigned, and was replaced by a new five-member State Council consisting of civilian and military leaders. It soon became evident that the resignation was forced, and that the Algerian Army had staged a coup d'etat. The second-round of elections in January were canceled, and a month later, the new Council imposed a year-long state of emergency on the public, under which virtually all constitutional rights were suspended.

As this Anthology goes to press, the situation in Algeria has not changed significantly since the above-described events; it remains uncertain and unresolved. But the lesson, for present purposes, is clear. The ruling elite of Algeria, in 1988, was willing to risk their governmental positions in a general election and thus point the way toward a new democratic republic. But what they did not foresee was the possibility of the emergence of an Islamic fundamentalist majority that would take over the country and establish a theocracy—a theocracy that could terminate the personal rights and freedoms of the former government elites and the rest of the non-fundamentalist minority in Algeria. In short, a process-based democracy of majority rule looks scary when you're in the minority and your personal rights and freedoms are not inviolate. It is even more frightening if the new majority has a religious fervor and wants to install a theocratic government that may end up ordering all aspects of your life and leaving you no personal space to resist the government's onslaught. If you are in such a situation, a process-based democracy doesn't solve your problem; in fact, it's part of the problem.

But maybe—just for argument's sake—you'd be better off becoming, heart and soul, a member of the majority. In Algeria, this might mean your willing conversion to Islamic fundamentalism. Suppose that your reason for converting is that you foresee an enhancement of your personal freedom, not its diminution. Perhaps by being a member of a group that has a religious answer for everything in your life—that provides you with religious security against the uncertainty of mortal existence—you'd be better off. In that case, you'd blend in to the majority group and find that your desires and the group's desires are one and the same. In such a situation, could it be said that you—as well as the group you are a member of—have achieved perfect democracy? Is the true meaning of democracy not the "process-based" engineering notion, nor the "rights-based" constitutional notion, but rather a third posssibility, namely, the "general will" totalitarian notion of democracy described by Jean-Jacques Rousseau?

Rousseau has arguably looked more closely into the soul of democracy than any other political theorist. His organizing question in *The Social Contract* was whether a people could govern itself the way a person can govern himself. Just as a mind can govern a body—a person's will asserts or attempts to assert control over the passions to which the flesh is heir—so too a democratic government is a kind of giant mind that somehow reflects the will of the people. But the complication Rousseau addressed is the existence of two kinds of popular will: the will of all and the general will. The will of all is the kind achieved either by direct popular referendum or, most often, through elected representatives. But it is only the aggregation of private interests. This aggregation can become, from the viewpoint of a dissenter, the tyranny of the majority. The dissenter is no better off because the tyranny is that of the crowd rather than a dictator; it is tyranny nonetheless. The ancient Greeks even preferred dictatorial tyranny to the mindless tyranny of the masses.[28]

For Rousseau, the "will of all" was not good enough as the mental engine of democratic government. Rousseau was a passionate believer in human freedom (he was a dissenter and a gadfly). He cared less about whether an entire representative democracy could function effectively than he cared about the loss of freedom of a single person tyrannized by the majority. Thus, he needed a better distillation of the will of the body politic than the aggregate will of all. And thus he invented the "general will," which he defined as the expression of the "common interest" of the people.[29] The common interest captures the interest of every single person in the state; hence, with respect to the

[27] Youssef M. Ibrahim, *Algeria Clamps Down Harder on Muslim Militants* (dateline Paris, Feb. 9), THE NEW YORK TIMES, sec. A, p. 3, col. 1 (Feb. 10, 1992).

[28] The United States Constitution achieved only a partial solution to the problem of tyranny of the majority in a representative democracy: it set up a countermajoritarian Bill of Rights and an unelected Supreme Court to interpret it. As every student of American constitutional history knows (e.g., the cases of the internment during World War II of Japanese-Americans), these safeguards against tyranny of the majority are not foolproof.

"general will" there is no theoretical possibility of dissent and no theoretical possibility of tyranny of the majority.

My repetition of the word "theoretical" in the previous sentence signals that there may be a closed loop in Rousseau's theory. If the general will is *defined* as that which expresses the common interest, and the common interest is *defined* as applying to everyone, then dissenters are ruled out by definition. Nevertheless, Rousseau was well aware that there was a practical possibility of dissent. Surely someone could stand up and proclaim himself to be in opposition to the general will. Rousseau had to deal with that practical possibility.

The key question is whether the dissenter is acting freely. A dissenter to the will of all can surely be acting freely; the sum of everyone else's private interests may be different from her own, and she is perfectly free to reject the self-defined self-interest of the majority. But if there is a general will, in Rousseau's terms, would the dissenter be acting freely if she rejected it?

Consider the famous opening words of Rousseau's *Social Contract*:

> Man is born free, and everywhere he is in chains. One who believes himself the master of others is nonetheless a greater slave than they. How did this change occur? I do not know. What can make it legitimate? I believe I can answer this question.[30]

Consider the analogy of government to the will of a man over the passions of his body. Assume we see a drunk stumbling down the street. Is that person "free"? If we asked him whether he is doing what he wants to do, he would probably say "yes." We might ascertain that he freely chose to drink a large quantity of alcohol, and that he knew in doing so that he would become intoxicated. Nevertheless, Rousseau might say that the man is clearly not free. He cannot really do what he wants; his actions are now governed by his state of intoxication. He may have chosen to drink alcohol, but in so choosing he lost the will power he needed to control his body. *What might Rousseau tell us to do if we want to free that person*? We should physically *prevent* him from drinking any more alcohol, and thus *force him to be free*.

The dissenter, like the drunk, may be mistaken about the exercise of her own freedom. The dissenter, in opposing the general will, may believe that she is acting freely, but in fact (like the drunk) she is not free. Thus the general will operates to *compel* the dissenter to abide by its terms. As Rousseau puts it:

> The constant will of all the members of the State is the general will, which makes them citizens and free. . . . Therefore when the opinion contrary to mine prevails [i.e., when the general will is ascertained], that proves nothing except that I was mistaken, and what I thought to be the general will was not. If my private will had prevailed, I would have done something other than what I wanted. It is then that I would not have been free.[31]

Let me suggest an illustration that I believe reflects the subtlety of Rousseau's reasoning in this passage. Suppose that a golden statue is found missing from a public park in a small state. A general meeting is called and all the citizens show up. An attorney points out that in this happy community there has never been any occasion to pass a law making theft a crime; no one has ever previously stolen anything. Someone then proposes legislation declaring that theft is a crime. Everyone is in favor except me, because, unknown to the others, I am the person who stole the golden statue. Surely it is in my clear self-interest to vote against the proposed legislation. It is also clear that my freedom will be greatly curtailed if the legislation passes, I am caught, and I wind up in prison. Thus, if I vote against the legislation, I am rationally acting in the furtherance of my own freedom. Nevertheless, Rousseau would surely conclude that I really did not want to defeat this proposed statute even if my single vote in opposition could veto it. He would say that all the assembled persons are voting to enact their common interest, that the proposed statute represents the general will of the assembly, and that I also am voting to enact the general will. The difference in my case is that I am mistaken as to what the general will should be. Once I think about it, I should come to the realization that I would not have been free if my own will had prevailed. Instead, I will be free if the statute is enacted and enforced and I wind up in jail.

This conclusion seems paradoxical, but in fact it is consistent with the deeper structure of Rousseauean democracy. The key premise in the argument is that I am a citizen of the state – a member of the community. It is by virtue of my membership in the community that I share, with all the other citizens, a common interest in having nice public parks with golden statues paid for by public funds. As a taxpayer, I contributed my share to these public funds. As a citizen, I enjoy frequent walks through the public park during which I can view the statuary. If I were not a member of the community, then none of these things would necessarily be true. As an outsider, I might well have an uncontaminated interest in stealing the statue; after all, it is not my tax money, it is not my park, and it's not my community. But once I am an insider, a member of the community, then I share in the general will that is expressed in the proposed legislation.

But there are still some steps remaining in the argument. I might argue at the meeting that it is morally worse to incarcerate a human being than it is to tolerate the theft of

---

29 ROUSSEAU, ON THE SOCIAL CONTRACT, bk. II, ch. iii. I regard decision-making by small groups through the process that we call "consensus formation" as probably coming closest to my understanding of what Rousseau meant by the general will.

30 SOCIAL CONTRACT, bk. I, ch. i.

31 SOCIAL CONTRACT, bk. IV, ch. ii.

the golden statue. As to this particular argument, I think Rousseau would say that he holds no substantive position. His *Social Contract* was not intended to dictate any substantive laws for society, but rather to investigate the democratic basis for substantive laws. If Rousseau had thought that there was a set of laws that would constitute the general will in all societies – including, for example, a law making theft a crime – then he would have suggested a constitution, perhaps with a bill of rights attached, setting forth those laws. Instead, Rousseau put his faith in the emergence of a general will, even if that general will would have a different content in different states.

Nevertheless, my proposed argument at the meeting would surely inspire someone there to take issue with me. That person would point out that the purpose of making theft a crime is not to put thieves in prison, but simply to deter people from stealing in the first place. Successful indictment, conviction, and imprisonment are not the hallmarks of success of the criminal law. Rather, a law that criminalized theft would be a total success if no theft ever occurs and no one was ever prosecuted for stealing.

I might reply that deterrence is inapplicable to the person who stole the golden statue, and thus with respect to that person there is a retroactivity problem in declaring theft to be a crime. But my objection can be overcome by the following considerations: First, the fact that this thief was undeterred is not atypical of deterrence theory – indeed, every person who ever committed a crime was in fact not deterred. Punishment is nevertheless imposed so as to send a message to the next would-be criminal that one can really be sent to prison for this kind of crime. Punishment under deterrence theory, in short, is not for the person who committed the crime but to deter all subsequent persons. Second, the person who stole the golden statue might attempt to mitigate punishment by restoring, or offering to restore, the statue to the park. Since there is a clear community interest in getting the statue back, the proposed legislation is rational. I lose the argument at the town meeting.

To draw a final lesson from my "mistake" in dissenting from the general will, let us change the small state from one in which theft occurred for the first time to one in which theft is endemic. Suppose a law is proposed that would make theft a crime. How could a thief be said to partake in the general will that would criminalize his chosen occupation? Rousseau's answer would surely be as follows.[32] The thief does not really have an interest in a society that has no laws against theft, because once he has stolen some property, the thief wants to be able to keep it and not have it stolen away from him. Thus the thief's real interest is not in decriminalizing theft, but in carving out an exception for himself from the law that criminalizes theft. In brief, he wants that law to exist and to be enforced, even though his own immediate personal interest is in breaking the law and getting away with it. If he can break the law and get away with it, then at that point he wants to enjoy the property he stole, and the way to enjoy it is to have a law on the books that deters others from taking his stolen property away from him. Thus, upon proper Rousseauean reflection, even the thief would have to concede that he partakes in the general will declaring theft to be a crime.

I said that none of these arguments would be applicable if the thief was an outsider. It is critical to Rousseau's conception of the general will that its premise is community membership. For it is only one's interest in the body politic that enables Rousseau to find, in that interest, the possibility of commonality that can be articulated in the general will. Although Rousseau perhaps does not make the premise of community membership as salient to the development of his argument as I have made it, he clearly recognized the implication of dissenting from the general will in his discussion of the criminal. A criminal is one who, by his actions, manifests his dissent from the general will (i.e., the criminal law). Thus he "wages war" against his homeland, and consequently "is no longer a member of the State."[33] Rousseau's solution is that the criminal be banished and exiled.[34] Exile is thus Rousseau's ultimate answer to democracy's dissenter.[35]

Banishing the dissenter is thus the ultimate way of safeguarding the general will. Resort to this drastic remedy will ensure that there is true democracy for everyone remaining. No one who remains a member of the community can be said to be forced to be free. But even if the remedy is logically required, it seems to raise a practical barrier to Rousseau's theory. The reader might well object that exile is too high a price to pay for achieving the general will, particularly if a significant number of people are exiled not because they engaged in criminal behavior but because their political viewpoints were inconsistent with those expressed in the general will. Surely there is something peculiar about a state that would expel many of its members for the purpose of achieving democratic single-mindedness.

Once the principle of banishing dissenters is allowed, where does it stop? Should the state banish all atheists? All agnostics? All followers of minority religions? What about banishing persons who want to change the government? Or those who argue that the government is corrupt? Or those who criticize the political leader? What about those who write books that the majority finds offensive?

---

32 In discussing the death penalty for murder, Rousseau says, "it is in order not to be the victim of a murderer that a person consents to die if he becomes one." SOCIAL CONTRACT, bk. II, ch. v. The particular example I give in the text of the thief who desires enforcement of the law against theft was originally presented, I believe, in Diderot's Encyclopedia.

33 SOCIAL CONTRACT, bk. II, ch. v.

34 If the crime is murder, Rousseau would impose the death penalty.

35 Of course, one can think of imprisonment as a form of banishment from civilized society.

What about those who advocate scientific doctrines that run afoul of the majority's view about how God created the human race?

Rousseau seems to have been acutely aware of the problem of dissenters and the undesirability of banishing them en masse. The final chapter to his *Social Contract* is entitled "On Civil Religion." The chapter begins almost as an afterthought, tracing for no apparent reason the history of the relationship between church and state. Whatever the historical relationship might be, it would seem to be a matter of contingency and not logical necessity. But then Rousseau's purpose gradually becomes clear, and we see how the "civil religion" becomes a part of his approach to the general will.

The first point Rousseau makes is that if a religion is separate from the state, it can divert a person from his duties as a citizen. Christianity is "manifestly bad" in this regard, as it "destroys social unity" by "giving men two legislative systems, two leaders and two homelands" thus preventing them from being "simultaneously devout men and citizens."[36] The state should therefore invent a civil religion, one which will cause the citizen to "love his duties."[37]

Rousseau's second point is the crucial one. We find a necessary connection between the civil religion and the general will. Rousseau writes:

> There is, therefore, a purely civil profession of faith, the articles of which are for the sovereign to establish, not exactly as religious dogmas, but as sentiments of sociability without which it is impossible to be a good citizen or a faithful subject. Without being able to obligate anyone to believe them, the sovereign can banish from the State anyone who does not believe them. The sovereign can banish him not for being impious, but for being unsociable; for being incapable of sincerely loving the laws, justice, and of giving his life, if need be, for his duty. If someone who has publicly acknowledged these same dogmas behaves as though he does not believe them, he should be punished with death. He has committed the greatest of crimes: he lied before the laws.

In brief, the civil religion is Rousseau's fail-safe solution to the problem of the dissenter. For despite all the arguments in his book up to the last chapter, Rousseau was aware that there would still be dissenters from the general will – people who for whatever reason were not persuaded by Rousseau's arguments that they "really" supported the general will. If there are too many dissenters, banishing all of them might be a cure worse than the disease. So, instead of banishing them, why not fit them into the system? If Rousseau's logical arguments of the general will do not do the job, then perhaps the metaphysical logic of religion can do it. The state may be able to appeal to the mystical aspect of the citizen's nature by promulgating a state-based set of religious dogmas. In short, if we can't persuade the dissenter through logic, maybe we can change her mind and bring it into conformity with the general will by using the techniques of religion. If we can't wash her out of the system, we can brainwash her into the system.

This does not mean, as Rousseau acknowledges, that all dissent will end. In the passage just quoted, Rousseau admits that anyone who does not believe the new statist dogmas can be banished. Exile thus remains the last safeguard of the general will. Only now that the civil religion has been introduced into the system, the Rousseauean hope is that the *number* of dissenters who must be banished will be drastically reduced. The end result is the same: a pure democracy where the general will of all the people constitutes the ruling engine of government.

In sum, Rousseau achieves a perfect democracy by a combination of brainwashing and banishment. There is no doubt that these two techniques, rigorously applied, will lead to a pure democracy, one in which the remaining citizens (those who haven't been banished) will agree on everything. We may ask, first, whether this isn't too high a price to pay for democracy. Second, we may ask whether we aren't already paying part of that price. Nearly everyone today lives in a country that is either democratic or calls itself democratic. For us, Rousseau's analysis points up the fundamental question whether or to what extent we've given up a portion of our human freedom in our acceptance of democratic governance.

The logic of democracy, as worked out by its most perceptive advocate, appears to lead directly to intolerance, conformity, and thought-control. I would not like to live in that kind of state; I think my personal freedom would be forfeit in such a society. Nevertheless, in rejecting the state that Rousseau describes, am I guilty of rejecting "democracy"?

I think that I am rejecting "democracy" in its mechanistic definition. If democracy means majority-rule, then, as Rousseau shows, the majority gets bigger and bigger until there is no minority left. All dissent has vanished. The process-based democracy described by Professor Franck seems to me to come perilously close to straight majority-rule democracy.[38] It is a curious point that many American governmental figures who were labelled "cold warriers" a decade ago – associated with a hard-line right-wing approach to American foreign relations – seem today to be in the forefront of those who want to forcibly export democ-

---

[36] SOCIAL CONTRACT, bk. IV, ch. viii.

[37] *Id.* In this respect, Rousseau emulates Hobbes, whom he cites with approval. Hobbes was the first modern political theorist to argue for the merger of church and state. *See* THOMAS HOBBES, THE LEVIATHAN, pt. III ("Of a Christian Commonwealth.") Rousseau agrees with Hobbes' sentiments, but disagrees that the state should be *Christian*.

[38] I applaud Professor Franck's insistence on freedom of speech. But I am skeptical about the extent that free speech is justified as a necessary component of a process-based democracy (free elections, open platforms, etc.).

racy to other countries. These people may see a deep affinity between their past support of Kissinger-style power politics that cared nothing for the rights of individual citizens, and the new democratic entitlement that could continue in Rousseau-like fashion to implant around the world a new popular totalitatianism. Professor Franck does not belong to this group, but I wonder, as a friendly critic, whether he may have inadvertently helped to give the old cold-warriers a new platform.

I'm certainly not against exporting human rights; I am simply skeptical that a process-based notion of democracy is a reasonable surrogate for the exporting of human rights. The American "democratic" experiment goes a lot beyond a process-based notion of democracy and yet not in the direction of a "general will" with totalitatarian overtones. Built upon the writings of Locke, Montesquieu, Rousseau, and others, the American democratic experience is that of a constitutional republic where power is separated at the national level (a very "democratic" branch – the executive; a somewhat "democratic" branch – Congress; and an undemocratic branch – the Judiciary), is divided federally between the central government and the state governments, and is dedicated (through the Bill of Rights) to minoritarian rule when certain enumerated rights of minorities are at stake. All of these values are rooted in what I have elsewhere called a "culture of indeterminacy."[39] If we take minoritarian guarantees out of the picture, if we take away a tolerant culture, if we take away divisions and separations of power, and we simply "export" to other countries a process-based democratic mechanism, I am not sure that in the long run we will be serving the noble cause of human freedom.

---

[39] See Anthony D'Amato, *Harmful Speech and the Culture of Indeterminacy,* 32 WM. & M. L. REV. 207 (1990).

16
Critical Perspectives

A. The Political Science Critique

1. Realist International Relations Theory[1]

Modern political realism is important to the intellectual history of power politics not only because it adapted power politics to the contemporary international political system composed of nation-states, but also because unlike Thucydides, Machiavelli and Hobbes, the modern realist imputation of a nationalistic definition to morality and legality achieved a psychic equilibrium acceptable to the conscience of its proponents. Political realism generated a psychological justification for the application of pure power politics to an international political environment composed of nation-states that would appeal to the psyche of modern man because of its proclivities to alleviate at least superficially the natural dynamic tension between the realist and idealist elements of the human personality.

Because a citizen considers his nation-state to be the political manifestation of the Rousseauistic general will, he believes in the necessity of power politics to protect that nation-state against both its internal and external enemies. The amount and extent of power politics applied by a nation-state against its own citizens depends upon the particular type of government chosen by the people to conduct its foreign and domestic affairs, with variations running between the two reputed extremes of liberal democracy and communist totalitarianism. But the amount and extent of power politics exercised by any one nation-state against another nation-state and the citizens thereof is said by the political realists to be independent of its particular type of government. In international politics, all governments, whether democratic, authoritarian, totalitarian, or any other type, are alleged to pursue what they believe to be in the national interests of their respective nation-states with equal vigor and by identical methods – power politics.

With a modern theory of political realism, both citizens and government decision-makers can all rationally justify to themselves the pursuit of power politics in the name of the national interest. Thus, in addition to the fact that the theory of political realism might conceivably be historically accurate under some circumstances, it also represents a fantastic psychological rationalization of universal political significance. Modern political realism invented the candy-coating of national interest/national self-determination/general will necessary to enable mid-twentieth-century foreign policy decision-makers and citizens to swallow the poisonous pill of power politics.

Due to the efforts of Hans Morgenthau, George Kennan and Dean Acheson, among others, this nationalized morality/legality of power politics obtained a status of intellectual hegemony over the American foreign policy decision-making establishment after the Second World War. Yet, the sophistic philosophy that might makes right is fine for the victor, but not for the vanquished. As Thucydides dramatically portrayed in his book, the Athenian democracy's adherence to the philosophy of power politics was ultimately responsible for the outbreak of the Peloponnesian War and eventually the defeat of Athens at the hands of authoritarian Sparta. Today, like Athens before it, blinded by hubris, America might very well lead the civilized world into another cataclysm. Only this time, there will be no Philip of Macedon around to pick up the radioactive pieces.

2. Liberal International Relations Theory[2]

"Liberal" international relations theory focuses not on state-to-state interactions, at least not in the first instance, but on an analytically prior set of relationships among states and domestic and transnational civil society. The "black box" of sovereignty becomes transparent, allowing examination of how and to what extent national governments represent individuals and groups operating in domestic and transnational society. Democracies, or, more precisely,

---

[1] By FRANCIS ANTHONY BOYLE, excerpted from: THE FUTURE OF INTERNATIONAL LAW AND AMERICAN FOREIGN POLICY 66–67 (N.Y.: Transnational Publishers, 1989). Reprinted by permission.

[2] By ANNE-MARIE SLAUGHTER BURLEY, excerpted from: *International Law and International Relations Theory: A Dual Agenda*, 87 AMERICAN JOURNAL OF INTERNATIONAL LAW 205 (1993). Reprinted by permission.

"liberal states," are presumed to behave differently from dictatorships, not only domestically but also internationally. Their relations with one another are shaped in important ways by domestic, transnational and international law, as are their relations with nonliberal states. Liberal international relations theory offers a way of conceptualizing the contributions of these bodies of law to the traditional goals of international order, while highlighting important patterns and breaks in current legal doctrines.

The Liberal agenda will require international lawyers to revise their most fundamental conceptions of the international system. The rewards are worth it, however; this approach permits the construction of a comprehensive legal framework that links factors and trends of interest to the widest possible spectrum of international lawyers, from traditional specialists on questions such as national self-determination, to human rights activists, environmental lawyers, trade experts and international litigators and deal makers.

Three fundamental assumptions shared by all Liberal theories are the following.

(1) "The fundamental actors in politics are members of domestic society, understood as individuals and privately constituted groups seeking to promote their independent interests. Under specified conditions, individual incentives may promote social order and the progressive improvement of individual welfare."[3] Here Liberal theory rejects a foundational premise of the previous international relations theories that have been called Realism[4] and Institutionalism[5]: that the structure of the international system, whether defined to take account of institutionalized state practices or not, is the primary determinant of state behavior. Liberals analyze state behavior primarily as a function of the constraints placed on state actors by being embedded in domestic and transnational civil society. Note that Liberals do not seek to rule out the state as the primary agent of international action; once state interests are determined, governments do pursue them in a rational unitary fashion. But the underlying source of those interests is social rather than systemic.

(2) "All governments represent some segment of domestic society, whose interests are reflected in state policy."[6] Here is the link between the individual and group actors in domestic and transnational society and state behavior. Liberals begin by identifying patterns of interests that are determined by the purposive actions of individuals and groups. The next step is to determine which particular interests – which segment of society – are represented by a particular state government. The answer depends on the type of government in question, ranging from military dictatorship or oligarchies to democracies.

(3) "The behavior of states – and hence levels of international conflict and cooperation – reflects the nature and configuration of state preferences."[7] The determination of the precise social interests represented by a particular government permits the specification of that government's "preferences" – the agenda that it will seek to promote in international bargaining. It is about the bargaining process that Liberalism makes its third fundamental assumption. Where Realists claim that power will determine bargaining outcomes, and Institutionalists argue that it is power as conditioned by institutionalized practices, Liberals claim, straightforwardly enough, that "what states do is determined by what they want." More formally, the strength and intensity of a particular preference will determine how much the state is willing to concede to obtain that preference, which in turn will determine its likelihood of success in achieving the bargaining outcomes it desires. This is a counterintuitive claim, here stated in a stronger form than is necessarily subscribed to by all Liberals. Nevertheless, its formulation here represents the Liberal antipode to Realist and Institutionalist claims about the determining power of the international system.

Liberal theory has important implications for the analysis of international institutions, including, although not limited to, customary and conventional international legal regimes and international organizations. On the one hand, a Liberal approach fills many of the acknowledged gaps in current regime theory by providing the tools to determine when there will be mutual interests that can be furthered by international cooperation, hence specifying the preconditions that Institutionalists hold necessary for strong and effective institutions. On the other hand, Liberal theory also suggests that in many instances institutions will be epiphenomenal; by pinpointing underlying interests, it will permit Institutionalists to isolate hard cases in which institutions caused an outcome that could not have been predicted by patterns of underlying interests. To the extent that the "institution" in question is a legal institution, a Liberal approach will permit a more rigorous demonstration of the impact of law.

---

[3] Andrew Moravcsik, *Liberalism and International Relations Theory* 6 (working paper, Center for International Affairs, Harvard University, 1992).

[4] Realism is typified by the skepticism of political scientists such as George Kennan, Hans Morgenthau and Kenneth Waltz that international law could ever play more than an epiphenomenal role in the ordering of international life.

[5] Institutionalism focuses upon the international system: the actors, the structure within which those actors act, and the process of their interaction.

[6] Moravcsik, *supra* n.3 at 9.

[7] *Id.* at 10.

This debate is a causal debate, of primary interest to political scientists. For international lawyers who wish to proceed from the assumption that international law exists and matters, Liberal theory offers an equally interesting, and, from a traditional international lawyer's point of view, heretical, proposition. From a Liberal perspective, regimes governing liberal states are likely to be more effective in accomplishing their professed aims than regimes governing liberal and nonliberal states (other than purely technical regimes such as international traffic agreements). This proposition generates a radical and stimulating research agenda, calling for a new comparative look at regimes ranging from the United Nations to the International Monetary Fund to, above all, the European Community. Indeed, one of the most powerful reorienting effects of Liberal analysis is the transformation of the Community from anomaly to archetype.

A Liberal approach to international relations and international law opens the door to a new normative agenda in international law that in turn could change the conceptual apparatus employed by international relations theorists. The evolution of what Henkin calls the "submerged rules of the game," fundamental concepts such as sovereignty and statehood, would result in a different analytical and operative construction of international reality. Liberal theory both buttresses and illuminates this agenda. [Consider] the nature of territorial and jurisdictional sovereignty among liberal states. Empirical evidence suggests that, as a practical matter, the higher volume of exchanges of all kinds among liberal states creates a web of interrelationships that in turn make judicial infringements or "violations" of sovereignty much more likely. Territorial boundaries become increasingly meaningless, so that situs analysis cedes its place to interest analysis. Indeed, the willingness to subject the matter in dispute to judicial scrutiny at all – even in the face of considerable political controversy – is significantly greater if the state in question is a liberal state.[8]

On the other hand, relations among liberal states are more likely to be conducted on a principle of "legitimate difference" or mutual recognition of each other's laws, on the implicit ground that sufficient commonality exists to render many country-specific differences along a wide range of policy choices irrelevant. In both directions, the figurative baseline of territorially defined absolute sovereign power seems increasingly inapposite. Within the liberal zone, then, the all-purpose powers and privileges currently denoted by sovereignty may in fact attach to different states in different issue-areas as a function of strength of interest and regulatory purpose. As the "dynamic density" of individuals and issues increases within this zone, rendering the inadequacy and irrelevance of traditional concepts of sovereignty apparent, Liberal analysis and prescription could highlight an alternative baseline for legal relations based on reciprocal recognition of mutual interest rather than exclusive zones of power.

Liberals operating within this framework must be able to deduce substantive theoretical propositions from its core assumptions. The leading example of such a proposition is the claim that liberal states do not go to war with one another.[9] Various hypotheses about how the legal relations of liberal states are likely to vary from legal relations between liberal and nonliberal states would also meet this requirement. Nevertheless, Liberal international relations theorists using this framework will be required by their Realist and Institutionalist colleagues to demonstrate its utility in generating a wider range of more specific propositions. To the extent they succeed, they will produce coherent empirical research programs from which international lawyers working within the same analytical framework stand to profit. Should they fail, the eclecticism, incoherence and utopianism that has long plagued Liberalism is likely to continue.

I suggest that Liberal insights will prove most fruitful in guiding the study of various kinds of legal relations among liberal states. Much Institutionalist scholarship, on the other hand, whether conducted by international lawyers or political scientists, will prove particularly applicable to the explanation and analysis of relations between liberal and nonliberal states. The world is likely to remain heterogeneous, and brutal, for centuries yet, and the painfully accumulated store of knowledge about how to ensure at least minimal regulation of the relations between competing sovereigns will serve diplomats and decision makers for a long time to come.

These caveats notwithstanding, we are on the edge of a new fault line in international relations. The emergence of this line emphasizes the transnational ties between states that share political and economic values and institutions, states that both permit independent action and initiative by individuals and groups in domestic and transnational civil society and provide the political mechanisms to ensure representation of the resulting patterns of interest. Political, economic and, ultimately, legal relations among such states will increasingly differ in their modalities, consequences and implications from political, economic and legal relations between liberal and nonliberal states. Liberal international relations theory provides international lawyers with a conceptual apparatus to understand and analyze this phe-

---

[8] Anne-Marie Burley, *Law Among Liberal States: Liberal Internationalism and the Act of State Doctrine*, 92 COLUM. L. REV. 1907 (1992).

[9] [Editor's Note: *See* Chapter 13, "Peace," in this Anthology.]

nomenon and gradually to build it into law.

Overall, international lawyers can ill afford to ignore the growing wealth of political science data on the world they seek to regulate. The measurements may be imprecise, the theories crude, but the whole offers at least the hope of a positive science of world affairs. As an adolescent discipline, international political science long rejected the insights of international law. As it grows, it rediscovers what international lawyers never forgot, but with added insights of its own. In the end, law informed by politics is the best guarantee of politics informed by law.

B. The Natural Law Critique

1. The Inevitable Circularity[10]

The main opposition to positivist international legal scholarship has always come from the proponents of natural law. Positivists asserted that the normative force of international law came from the fact that the sovereign had consented to it. The natural law thinkers claimed that this answer was insufficient. How could the sovereign bind itself to bind itself in the future? Why was the initial consent to law given higher normative status than some subsequent decision to renounce the applicability of international law? The natural lawyers argued that this circularity involved the positivists in an endless set of boot-strapping exercises in which they sought some higher source which could, in turn, imbue the sovereign's consent with the kind of normative force that they wanted. These "higher" sources generally had some kind of Latin tag, the most famous one being "pacta sunt servanda." Alternatively they relied on language of sublime generality, such as "states should act in such a way so as not to disappoint legitimate expectations." But neither Latin nor vagueness is protection against the realization that the process is endless. "Consent" must rely on a higher source if it is to bind the state to do something against its will. This higher source must rely on a still higher source and so on until one reaches something that can be called the "grundnorm," the "rule of recognition," or the "authority constituting social-legal construct," but which sounds like a definitional stop by any other name.

How did the natural law theorists themselves resolve this problem of the source of legal authority? Whereas the positivists relied on state consent (validated by some mysterious normative background), the natural lawyers relied on some putative normative deep-structure which emanated from the commands of the deity, or from the dictates of right reason, or from a discoverable teleology immanent in the natural state of affairs. I say this because the natural lawyer must walk a narrow line between saying that this normative deep-structure is already clearly evidenced by the actions of states (and thus implying that whatever states do is legal) and saying that the deep-structure is *not* evidenced by what states do (and thus implying that it is hopelessly irrelevant). In order to "privilege" the particular line that she chooses, the theorist must thus give some subordinate importance to the consent and the actions of states. Thus whereas the positivists started by positing consent as the source of international law and were driven to rely on some ever-receding normative background, the natural lawyers started by relying on a deep normative order and ended up depending on manifestations of consent in order to save their project from being branded as either hopeless idealism or craven apologetics.

When the positivists or the natural law theorists use their theory about the essence of law to make further claims about the binding nature of international law, or even to make doctrinal arguments, the inevitable oscillation between state consent and normative deep-structure makes their claims terminally unconvincing unless the indeterminacy of their analysis is concealed by a little judicious reification. For example, a positivist might claim that the essence of law is that it is a norm that stipulates a sanction.[11] International law is thus dependent on the right of a state to use sanctions, including force, if its legal rights have been infringed. Since this right of self-help is actually the basis of the binding quality of international law,[12] it cannot be abridged by international law; the state may make a political choice to revoke it, but it can never be legally alienated. The natural law theorist might respond by saying that the essential purpose of international law is to provide a stepping-stone to a peaceful world community, that its binding force depends on the fact that it serves this trans-historically valid normative goal of "world peace through world law," and thus, that states not only can, but should legally renounce their rights of self-help.[13] It is not simply

---

[10] By JAMES D. BOYLE, excerpted from: *Ideals and Things: International Legal Scholarship and the Prison-house of Language*, 26 HARVARD INTERNATIONAL LAW JOURNAL 327, 336–39 (1985). Reprinted by permission.

[11] [Editor's Note: This positivist theory was most lucidly and forcefully expressed by Hans Kelsen. According to Kelsen, a norm of law is one "in which a certain sanction is made dependent upon certain conditions." HANS KELSEN, GENERAL THEORY OF LAW AND STATE 45 (1945). Kelsen gives this example: "One shall not steal; if somebody steals, he shall be punished. If it is assumed that the first norm, which forbids theft, is valid only if the second norm attaches a sanction to the theft, then the first norm is certainly superfluous in an exact exposition of law. If at all existent, the first norm is contained in the second, which is the only genuine legal norm." *Id.* at 61.]

[12] [Editor's Note: See Chapter 3, "Is International Law 'Law'?" in this Anthology.]

[13] [Editor's Note: Would Vitoria, a classic natural-law theorist, have said that nations should renounce their right of self-help? *See* the section "Vitoria on 'Just Wars'" in this Anthology, Chapter 2.]

that positivists and natural lawyers disagree. Rather, their debates are entirely circular. One could argue from the same positivist premises with just as much logic that, *because* the sanction provided by the right of self-help is the foundation of international law, the state must *always* be able legally to renounce that right; otherwise it is not truly a state and international law is not binding on it. Or, to complete the symmetrical pattern, the natural law premises can be made to produce the argument that because the goal of international law is, in a sense, to annihilate itself by moving to a world community, the one peaceful act which a state cannot take under international law is to renounce its right to self-help. Such an act could only be "legally" accomplished in a binding way under a "higher" stage of law than international law–perhaps under "world law."

My point is not that international lawyers had bad arguments. In a sense it is the reverse: their arguments were too good. Theorists founded their discussion of sources on a definitional question. They claimed that the authoritativeness of their arguments depended on the "universal quality" of their definitions of law. Yet they could only be convincing when they covertly appealed to some "purpose," be it the operational perspective of practitioners, or the teleological perspective of internationalists. In order to maintain their arguments, they had to believe (or at least, seem to believe) that their purpose was woven into the essence of law. but once they had "reified" law in this manner (by incorporating their choice into the concept itself) they were left with arguments that were completely "flippable." As my example above may have shown, the arguments are so "essentialist" that they have been emptied of all content. In the end, both the natural law and the positivist arguments become blank assertions. One might just as well say, "Because." This fate is not particular to the theorists I have been discussing. It will always be the fate of any inquiry founded on the definition, the "essence," or the "nature" of law, or of any other phenomenon for that matter.

2. Natural Law As a Form of Dispute Resolution[14]

Natural law reasoning can be found in the classical writings of Suarez, Pufendorf and Grotius. But interpreting their works is hard for us today. Did they rely on the authority of the *content* of natural law, or its *terminology*, or its *meaning*, or its *method*? Difficult as these questions of interpretation are, finding determinable content to the notion of "natural law" is even harder.

For my part, I believe that no definite verbal content can ever be ascribed to natural law. As soon as you say natural law means X or Y, someone can "deconstruct" X or Y. Aquinas made the mistake, I believe, in attempting to provide content to natural law; the norms he formulated are sufficiently vague as to be capable of applying to both sides of any argument or dispute. Even worse, as soon as Aquinas reduced natural law to a set of norms, the method became positivistic–attempting to control real-world events and decisions by imperative language. But positivism is antithetical to natural law, and the result is that Aquinas' entire magnificent attempt results in an indeterminate set of prescriptions.[15]

If natural law has no substantive content, does it have meaning? I would say it does. But the meaning is not verbal, because a word doesn't "mean" anything. Nor does a definition of a word mean anything, because the definition is itself made up of words, and we would get into an infinite regress if we tried to chase down the meaning of a word by resort to other words. A word is nothing more than a sound that we have learned to associate with things we see or hear about–we learned words as a child when they were uttered as the names of things.[16] Plato was wrong in saying that words have intrinsic meanings (although in his early Cratylus dialogue–a neglected and most modern-sounding masterpiece–he deconstructs nominalism). The "meaning" of a word, then, is the set of real-world referents that we have learned to associate with the word. A word is a heuristic mental flash–it retrieves for us a set of associations in our memories that we have "wired in" to be associated with that word. But a word has no intrinsic "meaning."

Natural law can have a meaning, but not one that can be captured in words that are put forth as a definition of the term. Rather, I think it stands for a method of dispute resolution that we have learned to associate with the term "natural law."

"Law" in general is associated with a method of dispute resolution. Natural law is one of the methods of dispute resolution that is associated with the term "law." Law can only be a method of dispute resolution. For example, there is no such thing as statutory determinism because the words of a statute can be deconstructed at will whenever one purports to "apply" them to any real world situation. The dispute arises when the words are "applied"–one side says they govern the dispute, the other side contends that they do not, and the judge or other decision-maker has to decide one way or the other. (The judge then might be reversed on appeal.) The decision-making structure I have

[14] By ANTHONY D'AMATO, excerpted from: *Is International Law Part of Natural Law?* 9 VERA LEX 8 (1989). Reprinted by permission.

[15] For further discussion, *see* Anthony D'Amato, *Lon Fuller and Substantive Natural Law*, 26 AM. J. JUR. 202 (1981).

[16] For a more complete argument, *see* Anthony D'Amato, *Pragmatic Indeterminacy*, 85 NW. L. REV. 148, 182–87 (1990).

just briefly described is all that law "means." Thus, the important thing about law is not that words are applied correctly or incorrectly to situations (who knows what is correct? even the appellate court can get it wrong), but that there is a third-party dispute resolver in the form of the judge or other decision-maker. Their decisions are enforced. I contend that the method of dispute-resolution by judges is all that we mean by "law."

"Natural law" is a specialized form of legal dispute resolution, based on a conscious attempt to perpetuate past regularities in decisions. John Finnis calls natural law "practical reasonableness." The adjudicator uses her mind, her "reason," in the pursuit of what is "practical," namely, an appreciation of similar dispute-resolving processes that have worked in the past in cases similar to the one at hand.

"International law" has a deep affinity to the natural law method, because it consists of those practices that have "worked" in inter-nation claim-conflict resolution. Customary international law is a record of all those interactions between nations (and between individuals and nations) that have promoted systemic stability.

International lawyers make the Platonic-positivistic mistake when they attempt to formulate its norms in verbal terms. International law does not and cannot consist of verbalized norms (as much as it would seem convenient for us if it did), because the practices that gave rise to those norms and infuse them with meaning are the actions of states and not the words of states. At best, verbalized norms of international law are surrogates for—and poor generalizations of—the underlying methodological practices.

If we today read the dense prose of Suarez, Pufendorf, and Grotius, we have a hard time knowing whether they were reflecting natural law in the methodological sense I've been talking about, or were dragging in norms traditionally associated with international law just to support their own substantive positions. My sense is that Suarez came closest to the natural law method, but alas, of the three, he seemed to know the least about the customary norms of international law.

C. The Systems Critique[17]

The perception which dominates present conceptions of international law is of sovereign States which should cooperate but which are masters of their own destiny and which need not take into consideration, unless they wish to, the interests of others and those of the world community. They remain fully independent, self-sufficient and unrestrained unless self-limited. Scholars see such self-limitation in international treaties and customary international law, implemented according to the principle of pacta sunt servanda.

This picture, which results from a seventeenth century vision of the world, has not been reformulated in spite of a fundamental transformation of life in this century. New problems and the technological revolution which both creates them and supplies the means to address them have appeared in increasing numbers, especially since 1945: weapons of mass destruction, the need for the protection of human rights and for the satisfaction of basic needs, a regime for outer space, for Antarctica, and for the deep seabed, the depletion of the world's natural resources and that of the environment in general, the demographic explosion, the production of toxic substances, all represent but a partial listing of new challenges to international law.

Furthermore, world-wide phenomena demonstrate that there are organized forces which can take effective decisions at an international level and bend others to their will according to internationally-established rules and structures: multinational companies and terrorist organizations represent two examples of transnational efficiency. In a more positive way, the global campaign against starvation in Africa, as well as efforts to safeguard environmental and cultural values, often force governments to act in ways which are not in their immediate interests.

International lawyers have responded to these proliferating challenges with a piecemeal approach, placing new topics in the classic international law table of contents. The results have not been satisfactory. Neither as a practical matter nor conceptually have solutions been found to most recent international problems. In order to attempt such solutions, a new conceptual framework is necessary which is in accordance with present international realities.

The web of relations between States is the main characteristic of the present world. While the interdependent, dynamic character of modern society may first have been recognized by multinationals and terrorists, no government today can ignore it. All governments are obliged to recognize that the development of modern communications has unified the globe: the world has been transformed, in McCluhan's words, into a "planetary village." Any major event in any country of the world now produces world-wide immediate impact and reactions.

Moreover, there are global problems which cannot be solved by any single State. The demographic explosion of the last few decades, which shows few signs of decreasing, and the limited character of natural resources upon which

---

[17] By ALEXANDRE CHARLES KISS & DINAH SHELTON, excerpted from: *Systems Analysis of International Law: A Methodological Inquiry*, 17 NETHERLANDS YEARBOOK OF INTERNATIONAL LAW 45, 45–46, 51–53, 68–73 (1986). Reprinted by permission.

we are dependent, raise the question of our responsibility to future generations to ensure their continued vitality. This implies projecting into international legal norms a temporary, evolutionary factor heretofore generally ignored.

These realities argue for envisaging and applying a new approach to international law, developing concepts which can overcome the discrepancy between present rules and the behavior of States. The systems approach, with its focus on dynamic interrelationships, seems to offer the necessary theoretical foundation.[18] The nature of international law may be studied through its systemic response to problems such as the protection of human rights, the preservation of cultural property, the conservation of the environment, international traffic, communications, meteorology, exchange of persons and goods, the prevention of diseases, and the development of poor countries.

We must reconsider State sovereignty in functional rather than absolute terms. States must be seen within the system where their competences are determined according to the functions they perform. Such a "functional" approach to the concept of State sovereignty should not be considered shocking. As Brierly has noted,

> The truth is that States are not persons, however convenient it may often be to personify them; they are merely institutions, that is to say, organizations which men establish among themselves for securing certain objects, of which the most fundamental is a system of order within which the activities of their common life can be carried on.[19]

While the State was earlier viewed as a political entity in the service of sovereigns and, later on, as an abstract incarnation of lofty ideals for which all sacrifices could be demanded of its citizens, the present State *seen from inside* is a utilitarian one. Today, the State is deemed to exist to ensure the satisfaction of the needs of its citizens: security, justice, fundamental freedoms, a minimum economic level, education, culture, assistance to the poor and the sick, amenities, etc. The government of a State is judge according to its capacity to satisfy those needs. Any use of State power and means of action for other purposes is felt to be inadmissible, of discredit to public authority as well as bad organization or bad management of public affairs. This utilitarian concept and functional approach should be applied not only internally, but also in international society and international law.

Thus, States should be viewed in relation to the functions which they ensure in the world system. The adoption of not only the Universal Declaration of Human Rights, but also mandatory conventions with control mechanisms, is a recognition of the need for international supervision of the implementation of such universally accepted rules. In other fields, States cannot individually protect their cultural heritage or the environment and are obliged to cooperate with others. In these cases State competences must be determined by the functions they can and will perform.

Such a functional conception of the place and role of States may be generalized. It seems appropriate to analyze State sovereignty according to State functions. This entails considering State competences as relative values, rather than intrinsic ones. The first requirement is to identify and select the appropriate level for preventive and remedial action. For example, rule 10 of the Principles of a Community Environmental Policy, adopted by the Member States of the European Economic Community, provides:

> In each different category of pollution it is necessary to establish the level of action (local, regional, national, Community, international) that befits the type of pollution and the geographical zone to be protected should be sought. Actions which are likely to be the most effective at Community level should be concentrated at that level; priorities should be determined with special care.

Similarly, Articles 207–212 of the Convention on the Law of the Sea relating to pollution of the marine environment obliges the parties to harmonize their policies at the appropriate regional level and to establish global and regional rules, standards and recommended practices and procedures. Very clearly, the level for addressing problems will be selected according to the nature of the problem to be solved. It is characteristic that in a field like environmental protection the level at which problems should be addressed plays a paramount role in proposed solutions.

A systems approach can also explain recent trends in the drafting of international legal rules. If rules are considered as corresponding to determined functions, they must follow the evolution of those functions and adapt to the changes which may affect them. Thus, evolutive processes should be foreseen when treaty rules are drafted. As a consequence, the time which is necessary for evolution is taken into account so that the traditional rigidity of legal systems is replaced by dynamic conceptions.

Examples of the insertion of temporal elements in recent international instruments are frequent. Treaties relating to the protection of the environment are often drafted to allow or require modification in order to follow changes in the state of the environment or the evolution of our knowledge as to vulnerable species of wild fauna and flora threatened with extinction or the effects of determined pollutants. Such problems are frequently met by simplified revision tech-

---

[18] [Editor's Note: For an application of the systems approach to custom as a source of international law, see the section entitled "Seminar on Custom" in Chapter 4 of this Anthology.]

[19] JAMES L. BRIERLY, THE LAW OF NATIONS 54 (6th ed. 1963).

niques: the species to be protected or the pollutants whose discharge is prohibited are listed in annexes for which simplified procedures of revision are foreseen.[20]

In the classic period of international law, most treaties were aimed at the satisfaction of direct needs of States, through bargain and exchange, usually on a bilateral basis. Since 1919, international instruments have increasingly been drafted in the common interests of the whole world. They bring no direct advantage or disadvantage to any of the contracting parties. Such treaties are not based on reciprocity, but on the conviction that there are common goals which should be achieved world-wide by international cooperation, even if such cooperation does not include immediate benefit for any of the contracting parties.

D. The Critical Legal Studies Critique[21]

International lawyers are searching for the "real" story about what is going on. Faced with an international system that we cannot even describe without taking a political position, it is tempting to "simply look at what happens" without attempting to construct a descriptive or prescriptive international theory about it. The resulting attempt to construct theory-free statements about behavior relies for its authority on a claim to be describing an essence, which is supposed to be prior to ideological interpretation or factional polemic. Or, to put it another way, in their attempt to escape the circular arguments of positivists and natural lawyers,[22] behaviorist legal scholars actually rely on the same reification, the same essentialism, that was the cause of the very circles they were trying to avoid.

A most interesting example of the invidious effects that the dilemma of formalism and scientism can have is that of the *Yale Studies in World Public Order*, the series of books and research projects produced under the aegis of Myres McDougal. To reduce the study of international legal discourse to a technocratic means-end manipulation of strategically useful concepts seems unhelpful. The fact that this manipulation almost always ends up favoring the American national interest is disquieting. To claim that one can inject a universal value ("human dignity") into an avowedly means-end technique is a contradiction in terms. For this to become one of the dominant approaches to international law is a travesty.

It could be objected that I have deliberately chosen a dogmatic, scientistic example to make my point. In order to show that the contradictions I describe extend even to the non-scientistic forms of behaviorism, I will use Louis Henkin's influential work on national behavior and international law as a further example.

Henkin may seem a dubious example of a behaviorist. Admittedly, his book is called *How Nations Behave*, but he explicitly points out that he sees governments as being capable of "thought," "awareness," and other "internal" qualities that seem ill-suited to a theory which, in its most extreme forms, denies the reality of "consciousness." On the other hand, his central goal is to focus on "the influence of law on how nations behave," a subject to which jurisprudential discussion is only "incidental."[23] This sounds as though he believes that behavior can be stripped of its conflicting ideological "meanings" and analyzed from some independent standpoint. Let me say immediately that it is not so much that Henkin believes that he can provide a neutral or objective picture of what is going on, but rather that, like the legal realists, he thinks he can cut through the Gordian knots of formalist debate by presenting law as it appears in behavior. In order to make his project succeed, Henkin must claim that law is implicated in the actions of states, so that law is what states do. But, at the same time, he must maintain some residual picture that law is separate from, and critical of, state behavior. If he does not retain this residual picture of law as a set of apolitical rules, then it appears that anything that states do is legal. Thus Henkin would be contradicting the body of thought that forms the implicit background to his project, the ideology of the "rule of law" with its insistence on a sharp separation between law and politics. My point is not simply that Henkin's argument is contradictory. Rather, the search for the "stripped-down" reality of law leads us into a morass of question-begging, circular arguments.

Yet there is something liberating about international legal study. The thing that first attracted me to international law was the lure of internationalism. There was a hefty dose of an adolescent desire to be truly cosmopolitan, there was some connection to my membership in the Campaign for Nuclear Disarmament, and there was the burgeoning outrage against war, famine and pestilence that we condescendingly refer to as "youthful idealism." If you had asked me then whether these ideas were connected to my

---

[20] The CITES (Convention on International Trade in Endangered Species of Wild Fauna and Flora) annexes are a prominent example. [Editor's Note: *See* the sections on "Elephants" and "Whales" in Chapter 10 in this Anthology.]

[21] By JAMES BOYLE, excerpted from: *Ideals and Things: International Legal Scholarship and the Prison-house of Language*, 26 HARVARD INTERNATIONAL LAW JOURNAL 327, 343–45, 352–53, 358–59 (1985). Reprinted by permission.

[22] [Editor's Note: *See* "The Natural Law Critique" above in this Chapter.]

[23] LOUIS HENKIN, HOW NATIONS BEHAVE X (1979).

other political views I might have given a confused answer about monopoly capitalism, or the Judeo-Christian ethic, but in reality I would not have made a connection between, say, my opposition to the sexist Student Union at my university and my belief in world peace through world law.

Things at present look a bit different. I now spend a lot of time thinking about reification—the way we turn other people, or social systems, or institutional hierarchies into objects which we then confront as disempowered observers. And a sense of outrage at this "objectification"—this fateful separation from "the Other," who is seen as "a woman," or "a Professor" or "a foreigner," or "a famine victim"—seems to me to be the general purpose fuel for a commitment to internationalism as well as to the demonstrations outside an all-male pub. It is precisely because the utopian aims of international lawyers do express a hostility to the division of the world into Self and Other, North and South, Commie and Plutocrat, that their writing is still compelling even when it is covered over with medieval preoccupations about the "nature" of law. There is a plausible way of seeing internationalism as being inextricably intertwined with an opposition to sexism, racism and the calcification of authority.

E. DEBATE: The Feminist Critique of International Law

1. Affirmative[24]

By challenging the nature and operation of international law and its context, feminist legal theory can contribute to the progressive development of international law. We question the immunity international law has had up to now from feminine analysis. Our approach requires looking behind the abstract entities of states to the actual impact of rules on women within states. We argue that both the structures of international lawmaking and the content of the rules of international law privilege men; if women's interests are acknowledged at all, they are marginalized. International law is a thoroughly gendered system.

A feminist account of international law suggests that we inhabit a world in which men of all nations have used the statist system to establish economic and nationalist priorities to serve male elites, while basic human, social and economic needs are not met. International institutions currently echo these same priorities. By taking women seriously and describing the silences and fundamentally skewed nature of international law, feminist theory can identify possibilities for change.

Are women's voices and values already present in international law through the medium of the Third World? Sandra Harding has noted the "curious coincidence of African and feminine world views."[25] This world view is characterized by "a conception of the self as intrinsically connected with, as part of, both the community and nature."[26] The attribution to women and Africans of "a concept of the self as dependent on others, as defined through relationships to others, as perceiving self-interest to lie in the welfare of the relational complex," permits the ascription to these groups of an ethic based on preservation of relationships and an epistemology uniting "hand, brain and heart." These perceptions contrast with the "European" and male view of the self as autonomous, separate from nature and from others, and with its associated ethics of "rule-governed adjudication of competing rights between self-interested, autonomous others" and its view of knowledge as an entity with a separate, "objective" existence.[27]

An alternative, feminist analysis of international law must take account of the differing perspectives of First and Third World feminists. Third World feminists operate in particularly difficult contexts. Not only does the dominant European, male discourse of law, politics and science exclude the kind of discourse characterized by the phrase "a different voice," both female and non-European, but also feminist concerns in the Third World are largely ignored or misunderstood by western feminists.[28] Western feminism began as a demand for the right of women to be treated as men. Whether in campaigns for equal rights or for special rights such as the right to abortion, western feminists have sought guarantees from the state that, as far as is physically possible, they will be placed in the same position as men. This quest does not always have the same attraction for nonwestern women. For example, the western feminist preoccupation with a woman's right to abortion is of less significance to many Third World women because population-control programs often deny them the chance to have children. Moreover, "nonpositivist" cultures, such as those of Asia and Africa, are just as masculinist, or even

---

24 By HILARY CHARLESWORTH, CHRISTINE CHINKIN, & SHELLEY WRIGHT, excerpted from: *Feminist Approaches to International Law*, 85 AMERICAN JOURNAL OF INTERNATIONAL LAW 613 (1991). Reprinted by permission.

25 SANDRA HARDING, THE SCIENCE QUESTION IN FEMINISM 165 (1986).

26 *Id.* at 170.

27 *Id.* at 171.

28 The tension between some First and Third World feminists over the correct approach to the issue of female genital mutilation is an example. *See* Savane, *Why we are against the International Campaign*, 40 INT'L CHILD WELFARE REV. 38 (1979); R. MORGAN, SISTERHOOD IS GLOBAL 1–37 (1984); Boulware-Miller, *Female Circumcision: Challenge to the Practice as a Human Rights Violation*, 8 HARV. WOMEN'S L.J. 155 (1985).

more so, than the western cultures in which the language of law and science developed. Thus far, the "different voice" of developing nations in international law has shown little concern for feminist perspectives. The power structures and decision-making processes in these societies are every bit as exclusive of women as in western societies and the rhetoric of domination and subjugation has not encompassed women, who remain the poorest and least privileged.

In the context of international law (and, indeed, domestic law), then, Third World feminists are obliged to communicate in the western rationalist language of the law, in addition to challenging the intensely patriarchal "different voice" discourse of traditional non-European societies. In this sense, feminism in the Third World is doubly at odds with the dominant male discourse of its societies.

Feminists from all worlds share a central concern: their domination by men. Birgit Brock-Utne writes: "Though patriarchy is hierarchical and men of different classes, races or ethnic groups have different places in the patriarchy, they are united in their shared relationship of dominance over their women. And, despite their unequal resources, they are dependent on each other to maintain that domination."[29] Issues raised by Third World feminists, however, require a reorientation of feminism to deal with the problems of the most oppressed women, rather than those of the most privileged. Nevertheless, the constant theme in both western and Third World feminism is the challenge to structures that permit male domination, although the form of the challenge and the male structures may differ from society to society. An international feminist perspective on international law will have as its goal the rethinking and revision of those structures and principles which exclude most women's voices.

The international legal order is virtually impervious to the voices of women, because of the organizational and normative structures of international law.

The structure of the international legal order reflects a male perspective and ensures its continued dominance. The primary subjects of international law are states and, increasingly, international organizations. In both states and international organizations the invisibility of women is striking. Power structures within governments are overwhelmingly masculine: women have significant positions of power in very few states, and in those where they do, their numbers are minuscule. Women are either unrepresented or underrepresented in the national and global decision-making processes.

States are patriarchal structures not only because they exclude women from elite positions and decision-making roles, but also because they are based on the concentration of power in, and control by, an elite and the domestic legitimation of a monopoly over the use of force to maintain that control. This foundation is reinforced by international legal principles of sovereign equality, political independence and territorial integrity and the legitimation of force to defend those attributes.

International organizations are functional extensions of states that allow them to act collectively to achieve their objectives. Not surprisingly, their structures replicate those of states, restricting women to insignificant and subordinate roles. Thus, in the United Nations itself, where the achievement of nearly universal membership is regarded as a major success of the international community, this universality does not apply to women. Women are excluded from all major decision making by international institutions on global policies and guidelines, despite the often disparate impact of those decisions on women. Since 1985, there has been some improvement in the representation of women in the United Nations and its specialized agencies. It has been estimated, however, that "at the present rate of change it will take almost 4 more decades (until 2021) to reach equality (i.e.: 50% of professional jobs held by women)", a situation recently described as "grotesque."[30]

The silence and invisibility of women also characterizes those bodies with special functions regarding the creation and progressive development of international law. Only one woman has sat as a judge on the International Court of Justice and no woman has ever been a member of the International Law Commission. Critics have frequently pointed out that the distribution of judges on the Court does not reflect the makeup of the international community, a concern that peaked after the decision in the South West Africa cases in 1966.[31] Steps have since been taken to improve "the representation of the main forms of civilization and of the principal legal systems of the world" as Article 9 of the Court's Statute provides, but not in the direction of representing women, half of the world's population.

The normative structure of international law has allowed issues of particular concern to women to be either ignored or undermined. For example, modern international law rests on and reproduces various dichotomies between the public and private spheres, and the "public" sphere is regarded as the province of international law. One such distinction is between matters of international "public"

---

[29] Brock-Utne, *Women and Third World Countries—What Do We Have in Common*?, 12 WOMEN'S STUD. INT'L F. 495, 500 (1989).

[30] B. URQUHART & E. CHILDERS, A WORLD IN NEED OF LEADERSHIP: TOMORROW'S UNITED NATIONS 29 (1990).

[31] *See* E. MCWHINNEY, THE INTERNATIONAL COURT OF JUSTICE AND THE WESTERN TRADITION OF INTERNATIONAL LAW 76–83 (1987).

concern and matters "private" to states that are considered within their domestic jurisdiction, in which the international community has no recognized legal interest. Yet another is the line drawn between law and other forms of "private" knowledge such as morality.

At a deeper level one finds a public/private dichotomy based on gender. One explanation feminist scholars offer for the dominance of men and the male voice in all areas of power and authority in the western liberal tradition is that a dichotomy is drawn between the public sphere and the private or domestic one. The public realm of the work place, the law, economics, politics and intellectual and cultural life, where power and authority are exercised, is regarded as the natural province of men; while the private world of the home, the hearth and children is seen as the appropriate domain of women. The public/private distinction has a normative, as well as a descriptive, dimension. Traditionally, the two spheres are accorded asymmetrical value: greater significance is attached to the public, male world than to the private, female one. The distinction drawn between the public and the private thus vindicates and makes natural the division of labor and allocation of rewards between the sexes. Its reproduction and acceptance in all areas of knowledge have conferred primacy on the male world and supported the dominance of men.

How is the western liberal version of the public/private distinction maintained? Its naturalness rests on deeply held beliefs about gender. Traditional social psychology taught that the bench marks of "normal" behavior for men, on the one hand, and women, on the other, were entirely different. For men, normal and natural behavior was essentially active: it involved tenacity, aggression, curiosity, ambition, responsibility and competition—all attributes suited to participation in the public world. "Normal" behavior for women, by contrast, was reactive and passive: affectionate, emotional, obedient and responsive to approval.

Although the scientific basis of the public/private distinction has been thoroughly attacked and exposed as a culturally constructed ideology, it continues to have a strong grip on legal thinking. The language of the public/private distinction is built into the language of the law itself: law lays claim to rationality, culture, power, objectivity—all terms associated with the public or male realm. It is defined in opposition to the attributes associated with the domestic, private, female sphere: feeling, emotion, passivity, subjectivity. Moreover, the law has always operated primarily within the public domain; it is considered appropriate to regulate the work place, the economy and the distribution of political power, while direct state intervention in the family and the home has long been regarded as inappropriate. Violence within the home, for example, has generally been given different legal significance from violence outside it; the injuries recognized as legally compensable are those which occur outside the home. Damages in civil actions are typically assessed in terms of ability to participate in the public sphere. Women have difficulty convincing law enforcement officials that violent acts within the home are criminal.

In one sense, the public/private distinction is the fundamental basis of the modern state's function of separating and concentrating juridical forms of power that emanate from the state. The distinction implies that the private world is uncontrolled. In fact, the regulation of taxation, social security, education, health and welfare has immediate effects on the private sphere. The myth that state power is not exercised in the "private" realm allocated to women masks its control.

What force does the feminist critique of the public/private dichotomy in the foundation of domestic legal systems have for the international legal order? Traditionally, of course, international law was regarded as operating only in the most public of public spheres: the relations between nation-states. We argue, however, that the definition of certain principles of international law rests on and reproduces the public/private distinction. It thus privileges the male world view and supports male dominance in the international legal order. It also makes it possible to maintain repressive systems of control over women without interference from human rights guarantees, which operate in the public sphere. By extending our vision beyond the public/private ideologies that rationalize limiting our analysis of power, human rights language as it currently exists can be used to describe serious forms of repression that go far beyond the juridically narrow vision of international law. For example, coercive population control techniques, such as forced sterilization, may amount to punishment or coercion by the state to achieve national goals.

The public/private dichotomy operates to reduce the effectiveness of the right to self-determination at international law. The notion of self-determination is flatly contradicted by the continued domination and marginalization of one sector of the population of a nation-state by another. The treatment of women within groups claiming a right to self-determination should be relevant to those claims. But the international community's response to the claims to self-determination of the Afghan and Sahrawi people, for example, indicates little concern for the position of women within those groups.

The violation of the territorial integrity and political independence of Afghanistan by the Soviet Union when it invaded that country in 1979, and other strategic, economic, and geopolitical concerns, persuaded the United States of the legality and morality of its support for the Afghan insurgents. In deciding to support the rebels, the United States did not regard the policies of the mujahidin with respect to women as relevant.[32] The mujahidin are committed to an oppressive, rural, unambiguously patriarchal form of society quite different from that espoused by the socialist Soviet-backed regime. Indeed, Cynthia Enloe notes that "one of the policies the Soviet-backed government in Kabul pursued that so alienated male clan leaders was expanding economic and educational opportunities for Afghanistan's women."[33]

Morocco's claims to Western Sahara and the Polisario resistance to those claims have led to the establishment of Sahrawi refugee camps in Algeria that are mainly occupied by women and children. In these camps, however, women have been able to assert themselves: they have built hospitals and schools, achieved high rates of literacy, and supported women's rights and the fight for independence. The Sahrawis' only backing comes from Algeria, while Morocco is backed, inter alia, by France and the United States.

The international community recognizes only the right of "peoples" to self-determination, which in practice is most frequently linked to the notion of the independent state. Women have never been viewed as a "people" for the purposes of the right to self-determination. In most instances, the pursuit of self-determination as a political response to colonial rule has not resulted in terminating the oppression and domination of one section of society by another.

States often show complete indifference to the position of women when determining their response to claims of self-determination; the international invisibility of women persists. Thus, after the Soviet Union vetoed a Security Council resolution on the invasion of Afghanistan, the General Assembly reaffirmed "the inalienable right of all peoples to choose their own form of government free from outside interference" and stated that the Afghan people should be able to "choose their economic, political and social systems free from outside intervention, subversion, coercion or constraint of any kind whatsoever." The General Assembly's concern was with "outside" intervention alone. Women arguably suffer more from "internal" intervention: women are not free to choose their role in society without the constraints of masculine domination inside the state and are constantly subject to male coercion. The high-sounding ideals of noninterference do not apply to them, for their self-determination is subsumed by that of the group. The denial to women of the freedom to determine their own economic, social and cultural development should be taken into consideration by states in assessing the legitimacy of requests for assistance in achieving self-determination and of claims regarding the use of force.

Another example of the failure of the normative structure of international law to accommodate the realities of women's lives can be seen in its response to trafficking in women. Trafficking in women through prostitution, pornography and mail-order-bride networks is a pervasive and serious problem in both the developed and the developing worlds. These practices do not simply fall under national jurisdiction, as the ramifications of the trafficking and exploitative relationships cross international boundaries. They involve the subordination and exploitation of women, not on the simple basis of inequality or differences among individuals, but as a result of deeply ingrained constructs of power and dominance based on gender. To a large extent, the increase in trafficking in women in the Third World stems from growing economic disparities on the national and international levels. Once caught up in the trafficking networks, penniless women in foreign countries are at the mercy of those who arrange and profit from the trade.

Existing norms of international law could be invoked to prohibit at least some of the international exploitation of women and children. The international law on this issue, however, is incomplete and limited in scope. Just as the prohibition of the slave trade, and subsequently of slavery itself, did not occur until economic considerations supported its abolition, so a real commitment to the prevention of sexual trafficking in women is unlikely to be made unless it does not adversely affect other economic interests.

However, there is a question whether a rights-based approach to international law would advance women's equality. Feminist scholars have argued that, although the search for formal legal equality through the formulation of rights may have been politically appropriate in the early stages of the feminist movement, continuing to focus on the acquisition of rights may not be beneficial to women. Quite apart from problems such as the form in which rights are drafted, their interpretation by tribunals, and women's access to their enforcement, the rhetoric of rights, according to some feminist legal scholars, is exhausted.

Rights discourse is taxed with reducing intricate power relations in a simplistic way. The formal acquisition of a right, such as the right to equal treatment, is often assumed to have solved an imbalance of power. In practice, however, the promise of rights is thwarted by the inequalities of power: the economic and social dependence of women on men may discourage the invocation of legal rights that are premised on an adversarial relationship between the rights holder and the infringer. More complex still are rights designed to apply to women only such as the rights to reproductive freedom and to choose abortion.[34]

In addition, although they respond to general societal

---

[32] By contrast, the United States used the repression of women in Iran after the 1979 revolution as an additional justification for its hostility to the Khomeini regime.

[33] Cynthia Enloe, Making Feminist Sense of International Politics: Bananas, Beaches and Bases 57 (1989).

imbalances, formulations of rights are generally cast in individual terms. The invocation of rights to sexual equality may therefore solve an occasional case of inequality for individual women but will leave the position of women generally unchanged. Moreover, international law accords priority to civil and political rights, rights that may have very little to offer women generally. The major forms of oppression of women operate within the economic, social and cultural realms. Economic, social and cultural rights are traditionally regarded as a lesser form of international right and as much more difficult to implement.

A second major criticism of the assumption that the granting of rights inevitably spells progress for women is that it ignores competing rights: the right of women and children not to be subjected to violence in the home may be balanced against the property rights of men in the home or their right to family life. Furthermore, certain rights may be appropriated by more powerful groups: Carol Smart relates that provisions in the European Convention on Human Rights on family life were used by fathers to assert their authority over ex nuptial children.[35] One solution may be to design rights to apply only to particular groups. However, apart from the serious political difficulties this tactic would raise, the formulation of rights that apply only to women may result in marginalizing these rights.

A third feminist concern about the "rights" approach to achieve equality is that some rights can operate to the detriment of women. The right to freedom of religion, for example, can have differing impacts on women and men. Freedom to exercise all aspects of religious belief does not always benefit women because many accepted religious practices entail reduced social positions and status for women.[36] Yet attempts to set priorities and to discuss the issue have been met with hostility and blocking techniques. Thus, at its 1987 meeting the CEDAW Committee adopted a decision requesting that the United Nations and the specialized agencies

> promote or undertake studies on the status of women under Islamic laws and customs and in particular on the status and equality of women in the family on issues such as marriage, divorce, custody and property rights and their participation in public life of the society, taking into consideration the principle of El Ijtihad in Islam.[37]

The representatives of Islamic nations criticized this decision in ECOSOC and in the Third Committee of the General Assembly as a threat to their freedom of religion. The CEDAW Committee's recommendation was ultimately rejected. CEDAW later justified its action by stating that the study was necessary for it to carry out its duties under the Women's Convention and that no disrespect was intended to Islam.

Another example of internationally recognized rights that might affect women and men differently are those relating to the protection of the family. The major human rights instruments all have provisions applicable to the family. Thus, the Universal Declaration proclaims that the family is the "natural and fundamental group unit of society and is entitled to protection by society and the State." These provisions ignore that to many women the family is a unit for abuse and violence; hence, protection of the family also preserves the power structure within the family, which can lead to subjugation and dominance by men over women and children.

Nevertheless, the discourse of rights provides an accepted means to challenge the traditional legal order and to develop alternative principles. While the acquisition of rights must not be identified with automatic and immediate advances for women, and the limitations of the rights model must be recognized, the notion of women's rights remains a source of potential power for women in international law. The challenge is to rethink that notion so that rights correspond to women's experiences and needs.

In conclusion, international legal structures and principles masquerade as "human"—universally applicable sets of standards. They are more accurately described as international men's law.

Modern international law is not only androcentric, but also Euro-centered in its origins, and has assimilated many assumptions about law and the place of law in society from western legal thinking. These include essentially patriarchal legal institutions, the assumption that law is objective, gender neutral and universally applicable, and the societal division into public and private spheres, which relegates many matters of concern to women to the private area regarded as inappropriate for legal regulation. Research is needed to question the assumptions of neutrality and universal applicability of norms of international law and to expose the invisibility of women and their experiences in discussions about the law. A feminist perspective, with

---

[34] For a discussion of the feminist ambivalence toward gendered laws such as statutory rape laws, *see* Olsen, *Statutory Rape: A Feminist Critique of Rights Analysis*, 63 TEX. L. REV. 387 (1984).

[35] CAROL SMART, FEMINISM AND THE POWER OF LAW 145 (1989).

[36] *See, e.g.*, Arzt, *The Application of International Human Rights Law in Islamic States*, 12 HUM. RTS. Q. 202, 203 (1990).

[37] UN Doc. E/1987/SR.11, at 13. *Cf.* An-Na'im, *Rights of Women and International Law in the Muslim Context*, 9 WHITTIER L. REV. 491 (1987).

its concern for gender as a category of analysis and its commitment to genuine equality between the sexes, could illuminate many areas of international law; for example, state responsibility, refugee law, use of force and the humanitarian law of war, human rights, population control and international environmental law. Feminist research holds the promise of a fundamental restructuring of traditional international law discourse and methodology to accommodate alternative world views.

The centrality of the state in international law means that many of the structures of international law reflect its patriarchal forms. Paradoxically, however, international law may be more open to feminist analysis than other areas of law. The distinction between law and politics, so central to the preservation of the neutrality and objectivity of law in the domestic sphere, does not have quite the same force in international law. So, too, the western domestic model of legal process as ultimately coercive is not echoed in the international sphere: the process of international law is consensual and peaceful coexistence is its goal. Finally, the sustained Third World critique of international law and insistence on diversity may well have prepared the philosophical ground for feminist critiques.

A feminist transformation of international law would involve more than simply refining or reforming existing law. It could lead to the creation of international regimes that focus on structural abuse and the revision of our notions of state responsibility. It could also lead to a challenge to the centrality of the state in international law and to the traditional sources of international law.

The mechanisms for achieving some of these aims already exist. The Covenant on Economic, Social and Cultural Rights and the Women's Convention could be used as a basis for promoting structural economic and social reform to reduce some of the causes of sexual and other abuse of women. The notion of state responsibility, however, both under these Conventions and generally, will have to be expanded to incorporate responsibility for systemic abuse based on sexual discrimination (broadly defined) and imputability to the state will have to be extended to include acts committed by private individuals.

Is a reorientation of international law likely to have any real impact on women? Feminists have questioned the utility of attempts at legal reform in domestic law and warn against attributing too much power to law to alter basic political and economic inequalities based on sex. Could this reservation be made a fortiori with respect to international law, whose enforcement and efficacy are in any event much more controversial? Would an altered, humanized international law have any capacity to achieve social change in a world where most forms of power continue to be controlled by men?

Like all legal systems, international law plays an important part in constructing reality. The areas it does not touch seem naturally to belong within the domestic jurisdiction of states. International law defines the boundaries of agreement by the international community on the matters that states are prepared to yield to supranational regulation and scrutiny. Its authority is derived from the claim of international acceptance. International legal concerns have a particular status; those concerns outside the ambit of international law do not seem susceptible to development and change in the same way. To redefine the traditional scope of international law so as to acknowledge the interests of women can open the way to reimagining possibilities for change and may permit international law's promise of peaceful coexistence and respect for the dignity of all persons to become a reality.

2. Negative[38]

In this essay I shall show that while *liberal* feminism has important things to say about international law and relations, *radical* feminism is inconsistent both with the facts and with a view of international law rooted in human rights and respect for persons.[39] The Australian scholars Hilary Charlesworth, Christine Chinkin, and Shelley Wright conflate the divergent arguments of liberal and radical feminism, which coexist in uneasy tension throughout their article.

Liberal feminism is the view that women are unjustly treated, that their rights are violated, and that political reform is needed to improve their situation, that is, to allow them to exercise autonomous choices and enjoy full equal status as free citizens in a liberal democracy. *Radical* feminists agree with their liberal counterparts that the situation of women must be improved, yet believe that liberal institutions are themselves but tools of gender oppression, and that women are exploited by men in even the least suspecting ways. For radical feminists, existing states are hierarchically structured according to gender, infecting the process of legal reasoning itself. Actual choices made by

---

[38] By FERNANDO R. TESON, excerpted from: *Feminism and International Law: A Reply*, ___ VIRGINIA JOURNAL OF INTERNATIONAL LAW ___ (1993). Reprinted by permission.

[39] I am aware that there are other schools of thought within the feminist movement. Particularly noteworthy is relational feminism inspired by CAROL GILLIGAN, IN A DIFFERENT VOICE (1982). *See, e.g.*, Suzanna Sherry, *Civic Virtue and the Feminine Voice in Constitutional Adjudication*, 72 VA. L. REV. 543 (1986). However, I will confine myself to liberal and radical feminism, in part because they seem to me the two alternatives that are truly irreconcilable, and in part because Charlesworth and her associates refuse to adopt the "different voice" premise.

women only *seem* to be autonomous and free; in reality they are *socially* determined. Human beings are not, as liberals would have it, separate, rational entities capable of individual decision-making, but rather beings to some degree defined and determined by their social – and particularly gender – relationships. In the radical feminist's world, no woman is really free, not even in the "freest' of societies (radical feminists differ on whether or not *men* are free.)

I will start with the claim that women are underrepresented in international relations and thus deprived of the opportunity of participating in the creation of international law. There is no doubt that there are relatively few women heads of state, diplomats, or international organizations officials. But is this state of things an *injustice*? And how can the statistical underrepresentation (whether or not it is an injustice) be redressed? It is useful to distinguish between states, on one hand, and international organizations, on the other.

Let us consider first the case of illegitimate, undemocratic governments. Plainly, it does not make sense to criticize a dictator, say, for not appointing enough women to his government or as diplomatic agents. Indeed, it is a contextual *category* mistake to blame a dictator who has taken and held power by means of torture and murder for not appointing a woman as ambassador to the United Nations. That is like blaming a burglar ransacking our home at gunpoint for not having asked our permission to use the telephone. The normative context of a tyrannical state is one in which it does not make sense to ask the tyrant to appoint more women (or men, or blacks, or Catholics).

If an illegitimate government consists of a group of men who systematically exclude women, this is of course an injustice, but it is one that is subordinated to the greater injustice of tyranny, which by definition includes the illegitimacy of origin and the violation of human rights. It is true that discrimination against women aggravates the injustice of tyranny; it therefore makes sense to put pressure on *all* governments to refrain from sexist practices. But the analysis does not work the other way round: tyranny is not cured by the tyrant's celebration of diversity, as it were. Even in cases where human rights abuses (other than exclusion from government) are primarily directed at women, the suggestion that what we need is more women as international representatives of dictators is absurd on its face. The only remedy, here as elsewhere, is to get rid of the tyrants and secure human rights.

More interesting is the case of full members of the liberal alliance, that is, states with democratically elected officials where human rights are generally respected. Assuming a right to democratic governance,[40] a state may not discriminate against women in their exercise of that right.[41] The governing international principle, then, is the imperative of nondiscrimination and equal opportunity for women, along the lines suggested by the pertinent international instruments, themselves inspired in Articles 1(3), 8, and 55 of the U.N. Charter.

Radical feminists, however, seem to believe that there is a global injustice even where as a result of democratic elections held in independent, rights-respecting states, mostly men are elected to government, or if in such states mostly men traditionally seek admission to the diplomatic service. Would they impose a 50% gender quota for elected positions, or force women who do not want to run for office or to serve as diplomats to do so anyway? International law cannot go beyond mandating democratic governance and nondiscrimination in a general way. Local conditions will vary, and in states where women have been previously excluded from politics it may be permissible and desirable to adopt preferential electoral arrangements. Such measures, when properly tailored, do not do violence to the international law principle of nondiscrimination and the right of all citizens to participate in public life.

The next feminist claim is that the *content* of international law privileges men. For the great majority of positive international law rules, I find little plausibility in this claim. Positive international law is a vast and heterogeneous system consisting of principles, rules, and standards of varying degrees of generality, many of a technical nature. Rules such as the principle of territoriality in criminal jurisdiction, or the rule that third states should in principle have access to the surplus of the entire allowable catch of fish in a coastal states' exclusive economic zone, are not "thoroughly gendered" but, on the contrary, gender neutral. It cannot be seriously maintained that these norms operate overtly or covertly to the detriment of women. The same can be said about the great bulk of international legal rules.

However, feminists are correct in claiming that international law overprotects states and governments. International law, as traditionally understood, is formulated in exaggeratedly statist terms. Statism (understood as the doctrine according to which state sovereignty is the foundational concept of international law) repudiates the central place accorded to the individual in liberal normative theory,

---

40 [Editor's Note: *See*, Chapter 15, "Democracy" in this Anthology.]

41 *See* Articles 7–8, Convention on the Elimination of All Forms of Discrimination Against Women, adopted Dec. 18, 1979, G.A. Res. 34/180, 34 U.N. GAOR Supp. (No. 46) at 193, I.L.M. 33 (1980) (entered into force Sept. 3, 1981); Articles 1–3, Convention on the Political Rights of Women, opened for signature March 31, 1953, U.S.T. 1909, T.I.A.S. No. 8289, 193 U.N.T.S. 135 (entered into force July 7, 1954; art. 1, Inter-American Convention on the Granting of Political Rights to Women, opened for signature May 2, 1948, 27 U.S.T. 3301, T.I.A.S. No. 8365 (entered into force March 17, 1949).

and, by extension, it often results in ignoring the rights and interests of women within states.

But radical feminists seem to believe that even governments in liberal democracies are, to paraphrase Marx, mere committees to handle the interests of men. If part of the interests of men were to secure the continuing oppression of women, then the international law principles of sovereign equality and nonintervention would operate to the detriment of women. In that sense the content of international law would be male biased. Indeed, under such view there are currently no legitimate states or governments: all of them are simply men's devises to perpetuate their domination; international law compounds this oppression by securing the sovereignty of states and the external representativeness of governments.

There are fatal objections to this sweeping radical thesis. A first problem with the claim that states are patriarchal entities is that it is not subject to empirical testing. Like Marxists before them, radical feminists see their theory of gender oppression and hierarchy confirmed in every single social event, for the good reason that no single fact counts as a counterexample for the thesis. No improvement in women's condition counts as a move toward liberation; states remain patriarchal entities notwithstanding progressive legislation or significant conquests for women. Even in the freest societies (the Western liberal democracies) where most choices by women are apparently autonomous in the liberal sense, radical feminists insist either that such choices are not really autonomous because women have been socialized to make them, or that there is no such thing as autonomy anyway. So no amount of legal reform will placate the radical feminists; indeed, even consensual sexual intercourse is regarded by some of them as oppressive.

One choice that many women in fact make is to stay in the home. Because the radical feminists believe the homemakers' choices to be degrading, they conclude that those are not real choices, but are rather forced by socialization. Leaving aside the inexplicable disdain for family, motherhood, and heterosexuality associated with this claim, it is a highly suspect form of argument. One cannot just pick those choices that one approves of ideologically as being "real" choices, and discount those that do not fit one's preferred utopia as "apparent." Absent coercion or fraud, the choice of a homemaker to devote herself to the family ought to be valued and honored.

The thesis that states are inherently oppressive of women partakes of the weakness of all conspiratorial explanations. The feminist conspiratorial theory of the state attempts to explain social phenomena by claiming that men, who are interested in these phenomena taking place, have planned and conspired in more or less subtle ways to bring them about. Every social event and institution is the result of men having plotted to produce the event or create the institution, such as the state, with the purpose of perpetuating their domination of women.[42]

One cannot deny that there is something exhilarating in postulating a *total* explanation of society, or the universe, because then every occurrence can be effortlessly explained by reference to the Great One Conspiratorial Premise.[43] We are relieved of trying to find complex causal chains of social events.

If one looks at the modern liberal state, the explanation of it as a device created by men to ensure their domination appears impoverished and simplistic. Such a view overlooks the importance of the social forces that were unleashed once the universality of human rights was proclaimed by the "bourgeoisie." Feminists, radical and liberal, are right that many of the early liberals had the expressed or hidden belief that women be excluded from many of the benefits of liberty. This, however, was the result of a mistaken anthropology, not of a mistaken ethics. Once the prejudice against women was exposed, moral beliefs acquired a life of their own, as it were, and the universality of liberal moral theory, logically entailed by the belief in the inherent dignity of *all* persons, resulted in an astonishing improvement of the predicament of women in free societies.

The truth is that the assertion that a social arrangement is unjust or oppressive is contingent; it depends not only on the theory of justice that is presupposed, but on the facts as well. "Oppression" does not follow from the definition of "state"; it is not therefore inherent in the social organization we know as the modern state. Oppression may be defined as an individual or a group unjustly preventing others from exercising choices, and this may or may not occur in a particular case. So the sweeping definition of a state as inherently oppressive of women is, in my view, factually false because there are states where women are not oppressed, and morally irresponsible because it trivial-

[42] Thus, Catharine MacKinnon, Toward a Feminist Theory of the State 163–64 (1989). Not all feminists, however, endorse MacKinnon's conspiratorial explanation of the state. I follow here 2 Karl R. Popper, The Open Society and Its Enemies 94–95 (2nd ed. 1966). As Popper rightly points out, conspiracy theories are simply secular remnants of the superstitious belief that the Homeric gods determine the outcome of the battles.

[43] In radical feminist theory, men play the role that the capitalists, the Learned Men of Zion, the imperialists, the communists, etc., have played in various other conspiracy theories. Conspiracy theories, however, do become important when people who hold them are in power, for in that case they will spend most of their energies in a counter-conspiracy against nonexisting conspirators. Popper, *id.* at 95. For an almost pristine example of a conspiracy theory, the military Junta in Argentina (1976–1984) believed that the world's outrage over their human rights violations was the result of a "well orchestrated anti-Argentine campaign" waged by communists led by Amnesty International.

izes the notion of tyranny. States come in many moral shapes. In some states women are oppressed; in some others blacks are oppressed; whites are persecuted in a few; yet in other states members of a particular religion, or who speak a certain language, or who happen to be foreigners, may be mistreated, and in some states *everyone* is oppressed. The radical feminist's insistence on the inherent oppression of women by the state clumsily blurs the distinction between freedom and tyranny: radical feminists would have us believe that a state where the government murders and tortures its citizens is in the same category as one where there is a statistical gender imbalance in the public employees roster.

We have to distinguish two cases: violation of women's rights by *the government*, and violation of women's rights by *private* persons – notably abuse by men in the home and the workplace. From the standpoint of the international law of human rights, the violation of women's rights by governments does not present difficulties distinct from the violation of other human rights. Liberals and feminists are at one here in condemning discrimination against women. This is an unfair treatment of women in violation of international human rights law for which the state is internationally responsible.

The violation of women's rights by private persons or groups raises more difficult issues because, as feminists rightly point out, the boundaries between public and private action are blurred. Indeed, radical feminists contend that the very distinction between public or state action and private action is indefensible because it is male biased and harmful to women.

Let me discuss what seems to me the feminists' most persuasive point: that statism encourages an excessive legal protection to the family. This family "autonomy," considered to be part of the private law, the private social domain, has legitimized domination of women and children by the stronger family member: the man. This oppression ranges from outright brutality to subtle ways of socializing women within the family, for example, by more or less coercively convincing them that their place is in the home and thus preventing them from pursuing other options.

On the feminist view, the fact that the family is legally treated as a semi-enclosed unit to a greater extent than other legal relationships, and the fact that modern governments are, consequently, slow in intervening in internal family affairs, make states, in different degrees, accomplices in this injustice. A statist conception of international law, in turn, protects states by imposing a strong duty of nonintervention in internal matters. So there are two layers of legal immunity enjoyed by men who oppress women: domestic law, which treats the family as the man's castle; and international law, which likewise treats the state (with its many men's castles) as largely shielded from external scrutiny.

I think that feminists, radical and liberal, are right in decrying the excessive prerogatives enjoyed by men within the family. The law ought to punish the victimization of women and children; culprits should not be allowed to hide behind the "family unit." But this is not a failure of *liberalism*, nor does it show the bankruptcy of the private/public distinction. For *group* autonomy (state sovereignty, family autonomy) is an *illiberal* notion. Kantian liberalism insists that our moral principles derive from *individual* dignity and autonomy.[44] Every person holds individual rights which are not forfeited by membership in the family group. Therefore, a liberal state must recognize and enforce the rights of women and children within the family and protect them against risks of rights violations. A principle according to which families are treated as autonomous enclaves so that individuals within the family do not receive protection against rights violations by the strongest (i.e., men) cannot be called liberal: it is, to a large extent, a communitarian idea, a group's rights notion. Feminists are absolutely right that family autonomy is a suspect idea, but not because it is liberal, but because it is not liberal enough. The rights of women and children ought to be protected even (and maybe especially) against violations by family members. Just as the principle of state sovereignty must be set aside to protect the citizens whose rights are violated by their government, so the principle of family autonomy must be set aside to protect the rights of members of the family.

At this point, the international lawyer may raise an objection. Why cannot *domestic* law address the question of abuse of women? Why should *international* law provide a remedy for the acts of private individuals? Surely many offenses (i.e., murder or rape), heinous as they are, are not criminalized by international law. International law, the traditionalist would claim, is primarily concerned with rules of state behavior. These rules do include human rights standards, but these standards can only be violated by state officials. The international law of human rights regulates the relations between citizens and their governments (in particular, setting limits to governmental coercion), not relations among private individuals. Crimes committed by private individuals against their fellow citizens fall instead under the purview of the ordinary criminal law. It is true that, in special circumstances, certain crimes committed by private individuals are directly regulated by international law: piracy and genocide are examples. But most common offenses, including men's offenses against women, belong, it is argued, in the province of the state.

---

[44] *See* Fernando R. Teson, *The Kantian Theory of International Law*, 92 COLUM. L. REV. 53 (1992); *id.*, *International Obligation and the Theory of Hypothetical Consent*, 15 YALE J. INT'L L. 84 (1990).

It is the state, through its criminal and civil legislation, who has the power to prevent and redress those injustices.

This reply too readily accepts a statist conception of international law. To take an extreme example, suppose a state where rape is not criminalized. Unscrupulous men could go around taking advantage of women and terrorizing them; and everybody would live in constant fear. I am not sure we would even call this Hobbesian jungle a *state*; it would certainly not be a civilized state on any meaning of that word, and it would be ludicrous for the government to escape international scrutiny by arguing that, after all, the legally permitted acts of rape are not being perpetrated by state *officials*. So in this case liberal theory must postulate an affirmative obligation *in international law* on the part of the state to have a reasonably effective legal system where assaults against life, physical integrity, and property, are not tolerated. Thus a state is in breach of its international obligations not only if it violates human rights in the traditional sense, but also, I argue, if it fails adequately to protect its citizens – if it fails to punish enough, as it were.

There are of course cases where governments notoriously encourage or tolerate groups of private individuals who engage in the violation of the rights of women or other groups. Take the situation of women in some countries, where religious guards patrol the streets to make sure that women, under the threat of severe physical punishment, abide by a set of strict rules that ensure the women's official status as inferior citizens.[45] The state thus approves of the inferior status by allowing or encouraging the religious squads. In such a case, the situation is identical to direct human rights violations by state officials.

The question is then to determine what amounts to state complicity. The broad claim of feminists is that the government's reluctance to intervene in internal family affairs amounts to complicity. We saw that if domestic law fails to criminalize or punish the behavior of husbands who torment their wives the state should be held accountable by international law. But, of course, there are degrees of government negligence, and the traditional international law requirement that states take reasonable steps to prevent and punish crimes seems to me entirely appropriate. While even the most liberal states may have been remiss in the past in this regard (and there is surely much yet to be done, especially in the Latin American democracies), most democratic, rights-respecting states have laws that prohibit and punish the abuse of women. Where that legislation is enforced in good faith, holding such states nonetheless internationally responsible for the instances of abuse of women that still occur is like holding states internationally responsible for, say, murders that are committed every year notwithstanding the states' good faith efforts at crime prevention. It is one thing to hold the state in breach of international human rights law if it knowingly tolerates the behavior of wife-beaters (or death squads, or the Mafia), or if it fails to enact or enforce appropriate protective legislation, as in the Dutch case. It is a very different thing to hold a state responsible when, despite reasonable legislation and law enforcement, crimes are still committed by private persons.

I would go further: from a human rights standpoint, international law should *not* impose a requirement that states establish *perfectly effective* systems of crime control. For in such systems, effective deterrence would be achieved by criminal codes imposing very harsh punishments, such as death, for even minor offenses; and the law would be enforced by an aggressive and intrusive police with ample powers of arrest and seizure. Citizens in a liberal democracy, concerned with limiting rather than enlarging state power, would not rationally want legislation so severe and law enforcement machineries so efficient that would ensure the punishment of *all* wife-beaters, no more than they would want a system that would ensure the punishment of all murderers. The cost of such a system in terms of freedom would be intolerable. True, a law enforcement system that would *infallibly* ensure the punishment of criminals, without impinging on anyone's liberties (and in particular the *innocents'* liberties) would be optimal. But there is no such thing, and experience shows that, given human imperfections, the attempt to maximize efficiency in criminal repression will, more likely than not, lead to tyranny.

A number of radical feminists go deeper and reject the very idea of individual autonomy. They view the law's reliance on concepts such as autonomy, rights, and justice, as a masculine trait. The feminist critique is that this masculine jurisprudence has unduly emphasized rights over responsibilities, the individual over the community. Feminists may mean two things here: that the theory of autonomy was *created* by men, or that it is a reflection of how men typically *think* or feel and thus excludes women. In either version, this claim confuses the context of origin with the context of justification of a theory. It is perfectly possible to concede that the concept of autonomy is masculine in origin or mental make-up, but that it is also the *correct* position to hold. *Who* created the theory or *how* it came about or whether men or women think more about it may be interesting historical or anthropological questions, but they do not settle the issue whether or not the theory is justified. Dismissing liberalism as distinctively masculine because it was formulated by men or because it is a masculine way of thinking is like dismissing the theory of relativity as distinctively Jewish because it was formulated by Albert Einstein. Indeed, if I were persuaded by

---

45 *See* AMNESTY INTERNATIONAL, IRAN: WOMEN PRISONERS OF CONSCIENCE (1990).

radical feminists that the feminine way of thinking about political morality is illiberal, I would do my best to *keep* women from power. But, of course, the claim that women think about morality in less liberal ways is as false as the claim that men think about morality in more liberal ways. Liberals, it seems, give women more credit than do their radical counterparts.

The radical challenge is not so easily dismissed, however, because not all feminists allude to the origin or mental make-up of liberalism when they refer to it as being distinctively masculine. One can read this claim as simply holding that liberalism is metaphysically *wrong* and (maybe for that reason) *unfair* to women. These are claims about the philosophical truth or the moral legitimacy of liberalism and do not, therefore, confuse origin with justification.

Radical feminists, like communitarians and other radicals, believe that the liberal assumption of autonomy is mistaken because the self is not autonomous but rather socially constituted. This point (which for some reason has become almost undisputed among radicals and even among many of their detractors) is overdrawn. Among other things, this claim overlooks the undeniable capacity of human beings to overcome the constraints of history, tradition, and social pressures, including state coercion, to challenge existing values and follow their own lights. In addition, the claim is self-defeating, because if choices are socially constituted, presumably the choices of illiberal dissenters who challenge liberalism (the latter being the predominant philosophy in the West) are not excepted from this deterministic postulate. Radical feminists cannot just say that liberal society conditions everybody's choices *except the radicals' own choices*. Feminists and other radicals (unlike the rest of us liberal robots) are presumably endowed with the aptitude to make the autonomous choice of challenging autonomy. But one cannot hold a theory where the very act of formulating it is inconsistent with its central premise. The radicals' theorizing would not be possible if values and choices were socially constituted in its entirety: only people in Teheran, not in Berkeley, would be able to challenge liberalism.

Yet even if, *gratia argumentandi*, the claim that choices are socially determined is conceded, this does not affect the moral force of liberalism. The injunction to respect autonomy amounts to this: People make choices, they care about them, and we must respect them (within the framework of the coercion presupposed by the social contract), *even* if those choices are, in a Laplacean sense, biologically or socially determined. Liberals claim that, regardless of the response to the ultimate metaphysical question of social or biological determinism, a distinctive characteristic of human beings is their capacity for what for all purposes look like rational choices, and that such capacity *must be respected* by fellow citizens, and notably by the government. This is a moral, not a metaphysical claim.

A related feminist claim is that the liberal emphasis on autonomy does not leave room for an ethics of care and compassion. This is an unjustified charge against liberalism. As many writers have shown, rights-based liberalism is perfectly consistent with the flourishing of human emotions such as love and compassion.[46]

Radical feminist critics of international law would have to support the dismantling of international human rights law, since it relies expressly on liberal autonomy and the equal dignity of all persons, men and women. My suspicion (although this may be unduly optimistic) is that these critics do not want to take us all the way in this direction.

In any event, statism should be rejected. In consequence, we should examine critically the usual distinction between public and private social and legal domains. Feminists, after having discovered that the uncritical inclusion of the family in the private domain is often unfair to women, go too far in concluding that we should give up altogether the distinction between private and public law.

A first reply is that the concept of family privacy makes *some* sense provided one is clear that it is derivative of *individual* rights and autonomy (just as state sovereignty is derivative of individual rights and autonomy.) Liberals, unlike communitarians, ground this family privacy in autonomy and freedom, not in the primacy of the group over the individual. The duty of the state not to interfere with the family (provided the rights of their members are protected) is thus a simple extension of the duty to respect voluntary arrangements entered into by individuals. Even a radical feminist, I assume, would agree that if the state sent agents to take children away for re-education, or to make sure that sexual intercourse was practiced in the officially sanctioned manner, it would violate a private familial space. A consequence of accepting an autonomy-based family privacy is that the distinction between private and public may well reflect in many cases a rational division of labor between the sexes achieved through non-coercive, voluntary arrangements.

More generally, individual freedom *requires* separation between the private and public spheres, because the distinction is simply the legal consequence of the moral imperative of *individual* privacy required by any but the most totalitarian theories of law. For liberals, the power of the state is always limited, and individuals should be legally allowed to make choices in their personal and economic lives free of governmental coercion. This elementary idea (and not some conspiracy to oppress women), lies at the basis of the much maligned public/private distinction. Far from be-

46 *See* the excellent defense of Kant against radical objections by Barbara Herman, *Integrity and Impartiality*, 66 MONIST 233 (1983).

ing "an ideological construct rationalizing the exclusion of women from the sources of power," as Charlesworth and her associates say, the public/private distinction is a centerpiece of any constitutional system that protects human rights.

In the light of this obvious and, in my view, conclusive reply, how could radical feminists possibly suggest a conspiratorial explanation of the public/private distinction? One answer is possible: radicals do not care for human rights, for freedom. This may be true of some, but it is certainly not true of those who wish to improve the situation of women: by definition, they wish to free women from the bonds that prevent their fulfillment as autonomous human beings. The reason for the confusion is, once again, that the private autonomous sphere that the feminists challenge is but a travesty of liberalism's insistence on individual self-determination free from governmental coercion: the family conceived as a Dantesque place where the physically stronger husband victimizes the weaker members. Calling wife abuse an instance of "family autonomy" is as offensive as calling Saddam Hussein's genocide of the Kurds an instance of Iraqi "self-determination."

Moreover, the feminist claim that male domination is an inherent part of liberal discourse—or, as Charlesworth and her associates put it, "male, European discourse"—and that therefore liberal institutions are oppressive of women, is patently false. Their euphemistic assertion that "decision-making processes in [non-Western] societies are every bit as exclusive of women as in western societies" is just another example of the warped view that free societies and tyrannical ones are in reality morally equivalent. The truth is that the situation of women is immeasurably better in liberal societies, Western or non-Western. The most sexist societies, in contrast, are those informed and controlled by *illiberal* theories and institutions. These societies are much more exclusive of women than liberal societies (and most of the Western societies are liberal), not just "every bit as" exclusive. A failure to recognize these facts by those claiming to be concerned with the plight of women amounts to serious moral irresponsibility.

It is significant that Charlesworth and her associates do not emphasize violations of women's rights by *governments*, for if they did they would have to acknowledge that some countries are far worse than others—countries, for example, where women are officially discriminated against and even sometimes mutilated in unspeakable ways, with official endorsement and complicity.[47] Obsession with male dominance leads radical feminists to the grotesque suggestion that oppression of women is as serious in liberal democracies as in those societies that institutionally victimize and exclude women. Such a suggestion not only perverts the facts; it does a disservice to the women's cause.[48]

Indeed, at the global level there is no question that liberal institutions are the ones that have gone the farthest (although admittedly not far enough yet) in eliminating gender discrimination and other forms of unjust treatment of women. This salient fact should give pause to those who mindlessly echo the radical slogan that the way to improve the situation of women is to dismantle liberalism, human rights, and democracy.

F. DEBATE: The "Domestication" of International Law

1. Affirmative[49]

Like the positivists before them, many contemporary theorists perpetuate the conceptual framework of a unitary international law arching over an international community. This form of analysis helps make international law a marginal discipline. It perpetuates the image of international law's remoteness from the more important world of national politics and societies where most significant decisions are actually taken. The way to lend credibility and relevance to the international law discipline is to connect it with real communities with viable political foundations, arenas that have traditionally been categorized as "domestic."

Public international law should be reconceptualized. Instead of being seen as a single, unitary system applicable across the "world community," public international law should be imagined as a series of parallel systems, more or less convergent depending on the subject, separately applicable within the various nations of the world. Under this approach public international law resembles private international law, where each state has its own set of choice

[47] *See, e.g.*, Boulware-Miller, *Female Circumcision: Challenge to the Practice as a Human Rights Violation*, 8 HARV. WOMEN'S L.J. 155 (1985).

[48] Another reason for this "moral equivalence" thesis stems from a curiosity in the history of radical thought: feminists are leftists, and one of the mottoes of the left is solidarity with the Third World. Therefore, they feel more comfortable trashing the "imperialist" West rather than simply acknowledging that in many Third World societies women are seriously mistreated. The anti-Western bias of Charlesworth and her associates is clear in their brief reference to female circumcision. They delicately refer to "the tension between some First and Third World feminists over the correct approach to the issue of female genital mutilation." So, for feminists, liberal states are oppressive patriarchal entities, but the permissibility of that barbaric practice in some non-Western states is still open to debate.

[49] By PHILLIP R. TRIMBLE, excerpted from: *International Law, World Order, and Critical Legal Studies*, 42 STANFORD LAW REVIEW 811, 835–36, 839–45 (1990). Reprinted by permission.

of law rules (or other independently adopted rules) applicable to "private" controversies, but where those rules are similar in content and in fact provide a large measure of uniformity and predictability throughout the world.

The domestication of public international law would have three major advantages. First, it would provide a theory that more realistically describes international law as it actually works. Second, it would point the way to rhetorical strategies more persuasive to government officials, judges, and other decisionmakers. Validation of international norms by the same or similar processes that produce domestic law, and association of international law with domestic political theory, are important to the political support and therefore legitimacy of international norms. And legitimacy is the key to persuasiveness. My strategy would move the study of public international law to a more compelling position in the academic and practical worlds. Finally, it would alleviate the perennial difficulties in explaining whether international law is "really law" and why it is binding. It would accomplish this final advantage by simply abolishing the question. Everyone concedes that municipal law is "really law," and there are plausible explanations for its binding force. Thus, the ultimate persuasiveness of my case rests on the analysis of the first and second advantages.

A domestic approach in fact describes today's living international law. Law varies from culture to culture and from context to context, and international law is no exception. Most modern texts and casebooks include references to different "views" of international law, for example, to Socialist or Third World views. Although the differences are often overstated, important differences do exist with regard to several doctrines. For example, in response to United States hegemony, many Latin American states adopted the doctrine that a state's responsibility for injuries to aliens does not exceed its domestic standards and that only appropriate compensation determined under domestic law need be paid upon expropriation of foreign property. Latin American states also maintained that recognition of a government may not be denied for political purposes. These doctrines reflect a distinctive context, in which Latin societies reacted against foreign investment and the United States' use of recognition as a means of political coercion.

The existence of two approaches does not mean that there is *no* international law of state responsibility or of recognition of governments. It simply means that one rule would apply in Peru and another in Canada, just as different systems of constitutional law or contract law apply in those two countries. In the broad perspective, the particular rules may vary little from country to country, but the systems of law can be kept conceptually distinct. The development of new rules of customary international law provides another example. It is said that a state may opt out of an emerging customary rule by objecting to it in a timely manner.[50] This is simply another way of saying that a different rule applies in the jurisprudential culture of that state.

Professor Boyle reports that, in his efforts to use international law arguments in criminal defense trials in United States courts, he finds that lawyers often do not take such arguments seriously.[51] Constitutional and statutory arguments are preferred. To understand why this should be so, it is important first to look at the audience to which the argument is addressed. After all, the purpose of making a legal argument is to induce the decisionmaker – the prosecuting attorney or a judge in the United States criminal context – to decide the case a particular way. We should therefore analyze how an argument may "form attitudes or induce action in others."[52] A constitutional argument seems preferable not only because it is more familiar to these officials. It also appeals to their sense of duty and their identity as officials of the United States of America. They take an oath specifically to uphold the Constitution and laws of the United States, and they no doubt see themselves as part of the common enterprise of governance of the nation. Their appointment process reinforces a self-image of being part of the American political system.

Since international law has been portrayed as belonging to a distinct sphere of operation separate from politics and from domestic governments, it is easy to see why its arguments may not seem persuasive. Professor Frug suggests that arguments appeal to a person's psychic make-up and social role. The normal decisionmaker in an international law context is a government official or judge and consequently feels a duty to her government who identifies with it and its goals. It seems unlikely that she defines her character or role as a servant of the "international community." She may see herself as a servant of some generalized public interest, but she would probably define that interest in narrower terms, such as nation or class. The way to connect international law to the psychological world of decisionmakers is to bring it closer to home, not to preach to them about reforming their outlook. International law must be connected with the domestic political context. One way to do so is to validate it through a process similar to that used for regular, municipal law. Another way is to connect theoretically the norm or the process by which it was created with prevailing political theory, which will vary from culture to culture.

Ultimately, the decisionmaker must perceive the specific rule that is being invoked as legitimate. The rule's legitimacy can be enhanced, first, by the process by which it was created. Second, it can be connected with more general norms, rhetoric, or mythologies that are accepted within the society. Third, a rule's legitimacy can be enhanced by factors specifically applicable to the rule, such as its fairness, specificity, or obvious reciprocal applica-

---

50 Malcolm N. Shaw, International Law 74–76 (2d ed. 1986).

51 Francis Anthony Boyle, Defending Civil Resistance Under International Law 14–15 (1987).

52 Jerry Frug, *Argument As Character*, 40 Stan. L. Rev. 869, 872 (1988).

tion. The first two strategies connect the process or the rule in some way with prevailing political philosophy. For example, American political philosophy emphasizes popular sovereignty. Against that background customary international law which may be created entirely outside the "people's" political system, seems illegitimate. Treaty law, on the other hand, has explicit textual recognition in the Constitution, and it has been formally adopted by popular representative institutions – the President, the Senate, and, in the case of non-self-executing treaties, the House of Representatives. Thus, a treaty norm can be readily explained in terms of general political philosophy. In a state where treaties must be implemented by an act of the legislature, a similar foundation in popular sovereignty can be discovered.

In addition to philosophical support, the domestic implementation process assures that the rule's content has important practical political support. In the United States, a treaty may not become law until it passes formidable political hurdles, with all the publicity and consensus building that is entailed in the process. A ratified treaty has received formal endorsement by the President and the Senate or Congress, and has been scrutinized by the parts of the bureaucracy and public affected by its norms. Through this process of publicity, scrutiny, and political bargaining, the treaty attains symbolic legitimacy. Similar political benefits would accompany the implementation of international rules by the normal, domestic lawmaking process in any society.

A rule's legitimacy may also be enhanced by being connected with traditional ideologies, such as employing the concept of *jihad* to explain the meaning of self-defense contained in Article 51 of the United Nations Charter, or arguing that the concepts of fair treatment of foreign traders and humane treatment of prisoners of war can be rooted in Hindu tradition.

In stressing the importance of a sense of legitimacy in assuring compliance with international law, Professor Tom Franck emphasizes a third strategy of legitimacy enhancement including factors internal to the rules, such as determinance and coherence.[53] These factors may help in securing compliance, but it seems to me that a more important factor inducing a decisionmaker to follow a rule contrary to her short-term interest is her acceptance of the process by which the rule was promulgated and respect for the institutions that produced it. Thus, in Franck's example of the United States military's agreement not to interdict the introduction of Silkworm missiles into Iran because of the international laws of war, I would guess that the officer making that decision was influenced by respect for the treatymaking process and the political authority (and power) of the Senate and Congress, as well as the generalized interest in maintaining the overall system that would almost always be present in this situation.

When a person makes an international law claim, she is not only invoking self-interest, fear of possible sanctions, and an appeal to law abiding character. The appeal may also invoke respect for powerful political institutions – the President, Senate, and House – that have endorsed the norm and for accepted political theory. This approach to legitimacy will vary according to culture. Some societies are more dedicated to legalism and the "rule of law" than others. One might expect a greater receptivity to international law claims in bureaucratic governments within that tradition than in, say, China or Zaire. My claim that international law compliance may depend on acceptance of its legitimacy, which in turn can be enhanced by its domestication, may be difficult to prove empirically. In any situation several factors are likely to contribute to international law compliance, including the use of force by governments and self-interest. However, there is no orderly enforcement system, so that the availability of sanctions in any given situation is highly uncertain. Self-interest may superficially provide a more powerful explanation than legitimacy for international compliance. However, self-interest turns out to be either inadequate to explain some compliance behavior (such as the U.S. decision not to block transit of Cuban aircraft) or to be so broad that it explains nothing. As the "self-interest" of governments and government officials is characterized at higher and higher levels of generality – for example, expanding the U.S. "self-interest" in the above example from an interest in transiting Cuba, to an interest in transiting other states, to an interest in maintaining the overall air law regime – the concept becomes extremely elastic and ends up explaining any example of compliance behavior. Moreover, there are many different self-interests, within as well as among states. Conflict among them can be resolved in different and sometimes unpredictable ways. One could always find someone's self-interest served by any given course of compliance behavior. It therefore seems more precise and more persuasive to explain compliance by reference to a sense of law's legitimacy, which in turn can best be explained in terms of domestic political factors.

Finally, some might argue that by domesticating international law I have destroyed the value of the enterprise. For example, by making international law domestic it is always possible for a state to escape the obligations of international law simply by changing its domestic law. International law then becomes whatever states choose to do; the notion of law collapses into politics and behavior. Such a critique, however, is not as powerful as it might seem because it fails to take account of the extent to which state behavior is initially (and normally) shaped by law. Behavior does not exist in a pristine form untouched by law until it somehow runs against a legal barrier. That critique is merely another manifestation of the rigid separation of law and politics. It also neglects the formation and routine implementation process which structures state behavior in compliant forms. Under my domestic approach, the international law enterprise remains as important as ever, notwithstanding some deviations from its norms. Most behavior would regularly be "governed by the law" under a

[53] Thomas M. Franck, *Legitimacy in the International System*, 82 A.J.I.L. 705 (1988).

domesticated conception of international law for the reasons specified above.

The critique also assumes that international law may provide objective rules that may exist outside state behavior. But, as David Kennedy demonstrates, that is a false notion.[54] Still, international actors, like the World Court, intergovernmental arbitrators and international civil servants, as well as international law commentators, can come up with reasonably predictable conclusions of law in a wide variety of situations. If international law is conceptualized as domestic law, what happens to the work product of these people?

One answer might be that most international law is applied (or subverted) in a domestic context, so that we can simply ignore the international actors because they are few in number and unimportant in actual practice. That will not seem very satisfying to the international law profession, and also seems shortsighted in light of the growing interdependence that will increase the number and importance of international institutions.

Another answer might be that these "international" actors really only apply their own domestically conditioned versions of international law, so recharacterizing international law through a domestic prism simply reflects reality.

The most persuasive answer to the critique of domestically conceived international law is that in many, even most, situations there would be transnational agreement on the applicable rule of law. In some situations a genuine transnational subculture deals with particular functions, such as diplomacy, civil aviation, and monetary affairs. These people are likely to have contacts with counterparts abroad and be especially sensitive to claims involving the integrity of their particular regime. These situations produce genuinely universal norms. In other situations there may be generally accepted norms, at least at a high level of abstraction, so that the overlap among national conceptions of international law is broad enough (or the problem sufficiently insignificant) that states would be prepared to accept a decision on the basis of a general formulation, such as the "general principles of law accepted by civilized nations." In areas like terrorism, human rights, and environmental regulation, on the other hand, the overlap may be slight. But the force of observance is weak, so exposing the weak viability of the international law enterprise in these areas is no vice. That does not mean that the advocacy of human rights or environmental concerns should be subordinated. It means that the rhetorical approach should be adjusted to take account of the opposition to and the theoretical weakness of the claims in those areas. We need to figure out how to strengthen the political forces favoring the desired objectives, instead of engaging in futile law-talk.

Domesticating international law provides a theoretical framework that would enhance its legitimacy and hence its persuasiveness. Rhetorical strategies must be tailored to culture and subculture. They must take into account local political traditions, particular bureaucratic interests, and the rich variety of cultural contexts, especially the critically important domestic political context in which argument normally seeks to persuade.

[54] DAVID KENNEDY, INTERNATIONAL LEGAL STRUCTURES (1987).

2. Negative[55]

Professor Philip Trimble is a friend of international law. He very much wants it to work. However, like many teachers of that subject in American law schools, Phil seems frustrated because American students don't perceive international law as an independent, enforceable legal system. The students' perceptions in large part are shaped by offhand remarks of their favorite professors in other courses who tell them that international law isn't "real" law. It's just one of those "exotic" electives in the law-school curriculum.

Professor Abram Chayes has developed a strategy to deal with such perceptions in his introductory International Law course at Harvard Law School. Abe told me that he teaches international law only and exclusively as it appears as the rule of decision in cases in American courts. "That," he explained, "makes it real for the students." As with any truly great professor, there is a rationale behind his method. As I questioned him, the rationale was revealed. "You see, they get so interested in international law this way," he explained, "that they go on in later courses to study international law on its own."

In my view, what Professors Chayes and Trimble are really combating is not "international law" but rather the present curricular structure of American law schools. If they were teaching law in *any* foreign country, I daresay they would have an entirely different attitude. Foreign students study international law normally, as a regular—and not an exotic—discipline. Unlike this country where international law is an elective, foreign students are required to take it, they are required to pass examinations in it, and they are not admitted to the bar without competence in international law. As a result, they don't have a problem seeing international law as "real." It doesn't have to be sold to them as the rule of decision in, say, French courts or Finnish courts or Philippines courts.

When Professor Trimble argues that American lawyers and judges and governmental decision-makers respect arguments based on good old American law but are impatient with arguments based on external, international norms, he is simply discovering how the curricular structure of American law schools plays out in our culture at large. The law school curriculum has an absolutely enormous impact in the culture at large, because every state and federal judge

[55] By ANTHONY D'AMATO, written for this Anthology.

has gone through law school and has been steeped in, and socialized in, the law school curriculum. Many leading government officials, including many Senators, many Congresspersons, and most of our recent Presidents, have been socialized by law school education. Many of these people never even took a course in international law. As lawyers they tend to be conservative about the content of law—and by conservative I mean, here, that they don't refer to and don't apply anything that is unfamiliar to them. If international law is unfamiliar to them by virtue of the fact that they never took a course in the subject—and also by the disparaging remarks of professors in the so-called "hard" subjects—then naturally they are not going to be overwhelmed when someone like Professor Francis Boyle refers to international law in an argument in court.[56] The situation is, of course, different outside the United States. There, the judges and politicians have been trained in law schools where international law was an ordinary required course. As a result, they feel comfortable about applying its norms in cases and situations that come to their attention.

But I've said enough about psychology and perceptions. People see these things in different ways, and they are entitled to their own opinions. Let me talk instead about the cure that Professor Trimble proposes.

It is a cure that is vastly worse than the disease. In fact, it ends up reducing "international law" to vacuity. The following is the structure of Professor Trimble's argument:

> 1. The norms of international law have no independent force that they exert on decisions in American courts. They are not real norms of law.
>
> 2. When an American court in its discretion adopts an international law norm as a rule of decision in a case, then and only then does the norm become a rule of binding, enforceable law.
>
> 3. The norm of international law thus adopted acquires binding force not because it was originally part of international law, but because it has become part of American law by virtue of its adoption by a court.

Note that Professor Trimble could say exactly the same thing about lines from Shakespeare. The lines in Shakespeare's plays have no binding force in American legal decision-making. However, from time to time, judges quote some of them and weave them into their decisions. At that point, the immortal lines become part of the fabric of binding, enforceable American law. Shakespeare himself was not a source of law in the sense of writing lines that automatically became binding in American courts; rather, the only legal power in the United States that Shakespeare's lines can ever attain comes from their adoption, only if and when they are specifically adopted from time to time, by American judges.

It follows that we should not assume that we can predict what American courts will do by reading Shakespeare's plays. Similarly, Professor Trimble in effect is saying that we should not assume that we can predict what American courts will do in international cases by researching international law. The only "international law" that counts is that which has been transformed into American law by the discretionary powers of a court. Everything else that is part of external international law is just a bunch of prose waiting around to be adopted or rejected at the whim of a judge.

Professor Trimble is aware of the kind of argument I have just made. In his essay he acknowledges the contention that domesticating international law destroys the value of the enterprise. His answer is that it's not entirely destroyed. There's a little left. External international norms appear to have some sort of impact from time to time upon official behavior that could be interesting to comparative anthropologists or sociologists. But once having mentioned this will-o'-the-wisp behavioral impact, Professor Trimble hastily supplies us with a conclusion lest we evaluate the argument for ourselves. He concludes that "under my domestic law approach, the international law enterprise remains as important as ever." Really? "As important as ever"? It's like a judge saying to a defendant whom he has just sentenced to ten consecutive prison terms of 150 years each, "Believe it or not, your sad story really did have an important impact in my decision to mitigate the length of your sentence."

There is nothing *at all* important, from a legal point of view, about an "enterprise" that consists of a collection of rejectable prose—prose that's intrinsically a lot less interesting to read than Shakespeare. There may be something important from an anthropological or sociological point of view, helping us to find interesting regularities in the behavior of government officials (that we probably would just as easily have found if we didn't know about the norms in the first place.) But I presume that Professor Trimble wants to tell us something about the legal enter-

[56] Actually, the surprising thing is that it sometimes works quite the other way. Professor Boyle and I worked on a case where a number of Afro-Americans picketed the South African embassy in Chicago. We testified as experts on international law in court. The judge and jury actually seemed impressed—after all, this was an "international" case, wasn't it (it involved South Africa)? So obviously "international law" seemed quite relevant. Moreover, it seemed that the prosecutors knew practically nothing about it and didn't care, so Francis Boyle and I had pretty much an unobstructed time of it. (I must say that Francis did most of the testifying, and he did it extremely well.) The judge instructed the jury that the trespassing of the embassy was illegal under Illinois law. The facts of the trespass were not contested. The jury acquitted everyone.

What would Professor Trimble have done? Would he have argued that the norms of international law are "domesticated" in the Illinois trespass statute? I think that would have been frivolous on its face; the trespass statute is a purely local regulation. Would he have simply quit and gone home? Attorneys can't do that when their clients are facing fines and possible jail sentences. Francis Boyle and I argued that international law is part of our law (The Paquete Habana case, etc.) and that it simply overrides the local trespass statute. The prosecutors argued that nothing overrides the local trespass statute. And so there were two sides to the argument, and the jury made the final decision.

prise and not about the sociological or anthropological enterprise.

If that is what he is doing, let's assume further that the factor of importance has nothing to do with the case. If Professor Trimble has reduced international law to zero by making it entirely discretionary among states – by "domesticating" it – maybe it deserves to be reduced to zero. Let's examine whether the proposition is correct that international law does not exist outside of a state's specific, discretionary incorporation of its norms.

Our inquiry begins with a glitch in Professor Trimble's nimble assertion that under his approach "public international law resembles private international law, where each state has its own set of choice-of-law rules." Choice-of-law problems, of course, come up all the time in international business transactions. But a choice-of-law rule isn't easily characterized as each nation's "own." To illustrate, occasionally I get a phone call from a lawyer who is immersed in a complex choice-of-law question and is trying to get information on which choice-of-law rule applies – the law of the forum state or the law of the transaction state. The rules of both states are vague and seem to incorporate each other in a sort of infinite regress.[57] Now, if you want to be technical about it, you would say that of course the choice of law rule of the forum state applies, because that's the rule of the forum. That seems to be what Professor Trimble is saying when he says that "each state has its own set of choice of law rules." But it's a tautology that gets us nowhere. In fact, under the notion that all we have is a choice between the choice-of-law rule of the forum state and that of the transaction state, we are caught between a regress and a tautology.

What I usually advise over the telephone is that the attorney consult a third alternative – international law. "International law?" the attorney might typically say, "what's that got to do with it?" Well, I say, your forum state choice-of-law rule and your transaction state choice-of-law rule seem to be contradicting each other. International law is the neutral body of law that acts as a default rule in the case of conflict between two apparently equally authoritative rules of the forum state and the transaction state.

But *why* does international law act as the default rule? Is it because the forum state's law *incorporates* the international choice-of-law rule? I suspect Professor Trimble might say that, but it's a highly attenuated and technical position. We often don't have the vaguest idea whether the forum state has actually incorporated the international choice-of-law default rule (though there may be a slight psychological advantage in arguing that it has incorporated it). The fact is – after the exhaustive research that often goes into these questions because of the amount of money involved in the dispute – that no one can figure out whether the law of the forum state has incorporated the international law default rule. (Adding to the difficulty is the frequently invoked "against the policy of the forum" argument that, in my view, is just another surrogate for bringing in the international law default rule.) The advantage of the international choice-of-law rule is that it has been worked out over time by customary law (including the customary practice of the forum and transaction states and many other states as well) and thus has a lot going for it as a dispute resolution mechanism. With the proper argumentative preparation, a lawyer well versed in international law has a reasonable chance of convincing a judge to use the international choice-of-law default rule just because it is an independent, neutral rule that governs these otherwise intractable choice-of-law cases.

To be sure, you still have to convince the forum state judge to use the international norm. International law doesn't descend on us out of the blue, grab us and shake us, and tell us to obey its directives. International law is always a matter of persuasion. There's always a decision-maker, whether a government official, a judge, or just the other side's lawyer at the end of a bargaining table, who needs to be convinced that the governing rule of international law is such-and-such. My example from the preceding paragraph about convincing the forum state judge to apply the international law rule does not support Professor Trimble's thesis that international law rules exist only when they are incorporated into the decisions of the forum state. What *would* support Professor Trimble's position would be an argument to the judge that the rule of decision of the forum state already incorporates the international rule, and therefore should be applied. But that argument only works if in fact the international rule is already present in judicial precedent in the forum state. By hypothesis, it is not already present in any discernible form, and hence the Trimble Theory doesn't work here. The theory I would suggest is quite different: the judge should apply the international choice of law rule when there is no clear precedent on the books just because it is the default rule that is applicable to inter-state conflicts in such situations.

If we extend this example, we see the fatal flaw in Professor Trimble's entire argument. He would restrict an American lawyer (his own students when they become lawyers, for example) to arguing that any rule of international law applicable to a dispute must *already* have been incorporated into American law in a previous decision. Otherwise, the rule would not be part of domestic law at all. Therefore, when a lawyer follows Professor Trimble's advice, she is restricted to those rules of "international" law that in prior cases have become rules of American decisional law. She is otherwise disabled from arguing that the court should, as an original matter, pluck a norm out of the corpus of international law and insert it into the present case as the rule of decision. For if she makes such an argument, opposing counsel will cite Professor Trimble to the effect that the judge would not be following *law* at all in plucking out

[57] Not to mention the governing contract – and there usually is such a document – that specifies which law to apply. The question is how to interpret that clause in the contract and to what sorts of contractual problems it applies – a difficult task when the contract bargain is disrupted by, for example, the governmental action of the transaction state.

an external international norm and applying it to the case at hand; rather, the judge would be exercising unfettered discretion. The judge might as well cite a norm from *The Merchant of Venice.* Such unfettered discretion is inimical to the judicial enterprise, which relies for its authority on the application of real norms and not Shakespearean norms.

In short, if there's an international norm out there that can win a case for you, and that norm hasn't already been incorporated into an American case, Professor Trimble's thesis will not help you in winning the case for your client. The only way you can win a case where an international norm exists that hasn't already been incorporated into American case law is to reject Professor Trimble's thesis, and argue to the judge that international law is a body of norms that apply to all states when questions arise involving transboundary persons or events. And, you add, the United States is not alone here. All states, with varying degrees of specificity, have incorporated those international norms into their domestic law. With specific regard to the United States, its Supreme Court held in The Paquete Habana that

> international law is part of our law, and must be ascertained and administered by the courts of justice of appropriate jurisdiction, as often as questions of right depending upon it are duly presented for their determination.[58]

The Federal Republic of Germany is even more explicit about international law. Its Constitution provides, in Article 25:

> The general rules of public international law are an integral part of federal law. They shall take precedence over the laws and shall directly create rights and duties for the inhabitants of the federal territory.

Again, Professor Trimble might say that these citations just prove his point: that international law exists only to the extent that each state has or has not domesticated it, and The Paquete Habana and the German Constitution are examples of specific domestication, in different degrees, of international norms. And again my reply is that his point is technical and attenuated. For we must ask *why* and *under what authority* did the U.S. Supreme Court in The Paquete Habana hold that international law is part of our law. Was this simply an act of legislation by the Supreme Court? Or did it reflect a reality that was built up over years of jurisprudence led by Justice Marshall in applying international norms directly to the solution of numerous American controversies?

But let me put the point logically instead of historically. As a logical matter, Professor Trimble's thesis is a nonstarter. There is no international norm that can ever be correctly applied for the first time in any domestic case. The first time any court tries to apply the international norm, Professor Trimble's thesis can be cited to the effect that the norm is not already a rule of law because it hasn't been adopted by a previous court, and thus the norm must be rejected.

Professor Trimble's thesis leaves us in a most curious position. There is no external international law, he says, because it is not "law" until it is incorporated as the rule of decision in a domestic-law case. But there can be no internal international law either, because no court is warranted in taking a non-norm and making a norm out of it. Courts should apply the law, not make it up.

Yet I can hear in the back of my mind Professor Trimble accusing me of being an anti-realist. Of course courts make up law, he might say. They invent law all the time. The international norms that exist in domestic American law were all plucked out of the air at some time or other and converted by the brute force of judicial decision-making into good old solid American law.

Fine – I'll concede that argument as well. Courts make up law. They pluck norms out of international law books, out of Shakespeare's plays, out of Milton's *Paradise Lost*, out of Amy Vanderbilt's Book of Etiquette, and from lots of other places, and force them down the throats of unwilling litigants who are on the verge of losing. But then why *call* these norms "international" or "Shakespearean" or "Miltonian"? They're nothing more than ordinary common-law norms dressed in cultural costumes. For instance, what happens when Shakespeare is misquoted and the misquote becomes law? What happens when international law is misinterpreted, and that becomes law? To be consistent, Professor Trimble would have to say that the misquote and the misinterpretation are the "real" law. But then he's in a logical dilemma, because if he calls this "real" law Shakespearean or "international," he perpetuates the misquote and the misinterpretation! He disables us from going back to the original source and checking it out. But then, why *call* a norm "Shakespearean" when Shakespeare never said it, and why *call* a norm "international" if international law never knew of such a norm? Professor Trimble cannot even *care* whether an American court gets the international norm right or gets it wrong, because there is no room in his theory about getting it right – there's simply nothing out there to get. "International law" for him becomes real only at the moment of its transformation into American decisional law. But at that very moment it vanishes. It is no longer "international law" except in an arcane, academic, nominalistic, sociological sort of way. It is just simply a norm that may have originated once in some sentence in some book entitled "international law," or was a misreading of some sentence in such a book, or was an accurate reading of a sentence in a book that itself was a misinterpretation of international law.

Why does Professor Trimble insist upon such a vacuous thesis and believe, moreover, that it constitutes the very path to the salvation of international law as we know it? Like Professor Chayes, Professor Trimble did not concentrate on the study of international law as a law-school student or in graduate courses. Rather, both Professors Chayes and Trimble, subsequent to law school, had distinguished careers as high U.S. government officials in the

[58] The Paquete Habana, 175 U.S. 677, 700 (1900).

field of international relations and law. They then turned to the teaching of international law at the law-school level. As a result they both have, I think, a very "American" view of international law. An "American" view is not simply a nationalistic view (every country is more or less nationalistic in its view of international law), but it is the view of a huge superpower. The United States pretty much gets its way on the international scene; many people have called it the biggest bully on the block. When the United States acts stupidly in the international-law arena (and the litany of U.S. stupidities is writ plain for all to see in the editorial pages of journals such as the American Journal of International Law), the fact is that the public really doesn't notice it. If a little country makes an international law mistake, political heads roll. Some other country might even send over a bomb. But in the United States, international law errors are business as usual. We make some good decisions and some bad ones, and very few people either care about the bad ones or take the trouble to distinguish the bad from the good. We have become rather immune from bad-law feedback, which rolls off our national back like water off a duck.

An enormous, dull complacency sets in. American courts make all kinds of international-law decisions, often absurd ones, yet no one pays a price. There is no "market mechanism" that brings home the stupidity of some of our decisions. As a result, some American observers can conclude that "international law" doesn't exist, because if it did, we'd hear about it when we violated it. International law, to some American observers, is like the question "Where does an elephant sit?"; the answer of course is "Anywhere it wants to." No matter what our courts, and no matter even what our government officials, do about international law, the fact is that we are so big a country, and the television-blitzed public is so unaware of international law, that any semblance of international accountability is buried in the lower left hand corner of page 17 of the New York Times on one day and then never referred to again.

But to say that feedback is unnoticed is not the same thing as saying it doesn't exist. The United States does pay a price every time it violates international law, and if there were a genuine international market mechanism, I suggest that the price we pay in just about every case would exceed the benefit to us of the violation. If the United States were a private corporation, some corporation executive in charge of making the illegal decision would probably get fired. But the United States is a huge, sluggish political mechanism, and a governmental official has to do something gigantically stupid on the international scene before a question is even raised politically about his or her judgment. Was anyone in the United States Department of State blamed for wrongly deciding, in Lisbon in early 1992, to encourage the Muslim leadership to reverse itself and disavow the partition plan for Bosnia-Herzegovina the Muslims had already signed along with the Serbs and Croats? No. Yet seventeen months later, and over 150,000 dead people later, and tens of thousands of rapes later, and millions of displaced persons later, and the Muslims considerably worse off, a similar partition plan was accepted by the Serbs, Croats and United States. Nothing changed in the plan itself except that now it was *less* favorable to the Muslims. Was Warren Zimmerman, the U.S. State Department official primarily responsible for torpedoing the Lisbon plan in 1992, reprimanded for a disastrous decision leading to the loss of hundreds of thousands of lives? Warren Zimmerman? Who's he? If he were a serial killer in the United States, with fifteen murders to his credit, his name would be a household word.

Let me conclude with a concrete example of what, if a market mechanism were working, would be a disproportionate financial loss for the United States that resulted from a series of disastrously stupid international-law decisions. I refer to the abduction of Dr. Alvarez from Mexico. The facts of this case, and essays by Professor Malvina Halberstam and me, appear in an earlier chapter in this Anthology.[59] To recall that situation briefly, American officials bribed some Mexicans to abduct Dr. Alvarez from Mexico. At his trial, Dr. Alvarez pleaded a violation of the U.S.-Mexico Extradition Treaty, but eventually the Supreme Court held that the defense of treaty-violation was not open to him. Now, under Professor Trimble's theory, that's the end of the tale. The United States Supreme Court said that the treaty was not violated, and therefore the treaty was not violated. The highest authoritative interpreter of American law says the treaty was not violated, and hence there is nothing more to say unless you want to talk about the external "international law of treaty violation."[60] But that kind of talk counts for nothing, because it involves norms that are not be part of real "international law" as domesticated by the Supreme Court.

I think it is fair to criticize Professor Trimble on the basis of the Alvarez case, because he concedes that *treaties* are part of the law of the United States even though he thinks that international customary law is not part of the law of the United States. So I am using his strongest example—treaties—against him.

Must someone who rejects Professor Trimble's "domestication" theory also conclude that the U.S.-Mexico Extradition Treaty was not violated? Certainly not. As an individual, a commentator on international law, and someone who happens to be writing these words, I do not feel bound by the United States Supreme Court's view of the Extradition Treaty. I have not committed myself to the proposition that whatever a U.S. court says about interna-

---

59 *See* Chapter 8 "International Criminal Law" at the section on "Abduction."

60 Perhaps Professor Trimble would say that the internal law of Mexico might have a different view of the Alvarez matter. But that surely makes no difference, because Dr. Alvarez's case did not arise in Mexico, and no Mexican court had an opportunity to look at the facts and examine whether the treaty was violated. So, whether Mexico's internal law disagrees with the United States' view, or not, is a question that has not come up.

tional law constitutes the entire truth of the matter. Rather, I believe I can exercise a wholly independent judgment on the matter. And, looking at the Alvarez case, I can say that, without question, the treaty was violated. I say this because, unlike the U.S. Supreme Court, I look at extradition treaties in the context of customary international law, including the customary international law of the interpretation of treaties. That body of international law tells me that a treaty that specifies definite procedures for the international extradition of a national of one country to the courts of another country, for a crime committed in the national's own country, clearly excludes by implication any officially sponsored abduction. The U.S. officials who arranged for the abduction of Dr. Alvarez were acting in clear violation of the negative implication of the Extradition Treaty – a negative implication that is written plainly in international law. It is written in the international law of treaty interpretation which says that treaties ought to be given full effect in light of their purposes, and not dissected and deconstructed to serve the special (and in this case preposterous) interests of one of the parties. As the dissenters in the Supreme Court said, it is hard to imagine why there would be an extradition treaty at all if the parties could get around it by forceful abductions whenever they felt so inclined.

Now, my interpretation of the Extradition Treaty is the same interpretation of the international community as a whole. Nearly every state which commented on the matter supported Mexico's view that the treaty was violated. Nearly all states with which the United States has extradition treaties now are asking for revisions to exclude kidnappings and abductions – revisions that they thought were unnecessary, revisions that they thought were understood by good-faith interpretation, but revisions that they now have to demand due to the absurd decision by the U.S. Supreme Court.

In short, we are beginning to see the costs involved in the aftermath of the Supreme Court's decision. We may have to revise numerous bilateral extradition treaties. Our treaty partners will view us, and our Supreme Court, with suspicion. The immediate party to the case, Dr. Alvarez, went back to Mexico unscathed, where he is contemplating a multi-million dollar tort claim against the United States. The U.S. government squandered millions of dollars in taxpayers' money paying witnesses to appear in court against Dr. Alvarez, not to mention all the lawyers on the U.S. payroll who were employed in briefing and arguing the case as it went up the federal system to the Supreme Court.

The most important cost has been charged by Mexico. It has exacted stiff concessions from the United States in the NAFTA negotiations by complaining about the U.S. insult to Mexico in abducting one of its nationals and then having the highest court in the United States say it was O.K. to do so.[61] The government of the U.S. has had to promise to Mexico that there will be no more abductions. From now on, Mexico has good reason to distrust any interpretation of any agreement with the United States that is presented to the U.S. Supreme Court for interpretation. Mexico has good reason to distrust the Supreme Court itself.

Finally, consider the costs to the United States if someday a U.S. citizen is abducted from this country and tried abroad in the court of country X with which we have an extradition treaty. Will the U.S. public stand for it, or will people appear on television saying we should "nuke" the country X for doing such a thing? What will the U.S. government say? Will it try to hide the Supreme Court's interpretation of an extradition treaty in a similar situation in the Alvarez case? Of course, the media will cite the Alverez decision, and then the U.S. government will be in a bind. The government might then say, "Guess what, folks, the U.S. Supreme Court blew it. And so did we, because our own lawyers asked the Supreme Court to do what it did. So now we admit our mistake, and we disavow the Supreme Court result, and country X had better return our citizen pronto." Even if the U.S. government says and does all these things, the one thing it cannot do is get solace from Professor Trimble's theory, because his theory disables the government from arguing that the Supreme Court's interpretation of the treaty is wrong. In Professor Trimble's theory of "domestication," there was no right or wrong answer until the Supreme Court told us what the Treaty said about abductions. And, once the Court told us what the treaty said, that is what the "real" international law of the matter is. Anything any other country says – or even anything our own government might say in the event that an American citizen is abducted – is just irrelevant.

Professor Trimble wants to save international law by domesticating it. I can say from knowing him that he truly is a friend of international law. But, in the spirit of academic debate, I cannot resist concluding that if international law has friends like that, who needs enemies?

3. Affirmative Reply[62]

Professor D'Amato is correct to emphasize the pervasive importance of the law school curriculum in shaping beliefs and instincts of judges, officials and other practitioners of our profession. He is also correct to lament the inattention to international law in the curriculum. However, we disagree sharply on how to get proper respect for international law in the curriculum. Those differences in turn reflect our fundamentally different theoretical approaches to explaining international law. Professor D'Amato insists on projecting the discipline as a single, independent system

[61] I have been informed of this fact informally by a leading U.S. NAFTA negotiator.

[62] By PHILLIP R. TRIMBLE, written for this Anthology.

of law. I prefer to think of it as a collection of 150 or so separate, although largely congruent, systems. Professor D'Amato would presumably encourage or require all law students to study international law, as in European universities. Then the students would learn it first hand and would think of it like other subjects. Unfortunately the way the subject is now taught would probably have the opposite effect, since the course usually focuses on matters that are well removed from what students for the most part come to law school to do, viz., learn to practice a profession. My preferred alternative is to integrate the relevant aspects of international law into the mainstream curriculum (at least until that curriculum is fundamentally reformed). Thus when a student studies contracts, procedure, torts, securities regulation, antitrust, etc., she would learn the relevant international law and practice, and come to think like an international lawyer in all the contexts that students are faced with in their studies and eventually their practice.

My approach to curricular reform reflects my broader theoretical approach to international law, namely, to domesticate it. It is therefore not surprising that Professor D'Amato and I should differ on curricular reform, just as we differ on basic theory. In response to his comment above, I would first emphasize that I do not believe that international law is unimportant or unreal. It certainly exists and is becoming more, not less, important. For the most part it is not, however, independent and enforceable, apart from its roots in domestic political cultures. There is no international court with general, compulsory jurisdiction, no general legislative body, no universal monarch, and no international executive or administrative body with power to compel behavior through sanctions. Yet, of course, international law is made and obeyed, and sanctions (unilateral) are imposed. International law is largely self-enforcing, but is nonetheless important and real primarily because of its roots in domestic political cultures. From those roots it derives legitimacy and therefore enforcement.

Professor D'Amato's summary of my approach is incorrect, but more importantly it is seriously incomplete. I think, indeed I know, that international norms have an independent existence, like statutes. They are of course formed through different procedures, but they exist independently of ordinary judicial action, and they are sometimes (especially treaties) applied as a rule of decision or otherwise by a court. No one doubts that. The comparison with Shakespeare is fatuous because treaties and customary norms, unlike poetry, are created in a generally recognized law-making process. But more importantly my colleague's preoccupation with judicial decisions (all three summary points refer to judicial decisions as the exclusive source of law) yields a vastly incomplete picture. International law norms exist independently of judicial decisions, and are regularly observed independently of court order. Most international law is accepted and applied by officials in the executive branch of government, administrative agencies, and even Congress. The reason is that those norms, especially treaty norms, have political legitimacy. Treaties are blessed by the Senate, or Congress, and the President. They have more than "some sort of impact." They are regularly observed—because officials know treaty obligations are law, because the norms are reflected in executive regulations and administrative practice, and in all the other ways in which law influences behavior.

My point—that international law can be international in formation and domestic in implementation—is not controversial, even in the old-guard international law establishment. Looking at the law from a domestic perspective admittedly opens the way for each country to decide what law it will follow and seemingly opens the door for legitimate violations. Professor D'Amato says I make it "entirely discretionary among states." Of course states decide what treaties to join, and what customary norms to reject. Indeed, as Professor D'Amato has pointed out, that is how customary law changes. The more important inquiry is to examine compliance. That is the more normal practice, and is attributable to the political foundation of law's formation. In the United States treaties are taken seriously because the Constitution says so, because democratic law-making institutions endorse them, and there are sanctions (mostly non-judicial) for violating them.

Customary law is more difficult to defend, in large part because it often lacks formation in a traditionally recognizable law-making process. The Executive branch declares U.S. positions on customary international law, but the President is not usually thought of as a law-maker. The courts do not normally apply customary international law, notwithstanding the oft-quoted dictum of the Paquete Habana case.[63] The basic problem is weak political legitimacy. The Alvarez case illustrates my point.

I agree with Professor D'Amato that the abduction of the defendant was a violation of international law—the customary norm that prohibits extraterritorial law enforcement. However, the extradition treaty was not violated. The violation was of customary international law. Customary norms prohibit law enforcement activity, like an arrest, in another state's territory without its consent. Because of this fundamental rule of customary law, and because of the obvious need for law enforcement, extradition treaties are concluded in order to provide a consent-based procedure for law enforcement. The treaty does not prohibit general extraterritorial enforcement; it assumes such enforcement is prohibited. So technically the treaty was not

63 The story and an explanation can be found in my article, *A Revisionist View of Customary International Law*, 33 U.C.L.A. Law Rev. 665 (1986).

violated. This may seem a quibble about some niceties of international law, but the difference between treaties and customary law in America's jurisprudence is fundamental. Courts apply treaties; they do not apply customary law absent a signal from Congress or the President (as in the *Filartiga* case) that the political branches want the courts to do so.

Moreover, the courts defer to the political branches on issues raising foreign policy concerns. Violation of international law is such a concern. The courts have recognized that sometimes the United States may need to violate an international rule, just as a person may decide to breach a contract or drive negligently. The courts have permitted the President (and Congress) to do that, and, as Professor D'Amato points out, they are now taking the consequence. The courts have, so far as I know, never applied customary international law against an act of Congress or the President (at least in modern times). The reason lies in its lack of domestic political roots. A treaty at least has the political endorsement of the Senate, or Congress, and the President. Customary norms do not have such a secure base, often only having a Presidential declaration of their validity and, in cases like Alvarez, having the opposite of domestic political support. Paying attention to the domestic foundation of international law, as the Alvarez Case demonstrates, is crucial to understanding the role of international law in the real world.

17
The Future of International Law

Prediction is hard, but the hardest thing of all to predict is the future.

—Richard Falk

A. The Dysfunctional State[1]

What are the contemporary realities? To what extent are rising demands for protection and fulfillment satisfied? A cursory look at daily events around the world shows that deprivations and nonfulfillments continue to characterize the value-institutional processes of vast segments of the world's population. Though the nature, scope, and magnitude of the values at stake may differ from one community to another, the deprivations and nonfulfillments extend to every value sector.

Examples are dramatic. The demand for freedom of choice, for equality and for personal autonomy meets with persistent discrimination on such invidious grounds as race, sex, religion, and political opinion, massive invasion of the civic domain of personal autonomy, and the practice of apartheid. The demand to share power meets with the persistence of totalitarian regimes, politicide, one-party rule and military dictatorships, martial "law," arbitrary arrest, detention, censure, imprisonment, and torture in many police states; restrictions on emigration and immigrations; mass and collective expulsion of aliens. The search for enlightenment encounters suppression of political dissent, widespread censorship by official elites, inadequate education for children, and systematic indoctrination as an instrument of policy. The search for well-being is blunted by overpopulation, hunger and starvation, and deprivations of life because of war, oppression, revolution, terrorist activities, ecocide, and developing nations and the widening gap between rich and poor. The risk of nationalization without adequate compensation discourages the investment of private resources in local development. The demand for skill development must cope with consequences of skill obsolescence due to technological advances, the brain drain, unemployment, and underemployment. Pursuit of congenial personal relationships meets with prohibition of interracial and interreligious marriages, homelessness for millions of refugees and street people, and mutual suspicion and fear generated by networks of secret police and informers. Longings for a moral integrity meet with denial of freedom of worship, intolerance and persecution of religious minorities, and warfare involving religious fanatics.

Confronted with the unprecedented challenges of our planetary eco-system, the institutions and practices of humankind appear to be inadequate. Geographically, these value institutions and practices are too state-centered. Functionally, they are too tradition-bound to make timely responses and adjustments to the accelerated change, both in pace and dimension, as generated by the universalization of science and technology and the ever intensifying global interdependence. The problems in the contemporary world are global in nature and scale, yet the basic organizational framework to deal with them continues to rest on the problem-solving capacities of separate and highly unequal states and thus remains essentially partial and fragmentary. The ascendancy of the nation-state has been such that the search for common interest is more often than not distorted by the inordinate emphasis on national "sovereignty."

B. The Rhetoric of Expectation[2]

The early rhetoric of opportunity in the United States was country-building rhetoric, useful for luring the adventurous and the ambitious and for encouraging prodigious effort once they immigrated here. The New Deal iteration offered crucial reassurance—even when the bottom fell out

[1] By LUNG-CHU CHEN, excerpted from: AN INTRODUCTION TO CONTEMPORARY INTERNATIONAL LAW: A POLICY-ORIENTED PERSPECTIVE 441 (New Haven: Yale University Press, 1989). Reprinted by permission.

[2] By BARBARA STARK, excerpted from: *Postmodern Rhetoric, Economic Rights and an International Text: "A Miracle for Breakfast,"* 33 VIRGINIA JOURNAL OF INTERNATIONAL LAW 433, 458–59, 464–65 (1993). Reprinted by permission.

during the Great Depression, the state would make sure that everyone had a chance to get back to work and opportunity came again.

The previous iterations of the rhetoric of opportunity are no longer credible in the 1990s. We know that "opportunity" in apparently inexhaustible abundance will not come again to this planet. At the recent Earth Summit in Rio de Janeiro, the countries of the developing South as well as the developed North rejected the rhetoric of unlimited growth in favor of the rhetoric of "sustainable development."[3] It has been globally acknowledged that human needs must be met in a closed ecosystem. "Opportunity" can no longer be predicated on endless expansion.

Even as we enter an era of unprecedented internationalism, paradoxically, we increasingly seek particular, contextualized solutions to the problems of homelessness, hunger, unemployment, and poverty. The International Covenant on Economic, Social and Cultural Rights is an international text intended for local application. It requires those who adopt it to enter into it, as we enter into a poem, to contextualize it and make it their own. Article 11, for example, requires states to "recognize the right of everyone to an adequate standard of living for himself and his family, including adequate food, clothing and shelter, and to the continuous improvement of living conditions." What kind of food, clothing and shelter–and how much–is adequate? This obviously requires a series of complex, fact-specific determinations. The Economic Covenant could enable us to generate more coherent iterations of the rhetoric of opportunity, iterations that retain the rhetoric's vibrancy but channel it to meet the specific needs of diverse communities.

C. International Consciousness[4]

It is a speculation of the most profound human interest to consider what the human world would have become if international society had joined in the revolutionary development of national societies, if international society had had its 1789 or its 1917. It is a speculation which is not merely of intellectual and historical interest. It is actual and urgent.

Instead, what occurred was the misconceiving of international society as a system of closed sovereignties, externalized state-systems, undemocratized and unsocialized. This misconception spread throughout the world. As nations and peoples sought to establish themselves as social selves in their own right, to liberate themselves from what they regarded as alien state-systems, to actualize their self-determination in place of their other-determination, their aspiration to freedom and independence interacted with their need to establish a new social order. The theory of a naturally free, naturally equal, naturally sovereign statal society, whose external existence could be closely controlled in a world of other statal societies, seemed to be an excellent way to actualize the ideal of independence and to meet the need for a new internal order. And, like the ruling classes who had led the way along the same path, the ruling classes of the so-called new states also welcomed a theory which could give such a convincing supersocializing explanation of their own personal power.

Misconceived international society became, as national societies had at one stage of their development, a world sovereignty-state-system, a world fit for governments. It is an unsociety ruled by a collective of self-conceived sovereigns whose authority is derived neither from the totality of international society nor from the people but from the intermediating state-systems. International society has condemned itself either to stagnate in such a condition or to live again the experience of national societies in which the evolving statally organizing societies discovered, painfully, the dangers of their evolving sovereignty-systems, and discovered, painfully, how to redeem themselves in the name of democracy and justice.

The people of the world are not in a position to make an international revolution. Overwhelmed by the power of governments and their bureaucratic battalions, they have, in many cases, little enough hope of redeeming their own state-society in the name of democracy and justice. They know little enough of its constitution, its systems, its possibilities. They know too little of the social struggle at the level of the total social process, too much of the struggle of their own daily living. The idea of a misconceived international society is an idea formed in and for the reality of the ruling-classes of their state-societies.

But it is more than an interesting thought-experiment to consider how the people of the world would conceive of the human world if they could express their anguish and their aspirations. We may speak hypothetically for the people of the world who cannot speak for themselves. What follows is speculation. The speculation is that the people of the world, however cautiously and however tentatively, see in international society dangers that they, and their

---

[3] *But see* Martii Koskenniemi, *The Future of Statehood,* 32 HARV. INT'L L.J. 397, 403 (1991): "The official ideology of [the Earth Summit] compels diplomats to speak of environmental and developmental goals as if there were no essential conflict between them, by defining one in terms of the other. Poverty is pollution; environmental quality is an aspect of the standard of living. Such harmony is soon dispelled when concrete action is debated."

[4] By PHILIP ALLOTT, excerpted from: EUNOMIA: NEW ORDER FOR A NEW WORLD 249–53, 292–95 (N.Y.: Oxford Univ. Press, 1990). Reprinted by permission.

predecessors over the centuries, see and have seen in state-societies. Specifically, they see: (1) alienation – the alienation of humanity from itself; (2) corruption – the corruption, in particular, of an unsocialized international economy; and (3) tyranny – the tyranny of physical insecurity.

(1) *Alienation.* The people of the world understand the need for social organization, even for the remarkable energy-generating and energy-organizing capacity of the state-society. But the people of the world also know and respect and love the natural societies into which they are born and the societies which they make for themselves, societies whose limits frequently do not coincide with the limits of state-societies.

What they do not understand is their enforced alienation from each other, the surrender of their natural affections and natural loyalties, their subjection to state-societies which require that they treat other human beings as other, merely because they are subject to another state-system. The people of the world meet as friends in countless world-wide human activities but meet only as fellow-aliens in international society as presently conceived.

The people of the world feel a loving sympathy with their fellow human beings in their individuality, in their family-life, in all the striving of their personal lives. And they feel a loving sympathy with their follow human beings in all their suffering, the suffering at the hands of social power and of natural forces. And they feel their love distorted by an international system which demands from them perverted ideas and values, other forms of loyalty.

The peoples of the world are presented externally by their state-systems and by the governments which speak for them. But the idea and the ideal of democracy has evolved and the people have matured with it. They demand not merely to be represented but to participate in the willing and acting which is the willing and acting of their lives, their survival and prospering, their well-being.

(2) *Corruption.* As in the early days of statally organizing national societies, the most basic human social activity is alien to the system of international society as presently conceived. The world is a scene of economic activity of amazing energy, full of dynamic forces which are transforming the face of the earth and the lives of all the people of the world. And yet it is only the regulatory side of the international economy which is integrated into the international system. All the productive activity of farmers and manufacturers and traders, all agriculture and industry and commerce, is conducted on the periphery, in the interstices of an international system whose real business is conceived as being diplomacy and war.

Not integrated into the state-system of international society, the productive aspect of the international economy presents itself as a sort of natural world, an environment, in which nonsocialized forces produce natural effects. The supersocialization of the international economy is a supernaturalization. The consequence is that the people of the world feel locked into a natural system of unequal development. It is an unsocialized system in which natural energy seems to remain natural, not transformed into social power performing a social function. It is accordingly a system in which social justice is achieved, if at all, by good fortune rather than by good choosing.

The potentiality of the international economy has no known limits – a potentiality for good and for harm. The people of the world feel that the system, for all its remarkable achievements, is not making full use of its potentiality to generate human well-being and yet is imposing substantial burdens and costs on the physical world of the planet and on the moral world of humanity, burdens and costs which are growing rapidly but are beyond measurement and beyond control in the absence of systematic willing and acting by international society in the interest of the whole human race, including the interest of human beings yet to be born.

(c) *Tyranny.* The amoralization of international society has meant that so-called national interest may, one day, require the destruction of humanity itself. In other words, the self-conceiving international society leaves the possibility, and may even require, that one state-society or a collection of state-societies destroy not only their own men, women, and children by the million but also men, women, and children over wider and wider areas of the world, may even threaten the lives of all men, women and children everywhere. A society which conceives its survival as depending on threats of self-destruction is a society which misconceives its nature as a society. A society which conceives its own self-destruction among the possibilities which it might choose is a society which misconceives its potentiality as a society.

The people of the world live in a present-here-and-now in which they are obliged to see the future of humanity, its possibilities, in terms of these self-inflicted aberrations. An extraordinary effort of self-transcending is required from humanity, if it is to change the words and ideas and theories and values which are the reality-for-itself of a self-misconceiving international society.

In the twentieth century, and especially in the latter half of the twentieth century, it has begun to seem that the exclusive reality-forming of state-societies cannot be maintained for much longer. Governments are losing control of the minds of the citizens.

Through the international economy, through the mass-media of communication, and through travel, social reality now floods through the world's consciousness like the weather-systems of the earth's atmosphere. World social reality is a world climate, ultimately beyond the control of governments. Words and ideas and theories and values move round the world and make their way into human consciousness through a thousand unofficial channels. More and more, the people of the world are singing the same song. And it is a song that they have not learned at their mother's knee or in the classroom. Imagination and reason, the common inheritance of all human beings, are generating a common experience of all human beings, an international consciousness.

It is a consciousness which is acquiring distinctive features. It perceives the world as a unified environment, the shared arena of all human willing and acting, and an arena shared with all other living things. It perceives the humanity of human beings everywhere, responding with spontaneous human feelings to the experience of other human beings which it can recognize and understand, recognizing also wants and needs – physical, psychological, spiritual – shared by all human beings everywhere. It is beginning to conceive of standards, purposes, ideals which transcend the ideas of any particular society, but which are an amplification and an completion of the ideas which are the foundation of familiar, everyday values.

It is too soon to predict with any reasonable degree of assurance the consequences for the ordering of international society of the internationalization of human consciousness. It is possible already to discern a relative decline in the power of governmental systems, at least in relation to other forms of statally organizing society, especially industrial and commercial and financial corporations. It is possible, too, that politics in the form in which it has become familiar in recent centuries is in relative decline – that is to say, politics as a special part of the total social process devoted to a competition within a ruling class for control of certain legal powers under the real constitution of a society. Politics is apparently being assimilated to other forms of mass communication, with the mass of the people forming a political will to approve or disapprove potential power-holders and their programs in much the same way as they process any other form of choosing, including the willing and acting connected with the economy, the identifying and the satisfying of material wants.

The foregoing free-flowing speculation goes beyond the legitimate extrapolation of the new phenomenon of international reality-forming. But it is safe to predict, in the light of the present state of development of international society, that the structure-system of international society will not continue for much longer to be what it came to be in the modern period and especially in the period since the eighteenth century. As war and the use of force and self-centered self-defense wither away in the real constitution of international society, as diplomacy and international relations come to an end, as the international public realm comes to supersede the individual national public realms, as international reality-forming disempowers the reality-forming of state-societies, international society will have become new, whether or not it has chosen its newness in choosing new theories of its self-conceiving. Like any other society, international society will have created itself anew in its own present-here-and-now from the possibilities which it has itself found in its own self-conceived future.

D. Global Civilization[5]

There is these days an ever more widespread belief that a world map composed of sovereign states no longer provides (if indeed it ever did) a useful conception of how the world as a whole is constituted. In the spirit of popular commentary, Lewis Lapham, editor of an influential American monthly magazine, suggests that if someone were to try depicting "the new order," it would "look more like medieval France than nineteenth century Europe."[6] Lapham's image of the feudal precursor to the modern state system implies a multitude of overlapping types of authority, arising from royal, ecclesiastical, and economic sources, which were at once more centralized and less territorially exclusive than we generally imagine of our own age. Such a deconstruction of the modern state is a suggestive image of later twenty-first-century realities, perhaps, but it is surely premature and quite misleading as a descriptive basis for recasting our understanding of present international realities. An evocation of the feudal order helps us little to grasp what lies just beyond the horizon of an unfolding future. Territorial states remain the predominant political actors in our world, although their interactions are becoming bewilderingly complex and their operational reach increasingly extraterritorial even as their capacity for autonomy is cumulatively eroded.

Indeed, a strong case can be made for treating a map of states as more accurate than ever before. The global dynamics of nationalism in recent decades has created greater viability for many weaker states, at least in terms of resisting the most blatant forms of military encroachment by ascendant states. The actual situation is uneven and complicated, but it is certainly easier for many militarily subordinate territorial governments to organize resistance to interventionary diplomacy and thereby to safeguard their sovereign character against imperial designs. Even the superpowers have faced increasingly formidable challenges to their respective control over so-called "blocs" or

---

[5] By RICHARD FALK, excerpted from: EXPLORATIONS AT THE EDGE OF TIME: THE PROSPECTS FOR WORLD ORDER 196–205, 213 (Temple University Press, 1992). Reprinted by permission.

[6] Lewis Lapham, *Leviathan in Trouble*, HARPER'S MAGAZINE 8, 10 (Sept. 1988).

"spheres of interest." Military superiority is far more difficult to translate into political control than it was in the previous century, when mass mobilization around militant nationalist creeds was unusual. And economic penetration has become more difficult in its cruder forms, requiring elaborate arrangements to limit or disguise foreign capital. The need for indirection is a tribute to the potency of nationalism as a reigning political ideology. Governments can no longer sustain their full legitimacy—either in relation to their own society or with regard to the outer world—if they grant foreign allies special privileges within their territory. Foreign military bases are increasingly difficult to establish, and most of those that exist are under mounting political pressure from the local population. There are exceptions, either where a government lacks any autonomy (and any pretense of legitimacy) or where it is faced by a security challenge that makes a foreign military presence appear a genuinely necessary form of collective self-defense rather than a platform that serves the wider geopolitical strategy of a distant great power. Of course, whether these generalizations will hold up in the post-Cold War situation of international relations is uncertain, especially given the probability of consensus in the North and disunity in the South, as well as undisputed U.S. preeminence as the sole global actor.

Nor are all states adequate vehicles of nationalist claims. Many "nations" (self-consciously ethnic units) are "entrapped" within a sovereign space administered by a government that is controlled by a different nation. Such a state may be autonomous vis-a-vis the external world, but its internal legitimacy is constantly subject to interrogation, if not assault, by assertive and alienated national minorities. In such circumstances, crises of governability are evident. The state lacks the capability to produce either order, justice, or security against unwanted outside interference. Contemporary Lebanon is currently the most aggravated instance, but roughly analogous problems torment many societies to varying degrees, providing government with expedient justifications for abandoning democracy and human rights and exposing human populations to acute forms of daily insecurity with respect to basic human needs.

Can we portray the current shape of the world order by a conventional map of states? Or is it better to conceive of the world as a criss-cross of patterns based on different issues, regimes, and perceptions? I would argue that a sophisticated atlas is preferable to a map, that we need many different ways of looking at the planet as a whole, ranging from the photographs sent back from space satellites through geoeconomic presentations of resources, trade flows, arms trade, and military alliances, as well as space coordinated with population size and standard of living. Mapping differing expectations about the shape of the future would certainly disclose the priorities of a political vision based on world order values.

Hypotheses about a coming global civilization are put forward, partly descriptively, partly normatively, as an overlay upon this debate about the role, viability, patterning, and variety of sovereign states. The contention goes beyond either liberal formulations of interdependence or Marxist formulations of global class structure and international division of labor. In effect, an emergent global ethos suggests the reality of a shared destiny for the human species and a fundamental unity across space and through time, built around the bioethical impulse of all human groups to survive and flourish. Such an ethos has implications for the assessment of problems, the provision of solutions, and the overall orientation of action and actors. For most people and leaders, this sense of shared destiny does not displace a persisting primary attachment to the state as a vehicle for aspiration and as an absolute, unconditional bastion of security. As the "nuclear winter" imagery dramatizes, leaders of nuclear powers seem prepared to threaten the overall survival of civilization and even risk partial or total extinction if such a threat seems necessary to uphold the sovereign identity of a particular state or, more narrowly, the persistence of a particular regime type and governing elite. The logic of war in the nuclear age devours the self that is the object of protection and holds hostage the entire human race, including the idea and reality of unborn generations and indeed the whole life process. From a religious perspective, it is a blasphemy to creation, the sacred work of divinity, to contemplate as a deliberate and discretionary undertaking by human agency the destruction of the world; nuclearism is indefensible both in the most fundamental philosophical sense and in its practical relationship to human well-being.

There is thus at the base of our inquiry, a powerful set of paradoxical forces at work: As the territorial state becomes more vulnerable to what takes place beyond its sovereign reach, it acquires a capability that generates many varieties of extraterritorial harm as side effects of "normalcy." Such a loss of territorial moorings exposes the problem of the political organization of international life from the perspective of state sovereignty. It is difficult to avoid some degree of conceptual confusion at this point. If sovereignty inheres in the people, not the state, then a delegation of authority can be reinterpreted or even reclaimed by popular action. Sovereignty, by democratic theory, is not to be automatically identified with the state, yet in modern practice—especially in matters of international policy—the state, even the democratic state, has increasingly operated without encountering substantial challenges from "below" and generally without significant citizen participation; statist understandings of sovereignty tend to prevail.

In the discussion that follows, the inquiry into "evasions" starts from the empirical reality that "sovereignty" is perceived as concentrated in states. The recovery of sovereignty through the reinvigoration of democratic practice would work against the current tendency to identify sovereignty exclusively with the central governing process of territorial states enjoying international status. The notion of sovereignty rests on an overall congruence between authority, capability, territoriality, and loyalty. That is, at least conceptually and to varying degrees existentially, states claim, often credibly, the authority and capacity to provide security and welfare for the people within their territory in exchange for expectations of loyalty and obedience from the population. Such a practical adjustment has also been combined with the belief that war and conflict provide both a foundation for protecting diversity (or difference) at acceptable costs and, contrariwise, a legislative process for achieving change that is incidentally assimilated into the validating processes of international law by way of "the peace treaty" (even territorial changes achieved by "aggression" have been given full legal effect). Without war, the international status quo would arguably have been frozen with respect to the size and scale of operative units.

Patterns of incongruence take on such great significance at this historical moment because of their consequential character. The theoretical "discovery" of incongruence is by itself interesting; incongruence could over time weaken the loyalty and legitimacy claims of the state but would probably not be effectual on its own in the face of the capacities of the state to propagandize and coerce. But today, the human subservience imposed on citizens is quite extraordinary, especially under conditions of democracy where access to damaging information tends to be greater, and thus the vulnerability of people to breakdowns of international order cannot be disguised. The consequences of nuclear winter, of global warming and ozone depletion, of rainforest destruction, of air and ocean pollution are quite literally shattering to human prospects. This mismatch between capabilities and challenges is bound to cause severe tensions between state and society in the years to come.

Yet states will endeavor to fashion responses to these challenges, and over time the state has displayed a considerable capacity for adaption as well as resilience. State leaders have already given expression to the growing need for cooperation, including self-limiting standards. The impressive intergovernmental reaction to the prospects of harmful effects arising from ozone depletion is illustrative. With great haste and in a spirit of seriousness, once a consensus was formed as to cause and harmful effect, an international agreement was negotiated, the Montreal Protocol, whose central mandate is a commitment by treaty members, starting in 1989, to phase out by the end of the century 50 percent of those chemicals (especially chlorofluorocarbons) that deplete ozone. Subsequently, even before the treaty was in force, there were private and public acknowledgements that the plan, even if fully implemented, was woefully insufficient, and indeed, with the surprising help of Margaret Thatcher, a more stringent supplemental agreement on phasing out CFCs was accepted. Some corporate users voluntarily agreed to substitute more expensive components, beyond treaty requirements, and public officials called for more rigorous standards, asking that a commitment to the total elimination of CFCs be substituted for the present duty to cut down by half.

This regulatory process is a test of whether, in the face of vested economic interests unevenly distributed among state actors, it is possible to move toward an effective regime of prohibition even in a situation where the evidence of severe harm arising from the prohibited activity is substantially uncontested. The Montreal Protocol lacks an enforcement capability. If other states implement it, then a failure to implement will not seem so serious; if others cheat, then additional cheating will not matter that much, and why should some endure higher production costs if others don't? Such a structure, by its calculus of separate interests, is dominated by the pursuit of the well-being of the fragment or part, reinforced by the conviction that to forgo advantages merely shifts benefits to other state actors, as when a state withholds arms from warring parties. Can the aggregated interest of these separate and dissimilar perspectives be translated into policies that protect the well-being of the whole (which comprises all the parts, including itself) within existing structure? There is no assured answer at this point. There may never be a clear response. The conditions of each instance may shape a series of understandings not necessarily fully consistent with one another: How widely shared is the information about the probable gravity of the harm in the event of persistence? How deferred in time is the harm likely to be? How great are the economic costs of adjustment? Can they be shifted or otherwise offset? How aroused is both world public opinion and the practical climate of opinion in important countries? How easy is it to detect noncompliance with agreed standards? How likely are Third World countries to be guided by cost efficiency factors? To what extent will richer countries, especially those most responsible for the particular form of environmental harm, bear a proportional share of adjustment costs?

Ozone depletion may be an important test, both because of its own bearing on future health and well-being and because it presents an adjustment challenge that is significant in its requirements but not overwhelming. The nature of the test is severalfold: Can commitments of compliance be monitored and upheld in the absence of enforcement mechanisms? Can the depth of commitment be made responsive to the severity of the problem during an interval of time when successful adjustment is still possible? Is a regime of prohibition already too late in the sense that the process of harmful effects cannot be arrested or reversed by the time the political will is mobilized to take cooperative action? These are some of the general issues to be considered if our concern is with the adjustment capabilities of the state system by way of cooperative action. There is also the question of whether the more difficult adjustment required to arrest global warming can be agreed upon and then effectively implemented in sufficient time. Such an adjustment calls for a gradual shift away from burning fossil fuels as a primary source of energy for heating and transportation. What seems involved here is the nature of modern industrial society as it has evolved in the West.

The second dimension of resilience as a feature of statism concerns the affective loyalties of people. Given the way state and society interact in the modern world, the state is seen, increasingly in the postcolonial era, as a necessary (and desirable) from for advancing and safeguarding nationalist aspirations. Those nationals who have no state (Palestinians, Kurds, indigenous peoples) are exceptionally vulnerable to repressive tactics, especially as they are located within a state that is largely a vehicle for realizing the incompatible interests of a rival "nation." Since all territory belongs to existing states, and the loss of territory is generally considered an unacceptable encroachment on sovereign rights, the presence of rival nations within boundaries is regarded by established governments as an active or latent threat. The effect of nationalist energies is to fragment the world political structure to an even greater degree, but state resistance of these energies results in denial of self-determination and can be manipulated to restrict its relevance to existing territorial units as acknowledged by membership in the United Nations and other criteria. Conferring "nationality" by legal decree, or by issuing a passport, does not displace or overcome existential feelings of nationalist identity, and their denial. This nationalist creed seems, if anything, to be intensifying, although unevenly. It is primarily to satisfy nationalist aspirations that many people in different state settings are voluntarily risking their lives and displaying courage and commitment to alter existing political arrangements.

The significance of nationalist potency for my argument is this: Many state structures are being challenged by nationalist movements. The states generally resist these challenges by reliance on coercion, considering such resistance itself a sovereign right if exercised within territory. Consequently, the nationalist movements often seek the protective and assertive frameworks of the sovereign state, including a reliance on human rights. Although they are usually motivated by a territorial project, their political outlook often includes a sense of solidarity with other struggling nationalisms and a dependence for support on international institutions; it can be understood as a common quest for human rights within the existing statist structure. If our concern is with world order values—associated here with acting in response to a global ethos—then many of the various nationalisms are potentially capable of making positive contributions to an improvement of the relationship between human population groups and political institutions.

This contention can be specified to a further degree: attaining statehood would fulfill the process of self-determination of peoples for certain national movements, itself a normative accomplishment; increasing the congruence between nation and state would reduce violent conflict and presumably allow more political attention to be devoted to the global agenda.

But there are several structural problems. By 1990 there were more than 800 nationalist movements in the world but fewer than 200 states. Many among these 800 claimants are small, weak, dispersed, nonviable, but not necessarily resigned to their fate. There is no prospect that all these nationalisms cab be accommodated by grants of statehood. In fact territorial claims are often layered in such a way that the vindication of one nationalist destiny would displace another. As a result, sovereignty is difficult to evade, even if political self-determination is accepted as an authoritative norm. Its application necessarily involves tensions, contradictions, and conflict. Also, states that are inherently incapable of mobilizing resources to meet the needs of their population present serious problems of viability, even if their political structure is accepted as legitimate.

Could one imagine denationalized states as a basis for a more constructive role of sovereignty? Of course, most modern states already claim to be secular entities that confer nationality by legal, not ethnic, criteria and govern on a nondiscriminatory basis. But the secularization of sovereignty has not succeeded in extinguishing the primacy of nationalist identities or their perception of many existing states as repressive vehicles of ascendant forms of nationalism. Hence, unfortunately, at a time of long-range, global-scale challenge it is likely that the political energies of many states and discontented nations will focus on immediate struggles over autonomy, human rights, and contested movements for statehood.

What is the overall prospect for cooperative undertakings in a world menaced by disintegrative forces associated with the limits of "carrying capacity" and an absence of sufficient capabilities to define and protect global interests? These limits must be tested, stretched, and, one hopes, relocated; the intellectual and political significance of a global integrative process is to identify the limits as they bear upon the challenges and capabilities of political actors in our world, premised on a shared affirmation of the value of sustaining, and even enhancing, the quality of life for the peoples of the world, including those of future generations. With such a normative premise, the collaborative endorsement of an emergent global civilization seeks to expand the resources of both citizens and leaders by making public opinion more attuned to the dangers and to possibilities for constructive action, by abolishing destructive polarities between ''us'' and ''them'' without losing the special qualities of diversity that give the particularities of human existence their special glow of enchantment.

States do participate cooperatively in wider political communities that fall into three general categories: (1) hegemonic ''communities,'' in which most of the glue is supplied by the dominant state, and the weaker participants have had their autonomy gravely compromised, and their legitimacy as well, to the extent that a governing elite in subordinate countries loses control over vital sectors of policy and acquiesces in such arrangements: (2) alliance ''communities,'' especially during wartime, periods of high international tension, and in reaction to expansionist drives of antidemocratic and imperialist states: (3) cooperative ''communities,'' in which the mutual benefits of economic integration or common regimes for environmental protection and technical relations provide rational incentives for weakening state boundaries. These arrangements are extensions of ordinary diplomacy, fulfilling goals of state actors. Their scope is normally regional, motivated either by domination, fear (of an enemy), or calculations of gain. Such patterns do not as yet respond directly to either the affirmative reality of a global ethos or the more negative dangers associated with the deterioration of the global commons. From the perspective of world order values, such extended political communities can be either regressive or positive, depending on the circumstances. The normative effects can be complex, as is illustrated by debates about the impact of the 1992 plans for further economic integration in western Europe or the recently concluded free trade treaty between the United States and Canada. Even when the economic effects suggest mutual benefit, a weaker state that participates in such a widening process risks its autonomy and often gives up political space in which to explore alternative lines of policy. Wider frameworks do not necessarily represent a positive adjustment from the perspective of world order values. Quite the contrary, the most prevalent patterns of ''suprastatism'' often jeopardize some of the most desirable features of national identity that are preserved by states operating on a secure basis of legitimacy: that is, providing their people with human rights, political democracy, a sense of community and tradition, and overall security.

One focus of this effort to adapt political behavior to the global setting is to reinterpret sovereignty, weakening its conflictual preoccupation with threats to territorial space, without depreciating its role in safeguarding to the extent possible the autonomy of particular nations (or, more problematically, of groups of nations joined together as a single state beneath a common flag). Changing the perceptions of the character of the threat – from ''the other'' as enemy to the current enfeebled arrangements of ''the whole'' as menacing – can change the choice of instruments for upholding autonomy (that is, the exercise of sovereignty), especially if these instruments of political assertion become denuclearized and demilitarized. Such a process centers, of course, on rethinking ''security,'' shifting the locus from ''national security'' (part versus part) to ''common security'' or ''comprehensive security'' (parts depending on the whole), but it also involves adapting the agenda and priorities of states so that they respond by the most effective means available to challenges directed at their citizenry. The assumptions here are decidedly selfish rather than altruistic, presupposing that a collective response to ozone depletion, for example, is necessary for the sake of national well-being. In this regard effective sovereignty entails establishing an ambitious regime of prohibition on the basis of negotiation and cooperation among states rather than on the typical basis of a threat posed by an external enemy which can be countered only be counterthreats and capabilities. It may be better to grasp the integrative tendencies of international life as a challenge to a militarized and highly spatial orientation toward sovereignty rather than to sovereignty per se. Part of the analysis being made rests on the diminished ability of territorial boundaries, as defended by military capabilities, to keep a given society free from external penetration. Increasingly, even the most impressively protected boundaries cannot keep out unwanted drugs, persons, ideas, or polluting substances.

Part of the resilience of political life in general derives from the multiplicity and interaction of forms for acting in the world. The role of independent voices is crucial in placing problems on the main political agenda, because vested interests are often mobilized to keep as ''invisible'' and ineffectual as possible any such challenges to current patterns of ''profitable'' practices. To initiate action requires an acknowledgment of the gravity of a problem, as well as enough time to overcome destructive patterns of practice. The existence of democratic space is indispensable, as is the protection of those who are the messengers of bad news. Yet individuals who break ''the silence'' of institutions are vulnerable to severe forms of abuse. Their voices are stilled by the oppressive reflect action of even democratic political traditions under such labels as ''treason,'' ''espionage,'' or ''national security.'' When Mordechai Vanunu disclosed and verified the extent of Israel's nuclear weapons program in 1986, he breached Israel's official silence and was abducted abroad by Israeli secret agents, prosecuted, convicted of treason, and sentenced to eighteen years in jail. With such rigid bureaucratic reflexes the state damages its own resilience by responding severely to challenges, especially those associated with ''national security'' at the core of its militarist orientation toward sovereignty. Exposing the state to such challenges on ground of policy and practice, from within and without (transnational democracy), is part of what might enable sovereignty to become potentially more adaptive. Such constitutional conceptions as ''checks and balances,'' ''separation of powers,'' ''inalienable rights,'' and periodic elections to obtain ''the consent of the governed'' are part of an effort to make government more flexible in the face of changing conditions and values but not so fluid as to be able too easily to transgress limits on the exercise of power. Notions of ''civil disobedience'' and, more recently, ''civil resistance'' are ways of underscoring the relevance of conscience to the assessment of official policy. After World War II the notion of moral assessment was given an obligatory character in the course of the Nuremberg trials and the subsequent formulation of a notion of responsibility to uphold international law in the war/peace area, even as against direct commands by the head of state. There are, then, many connections between a revitalized political democracy, positive sovereignty, and a relatively smooth transition to a more integrative, less territorial stage of international relations.

The state has demonstrated a remarkable degree of resilience over the several centuries of its existence, but whether it can significantly reorient its sense of sovereign prerogative from space (protecting territory) to time (contributing to a viable and desirable future) is uncertain in the extreme. The realization of such a possibility depends on abandoning the realm of reification. Only if specific persons, acting on behalf of the state, can develop the sort of understanding and backing needed can states be led away from their boundary-obsessed territorialism to a more formless contouring of authority that responds to the bewildering array of dangers and opportunities in the world today.

To make this shift at all viable requires an active civil society that gives its citizens ''the space'' to explore ''adjustments,'' including transnational initiatives, and depends on the secure establishment of human rights and democracy, and further depends on the internal accountability of leaders for violation of international law. Citizens need an enforceable right to a lawful foreign policy if initiatives from below are going to be protected in sensitive times. The natural flow of political life in response to the agenda of global concerns is to encourage evasions as a matter of deliberate tactics. Is the state flexible enough to preside over its own partial dissolution, circumvention, and reconstitution?

Index